The media's watching Vau
Here's a sampling of our coverage.

"With admirable directness, the Vault.com 50 tries to measure prestige by prestige."
— *National Law Journal*

"With reviews and profiles of firms that one associate calls 'spot on,' [Vault.com's] guide has become a key reference for those who want to know what it takes to get hired by a law firm and what to expect once they get there."
— *New York Law Journal*

"The well-written profiles make Vault.com the next best thing to camping out in a company rest room."
—*Yahoo! Internet Life*

"For those hoping to climb the ladder of success, [Vault.com's] insights are priceless."
— *Money Magazine*

"Vault.com is indispensible for locating insider information."
— *Metropolitan Corporate Counsel*

"The granddaddy of worker sites."
— *US News and World Report*

"Vault.com is another killer app for the Internet."
— *New York Times*

VAULT.COM GUIDE TO THE TOP 50 LAW FIRMS

© 2000 Vault.com Inc.

ACKNOWLEDGEMENTS

Vault.com would like to take the time to acknowledge the assistance and support of Geoff Baum, Ken Cron, Matt Doull, Glenn Fischer, Mark Hernandez, Ravi Mhatre, Tom Phillips, Jay Oyakawa, Carter Weiss, the folks at Hollinger Venture, Ingram and Globix, and our loving families and friends.

This book is the result of the extraordinary efforts of Kofo Anifalaje, Alan Audi, Greg Gartland, Nayana Kulkarni, Clarissa Londis, Sumiya Nowshin, Rachel Penski, Kathleen Pierce, Chris Prior, Jeremy Root, Rob Schipano, Rose Schipano, Nikki Scott, and Ed Shen. Thanks to Cliff Cook, Regina Kent, and Todd Kuhlman for providing technical support for the surveys.

Special thanks to all of the law firm recruiting coordinators and hiring partners who helped with this book. We appreciate your patience with our repeated requests and tight deadlines.

We at Vault.com dedicate the *Vault.com Guide to the Top 50 Law Firms* to the 4,880 associates who took the time to be interviewed or complete our survey.

[they told him it was a "lifestyle" firm]

AOL Keyword: Vault.com

Industry Channels
Insider Research >
Message Boards
News
Find a Job

Company Profiles
Find out what the firm is really like before you accept the offer.

VAULT.COM

[The truth is in the VAULT]

© 2000 Brobeck, Phleger & Harrison LLP

FIRMS MENTIONED MOST OFTEN

1. Brobeck, Phleger & Harrison

2. Wilson Sonsini Goodrich & Rosati
3. Cooley Godward
4. Fenwick & West
5. Gibson, Dunn & Crutcher
6. King & Spalding
6. Orrick, Herrington & Sutcliffe
8. Hale and Dorr
8. Morrison & Foerster
8. Skadden, Arps, Slate, Meagher & Flom

FIRMS MENTIONED MOST OFTEN AS CORPORATE COUNSEL

1. Brobeck, Phleger & Harrison

1. Hale and Dorr
3. Davis Polk & Wardell
3. Gibson, Dunn & Crutcher
3. Skadden, Arps, Slate, Meagher & Flom
3. Venture Law Group
3. Wilson Sonsini Goodrich & Rosati

FIRMS MENTIONED MOST OFTEN AS LITIGATION COUNSEL

1. Brobeck, Phleger & Harrison

2. Orrick, Herrington & Sutcliffe

FIRMS MENTIONED MOST OFTEN AS SECURITIES COUNSEL

1. Brobeck, Phleger & Harrison

1. Wilson Sonsini Goodrich & Rosati
3. Gibson, Dunn & Crutcher
3. Willkie Farr & Gallagher

Excerpted from the September 1999 issue of *The American Lawyer*. Copyright © 1999 NLP IP Company.
(Duplicate numbers indicate a tie in the ratings)

Brobeck. When your future is at stake.℠

ATTORNEYS AT LAW ▶ www.brobeck.com

AUSTIN · DALLAS · DENVER · IRVINE · LONDON · LOS ANGELES · NEW YORK · PALO ALTO · SAN DIEGO · SAN FRANCISCO · WASHINGTON, D.C.

INTRODUCTION

Introduction 1
The State of the Law: 2000-2001 2
A Guide to this Guide 7

THE VAULT.COM PRESTIGE RANKINGS

The Vault.com Top 50 13
Prestige Rankings by City 16
Departmental Rankings 21

QUALITY OF LIFE RANKINGS

The Best 20 Firms to Work For 30
Quality of Life Rankings by Category 33

THE VAULT.COM 50

1	Cravath, Swaine & Moore	60
2	Wachtell, Lipton, Rosen & Katz	76
3	Sullivan & Cromwell	90
4	Davis Polk & Wardwell	104
5	Skadden, Arps, Slate, Meagher & Flom	116
6	Simpson Thacher & Bartlett	130
7	Cleary, Gottlieb, Steen & Hamilton	142
8	Shearman & Sterling	156
9	Latham & Watkins	170
10	Wilson Sonsini Goodrich & Rosati	182
11	Kirkland & Ellis	194
12	Williams & Connolly	204
13	Weil, Gotshal & Manges	214

THE VAULT.COM 50 (cont'd)

14	Covington & Burling	226
15	Paul, Weiss, Rifkind, Wharton & Garrison	236
16	Sidley & Austin	250
17	Gibson, Dunn & Crutcher	262
18	Debevoise & Plimpton	274
19	O'Melveny & Myers	284
20	White & Case	298
21	Arnold & Porter	308
22	Morrison & Foerster	320
23	Wilmer, Cutler & Pickering	330
24	Brobeck, Phleger & Harrison	340
25	Mayer, Brown & Platt	352
26	Milbank, Tweed, Hadley & McCloy	364
27	Hale and Dorr	374
28	Ropes & Gray	386
29	Fried, Frank, Harris, Shriver & Jacobson	398
30	Jones, Day, Reavis & Pogue	410
31	Dewey Ballantine	422
32	Cooley Godward	432
33	Clifford Chance Rogers & Wells	444
34	Morgan, Lewis & Bockius	456
35	King & Spalding	468
36	Willkie Farr & Gallagher	478
37	Venture Law Group	488
38	Gunderson Dettmer Stough Villeneuve Franklin & Hachigian	498
39	Hogan & Hartson	510
40	Munger, Tolles & Olson	522
41	Paul, Hastings, Janofsky & Walker	532
42	Orrick, Herrington & Sutcliffe	544
43	Akin Gump Strauss Hauer & Feld	554
44	Winston & Strawn	566

THE VAULT.COM 50 (cont'd)

45	Baker & McKenzie	578
46	Vinson & Elkins	590
47	Cadwalader, Wickersham & Taft	600
48	Proskauer Rose	610
49	Baker Botts	622
50	Cahill Gordon & Reindel	634

NEARLY AND NOTABLE

Alston & Bird	648
Chadbourne & Parke	658
Choate, Hall & Stewart	670
Dechert Price & Rhoads	682
Fulbright & Jaworski	694
Gray Cary Ware & Freidenrich	704
Irell & Manella	714
Jenner & Block	724
Kilpatrick Stockton	736
LeBoeuf, Lamb, Greene & MacRae	746
McDermott, Will & Emery	756
Perkins Coie	770
Pillsbury Madison & Sutro	782
Preston Gates & Ellis	794

THE BEST OF THE REST

Arent Fox Kinter Plotkin & Kahn	807
Ballard Spahr Andrews & Ingersoll	808
Bingham Dana	809
Blank Rome Comisky & McCauley	810

THE BEST OF THE REST (cont'd)

Bracewell & Patterson 811
Drinker Biddle & Reath 812
Duane, Morris & Heckscher 813
Fenwick & West 814
Fish & Neave 815
Fish & Richardson 816
Foley, Hoag & Eliot 817
Foley & Lardner 818
Gardere & Wynne 819
Goodwin, Procter & Hoar 820
Haynes and Boone 821
Heller Ehrman White & McAuliffe 822
Howrey Simon Arnold & White 823
Hunton & Williams 824
Jenkens & Gilchrist 825
Katten Muchin Zavis 826
Kaye, Scholer, Fierman, Hays & Handler 827
Kelley Drye & Warren 828
Loeb & Loeb 829
Long Aldridge & Norman 830
Manatt, Phelps & Phillips 831
Mintz, Levin, Cohn, Ferris, Glovsky and Popeo 832
Montgomery, McCracken, Walker & Rhoads 833
Palmer & Dodge 834
Pepper Hamilton 835
Piper Marbury Rudnick & Wolfe 836
Saul, Ewing, Remick & Saul 837
Schiff Hardin & Waite 838
Schulte Roth & Zabel 839
Shaw Pittman 840
Sheppard, Mullin, Richter & Hampton 841

THE BEST OF THE REST (cont'd)

Sonnenschein Nath & Rosenthal 842

Squire, Sanders & Dempsey 843

Steptoe & Johnson 844

Stroock & Stroock & Lavan 845

Swidler Berlin Shereff Friedman 846

Testa, Hurwitz & Thibeault 847

Thelen Reid & Priest 848

Thompson & Knight 849

Troutman Sanders 850

Winstead Sechrest & Minick 851

Winthrop, Stimson, Putnam & Roberts 852

Wolf, Block, Schorr and Solis-Cohen 853

APPENDIX

Alphabetical Index of Law Firms 857

Firms by Main Office 860

People Index 864

Company/Organization Index 873

About the Authors 883

Latham & Watkins

> **Taitt Sato**
> UC Berkeley, Class of 1997

Loves: *Iced coffee, digital art, cool shoes, riding her carbon fiber road bike*

Hates: *Bubble gum, bad handwriting, slow modems, listening to country music*

Deals: *Advised Safeway, NorthPoint and Cordant Technologies on their public offerings*

Quote: *"At Latham there's such a variety of interesting projects to choose from, I feel like a kid in a candy shop!"*

Make your mark.

Choosing your first firm is a big deal. You don't really want to be doing case research for the next three years, do you?

At Latham & Watkins, we offer remarkable opportunities for young lawyers. Our associates get challenging assignments from day one—in high tech, corporate and finance, complex litigation, international, environmental and tax— along with full support to do their very best work.

Ready to make your mark? Check us out on campus or on the Web at www.lw.com.

Oh yeah—our pay and benefits are pretty good too!

www.lw.com

Chicago   Los Angeles   New Jersey
New York   Orange County   San Diego
San Francisco   Silicon Valley
Washington, D.C.   Hong Kong   London
Moscow   Singapore   Tokyo

Introduction

Welcome to the third year of the *Vault.com Guide to the Top 50 Law Firms*. (You may notice a title change; that's because this year we considered top firms based outside the United States as well.) We created this guide in 1998 because there was no unbiased ranking of the most prestigious law firms in the country. Today, the *Guide* serves not only as the best resource for discovering the top 50 firms in the country, but also as an unbiased, comprehensive, investigative counterpoint to glossy firm recruiting literature and law firm web sites.

This year, we surveyed 4,880 lawyers — more than twice as many as last year — to come up with our Top 50 list. We asked them to tell us what they knew and thought of their peer law firms by asking them to score each firm based on its prestige. We took these scores and calculated the Vault.com Top 50.

It's a fact of business and life — clients gravitate toward firms with the best reputations, just as law firms care about the prestige of law schools when they recruit new attorneys. Not only do the most highly regarded law firms attract a higher volume of work, but the cases and deals you'll work on at these firms will likely be more prominent and far-reaching. Most importantly, your firm's reputation will continue to mark your resume and follow you throughout your career. Proving yourself at one top-notch firm can make it easier to get another great job.

At the same time, even the most competitive lawyers should look for more fulfillment in their work than a big name. We hope you'll be able to use the information contained in the *Guide* to choose the firm that works for you, whether that means prestige, perks, interesting work or flexible schedules. You may be especially interested in our Best 20 Firms to Work For, which weighs our surveys to bring you a list of the firms we feel may be most amenable to an enjoyable lawyerly existence.

The *Vault.com* 2000 *Guide to the Top 50 Law Firms* provides in-depth information about more firms than ever before. We at Vault.com are proud to bring you the most current information for each and every one of the top firms (plus a few other notable firms). This year we include department rankings and rankings by region, as well as our detailed, honest, investigative law firm profiles — 64 this year.

We're confident that the *Guide* is your best resource on the top law firms.

The Editors
Vault.com
New York, NY
September 2000

The State of the Law: 2000-2001

It's been another crazy year in the law — crazy in a good way, if you're a lawyer looking for a job. (If you're a hiring partner or a recruiter, you'll probably just find the market crazed.) The appetite for brand-new lawyers and laterals continues unabated, and law firms have resorted to paying ever-escalating salaries and bonuses to attract and retain associates. And for the first time, those pay raises don't originate in New York within the stolid confines of a Cravath or a Cadwalader — they're emanating from trendy West Coast tech meccas, like Menlo Park and Palo Alto.

At the same time, law firms are expanding their operations, both in number of associates and offices, in the United States and in other countries. According to the National Association for Law Placement (NALP), entry-level hiring increased 13 percent in 1999. If you're one of those lawyers looking for a new home, you've hit the right legal market. Law firms are attempting to expand operations to meet the demands of a superhot economy — while their associates receive increasing numbers of offers to go in-house or try their luck with the latest startup.

It's a strong year for lawyers — and perhaps an atypical one. Even more so than last year, associates welcome their good fortune in the form of skyrocketing salaries and tempting perks while simultaneously wondering just how long their good fortune can last. (Anyone remember the layoffs of the early 1990s after the boom legal years of the late 1980s?) Let's have a look.

Dot com dandy

Perhaps one of the most interesting aspects of the law this year is the infiltration of Internet influence into unexpected niches of law careers. While a few years ago casual Fridays were a treasured perk, today even the famously conservative Cravath permits casual Fridays (albeit in summer only). The impetus? Dot com clients and dot com competition. Gunderson Dettmer, a tech-focused firm based in California, not only permits business casual dress every day, it allows completely casual dress — meaning T-shirts and jeans. More typical of the trend is New York's Cadwalader, which permits business casual dress all year round — essentially, polo shirts and khakis for men, tasteful Banana Republic-esque garb for the women.

"A war of attrition"

While dressing like a dot commer may be appealing, for many associates working *for* a dot com is even more attractive. As the number of Internet startups looking for savvy hires with contract and negotiation experience increases, associates find themselves besieged on a daily basis by headhunters offering tempting positions at tech companies, complete with stock options. Many associates are also drawn to the opportunity to get involved in aspects of business other than law — many lawyers are drafted to do Internet business development, for example. Attorneys surveyed often attribute turnover at their companies to poaching by Internet companies — companies that are sometimes clients of the very firms they steal from. "It's becoming a war of attrition," says a lawyer at Cravath, with lawyers being "steadily plucked away to dot coms." Other associates point out that their chances of making partner have improved with the defection of their peers, though many wish they weren't "left behind with the hours and the work."

In May 2000, Brobeck became one of the first firms to actively fight the tide of lawyer defections. That month, the firm began to ask clients who lure away its associates to pay a fee — a headhunting fee. Brobeck got the idea from its high tech clientele, some of whom include similar protective clauses in their contracts with their clients. Brobeck's new contract clause now requires clients who can't resist poaching one of Brobeck's lawyers to pay the firm 25 percent of the lawyer's salary to the firm. Many legal recruiters routinely charge 30 percent of starting salary to their clients.

But the tide of defections may be slowing. With the spring 2000 downturn in the market, jumping ship to a dot com has become a riskier proposition, and the secure realm of lawyerdom once again holds appeal. Still, as one insider puts it in an only mildly mixed wildlife metaphor: "It's an inescapable fact of being a lawyer that the higher you go up the food chain, the smaller the number of fish."

Fight back with cash

How do you fight the allure of potential Internet riches? Two options: pay associates more money or allow them the thrill and risk of investing in an Internet company without losing them to one.

Let's start with cold hard lucre. This year, salaries at Menlo Park tech boutique Gunderson Dettmer rose to $125,000 for first-year associates, with a guaranteed bonus. The news traveled at the speed of e-mail. Within days, New York-based firms scrambled to match their Silicon Valley counterparts. When the dust settled, most New York firms set base salaries at $125,000. Skadden Arps Slate Meagher & Flom led the East Coast pack with a base salary of $140,000. Summer associates benefited as well, earning an average of $2,400 per week. Firms that don't pony up to the pay raises swiftly attract protest from their associates, who mutter darkly about firms that are "slow to match."

One unusual aspect of the latest wave of raises is that it began in California instead of New York, the traditional home of attorney pay hikes. Some see the money flow's change of direction as evidence of Silicon Valley's new importance in the legal world.

(Keen observers of this year's Top 50 will note the upward surge in rankings of many California-based and West Coast-based firms, such as Brobeck, Gunderson Dettmer, Cooley Godward and Venture Law Group.)

It's also worth noting that, unlike in previous years, pay raises are not dependent on city. That means a Boston or Washington associate will often make the same salary as an associate living in New York City even though the cost of living in those cities is dramatically different.

Stocky clients

In a further effort to put the kibosh on the allure of the dot coms, firms have started to let associates in on the equity game. A little Internet primer first: as law firms increasingly represent Internet firms long on flipbooks and buzzwords but short on operating capital, they've begun to accept equity in place of at least a portion of their normal legal fees. Firms that take a chunk of clients include Proskauer Rose, Morrison & Foerster, and Winthrop Stimson. Venture Law Group bases much of its business model on this very practice.

Other firms prefer to invest directly in promising clients. Firms like Wilson Sonsini and Brobeck have established investment funds — and permit participation in them by associates. Firms hope that the chance to earn money from these risky dot coms, without actually having to work for one, will help keep associates from leaving. (Consulting firms and investment banking firms are adopting similar strategies.)

Perk-enhanced lifestyle

While inflated salaries and the chance at further equity riches may be new tactics in the law firm's retention portfolio, firms continue to rely on enhanced "goodies" to keep associates as well. Standard perks at many firms already include car service, subsidized gyms, free tickets to shows and sporting events, and free meals for associates working late, but firms are increasing their arsenal of perks to keep their valuable associates. One unusual trend: a focus on wellness and relaxation. For instance, associates at Debevoise can slip away for a firm yoga class. Davis Polk & Wardwell's New York office has a new relaxation room where associates can escape to de-stress. Fenwick & West flies its associates to Maui and Park City, Utah for vacations in the firm's condos.

Summer associates are extremely valuable commodities in this era where Internet companies, prestige-laden consulting firms like McKinsey, and investment banks exert their pull on the career plans of budding lawyers. When an individual accepts a full-time offer, firms shower them with gifts that range from the basic clothing, cookies, or chocolates inscribed with the firm's name to more elaborate enticements.

At Dewey Ballantine's Los Angeles office, new hires receive Coach leather planners, while newcomers at New York's Paul, Weiss, Rifkind, Wharton & Harrison scored subscriptions to *Time Out New York* magazine (a $39.95 value).

The number of summer associates is on the upswing as well — even from 1999, when summer classes routinely broke the 100-lawyer mark. Hot sports law firm Proskauer Rose has almost doubled its 2000 summer associate class to 80 lawyers while Sullivan & Cromwell (No. 3 this year on the Top 50 survey) hosts a class of 119 associates, up from 102 in 1999. Summer associates routinely get paid $2,400 at most of Vault.com's Top 50 law firms.

The day stretches

But the extra cash often comes at a price. Most firms accompanied their increased salaries with increased billing requirements, ranging from 2,000 to 2,200 hours. Other firms have developed multi-tier salary and bonus structures that directly tie associates' fortunes to their hours. That means that as associates earn greater salaries and the work level increases, the number of hours expected of them rises as well. At Hogan & Hartson, for example, first-year associates have the option to bill 1,800 hours and earn $120,000 or to bill over 1,950 and earn $135,000.

Some associates bemoan the increasing emphasis on billable hours and the corresponding lack of emphasis placed on pro bono work. Lawyers across the board tell Vault.com that the raises mean "the loss of a formerly pleasant environment." "I believe that the partners now watch us to make sure we are earning our salaries," laments one associate. Another lawyer went so far as to say that he wishes he'd had the chance to vote against pay raises at his firm!

While most minimums top out at about 2,200, many lawyers report billing up to 3,000 hours. At the top of that range, associates are looking at nearly 12 hours a day, every day, not including other, non-billable tasks or the necessities of life. The continuing defection of mid-level associates to dot coms and in-house legal positions holds little hope for associates hoping to reduce their hours.

Trading coasts

There's gold in them there hills — on both the East and West coasts. While firms have been expanding internationally for many years, they are now following their clients whose attention is focused on the Valley. Realizing the potential for expansion in the high tech Valley, New York firms plan to capitalize on their high-end dealmaking and litigation capabilities. At least seven of the largest New York firms opened offices out west in 1999 and 2000, including Simpson Thacher & Bartlett and Davis Polk & Wardwell (both among this year's top 10). At the same time, West Coast firms, such as Brobeck and Orrick, made strong forays into New York City in 1999. Brobeck in particular, through an aggressive and innovative marketing campaign, succeeded in grabbing business in New York City's burgeoning Silicon Alley sector from underneath the noses of that city's top law firms — clients include Doubleclick and About.com.

Merger mania

Investment banks aren't the only mergers and acquisitions enthusiasts. In order to rapidly expand into hot domestic and international markets and quickly acquire squadrons of experienced lawyers, law firms are taking over competitors. The standout merger of 1999 was the marriage of U.K.-based Clifford Chance with New York-based Rogers & Wells to create the 2,400 lawyer Clifford Chance Rogers & Wells. The merger enhanced interest in joining law firms from the superheated legal market of London, though few firms have followed in their footsteps to date; Latham & Watkins is among the firms that have turned down a possible merger with a U.K.-based firm.

Nonetheless, other top firms are setting their sights on growing through combining. Taking the lead in the merging field is internationally-oriented New York-based Coudert Brothers, who joined with Australia's Norton Smith & Co. and added the German firm Schurmann & Partners, giving the firm a grand total of 300 lawyers in Australia, Europe and Asia. In June 2000, California-based Paul, Hastings, Janofsky & Walker (number 41 in our survey this year) swallowed up New York's Battle Fowler. Interestingly enough, the acquisition of Battle Fowler makes New York Paul Hastings' largest office.

A strange footnote to the emphasis on internationalization and expansion among law firms: Vault.com has noticed that many firms, presumably in an attempt to give equal prominence to all their offices, now insist that they do not have a headquarters or branch offices. Morgan Lewis was a forerunner in the no-HQ trend, one now adopted by other firms, among them Kilpatrick Stockton, Cleary Gottlieb, Latham & Watkins, and Jones Day.

If you've read this far, you're probably eager to start reading about which of these firms rank tops in prestige — and which may be the best to work for. Any feedback? Let us know at law@staff.vault.com. Enjoy!

Guide to This Guide

If you're wondering how our entries are organized, read on. Here's a handy guide to the information you'll find packed into each entry of this book.

THE BUZZ

Our surveys aren't just cold hard numbers — we also asked our respondents to detail their opinions and observations about other law firms. We've collected a sampling of these comments in "The Buzz."

When selecting The Buzz, we included quotes representative of the common outside perceptions of the firms, even if in our opinion the quotes did not accurately describe the firm. We should note that we were shocked — shocked! — at the nastiness of some of the impressions attorneys had of other law firms. This general mean-spiritedness is reflected by the sometimes negative comments in The Buzz. Please keep in mind when reading The Buzz that it's often more fun for outsiders to trash than praise a competing law firm. Nonetheless, we have found The Buzz to be another valuable means of gauging a firm's reputation in the legal field or at least to detect common misperceptions.

FIRM FACTS

Locations: A listing of the firm's offices, with the headquarters bolded. (You may see a few firms with no bolded location. This means that these are self-proclaimed decentralized firms without official headquarters.)

Major Departments/Practices: Practice areas that employ a significant portion of the firm's headquarters' attorneys as reported by the firms.

Pay: The firm's pay at its headquarters. Pay at other offices is given when available. Pay is for 2000 except where noted.

Notable Perks: A listing of perks and benefits outside the norm. (For example, we do not list health care, as every firm we surveyed offers health care plans.)

Uppers and Downers: Good points and bad points of the firm, as gleaned from associate interviews and surveys. Uppers and downers are the impressionistic perceptions of insiders and are not based on statistics.

Key Competitors: A firm's competition in the legal community in both recruiting and business, according to the firm's associates.

Employment Contact: The person that the firm identifies as the primary contact in the firm's main office to receive resumes or to answer questions about the recruitment process.

THE STATS

No. of attorneys: The total number of attorneys at a firm in all offices as of May 2000.

No. of offices: The firm's total number of offices worldwide.

Summer associate offers, 1999: The number of second-year law students offered full-time associate positions at the firm's headquarters in 1999. In some cases, we report firm-wide figures.

Chairman, Managing Partner, etc.: The name and title of the leader of the firm. Occasionally, more than one name may be given.

THE QUALITY OF LIFE METERS

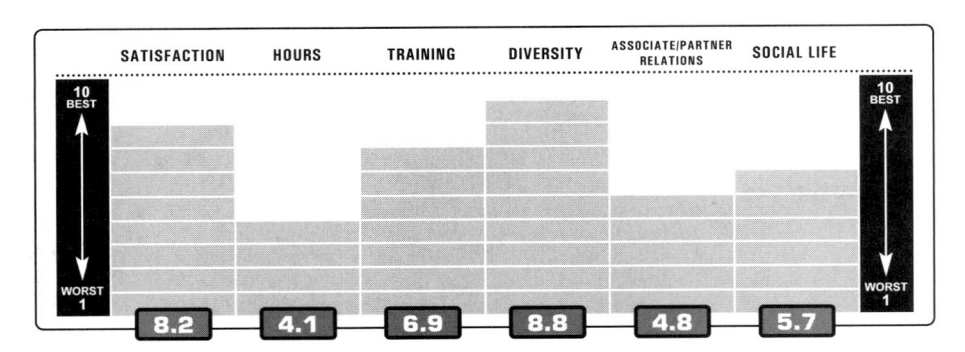

SATISFACTION	HOURS	TRAINING	DIVERSITY	ASSOCIATE/PARTNER RELATIONS	SOCIAL LIFE
8.2	4.1	6.9	8.8	4.8	5.7

Our meters are based on our surveys of 4,880 law firm respondents. Associates surveyed were asked to rate their firm in a variety of categories (13 categories in all) on a 1 to 10 scale. The firm's score in each category is simply the average (mean) of the scores its associates gave in that area. We have highlighted the following categories for our meters:

Satisfaction: Associates rank their satisfaction with their firm on a scale from "unsatisfactory" to "entirely fulfilling."

Hours: Associates rank how they feel about their hours on a scale from "overwhelming" to "very livable." Please note the hours score is based on the subjective perceptions of associates, not on the actual hours they work.

Training: Associates rank the level of training their firm provides.

Diversity: Associates rank their considerations of all diversity issues, including the situations of minority group members, gays and lesbians, and women.

Associate/Partner Relations: Associates rank how well they feel they're treated and mentored by the partners at their firms.

Social Life: Associates rank the social interaction between attorneys at the firm.

If you see a star above a certain meter score, you'll know that the firm was one of the top 3 scorers in the category.

It is important to note that firms that did not distribute surveys were not rated by our quality of life meters. The five firms in our Top 50 that did not distribute surveys are: Gunderson Dettmer Stough Villeneuve Franklin & Hachigian; Jones, Day, Reavis & Pogue; Venture Law Group; Vinson & Elkins; and Wachtell, Lipton Rosen & Katz.

THE PROFILES

Each of our profiles is broken up into three sections: The Scoop, Getting Hired, and Our Survey Says.

The Scoop: The firm's history, clients, recent deals, recent firm developments, and other points of interests.

Getting Hired: Qualifications the firm looks for in new associates, tips on getting hired, and other notable aspects of the hiring process.

Our Survey Says: Actual quotes from surveys and interviews with current and former associates of the firm on topics such as the firm's assignment system, feedback, partnership prospects, levels of responsibility, summer associate program, culture, hours, pay, training, and other matters.

Beyond the Top 50

We have also included additional firm profiles in the Nearly and Notables section. We chose these firms for a variety of reasons, including strong quality of life scores and regional prominence.

Best of the Rest

We've also included basic information on other law firms that did not make our list this year.

careers.martindale.com

The Only Legal Career Center That Was 130 Years in the Making

For over 130 years, Martindale-Hubbell® has been the provider of trusted and reliable information about the legal community.

Introducing a new service to help legal employers and candidates like you find each other. It's the *Legal Career Center* at **careers.martindale.com**.

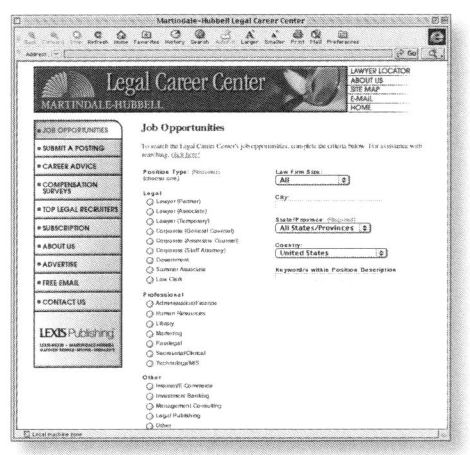

This important site harnesses the power of **martindale.com**, which reaches qualified candidates, legal recruiters, lawyers, corporate counsel and others who make it one of the most frequently visited sites on the Web now averaging two million searches monthly.

An Efficient, Effective Way to Reach Qualified Legal Candidates

- Reach a highly qualified online community comprised of lawyers and legal professionals.
- Enhance your legal-recruiting strategy online in a highly cost-effective way.

A Great Tool for Legal Candidates

- Search for legal jobs, get career advice and insight and use **martindale.com** to conduct additional research on prospective law firm and corporate law department employers.
- Rely on the **Legal Career Center** for the focus on legal careers you won't find anywhere else.

Visit the site today at **careers.martindale.com** or call **1-800-526-4902, ext. 6952** for information.

If you're a Martindale-Hubbell subscriber you'll get **3 FREE job postings**—a $450 value!

careers.martindale.com
Your Source for Qualified Candidates & Legal Careers

MARTINDALE-HUBBELL®
A Member of LEXIS Publishing™

LEXIS, NEXIS, SHEPARD'S and Martindale-Hubbell are registered trademarks, and LEXIS Publishing and MICHIE are trademarks of Reed Elsevier Properties Inc., used under license. Matthew Bender is a registered trademark of Matthew Bender Properties Inc.
© 2000 Martindale-Hubbell. All rights reserved.

LEXIS Publishing™
LEXIS-NEXIS • MARTINDALE-HUBBELL
MATTHEW BENDER • MICHIE • SHEPARD'S

THE VAULT.COM PRESTIGE RANKINGS

THE RANKING METHODOLOGY

Top 50

Getting 4,880 lawyers to rate the top 50 law firms — and tabulating and analyzing the ensuing surveys — was a long and painstaking process. For 2000 we started with the 100 most renowned law firms. Vault.com compiled this initial list by reviewing the feedback we received from previous surveys, consulting our previous Top 50 lists, and talking to lawyers in the field.

We asked these 100 law firms to distribute a written survey to their associates. In total 4,880 attorneys from 77 law firms around the country returned surveys to Vault.com. We surveyed associates at offices in New York, Los Angeles, Chicago, Boston, Philadelphia, Houston, Washington, DC, and San Francisco among other locations (including international locations). The written survey asked attorneys to score each of the 100 law firms on a scale of 1 to 10 based on its prestige. Associates were asked to ignore any firm with which they were unfamiliar.

Vault.com collected all surveys and averaged the score for each firm (excluding the attorneys' ratings of their own firms). The firms were then ranked in order, starting with the highest average prestige score as No. 1 (Cravath for the third year in a row) on down to determine the Vault.com Top 50.

We understand that there are problems inherent in any prestige ranking. However, we found that the rankings typically paralleled conventional wisdom — with a few interesting exceptions. Remember that in the Top 50, Vault.com is not assessing firms by profit, size, lifestyle, or quality — we are ranking the most prestigious law firms based on the perceptions of currently practicing lawyers at peer firms.

The more things change, the more they stay the same, right? Well, yes — and no. It's true that our top eight firms have remained static for the past three years. As in previous years, the top eight firms are all headquartered in New York City. But for the real story, look just a little bit further down the list. California firms make an increasingly strong showing, with Latham & Watkins holding steady at No. 9, and Palo Alto VC wunderkind Wilson Sonsini Goodrich & Rosati breaking into the top 10 for the first time. Look just below the top 10, and you'll detect the upwards surge of firms like Williams & Connolly and Brobeck, Phleger and Harrison. At the same time, other New York firms, such as Paul Weiss and Debevoise and Plimpton, have been pushed down in the ranks.

The Vault.com 50　　　　　　　　　2000

[The 50 most prestigious law firms]

2000 RANK	LAW FIRM	1999 RANK	1998 RANK	PRESTIGE SCORE	LARGEST OFFICE/ HEADQUARTERS	NUMBER OF ATTORNEYS
1	Cravath, Swaine & Moore	1	1	9.031	New York	408
2	Wachtell, Lipton, Rosen & Katz	2	2	9.006	New York	165
3	Sullivan & Cromwell	3	3	8.655	New York	523
4	Davis Polk & Wardwell	4	4	8.597	New York	580
5	Skadden, Arps, Slate, Meagher & Flom	5	5	8.326	New York	1,424
6	Simpson Thacher & Bartlett	6	6	8.047	New York	571
7	Cleary, Gottlieb, Steen & Hamilton	7	7	7.889	New York	618
8	Shearman & Sterling	8	8	7.690	New York	867
9	Latham & Watkins	9	10	7.684	Los Angeles	1,001
10	Wilson Sonsini Goodrich & Rosati	15	12	7.611	Palo Alto	613
11	Kirkland & Ellis	11	15 (tie)	7.484	Chicago	691
12	Williams & Connolly	16	22	7.389	Washington, DC	175
13	Weil, Gotshal & Manges	10	17	7.344	New York	793
14	Covington & Burling	14	9	7.343	Washington, DC	422
15	Paul, Weiss, Rifkind, Wharton & Garrison	13	11	7.244	New York	437
16	Sidley & Austin	20 (tie)	15 (tie)	7.178	Chicago	862
17	Gibson, Dunn & Crutcher	19	18	7.087	Los Angeles	749
18	Debevoise & Plimpton	12	13	6.994	New York	419
19	O'Melveny & Myers	17	19	6.983	Los Angeles	752
20	White & Case	18	20	6.978	New York	1,000+
21	Arnold & Porter	20 (tie)	14	6.905	Washington, DC	540
22	Morrison & Foerster	25	29	6.852	San Francisco	844
23	Wilmer, Cutler & Pickering	23	NR	6.837	Washington, DC	344
24	Brobeck, Phleger & Harrison	NR	48	6.761	San Francisco	750
25	Mayer, Brown & Platt	26	27	6.740	Chicago	931

NR = Not Ranked　　*Source: Vault.com 2000 Associate Survey*

Vault.com Guide to the Top 50 Law Firms • 3rd Edition

The Vault.com Prestige Rankings

2000 RANK	LAW FIRM	1999 RANK	1998 RANK	PRESTIGE SCORE	LARGEST OFFICE/ HEADQUARTERS	NUMBER OF ATTORNEYS
26	Milbank, Tweed, Hadley & McCloy	22	23	6.682	New York	417
27	Hale and Dorr	31	31 (tie)	6.653	Boston	407
28	Ropes & Gray	30	24 (tie)	6.574	Boston	392
29	Fried, Frank, Harris, Shriver & Jacobson	27	24 (tie)	6.572	New York	491
30	Jones, Day, Reavis & Pogue	24	30	6.565	Cleveland	1,289
31	Dewey Ballantine	28	28	6.522	New York	486
32	Cooley Godward	NR	NR	6.521	Palo Alto	553
33	Clifford Chance Rogers & Wells	46	46	6.500	New York (US)	2,531
34	Morgan, Lewis & Bockius	34	38	6.460	Philadelphia	1,010
35	King & Spalding	39	37	6.398	Atlanta	558
36	Willkie Farr & Gallagher	29	26	6.395	New York	424
37	Venture Law Group	NR	NR	6.359	Menlo Park	97
38	Gunderson Dettmer Stough Villeneuve...*	NR	NR	6.344	Menlo Park	110
39	Hogan & Hartson	42	NR	6.232	Washington, DC	737
40	Munger, Tolles & Olson	NR	21	6.229	Los Angeles	133
41	Paul, Hastings, Janofsky & Walker	35	35	6.213	Los Angeles	729
42	Orrick, Herrington & Sutcliffe	33	31 (tie)	6.179	San Francisco	540
43	Akin Gump Strauss Hauer & Feld	37	NR	6.096	Dallas/DC	908
44	Winston & Strawn	40	42	6.086	Chicago	725
45	Baker & McKenzie	36	41	6.037	Chicago	2,700
46	Vinson & Elkins	NR	40	6.016	Houston	658
47	Cadwalader, Wickersham & Taft	41	NR	5.995	New York	411
48	Proskauer Rose	43	43	5.986	New York	501
49	Baker Botts	44	NR	5.964	Houston	546
50	Cahill Gordon & Reindel	38	34	5.947	New York	219

*Gunderson Dettmer Stough Villeneuve Franklin & Hachigian

Visit Vault.com for the latest news, salary discussion, and insider messages on every law firm in this book — and hundreds more.

REGIONAL RANKINGS

This year Vault.com expanded its regional rankings. We took only the votes from firms in each regional area to determine the most prestigious regional firms. Firms only qualified for a regional listing if their headquarters or their largest office was located in that area. No firms were entered into candidacy for more than one regional ranking. Associates in Atlanta, Boston, Chicago, Philadelphia, Southern California, Texas and Washington were able to vote for some additional firms that were not candidates for the national Top 50 rankings.

In most cases, firms that ranked high locally also made the Vault.com Top 50 list, though the order of the firms in the regional ranking differs in some interesting ways from the order of the firms in the Top 50.

New York

RANK	FIRM	SCORE
1	Wachtell, Lipton, Rosen & Katz	9.303
2	Cravath, Swaine & Moore	9.142
3	Davis Polk & Wardwell	8.850
4	Sullivan & Cromwell	8.775
5	Simpson Thacher & Barlett	8.291
6	Cleary, Gottlieb, Steen & Hamilton	8.197
7	Skadden, Arps, Slate, Meagher & Flom	7.965
8	Shearman & Sterling	7.743
9	Paul, Weiss, Rifkind, Wharton & Garrison	7.386
10	Weil, Gotshal & Manges	7.299

Source: Vault.com 2000 Associate Survey

REGIONAL RANKINGS (cont'd)

Southern California

RANK	FIRM	SCORE
1	Latham & Watkins	8.050
2	Gibson, Dunn & Crutcher	7.526
3	O'Melveny & Myers	7.523
4	Munger, Tolles & Olson	7.236
5	Irell & Manella	6.871
6	Paul, Hastings, Janofsky & Walker	6.153
7	Gray Cary Ware & Freidenrich	5.560
8	Sheppard, Mullin, Richter & Hampton	5.379
9	Manatt, Phelps & Phillips	5.098
10	Loeb & Loeb	4.982

Source: Vault.com 2000 Associate Survey

Northern California

RANK	FIRM	SCORE
1	Wilson Sonsini Goodrich & Rosati	7.801
2	Gunderson Dettmer Stough Villeneuve...	7.302
3	Venture Law Group	7.189
4	Cooley Godward	7.183
5	Brobeck, Phleger & Harrison	7.089
6	Morrison & Foerster	6.972
7	Orrick, Herrington & Sutcliffe	6.484
8	Fenwick & West	6.459
9	Heller Ehrman White & McAuliffe	6.138
10	Pillsbury Madison & Sutro	5.895

Source: Vault.com 2000 Associate Survey

REGIONAL RANKINGS (cont'd)

Texas

RANK	FIRM	SCORE
1	Vinson & Elkins	8.275
2	Baker Botts	7.913
3	Fulbright & Jaworski	7.001
4	Akin Gump Strauss Hauer & Feld	6.750
5	Bracewell & Patterson	5.951
6	Haynes & Boone	5.475
7	Jenkens & Gilchrist	4.922
8	Thompson & Knight	4.857
9	Winstead Sechrest & Minick	4.677
10	Gardere & Wynne	4.574

Source: Vault.com 2000 Associate Survey

Philadelphia

RANK	FIRM	SCORE
1	Morgan, Lewis & Bockius	8.476
2	Dechert Price & Rhoads	8.270
3	Ballard Spahr Andrews & Ingersoll	7.410
4	Pepper Hamilton	7.110
5	Drinker Biddle & Reath	6.644
6	Wolf, Block, Schorr and Solis-Cohen	6.036
7	Blank Rome Comisky & McCauley	5.881
8	Duane, Morris & Heckscher	5.839
9	Saul, Ewing, Remick & Saul	5.441
10	Montgomery, McCracken, Walker & Rhoads	5.439

Source: Vault.com 2000 Associate Survey

REGIONAL RANKINGS (cont'd)

Boston

RANK	FIRM	SCORE
1	Ropes & Gray	8.512
2	Hale and Dorr	8.458
3	Goodwin, Procter & Hoar	7.339
4	Testa, Hurwitz & Thibeault	7.327
5	Foley, Hoag & Eliot	6.314
6	Mintz, Levin, Cohn, Ferris, Glovsky and Popeo	6.256
7	Bingham Dana	5.809
8	Palmer & Dodge	5.566
9	Choate, Hall & Stewart	5.526
10	Fish & Richardson	5.270

Source: Vault.com 2000 Associate Survey

Washington DC

RANK	FIRM	SCORE
1	Williams & Connolly	8.720
2	Covington & Burling	8.351
3	Wilmer, Cutler & Pickering	8.216
4	Arnold & Porter	7.903
5	Hogan & Hartson	7.569
6	Steptoe & Johnson	5.944
7	Shaw, Pittman, Potts & Trowbridge	5.806
8	Howrey Simon Arnold & White	5.630
9	Arent Fox Kintner Plotkin & Kahn	5.249
10	Swidler Berlin Shereff Friedman	5.224

Source: Vault.com 2000 Associate Survey

REGIONAL RANKINGS (cont'd)

Chicago

RANK	FIRM	SCORE
1	Kirkland & Ellis	8.501
2	Sidley & Austin	8.130
3	Mayer, Brown & Platt	7.946
4	Winston & Strawn	7.175
5	McDermott, Will & Emery	6.697
6	Jenner & Block	6.629
7	Baker & McKenzie	6.193
8	Katten Muchin & Zavis	6.182
9	Sonnenschein Nath & Rosenthal	6.104
10	Schiff Hardin & Waite	5.413

Source: Vault.com 2000 Associate Survey

Atlanta

RANK	FIRM	SCORE
1	King & Spalding	7.922
2	Alston & Bird	7.201
3	Kilpatrick Stockton	6.363
4	Troutman Sanders	6.065
5	Long Aldridge & Norman	5.966

Source: Vault.com 2000 Associate Survey

DEPARTMENTAL RANKINGS

Associates were allowed to vote for up to three firms as the best in each practice area. We indicate the top firms in each area, as well as the total percentage of votes cast in favor of the firm. (Each associate surveyed chose three firms; the maximum percentage of votes per firm is 33.3 percent.)

Litigation

RANK	FIRM	% OF VOTES
1	Cravath, Swaine & Moore	9.6
2	Williams & Connolly	7.2
3	Paul, Weiss, Rifkind, Wharton & Garrison	6.6
4	Kirkland & Ellis	5.2
5	Skadden, Arps, Slate, Meagher & Flom	3.5
6	Sullivan & Cromwell	3.2
7	Covington & Burling	3.1
8	Wachtell, Lipton, Rosen & Katz	3.0
9	Davis Polk & Wardwell	2.9
10	Jenner & Block	2.5

Source: Vault.com 2000 Associate Survey

DEPARTMENTAL RANKINGS (cont'd)

Corporate

RANK	FIRM	% OF VOTES
1	Cravath, Swaine & Moore	13.3
2	Skadden, Arps, Slate, Meagher & Flom	12.0
3	Wachtell, Lipton, Rosen & Katz	10.5
4	Sullivan & Cromwell	7.8
5	Davis Polk & Wardwell	6.4
6	Wilson Sonsini Goodrich & Rosati	5.4
7	Simpson Thacher & Bartlett	2.8
8	Latham & Watkins	2.4
9	Cleary, Gottlieb, Steen & Hamilton	2.3
10	Shearman & Sterling	1.9

Source: Vault.com 2000 Associate Survey

Real Estate

RANK	FIRM	% OF VOTES
1	Skadden, Arps, Slate, Meagher & Flom	3.5
2	Fried, Frank, Harris, Shriver & Jacobson	2.8
3 (tie)	Stroock & Stroock & Lavan	2.7
3 (tie)	Shearman & Sterling	2.7
4	Cadwalader, Wickersham & Taft	2.5
5	Paul, Hastings, Janofsky & Walker	2.4

Source: Vault.com 2000 Associate Survey

DEPARTMENTAL RANKINGS (cont'd)

Securities Offerings/Corporate Finance

RANK	FIRM	% OF VOTES
1	Wilson Sonsini Goodrich & Rosati	10.0
2	Sullivan & Cromwell	8.1
3	Skadden, Arps, Slate, Meagher & Flom	7.2
4	Davis Polk & Wardwell	6.9
5	Cravath, Swaine & Moore	6.5

Source: Vault.com 2000 Associate Survey

Intellectual Property

RANK	FIRM	% OF VOTES
1	Fish & Neave	14.9
2	Wilson Sonsini Goodrich & Rosati	12.0
3	Brobeck, Phleger & Harrison	7.5
4	Cooley Godward	3.8
5	Fenwick & West	3.3

Source: Vault.com 2000 Associate Survey

M & A

RANK	FIRM	% OF VOTES
1	Wachtell, Lipton, Rosen & Katz	19.3
2	Skadden, Arps, Slate, Meagher & Flom	18.0
3	Cravath, Swaine & Moore	11.2
4	Sullivan & Cromwell	4.7
5	Simpson Thacher & Bartlett	4.6

Source: Vault.com 2000 Associate Survey

DEPARTMENTAL RANKINGS (cont'd)

Tax

RANK	FIRM	% OF VOTES
1 (tie)	Cleary, Gottlieb, Steen & Hamilton	6.1
1 (tie)	Cravath, Swaine & Moore	6.1
2	Skadden, Arps, Slate, Meagher & Flom	5.2
3	Davis Polk & Wardwell	4.1
4	Sullivan & Cromwell	4.0
5	Baker & McKenzie	2.9

Source: Vault.com 2000 Associate Survey

Bankruptcy

RANK	FIRM	% OF VOTES
1	Weil, Gotshal & Manges	22.6
2	Wachtell, Lipton, Rosen & Katz	7.7
3	Skadden, Arps, Slate Meagher & Flom	4.5
4	Willkie Farr & Gallagher	2.0
5	Davis Polk & Wardwell	1.9

Source: Vault.com 2000 Associate Survey

Connected Creative Intuitive

"Pillsbury - elegant solutions to difficult problems"

"Resources to succeed"

"I work for a winning team"

"Sophisticated, diverse...that's my work at Pillsbury"

"Top-notch clients"

"...Algorithms to zoom lens systems, and everything in between"

Pillsbury Madison & Sutro LLP

one FIRM
many opportunities

Our attorneys are online at
http://www.pillsburylaw.com

QUALITY OF LIFE RANKINGS

Quality of Life Rankings

Methodology

This year 78 law firms participated in our associate survey process. Associates were asked to rate their firm on a 1 to 10 scale for each of 13 quality of life categories. The firm's score in each category is simply the average of the scores its associates gave in that area.

It is important to note that firms that did not distribute surveys were ineligible to appear in these rankings. The five firms in our Top 50 that did not distribute surveys are: Gunderson Dettmer Stough Villeneuve Franklin & Hachigian; Jones, Day, Reavis & Pogue; Venture Law Group; Vinson & Elkins; and Wachtell, Lipton, Rosen & Katz.

The Best 20 Firms to Work For

We feature our Top 50 firms ranked in terms of prestige. However, the question rages — which are the best firms to work for?

To determine our Best 20 firms, we analyzed the 100 firms that were candidates for the Top 50 using a new formula that weighed the most relevant categories for an overall quality of life ranking. Each firm's overall score was calculated using the following formula:

- 40 percent satisfaction
- 10 percent hours
- 10 percent partner/associate relations
- 10 percent training
- 5 percent social life
- 5 percent diversity (the average of the firm's scores for three diversity categories: diversity with respect to minorities, women, and gays & lesbians)
- 5 percent offices
- 5 percent support services
- 5 percent pay
- 5 percent retention

Like our Top 50 rankings, our Best 20 is meant to be the subjective opinion of associates. By its nature, the list is based on the perceptions of insiders. For some context, compare how associates rank their firms in terms of hours with the average amount of hours the associates report working.

BEST 20 LAW FIRMS TO WORK FOR

RANK	FIRM	SCORE	LARGEST OFFICE/ HEADQUARTERS
1	Cooley Godward	8.147	Palo Alto
2	Jenner & Block	8.079	Chicago
3	Winston & Strawn	7.984	Chicago
4	Morrison & Foerster	7.962	San Francisco
5	Gray Cary Ware & Freidenrich	7.853	Palo Alto
6	Covington & Burling	7.784	Washington, DC
7	Choate, Hall & Stewart	7.654	Boston
8	Arnold & Porter	7.614	Washington, DC
9	Hogan & Hartson	7.591	Washington, DC
10	Preston Gates & Ellis	7.569	Seattle
11	Alston & Bird	7.544	Atlanta
12	Brobeck, Phleger & Harrison	7.515	San Francisco
13	Baker Botts	7.494	Houston
14	Wilson Sonsini Goodrich & Rosati	7.474	Palo Alto
15	Perkins Coie	7.473	Seattle
16	Kirkland & Ellis	7.459	Chicago
17	Irell & Manella	7.449	Century City
18	Wilmer, Cutler & Pickering	7.445	Washington, DC
19	Ropes & Gray	7.438	Boston
20	Davis Polk & Wardwell	7.381	New York

Source: Vault.com 2000 Associate Survey

Focus on the top three firms to work for

1. Cooley Godward

"Explosive" would probably be the best adjective to describe this Palo Alto firm, which rockets to No. 1 in our best 20 rankings this year. The firm has also been experiencing explosive growth, adding over 150 new lawyers in the past two years. Cooley Godward boasts a high-profile high-tech practice with such clients as Qualcomm and Sun Microsystems, as well as prestigious corporate and litigation departments, which may add to the associate satisfaction rate.

The firm ranks in the top 10 in six of our quality of life categories, including five rankings in the top five. How does the firm manage this feat? Besides maintaining an active and respectful social atmosphere and sponsoring outstanding training programs, the firm demonstrates a "commitment to associate contentment." Having a "management committee that does the right thing most every time" doesn't hurt. One associate summarizes, "I am confident that there is no law firm in which I would rather work than Cooley."

Cooley partner Bob Jones tells Vault.com, "I have always thought that the best reasons to be in private practice, and to stay in private practice, are because you really, truly have a fun and interesting job and enjoy the people you work with. Goodness knows there are easier ways to make a living. So I am delighted to learn that so many of the associates at Cooley are having as good a time as I am. That's what keeps me here and I hope will keep them here as well."

2. Jenner & Block

According to its own associates, Jenner & Block is nearly perfect in every way. New to Vault.com's quality of life rankings, Jenner associates heap praise on their firm, calling it "truly an outstanding place to work." If there is any one key to Jenner's success, say insiders, it is the "exceptional" associates. Asked to describe the best aspect of working at Jenner & Block, associates point to "the people" in nearly automatic fashion, calling them "fabulous," "smart," "great," "talented," and "absolutely tremendous." Jenner & Block did not earn its place in the top three for its employees alone — associates rave about virtually every aspect of their workplace. High marks were given for "very satisfying," "complex and exciting" legal work, pay at the "the top of the market" with potential for "extraordinary bonuses," and "excellent partnership prospects."

Theodore Tetzlaff, co-chairman of the firm, tells Vault.com: "A law firm should be a place where dedicated professionals look forward to coming to work each day to confront the many intellectual challenges presented by practicing law. Jenner is that kind of place. Beyond the professional rewards of practicing law here, Jenner has a community of lawyers and staff second to none. Life-long friendships formed between partners, associates, and staff make each of us look forward to each day."

3. Winston & Strawn

Winston & Strawn moves up one slot from last year to No. 3 in the race to be the Best 20. The firm had strong showings in the social life, offices, support services, and retention categories. Of course, no firm can make it as one of the Best 20 without satisfied attorneys. And Winston & Strawn has them aplenty. "This is the best firm to work at. The partners are respectful, the work is high-quality, and the associates make the work entertaining," raves one lawyer. Another Winston & Strawn attorney explains to Vault.com, "I chose Winston because I thought the people were great and the work cutting-edge."

Indeed, Winston & Strawn associates are particularly enthusiastic about their colleagues. "There is a lot of camaraderie among associates. Also, many partners will look out for you and take you under their wing."

The partners agree that the combination of personable lawyers and quality work contributes to the firm's high ranking. James M. Neis, the firm's managing partner, tells Vault.com, "We're especially pleased to be thought of as one of the best firms to work for. It's important both to have an interesting practice and to like the people with whom you work."

SATISFACTION

Average score = 7.49

RANK	FIRM	SCORE
1	Cooley Godward	8.72
2	Morrison & Foerster	8.59
3	Fish & Richardson	8.49
4	Gray Cary Ware & Freidenrich	8.45
5	Jenner & Block	8.41
6	Covington & Burling	8.32
7	Preston Gates & Ellis	8.17
8	Winston & Strawn	8.13
9	Hogan & Hartson	8.09
10	Brobeck, Phleger & Harrison	8.02

Source: Vault.com 2000 Associate Survey

Focus on the top three in satisfaction

1. Cooley Godward

Called "almost too good to be true" by those who work there, Cooley Godward makes a shocking leap in our satisfaction poll this year, cracking our top three. "Confident that there is no law firm in which [they] would rather work" and unwilling to "consider leaving to go to another firm," Cooley associates are some of the happiest we polled. Associates love their firm's "challenging work" and they give kudos to the "best people" in the industry.

Partner Mark Tanoury comments, "I am delighted that the Vault.com survey reflects what I have been saying for the past 18 years about Cooley — that there is no better place for young lawyers to develop their legal skills. Cooley offers the chance to work with cutting-edge companies in a teamwork oriented environment."

2. Morrison & Foerster

There's got to be more than San Francisco sunshine to explain MoFo's satisfied barristers. Many associates say the key is co-workers: "I can honestly say that I cannot imagine working anywhere else. I don't really like the big firm politics, but find the people I work with to be the best," insists one lawyer. High-quality work doesn't hurt either, of course. "The cases I've gotten on so far have been interesting and somewhat complex," says another attorney. "I have heard from other associates that we don't always get the most complex, large cases because of the relatively small size of our litigation group here, but I haven't seen that for myself yet."

3. Fish & Richardson

They may not be at Skadden or Cravath, but Fish & Richardson attorneys declare that they are happier than most of their big shot brethren. Associates at Fish say they feel little temptation to seek out a dot com or in-house position. "I have no desire to check out other positions, despite the numerous headhunter calls each week," asserts a San Diego second-year. A first-year colleague in Boston enthuses, "I get to do what I always wanted to do, every day. I really enjoy the working environment and the people. This is presently my ideal job."

HOURS

Average score = 5.58

RANK	FIRM	SCORE
1	Jenner & Block	6.99
2	Winthrop, Stimson, Putnam & Roberts	6.86
3	Munger, Tolles & Olson	6.84
4	Fish & Richardson	6.66
5	Howrey Simon Arnold & White	6.64
6 (tie)	Ballard Spahr Andrews & Ingersoll	6.63
6 (tie)	Fish & Neave	6.63
7	Choate, Hall & Stewart	6.56
8	Kaye, Scholer, Fierman, Hays & Handler	6.53
9	Hogan & Hartson	6.49
10	LeBoeuf, Lamb, Greene & MacRae	6.48

Source: Vault.com 2000 Associate Survey

Focus on the top three in length of hours

1. Jenner & Block

Associates at Chicago's Jenner & Block rate the firm highly for hours that "aren't overly demanding" and associates who are "allowed to work [their] hours when [they] want." While some may balk that Jenner employs a minimum billable hours assignment, associates are happy to point out that it "has always been seen as both a floor and a ceiling," and even associates who bill their minimum "routinely make partner."

According to Theodore R. Tetzlaff, co-chairman of the firm: "Jenner has always believed that the quality of work, not the quantity, is the hallmark of an excellent professional. For this reason, and because the firm believes that an attorney needs a lifestyle that is balanced between work, family, and community, the firm makes sure attorneys are being professionally challenged while having ample time to devote to outside endeavors. Jenner has never been, and never will be, one of the so-called 'sweatshops.'"

2. Winthrop, Stimson, Putnam & Roberts

Can this really be a New York firm? Associates at competitor firms, read this and weep: "Hours at Winthrop definitely permit a life outside of work," crows a second-year IP attorney. A first-year in trusts and estates insists, "When I work late or on weekends, it's because I choose to. There is little to no face time here as long as you get the work done — that's all the firm cares about." The firm is "the antithesis of sweatshop" but "you will need to learn how to say no to work," explains another associate.

3. Munger, Tolles & Olson

Despite high-pressure workloads and demanding clients, Munger associates still insist they are not overworked. Manageable, if unpredictable, schedules put the firm in the top three for this quality of life ranking. "Hours are up and down. Sometimes it is very demanding, other times it is very reasonable," assesses a fourth-year litigator. "You have a lot of control over your caseload, but any case can explode."

According to Marc Becker, co-chairman of the recruiting committee, Munger "recognizes that its ability to attract and retain the highest quality lawyers depends on its continued flexibility with respect to work schedules. Because our compensation structure does not incorporate any minimum hours requirements, we have lawyers who choose to work fewer hours than average to accommodate family and other commitments and we also have lawyers who have chosen to work part-time. These policies supplement the firm's generous maternity and paternity policies and its sabbatical program."

We asked associates: How many hours, on average, do you work per week? We averaged their answers. Note that this is not an "official" count, but how much associates feel they work in the average week.

Average hours as reported by associates

FIRM	HRS	FIRM	HRS
Akin Gump Strauss Hauer & Feld	55.3	Kirkland & Ellis	55.5
Allen & Overy	55.0	Latham & Watkins	54.4
Alston & Bird	56.3	LeBoeuf, Lamb, Greene & MacRae	46.5
Arent Fox Kinter Plotkin & Kahn	51.2	Mayer, Brown & Platt	54.5
Arnold & Porter	48.2	McDermott, Will & Emery	52.2
Baker Botts	51.6	Milbank, Tweed, Hadley & McCloy	53.5
Baker & McKenzie	52.6	Mintz, Levin, Cohn, Ferris, Glovsky and Popeo	56.9
Ballard Spahr Andrews & Ingersoll	53.1	Morgan, Lewis & Bockius	55.7
Brobeck, Phleger & Harrison	56.0	Morrison & Foerster	56.0
Cadwalader, Wickersham & Taft	52.5	Munger, Tolles & Olson	50.0
Cahill Gordon & Reindel	58.0	O'Melveny & Myers	54.5
Chadbourne & Parke	52.5	Orrick, Herrington & Sutcliffe	56.1
Choate, Hall & Stewart	53.0	Paul, Hastings, Janofsky & Walker	56.9
Cleary, Gottlieb, Steen & Hamilton	62.4	Paul, Weiss, Rifkind, Wharton & Garrison	59.1
Clifford Chance Rogers & Wells	53.4	Pepper Hamilton	52.4
Cooley Godward	53.8	Perkins Coie	50.8
Covington & Burling	56.3	Pillsbury Madison & Sutro	58.4
Cravath, Swaine & Moore	61.4	Piper Marbury Rudnick & Wolfe	56.3
Davis Polk & Wardwell	55.1	Preston Gates & Ellis	51.6
Debevoise & Plimpton	57.2	Proskauer Rose	55.8
Dechert Price & Rhoads	53.5	Ropes & Gray	56.7
Dewey Ballantine	58.5	Schulte, Roth & Zabel	52.8
Fenwick & West	58.0	Shaw, Pittman, Potts & Trowbridge	53.3
Fish & Neave	50.8	Shearman & Sterling	58.9
Fish & Richardson	53.0	Sidley & Austin	54.9
Foley & Lardner	51.0	Simpson Thacher & Bartlett	57.4
Fried, Frank, Harris, Shriver & Jacobson	57.8	Skadden, Arps, Slate, Meagher & Flom	56.8
Fulbright & Jaworski	54.5	Squire, Sanders & Dempsey	56.6
Gibson, Dunn & Crutcher	53.0	Stroock & Stroock & Lavan	57.2
Gray Cary Ware & Freidenrich	54.1	Sullivan & Cromwell	66.5
Hale and Dorr	59.4	Thelen Reid & Priest	53.3
Hogan & Hartson	50.8	Weil, Gotshal & Manges	54.5
Howrey Simon Arnold & White	51.7	White & Case	56.3
Hunton & Williams	53.7	Williams & Connolly	53.8
Irell & Manella	54.6	Willkie Farr & Gallagher	51.3
Jenner & Block	51.0	Wilmer, Cutler & Pickering	53.8
Kaye, Scholer, Fierman, Hays & Handler	48.9	Wilson Sonsini Goodrich & Rosati	52.0
Kelley Drye & Warren	57.2	Winston & Strawn	52.6
King & Spalding	55.9	Winthrop, Stimson, Putnam & Roberts	56.9

Source: Vault.com 2000 Associate Survey

PAY

> Average score = 8.18
>
> | RANK | FIRM | SCORE |
> |---|---|---|
> | 1 | Brobeck, Phleger & Harrison | 9.49 |
> | 2 | Cooley Godward | 9.43 |
> | 3 | Gray Cary Ware & Freidenrich | 9.31 |
> | 4 | Gibson, Dunn & Crutcher | 9.20 |
> | 5 | Kirkland & Ellis | 9.18 |
> | 6 | Hogan & Hartson | 9.16 |
> | 7 | Hale and Dorr | 9.14 |
> | 8 | Arnold & Porter | 9.08 |
> | 9 | Covington & Burling | 9.08 |
> | 10 (tie) | Latham & Watkins | 9.06 |
> | 10 (tie) | Winston & Strawn | 9.06 |
>
> Source: Vault.com 2000 Associate Survey

Focus on the top three in pay

1. Brobeck, Phleger & Harrison

San Francisco's Brobeck, Phleger & Harrison ranks first in regard to associate pay. Why, if other firms pay similar salaries to Brobeck, does its associates rank it higher than others? Firm Managing Partner James E. Burns, Jr. attributes his firm's high rankings to fairness and predictability.

"We thought it would be unfair and divisive to give some offices the raises while denying them to others," says Burns. "Our associates appreciated this sense of fairness, and our action led the market in the many regions in which we have offices, and caused many large firms to follow our lead or be left behind. Moreover, our new salary schedule includes generous bonuses that are to be paid on the basis of clear, objective criteria. Our associates and recruits who have come to us appreciate the predictability and credibility of our compensation package."

But there's more. Burns continues, "We also have many attractive benefits that other firms can't or won't offer, such as an associate venture fund, which invests in our clients for the benefit of our associates, and a home mortgage assistance program that enables our associates to purchase homes in some of the most overheated markets in the country. Taken as a whole, our compensation package is unbeatable and we have demonstrated that we intend to lead the market."

2. Cooley Godward

Cooley's salary structure seems pretty normal for Silicon Valley — what sets this firm apart from the crowd? Associates claim that Cooley was one of the first Bay Area firms to follow Gunderson Dettmer's pay raises in January 2000. Moreover, a simple compensation structure, "investment funds which offer additional bonus opportunities," and "spot bonuses which are sometimes given in particularly busy times or for exceptionally hard work or strong performance on a deal" are also cited as extra pay perks.

Partner Mark Pitchford tells Vault.com, "We have always felt that our compensation package more than competitively rewards the high caliber associates who are so critical to the firm's success in the markets in which we practice. The Vault.com survey validates both our perceptions and our approach."

3. Gray Cary Ware & Freidenrich

Gray Cary, another heavy-hitter in pay, is headquartered in Silicon Valley. Gray Cary managing partner Maggie Kavalaris reports that the firm's high ranking in this category is due to factors not entirely related to pay. "When you make a lot of money doing something you like, it seems like high pay. Our lawyers love what they do. I think the reason they perceive the firm to be so good is because of the interesting work and the interesting clients as well as the great people they have a chance to work with."

Base salary for firm HQ or main office* [as of July 2000]

LAW FIRM	1ST YEAR	2ND YEAR	3RD YEAR	4TH YEAR	5TH YEAR	6TH YEAR	7TH YEAR	SUMMER (WEEKLY)
Akin Gump Strauss Hauer & Feld	$125,000	$135,000	$150,000	$160,000	$170,000	$185,000		$2,400
Alston & Bird	100,000	105,000	110,000	115,000	122,000	130,000	137,000	1,750
Arent Fox Kinter Plotkin & Kahn	110,000							1,925
Arnold & Porter	125,000	135,000	145,000	155,000	165,000	175,000	185,000	2,400
Baker Botts	110,000	114,000	121,000	130,000	140,000	145,000	155,000	1,700
Baker & McKenzie	125,000	130,000	140,000	150,000	170,000	180,000	185,000	1,520
Ballard Spahr Andrews & Ingersoll	100,000							1,900
Bingham Dana	125,000	130,000	135,000	160,000	180,000	190,000	200,000	2,400
Blank Rome Cominsky & McCauley	105,000							2,000
Bracewell & Patterson	105,000	105k-115k	107k-120k	110k-125k	113k-135k	121k-145k	131k-155k	1,650
Brobeck, Phleger & Harrison	125,000	135,000	150,000	165,000	185,000	195,000	205,000	2,400
Cadwalader, Wickersham & Taft	125,000	135,000	150,000	170,000	190,000	200,000	205,000	2,400
Cahill Gordon & Reindel	125,000	135,000	150,000	170,000	190,000	210,000	220,000	2,400
Chadbourne & Parke	125,000	135,000	150,000	170,000	190,000	205,000	210,000	2,403
Choate, Hall & Stewart	125,000	135,000	145,000	155,000	170,000	175,000	175,000	1,730
Cleary, Gottlieb, Steen & Hamilton	125,000	135,000	150,000	170,000	190,000	205,000	220,000	2,404
Clifford Chance Rogers & Wells	125,000	135,000	150,000	165,000	185,000	195,000	205,000	2,404
Cooley Godward	125,000	135,000	150,000	165,000	185,000	195,000	205,000	2,400
Covington & Burling	125,000	135,000	150,000	155,000	165,000	175,000	185,000	2,400
Cravath, Swaine & Moore	125,000	135,000	150,000	170,000	190,000	205,000	220,000	2,500
Davis Polk & Wardwell	125,000	135,000	150,000	165,000	180,000	205,000		2,400
Debevoise & Plimpton	125,000	135,000	150,000	170,000	190,000	205,000	220,000	2,400
Dechert Price & Rhoads	105,000	110,000	117,500	125,000	132,500	140,000		2,000
Dewey Ballantine	125,000	135,000	150,000	170,000	190,000	200,000	205,000	2,403
Drinker Biddle & Reath	105,000							2,019
Duane, Morris & Heckscher	100,000							1,730
Fenwick & West	125,000	135,000	150,000	165,000	185,000	195,000	205,000	2,400
Fish & Neave	125,000	135,000	150,000	165,000	185,000	200,000	215,000	1,925
Fish & Richardson	125,000	135,000	140,000	150,000	160,000	165,000	175,000	2,400
Foley & Lardner	100,000	105,000	110,000	115,000	125,000	135,000	145,000	1,925
Foley, Hoag & Eliot	125,000	135,000	145,000	155,000	170,000	175,000	180,000	1,730
Fried, Frank, Harris, Shriver & Jacobson	125,000	135,000	150,000	168,000	190,000	205,000	215,000	2,400
Fulbright & Jaworski	110,000							1,700
Gardere & Wynne, L.L.P.	86,000							
Gibson, Dunn & Crutcher	125,000	135,000	150,000	165,000	185,000	195,000	205,000	2,404
Goodwin, Procter & Hoar	110,000							1,730

Source: Vault.com 2000 Associate Survey
* Does not include bonus

Base salary for firm HQ or main office* [continued]

LAW FIRM	1ST YEAR	2ND YEAR	3RD YEAR	4TH YEAR	5TH YEAR	6TH YEAR	7TH YEAR	SUMMER (WEEKLY)
Gray Cary Ware & Freidenrich	$125,000	$135,000	150,000	165,000	185,000	195,000	205,000	$2,200
Gunderson Dettmer Stough Villeneuve...	125,000	135,000	150,000	165,000	185,000	195,000	205,000	2,400
Hale and Dorr	125,000	135,000	145,000	155,000	170,000	175,000		2,400
Haynes and Boone	110,000	110,431	111,569	118,333	127,059	136,863	144,667	1,700
Heller Ehrman White & McAuliffe	125,000							2,400
Hogan & Hartson	125,000	135,000	150,000	165,000	180,000	190,000	200,000	2,400
Howrey Simon Arnold & White	125,000	135,000	145,000	155,000	165,000	175,000	185,000	2,000
Hunton & Williams	90,000							1,500
Irell & Manella	130,000	135,000	150,000					2,400
Jenkens & Gilchrist	110,000	114,000	121,000	130,000	140,000	145,000	155,000	1,650
Jenner & Block	125,000							2,400
Jones, Day, Reavis & Pogue	110,000							
Katten Muchin Zavis	125,000	135,000	150,000	165,000	175,000	185,000	195,000	2,400
Kaye, Scholer, Fierman, Hays & Handler	125,000	135,000	150,000					2,400
Kelley Drye & Warren	125,000	135,000	150,000	165,000	180,000	195,000	205,000	2,403
King & Spalding	100,000	105,000	110,000	115,000	122,500	130,000	137,500	1,750
Kirkland & Ellis	125,000	135,000	150,000	165,000	185,000	195,000		2,404
Latham & Watkins	125,000	135,000	150,000	165,000	185,000	195,000	205,000	2,400
LeBoeuf, Lamb, Greene & MacRae	125,000	135,000	150,000	170,000	190,000	200,000	205,000	2,403
Loeb & Loeb	125,000							1,700
Long Aldridge & Norman	100,000							1,500
Manatt, Phelps & Phillips	115,000	120,000	130,000	135,000	145,000	150,000		2,200
Mayer, Brown & Platt	125,000	135,000	150,000					2,400
McDermott, Will & Emery	125,000	135,000	145,000	155,000	170,000	175,000		2,400
Milbank, Tweed, Hadley & McCloy	125,000	135,000	150,000	165,000	190,000	205,000	215,000	2,047
Mintz, Levin, Cohn, Ferris, Glovsky...	125,000	135,000	145,000	155,000	170,000	175,000	180,000	2,400
Montgomery, McCracken, Walker & Rhoads	100,000							1,730
Morgan, Lewis & Bockius	110,000	110,000	110,000	120,000	120,000	130,000	130,000	1,900
Morrison & Foerster	125,000							2,400
Munger, Tolles & Olson	125,000	135,000	150,000	165,000	185,000	195,000		2,400
O'Melveny & Myers	125,000	135,000	150,000	165,000	185,000	195,000	205,000	2,400
Orrick, Herrington & Sutcliffe	125,000	135,000	150,000	165,000	185,000	195,000	205,000	
Palmer & Dodge								1,730
Paul, Hastings, Janofsky & Walker	125,000	135,000	150,000	165,000	185,000	195,000	205,000	2,400
Paul, Weiss, Rifkind, Wharton & Garrison	125,000	135,000	150,000	170,000	190,000	210,000	220,000	2,400
Pepper Hamilton	100,000							

Source: Vault.com 2000 Associate Survey
* Does not include bonus

Base salary for firm HQ or main office* [continued]

LAW FIRM	1ST YEAR	2ND YEAR	3RD YEAR	4TH YEAR	5TH YEAR	6TH YEAR	7TH YEAR	SUMMER (WEEKLY)
Pillsbury Madison & Sutro	$125,000	135,000	$150,000	$165,000	$180,000	$185,000	$185,000	$1,650
Piper Marbury Rudnick & Wolfe	125,000	$135,000	145,000	155,000	170,000	180,000	190,000	1,850
Proskauer Rose	125,000	135,000	150,000	165,000	185,000	195,000	205,000	2,404
Ropes & Gray	125,000	135,000	145,000					2,400
Saul, Ewing, Remick & Saul	100,000							1,925
Schiff Hardin & Waite	125,000	135,000	145,000					2,000
Schulte, Roth & Zabel	125,000	135,000	150,000	170,000	190,000	205,000	215,000	2,403
Shaw Pittman	125,000	135,000	145,000	155,000	175,000	185,000		2,000
Shearman & Sterling	125,000	135,000	150,000	165,000				2,538
Sheppard, Mullin, Richter & Hampton	110,000	120,000	130,000	140,000	145,000	150,000	150,000	2,000
Sidley & Austin	125,000	135,000	150,000	165,000				2,400
Simpson Thacher & Bartlett	125,000	135,000	150,000	170,000	190,000			2,404
Skadden, Arps, Slate, Meagher & Flom	140,000	150,000	170,000	185,000	200,000	212,000	220,000	2,400
Sonnenschein Nath & Rosenthal	125,000	135,000						1,865
Squire, Sanders & Dempsey	110,000							
Steptoe & Johnson	110,000	116,000	123,000	130,000	140,000	150,000	157,000	2,000
Stroock & Stroock & Lavan	125,000	135,000	150,000	170,000	190,000	200,000	205,000	2,400
Sullivan & Cromwell	125,000	135,000	150,000	170,000	190,000	205,000	220,000	2,404
Swidler Berlin Shereff Friedman	125,000	135,000	145,000	160,000	170,000	185,000	200,000	2,115
Testa, Hurwitz & Thibeault	140,000	155,000	167,500	180,000	192,500	205,000	217,500	2,600
Thelen Reid & Priest	125,000							2,400
Thompson & Knight	100,000							1,650
Troutman Sanders	100,000							1,400
Venture Law Group	125,000							2,400
Vinson & Elkins	110,000	114,000	121,000	130,000	140,000	145,000	155,000	1,700
Wachtell, Lipton, Rosen & Katz	140,000	150,000	165,000	180,000	195,000			2,404
Weil, Gotshal & Manges	125,000	135,000	150,000	165,000	190,000	205,000	215,000	2,400
White & Case	125,000	135,000	150,000	170,000	190,000	200,000	205,000	2,403
Williams & Connolly	130,000	140,000	150,000	160,000	170,000	180,000	190,000	2,450
Willkie Farr & Gallagher	125,000	135,000	150,000	170,000	190,000			2,000
Wilmer, Cutler & Pickering	110,000	120,000	130,000	140,000	150,000	160,000		2,400
Wilson Sonsini Goodrich & Rosati	125,000	135,000	150,000	165,000	185,000	195,000	205,000	2,400
Winstead Sechrest & Minick, PC	96k-105k	98k-115k	102k-126k	103k-132k	131k-145k	134k-148k	148k-155k	1,700
Winston & Strawn	125,000	135,000	150,000					2,400
Winthrop, Stimson, Putnam & Roberts	120,000	127,000	135,000	152,000	170,000	175,000	185,000	2,404
Wolf, Block, Schorr and Solis-Cohen, LLP	100,000							1,725

Source: Vault.com 2000 Associate Survey
* Does not include bonus

RETENTION

Average score = 5.28

RANK	FIRM	SCORE
1	Winston & Strawn	6.80
2	Ballard Spahr Andrews & Ingersoll	6.64
3	Williams & Connolly	6.60
4	Covington & Burling	6.55
5	Baker Botts	6.51
6	Mintz, Levin, Cohn, Ferris, Glovsky and Popeo	6.47
7	Fish & Richardson	6.31
8	Hogan & Hartson	6.30
9	Munger, Tolles & Olson	6.26
10	Arent Fox Kinter Plotkin & Kahn	6.12

Source: Vault.com 2000 Associate Survey

Focus on the top three in retention

1. Winston & Strawn

Winston & Strawn has moved up to the number one spot in the retention category. That is quite a feat in a year in which many associates were scrambling for the exits. "Most associates are satisfied with their employment and turnover is extremely low in comparison to other firms," says a mid-level attorney.

According to the firm's hiring partner, Paul Hensel, "The firm's attrition rate has remained low in part because of the substantial training and other work-life programs implemented by the firm."

2. Ballard Spahr Andrews & Ingersoll

Philly's Ballard Spahr must have cornered the market on brotherly love. Associates report low turnover, even in the face of today's overheated market. And those who do leave are forgiven since they "often go off to neat jobs — one guy went in-house at the NBA and another mid-level went to become General Counsel to a medium-size client she had worked with."

Geoffrey Kahn, litigation and firm-wide Professional Personnel Manager, suggests that "the biggest challenge facing firms like us is making associates feel like part of the enterprise as opposed to the all-too-prevailing sentiment that associates feel like they are a fungible commodity." Associates find the firm succeeds in reaching Kahn's goal of making them "feel invested" in Ballard Spahr's future.

3. Williams & Connolly

In today's tight employment market, most attorneys are resigned to huge turnover at the office, often losing co-workers to peer firms. Not Williams & Connolly in DC. "Like all big firms, people leave, but W&C has an extremely small number of people go to other DC firms — most go to government or make a geographic move," observes an associate. No hard feelings towards those who hit the road, either. According to one contact, "People leave because they have great opportunities in other areas of the law."

TRAINING

Average score = 7.00

RANK	FIRM	SCORE
1	Kirkland & Ellis	8.70
2	Cooley Godward	8.65
3	Ropes & Gray	8.63
4	Jenner & Block	8.41
5	Davis Polk & Wardwell	8.18
6	Cravath, Swaine & Moore	8.15
7	Shearman & Sterling	7.92
8	Winston & Strawn	7.81
9	Choate, Hall & Stewart	7.75
10	Hale and Dorr	7.73

Source: Vault.com 2000 Associate Survey

Focus on the top three in training

1. Kirkland & Ellis

Kirkland & Ellis has stayed on top of the training rankings. For litigators, the firm offers the Kirkland Institute of Trial Advocacy (KITA), a year-round program aimed at improving lawyers' skills, as well as a two-day jury trial practice session. Other offerings include the Kirkland Institute of Corporate Practice (KICP) and the Kirkland Intellectual Property Institute (KIPI). "The firm is maniacally devoted to training," according to one attorney. "They have many formal training programs, but the best thing is that the senior partners take the time to get you involved in all aspects of a deal or trial, let you know what is going on, and explain things to you."

2. Cooley Godward

"Cooley can't be topped for training," raves one associate. Well, it can, but coming in second isn't bad at all. The firm's Cooley College program is an 80- to 100-hour program, covering all of the firm's practice areas. Individual practice groups also hold monthly training sessions. Firm hiring partner Rick Climan tells Vault.com: "Associate training has been an integral part of Cooley Godward's culture for decades, and we devote substantial resources — millions of dollars and thousands of attorney hours — to our efforts in this area. Our success as a firm depends on having savvy associates with well-developed legal skills interacting with our increasingly sophisticated, quality conscious clients."

Climan says the firm does not believe in the "sink or swim" or "throw them into the fire" approach to training associates. "Even though this approach may be less costly in the short run from a pure dollars-and-cents perspective, we have consciously rejected this approach because we view it as an abdication of our fundamental responsibilities to our clients and our associates. We want our associates to feel confident in taking on substantial responsibility early in their careers and our training programs make this possible while enabling us to maintain our reputation for producing consistently high quality legal work."

3. Ropes & Gray

Taking the bronze medal for the second straight year is Boston's Ropes & Gray. Associates claim the firm has "the best training program in Boston — hands down!" And Douglas Meal, the firm's Hiring Partner, thinks he knows the reason: "[Our distinction in training] is a function of two factors. The first is that the firm has a very substantial commitment to, and makes a substantial investment in, formal training. The second and more important factor is the fact that our firm has one of the lowest partner-to-associate ratios on [Vault.com's] list. This allows a lot of opportunities for partner-associate interaction, which is invaluable in training."

ASSOCIATE/PARTNER RELATIONS

Average score = 8.20

RANK	FIRM	SCORE
1	Jenner & Block	9.19
2	Munger, Tolles & Olson	9.11
3	Cooley Godward	9.10
4	Morrison & Foerster	9.06
5	Covington & Burling	8.95
6	Preston Gates & Ellis	8.87
7	Gray Cary Ware & Freidenrich	8.82
8	Latham & Watkins	8.76
9	Winston & Strawn	8.75
10	Choate, Hall & Stewart	8.72

Source: Vault.com 2000 Associate Survey

Focus on the top three in associate/partner relations

1. Jenner & Block

As a firm, Jenner & Block seems to take the term "partnership" seriously. Even with 200 partners, associates "rarely encounter a partner who does not respect the fact that personal plans and obligations sometimes conflict with work." Describing them as "great people and great lawyers," associates tell us that the partners at Jenner & Block are "the principal selling point of our office," a rare claim indeed.

Hiring partner John H. Mathias, Jr. tells Vault.com, "It's gratifying to learn that our associates share our affection for this great law firm. Our partners try hard to make this into a place that is professionally rewarding for everybody. It looks like we're getting the job done."

2. Munger, Tolles & Olson

Partners don't have to be monsters, according to Munger Tolles associates. The fearless leaders of the California firm make sure that "high-quality or especially hard work is recognized," says one of the troops. Also, "the partners here value their own life outside the firm" and "hold that value for associates' outside life as well."

Partner/associate respect is built into firm structure, points out another underling. "Munger's reverse leverage and free-agent system for associates' work means that partners have to treat associates with respect."

Co-chair of Munger's recruiting committee Marc Becker notes that Munger "has always viewed lawyers as colleagues from their first day at the firm and has sought to minimize any associate/partner hierarchical distinctions. This is demonstrated by the role associates play in firm decision-making and governance and the sharing of financial information with associates."

3. Cooley Godward

The "great" partners at Cooley and the "professional and collegial atmosphere" they create help Cooley Godward jump into the top three in partner/associate relations after not even placing in the top ten last year. Laterals rave that they have "never been treated better" while senior associates note that "the mentoring is the best" in the industry. "Our partners are fantastic — always telling us how they appreciate how hard we work." The feeling is apparently mutual.

Cooley business partner Deborah Marshall tells Vault.com, "I really like our associates — they are smart, dedicated, fun, and they have a wide variety of interests."

DIVERSITY — MINORITIES

Average score = 6.43

RANK	FIRM	SCORE
1	Arnold & Porter	8.37
2	Morrison & Foerster	8.29
3	Covington & Burling	8.09
4	Kilpatrick Stockton	7.59
5	Winston & Strawn	7.54
6	Hogan & Hartson	7.53
7	Akin Gump Strauss Hauer & Feld	7.51
8	Simpson Thacher & Bartlett	7.41
9	Pillsbury Madison & Sutro	7.35
10	Davis Polk & Wardwell	7.31

Source: Vault.com 2000 Associate Survey

Focus on the top three in minority diversity issues

1. Arnold & Porter

"They put their money where their mouth is. Lots of minority recruiting," explains an Arnold & Porter associate. More than one has observed "a genuine desire to make Arnold & Porter more ethnically diverse" and notes that organized diversity training has "positively enhanced firm relations." All of this helps make Arnold & Porter the highest-rated firm in our poll for diversity with respect to minorities.

Regarding this ranking, Managing Partner Jim Sandman comments, "We try hard to solicit and be responsive to the suggestions and concerns of our colleagues, and that has been especially helpful to us in addressing the concerns of minorities."

2. Morrison & Foerster

Perhaps the reason MoFo associates rate their firm so highly simply because they are so very aware of the difficulties of diversity. Even though those surveyed give the California-based firm high marks, many still worry about recruiting efforts falling short. "I understand that [the firm] has a program in the headquarters for minorities in all offices, but I am not sure what it entails," admits a DC fourth-year. "I don't know that we really 'walk the walk' as much as we could because our emphasis on excellence sometimes leads us to ignore differences that are an asset to a practicing attorney. But that doesn't always translate to objective criteria (such as high grades)."

3. Covington & Burling

In spite of dropping down one place from No. 2 last year, Covington & Burling again places highly in our survey for diversity with respect to minorities. According to one attorney at the firm's Washington, DC headquarters, the firm does not tolerate racism of any kind. "There is absolutely no overt discrimination here, and I'm confident that any overt discrimination would be dealt with harshly."

DIVERSITY — WOMEN

Average score = 7.30

RANK	FIRM	SCORE
1	Arnold & Porter	8.79
2	Morrison & Foerster	8.70
3	Hogan & Hartson	8.51
4	Choate, Hall & Stewart	8.45
5	Gray Cary Ware & Freidenrich	8.39
6	Covington & Burling	8.34
7	Pillsbury Madison & Sutro	8.32
8	Cooley Godward	8.19
9	Debevoise & Plimpton	8.07
10	Jenner & Block	8.03

Source: Vault.com 2000 Associate Survey

Focus on the top three in women's diversity issues

1. Arnold & Porter

Arnold & Porter receives high praise for their treatment of female attorneys. Associates rave about "excellent" part-time hours, on-site day-care, and 12 weeks maternity leave, which associates are encouraged to take.

Managing Partner Jim Sandman notes that the firm's "management philosophy is to promote a work atmosphere that values individuality and that enables all of our colleagues to feel comfortable being themselves."

2. Morrison & Foerster

MoFo climbs from seventh place for its treatment of female associates to second this year, the result of enthusiastic ratings from its lawyers. "The numbers speak for themselves in relation to other firms," declares a DC fourth-year associate who guesses that "about 22 percent of partners are women." A number of colleagues mention the "liberal maternity leave policy." One senior associate makes it personal: "I am six months pregnant and have found the maternity leave policies to be first-rate. The attorneys I work with have been extremely supportive, understanding and flexible."

3. Hogan & Hartson

Although Hogan & Hartson dropped from second place to third in the poll on women's diversity, the Washington, DC firm maintains its position as one of the nation's best law firms in this category. Associates were proud to proclaim that their firm is "probably is best in the city and maybe the country. Women are integrally involved in the success of the firm and are well-represented on associate and partner levels." Another associate tells Vault.com that Hogan & Hartson is "such a woman-friendly place" that equality is never even a question.

DIVERSITY — GAYS & LESBIANS

Average score = 7.49

RANK	FIRM	SCORE
1	Irell & Manella	9.41
2	Morrison & Foerster	9.19
3	Arent Fox Kintner Plotkin & Kahn	9.00
4	Arnold & Porter	8.93
5	Preston Gates & Ellis	8.81
6	Jenner & Block	8.78
7 (tie)	Covington & Burling	8.65
7 (tie)	Munger, Tolles & Olson	8.65
8 (tie)	Cooley Godward	8.56
8 (tie)	Milbank, Tweed, Hadley & McCloy	8.56
9	Akin Gump Strauss Hauer & Feld	8.37
10	Gray Cary Ware & Freidenrich	8.29

Source: Vault.com 2000 Associate Survey

Focus on the top three in gay & lesbian diversity issues

1. Irell & Manella

Leading the pack in terms of firm diversity for homosexuals, California firm Irell & Manella has long been heralded as "a very gay-friendly place to work," according to one source, and a firm where same-sex partners attend firm events. The firm puts its pro bono money where its mouth is: Irell represented gay high schools students who were banned by their school from forming a club.

2. Morrison & Foerster

In addition to standard benefits for domestic partners, MoFo fosters an accepting work environment that draws praise from its gay and lesbian attorneys. "[It] seems like there are a lot of gay people at the firm who are comfortably being open about their sexuality," one contact says.

3. Arent Fox Kinter Plotkin & Kahn

The key to DC-based Arent Fox's success in recruiting and retaining gays and lesbians lies in the "well-established and highly visible group of gay and lesbian attorneys" at the firm, according to one associate. There are at least five openly gay partners at the firm and numerous openly gay associates and summer associates. "It is perfectly routine to see multiple gay couples at firm social events and outings." Others point out same-sex domestic partner benefits as indicative of Arent Fox's commitment to "a single unified community." This is a place where "having a picture of you and your partner on your desk never elicits more than a 'aren't you guys cute.'"

SELECTIVITY

Average score = 8.04

RANK	FIRM	SCORE
1	Munger, Tolles & Olson	9.79
2	Williams & Connolly	9.70
3	Covington & Burling	9.50
4	Davis Polk & Wardwell	9.17
5	Irell & Manella	9.16
6	Cravath, Swaine & Moore	8.95
7	Arnold & Porter	8.88
8	Hogan & Hartson	8.87
9	Ropes & Gray	8.86
10	Gibson, Dunn & Crutcher	8.78

Source: Vault.com 2000 Associate Survey

Focus on the top three in associate selectivity

1. Munger, Tolles & Olson

You might have gone to Yale or Stanford, but that doesn't mean you'll go to Munger. "Even a Supreme Court clerkship doesn't guarantee you a job here," sniffs one associate who made the cut. Landing at the top of the heap for selectivity is no coincidence for this L.A. firm. "I've heard people go back and forth on the topic of which firm on the West Coast is the most prestigious [or] most elite," notes another associate, "but I don't think many people have argued against the notion that Munger Tolles is the most selective law firm on the West Coast. With almost one out of every eight lawyers here being a former Supreme Court clerk, I think the selectivity bar is in fact quite high."

The firm seems to agree. Marc Becker, co-chairman of the firm's recruiting committee, comments to Vault.com that "one of the most important aspects of the firm's philosophy has been its commitment to hire only the highest-caliber lawyers. Although law school record and clerkship are among those indicators the firm looks to, ultimately our goal is to hire those individuals who are most likely to succeed at the firm and add something to what is a very unique group of people."

2. Williams & Connolly

Although there is "no hard-and-fast grade cutoff," DC's Williams & Connolly manages to attract only the very best. And while there is "no paid clerkship bonus, except for Supreme Court clerkships," one associate admits that "pretty much everyone here clerks." Insiders insist the firm comes out near the very top for selectivity because it chooses only those who "like dealing with legal issues and are excited by them. If you don't have that kind of enthusiasm for the law, it shows easily."

3. Covington & Burling

Covington & Burling cracks our top three this year. According to its associates, the prestigious Washington, DC firm "is extremely selective in its hiring process and prides itself on identifying the most impressive, thoughtful candidates." Although it is possible to get hired from a lesser school if you have great credentials, insiders tell us that your best bet for a job is a diploma from the cream of the Ivy crop. "There are a few people from lower top-20 schools who had good clerkships but Covington continues to attract primarily Harvard/Yale-type pedigrees."

OFFICES

Average score = 7.19

RANK	FIRM	SCORE
1	Winston & Strawn	9.30
2	Cleary, Gottlieb, Steen & Hamilton	8.80
3	Dewey Ballantine	8.68
4	Simpson Thacher & Bartlett	8.61
5	King & Spalding	8.59
6	Arnold & Porter	8.58
7	Wilson Sonsini Goodrich & Rosati	8.56
8	Hale and Dorr	8.35
9	Baker Botts	8.22
10	Ballard Spahr Andrews & Ingersoll	8.13

Source: Vault.com 2000 Associate Survey

Nicest offices

1. Winston & Strawn

With its breathtaking views, Winston & Strawn's Chicago home earns the firm the top spot in the offices category. The offices occupy the top 12 floors of the Leo Burnett Building located downtown in "the Loop." From there, associates get views over Lake Michigan and the Chicago skyline. One lawyer explains that Winston toil "is made a lot easier by feeling like you're in a setting made to show you that hard work has paid off." Another attorney boasts, "Without a doubt, the offices are the most beautiful in the city."

2. Cleary, Gottlieb, Steen & Hamilton

When Cleary's Manhattan offices were redesigned in 1992, the design firm in charge of the project received an award ("Best in Law Office Design") from *Interiors* magazine. Associates at the firm appreciate the award-winning effort. "Our views are unparalleled, the decor and art are peaceful, and I don't think I know another firm in New York that gives first-years their own offices," notes one attorney.

3. Dewey Ballantine

Dewey Ballantine's "very attractive, spacious and well-appointed offices" are ranked third by the firm's associates. Many rave about the space, calling it "among the nicest in New York." Attorneys praise the firm for moving associates into their own office after only six months as well as maintaining the "attractive" appearance of the space.

Lovers of both historicism and modernism will find their nirvana at Dewey Ballantine. According to the firm: "To unify all interrelated functions, Dewey Ballantine and architect Butler Rogers Baskett created a visual environment in wood, stone and carpet that is delicately poised between 18th-century historicism and International-style modernism."

SUPPORT NETWORKS

Average score = 7.30

RANK	FIRM	SCORE
1	Winston & Strawn	9.00
2	Wilson Sonsini Goodrich & Rosati	8.89
3	Jenner & Block	8.63
4	Alston & Bird	8.61
5 (tie)	Davis Polk & Wardwell	8.60
5 (tie)	Irell & Manella	8.60
6	Ropes & Gray	8.37
7	Skadden, Arps, Slate, Meagher & Flom	8.34
8	Mayer, Brown & Platt	8.24
9	Paul, Weiss, Rifkind, Wharton & Garrison	8.12
10	Baker Botts	8.08

Source: Vault.com 2000 Associate Survey

Focus on the top three support networks

1. Winston & Strawn

Winston & Strawn has improved its ranking from last year in most quality of life categories. Support services is no exception. The firm's 24-hour secretarial help, copy center, and paging system for IT problems has helped put Winston on top. One Winston lawyer claims the firm has "support services for just about every attorney need."

Firm chairman Paul Hensel tells Vault.com: "We're particularly proud that in this tight job market, people understand the importance of their role in contributing to the services we provide our clients."

2. Wilson Sonsini Goodrich & Rosati

Shooting into the top 10 for the first time this year, Wilson Sonsini places second this year for its support services. One associate remarks, "The infrastructure at WSGR operates like a well-oiled machine. No other firm in the area has support services that are as helpful."

J. Robert Suffoletta, Wilson Sonsini's Law School Hiring Partner, offers the following: "The high rating we received for our support organization reflects our emphasis on providing our attorneys with the tools that are necessary to service our high technology client base and the high quality of our support personnel."

3. Jenner & Block

Jenner associates took the opportunity afforded by their first quality of life survey to rave about "fantastic" support services, gush over having "everything at your disposal" and enthusiastically report that the firm employs "people to help with anything" — be it travel, document production, or lunch.

Theodore R. Tetzlaff, co-chairman of Jenner, tells Vault, "Jenner believes that attorneys — and the clients we serve — deserve the very best support possible. For that reason, the firm has invested heavily in technology to insure that we are on the cutting edge of progress in making our attorneys mobile and efficient. We also hire the best legal assistants, secretaries, and professional staff to support our practice. These committed professionals make Jenner's support service excel on a day-to-day basis."

SOCIAL LIFE

Average score = 6.44

RANK	FIRM	SCORE
1	Winston & Strawn	8.22
2	Alston & Bird	7.85
3	Fenwick & West	7.70
4	Cooley Godward	7.68
5(tie)	Choate, Hall & Stewart	7.63
5(tie)	Gray Cary Ware & Freidenrich	7.63
7	Akin Gump Strauss Hauer & Feld	7.53
8	Jenner & Block	7.52
9	Willkie Farr & Gallagher	7.46
10	Wilson Sonsini Goodrich & Rosati	7.36

Source: Vault.com 2000 Associate Survey

Focus on the top three firms in the arena of social life

1. Winston & Strawn

Moving up from last year's number two spot, Winston & Strawn comes out on top of the social life category in this year's survey. Most Winston & Strawn associates think highly of their colleagues. "Winston is a very enjoyable place to work because of its associates. There is a great deal of social interaction between attorneys outside the firm, particularly those who live in Chicago as opposed to the suburbs," reports one Winston associate.

Firm chairman Paul Hensel says, "People seem to enjoy working at Winston & Strawn. It reflects well on the caliber of people who have joined us over the years."

2. Alston & Bird

The key to the booming social life at Atlanta's Alston & Bird, according to the firm's Managing Partner, Ben Johnson III, is that attorneys like each other. They really do. "Because there is a substantial emphasis on teamwork and team building," notes Johnson, "people genuinely enjoy working with the other people here. This translates into social interaction that really isn't organized by the firm."

3. Fenwick & West

A newcomer to the Quality of Life rankings, it appears that firm-sponsored "chips and salsa" Friday afternoons and trips to Yosemite have made an impression on the hungry, happy hordes of Fenwick. Associates at Fenwick & West give high marks to their firm's social environment and the "friendly and social" attorneys. One associate observes that "Fenwick's firm culture fosters mutual respect and a sense of humor about oneself. The partners don't take themselves too seriously, and the associates generally get along very well with each other and the partners."

Hiring Partner John Steele comments: "Our esprit de corps as lawyers for the new economy and our various social events lead to a particularly collegial atmosphere."

mofo.com

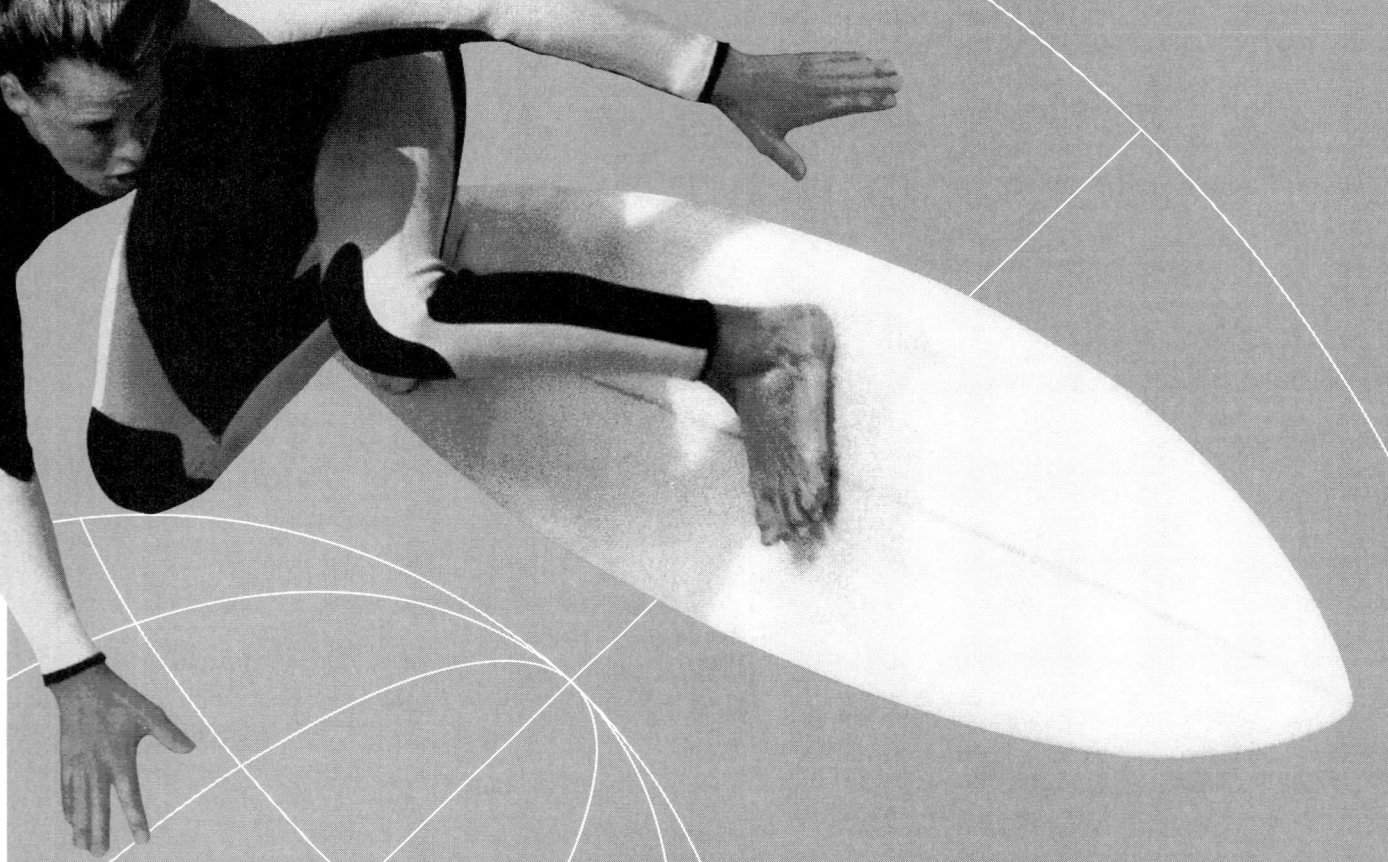

Cutting Edge Practice — A Great Place To Work

MORRISON & FOERSTER LLP
Lawyers for the global e-conomy℠

THE VAULT.COM 50

VAULT.COM

1 PRESTIGE RANKING

Cravath, Swaine & Moore

Worldwide Plaza
825 Eighth Avenue
New York, NY 10019
(212) 474-1000
Fax: (212) 474-3700
www.cravath.com

LOCATIONS

New York, NY (HQ)
Hong Kong
London

MAJOR DEPARTMENTS/PRACTICES

Corporate
Litigation
Tax
Trusts & Estates

THE STATS

No. of attorneys: 408
No. of offices: 3
Summer associate offers: 86 out of 86 (New York, 1999)
Presiding Partner: Robert Joffe
Hiring Partners: Stephen L. Burns, Elizabeth L. Grayer

PAY

New York, 2000
1st year: $125,000
2nd year: $135,000
3rd year: $150,000
4th year: $170,000
5th year: $190,000
6th year: $205,000
7th year: $220,000
8th year: $235,000
Summer associate: $2,500/week

NOTABLE PERKS

- Numerous free sports and theater tickets
- Relocation expenses
- Gym subsidy
- On-site emergency child care
- Paid parental leave

THE BUZZ
What attorneys at other firms are saying about this firm

- "The best"
- "Whitest shoe"
- "Corporate takeover kings"
- "The essence of sweatshop"

UPPERS

- Opportunities to work on exceptionally important deals
- Matchless reputation
- Tremendous associate responsibility

DOWNERS

- The hours, the hours, and the hours
- Sink-or-swim work environment
- Social chasm between partners and associates

KEY COMPETITORS

Davis Polk & Wardell
Simpson Thacher & Bartlett
Sullivan & Cromwell
Wachtell, Lipton, Rosen & Katz

EMPLOYMENT CONTACT

Ms. Lisa A. Kalen
Assistant Director of Legal Personnel and Recruiting
(212) 474-3215
lkalen@cravath.com

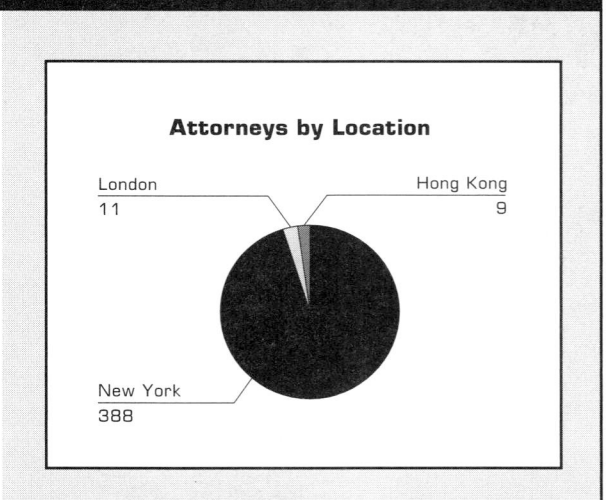

Attorneys by Location

- London: 11
- Hong Kong: 9
- New York: 388

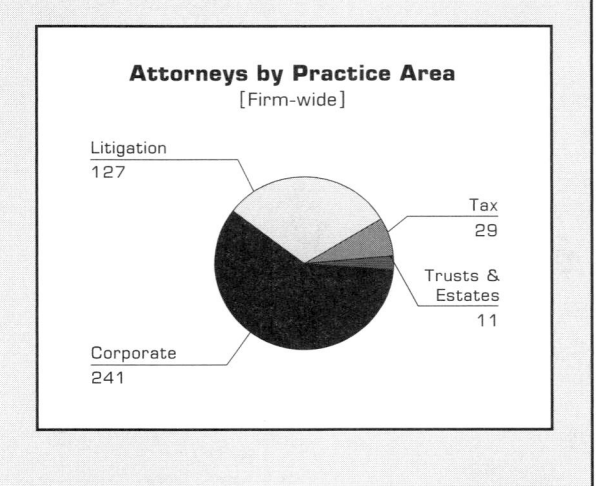

Attorneys by Practice Area [Firm-wide]

- Litigation: 127
- Tax: 29
- Trusts & Estates: 11
- Corporate: 241

QUALITY OF LIFE RANKINGS [ASSOCIATES RATE THEIR OWN FIRM]

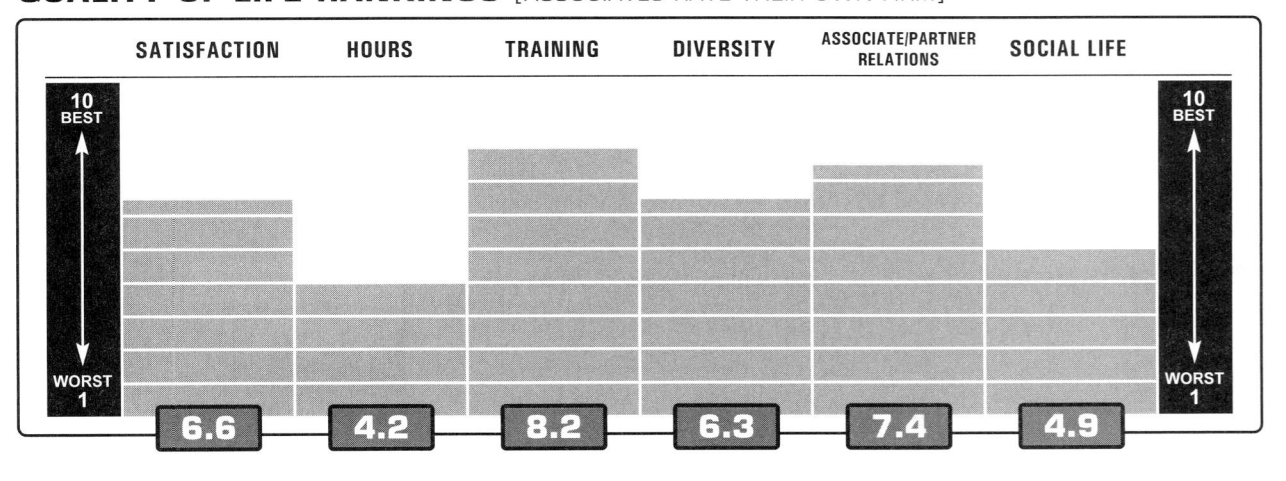

Satisfaction	Hours	Training	Diversity	Associate/Partner Relations	Social Life
6.6	4.2	8.2	6.3	7.4	4.9

THE SCOOP

When other law firms grow up, they want to be Cravath, Swaine & Moore. Old-fashioned and exclusive, Cravath has also been chosen in the Vault.com Top 50 survey as the most prestigious firm in the nation for the third year in a row. If you're looking for a firm where "your reputation precedes you" and you don't mind very long hours and an antiquated lockstep compensation system, search no further than Cravath.

A truly proud history

The august Cravath, Swaine & Moore is the product of two firms, one in New York City, the other in Auburn, NY. The New York City parent was founded in 1819, the Auburn firm in 1823. Early activities of the New York City practice included representing the liquidated Bank of the United States (closed when the truculent and ill-advised Andrew Jackson vetoed a bill extending the charter of the bank). Prominent early members included William Seward, who would become the Secretary of State under Abraham Lincoln. The two firms merged in 1853.

In the early 1900s, Paul Cravath envisioned a firm that would draw on the labor of many junior attorneys who would strive to join a small partnership and leave the firm if they failed in this goal. Most law firms follow this model today. The "Cravath Way" (or "Cravath System") also provides that Cravath lawyers should be promoted only from within the firm. Cravath is unusual in its adherence to this strict dictum and it is still a very unusual thing within the Cravath culture for a lateral to be promoted to partner.

The "Cravath Way"

The "Cravath Way," elucidated by name partner Robert Swaine in 1948, captures Cravath's philosophy. Many of these tenets can still be observed at Cravath today — there are still no merit bonuses at the firm, new associates effectively rely on the efforts of partners and senior associates for their training, and lawyers are still "promoted from within the firm, not from the outside." A rare exception to this ironclad rule occurred in November 1997, when Jeffrey Smith (an environmental associate hired laterally in 1992) was promoted to partner. Despite being told outright that his position would not lead to partnership, Smith went on to build an enormously successful environmental law practice from Cravath's existing client base, earning him the coveted brass partner ring.

Cravath has tried to buck the trend of training lawyers as specialists. Lawyers in both the litigation and corporate department rotate among different partners within the group to ensure that they get a taste of different types of work. The firm claims this system produces generalists within a practice area.

Cravath has also traditionally shunned marketing. The joke once went that the Cravath notion of marketing was picking up the phone on the third ring instead of the fourth. However, the firm has been increasing its marketing efforts, participating in so-called "beauty contests" in competition with other law firms. Despite Cravath's attempt to be more accessible, insiders say the firm still gets most of its business through its peerless reputation. As one Cravath partner once sniffed to *The Wall Street Journal*, "We don't do cold calls." So far, these modest changes seem to be enough to keep Cravath at the top of its profession.

Moving in lockstep

Cravath deals with its internal issues in an ad hoc "town meeting" style. "We discuss everything at lunch," says a partner. There are no controlling committees, and all-important decisions are made by consensus, a system that one partner says "borders on chaos" but emphasizes the integral nature of each partner at the firm. Only about two or three members of each entering class will join the 83 partners of Cravath, Swaine & Moore. Thus, partners are rare and special — "like senators," according to one former associate. Cravath legend has it that when a partner dies, every other partner attends the funeral, forming a two-by-two procession called "the Cravath Walk." "It's right that we should be right there with the family," one partner once noted to *The American Lawyer*.

Cravath partners are bound together by a lockstep compensation system, a pay structure common to English firms but largely abandoned by Americans in favor of more merit-based regimes aimed at increasing retention. As the system has nothing to do with individual merit or rainmaking, no partner receives a bonus, and extraordinary partners are paid the same as their less-celebrated colleagues. Perhaps the payouts are lucrative enough to still potential dissent. The average partner at Cravath makes well over $1 million a year (over $1.5 million in 1997). Similarly, while associates may (and do) get fat bonuses, these bonuses are never, ever based on merit.

The granddaddy of the associate pay hike

Cravath touched off the first associate salary race in 1968 when it nearly doubled its starting salary to $15,000. This raise ended up setting the pay scale for New York City firms and for many firms across the country. Cravath rocked the legal world again in 1986 when its first-year associate salaries jumped from $53,000 to $65,000, a stunning 23 percent increase. Cravath's rivals quickly followed suit.

But in 2000, Cravath declined to lead the field in pay raises, leaving it to Silicon Valley newcomer Gunderson Dettmer to place its associate salaries at the head of the associate pay pack. To date Cravath has been keeping pace with associate salary raises, but it no longer offers the highest starting salaries in the United States.

Superlative corporate department

Cravath's corporate department is divided into 17 small groups of two to four partners. These groups may be centered around specific areas of practice, such as mergers and acquisitions, banking, securities underwriting, and real estate. Others are focused around a particular corporate or international practice, even a client. For example, Cravath has a Time Warner group, a real estate group, and several securities offerings groups. Many corporate lawyers work on international transactions and with non-U.S. corporations and clients. More than a third of Cravath clients are based outside the United States, but nearly all lawyers are trained at Cravath's New York headquarters. The corporate department is home to about 220 lawyers.

Vacation interrupted by merger

In January 2000, Cravath partner Robert A. Kindler decided to take a break from the New York winter by heading to the Caribbean. But his vacation was rudely interrupted when he received a phone call that Cravath client Time Warner was joining forces with AOL (or rather, being acquired by the chipper online giant). He chartered a plane to New York and went right to work, arriving with such alacrity that he had no time to change — Kindler wasn't even wearing socks when he met with the Time Warner board.

Cravath's involvement in the deal was something of a gamble; it represented Time Warner on a contingency basis, meaning if the merger failed it would receive nothing. (Typically, fees for M&A are based on billable hours, with a bonus premium if the deal goes through and a discount if it doesn't.) The deal, worth a record $165 billion if officially completed, will garner Cravath a whopping $35 million, one of the largest transaction fees ever for a law firm. Unfortunately for Cravath, Kindler won't be able to top his record any time soon, as he left the firm in June 2000 to become a managing director at Chase Manhattan Corp. No word on whether he plans to return to the beach any time soon.

There was more than the AOL deal to keep Cravath busy in January 2000. The firm also handled Time Warner's music business' $20 billion joint venture with EMI Music to form the world's largest record company. Cravath lawyers had to figure out how the new gigantic music company would navigate between U.S. and U.K. law. Despite its involvement in these high-profile business dealings, Cravath lawyers have taken their prominence in stride. "This is just not remarkable," corporate partner Richard Hall told *The New York Law Journal*. Hall's comment is particularly striking since he worked on both the AOL and EMI deals while helping Royal Bank of Scotland with its 23 billion pound effort to take over National Westminster Bank.

In other media

Cravath has been on the forefront of other changes in the media world, including work on Viacom's $40 billion bid to purchase CBS. The deal involved complicated issues concerning the division of power between officers of a corporation and its board of directors. Sumner Redstone of Viacom had his eye on the CEO position of the resulting company, with majority control over the board, but Mel Karmazin of CBS wanted control of the company's operations. Cravath lawyers came up with a unique corporate charter that circumscribes the power of the board of directors for a three-year period. "The Viacom board was very concerned that they were not just turning over the ship, lock stock and barrel," Cravath partner Allen Finkelson told *The New York Law Journal*.

MCI WorldCom has also been keeping Cravath M&A lawyers busy. In May 1999, MCI WorldCom signed an agreement to acquire SkyTel for a $1.2 billion stock exchange. Through the deal, MCI WorldCom will enter the world of wireless communication, since SkyTel's main products include e-mail and Internet paging services. Cravath also helped MCI WorldCom with its proposed $115 billion purchase of Sprint Corp.

In 1998 Cravath had a part in reducing the "Big Six" accounting firms to the "Big Five." The firm handled the corporate issues for Price Waterhouse when it merged with fellow accounting giant Coopers & Lybrand to form PricewaterhouseCoopers. Other notable Cravath M&A activities include representing Atlantic Richfield in its $53 billion merger with British Petroleum and helping Peco Energy in its proposed merger negotiations with Unicom Corp.

Finicky litigation squad

Cravath is one of the most prominent litigation firms in New York. "While Cravath is known as a corporate firm, and it does have the top floors of the building in a kind of metacommentary," says one associate, "the litigation department is excellent and not considered a step down, except literally." There are approximately 125 lawyers in Cravath's litigation department. Cravath's litigation expertise spans from antitrust and IP to white-collar crime and securities actions.

Cravath can be quite finicky in the cases it takes, passing up potentially lucrative assignments that other firms have leapt at. On Cravath's nix list: breast-implant cases against Bristol-Myers Squibb, repetitive stress cases for IBM, and cigarette cases for Phillip Morris and BAT Industries. To explain the rejection of these cases, the firm has suggested the work would put severe strains on the litigation department and involve hiring large numbers of additional attorneys — some they might not otherwise hire.

Cravath's choosiness has not prevented it from handling more than a few prominent cases. Cravath, along with Philly firm Morgan, Lewis & Bockius, brought an action on behalf of Priceline.com against Microsoft. The suit alleges that Microsoft violated Priceline's process patent that enables buyers to name their price on airline tickets, hotel rooms, and other goods and services. According to the complaint, Microsoft gained access to Priceline.com's source code by offering the company technological help.

On the other end of the litigation spectrum, Cravath took on Robert Maurer as a pro bono client. As a prisoner at Sing Sing, Maurer was written up for false violations and put in isolation after he reported that a prison official was throwing away grievances. Maurer decided to bring a lawsuit (written by hand). Cravath lawyers took the case pro bono. They were able to win $100,000 for Maurer, one of the largest jury awards of its kind for a prisoner

Few offices, big business

In their efforts to establish themselves as "global" firms, Cravath's competitors have hastened to open up branch offices around the world. By contrast, Cravath offers only three offices: New York, London (founded in 1973), and Hong Kong (started in 1994 after much dissension among partners). The firm plans to expand its London office.

The dearth of branch offices is no reflection of the firm's international expertise or clientele. International companies that have turned to Cravath include Bayer, Nestle, Unilever, and Salomon Brothers Hong Kong. Perhaps the firm's most impressive international work has been for the various entities devoted to creating Europe's economic, political, and social convergence (The European Community, European Investment Bank, Euratom, and so on). Here, Cravath has done extensive finance work, handling the first ECU and euro offerings registered with the SEC.

GETTING HIRED

Top tier only

Despite the extremely hot job market for law students, Cravath can still afford to be very picky. Insiders report that law students who don't hail from a top-10 law school have a tough time getting an offer at Cravath. But given the need for lawyers at most large law firms, now may be a good time to apply. One lawyer says, "Comparatively, [Cravath is] one of the most selective firms, but right now it's a law student's market, no matter where you're looking." Insiders also report that Cravath is bringing on a larger class of summer associates than usual.

During on-campus interviews, Cravath interviewers look for more than just outstanding grades and law review. "They also prize confidence and personality," say insiders, "as well as some prior experience in business or finance." Cravath is extremely selective about making callback invites, perhaps because only Cravath's busy and high-billing partners interview second-round applicants. As a result, those invited for callbacks at Cravath have better odds of receiving an offer than at most other firms.

Full day of interviews

Cravath breaks the callback interview mold in several respects. First, the firm requires a full day of interviews rather than the typical half-day. Applicants arrive at Cravath in the morning and check in with the legal recruiting staff. They are then asked to sit in the reception area with other applicants who are interviewing that day. "Everyone sits around looking nervous," say associates who have gone through the process. Eventually, when a partner's schedule frees up, an applicant is escorted to his office. There's no exquisite science to it, say insiders, except that "usually if you're interested in corporate they'll try to have mainly corporate partners interview you."

Also unique to Cravath is the fact that each interviewee has no set schedule and, therefore, there is no time limit for each interview. "You just sort of interview with a partner until he decides he's had enough and then sends you back to the holding pen," explains one associate. "My first interview was only fifteen minutes long, so I thought the partner hated me. Then my next partner interview was nearly two hours long."

At some point, the applicant breaks for lunch with two Cravath associates. "These are the only Cravath associates you will speak to all day," says an insider. The two associates later report to the firm on how the lunch went. Although Cravath professes to value associates' opinions of recruits, one source tells Vault.com, "After lunch you fill out an assessment form, but I don't think the partners care at all. Associates essentially have zero input into Cravath hiring." If it's free food you're after, make sure to put on a happy face: "The lunch-host associates are chosen by legal recruiting — and they look for personable people. If they think you hate Cravath, you will not be asked to take a candidate to lunch."

After each interview, the legal recruiting staff confers with each partner, debriefs him, and tries to collect a consensus among all the partners. Insiders say that in most cases all partners must unanimously agree to extend an offer. According to one associate, "The full day of interviews can either be fun or torture — it's all in the luck of who ends up being free to interview you." The majority of successful Cravath applicants receive an offer within 24 hours.

OUR SURVEY SAYS

Cravath boot camp

One insider describes Cravath as a "respectful military base" — an unusual and strangely apt metaphor. Like the military, Cravath is an institution that thrives on tradition and stability. Another source took a few moments to psychoanalyze the distinguished firm: "This firm's culture is rooted in being at the top of the status quo. As a symbolic example, Cravath was one of the last [law firms] to go casual — and then only on Friday, and during the summer only. There is a civility and old-time professionalism that still governs and yet there is an all-business feel. Cravath is just starting to relax a bit, which feels like a welcome relief."

Like most military outfits, Cravath's decision-making process is top-down. Decisions are made at the partner level, according to associates, with information filtering from partners on an ad hoc basis "until a memo greets you some morning." "Interpreting the firm's management structure and decision-making process is a little like the Kremlin-watching that took place during the Cold War," suggests one source.

Blind devotion to the greater cause is a must as well. Don't count on lunchtime mingling to get the dirt — "partners eat in a separate room."

Strong meritocracy

For all its Star Chamber decision-making and its flat bonus system, Cravath is a strong meritocracy. Results matter, "not face time" or background. "The culture is one that is very eclectic with a focus on merit and ability," says one associate in the corporate group. "Nobody cares how you dress or what music you listen to, as long as you can get the job done, and get it done correctly. I find the achievement-based culture here inspiring but not for the faint-hearted." Other associates concur that "the partners care about results and little else." This focus results in a "collegial" and "surprisingly casual" atmosphere, as associates compete only with their own potential. As one litigator summarizes, "If you work hard and well, you will be respected. If not, you will not be respected."

This militaristic meritocracy reportedly extends to women, minorities, and gays and lesbians, though Cravath does not seem to be making unusual efforts in the area of diversity. The "number of woman partners has gone up dramatically in the past five years," but the Cravath system is still "laissez-faire." The firm has a part-time policy, although some associates appear unaware of its existence. "When you're expected to be available 24/7, working part-time is difficult," explains one insider. As for minorities, the partnership is still "monochromatic" but "hiring efforts have made great strides." Gays and lesbians find a welcoming environment. The firm has "several openly gay partners" and "seems relatively open, which is surprising for a firm that's supposed to be the utmost in formality."

Time to rotate

Cravath uses a rotation system that "marries" associates to a few partners for one year. During that year, associates work with these partners almost exclusively and receive their assignments from these partners. A corporate associate suggests that "because of the rotation system, there are two firm cultures. The first is that of the oppressed, who work at all hours of the day and night and barely have time to pick up their heads and watch life go by. The rest work for partners with a light caseload, who skip out at 8:30 p.m. and never come in on weekends. The first group doesn't like the second. The second doesn't notice the first." Associates suggest that their experience at Cravath depends significantly on the partners they are assigned to. One insider warns that prospective Cravath lawyers should "definitely think about the rotations. As people imagine shorter and shorter careers, there is some real downside to being locked into a non-marketable rotation for a year and a half." On the other hand, another attorney points out the value of "not being forced to specialize early on."

Opening doors

Many associates cite the firm's stellar reputation as their favorite thing about Cravath. One associate asks, "If you really want to be a high-powered Wall Street lawyer, why would you want to go anywhere else?" Many insiders comment that they thought Cravath would do wonders for their resume and open doors down the road. One source raves, "Undoubtedly the best thing about working for Cravath is the range of opportunities available to you when you leave. Cravath's reputation extends far and wide, and you can count on being able to name your price at a law firm anywhere in the country or even outside it."

Most associates also applaud the lack of a billing requirement. "Associates do not compete for work, there is no need for associates to prove they are smart, and there are no cut throats," one source says. Another adds, "Most of us don't know and don't care how many hours we have billed because there is no bonus or other advantage tied to billables. There is, however, always a lot of work."

Grub complaints

Several associates indicate great dissatisfaction with Cravath's after-hours dining policy in the New York office. Insiders say that they're "supposed to use the cafeteria for meals if it's open," which means "no ordering out until after 9:30." "You can spend whatever you want to in the cafeteria," shrugs one lawyer, "though it's hard to imagine spending more than $10." When the cafeteria is closed, "you must order from a few restaurants the firm has accounts with," none of which, according to one associate, "are any good" although "you could feed a horse [at them] without spending very much." London seems to have a slightly more flexible policy: "Daily meal allowance is 15 pounds if you're working past 9 p.m."

Trial by fire

Although formal training classes are increasingly numerous at Cravath, learning to be a true Cravath lawyer is, at heart, a hands-on task. Most sources think this is the best way to learn the ropes. "The firm runs training programs that are decent. Better training comes by doing," announces one insider. "Cravath's trial-by-fire method of training really forces associates to learn what they need to because they will not make it here for very long if they don't," says one associate. Working at Cravath is "a great but scary learning experience," according to another insider. Deal teams almost never comprise more than two associates and a partner, even when there may be double that number or more on the teams of other law firms involved.

A corporate associate tells Vault.com, "On my first day here I was on the phone discussing a deal with clients." As for the litigation department, insiders report: "While associates get little training in certain areas, we do work on the biggest, most complex cases anywhere. Having learned how to litigate by working on such big cases, I feel that I could easily handle anything that comes up in a smaller-scale litigation practice." Another corporate attorney warns that "some associates will enjoy closing a billion-dollar deal without much direct oversight from a partner; other associates will find this painfully stressful. In either case, it's the quickest way to get good experience. Also, the adage is true — a mid-level Cravath associate will often end up interacting with partners at other law firms on a relatively equal basis in terms of deal responsibility."

While most rave about the lawyerly skills they picked up at Cravath, an associate says the partnership needs to provide more personal mentoring. Some Cravath associates think formal reviews are lacking. "Feedback, in terms of formal reviews or otherwise, is extraordinarily limited," gripes one lawyer. Cravath is a do-or-die law firm. "You sometimes feel like you're left out to sink or swim on your own, and you only hear about it when you sink," one lawyer says.

Respect and civility . . . but where's the charm?

According to insiders, "partners are generally respectful but often not chummy." One corporate associate says, "I have never been treated with anything other than the utmost respect and professional courtesy by any partner here." While many associates describe the partnership as "civil," one suggests that partners "fall short in terms of respecting our private lives and our time. But they are very busy." Cravath associates say how one is treated by partners may be up to the luck of the draw. "It depends on the partner. Some have not gone to charm school." On the other hand, one associate suggests that partners are very friendly "once they get a chance to know you."

Not a singles bar

Cravath associates give the firm low ratings in terms of social life. As one lawyer put it, "People do their work and go home." Another says, "Cravath is not a singles bar but the firm does sponsor elegant dinners and parties now and then." Associates say Cravath lawyers tend to go home to their families or they go out with their non-Cravath friends. Many attorneys don't seem to mind the lack of socializing at Cravath. "You work long hours with these people. Why hang out with them too?"

But life at Cravath is not a friendless proposition. "Many of my good friends are people I've met at Cravath," an associate reports. Another opines, "There are enough people here that you are sure to find at least a few you click with." According to another insider, Cravath "is very hands-off in terms of associates' personal time. It just so happens that many people here are friends and spend time together out of work. But the firm neither encourages nor discourages such interaction."

Looking forward to bonus time

Despite a $125,000 starting salary for first-year associates, associates gripe about their pay. Many seem personally hurt that Cravath is no longer a "salary leader." "Frankly, we are more profitable than all but a handful of firms. We should be paid above market," says one irritated insider. A corporate lawyer puts it this way: "Cravath should be paying a premium over what other New York law firms are paying because associates here are expected to assume significantly more responsibility than associates in the same class at other New York firms." "It doesn't make sense that Skadden associates make more money than we do," sighs another associate. Some duly note that the final amount Cravath associates will bring home remains uncertain because bonuses have not been announced. According to one source, "The general view among associates is that bonuses should be substantial this year."

In and out

Cravath associates report a relatively high turnover rate at the firm. "Everyone seems to leave after a year or two," attorneys say. As one lawyer puts it, "There are revolving doors out front for a reason." According to insiders, by mid-2000 the fourth-year associate class in Cravath's corporate department — originally 40 in number — was down to nearly single digits.

But associates aren't blaming the firm. "We seem to be living in exceptional times, and it appears that a significantly larger number of associates have left this year than historically has been the case — mostly for dot coms." Many Cravath lawyers see the low retention rate as a positive reflection on the firm. Along with the hot job market, associates claim the revolving door is "partially due to fact that Cravath associates are prized by other employers, so typically people can leave whenever they want to." Another source says, "There are some incredible job opportunities upon leaving Cravath, and the phone rings daily." One associate claims to have been called by headhunters "from day one."

A push on hours

Hours are long for hardworking Cravath associates. "Billables of above 300 hours a month are common" though "hours change — one week you may struggle to bill 15 hours, the next week you're in the office for 100 hours." Many say that hours depend on the partner. "If your partner is in the office all night, you're there with him;" others "try to push work out the door." Still, when "it rains, it pours," and Cravath associates cite more than their share of "ruined weekends" — "things tend to come up at the last minute often." "I feel awkward leaving at 8 p.m.," confesses one associate. Others point out that "there's no bonus or other incentive tied to billable hours" and "in this market, the partners are staying weekends too."

Life in the office

First-, second-, and third-year associates must share offices at Cravath. Insiders say that "the offices themselves are fine — but sharing an office gets old after a while." Lawyers describe their working environment as "pleasant" and "functional," but one associate points out that "the offices are now over a decade old" and "aging a bit."

The support services get mixed reviews. One source says, "You really get spoiled here." But junior lawyers say things aren't so hot for beginning associates. "I have been consistently disappointed with the quality of secretarial support available to junior and mid-level associates," says one insider. Lawyers applaud the Cravath paralegals, but some associates note high turnover and low motivation among the secretarial staff. Sources report that Cravath pays secretaries less than many of its competitors, but one insider reports the firm is "addressing the situation."

Perks for Cravath associates include a "three-dollar shoe shine," "discount gym membership," and "sports tickets, which the partners are pretty good about giving out." One associate says that partners occasionally bestow ad hoc benefits: "When I was a first-year, a partner paid to upgrade my tickets to first-class when I was going home for Thanksgiving." Another mentions a barber who works in the Cravath office complex. "Many people don't think he's very good, but a lot of partners use him."

Partnership a distant dream . . . or is it?

If you want to reach the elite partnership of Cravath, you have a shot. Chances may be "slim" but are "improving for people willing to stick it out and work hard. The myths of impossibility are simply not true." And the myths abound — one associate says the rumor at this office is that the chances of making partner for a first-year associate are "less than one percent." While the criteria for partnership are "a riddle to which only initiates — a.k.a. partners — know the answer," insiders have several suggestions along the lines of "work hard," "work for the right partners," "know what you're doing and do it very well," "become clairvoyant," "show moxie," "don't piss off partners or clients," and — oh, yes — have that "something extra." Another claims that at this point "partnership decisions have been so random that anyone can make partner if the stars are aligned correctly."

Pro bono often non grata

Contacts say pro bono work at Cravath is done almost exclusively by litigators "as a way to get trial experience." Although Cravath has worked on some headline-grabbing pro bono cases (such as the Boy Scouts anti-discrimination suit), some associates say the paying work always takes precedence. "When push comes to shove," says one associate, "if you have an 'insignificant' prisoner case, the partners are going to get pissed off when you have to be out for a day to take a deposition or when you tax the firm's resources." Partner approval is apparently required to do pro bono work and is usually granted "as long at the work doesn't interfere with paying work." Still, one associate fears his partner "will think I don't have enough work to do if I ask for a pro bono case."

Simply the best

While it's not always easy, Cravath associates are confident that they practice at the best law firm in the country (and the associates we surveyed at other firms agree with them). "I think [Cravath] is regarded as the best law firm, and we are," says one associate proudly. "In each area we practice in, our reputation is superb," volunteers another insider. Recounts one associate: "In law school, this firm was the name to use when describing a firm. 'If you want to go work at Cravath...' Other firms are the Cravaths of the South or the West. It always seems to come back to Cravath."

INTERVIEW TIP #1

DO make sure you walk into the interview with a firm grasp of the firm's history and its recent engagements — knowledge that will help you target your questions. "How many associates work on these wonderful pro bono projects your firm is known for?" won't impress your interviewer if you can't name any pro bono work the firm does!

VAULT.COM

PRESTIGE RANKING: 2

Wachtell, Lipton, Rosen & Katz

51 West 52nd Street
New York, NY 10019
(212) 403-1000
Fax: (212) 403-2000
www.wlrk.com

LOCATIONS

New York, NY (HQ)

MAJOR DEPARTMENTS/PRACTICES

Antitrust
Creditors' Rights
Corporate
Exec. Compensation & Employee Benefits
Litigation
Real Estate
Tax
Trusts & Estates

THE STATS

No. of attorneys: 165
No. of offices: 1
Summer associate offers: 24 out of 25 (New York, 1999)
Executive Partner: Richard D. Katcher
Hiring Partner: By committee

PAY

New York, 2000
1st year: $140,000
2nd year: $150,000
3rd year: $165,000
4th year: $180,000
5th year: $195,000
(Associates also receive a substantial bonus)
Summer associate: $2,404/week

NOTABLE PERKS

- Huge bonuses
- Free breakfast and catered dinners from top restaurants
- Cell phone account
- Free laptops and palm pilots
- Installation of second home phone line
- Two words: frozen yogurt

THE BUZZ

What attorneys at other firms are saying about this firm

- "In a league by itself"
- "Insanely hard-core"
- "Eliminate your student debt quickly"
- "Super arrogant"

UPPERS

- Astronomical bonuses
- Small firm with big firm benefits
- Sense of security as best M&A boutique ever

DOWNERS

- Hours require devotion of life to firm
- Workaholism a plus
- Ulcer-provoking intensity

KEY COMPETITORS

Cravath, Swaine & Moore
Davis, Polk & Wardell
Simpson Thacher & Bartlett
Skadden, Arps, Slate, Meagher, & Flom
Sullivan & Cromwell

EMPLOYMENT CONTACT

Ms. Ruth Ivey
Recruiting Director
(212) 403-1374
rmivey@wlrk.com

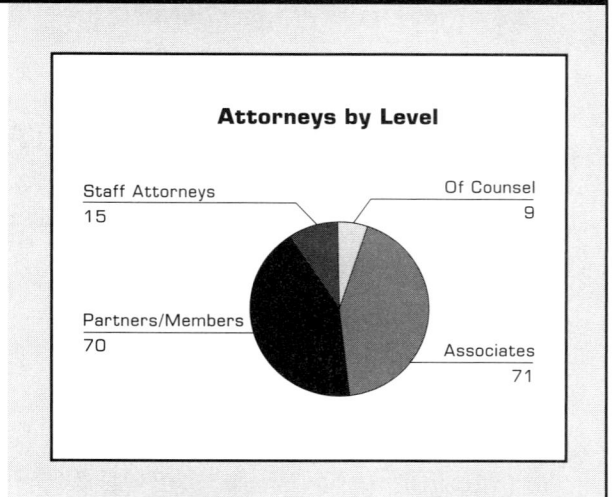

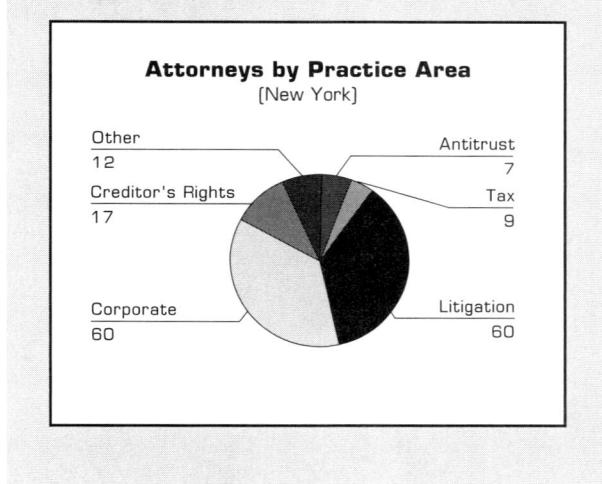

Attorneys by Level
- Staff Attorneys: 15
- Of Counsel: 9
- Partners/Members: 70
- Associates: 71

Attorneys by Practice Area
[New York]
- Other: 12
- Antitrust: 7
- Creditor's Rights: 17
- Tax: 9
- Corporate: 60
- Litigation: 60

THE SCOOP

In three short decades, the M&A firm founded by four guys from NYU Law School has become one of the most prestigious and sought-after tickets in law. "We don't do a lot of green-grocer legal chores," says an insider. "We are a small firm that takes on super-elite matters," explains another Wachtell lawyer. Wachtell is tiny compared to its competitors (about 165 attorneys and a nearly even partner-associate ratio) but very profitable — and generous. The firm is known as a compensation leader, and it has doled out extravagant bonuses in recent years.

Young firm with interesting work

For the elite corps of lawyers at Wachtell, Lipton, Rosen & Katz, history isn't a melange of mustachioed clerks and railroad baron bailouts. Of the four name partners — Herbert Wachtell, Martin Lipton, Leonard Rosen, and George Katz — three are still alive and have their names on the door. (George Katz has passed on to his eternal reward, and Leonard Rosen is now of counsel.) The four graduated from New York University Law School, where they worked together on law review, and started their own firm in 1965. Ironically, the firm's founders at first sought "interesting work," not necessarily lucrative work.

The primary goal of the partners was to create a non-hierarchical law firm. Lawyers would write their own first drafts of briefs and do their own research. The firm's partners agreed that they would do all their work through transactions; they would not have "retainer relationships" or serve as general counsel. (This policy means that Wachtell has fewer conflicts of interest.) The young firm attracted mostly Jewish and other ethnic lawyers at a time when the large New York firms were not open to them.

Startling early success

Wachtell attracted a lot of notice from the start, especially after its handling of Loews Corporation's nine-month struggle to take over CNA Financial Corp. in 1974. By 1980 Wachtell was the preferred M&A ally of those defending against corporate raiders. Wachtell, in fact, was known for its constant avowal that hostile takeovers were an evil that destroyed companies and ruined the economy. Brilliant innovator Marty Lipton invented the "poison pill" defense against takeovers in 1982, which more than 250 leading corporations quickly adopted. (This defense discourages a hostile takeover by allowing current shareholders to acquire shares of the target or the would-be raider at a discount, thereby diluting the would-be raider.) In 1984 Phillips Petroleum hired Wachtell to defend against takeover attempts by both famed corporate raider T. Boone Pickens and TWA chairman/hostile bid aficionado Carl Icahn. In 1986 the firm represented Beatrice Companies in its dazzling $6.2 billion takeover by Kohlberg, Kravis and Roberts (KKR).

In the 1980s, the golden decade of the hostile takeover, Wachtell began discounting its M&A work to attract clients. Wachtell, along with Skadden, was one of the first law firms to begin to charge firms involved in takeovers on a contingency-fee basis. Fees were based on the result achieved and the firm's contribution to the ultimate result. (This is now the payment scheme followed by many New York firms.)

Wachtell soon attracted notice for charging clients enormous fees, including a $20 million dollar tab given to Kraft, which Wachtell represented in its 1988 takeover by tobacco giant Philip Morris. Kraft was happy to pay — Wachtell was credited with obtaining a significant increase in the final price Kraft shareholders received. Legal eyebrows were raised in 1993 when Wachtell hopped to the takeover side and opted to represent QVC, which was attempting a hostile takeover of Paramount. Herbert Wachtell argued the case himself.

Takeover targets: your last resort

Hostile bidders breathing down your neck? Who you gonna call? Most likely, Wachtell. Wachtell is mainly known as a mergers and acquisitions firm — but, oh, what an M&A firm it is! Because the firm traditionally represents a lot of M&A targets Wachtell does not have a long list of constant clients. This forces the firm to rely on its expertise alone for new business. "It is a risky business model, but so far it has paid off," claims a Wachtell lawyer.

In an industry where pay scales and fees tend to move, if not in lockstep, then in a closely aligned fashion, Wachtell busts all barriers. The firm typically charges as much as 1 percent of the total dollar value of a deal, depending on the complexity of the transaction and the result. Don't like paying tens of millions of dollars, as happy clients such as Banc One and Kraft (in its merger with Philip Morris) have done? Then take a pass on Wachtell. It's not as if Marty Lipton and his cohorts will miss the business — one insider estimates that the firm turns away five engagements for each one it accepts. Similarly, associates garner huge bonuses that bring them far above their peers at law firms of comparable prestige.

Though Wachtell has a powerful M&A practice, it would be a mistake to overlook its other practices. In addition to M&A, Wachtell's other practice groups include litigation, tax, real estate, antitrust, and creditors' rights (also known as bankruptcy). The firm's litigation department has handled many high-profile cases in recent years, such as the NFL's dispute with Cowboy's owner Jerry Jones and litigation surrounding Hilton's attempted takeover of ITT. Insiders say other departments such as tax and real estate largely function as support departments, working almost exclusively on the

M&A deals that the firm handles. An exception is Wachtell's creditors' rights group (a.k.a. bankruptcy), which represents most of the world's major financial institutions. Wachtell confines its practice to the creditor side.

Small and busy

Wachtell is unusually small for a major law firm, with about 165 lawyers total (not much larger than the entering associate classes of huge firms like Skadden). This means that staffing teams are often partner-heavy, pleasing clients who want top-flight talent on their cases. Clients get what they pay for. Wachtell is an around-the-clock business, ever ready to fight an injunction or give an opinion at any hour of the day or night. Wachtell is also a perfectionist firm, insiders tell Vault.com. "We don't cut corners," say sources. "We will do anything to perfect our work. That's why we can charge exorbitant fees, because we get the job done." Even with Wachtell's cost, "we still turn down lots of work." Some critics of the firm say that its lawyers are obsessive and devote their lives to building the practice. A few partners have resigned partnerships at Wachtell; one to loll on a Costa Rican beach, another to teach law at Harvard Law School. The latter left only eight months after making partner. "Wachtell is the best firm there is," the Wachtellite-turned-professor John Coates told *The National Law Journal.* "But making partner is like winning a pie-eating contest. The prize is more pie."

The cigarette-smoking men

Wachtell has been helping tobacco firm and popular lawsuit target Philip Morris navigate the cloudy landscape of tobacco litigation. In November 1999, Herbert Wachtell, Peter Hein, and Barbara Robbins protected the tobacco company from a suit by union trust funds and health insurers. The plaintiffs had tried to bring a RICO and antitrust case against the tobacco company. But Wachtell successfully argued before the 7th Circuit that the damages to those plaintiffs were too remote. (Wachtell has also succeeded before four other federal courts of appeals on this same point.) The court agreed and held that allowing the suit to proceed would risk double recovery because the smokers could file their own suits. In 1995 Herbert Wachtell spearheaded the attack on ABC's *Day One* news program for broadcasting a misleading report on alleged manipulation of nicotine by the tobacco industry.

For and against Clinton

Another client in extremis (in a sense) was Paula Jones, President Clinton's infamous accuser. A Wachtell lawyer, George Conway, helped Paula Jones' lawyers write the brief that led to the 1997 Supreme Court ruling that President Clinton was not immune from the Jones lawsuit. But Jones was considered a private client of Conway, not a client of the firm. Wachtell partner Bernard ("Bernie") Nussbaum had previously served a stint as Clinton's legal counsel, returning to the firm in 1994.

The road to the top is lined with mergers

Wachtell isn't known as M&A central for nothing. Wachtell worked on about $395 billion of financial M&A deals in 1999 (the firm's estimate), making it the top law firm in M&A in that year. The firm represented cell phone maker Motorola in its acquisition of General Instruments Corp. General Instruments was the leading maker of cable set-top boxes, so the acquisition will now allow Motorola to develop products for cable web access. Wachtell also advised Warner-Lambert Co. during the bidding war for the pharmaceutical company. From a choice of two suitors, Warner Lambert ended up joining with Pfizer Inc. in a deal worth over $90 billion.

When AT&T decided to take control of MediaOne Group Inc. in March 1999, the telecom monolith turned to Wachtell for the $58 billion transaction. The AT&T bid put an end to MediaOne's planned merger with Comcast. The deal makes AT&T not only the country's largest telephone company but also America's biggest player in the cable arena. Wachtell also advised AT&T in its $68 billion megamerger with TCI. In addition, Wachtell helped Reynolds Metals Co. rise to the top of the aluminum world. Marty Lipton, Andrew Brownstein, Karen Krueger, Michael Byowitz, and Steven Cohen worked on the company's merger with Alcoa, the world's largest producer of the metal, announced in September 1999.

Big banking deals

Wachtell is the happy home of one of the most sought-after lawyers in the business, Edward D. Herlihy, who's a member of its M&A group. Herhily has led the firm to prominence in the area of large-scale bank mergers. In April 1998, BankAmerica turned to Wachtell as its advisor in its $60 billion merger with NationsBank. NationsBank used its own counsel. But as a longtime Wachtell client, the bank was happy to see its old firm involved as well. That same month, the firm scored a coup when Banc One and First Chicago opted to merge. Wachtell, led by Herlihy, represented both Banc One and First Chicago in the $30 billion merger, netting upwards of $10 million in fees. Though even a first-year law student could discern that representing both sides in a deal normally howls "conflict of interest," both First Chicago and Banc One agreed jointly to use Wachtell because of the firm's expertise.

Just a couple of months later, Herlihy and Wachtell duplicated the feat by serving as counsel to both Wells Fargo and Norwest Corp. in their $34 billion deal. The firm continued its dominance of the field in 1999, representing Bankers Trust in its $10.1 billion sale to Deutsche Bank AG.

Despite their involvement in some of the biggest combinations in the banking world, Herlihy and Wachtell have tried to keep a low profile and avoid the press. But one client told *The American Banker* that Herlihy keeps frequent contact with clients, sending them not only the analyst reports and the like but also other valuable information. "My entire library of golf literature is thanks to Ed Herlihy," one client said.

Counsel to Air Jordan

Wachtell doesn't just limit itself to the world of banks and finance — it plays ball too. The firm is part of the noble effort to breathe new life into the ailing Washington Wizards basketball team. In January 2000, Michael Jordan relied on the advice of Wachtell partners Mitchell Presser and David Silk to guide him through his deal to become chief of basketball operations for the Washington Wizards. The deal gives the former Chicago Bull control over trading players and hiring the coaching staff. Jordan also got a generous equity stake in the Wizards, Capitals, and the MCI Center. The firm has also advised Jordan and other sports figures on corporate investments.

GETTING HIRED

Very picky

Because of its tiny size, prestige, and high pay, getting an offer at Wachtell may be more difficult than at any other firm. The ratio of partners to associates is almost even, and the firm fully expects that every associate it hires will become a partner. Wachtell is small enough that the firm can afford to be extremely selective. The small size is a deliberate decision — larger firms make most of their money on their "excess" associates, most of whom have no chance at making partner.

Wachtell recruits from "the usual suspects," including Harvard, Yale, Columbia, Chicago, Penn, Stanford, and NYU. "Occasionally the firm will hire someone from the second tier but it's uncommon. They usually need to stand out for one reason or another," says one insider. The firm places the most emphasis on grades when making its hiring decisions, according to Vault.com's sources. "No one has surmounted bad grades with their personality or interesting background," explains one Wachtell lawyer. Another contact says a typical Wachtell hire is "the nerdy guy in law school who was managing editor of law review." The firm also wants candidates who seem committed to their practice area. "We are looking for people who want a lot of responsibility — not people who are looking to hide for a couple of years and get out."

Two or three partners and two associates typically handle call back interviews at Wachtell. Even if you get an interview, it is far from a foregone conclusion that you will get an offer. During the interview, anything on your resume is fair game, insiders report. Sometimes interviewers will ask an applicant's opinion on a recent development in the law. "The type of person we're looking for is intelligent and can think on their feet. [The interview] can be pretty grueling and you have to be able to handle it. You need to be more than just friendly," warns one Wachtell attorney. An insider who received an offer from the firm reports that Wachtell interviews "were the hardest I had." The same insider reports receiving substantive legal questions during one of his interviews. Interviewers don't mind candidates asking about hours "but we'll tell them it's a lot of hours. We want people who aren't willing to work to select themselves out."

One contact says: "It's very important to do a summer internship at Wachtell, and it's extremely difficult to get an offer here if you turn one down for the summer. We wonder, if you wanted to work here, why wouldn't you take our offer the first time?" But another source says the summer associate prerequisite is just a "myth." Cravath and Sullivan & Cromwell are the firm's favorite sources for its few lateral hires, according to associates.

OUR SURVEY SAYS

One-to-one relationships

The philosophy at Wachtell is that "it's a team" or "an extended family." Deals and cases at Wachtell are often staffed with just one partner and one associate. This close relationship avoids the hierarchy that exists at many other firms, associates report. "You're basically treated as equals," one source tells Vault.com. "Partners see you as colleagues and they want to hear what you think," says another Wachtell lawyer. Partners both ask for and value associates opinion, insiders say. "You very much feel on an equal footing with the partnership," boasts one Wachtellian. "Because the ratio between partners and associates is basically even, you work very closely with partners."

Reportedly, "doors are always open at Wachtell," and "partners call you directly. They call you by your first name, and they know who you are." Even the august Herbert Wachtell "has breakfast with associates and summer associates and he calls them into his office." Marty Lipton is said to "work with associates all the time." Most partners are "not screamers," though Herbert Wachtell "definitely raises his voice." "A month after I started here," says an associate, "a partner I was working with called me and asked me what my opinion was on an aspect of the case we were doing. I was flabbergasted, first of all, that a partner would call me, and second, because I had no idea what was going on." But the close associate/partner relationship can put a lot of pressure on associates. "You're expected to carry your load. If you live up to that, the relationship with the partners is terrific. If not, it will be a little harder."

Because associates work so closely with partners, say insiders, there is almost no competition between associates. There are also no associate committees or formal channels for associate feedback at Wachtell. But associates say they don't need them because their access to partners provides ample opportunity for informal feedback. "People feel open to talk to partners and tell them how they feel and partners are constantly asking what you think," an associate says.

An old-fashioned meritocracy

Associates continually point out that Wachtell was founded as a meritocracy. Insiders describe Wachtell as "professional," "formal," and "a bit old fashioned." "Formality is the way of Wachtell," according to an attorney. "Let's put it this way — I can't see the firm going casual," says another associate. In fact, women associates first started wearing pants to work only two years ago. But others point out that Wachtell is "not a typical white shoe firm" and the firm is "not necessarily prim and proper." "There are few distinctions between partners and associates or even associates and our staff," raves a Wachtell attorney. Another associate explains, "Collegiality at the firm crosses partner/associate lines." But others say the firm is hierarchical in that it treats its senior partners with a great deal of veneration, even adoration.

Wachtell reportedly does not give its associates a lot of grunt work. "They throw you right in there. We try to hire the best people and once you get here, there is an assumption that you will be able to do the work," an associate explains.

Not a rah rah social scene

Insiders say lawyers at Wachtell are "pretty focused on their work and don't have much of a life outside the firm." (Then again, how much of a social life can you have in 68 hours a week outside the office?) "There is not a rah rah social scene," shrugs one lawyer. "People pretty much work hard and then go home to their family and friends outside the firm. They aren't standing in the hall and talking about the Yankees," according to another associate. "The dearth of massive gala events and general hobnobbing is due to the fact people are working very late and many lawyers have families waiting at home," one source opines. But life at Wachtell is not completely devoid of human interaction. Attorneys often eat lunch or even dinner together as part of a large group. Partners will invite summer associates and new permanent hires out to dinner.

Training for self-starters

Wachtell does not have many formal training programs, although the firm does now offer more CLE in-house classes than it did in the past. Associates say most of their training at Wachtell occurs by "being thrown into things head-on. If you encounter something you don't know how to do you are expected to go find someone to help you." "We hire very smart people who will figure out what to do. Certain people thrive in this type of environment and those are the people who do well at Wachtell," observes one insider. Many Wachtellian attorneys don't mind the lack of formal training: "It encourages you to be a self-starter." But some lawyers report that partners will "take the time to discuss work with you like a professor." One associate thinks the firm could benefit from a tiny bit of structured training. "I wouldn't mind just a little hand-holding," he says plaintively.

At your desk around the clock

Wachtell is notorious for brutally long hours, and the insiders contacted by Vault.com did nothing to discredit that reputation. Associates describe the hours at Wachtell as "unbelievable." "I love what I do, but I do it too much," gripes one lawyer. Insiders report that it is not unusual for attorneys at Wachtell to bill perilously close to 3,000 hours per year. "Not everyone is billing 3,000 hours, but it is not a shock here if you do," according to an associate. Many Wachtell lawyers take their extraordinary workload in stride. "There are long hours, but people come here expecting that there will be long hours," states a third-year attorney. On the other hand, Wachtellians say their hours are not filled with drudgery. "You don't get a lot of document-intensive matters, so they're substantive hours," explains one attorney. While all Wachtell associates bill long hours, "the corporate associates are the ones who really suffer." Associates do say that they "retain a great amount of control over assignments." "As a first- or second-year associate you'll be reporting to a partner, but really your work is dictated by the clients, not the partners," says one associate. Another contact says that despite the intense hours, people do take vacations and are even encouraged to do so.

Don't expect the hours to lessen as you progress in your Wachtell career, either. Says one associate, "Essentially, you become more and more efficient but they just give you more and more deals." And what if you make partner? "The partners are somewhat mixed, but in general the partners work quite hard," asserts one insider. "Some kind of take a free ride, but that's the exception. That's the tradeoff. You'll make the money, but you're going to work. You have to work hard even as a partner."

Assignments & feedback: partnership with partners

Each department at Wachtell has an assigning partner who is primarily responsible for giving out case assignments. Partners will occasionally approach associates they have worked with previously and ask them for help on a case, insiders tell Vault.com. Every week, Wachtell sends around a sheet of paper on which associates are expected to estimate how much time they have to spare. Because there is such a low partner-to-associate ratio, say insiders, "everyone knows about how hard you are working anyway, so they are not going to give you work if you already have tons."

Lavished with goodies — healthy and otherwise

Wachtell lawyers are enthused about their offices and support services. "There is not a huge difference between partner and associate offices. Partner offices are, of course, a little bigger and may have a couch. But it is not like some firms, where the partners are sitting in offices twice the size [of associates' offices]," states a contact. The firm recently opened new floors, obtaining enough space to give everyone their own office.

Wachtell spends some of its impressive profits on making the lives of its associates a bit easier. "Anything you need, you get," at Wachtell. When it comes to giving perks, the firm "doesn't nickel and dime you," a contact notes. Wachtell associates are treated to a "full breakfast spread every morning." When the evening rolls around, "there is a catered dinner." "Anyone who is around comes to the cafeteria and has dinner together," explains one source. What kind of food do attorneys at Wachtell eat for dinner? Not the pizza and sub dinners some of their attorney friends are having. "They order from a good, fatty restaurant or one of the healthy restaurants. There's always a healthy option," reports one insider. "One of the restaurants is Hatsuhana, which is one of New York's top sushi restaurants. I've gone there by myself and it's like $60 to $70 a night. I hate to think about how much they're spending." The firm also sponsors bi-weekly lunches, which increase to once a week in the summer. The food at the luncheons is not quite at the same level as the catered dinners, Wachtell associates say. "You go up to the buffet and it's either a chicken product or a fish product," says one insider. "It's one step above the high school cafeteria."

Wachtell also has full-time kitchen staff "who dress in little kitchen outfits. They walk around and bring you coffee and take your soda cans." Each floor has a pantry with "cookies and drinks" and "fresh fruit." The firm also boasts espresso machines and a yogurt machine. "It's all free!" raves one associate. Some insiders dispute Vault.com's report from last year's *Guide* that Wachtell associates have, by and large, fattened up through access to endless free food and lack of a firm gym, noting that Wachtell subsidizes membership in area gyms.

Wachtell outfits its lawyers with laptops and an extra phone line at home to dial into the office (soon to be replaced by super-speedy DSL lines). Additionally, Wachtell "provides all associates with a cell phone and 600 minutes paid for by the firm." But the high tech gadgets do not end there: "A Palm Pilot is given to any associate who asks for one." The tech perks should come in handy during the few hours a week

Wachtell insiders actually leave their office. "Wachtell is a little bit more generous about everything," says a source. "The car service is paid for from an earlier hour. We fly first class. The firm spends extra money to make associate life comfortable."

Wachtell associates aren't saving money on their wardrobe or dry cleaning bills, though: The firm still doesn't have a casual Friday dress code. "It's suit and tie, or the equivalent for women." Wachtell attorneys can dress down on the weekends. So how do Wachtell attorneys dress? "There are a couple of fashion plates, but the vast majority of us look fairly dorky," admits one insider.

Support me

"The support is tremendous here, from car service home to 24-hour-a-day support staff. I don't have to worry about logistics. I get total logistical support from paralegals, from travel agents, from whomever. If you have to go on the spur of the moment and get your suit cleaned, there's support here to do that," says one insider who credits the outstanding support to the willingness of the firm's management to pay support staff well. "There's this entire support structure that's built up. These are people who have been here for 20 to 25 years and are paid very well," says that insider. The firm also places a great emphasis on training the support staff well, according to associates. Another source explains that support staff are just another part of the Wachtell "family." In fact, the support staff get bonuses along with the attorneys. One lawyer says that most staff members know the attorneys by name. Many of the secretaries have been around long enough to get their 10th or even 20th anniversary commemorative Wachtell plaque. The turnover rate for paralegals is reportedly high, however.

Little green lawyers

"We don't care if you're from Mars, as long as you get the job done and do it right," says one associate. But most of those Wachtell lawyers who are "doing the job right" are of the male persuasion. Many insiders observe that there are many more men than women among the associate ranks at Wachtell. "The firm used to have a rap about not being good for women. It was undeserved," says one source, who goes on to admit "the hours are heavy and not conducive to raising a family."

Mazel tov

Insiders report that Wachtell has a "Jewish family culture." For example, "kosher food is always available" for luncheons and catered dinners. Religious associates "have no problem taking Saturdays off." And on Fridays "everyone clears out." But there are few other minority lawyers at the firm. Wachtell attorneys say that has nothing to do with the atmosphere at the firm. "The firm would never look down on someone of a different race or religion," insists an insider. The firm reportedly has some openly gay attorneys, and Wachtell partners "publicly support hiring gays and lesbians."

Pro bono sometimes takes a back seat

Many sources tell Vault.com that Wachtell does not put a lot of effort into promoting pro bono work. "Pro bono is more of an individual effort here," explains one contact. Wachtell lawyers also say that they often don't have the time to devote to pro bono matters. "We are so busy with paying clients it's hard to even imagine choosing to do pro bono work," another associate states. But Wachtell partners and associates do provide pro bono litigation and corporate advice, including advising on the merger negotiations for NYU Medical School.

Sharing the (considerable) wealth

Though clearly some departments (like M&A) are much bigger moneymakers than others, associates in all departments receive the same pay and the same bonus (calculated as a percentage of salary). "Everything is lockstep," reports one insider. Wachtell reportedly matches the highest New York base salary (as of June 2000, set by Skadden Arps at $140,000 for first-year associates). However, in addition Wachtell pays its associates a bonus that puts the firm at the very top of the compensation heap. Associates says the firm tries to treat associates almost like partners by sharing a good chunk of the firm's earnings. In 1996 the bonus was 50 percent of salary; in 1997 it was a titanic 80 percent. Bonuses at Wachtell over the last two years have been 100 percent of the base salary. The greedy beware — one lawyer warns, "Don't come for money because if that is your only motivation it won't be enough. You have to want to work this hard."

Howdy, (future) partner

The party line at Wachtell is that the firm only hires associates they believe will make partner. Indeed, insiders believe the chances of making partner at Wachtell are better than anywhere else. "The hiring decision is usually a decision that this person is partnership material," says one Wachtell lawyer. "You have about a 50 percent chance if you stick it out," estimates another attorney. "You just have to do the job right." Another source says that in order to make partner you have to take on even more responsibility than the average workaholic Wachtellian. "You really have to act like you want to make partner from the get-go," he advises.

Associates who are still at the firm in their seventh year "generally know they're going to make it, because if they're there that long, they've already been told that they have a good chance." The mere fact that there are so few associates per partner means that statistically, associates who go the distance have a better chance of making partner at Wachtell than at other firms. "Associates used to make partner in their sixth year," say insiders, "now the cutoff is year seven." How do you become a Wachtell partner? "Work your ass off!"

However, insiders note that part of the reason partnership prospects are so good for those who make it through seven years is that the firm has an up-or-out environment and will "push people out." "They are what some might call brutally honest," reports one insider. "They'll give you a chance to improve, but at some point they'll tell you it's not a good fit. There's no firing unless you're found guilty of insider trading, but they'll tell you to start looking." However, notes that contact, "the firm is extremely generous. There are people who have hung around for several years after being told that they should look elsewhere."

The few, the proud, the summer associates

Wachtell hires "four or five" 1Ls every summer as well as a 2L summer associate class. Summer associates typically rotate through at least three of Wachtell's departments. Because most of these departments are small, associates spend four weeks each in two departments, then a week or two in the third department. Some summer associates may opt to spend a four-week rotation in a smaller department like real estate or creditors' rights (bankruptcy). Each department has a partner who gives out summer assignments. Summer associates say they get an enormous amount of responsibility. "What we do here is like what a fourth or fifth-year does at other firms," reports one insider. "Summer associates write briefs here on their own. It is incredibly satisfying."

By most accounts, the 20-odd summer associates at Wachtell are treated well during their brief stay. A former summer associate estimates he was taken out to lunch "maybe twice a week." Other events include a picnic at a partner's home in Larchmont (a suburban town near New York City) and another event at a partner's house in the Hamptons, the popular Long Island resort area. There is also a night when summer associates are split up and taken out to various restaurants by associates and partners. Each summer associate is assigned two "buddies," one an associate, the other a partner. Summer associates have a "partners night out," when, according to one associate, summers get to do "whatever they want." One summer associate requested — and got — "a trip to the Knicks playoffs."

Sullivan & Cromwell

PRESTIGE RANKING: 3

125 Broad Street
New York, NY 10004
(212) 558-4000
Fax: (212) 558-3588
www.sullcrom.com

LOCATIONS

New York, NY (HQ)
Los Angeles, CA
Palo Alto, CA
Washington, DC
Frankfurt
Hong Kong
London
Melbourne
Paris
Tokyo
Beijing
Sydney

MAJOR DEPARTMENTS/PRACTICES

Estates & Personal
General Practice (Corporate)
Litigation
Tax

THE STATS

No. of attorneys: 523
No. of offices: 12
Summer associate offers: 102 out of 102 (Firm-wide 1999)
Managing Partner: H. Rodgin Cohen
Hiring Partner: Francis J. Aquila

PAY

All Domestic Offices, 2000:
1st year: $125,000 + bonus
2nd year: $135,000 + bonus
3rd year: $150,000 + bonus
4th year: $170,000 + bonus
5th year: $190,000 + bonus
6th year: $205,000 + bonus
7th year: $220,000 + bonus
8th year: $235,000 + bonus
Summer associate: $2,404/week

NOTABLE PERKS

- Subsidized gym at NYC headquarters
- Emergency day care center
- Four-week paid child care leave
- Home down payment assistance
- Tickets to sporting and cultural events
- Adoption assistance plan
- Opportunities for part-time work

THE BUZZ

What attorneys at other firms are saying about this firm

- "Old money, old line"
- "Classic white shoe firm"
- "Corporate monsters"
- "Nirvana for corporate securities types"

UPPERS

- Elite firm with top work
- Responsibility that comes early and often
- Deals talked about in the *Wall Street Journal*

DOWNERS

- Grueling hours
- Secretive about decisions
- Blah beige decor

KEY COMPETITORS

Cravath, Swaine & Moore
Davis, Polk & Wardwell
Wachtell, Lipton, Rosen & Katz
Williams & Connolly

EMPLOYMENT CONTACT

Ms. Sarah K. Cannady
Manager of Legal Recruiting
(212) 558-4847

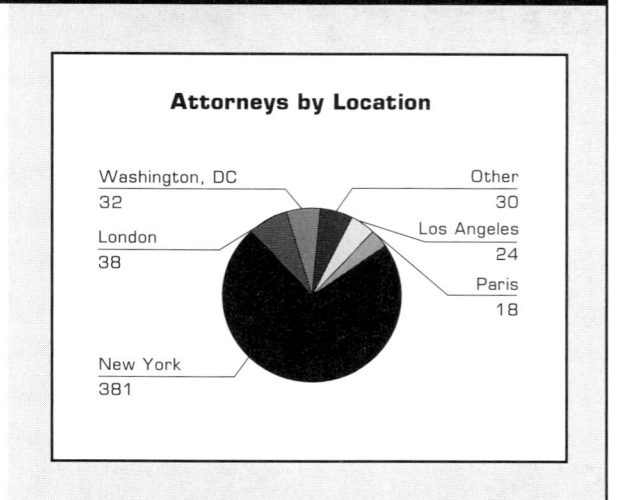

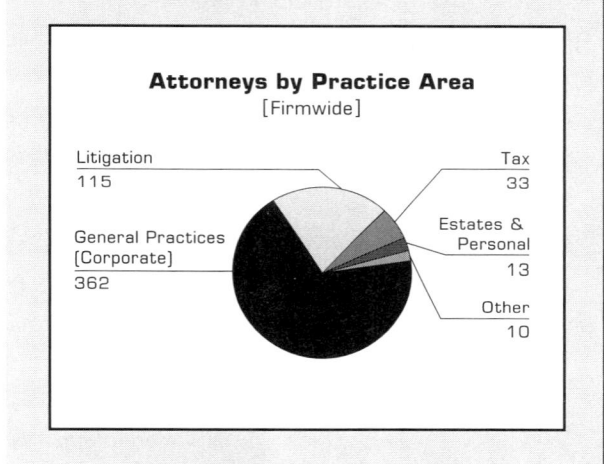

Attorneys by Location
- Washington, DC: 32
- London: 38
- New York: 381
- Other: 30
- Los Angeles: 24
- Paris: 18

Attorneys by Practice Area [Firmwide]
- Litigation: 115
- General Practices (Corporate): 362
- Tax: 33
- Estates & Personal: 13
- Other: 10

QUALITY OF LIFE RANKINGS [ASSOCIATES RATE THEIR OWN FIRM]

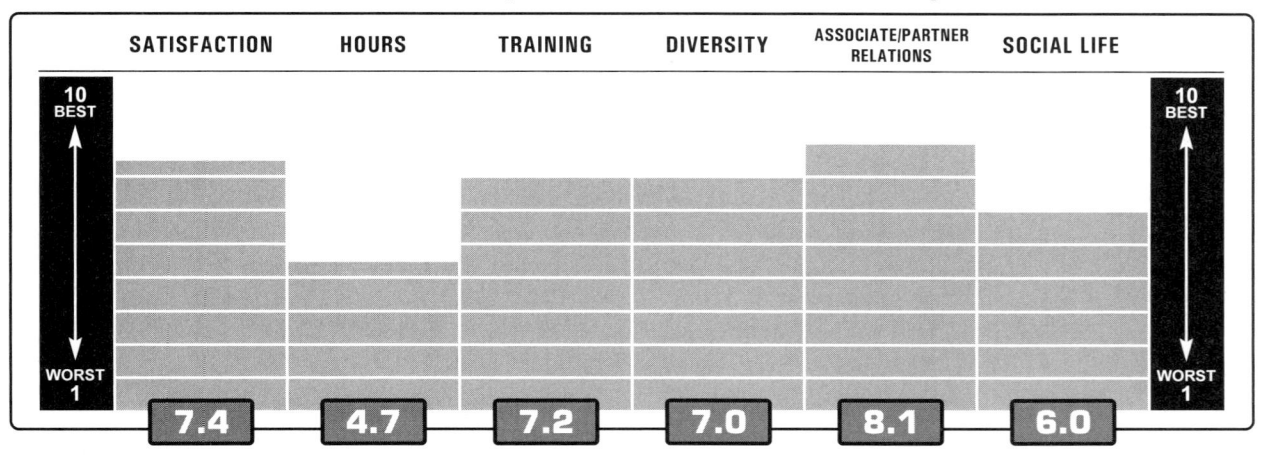

Satisfaction	Hours	Training	Diversity	Associate/Partner Relations	Social Life
7.4	4.7	7.2	7.0	8.1	6.0

THE SCOOP

From intense cases and deals to a hushed office culture, Sullivan & Cromwell is all business. A serious mien and "tomb-like" silence pervading the hallways haven't impacted the firm's bottom line — average partner compensation at the firm has exceeded the $1 million mark for more than a decade, S&C's corporate practice is among the very best in the legal field, and the firm maintains a reputation for expertise and professionalism in all of its endeavors.

An unsullied history

Sullivan & Cromwell gets its name from its founders, Algernon Sullivan and William Cromwell, who founded the firm in New York in 1879. The firm took on some of the blockbuster deals of its day, such as the formation of Edison's General Electric Company in 1882 and the United States Steel Corporation in 1901. Sullivan & Cromwell also took an early lead in the international finance market. The company represented European financiers of America's railroads and the builders of the Panama Canal. By 1928 Sullivan & Cromwell had offices in Buenos Aires, Berlin, and Paris. Even the Great Depression didn't stop S&C — the firm was an early player in the field of federal income tax and developed expertise in antitrust and shareholder litigation law.

Partners John Foster Dulles and Arthur Dean ensured that Sullivan & Cromwell continued its prestige and prominence on the international scene. Riding the waves of international capital flows and the development of the European, Asian, and Latin American markets, Sullivan opened offices in London in 1972, Washington, DC in 1977, Melbourne in 1983, Los Angeles in 1984, Tokyo in 1987, Hong Kong in 1992, Frankfurt in 1995, Beijing in 1999, and Palo Alto and Sydney in 2000. The firm now boasts 523 lawyers in 12 cities around the world.

Changing of the guard

All good things must come to an end, and one of those good things is the reign of current Sullivan chair Ricardo Mestres. Mestres, who led Sullivan for five years, stepped down on July 1, 2000. Firm rules dictate that a chairman must hand over his power when he turns 67, and Mestres's time has come. During Mestres's tenure, the firm has maintained its prominence on Wall Street while gradually expanding its overseas practice. (It's held steady at No. 3 on Vault.com's Top 50 survey, however.)

The firm has named H. Rodgin Cohen, an M&A and banking partner, as his successor. The 55-year-old Cohen has been with Sullivan since 1970 and has been a partner at the firm since 1977. In 1981 Cohen negotiated with U.S. banks to release Iranian assets, a key part of the deal that freed the American hostages in Iran. Cohen has worked on several historic transactions, including Mellon Bank's 1994 acquisition of Dreyfus, valued at $1.8 billion, the largest combination of a bank and a mutual fund ever. He also played a role in bank mergers like Northwest Corp.'s 1998 acquisition of Wells Fargo & Co. and Chemical Bank's 1996 deal with Chase Manhattan Corp.

Cohen plans on spending 75 percent of his time on client matters and 25 percent on running the firm — a daunting ratio, considering the size and prominence of Sullivan. But Cohen won't be running matters by his lonesome. He has stated that he intends to give Sullivan partners more delegated decision-making power. Cohen also intends to revisit the issue of hiring lateral partners — Sullivan has never hired a partner laterally (or at least not as of January 2000).

M&A around the world

If you are a company and you want to merge, Sullivan will probably consider the deal. In terms of the number of deals it has worked on, Sullivan ranks as one of the top three mergers and acquisitions law firms in the United States. Sullivan's M&A prowess, however, stretches overseas as well. Sullivan participated in the largest corporate takeover in history, British wireless communications company Vodafone AirTouch's $183 billion purchase of the Germany's Mannesmann AG in spring 2000. The size of the European deal broke the record set in January 2000 by the Time Warner-AOL deal.

As if building the legal underpinnings for a massive international wireless communications company weren't enough, Sullivan took part in the creation of the world's second-largest chemical company. The firm represented Union Carbide in the $11.6 acquisition by Dow Chemical announced in August 1999. The new entity will operate in 168 countries and employ over 49,000 people. Sullivan also advised oil and gas powerhouse BP Amoco on its merger with ARCO, completed in April 2000.

When French company Societe Generale bid on its domestic competitor Paribas, it was challenged by a hostile bid from Banque Nationale de Paris. To guide it through the battle, SocGen looked across the Atlantic and chose Sullivan & Cromwell. Sullivan needed to get regulatory clearance for SocGen in 64 jurisdictions, including the United States. Rodgin Cohen and his team had eight days to steer the company clear of the various legal pitfalls and get the bid ready.

Internal mergers

Never say that Sullivan doesn't plan ahead. At the end of 1999, President Clinton signed the Financial Services Modernization Act into law — an event that is expected to prove a windfall for many law firms. The new law overturned the Depression-era Glass-Stegall Act, permitting the creation of companies that provide services that include both bank loans and investments as well as insurance policies. Under the

FSMA, banks may trade securities, and insurance companies may own banks. The FSMA is expected to lead to many more mergers and combinations along the lines of the prescient Travelers-Citibank-Salomon Smith Barney rollup — and bring more work for Sullivan & Cromwell. The firm has readied itself for the new merger-friendly environment by doing a little internal merger of its own, combining its banking, insurance, and asset management attorneys into a 75-lawyer financial institutions group.

Au revoir, le partner

In February 2000, Sullivan lost one of its partners to a rival firm for the first time in its history. Pierre Servan-Schreiber is one of France's top M&A lawyers and was Sullivan's first non-English speaking partner. He was also one of the first partners not to spend any time in the New York office. Sullivan should have perhaps kept a closer eye on him — Servan-Screiber has moved to Skadden, Arps, Slate, Meagher & Flom's Paris office. Servan-Schreiber told *The Lawyer* that he was leaving because he thought Skadden was more committed to European growth.

Massive corporate finance

Sullivan consistently handles some of the largest corporate finance deals in the world. Sullivan was one of three U.S. firms to get in on the $18.6 billion sale of shares in Italy's electric company Enel. (The other firms were Shearman & Sterling and Skadden Arps.) Sullivan partner William Plapinger advised Enel in the offering. The IPO was quite complex because of its size, changes in regulations, and the need to coordinate between the U.S. and Italy. The offering was the second-largest in history, after the 1998 offering by Japanese cellular company NTT DoCoMo (with which Sullivan was also involved).

This IPO is as good as gold

After much anticipation, S&C mainstay client Goldman Sachs became the final investment bank to go public in May 1999, with Sullivan serving as issuer's counsel. In the IPO — the nation's second-largest ever — Goldman sold 69 million shares (slightly over 11 percent of the firm), raising $3.66 billion.

The crusaders of litigation

With 115 lawyers, litigation is Sullivan's second-largest department. In October 1999, Sullivan litigators represented British Airways in its battle with Virgin Atlantic. Virgin Atlantic claimed that BA engaged in anticompetitive conduct by maintaining a stranglehold on air routes originating at London's Heathrow Airport and manipulating travel agent bookings. The district court held that there wasn't enough evidence to keep the case alive and dismissed the suit. But Sullivan's work is not finished quite yet — Virgin has appealed to the Second Circuit.

Sullivan lawyers helped client Norelco through a close shave with rival razor company Gillette, which sued Norelco for libel. Gillette claimed that Norelco's advertisements for its electronic shavers were false and disparaging. But in Norelco's defense, Sullivan lawyers pointed out to the court that Gillette engaged in a strategy they described as "sue first, test later." The same Gillette people who decided to bring the suit later designed the tests used to prove the ads were false. In October 1999, the judge sided with Norelco and held that Gillette had failed to show how consumers interpreted Norelco's ads. Sullivan lawyers Richard Carlton, Bob Giuffra, Timothy Helwick, John Stellabotte, and Michael Steinberg worked on the case.

Big companies aren't Sullivan's only clients. In October 1999, the firm filed a suit on behalf of the Gay Men's Health Crisis. The dispute began when four men were arrested while attending a rally for slain gay University of Wyoming student Matthew Sheppard. According to the complaint, the New York police kept the four from getting vital prescription medication while they were being detained. The plaintiffs say the New York police violated their civil rights, caused them emotional distress, and chilled their willingness to participate in civil demonstrations. As of the time this book went to print, the case was unresolved.

Mondo Microsoft

Working with Microsoft may be giving some Sullivan lawyers a splitting headache. Sullivan's many successes have been overshadowed somewhat by the setbacks it suffered in the federal Microsoft antitrust suit, the most highly publicized antitrust case in recent years. The trial has presented cutting-edge issues in the antitrust field, as that area of law struggles with the new Internet economy. One issue is that of "technological tying" — which in this case consists of Microsoft's incorporation of a web browser into its Windows 98 operating system. The Justice Department alleged that this tying was an anti-competitive scheme aimed at crushing rival Netscape Communications.

The DOJ's lead counsel, David Boies, poked serious holes in Microsoft's defense. Boies introduced e-mail after e-mail from Microsoft executives discussing their desire to destroy competing companies. In addition, Boies brought a number of witnesses to the stand to argue that Microsoft had bundled Internet Explorer with Windows to cement its operating system monopoly. Sullivan, on the other hand, had to give its lead counsel Richard Urowsky a back seat due to his acrimonious relationship with the presiding judge, District Judge Thomas Penfield Jackson. Sullivan did achieve some early success in the suit: the appeals court found in June 1998 that District Judge Jackson had wrongly issued a preliminary injunction against Microsoft.

But Sullivan lawyers must have realized things were taking a turn for the worse in November 1999 when Judge Jackson came out with a finding of fact that labeled Microsoft a predatory monopolist. After settlement discussions with the software giant fell apart in April 2000, Judge Jackson definitively ruled that Microsoft violated antitrust laws and kept "an oppressive thumb on the scale of competitive fortune." In June 2000, Judge Jackson ordered Microsoft be broken into two companies. Microsoft has appealed the decision and remains a committed client of S&C.

Transmission problems

When the Bank of New York had to go before Congress in September 1999 to talk about its role in Russian money laundering, it turned to Sullivan & Cromwell lawyers to help prepare and to scrutinize the bank's records. The government discovered that around $10 billion had passed through the bank in perhaps the biggest illegal money transmission operation ever uncovered. BONY employees came up on the Justice Department's radar screen because one of the bank's vice presidents, Lucy Edwards, handled accounts that were the focus of the investigation. Edwards and her husband Peter Berlin pleaded guilty to charges of conspiracy to operate an illegal funds transmission, fraud, and tax evasion. The government has not accused the bank of any wrongdoing, and the bank has cooperated in the government investigation. BONY also reportedly fired two employees over the scandal.

Going where the clients are

To keep up with the firm's growing business around the world, Sullivan has been expanding the number of its outposts. The firm opened an office in Beijing with three lawyers in 1999. S&C plans on representing outside investors in China as well as helping Chinese companies raise cash. In March 2000, Sullivan announced that it would set up shop in Silicon Valley. Sullivan plans on relocating four partners to the new office, and will transfer and hire up to 10 associates in the high-tech hotspot.

GETTING HIRED

High emphasis on grades

Although Sullivan is very choosy when it comes to picking new hires, the firm has lawyers from more than 70 law schools in its ranks. "Of course, law school grades form the cornerstone of the recruiting process, particularly with law schools outside of the top ten," insiders say. In fact, S&C puts such an emphasis on grades that the firm routinely bounces law review applicants. According to one source, however, "the firm is also looking for nice people who have interesting backgrounds." S&C lawyers report that although standards remain high, it is much easier to get hired as a lateral than straight out of law school. S&C itself disputes this, claiming that it may actually be more difficult for laterals to get in the door.

Sullivan looks for candidates "who can both analyze information and articulate their findings." "At Sullivan, we don't do a lot of memos," adds another insider. "You're just given a problem and asked to figure out what's going on and report back. So if you can do a brilliant analysis but can't communicate it clearly, no dice." The other factor is "how dedicated you will be. We use a test where we ask ourselves, if you got a call from an important client, would this person be a handicap or a benefit if added to your team over the weekend?" Insiders say the reason for this is the simple fact that "Sullivan is a wonderful firm, but not for everyone. If you're really busy, you can't clear out at 7:00 to go meet friends for dinner." Evidence of "dedication and perfectionism, such as athletic performance," thus becomes an advantage.

OUR SURVEY SAYS

Partners confidential

"The professional confidence that partners express in their associates is special," one S&C lawyer raves. A second-year associate also comments on the amount of trust partners place in associates. "I've been asked by the partners on many occasions what I think about difficult issues. If they find that you have proven your capability, the partners will value your judgment and treat you with respect." Another associate says that he feels free to speak his mind to his bosses. "It's accepted and often encouraged to engage your fellow attorneys, including partners, in debate regarding the best business or legal strategy to pursue both inside the walls of S&C and in front of clients. Good ideas are good ideas regardless of their source."

A corporate associate adds, "While not every partner is charming and delightful, even the worst at least appreciate my input and hard work. The best have shown interest in my career and training and have taken me to lunch, thanked me, and occasionally even said 'good job.'" But a respectful partnership doesn't necessarily translate into a warm and fuzzy partnership. Says one source, "Partners are generally very formal — almost to a fault, especially the older generation." In order to bridge this gap, new chairman Rodgin Cohen and partner Frank Aquila hold a weekly lunch with small groups of associates to discuss firm issues.

Buttoned-down environment

Insiders describe S&C as "intense" and "formal." "This firm is stuffy," opines one lawyer. "It is not hostile or a place of closed doors, but it is questionable whether I would ever enter an open one unless I knew the lawyer." Another lawyer reports, "It's the buttoned-down, Wall Street culture that you'd probably expect from a buttoned-down, Wall Street firm." But things may be changing, if a bit slowly. Straying from the buttoned-down image, the firm recently adopted a business casual policy for the summer and Fridays the rest of the year. "The firm is far from stuffy or even very white shoe," one associate claims. "People are very down to earth and they respect diversity of opinions."

Despite the image, insiders report a sense of camaraderie. "There is a clear promotion of the firm and teamwork over individual achievement," says an associate. Another attorney explains, "The culture is extremely supportive. The combination of essentially lockstep compensation for associates and partners limits competition."

To paint the town red, look elsewhere

While insiders describe S&C as collegial, many emphasize that "this is not a party firm." One source tells Vault.com, "Associates will talk on the phone with each other and send e-mails to keep in touch with friends. But mostly they work too hard to find time to play. When they have time to spare, they'd rather go home to spouses or sleep." Insiders cited their busy schedules as one of the main reasons behind the lack of out-of-office socializing. "Free time is very rare and I don't see a lot of people spending it with other S&C lawyers, unless you count lunch on Saturday at the corner deli." According to another S&C lawyer, "S&C is by and large a very professional, non-social environment. Small groups of lawyers may spend time together, but the environment is geared to working and not socializing."

Still, the motivated will always find time to enjoy their co-workers. An S&C associate claims, "Ultimately the social life of the firm is what makes the job worthwhile. In my experience, at least once — and usually twice — a week in the evenings or on weekends I will get together with other associates and sometimes partners from the firm outside of the office."

A commitment to pay the piper

"Setting aside Wachtell's bonus structure, S&C has made a commitment to pay the highest salary in New York," according to one source. Indeed, Sullivan & Cromwell has kept pace with the salary raises in the legal market. "S&C keeps up with the salary requirements to attract and retain top associates and tends to give raises retroactively after studying the compensation market," associates say. S&C provides lockstep compensation and bonuses are not tied to hours.

Although most associates are pleased with the money they are bringing home, some say they deserve more than their competitors. "Associates feel that S&C asks more from them than other firms, especially firms in San Francisco, DC, or Boston, and as a result they should be compensated more than other firms, especially firms in other regions," one lawyer says.

Training is improving

Associates have mixed views on the firm's training. "S&C has a very comprehensive official training program that is very good," according to one lawyer. Others say, "There are numerous training sessions afforded to young associates but they are generally presented by senior partners and do not provide practical lawyering skills." Another associate adds, "The formal training programs are lacking, but the firm is attempting to improve the training through meetings with associates." S&C will institute a new formal training program for associates of all levels in late 2000.

Most associates feel they are gaining valuable skills from their daily work experience. "Associates are given as much responsibility as they can handle and there is no better way to learn than on the job," reports one lawyer. "The flip side of having tremendous responsibility is that you do not have as much informal training," opines another attorney.

Erratic hours — long or longer

Although hours can be erratic, most associates report billing between 60 to 70 per week on average. But the firm reports that associates averaged less than 2,250 total hours in 1999. According to one source, "Hours worked is the greatest quality-of-life problem this firm faces, and it's unclear if the partners recognize the seriousness of the problem. The brightest young associates realize that the cost/benefit equation of being a young associate does not make financial or quality-of-life sense and they leave." Another typical comment: "The work is amazing and the people are brilliant. I just wish there were fewer hours." As at most large firms, another problem is the unpredictability of associates' schedules. "The hours can be pretty tough. In addition, there is an expectation that you are available at any moment. This is driven by the senior associates when you are a junior attorney and then by the clients once you are a senior associate." But one source says associates gain a little more control over the schedule as they progress through the ranks. "By the time you're a third-year associate, you manage your workload and generally can make time for one or two important things — like family and exercise."

"Small things make a big difference"

Most associates describe the offices as "professional," "spacious," and "functional." But some find them a little drab. "The offices are very nice — and very beige," one associate says. (But isn't beige the new black?) New associates may have to share offices for up to two years. Others point out that the firm is generous on small details. "They do not skimp on little things. For example, we don't have to punch in billing codes on the phones when making a call, we have local fax machines in each secretary area, and copiers on the floor which do not require billing codes. These may seem like small things, but when you are busy, small things make a big difference."

Associates give kudos to most of S&C's support services. Paralegals and the library staff are singled out as particularly exceptional. But some of the secretaries draw criticism. "There are some excellent secretaries but in many cases there is no value added," one associate says. Often two to three associates share a secretary. Some junior attorneys find that they are low priority in the eyes of some secretaries. "Support staff often does not understand that they work for associates as well," according to one lawyer. One associate also claims the duplicating department is "hostile" at times; the firm claims that it has remedied this problem, however.

S&C lawyers in demand

S&C has not been spared the high turnover rate endemic to the legal industry over the past few years. "The majority of associates leave within three to five years, but of those there are a large number who never planned to stay any longer in the first place," according to one S&C lawyer. Another associate says, "Turnover is fairly high, but what do you expect? We have headhunters calling us weekly, and quite often the opportunities presented are pretty good." In recent years lateral moves by associates have been evenly distributed between Internet startups, investment banks, and other law firms, associates report.

A comfortable zone for diversity

"S&C is the truest meritocracy I've witnessed," says one associate. "Sex, sexual orientation, religion, race, political affiliation, and social preferences are irrelevant. What matters is whether you're an effective attorney." Most associates seem to agree that S&C is a comfortable place for minority lawyers, but the firm has not taken any special initiatives in that area. One source reports, "I have not noticed any recognition of minority issues in either a positive or negative way." "The efforts to enhance ethnic diversity are less visible. But because this is a meritocracy where you will fit in if you work hard, anyone can succeed," says an associate. Yet another points out that, "because there are few minority partners and senior associates, mentoring is not widely available."

To its credit, Sullivan is trying to address diversity issues head-on, announcing three brand-new diversity programs. The first is the establishment of a Diversity Committee, headed by litigation partner and former President of the New York City Bar Association Mike Cooper. It has also designated fifth-year associate Kandance Weems Norris as coordinator of the firm's minority recruitment and retention efforts. Finally, S&C will fund six $10,000-per-year scholarships for minority students at Howard Law School.

Most of Vault.com's sources say the firm treats men and women as equals. Four women made partner in 1999 and S&C's management has made it clear that Sullivan lawyers who work part-time (mostly women) can make partner. "S&C is extremely flexible in terms of telecommuting and part-time work. In this respect S&C is way out in front of many of its clients," says one lawyer.

Associates report that there are openly gay partners and associates at S&C and the firm has an accepting attitude toward gays and lesbians. The firm provides domestic partnership benefits and generally treats homosexual partners the same as heterosexual partners at social events. "As I said before," one source explains, "S&C is a place where people don't care who you are as long as you get your work done."

Pro bono available but not pushed

Along with the Microsoft trial and the high-profile mergers, S&C has also been active in defending prisoners' rights. The firm annually offers up a member of its incoming class to work exclusively on prisoners' litigation on a pro bono basis for an entire year. The firm also donated between $5,000 and $20,000 to the Prisoners' Legal Service after New York's Governor Pataki vetoed the organization's budget. Additionally, Sullivan lawyers Michael Lacovara and Theodore Edelman took a Georgia prisoner's habeas corpus case and got the Georgia Supreme Court to set aside the man's death sentence. The attorneys successfully showed that the court-appointed trial counsel had done almost no work until just before trial. Unlike the trial counsel, the Sullivan lawyers recorded thousands of hours on the case.

Insiders say S&C is very supportive of pro bono work and the firm treats pro bono matters like billable work. One typical response suggests that "the firm is committed to pro bono. But it's the individual lawyer's commitment that counts. If you want to support a cause, from defending death penalty cases to protecting community gardens from development, you have the full resources of the firm behind you." Many attorneys say that S&C has a hands-off attitude toward pro bono. "There are people here dedicated to pro bono matters; however, I have not been encouraged to do any pro bono work and the firm seems to neither encourage or discourage it."

INTERVIEW TIP #2

DO turn the focus toward your interviewer. Always keep in mind that lawyers are not professional interviewers — "In fact, some of them are kind of uncomfortable," confides one Simpson Thacher lawyer. However, "if interviewers talk through most of the interview, they'll think it went well."

How do you do this? Keep your ears open and ask personal questions. One first-year associate suggests, "Ask how they got interested in their firm. And when you hear something you can extend a bridge to, take advantage of the opportunity. Perhaps your interviewer went to Dartmouth — hey, so did your brother — it might be an excellent way to get the conversation rolling."

Davis Polk & Wardwell

PRESTIGE RANKING: 4

450 Lexington Avenue
New York, NY 10017
(212) 450-4000
Fax: (212) 450-4800
www.dpw.com

LOCATIONS

New York, NY (HQ)
Menlo Park, CA
Washington, DC
Frankfurt
Hong Kong
London
Paris
Tokyo

MAJOR DEPARTMENTS/PRACTICES

Corporate
Litigation
Tax
Trusts & Estates

THE STATS

No. of attorneys: 580
No. of offices: 8
Summer associate offers: 86 out of 86 (New York, 1999)
Executive Partner: John R. Ettinger
Hiring Partner: Gail A. Flesher

PAY

New York, 2000
1st year: $125,000
2nd year: $135,000
3rd year: $150,000
4th year: $165,000
5th year: $180,000
6th year: $205,000
Summer associate: $2,400/week

NOTABLE PERKS

- Subsidized cafeteria
- Domestic partner benefits
- Emergency child care
- Free Starbucks coffee

THE BUZZ
What attorneys at other firms are saying about this firm

- "Where everyone wants to work"
- "Intellectually powerful"
- "Stuffy"
- "High on the food chain"

UPPERS

- Outstanding food in cafeteria
- Interesting legal work
- Courteous culture

DOWNERS

- Sharing offices wears thin quickly
- Some passive-aggressive senior associates and partners
- Habit of "assigning" people to specialty practice groups

KEY COMPETITORS

Cleary, Gottlieb, Steen & Hamilton
Cravath, Swaine & Moore
Simpson Thacher & Bartlett
Sullivan & Cromwell
Wachtell, Lipton, Rosen & Katz

EMPLOYMENT CONTACT

Ms. Bonnie Hurry
Director of Recruiting & Legal Staff Services
(212) 450-4144

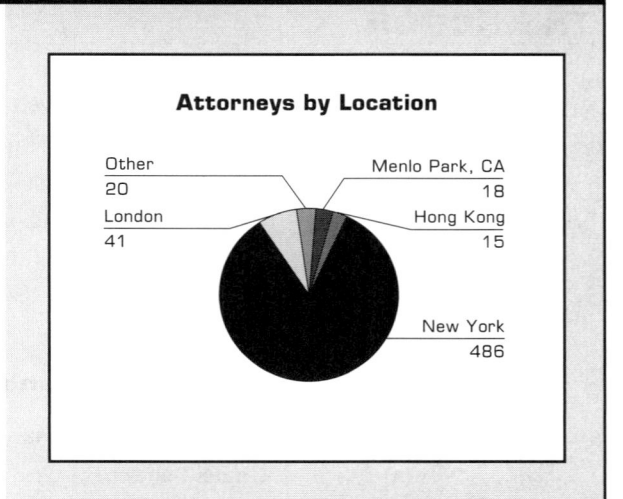

Attorneys by Location
- Other: 20
- Menlo Park, CA: 18
- London: 41
- Hong Kong: 15
- New York: 486

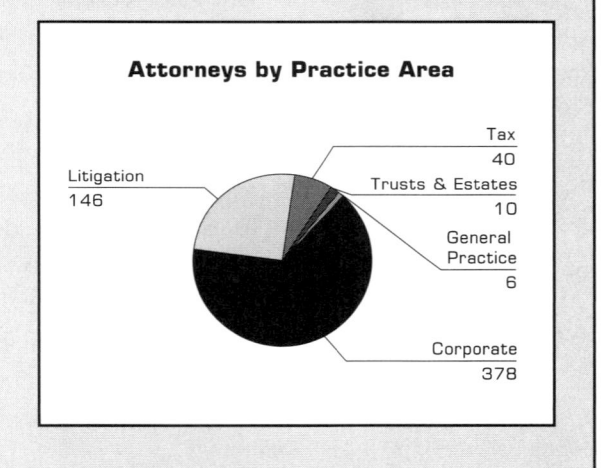

Attorneys by Practice Area
- Litigation: 146
- Tax: 40
- Trusts & Estates: 10
- General Practice: 6
- Corporate: 378

QUALITY OF LIFE RANKINGS [ASSOCIATES RATE THEIR OWN FIRM]

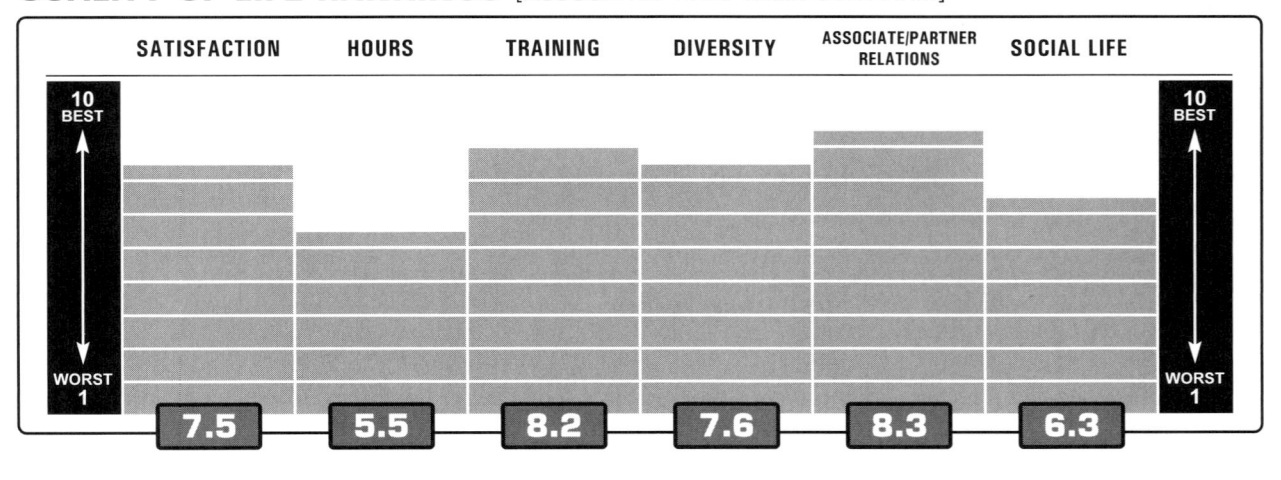

SATISFACTION	HOURS	TRAINING	DIVERSITY	ASSOCIATE/PARTNER RELATIONS	SOCIAL LIFE
7.5	5.5	8.2	7.6	8.3	6.3

THE SCOOP

Davis Polk & Wardwell is not only one of the most prestigious law firms in the world — it is also one of the nicest. Davis is evenhanded in its success. The firm brings in record revenues with a rock-solid securities practice and possesses an equally reputable litigation department that's renowned for its white collar defense work. Civil behavior has its rewards — Davis Polk once again takes the No. 4 slot in the Top 50 survey.

The distinguished Davis Polk

Davis Polk's origins date back to 1849, making it one of the oldest law firms in the United States. How would you like to work for the firm of Bangs & Stetson? Davis Polk's lawyers opted for a different set of names for the firm from those of its original founders, and today Davis Polk & Wardwell is one of the most prestigious and most successful law firms in the world, with offices in New York, Washington, DC, Menlo Park, London, Paris, Frankfurt, Tokyo, and Hong Kong. Francis Bangs was a litigator who made his name opposing William Tweed and his ring of corrupt lawyers, judges, and other sinister hirelings. Bangs was succeeded by his partner Francis Stetson, who had abandoned the field of litigation to cash in on the growing importance of corporate work. In 1887 J. Pierpont Morgan selected Stetson to be chief counsel for his banking business. The crafty Stetson soon proved his worth, stringing together several newfangled electrical companies for Morgan to create an entity called "General Electric." Stetson's firm also worked around the clock to create corporate structures for huge corporations like U.S. Steel, International Paper, and ITT.

Litigator John Davis assumed management of the firm after Stetson's death in 1921. Davis, once a Democratic presidential candidate, argued before the Supreme Court 141 times during his lifetime. Frank Polk, a corporate lawyer, led the U.S. delegation to the Paris Peace Conference that created the ill-fated Treaty of Versailles. The third name partner, Allen Wardwell, was a banking specialist who worked in Russia during that country's 1917 revolution. In fact, Davis Polk handled international matters as early as the 1890s, working on J.P. Morgan's behalf in Europe, Africa, and Asia. To this day, Davis Polk is one of J.P. Morgan's primary counsels. The firm also works extensively for securities firm Morgan Stanley Dean Witter.

New offices, new faces

Davis Polk is part of the new California firm rush, opening an office in Menlo Park. To get the new outpost off on the right foot, Davis Polk hired top technology lawyers Frank Currie and Bill Kelly. In exchange for jumping ship to Davis Polk, the firm promised Currie it would eventually send him to one of its international offices. The defection ended Currie's 14-year tenure with Wilson Sonsini, while Kelly left his post as senior vice president at Silicon Graphics. The new office is also staffed by Sally Brammell, who is returning to Davis Polk after spending six years at Pillsbury Madison & Sutro, as well as three other Davis Polk partners.

Earning bucks from Davis Polk

On January 31, 2000, Davis Polk became the first New York firm to match the Silicon Valley salary raises, agreeing to start its first year associates at $125,000. In case you're looking for further financial rewards, the firm offers another way to make a little extra money: get hitched. When Davis Polk associates marry each other, each receives a gift from the firm.

Davis Polk associates have the chance to directly impact the compensation of partners as well. Jumping on a burgeoning law firm trend, Davis Polk now allows associates to help determine partners' fortunes through written reviews. The evaluations are more than just an avenue to vent complaints — they are factored into the partner's compensation considerations.

Oh-so-techie

Davis Polk has kept ahead of the technology curve, maintaining a company intranet for the past five years. The system keeps lawyers up to date on regulatory changes, news about practice areas, and clients. The intranet also eases previously time-consuming data searches. Davis Polk has devoted a lot of attention to its office services — *The New York Law Journal* reports that even competitors want to follow the example of DPW director of professional services and systems Michael Mills. In addition, the firm has put a few of its attorneys into full-time practice resource positions. These lawyers forgo billables to provide standard forms and other services for various transactions.

Davis Polk was one of the first firms to offer virtual legal services to clients. The firm runs the Global Collateral Project, a tool aiding cross-border financing. It allows clients to enter the variables for a specific transaction and pull up legal analysis the firm has rendered. The computer system's preliminary advice can then be fine-tuned later by a flesh-and-blood DPW lawyer.

Big IPOs and beastie mergers

"You couldn't do any better for finance, securities and transactional work," insiders opine. Indeed, many regard Davis Polk's securities as the finest in the country. In a year known for IPOs, Davis Polk worked on $5 billion of offerings, putting it at the top of *The National Law Journal*'s 1999 IPO list. That year, the firm advised Morgan Stanley, the underwriter for UPS's offering, the largest American IPO at the time.

The firm continues to take part in headline-grabbing mergers. Davis Polk scored a bit of a coup in the M&A world by representing Network Solutions when VeriSign acquired the assignor of Internet domain names. Network Solutions skipped over Pillsbury Madison & Sutro, its longtime corporate counsel, for help on the deal. DPW also took part in the creation of the largest railroad in North America by representing Canadian National Railway Company in its $6 billion merger with Burlington Northern Santa Fe Corp. The new railway company encompassed 50,000 miles of track reaching from Nova Scotia to Los Angeles and the Gulf of Mexico.

Davis Polk counts the nation's third-largest cable television provider, Comcast, among its clients. In January 2000, the firm advised Comcast on its purchase of the 45 percent of Comcast MHCP that the company did not already own. The deal gives Comcast 642,000 additional subscribers in Michigan, New Jersey, and Florida. A month earlier, Davis Polk also helped Comcast in its efforts to acquire cable company Lenfest Communications from AT&T.

DPW is taking part in creating the world's second-largest music business. The firm is advising EMI Group as it merges its music business with that of Time Warner. The new mega-music business will represent 2,500 musicians. The joint venture also means that EMI's Beastie Boys, Janet Jackson, and Spice Girls will be under the same roof as Time Warner's Metallica, Madonna, and REM. Together the two companies will hold 20 percent of the music market.

Davis Polk has maintained a huge presence on the Spanish Bank market, having worked on the $36 billion merger of Banco de Credito Hispanoamerica and Banco Santander, and the $11.5 billion merger of Banco Bilbao Vizcaya and Argentaria Caja Postal & Banco Hipotecario. The firm has also been heavily involved in the process of privatizing the banks in Spain.

So sue you

While DPW may have notable corporate work, the firm offers an equally prestigious litigation practice. The firm's litigation group encompasses such fields as securities litigation and compliance (Davis Polk is often called upon to assess clients' compliance practices), antitrust law, and products liability. Another particularly lucrative if somewhat controversial source of revenue has been Big Tobacco. Davis Polk has represented the parent company of RJR Nabisco's tobacco business.

The firm also possesses a fine white collar criminal litigation practice, led by original Whitewater independent counsel Robert Fiske. Many of its other litigators were previously government prosecutors or agents as well. Clients Davis Polk represented in the 1990s include Philip Morris in its many federal grand jury investigations; Prudential in its successful effort to elude criminal liability in its limited partnership fiasco; and Exxon in federal and state grand jury investigations of potential environmental violations stemming from the Valdez oil spill. Davis Polk also represented the crafty, superannuated Washington lobbyist Clark Clifford in connection with his involvement in the BCCI banking scandal.

When the former chief executive officer of investment bank Keepe, Bruyette & Woods, Inc. was arrested for allegedly leaking confidential information to a Miami porn star, he turned to Davis Polk. The U.S. Securities and Exchange Commission accused James McDermott of leaking information concerning at least six mergers to the "performer" with whom he supposedly had an intimate relationship. But a conflict of interest developed for the firm — Davis Polk lawyer Gary Lynch had represented McDermott in May 1999 when he went before a bank board to confess only that he had passed on public non-material information to a friend. Lynch now may be called as a witness to testify about McDermott's statements before the KBW board and has agreed not to participate in the defense. But Davis Polk's Scott Muller continues to vigorously defend McDermott.

Judging the judge

In January 2000, Davis Polk found itself not just arguing in front of a judge but arguing against a judge. The firm represented the Judicial Council of the 5th Circuit, which had sanctioned federal judge John McBryde. The Council banned the judge from hearing cases for a year due to his courtroom demeanor, his fights with other judges and members of the bar, and some of his decisions. McBryde struck back at the Council by bringing a legal challenge to the sanction, arguing that the Council did not have the authority to sanction him under the Judicial Conduct and Disability Act. The district judge didn't buy it, however, and left the punishment in place.

The sting

Davis Polk has provided plenty of high-quality legal advice to client Morgan Stanley Dean Witter. But the firm took some heat for its role in the investment bank's infamous Christian Curry affair. In April 1998, MSDW fired Curry after nude photographs of the junior analyst appeared in *Playguy*, a gay men's magazine. Morgan Stanley insisted that it fired Curry for abusing expense accounts. In August 1998, the situation was complicated when Curry was arrested for allegedly conspiring to plant racist e-mail messages in Morgan Stanley's computer system to use as evidence in an anticipated discrimination suit.

In May 1999, things took another weird turn with the revelation that the bank had paid Curry's friend Charles Luethke $10,000 for help in catching Curry's alleged e-mail plants. It was further revealed that, before making the payment, Morgan Stanley's in-house counsel had sought advice from longtime outside counsel Davis Polk. The firm advised that such a payment would be legal, on the grounds that it was a simple reward for Luethke's services as a whistleblower. Davis Polk took its share of criticism, but partners quickly expressed their confidence that the scandal would not damage relations between Davis Polk and Morgan Stanley. "From our point of view, the relationship is a strong one," managing partner John Ettinger commented shortly after news of the payment broke. "It's absolutely solid. I feel very confident of that."

Award-winning pro bono

Davis Polk has long demonstrated a dedication to pro bono work. Recently the firm sponsored a fellow at the Lawyers Alliance for New York to spearhead the Public School Reform Project. The fellow will help provide legal services to educational reform organizations striving to improve schools in low-income communities. In October 1999, the Minority Corporate Counsel Association honored Davis Polk for its efforts to increase diversity in the profession. Additionally, Columbia University awarded Davis Polk a prize for social responsibility for its pro bono work in the area of political asylum law.

Davis Polk has also been a leader in the founding of Probono.net, a web site that provides resources to attorneys seeking to get involved with pro bono cases. The site features everything from potential assignments and training materials to background research and online assistance. Davis Polk's pro bono coordinator, Mark O'Brien, founded the site, launched in December 1998, along with a partner at Latham & Watkins.

GETTING HIRED

The ordinary need not apply

One source says the door to Davis Polk is closed to candidates who are not from the nation's top law schools, "unless you have something outstanding in your background, such as your undergraduate school or work experience." Although stellar credentials may get you past the on-campus interview, insiders say that getting good grades at a prestigious law school does not guarantee a job at Davis Polk. "Grades only get you in the door. Personality gets you the job." Other insiders imply that Davis Polk has a taste for "blue blood" and "prefers people from Harvard and Yale." More than 20 different law schools were represented in the 2000 summer class, however.

After candidates are called back to headquarters to interview, "grades aren't as important, though they still matter." Prospective Davis Polk attorneys have four or five interviews in the second round — two with partners and two or three with associates. Many candidates also have lunch with two junior associates. Insiders report that after each interview or meeting, the interviewers fill out an evaluation sheet, assessing the candidate on "analytical and communications skills" and "deciding whether they would like to work with that person." Some associates also told Vault.com that Davis Polk will take into account a candidate's language skills and willingness to work in foreign offices.

The hiring committee meets weekly to make its decisions. Those who are hired normally get a call shortly after the day of the meeting from a partner, though some associates point out that "if they're missing a few evaluation sheets or the meeting is delayed for some reason, they can skip a week." After an offer is made, one of the associates follows up with phone calls "to help sell the firm."

One insider muses, "At some New York firms, getting the 'flyback' is tantamount to receiving a summer offer. Davis Polk, on the other hand, relies more heavily on the flyback interviews and regularly rejects people after a full round of interviews at the firm. Those found haughty or conceited often get harshly reviewed and fail to receive summer offers."

OUR SURVEY SAYS

An early lead in the salary race

In February 2000, Davis Polk raised first-year salaries to $125,000. Associates were excited not only by the raise itself but also by Davis Polk's decision to be one of the first New York firms to offer the increase. Says one corporate associate, "DPW surprised us by leading the last salary charge. It gave the associates here a new feeling that the partners were watching out for us. They bought themselves some new loyalty." Associates also compliment the firm on not tying salaries to billable hours. Some of the more senior associates are not quite as impressed. "The first-year associates were bumped up to $125K, but the mid-level associates received comparatively meager raises," reports one. Many lawyers are also waiting to see their bonus at the end of 2000 before they start celebrating, "We are hoping for $20,000, but $10,000-$15,000 wouldn't cause a revolt."

"No screaming, no insults, no hugs"

Davis Polk lawyers describe the partners as "very nice and cordial, but you don't forget who is boss." "Although the atmosphere at Davis Polk is extremely civil and polite, it can be rather impersonal," comments one insider. Another common sentiment rings, "They don't shout and scream, but they don't invite you out for drinks or dinner or take an interest in your career or personal life." Although there are a few associates who feel they are treated as "cannon fodder," many Davis Polk lawyers find their bosses to be good mentors. "Some of them very clearly put an emphasis on teaching young associates." Another adds that "the partners will typically bend over backwards to make sure that associates get to take their vacations."

Amazing associates and hierarchical social scene

If you're looking for love — or at least a good time — you may very well find it at Davis Polk. Lawyers say there is "lots of firm dating" at Davis Polk. One associate tells Vault.com, "I've met some of my best friends through the firm. I've taken vacations with them. I always go out for drinks, dinner, and karaoke with them. The associates here are amazing!" Still, another source remarks that "there are those who get together and do things outside of the firm, but it is not generally prevalent and is certainly not required or expected." Davis Polk isn't a social utopia; several insiders describe the social scene at Davis Polk as "hierarchical — partners with partners, mid-levels with mid-levels, and juniors with juniors," and other associates term the firm "cliquish."

Top-notch training

Those thirsting for education above the law school level may find Davis Polk right up their alley. Associates gush that the training they get at Davis Polk is "fantastic" and "top-notch." "A tremendous amount of time, energy, and money is put into training," according to insiders. "The firm clearly cares about the development of its associates," says a corporate attorney. Davis Polk offers a wide range of training activities, including a one-week introductory course called "Lawyering 101," and other courses for mid-level and upper-level associates. The firm also provides departmental training sessions. "My experience is that they have a 'no questions asked' policy when an associate requests training outside the firm. Overall, this is one of most appealing aspects of the firm," offers one associate. One of her colleagues, however, comments that it's hard to get permission to go to any courses other than those offered by PLI.

Relaxed white shoes

Associates say the DPW culture is "reserved" and "traditional." "We are no doubt a white shoe law firm," explains one associate, "but we are as relaxed as such a firm can possibly be." Adds another, "Good judgment and plain old courtesy are prized qualities." Some insiders describe a "middle-of-the-road" culture. Associates note, "Fierce passions about almost anything or quirkiness are generally discouraged." "People are smart and work hard, but they are civil and try to have lives outside the firm," lawyers say.

Although associates give Davis Polk only average marks in terms of hours, most agree that "DPW is not a sweatshop." "People take their vacations and are not overworked purposely." "DPW is good about spreading the work out," one corporate lawyer tells Vault.com. "There is no face time here — which is good. If the firm is busy then you work. Otherwise you go home." Another lawyer comments, "I may at times be working long hours, but it is not because of poor management by the person senior to me. There is just work to be done. Davis Polk turns away a fair amount of appealing work in order to maintain a livable balance."

Diverse clients, diverse problems

One of the biggest draws for most associates is DPW's prestige. Insiders also praise the interesting legal work and the opportunity to get deeply involved in deals and cases at an early stage in a lawyer's career. "There is some great work to be done here," says a litigator. "Things are staffed leanly and you have great opportunities that you cannot get anywhere else. The clients are as diverse as their problems."

A well-fed lawyer is a happy lawyer

A surprising number of Davis Polk insiders in New York praise the "gourmet" cafeteria. "Most often attorneys choose to eat dinner from the cafeteria and not purchase food from outside. In addition, the cafeteria food is subsidized so these delicious meals are not expensive," raves one source. "Amazing food at dirt-cheap prices," adds another budget gourmet. "Pretty fishies in the fish tank, too," adds one associate, though it is unclear whether or not she thinks the creatures were on the cafeteria menu.

Who wants to go to Hong Kong?

Insiders warn that DPW associates have to be careful about expressing interest in specialty practice areas or foreign offices. "You mention one thing offhand to a partner, and the next thing you know you're working in Hong Kong," explains one lawyer. Another source reports that junior associates typically get forced into spending six months in one of the specialty practice groups. "It wouldn't be so bad if they told you this up front. The problem is that most people don't expect it and then get very disappointed when they are 'asked' to do the rotation."

Beautiful and cramped

Associates are generally pleased with their surroundings in all of Davis Polk's U.S. offices. "The offices are incredible and the cafeteria is amazing!" exclaims one New York attorney. "[The] best offices in New York City, hands down," says another. But those in the New York office say that DPW is pressed for space. One respondent tells Vault.com, "Most associates share offices through the third year — it's ridiculous and hampers productivity. You have zero privacy and you end up spending way too much time around the other person. Once you have your own office — if you make it that long — you are king." The firm got two new floors ready in June 2000 and expects that all associates from the class of 1997 will have their own office by the fall. But some associates don't believe the extra square footage will alleviate all space concerns. London associates don't have to wait. "We have more offices than attorneys," says one associate at that location.

Adding to the beauty of Davis Polk's surroundings are, apparently, the lawyers themselves. More than one insider claims that "most of the associates at Davis Polk, particularly the women, are better looking than at other firms."

Support draws praise

Associates have positive things to say about the DPW support services. "There are services for everything short of helping you go to the bathroom," one insider jokes. Associates shower particular praise on the paralegals. "Paralegals are the best in the city," exclaims one source. But some are not thrilled with the secretarial service. "Some of the secretaries aren't very well trained and don't seem to be able to get around the computers very well, which is a problem when you're constantly working on complicated documents," according to one insider. "All some do is answer the phone."

Perks fall short

While they cherish their cafeteria, Davis Polk attorneys are less than delighted with the array of perks the firm offers. "The firm is strangely cheap," carps one associate. Another laments, "No gym membership, which can be a real downer." Other associates hasten to add that Davis Polk gives them no free PCs or cell phones either. On the other hand, the assessment of the perk situation may depend on the associate's perspective. "Car service is great," says one New York lawyer, "with cars waiting from 7:00 on." Sports tickets to Yankees and Mets games are sometimes available "through lottery or coin toss." A firm contact contends that games of chance to acquire tickets is only necessary "when it's a big game." Tickets are usually "readily available," to the point where they often go to support staff due to a lack of demand on the part of associates. Several associates genuinely appreciate the month of paternity leave, "which is taken." Plus, coffee is free.

Intellect matters, not race or gender

Insiders say that neither race nor gender factors into the hiring process. "My impression is that people are not evaluated based upon race or gender here but upon perceived intellectual capacity and articulate speech," according to one lawyer. But associates say that there are no special efforts made to mentor minority lawyers. "I've noticed that people in general tend to mentor those who remind them of themselves when they were wet behind the ears. The less you look or seem like them, the less likely it is that they will mentor you." One insider says despite the presence of minority attorneys, the firm is still "WASP-y." In 1998 DPW promoted an African-American lawyer to partner for the first time.

Sources say DPW has more women partners than many of its rival firms. The firm also offers a part-time program intended to help women lawyers with families. While some sources describe the part-time policy as "very flexible," one lawyer says that only senior associates feel comfortable enough to take advantage of it. The firm is reportedly revamping the policy.

Davis Polk does not engage in mentoring specifically aimed at women attorneys, insiders say. "There are no special efforts made to make the women feel more accepted. On the flip side, the firm doesn't have a boys' club mentality."

Committed to pro bono work

Associates give the firm's commitment to pro bono work high marks. "It is not possible for a firm to be more committed to pro bono work," opines one attorney. "The firm recognizes its importance to the public interest as well as its benefit in the development of associates." Sources say the firm's policy is that pro bono work is "real" work, but that doesn't always seep through to individual partners. One litigator tells Vault.com, "You can do almost anything you want. I will have written several briefs and had three arguments within my first nine months here. At least 40 percent of my hours have been pro bono, and nobody has complained — yet."

Skadden, Arps, Slate, Meagher & Flom LLP and Affiliates

VAULT.COM PRESTIGE RANKING: 5

4 Times Square
New York, NY 10036
(212) 735-3000
Fax: (212) 735-2000
www.skadden.com

LOCATIONS

New York, NY (HQ)
Boston, MA
Chicago, IL
Houston, TX
Los Angeles, CA
Newark, NJ
Palo Alto, CA
Reston, VA
San Francisco, CA
Washington, DC
Wilmington, DE
11 other offices worldwide

MAJOR DEPARTMENTS/PRACTICES

Antitrust • Complex Mass Tort and Insurance Litigation • Corporate Restructuring • E-Commerce • Employment Issues • Energy • Finance • Intellectual Property • International • Litigation • Mergers and Acquistions • Privatizations • Products Liability• Real Estate • Tax

THE STATS

No. of attorneys: 1,424
No. of offices: 22
Summer associate offers: 72 out of 73 (New York, 1999)
Executive Partner: Robert C. Sheehan
Hiring Partner: Wallace L. Schwartz (New York)

PAY

New York, 2000
1st year: $140,000
2nd year: $150,000
3rd year: $170,000
4th year: $185,000
5th year: $200,000
6th year: $212,000
7th year: $220,000
8th year: $225,000
Summer associate: $2,400/week

Chicago, 2000
1st year: $140,000
2nd year: $150,000
3rd year: $170,000
4th year: $179,000
5th year: $190,000
6th year: $200,000
Summer associate: $2,400/week

Boston, Houston, Palo Alto, Los Angeles, San Francisco, Wilmington, and Washington, DC, 2000
1st year: $140,000
2nd year: $155,000
3rd year: $170,000
4th year: $185,000
5th year: $200,000
6th year: $212,000
Summer associate: $2,400/week

NOTABLE PERKS

- $3,000 toward home office
- Catered attorney lunch
- Firm gym with workout clothing available
- Emergency child care

THE BUZZ
What attorneys at other firms are saying about this firm

- "The quintessential legal machine"
- "I'm sweating just thinking about it"
- "Great corporate work, aggressive"
- "Forward-thinking, law firm of the future"

UPPERS

- Excellent place to learn
- Fascinating and challenging work
- Skadden name on your resume shines

DOWNERS

- Huge firm means your mileage may vary
- Wave bye-bye to social life
- "Shark tank on speed"

KEY COMPETITORS

Cravath, Swaine & Moore
Latham & Watkins
Paul, Weiss, Rifkind, Wharton & Garrison
Sullivan & Cromwell
Watchell, Lipton, Rosen & Katz

EMPLOYMENT CONTACT

Ms. Carol Lee H. Sprague
Director of Legal Hiring
(212) 735-3815
csprague@skadden.com

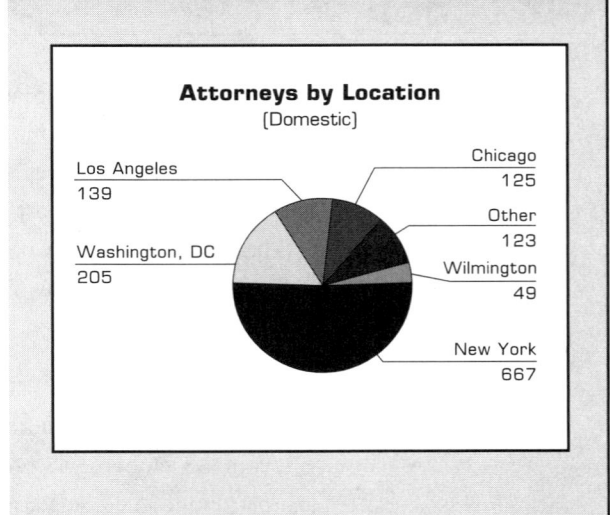

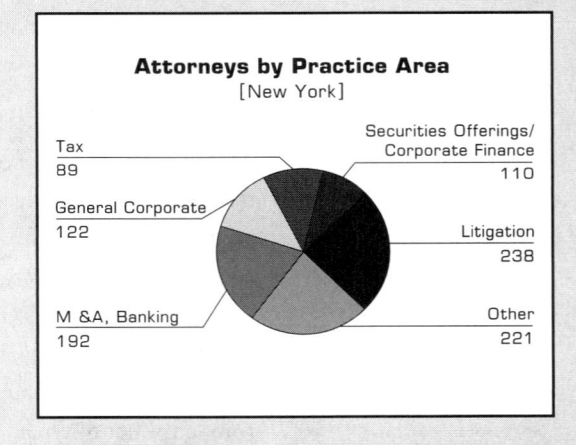

Attorneys by Location (Domestic)

- Los Angeles: 139
- Washington, DC: 205
- Chicago: 125
- Other: 123
- Wilmington: 49
- New York: 667

Attorneys by Practice Area [New York]

- Tax: 89
- General Corporate: 122
- M&A, Banking: 192
- Securities Offerings/Corporate Finance: 110
- Litigation: 238
- Other: 221

QUALITY OF LIFE RANKINGS [ASSOCIATES RATE THEIR OWN FIRM]

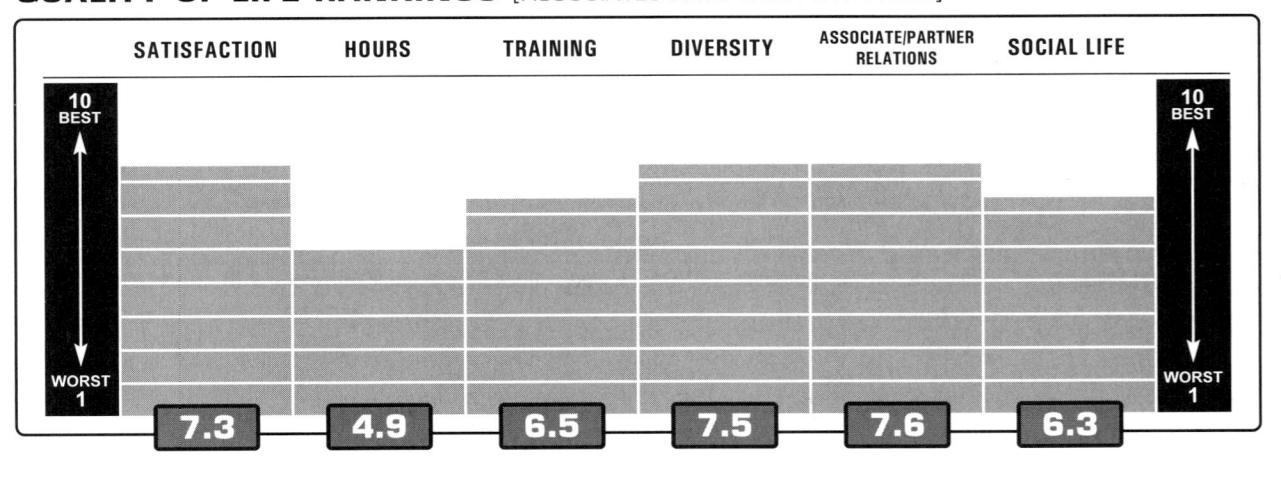

SATISFACTION	HOURS	TRAINING	DIVERSITY	ASSOCIATE/PARTNER RELATIONS	SOCIAL LIFE
7.3	4.9	6.5	7.5	7.6	6.3

THE SCOOP

One Skadden, Arps, Slate, Meagher & Flom partner reportedly described the firm as the greatest accumulation of talent in history. Starting from humble roots back in 1948 — when Joe Flom was the firm's only associate — Skadden Arps has grown into one of the biggest and most profitable law firms in the world. Based in New York, it has branch offices everywhere from Sydney to San Francisco, and may be one of the most widely recognized law firms in the world.

A distinguished 20th-century history

Joseph Flom was Skadden's first associate. A graduate of Harvard Law, he joined the firm in October 1948. According to one Skadden legend, the firm could not afford to pay Flom when he started, so they had a pinochle game every Friday afternoon and gave him the pot. Another story claims the partners paid Flom instead of themselves, making him the highest-paid lawyer in the firm. Flom made partner in 1954, six years after joining Skadden.

Today, most partners hold Flom (who is still with the firm) in the highest esteem, and many call him a genius — at the very least, the best lawyer of his generation. He is credited as the major force in establishing the firm's dominance in mergers and acquisitions, and is largely responsible for establishing the firm's intense work ethic. According to Lincoln Caplan's book *Skadden: Power, Money and the Rise of a Legal Empire*, Flom purchased an engagement ring for his fiancée from fellow name partner Les Arps, who had bought it for his former fiancée. Flom had his fiancée stop by the firm, gave her the ring, and then went back to work. When complimented on the ring, Mrs. Flom replied, "Thanks, Les Arps picked it out for me."

The beginning of the legend

Skadden first made its name in mergers and acquisitions. The firm was involved in some of the biggest mergers of the fast-paced 1980s, helping to construct elaborate support structures of revolving credit and junk bonds. Throughout the 1970s and 1980s Skadden was involved in nearly every major M&A deal in America. Still, at the peak of its success Flom insisted on investing Skadden's huge profits in new practice areas rather than distributing them as partner compensation. The huge law firm hit a speed bump in the early 1990s as a deep recession shrunk partner profits to $620,000 in 1991, almost half of what they had been the year before. In 1990 M&A work represented a full quarter of Skadden's revenue, and the slump in that area hit Skadden like a ton of bricks. Ten dispirited partners fled to other firms.

To counteract the loss of earnings and morale, Skadden partners tightened their belts and shrunk the size of entering associate classes. Yet Flom's emphasis on diversification in the 1980s paid dividends. Non-M&A practices, like project finance, product liability, and (not surprisingly) bankruptcy, thrived. By 1994 Skadden had rebounded. Its M&A work returned to 1980s levels, and other categories like REITs, project finance, and corporate high-yield debt proved strong as well.

Skadden pride

A 1996 survey of corporations put Skadden on top as the most-used law firm (with 20 percent of surveyed corporations saying they had turned to Skadden at some time). Skadden also received top marks for "service" and "clout." However, respondents critiqued Skadden for "overstaffing," "going over budget," and "arrogance." In fact, New York corporations named Skadden as the most arrogant law firm, attracting 11 percent of the "arrogance" vote. Caplan reports in his book on Skadden that at the firm's 40th anniversary black tie gala, guests heard their names announced by herald and a trumpet when they entered. A number of Skadden partners entered and re-entered several times in order to hear their names and trumpet call again and again. In response to the results of the poll, executive partner Robert C. Sheehan said, "I am sure we are not [the most arrogant]. Further, I will not comment."

Hey big spender

Skadden has always kept up with the market when it comes to pay. Therefore, when California boutique law firm Gunderson Dettmer Stough Villeneuve Franklin & Hachigian touched off a wave of salary hikes, Skadden was naturally expected to follow suit. But in February 2000, Skadden went one better than the market, offering its first-year associates a $140,000 starting salary — a top-of-market figure that prompted discontented mewlings from associates at less fortunate top-tier law firm rivals.

The new pay represented not only a 40 percent raise on associates' base salary, but it was also significantly more than the $125,000 level to which most firms had raised their first-year associate salaries. According to Sheehan, the raise is not an attempt to top the other firm's salaries. Skadden intends to give correspondingly smaller bonuses.

A case of billables

While Skadden has been willing to spend big for talent, the firm has gotten into hot water by billing extensively as well. In January 1998, clients from the estate of San Diego company Golden Eagle appeared in court to challenge Skadden's fees in the case of *Insurance Commissioner v. Golden Eagle Insurance Company*. Skadden attorneys appeared to explain hourly rates of $495 and charges of up to $120 an hour in paralegal fees for what appeared to be secretarial work. A legal firm auditor, upon reviewing the charges of $1.3 million, reduced them to $800,000. The judge on the case, William Cahill, told Skadden partner James Lyons that he didn't approve of Skadden's charging for secretarial work in addition to its regular attoneys' fees of more than $330 an hour.

One of the finest for M&A

Skadden topped the December 1999 *National Law Journal* list of "Who Represents Corporate America" for the fourth consecutive time. The firm advised prominent acquisition targets in some of the most important deals of the year. Partners Scott Simpson and Michael Hatchard from the London office became involved in the largest corporate takeover in history, representing Germany's Mannesmann when Britain's Vodafone AirTouch proposed to buy the company. In February 2000, Vodafone, a wireless communications company, offered to pay a whopping $183 billion for Mannesmann, breaking the merger record set the month before by the Time Warner-AOL deal.

More than paper wealth

The rapid consolidation in many major industries has meant lots of work for Skadden. Take the paper industry, for example. Skadden attorneys counseled Champion International when Finnish paper giant UPM-Kymmene acquired it for $6 billion in stock. Skadden also stands behind Sterling Software as it works out a possible $4 billion acquisition by Computer Associates International. The deal would be the software industry's largest acquisition ever. Skadden represents energy company Coastal Corp., which is being wooed by El Paso Energy to the tune of $16 billion. If all goes well with the stockholders and government regulatory agencies, the deal will close at the end of 2000.

Record-breaking securities

Skadden Arps's corporate prowess is by no means limited to mergers and acquisitions. The firm also offers a top-flight securities practice. Skadden had a hand in the world's largest public offering, advising the Italian government when it sold $18.6 billion worth of shares in the Italian state-owned electricity company Enel. Fellow securities powerhouse Sullivan & Cromwell advised Enel. The parties involved turned to American firms because a large number of shares were sold on the New York Stock Exchange. On the new media front, the firm handled Priceline.com's closely watched $160 million initial public offering in April 1999. Priceline.com went on to rack up an initial market cap of $2 billion, then the largest ever for an Internet company.

First firm

Fully a third of Skadden's lawyers (about 385) are devoted to litigation. Skadden litigators have crusaded in the Supreme Court, all 13 U.S. Circuit Courts of Appeal, and most of the U.S. District Courts. In order to bolster its presence in Northern California, Skadden's San Francisco office stole away star litigator Raoul Kennedy from Morrison & Foerster. One of the factors influencing Kennedy's move was the chance to work with product liability guru Sheila Birnbaum, the so-called "Queen of Toxic Torts."

Skadden grabbed its share of the spotlight for its defense of President Clinton against claims of sexual harassment brought by Paula Corbin Jones. The firm helped get the case dismissed on the grounds that Clinton's alleged behavior towards Jones did not meet the standard for sexual harassment under federal law. Jones' lawyers appealed, and the two parties settled in November 1998 for $850,000.

Wisconsin gay rights case

David Springer, a partner at Skadden, took a pro bono case on behalf of Jamie Nabozny, a gay Wisconsin man. Nabozny alleged that the public school district in his tiny hometown of Ashland, Wisconsin had violated his right to equal protection by allowing fellow students to harass and molest him. Springer, who is himself gay, took the case after returning to Skadden from a five-month HIV-related medical leave of absence. Springer conducted an extremely thorough voir dire to tease out any jurors who were prejudiced against gays. The Skadden attorney commented that his selection was helped because the jury trial took place during deer hunting season, when the "deer hunting types," as he called them, were not available for jury selection. The school district eventually settled for $900,000.

Go for broke

Skadden Arps is a leader in the bankruptcy field, and it's no wonder — the L.A. office's Richard Levin has literally written the book on bankruptcy. Skadden partner Levin authored the Bankruptcy Code and the Bankruptcy Reform Act of 1978. Legal publisher Matthew Bender has also selected Levin to be a member of the Collier on Bankruptcy Editorial Board, where he will help the company expand and enhance its bankruptcy treatises.

Skadden.com

Like many firms these days, Skadden has been seeking to expand its intellectual property practice (which currently boasts 15 lawyers). Skadden brings a unique perspective to Internet law, having been an actual litigant in an Internet case. When the firm tried to find some cyber real estate for the its web page, it found that a cybersquatter had already snatched up Skaddenarps.com. Rather than paying for it, the firm took the cybersquatter to court and won the domain.

GETTING HIRED

Beyond Ivy

Although Skadden remains an extremely selective firm, don't completely count yourself out if you're not from a top-tier law school. One New York associate explains, "To its credit, Skadden is willing to look past *US News*' idea of the top six law schools. While this may hurt its selectivity rating, it's a boon in terms of the diversity of viewpoints and geographic identities we get here. As a graduate of an Ivy League college and law school, I can tell you with certainty that too many Ivy Leaguers in one place really spoils the soup." But one source opines that those from second-tier schools only have a hope of getting in the door if they have a GPA of 3.6 or higher. A corporate lawyer says, "If you have the grades to pass the screening process, getting hired is just a matter of getting along with the people that interview you."

A source in the Los Angeles office tells Vault.com that nearly all Skadden summer associates receive offers. A Chicago associate recommends candidates target themselves to a rapidly growing area such as banking, restructuring, or litigation. According to insiders in the Washington litigation department, that office prefers former judicial clerks. Those in smaller Skadden outposts such as Houston emphasized that more than a stellar resume is needed to get hired — a little personality helps, too.

The Skadden interview

Typically, the firm likes to send alumni interviewers from the schools where it conducts the first round of screening interviews. Candidates invited back after the initial meeting interview at the branch where they wish to work. While scheduling the second round, candidates are asked about their department of interest. During callbacks, at least half of their interviewers will be members of their preferred department or related departments.

Candidates typically have four interviews, either in the morning or in the afternoon, and are taken out to lunch by two first-year associates. "They want you to have someone to relate to," say insiders. Some recent interviewees say they have interviewed with one junior associate, one mid-level or senior associate, and two partners. Different offices will dispatch different recruiting teams to schools, mostly from New York, Chicago, Los Angeles, and DC, though the little Wilmington office does some in-field recruitment as well. The firm's hiring committee meets once a every Friday, so candidates may hear the good (or bad) news from a member of the hiring committee anywhere from two to five days after interviewing.

OUR SURVEY SAYS

Salary leader

Money talks, Skaddenites applaud. And it's not just the New York office that's thrilled. One attorney raves that Skadden offers the "best pay in Chicago — period." According to another insider, "Skadden is one of the few firms in DC that pays full-fledged New York salaries. Also, unlike many DC firms, Skadden's salary curve maintains a strong upward trend long after the initial year."

Insiders' faith in Skadden seems to be more than just a fleeting infatuation with their newfound wealth. "Skadden attorneys feel that they will never be underpaid for long, and even if the market shifts up either Skadden will be the leader of that move or it will catch up shortly thereafter," says one source. But some senior associates complain their raises were small compared to those of junior attorneys. "The firm does not recognize the efforts of senior associates from a compensation standpoint," one lawyer grumbles.

Dig the new digs

Though Skadden's traditionally been known for utiliarian offices, this is one firm that's changing its architectural ways. In January 2000, after thirty years on Third Avenue, Skadden picked up and moved its New York office to a new home in the resurgent and Disneyfied Times Square. The modern-looking building gives lawyers visiting the cafeteria a sweeping view of the Hudson. Skadden shares the building with Condé Nast, the chi-chi publishing house. Skadden will eventually occupy the 24th floor all the way up to the 48th. Associates in New York seem to enjoy their new neighborhood. "The new offices are great. The gym is great. The cafeteria has a great view," beams one lawyer. Views from offices include, depending on the side of the building, "the Hudson River, Times Square, the Empire State Building, or Rockefeller Center." Don't expect velvet drapes and mahogany panelling, though — one associate in New York notes that "Skadden's image as a roll-up-your-sleeves firm keeps it from indulging and decorating its offices with the lavishness and opulence of a Davis Polk or Sullivan & Cromwell."

Skadden has new office space in Washington, DC, too. But rather than looking for a brand-new home in the nation's capital, Skadden merely expanded to three neighboring buildings. The firm's reluctance to move is understandable, as its offices face the Treasury and the White House, home to several high-profile clients. DC associates, in the meantime, are less than enthused with their own interior décor, which associates say is "ugly" and "not terribly fancy." Insiders note that the offices are being renovated and "hope the results will be as positive as the new offices in New York."

The Chicago office is also undergoing renovations and new associates are getting new furniture. "With the new remodeling, things should improve greatly. Still, the new New York offices take the cake," according to a Chicago Skaddenite. The Houston offices are also undergoing a makeover. The changes taking place at other offices leave at least one L.A. associate envious. "When I visit another firm's office, they are usually much nicer," the source explains. Some L.A. associates predict that Skadden will give the office a face-lift now that the firm has renewed its lease on its current L.A. locale.

Love and live to learn

Our contacts praise the learning curve as well. One lawyer reports, "I learn new things every day, and so I can't think of a better place to learn the ropes of corporate law." Another associate tells Vault.com, "There's something to be said for working two days straight on a multi-billion dollar deal. I'm not saying what, but it's definitely something."

Skadden associates express enthusiasm about working on high-profile transactions but they recognize the spotlight comes with its cost. "The deals and litigation matters are almost always front-page transactions, and there's a degree of additional pressure attached when the stakes are so high. It's just an intense place to work where you are surrounded by not only very smart people but very good lawyers all the time." "It is important to do good work, and beyond that, not much matters," says one associate.

One DC associate had nothing but praise for his own learning experience. "There are plenty of associates here who started at other well-known law firms in DC only to find that the other firms' "first-rate" experiences just didn't hold up."

Social Skadden

Skadden offers a booming social scene in its bigger offices. "Obviously, there is no pressure to spend time with your colleagues outside of work. But most associates have many friends at the firm and we go out a lot," a New York associate reports. "Many of my best friends are co-workers," another lawyers reports. The word from the Windy City is that "associates are more friendly to each other than at other large law firms in Chicago. The environment is collegial and supportive, not cutthroat or competitive." But Chicago insiders stress that the firm does not strong-arm them into making friends. "It is in no way expected or demanded that one hang out with fellow Skadden attorneys," says one mildly antisocial type.

According to a Washington insider, Skadden DC makes "a lot of effort to create opportunities for social interaction." But some DC Skaddenites say the socializing is limited to a small group of single lawyers, and one lawyer says the layout of the Washington offices does not promote a lot of socializing. Another DC attorney says, "People pretty much keep to themselves." A lawyer down in Texas says that being hitched is not an obstacle in his office. "Attorneys know each other's spouses and kids and often socialize."

Respectful, demanding partners

Many insiders feel most of the Skadden partners treat them well and value their input. "They are incredibly respectful and friendly. There are no partners whom I dread working for. In addition, I feel like I am a personal friend to some of them," an associate in the Washington office offers. Attorneys in the L.A. office describe the partnership there as "young and dynamic." Another source says, "There is a real aura of respect. I could not imagine any of the partners ever really screaming at anyone."

But another lawyer doesn't need to use his imagination. "We are interchangeable and replaceable parts. The partners expect us to work into the ground — over and over and over again with no end in sight," moans this lawyer. One associate reports that although partners usually treat associates with respect, "junior attorneys must have a thick skin. Because our work is so high-profile, so time-sensitive, and so expensive for our clients, partners can be demanding and occasionally get very intense if work is not completed." A corporate associate claims partners "will write off" associates who are not perfect from the start, leaving them with very little work. An M&A lawyer has a mixed review of the partnership: "Nearly every partner is a pleasure to work with. Some are less socially skilled, but what can you do? These are people who spend too much time with lawyers."

Training with wolves

Skadden hosts in-house CLE programs and luncheon lectures. In addition, the firm willingly pays for outside training classes. But insiders tell Vault.com they mostly learn by doing. According to one Skaddenite, "Most of my training is of the on-the-job variety. No complaints about that." "I feel a bit thrown to the wolves at times, but when I need help, [the firm] always provides it," says another source. A tax lawyer claims that assignments are structured so that attorneys can develop the skills they need. "Someone looking for a regimented program of training should probably look somewhere else," advises another insider.

The story from Skadden litigators is somewhat different. Skadden runs National Institute for Trial Advocacy (NITA) training programs and provides (reportedly sporadic) deposition training for its litigators. According to a California Skadden associate, "The formal training is extensive for litigators. In the six months that I have been there I have accumulated at least 45 CLE credits, most of which were very useful."

No billing requirement, but still

Skadden has no official billing requirements. But some associates reportedly were told they weren't carrying their weight after putting in over 2,200 billable hours. Although insiders say their workload varies greatly, many associates in larger offices reported billing between 50 and 60 hours per week. One New York associate claims the associates' motto is "What lives?" "There is no apology when one is called in to work, even if it is a weekend night or a holiday," according to a Skadden litigator.

Some Skaddenites are not bothered by their intense schedules. "I get paid a lot and work on very significant matters. I expect to work hard," says one. Others say it is not so much the hours but the inability to predict their schedule that bothers them. "The number of hours alone tells, at the margin, something about how much sleep one can get, but it does not describe whether it is feasible to make dinner plans or to go out of town on a weekend."

Perhaps all that's necessary is the right perspective. One lawyer philosophizes, "There's no such thing as a lifestyle firm. So why not kill yourself for one of the top firms in the world?"

Round-the-clock support services

Insiders give Skadden high marks in the support services department. "The firm's biggest strength is its support services. You can get help 24 hours a day, 7 days a week, 365 days a year," according to another source. A New York lawyer reports that each department has "its own cadre of dedicated legal assistants just for that department." Our Skadden insiders say the computer services and library are praiseworthy as well.

Exodus

Insiders say, like many law firms these days, Skadden is having trouble holding onto its talent. Recalling the biblical exodus, one lawyer inquires, "When did they put Moses in charge of hiring here?" One M&A lawyers reports, "There are so many opportunities out there right now" that "recruiters incessantly try to pluck away Skadden associates."

Associates say that Skadden is losing lots of good people to new economy companies, other law firms and, particularly in the Washington office, government agencies.

But some sources say that the high turnover rate is a testament to the quality of the firm. "The high turnover rates at Skadden are attributable to the fact that many view Skadden as a desirable pool of intelligent and well-trained individuals from which to recruit. In fact, many associates arrive with the view that the firm will serve as a springboard to investment banks, in-house counsel, and other career opportunities," opines one associate optimistically. Another associate states that "generally, Skadden attorneys leave to pursue 'opportunities of a lifetime' and not because they're unhappy with the firm. Headhunters started calling me during my first month at Skadden."

Pushing pro bono

Despite its high-billing lawyers, Skadden has found time to sponsor pro bono work. Those in public interest circles are most likely familiar with the Skadden Fellowship, the pro bono lawyer's brass ring. Skadden puts up about $25 million to fund a two-year fellowship program for 25 new lawyers who wish to better society. The firm also lends its associates to nonprofit organizations on a temporary (but full-time) basis. During the hiatus Skadden retains the associates on the payroll. These externships help the poor and also help the firm recruit, train, and retain the associates. In addition, Volunteer Lawyers for the Arts presented Skadden with an Award for Excellence for the firm's pro bono work at its 1999 benefit and pro bono awards ceremony.

Insiders report, "A range of excellent pro bono projects always exists and associates receive full credit as if they were working on a paying client's project." Reportedly pro bono work is not limited to litigators, and the corporate department is encouraged to take on non-paying matters as well. Sources also claim that Skadden does not shy away from controversial pro bono cases. But not everyone is thrilled with the firm's emphasis on pro bono. "The firm pushes pro bono a little too much. If you are already exhausted from your regular clients, you don't want to hear how you can work more for a pro bono client. It may sound selfish, but we need some time to ourselves also," one lawyer complains.

Multi-culti Skadden

"The firm is a true melting pot," according to sources in the Chicago office. That seems to be the sentiment at most of Skadden offices. Skaddenites in New York have "gotten a real sense that hiring here is done on a race-blind basis." But others claim that "the firm tries — but there are not all that many minorities, especially African-

Americans." Sources tell Vault.com that Skadden does have some minority partners but the numbers are still pretty low.

"I honestly think the firm is gender-blind," says one Skaddenite. Indeed, most sources believe women are treated no differently than their male counterparts at the firm: "I've never felt that people evaluate my work with the frame of reference that I'm a woman. At Skadden, you are an attorney — end of story." Insiders report that Skadden hosts some programs aimed especially at women and offers a part-time policy. Sources also tell Vault.com that female partners and senior associates go out of their way to support junior women attorneys.

But some attorneys indicate a dearth of women in the partnership. One attorney says, "The work schedule is grueling, so it is virtually impossible to be a mother and a full-time attorney. Therefore, there are fewer women partners and very few of them have balanced family lives. The result is a firm which has a minority makeup not too different from that of my law school. Although it is not truly representative of New York City as a whole, it is about as good as one can expect in this day and age."

Insiders say there are quite a few openly gay lawyers at the firm. One lawyer says that Skadden's openness to gays and lesbians is not just part of the fashion. "Skadden has always been open to gays and lesbians, even before it was considered cool to be so." Sources say gay lawyers' life partners are always included in firm events where the family is invited. Associates also point out that the firm has done a lot of work for gay rights.

The myths of Skadden — and the reality

Skadden associates acknowledge that their firm is often rumored to be a "sweatshop" with "screamers," but the truth is much more complex. "I think the sweatshop label comes from the 1980s," contends one New York associate. Most of the associates tell Vault.com that because Skadden is such a large law firm with so many different practices, personal experience varies by office and department. "My department is like a small law firm or even a judge's chambers. We are very close and have lunch together several times a week," says a Skaddenite who works in intellectual property. A DC associate terms that office "relaxed" and adds that "people take their work, not themselves, seriously." An M&A associate in New York, on the other hand, terms that practice "intense" and "macho — very confident and very inspiring of confidence."

At the same time, there are some commonalities to Skadden culture. The firm has an "independent, eclectic-minded culture" that "makes allowances for the exceptional and unusual." Most associates would agree that this diverse firm nonetheless universally experiences "intense pressure" and is "very focused on making money." "There is a single-minded focus on delivering bottom line results for clients that other firms find impossible," says a Chicago associate. Though the firm only recently went summer casual, several associates say they dressed down before the change; the reason being that "no one cares what you wear, just [that you] get the work done." The zeal to do well can produce a "billing-er than thou" attitude among some associates. Nonetheless, insiders agree that the firm remains "progressive," "tolerant," and "the blue suede shoes of the white shoe law world."

VAULT.COM

PRESTIGE RANKING: 6

Simpson Thacher & Bartlett

425 Lexington Avenue
New York, NY 10017
(212) 455-2000
Fax: (212) 455-2502
www.simpsonthacher.com

LOCATIONS

New York, NY (HQ)
Columbus, OH
Los Angeles, CA
Palo Alto, CA
Hong Kong
London
Singapore
Tokyo

MAJOR DEPARTMENTS/PRACTICES

Bankruptcy
Corporate (Banking, M&A, Securities)
Employee Benefits & Compensation
Exempt Organizations
Litigation
Personal Planning
Real Estate
Tax

THE STATS

No. of attorneys: 571
No. of offices: 8
Summer associate offers: 87 out of 90 (New York, 1999)
Chairman: Richard Beattie
Hiring attorneys: David L. Williams and Marissa Wesely

PAY

New York, 2000
1st year: $125,000
2nd year: $135,000
3rd year: $150,000
4th year: $170,000
5th year: $190,000
Summer associate: $2,404/week

NOTABLE PERKS

- Three months paid maternity leave
- One week paid paternity leave
- Broker's fee
- Subsidy for any gym
- Paid moving expenses
- Free pizza every other Friday
- Freeflowing Starbucks coffee and Poland Spring water

THE BUZZ
What attorneys at other firms are saying about this firm

- "Corporate but friendly"
- "Straightforward and solid"
- "One of the top"
- "Not so kind; not so gentle"

UPPERS

- Friendly culture
- Opportunity for lots of responsibility
- Cookies!

DOWNERS

- Almost no chance of making partner
- Growth at the cost of niceness
- Not much social interaction with other associates

KEY COMPETITORS

Cleary, Gottlieb, Steen & Hamilton
Cravath, Swaine & Moore
Davis Polk & Wardell
Sullivan & Cromwell
Wachtell, Lipton, Rosen & Katz

EMPLOYMENT CONTACT

Ms. Dee Pifer
Director of Legal Employment
(212) 455-2687
d_pifer@stblaw.com

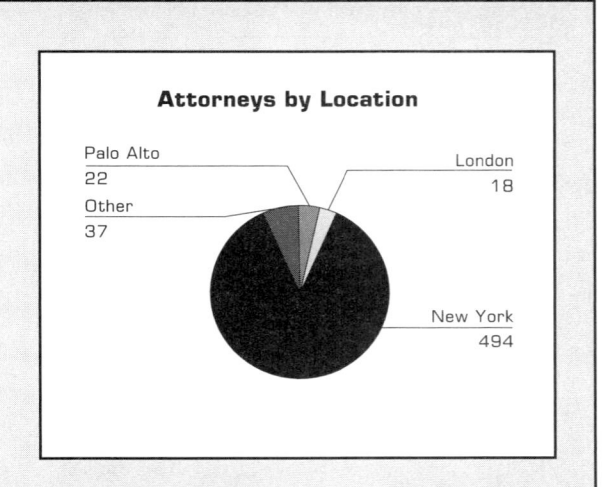

Attorneys by Location
- Palo Alto: 22
- Other: 37
- London: 18
- New York: 494

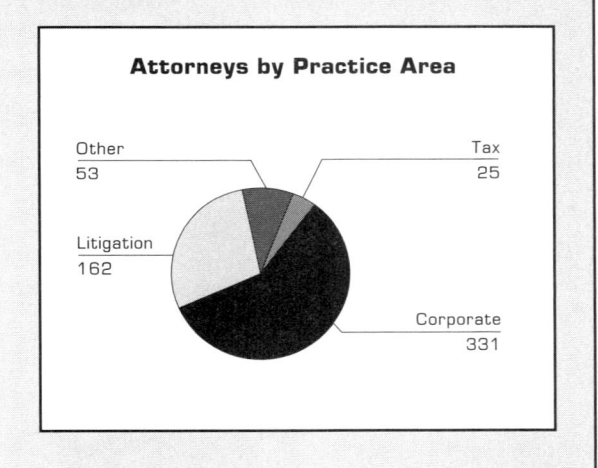

Attorneys by Practice Area
- Other: 53
- Tax: 25
- Litigation: 162
- Corporate: 331

QUALITY OF LIFE RANKINGS [ASSOCIATES RATE THEIR OWN FIRM]

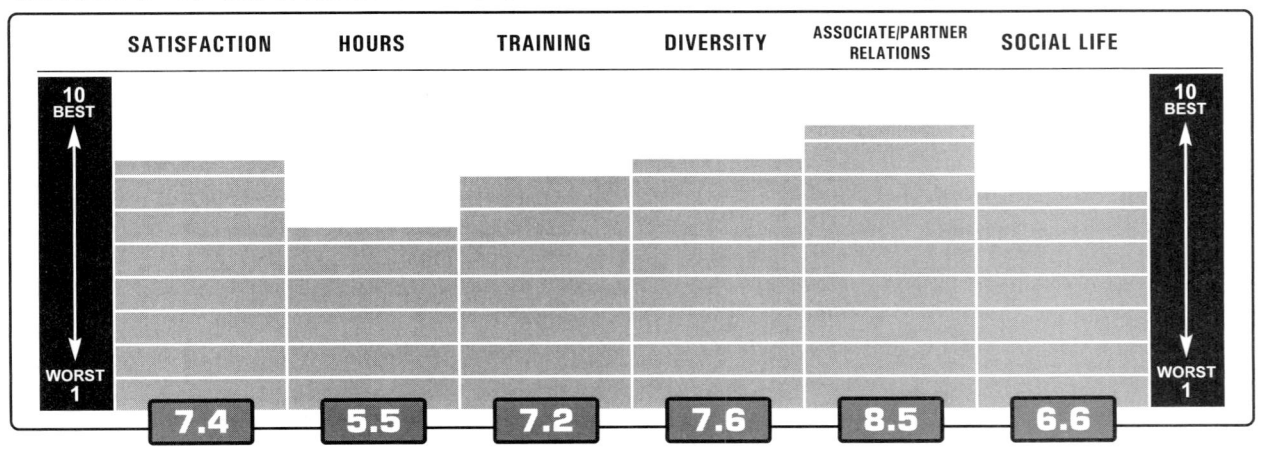

SATISFACTION	HOURS	TRAINING	DIVERSITY	ASSOCIATE/PARTNER RELATIONS	SOCIAL LIFE
7.4	5.5	7.2	7.6	8.5	6.6

THE SCOOP

Among New York's top firms, Simpson Thacher & Bartlett has established a reputation as one of the nicest in its class. Good manners haven't kept Simpson Thacher from competing in the rough-and-tumble legal world, routinely making national headlines, or once again hitting the No. 6 spot in the Vault.com Top 50.

A very pleasant history

Simpson Thacher & Bartlett was founded 116 years ago and has represented a long string of well-heeled corporate clients ever since. Investment bank Lehman Brothers has been a client since the 1930s, and the firm led Paramount Communications (then called Gulf & Western) through its acquisitions in the 1960s and 1970s. But perhaps the more important deal for Simpson Thacher occurred in 1952, when the firm scooped up about ten lawyers from a little Manhattan law firm, Newman & Brisco, which represented a company that would soon become Manufacturers Hanover Trust. In another prestige deal, Simpson Thacher hired Cyrus Vance as an associate in 1947. The renowned diplomat, who later served as Secretary of State in the Carter administration, became a partner at Simpson in 1956 and repeatedly moved between public service and private practice at the firm before retiring in 1997.

Manufacturers Hanover became an increasingly important client to Simpson Thacher. In the early 1980s, fees from Manufacturers Hanover represented nearly 30 percent of the firm's income. Until moving offices in 1988, 110 Simpson Thacher lawyers in banking, real estate, project finance, and bankruptcy worked directly out of Manny Hanny headquarters, filling three floors of the building (though not all the lawyers worked for Manufacturers Hanover all the time). Another client that has paid dividends — a small buyout firm Simpson Thacher first began representing in 1976 called Kohlberg Kravis Roberts & Co. (KKR). KKR would acquire RJR Nabisco in 1989, paying Simpson Thacher a fee said to have been near $30 million.

Growing at home and abroad

Like many other prestigious New York firms, Simpson Thacher is tightly knit. The vast majority of its partners started as associates with the firm. For most of its history, ST&B has been known as a New York firm, notwithstanding its small satellite offices in London (opened in 1978) and Columbus (in 1980). But the 1990s have seen a wave of domestic and international expansion at Simpson Thacher. On the home front, Simpson Thacher opened a Los Angeles office in 1996 and launched a Silicon Valley branch in 1999. In addition, the firm has opened offices in Tokyo (in 1990), Hong Kong (in 1993), and Singapore (in 1997).

Simpson on the bleeding edge of law tech

Keeping Simpson on the cutting edge of technology starts right at the top. Richard Beattie, chairman of the executive committee, heads up Simpson's new knowledge management system. The updated information system organizes information around practice areas using specialized software, and each practice group controls its own intranet space. The firm's intranet gives lawyers links to specific deal documents and briefs (which must be a source of relief to associates tired of hunting through stacks of paper). These documents are password-protected so only authorized viewers can access them (which must be a source of great relief to Simpson Thacher clients).

Aggresssive corporate deals from a nice firm

While Simpson Thacher & Bartlett may have a genteel reputation, the firm has been involved in some pretty aggressive deals. Thanks in part to the assistance of steely-eyed head partner Richard Beattie and aggressive M&A leader Charles Cogut, Simpson Thacher has become a top M&A advisor. Financial Securities Data placed ST&B on top of the M&A world for all 1999 U.S. mergers and acquisitions in terms of deal value. The report listed ST&B as advisor on 142 deals with a total value of more than $615 billion. The past year kept Simpson M&A lawyers busy overseas as well with 34 European transactions. The firm also features strong international and domestic capital markets, banking, and project finance practices. Its corporate practice is its largest department, with approximately 73 partners and over 250 associates.

E-merging

Simpson grabbed headlines in January 2000 for advising AOL on its merger with entertainment giant Time Warner. The deal, worth $150 billion, was the largest ever at the time of its announcement. The acquisition was negotiated in extreme secrecy, and the final touches were put together in one frenetic week. But in order to create the new media monolith, Richard Beattie, Philip Ruegger and the rest of the Simpson team, along with Time Warner's outside counsel Cravath, Swaine & Moore, still must guide the companies through both American and European regulatory approval processes. They also have to get the OK from about 40 local authorities in the United States.

Simpson's involvement in e-biz goes beyond AOL. Partner Gary Horowitz from Simpson's New York office and partner Michael Nooney from the Silicon Valley branch represented Internet travel agent Preview Travel Inc. in its merger with Travelocity. The deal creates a single online travel agent called Travelocity.com. Preview stockholders walked away with 30 percent of the new travel powerhouse, and undoubtedly Simpson enjoyed the fruits of the lucrative deal as well.

The Simpson project (finance)

Another mighty Simpson Thacher practice area is project finance. For more than 30 years, the firm has represented construction firms, insurance companies, commercial and investment banks, and major corporations in various projects all over the globe. Simpson represented senior bank lenders CIBC and Barclays in the "FLAG project." FLAG involved the financing and construction of 27,000 miles of submarine fiber optic cable stretching from the United Kingdom to Asia, the largest such cable system in the world. In another telecom deal, the firm was involved in the building of over 400,000 phone lines in central Java. Power projects are also an area of expertise for Simpson Thacher. Examples include work on a $1 billion natural gas processing facility; counseling General Electric Capital Corporation on its ownership of a coal-fired electric generating facility in Asia; and representing Citibank in a first-of-its-kind gas and electric plant project in Mexico.

So sue me

Although big corporate deals often garner much of the firm's press coverage, Simpson Thacher's litigation practice is no less impressive. The firm handles hundreds of cases at any given time, across a wide variety of areas. The litigation department adopts a generalist approach with an emphasis on trial skills but also has several loosely-organized practice groups: antitrust; government investigations and business crimes (a.k.a. white-collar defense); insurance and reinsurance coverage; intellectual property; international arbitration; product liability; and securities and shareholder litigation. The practice is one of New York's largest, with approximately 35 partners and over 125 associates.

The firm has gotten in on the wave of tobacco litigation. Simpson's Roy Reardon heads a team representing B.A.T. Industries, the British owner of tobacco company Brown and Williamson.

Partner Thomas Rice and his Simpson team also defended American Home Products against various New York actions brought due to heart injury from the diet drug fen-phen. The firm successfully got a number of the cases filed in New York by non-New Yorkers dismissed in October 1999. Nonetheless, Simpson is still handling more than 1000 claims against AHP filed by unhappy would-be dieters.

Simpson also takes the side of the plaintiff on occasion as well. The firm recently filed a multibillion dollar lawsuit on behalf of client Global Crossing, a developer of undersea fiber optic cable systems, against Tyco Submarine Systems for fraud, theft of trade secrets, and breach of contract.

Challenging the structure of public education

In one of New York's most highly publicized cases in 2000, Simpson Thacher is representing a coalition of parent organizations, community schools, and advocacy groups challenging the legality of the state's public school funding. Partner Joseph F. Wayland is lead counsel for *Campaign for Fiscal Equity v. State of NY*, the largest and longest pro bono effort that the firm has tackled. The plaintiffs are trying to get the state to change its funding structure and allocate more money to city schools. Since the trial began in October 1999, Simpson lawyers have argued that New York City schools are crumbling, classes are overcrowded, teachers are not properly trained, and the children lack adequate support services. According to the suit, these deficiencies violate the New York constitution's requirement for a "sound, basic education."

Wayland has described the case as a once-in-a-lifetime opportunity. "It's the type of case that many people dream of doing in law school," he told *The New York Law Journal*. Associates have gotten ample opportunity to get in on the action as well. Jonathan Youngwood, a sixth-year associate, questioned seven witnesses, and four of the other associates working on the case have also questioned witnesses in court. Despite the amount of free hours spent on the matter, Simpson presses on with the suit. Firm chairman Richard Beattie, who has served as a member of New York City's Board of Education, says the firm is committed to litigating the case to its final resolution.

Pro-gram

Simpson associates don't have to resort to watching *Judge Judy* to get their fill of courtroom exposure. Simpson gives junior litigation associates hands-on pro bono training — and offers them the choice of either housing court matters or family court actions. These do-gooder go-getters gain significant experience that their regular work might not afford them, including extensive client contact and courtroom exposure in the Housing Court Project and Family Court Projects. Each class that takes part in the program serves as mentors for the next class of associates. Simpson Thacher stresses that the program is voluntary (as is the case with all of the firm's pro bono work) but strongly encourages its lawyers to take part. Feedback from the program's recipients has been positive as well. In March 1999, the Network for Women's Services — a referral agency for indigent women seeking help with family law matters — honored Simpson for its pro bono work with the organization.

GETTING HIRED

Nice firm, tough standards

As a top New York firm, Simpson Thacher must maintain tough hiring standards. One source says, "If you haven't graduated from a top 10 law school or at the top of your class from a respected top 20 law school, you pretty much can rule out getting hired here." Another source thinks making it to the callback is the biggest hurdle. "Once you get an interview, I think that it is fairly easy to get hired if you are a nice person who can maintain a conversation," he says. (There's the niceness again.) An attorney advises applicants in limbo, "Don't give up — pursue your application." Some insiders say the firm has a soft spot for the Ivy League, Stanford, and Southern schools. Must be that Southern charm.

OUR SURVEY SAYS

Friendly and conservative culture

Simpson's reputation for niceness is born out in the words of associates. No matter what, Simpson associates feel that they're highly respected. Insiders describe Simpson as "friendly," "reserved," "family-oriented," and "conservative." "People treat each other very well," claims one lawyer. Another gratified source comments, "Simpson is true to its reputation. You are thanked for your work, no matter whether it's a fifteen-minute research project or a heavy all-nighter. The hallways are quiet and people are polite and nice." Any meanies? "It is surprising to find a handful of less than friendly people," contends one laywer.

While Simpson lawyers seem to appreciate each other's company, they don't necessarily pursue it outside the office. "During office hours, everyone is incredibly friendly," says one insider. "After work hours, it is a family-oriented rather than a 'happy hour' firm." While Simpson is not a "going-out firm," summers are said to be "naturally a little looser." Another contact sums up his experience at Simpson this way: "The job is demanding and challenging but has taught me to be an excellent attorney."

Like the sands through the hourglass, so are the days of Simpson lives

Like their colleagues at other New York firms, Simpson associates express widespread dissatisfaction with their hours, which tend to hover between 60 and 70 hours a week. "Crazy and inhumane," says a corporate contact. Another finds that "the hours worked are the main problem with this job." Other corporate attorneys offer some words in their firm's defense. "I work a lot of hours," says one, "but so do other associates in firms like this." Another adds: "Everyone works hard, but people are generally respectful of real personal obligations like weddings and vacations."

Litigators also bemoan the hours regime but like litigation associates across the country insist that their hours "vary greatly depending on which cases you are assigned to." Another finds hours are "cyclical. Some months are intense, others are quite livable."

Accessible partners

Associates say that most of the Simpson partners treat them very well. A corporate lawyer says the partners are "very accessible, down-to-earth and great teachers while also being good colleagues." Sources say most partners go out of their way to thank associates for a job well done. But one lawyer says there are "one or two notable exceptions" and "a certain level of horrible partner behavior is tolerated."

Get done and go home

Although associates say their colleagues are "extremely civil toward each other," Simpson is not the place to go for galas and debauchery after hours. One contact explains, "I like the people I work with, but I already have a lot of friends. I'm at Simpson to work, bottom line." Another Simpson associate says, "Some people think it's OK to leave their personality at the door and come to the office. It's very clear they only want to get their work done and leave." Many attorneys are relieved that the firm is respectful of their personal time and does not obligate them to attend firm social events.

Competitive pay

Most lawyers at Simpson feel the firm is "extremely competitive" when it comes to pay. "One of the best things about Simpson is that there is never a question of whether we will get top pay," boasts one well-compensated associate. Some associates say although the firm is not at the tippy-top of the salary heap (leave that to the Skaddens and Gundersons of the world), the firm plays catch up come bonus time. "We're not quite at the top of the ever-increasing pay scale. But at the end of the year, bonuses may even things out," speculates one insider hopefully. But not every lawyer thinks Simpson is doing a good job of keeping salary competitive. "I would have gone to Skadden or L.A. or Boston if I had known about this most recent round of hikes. We are definitely below market, as are most NY firms," complains one lawyer. (The firm has since matched the top level of New York salaries.) On the other hand, some sources express relief at the fact Simpson does not tie compensation to hours.

Training as you go

If you're not proactive, you might not find Simpson's training entirely to your liking. One lawyer finds the training at ST&B to be "ad hoc," although most sources say there are training programs for all levels and all subjects. The credit and banking group sponsors classes on various topics every Wednesday morning. Associates also say that partners do a good job of giving on-the-job training. "Partners generally make a point of using assignments to point out other useful information," according to one lawyer. Another associate boasts, "I have gotten more opportunity and experience as a junior associate than I could have imagined possible." But one attorney complains, "The partners are extremely busy, which translates into little time for training or mentorship." One associate sagely points out that any prospective Simpson lawyers should not be "lacking in common sense. People will expect you to figure some things out for yourself."

Mixed accounts on support

Some lawyers have complaints about Simpson's support services. One lawyer warns, "Delegate at your own risk. The general rule is that secretaries are good for copying and faxing, maybe. It is an embarrassment that Simpson cannot hire better secretaries." Another contact gripes, "It's impossible to get good help during the day. I think there are usually four operators in word processing during the day — an example of ridiculous cost-cutting at a firm this size." (According to the firm, that pool expands significantly during evening hours.) But other sources claim "very good help exists, and most [of it is] quite professional." One insider who habitually works late hours has reason to love Simpson support, telling Vault.com, "Simpson is set so that support is available, for better or for worse, 24-7, 365 days of the year. The night paralegals have saved me a number of trips back to the office after midnight." One sensible associate recommends, "Treat your secretary with respect, and you will get it back."

Diversity: always room for improvement

The firm gets mixed reviews in the diversity area. One contact reports, "It seems like half of the women in the litigation department are on maternity leave. The firm appears to be fine about it." Another source claims there is only one female partner in the Credit & Banking group (out of 19 partners), but the group has many female associates who work part-time. Sources say there are few senior female associates in the corporate department, though reportedly two female associates have made partner in that group. One insider says that "litigation and tax are best" for women, while "securities and banking are improving."

Insiders say that Simpson strives to create an ethnically diverse work place. "Like all firms, I'm sure we can do better, but it appears the firm makes a strong effort and achieves good results in terms of numbers hired and retained." But others think the firm's efforts have lessened in recent years. "Appallingly poor recruitment effort last year," remarks an associate. Another lawyer thinks the firm's efforts to recruit minorities is "great" but thinks Simpson "needs to see more minorities sticking around long enough to even come up for partner." One associate charitably says that the firm had been "resting on its laurels" and is "now starting to pay more attention again."

What lovely offices you have, my dear associate

Simpson Thacher, by all accounts, offers comfortable and charming work environs. "Tasteful," says a corporate contact, who characterizes the firm's New York offices as "exquisite and among the top five in city." Another source in corporate agrees that "very few offices compare." A litigator praises the "great facilities" and notes that "all attorneys have exterior offices with windows — I got my own office after about a year and a half."

As the prior comment indicates, Simpson does double up, a fact that irks some of our insiders. A corporate contact explains: "First-years share an office with second-years until the following spring, then with a summer associate. I'd prefer my own office." A colleague agrees, "Once you have a single, great! Until then, life sucks for first- and second-years and especially for summers." Apparently the firm is taking steps to ease the situation. A litigator explains that "the expansion to additional floors should reduce overcrowding, but elevators were never meant to handle this many people."

Splashy pro bono — if you have time for it

Sources say that Simpson is very supportive of pro bono work. "Opportunities are widely and easily available and often sponsored by a partner. The firm does not penalize associates in any way for time spent on pro bono matters," according to a litigator. But one associate says, "I don't think assigning partners take into consideration pro bono work." Perhaps part of the reason for this lack of consideration is that "no one keeps track of whether you do [pro bono] or not." Another contact says that pro bono is "very much encouraged, but where the hell do you find the time?"

Simpson springboard

Associates believe that ST&B has a high turnover rate. "People use ST&B as a training ground — a springboard to getting a position anywhere else in the world with better hours and lifestyle," says one lawyer. Insiders observe associates packing their bags after their second year at the firm. But one lawyer indicates that "people seem to leave for interesting work." They also come back. Over the last two years, nearly a dozen associates have left Simpson and returned.

Hours all over the map (or is that clock?)

Simpson associates emphasize that the hours can be very volatile. Some attorneys think the firm is on par with its peers. "If you want to practice law, you must expect to work. Litigators at Simpson work no harder (or less for that matter) than [other firms.]" One associate claims, "People definitely respect that you have a life outside the firm and will work with you so that everyone's schedules can be accommodated." But another source advises, "Just hope and pray you aren't working for someone who is up for partner. They keep ridiculously long hours."

Pray for partnership

Insiders say their chances of making partner range from "dim" to "nil." One insider tells Vault.com, "You have virtually no chance at partner. If you believe in a God, you can pray. That's the only way to improve your chances." But not everyone thinks their prospects are so bad. "If you do great work and are willing to stay around long enough, chances are reasonable. Most associates, however, are not interested." Another contact concurs, "I think [chances] are OK because so few associates wait the eight to nine years to be considered."

Attorneys describe the requirement for making partner as "a complete mystery." Another source says that associates in the M&A group have a better shot at the top. Others claim that making partner is a political matter at Simpson because associates need a "backer" to be promoted.

Perkfest for Simpson

Aside from tasty treats like pizza (every other Friday), cookies and aromatic Starbucks coffee, Simpson Thacher associates pick up other perks as well. These include the always much-appreciated car service home, a subsidy of gym membership by two-thirds (up to $1000/year), use of an at-home laptop, and the occasional cocktail party. Another perk is casual dress — the firm is said to be "going full-time casual at the end of the summer." This doesn't mean Simpson lawyers will start shuffling in wearing tattered jeans, sneakers, T-shirts and tank tops. The de facto dress code is said to be "no jeans, no sneakers, no T-shirts. Men have to wear long sleeves and collared shirts." Women's dress, however, "runs the gamut," and "the firm is becoming more casual every day."

INTERVIEW TIP #3

DO ask what practice area your interviewer works in, and what attracted them to the practice. Ask about deals they're working on.

INTERVIEW TIP #4

DON'T brag about your mastery of the law. Our recruiting contacts advise interviewees to "avoid legal issues unless the interviewer brings them up."

Cleary, Gottlieb, Steen & Hamilton

VAULT.COM PRESTIGE RANKING: 7

One Liberty Plaza
New York, NY 10006
(212) 225-2000
Fax: (212) 225-3999
www.cgsh.com

LOCATIONS

New York, NY • Washington, DC • Brussels • Frankfurt • Hong Kong • London • Paris • Rome • Tokyo

MAJOR DEPARTMENTS/PRACTICES

Antitrust
Banking
Corporate and Finance/Securities
Employment Benefits
International/Foreign Sovereign Debt Restructuring
Litigation
Mergers and Acquisitions
Project Finance
Real Estate
Tax
Trusts & Estates
Workouts & Bankruptcy

THE STATS

No. of attorneys: 618
No. of offices: 9
Summer associate offers: 67 out of 67 (New York, 1999); 14 out of 14 (Washington, 1999)
Managing Partners: Peter Karasz (New York)
Hiring Partners: Jeffrey S. Lewis (New York); Michael Lazerwitz (Washington, DC)

PAY

New York, 2000
1st year: $125,000 + $5,000 bonus
2nd year: $135,000 + $9,000 bonus
3rd year: $150,000 + $12,000 bonus
4th year: $170,000 + $13,500 bonus
5th year: $190,000 + $15,000 bonus
6th year: $205,000 + $20,000 bonus
7th year: $220,000 + $20,000 bonus
8th year: $235,000 + $20,000 bonus
Summer associate: $2,404/week

NOTABLE PERKS

- Casual every day during the summer and Fridays the rest of the year
- $2,500 brokerage fee
- Four weeks paternity leave
- Free local health club memberships
- Reduced schedule option for all attorneys

THE BUZZ

What attorneys at other firms are saying about this firm

- "Superb international corporate practice"
- "Eccentric"
- "Groovy on the outside, stuffy on the inside"
- "Excellent, somewhat 'cool' firm"

UPPERS

- Fabulous office space
- Wine and cheese every Friday
- Cheerily eclectic atmosphere
- Inclusive "Athenian-style democracy"

DOWNERS

- Haphazard assignment process
- "Athenian-style democracy" can be sluggish
- Too many hours, too little praise

KEY COMPETITORS

Cravath, Swaine & Moore
Davis Polk & Wardwell
Shearman & Sterling
Skadden, Arps, Slate, Meagher & Flom
Sullivan & Cromwell

EMPLOYMENT CONTACT

Ms. Norma F. Cirincione
Director of Legal Personnel
(212) 225-3150
Nyrecruit@cgsh.com

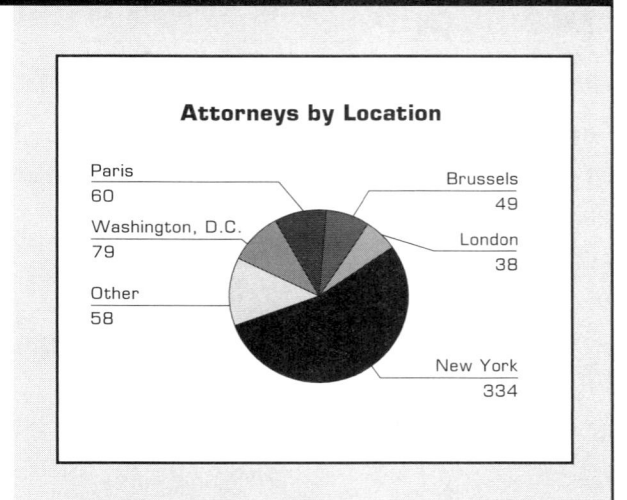

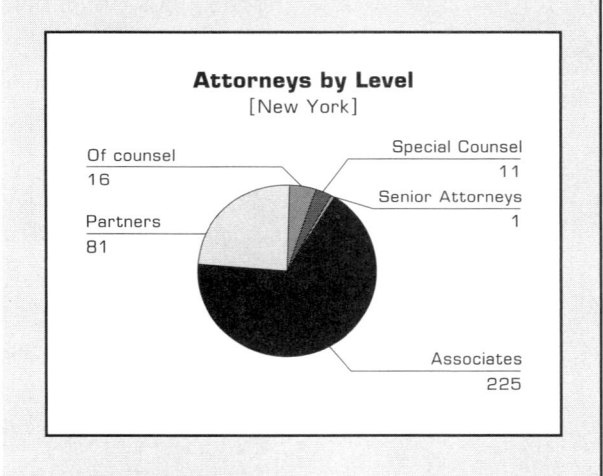

Attorneys by Location
- Paris: 60
- Washington, D.C.: 79
- Other: 58
- Brussels: 49
- London: 38
- New York: 334

Attorneys by Level [New York]
- Of counsel: 16
- Partners: 81
- Special Counsel: 11
- Senior Attorneys: 1
- Associates: 225

QUALITY OF LIFE RANKINGS [ASSOCIATES RATE THEIR OWN FIRM]

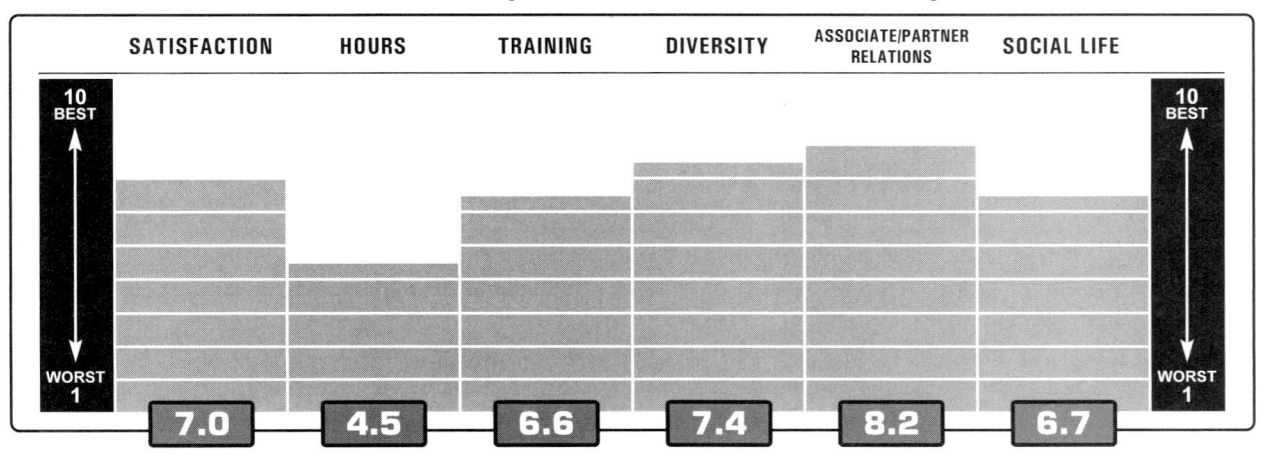

SATISFACTION	HOURS	TRAINING	DIVERSITY	ASSOCIATE/PARTNER RELATIONS	SOCIAL LIFE
7.0	4.5	6.6	7.4	8.2	6.7

THE SCOOP

Cleary Gottlieb may be a big-time New York law firm — it resides comfortably among the top 10 law firms in the world by most measures (and ranks No. 7 in the Vault.com Top 50). The firm views itself as distinct from its New York peers. Don't be fooled, however — beneath a "funky" image, Cleary remains large, well-connected, and focused on profits.

Rebellious history

Founded in 1946, Cleary, Gottlieb, Steen & Hamilton is the product of a 1940s rebellion at Root, Clark, Buckner & Ballantine. Four Root lawyers — George Cleary, Henry Friendly, Leo Gottlieb, and Mel Steen — bolted from their "roots" after their parent firm set up a partner compensation system based on hours billed and clients ensnared. The group felt that the noble work of law should be built around the principles of cooperation and that setting up a system in which lawyers would compete against others at the same firm was simply wrong. So they started their own firm, where associates and partners would be compensated by seniority alone. Some of Cleary's founders went on to achieve tremendous prominence: Henry J. Friendly, for example, became one of the Second Circuit's most famous judges, and George W. Ball became Undersecretary of State and Ambassador to the United Nations. The upstart firm got lucky early on when it acquired Salomon Brothers, then just a bond trading house, as a client. As Salomon developed into a big player in the capital markets, so did Cleary.

Overseas expansion

The firm, which initially set up two domestic offices in New York and Washington, DC, soon expanded overseas. It established a Paris office in 1949, a Brussels office in 1960, and a London office in 1971. The firm entered Asia in 1980 with a Hong Kong office and set up an office in Tokyo in 1987. In fact, the firm's resident partners were the first foreign lawyers to be licensed under Japanese law. And in 1989, Cleary became the first firm to promote Japanese attorneys. The firm also opened an office in Frankfurt in 1991, which today represents Treuhandanstalt, the agency responsible for privatizing companies in the former East Germany. Cleary's five European offices also engage in privatization, investment, and governmental counsel in Russia and Eastern Europe. In 1998 Cleary became the third major U.S. firm to open an office in Italy. Cleary's international orientation bears great benefits for associates who hanker to work overseas. Insiders say that there are few language requirements "except for Germany and maybe France." The firm is said by associates to be "the best place to work if you want to go overseas."

New leadership and new titles

January 1, 2000 brought more than a new millennium to Cleary. It also brought a new man at the top — Peter Karasz, the firm's new managing partner. Karasz succeeds Ned Stiles, who had led the firm since 1988. Karasz is a corporate lawyer whose expertise is in project finance, infrastructure projects, and international M&A. Recently he has been spending much of his time working on Latin American energy projects.

Cleary's clearly concerned about retaining its top lawyers — and has a new plan and a new position to keep valuable associates. In 1999 the firm created a new position of "senior attorney," available to seventh-year attorneys who have been with the firm for two or more years. Associates reveal that those qualifying for the position can negotiate hours and pay. One source told *The New York Law Journal* that the job seems to be designed for people who want to work more than part-time but less than the rigorous schedule that large firms like Cleary often require.

The English (and Germans) are coming

Cleary has an extensive international M&A practice in Asia, Europe, and Latin America. The firm participated in two of the most important bank consolidations of the past year. In May 1999, Cleary Gottlieb was tapped to represent Great Britain's HSBC Holdings in the bank's largest deal yet — a $10.3 billion takeover of Republic New York Corporation and its Luxembourg affiliate, Safra Republic Holdings. At the time of its announcement, the deal was the largest-ever foreign acquisition of an American bank. HSBC used no in-house counsel, relying solely on Cleary attorneys.

Longtime client Deutsche Bank also turned to Cleary as outside counsel in its controversial $10.1 billion purchase of Bankers Trust. The deal, closed in June 1999, combined Germany's largest bank with the eighth-largest financial institution in the United States, creating an entity counting over $800 billion in assets.

But Cleary's work in the financial services area isn't just limited to M&A. The firm is also helping the government of Indonesia get back on its feet after that country's economic turmoil and political unrest at the end of the 1990s. Cleary is helping the country with a $7 billion Indonesian bank debt restructuring program. Cleary has also been counseling the governments of Mexico, Argentina, Chile, Columbia, Ecuador, Russia, Korea, and the Philippines on debt management.

Vive le Coca-Cola!

Cleary Gottlieb has long represented The Coca-Cola Company. In spring 1999, the firm busied itself with Coca-Cola's continuing attempts to acquire the Orangina brand from Pernod-Ricard, a French beverage company. PepsiCo, Coca-Cola's nemesis, has been fighting the acquisition for several years, particularly since PepsiCo uses the Orangina infrastructure for its own product distribution in France. Soon after the acquisition agreement between Coke and Orangina was announced in late 1997, PepsiCo filed a motion seeking to block the deal, appealing to a French law which bars mergers resulting in a single entity dominating 25 percent or more of the market. In 1998 PepsiCo successfully convinced a French court that acquiring Orangina would indeed allow Coca-Cola to dominate the French beverage market.

The last bank standing

Cleary is a self-described pioneer in the area of mortgage-backed securities and continues to be active in the formation of new asset-backed financial products. It is the principal underwriter on public offerings of mortgage-backed securities and debt for the Federal Home Loan Mortgage Corporation (Freddie Mac). The structured finance practice is especially active in France, Germany, and Latin America.

After much private debate and public scrutiny, ultraprestigious Goldman Sachs became the final major investment bank to go public in May 1999. Goldman raised a cool $3.66 billion from the IPO, selling 69 million shares of stock in the company (just over 11 percent). Cleary Gottlieb was closely involved in the IPO, serving as underwriter's counsel for Goldman. Sullivan & Cromwell, also longtime attorneys for Goldman, served as issuer's counsel.

Deutsche Telekom through the years

Cleary scored a great coup in 1995 when it beat out other major law firms for the business of German telephone monopoly Deutsche Telekom AG in its $10 billion international IPO (which actually took place in 1996). Cleary's major competition proved to be Skadden, which Cleary beat out in a Bonn-based beauty contest. In 1999 Deutsche Telekom again turned to Cleary, this time for merger discussions with Telecom Italia. Cleary is no stranger to Telecom Italia either — in 1997 the firm represented the Italian government in Telecom Italia's privatization and has since advised the company on regulatory matters.

Inside the Beltway

Cleary has a bustling Washington, DC practice, established the same year as the firm's New York office. Cleary's outpost in the nation's capital is essentially an independent entity in relation to the firm's New York operations. The office's management and hiring are separate, and its practice areas and client base are distinct. The office houses about 70 lawyers, and a few of the firm's Washington lawyers are actually resident in foreign offices. The office's practice is primarily business-related and is engaged in significant transactional work. Its work extends far beyond the boundaries of Washington, DC — its attorneys advise clients in Europe, the Middle East, Latin America, the Russian Federation, and the Far East. The office's client list includes such international organizations as the Asian Development Bank, the European Bank for Reconstruction and Development, and the International Bank for Reconstruction and Development (the World Bank).

Fighting for a scout's honor and the MoMA's art

Though Cleary insiders concede that the firm is more known for corporate work than for litigation, the firm has been involved in some headline grabbing cases.

Cleary is serving as co-counsel with the Lambda Legal Defense and Education Fund in a high-profile New Jersey case involving the right of a gay man to serve as a scout leader in the Boy Scouts. The New Jersey Supreme Court ruled that the Boy Scouts' ban on homosexuals violates New Jersey's anti-discrimination law. In a unanimous 89-page decision, the court ruled that the Boy Scouts organization qualifies as a "place of public accommodation." The Boy Scouts have appealed, and as of May 2000, the United States Supreme Court was still mulling the case.

Cleary successfully represented the New York Museum of Modern Art when Manhattan prosecutors tried to prevent the museum from returning two paintings to an Austrian foundation. Prosecutors wanted to stop the art transfer as part of their investigation into art thefts by Nazis. The museum was preparing to fulfill its contractual obligation and return the paintings to the Leopold Foundation when the heirs of two Austrian Jews claimed ownership of the paintings. MoMA argued that New York's Arts and Cultural Affairs Law provided that the paintings could not be seized. The Court of Appeals ruling in MoMA's favor came as a relief to many art institutions, who feared an adverse decision would discourage owners from exhibiting their art in New York.

Litigation leader

A source of pride for Cleary is litigation partner Evan A. Davis, the new president of the Association of the Bar of the City of New York. The 61st person to hold the post, Davis brings a history of public service to the job. He served as counsel to Governor Mario Cuomo from 1985 to 1991 and in 1974 held the position of Watergate Task Force Leader for the Nixon Impeachment Inquiry of the U.S. House of Representatives Judiciary Committee.

GETTING HIRED

Be unique

Many insiders say that a "diverse or unusual" background will bolster a candidate's chances of getting hired at iconoclastic Cleary. Of course, you need good grades to get in the door. "You are doomed, even as a lateral, without sufficient A's on your transcript," a litigator reports. "In short, if you have stellar academic credentials and are good at making interesting cocktail party conversations, you'll do fine in the interviews," advises one source. Associates also say the firm puts a lot of emphasis on law review or participation with other journals. The firm is said to favor former judicial clerks. And given the firm's international bent, Cleary is especially interested in candidates with foreign language skills.

One lawyer proposes that the on-campus interviews are where Cleary makes most of its cuts. "Once you get an invite to come to the firm for a second interview, it's hard to blow it." Sources report that the firm has been increasing its summer associate classes to keep up with its increased workload — but recruitment still proves problematic, even at this top firm. "We now hire at schools where we once did not interview, and we still don't seem to get enough people in the door," laments a Cleary lawyer.

OUR SURVEY SAYS

Caring Cleary

Cleary associates most often term their firm's culture "friendly." "The firm's strong rhetoric is that it values its associates, and the general personal interactions between partners and associates is completely consistent with that," one contact reports. One associate gushes, "The people are really sweet, quirky and caring." But a less-impressed corporate associate describes the firm as "disingenuously friendly." "There is a very real hierarchy based on seniority, lurking beneath the friendly exterior. Consequently, interactions often involve a strained effort at casualness that conceals the instrumental nature of workplace relationships. In short, they're very nice about asking you to cancel your vacation or spend the weekend at the printer," he explains.

Associates believe the lack of billing requirements and the lockstep compensation system prevent Cleary from becoming more competitive. "Since there is no billable hours requirement, and each associate makes exactly the same amount as other associates at his or her seniority level, there is no competition, and thus no friction, among associates."

"I'm surprised to find myself saying this, because I never thought I'd like a commercial practice, but the work here has been fascinating, and I've been treated well," confesses another attorney. One associate reports that "one of the strengths of Cleary is that it hires lawyers with outside interests other than the law. This is also a drawback because we are not one-dimensional, so a lot of us feel unfulfilled as human beings."

Socialistas

Social butteflies will find a comfortable perch at Cleary. The New York office has three main outings. One is a holiday party, which takes place either at Cleary or at a restaurant like the elegant Windows on the World. The entire firm is invited to the party, but dates are only allowed when it is held at the firm's offices. In March Cleary has a firmwide event at Wranglers, intended to introduce new associates to the firm. "Mild hazing takes place then," a source says. "Partners and associates will be made fun of. New associates will have to stand up and introduce themselves." Shy associates should practice public speaking in advance.

Finally, in lieu of its traditional summer country club outing, in 2000 the firm is experimenting with a community service day at a local public high school. Cleary lawyers will tutor students, play sports with them, and clean up the school. The day's activities also include a lunch reception with students and a dinner with the school's faculty and staff.

Psst! We've got your next assignment right here!

Cleary, for better or for worst, is a decentralized organization, and associates have great latitude to move between practice areas. There are no rotations, allowing associates to either specialize early or remain a generalist for some time. "People are free to whatever work is in the office," explains one associate. Another lawyer elaborates, "Each associate is responsible for managing and arranging his docket. Partners in need of staffing a team call around to see who is available. It is within each associate's discretion to say yes or no."

Decentralization by its nature, however, rewards proactivity and initiative. While many Cleary associates rave about the type of work the firm does, some think the quality assignments are not evenly distributed. "It seems like if the assigning partner likes you, you're in. If not, too bad," theorizes one contact. Another attorney explains, "Although some assignments are given out by partners through the gray market of Cleary assigning, many come through the assigning partner. As a result, many of the choice assignments are filled when the assigning partner calls. If you are unfortunate enough to have time in your schedule, he will assign you to whatever is left." "If you just sit back," warns a New York associate, "you're not going to be taken care of," presenting the danger that "you can slip through the cracks and get stuck doing the same kind of deal over and over again."

Working for and with the partners

Many associates report a positive and "open door" relationship with partners — a priority at Cleary. "It's definitely a 'work with,' not a 'work for,' atmosphere," according to a corporate attorney. "Generally partners treat associates very well — a few partners yell, but this is frowned upon," says another lawyer. One associate raves that Cleary partners are "more accessible than my law professors were!"

Another contact offers this insight: "The partners are very pleasant to work with generally, but they view themselves as superior in the Cleary hierarchy. Some of them seem to actually care about the associates, and some just think of us as revenue generators." A litigator disagrees with the hierarchical view of Cleary. "Not only do I find that partners treat associates with great respect, I find relatively few lines drawn between the different tiers. I can honestly say that I count some of the partners I work with as close personal friends."

The open-door policy has its drawbacks, according to some associates surveyed by Vault.com. "Decentralized means disorganized. It is sometimes difficult to get partners to agree on how to share your time," says a New York associate. Another insider from that office states that "firm management is an afterthought. Managerial duties are allocated to a diffuse committee structure. Consequently, decisions are slow to emerge and reflect compromise and consensus rather than executive leadership."

Wine and cheese

Many insiders count their fellow associates as one of Cleary's best selling points. "Associates talk to each other a lot at work and, if they have time, have lunch or dinner together or sometimes go out after work. People are very friendly and helpful." But insiders emphasize that Cleary is not party central. An associate in the Washington office claims, "People are very friendly, but it is definitely a 'geek' firm. Lots of value hung on intellectualism and very little on social skills." Associates can find colleagues at Cleary to hang out with after work. But one insider claims, "Some associates spontaneously get together, but most associates have no time for such frivolities as a social life or dating, intrafirm or otherwise." The New York office sponsors wine and cheese parties every Friday. These social events are reportedly well attended, but one lawyer believes them to be "a thinly veiled way to identify the few associates who do not yet have weekend assignments."

Better late than never?

Cleary has remained competitive in the law firm salary wars. The firm has a lockstep compensation system and no merit-based bonuses, though the firm has paid boom year bonuses in the past. But some associates think the firm is just a "follower" when it comes to compensation. "The firm's slowness in responding to pay raises and bonuses at comparable firms is a source of frustration and anxiety for associates," an insider reports. Cleary does not claim to set the market but does assert that it was among the leaders during the last round of salary hikes.

And not everyone thinks the money is enough. "In the abstract, the pay is great, but when you factor in the hours and cost of living in New York, it doesn't seem so good any more," says one associate whose salary easily tops $130,000 annually. Some attorneys also are unsatisfied with Cleary's inclusion of a 3 percent 401(k) contribution as part of their salary. "Many associates view this structure as paternalistic and would rather have the cash to allocate as they see fit, which often means paying off student loans," snipes one associate.

Billing outside the cracks

Associates report hours that average between 50 to 80 hours per week. A New York associate says that associate gossip pegs the range of billing in the corporate department as between 1,600 and 2,500, with a few enthusiastic associates in the 2,800 to 3,200 range. "If you are semi-responsible, the job dominates your life. The firm generally does respect vacations, though," comments a Vault.com source. Many Cleary lawyers feel the work burden at the firm is unevenly distributed. "Cleary's reputation for being humane on the billing issue derives from the fact that there is no oversight here. Some associates fall through the cracks, and others bill," one insider opines. Folks in the DC office say the litigation and anti-trust practice areas work a few more hours on average per week than the rest of the firm.

"Figure it out and call me back"

Some Cleary attorneys express complaints about the level of training and mentoring at Cleary. "Training equals 'throw associate into difficult situation and see what happens,'" claims a Cleary lawyer. One associate cites an overheard directive from a partner to a junior associate that "sums up the reality" at Cleary. The overheard statement? "I don't have time to train you, just figure it out and call me back (click)." But a corporate lawyer describes the amount of training as "unbelievable" (in a good way), pointing to Cleary's practice group lunches and the firm's CLE offerings. Others report that Cleary is making efforts to improve its training. "For a long time, partners had the attitude that smart people would learn on their own and those who didn't catch on were not worth the time and effort to train. The mindset is slowly changing, as partners realize the need to train and maintain associates," one lawyer explains. The firm reportedly is in the midst of setting up an intranet site with training materials.

The price of ambition

Associates believe that Cleary has a very high turnover rate, though everyone Vault.com surveyed insists associates are not leaving for rival firms. "Because Cleary attracts interesting people, a lot of people leave to do other, more interesting jobs, or simply to get out of a job that requires such a great time commitment," one lawyer explains. "The firm attracts very ambitious people. It's no wonder many move on after learning the legal ropes," another contact concurs.

Peaceful offices, surly support

Ah, the lovely vista of Lady Liberty. "I'm looking out on the Statue of Liberty's harbor boats — what more can you ask for?" inquires one statue-loving Cleary associate. According to another New York contact, "the carpets are starting to fray a bit after ten years, but our views are unparalleled. The décor and art are peaceful." Cleary officials assure Vault.com that the carpets are in fact replaced regularly. "Unlike other white shoe New York firms whose décor is stuffy and formal, Cleary has eschewed colonial paintings and mahogany for streamlined furniture and architecture and a first-rate modern art collection," notes another attorney approvingly.

DC associates also like their (admittedly less dramatic) offices and are particularly impressed with the firm's location in Washington. Cleary gives most first-years their own office within a month or two of coming to the firm.

Associates also seemed pleased with the support services at Cleary. "Most people I know are very happy with the support staff and have a good relationship with their secretaries. The word processing staff is often surly, but their work is competent," says one contact. The New York office has a 24-hour duplicating, fax and word processing centers, though some hardworking associates complained about a lack of secretarial help during the weekends. "The word processing staff have attitudes and won't do things like copying and mailing labels," gripes one attorney. The Washington office only has full-time word processing until 3 a.m. and other support services close up around 11. Although the computer system has gone through sundry upgrades, attorneys in some offices say it's still a touch antiquated.

Working 9 to 5 — maybe 9 to 9

Associates report that Cleary hires about the same number of women as men. According to a Cleary litigator, "The firm is very conscious and in my personal experience could not try harder to make things work for women." Another source says hesitantly, "It is not bad to be a woman associate at Cleary. But women seldom make partner and don't have very good long-term prospects at Cleary. The few who do make partner dress and act like men to fit into the partners' boys' club." Cleary denies this claim, and openly offers support to its female associates. It hosts a "Working Women" group that meets monthly to discuss women's issues and has increased schedule flexibility for mothers. Some insiders have doubts about these initiatives. "A new senior attorney track has just been created, and the firm is now allowing more associates to take a reduced schedule for parenting. But many women are worried that this will produce a 'mommy track' and that women who take a reduced schedule will be shunted to a senior attorney position rather than seriously considered for partner. Preliminary evidence suggests that they're right." According to the firm, the two attorneys who have thus far moved to the senior attorney track are both women. One of the two has children.

Minorities: what the *NYLJ* says and what associates think

Cleary has been called a leader in diversity by *The New York Law Journal*, promoting two Asian partners and one Hispanic partner in 1999. Minorities have accounted for 20 percent of the firm's partners since 1992 and more than 25 percent of Cleary's associates are minorities. But some associates believe that ethnic minorities, particularly African-Americans, leave in disproportionately high numbers. "I think the firm works very hard on this. I can see, though, why African-American associates find it dismaying that there are no African-American partners," says one contact.

"Pronounced gay contingent"

Insiders say Cleary has a "very pronounced gay contingent." "You don't hear gossip about people's sex lives here. We have lots of open partners and associates and no one seems to care," reports one source. One openly gay Cleary lawyer reports that "no one seems fazed by my sexual orientation." Cleary provides benefits to domestic partners and the firm also boasts a gay and lesbian group that has lunch meetings. Reportedly gay associates' significant others can attend firm social events without getting any "flak."

Personally for pro bono

Associates' experiences with pro bono work at Cleary differ greatly. "Some people do it, but it's more of a personal commitment than something everyone is encouraged to do," reports one lawyer. Another insider says, however, "I have been encouraged to take on pro bono projects and have been commended for my involvement." "Pro bono, as far as I can tell, is treated exactly like billable work for all purposes," says another source.

As Cleary as day

Despite any complaints, most Cleary insiders seems cognizant that their firm differs from other law firms in important ways. Several associates tell Vault.com they "never thought they would like a large commercial firm" but appreciate Cleary for the "freedom," "collegial atmosphere," "the opportunity to spend time in a foreign office" and "intelligent, cool and well-rounded" co-workers. "No matter how junior you are," comments one associate, "you do feel your opinion counts here."

INTERVIEW TIP #5

DO ask about training, both formal and informal, as well as mentoring. It shows that you are interested in learning.

INTERVIEW TIP #6

DON'T bring up your LSAT score — it's tacky. Maybe you got a perfect score — but what if your interviewer didn't?

VAULT.COM

PRESTIGE RANKING 8

Shearman & Sterling

599 Lexington Avenue
New York, NY 10022
(212) 848-4000
Fax: (212) 848-7179
www.shearman.com

LOCATIONS

New York, NY (HQ)
Menlo Park, CA • San Francisco, CA • Washington, DC • Abu Dhabi • Beijing • Dusseldorf • Frankfurt • Hong Kong London • Paris • Singapore • Tokyo • Toronto

MAJOR DEPARTMENTS/PRACTICES

Antitrust
Bank Finance & Bankruptcy
Corporate Finance
Exec. Compensation & Employee Benefits/Private Clients
Leasing
Litigation
Mergers and Acquisitions
Project Development & Finance
Property
Tax

THE STATS

No. of attorneys: 867
No. of offices: 14
Summer associate offers: 78 out of 78 (New York, 1999)
Chairman: Stephen Volk
Managing Partner: Whitney D. Pidot
Hiring Partner: Stephen Fishbein

PAY

New York, San Francisco, and Washington, DC, 2000
1st year: $125,000 + $7,000 bonus
2nd year: $135,000 + bonus
3rd year: $150,000 + bonus
4th year: $165,000 + bonus
Summer associate: $2,538/week

NOTABLE PERKS

- Longevity bonuses
- Mandatory one-month sabbatical or three-month transfer assignment for all fifth- or sixth-year associates
- Laptop computers for associates and summer associates
- Senior associates' "slush funds" to spend on associate morale
- Monthly drawing for several pairs of theatre tickets and one $150 voucher for dinner at a restaurant of choice

THE BUZZ
What attorneys at other firms are saying about this firm

- "Basic old-line New York"
- "Desperately trying to change its image"
- "I'd take an offer from them!"
- "International dealmakers"

UPPERS

- Keen attention, monetary and otherwise, to associate satisfaction
- No "cookie cutter" work
- Lush and lovely lawyer's dining room

DOWNERS

- Long hours
- Vomit-colored carpets
- Up-for-grabs weekends

KEY COMPETITORS

Cleary, Gottlieb, Steen & Hamilton
Cravath, Swaine & Moore
Davis Polk & Wardwell
Skadden, Arps, Slate, Meagher & Flom
Simpson Thacher & Bartlett
Sullivan & Cromwell

EMPLOYMENT CONTACT

Ms. Halle Schargel
Manager, Professional Recruiting
(212) 848-7456
hschargel@shearman.com

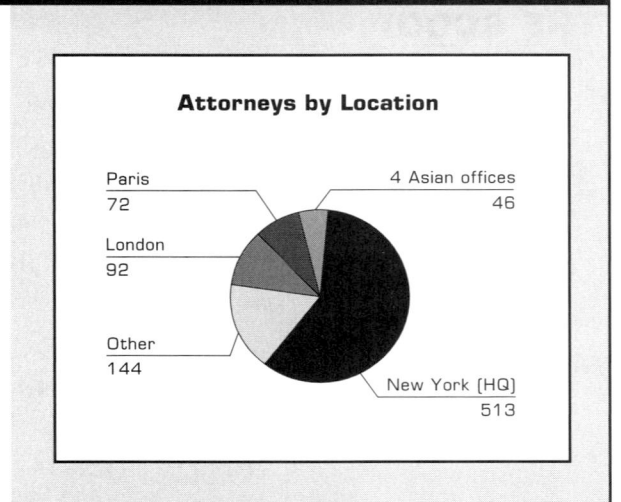

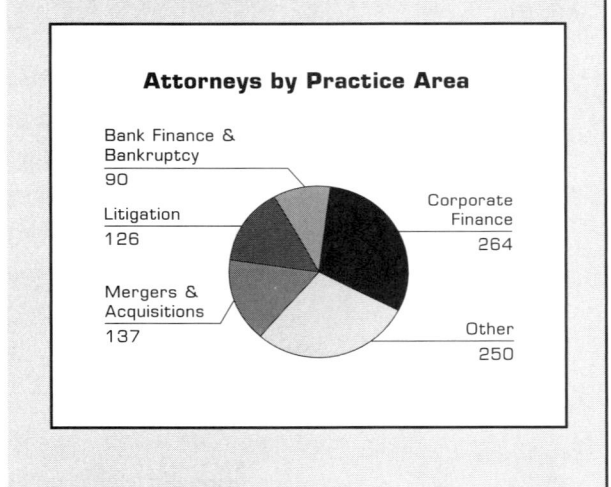

Attorneys by Location
- Paris: 72
- 4 Asian offices: 46
- London: 92
- Other: 144
- New York (HQ): 513

Attorneys by Practice Area
- Bank Finance & Bankruptcy: 90
- Litigation: 126
- Corporate Finance: 264
- Mergers & Acquisitions: 137
- Other: 250

QUALITY OF LIFE RANKINGS [ASSOCIATES RATE THEIR OWN FIRM]

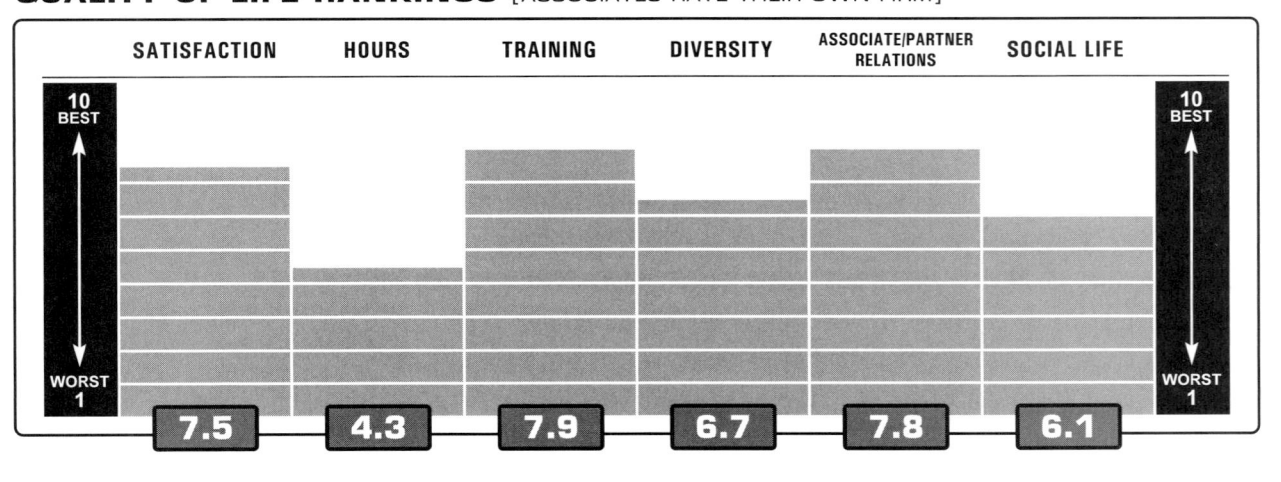

SATISFACTION	HOURS	TRAINING	DIVERSITY	ASSOCIATE/PARTNER RELATIONS	SOCIAL LIFE
7.5	4.3	7.9	6.7	7.8	6.1

THE SCOOP

Founded 127 years ago, Shearman & Sterling is one of the oldest and largest law firms in the world. Shearman has built up a top-notch mergers and acquisitions department and formed relationships with numerous financial institutions. The firm plans to continue its impressive international expansion but not at the expense of associate happiness. In 1999 Shearman unveiled a set of groundbreaking retention policies designed to improve its somewhat "sweaty" reputation.

Marching through history

Shearman & Sterling's story began on November 17, 1873 when Thomas Shearman, 34, and John Sterling, 24, opened a law practice together at No. 20 Nassau Street in New York's Fourth National Bank Building. The offices had a staff of seven — two partners, three law clerks, a bookkeeper, and the ever-helpful office boy. Shearman, a former law reporter for *The New York Times*, and Sterling, who graduated No. 1 in his class from Columbia Law School, had both previously worked for David Dudley Field, head of the New York bar. Together they brought over a major client from Field's law firm, industrialist Jay Gould, who would become Shearman & Sterling's principal client. Other high-profile 19th century clients included Jonathan Thome, a wealthy Quaker merchant; Charles Osborn of Osborn & Chapin, one of the largest Wall Street brokerage houses; railway magnates George and Donald Smith; and the Rockefellers. Soon Shearman & Sterling began representing banks, including the corporate ancestor of Citibank, thereby firmly establishing itself as a player in the New York legal community.

Shearman opened its first branch office in Paris in 1963, followed by offices in London (1972), Abu Dhabi (1976), and Hong Kong (1978). In 1979 the firm began its domestic expansion with a San Francisco office. In 1987 it established a Washington, DC branch, and in fall 1998, it opened a Menlo Park outpost to cater to the needs of Silicon Valley clients. Within the last decade or so, Shearman has pushed its international presence to new heights, setting up offices in Tokyo (1987), Toronto (1989), Frankfurt and Dusseldorf (1991), Beijing (1993), and Singapore (1995). At the end of May 2000, the firm stood poised to acquire most of the German firm Schilling, Zutt & Anschutz (which counts Daimler-Chrysler AG, BASF AG, and SAP AG as clients) in another step towards globalization.

Perky Shearman

In January 1999, Shearman announced a new set of perks for its lawyers. First, the firm set aside a minimum of $2 million annually for an associate benefit fund. Associates will accrue bonus shares after three years at the firm and start getting payoffs in their fourth year. But Shearman's reforms aren't just centered around money — they also affect quality of life issues, often regarded as a notoriously weak aspect of the New York law firm experience. The new initiative allows any associate who has spent at least two years at S&S to shift to a part-time or flextime schedule without hurting his or her partnership chances.

And speaking of that coveted partner status, Shearman is pledging to demystify the process by giving all senior associates a comprehensive review and appraisal of their partnership prospects. If a particular associate shows a reasonable likelihood of a long-term career with the firm as partner or counsel, the firm will provide a $50,000 bonus as an extra incentive to stick around. Finally, in order to prevent associate burnout, the reforms mandate that fifth-year or sixth-year associates choose between taking a one-month sabbatical devoted to career development or spending three months in another S&S practice group or office. Options for the month-long sabbatical range widely, from community service, to an intensive language course, to working in a prosecutor's office.

Partner raid

Shearman has been hiring lateral partners to beef up its international M&A and securities practices. The firm successfully lured Adrian Knight, the former head of the investment banking group at London's Ashurst Morris Crisp, in May 1999. Five months later Shearman made its largest talent grab, adding 13 French M&A lawyers to its ranks, thus giving the firm a strong M&A presence on both sides of the Atlantic. Shearman also picked up securities and cross-border financing lawyers Marke Raines from Allen & Overy and Gary Barnett from O'Melveny & Myers.

...and losses

But turnabout is fair play in the land of lawyers — and accountants. In March 2000, accounting giant Ernst & Young poached Shearman litigation counsel Eric Teynier plus two senior assistants and a paralegal. Teynier and his team will be setting up a litigation and arbitration department for E&Y. October 1999 saw the New York office of Lovell White Durrant snag Shearman tax associate Joseph Gruber. That same month, Rogers & Wells grabbed Shearman executive director Douglas Benson to manage the firm's merger with Clifford Chance.

Corporate powerhouse

Shearman & Sterling has become a leader in all facets of corporate law. The firm's corporate lawyers represent U.S. and international companies in everything from mergers to proxy contests to joint ventures. The firm's global reach and its solid reputation abroad enable it to handle complex cross-border transactions, including those involving multiple jurisdictions and practice areas. In fact, Shearman helped negotiate NAFTA and played a key role in a number of legislative developments in Central and Eastern Europe. In October 1999, Privatisation International and Thomson Financial Securities Data ranked Shearman the number one firm in terms of the value of closed projects, with 21 completed deals valued at a total of $13.9 billion.

Marrying off SmithKline

An insider describes the M&A department as "a fraternity of tough guys and girls that work hard and feel like tough guys because of it." In one major deal, Shearman lawyers Creighton Condon, Stephen Volk, Michael DeFranco, and Mark Roppel advised pharmaceutical giant SmithKline Beecham on its $76 billion merger with Glaxo. Merger negotiations were thrown off course in 1998 due to a power struggle between top executives, but the deal finally got back on track in January 2000. The new entity, Glaxo-SmithKline, will be the world's largest drug maker, providing stressed-out lawyers with such products as Tums antacids and the ulcer medication Zantac. S&S also represented Viacom in its $40 billion acquisition of CBS in September 1999.

Other deals in which Shearman played a role include chemical company BASF's $3.8 million purchase of American Home Products' chemical unit in March 2000 and Gambro's May 1999 sale of its cardiovascular medical device company, COBE, to Italy's Sorin Biomedica.

The biggest IPO

The Shearman corporate finance team represents companies and governments who have been in the markets for years as well as those entities seeking to enter the capital markets for the first time. In 1999 S&S topped European equity rankings, working on 42 transactions totaling $31.8 billion. Partner Bob Treuhold advised Merrill Lynch on its role in the world's largest IPO. Merrill served as a global coordinator (with Mediobanca) in the $18.6 billion sale of shares in Italian state-owned electricity company Enel at the end of 1999. Treuhold also advised French bank Credit Lyonnais on its 1999 privatization and stock exchange listing. According to Treuhold, the bank's privatization presented complications because 90 percent of the bank — a much larger portion than usual — needed to be sold.

Shearman lawyers also took part in the first project financing in the United Arab Emirates, a $750 million water desalination project. The project is part of the UAE's plan to privatize and restructure its water and electricity sectors. The firm's other headline-making work includes representing Morgan Stanley Dean Witter, the underwriter of Amazon.com's $325 million high-yield debt offering, and representing Goldman Sachs, the underwriter of eBay's initial public offering.

Global litigation

Shearman's litigation and dispute resolution practice handles trial and appellate work in federal, state, tax, and bankruptcy courts throughout the United States, France, and Germany. The group has argued cases before a wide range of arbitration panels and tribunals worldwide, including the International Chamber of Commerce, the London Court of International Arbitration, and the Iran-U.S. Claims Tribunal at the Hague.

In the spring of 2000, Shearman lawyers helped clear the legal hurdles to a $40 billion plan to unite the operations of Viacom and CBS Corp. Chris-Craft Industries, Viacom's partner in the United Paramount Network (UPN), brought a challenge to the scheme, arguing that by engaging in the CBS merger Viacom would be violating its contractual duties to UPN. (Viacom had promised to build up UPN as a fifth major network.) In March 2000, Shearman's Stuart Baskin successfully persuaded the court that Viacom had both properly structured the merger and honored its obligations to UPN. The ruling paved the way for Viacom to buy out Chris-Craft's 50 percent stake in UPN, making Viacom the first-ever owner of two broadcast networks.

The firm is also defending Lexis-Nexis owner Thomson from an antitrust suit brought in March 2000 by small-firm lawyers. The suit claims that Lexis-Nexis is in cahoots with fellow electronic legal research powerhouse West Group in a plot to inflate the cost of legal research. Dale Collins, an antitrust partner from Shearman's New York office, is handling the case.

Shearman & Sterling boasts an active white collar criminal defense pratice as well. The group is led in New York by five former federal prosecutors and recently took part in the defense of a vitamin manufacturer against allegations of price fixing, the largest criminal case ever brought by the Justice Department.

Shearman and the big blue bank

Shearman's century-long relationship with Citigroup, one of the world's largest banking institutions, has propelled the firm to first-tier status. For decades Shearman relied on Citigroup for a significant portion of its revenue, and the bank remains one of the firm's top five clients. Shearman is currently defending Citicorp in a more than $80 million lender liability case brought by two architects in Oakland, CA Superior Court. The suit alleges that Citicorp committed fraud in connection with the construction loan agreement for a renovation project. On the first go-round in December 1999, the jury deadlocked. Partner Paul Wickes is leading the Shearman litigation team and is assisted by associates from the firm's New York and San Francisco offices.

Tech smarts

Shearman handled a large number of technology-related transactions in 1999. On the M&A front, the firm took part in Beyond.com's $140 million purchase of BuyDirect.com in March, Synetic's $1.3 billion purchase of Medical Manager Group in July, and Raychem's $2.97 billion acquisition of Tyco International Ltd. in August. It also worked on public offerings of Looksmart, Active Software, and eBay, among others. But the firm's tech focus is not limited to its clientele. Shearman was one of the first large law firms to give its attorneys laptop computers and stays on the cutting edge by replacing them every year and a half. Under the guidance of Director of Information and Professional Systems Eugene Stein, it has also built an extensive technology infrastructure that can be suited to every Shearman lawyer's unique preferences and work style.

Shearman to the rescue

When refugees were amassing on the Macedonian border in April 1999 during the war in Kosovo, Shearman lawyers helped them get into the U.S. while avoiding bureaucratic red tape. The U.S. had agreed to let in 20,000 refugees, but they first had to apply, interview, and go through medical and security checks. Because time was of the essence for the homeless Kosovars, partner Cornelius Dwyer, litigation associate Helen MacFarlance, and other Shearman lawyers went to work poring over the refugee and asylum sections of the applicable immigration law. They submitted a memo to the U.S. government concluding that the Kosovars could avoid lengthy policy delays by entering the country under refugee status rather than as asylum seekers. This policy averted lengthy delays at a time when Macedonia was periodically closing its borders.

Moving on

In 1994 Shearman & Sterling lawyers successfully ended their fight to get Shannon Faulkner admitted to The Citadel, a prestigious military institute in South Carolina. Although a federal judge ordered the school to admit Faulkner, she ended up dropping out after less than a week. (The fact that the first week is referred to as "Hell Week" may have had something to do with it.) It seems that Shearman and The Citadel are ready to let bygones be bygones — as the firm plans to donate a portion of its fees from the case to the university in order to help female cadets.

GETTING HIRED

Grades matter

Even in this tight job market, insiders report that Shearman is still highly selective. Sources tell Vault.com that grades are more important than the candidate's law school. "I know people who went to better schools but did not get interviews here because they had mediocre grades," says one source. A litigator notes the presence of "lots of smart people in litigation" with both law review and clerkships on their resumes.

One DC insider, however, sees more flexibility. "The firm sets high standards in recruiting but sometimes compromises them to get people they like. The firm finds it has to compete hard for the best candidates." Another associate provides this sound advice: "If you know of a department which is especially short of associates at the time you interview, expressing interest in that department may help balance out areas of your resume where you are relatively weak." One source comments that "it helps to be Australian. The firm is now recruiting many male associates from down under."

As for specific schools, the firm officially targets Chicago, Columbia, Cornell, Fordham, Georgetown, Harvard, Michigan, NYU, Penn, Stanford, Virginia, Yale, and about 15 additional schools in the U.S. and Canada. A contact in corporate finance remarks that "Shearman & Sterling hires from a wide variety of law schools, including those typically considered 'third' or 'fourth' tiers." That contact, however, stresses Shearman's "extremely high GPA requirement" and recalls seeing one candidate with a B average from a top law school denied an interview.

In fact, several associates note that the firm seems to prefer "to take top candidates from second-tier law schools." One M&A contact explains, "They are hungrier, need the job more, and tend to work harder." A corporate finance contact agrees that "the firm seems to prefer to hire someone at the top of a second-tier law school than in the middle or bottom of the so-called five top-tier schools." That insider qualifies that "there is, however, a consensus that the last few summers have brought more intense recruiting of Harvard students from many levels."

Mechanics: in and out

For prospective new associates and summer associates, the first interview is typically on campus with a partner or an associate. The firm is big enough to have several alumni from each school who are organized into teams to conduct recruiting. Says one contact, "I think they just want to get a sense of who you are and whether you meet certain requirements like being able to speak well and having a good attitude."

According to the firm, about 50 percent of candidates get a callback invitation to the firm's offices. There are two shifts for the firm's interviews: the 9:30 to 1:30 morning session and the 2:30 to 5:30 afternoon shift. At the beginning of the interview process, you will be greeted either by a recruiting delegate or a first-year associate. This person will guide you through your session, which generally consists of five or six interviews of about 30 minutes each. Interviews will be split between partners and associates — if you have five interviews, expect a three partner/two associate breakdown. Interviewees taking part in the morning session go to lunch with two associates from the firm.

Following interviews, interviewers will submit an evaluation form, which is submitted to the hiring partner with resumes and transcripts. The hiring partner then decides whether to extend an offer.

Offers: please, please, please accept

Job offers are given anywhere from a few days to a week after the interview. If you are lucky enough to receive an offer, expect to be "hounded" until you tell the firm whether you accept or not, according to sources. "The contact person will call you every week until you accept or decline," an applicant who turned down an offer from the firm says. "They'll ask you, 'Well, why can't you accept?'" "I told the firm I couldn't decide on the offer yet because I hadn't spoken with an M&A associate, my preferred department," another offeree recalls. "So the firm had a third-year M&A associate call me almost daily, often past 11 p.m., from the office — I don't know how that helps sell the firm. Since I was stalling for more time, I played strategic phone tag, which was difficult since this associate seemed to be at work all the time. I called at 3 a.m. and left a message, 'Oh, I must've just missed you.'" Another applicant who turned down Shearman reports that the firm did not take the rejection well. "They told me that I was giving up an incredible opportunity," the source says. The firm contends, however, that the associates who make follow-up calls usually get the job done and typically with less of a hard sell.

Lateral hires: short and sweet

For lateral hires, there is an initial screening interview with a partner at her or his office. "They discuss your past experience," a source says. "They ask you some substantive questions, to see how much you know about your purported area of specialty. They ask you, 'Why Shearman and Sterling?' and 'What other firms are you looking at?' They try to make the interview feel like a conversation."

Lateral applicants who pass the screening interview are called back for a second interview session in which they meet with four or five attorneys, typically two or three partners and two associates. "They ask you the same questions they asked in the screening interview," one insider says. Another source says that the lateral interview is "experience-based." Says the source, "Partly what they are looking for is people they want to work with, people who handle themselves well, since there is a lot of client contact at the firm. They want attorneys who are well-rounded and have a sense of humor. There are no curveball questions at all." Note that one litigation associate reports that a "phenomenal amount of lateral hires have been made."

OUR SURVEY SAYS

International feel

Attorneys describe Shearman as an "old-school," "white shoe" firm. But Shearman attorneys say they can't imagine practicing law anywhere else. "For the most part I have enjoyed my time at S&S. The work is very challenging and most of the people are very supportive," a Shearman attorney reports. A New York lawyer says the firm is "professional yet open and approachable." Associates also say Shearman has "a very international feel, even in the U.S. offices." Naturally an attorney's take on Shearman depends a lot on their department. One corporate lawyer characterized some of Shearman's different groups this way, "M&A people tend to be aggressive and cocky (they demanded a meeting with the Executive Group to find out when salaries would be raised), Project Finance people are very international and stylish, Corporate Finance people are all about business, and Leasing people are extremely smart but low-key."

Grading the boss

Shearman partners generally treat their associates in a polite and cordial manner, according to Vault.com sources. "Partners are extremely respectful and conscious of the demands they put you under," says a corporate associate. Adds a litigator, "there are a few who snap under pressure. Some are more sensitive to weekends and evenings than others. None are screamers. I do not feel subjected to hazing by partners." One insider calculates, "There are only one or two ogres among the 45-plus partners in my department. That's an ogres-to-human-beings ratio I'm happy with."

Associates also rave about the upward review process that gives them an opportunity to review partners anonymously. Shearman has had associates rate partners since 1997. The reviews may actually have made a difference in the lifestyle at the firm — the attrition rate decreased from 24 percent to 17 percent within a year of the first review. "This seems to have made a real difference," opines one insider. "After all, nobody wants to be the guy that everybody hates." In 1998 Shearman added a little bite to the review process by making the evaluations a factor in partner compensation.

Neither nightclub nor monastery

Most associates say their social lives do not revolve around the firm. "Everyone has lives outside the firm, and when they have time off they would rather not spend it with their co-workers," remarks one lawyer. A source in the New York office says, "The atmosphere is friendly but a little distant. People tend to want to do their work and go home." Others note that some associates will make efforts to have lunch together and go out after work every once in a while. One insider summed the social scene up this way: "It's not like we're at a nightclub, but it's not like we're in a monastery either. Overall, though, I think it could be more sociable."

Shearman ponies up

Shearman has gotten in on the salary race and boosted first year pay to $125,000. One source says, "It's hard to complain about salary after the latest increases." But others do not have such a difficult time. Several Shearman lawyers grumble that the firm does not match market leader Skadden Arps in terms of pay. One dissatisfied soul explains, "In comparison to other top U.S. and New York firms, Shearman is not the leader in compensation packages. It claims to be on par with its peer firms — however, that is not the case." Shearman has taken steps to augment associates' pay, in the form of a long-term bonus and certain "special recognition bonuses."

Turnover turns low

The turnover rate at Shearman has dropped significantly in recent years, insiders report. They have numbers to back up this assertion: according to *New York Lawyer*, 11 percent of associates left the firm in 1999, down from 17 percent the previous year and 24 percent in 1997. Sources say the perks and programs such as the retention bonus and rotation program have successfully stemmed the tide of defection. "Part-time arrangements are skyrocketing," according to one lawyer. "I think the retention package works, not only because of the economic incentive to stay, but also because it shows that the firm is aware and concerned about the (former) problem and ready to act on it. It shows a lot better management than the general whining about uncommitted associates heard at some other places in the city," according to another associate. In addition, insiders report that most defectors do not leave to go to other firms but to work in-house for investment banks or at startups.

Hardcore training

Shearman takes its training programs very seriously. In fact, the firm hired an associate dean from Northwestern University law school in February 2000 to head up its continuing legal education program. J. William Elwin, Jr. will coordinate the CLE program from New York, though each of Shearman's 14 offices has control over its own CLE classes.

Shearman & Sterling was one of the first law firms to implement an in-house CLE curriculum with a full-time professional director. In 2000 associates will be able to choose from around 80 programs featuring both lecture-style and hands-on classes. The courses cover everything from corporate finance to ethics. In the summers, Shearman runs a "deal-a-rama" program in which teams of summer associates and other attorneys take on different roles and walk through corporate transactions.

Associates rave about Shearman & Sterling's "phenomenal" formal training programs. One source boasts, "S&S has a well-deserved reputation for great training (both formal and informal). There are seminars on some subject or another just about every week and the individual practice groups have bi-weekly meetings where someone talks about something related to the practice group. This is always informative, usually useful, and sometimes interesting." "I don't think the training here could possibly be any better. Anything you need to learn, develop, or understand can easily be taken care of via the firm's numerous lectures, department meetings, seminars, and videos," says another lawyer.

But some are not thrilled with the on-the-job training. "Associates do work, it gets revised, and that's it. There is little mentoring. Day-to-day training is almost exclusively by observation," says one litigator. A corporate attorney adds, "It may take months before an associate actually gets to work on a transaction, thus putting to use the knowledge gained by any training seminars."

Hours grow more manageable

Although insiders report working long hours, many associates now find Shearman to be livable. "Associates at Shearman work a lot, but it is manageable. It is still possible to have a life outside the office if you are focused and efficient. There is no face time requirement. Just get your work done." The firm does not have a minimum hours requirement, and bonuses are not tied to hours. Another attorney reports, "S&S used to have a reputation as a sweatshop. Nowadays, it's nice to see how few people are around after 7:30 to 8:00 each night." But one lawyer says it's hard to keep the work from piling up. "No is the wrong answer to a new assignment request."

Lousy layout

Some New York Shearman associates are far from excited about their surroundings. "The average carpet at the average fraternity house is in better condition that at this white shoe establishment," rants a New York associate. "The only good thing about the worn out puke-beige rug is that it hides coffee stains. The offices are generally sterile, with a hospital-like feel." Another lawyer points out, "It is necessary to change elevator banks to get from the conference center to your office, and you have to cross the street to get to most of the administrative offices — all in all, not the most convenient layout." Others don't mind the décor and layout but want more space. "Many associates are sharing former conference rooms due to lack of available office space," reports one attorney. Insiders say first- and second-years share offices and then get their own digs in their third year.

Delight of the librarians

While the New Yorkers are less than thrilled about the offices, most associates compliment Shearman's support services. "I have been highly impressed by the level of support services — not only secretarial and word processing but also the distribution center, library, and proofreading," reports one insider. One source is particularly impressed with the library staff. "The library staff goes out of their way whenever possible to help in any type of research request associates may come to them with." But sources in the DC office say, "We have had huge secretarial turnover lately, with some associates going months at a time with different temporary secretaries."

Diversity on the upswing

Most associates report that Shearman is a comfortable place for minorities, though the firm has few minority attorneys in its ranks. "There are so few minorities, it is hard to tell," a source remarks. "That said, I don't think this place is unwelcoming to minorities. Based on summer associate classes, it appears that minority hiring is on the rise." Attorneys have divergent views on the firm's commitment to diversity. One says, "The firm appears to be making an effort in this respect." Supporting this claim, Shearman has established a scholarship program for African-American law students that provides for joint summer internships with the firm and the NAACP Legal Defense and Educational Fund. In spite of such measures, another associate reports, "While recruiting seems to be an ongoing process in which the firm is looking to improve, members of the firm are not very active in fostering a more supportive environment."

Associates give Shearman satisfactory marks in the gender diversity area. "I just haven't come across any situation where gender seemed to be an issue," says one attorney. But another lawyer complains, "To me this is a weak point of S&S.

Although at a policy level several initiatives have been taken, in day-to-day life it is still very much a boys' club."

Pro bono barrage

Shearman has a full-time pro bono attorney who farms out projects to the firm's attorneys. Insiders report that e-mails go around everyday with new pro bono assignments for those who are interested. "All firms say they are committed, but Shearman actively solicits its associates on a regular daily basis to take on pro bono matters," boasts an attorney. In addition, pro bono is treated like billable work. One attorney reports that he spends 20 percent of his time on pro bono work and the firm has been supportive of his efforts.

Latham & Watkins

VAULT.COM PRESTIGE RANKING: 9

633 West Fifth Street
Suite 4000
Los Angeles, CA 90071-2007
(213) 485-1234
Fax: (213) 485-8763
www.lw.com

LOCATIONS

Costa Mesa, CA • Chicago, IL • Los Angeles, CA • Menlo Park, CA • Newark, NJ • New York, NY • Reston, VA • San Diego, CA • San Francisco, CA • Washington, DC • Hong Kong • London • Moscow • Singapore • Tokyo

MAJOR DEPARTMENTS/PRACTICES

Corporate
Environmental
Finance and Real Estate
International
Litigation
Tax Law

THE STATS

No. of attorneys: 1,001
No. of offices: 14
Summer associate offers: 22 out of 23
(Los Angeles, 1999)
Managing Partner: Robert M. Dell
Hiring Partner: Mary Rose Alexander

PAY

All Domestic Offices, 2000
1st year: $125,000
2nd year: $135,000
3rd year: $150,000
4th year: $165,000
5th year: $185,000
6th year: $195,000
7th year: $205,000
Summer associate: $2,400/week

NOTABLE PERKS

- Annual firm business meeting in fun locale
- Brand new gym in New York office
- "The Yard" in San Francisco
- Pick-up and delivery of dry cleaning in Orange County and Los Angeles
- Child care program

THE BUZZ
What attorneys at other firms are saying about this firm

- "Surging sweatshop"
- "Very California"
- "A cult — but a happy cult"
- "Arrogant but effective"
- "Big hours, big dollars"

UPPERS

- Low ratio of associates to partners
- Open sharing of firm's financial information
- No screamers

DOWNERS

- New York hours (even outside New York)
- Rapid expansion making firm less cohesive
- Money overshadowing other firm values

KEY COMPETITORS

Davis Polk & Wardwell
Gibson, Dunn & Crutcher
Simpson Thacher & Bartlett
Skadden, Arps, Slate, Meagher & Flom

EMPLOYMENT CONTACT

Ms. Debra Perry Clarkson
National Recruiting Administrator
debra.clarkson@lw.com
(619) 236-1234

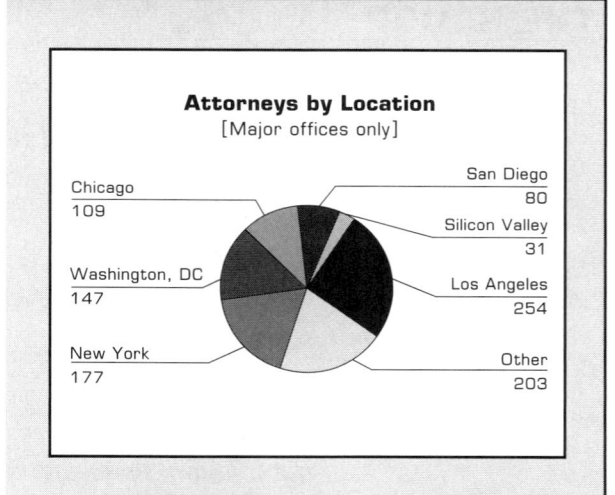

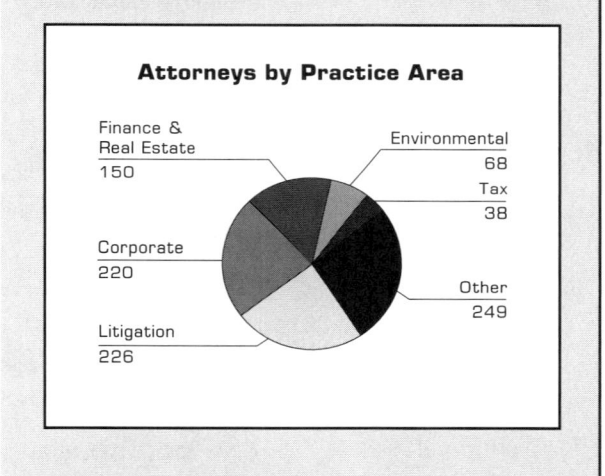

Attorneys by Location [Major offices only]

- Chicago: 109
- Washington, DC: 147
- New York: 177
- San Diego: 80
- Silicon Valley: 31
- Los Angeles: 254
- Other: 203

Attorneys by Practice Area

- Finance & Real Estate: 150
- Corporate: 220
- Litigation: 226
- Environmental: 68
- Tax: 38
- Other: 249

QUALITY OF LIFE RANKINGS [ASSOCIATES RATE THEIR OWN FIRM]

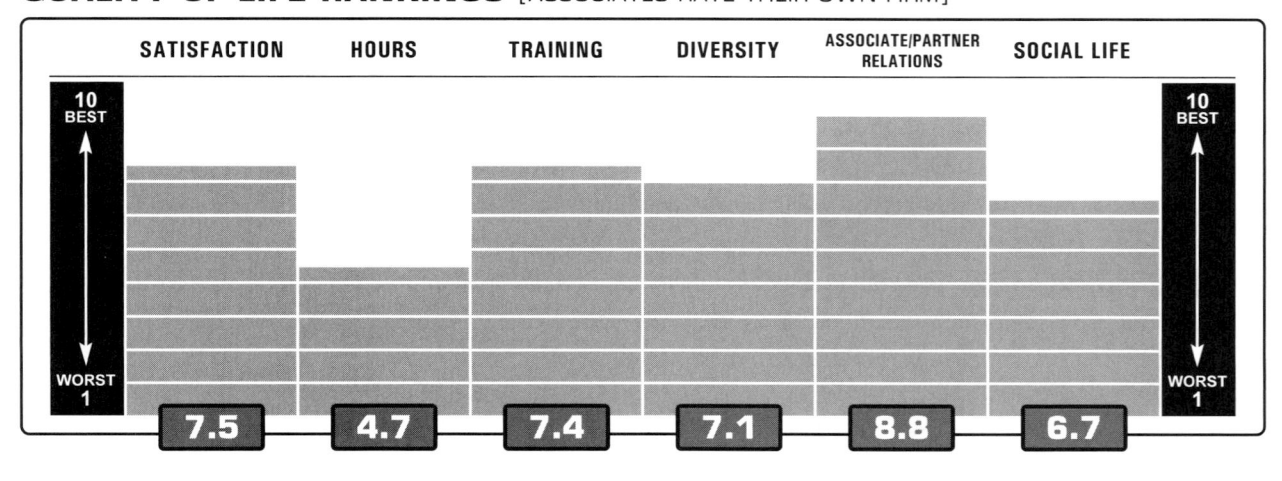

SATISFACTION	HOURS	TRAINING	DIVERSITY	ASSOCIATE/PARTNER RELATIONS	SOCIAL LIFE
7.5	4.7	7.4	7.1	8.8	6.7

THE SCOOP

Fans of the 1980s TV series *L.A. Law* may be able to live out their Corbin Bersen fantasies working at Latham & Watkins, the top-ranking L.A.-based firm in this year's Vault.com Top 50. This prestigious firm was the fourth highest-grossing law firm in the country in 1999.

History: the Big Bang theory

Founded in Los Angeles in 1934 by Dana Latham and Paul Watkins, the firm grew steadily over the years, employing 42 attorneys by 1969. It is Latham's relatively recent growth explosion that explains its perceived youth. The firm has doubled in size since 1987. And while the L.A. office remains its largest with 254 lawyers, the firm now counts a total of 1,001 attorneys in offices all over the world.

Latham made a name for itself in the 1980s with its work on high-yield debt structuring for the infamous junk bond king Michael Milken and his firm, Drexel Burnham Lambert, as well as for advising on Kohlberg Kravis Robert's (KKR) takeover of RJR Nabisco in 1988. But once the takeover boom went bust at the end of that decade, so too did much of Latham's business. The firm lost billing from major clients like GM Hughes Electronics Corp. and Drexel, which went bankrupt. In 1991 the firm lost its suit against a former client for alleged unpaid legal fees — and ended up paying an extra $150,000. Several months later 41 associates were laid off and partners' bonuses were slashed.

The comeback kids

But in the last few years, Latham has made a true superstar turn. Amidst troubled times, Latham pushed back, vigorously pursuing new clients before many other large firms did. It endeavored to establish a higher profile among community leaders and charitable organizations, while developing sophisticated data systems to tailor presentations to prospective clients. The firm relied on several recognizable personalities to give a face to Latham & Watkins, such as erstwhile chairman of the San Fernando Valley Board of Economic Alliance and Commissioner of the L.A. Fire Department David Fleming and the former chair of Rebuild Los Angeles, Barry Sanders. Another notable attorney is Alan Rothenberg, whose visibility in the legal field is rivalled only by his celebrity on the playing field — the Alan Rothenberg Trophy for Major League Soccer was named in recognition of his tenure as United States Soccer Federation president.

You'll get yours

The team effort has paid off in spades. The 1999 *American Lawyer* survey of the top 100 law firms reporting revenue for 1998 ranked Latham fourth in gross revenues with a total of $502 million, a 19.2 percent increase over the previous year. Nineteen ninety-nine brought a 15 percent increase in revenues, to $581,300,000, and $1,014,000 in profits per partner. Partners are not the only ones to profit from success; first-year salaries rose from $97,500 to $125,000 last year in all of Latham's U.S. offices. Although Latham's second-largest office is in New York (with 177 attorneys), its L.A. roots have caused many elite firms to relegate it to "outsider" status in the past. Now it seems poised to trump its East Coast competition and set its own standard.

Bonuses remain a huge Latham plus — the firm pays out a minimum of $5,000 once an associate bills 1,900 hours. The "range of [the] first-year bonus is anywhere from $0 below 1,900 hours to $40,000 if you are a rock star," explains one newcomer. Others appreciate the firm's commitment to "high performance-based bonuses for associates." One first-year in IP enthuses that "bonuses are theoretically tied not only to hours but to quality of work."

Venice in Vegas and crimes in Croatia

In the last few years, Latham has consistently ranked among the nation's top 10 law firms in the equity, REIT, high yield, and M&A sectors. The firm worked on a number of massive deals in 1999, many of them representing blockbuster underwriters such as Goldman Sachs. Latham played a key role in engineering Goldman's financing package for the $1.5 billion Venetian Resort Hotel and Casino in Las Vegas, which opened in May 1999 complete with a quarter-mile long "Grand Canal" navigated by a fleet of singing gondoliers passing under Venetian-style bridges.

Latham's attorneys were already very familiar with real estate deals in Vegas, having also worked on the MGM Grand Hotel Theme Park financing in 1993. The winning streak continued when Park Place Entertainment Corp. hired the firm to handle its $3 billion purchase of the Caesars World Inc. hotel and casino business from Starwood Hotels & Resorts Worldwide Inc.

Latham litigators attract monster clients, such as AOL, Apple, and Silicon Graphics. They win crucial decisions, such as the reversal of a $64 million damage award slapped on Raychem Corp. in an antitrust case against Bourns Inc. And they take on unique — if occasionally unpopular — cases. In one notable example, L.A.'s Russell Hayman recently defended Tihomir Blaskic, a former general in the Croatian Army indicted on three counts of crimes against humanity committed during the war in Bosnia five years ago.

Technology-oriented firms have proved a rich clientele for Latham lately. Latham's Global Venture and Technology group represents star clients such as local incubator idealab!; venture capitalists extraordinaire Accel Partners; Kleiner, Perkins, Caulfield & Byers; and the Mayfield Fund. Dot com clients include Homestore.com and quirky online currency company Beenz.

Poaching for gold

One wonders if Latham attracts the clients it does because of its attorney roster or if it attracts its attorneys because of its client roster. Whatever the answer to this chicken-and-egg question, Latham has managed to leverage its reputation to hire a number of talented attorneys away from other elite firms. As part of its phenomenal growth in San Francisco (from four attorneys in 1990 to a projected 116 by the end of 2000), the firm announced the hiring of two new partners, Daniel Wall and Karen Silverman Johnson, both formerly of McCutchen, Doyle, Brown & Enersen. The move was a strategic one, bulking up Latham's antitrust practice in technology and health care. Wall is an internationally-known antitrust litigator with clients including Intel, Microsoft, and Compaq. Silverman Johnson is equally accomplished in antitrust matters, having represented Intel, Microsoft, and First Data Corporation, in addition to having extensive Hart-Scott-Rodino experience. More recently, Latham lured Alan Mendelson, Cooley Godward's top rainmaker, to its Menlo Park office.

The intellectual property departments have been stepped up, too. The firm scored a hat trick last summer when the L.A. office hired prosecutor David Schindler away from the city's U.S. Attorney's office, and the Silicon Valley branch snagged Vernon Winters from Day Casebeer Madrid Winters & Batchelder as well as Charles Crompton III from McCutchen. The three will further boost Latham's ever-improving litigation reputation. London's Michael Immordono and Olof Claussen recently bolted from corporate partnerships at Clifford Chance Roger & Wells to join Latham.

Partners and summers schooled

As befits an L.A.-born firm which has succeeded as an outsider in the tight New York club, Latham prides itself on its innovative approach to reviews and training programs. Twice a year, paralegals and associates are asked to complete a two-page questionnaire about every lawyer who has overseen them. Participants are guaranteed anonymity in exchange for their honest assessments of their supervisors' abilities to communicate assignments effectively, provide helpful feedback, answer questions, and handle other managerial duties. The brutal truths generate two lists: the "best" and the "worst." Making the former ensures accolades as a result of firm-wide memos and e-mails; ending up on the latter means circulation of complaints to executive committee members and office heads. Indeed, the lists can make a major impact. According to a seventh-year associate who has both filled out reviews and been the subject of them, "There were several notable instances where supervisors had very negative comments in their reviews and would modify their behavior and sometimes even make the 'best' list."

But long before their names are bandied about on supervisor ratings lists, future Latham attorneys are introduced to the firm's distinct brand of training. Summer associates ship off to Latham & Watkins University — a four-day retreat designed to prepare summers for different practice areas and the realities of the corporate law world through a variety of pre-registered classes. The firm's partners and associates join them. The retreat is run completely by Latham's own, with no outside consultants or speakers. Work is broken up with social events such as inner-tube water polo tournaments as well as casino parties and cruises along the beach. The program has been a resounding success — summers rave about the instruction they've received, and firm attorneys say that participation is extremely satisfying and productive in terms of hiring qualified graduates. Latham commits $2 million to its annual training budget, which is a testament to the value of funding education.

GETTING HIRED

All-day interviews

Potential summer associates usually have a 20-minute interview with an associate or partner on campus. Callbacks take place at the office to which the candidate has applied and involve a series of eight or more interviews. These last from 10 in the morning to 3 or 4 in the afternoon and are broken up with a lunch with one or two associates. "You get here in the morning, and there's an informational session to kind of go over all the basics of the firm, so you don't have to waste time going over salary or salary structure," one insider explains.

Tough to clear the 'credential hurdles'

Latham is "very picky about who is hired," according to those who made it through the process. "Not only do we look for excellent credentials, but we look for people who are self-confident, have a positive outlook, and make a good impression," offers a San Francisco associate. Others stress the importance of coming from a "name" school. "If you have some personality and graduated from a top-five school, you're a shoo-in." The opposite is true as well. One associate says, "Our new theme is 'you have to be an adult' to work here. With so many opportunities for recent law school grads, the applicants have become increasingly arrogant and self-righteous. It's annoying and insulting. It's the one thing that will have me tell the recruiting committee 'over my dead body hire this person,' and the recruiting committee listens to the associates."

While it's "obviously worse right out of school," even "laterals with strong track records often cannot clear the credential hurdles," says a New York associate. Firm leaders "will choose the bottom of the class from Harvard over top candidates from mid-tier schools," huffs an Orange County fourth-year.

Some associates wonder if the firm's stringent standards have been loosened due to the avalanche of legal work from the busy market. "Latham really needs people and has become less selective," claims a DC litigator. A corporate attorney in New York gripes that "like all firms, with the hot economy and crushing amounts of work, Latham is somewhat less exacting with its standards" as of late. The firm points out that 69 percent of the entering class is hired from the recognized top-tier law schools and that it has not changed its grade cuts since the early 1990s. The firm's methods of evaluation remain cutting-edge, however — interviewers give feedback on the candidates through an electronic evaluation process.

OUR SURVEY SAYS

What goes around comes around

Latham recruiters may have managed to lure some of the best and brightest from other firms, but they are not above feeling the pinch themselves. As in many other firms, "dot com and in-house counsel mania has swept" Latham — attorneys in several offices characterize turnover as "very high." The attrition "varies by region — the Chicago office is more stable than, say, San Francisco," says a first-year in the Windy City. A corporate associate from the Bay area agrees that "dot coms, in-house positions, and other firms have recruited away many of our attorneys — decimating our ranks [by] over 30 people in the last couple of years in an office that has about 75 lawyers." A colleague adds that "it is less Latham than it is the fact that we are in San Francisco where all the firms compete with dot com companies." But the West Coast is not alone — real estate attorney in New York says that retention "was pretty good compared to other big New York firms until the dot coms [sprung up]. Now the place seems to be bleeding pretty badly."

Despite some high numbers marching out the door, some associates don't seem overly concerned. An Orange Country litigator suggests that "a lot of people join the firm for the initial experience and prestige, so the turnover is planned, so to speak." An IP attorney in New York wonders, "Does anyone work for firms longer than a couple of years these days?"

One for all and all for one

Again and again, Latham associates emphasize the firm's commitment to a unified identity among its many far-flung offices. "For a very large firm with offices all over the world, Latham does an incredible job of maintaining a 'one firm' ethos," compliments a DC fifth-year. This philosophy "means that we are all part of the same team," says a co-worker, "and I can get staffed on a deal out of New York almost as easily as I can get staffed on a deal out of Washington. This allows for the firm to draw on greater resources and expertise. It also allows for attorneys to gain experience on other types of deals that are done out of another office."

To frat or not to frat?

Some lawyers argue that the "one-firm" mentality extends itself to a herd mentality when it comes to the firm's social scene. A number of associates suggest that Latham is "fraternity-like," although "socializing is more playing golf than [going to] bars." Many attorneys say they have some of their closest friendships with their co-workers. A corporate attorney says, "we are great friends and truly like each other in my department. It's the thing that keeps me here past all levels of disgust with the hours." A colleague in Gotham admits that "we even hang out over the weekends — for hiking, biking, shopping, going to restaurants — and yes, it's all voluntary. We genuinely like each other, and people are extremely supportive here."

Not everyone takes part in the thriving Latham social life. "We used to be a big 'fraternity' firm, but that has died down considerably," insists a San Francisco corporate associate. There are "plenty of social events if you want to attend but really no pressure anymore." Someone else in the department agrees that "Latham — or at least the San Francisco office — is moving away from its stereotype [as a] 'frat' firm. Although it does place emphasis on picking well-rounded types who are a good fit with other Latham-ites, it definitely is no longer a firm for only good-looking *L.A. Law* types." A Chicago counterpart says that there are "stable peer groups within the firm" but "happily, it's no frat house. We have our own social lives, thank you."

One big happy family

Some attorneys attribute the warm-and-fuzzy Latham atmosphere to partners who treat associates "basically as colleagues" or "as equals, but with less experience." A San Francisco corporate lawyer says he "always feels like a member of a team, never like a slave." On the other coast, a New York counterpart maintains that "partners and associates are on a first-name basis, and the open-door policy really is open-door." In Chicago, one source declares that "even in the most difficult and emotionally charged moments, professionalism, courtesy, and client service come before ego, hierarchy, and ass-covering." When it comes down to the basics, the partners "work as hard as you do, are never too tired to train you, and always buy the drinks."

Maybe the partners are just relieved to have made it. Although the chances of making partner at Latham may be "better than at most big firms," they are "still not something to bank on." Several associates mention that "there is a lot of emphasis on business development — not actually getting clients but getting your name out there and trying." Those panting for partnership would do well to "find a growth trend and grow with it" or "better yet, lead the growth."

Aspiring partners should also "illustrate their capability to manage all aspects of a deal or case on your own, plus show your commitment to the firm outside of billable hours — whether by serving on committees [or] taking on office projects." Odds also depend on the office. A litigator in New York says his office's partners are "fairly young and there are few opportunities" for more to make it.

All the advice in the world might not make the difference for some. "They sit down and explain all of this to us at Fourth-Year Academy," shrugs a DC associate, "but it went in one ear and out the other." In general, "you do have to toe the party line, indicate that you are not considering leaving, and talk the Latham culture talk," says a New York first-year. Anything other than that? "Sacrifice, sacrifice, sacrifice," warns someone in DC. A New York peer suggests that you "pray."

Heavy demands on hours

No matter the office, Latham lawyers acknowledge that hours are a concern. While some associates say they have "never thought Latham's reputation as a sweatshop was well-deserved," the firm does have "its share of workaholics," and "client demands are very heavy." "Don't be fooled," cautions a San Francisco corporate associate. "No matter what other firms say, we are all working a lot because there is too much work and not enough associates willing to stay in law firms." Associates say the average billable hours per year is 2,200.

They train for the pain

Even when the hours are "killer," many associates feel that they are well prepared by the firm's training. There is "a lot of training by fire," according to a San Diego litigator, "but with appropriate supervision." A Chicago attorney points out that "in this market the pace sometimes precludes ideal emphasis on training." However, given the market, he is "impressed with the time that is taken" and is "satisfied with the rate at which [his] skills are developing." In Orange County, the corporate practice has instituted more lunch teleconferences and "boot camps" for certain practice areas and associate levels as well as half-day and day-long training events. Still, there are complaints that although "Latham offers a lot of training opportunities," not many are "geared towards mid-level or senior associates."

Decorate your heart out

One of Latham associates' favorite perks is the $500 decorating stipend they receive for their individual offices. Aside from this "wonderful benefit," assessments of facilities are all over the place. Chicago attorneys deem their space "moderate and somewhat functional but not fancy," though the "views are great." Orange County offices are "nice and the decor is new and tasteful," while neighboring inhabitants in Palo Alto laud their "large offices" and "great workstations — it's hard to tell the difference between a partner's office and an associate's office." DC associates will be moving to a new building in winter 2001 which will alleviate some of the complaints that the current conditions are "old and tired." Even New Yorkers, with offices that are "probably the least nice in the firm," "on low floors with no views," can't complain about the amount of space. Some of them even rate the place as "definitely nice."

Supporting evidence?

To each associate, his own gripe about support services. No one seems to agree on which service is weakest, but everyone seems to have a horror story. In DC "certain of the floater secretaries are incompetent" and the "fax and copy department should be available later during weeknights." A Chicago associate says that "secretarial assistance is mediocre in general" and "getting night help can prove to be a battle." Some Orange County lawyers say they "often find it difficult to get adequate paralegal staffing," although "the library staff is excellent," and "secretarial services are well above average." In New York "word processing sucks, and there are not enough tech-proficient employees," in the opinion of one attorney. "If I quit this job, which I largely love, it will be because the staff will drive me out."

Some try to go a bit easier on the criticism. In Palo Alto, "being a relatively new office, it's hard to find the support system that's in place at much more established places," sighs a second-year. A DC associate ventures that the firm "could take a step up in terms of secretarial and word processing support." Others have thrown up their hands. "I do not feel like the administration provides me with the support that I need to do my job, particularly in the secretarial area," complains one frustrated DC insider. "I also do not feel that the administration listens to me when I tell them what I need."

How many female associates does it take to make a partner?

Latham hires large numbers of female associates and has put in place extensive part-time work options, but many at the firm wonder how Latham is putting the rules into practice. A San Diego litigator says she sees "more and more women taking advantage of part-time schedules to accommodate their family lives" but has yet to see "any women who have worked part-time make of counsel, income partner, or equity partner." A DC comrade feels that she's "treated equally" but "there are no women who are more senior than [she is] who do the same type of work. There has to be a reason for that." Several women express that the firm is "doing what [they] would expect of it, but not much more."

However, an Orange County hopeful points out that "throughout the firm at all levels, women are on important committees and have taken substantial leadership roles." In the Silicon Valley office, "there are more women attorneys than men," according to a first-year, and "Ora Fisher heads the venture and technology group," a "very influential" practice area.

Can't hold on to minorities

Retention problems plague the firm's minority recruiting, although the firm points out that attorneys are increasingly sought for choice in-house slots. Some associates celebrate the perception that "the firm is a meritocracy and does not place special emphasis on recruiting minorities" and feel that "de facto treatment is effective without the need for pervasive monitoring and program implementation." Others lament that Latham hires "very diverse first-year classes and then can't hold onto them." Several Palo Alto associates mention a "large Asian representation" but "not many other groups." A third-year in New York opines that "if they're doing anything, it isn't working." Says a Chicago newcomer, "Man, is this place vanilla."

Reception of gays and lesbians seems to depend on the branch. An IP associate in New York finds "very few openly gay employees" in his office, and although "many are tolerant [and] accepting, there is a lot of hush-hush homophobia, like jokes quietly made and insensitive remarks, leaving large vacant space for improvement." A real estate attorney in the same building deems it a "kind of 'don't ask-don't tell' environment. There are gays here, but it's just not openly discussed. I cannot imagine a gay attorney ever bringing a date to a firm function."

But in Orange County, "there are numerous openly gay attorneys in the firm" and one lawyer says he has "not seen any signs of discrimination against gays, either direct or covert." From the "actions speak louder than words" department, the DC office "just had a firm party to celebrate an openly gay associate's commitment ceremony, and the partners paid out of their own pockets."

Down with the Valley

Besides championing the opinion that "Latham is viewed as one of the top full-service law firms in the country," a number of associates choose to be at Latham for other quality of life factors. Gushes one associate, "It's exciting to be in the Valley and the deals here are really stimulating. And to be able to do it all in the gorgeous natural setting of Northern California is an extra bonus. It's not perfect, but it's as good as a lawyer's job is going to be!"

It seems that everyone at Latham has some strong opinions about the firm. An associate in New York complains that there are "few mid-level associates, many of whom are lousy supervisors." A colleague emphasizes the flip side: "There is tremendous opportunity for young associates who want to get experience quickly, and there is lots of contact with partners." Then again, there may be a flip side to that, according to a corporate first-year in DC. "Because associates are given so much responsibility, some associates on occasion tend to grow large egos."

A corporate player in Silicon Valley is blunt about the firm culture: "You either love it or you hate it. You fit in or you don't. Because we are a fairly close-knit group, I think that it would be hard if you didn't somehow fit into the group. Of course, the group is comprised of all kinds of different people — of different races, ethnicities, gender, and sexual preference — but you have to be willing to be a part of the team and be a team player." That said, a New York litigator still crows that "on a national level, we rock." Indeed, most attorneys revel in Latham's rep: "If you want to work at a big, national firm, it would be borderline insanity to go anywhere else."

Wilson Sonsini Goodrich & Rosati

VAULT.COM PRESTIGE RANKING: 10

650 Page Mill Road
Palo Alto, CA 94304-1050
(650) 493-9300
Fax: (650) 493-6811
www.wsgr.com

LOCATIONS

Palo Alto, CA (HQ)
San Francisco, CA
Austin, TX
Kirkland, WA
McLean, VA

MAJOR DEPARTMENTS/PRACTICES

Antitrust
Corporate and Securities
Employee Benefits and Executive Compensation
Environmental and Real Estate
Intellectual Property
Life Sciences
Litigation (Securities, Intellectual Property, Business, and Employment)
Mergers and Acquisitions
Patent Prosecution
Tax
Technology Transactions
Trademark and Advertising
Venture Capital
Venture/Investment Funds
Wealth Management

THE STATS

No. of attorneys: 613
No. of offices: 5
Summer associate offers: 45 out of 47 (Palo Alto, 1999)
Chairman: Larry Sonsini
Hiring Partners: Keith E. Eggleton & Robert Suffoletta

THE BUZZ
What attorneys at other firms are saying about this firm

- "Entrepreneurial"
- "Terrible working environment"
- "Great IP firm"
- "800-pound gorilla"

PAY

Palo Alto, 2000
1st year: $125,000
2nd year: $135,000
3rd year: $150,000
4th year: $165,000
5th year: $185,000
6th year: $195,000
7th year: $205,000
8th year: $215,000
Salaries for 4th through 8th year associates are at the top of the range.
Summer associate: $2,400/week

NOTABLE PERKS

- Free dinner after 7 p.m.
- Free on-site gym
- Underground parking
- Discounts on cell phone (1/2 off)
- Lavish annual retreat at Pebble Beach

UPPERS

- Entrepreneurial culture
- Potentially lucrative investment opportunities
- Top player in Silicon Valley

DOWNERS

- Long hours, even for a law firm
- High turnover due to dot com flight
- Entirely unimpressive diversity

KEY COMPETITORS

Brobeck, Phleger & Harrison
Cooley Godward LLP
Gunderson Dettmer Stough Villeneuve Franklin & Hachigian
Morrison & Foerster
Venture Law Group

EMPLOYMENT CONTACT

Kelly McHaffie, Esq.
Director of Attorney Recruiting
1(888) GO2-WSGR
attorneyrecruiting@wsgr.com

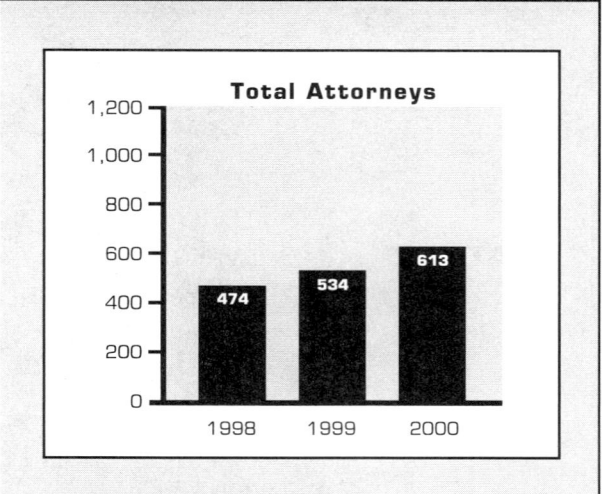

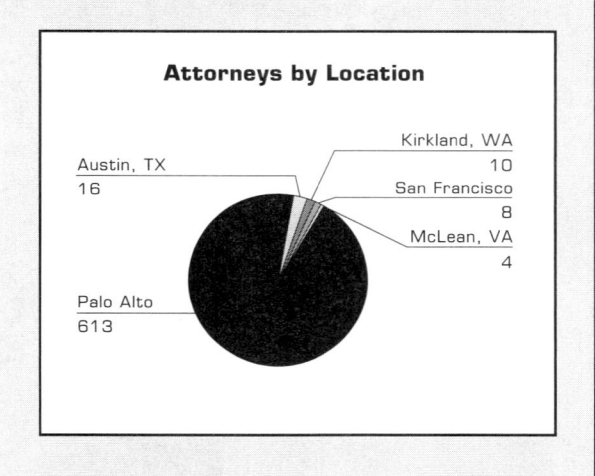

Total Attorneys

Year	Attorneys
1998	474
1999	534
2000	613

Attorneys by Location

- Palo Alto: 613
- Austin, TX: 16
- Kirkland, WA: 10
- San Francisco: 8
- McLean, VA: 4

QUALITY OF LIFE RANKINGS [ASSOCIATES RATE THEIR OWN FIRM]

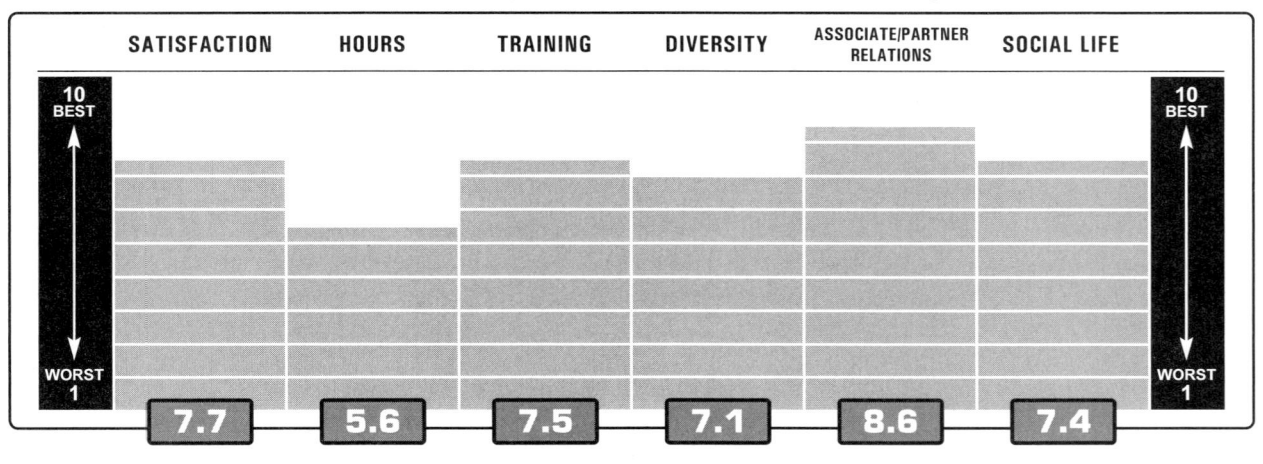

Satisfaction	Hours	Training	Diversity	Associate/Partner Relations	Social Life
7.7	5.6	7.5	7.1	8.6	7.4

THE SCOOP

History: a mere youngster

Wilson Sonsini was founded in Palo Alto in 1961 as McCloskey, Wilson, Mosher & Martin. Founding partner John Wilson recognized that the young inventors and financiers in the area would need a law firm to represent their interests. The firm began by helping clients connect with the Valley's venture capital community. Wilson recruited partners Larry Sonsini in 1966 and Mario Rosati in 1971. In 1978, Sonsini took over as leader of the firm. Two years later, Apple tapped the firm to handle its much-publicized IPO. After that deal, the firm was still a relatively minor player with only 32 attorneys. But by 1986, the firm had tripled in size, and its growth has continued unabated. The firm employs over 550 attorneys, with a support staff that is twice that size. Silicon Valley's Wilson Sonsini busts into the Top 10 for the first time this year.

Founding partner no more

On December 15, 1999, John Wilson, a founding partner of Wilson Sonsini, died at the age of 83. While most observers have credited managing partner Larry Sonsini with building the firm into the technology titan it is today, Wilson's death nevertheless is a major event in the history of the firm. Retiring in 1983, Wilson remained with the firm in an advisory role until just months before his death. Craig Johnson, a partner who left Wilson Sonsini in the early 1990s to form the law firm/venture capital firm hybrid Venture Law Group, told *The Recorder* that he models his own firm on Wilson's values. "Clients came to look at John in a very special way, as a person who could help bring people together," commented Johnson.

Another record year

Wilson Sonsini enjoyed a tremendously successful year in 1999. The firm refuses to allow a year to pass without posting record revenues and partner profits. Riding what *The Recorder* called "a tsunami wave of corporate securities work," Wilson Sonsini's revenue leapt to $296 million in 1999, a 38 percent increase over the previous year. Partner profits also increased by 35 percent, going from $620,000 in 1998 to $838,000 in 1999. Handling more initial public offerings than any other law firm, Wilson Sonsini continues to earn its reputation as a premier California law firm in the burgeoning technology industry.

The IPO wave washes over Wilson

Wilson Sonsini ushered 47 young companies to their IPOs in the first half of 1999, more than double the number it introduced the previous year. While the bulk of its securities deals came early in the year, the biggest IPOs (in terms of profits) came during the second half of 1999. Unless the ABA puts an outright ban on investing in clients, Wilson Sonsini will continue to enrich its portfolio in this manner. During the period from July to December 1999, Wilson Sonsini brokered three IPOs that brought in significant profits for the firm: VA Linux, Ask Jeeves, and Webvan.

Wilson Sonsini hits the jackpot

On December 9, 1999, VA Linux, a software company that bases its products on an operating system with the potential to compete with Microsoft's Windows, went public with an initial share price of $30. Judith O'Brien, the first woman to make partner at Wilson Sonsini, led the deal as issuer's counsel. When the stock closed at $239.25, Wilson Sonsini, the company's longtime counsel, sat on 102,584 shares that were suddenly worth $24.5 million. The 698 percent increase in stock price remains a first-day record. The Ask Jeeves IPO in July, also managed by Wilson Sonsini, had set the previous record — Ask Jeeves stock rose from $14 to $186 on the first day of trading. The firm's 275,000 shares were pushing $18 million in value by the end of the day. In terms of absolute gains, though, the November 1999 Webvan IPO led the way. Wilson Sonsini owns more than a million shares in the online grocer. Combined with the personal stake that partner Jeffrey Saper has in the venture, the law firm holds over 2 million shares. The value of those shares at the close of trading was $51,475,327 — not bad for a day's work. (Since that time, the value of these shares has fallen significantly.)

Client investment, for better or for worse

The practice of investing in clients is certainly not new; Wilson Sonsini has been doing it since the 1960s. It does raise some thorny ethical dilemmas, however. When an attorney or a law firm has an equity stake in a client company, conflicts between the legal interests of the company and the economic interests of the law firm can easily come about.

As long as IPOs continue to be profitable, such issues tend to remain hypothetical. "It's when the market turns that the problems will arise," reports Ronald Mallen, a San Francisco lawyer and legal ethics consultant, in *The ABA Journal*. "You not only have the opportunity to become a multimillionaire, you have the opportunity to get sued." The current Nasdaq instability should make this an interesting time for Wilson Sonsini.

Another way Wilson Sonsini protects its independence is through the use of an outside partnership to handle its investments. "The whole thrust of our investment partnership is geared toward not having an investment in a startup that would interfere with a lawyer's independence," Wilson Sonsini general counsel Donald Bradley told *The ABA Journal*.

On the cutting edge in litigation

It may come as a shock, but Wilson Sonsini has a life beyond the IPO. In June 1999, litigation partner Susan Creighton and her team won a patent fraud case brought by the Federal Trade Commission. The FTC alleged that VISX, Inc., a laser manufacturer, conspired with a competitor to pool their patents and share the royalties. The patents at issue governed the use and availability of laser technology for the increasingly popular laser eye surgery. After spending a grueling Christmas in 1998 working on the case, the trial victory came as a sweet relief. It was the first patent fraud suit the FTC had brought in over two decades, so a loss could have ushered in a new era of difficult intellectual property litigation.

The firm is also a leader in the area of securities litigation, representing a number of high-tech companies in securities fraud cases. In August 1999, the firm successfully represented Silicon Graphics in the first appellate decision under the Private Securities Litigation Reform Act of 1995.

Salary, retention, and expansion

Like most firms at the pinnacle of the legal profession, Wilson Sonsini increased associate salaries significantly in 1999. First-year associates can now earn up to $130,000 (including merit-based bonuses), and fourth-years can earn between $150,000 and $223,500. Despite the ever-rising pay scale, associates and partners alike have been leaving Silicon Valley law firms to take even more (potentially) lucrative positions in the technology industry.

What might help is a new plan to provide associates quarterly "productivity adder" bonuses of $2,500 to reward those putting in an extra effort. Senior associates have also recently been allowed to participate in the investment pools created with the firm's profits. This gives associates an opportunity to get equity in their clients, enabling them to try their luck with Internet IPOs.

As for the partnership ranks, partners Peter Chen, James Strawbridge, and Jeff Herbst all left the firm in 1999 for positions with Internet companies. Fortunately Wilson Sonsini can bank on its reputation to poach lawyers from other area firms to fill the gaps those departures have created. Katherine Martin, Michael Kennedy, Steve

Camahort, and Michael Dorf all left other Bay Area law firms to take lateral partner appointments in M&A at Wilson Sonsini in fall 1999.

As salaries and profits balloon, Wilson Sonsini continues to expand and grow. After establishing Seattle and Austin outposts in 1998 and 1999 the firm went bi-coastal in spring 2000 with a new office in northern Virginia. The development of the tech industry in the Dulles corridor near Washington, DC inspired the firm's newest location. Don't look for the expansion to stop there, either. Larry Sonsini, the firm's chairman, has said the firm is "continuing to evaluate the placement of other offices, including the possibility of opening an office in New York."

GETTING HIRED

"Desperate for attorneys"

Since Wilson Sonsini represents companies growing in the New Economy boom, the firm has to grow with them. That means hiring more associates — a lot more. "Silicon Valley has tons of legal work — WSGR is desperate for attorneys," says one contact. The desperation benefits lateral hires the most, and Wilson has developed a reputation for poaching other firms' associates and partners.

Pedigree still matters; so does interest in tech

Despite its need for more manpower, the firm apparently still insists on pedigree in its hiring of law students. "The firm tends to only look at the top schools," one insider says. The firm reports that along with local elites such as Stanford and Boalt Hall, many associates come from Harvard, Columbia, and NYU. One associate reports that the "law school attended is important." Says another, "It can be very snooty around here because of all the pedigrees." One associate without such a pedigree remarks: "When you're talking about firms like this and you don't have it on paper, you have to show it in the interview. In my interviews either I brought it up or they did, so I inevitably got into a large discussion about the law."

Other contacts at Wilson say that this quizzing isn't just directed at those graduating from less-distinguished institutions. "We ask the 'Why do you want to work here?' question, and we need to see that they really get the Silicon Valley difference," says one associate. "We don't want to hear, 'Well, you're prestigious.' You've got to love the business and be excited about the Valley." Also, that contact says, "It seems that there are a lot of people who have different degrees — JD/MBAs and people with engineering backgrounds — because it's such a business-oriented law firm." Another insider agrees on the need to emphasize an interest in Wilson's client base. "So much of our practices focuses on high tech," says another insider, "that it would help to be able to tie your own background to that."

OUR SURVEY SAYS

Entrepreneurial meritocracy

The terms "meritocracy" and "entrepreneurial" come up often when describing the tech-focused Wilson Sonsini. "The firm is very Silicon Valley," reports one contact. "We have a business casual dress code, people are hardworking and innovative, and it is a meritocracy." Another associate terms the firm "a pure Darwinian meritocracy. It is great if you succeed, and not as great if you don't. In other words, for the associates perceived as stars, there is lots of attention from senior partners, good projects, and lots of mentoring. For others, life is tolerable but not as pleasant."

The downside to such a hard-driving atmosphere, says some associates, is that money seems to be a prime motivator. "Make money, make it now, and make a lot of it," is how one attorney describes Wilson. "Everyone here is lusty with the smell of money."

Pick your partner

Treatment by Wilson Sonsini partners is good in general because of a free-market system. "There is an open market here," reports one associate. "If a partner doesn't treat you well you can either leave that section of the firm and go somewhere else or go to some other firm or a client. Partners who don't treat associates well don't have many associates for very long." Another contact says that "partners will chat like equals, will discuss points of law or business, and no one seems to be afraid of them at all." That associate reports that "I've never been yelled at or combed down, and when I make a mistake or have a client problem I have always been backed up." One associate concedes that "we have some partners who have absolutely no idea how to manage people," but most agree with the attorney who says "the partners treat associates with great respect and expect the associates to treat everyone with the same respect."

Moderate social life

Due to the busy nature of the practice, Wilson attorneys report having little time for fun. "We go out periodically and have a great time when we do," says one contact. However, "due to the busy nature of the practice, most of the time attorneys want to get home to their families." Another associate notes that "the firm is so large that there are many people who choose to socialize together after hours but many more who do not."

Busy, but things are getting better

In a burgeoning practice such as Wilson, hours are as crazy as one might expect. One associate claims to often work 12-hour days Monday through Friday, with an extra five on weekends. However, the firm is reportedly trying to accommodate the lifestyle needs of its attorneys. "The firm has made a real commitment to reduce hours by being very selective in any new business and managing the clients' expectations on timing of transactions," says one insider. Another associate says, "Everyone here is concerned about making sure we have balanced lives." "The hours can be tolerable if you work hard to make them that way," concludes one associate. "It is possible to draw the line."

Pay: investment opportunities, too

Most associates seem happy with their pay — "very, very happy" in one case. "Wilson's pay is among the best the Valley has to offer," says one contact. Wilson has been one of the first firms to permit the controversial practice of allowing associates to invest in the companies they represent. "We get great opportunities to invest in Wilson Sonsini clients that we work on," says one lawyer. "This benefit shouldn't be underestimated."

Between market pressures and investment opportunities, attorney salaries have grown quickly. One associate reports the third-year salary to be 175 percent of that of a first-year. However, some complain that the firm has stopped leading the pack when it comes to salaries, saying Wilson is "no longer willing to set the pace in Silicon Valley anymore despite partner take-homes well above the rest, due to WSGR stock investments."

A decadent retreat

Wilson associates list the company's retreat to the Pebble Beach golf resort as one of the best perks. Associates are permitted to bring a spouse or other guest. One insider says the retreat "is highly decadent" though it has been "clamped down a bit in past years [due to] early excesses." Additionally, the firm offers the other typical perks — dinners and cars after 7 p.m., gym membership, and event tickets, to name a few. In Palo Alto, the litigation department apparently has weekly beer bashes.

Training: you have to ask

Insiders are generally pleased with both the formal and informal training but say much of the responsibility for arranging training falls to the associate. "There is a good initial training program, and I can always go ask about things," says one associate. "Day-to-day mentoring working on the same deal isn't much. In some ways this is great because I learn by doing and I know that there are always people willing to help. The trick is that you have to ask." Another lawyer says, "The mentoring and training I get from the partners and senior associates in my group is great. I am given a lot of responsibility, but someone is always there to help answer questions and give guidance if I want it." One confused associate gripes, "The firm has a training program and lots of institutional knowledge from the extensive deal flow. I still don't feel like I know what I'm doing, though."

"I love my office"

WSGR insiders rave about their workplace. One says simply, "I love my office" while another offers, "I like my office a lot — it's open, new, and contemporary." Opinions about support staff are more varied. One associate compares the infrastructure to "a well-oiled machine." Another blasts the support staff as "totally lacking training and professional commitment" and says "if you have a pulse you've got [a] job" as a secretary. Another contact, while grateful for the 24-hour support, gripes that "the computer [system] has some serious reliability issues, and the person in charge won't take responsibility."

Revolving door

In a fertile land of opportunity, it's not surprising that many Wilson associates leave in pursuit of other positions. "It's a revolving door," says one insider. "I don't think it's because life is so miserable here, but because the market is good and people have more choices than they're used to." The Internet firms that make up Wilson's clientele often poach talented associates. "People go to great in-house positions, not other law firms," reports one associate. "I think the turnover is a symptom of the great opportunities we have, not that we're not a good place to work."

Partnerships going to the dogs

Those who do stick around have an excellent chance to make partner. "Almost everyone that is eligible makes partner in year seven," according to one contact. "One of the partners here said he'd put up his dog for partnership next year since it was so easy to make it," says an attorney. "I don't know about that, but they don't seem to worry about making too many partners, which is nice." Unlike at many firms, partnership seems to hinge strictly on quality of work, not the amount of business you bring in. "WSGR doesn't care if you're not a rainmaker — we have plenty of work without spending a lot of time going out looking for more."

A solid pro bono commitment

Wilson seems to encourage its associates to pursue pro bono work. "[Wilson] has a partner-level person who is responsible for coordinating [pro bono] and making it easier to do, and it counts towards billing," says an associate. Another attorney reports, "I have spent up to 50 percent of my time some months on large pro bono cases and have received nothing but good feedback at reviews." The firm has handled pro bono matters for charities and community groups including the East Palo Alto Community Law Project, the AIDS Legal Referral Panel, and the Legal Advocates for Children and Youth Guardianship Project.

Male-skewed

One area where Wilson Sonsini gets low marks is diversity. "They hope to ignore it and think it will fix itself," says an associate. "Again, there are some well-respected and powerful minorities, but no effort is put forth." Another contact says, "I feel that the firm is less successful generally at integrating minorities in the more senior associate and partnership ranks," but adds that the situation is reflective of problems in society at large as opposed to issues specific to the firm.

"At the end of the day it's a place run by men," complains one woman associate. She goes on to say that the firm investigated why associate classes so often had more men than women and found that the hiring wasn't out of proportion with the on-campus interviewing Wilson recruiters were doing. "So they dropped it there, rather than investigating why women didn't seem to be interested in working here, much less staying." On the flip side, at least one attorney feels that "my opportunities [have not] been limited because I am female."

No California dreamin'

Surprisingly, associates seem unhappy with the Silicon Valley area in general. "Although the beach is only 45 minutes away, the Pacific Ocean is cold," complains one associate. "Silicon Valley housing is ridiculously expensive." A single associate says that one of the drawbacks of working at Wilson is "living in Palo Alto — the worst area on the planet for young bachelors." Another popular gripe, more specific to the firm, is the workload — one insider sums up by saying that "the hours are just too long."

Why Wilson?

"I know it's unpopular to admit this," one attorney says, "but I'm actually very happy here. They treat me well, pay me absurd amounts of money, give me free rein to do whatever I want, and I'm learning an amazing amount." Another associate remarks, "I like the work, the people I work with, and being at the center of the Silicon Valley deal flow."

Wilson is definitely near the top in the tech world. Associates list Wilson's stature in Silicon Valley as one of the best things about the firm and many cite it as a factor in choosing their offer. Wilson has "the most exciting client base of any law firm, exciting deals, and tremendous levels of responsibility," says one associate. Other insiders say the people and atmosphere were important criteria and that the majority of summer associates receiving offers choose Wilson, most without seriously considering another firm. "There is no better place at which to practice law in Silicon Valley," sums up one associate.

INTERVIEW TIP #7

DO bring extra copies of your resume, and be prepared to discuss the most arcane parts of your resume. Have a story or some other kind of conversational springboard from every entry. If you wrote on your resume that you did extensive research on WWI literature, be prepared to chat about the poetry of the trenches.

VAULT.COM PRESTIGE RANKING 11: Kirkland & Ellis

200 East Randolph Drive
Chicago, Illinois 60601
(312) 861-2000
Fax: (312) 861-2200
www.kirkland.com

LOCATIONS

Chicago, IL (HQ)
Los Angeles, CA
New York, NY
Washington, DC
London

MAJOR DEPARTMENTS/PRACTICES

Bankruptcy
Corporate
Employee Benefits
Environmental
Intellectual Property
Litigation
Real Estate
Tax
Trusts and Estates

THE STATS

No. of attorneys: 691
No. of offices: 5
Summer associate offers: 47 out of 47 (Chicago)
Member, Firm Committee: Jack S. Levin
Hiring Partner: John Donley

PAY

All Domestic Offices, 2000
1st year: $125,000 + $10,000 summer stipend
2nd year $135,000
3rd year: $150,000
4th year: $165,000
5th year: $185,000
6th year: $195,000
Year-end merit-based bonus for all classes
Summer associate: $2,404/week

NOTABLE PERKS

- Moving expenses
- House-hunting trip
- Paid parental leave
- Dependent care plan
- Emergency child care
- Pre-tax reimbursement program

THE BUZZ
What attorneys at other firms are saying about this firm

- "Aggressive litigators without a life"
- "Very cutthroat and competitive among associates"
- "Some of the best lawyers around"
- "THE Chicago firm"

UPPERS

- Major prestige, especially in Chicago
- Top-notch litigation department
- High pay scale
- Good support staff and services
- Early on-the-job and formal training

DOWNERS

- Spotty pro bono record
- Limited social interaction among peers
- Diversity not delightful

KEY COMPETITION

Jerner & Block
Mayer, Brown & Platt
Sidley & Austin
Skadden, Arps, Slate, Meagher & Flom
Latham & Watkins

EMPLOYMENT CONTACT

Ms. Kimberley Klein
Attorney Recruiting Manager
(312) 861-8785

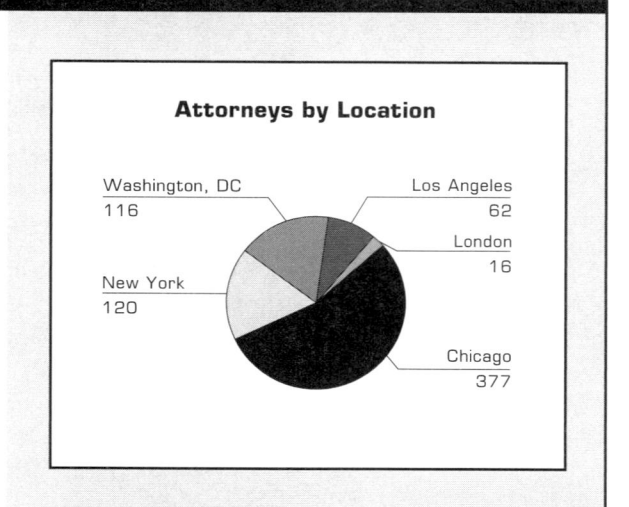

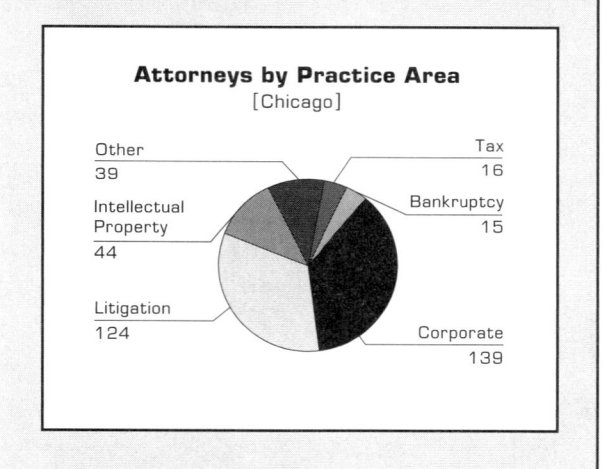

Attorneys by Location

- Washington, DC: 116
- Los Angeles: 62
- London: 16
- New York: 120
- Chicago: 377

Attorneys by Practice Area [Chicago]

- Other: 39
- Tax: 16
- Bankruptcy: 15
- Intellectual Property: 44
- Litigation: 124
- Corporate: 139

QUALITY OF LIFE RANKINGS [ASSOCIATES RATE THEIR OWN FIRM]

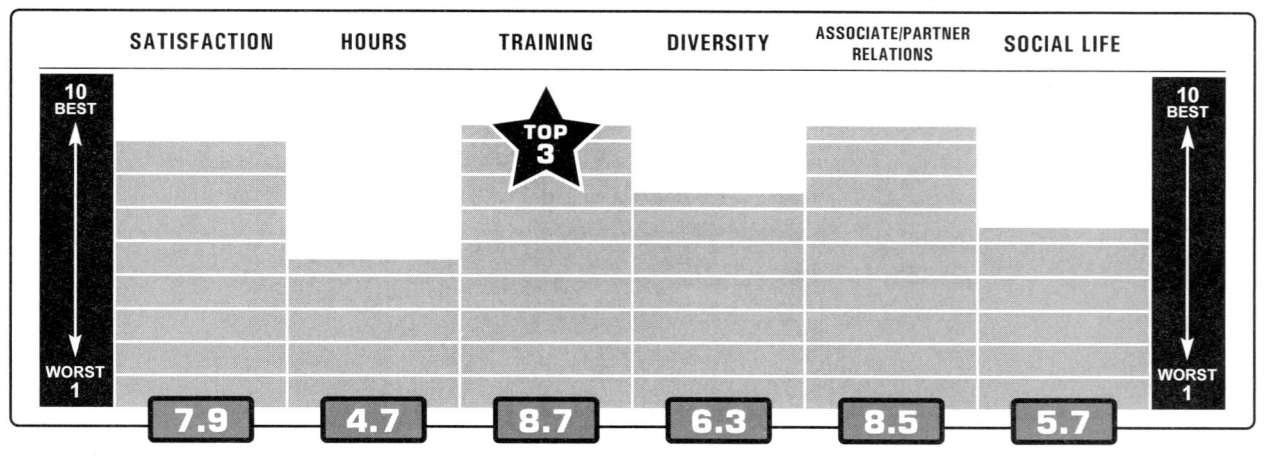

SATISFACTION	HOURS	TRAINING	DIVERSITY	ASSOCIATE/PARTNER RELATIONS	SOCIAL LIFE
7.9	4.7	8.7 (TOP 3)	6.3	8.5	5.7

(10 BEST / 1 WORST)

THE SCOOP

Founded in 1908, Chicago's Kirkland & Ellis has made its name by handling antitrust litigation and other matters for Midwest-based clients such as International Harvester, Firestone, Santa Fe Industries, Inland Steel, and Marshall Field. Kirkland's noted litigation and transactional departments have since cultivated close relationships with a number of blue-chip companies, including Dow Corning, Motorola, and BP Amoco. Under the leadership of Jack Levin, a respected tax attorney, the firm has created one of the nation's top venture capital/private equity practices, representing over 40 private investment groups.

Placating Chicago associates

When the 2000 salary race began, there were rumors that associates were ready to revolt in the firm's Chicago headquarters. In addition, *The Legal Times* ranked Kirkland "a lowly 17th place in overall mid-level job satisfaction." A quarter of the associates polled reported dissatisfaction with their compensation in particular.

K&E has since raised its salaries. Perhaps as a response to the brewing discontent, the firm management showed signs of loosening its historically staid image when it sanctioned business-casual dress for its Chicago employees in the summer of 1999. When the fall came around, the firm opted not to revert back to more formal attire. "Many firms tried to put the genie back in the bottle [after the summer]," Kevin Evanich, a member of the committee, commented to *The National Law Journal*. "Once you've given a person a taste of the good life, why take it away?"

Happy on the coasts

K&E hopes that these changes will make the Chicago associates as happy as their New York counterparts. In 1999 the New York office earned the highest ratings for mid-level and summer associate satisfaction in *The American Lawyer* survey for the fifth year in a row. In a city where associates are notorious for grousing about their jobs, Kirkland lawyers in New York seem more than satisfied with the firm. This may be due to the relatively high level of autonomy that Kirkland grants to its young attorneys. They are given the freedom to choose their assignments and the responsibility to shoulder a major portion of the deals. One associate remarked, "I'm treated like a smart adult." In most fields, being treated like a smart adult would not be something to brag about, but such respect is apparently a real perk to lawyers at New York firms. Meanwhile on the opposite coast, K&E mid-level associates in Los Angeles also ranked their office No. 1 in the city. The branch received especially high marks in the areas of training and feedback.

Nerd alert

Kirkland was recently involved in a major case that had civil procedure geeks foaming at the mouth. Frank Cicero, Jr., one of the firm's most prominent litigators, represented Abbott Laboratories before the Supreme Court in a class action suit that attracted major attention from the scholarly community. Interest in the case, which alleged that Abbott and two other companies had conspired to fix prices of baby formula, was strong because its decision could have had an enormous impact on the accessibility of federal courts for class action suits. Under current law, any lawsuit between citizens of different states can be tried in federal court provided that the claim seeks at least $75,000. Because this was a class action suit, the question was whether every member of the class had to be making a claim of that sum. This was the first case that the Supreme Court had accepted that confronted the supplemental jurisdiction statute directly. If the court had found that every person involved did not have to be claiming $75,000, more class actions could have moved into federal courts. In March 2000, though, the Court split 4-4 in its decision, thereby upholding a lower court's ruling that had allowed the case to be moved to federal court. It was a victory for K&E and Abbott, since the federal court had dismissed the case, but the civil procedure issue remains unresolved.

Counsel to GM

General Motors was an early Kirkland client, and the company still provides the firm with a steady stream of business. With Tom Gottschalk, a former K&E partner, heading up the legal department at GM, this relationship is unlikely to change in the near future. In 1999 Kirkland's litigation department represented the auto manufacturer in a number of controversial suits involving fuel-fed fires in GM vehicles.

IP for allergy sufferers

The intellectual property unit of Kirkland and Ellis was also involved in some noteworthy litigation in 1999. It continues to represent Schering-Plough Corporation, a pharmaceutical manufacturer, in a patent dispute that will govern the future availability of the widely advertised allergy wonder-drug Claritin. Allergy sufferers are waiting with bated breath for the outcome — if Schering-Plough loses the case, Claritin could become available in syrup form at a significantly discounted price.

Clamshell phone patent

In the fall of 1999, K&E successfully represented Lucent in a patent infringement suit against Newbridge Networks. The case, which surrounded Lucent's data networking patents, netted the company $9.6 million in damages, a figure that could be tripled by the court. Also in the tech industry, Kirkland client Motorola settled a protracted patent lawsuit against competitor Qualcomm in March 2000 over the manufacture of its "Q phone," a wireless folding telephone in a clamshell shape. After two years of litigation, the two companies agreed to a three-year moratorium on patent infringement suits between them, protecting the highly sought-after clamshell-shaped phones until at least 2003.

"You've got Cappuccio"

One of the most promising technology-related events of the last year for Kirkland & Ellis came as something of a surprise — the departure of Paul Cappuccio, a Kirkland partner that had managed its appellate and telecommunications groups. Mr. Cappuccio left Kirkland to take the general counsel position at America Online in August 1999. Steven Bradbury, Cappuccio's replacement, told *The American Lawyer*, "Not only are we very proud of Paul, but we're very excited about the relationship we will have with the largest Internet service provider in the business."

Merger shootout

K&E is facing a major antitrust battle with the Federal Trade Commission over a scheduled merger between Amoco BP and Atlantic Richfield Co. (ARCO). Commentators described the confrontation as the antitrust equivalent of the "showdown at the OK corral." The last time these two competitors went head to head — over the proposed merger between Office Depot and Staples — Kirkland went home a loser. This time around, the firm played Wyatt Earp to the FTC's Ike Clanton — the BP Amoco-Arco merger was approved in April 2000.

GETTING HIRED

Wanted: more than just a pretty transcript

"Like most large law firms, K&E hires students from the top law schools and top students from the other law schools," says a Kirkland insider. Another contact comments, "I would say that the selectivity is among the highest in the country, although, to the firm's credit, it is not a slave to the national rankings."

Drive, energy, and leadership skills are also important to K&E. "Grades and intellectual power are a must, but they do not, by themselves, cut it," according to one associate. "A few summers ago the only summer associate not to get an offer was the one who had a Supreme Court clerkship lined up. Nobody could stand the guy, and in those circumstances it did not make sense to hire him." The firm adds intellectual curiosity, drive, and team play to the list of desirable attributes.

Hiring can vary according to practice area. "It depends on the department," one contact says. "Right now, corporate is very busy, so it is easier to be hired by the corporate department as opposed to the litigation department." That applies to those hoping to get in from other firms as well. "Lateral hiring in this market is approaching 'any warm body,'" says one tax attorney.

OUR SURVEY SAYS

All work and no play

Kirkland insiders say the firm is a pleasant place to work, but that there is little interaction outside the office. "It is an all-work, no-play kind of place," remarks one associate. But in the workplace, attorneys are said to be friendly and helpful. "I'm always surprised at the willingness of other associates and partners to drop what they are doing to answer a question, help you find something, or teach you how to do something," says a young associate. Beware of a high-intensity workplace, though. "It is a hardcore, very male type of firm with lots of confident and assertive attorneys," notes one contact. "Consequently, the atmosphere is pretty tight." Another associate says that confidence runs so high in the firm that the attorneys border on "cocky."

Insiders also call the firm a meritocracy and remark that the workload often depends on how much the associate wants to take on. "While it usually takes associates a year or two to figure it out — and some never do — you are really in control of how much you work at this firm," observes an attorney. "If the partners have faith in you, watch out," says a contact. "They will give you a ton of responsibility. That, of course, means you won't make it home until after primetime TV is over." The upside is that there's no "face time" required. "When there is no work to be done, nobody will fault you for being in the bleachers at a Cubs game," says one Chicago associate.

Partners: no screamers

K&E partners are, for the most part, easy to get along with, and one associate reports that there are "no screamers." "There is a lot of variation, but because associates have a lot of control over their assignments, partners have to cultivate good relations," says a source. Interaction and cooperation are common. "The partners that I work with are always willing to answer questions and teach you how to do what you need to do to get the job done," according to an associate. Another remarks that "partners often ask for associates' opinions, and are extremely concerned and receptive about how associates are feeling." Tyrannical partners, a peril of any law firm, do exist at K&E, however. "As anywhere, there are some partners who think they have a God-given right to have associates at their beck and call, but we're much, much better than a lot of firms in that respect."

Separate social life

One area where Kirkland associates say the firm lags behind others is social interaction. While the atmosphere at work is friendly, K&E lawyers say there's little informal outside socializing and virtually no firm-sponsored events. "I wouldn't describe it as a place for someone looking for a thriving social life with people at work," says one contact. Another reports that "I've made good friends here, but it takes effort — there are no weekly happy hours or other firm-sponsored events." K&E attorneys seem to want to keep a separation between home and work. "I'm sure there would be more if I felt like interacting socially, but really — why not have an actual social life instead?" asks one associate.

Pay: in Chicago, a market leader

Kirkland attorneys now seem more content with their pay, and say the firm makes an effort to keep up with market movement. "Unlike many of its competitors in Chicago, Kirkland did not hesitate to meet the recent market changes in associate compensation," reports a Windy City lawyer. "One thing Kirkland does well is pay its associates," says another attorney.

While K&E has matched base salary, insiders report a little uncertainty regarding the bonus structure. "The new salary structure was only recently implemented and will likely affect the bonus structure," says one source. "There is no track record under the current salary structure to estimate the likely bonus amount."

Weak perks

K&E seems to be behind other firms in the perks area. Anyone working after 7:30 can expect dinner and a ride home at the firm's expense. Sports tickets, common at many firms, vary by location at Kirkland; DC associates report "occasional" Orioles tickets, while Los Angeles and Chicago lawyers get more frequent access to those cities' sports venues. Chicago associates also get dressed up for an annual formal dinner dance. In general, insiders say that most perks are reserved to hook in summer associates.

"Maniacally devoted to training"

What the firm lacks in perks it may make up in training. For litigators, it offers the Kirkland Institute of Trial Advocacy (KITA), a year-round program aimed at improving lawyers' skills, as well as a two-day jury trial practice session. Other offerings include the Kirkland Institute of Corporate Practice (KICP) and the Kirkland Intellectual Property Institute (KIPI). "Training is a priority at K&E," says an associate. "One-on-one, on-the-job training from partners is great," adds another contact. "The in-house training program is very good, too." "The firm is maniacally devoted to training," according to one attorney. "They have many formal training programs, but the best thing is that the senior partners take the time to get you involved in all aspects of a deal or trial, let you know what is going on, and explain things to you."

Offices: functional, but bland

Attorneys at K&E have some problems with their office space, but agree that it is functional and provides good views. "Ugh. The architecture of the building, while impressive in appearance, allows for only small windows in all of the offices," complains a Chicago associate. "On the plus side, the individual offices are quite spacious and functional, if rather bland." A DC associate can expect a direct line to Bill Clinton. "In Washington, associates have the opportunity to score spacious offices with White House views. That's hard to beat." Movie trivia buffs, take note: the conference room in the Los Angeles office was used in the Andy Kaufman biopic *Man on the Moon*.

K&E associates, for the most part, blast the support staff. "It's hard to describe the support services here, because there aren't any," says a DC lawyer. In the Los Angeles office, support staff hasn't grown as quickly as the practice, which insiders say is becoming a problem.

Smooth road to partnership

According to insiders, turnover at K&E is no worse than at other large firms, and attorney departure to other firms is rare. "We have lost many junior corporate associates to investment banking, venture capital, and dot com jobs, but in general people never leave to go to another firm," says one source. Firm clients often poach attorneys for corporate counsel positions. "K&E attorneys seem to leave for in-house positions at Fortune 500 companies or for government positions," says an associate.

K&E offers associates a fair chance to make partner. "An associate has good prospects for becoming a non-share partner here after six years," says one lawyer. "And the prospects of becoming a share partner are pretty good after another couple of years." Additionally, you'll know how you're doing. "K&E recently instituted a new review process which helps an associate track his or her chances of making partner," says a contact.

Diversity: room for improvement

Attorneys at K&E believe the firm makes an effort at diversity in recruitment and retention, but say the results have been fair at best. "It's hard to rate the firm's efforts — I'm sure they're trying," concedes an associate. "But the end result is that there's almost no diversity." The firm cites a few statistics to dispute this claim: 18 of the 41 associates who joined K&E's Chicago office in fall 1999 are members of minority groups, as are nine of the office's 48 summer associates in 2000. The firm sponsors minority fellowships at universities, and asserts that several clients — General Motors, Monsanto, and Dow Corning among them — are "committed to minority lawyer advancement."

Kirkland has been criticized for gender diversity issues as well, although there appears to be some dispute in this area. "K&E is sometimes tagged as not being woman friendly," says one associate. "I see no evidence of this." "As a woman, I have never felt any difference in treatment, training or otherwise, from my male peers," says another woman associate.

Happy scriveners

K&E lawyers seem satisfied with the firm, and most complaints are directed towards the legal profession in general. One attorney claims to get "as much [satisfaction] as one can reasonably expect out of being a scrivener." "I am very happy here," one contact notes. "Compared to other firms it's a 10. Compared to other professions..." It looks like the jury is still out.

Pluses include the quality of work and the talented peers. "The lawyers, particularly the more senior partners, are tremendously talented," says one associate. Other uppers include pay, training, and tremendous responsibility bestowed upon associates. In fact, responsibility, prestige, and pay are often cited as reasons associates chose K&E.

Of course not all is sunny in Kirkland's neck of the woods, particularly in the litigation department. "The dirty little secret is that Kirkland litigation associates don't really make it to court as often as people are led to believe," reveals one source. Attorneys say they often do hours upon hours of grunt work for a case only to see it settled "before the real fun starts."

INTERVIEW TIP #8

DON'T talk about your weaknesses. "Give them a strength wrapped in words of weakness," but don't be too obvious. The right way: "I'm kind of anal about checking things over." The wrong way: "I work too hard. Sometimes I'll work all night and I still don't feel satisfied." The human body does have its limits.

Williams & Connolly LLP

PRESTIGE RANKING: 12

The Edward Bennett Williams Building
725 12th St. NW
Washington, DC 20005
(202) 434-5000
Fax: (202) 434-5029

LOCATIONS

Washington, DC (HQ)

MAJOR DEPARTMENTS/PRACTICES

Corporate
Litigation
Tax

THE STATS

No. of attorneys: 175
No. of offices: 1
Executive Director: Richard W. Goodale

PAY

Washington, DC, 1999
1st year: $130,000
2nd year: $140,000
3rd year: $150,000
4th year: $160,000
5th year: $170,000
6th year: $180,000
7th year: $190,000
Summer associate: $2,450/week

NOTABLE PERKS

- Free lunches in the dining room
- Twelve weeks of maternity leave
- Unlimited paid sick leave
- Unlimited vacation

THE BUZZ

What attorneys at other firms are saying about this firm

- "The place to work if you're a litigator"
- "Lawyer's cult; ancestor worship of EB Williams"
- "Good writers, good fighters"
- "IMPEACHMENT!"

UPPERS

- The litigation star of DC
- Nonexistent billable hours requirement
- "Darn good" partnership track

DOWNERS

- Dearth of formal training
- No bonuses, no matter how many hours you work
- Free market system sometimes causes associate tension

KEY COMPETITORS

Arnold & Porter
Covington & Burling
Cravath, Swaine & Moore
Kirkland & Ellis
Paul, Weiss, Rifkind, Wharton & Garrison
Wilmer, Cutler & Pickering

EMPLOYMENT CONTACT

Ms. Donna M. Downing
Recruiting Coordinator
(202) 434-5605

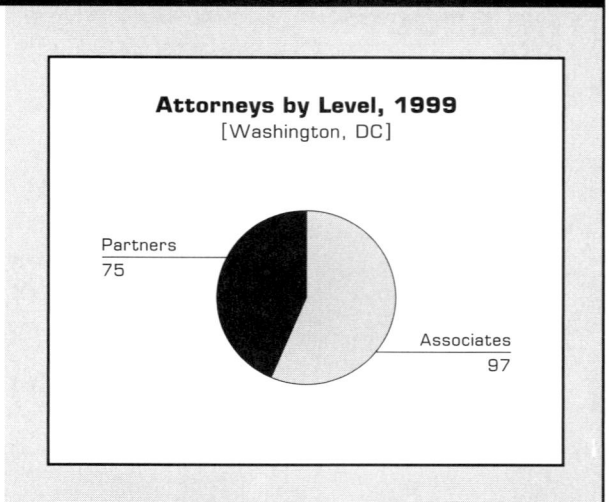

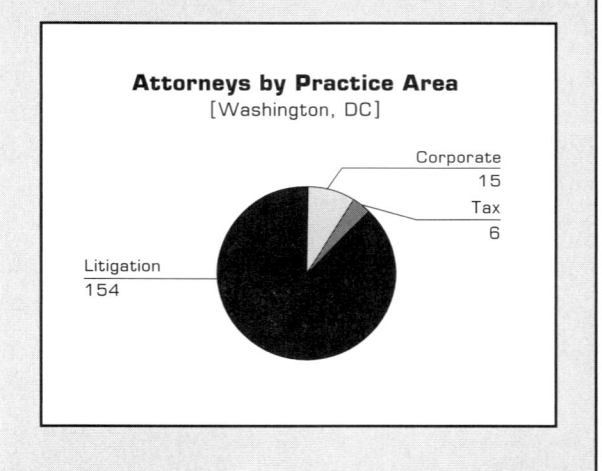

Attorneys by Level, 1999
[Washington, DC]
Partners 75
Associates 97

Attorneys by Practice Area
[Washington, DC]
Litigation 154
Corporate 15
Tax 6

QUALITY OF LIFE RANKINGS [ASSOCIATES RATE THEIR OWN FIRM]

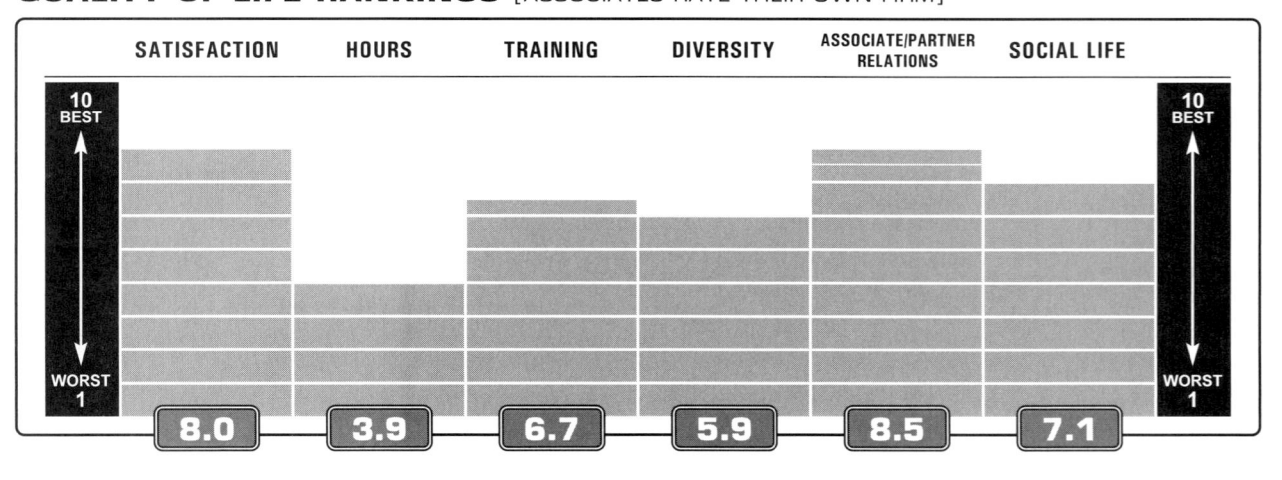

SATISFACTION	HOURS	TRAINING	DIVERSITY	ASSOCIATE/PARTNER RELATIONS	SOCIAL LIFE
8.0	3.9	6.7	5.9	8.5	7.1

THE SCOOP

Washington, DC-based Williams & Connolly LLP is one of the more prestigious firms in the nation — and one of the most tight-lipped. The firm almost never speaks to the press about its clients and actively attempts to keep a low profile. This low profile is evidently attractive to well-known clients such as President Bill Clinton, hotel tycoon Leona Helmsley, former army colonel Oliver North, and junk bond king Michael Milken. Williams & Connolly LLP has over 170 attorneys on staff.

Legendary founder

Williams & Connolly LLP was founded in 1967 by the late Edward Bennett Williams and Paul Connolly. Williams was famous for defending Teamsters union head (and alleged mob associate) Jimmy Hoffa in 1957. (Other notorious Williams clients include Joe McCarthy, Frank Costello, Richard Helms, and Michael Milken.) He later argued successfully in front of the Supreme Court for limitations on the power of the police to search and seize evidence from criminal defendants. Supreme Court Justice William Brennan once praised Williams as one of the greatest advocates ever to appear before the nation's most powerful judicial body. As the firm's reputation grew, top Washington lawyers joined the practice, including Joseph Califano, who brought the Democratic National Committee to Williams & Connolly LLP as a client. Williams & Connolly LLP now has an established reputation as one of the nation's premier litigation defense firms.

All over Washington

While Williams & Connolly LLP has recently attracted notice for defending the First Family, it has been involved in numerous other high-profile Washington cases spanning the political spectrum. Partner Terrence O'Donnell has represented the Republican National Committee, and partner Jack Vardaman has advised former vice president Dan Quayle. Another well-known partner, Brendan Sullivan, defended Oliver North during the 1980s Iran-Contra scandal and four FBI agents involved in the controversial 1992 Ruby Ridge shootout. More recently, he defended former Housing and Urban Development Secretary Henry Cisneros against allegations of making false statements to the FBI during a background check. Perhaps following the famous advice of founder Edward Williams — who once said that a delay is as good as an acquittal — Sullivan fought for and earned numerous delays, pushing the trial back almost a year and a half. Despite the millions of dollars spent by the independent counsel on his prosecution, Cisneros ultimately walked away with a plea to one misdemeanor count and a small fine.

Turnabout is fair play

In light of its frequent defense of government targets, it was with some irony that Williams & Connolly LLP went after the government in November 1998. The firm represented Department of Justice attorneys in a class action suit against the government. The DOJ lawyers claim that they were denied overtime pay entitled to them under the Federal Employees Pay Act of 1945. A 1994 study found that although DOJ lawyers put in a combined 1.9 million overtime hours that year, they were only compensated for 62 total hours, a paltry .003 percent. The overtime tab has been estimated at over $40 million per year. The case has yet to be decided.

Hola

Williams & Connolly LLP partner Gregory Craig (who helped represent President Clinton during his impeachment trial) represented Juan Miguel Gonzalez, father of Cuban refugee Elian Gonzalez, in his dealings with the Immigration and Naturalization Service and the Department of Justice (not in his dispute with Elian's relatives in the U.S.). While he might belong to a low-key firm, Craig could hardly avoid publicity when the INS recovered Elian from his relatives in April 2000. Craig's previous experience with well-known clients includes serving as one of two lead lawyers in the representation of would-be assassin and Jodie Foster enthusiast John Hinckley, Jr. Craig won an acquittal for Hinckley, Jr. on an insanity plea.

The firm's Washington reputation grew when political news web site Voter.com named senior partner Brendan Sullivan to its list of the "100 Most Powerful People in Politics" in May 2000; the list also included Attorney General Janet Reno and William Rehnquist, chief justice of the Supreme Court.

It's not all DC

Although Williams & Connolly LLP is reknowned for handling government cases, the firm does have many other clients. Corporate clients include Archer Daniels Midland, General Electric, Norplant manufacturer American Home Products, and Lockheed Martin. The business practice group accounts for 20 percent of revenues. In a holdover from the days of Edward Bennett Williams, the firm represents the Teamsters' union as well.

The firm also has an impressive list of media clients. Partner Robert Barnett represents over 350 television correspondents and producers, including ABC news personalities Sam Donaldson, George Will, and Cokie Roberts. Williams & Connolly LLP has represented several big-name print media clients, from respected daily *The Washington Post* to the celebrity-obsessed tabloid *The National Enquirer*. The firm successfully defended *Newsweek* in a libel case filed by anti-rap crusader C. Delores

Tucker. (The case was dismissed by a U.S. district judge in February 1999). On the other side of the journalistic spectrum, Williams & Connolly LLP represented supermarket tabloid *The Star* in a libel suit filed by the parents of Jon Benet Ramsey. *The Star* reported that Jon Benet's brother Burke was a suspect in her murder. The suit was settled in March 2000 for an undisclosed sum; *The Star*, continuing its commitment to journalistic excellence, printed a retraction.

Williams & Connolly LLP is proud of its distinguished sports law practice. The firm represents athletes at both the professional, and amateur levels, as well as sports teams, player unions, coaches, leagues, and owners. Notable athletic clients include NBA players Patrick Ewing and Grant Hill and WNBA star Chamique Holdclaw.

Law firms defending law firms

Williams & Connolly LLP is currently representing a legal peer. DC law firm Steptoe & Johnson is facing a law suit by Moore Publishing that accuses the firm of hacking into Moore computers and trying to launch a denial-of-service attack similar to those that crippled several major web sites in 1999. Williams & Connolly LLP is representing Steptoe in the case, which is being heard by Thomas Penfield Jackson, the same judge overseeing the Microsoft antitrust case. Williams represents 14 law firms in total.

Steptoe can only hope Williams & Connolly LLP does a better job than it did for itself. Former clients Michael Viner and Deborah Raffin Viner won a $13.3 million jury verdict against the firm in November 1999. According to *The American Lawyer*, the Viners were represented by the firm in the divestiture of their stake in a publishing business; among other things, they claim that Williams failed to secure them dividend payments to which they were entitled. The firm, which represented itself along with some outside counsel, appealed the verdict.

The granddaddy of all clients

Williams & Connolly LLP's biggest client is perhaps the biggest of them all — the firm has represented President Clinton since 1992. Partner David Kendall guided him through the Whitewater affair, and the firm continued to represent him during his 1999 impeachment trial. Many legal analysts speculated that Clinton's response to the Monica Lewinsky scandal — including his terse public denial — was the result of Kendall's advice. Kendall's tough questioning of independent counsel Kenneth Starr in front of the House Judiciary Committee, in which Kendall questioned the investigation rather than its findings, unsettled Starr but was nonetheless criticized. In the end, Williams & Connolly LLP won a public victory when the Senate acquitted

Clinton. Williams & Connolly LLP will keep the Clintons as clients — partner Robert Barnett agreed to represent them in all matters after the president leaves office in 2001.

GETTING HIRED

"Pretty much everyone clerks"

Associates say that although there is "no hard-and-fast grade cutoff." Successful candidates at Williams & Connolly LLP normally come from a "real top school or are people with extraordinary resumes from outside the top 10." The school has a "strong history" with Georgetown University, from which name partner Edward Bennett Williams graduated. Additionally, the firm has "a lot of partners from Harvard and Yale." Other popular schools at the firm are Chicago, UVA, Texas, and Stanford.

Although the firm favors law review members and clerks, an insider notes that there is "no paid clerkship bonus, except for Supreme Court clerkships." (When considering partnership track and compensation, however, the firm gives credit for clerkships.) "Pretty much everyone here clerks," reports one associate, although she is quick to point out that the firm is not "snobby" about clerkships and does not necessarily favor those with federal circuit or appellate clerkships over those who clerked for federal districts. (Supreme Court clerkships, of course, are a different story.)

Interviewers are sure to ask applicants: "Why are you interested in the firm?" Says an insider, "The attorneys at this firm are interested in the law and in litigation. They like dealing with legal issues and are excited by them. If you don't have that kind of enthusiasm for the law, it shows easily."

Summer program does not mean sure thing

"Basically, I'd say we get about half of the associates from the summer program; the rest are people who contact us, often while doing a clerkship," says one insider. That contact warns that landing a summer position with the firm can be extremely difficult: "It's a lot harder to get a job here as a summer associate. The summer program is still fairly small and because we interview at 12 to 15 schools, the firm likes to get somebody from each of those schools. So you really only have one or two from each school and because of that it's really artificially restrictive. There are lots of people walking around the office who interviewed for the summer program but didn't get in. They went back to school, got clerkships, and now work here."

Those applying for the firm's summer program can expect four to six interviews in the callback round in DC with "half-and-half partners and associates." After the interviews, the candidate will generally be taken to lunch with two associates. The format is similar for those applying laterally or from clerkships. A contact tells us that the firm "doesn't hire a lot of laterals. When they do, they are mainly people a couple years out. More than three years out, it's really not many people."

OUR SURVEY SAYS

There is no "I" in Williams & Connolly LLP (Well, there is, but you get the idea)

One third-year associate at Williams & Connolly LLP says the firm "feels more like a team than a corporation." Other insiders say W&C has a "pervasive team spirit" and "a very unstructured environment." The personalities of the firm's lawyers shine through and shape the corporate culture.

"One summer associate once told me, 'People here are very confident,'" says a litigation associate. "In general, people are fairly gregarious and self-confident, with good senses of humor. You don't have to be intensely outgoing to succeed here, but even the quiet, reflective, genius types are not shrinking violets or timid. The firm tries to weed out arrogant jerks in the hiring process," that contact continues. "[The firm] gives a tremendous amount of say to non-partner, non-hiring committee associates with whom applicants interview, so the result ends up being a very likable group of people."

Among the criticisms of the Williams & Connolly LLP culture is the perception that "the firm is very litigation-oriented and fairly aggressive." Also, one source says the firm is "very sink-or-swim."

No fungible units

Insiders report few problems with W&C partners. "I have had a terrific working relationship with Williams & Connolly LLP partners," comments one litigation associate. "From my first year at the firm, my opinion was valued and sought after. Maybe this is because Williams & Connolly LLP raises 99 percent of its partners from within, so it makes sense to treat associates as valued colleagues and potential future partners, not the 'fungible billing units' of Wall Street law firm fame."

Nearest and dearest

"I've made some of my dearest friends at the firm," gushes one lawyer. "I would say that 85 percent of my social life involves at least one of my fellow associates." Indeed,

Williams & Connolly LLP appears to be a place where attorneys get along, both during and after work. There are "lots of party invitations sent to all associates and a lot of informal happy hour forays," says an attorney. Wedding bells are often in the air. That insider reports that there are "a pretty high number of intra-firm engagements and marriages" which are all, at this point, happy relationships. It's likely these firm lovebirds met over lunch. "The dining room helps develop a camaraderie between all associates," says a third-year lawyer. "You can go downstairs and effortlessly have a bunch of folks to eat lunch with."

"You might beat us but you won't outwork us"

As at most firms, hours at Williams & Connolly LLP are cyclical, with a significant spike around trial time and deal time. "Everything comes in waves, but the hours are somewhat longer than at other DC firms," says an insider. Another associate begs to differ, laying out a well-reasoned argument to support his view. "Although a lot of people work hard here, the sweatshop label is misplaced," says that source. "There is simply no concept of face time, and if you walk around on a weeknight after 7:15 p.m. or so or on a weekend there are not a lot of people around." That insider continues: "The really high billers are either people who are workaholics by nature or people who said yes to a case that put them over the top hours-wise because it was too juicy to pass up — a good white collar case, libel/First Amendment, good travel, working with a cool partner — or those who are in trial. In trial, all bets are off; you might beat us but you won't outwork us."

Pay: no bonuses, but that's OK

While most at Williams & Connolly LLP are satisfied with the pay structure, there is some controversy over the lack of bonuses. "Williams & Connolly LLP does not award hourly-based bonuses," reports one fourth-year associate. "There is resistance, among both partners and associate, to such a system. The rationale is that it would encourage both inflated billing and inefficiency and would pressure associates to spend more time in the office than they otherwise would." Another source says, "I am okay [with the lack of bonuses] because first, I don't want to work the extra hours to get them; second, we have a cohesive bunch of associates, and I'm just as happy not to have what is likely to be at least the mildly divisive issue of who-gets-what bonus; and third, W&C has always made a lot more partners than other DC firms so the ultimate payoff is more assured."

Lunch and tickets

In addition to the dining hall, which provides free lunch and the opportunity to meet that special someone, the firm has choice seats at DC-area sports teams, including the

Baltimore Orioles and Washington's Wizards, Redskins, and Capitals. When traveling, it's "firm policy that we fly first class — the firm will pay the difference if a client doesn't pay for first class." Also available for associates: a gym described as "small" and "mediocre" and access to the firm's Manhattan apartment when traveling to New York.

Training by fire

Associates at Williams & Connolly LLP say formal training is a bit scanty; the firm believes in learning as you go. "There is a lot of training by fire," says a third-year associate who feels such training "is not necessarily a bad thing." Another lawyer says the litigation department has a "see-one-do-one" approach to training. "There is training in the sense that I get a lot of stand-up experience in doing depositions and so on," says one senior associate. "If I leave here, it will be as a well-trained, competent, and confident litigator. There is not as much training in the sense of NITA-like fake trial advocacy courses and things of that nature, but sometimes I think the firms that have all that do it because their associates are never going to get witnesses in a real trial."

Stand by me

"Like all big firms, people leave, but Williams and Connolly has an extremely small number of people [who] go to other DC firms — most go to government or make a geographic move," says a lawyer. Another insider concurs, saying that "people leave because they have great opportunities in other areas of the law."

Partnership track "pretty darn good"

Partnership prospects at Williams & Connolly LLP are described as "pretty darn good" by insiders. Decisions are made in the eighth year and chances are "excellent compared to just about any firm in town," says a senior associate on the cusp of partnership. "Traditionally, any good attorney who stayed made partner regardless, for instance, of whether they bring in business." That associate also notes that W&C doesn't have the "phony 'non-equity' partnerships that some firms have." Additionally, insiders report that "if prospects look grim for a given associate, the firm probably lets him or her know before the decision is made." One associate warns that "there is a concern that the dynamic may change given the recent salary hikes."

The normal good-faith efforts toward diversity

The firm generally makes the typical effort to hire minorities, say insiders, but as at many firms, the results have yet to show up. For women, there are "excellent" part-time and maternity policies. "Williams & Connolly LLP enthusiastically tries to get women associates in the hiring process," says one associate. "Although there is a formal process, it generally works best informally; senior associates in particular really look after young women associates." "The firm is very welcoming" towards gays, say insiders. "There are openly gay partners, and they and their partners are a part of the social fabric of the firm, so it sets a good example."

The stresses on Williams worklife

"Because of the so-called 'free market' work distribution system, it happens too often that you're caught in a conflict between multiple cases and multiple partners who aren't always ready to compromise," complains one lawyer. "In that situation, the lack of structure to provide a referee can be intensely frustrating to associates." Another insider complains about the "poor support structure," including the lack of after-hours secretarial or document processing services. The absence of formal training is also a negative, there's "no hand-holding — you have to be a self-starter."

(Almost) everybody's happy

Those who love to litigate may find Williams & Connolly LLP as close to nirvana as one can get on Earth (and certainly in DC). One associate calls Williams & Connolly LLP "a fantastic place to work if you like litigation and find it challenging and fulfilling." The pluses include "very funny, very likeable colleagues." At Williams & Connolly LLP, lawyers get "lots of responsibility early [and] associates keep their own schedule with little oversight or second-guessing of workload," highlighted by a lack of a billable hours requirement.

"I picked this firm because I thought it was the best in litigation in DC and had the best white-collar practice," says one source. The reputation of the litigation practice was mentioned several times as a factor in choosing Williams & Connolly LLP. The other main factor cited by many sources was the responsibility awarded to associates.

VAULT.COM

13 PRESTIGE RANKING

Weil, Gotshal & Manges LLP

767 Fifth Avenue
New York, NY 10153
(212) 310-8000
Fax: (212) 310-8007
www.weil.com

LOCATIONS

New York (HQ)
Dallas, TX • Houston, TX • Menlo Park, CA • Miami, FL • Washington, DC • Brussels • Budapest • Frankfurt • London • Prague • Warsaw

MAJOR DEPARTMENTS/PRACTICES

Business and Securities Litigation
Business Finance and Restructuring
Corporate
Corporate Governance
Litigation
Real Estate
Tax
Trade Practices and Regulatory Law
Trusts & Estates

THE STATS

No. of attorneys: 793
No. of offices: 12
Summer associate offers: 69 out of 69 (New York, 1999)
Executive Partner: Stephen J. Dannhauser
Hiring Partners: D. Pearlstein, J. Tabak, and J. Tanenbaum

PAY

New York and Menlo Park, 2000
1st year: $125,000
2nd year: $135,000
3rd year: $150,000
4th year: $165,000
5th year: $190,000
6th year: $205,000
7th year: $215,000
Summer associate: $2,400/week

Dallas, 2000
1st year: $125,000
2nd year: $135,000
3rd year: $150,000
4th year: $165,000
5th year: $190,000
6th year: $205,000
7th year: $215,000
Summer associate $1,750/week

Washington DC, 2000
1st year: $115,000
2nd year: $130,000
3rd year: $145,000
4th year: $155,000
5th year: $165,000
6th year: $185,000
7th year: $200,000
Summer associate $2,212/week

Houston, 2000
1st year: $115,000
2nd year: $130,000
3rd year: $140,000
4th year: $150,000
5th year: $165,000
6th year: $180,000
7th year: $190,000
Summer associate: $1,750/week

THE BUZZ
What attorneys at other firms are saying about this firm

- "Slave drivers"
- "Aggressive firm clients want in their corner"
- "Tenacious little pit bulls"
- "High-powered, hard-working meritocracy

NOTABLE PERKS

- Knicks and other athletic tickets
- Health club membership subsidy
- Twelve weeks of maternity leave
- Four weeks of paternity leave

Weil, Gotshal & Manges LLP

UPPERS

- Top bankruptcy department
- High-profile clients
- Friendly atmosphere
- Prime real estate for HQ

DOWNERS

- High-volume environment
- Complaints about support staff
- Problems with retention
- Lack of partner mentors

KEY COMPETITORS

Cravath, Swaine & Moore
Paul, Weiss, Rifkind, Wharton & Garrison
Proskauer Rose
Shearman & Sterling
Sullivan & Cromwell

EMPLOYMENT CONTACT

Ms. Donna J. Lang
Manager of Legal Recruiting
(212) 735-4553
donna.lang@weil.com

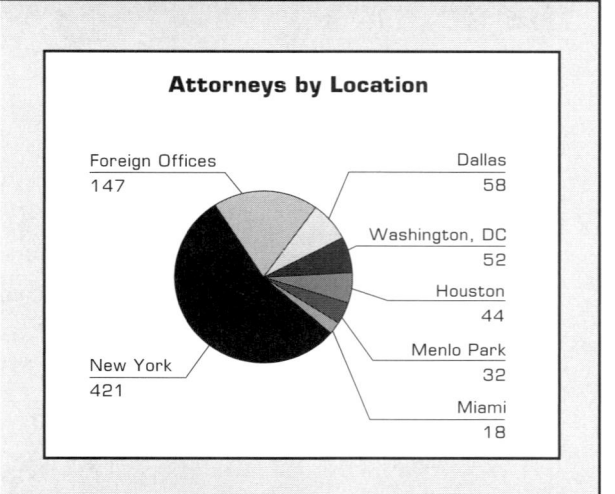

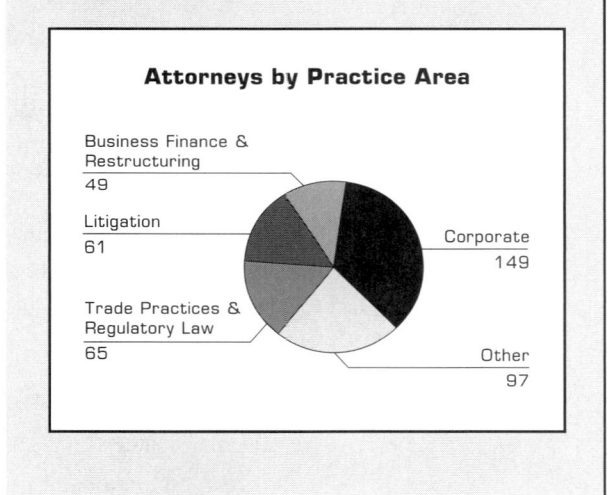

Attorneys by Location
- Foreign Offices 147
- Dallas 58
- Washington, DC 52
- Houston 44
- Menlo Park 32
- Miami 18
- New York 421

Attorneys by Practice Area
- Business Finance & Restructuring 49
- Litigation 61
- Trade Practices & Regulatory Law 65
- Corporate 149
- Other 97

QUALITY OF LIFE RANKINGS [ASSOCIATES RATE THEIR OWN FIRM]

SATISFACTION	HOURS	TRAINING	DIVERSITY	ASSOCIATE/PARTNER RELATIONS	SOCIAL LIFE
7.2	5.1	7.2	7.2	7.9	6.3

THE SCOOP

With almost 70 years of history behind it, Weil, Gotshal & Manges LLP is one of the most respected law firms in the world. The New York-based firm has over 750 lawyers in 12 offices worldwide, including outposts in London, Brussels, Frankfurt, and Warsaw. Weil Gotshal specializes in corporate law — but perhaps its more unique, and strongest, departments are bankruptcy and sports law. Weil is renowned for its prestigious bankruptcy practice, and the firm regularly represents sporting clients, such as the National Basketball Association Players Association.

History: from exclusion to a worldwide presence

Weil, Gotshal & Manges was founded in 1931 by a group of Jewish lawyers who had suffered discrimination at New York law firms. The firm started out by representing retail and textile companies, and grew rapidly. In the 1960s, Weil Gotshal established one of the nation's first antitrust practices, and in 1968 picked up and moved to its current location in the General Motors Building at Trump International Tower, overlooking Central Park. When the economy slumped in the 70s, Weil Gotshal hired lawyers while other firms were laying them off. The reason — the firm's bankruptcy practice. Large companies seeking bankruptcy protection meant a steady deal flow for the firm, allowing its expansion to continue virtually unimpeded. Today it employs more than 750 attorneys.

Also in the 1970s, Weil, Gotshal & Manges opened its first satellite office, in Washington, DC (1975). That was followed by offices in Miami (1981), Houston (1985), Dallas (1987), and the first major law office in Silicon Valley (1991). The firm grew internationally as well, adding branches in Budapest and Warsaw in 1991, and Prague and Brussels the following year. Until 1995 Weil, Gotshal & Manges linked its London operations to British firm Nabarro Nathanson. The firms split, however, and Weil, Gotshal & Manges now has over 100 attorneys practicing in its London office. The firm has also broached the idea of expanding into Italy and Singapore. In May 2000, the firm added a branch in Frankfurt, and in June 2000 announced an affliliation with a Paris law firm.

Brawlin' at the top

Stephen Dannhauser has spent 25 years with Weil Gotshal and was elected executive partner (essentially the firm's CEO) in 1989. Dannhauser's reign has not been without some controversy — in 1998 Dennis Block, a prominent business and securities litigation partner who had been with Weil for 27 years, left the firm. Reportedly, Block had objections to the general direction of the firm, including the opening of the London office. The initial break up was amicable, at least publicly. Block told *The*

Wall Street Journal that "we had differences regarding how fast the growth is, how disorganized the growth is." Firm management commented only that Block's departure was a "mutual decision."

The split proved to have more to it, courtesy of a June 1999 *New York* magazine article exposing the dark side of New York law firms. Block claimed he received no support at Weil Gotshal and that his clients "didn't select Weil, they selected Dennis Block." Dannhauser disputed that claim, saying Block's former clients had, by and large, stayed at Weil. The firm followed up with a letter to the magazine, claiming that Block had a "long history of inappropriate conduct" while at Weil and that he was asked to leave before the other partners expelled him.

The firm added two high-profile lawyers in February 2000. Stanley Sporkin, a retired U.S. District Court judge from Washington, DC who served as director of enforcement for the Securities and Exchange Commission in the 1970s, joined as a partner. Harvey Goldschmid, a professor at Columbia Law School and former general counsel of the SEC, joined as counsel. In June 2000, Catherine Dixon, chief counsel of the Division of Corporation Finance of the SEC, joined as a partner.

Going broke? Call Weil

Weil, Gotshal & Manges is probably best known for its bankruptcy practice, considered one of the best in the world. The bankruptcy practice group is called "Business Finance and Restructuring" and has almost 20 partners in the U.S. The group head is partner Harvey Miller in New York.

The bankruptcy client list reads like the Who's Who of firms that have gone broke or nearly so in the U.S. Included are: Continental Airlines, Drexel Burnham Lambert, Dow Corning, Empire Blue Cross/Blue Shield, Federated and Allied Department Stores, Eastern Airlines, Greyhound, Macy's, and Texaco. If a large firm sought bankruptcy protection in the U.S., chances are that Weil Gotshal represented it.

Weil Gotshal has also represented several real estate investment trusts (REITs) in restructuring efforts for over 20 years, most notably that of the former owners of Rockefeller Center in New York.

Regional offices

Weil, Gotshal & Manges's regional offices have been marked by rapid growth. For example, the Dallas and Houston offices, established in the mid-1980s, have grown to over 100 attorneys combined. The Texas outposts practice mainly in the litigation, corporate/securities, business finance and restructuring, tax, and technology and intellectual property areas.

Weil went further west in 1991, opening up an office in Menlo Park, California, the first Silicon Valley office of any major New York firm. The Menlo Park outpost has grown from three to 30 lawyers since its founding. It focuses on the high-tech firms that dominate the Silicon Valley area, specifically on patent and intellectual property matters.

Goodbye, old chap

As previously noted, Weil Gotshal's presence in London prior to 1995 was limited to a joint venture with British law firm Nabarro Nathanson. In August 1995, Weil started a banking and capital markets practice in the city (the first U.S.-based law firm to do so), attracting SBC Warburg, Bankers Trust, and NatWest Capital Markets as clients.

The London office experienced a bit of a shake-up in February 2000. Maurice Allen, co-head of the London office, resigned after four years, reportedly due to disputes with headquarters over strategy and management. The firm immediately announced pay hikes for London attorneys, and the office's business remains robust. London co-head Mike Francies was named the office's official head after Allen's departure.

One of the London office's most notable clients was MediaOne, whom Weil advised on its sale of One2One to Deutsche Telekom in August 1999. Also, the London branch worked with U.S. investment bank Morgan Stanley Dean Witter on the first euro-denominated collateralized debt obligation, raising 416.5 million euros in September 1999.

Slam dunk

Among the firm's highest-profile clients are the players' associations of three of North America's largest sports leagues — the National Basketball Association, the National Football League, and the National Hockey League. James Quinn, head of Weil Gotshal's litigation department, represented the NBA Players' Association for nearly 20 years, winning an antitrust suit against the league on behalf of superstar Oscar Robertson in 1976. In 1983 he negotiated a collective bargaining agreement which secured the players 53 percent of league revenues in the salary cap. The NBA was later passed on to Jeffrey Kessler, who had won free agency for NFL players in the Freeman McNeil case. Kessler took on several high-profile cases on behalf of NBA players, including challenging the suspension of Latrell Sprewell of the Golden State Warriors for choking his coach. (Kessler won a reduction in Sprewell's punishment.) Weil went to battle with the NBA once more in 1999, negotiating a new collective bargaining agreement after a six-month lockout threatened to wipe out the entire 1998-1999 season.

Big-time practice areas

Weil, Gotshal & Manges's practice areas are many. The corporate department, however, is Weil, Gotshal's largest in terms of number of attorneys (approximately 150). The department covers capital markets, finance, general corporate, international, mergers and acquisitions, private equity, and investment management and structured finance/derivatives. Weil represented Chancellor Broadcasting in its merger with Evergreen Media, and later advised the combined Chancellor/Evergreen in its $1.075 billion purchase of Viacom's radio stations. Other noteworthy corporate deals include advising NYNEX in its $31 billion merger with Bell Atlantic, and MediaOne in its purchase by AT&T.

Weil Gotshal's litigation practice has also seen its share of well-known clients. The firm successfully represented Avon Products in a wrongful termination suit filed by a former employee. Weil also represented New York State Assembly Speaker Sheldon Silver in his suit against Governor George Pataki. Silver alleged that Pataki had wielded his line-item veto power in an unconstitutional fashion. The suit is still pending.

In other cases, Weil, Gotshal & Manges represented the New York Museum of Modern Art (MoMA) in a lawsuit filed by the original owners of two works of art pilfered by Nazi agents. The paintings were seized by the Manhattan District Attorney as part of a criminal investigation, and the seizure was upheld by an appellate court. Weil partner Rusty Wing represented British attorney David Sandy on charges that he suppressed evidence related to the 1991 collapse of the Bank of International Credit and Commerce. American Airlines is also a client — Weil partners Helene Jaffe, Ira Millstein, and Debra Pearlstein represented the airline when USAir (now US Airways) filed a lawsuit targeting an alliance between American and British Airways. Finally, the firm is advising Sotheby's in a Justice Department investigation surrounding collusion in the auction industry.

GETTING HIRED

In a hot economy, an expanding reach

Weil focuses its search on top law schools, say insiders. "Hiring is limited to name-brand schools," says one contact bluntly. But some disagree, saying that getting hired "greatly depends on the law school you went to, although regional offices do hire from top tiers of regional schools." "Weil is not as status-conscious as some other firms in the law schools it recruits from," adds a source. "While the top national schools dominate, there are many attorneys from schools such as Cardozo, Brooklyn, St.

John's, and so on," comments a New York associate. Seventeen schools in all are represented in the 2000 summer program.

Lateral hiring is most sensitive to economic conditions: "It of course depends on the condition of the economy in general and the capital markets in particular." Says one contact, "These days laterals who would not even have received an interview while in law school get on-the-spot job offers."

The firm is reportedly very generous when it comes to hiring summer associates. "The firm extends offers to virtually every summer associate," notes a source. "Once a summer associate has an offer for the summer, it's very difficult not to get a permanent offer."

The initial interview is everything

Weil's interview process generally starts with an on-campus interview, which is conducted primarily by partners. According to insiders, the interview is conversational in tone and lasts about 20 minutes. Not to put on any pressure, but one insider insists that the "initial interview is everything."

Applicants are notified within a week if they will receive a callback interview. For those that do, "the firm will pay for everything — airfare, the hotel, [and] food." For the callback session, members of the recruiting staff first greet the applicant "for a bit of a schmooze." Next, a member of the recruiting staff takes the applicant to the first of his or her four interviews, each of which lasts about 30 minutes. Interviews are divided equally between two partners and two associates. Insiders indicate that associates generally focus on personality and fit issues, while partners tend to explore whether the firm can "rely on you to do what you need to do at your level." At the end of the first interview, the attorney calls the next interviewer, and walks the applicant to the next office. After the interviews are done, two junior associates (generally in their first or second year) take the applicant to lunch.

OUR SURVEY SAYS

Competitive intensity

Weil associates generally describe the firm's culture as intense without being stuffy. One attorney calls it "a strange mix of competitive intensity on the one hand and left-liberal permissiveness and laxity on the other." Another associate calls it "very aggressive and loud — not a gentle place. The nickname of 'we'll get ya and mangle ya' about sums it up." (Firm management vehemently denies that the nickname still lingers among Weil Gotshal associates, though several lawyers from other firms that Vault.com surveyed used it in their descriptions of Weil.)

The New York office is by reputation more intense than the DC or Silicon Valley offices. "The Silicon Valley office is a 'work hard, play hard' casual environment," says a Menlo Park lawyer. Be warned, however: "Don't let the casual atmosphere fool you," says a DC associate. "The work that we do is top notch, and half-assed work won't cut it." In the end, a strong work ethic pervades the firm. "I often feel like I'm hanging out with my friends, only we have to get a lot of work done, and fast," reports one contact.

Contacts reveal that the partner-associate relationship varies greatly. "Partner treatment of associates leaves much to be desired," gripes one attorney. "I have seen associates literally reduced to tears," says an associate who claims that his general experience has been good. That associate concedes, though, that, "I have met senior partners who talk to me as if I am a worm." Other sources say that associates have been treated well and that the firm works to rein in problem partners. "In the event you are badly treated, there is a system in place for complaints, and I have even heard of other partners running to the rescue if they thought you were being unduly yelled at."

Less work, more play

Weil associates are critical of the social interaction among attorneys. "We need to have more events and social occasions that do not involve bi-monthly consumption of alcohol," says one teetotalling associate. "The biggest problem I have with the firm is that a true camaraderie among associates seems to be lacking." Another associate complains that "people are so busy they don't have time to talk to you. When I leave this firm, it's going to be because of the impersonal way we are treated." One associate claims that at Weil there exists a "billing code for partners to bill social time spent with associates. I'm not kidding!"

Other associates disagree, saying that the opportunity to socialize is there for those who want it. "In my department you can always find people to go out with either for lunch or after work, but you never feel pressured to go," says one contact. "Lawyers in this office are very social during work hours," chimes in another. "A closed door is fairly unusual and tends to signal either a very busy day or a confidential discussion." The Palo Alto office is said to be especially social, with associates "going shopping, going out for drinks, and seeing games together."

Acing the spelling test

Hours at Weil are longer than at most other large firms, according to associates. "The work assignments can come in late and that means wasted, non-billable time in the morning and late nights, which makes for unhappy significant others," says one associate. "Work can swallow you up whole here," warns another contact. "However, it is as much a function of the type of people who work here — that is to say, 'A-type' personalities — than the actual press of business. Most WG&M associates were the kids in your elementary school class who lost sleep for fear they had not studied enough for that upcoming spelling test." Not everyone is complaining though. "The hours are not bad as far as firms go — the billable target is 2,000, but not everyone hits it." Weil Gotshal says it does not have a target for billable hours. Other associates remark that "pro bono hours are counted as billable."

Pay: no trendsetter, but on the ball

Associates say that though Weil will never be the firm to spark a bidding war with attorney salaries, it will always keep up with the industry average. "Like firms across the country, Weil responded to the salary increases that started in California earlier this year," explains an associate. "As a result, associate pay dramatically increased across the board in February — though still not dramatically enough for many associates who feel overworked and undervalued." The firm now offers a long-term bonus plan to enhance associate retention. Observes one source contentedly, "I have no doubt that at the end of the year, my total compensation will meet or exceed that of any other firm for an associate performing at my level."

Another lawyer accuses the firm of playing games when calculating bonuses, essentially counting the first 15 months with the firm as one year. "Your second fall at the firm, your salary actually drops because you are still earning the base and there is no extra guaranteed bonus. It captures the Weil compensation strategy: Give you something extra that makes them look good by comparison, but then cut corners in places it would never occur to you someone would."

Perks seem to be at least on par with other top law firms. Company-sponsored gym memberships, meals and cab rides for late nights, and sports tickets are common. "The summers are jammed with social events where getting drunk seems to be the norm," says a New York attorney. Associates also get a $2,000 technology stipend in their first two years, according to insiders.

Training: both formal and informal

Weil attorneys are pleased with the firm's training program, both formal and informal. "Associates getting ready for oral argument and the like are mooted in-house," says one attorney. "The firm has great training opportunities," says a contact. "In addition to excellent in-house opportunities, the firm will send interested associates to outside training programs." Additionally, "many associates and partners go out of their way to spend time with and train junior associates."

"Breathtaking" New York office

Office quality seems to vary by location — and sometimes by department. "The offices are nice and the views of Central Park are breathtaking," says a New York lawyer. "Great location. Nice design. Great location. Comfortable. Great location." another New York associate declares.

While the New York office is pretty, it can get pretty cramped for corporate attorneys. "All second-years and first-years in corporate are still sharing offices. We now have third-year corporate associates who are still sharing double offices," says one source. "In most other departments at the firm, first-years get their own window offices. Needless to say, the corporate associates are most annoyed." Insiders report that Weil is adding more space for the corporate department, which should alleviate the crowding.

"Office space is nothing special — certainly more utilitarian than posh," says a DC attorney. Menlo Park attorneys are more excited about their space. "Offices are very large compared to others in Silicon Valley, and [there are] no shared offices," says an insider. The "award-winning interior feels more like an advertising agency than a law firm."

Mixed reviews for support staff

Opinions on support staff vary. "Support services are either excellent or plain bad — there doesn't seem to be an in-between," says an associate. "Most of the support services are fantastic," reports another attorney. "[But] the MIS department is sub-par." One lawyer reports that "there is definitely a prevalent 'don't make me do too much work' attitude among most support staff."

Captains of the JV team

Weil attorneys agree that the firm has a lot of work to do to improve retention. Weil has recently instituted a retention bonus, but for some that's not enough. "The firm has instituted various associate retention initiatives, but they seem to fail to understand that throwing money at the problem will not solve it," says one contact. "Sincere efforts toward retention have been made over the past year or two," concedes a lawyer. (These initiatives include the appointment of a Director of Associate Retention, the creation of a retention committee, and the appointment of career development partners.) "Unfortunately, many of the 'new' partners grew up in the 'old' Weil, Gotshal and harbor many of the old despotic management creeds." The new economy may be partially to blame for turnover. "Several associates have left or are leaving for dot coms, as [has one] corporate partner," says one attorney.

The partnership track is another frequent complaint. "Not good," one associate says of the chances of making partner. Another says it's "easier for a camel to pass through the eye of a needle" than for a Weil associate to make partner. To make up for the scant partnership opportunities, insiders report that Weil has made use of the "of counsel" title, a move that does not sit well with many associates. "Of counsel is sort of like being the captain of your high school junior varsity team," complains one contact. Still, associates do offer advice for those seeking a partnership. "Stick it out and you will make it," advises one attorney. "It might take time, but it can be yours." In the past two years, according to Weil, the firm has elected 59 partners, including laterals.

Steps towards increased diversity

Associates feel that Weil has taken steps to promote diversity but needs to do more. "The firm has really been trying to hire more minority attorneys," says one contact. "Minority retention seems to be a problem at all the firms in New York." "My firm's idea of diversity is the mailroom staff," another associate says.

Weil also has work to do for women, say some attorneys. "Mentoring is the downfall in this department," laments a litigation attorney. "There is definitely equality in hiring, but mentoring is non existent." The firm has formalized a part-time policy, insiders say, and has made improvements. Women lawyers serve on Weil's management committee, co-chair the hiring committee, and hold important posts in a number of other firm committees and practice groups. However, some female associates feel they're on the outside looking in. "The firm has a strong commitment to [diversity], but my department is very male-heavy and I still feel like I am trying to break into a boys' club."

The firm reportedly fares better in its treatment of gays. Insiders report the firm has excellent domestic partner benefits and that sexual orientation has not been an issue. "[I've] never seen any problems — and I have noticed latent homophobia in other places I have worked," says one insider.

Round up the usual complaints

In total, Weil associates seem fairly satisfied with the firm, and their complaints are typical of large law firms. "All in all, I have been happy working here," remarks one associate. "On balance, the positives outweigh the negatives. Another attorney says, "I am as satisfied at Weil Gotshal as I can be at any large law firm."

Weil's clientele is frequently mentioned as one of the positives of working for the firm. "It is an absolutely incredible client base that keeps expanding into every area of the law — which means that associates are constantly challenged and doing, on the whole, substantial lawyering," gushes one source. The quality of people was another plus. "I expected to work with a bunch of dorks, so I was pleasantly surprised to find myself working with people I could hang out with after work as well," says a jock/attorney, adding that, "The high-profile sports-related work is also a major factor in my career choice."

Again, diversity issues come up when assessing the firm's negatives. "As a woman and a minority I feel that the firm does not do enough to make you feel like you belong," complains one attorney. "You are faced with a culture of white male egotism." Other lawyers feel overwhelmed by the hours and the commitment to the client. "At Weil, the firm is first, God is second, and your family is third," assesses one contact. Another grouses, "The firm's attitude is to meet any client need, no matter what resources are necessary. This can sometimes mean late nights rushing to meet a deadline or to do a task in short order."

Covington & Burling

VAULT.COM PRESTIGE RANKING: 14

1201 Pennsylvania Ave., NW
Washington, DC 20004-2401
(202) 662-6000
Fax: (202) 662-6291
www.cov.com

LOCATIONS

Washington, DC
New York, NY
San Francisco, CA
Brussels
London

MAJOR DEPARTMENTS/PRACTICES

Antitrust • Arbitration/ADR • Communications • Corporate, Securities, Insolvency & Real Estate • Employee Benefits/Employment • Environmental • Financial Services • Food & Drug and Health Sciences • Information Technology, Internet & E-Commerce • Insurance • Intellectual Property • International • Legislation • Litigation (Trial & Appellate) • Mergers & Acquisitions • Patent Advice and Litigation • Sports • Tax • Transportation & Energy • White Collar Defense

THE STATS

No. of attorneys: 422
No. of offices: 5
Summer associate offers: 54 out of 56 (Washington, 1999)
Chairman, Management Committee: Jonathan D. Blake
Hiring Partner: Neil K. Roman

PAY

All Domestic Offices, 2000
1st year: $125,000
2nd year: $135,000
3rd year: $150,000
4th year: $155,000
5th year: $165,000
6th year: $175,000
7th year: $185,000
8th year: $195,000

Summer associate: $2,400/week
Base salary includes pension contribution for Washington associates

Two bonus pools: one based on pro bono and client development contributions (up to $15,000) and the other on billable hours ($8,500 to $62,500).

NOTABLE PERKS

- 4 weeks vacation
- "Pretty decent gym"
- Cafeteria meals for about $4
- Outstanding pension plan
- Great health insurance plan ("I pay almost nothing")

THE BUZZ
What attorneys at other firms are saying about this firm

- "Politically connected"
- "The Cravath of DC"
- "Secret society"
- "Crazy lefty litigators"

UPPERS

- Never a dull intellectual moment
- Wide berth to develop practice interests
- Tremendous independence

DOWNERS

- Challenging workload management
- Archaic computer system
- Intellectual elitism

KEY COMPETITORS

Davis Polk & Wardwell
Hogan & Hartson
Paul, Weiss, Rifkind, Wharton & Garrison
Sullivan & Cromwell
Williams & Connolly LLP
Wilmer, Culter & Pickering

EMPLOYMENT CONTACT

Ms. Lorraine Brown
Director of Legal Recruiting
(202) 662-6200
legal.recruiting@cov.com

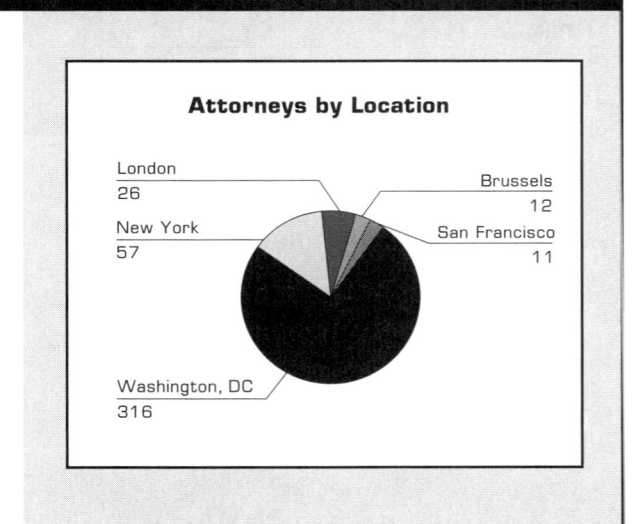

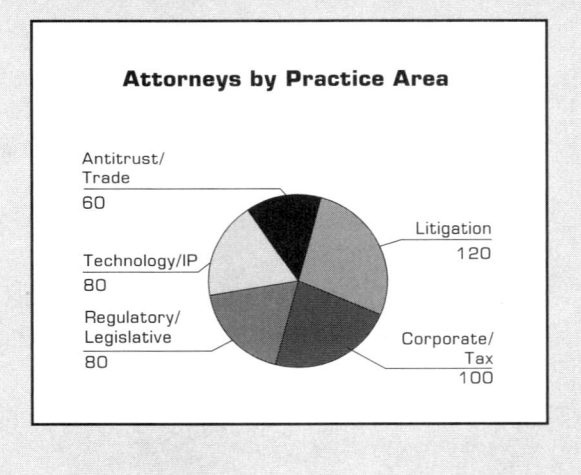

Attorneys by Location

- London: 26
- New York: 57
- Washington, DC: 316
- Brussels: 12
- San Francisco: 11

Attorneys by Practice Area

- Antitrust/Trade: 60
- Technology/IP: 80
- Regulatory/Legislative: 80
- Litigation: 120
- Corporate/Tax: 100

QUALITY OF LIFE RANKINGS [ASSOCIATES RATE THEIR OWN FIRM]

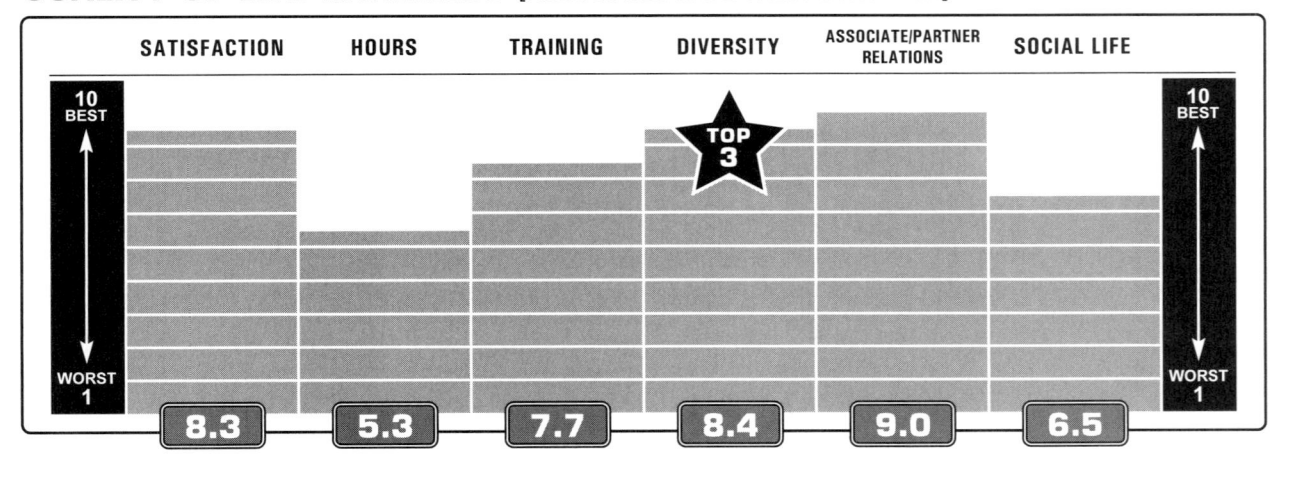

SATISFACTION	HOURS	TRAINING	DIVERSITY	ASSOCIATE/PARTNER RELATIONS	SOCIAL LIFE
8.3	5.3	7.7	8.4 (TOP 3)	9.0	6.5

THE SCOOP

By the summer of 1918, J. Harry Covington and Edward Burling had already established themselves in legal circles. Covington had served in Congress, pushing through litigation to create the Federal Trade Commission and sat on what was then known as the Supreme Court of the District of Columbia as chief justice. Burling had co-founded the successful Chicago firm of Bentley & Burling. But after meeting through mutual friend George Rublee, the two men had a new vision — to build a firm specializing in federal law.

What's in a name?

Covington & Burling opened its doors on January 1, 1919. By the 1930s the firm's name had grown along with the firm itself — Rublee and Dean Acheson, who would later become the Secretary of State under President Truman, added their names to the door, followed by Paul Shorb and John Lord O'Brian by 1950. The following year the firm reverted to its original name. In 1989 Covington set up shop in London, its first outpost outside the Washington area. The firm now has about 40 attorneys in its London and Brussels offices. And in December 1997, the firm announced that it had reached an exclusive cooperation agreement with the 60-lawyer French law firm August & Debouzy. Covington opened an office in San Francisco in March 1999 to service and expand its intellectual property and technology practices and merged with tech-savvy New York firm Howard, Smith & Levin in October 1999.

Big battles with big brother

Covington's client list features some very notable names that have been at the center of high-profile legal conflicts. The firm is tobacco happy — for years, it has been the lead counsel for the Tobacco Institute. Where there's smoke, there's fire — in 1996 the firm took heat for alleged abuse of the attorney-client privilege while representing tobacco clients. That same year, *The Washington Post* reported that Covington permitted client Philip Morris to funnel more than $1 million into an air-quality firm that testified repeatedly that the secondhand effects of smoking indoors were minimal. (Covington denies that any illegal activities took place.) Covington continues to represent Philip Morris on some controversial issues; in May 1999, the firm challenged regulations issued by the Massachusetts Attorney General which restrict tobacco sales and advertising, charging violations of First Amendment rights as part of the suit.

Tobacco giants are not the firm's only mega-clients with extensive legal concerns. Charles (Rick) Rule, a Covington partner and former U.S. Department of Justice antitrust head during the Reagan administration, has been a zealous advocate for

Microsoft in its antitrust proceedings, arguing forcefully against the government and Microsoft detractors such as Robert Bork. The firm also helped represent Dow Corning in silicone breast implant suits and led several Missouri utility companies in a successful defeat of the EPA's statewide Clean Air Act, which was intended to impose controls on ozone emissions.

Pro bono props

Even the firm's public service efforts are high-profile. The firm does work for the Association of American Medical Colleges, serves as special intellectual property counsel to the Smithsonian Institute and advises PBS on intellectual property and Internet-related issues. All these heavy hitters can't keep Covington from committing to clients with less cash or clout, though. Covington has far and away led all large firms in the DC area in pro bono hours (prompting one associate to refer to its "long-standing tradition of being the 'pro bono firm on steroids'") and in recent years has topped national pro bono rankings in *The American Lawyer*'s annual survey. Covington's pro bono program focuses on civil rights/civil liberties, child welfare initiatives, criminal and court-appointed cases, environment, historic preservation, and intellectual property.

The firm made headlines in April 2000 when it filed a wrongful death suit against the U.S. Army on behalf of Patricia Kutteles, the mother of Private Barry Winchell, who was beaten to death while asleep in his army barracks a year earlier. The two soldiers convicted in connection with Winchell's death were said to have attacked the sleeping private because they thought he was gay; Covington attorneys want the army to accept responsibility for the events leading up to the murder.

Of course, with a new salary scale and billable hours targets instituted in 2000, many associates fear that the pro bono commitment "will suffer significantly." Pro bono hours count towards bonuses but not towards billable hours; the "increasing pressure to make more money" will likely take its toll, since "somebody has to pay" for the "huge salary structure." Different partners give different messages as to the importance of pro bono work (some are "so supportive that they are inspirational"); associates "know the firm is struggling with this issue."

We've got it covered

While Covington has earned a solid reputation for regulatory matters and litigation, its strengths are many. The firm boasts a strong food and drug practice — its 5,000 volumes on food, drugs, and cosmetics are the centerpiece of its impressive library. In April 1998, Covington was tapped to handle the $1.93 billion sale of Dewar's Scotch whiskey and Bombay gin brands by Diageo PLC to Bacardi Ltd. In other M&A news, the firm represented Computer Associates in its $4 billion February 2000 acquisition of Sterling Software.

Covington also has a prominent health care practice. The firm handles regulatory issues involving the development of AIDS drugs, cancer drugs, and recombinant DNA products. It is well known for its popular sports practice as well: Covington represents the National Football League, National Basketball Association, and National Hockey League. NFL commissioner Paul Tagliabue is a Covington alumnus, and in October 1999 his former firm advised his current organization on the sale of Houston's expansion team. In early 2000, Covington advised the NFL and NBA on a copyright suit against TVRadioNow Corp., a Canadian Internet company that rebroadcast some of the leagues' games over the Web.

In the summer of 1998, firm officials indicated three major growth areas for the firm: intellectual property, communications, and Internet law. Accordingly, in February 1999 Covington opened shop in San Francisco, thereby taking on tough competitors such as Wilson, Sonsini; Brobeck, Phleger & Harrison; and Orrick, Herrington & Sutcliffe. Responding to doubts about the firm's readiness to compete with such tech titans, San Francisco's managing partner James Snipes cited Covington's ability to act as an all-purpose firm with more than just tech resources. "There's a lot of appeal for one-stop shopping on regulatory and corporate and commercial work," he told *The Recorder*. "It's always more efficient and cost-effective if you can get that all under one roof."

Merger away!

Though it has traditionally shunned lateral growth, in October 1999 Covington joined the fin-de-siècle consolidation craze when it announced a merger with New York's 60-lawyer Howard, Smith & Levin. The deal boosts Covington's transactional expertise considerably and combines the two firms' well-known litigation and white-collar practices. Howard Smith has cultivated an impressive Wall Street clientele, including UBS and The Bank of New York. Andrew Friedman, a Covington partner, told *The Washington Post* that "a lot is at stake...but when we started talking to Howard Smith, we felt like we found our soul mates." Covington is counting on the marriage of its established antitrust and regulatory practice to Howard Smith's experience with high tech mergers to further increase its reputation in the New York market.

Where's the party?

After their fifth year, Covington associates benefit from comprehensive reviews regarding partnership prospects. The firm says that complete reports from the evaluation committee typically run between 1,000 and 1,200 words. It's certainly no cakewalk — one associate characterizes the chances of making partner as "pretty grim." Those who do make it, however, shouldn't expect too much fanfare. Covington partner-elects are summoned to a conference room, where they are congratulated and asked to sit through a year-end fiscal review.

Covington has been recognized as a leader in promoting members of minority groups to partnership (though it traditionally has not received much competition from other large firms in this area). As of December 1998, five percent of the firm's partners were African-American.

Some of the common folk find the anointed to be a "mixed bag" and wonder if the "atmosphere of the firm in general soured following the recent salary increases." But others find the partners "great to work with," offering "tremendous independence and client contact," "excellent treatment," and "respect" across the board. "Of course, you need to be a little bit crazy to be a partner at any large law firm," opines one watcher. "That said, the craziness here tends to manifest itself in quirkiness, but it makes working with the various partners more interesting."

Hi-ho, hi-ho, it's off to work we go

Attorneys remain determinedly cheery, in large part as a result of the firm's benefits and the relatively minimal pressure to work late nights and weekends. In an attempt to keep its troops content, the firm has extended generous maternity leave, part-time partnership track options, and other perks such as an on-site fitness center and weekend retreats every three years for all attorneys and their guests. The 401(k) plan is also a major plus — the firm contributes approximately 10 percent of base salary annually for attorneys with two or more years of service, while attorneys hired after January 1, 2000 will be paid an equal amount directly instead of receiving the contribution. Salaries "keep pace with other large firms in the city," and there are substantial performance bonuses — from a low of $8,500 at the first pay level to a potential high of $62,500 at the top level — as well as "a bonus of [up to] $15,000 for associates who perform significant non-billable work." While the decision to raise the firm's billable hour benchmark to 1,950 has caused concern among some associates, others insist that "much care went into the decision" and that "the management committee truly agonized over how to restructure salaries." The attention seems to be paying off — Covington was ranked fourth nationally among extra-large firms and first in DC in *The American Lawyer*'s October 1999 satisfaction survey. As one content attorney comments, "They pay us all too much."

GETTING HIRED

Not your father's interview

Covington's DC office is known for its unconventional hiring process. Summer associate candidates are given offers based on campus interviews and reference checks alone. Insiders report that the firm structures the round so that the last interview is with a high-ranking firm official who has heard from others and can say something along the lines of, "It's very likely you will be given an offer." Post-offer interviews are simply informational sessions. The New York office's process is more traditional, however, featuring a second round similar to most large firms.

Making the list, checking it twice

First-round interviews at Covington are more intense than your average "So do you like sailing?" law firm interview. "They're longer than any other interviews I had at other law firms," says one associate, describing his full day of interviews. "Any given interview lasted at least half an hour, rather than 15 minutes. I would say they were more substantive — usually the interviewer would address some substantive legal topic. They want to figure out how you will discuss legal matters, rather than check your social graces." Covington also requires a writing sample and references from all potential hires. The writing sample is usually a JD note or a case comment. The references are generally law school professors or previous legal employers. "And they do call them," says one associate. "Sometimes the references will call you and say, 'Hey, I got a call from Covington.'" Reports another insider, "The firm places great weight on references and questions references carefully." Candidates should pay attention to the writing sample they submit. Says one associate who submitted a piece written for a law journal, "During my interviews, one or two people asked me about it and argued with me about my conclusions. I didn't expect that I would be challenged."

Harvard, clerkship heavy

Long known as a Harvard grad stomping ground, Covington has retained its stringent standards. One contact tells us that serious candidates "need to come from a big-name law school or have some other unusually outstanding quality on their resumes." That prized quality is often clerkship experience. "I would say the overwhelming majority of people here have clerked. It may be a Covington thing," says one associate. "They hire folks that go through the summer associate program, but graduates in clerkships are a major secondary source of hires. Not nearly as large but a substantial one." Another insider cautions against playing the clerkship card too heavily without the degree to back it up, however: "There are a few people from lower top 20 schools who had good clerkships, but Covington continues to attract primarily Harvard- and Yale-type pedigrees."

OUR SURVEY SAYS

Where do you think you're going?

Perhaps because it's so difficult to get into Covington, not too many associates try to get out or at least not to go to other firms. Most "associates who leave move on to government or in-house positions," says a DC corporate observer. In fact, "many return after serving in government, and the firm is very accommodating." A litigation colleague agrees, pointing out that while "a few people have left to chase the pot of gold at the end of the dot com rainbow," most Covington associates who depart are "more likely to go into academia or government."

Your work is what counts

When it comes to the question of gender, Covington ranks highly. Most associates feel that the firm is "extremely dedicated to fostering an atmosphere that treats women and men equally on a professional track." One lawyer chose "C&B as a lateral specifically because I was looking for a place where gender was not an issue" and has "not been disappointed." Some lawyers leave it at that, confident that "for all of these issues — gender, race, sexuality — your work is what counts. C&B is a meritocracy."

But some others are troubled by what they perceive as a hands-off approach to diversity in the office. While insiders comment that Covington's "Diversity Committee has an extremely low profile," there are both informal and formal women's groups at the firm.

Lip-service to minorities and gays?

As for the presence of ethnic minorities and gays and lesbians, a DC litigator says that "in some respects, the firm is very receptive." Covington is known for its commitment to promoting minorities to partner (more so than other peer firms, anyway) and was the first in Washington to offer health benefits to same-sex domestic partners. But while there may be "absolutely no overt discrimination here," and associates are "confident that any overt discrimination would be dealt with harshly," there are "preciously few people of color here, and openly gay attorneys are an endangered species."

One associate suggests that "Covington aspires to be a gender-free, color-free, and sexual orientation-free firm with regard to hiring and retention."

A colleague, who says there are only two openly gay attorneys in an office of over 300, mentions another caveat, "Because attorneys are far too intelligent — usually — to be overtly homophobic, the effect of being out on [one's] long-term future remains to be seen."

Home sweet home

It's common to kvetch about offices, but Covington associates seem pretty pleased with the place where they spend the majority of their waking hours. "Our offices are quite acceptable, particularly with the new remodeling that allows better working interaction between lawyers and secretaries," says one. Another concurs, saying that the firm has "nice, if formal, offices, especially since the new renovations to get rid of the suite system." Even better, "the bathrooms are rather posh." There have been "substantial improvements, particularly with regard to the lighting" as well. But you've always got at least one eye-roller in the bunch: "Between the furnishings, the art, and the oriental rugs, it's like working in the middle of an episode of *Antiques Roadshow*. You can just sense that Covington lawyers watch a lot of public television."

Support for support

Even support services get applause, a rare thing indeed in most firms. One litigator says the paralegals are "excellent," "secretarial support varies but is good overall," and "word processing and practice tech support are very good." The one thorn is the computer system, which is "not state-of-the-art and fails frequently." The firm has "not implemented document management software. The computer network, or lack of the same, is one of C&B's primary weaknesses." Some associates remain optimistic, sure that "the new CIO the firm hired a couple of months ago is definitely working this out."

It's all about balance

Covington associates value their working relationships, but not at the expense of their outside lives. "Many single associates spend a good bit of time socializing outside of the office while those with families tend to head home after work," says an associate. "But most associates have several good friendships with other C&B attorneys." While "social life tends to be on the slight side," as another attorney complains, "the 1999 associates seem to be a rather sociable group. I think the firm has recognized that it needs to play a role in fostering a social, warm atmosphere, so it has made some slight changes. There's still work to be done, however." Some might disagree, though, since "the firm at times can seem slightly cliquey." The firm asserts that it has been making an effort to improve its attorneys' social lives for years and that it has recently held a number of team-building retreats, dinners, and other events.

Proud to be at Covington

When asked, Covington associates point to their firm's antitrust, regulatory, and IP/high tech practice areas as those that set it apart from other top firms in the city. In these areas and others, "the quality of work available to young lawyers who seek it out is simply extraordinary." The quality of the firm's reputation makes its attorneys a wee bit defensive about any perceived slights to their individual characters. Its players insist that the firm is "not nearly as staid as the reputation would suggest — younger associates hang out at happy hours and weekends but also work quite hard." "Genteel and stoic," Covington & Burling "attracts very intelligent, professional, and perhaps slightly right of center but generally non-ideological attorneys," assesses one lawyer. "There is an assumption of exceptional competence and creativity."

There can be a flip side, of course. "There is also a passive-aggressive element," continues that same attorney, "that comes with an insistence on always doing things correctly — management is not always responsive to genuine associate problems or concerns but rather follows its own agenda." And you do occasionally run into some "intellectual elitism," though the firm is "starting to realize that it can hire smart, hardworking associates who didn't graduate from Harvard, Yale, or the like."

Generally, though, associates practically glow about their "genuinely nice and extremely smart" co-workers, "fascinating" work, and a firm culture that is "characterized first by its commitment to excellence." Most comments seem to point to the fact that "it is an intense place and the level of play is consistently high." A litigator seems to sum up many of her colleagues' sentiments when she says emphatically that she "can imagine leaving private practice some day" but doesn't think she "would ever leave Covington for another firm."

Paul, Weiss, Rifkind, Wharton & Garrison

VAULT.COM PRESTIGE RANKING: 15

1285 Avenue of the Americas
New York, NY 10019-6064
(212) 373-3000
Fax: (212) 757-3990
www.paulweiss.com

LOCATIONS

New York, NY (HQ)
Washington, DC
Beijing
Hong Kong
Paris
Tokyo

MAJOR DEPARTMENTS/PRACTICES

Bankruptcy
Corporate
Employee Benefits and Executive Compensation
Entertainment
Environmental
Litigation
Personal Representation
Real Estate
Tax

THE STATS

No. of attorneys: 437
No. of offices: 6
Summer associate offers: 81 out of 81 (New York, 1999)
Chairman of Management Committee: Alfred Youngwood
Hiring Partner: Bruce Gutenplan, Esq.

PAY

New York and Washington, 2000
1st year: $125,000
2nd year: $135,000
3rd year: $150,000
4th year: $170,000
5th year: $190,000
6th year: $210,000
7th year: $220,000
8th year: $235,000
Summer associate: $2,400/week

NOTABLE PERKS

- Weekly cocktail hour
- Potential to work overseas
- Spring "prom"
- Monthly supper club

THE BUZZ
What attorneys at other firms are saying about this firm

- "Tough place to work"
- "Excellent reputation in litigation"
- "Relaxed tyranny"
- "Top-flight but unbearable"

UPPERS

- Tremendous amount of training and responsibility
- Top-notch litigation practice
- Substantial pro bono work

DOWNERS

- Negativism
- Lack of mentoring for women
- Some difficult partners

KEY COMPETITORS

Cleary, Gottlieb, Steen & Hamilton
Cravath, Swaine & Moore
Debevoise & Plimpton
Davis Polk and Wardwell
Simpson Thacher & Bartlett

EMPLOYMENT CONTACT

Ms. Patricia J. Morrissy
Legal Recruitment Director
(212) 373-2548

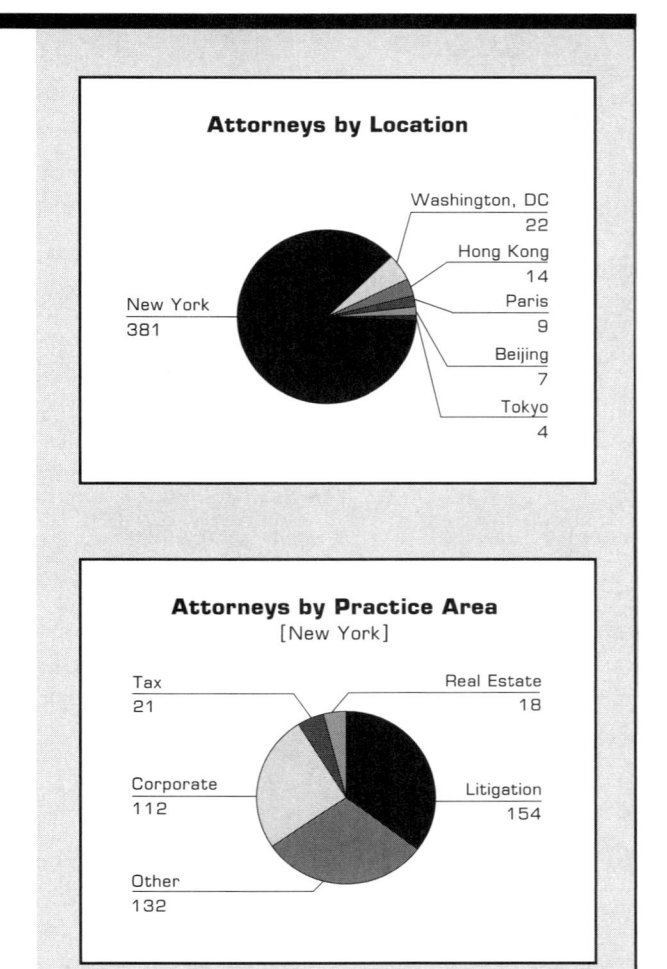

Attorneys by Location
- New York 381
- Washington, DC 22
- Hong Kong 14
- Paris 9
- Beijing 7
- Tokyo 4

Attorneys by Practice Area [New York]
- Tax 21
- Real Estate 18
- Corporate 112
- Litigation 154
- Other 132

QUALITY OF LIFE RANKINGS [ASSOCIATES RATE THEIR OWN FIRM]

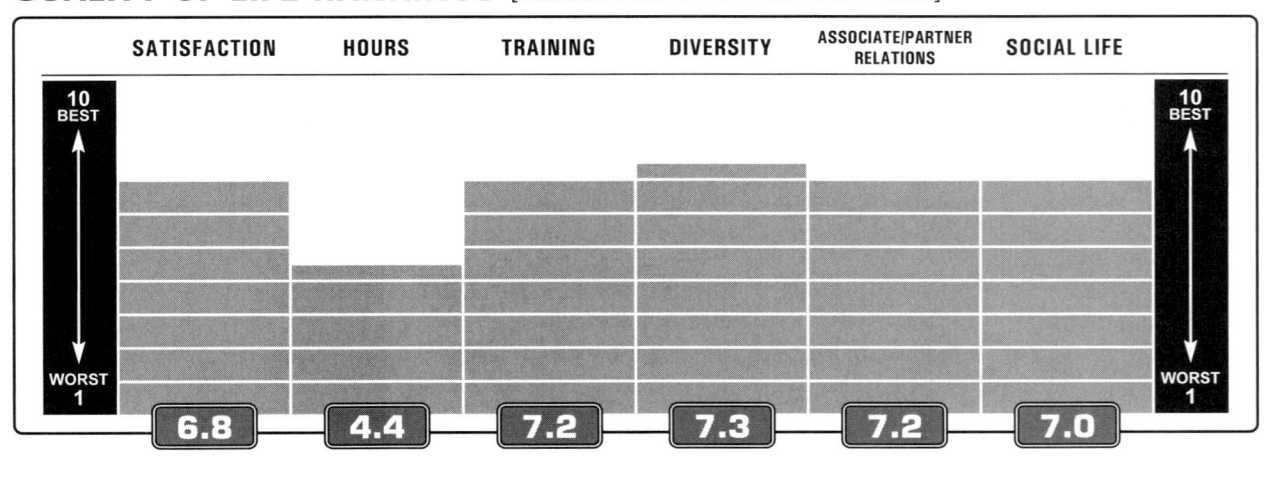

Satisfaction	Hours	Training	Diversity	Associate/Partner Relations	Social Life
6.8	4.4	7.2	7.3	7.2	7.0

THE SCOOP

Paul, Weiss, Rifkind, Wharton & Garrison celebrated its 125th birthday this year. A New York-based litigation all-star Paul Weiss drops two spots to number 15 in 2000.

The times they are a changin'

When proud Paul Weiss partners say their firm leads the pack in championing change, they put their names on the line — literally. Since its founding in 1875, Paul, Weiss, Rifkind, Wharton & Garrison has changed its name six times. The firm settled on its current moniker in 1946 when tax titan Randolph Paul and litigator Lloyd Garrison partnered with lawyers Louis Weiss and John Wharton. With both Christian and Jewish founders, the firm stood apart from the beginning in its sensitivity to religious and ethnic diversity. In 1949 Paul Weiss became the first major New York firm to hire a black attorney.

The firm's management aimed for an equally egalitarian style. In 1963 Paul Weiss announced its "Statement of Firm Principles," written by Judge Simon Rifkind. Its key tenet lay in democracy "with a small 'd'." To this day, each partner at the firm gets one vote — and one vote only. Important decisions are determined by consensus. Rifkind sat on the central committee, the "Committee on Committees" (internally known as the "C on C"), until 1973. In May 1999, however, the firm made a different sort of change by shifting towards a more typical central administrative structure. It elected partner Alfred Youngwood to a five-year term as chair of the management committee and the entire firm. While members of the firm continue to vote on significant matters, the 11-member management committee deals with daily business matters and individual department chairs report to the committee. Even though Paul Weiss' denizens celebrate its individualistic culture, many were reportedly relieved by the move towards centralization.

Ups and downs

Change isn't always easy, of course. Like many big New York law firms, Paul Weiss embraced the barrage of late 1980s insider trading work and overexpanded as a result — one year admitting a class of 97 new associates (today the firm has a total of just over 400 attorneys worldwide). Despite belt-tightening efforts, the firm was still forced to lay off 40 associates in 1991. The firm learned its lesson well: realizing that clients at times would not be willing or able to pay its regular rates, in 1998 it instituted a "staff attorney" program for associates whose educational backgrounds would not normally have landed them a plum position at Paul Weiss. The positions pay less than associate salaries (although "more than half," according to one placement director) and staff attorneys are not placed on partnership track.

The firm has rebounded since the early 1990s, now ranking as one of the 15 most profitable law firms in the country. Morale has risen with salaries; Paul Weiss upped its first-year pay in its New York and DC offices to $125,000 a year as of February 2000. As at many firms, the robust economy has paid dividends across the board. Last year brought boom-year bonuses ranging from $8,000 for first-year associates to $20,000 for eighth-years. There is some grumbling about the new salary structure because "the 'guaranteed' bonus became part of [the] salary, making the 'raise' seem larger than it actually was," according to one cash-minded insider. Some associates wonder if the "totally insane" raises will force "negative repercussions in a couple of years — like layoffs." But really, "who's kidding whom?" asks one attorney. "We're all ridiculously overpaid."

All that glitters IS gold

Paul Weiss has historically been known as a litigation firm, most notably for work such as defending Michael Milken and counseling the Senate during the Iran-Contra hearings in the 1980s. But today the firm has a nearly equal number of corporate and litigation attorneys and has garnered headlines for an assortment of flashy deals. The firm's entertainment practice stands out in particular. Glamorous individuals spotted strolling through the halls include, say insiders, "Sigourney Weaver, Spike Lee, and Calvin Klein."

Prestige spills over into the M&A practice as well. In 1998 Paul Weiss represented Revlon in its acquisition by MacAndrews & Forbes as well as British Telecommunications, plc in its attempt to acquire MCI. The following January, the firm advised the Washington Redskins on the team's sale for a reported $750 million to a group headed up by New York investor Howard Milstein. Summer 1999 saw CBS acquire King World Productions, Inc., with Paul Weiss working out the deal for King World. And the M&A practice has continued to flourish in 2000 — the firm is representing Morgan Stanley, Time Warner's financial advisor, in the media giant's acquisition by America Online.

It's a small world

Ted Sorensen, President Kennedy's special counsel, kicked off Paul Weiss' overseas growth in 1966 when he joined the firm and developed several international clients. In an effort to further its Asia-Pacific interests, the firm hired laterals such as Harvard Law School East Asian expert Jerome Cohen in 1981. With him came Toby Myerson, an attorney with significant experience in Japanese legal issues (Myerson is now a partner and co-chair of the firm's corporate department). While work in Hong Kong and Beijing is said to consist of an eclectic assortment of ventures, the Tokyo branch's work is mostly derived from Japanese companies doing business in the United States.

But as the political structure of the Pacific Rim nations shifts, Paul Weiss's role does as well. While Hong Kong was under British authority, American lawyers were effectively restricted to practicing offshore law. But since Beijing has been in charge, the playing field has been leveled and Paul Weiss has benefited from the open legal market. A prime example is Hong Kong's selection of the firm as counsel in the deal to bring Disneyland to the city. While some Hong Kong lawyers expressed surprise that an American firm was chosen for the project, Paul Weiss' G. Frederick Kinmonth told *The American Lawyer* that it shouldn't have been so shocking. "The truth of the matter was that the Hong Kong government had to have a firm with both U.S. and Hong Kong experience." That turned out to be Paul Weiss.

While Paul Weiss' Asian focus is evident, its European practices are also expanding rapidly. In addition to its Paris branch, a London office is in the planning stages. This newest location will cover corporate, litigation, bankruptcy, tax, and real estate transactions. The option of a U.K. merger to complement the new office has not been ruled out.

Bright lights, big names

The turn of the millennium brought with it more press for Paul Weiss when nationally-renowned litigator Theodore V. Wells, Jr. joined the firm as partner and co-chair of the litigation practice. Experienced litigator Wells has in the past won several major acquittals for clients such as Mike Espy, the Secretary of Agriculture charged with 30 counts of illegally accepting gratuities, and Franklin Haney, the Tennessee financier and friend of Al Gore, accused of 42 violations of campaign contribution laws. *The National Law Journal* named Wells one of the 100 most influential lawyers in America in 1991, 1994, and 1997. His relationship with Paul Weiss is not a new one — he worked in tandem with the firm to represent Michael Milken. And as Treasurer for Bill Bradley's campaign and an active member of many social, political, and community boards, Wells brings with him political connections and an impressive commitment to public service. Bradley himself said that "Ted is one of the best trial lawyers in America and one of my closest advisors and friends."

The firm scored another coup in March 2000 when it beat out several other firms for the services of Mark F. Pomerantz, a highly regarded trial lawyer from Rogers & Wells. Prior to his big-firm experience, Pomerantz had served as the chief of the criminal division of the venerable U.S. Attorney's Office for the Southern District of New York.

Pro bono presence

Paul Weiss is well regarded for its pro bono work, with specialties in death penalty cases, prisoners' rights, rights of asylum, treatment of the homeless, and the teaching of creation science in public schools. The firm's real estate department also lowers its fees for certain community groups, although this work is not included in the firm's official pro bono figures.

In February 1999, Paul Weiss kept in the pro bono news when partners Maria T. Vullo and Martin London prevailed in the firm's three-year representation of a group of abortion providers (four doctors as well as two women's health clinics) in its suit against 12 anti-abortion protestors who had posted personal information about the doctors on handouts and on the Internet. (The handouts were designed to resemble an Old West "wanted"-style poster.) The jury awarded $107 million in compensatory and punitive damages to the Paul Weiss clients, and the trial judge followed with an injunction. The case made *The American Lawyer*'s "Top Pro Bono Cases" for 1999.

To encourage pro bono, Paul Weiss grants pro bono hours the same weight as associates' billable hours. Many associates say that "the support for pro bono is tremendous" and that the firm "is very involved in pro bono projects." Some caution, though, that unless you are "working with a partner on a pro bono matter to which that partner is very committed," there is "inescapable pressure to put billable matters first." According to insiders, even though the firm is "committed in philosophy" to the pro bono policy, "the problem is that people are often so busy it is difficult to take advantage of it." Paul Weiss officials point out, however, that the firm billed a total of 44,125 pro bono hours in 1999 and that pro bono billables have increased by 60 percent over the past three years.

Can't keep a good woman down?

The legal profession's struggle for gender equality has been particularly evident at Paul Weiss. In a 1997 survey of women lawyers' perceptions of their treatment at 77 top firms, Paul Weiss came in close to last. According to the survey, 16 out of 18 women gave Paul Weiss black marks for advancement opportunities, 14 out of 17 thought they were not mentored as thoroughly as men at their firm, and 17 out of 18 reported low job satisfaction. In the wake of the survey, the firm took substantial steps to improve its gender record, notably by bringing in a consultant to evaluate problems.

Since then Paul Weiss has further grabbed headlines for its efforts at gender equality. Over 50 percent of associates are women, leading one associate to speculate that there isn't "any firm in the city that takes women's issues...more seriously." One M&A lawyer comments that "women here recognize that the squeaky wheel gets the grease. The firm has responded to the terrible reviews by trying to reform some of the macho habits." Policy changes have been implemented as well, including a part-time program (80 percent of average hours for 80 percent of salary) for maternity reasons. As part of the Women's Issues Committee's networking program, the firm has held dinners (Hillary Clinton was a recent speaker) and other networking opportunities for Paul Weiss associates, partners, alumnae, clients, and friends (read: potential clients). Other firms have already begun to emulate the networking program.

The natives seem restless nonetheless. Even though "lip-service efforts are pretty good," there's still "no genuine feeling of encouragement from power partners." This may have to do with the makeup of the power partners themselves, at least in the litigation department, where there are only three female partners (two of whom were just tapped in 1998). And the part-time policy isn't uniformly celebrated — associates mention "women with children who feel like they have been offered less work and given less desirable assignments because they were perceived as less available — or perhaps less committed." In general, "the women on part-time status seem to work more than they commit to doing."

Beefing up training

Paul Weiss is extremely proud of its recent efforts to train its attorneys. In 1999 the firm created a Professional Development department to oversee its formal training programs. It now offers two such programs a week in addition to informal group and department development initiatives. Other events, including an orientation week and a retreat for new associates, are also in the offing. All told, Paul Weiss reports that corporate associates will receive about 35 hours of training in their first year, while their counterparts in litigation will receive about 30. But the programs are not just for the newbies — the firm also plans to train senior lawyers in management skills such as mentoring and offering feedback to their young charges.

GETTING HIRED

Pedigree fetishists

No matter how you cut it, getting into Paul Weiss isn't easy. "You pretty much have to be from a top school unless you interview for one of the smaller departments," advises one insider. "Bankruptcy and Real Estate seem to have more associates and partners from 'lesser' schools." The firm is known to have "a fetish for Ivy League pedigrees," with a "particular focus on the usual schools — Columbia, Yale, Harvard, NYU, Stanford, and so on." The difficulty seems to depend on the department to some degree; it's said to be "much harder to get hired into the litigation group than in corporate, and it's almost impossible to get into the elite entertainment group."

Besides the basic transcript scrutiny, say associates, Paul Weiss truly cares about the personality and background of its hires. Opinions vary, but most contacts agree that "Paul Weiss looks for people who have done something besides school, who have a breadth of experience." One associate opines, "Paul Weiss works with a lot of entrepreneurial clients, so the firm likes to see people who have either started businesses or who have a business background, or even those who have majored in economics." Other insiders point out that "a fair amount of associates are older, in their mid-thirties. It's not a huge number but significant". These elder sorts have "generally done something idealistic, like Peace Corps or international travel." Another contact notes that "there are more artistic types than you would expect. They want people with a lot of life experience." "In retrospect," muses an associate, "they're looking for good conversationalists. That's especially important in litigation, because litigators tend to be very outgoing. They call themselves crazy. They are loud and brash — not rude — but at firm functions, you know who the litigators are. They're the ones dancing on the tables." Also, "almost everyone in litigation has clerked, and a lot of people in bankruptcy [have too], but it's not important for other practices."

The process

Paul Weiss does half-hour screening interviews (depending on the school), generally with partners. Callback interviews last half a day and can be scheduled either in the morning or the afternoon. A representative from legal recruiting meets candidates and guides them to their first interview. "The interviews tend to last anywhere from half an hour to forty-five minutes," says an associate. "They strive for a mix of men and women, partners and associates. In general, you should interview with two men and two women." "Because personality matters to Paul Weiss, it's really a conversation. There is no form to go over. I think what they encourage during the interviews, at least from the perspective of an interviewer, is selling the firm, answering questions, and having a conversation. We are building a team environment. We spend a lot of hours together and we want to get along," says an associate. After each interviewing session, the interviewer escorts the candidate to the next office. At the end of the interview rounds, the candidate once again returns to legal recruiting. One survivor deems it "one of the toughest interviews in town in the sense of intellectual evaluation."

The hiring committee meets every week. According to an associate, "if you interview right after they've met, you may not hear from them for some time. But if they don't immediately neg or want you, they'll retain your file until they fill all the slots." Those offered positions first receive a call from a member of the recruitment committee, then a letter from the chair of the recruiting committee. Afterwards, partners and associates make follow-up calls, often to their alumni universities. Those rejected "eventually get a ding letter."

OUR SURVEY SAYS

Fight or flight

Once you get in, though, the question might become whether you'll want to get out. While some associates say that "the turnover rate is comparable to any large New York law firm," others say Paul Weiss is a "tough place to stay at for a long time" and that "all the good associates are leaving," particularly in the corporate and litigation departments. "I once went on vacation for a week and found four departure memos in my inter-office mail when I returned," sighs one veteran. Many of the defections have less to do with Paul Weiss than the "recent boom in the Internet field," argue some attorneys. "There's been a recent flight to dot coms by a lot of senior corporate associates. However, there are a lot of people who leave the firm for a few months and then come crawling back." The firm claims that its attrition rate is close to zero.

Those who stay cite the "aggressive, fast-paced" nature of life at the firm as a major draw, reveling in the "frenetic" atmosphere. "Paul Weiss is a loud place and not for the overly timid," stresses a boisterous litigator. "It's not that people are 'screamed at' as often as reported — you just have to yell loud to get your message heard." An officemate concurs: "The firm is a loud, hectic place. It can be exciting and stressful at the same time. I would not recommend it for wallflowers, but those who can stand up for themselves will thrive."

Casual culture

This anything-goes attitude shines through in a number of different respects. "This firm has a nearly flat hierarchy. On an interpersonal level there is no discernable difference between partners and associates. Everyone is known by his or her first name and everyone keeps his or her door open," according to a corporate associate. "People don't care if you are a first-year associate or an eighth-year associate. They are interested only in what value you can add to the transaction. In that sense this is a very output-oriented firm."

It makes sense, then, that the firm has picked up on the trend of casual dress Fridays and is instituting an all-casual summer dress code. While "the women are pretty fashion forward," they're "not particularly flashy" and "the men are part of the

Dockers generation." As a litigator warns, the firm "is not big on gentility, manners or formality, so blue-bloods beware."

Partners on parade

Playing with the partners is a whole different ballgame, however. While most associates praise their peers, they find partner/associate relations a bit strained. One associate finds that "partners are cordial but won't go too far out of their way to make sure you feel loved." Another says that there are "some nice ones" but that partners are "on the whole very inaccessible."

Other assessments are more brutal. "The biggest problem Paul Weiss has is that, despite the good work an associate can get here, the partners are so unremittingly awful to work for and are so needlessly rude and dismissive of associates that most good associates leave the moment it's feasible to do so," complains a put-upon attorney. A colleague is even more specific: "Because many of the partners in this department have devoted their life to their work with monomaniacal drive, they have no ability to relate to associates except as workhorses, devoid of feelings or private lives. I've analogized the situation to someone using a battery — it makes no difference to the user whether the battery is used six hours a day in ideal circumstances, 12 hours a day in moderate circumstances, or 24 hours a day in stressful and unhealthy circumstances. It only matters how much work you can get out of the battery before it burns out."

Some insiders insist that "things are getting better" and that the partners "are tossing out the bad apples and are trying to foster a more professional adult atmosphere." One finds that the partners "are all appreciative of the quality and quantity of my work, and besides, at how many other firms would I feel comfortable trading 'yo mama' jokes with a partner?"

And what if you want to be the battery operator? If you "hold out the eight years" necessary and "really, really want it," you might "have a reasonable shot" at making partner. Or maybe not — some associates say the chances of partnership are "so tiny it's funny" and that you might as well "dream on if you want to have children before making partner." No matter what, the prospect requires knowing how to "form relationships with key partners, get good assignments" and "how to run a case." It's a given that you'll "work a trillion hours" and you "must do great work, be confident and know how to schmooze with the partners." Some attorneys suggest that factors other than hard work come into play: "In litigation it looks like you have your best shot at partner if you are a male and you graduated from either Harvard, Columbia, or NYU."

Are we in this together?

The social life at Paul Weiss seems to be whatever associates make of it. "People here are generally very friendly," but "social interaction is influenced by hierarchy. Except in rare instances, associates do not go out drinking with partners, for example." Several attorneys mentioned "some rather tight-knit groups of associates, usually female," but a bankruptcy lawyer suggests "there's little pressure if you would rather bond with your spouse, cat, or exercise equipment."

A cocktail party every Friday night seems to have been a success, a "well-attended" event that seems to "promote some mixing." But overall, "things are busy enough that people don't really want to spend any more time with the firm than they have to." There's at least one cynical litigator who might disagree, arguing that "the associates here generally form close friendships with one another, much in the same way I suspect members of the same army platoon are drawn together by their shared unpleasant experiences."

This space ain't bad

Paul Weiss associates are relatively content with their office space. "Renovations are underway" as is office expansion, so for now attorneys are putting up with the "terrible lighting." All associates have window offices, and only first-years share them. With the "decorating 'facelift'" underway and an "excellent collection of photography and modern oil paintings," the "firm's offices are better than most." And it's the little things that count, as one associate illustrates with her furniture enthusiasm: "I just got a new chair I am very excited about."

As for the services that come along with the space, associates find the "solid support staff" to be extremely accessible. The "services are extensive," and "24-hour secretarial support is a huge help." Quality can be "spotty," though, and "attitudes and competence among secretaries and word processors vary from outstanding to surly, but the resources are there." One pleased associate offers the slogan "they've got it all, all the time" to describe the "unbelievable" support he gets at Paul Weiss.

Women before minorities?

The firm has struggled to improve its hiring, retention, and promotion of women since the dismal results of the 1997 survey on the subject, but its efforts seem not to have generated many results with respect to minorities. Some observers comment that "it is clear that the firm is committed to recruiting and mentoring African-American associates," but "there is certainly not enough diversity among partners. There is [only] one black partner" and "there remains something of a boys club culture, particularly in the corporate department." But at least one associate wonders if it even matters, since "if you want to help document transactions where one box that is owned by another box is merging with yet another box, it doesn't matter what your ethnic identity is."

On the other hand, Paul Weiss associates seem to feel that firm is "very supportive of its gay associates and partners." A corporate attorney thinks that "homophobes would probably feel less welcome here than gay people," and others agree that "the firms seems to be receptive" to the concerns of the "several 'out' gays and lesbians" in various departments. Still, "the firm, while not discriminating and while offering domestic partnership benefits, does not affirmatively seek to hire gays and lesbians," and might not "be overly receptive to pressure in that regard."

Less is more

Paul Weiss associates really want to like their jobs. They offer up testimony to the "exceptional litigation" practice, "work of the highest caliber" and "incredibly smart lawyers with a diverse range of interests." But many of them feel beaten down. One attorney seems to sum up many of his colleagues' sentiments when he says, "I love the work, I'd just like less of it. I love the people, I'd just like to see less of them."

Hours "vary widely," but not all attorneys feel like their schedules are out of control. One lawyer attests to having "seen the spreadsheet of average hours worked by a corporate associate here" and swears "that the average billables for a corporate associate in 1999 was just under 2,000, which is well under the average at any other major New York law firm." A corporate attorney who "can't imagine a better place to work" finds the work "exciting and challenging" but doesn't "feel overwhelmed." One asociate who says that "the only thing keeping" him from "rating the firm a 10" in terms of satisfaction "is the hours," although he insists the late nights are "common to the industry and not particular to this firm."

At the same time, there remain "many unhappy people." For some people, "it comes down to the way partners here treat associates. It creates a pervasive misery that is hard to fully describe." "The morale at Paul Weiss has steadily deteriorated," gripes one litigator. "The hours are grueling, the level of respect from partners is generally unsatisfactory, and there is a pervasive sense that no one is willing to look beyond their own immediate self-interest to promote the good of the firm as a whole. Despite the fact that Paul Weiss's clients and cases remain fascinating, I don't believe that top-level legal work can effectively substitute for a tolerably pleasant working environment."

'I can really be my true self here'

Paul Weiss has long established itself as a litigation leader. Its reputation is "outstanding" and "absolutely top-tier," particularly in securities, white collar crime, and intellectual property and is known as a "diverse practice that 'still goes to trial.'" The firm is also "extremely strong in private equity," especially LBO funds and venture capital funds. Many of its associates chose to join the firm on the basis of these strengths and the sense that "the firm has the most interesting client base of any firm in the city."

Others find its "un-stuffy" culture appealing. "I like the informality, cynicism, and humor of the office," says one lawyer. "It's okay to have a messy office here." A female litigator enjoys fulfilling a cliché: "I felt I could really be my true self here. I can wear pantsuits every day, curse like a sailor, pursue police brutality cases, just go for it in terms of litigation." Someone else in the department seconds her, offering the example that if she decides she's "really into a new age Hindu guru, people think that's cool."

Associates say there is responsibility for the taking, with "little oversight and no face time" and a "lot of client contact." Even better, the "mix of work includes smaller transactions where ambitious first- and second-year associates can run the deals."

The cost of greatness

Many associates feel they pay a high price for the Paul Weiss name. It's "NOT a lifestyle firm," is "very difficult for associates who are also mothers," and can be "very impersonal at times," fomenting "horrible insecurity" for young associates. More insidiously, "once you agree to help out on a matter for a client, partners circumvent the assigning partner system and stick you on other unrelated matters for that client without asking you about your other commitments, availability, and workload."

Advice comes fast and furious for those considering accepting an offer at the firm. One attorney suggests that you ask yourself, "Do I want to put up with the stress, annoyance, and fatigue of working with some very demanding and difficult people in order to do rewarding work with the best lawyers in the business?" Another says emphatically, "Know what you are getting into. Do not trust the summer program to give you a feel for what it's like to be an associate." An even more vehement associate adds, "Honestly, unless you don't mind being screamed at, at the drop of a hat, go elsewhere. I came to Paul Weiss because I liked how eclectic and unusual the people were here — but now that I work here I see that although they are perhaps very intelligent and interesting, they are also horrible to work for."

Perspective may be the key. "If you want to do corporate work, this is a great place to be," according to a content associate. "And if you want to litigate, this is unquestionably the place to be. No other firm has our breadth of litigation practice. Where else can you litigate a multi-billion dollar, international corporate dispute one day and represent Hollywood or record industry moguls the next?"

INTERVIEW TIP #9

DO try your hardest to remember everyone's name. "At the end of the interview, you should be able to say 'you know, X, it was great to meet you,'" says an L.A. lawyer. Name recall is especially impressive when you're out to lunch with a large group; your dining companions will notice that you remembered all of their names.

Sidley & Austin

VAULT.COM PRESTIGE RANKING: 16

Bank One Plaza
10 South Dearborn Street
Chicago, Illinois 60603
(312) 853-7000
Fax: (312) 853-7036
www.sidley.com

LOCATIONS

Chicago, IL (HQ)
Dallas, TX • Los Angeles, CA • New York, NY • Washington, DC • London • Singapore • Tokyo • Hong Kong/Shanghai

MAJOR DEPARTMENTS/PRACTICES

Commercial, Financial, and Banking • Constitutional & Appellate • Corporate & Securities • Corporate Reorganization and Bankruptcy • Employment & Labor • Environmental • Health Care • Intellectual Property and Patent • Litigation • Real Estate • Tax • Trusts and Estates • White Collar Criminal

THE STATS

No. of attorneys: 862
No. of offices: 9
Summer associate offers: 82 out of 86 (Chicago, 1999)
Chairman, Executive Committee: Thomas A. Cole
Chairman, Management Committee: Charles W. Douglas
Chairman, Recruiting Committee: John G. Levi
Hiring Partners: D. Cameron Findlay (Chicago)
Kelley Cornish (New York)
Richard Grad (Los Angeles)
Elisabeth Evert (Dallas)
Peter Keisler (Washington, DC)

PAY

All Domestic Offices, 2000
1st year: $125,000
2nd year: $135,000
3rd year: $150,000
4th year: $165,000
Summer associate: $2,400/week

NOTABLE PERKS

- Health insurance for same-sex domestic partners
- 12 weeks paid maternity leave
- Transportation costs
- Wellness programs (including Weight Watchers membership)
- Subsidized chair massages (Dallas)
- Confidential phone counseling for employees and families
- Emergency back-up child care

THE BUZZ

What attorneys at other firms are saying about this firm

- "Generic"
- "Very good to associates"
- "Horrible towards opposing counsel"
- "The feudal kingdom is about to collapse"

UPPERS

- Good advancement opportunities for women
- Excellent pro bono record
- Meritocracy
- Nice computers

DOWNERS

- Dog-eat-dog world when trying to get good assignments
- Poor support services
- Low bonus pay
- The offices

KEY COMPETITORS

Baker & McKenzie
Jones, Day, Reavis & Pogue
Kirkland & Ellis
Mayer, Brown & Platt
McDermott, Will, & Emery

EMPLOYMENT CONTACT

Ms. Jennifer C. Hernandez
Recruiting Team Leader
(312) 853-7495
jherna01@sidley.com

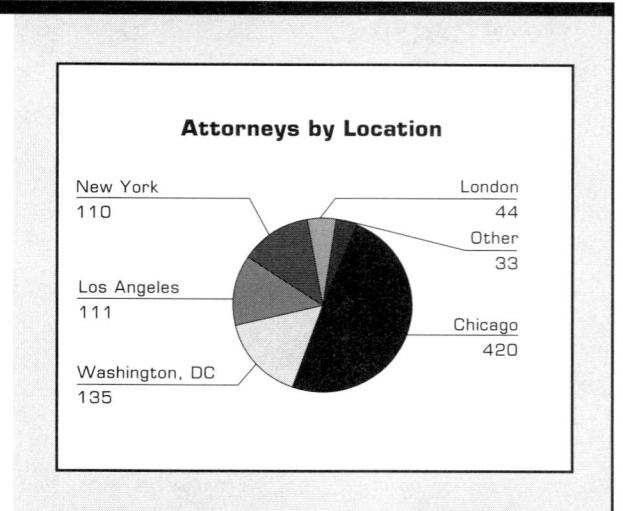

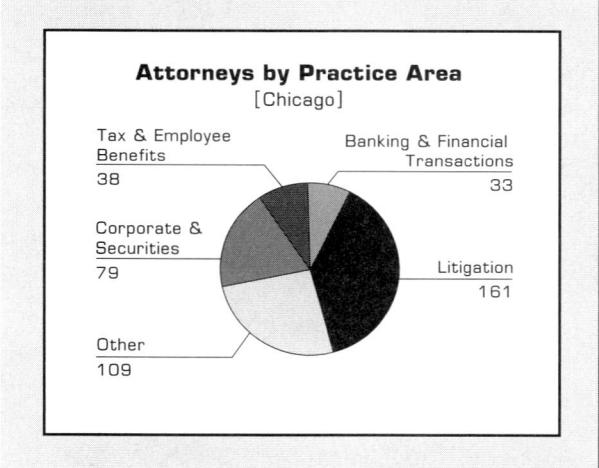

Attorneys by Location

- New York: 110
- London: 44
- Other: 33
- Los Angeles: 111
- Washington, DC: 135
- Chicago: 420

Attorneys by Practice Area [Chicago]

- Tax & Employee Benefits: 38
- Banking & Financial Transactions: 33
- Corporate & Securities: 79
- Litigation: 161
- Other: 109

QUALITY OF LIFE RANKINGS [ASSOCIATES RATE THEIR OWN FIRM]

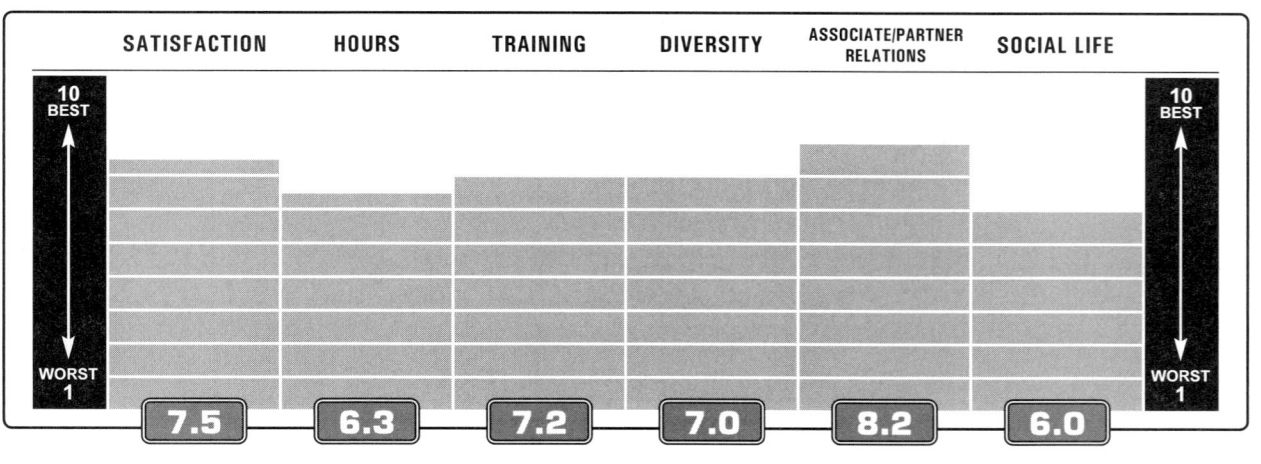

SATISFACTION	HOURS	TRAINING	DIVERSITY	ASSOCIATE/PARTNER RELATIONS	SOCIAL LIFE
7.5	6.3	7.2	7.0	8.2	6.0

THE SCOOP

Having been located in the city for over 130 years, Sidley & Austin can be considered as much of a Chicago institution as bratwurst, deep dish pizza, and snow. The firm features a strong litigation practice and a top-notch corporate department.

History: branch explosions

Sidley & Austin, founded right after the Civil War in 1866, has developed into one of the largest and most profitable law firms in the world. The firm's history has been punctuated by a series of occasional growth spurts. In 1972, for example, Sidley merged with national law firm Leibman, Williams, Bennett, Baird, and Minow, vastly increasing its presence in both Chicago and Washington, DC. The firm pulled off another merger in 1996, taking in 21 new lawyers from Richards, Medlock, & Andrews, a move that both enabled Sidley to double its patent and intellectual property practice and to open a fully-functioning branch office in Dallas. Major offices outside Chicago include Los Angeles (opened in 1980); New York (1982); Washington, DC (1963 — the largest branch outside Chicago); London (1974); Singapore (1982); and Tokyo (1990). In the spring of 1999, Sidley further capitalized on its global reputation when it opened an office in Hong Kong to cover project finance, securitization, and corporate finance transactions in China. Two weeks after announcing the new branch, the Ministry of Justice of the People's Republic of China approved another office in Shanghai, China. Sidley & Austin was one of only six U.S. firms to receive a license.

Bigger is better

Sidley & Austin proves the old adage that "size matters." The firm has nearly 900 lawyers (making it the 13th-largest firm in the world) on three continents and handles issues in every legal field extant. Sidley's largest office, home to well over 400 attorneys, has emerged over the years as a force on the Chicago, national, and international legal scenes. The reputation of the Sidley corporate department is unparalleled in Chicago, and the Sidley name carries significant weight on both coasts and abroad. Clients turn to the department for a wide variety of dealings. Securities offerings are a major area of expertise — while the firm dropped the top spot to Cadwalader in 1999, Sidley still ranked second overall for public commercial mortgage backed securities (CMBS) deal activity, according to a survey by *Commercial Mortgage Alert*. The mergers & acquisitions practice has held its own as well. In March 2000, the department represented Tribune Co. in its $8 billion bid for L.A.-based Times Mirror Co. as well as Lucent Technologies in its agreement to buy cable TV tech developer Ortel Corp. for $2.95 billion.

No-smoking zone

Sidley's excellent litigation practice maintains longstanding relationships with many corporate clients, such as Citicorp and the aforementioned AT&T, for which the firm has tried a number of antitrust and breach of contract cases. The litigation department has experienced major growth recently, particularly in the area of intellectual property. Lawyers at the firm have argued a number of cases before the Supreme Court, and a sizeable proportion of the associate ranks have experience as Supreme Court clerks. In the spring of 2000, the firm took on Storage Computer Corporation as a client, handling matters like licensing agreements. About the only industry whose litigation Sidley will not touch is tobacco, an industry that has proven to be a source of countless billable hours and huge fees for other firms.

In January 2000, Sidley & Austin won a significant U.S. Supreme Court victory on behalf of the State of Missouri. The court ruled in *Nixon v. Shrink Missouri Government PAC* that Missouri's limits on individual contributions to political candidates prevented corruption and did not violate free-speech rights under the First Amendment.

The office euphoria was tempered, though, by a March 2000 settlement that forced Sidley to pay boxer Mike Tyson $20 million in damages for conflict of interest. Tyson charged that his interests weren't protected sufficiently because the firm had represented both the pugilist and his promoter, Don King, at the same time when Tyson was boxing under a promotional agreement with King. The firm denies any wrongdoing in the matter.

Brave new world

Times are changing at Sidley. In February 1999, the firm announced that litigator Charles W. Douglas would succeed R. Eden Martin as chairman of the Management Committee, the body that handles Sidley's day-to-day operations. Douglas inherited the title in April 1999. By the end of the year, some major structural changes were instituted at the firm, most controversially de-equitizing up to 33 partners and creating a new retirement policy (which lowered attorneys' required retirement age). The moves are part of an effort to keep up with what Thomas Cole, the chairman of Sidley's 30-member executive committee, called "an increasingly competitive environment."

As its IP practice has gained muscle, Sidley has begun to pay particular attention to its Internet law work. The firm has handled IP and bank regulatory matters for NextCard and has represented RadioWave.com, BroadcastSports.com, DigitalCars.com and Edmunds.com in private equity financings. S&A represented First Data Corporation in the $460 million merger between iMall (in which First Data had invested) and Excite@Home. In May 1999, the firm established CyberLaw@Sidley to cover

Internet law issues within the firm's general web site. In addition to posting Sidley & Austin's own work such as position papers and policy statements regarding major Internet issues, the site offers links to important Internet news.

Minority house leader

Sidley has also begun to see progress in its ethnic diversity efforts. Several years ago, Sidley undertook a strategy designed to diversify its ranks. The firm developed a task force that works with the firm's recruiters to set goals and attract potential candidates early in the hiring process. It also strengthened relations with minority law student organizations. Once more minorities were employed at the firm, it adopted policies intended to increase retention. Most notably, individual associates are assigned to task force members (in addition to their regular mentors) to help them assimilate into the firm culture. In 1998, the efforts began to bear fruit: Sidley promoted three African-Americans from the associate class of 1990 to partner, bringing its total to five, three more than any other major Chicago firm. As of mid-1999, Sidley had 34 minority lawyers overall, 7.7 percent of the attorneys in the Chicago office.

Sidley's efforts to bring in more members of minority groups complements its relatively solid record for gender diversity. The firm is home to more than 70 women partners and about 250 women lawyers in total — about 28 percent of the entire firm. The Chicago office leads the city in the number of women attorneys at 130, 34 of whom are partners. Many women currently serve on Sidley's most important administrative committees. Two women, Virginia L. Aronson and DeVerille A. Huston, are members of the firm's executive committee. (Aronson is also head of the real estate group and a member of the firm's management committee.) Insiders attribute Sidley's success in this area in part to the firm's "flexible policy on part-time work." Indeed, Sidley has promoted numerous women associates to partner while they were working in a part-time capacity. In recent years, several women attorneys have left to become general counsel at major corporations. (Women serving as general counsel are still a rarity in the legal universe.)

Public notice for public service

Sidley possesses an impressive pro bono record as well. "The firm as a whole encourages" pro bono work by counting it towards billable hours and giving out an award for the top pro bono contribution each year. Sidley lawyers have racked up more than 24,000 hours in each of the last five years, providing assistance to a number of worthy organizations including the American Civil Liberties Union, the AIDS Legal Counsel, and the National Veterans Legal Services Project. The firm also furnishes the Uptown Hull House Legal Clinic with legal personnel and in late 1998 created a public interest fellowship for summer associates in conjunction with Columbia University Law School and New York University Law School.

In recognition of its charitable contributions, the firm has received awards from such groups as the Legal Clinic for the Disabled, the Chicago Volunteer Legal Services Foundation, and the State Bar of California. Still, associates are concerned that the new push for billable hours will take away from the firm's commitment to pro bono work. Don't tell the associate who worked "over 700 pro bono hours last year" in Chicago, though — "every one of them counted."

GETTING HIRED

Names and numbers

For recruiting purposes, Sidley & Austin targets the usual schools, with several solid Midwesterners thrown in for good measure: Boalt, Chicago, Chicago, Kent, Columbia, DePaul, Duke, Georgetown, Howard, Illinois, Indiana-Bloomington, Iowa, John Marshall, Loyola-Chicago, Michigan, Minnesota, NYU, Northwestern, Notre Dame, Pennsylvania, Stanford, Virginia, Wisconsin, and Yale. The firm reports that in 1999 the top six schools from which the Chicago office drew were Northwestern, Yale, Duke, Chicago, Michigan, and Illinois.

The name game is alive and well at Sidley; attorneys say law schools' reputations still carry more weight than any other factor in the hiring process. A litigator in Chicago puts it bluntly: "Sidley only interviews the best at the best schools. Unless you are in the top of your class (Nos. 1 through 5) at a regional law school, Sidley pretty much won't look at you." Another agrees that the firm "draws most heavily from top Chicago schools." But even with the pedigree of a top law school, grades still make or break candidates. An IP/Trademark practitioner in the Dallas office gripes that "hiring is *very* much tied to grades, sometimes to the exclusion of other very meaningful qualifications. As a result, some deserving candidates have been overlooked." Another litigator in the main office affirms the narrow window of opportunity; getting an offer at "most schools...means being in the top 10 percent of your class." This is not to say the system doesn't keep insiders guessing. Another Dallas IP/Trademark practitioner finds it "strange — and a bit unfair — that [the firm] will sometimes allow people to come in for interviews, even knowing that they do not meet the minimal standards and therefore cannot be hired."

Charm works

Others insist that additional factors come into play in deciding the fate of future lawyers. "One of Sidley's best features are its people. Hiring is competitive because Sidley not only seeks to hire smart people but also hires people with whom it is a pleasure to work," says another Chicago litigation associate. A counterpart in L.A. echoes that assessment, mentioning that "Sidley is selective as far as law school attended and journals go, but it tries to get the best and brightest and most well-rounded out of that 'smart group.'" For those interested in IP, note that "qualified candidates with the necessary scientific background are very much in demand." In fact, one patent attorney alerts Vault.com that the firm will be "less grade-conscious" when it comes to hiring. "Top five percenters with an engineering degree are not easy to come by," says that contact. Another agrees that "experience in technology is just as important as outstanding law school performance."

Long on interviews means short on turn-around

Adhering to standard operating procedure for a large law firm, "the interview process usually begins with a 20-minute on-campus interview, which is followed by a callback interview." Sidley pays for "reasonable airfare and hotel accommodations," except for first-year law students, who pay their own way. The entire callback session tends to be a slightly longer than average, "usually lasting five or six hours," a timespan that includes lunch. Candidates have between eight and 10 interviews of 30 minutes each with senior partners or associates; the firm tries to use interviewers from a fairly broad cross section of departments and practice areas.

Breaking up the long interviewing day is "lunch, usually with junior associates." This gives the candidate a chance to meet prospective peers as well as to "ask questions on a more informal basis." Sidley does not dawdle when it comes to deciding whether to extend an offer. After the hearty meal, the payoff awaits for those who made the grade (or to be more precise, those who made the grades). The few, the proud, the winners, are "given their offer by the hiring partner."

OUR SURVEY SAYS

Social life and work shall not meet

Associates express great respect for each other as colleagues, but most seem to draw the line at pursuing social connections outside of the office. Some attribute this to the fact that the firm is "extremely oriented towards ensuring that the associates are well-rounded persons and do not sacrifice their family and personal lives." This is "not a face-time firm;" attorneys want to get their work done and get out of the office. "Most attorneys are pleasant and professional but want to get home to their families," says a DC litigator. "This is not a firm where people spend a lot of time socializing with one another." This division between work life and social life brings mixed reviews. Many Sidley lawyers are relieved by the lack of pressure to schmooze outside of the office with their co-workers, but others wish there was a little more camaraderie in the evenings. Overall, most seem to appreciate the hands-off attitude associates find the atmosphere to be "collegial" and "warm" and note that "Sidley...does not strive to be the center of an attorney's social circle. Most attorneys have close friends here, but there is not an imperative to belong to a group." Or in other words, "this firm is not a frat house."

'This is not a frat house'

That said, associates still rave about firm culture, citing "the great people" and the "quality of life" as major reasons for their decisions to accept offers at Sidley. Some say it simply — "I love what I do" — and others more specifically — "While there are things that frustrate me about working here, I am convinced that Sidley is as good as big firms get. Great people, relatively interesting work, nice facilities. I would never leave here to go to another large firm." The atmosphere is often described as "relaxed" (if "very male"), "friendly," "collegial," and "intellectual." Lately there have been some rumblings of discontent, though, much of it stemming from the de-equitization of partners the firm undertook last year. A Chicago IP/Trademark attorney says he is disillusioned, having chosen this firm because "it was known as the 'kinder, gentler' firm, where hours were not unreasonable, pay was fair, and partner prospects were good. None of these aspects are true anymore."

We're moving, we're moving already

It's a good thing that Sidley lawyers are so satisfied with each other's company — it must help distract them from complaining about their offices and support staff. Many try to keep a stiff upper lip in the face of furniture old enough to be uncomfortable but not vintage enough to be charming. "The offices are functional but old and in need of refurbishment. The furniture is ugly and battered, the equipment outdated. The firm needs to spend some money in this area," sighs an IP associate. Although the Chicago office is reported to have "tremendous views," everyone in DC is waiting with great anticipation for new digs: "A new building is being built and should be great. Right now, we are just waiting for it to get finished." Well, not everyone is waiting hopefully — some aren't holding their breath for much improvement at all, even with the new building. "The Sidley offices are repulsive. They are decorated in ugly brown '70s décor and furniture. They are unpainted. The fixtures are incredibly old. The management refuses to spend any money bettering the place. The word is that the old furniture will be taken along [to the new office] — and in my opinion, this alone will destroy any inherent architectural attractiveness. I personally believe that most people who decline offers to this firm do it because of the atrociousness of the space."

Support services: 'from acceptable to abysmal'

Support services draw criticism, although many lawyers are quick to assert that their secretaries are "wonderful," "excellent," even "a dream." The other in-house help can draw immediate fire for being "generally lazy and unskilled," yet the firm "does not actively terminate or replace poor performers despite their poor reviews." Word processing can be "unreliable," although that may be due in part to the fact that it is supported by a vendor.

Follow the leader

Sidley associates tend to measure their own circumstances against those of other firms. Nowhere is this more true than in the realm of salary. As a major player in the legal world, Sidley & Austin has been forced to keep up with the upward spiral of law salaries. While not a leader in the paycheck wars, S&A keeps up with the Joneses well enough; Sidley met other top firms in offering $125,000 a year to first-years in spring 2000. Some associates are more enthusiastic than others, exclaiming that "pay is excellent for hours worked and Chicago cost of living" or insisting that "the slightly lower salary at Sidley, as compared to other large firms, is a reasonable trade-off for the superior quality of life offered by the firm."

Even those who delight in the leapfrogging salaries have questions about the bonus system. While not all the attorneys are clear on the billing requirements — the process seems a bit mysterious to some of them — most agree that bonuses are not awarded for fewer than 2,000 billable hours a year. And those who do make the cut feel less than fairly compensated at times. An IP/Trademark attorney in Chicago laments that "Sidley does not reward hardworking associates. [The firm's] bonus structure is very compressed, with high billers (2,500 hours) receiving only about $25,000 in bonus, extremely low compared to other firms of Sidley's caliber in the city paying an average of $55,000 for the same hours worked. It seems Sidley is rewarding sloth." A Dallas colleague comments that "although current salaries are certainly competitive, the firm is slow to react to changing market conditions. Just two months ago, our salaries were so far behind the market that attorneys in my class received an upward adjustment of over 50 percent — along with an increase in billable requirement). This came too late to recruit a summer class. In this office, we have zero clerks scheduled for summer 2000. We usually have between 8 and 12."

All's fair in quality and quantity?

The de-equitization of a number of partners had a profound impact on everyone at Sidley. Associates say they have to fight much harder to get quality work, because now the partners are running scared and taking the interesting material with them. Since the partner "restructuring," complains a Dallas associate, the partners "have been motivated to maintain their own billable hours, thus the quality of work and the quantity of training for the associates has been severely limited." Attorneys insist that the work the firm does is consistently "top-notch" — it's just not easy to get. You have to "be aggressive in asking for work you want to do. No one will hand you the good stuff."

The resulting change in culture and attitude has led to higher turnover in all offices, according to several lawyers who fault the firm for "attempting to become a stereotypical New York-style firm." Other fallout from the structural changes is tied into the salary increases. While most attorneys are thrilled about getting paid more, the deal with the devil has deepened in some ways. In DC, some feel "the increased salaries have actually hurt morale. One partner commented that he no longer cares about associate development, he just wants his work done. Generally, the partners seem more willing to destroy your weekend plans on Friday afternoon." Dallas backs its East Coast brethren on this one. Says one lawyer, "The attitude from partners since the adjustment has been, 'You got your pay increase, now we don't want to hear any complaints of any kind.' This includes grievances about billable hours, quality of work, mentoring, and firm-sponsored social activities — all of which have suffered recently."

Getting even lonelier at the top

Some underlings still jump to defend the majority of the firm's partners, though. One says he has "a hard time believing that partners at other large firms treat their associates with as much respect as they generally do here." It's a relief to find partners who "do not have major egos that must be fed with the blood of associates." Depending on the practice group, associates say partners seem to offer as much mentoring as possible — the FDA group is particularly known for its guidance.

Not that the associates are kidding themselves about their chances of making partner themselves. While the partnership track has traditionally been about eight years, Sidley insiders say the path to partnership has been stretching to nine or 10 years (at least for some) recently. If you "develop a good relationship with an established client bring in business or show you can manage a big case," you'll have an advantage, but there are few guarantees. One cynic suggests that his comrades "bill, bill, bill...and have an old law school friend that happens to be general counsel for a potential client."

Behind every great man...

Sidley & Austin gets consistently high marks for its recent efforts to hire, retain, and promote women in its ranks. The firm prides itself on having a part-time program that really works. While some firms have such programs in name but penalize those who take advantage, this is not the case at Sidley, say many men and women. "Look at this year's partnership class — two women in Chicago," points out one litigator in that city. "One has four kids and worked part-time for four years and still made partner with her class; the other has five kids. She was set back one partnership class but took three- to seven-month leaves and worked part-time some of the time. I doubt if there is another firm that can match that history."

Most attorneys support the firm's efforts to remain vigilant as to gender issues that face the legal profession in general and Sidley in particular and think their firm "does a better job than most" at addressing them. But sometimes initiatives backfire. When the "women's issues committee" disclosed that women associates are still generally reviewed lower than male associates — and so paid less — the firm's response was to schedule a series of luncheons to "help" women with their negotiation and lawyering skills. As one lawyer pointed out, some associates found this "insulting, suggesting that the women were the problem, not the men doing the reviewing."

Top-heavy minority presence — but limited gay and lesbian visibility

While Sidley's Chicago office has been recognized consistently for its high number of minority attorneys compared to other firms in the city, particularly African-American partners, insiders suggest the firm's commitment is not what it could be. While the firm "tries and has had some success," some associates think it "could do better." Partners stand out, certainly, but recruiting is weak, with only a handful of minority associates in most offices. Pointing out that the strong minority presence in the partnership is "threatened without recruitment," an L.A. litigator suggests that "Sidley put pressure on UCLA, Berkeley, and other schools that have gotten rid of affirmative action. It would make their diversity spiel seem a lot more genuine."

Few Sidley associates know how to address the issue of gays and lesbians at Sidley, stating that "there isn't much discussion of the issue" and there are "so few openly gay attorneys that it is impossible to discern a pattern one way or the other." Others felt that "sexual orientation doesn't seem to be a big issue at Sidley. The firm offers benefits to domestic partners" and "gay and lesbian attorneys involve their partners in social events and chat about life outside the office just like heterosexual attorneys." One attorney summed up the attitude "as welcoming as any Chicago firm of blue-bloods can be."

Perk up, kids, and buy some khakis!

While some associates complain that there are "very few" perks or "almost none" at Sidley, the list actually sounds pretty standard. Besides the usual 401(k) plan, health and dental benefits, and life insurance, the firm offers up a hodgepodge of meals, social events, subsidized gym memberships, laptops, the occasional happy hour, and the like. One attorney says he enjoyed a "chair massage" on the firm; his officemates routinely enjoy tickets to professional sports events, ballets, operas, and even theme parks. Besides meals and car service home after working late, the firm supports a "good transit program — supplemental checks to cover the cost of commuting via train, bus, or subway which do not count against income as at some other firms." In another nod to its family-oriented philosophy, Sidley administers a family crisis program called Carebridge for its employees.

Casual dress may soon become a full-time perk, or at least full-time during the summer months. Fridays are casual all year and every day is laid-back in the summer, although most associates lean towards the "conservative." While the scene is definitely "not flashy," it's "not frowned upon" to experiment as long as it's "tasteful." Most male attorneys have resigned themselves to "khakis and a short-sleeved sports shirt [with a] sweater in winter," while women wear the "functional equivalent."

VAULT.COM
17 PRESTIGE RANKING
Gibson, Dunn & Crutcher LLP

333 South Grand Avenue
Los Angeles, CA 90071
(213) 229-7000
Fax: (213) 229-7520
www.gdclaw.com

LOCATIONS

Los Angeles, CA (HQ)
Century City, CA
Dallas, TX
Denver, CO
Irvine, CA
New York, NY
Palo Alto, CA
San Francisco, CA
Washington, DC
London
Paris

MAJOR DEPARTMENTS/PRACTICES

Corporations
Labor
Litigation
Real Estate
Tax/Probate

THE STATS

No. of attorneys: 749
No. of offices: 11
Summer associate offers: 145 out of 157 (1999)
Managing Partner: Wesley Howell Jr.
Hiring Partner: Kevin Rosen

PAY

All Domestic Offices, 2000
1st year: $125,000
2nd year: $135,000
3rd year: $150,000
4th year: $165,000
5th year: $185,000
6th year: $195,000
7th year: $205,000
8th year: $210,000
Summer associate: $2,404/week

NOTABLE PERKS

- Free lunches for new attorneys
- Generous business development budget
- $300 book-buying budget

THE BUZZ
What attorneys at other firms are saying about this firm

- "Snobby; arbitrary cutoffs for hiring depending on your law school"
- "Probably THE L.A. firm"
- "Cravath wannabe"
- "Classy place; great appellate practice"

UPPERS

- Free-market system that allows associates to choose their work
- Top-notch clients
- Early associate responsibility

DOWNERS

- Terrible support staff
- Little to no diversity
- Tension between partners and associates over raises

KEY COMPETITORS

Latham & Watkins
O'Melveny & Myers
Paul, Hastings, Janofsky & Walker
Skadden, Arps, Slate, Meagher & Flom

EMPLOYMENT CONTACT

Ms. Leslie E. Ripley
National Recruiting Manager
(213) 229-7273

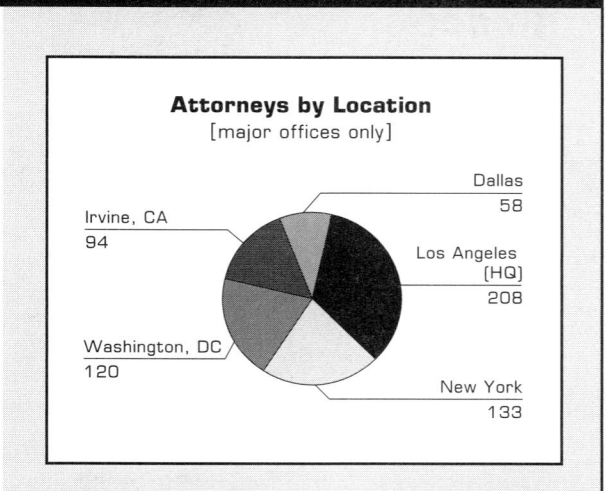

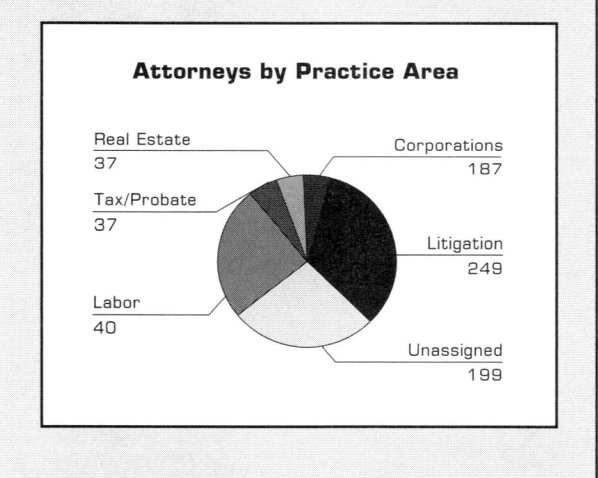

Attorneys by Location
[major offices only]

- Dallas: 58
- Los Angeles (HQ): 208
- New York: 133
- Washington, DC: 120
- Irvine, CA: 94

Attorneys by Practice Area

- Corporations: 187
- Litigation: 249
- Unassigned: 199
- Labor: 40
- Tax/Probate: 37
- Real Estate: 37

QUALITY OF LIFE RANKINGS [ASSOCIATES RATE THEIR OWN FIRM]

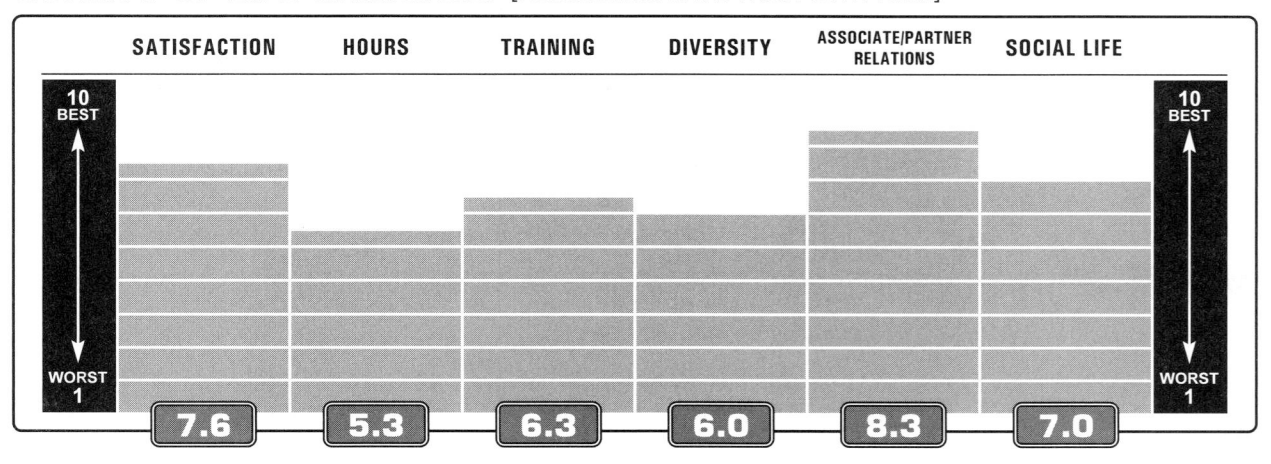

SATISFACTION	HOURS	TRAINING	DIVERSITY	ASSOCIATE/PARTNER RELATIONS	SOCIAL LIFE
7.6	5.3	6.3	6.0	8.3	7.0

(10 BEST / 1 WORST)

THE SCOOP

Gibson, Dunn & Crutcher is a Hollywood superstar. One of L.A.'s "Big Three" law firms, GD&C has long been a player on the international scene.

History: L.A. player

Gibson, Dunn & Crutcher was founded in 1890 in Los Angeles and has become an international firm with approximately 700 lawyers in eleven offices. Gibson was the first of L.A.'s "Big Three" to establish a New York office and the second to open an outpost in Washington, DC. In 1967 the firm branched out internationally, opening for business in Paris. Unfortunately, Gibson is perhaps most famous for offering the top Stanford law graduate of 1952 a job as a legal secretary. That Stanford grad, Sandra Day O'Connor, was later appointed to the Supreme Court.

The firm, like all other California law firms, suffered financially when the California economy went into a tailspin in the early 1990s. While other firms laid off associates, Gibson responded by closing its smaller offices: San Jose in 1992, then Brussels, Moscow, and Seattle in 1994. The trend has carried over into the recent boom economy — the firm announced the closing of its San Diego office in April 2000.

Grabbing associates, anywhere it can

As Gibson's business rebounded in the mid-1990s, the firm starting swiping partners from other California powerhouses, including Brobeck, Phelger & Harrison and Morrison & Foerster. In December 1997, Gibson picked up the six-person structured finance team from Orrick Herrington in New York. Six months later, partner Randy Mastro, who had left Gibson to become deputy mayor of New York, returned to the firm. Mastro took on more work for the city's mayor, Rudy Giuliani, in March 1999 when he assisted an attempt to reform the city's charter. (Charter reform was defeated in the November 1999 election.) In April 2000, Stephen Glover, a respected M&A attorney from Fried, Frank, Harris, Shriver & Jacobson, jumped to Gibson's DC office. And that same month, Stephen Ball, formerly chief general counsel at Nomura International, joined the firm's London branch.

More star partners

Gibson is chock full of powerful lawyers. Partner John Olson, a respected securities lawyer, has served on the legal advisory committee of the National Association of Securities Dealers and currently serves on the legal advisory board for the New York Stock Exchange. Additionally, he serves as a member of the Council of the American Bar Association's Business Law Section.

Partner Theodore Olson served as an assistant attorney general in the Reagan administration and recently represented several telecom industry associations in a lawsuit against the Federal Communications Committee regarding wiretapping. Joseph Kattan, a partner in the Washington, DC office, represented Intel during an antitrust investigation by the Federal Trade Commission. And Theodore Boutrous Jr., who moved from the firm's Washington office to L.A. to become co-chair of Gibson's Appellate and Media Law Practice group, has won reversals of more than $1 billion in jury awards, including a $200 million award against *The Wall Street Journal*.

Invading M&A turf

GD&C is one of the few firms based outside of New York that dares to challenge Big Apple-based firms for M&A advisory work. Gibson ranked third (in terms of number of deals) among law firms in 1999, advising on 189 deals worth a total of $69.6 billion. Notable transactions include representing the Chandler family, part-owners of publisher Times Mirror, in that company's merger with the Tribune Co. The deal was quite controversial for Gibson — William Steinhart, the Gibson partner who represents the Chandlers, is a Times Mirror board member and negotiated the deal on behalf of the Chandlers without telling his fellow board members. Another notable client was Computer Science Corp., which GD&C defended against a hostile takeover bid from Computer Associates.

Pro bono: adoption and prison brutality

Gibson is also proud of its pro bono efforts, which have come on behalf of a range of clients. In 1998 the firm's L.A. headquarters hosted Adoption Saturday, which brought together foster children, adoptive parents, and adoption authorities in an attempt to expedite the process. In March 2000, the firm won a $54,000 jury verdict for a L.A. county prisoner who claimed he had been assaulted by a corrections officer in retaliation for filing complaints against the officer.

Firm insiders seem to agree that the firm has a strong commitment to pro bono. "I know one attorney who billed over 300 hours to a pro bono case her first year and over 250 the next year," says one contact. "Her time was never called into question and she received full credit for all of the hours." While pro bono hours do not count towards the firm's minimum billable hours requirement, once an associate meets that requirement, time spent on pro bono cases does count towards his or her bonus.

Other practice areas

Gibson Dunn has a strong corporate practice beyond its M&A clientele. The firm delves into areas such as antitrust, taxation, intellectual property, employee benefits, and securities law. Ironically, Gibson received some press for an IP case it couldn't argue. NextWave Telecom selected the firm to represent it in a lawsuit against the FCC regarding control of licenses after Nextwave went bankrupt. Too bad for Gibson that Judge Robert Sack, a former Gibson partner, was part of the three-judge panel hearing the appeal of the case. In March 2000, the U.S. Court of Appeals prohibited Gibson from taking the case, saying Sack had been assigned first and NextWave should have sought other counsel.

Molding the minds of young associates

While associates give training at Gibson mixed reviews, the firm states that it has a strong commitment to both informal and formal training. The firm pays for outside training programs and buys passes for all PLI seminars around the country, which associates are encouraged to use. A recent survey of associates indicated that in-house training needed improvement, and in response the firm has hired a training coordinator. The training coordinator will set up intranet-based training modules, and partners in charge of local offices have been tasked with the responsibility of overseeing training in their respective offices.

GETTING HIRED

Don't even think about it

Firm insiders say Gibson "has strict grade point cutoffs." The grade requirements "apply to every potential hire [and] make it difficult for otherwise attractive candidates to get their feet in the door." According to one associate, the grade cutoffs vary by school, but everyone agrees the firm sticks to them religiously. One lawyer criticizes this practice, saying that the firm adheres to it "blindly."

Centralized hiring process

Gibson undertakes a massive annual recruiting effort — the firm conducts on-campus interviews at about 40 law schools. Unlike other large firms, hiring is done on a national level, as opposed to by individual office. "In order for you to get an offer, the recruiting committee, which is made up of all the different offices, has to agree," explains one contact.

Identical process

Because of this centralized process, the callback round is nearly identical. For summer associates, the firm conducts four interviews, usually with partners. The candidate is then taken to lunch with associates. If all goes well, the candidate is asked to dinner. In the break between lunch and dinner, everyone who has met the candidate compares notes, and if they like what they see, an offer can be extended at dinner. (Don't fret if you don't get a dinner offer. Outside circumstances, such as a scheduling conflict with a partner, can cause a delay.)

Looking for initiative

One associate who conducts interviews says that Gibson's free market assignment system influences what she looks for in a candidate. "I'm looking for somebody who's got initiative, who's pretty outgoing," says that contact. "People who are sort of shy are probably going to have a difficult time here. If I'm the one asking question after question, it's probably not going to work out well. If I start a topic and they go off on their own, that's probably not good." Job seekers can visit Gibson's web site, which lists recruiting contacts and features a firm brochure.

OUR SURVEY SAYS

They hate New York (at least the culture)

"The culture used to be laid-back and somewhat attuned to lifestyle issues," says one New York associate. "Now, for some reason, Gibson has decided to become like the New York firms, pushing associates to work harder and being far less interested in ensuring that associates have lives outside of the office." Indeed, several Gibson attorneys comment on a perceived clash between the firm's California roots and its New York aspirations. "The firm wants to be a laid-back, California-type lifestyle firm," another contact says. "This tends to conflict with the firm's desire to have the profits of a New York firm."

Walk softly and carry a briefcase

Many feel that the firm values independence in its associates, but that that independence comes with expectations for aggressiveness and, ultimately, results. One contact assesses the firm: "Hobbesian would be too harsh — maybe like Teddy Roosevelt. The firm treats everyone as a rugged individual. From training to work assignments to scheduling, we are given opportunities and left to our own devices." That contact concludes, "I am neither coddled nor stifled."

Teddy Roosevelt in khakis and a polo shirt

Even while the firm is preparing its associates for the proverbial charge up San Juan Hill, a relaxed atmosphere is retained. "Although a traditional firm, the culture is very informal," notes one associate. "I can't imagine a big law firm with a more easygoing culture," adds a Dallas lawyer. "The firm's California roots are readily apparent in the casual demeanor of most of the office's lawyers. We have recently adopted a full-time business casual dress code."

Partners in a free market

Given the free market system, Gibson partners have an incentive to treat associates well. Indeed, most insiders say that partners treat them with respect and "quickly come to rely" on them. That doesn't mean all partners do so. "The partners could be a little more friendly," one associate complains. "When I say 'Good morning,' I don't expect to be stared at in response." Another contact reports that the attitude towards associates "varies from partner to partner. Some are respectful; others border on unprofessional." A Los Angeles associate says, "I am concerned that the associate pay increases will have a negative effect on partner attitudes," as it has in some other firms. Other insiders point out that "with the free market system, negative partners find it hard to get people to do their work."

Social life lacking

Gibson associates report that while there is some attempt made — both formally and informally — to foster a social life, the end result comes up a little short. "We have firm happy hours inside and outside the office, firm sports teams, and an active lunch scene," reports one source. Says another associate: "My department is too busy for anyone to interact socially with anyone," noting that if one does want social interaction, "you can find it." Don't expect much contact with the partners, though. "[They] barely talk to you here," fumes one lawyer.

Hours: thanks for not trying to kill me off

"I find the hours pretty livable, but I do not have children," says a source. "If I did, I would probably find them to be unmanageable." In general, Gibson attorneys work hours typical of a large firm, with the work varying depending on department and the cyclical nature of deal flow. "I travel a lot," says one corporate associate, "which makes for long hours, and I work hard close to deals, but I went to opening day at

Dodger Stadium and I played in a golf tournament last week. It all depends on how you structure your schedule." Another contact points out that "Gibson attorneys work hard," as do most lawyers, "but the firm tries not to kill off or burn out its attorneys — partners or associates."

Market pay

"There's never any doubt Gibson, Dunn will pay market," says an associate. Another says "GD&C always pays enough to stay exactly where the New York market is paying but is never a salary leader." The firm has the unusual policy of paying associates in all offices on the same scale, regardless of the cost of living. That leads to happy lawyers, or at least well-compensated ones, in smaller markets. "Los Angeles pay and Dallas cost of living: the best of both worlds!" enthuses an associate.

Despite that unbridled joy, there are some areas where Gibson trails the market. "[The firm] does not have an associates' investment fund as do other firms in the Bay Area," says one contact. "This means that GD&C's overall compensation may be somewhat lower than these other firms, even though GD&C's base salaries and hours-based bonuses are very high." Speaking of bonuses, the exact amount has been unclear after the recent pay raises that swept through the legal profession. "The bonus policy has not been clearly laid out for this year as we, like most firms, are in transition," says an associate.

The firm points out that its bonuses are not set until late in the year since they are based on profitability. This year, according to Gibson, "looks to be very strong, and we fully expect that our bonuses will be at the top of the pay scale."

Typical perks

Gibson associates receive all the usual perks — "free working dinner, access to firm sports tickets, [and] free transportation home." DC associates have a "small gym" at their disposal. Additionally, "we receive $1,000 a year for client development," says one attorney. "This can be used for any activity that we do with a legitimate potential future client (including classmates from college or law school). We [also] receive a $300 annual book budget to buy any books we want." Finally, that associate reports that "every year the firm has a retreat in California — usually San Diego or Palm Springs."

Learning by doing

"Simply put, training is non-existent," one lawyer reports. "It's learn by doing or don't learn." Gibson insiders say there are "very few formal training programs aside from the occasional lunch lecture, and the amount of individual training one receives from superiors varies considerably. If you are lucky enough to work for a partner with an interest in training, you will get a lot of hands-on training. If you are not, you will get very little." Another associate complains, "I receive training from exactly one person. No one else has taken an interest, except for one partner who has insisted on setting up seminars that are really useless."

Gibson's atmosphere may make the training issue moot. "[The training question] is a hard question to answer at Gibson," claims one lawyer. "The in-house formalized training is almost non-existent, but most attorneys want it that way." A different source sums up the training situation: "The short answer is, if you want training around here, you just go out and get it — it's free and available in abundance."

Beware the 47th floor

Office aesthetics seem to vary by location but are in general very good. "We just moved into new offices and they are convenient [in terms of commuting and parking] and attractive," reports a Dallas associate. "The individual offices aren't huge, but we have glass doors so even if we need to shut doors during conference calls the offices don't seem too small. Almost all of the associates received new furniture, too, and that has been very popular." Another Dallas associate complains that the new layout places some associates far away from their secretaries.

"The DC office décor simply does not reflect that this is a top national firm," laments another associate. "The DC office is moving soon and it is reflected in the décor." Comments another lawyer in the nation's capital, "the office has a legendarily bad design, but this doesn't affect my life very much."

One source offers this warning about the New York office. "The 47th floor of the New York office is a pit. Everybody who can move off 47 does. Unfortunately, the firm has realized this and inter-floor mobility has been terminated. The managing partner moved to the 47th floor for morale purposes and even he admits it's a dump."

According to the firm, Gibson is "committed to maintaining offices appropriate to our stature as a firm and where our attorneys will enjoy working. In that regard, we recognize the need to improve the Washington, DC and New York facilities. We are committed to either remodelling the 47th floor of our New York office and our Washington office or moving to different space. Either way, we recognize the need to improve the offices in those locations and are committed to doing so quickly." In the last three years, the firm has remodeled the 48th and 49th floors of the New York office.

Unsupportive staff

Gibson associates are nearly unanimous in panning the support staff. "Ha! Ha! Ha! That's a good one," a New York attorney cracks about the staff. "Simply stated, poor to none." Another lawyer says that support staff is "terrible. Virtually no paralegal help and many secretaries border on incompetent." "This is our greatest weakness," says one contact. Another offers this mathematical equation for secretarial support: "Sharing a secretary with a senior partner equals no secretary."

The paralegals and secretaries aren't the only members of the staff Gibson attorneys feel are lacking: "Word processing is OK unless they're busy, at which point they commence making mistakes." "The computers are miserable," one lawyer gripes. "The firm had a clever idea in 1997 to use laptops, and those 1997 laptops are dying under 2000 software. New computers are coming but not soon enough." The firm expects to have the new computers by summer 2000.

Mass exodus on the way?

Gibson Dunn seems to have the same retention issues as other large firms. "Associates leave, but I think it is primarily because the opportunities that GD&C associates are exposed to are too good to pass up." Remarks another associate, "Gibson Dunn's New York office seems to experience turnover in waves, with no one leaving for quite a while and then several associates leaving all at once." One of those waves might be coming soon. "There is about to be a mass exodus from the litigation department as the character of the firm is changing for the worse," claims one insider.

Partnership prospects

Though one associate says partnership prospects are equal to a "snowball's chance in hell," most seem to feel that Gibson lawyers have at least a fair chance at the brass ring. "Probably better than at most New York firms if one is committed but generally somewhat difficult," rates an attorney. "If an associate wants to make partner and puts in the time, the prospects are not bad," says another lawyer. Finally, firm insiders report there is a "complex rating system that lets you know where you stand."

Diversity: white-bread?

Gibson seems to have issues regarding diversity. One associate calls the firm's efforts to recruit and retain minorities "abysmal. I would say the partnership has almost no interest in racial diversity." A Dallas lawyer remarks that "the level of minority attorneys here is embarrassingly low." "The firm is incredibly white-bread," an associate summarizes. "The firm doesn't do much to change it either."

Insiders are more mixed on the firm's efforts with respect to women. While many say that the firm works to make the atmosphere conducive to women, the results are poor. "We have two female partners in the whole New York office," one insider reports. "I have had one partner tell me that 'women just make choices like having children' that don't work well with partnership." Another associate complains that "there is a lot of lip service paid to women's issues, but [there are] very few women partners and no real recognition that the attrition rate among women is much higher than with men." Finally, an attorney predicts that the "firm will lose women partners and associates until it lets them work part-time." The firm does have at least one women-friendly policy, covering the cost of on-site emergency day care for attorneys and staff in its New York office.

"GD&C is a surprisingly gay-positive firm, given their seeming lack of interest in promoting women and hiring minorities," says one contact. Most insiders feel Gibson makes sexuality a non-issue and that gay and lesbian attorneys are welcome. A lawyer noted that the firm filed an amicus brief in *Dale v. Boy Scouts of America*, the case in which the youth organization barred a gay scoutmaster.

"Lucky" associates

Many Gibson lawyers, despite their complaints, seem satisfied with the firm. "I feel lucky to work for this firm," an insider gushes. "It's been a great experience." Another associate claims, "I have had a much better experience than I ever imagined possible while in law school."

But the feeling is far from unanimous. At least one associate predicts impending doom for the firm. "In the last year the character of the firm has changed a great deal for the worse. I think the partners' greed means that new work is never turned down, whether or not the staffing exists to undertake [it]." Additionally, that insider reports that "a small group of partners — ones that are generally disliked by associates and thus, find it difficult to staff their cases — are trying to change the free agent system so that they will have associates assigned to permanent misery with them."

The quality of work is mentioned most often when discussing the pluses of working for Gibson. "You can do everything from venture capital to leveraged buyouts to IPOs," one associate says. The people and the experience that come with Gibson's culture are also popular. And, as an associate points out, "the compensation ain't bad either." On the downside, in addition to the reportedly lagging support staff, insiders cite "abusive partners and billing pressure."

"I chose GD&C for the culture," says one associate. Another mentions the free market system as his reason for joining, while others chose Gibson because of the clientele. The lawyer offers a warning, though: "The culture is rapidly disappearing and a lot of homegrown GD&C people will probably leave in the next year or so if the trend is not arrested."

INTERVIEW TIP #10

If you're taken to a meal during the interview, DON'T order a hamburger, spaghetti or anything else that could get messy. Avoid drinking alcohol, even if you're at a recruiting dinner where everyone's drinking. (If you're self-conscious, consider getting seltzer or something that can masquerade as alcohol.)

Debevoise & Plimpton

VAULT.COM PRESTIGE RANKING: 18

875 Third Avenue
New York, NY 10022
(212) 909-6000
Fax: (212) 909-6836
www.debevoise.com

LOCATIONS

New York, NY (HQ)
Washington, DC
Hong Kong
London
Moscow
Paris

MAJOR DEPARTMENTS/PRACTICES

Corporate
International
Litigation
Real Estate
Tax
Trusts & Estates

THE STATS

No. of attorneys: 419
No. of offices: 6
Summer associate offers: 88 out of 88 (New York, 1999)
Presiding Partner: Martin Frederic "Rick" Evans
Hiring Partner: Seth L. Rosen

PAY

New York and Washington, 2000
1st year: $125,000
2nd year: $135,000
3rd year: $150,000
4th year: $170,000
5th year: $190,000
6th year: $205,000
7th year: $220,000
8th year: $235,000
Summer associate: $2,400/week

NOTABLE PERKS

- Spousal benefits for same-sex domestic partners
- Parental leave: paid (10+ weeks maternity; 2 weeks parenting time) & unpaid
- Emergency child care
- Bi-weekly "lawyers' tea"
- Museum of Modern Art membership

THE BUZZ
What attorneys at other firms are saying about this firm

- "Some pretty exceptional people"
- "Pompous without reason"
- "Humane & smart"
- "Takes itself seriously"

UPPERS

- Screamer-free
- Lack of irksome micromanagement
- Strong and visible commitment to pro bono

DOWNERS

- Slow to respond to market trends
- Relatively little responsibility for junior associates
- Culture discourages feedback

KEY COMPETITORS

Cleary, Gottlieb, Steen & Hamilton
Davis Polk & Wardwell
Shearman & Sterling
Sullivan & Cromwell

EMPLOYMENT CONTACT

Ms. Ethel F. Leichti
Manager of Associate Recruitment
(212) 909-6657
recruit@debevoise.com

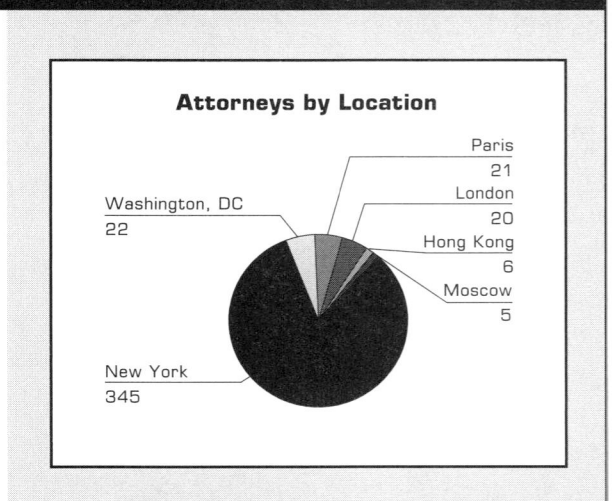

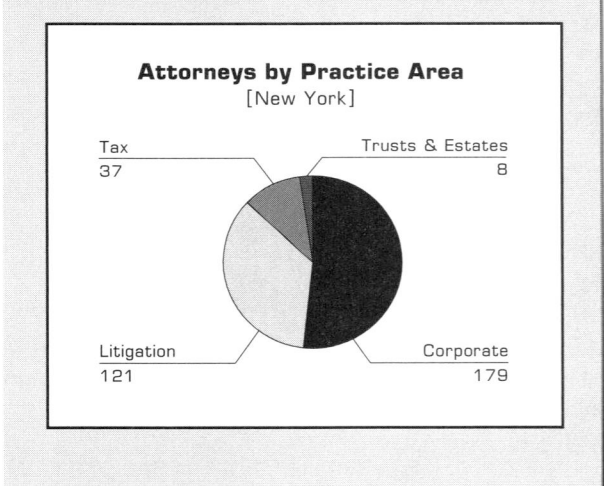

Attorneys by Location

- Paris: 21
- London: 20
- Hong Kong: 6
- Moscow: 5
- Washington, DC: 22
- New York: 345

Attorneys by Practice Area
[New York]

- Tax: 37
- Trusts & Estates: 8
- Corporate: 179
- Litigation: 121

QUALITY OF LIFE RANKINGS [ASSOCIATES RATE THEIR OWN FIRM]

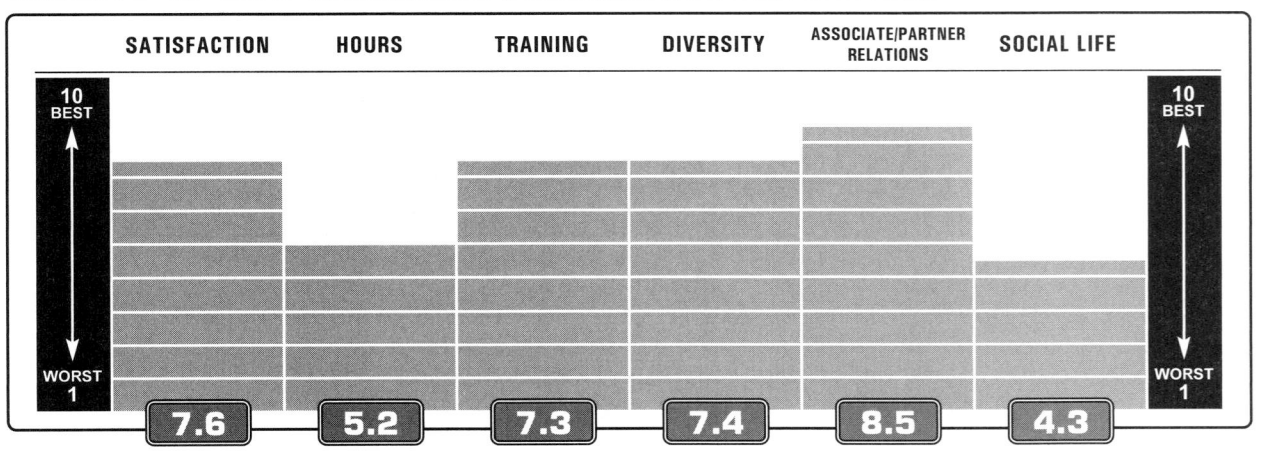

SATISFACTION	HOURS	TRAINING	DIVERSITY	ASSOCIATE/PARTNER RELATIONS	SOCIAL LIFE
7.6	5.2	7.3	7.4	8.5	4.3

(10 BEST / 1 WORST)

THE SCOOP

Debevoise & Plimpton is a rare specimen: a powerful New York law firm with a strong commitment to pro bono work. The firm also has prestigious litigation and corporate departments which attract an impressive lot of clients.

Following in historical footsteps

Despite lending their names to what would become one of the nation's most prominent law firms, the founders of Debevoise & Plimpton each have family members far more famous than themselves. Eli Whitney Debevoise was a descendant of Eli Whitney, the inventor of the cotton gin, and Francis T.P. Plimpton was the father of George Plimpton, the renowned aesthete and humorist. But along with William Stevenson, Debevoise and Plimpton made good on their names, building the firm's reputation through their government careers. Eli Debevoise became counsel to the High Commissioner for Germany in the early 1950s, while Francis Plimpton served as a delegate to the United Nations for Presidents Kennedy and Johnson. The New York office opened in 1931, and the firm began to expand in 1964 with its first foreign branch in Paris. The 1980s witnessed tremendous growth, with offices in Washington, DC (1982), Moscow (1988, receiving official accreditation in 1998) and London (1989). Most recently, the firm established a Hong Kong branch in 1994 and is currently in the process of opening an office in Frankfurt, further cementing its reputation as an international force. In the past year, more than 50 percent of the firm's work has been for non-U.S. matters or non-U.S. clients.

Show me the clients

With 345 attorneys in New York (419 firm-wide), Debevoise & Plimpton is statistically one of the smaller power players in the city. But its client list more than makes up the difference. American Airlines, PricewaterhouseCoopers, MetLife, and J.P. Morgan all come to Debevoise, as do the Democratic National Committee, *The New York Times*, and Goldman Sachs. The firm has made also its niche in entertainment and sports, representing Oxygen Media, the National Football League, and the National Hockey League, as well as working on the $320 million private purchase of the Cleveland Indians by Ohio attorney Lawrence Dolan in November 1999. The firm also represented Hasbro, Inc. in the toy industry's largest licensing transaction (Hasbro won worldwide toy and game rights to the *Star Wars* prequels) and the company's acquisition of Wizards of the Coast, Inc. (makers of the Pokemon trading card game and Dungeons & Dragons).

The firm has built its name primarily on its corporate work, and mergers & acquisitions are the corporate department's specialty. In 1999 the firm handled over

130 M&A transactions with a total value of over $430 billion, and stood up for some big names. D&P attorneys represented The Jim Henson Company, Inc. (creator of *Sesame Street* and the Muppets) in its over $900 million sale to the German media group EM.TV & Merchandising AG in March 2000. The firm is currently working for the financial advisors to AT&T's pending $58 billion acquisition of MediaOne Group, transacted in April 1999, and its $70 billion purchase of Tele-Communications, Inc. It is also counseling the financial advisors to Bell Atlantic's $53 billion merger with GTE and Telecom Italia in its April 1999 $82 billion merger with Deutsche Telecom. These numbers follow a year in which Debevoise represented Chrysler in its $38 billion merger with Daimler-Benz and served as advisor on the building of the $1.2 billion international terminal at JFK Airport, the largest U.S. airport privatization to date.

The litigation department has also gained attention in recent years. D&P successfully defended PricewaterhouseCoopers LLP in a trial involving allegations of professional liability and potential damages of over $50 million and is representing *The National Law Journal* in a defamation claim brought by Larry Klaman, chairman of the organization Judicial Watch, a conservative advocacy organization. Other cases involve Lever Brothers' trademark suit challenging the unauthorized use of its "Snuggle Bear" character as part of a violent video game as well as the Democratic National Committee's connection with government investigations into fundraising activities. Add to the list the representation of sexy firms John Hancock Mutual Life Insurance and Metropolitan Life Insurance in their demutualizations and IPOs as well as ongoing representation of Waste Management, Inc. in more than 30 class actions.

Bringing compensation up to speed

Despite such an impressive client roster, in the past there were muted complaints from associates' quarters about D&P's compensation packages. The firm has taken aggressive measures to silence such grievances in the past year or two. When Davis, Polk & Wardwell and Cravath, Swaine & Moore bumped up first-year salaries in February 2000, Debevoise quickly followed suit (offering first-years $125,000 a year in salary) in an ongoing effort to compete for the most sought-after law school grads. Lockstep bonuses are paid annually (not to be confused with boom year bonuses); generally the firm announces each class's bonus ahead of time, but this year "the firm has not been as forthcoming as to what the bonuses will be." Associates say they are "satisfied with the pay" since it is "generally competitive with other New York City firms." Still, at least one attorney suggests that the firm's "slowness in reacting to industry salary increases and reluctance to take a lead can cause associates to question the goodwill of the firm and at least temporarily hurts morale."

Name dispute

Apparently success has made the Debevoise moniker a valuable one in cyberspace as well as the legal world. In February 2000, the firm filed *Debevoise & Plimpton v. Moore*, winning damages from a cybersquatter who registered the firm's name as an Internet domain and then attempted to sell it back to the firm. Fellow plaintiffs include several other well-known firms across the country whose names were also registered. They charge that the squatter made "a bad-faith attempt to profit from the names and trademarks of these firms and then offered to sell those names [to the firms] or use them to promote his own interests," according to David Bernstein, the Debevoise & Plimpton partner who led the plaintiffs' case.

For the people

Another area in which Debevoise has marked its territory is public service work. The firm has received numerous accolades from various pro bono groups for its commitment to providing quality legal work to those in need. Most recently, Network for Women's Services honored the firm with its Commitment to Justice Award. The firm continues to handle more asylum cases for the Lawyers Committee for Human Rights than any other law firm, serving as counsel in litigations under the Torture Victims Protection Act and Alien Tort Claims Act involving human rights abuses around the world. *The American Lawyer* ranked the firm sixth out of its top 100 firms for pro bono work over the past five years — during that period, Debevoise topped the public service list in New York, logging 36,400 hours, four times as much as other firms of the same size. Again and again, Debevoise attorneys praise the firm's "remarkable level of public spiritedness," to the point that "many of the litigation partners seem more committed to doing good than to doing well." One attorney who dedicated over 75 percent of his time to pro bono last year says his experience is "unusual but not unheard of" and insists that "this is one area where D&P cannot be faulted."

The firm has demonstrated its pro bono commitment recently in several high-profile cases. Last fall, senior associate Natalie Williams led the firm in a class action against the City of New York, alleging that the police department's Street Crimes Unit has a policy of stopping and frisking black and Latino men, in violation of their constitutional rights. A few months earlier, the firm settled (in conjunction with the Center for Social Justice at Seton Hall University School of Law) a lawsuit against the New Jersey Department of Corrections on behalf of more than 2,000 New Jersey prisoners suffering from mental health disorders. The settlement will secure the mental health treatment and facilities the prisoners had been desperately lacking.

GETTING HIRED

Choice schools

When it comes to hiring new associates, Debevoise sticks with a core group of law schools — "Yale, NYU, Harvard, or Columbia." Even with a degree from those schools, though, the firm is "pretty picky" — there's a "cutoff in terms of grades even for top-tier law schools" — and will only tap Ivy League kids or the "equivalent with top 25 percent grades." Stanford, Cornell, and the University of Chicago send a few graduates D&P's way each year as well.

But there's more to the selection process than just prestigious diplomas and standout GPAs. Getting in requires "more than just being a workhorse," says one insider. "We're interested in finding people who are interesting, who lead interesting lives. Someone who knows things about the outside world — not just books." A New York litigator suggests that "people who've held jobs before law school tend to do better" due to expectations to "conduct yourself as a professional in an office." Another attorney says that "once you are over the bar on grades, you are then chosen on personality and 'would I want to work with you' factors." The interview process is in-depth, requiring each interviewer to fill out a detailed evaluation form in an effort to find just the right fit between the firm and its candidates. And while being "full of yourself" is relative "in reference to the population as a whole," don't be surprised that "oversized ego is generally not appreciated."

OUR SURVEY SAYS

Friendly but not forward

A number of Debevoise associates cite "never raise your voice" as the firm's golden rule, unwritten but understood. "No one will yell at you here," says one attorney, pleased that this is "not a place for shouters or obnoxious people — although some slip through the cracks." While this fosters a surprisingly "genteel" atmosphere and "reduces tension dramatically," some more outspoken attorneys worry that it also encourages "passive-aggressive" behavior. "D&P retains its WASPy roots in that people are reluctant to probe your personal life, don't really yell, and criticism is usually indirect," comments an insider from the corporate department. "While this reduces tension dramatically, it makes it hard to understand when you've done something wrong because everything is couched." A co-worker agrees, finding the office a "very nice and positive atmosphere" but one where "sometimes it's hard to get constructive criticism…because everyone is so worried about being nice."

The firm-wide respect for personal space impacts on social life as well, with "less mingling and socializing" than some associates would prefer. By and large, however, it seems that the attorneys heave a collective sigh of relief at the lack of pressure to hang out with other officemates after hours. The firm "doesn't send hordes of associates out drinking every night. People seem to have lives and interests outside the firm, and associates don't look to the firm as the source of their social life." This doesn't mean that there is infighting among the professional family, though; it just indicates that "there is no expectation that you'll socialize with your colleagues."

The family-first philosophy is pervasive regardless of gender or seniority, and attorneys put their money where their mouths are. An associate tells the story of a first interview in the New York City office: "When I interviewed at Debevoise, one of the partners had his kid in the office. He explained that his babysitter had gotten sick, so his kid was visiting Daddy's office for the afternoon. Debevoise was the only place I interviewed where such a thing would ever happen."

Hope springs eternal

Debevoise & Plimpton attorneys in New York perhaps should think about getting out together more often, since many of them seem pretty darn cranky about their office environs. Some are more critical than others: "The air-conditioning sucks — I'm sweating right now — and the office furniture is cheap and ugly," grouses one. Others exhibit a don't-hold-your-breath attitude: "Offices are not good. New offices are coming. We'll see." In light of the anticipated move in 2001, one corporate lawyer finds it understandable that "very little effort" has been made "in the way of decorating, or even maintaining our offices, which are small, poorly laid-out, unkempt, and crumbling." As a result, though, there is not "a single healthy plant on any of the 12 floors" the firm occupies.

But the glass-is-half-full contingent is holding out "hope, though, that the new offices will be presentable, if not quite 'posh.'" It may have good reason, according to a colleague: "I have been working on the planning committee for the new space and I can say with certainty that the new offices will be nothing short of swank."

So-so support staff

Will the new digs come equipped with new support services? The "quality of the staff varies greatly," according to insiders. While "the litigation support people and the legal assistants tend to be excellent," tech support suffers a bit and secretarial help is widely derided. "The folks who manage the secretarial pool should be dumped post haste," cries one beleaguered litigator. An associate in M&A huffs that "secretaries regularly refuse to do certain basic tasks for more junior associates, and the overall quality of secretarial services is quite poor."

Women on the way up

Debevoise continues to fight the good fight to promote gender equality in its ranks. A number of associates rave about the part-time program, "from which part-time associates actually make partner," and the generous family leave. "One of the most recent people to make partner is a woman who works part-time, and she isn't the first."

But other associates worry she may be the exception rather than the rule, because "while the firm does attract a substantial number of female attorneys," women "appear to have difficulty advancing at the firm. Many factors contribute to this difficulty, including limited access to female mentors, the perception that part-time takes certain women off the partnership track, and different messages from senior attorneys with respect to workload, public-speaking opportunities, and other professional development opportunities."

Minorities? What minorities?

Women's issues might gain the spotlight occasionally at the firm, but the same cannot necessarily be said for minority representation. While "on the associate level, the firm is fairly diverse," there are no specific mentoring programs or other programs for attorneys of color and "very little is said about the specific problems that attorneys of color might face." This takes its toll eventually, as "diversity among partners is non-existent." Currently Debevoise has only one minority partner at the firm, prompting associates to observe that "possibly the firm is trying hard, but it is not succeeding very well."

At the same time, associates don't question the firm's receptiveness to gays and lesbians. Many say they have "no idea" where the firm stands because it "simply isn't an issue here positively or negatively." With a "number of openly gay attorneys and support staff," associates seem comfortable enough. "No one seems to have a problem with that and the policies are great," notes one source.

Do-si-do your partner round

As befits an institution that prides itself on civil tones, associates are somewhat reluctant to criticize partners' treatment of them. Most say that they've had "really good experiences with partners here so far." Partners are "usually polite" and "generally take their responsibilities in mentoring seriously." Even if "'great respect' is too strong a term," the good ones "tend to be extremely helpful and caring." But sometimes frustration seeps through, as with one New York securities associate: "Although I work part-time, I don't get any consideration for the fact that I can't do all the work that I'm asked to do in the time I have to do it. God forbid if anything falls through."

As for those who aspire to the whip-cracking partnership themselves, chances are typically "slim to non-existent," although some would say the prospect "doesn't seem impossible if one is a well-rounded lawyer — genial and skilled." Others liken prospects to "the odds of winning the New York Lotto." Most say it's important to connect with the right mentor (read: "sucking up to the right people") and do "excellent work for some of the firm's bigger and more well-known clients." But when push comes to shove, it has as much to do with being a "kick-ass lawyer" and putting in "a lot of hours" — knowing, however, that "the latter won't do that much good without the former" — as with "not pissing anyone off."

Making a name for itself

"Traditionally, Debevoise was regarded as a corporate powerhouse, with reliable blue-chip clients like American Airlines and Chrysler," says an in-the-know attorney. "In recent years, the reputation of the litigation department has been increasing to the point where now law students seem to regard the firm as more of a destination for would-be litigators than for aspiring Barbarians at the Gate." Indeed, the firm has truly spread its wings in litigation in recent years (particularly relating to International Arbitration and class action suits) and is gaining attention for its IP/new media work. Although D&P's reputation remains "less flashy than [at] some other firms" and "not a firm that seeks headlines," its internal community considers it "a big name in its own quiet way."

You wish you could be us

It seems most would like to keep it that way and would send the sharks somewhere else. "If you want to work in a civil environment with decent, intelligent colleagues… think seriously about Debevoise & Plimpton. If you prefer a take-no-prisoners approach, consider Skadden or Paul Weiss," intones one happy camper. "Do not come here if you want a super-aggressive, high-drama environment," warns another.

Of course, attrition is similar to most large firms in the city. Debevoise has been characterized as having experienced a "mass exodus since the beginning of the year," though the firm claims that the departure rate is no worse than it has been in the past. The situation "doesn't seem to have as much to do with associate dissatisfaction as it does with better opportunities elsewhere — and in some cases outside of law altogether." As another philosopher puts it, "Hey, it's a job. There are going to be problems. But D&P has a good and interesting group of people, good clients, practices law very seriously, and does a lot of pro bono work — you have to take the rough with the smooth."

INTERVIEW TIP #11

DON'T seem tired. "Be fresh-faced and interested, even if it's your seventh interview of the day. Never admit that you're exhausted. If you can't make it through a day of interviews, they'll wonder how you'll make it through a week at work," advises one lawyer.

19 O'Melveny & Myers LLP
PRESTIGE RANKING

400 South Hope Street
Suite 1576
Los Angeles, CA 90071-2899
(213) 430-6000
Fax: (213) 430-6407
www.omm.com

LOCATIONS

Los Angeles, CA (HQ)
Century City, CA • Irvine, CA • New York, NY • Newport Beach, CA • San Francisco, CA • Tysons Corner, VA • Washington, DC • Hong Kong • London • Shangai • Tokyo

MAJOR DEPARTMENTS/PRACTICES

Corporate Reorganization and Restructuring
Corporations
Entertainment and Media
Intellectual Property
International Trade
Labor and Employment Law
Litigation
Real Estate, Environmental and Natural Resources
Tax and Estate Planning

THE STATS

No. of attorneys: 752
No. of offices: 12
Summer associate offers: 151 out of 153
Managing Partner: Charles Bender
Hiring Partner: A. B. Culvahouse
National Recruiting Partner: Mark Steinberg

PAY

All Domestic Offices, 2000
1st year: $125,000
2nd year: $135,000
3rd year: $150,000
4th year: $165,000
5th year: $185,000
6th year: $195,000
7th year: $205,000
8th year: $210,000
Summer associate: $2,400/week

Figures are "base" figures; in compensation year 2000 lawyers are eligible for discretionary and productivity bonuses.

NOTABLE PERKS

- "Doughnut days" every other week
- Tickets to sporting events
- Take-a-partner to lunch program
- Connections to the movie industry; occasional invitations to premieres and Oscar screenings
- Attorney dining room catered by the Four Seasons Hotel

THE BUZZ
What attorneys at other firms are saying about this firm

- "Would the last associate to leave please turn off the lights?"
- "First-rate West Coast and East Coast firm"
- "Entrenched — don't count them out"
- "Spartacus would have been at home"

UPPERS

- L.A. office ocean views
- More outgoing attorneys than your garden-variety big-firm lawyers
- Kick-ass work and brilliant attorneys
- Excellent resume-builder

DOWNERS

- Poor communication between partners and associates
- Out-of-date technology infrastructure
- Late arrival to the new economy
- Not much partner supervision

KEY COMPETITORS

Gibson, Dunn & Crutcher
Latham & Watkins
Paul, Hastings, Janofsky & Walker

EMPLOYMENT CONTACT

Ms. Michele Marinaro
Recruiting Manager
(213) 430-6677
mmarinaro@omm.com

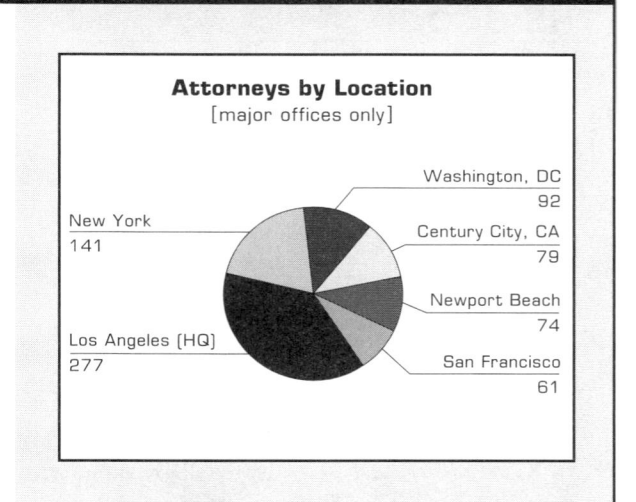

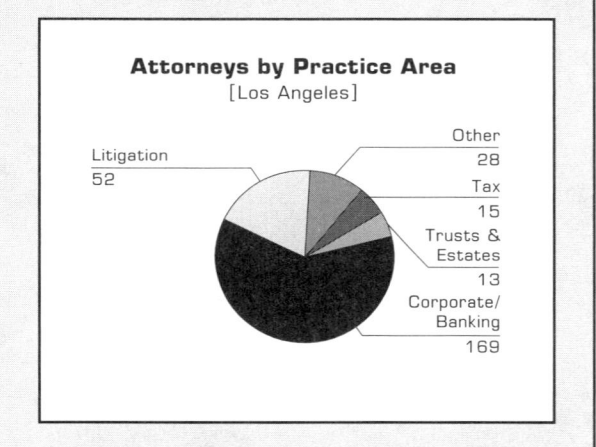

Attorneys by Location [major offices only]

- Washington, DC: 92
- Century City, CA: 79
- Newport Beach: 74
- San Francisco: 61
- Los Angeles (HQ): 277
- New York: 141

Attorneys by Practice Area [Los Angeles]

- Other: 28
- Tax: 15
- Trusts & Estates: 13
- Corporate/Banking: 169
- Litigation: 52

QUALITY OF LIFE RANKINGS [ASSOCIATES RATE THEIR OWN FIRM]

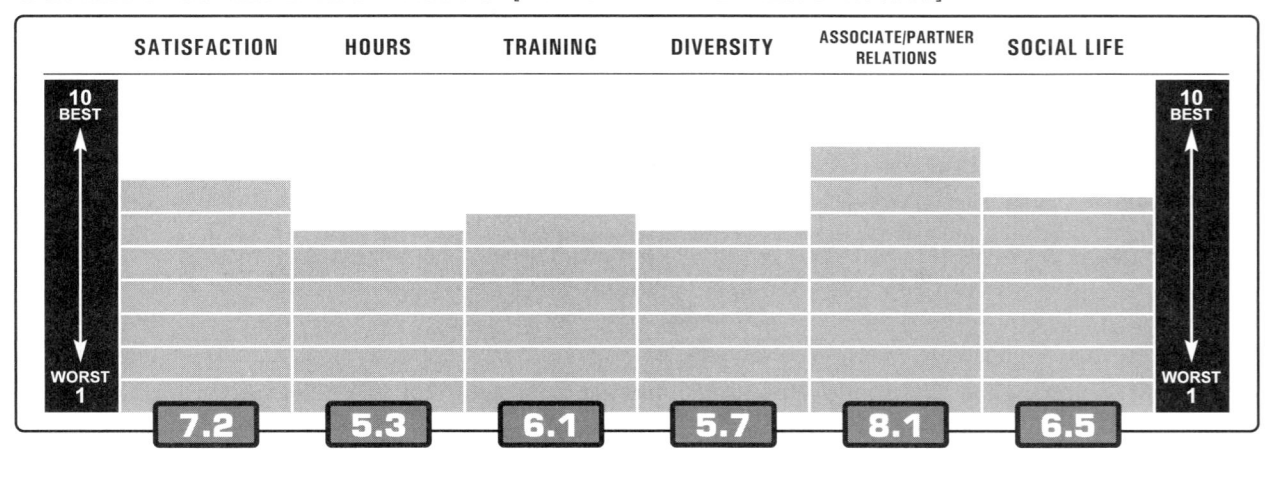

SATISFACTION	HOURS	TRAINING	DIVERSITY	ASSOCIATE/PARTNER RELATIONS	SOCIAL LIFE
7.2	5.3	6.1	5.7	8.1	6.5

THE SCOOP

One of the "Big Three" Los Angeles-based law firms, O'Melveny & Myers boasts a global practice known for its strength in litigation and a stable of corporate clients including Ford, Citigroup, Disney, Marriott, and CIGNA Corp. Yet insiders say the firm is facing an identity crisis, unsure whether to focus more on profitability and billable hours or its traditional law practice.

L.A. law

O'Melveny is quite conscious of its own history — a curator oversees the firm's artwork, historical archives, and small O'Melveny museum in Los Angeles (with tours available by appointment). The history begins with the firm's founding by Jackson A. Graves and Henry O'Melveny in 1885, at which time the population of the City of Angels had ballooned to all of 15,000 souls. Nonetheless, legal business was brisk as land speculators relied on lawyers to accomplish their sometimes less-than-savory deals. Thus the firm enjoyed early success and quickly rose to prominence in the community. In fact, founder Henry O'Melveny was the third Angeleno to get a telephone installed in the city. As L.A. began to resemble its present sprawl, the firm grew, taking on bigger clients such as Goodyear Tire & Rubber and Pacific Mutual Life Insurance. An important O'Melveny milestone came in 1969 when the firm hired Diana Walker, one of the firm's first women lawyers and later its first female partner.

Jack O'Melveny, son of founder Henry, took an early lead in developing the firm's entertainment clientele. High-rolling clients included Mary Pickford, Bing Crosby, Jack Benny, Jimmy Stewart and Gary Cooper as well as institutional clients such as CBS, Paramount, and Walt Disney Productions. Indeed, O'Melveny was so involved with the entertainment industry that it opened a small office in 1951 right on Sunset Boulevard (the office was relocated in 1970 to Century City).

O'Melveny muscle

Ever since O'Melveny represented the bank group that financed Kohlberg Kravis & Roberts' (KKR) spectacular $24.8 billion buyout of RJR Nabisco in 1988, O'Melveny has been a force to be reckoned with in the legal world (particularly in the corporate sphere). Left Coast-based O'Melveny, unsuprisingly, has strong ties to the media and entertainment industry. In addition to representing Disney in its major investment in Infoseek in 1998, the firm has moved into the wide world of sports. OMM attorneys advised Peter O'Malley in that year's sale of the Dodgers to Fox Inc.; in more controversial matters, the firm is currently representing the International Olympic Committee in the bribery scandal surrounding the 2002 Winter Olympics in Salt Lake City. It's also worth noting that O'Melveny is lead counsel in a current federal court challenge to the legality of the managed care industry — a suit originally brought by star litigator David Boies (formerly of Cravath).

Of course, no California firm would be complete without high tech clients. The ball really got rolling in August 1998 when longtime client GTE Corp. tapped O'Melveny to represent it in its $70 billion merger with Bell Atlantic. At the time of its announcement the merger was the fourth-largest in U.S. history. Another indicator of O'Melveny's M&A prowess was its selection in November 1998 by Lockheed-Martin Corp. to work on its plan to acquire Comsat Corporation, a government-created satellite telecommunications company. Both companies anticipate at least two years of intense legal and lobbying work to complete the $2.7 billion transaction since closing the deal will require revision of the 1962 federal law that created Comsat. Since then, O'Melveny has also garnered attention for its representation of the lead underwriter in MP3.com's IPO (the popular and controversial online music company went public in May 1999). OMM was the first L.A. law firm to follow the Silicon Valley practice of accepting equity in start-up clients in lieu of legal fees.

Identity crisis

Despite these successful ventures, O'Melveny & Myers has had a few issues in the past few years, particularly with its corporate practice. Over the course of the 1990s, a number of OMM's major clients, such as Security Pacific National Bank and First Interstate Bank, abandoned their work with O'Melveny due to consolidations, bankruptcies, and relocations. The firm didn't bounce back quickly. When the other big L.A. firms like Latham & Watkins and Gibson, Dunn & Crutcher saw the writing (or programming?) on the wall and established new offices in Silicon Valley, O'Melveny was slower on the draw and has trailed the other firms in profits ever since. The firm has also lagged behind its competitors in the corporate M&A scene. John Beisner, a member of O'Melveny's 12-person management committee, told *The American Lawyer* in February 2000 that the firm had gotten too complacent and didn't articulate a specific vision, stating "[that OMM had] become too insular and failed to make little changes to keep up with the market."

In the face of spiraling associate salaries, the firm has been forced to step up to the plate. While "O'Melveny has shown its commitment to matching the salaries of the top-paying firms," some associates feel that "the partnership has been fairly vocal about its bitterness in having to give [associates] these raises." Still, O'Melveny has been awarding bonuses regularly; the firm gives discretionary bonuses of $5,000 and productivity bonuses of up to $37,500. O'Melveny claims that in 2000, more than 60 percent of all associates received "exceptional bonuses."

Once profits declined the firm committed itself to major changes. It christened a new office in Virginia's high tech corridor last year and opened another office in high tech paradise Menlo Park in summer 2000, employing a total of 760 lawyers worldwide. (O'Melveny also opened an office in Irvine, California in April 2000.) Firm revenues increased by an estimated $380 million by the end of the 1999 fiscal year, an increase of 16 percent from the previous year.

Much of this growth is attributed to a shakeup in leadership; the firm's first new chairman in eight years was to be named by summer 2000. Semi-celeb Warren Christopher, who left the post in 1992 after 10 years at the firm to become President Clinton's Secretary of State, has proven a tough act to follow. According to C. Douglas Kranwinkle in *The American Lawyer*, "Chris had the moral authority of God." Though perhaps not filling the void left by Christopher's departure, the firm did receive a new addition from the political world recently — politico Ronald Klain, chief of staff to Al Gore and Janet Reno, joined the DC office as a partner in August 1999. The adept Klain is now counselling AOL in its proposed merger with media behemoth Time Warner.

Quick, call O'Melveny & Myers!

O'Melveny's litigation practice remains strong and prestigious. Once again, the firm's ties to the media biz are evident. In 1998 the firm successfully defended *Time* magazine in a libel case brought by Kato Kaelin's former girlfriend over the publication's coverage of the O.J. Simpson trial. Time, Inc. selected O'Melveny again in March 1999 to represent it in connection with congressional hearings on sweepstakes promotions, an allegedly shady practice that nevertheless brought the magazine no less than 1.4 million new subscribers in 1998. On the IP side, O'Melveny was tapped by Connecticut's Bristol Technologies, a software producer suing Microsoft on — guess what — antitrust grounds.

In December 1999, the firm defended Ford in a $3 billion California class action suit charging the company with installing a defective ignition system in 1.7 million vehicles between 1983 and 1995. Fresh from the fight, O'Melveny lawyers kicked off the new millennium by leading Apple Computer's legal assault on iMac knockoffs. Guess not everyone "thinks different!"

Law everywhere

O'Melveny & Myers first ventured abroad in the mid-1960s when the firm established a Paris office. Since entering the U.K. market through a partnership in the late 1980s, the firm has established a solid presence with its London office. O'Melveny has fared well in other regions, too, especially Asia. The firm set up shop in Japan in 1987, becoming one of the first American firms to do so. In 1996 it became the second firm to be admitted to practice in China. (The firm also has a partnership in Beijing with the Chinese law firm King & Wood.) OMM was also admitted to practice law in China-controlled Hong Kong. Moreover, O'Melveny has cultivated its contacts in Latin America and in August 1998 represented Telecom Italia in its $3 billion bid for three Brazilian telecom companies. O'Melveny counts as clients public entities from such far-flung locales as Ecuador, Mexico, Canada, and even the Federated States of Micronesia.

Public counsel

O'Melveny has a distinguished history of pro bono work. In March 1998, the firm took on pro bono representation of the City of Los Angeles in connection with its attempt to use "statistical sampling" techniques at the U.S. Census bureau. The engagement was the firm's most significant pro bono matter in 1998 and 1999. Clients represented in the case included not only L.A. but the states of Texas and New Mexico, the U.S. Conference of Mayors, 20 members of Congress, and other cities such as Chicago, New York, and San Francisco.

The firm finally won a long-time pro bono case in 1999. O'Melveny took the case on behalf of local residents who were swindled in a housing scam, winning a settlement of about $400,000 — and prompting teary thanks from many elderly plaintiffs who thought their case had long been forgotten. They had reason to think so — O'Melveny had been handling the case for 18 years.

Beautiful Belmont

The firm has also made waves in the L.A. area for its involvement with the controversial development of the Belmont Learning Complex a school. O'Melveny lawyers (including real estate attorneys David Cartwright and Lisa Gooden) were hired by school district administrators to assist in an ambitious project to tie the school construction with various community and business initiatives. The firm, however, found itself on the wrong end of conflict-of-interest accusations, as it represented the school district in the project despite having had advised the project's construction company, Kajima Corp, on an unrelated matter. Although the school board and contractor waived any conflicts, it later removed Cartwright as counsel on the matter in February 1999. To complicate matters, controversy arose over an environmental problem at the school's construction site (which was atop abandoned oil fields.) The L.A. Unified School District filed a suit charging that OMM gave faulty advice on the project regarding environmental conditions. In response, O'Melveny began conducting tests at the nearby Belmont High School in March 2000 hoping to demonstrate that conditions at the high school, which operates safely, are comparable to those at Belmont Learning Complex.

Other local matters include the firm's counsel to the ports of L.A. and Long Beach (along with the Alameda Corridor Transportation Authority) to negotiate the $2.4 billion Alameda Corridor, an infrastructure project connecting local ports with transcontinental railroad lines.

When the firm recently raised salaries and bonuses to match competing firms' increases, there was some debate about which hours would count towards an associate's minimum hours requirement and which hours would be counted for calculating an associate's bonus. Says an insider who was around for the process, "Throughout this debate, there was never a question raised — at least publicly — about whether pro bono hours would continue to be included for both." They are. But some associates still feel that "the commitment is more lip service than actuality with the increased pressure on all attorneys to bill more." One comments that "the feeling definitely is that pro bono that will be high-profile (impact litigation) for the firm is actually more valuable than individual representation of indigent or disadvantaged folks." Another caveat is that all pro bono work must be approved in advance for each associate involved.

GETTING HIRED

O'Melveny likes A's

Most contacts at O'Melveny & Myers tell us that the firm looks closely at applicants' grades when making hiring decisions. "OMM seeks to hire top students from the top schools. If you met [the firm's] minimum requirements, you have a personality and you do not offend anyone, then you have a very good chance of getting hired. Otherwise, forget it." An associate in the capital city office says that while fit matters, "unless a student is in a top-tier school, our office doesn't really look beyond the top five percent, even at DC schools." And since "OMM does not hire very many laterals," the "focus is on the summer recruitment program," which means prospective candidates have to sell themselves to the firm early on.

A beautiful mosaic of schools

Second-tier residents take note — O'Melveny has been known to select people with top-notch credentials from less famous or prestigious schools, "demonstrating its recognition that great lawyers don't all come from Stanford, Harvard, and Yale," according to one associate. Slackers can take some small comfort in this fact: with the booming legal market and high turnover, the firm has been known to waiver from its high standards. "They have pretty stringent law school and grades criteria here," says one associate, "but those can change if a particular candidate fits a perceived need." Another agrees: "In recent years OMM has interviewed at more schools — more than 30. And while the firm is selective at each school, I would say the sheer number of schools has led to a decrease in selectivity."

Interviewing with "a friendly face"

The first step in the O'Melveny hiring process is the on-campus interview. Generally, one partner and one associate from the hiring committee conduct the interview, although the number might vary from school to school. Candidates who pass O'Melveny muster on campus are then assigned a hiring attorney, who telephones one week after the interview to call back for the next round. For callbacks, the firm will pay for lodging and expenses.

The second round lasts half the day, either in the morning or the afternoon. The hiring attorney, "a friendly face," greets the candidate and spends 15 minutes explaining the order of events and interviewers and taking any last minute questions from the candidate. Candidates then interview with both associates and partners, each interview lasting about half an hour. Note also that the candidate will most likely interview with attorneys from the particular practice group in which they have expressed an interest. At the end of the morning or afternoon, the firm takes the candidate out to eat, accompanied by either an associate or partner. Third-years who interview go out for both lunch and dinner.

OUR SURVEY SAYS

Partners from on high

While many attorneys say that they are "generally impressed with partner/associate interaction" and that "some partners are always nice and take the time to discuss an issue or a project," there remain significant dissatisfactions among associates. In addition to a perception of bitterness on the partners' part in response to salary raises, "most partners do a poor job of giving guidance and making younger associates feel like they are part of the team on transactions," according to an L.A. lawyer. Others agree that "there is no pretense of mentoring unless you happen to be handpicked by a certain partner. Otherwise, you're totally on your own to figure out what to do with your career here and beyond." A litigator mentions that the DC office is a "very masculine" one and that "the managing partner chats with white, clean-cut male associates in the hallways but barely acknowledges the female associates; it is not an accident that the DC office has not had a female partner in years."

'Many are called, few are chosen'

Several associates mention that partnership prospects might be vastly improved "if you are male." According to a DC associate, "many of the male partners married only after they were made partners. Although several of the senior male associates were married before they joined the firm, most of the female associates are either unattached or ended a serious relationship after they joined the firm. One partner joked that you 'cannot be a female litigation associate and have a social life.'"

Of course, many other factors come into play. An associate eyeing the top spot would do well to "bring in business, develop a name in the community, and devote himself totally and completely to the practice of law and the firm." It wouldn't hurt to "stay out of politics" and hope that "the market is as good as it is today." An associate offers this set of directions: "First, you have to be a golden boy. Then you have to manage to STAY one and not piss anyone off for eight or so years. It's basically like trying to get yourself through the eye of the needle." It's all about the "marketing, baby."

As you like it

Social life at the firm seems to depend on branch office and department. The L.A. litigators rave about their "very cohesive" group which "eats lunch together on most days" (the partners "rarely go to the dining room for lunch but they do show up at social events now and again") and has "happy hour on most Friday evenings." Other departments in that office are a bit less effusive. While the corporate "people are very nice and everyone takes time to go to lunch with other attorneys," associates "go their separate ways after work and the firm basically has NO social events outside of the summer program." A labor/employment attorney adds that "everyone gets along with respect but this is not a fraternity where everyone goes out drinking after work."

DC litigators seem to cultivate a cozy camaraderie. "Sure, we have lives and friends outside the firm," says one, "but people really seem to enjoy seeing each other socially. It's a very friendly, very open and yet tight-knit group." Another DC O'Melveny associate finds the firm "much more social than my last firm" and has been "to any number of parties/events with friends from work." Some associates still bemoan a lack of opportunity for socializing, finding that "there are chances to get to know colleagues in non-work settings — including the running club, summer associate events, and the attorney dining room" but that "few take advantage of those opportunities except the attorney dining room."

Regardless of the degree of social interaction outside the firm, most associates seem relieved that "it is all up to the individual" and that "nobody is forced to do anything," in the words of a New York lawyer. Well, with some notable exceptions — a colleague complains that "lately it seems that most of the social interaction among associates occurs at farewell parties."

Can we get some training around here?

Associates are lukewarm in their praise for O'Melveny's training programs. "Training tends to be informal," says one DC litigator, "although formal training opportunities do exist. We're formalizing as we go." Most associates seem to agree that "training is mostly by experience;" even though "the orientation program gives some training, like the mock deposition program," newly-minted attorneys "mostly learn by doing it." A New York real estate associate suggests that "most learning occurs by working closely with partners and senior associates to get transactions closed." And herein lies the problem for many associates who feel that training by partners "is an area in which the firm has been traditionally been weak." An L.A. associate says that "the most important source of training — partners giving guidance in specific situations — is sorely lacking." An officemate backs him up: "Often a partner's need to get work done trumps an associate's need to improve skills by attending training." A DC colleague counsels patience, certain that "the partnership is keenly aware of this and lately has taken steps to improve training. So far, so good. But it's still early for a final verdict."

Our house is a very, very, very fine house

OMM attorneys wax eloquent when talking about their offices. In Orange County, "the joke is that the partners had an unlimited budget when they built this office and they exceeded it. All offices look out at either the ocean and Newport Harbor or the Big Canyon Golf Course. Our attorney dining room is catered by the Four Seasons Hotel. Things are definitely first-class." In L.A., "the Century City office recently added a new floor (making for a total of four floors)." Even if "the offices are a little old-school and traditional," with "dark wood," the "art collection is impressive" and "the new floor has all new furniture and looks great." In New York, O'Melveny is "one of the only firms that give first-years their own offices" which "makes a great difference in how much work you can get done." Some spatial issues can never be resolved, though, as a DC associate gripes that his "office is small compared to the stacks of paper that inhabit it."

We need more help!

Keeping the house in order seems a more daunting task at O'Melveny & Myers these days. While there is "24/7 word processing and proofreading help," attorneys wish they could have "additional tech support:" "What we have is good, we just need more." Same goes for paralegal staffing — the firm "could use more and better paralegal help" since "the support needs to grow to match the size of the office."

Associates aren't holding their collective breath, however; the firm "can't keep paralegals because OMM doesn't pay them dirt." Some don't hold back on their criticisms, expressing that "the secretaries often suck" and "support staff personnel are not very competent and generally not very willing to go out of their way at all to be helpful." Across the board, "there is definitely a perception that O'Melveny does not hire the best secretaries."

A litigation attorney in DC offers an analysis of the problem. "A lot of our long-time secretaries left in the last five years because other firms pay their staff more. As a result, lots of attorneys have had to work with floater secretaries for long stretches. The firm's salary for legal assistants is also below market. Thus legal assistants leave before their unenforceable two-year commitment is up, causing associates to work with inexperienced legal assistants and often doing the work of legal assistants. Partners are then forced to write off associates' times which decreases their own productivity rating and cuts into their partners' bonus." Never let it be said that lawyers can't reason.

Women in the (low) ranks

Women tend to leave O'Melveny before reaching the firm's upper echelons, according to insiders. While "management seems genuinely committed to hiring, training and keeping women in the department" and perhaps "the problem with the gender disparity is more one of benign neglect than any outward hostility or animosity," associates still tend to believe that "women come here but they don't stay." The L.A. office counts "one female litigation partner" among its own and "only a few others firm-wide." A DC litigator says there is "not one woman partner" in that neck of the woods.

Insiders speculate that the situation is rooted in the fact that "part-time work is de facto discouraged." Some associates suggest that "there's no such thing as part-time here — not if you really want to stay on track with your career." With the recent increase in salaries, it may "be very difficult for women attorneys to go part-time in order to meet the needs of their young families." Informal mentoring is "theoretically the same for women and men but it's hit-or-miss, and with no women partners it's a little more challenging." Furthermore, some attorneys have the "impression that females are treated like 'worker bees' or 'fill-in people.'" One DC litigator attributes the atmosphere to the leadership, not other associates: "The male associates here are great. They have bemoaned the [discrepancies in treatment between men and women] as much as I have. They feel it's unfair. It's the partners. It's not that they discriminate against women, it's just that favoritism abounds here and the favorites have never been female."

Everybody in white?

Nobody is thrilled with the firm's efforts to recruit and promote minority attorneys, either. Several attorneys say they "see no effort at all. The firm certainly does not intentionally discriminate against minorities but there is no affirmative effort to encourage diversity." Others say that while the firm has "made great efforts to hire more attorneys who are not white," it's a "vicious cycle — we don't yet have enough minority attorneys here to convince others that it is a good place to work." A New York litigation associate points out that "there are no African-Americans in the New York office and few elsewhere in this firm (oh, unless you count the staff!)" — "good efforts but mediocre results."

Associates are more reluctant to comment on OMM's reception of gay and lesbian attorneys, mostly because they simply find it "hard to say" where the firm stands. Many say they "have no idea what the policies are" (for the record, the firm does offer same-sex domestic partner benefits) and "don't know of any openly gay associates or partners." (The firm currently has three associates who publicly identify themselves as gay.) One cynical Bay Area associate suggests that while "hiring and advancement are strong," the firm "went to domestic partner benefits only because we do business with the City of San Francisco, which requires it of city contractors." An L.A. associate sums up the general vibe that the firm isn't "homophobic in general but for some reason gay and lesbian associates are not very comfortable with either coming to work here or being out of the closet once they get here. This is a problem that is endemic to the legal profession and not just O'Melveny."

An intriguing culture

When it comes to catchphrases to sum up O'Melveny's atmosphere, the firm seems to be at a crossroads. Some associates describe OMM as a place that "clings strongly to its history" while others say it is "on the cutting edge;" it is alternately "uptight" and "relaxed," a "flat organization" at the same time it is described as "hierarchical." Even in the same office, associates contradict each other's assessments; one says there is "too much factionalism" while another says that the firm is very "team-oriented." But there is consensus on certain contradictions — many attorneys say O'Melveny is "laid-back for a law firm" even if it is "definitely conservative."

One critic says that "everything is subtext here. The rules are unclear. You find them out the hard way when you've done the wrong thing. Associates navigate their career here in the dark. A few get mentored and told what's what behind closed doors but the rest have to try to read the subtext." A San Francisco colleague also finds the culture "odd" and thinks there is "lots of distrust between associates and partners (as groups, not individually). Management is stiff and inflexible much of the time." But others would argue that even though "the firm does not go out of its way to coddle all the associates," it does "recognize, train, encourage, and reward people with skill and who work hard."

Perhaps the firm is best described right now as "confused, switching from L.A. laid-back to New York corporate" in terms of atmosphere. Indeed, there seems to be a "movement among the younger partners to make O'Melveny more aggressive and more business-like." This evolution from an "old line, white shoe" firm brings with it the "struggle to move forward." Some attorneys worry that even though "many of these changes are much needed," there is also a sense of loss that some of the firm's long-standing values are changing. But no matter how "in flux" the firm may be, at the end of the day O'Melveny values "smart lawyers who aren't smart asses."

Dressing the part

O'Melveny takes its "laid-back" image seriously enough to have instituted all casual dress, all the time, except in the DC office (where an insider states that casual days are "only when the senior partner is out of town," though the firm says it's simply confined to Fridays in the summer months) and New York City (which is also business casual only in the summertime). For most this translates into "basic, preppy, unimaginative dress — khaki pants and polo shirts for guys," with "most dressing comfortably but not trashy." The dress code is "more an issue for the men" than for the women as "partners have approached the men to tell them they must wear a collared shirt under any sweater." One associate says that "women dress in a style I like to call 'Ann Taylor Lite.' The men wear Dockers and golf shirts although some wear Banana Republic."

The rep is right

Many of O'Melveny & Myers associates came to the firm for "exciting work," particularly its "power base" litigation practice as well as its "outstanding" entertainment work and "very strong international presence." They cite the firm's "flexible practice areas" and its "reputation in the community as a great stepping stone" as well. But many have stayed because "the mix of people here is its true strength" and because O'Melveny seems "more committed to leading a balanced family life than many competing firms." One litigator says he came because he "didn't sense any fear in the atmosphere" and a co-worker perceived OMM "as a kinder, gentler big-firm practice — intense and demanding but humane."

Some associates worry that the qualities that first drew them to O'Melveny are eroding. An associate in DC laments that when he was hired "the firm was much less hours-conscious than it is now. It was also less inclined to eat its own." He recalls that "the firm was proud that it did not lay off any attorneys during the 1980s recession. Now the younger partners are determined to make the firm more lucrative."

INTERVIEW TIP #12

DO know the culture of the firm. If you are interviewing at a high-powered firm, you should project a high-powered image. For example, we hear that one law firm administers a "weekend test." Confides a veteran of the interview process: "They will ask you if you would work all weekend if they handed you a project on Friday. If you are serious about working there, the answer is yes."

White & Case LLP

VAULT.COM PRESTIGE RANKING: 20

1155 Avenue of the Americas
New York, NY 10036-2787
(212) 819-8200
www.whitecase.com

LOCATIONS

New York, NY (HQ)
Los Angeles, CA
Miami, FL
Palo Alto, CA
Washington, DC
28 other offices worldwide

MAJOR DEPARTMENTS/PRACTICES

Corporate and Financial
Intellectual Property
Litigation
Tax
Trusts & Estates

THE STATS

No. of attorneys: 1,000+
No. of offices: 33
Summer associate offers: 65 out of 65 (New York, 1999)
Managing Partner: Duane Wall
Hiring attorney: David N. Koschik

PAY

New York, Los Angeles, and Washington, 2000
1st year: $125,000
2nd year: $135,000
3rd year: $150,000
4th year: $170,000
5th year: $190,000
6th year: $200,000
7th year: $205,000
8th year: $210,000
Summer associate (New York): $2,403/week
Summer associate (Los Angeles): $2,403/week
Summer associate (Washington): $2,400/week
Summer Associate (Palo Alto): $2,403/week

Miami, 2000
1st year: $105,000
2nd year: $110,000
3rd year: $120,000
4th year: $140,000
5th year: $155,000
6th year: $165,000
7th year: $170,000
8th year: $175,000
Summer Associate: $2,019/week

NOTABLE PERKS

- Back-up day care centers
- Firm gym (firm supplies clothes and does laundry)
- Season tickets for sporting events (for entertaining clients)

THE BUZZ

What attorneys at other firms are saying about this firm

- "White and Whiter"
- "Fading fast"
- "Well-rounded practice"
- "Good thing they're not merging with Brown & Wood"

UPPERS

- Attractive attorneys
- Good feedback
- Low dweeb ratio

DOWNERS

- Offices need a facelift
- Lagging pay
- Training is a joke

KEY COMPETITORS

Clifford, Chance, Rogers & Wells
Jones, Day, Reavis & Pogue
Mayer, Brown & Platt
Milbank, Tweed, Hadley & McCloy
Shearman & Sterling

EMPLOYMENT CONTACT

Ms. Dana E. Stephenson
Director of Attorney Recruiting & Employment
(212) 819-8200
recruit@whitecase.com

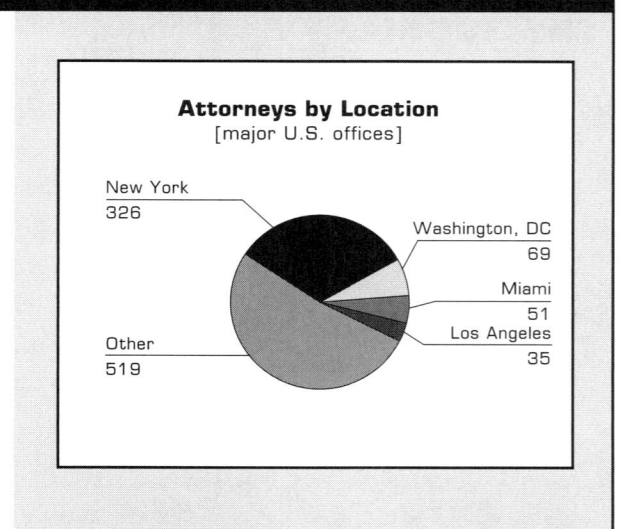

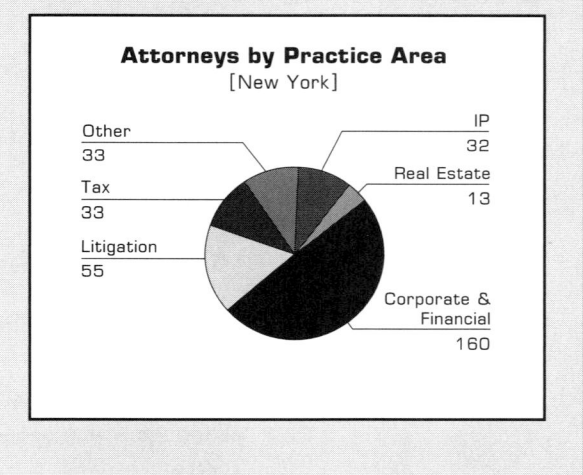

Attorneys by Location [major U.S. offices]
- New York: 326
- Washington, DC: 69
- Miami: 51
- Los Angeles: 35
- Other: 519

Attorneys by Practice Area [New York]
- Other: 33
- IP: 32
- Real Estate: 13
- Tax: 33
- Litigation: 55
- Corporate & Financial: 160

QUALITY OF LIFE RANKINGS [ASSOCIATES RATE THEIR OWN FIRM]

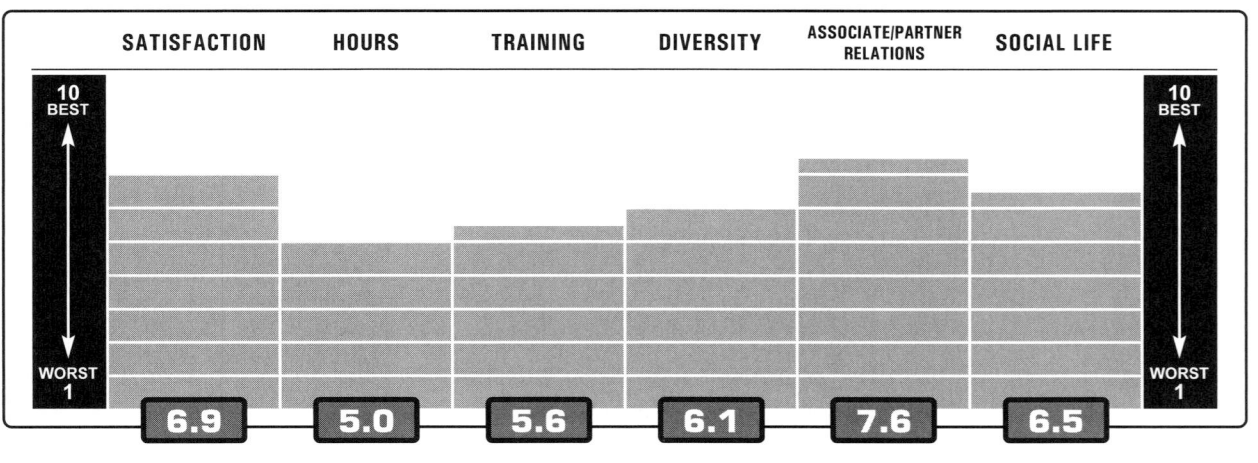

SATISFACTION	HOURS	TRAINING	DIVERSITY	ASSOCIATE/PARTNER RELATIONS	SOCIAL LIFE
6.9	5.0	5.6	6.1	7.6	6.5

THE SCOOP

Associates say White & Case offers challenging international work along with people who are "very bright and pleasant to work with." With more than 1,000 lawyers of 30 nationalities in 23 countries, W&C is one of the world's premier international law firms. One insider tells us, "Whenever I've been abroad in Asia, White & Case is the only American law firm that anyone knows." The firm has established itself as a preeminent player in many legal fields that involve the globalization of financial and securities markets, such as bank finance, project finance, equipment finance and leasing, international capital markets, and bank regulation. The firm is also attempting to move into new areas, such as helping emerging government markets establish rules for their securities operations.

Associates also boast about the firm's reputation in the areas of antitrust, litigation, banking, and general corporate work. In the United States, White & Case boasts five offices: its New York headquarters; a Washington office that serves as the headquarters for the firm's international trade practice; a Los Angeles branch; a Palo Alto office; and a Miami base that is the center of the firm's booming Latin American and Caribbean practice.

History: building an international power

Founded in 1901, the New York-based firm began its history by providing legal services to banks and other clients. In the 1920s, White & Case opened up a Paris office, which it closed at the start of World War II. This would be the first in a series of foreign office openings and closings. The firm re-established its Paris branch in 1960 and later added offices in London (1971), Washington, DC (1974), and Hong Kong (1978).

Changing of the guard

In 1980 the firm elected James B. Hurlock as its managing partner. Hurlock built White & Case into an international power, adding 10 foreign offices by 1990. Hurlock stirred up a whirlwind of controversy in 1989 when he hired Rudy Giuliani, the former Manhattan U.S. Attorney, as a partner — despite Giuliani's apparent lack of interest in doing any work. Giuliani left the firm in 1990, saying the firm was too contentious. The firm received further negative publicity as attention focused on its list of foreign clients, which included the government of Panama and Banco Nacional de Panama.

After two decades at the helm, James Hurlock stepped down as the managing partner of White & Case in 2000. The W&C partner committee elected 60-year-old Duane Wall to serve a four-year term beginning April 1 of that year. Wall had been in charge of W&C's banking practice group since 1981 and had a hand in Deutsche Bank's acquisition of Bankers Trust and Swiss Bank's merger with Union Bank of Switzerland.

We are the world

White & Case's has engaged in dramatic international expansion. The firm added more than 185 lawyers to its foreign offices between 1990 and 1996. In Latin America, it established a sizeable branch in Mexico City and a presence in Sao Paulo, Brazil. The firm also has significant offices in Turkey (with offices in both Istanbul and Ankara), London, Moscow, Budapest, Hong Kong, Singapore, Tokyo, Paris, Prague, Brussels, Stockholm, and Warsaw. With its early entry in Eastern and Central Europe, the firm ably positioned itself to take advantage of the interdependent nature of the global economy and became a leader in a trio of new practice areas in the formerly communist countries: project finance, privatization, and law reform. White & Case will often establish a presence in countries prior to official certification. For example, the firm first ventured into Kazakhstan in 1992, but did not become officially licensed there until March 1998.

W&C's international growth shows no signs of slowing. In April 2000, White & Case took over a 40-lawyer Thai corporate law firm, Nopadol & Khaisri, to boost its presence in Asia and two months later reopened its Frankfurt office. In November 1999, W&C took a partner from a disintegrating firm in Indonesia to re-establish its Jakarta outpost. The firm also has fostered a relationship with a Middle Eastern firm to get a foot in Bahrain.

Debate and defections

Not everyone is thrilled with the overseas growth. Critics have pointed to the firm's habit of opening and closing its foreign offices as evidence that it has overextended abroad. Some White & Case insiders snipe that the frantic push to expand internationally has hurt profits. The issue came to a head in March 1995, when eight of White & Case's litigation partners bolted for New York's Dewey Ballantine — a major blow to the firm's 24-partner New York litigation department. But in May 2000, four defectors from Weil, Gotshal & Manges and two from Clifford Chance bolstered White & Case's partnership ranks in London. In addition, former U.S. Deputy Attorney General George Terwilliger joined the Washington office, adding to the white collar crime practice there.

"Backhanded compliments"

In August 1999, David Llewelyn, co-founder of the London firm Llewelyn Zietman, and five other lawyers from that firm joined White & Case's London IP practice. The additions were part of W&C's efforts to expand the lucrative practice in several of its branch offices. At the end of the year, however, the firm took some hits in the IP area. W&C lost the chairman of the intellectual property practice, Edward Filardi, and four of the group's lawyers to Skadden, Arps, Meagher & Flom. IP partner Nels Lippert also jumped ship to help launch Hale & Dorr's New York office, bringing eight other attorneys with him. But new chairman Wall took it in stride, telling the *New York Law Journal* that he took the defections as a "backhanded compliment" that just proves the strength of W&C's IP lawyers.

The international paper chase

White & Case is currently taking part in the creation of the largest paper producer in the world, representing Finnish paper giant UPM-Kymmene in its merger with U.S.-based Champion International Corporation. The deal, announced in February 2000, is the first substantial cross-Atlantic merger in the paper industry.

The following month, White & Case advised the National Property Fund of the Czech Republic on the privatization of the second-largest Czech bank, Ceska sporitelna. The W&C lawyers took a large role in drafting and negotiating the sale of shares, the first of its kind in the nation. The firm also worked with the other half of the former Czechoslovakia, advising the Slovak cabinet on the privatization of three financial institutions in that country in December 1999.

In May 1999, the firm finished a huge project finance deal in India, funding a power generation facility called Dahbol. Worldwide energy corporation Enron sponsored the deal. White & Case's other international deals include representing Royal Ahold, a Dutch supermarkets group, in a $750 million joint venture with Argentina's Velox Retail Holdings; closing four leasing transactions for Austrian utility Verbund; and representing the Venezuelan Government in a successful privatization of Sidor, the state-owned steel company.

Friend to football

Back at home, the firm represented the estate of Leon Hess when it sold the New York Jets to pharmaceutical heir Robert Wood Johnson IV in January 2000. The firm later successfully defended the Jets against a lawsuit brought by its former assistant coach Bill Belichick. Belichick brought suit against the football club and the NFL in order to be let out of his contract with the team and move on to the New England Patriots. The two sides eventually settled their dispute with Belichick heading off to New England in exchange for a first-round draft pick. In February 2000, the firm successfully represented NFL Properties and the Green Bay Packers in post-trial motions in the trademark infringement case against ProStyle, Inc.

Friend to foreign governments

With around 200 lawyers worldwide, White & Case arbitrators and litigators handle everything from antitrust and banking cases to securities litigation and IP disputes. White & Case lawyers have been called upon to represent international entities both in the U.S. and abroad.

White & Case represents the government of Colombia in a suit against Banco Popular de Ecuador stemming from the bank's alleged plot to take millions from Colombian investors and taxing authorities. The suit claims that the bank collected funds in the Colombian branch on behalf of the Colombian government but never handed over the money. Instead it moved the cash around the bank's branches in the Caribbean and Miami to hide the fact that it was public funds. White & Case successfully got the bank's U.S. assets frozen. The firm also successfully defended the Republic of Costa Rica and two of its state-owned agencies in a $400 million suit filed by Millicom, a large multinational cellular telephone company.

GETTING HIRED

A window of opportunity

Insiders report that White & Case is very selective when choosing its lawyers. But some believe that the standards for getting hired at White & Case have eased a bit due to the hot legal job market. "The firm now accepts lower grades and much less selective law schools," one source opines. Some lawyers report lower-than-normal representation in the W&C summer class from the country's top schools. According to one lawyer, some candidates for summer positions have gone to other firms because of the W&C's slow response to the salary wars in New York and a perceived lack of marquee practice areas. Nonetheless, getting a job at White & Case is no cakewalk, and things could become even more difficult in a tighter legal job market.

White & Case's summer program offers a rotation system that gives law students a chance to spend three to six weeks in various practice areas. Summer associates are not encouraged to split their summer between two firms and are expected to work at W&C for at least the first nine weeks of the summer.

Grades are by far the most important factor for getting a job at White & Case, associates say. But the firm also looks for candidates who have interesting resumes. "Recruiting looks at the overall person, not just grades," says one source. Insiders say that a candidate should present himself or herself as "someone who takes initiative" — since the firm has an unstructured assignment system — as well as someone who "can handle a great deal of responsibility at an early stage of their career." Another associate suggests that "an interest in the international practice, language skills, and broad travel are pluses but not mandatory."

OUR SURVEY SAYS

The proof is in the people

What is associates' favorite thing about the firm? "The people, by far." "I have a great deal of respect for the people I work with and for the individuals at my firm generally. It is a great working environment in that respect," opines one associate. Another source comments: "People work very hard here, but most know when it's time to go home, go out for a drink, or take a vacation."

Camaraderie seemed to be the operative word when describing the W&C social scene. Associates report that W&C lawyers take time out of their day to celebrate birthdays, baby births, and other occasions. "Associates often push tables together at lunch in the cafeteria to make room for a large, fun crowd," says one associate. Lawyers in the New York office say that some departments have frequent dinners and outings, though this is "not so in the corporate department, which is unfortunate because we are probably much more fun and generate all of the money essentially."

Less stuffy than most

"Of the big firms, W&C is less stuffy than most. Not everyone here is from an Ivy League school, but everyone is an excellent lawyer," according to one associate. Although White & Case's size makes it difficult to put a single label on the culture of the firm, most associates find it a pleasant place to work. An insider says, "White & Case associates tend to be better rounded than those at other big New York firms. Most people have interesting backgrounds and most have lived outside of the U.S. The office is very international and very social."

Others remark about the entrepreneurial spirit at White & Case. "The culture supports people who take the initiative and ownership of situations, sometimes too much," says one associate. Opines another, "Associates who seek out opportunities with enthusiasm and commitment are duly rewarded. If you are not interested in doing high-level work, you can float through this place, but you will not find it a fulfilling experience." Compared to corporate, the New York office's litigation department has "a small-firm feel" insiders report. "Corporate is probably more similar to what one would expect of a New York corporate law firm," the lawyer notes.

Friendly and respectful partners

Associates have glowing things to say about their relationship with the partnership. Says one lawyer, "As long as I'm willing to speak up, partners are willing to listen to my needs and try to work around scheduling conflicts." Observes another, "Very few partners here are not nice. [There are] only one or two to avoid." According to one associate, "There has been a strong effort in the past year or two to be responsive to associates' needs, and it is definitely working."

Insiders describe most of the W&C partners as "friendly" and "respectful." "The partnership is generally genteel and engaging, and high expectations are placed on associates." But "respectful" doesn't necessarily translate into "social." Lawyers in the New York office say many of the White & Case partners live in the suburbs and don't stick around to socialize.

One junior lawyer reports that it is easy for first-years to get lost in the crowd and remain "nameless and faceless" in the eyes of the partnership. "As a first-year, it is difficult to be recognized by the partners, which is both good and bad. If you know what you're doing, however, you can get a great deal of substantive work early on."

Growing pains

Associates are enthusiastic about White & Case's strong focus on the international arena. "It is rare that a matter does not involve foreign offices and clients," comments one attorney. Many insiders cite the firm's international focus as the reason they chose White & Case. But the firm's global expansion has translated into growing pains for a few lawyers. Some New Yorkers worry that much of the "deal of the year" work is done abroad, while an associate in the DC office complains that that branch is too dependent on other offices for work. Some insiders also lament the poor communication between attorneys.

More money = more hours?

In the New York, Washington, and California offices, White & Case joined the firms paying $125,000 starting salary. W&C hands out bonuses to associates who bill over 2,000 hours, but the firm has not revealed the amount of the bonuses. Although some associates say they do not believe White & Case was a leader when it came to raising pay, associates in the Miami office aren't complaining. W&C was the first South Florida firm to raise its starting salary by 35 percent. Along with the usual free meals and car service at night and occasional free theater and sports tickets, the firm provides its associates with a gym, complete with a trainer. White & Case also has a year-round casual Friday policy and an all-summer casual policy.

Most associates are pretty satisfied with the new pay structure. But some are left cold by the way the firm unveiled the raises. "Unlike other law firms, the management made it clear to associates that the salary increase was not because we earned it but rather because they were forced to do so," said one associate.

Like attorneys at many of the high-paying firms, W&C lawyers are also concerned about the consequences of the new salaries. According to one insider, "Although salaries have increased significantly in the past few months, the expected work level for associates has unfortunately also increased. Associates generally feel underpaid for the level of work expected of them — consequently, an increase in salary that is also met with increased workload expectations will do nothing to alleviate the problem." Another attorney says, "The firm is becoming increasingly more concerned with billable hours and maximizing its use of associates. This change is affecting morale throughout the firm."

Improved training

Associates describe a renewed emphasis at W&C on formal training programs and CLE. "The firm has undertaken a laudable initiative to increase the amount of institutional training attorneys receive, probably in part because of the recently-enacted CLE requirements for all attorneys. Whatever the motivation, the firm is doing a respectable job of increasing the quality and quantity of training," one associate opines. But most of the professional development at W&C takes place on the job. One associate says succinctly, "Sink or swim."

Associates like the broad-based exposure they get at W&C: "There is an emphasis on interdisciplinary lawyering. White & Case encourages young lawyers to be generalists more than other big firms." W&C does not use a strict assignment system — associates can solicit the work they prefer from the partners.

White shoe firm in white shoe offices

White & Case's offices get mixed reviews. One lawyer says, "The dated earth and desert tones and dowdy furnishings make our office comfortable, but not entirely modern or attractive." Some say the offices match the firm's personality. "Very old and white shoe décor. However, it fits with the history of the firm and the majority of its attorneys." In the New York office, pairs of first-years and second-years share offices. One insider reports that White & Case's lease on its New York office is up for renewal in two years and the firm is considering a renovation.

White & Case receives mostly high marks for its support services, although there are some complaints from junior lawyers who don't get their own secretary. One insider reports, "First-years wait a bit too long to have secretaries. Once you pass that hurdle, support services are generally pretty decent."

International diversity

According to insiders, White & Case has made great strides in recent years in terms of diversity. Comments an attorney in the New York office, "The firm's global practice attracts a relatively diverse group of attorneys, not only in terms of race but national origin as well. It is not uncommon to hear three or four languages in the office on any given day. However, the firm does not maintain a formal affirmative action policy."

Hiring of female associates seems to be close to that of male associates, but associates claim women in the senior ranks have yet to catch up and there remain relatively few female partners. Says one associate, "[White & Case is] weak on mentoring but very strong with respect to accommodating women who wish to either work part-time or work from home." Another lawyer says she thinks the firm is a great place for women without children but tough for mothers.

The atmosphere is reportedly comfortable for gay and lesbian lawyers, too. One attorney says the situation is getting "better and better — mostly as a result of more prominent gay partners." The firm's domestic partner benefits are reportedly in line with marriage benefits. Another associate reveals, "As a gay man, my relationship with my life partner is given the same respect as any married or long-term straight couple."

Pro bono: if you build it, they will come

White & Case's pro bono work includes working on asylum cases for refugees forced to flee their countries and assisting several nonprofit organizations in incorporating and filing for tax exempt status. Although W&C counts pro bono hours toward billing requirements, it keeps pro bono in a separate category in hour reports. On associate complains that his pro bono hours were "filtered out" during his performance reviews. Another lawyer remarks, "Some partners have made it quite clear that they have no regard for pro bono work. If you seek it, they will let you do it. [But] I have not heard any partners encouraging it." Others report that the litigation department is more receptive toward pro bono than the corporate department.

Arnold & Porter

VAULT.COM PRESTIGE RANKING: 21

555 12th Street, NW
Washington, DC 20004
(202) 942-5000
Fax: (202) 942-5999
www.arnoldporter.com

LOCATIONS

Washington, DC (HQ)
Denver, CO
Los Angeles, CA
New York, NY
London

MAJOR DEPARTMENTS/PRACTICES

Antitrust & Trade Regulations
Bankruptcy
Benefits & Employment Law
Corporate & Securities
Environmental
Financial Institutions
Food, Drug & Medical Devices
Government Contracts
Intellectual Property and Technology
Litigation
Life Sciences
Product Liability
Public Policy
Real Estate
Tax
Telecommunications

THE STATS

No. of attorneys: 540
No. of offices: 5
Summer associate offers: 32 out of 33 (Washington, 1999)
Managing Partner: James J. Sandman
Hiring Partner: Ms. Claire E. Reade

THE BUZZ
What attorneys at other firms are saying about this firm

- "The definitive DC sweatshop"
- "A Washington powerhouse"
- "Very Beltway"

PAY

Washington, DC, 2000
1st year: $125,000
2nd year: $135,000
3rd year: $145,000
4th year: $155,000
5th year: $165,000
6th year: $175,000
7th year: $185,000
8th year: $195,000
Summer associate: $2,400/week

Denver, 2000
1st year: $110,000
2nd year: $120,000
3rd year: $130,000
4th year: $140,000
5th year: $150,000
6th year: $160,000
7th year: $170,000
8th year: $180,000
Summer associate: $2,100/week

Los Angeles and New York, 2000
1st year: $125,000
2nd year: $135,000
3rd year: $150,000
4th year: $165,000
5th year: $185,000
6th year: $195,000
7th year: $205,000
8th year: $210,000
Summer associate (Los Angeles): $2,400/week
Summer associate (New York): $2,404/week

NOTABLE PERKS

- Health insurance for domestic partners
- 12 weeks paid maternity leave; 6 weeks paid paternity leave
- Free on-site athletic facility and child care center
- Options for leave of absence and part-time
- 5 percent contribution to associates' retirement accounts
- Confidential counseling for employees and families

UPPERS

- Good advancement opportunities for women
- Excellent pro bono record
- No minimum billable hours requirement

DOWNERS

- Some less than exemplary support staffers
- Workload can be overwhelming

KEY COMPETITORS

Covington & Burling
Williams & Connolly LLP
Wilmer, Cutler & Pickering

EMPLOYMENT CONTACT

Ms. Lisa Pavia
Manager of Attorney Recruitment
(202) 942-5059
Lisa_Pavia@aporter.com

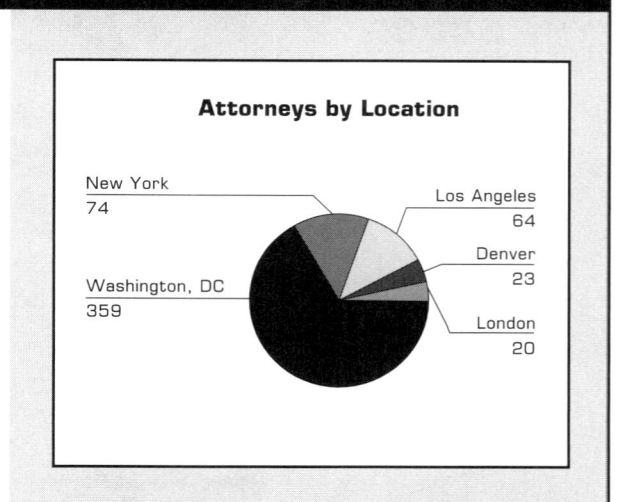

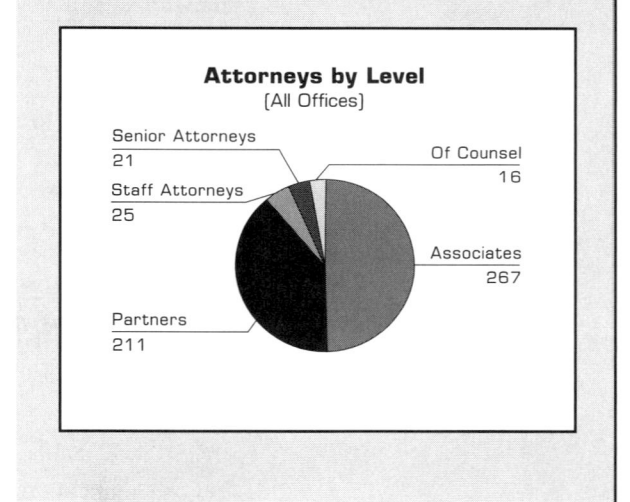

Attorneys by Location

- New York: 74
- Los Angeles: 64
- Denver: 23
- London: 20
- Washington, DC: 359

Attorneys by Level (All Offices)

- Senior Attorneys: 21
- Of Counsel: 16
- Staff Attorneys: 25
- Associates: 267
- Partners: 211

QUALITY OF LIFE RANKINGS [ASSOCIATES RATE THEIR OWN FIRM]

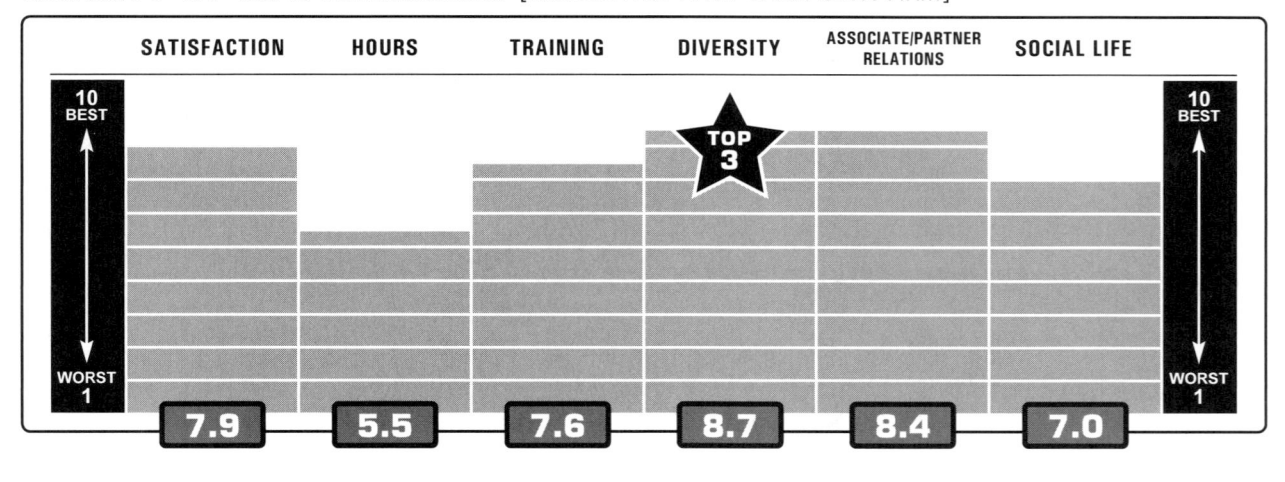

SATISFACTION	HOURS	TRAINING	DIVERSITY	ASSOCIATE/PARTNER RELATIONS	SOCIAL LIFE
7.9	5.5	7.6	8.7 (TOP 3)	8.4	7.0

THE SCOOP

Arnold & Porter has a long history of antagonizing. The firm has represented an unusual mix of clients, from the Black Panthers to tobacco giant Philip Morris. Today, Arnold has over 500 attorneys in five offices. Besides the Washington, DC headquarters, the firm has operations in New York, Denver, Los Angeles, and London. The firm has an impressive corporate practice and is also well-known for its pro bono work.

A Presidential-level history

Arnold & Porter was founded in 1946 by three former members of President Franklin Roosevelt's administration. Paul Porter was a former Federal Communications Commission chairman; Thurman Arnold was a U.S. Court of Appeals judge; and Abe Fortas was Roosevelt's Undersecretary of the Interior. Fortas was later appointed to the Supreme Court, and in 1963 argued *Gideon v. Wainwright*, a landmark case that reaffirmed the right to an attorney for all criminal defendants. The firm is currently led by Managing Partner James Sandman, who works on commercial litigation and product liability from the Washington office.

Arnold & Porter University: a school for government commissioners

The firm has a history of sending its attorneys on to posts in various government organizations. Robert Pitofsky, formerly of counsel at the firm, is chairman of the Federal Trade Commission. William Baer served under Pitofsky, directing the FTC's Bureau of Competition before returning to Arnold & Porter in January 2000. (The FTC contacts come in handy, as the firm has defended numerous large companies, including Xerox, Intel, and General Electric, in antitrust matters.) In 1996, A&P partner Brooksley Born was named chair of the Commodity Futures Trading Commission, holding the post until returning to the firm in 1999. And in May 1998, Harvey Goldschmid, of counsel at Arnold, was named general counsel at the Securities and Exchange Commission. Goldschmid has since left to become of counsel at Weil, Gotshal & Manges.

Corporate practice: touching all the bases

Arnold & Porter has a large corporate practice with operations in all areas relevant to corporate law, including mergers and acquisitions, product liability, taxation, bankruptcy and restructuring, benefits and employment, and securities.

The firm has handled numerous large M&A clients. It represented PNC Bank in its acquisition of BlackRock Financial Management in 1994 and again in 1996 when PNC bought Midlantic Bank. The firm represented another bank, First Empire State, in its acquisition by ONBANCorp. A&P has often handled the antitrust and competition concerns related to large mergers, including the November 1998 union of Kroger Co. and Fred Meyer, Inc. and BP Amoco's April 2000 acquisition of ARCO.

Too big? Not if Arnold & Porter has its way

In addition to merger cases, Arnold & Porter handles other antitrust matters. The firm represented Xerox in a lawsuit stemming from the company's refusal to sell replacement parts to non-Xerox service providers. As co-counsel, A&P successfully defended GE against charges that it conspired to fix the price of diamonds used for industrial purposes. It represented Continental Airlines in a suit filed by travel agents alleging Continental, along with other airlines, illegally reduced agents' commissions.

Out of money

Arnold & Porter has handled several high-profile bankruptcy clients. Braniff Airways retained the firm when it filed for Chapter 11. Arnold has also represented Maryland Deposit Insurance Fund, a savings and loan company, in over 350 bankruptcy proceedings. Other A&P bankruptcy clients include Mission Insurance, Washington Bancorporation, Bankeast Corp., and Guinness PLC.

You're liable to like this practice

Product liability has been a particularly lucrative area for the firm. It represents American Home Products in suits surrounding complications arising from fen-phen, a diet drug that caused heart problems along with slimmer thighs. Another Arnold & Porter client, tobacco company Philip Morris, has faced a host of lawsuits from government agencies and private individuals over the dangers of cigarettes. A&P has also represented a blood bank in a number of cases alleging that patients contracted the AIDS virus from blood transfusions at the bank.

On the frontlines of intellectual thought

Another notable practice area for Arnold & Porter has been intellectual property. The firm published a two-volume treatise on intellectual property in 1988 and three years later opened an information technology practice, in part to deal with copyright and patent issues. It also lobbied on behalf of the Recording Industry Association of America for legislation on digital home taping and transmission of recordings over the Internet. The firm handled the copyrightability of a manuscript of the Dead Sea

Scrolls in two countries. Additionally, Arnold & Porter has argued trademark cases for the American Red Cross, Bell Atlantic, and the Professional Golfers' Association of America. America Online has tapped the firm to help set up and protect Digital Cities, a network of interactive online content sites centered around local communities.

Pro bono restitution

Perhaps the area A&P is most proud of is its pro bono practice. In 1999 Arnold & Porter was named the pro bono firm of the year by the District of Columbia Bar. In August 1999, it was awarded The Whitman-Walker Clinic's Outstanding Pro Bono Publico Law Firm Award. Whitman-Walker is a DC-based legal clinic for people with HIV and AIDS. The award and the work inspired warm feelings among A&P lawyers. "Doing the work for Whitman-Walker has been a very personally rewarding experience," associate Laura McNally told *The Legal Times*. "It's enabled me to bring the resources of this firm not just to big-impact matters but to people in this community who need the help."

That same year, Arnold & Porter won a major pro bono victory. In 1881 Lieutenant Henry O. Flipper, a former slave and the first African-American graduate of the U.S. Military Academy at West Point, was convicted of conduct unbecoming an officer in connection with $1,440 that had turned up missing while he was in command. Flipper was dishonorably discharged, and the conviction was upheld by President Chester A. Arthur. In 1976, 30 years after Flipper's death, his family convinced the Army that the charges had been fabricated and racially motivated and Flipper was posthumously granted an honorable discharge. The Army, however, was powerless to deal with President Arthur's decision. Arnold & Porter partner Jeffrey Smith took up the case and lobbied to have Flipper's conviction overturned. President Bill Clinton pardoned Flipper in February 1999, and the case was cited by the DC bar in its presentation of the pro bono award to the firm.

GETTING HIRED

Beyond the top 20

A&P associates in general rate their firm as fairly selective. Like most firms, Arnold & Porter puts a premium on graduates of top law schools. "I would say that for applicants who have attended top law schools and have decent grades, getting in can be quite easy," notes one contact. "If you did not go to a top school and were not in the top percent or percent of your class, it would be difficult or impossible to get a position here," says another associate, offering little encouragement to law slackers everywhere. According to one associate: "The firm looks for grades and school and then focuses very hard on finding interesting people with varied backgrounds."

Despite the emphasis on top-tier law schools, those from less prestigious schools can land a position at the firm. "Arnold has extremely high hiring standards. However, the firm does historically take the top people from second-tier law schools," says an associate. "The firm does NOT limit itself to the top 10 schools," according to one contact. "We have associates from the top schools but also many from the lower-ranked schools."

Summer associates: careful who you cc

Summer associates are all but assured of getting a full-time offer. "Once you get a summer associate position, you are effectively guaranteed an offer for an associate position." Almost every summer associate has received an offer in the past five years; one who did not "repeatedly harassed his fellow summer associates and cc'ed the entire office on e-mails," says one contact.

Laid-back callbacks

Invited candidates are brought to the firm for a half-day of callback interviews. "It's very laid-back," says one associate. "Sometimes you talk about the law, sometimes not. I think people just want to get to know the person, share the laid-back atmosphere of the firm, and find new people that everyone can get along with." "It was standard stuff," recalls a recent interviewee. "They were chit-chatty. At that stage, the firm just wants you to meet people, so you know they're not shackled to their desks." Associates report getting an offer "about a week" after the callbacks.

Quirky recruitment process

A quirk about Arnold & Porter's recruiting process: third-year students who are summer alums will be taken out to a "fancy-schmancy dinner" with candidates from the school and recruiters. "It's kind of like 'Hey, we're in town, let's get together.'" And while the firm in the past was not known for being flexible about some aspects of the hiring process, incoming associates do have some flexibility when it comes to their start date.

OUR SURVEY SAYS

Corporate culture: "mavericks and visionaries"

Most Arnold insiders describe the corporate culture as "laid-back" or "collegial." "The standard firm bullshit line is 'mavericks and visionaries,'" says one associate. "But like all standard firm bullshit lines, there's actually some truth to it. What matters here is doing great work and not being a jerk. Any other personality quirks really don't matter much." That's a good thing, as another associate described the firm as "very smart, but nerdy."

Attorneys describe a comfortable atmosphere. "Arnold's very laid back with a lot of room for individuality," notes one contact. "There's not a partner in the firm whose office I wouldn't feel completely comfortable walking into." Another associate says "Many of the partners are rather eccentric — though brilliant — leaving the impression that you can be whoever you want to be, provided you get the job done. For example, Harry Katz is a *Star Wars* fanatic, wearing Luke Skywalker ties and displaying a larger-than-life Darth Vader in his office." Jim Sandman, the managing partner, is said to be not only a highly-skilled attorney but "a committed managing partner."

"Everyone likes to think of themselves as 'anti-big-firm people,' which is kind of ironic," says one associate. "The top management is very accessible and no one cares what you wear or when you [show up] in the morning." Another associates opines that the firm in general "follows the Democratic platform" though others point out the firm has "Republican ties as well." (A firm based in DC could hardly avoid a certain level of bipartisanship.)

The firm's pay policy, which is not based on billable hours, fosters a spirit of cooperation. "Your fellow associates here are friends who will help you out, not competitors trying to out-bill you," according to one contact. "The firm tries hard to avoid a sweatshop atmosphere and rejecting a move to targeted hours supports that," says another associate. That contact concedes, though, that "the reality doesn't always meet the ideal."

Partners: mixed reviews

Arnold associates say treatment by the partners varies greatly. "It's difficult to speak generally about partners, because they can be quite different from each other," offers a contact. "The partners in my group are fairly cool," says one person. Another agrees that partner personalities vary, but says the firm could do a better job of ensuring that associates receive good treatment. "It is a big place and some partners treat you very well and others treat you poorly. Unfortunately, there are far too many partners who do not treat associates well and many of them are horrible." To help avoid such problems, the firm does allow associates to evaluate the partners with whom they work.

Another associate gives partners grades all over the spectrum. "Some are great to work with and I would rate them a 10, other are difficult to work with or have unpredictable mood swings and would get a three."

But others disagree strongly. "The partners are so glad to have us and so badly want us to stay that it is amazing how nicely they treat us," raves an associate. "I get asked almost weekly how I'm doing and am never given an assignment without being asked first whether I have the time to do it."

Social life for "nerdy kids"

Firm insiders describe significant social activity for those Arnold insiders willing and able to take advantage. "People are friendly and easy to be with," says one associate. "There are all types here so everyone can make friends," reports another insider. "Most of the people here were nerdy kids from high school, though." "It's all about you," notes an associate. "I tend to socialize a lot with my colleagues. Others have families and other social outlets. It all depends on the person, but it's there if you want it."

The firm isn't stuffy about romantic relationships either, "Intrafirm dating is rampant," gossips one source, "including associates [with] associates, associates [with] partners and associates [with] legal assistants. Everyone is professional about it and the only guideline is to make sure you don't work with someone you are dating."

NACHO man

In addition to informal social activities, the firm makes an effort to structure activities for the partners and associates to get to know each other. "I was the 'Lunch Czar' this past fall, whereby I set up new associates with more senior attorneys for lunch," says one enterprising attorney. "The firm has a dedicated New Associates Committee (NACHO) that is given a very substantial budget to plan both formal and impromptu social events."

"Arnold tries very hard to encourage interaction among lawyers, with snacks and drinks every night, pizza on Friday nights, plus numerous out-of-office social events," says one associate. "Nonetheless, the place seems to be getting a little colder each year as it gets bigger and lawyers work harder." One of the colder attorneys had this to say: "One of the big issues is actually finding time away from the lawyers."

Hours: from "humane" to "horrific"

Arnold associate schedules tend to vary, say insiders. "With litigation at Arnold, hours tend to go in cycles. Associates may go a few months working a fairly humane schedule, followed by a few months of late nights and weekends," reports one insider. "I've gotten complaints from my friends that I spend too much time at work," says another contact. "Maybe that's true, but if I didn't like what I was doing I would place more limits on the hours I was working." "Work is not evenly distributed," complains one associate. "Some people work horrific hours and others get off easy."

Paying on par

Most Arnold insiders are satisfied with their pay, saying it is as good or better than industry average. "The pay is comparable to other places," says an associate. "If you can get away with working less, or have a lot of pro bono work, it is clearly better than other places; if you work a ton, it is comparable or better than other places; if you have a little pro bono and work hard but are not killing yourself — in the 1,950 hours to 2,350 hours range. The pay is not as good as elsewhere."

Other associates celebrate the lack of a billable hours requirement, plus the fact that those working a large number of hours get rewarded. "I think our salary system is great," says one insider. "Although it is slightly lower than at the big New York City and California firms at the mid- and upper-levels, the fact that we don't have a minimum billables or hours-based bonuses — with the exception of a 2,400-hours apology bonus — helps a lot."

Like all associates at large firms, Arnold lawyers have benefited from recent competition. "In the wake of recent associate salary hikes, the firm, under the leadership of Jim Sandman, came up with an excellent salary package that allows the firm to compete with other firms yet does not put additional burdens on associates nor jeopardize the financial health of the firm."

Top-notch training, especially in litigation

"The partners take training very seriously," says one associate. "In litigation alone, we have hands-on deposition and trial training lasting several days each, monthly breakfasts with speakers, an 'emergency litigation' training, and a dozen other subject-matter training [programs]." "Litigation training is great," says another in the department. "There is an effort to have other training, but the problem is that the lawyers are all so busy there's very little time to prepare for meaningful in-house training." Other contacts warn that the onus is usually on the associate to get training. "You can get great training, but you should be aware that certain partners do not communicate as well as others and are not the best trainers. You need to be self-motivated."

Perks: tickets, lunches, gyms and more

Associates enjoy the typical perks: free lunches, company laptops, free food and tickets to Washington-area sports teams, including the Capitals and the Wizards (if you call that a perk). "Associates get to have lunch for free (up to $25 per person) with their associate mentors anytime, forever," says one source. Another says that with the proliferation of free food, "it's real easy to get fat here." It's not too difficult to work off the fat at the Washington office; insiders point out that the company has a small gym on site and reduced memberships at two area gyms. Finally, the company sponsors "free emergency back up child care," as well as full-time child care available on site for market tuition.

Peripherals: great offices, so-so support

Associates rave about Arnold's offices, calling them "large, sunny, and light." Science fiction is a common theme. "The atrium reminds me of *Gattaca*," says one insider. "We have our own modern building that is very space-age — it was in the movie *Contact* with Jodie Foster," says another.

Attorneys were more critical of the support staff. "Support staff varies a great deal," says one associate. "I've found most secretaries here to be really good at what they do and always professional," says an insider. Another rips into the staff, saying, "My secretary has yet to make accurate document edits and has problems following simple instructions. Also, they hire 'legal assistants' straight out of college rather than more experienced 'paralegals,' which tends to burden new associates with training and oversight." "The computer system is a nightmare and secretarial support is hit-or-miss, but the library is great and numerous legal assistants are available to help out with projects," says one contact.

Retention: "bleeding like crazy?"

"We've had a lot of departures recently, including to other firms, but in the past few years retention has been very good," reports one associate. Another insider disagrees: "We're bleeding at the mid-level range like crazy." That kind of turnover may be inherent in the kind of attorneys the firm attracts. "A lot of people come to Arnold because of its commitment to public service and they will leave after two to three years to pursue public service," according to one source. "Associates don't typically leave Arnold for other law firms," claims another associate. "Decisions to leave Arnold usually mean the individual wants to do something quite different."

Partnership track: stick around and you'll be OK

Insiders say that those who stay at Arnold have a good chance to make partner. "If you stick around and do good work, you'll make partner," says one associate. "Most people self-select out of the partnership track by leaving the firm." Insiders differ on the role of politics in the selection process. "Lots of people make it who have outrageous hours and who are not aces in the personality/politics/schmoozing department," says one. "Not everyone agrees on the criteria for making partner, however. Associates have a fair chance at making partner at Arnold if they stay the requisite 7.5 years. However, making partner can be highly political," states another attorney.

Pro bono powerhouse

Associates echo the firm's commitment to pro bono work. "Arnold encourages all attorneys who have been with the firm for at least six months to spend at least 15 percent of their time on pro bono." However, some say pro bono work is meant to be in addition to regular duties. "The firm is very positive toward pro bono work, but the reality seems to be that in many instances the work is not in place of your other work, but in addition to that work," reports one contact. "The only caveat is that partners are very receptive when you say that you can't get to their matter immediately [because of a pro bono case]."

High marks for diversity

All told, Arnold & Porter associates give their firm high marks for diversity. "They put their money where their mouth is," says one associate, "with lots of minority recruiting." "My sense is that the firm tries every method imaginable to promote a diverse workplace," says one contact. "Diversity training is mandatory, and a sub-committee of the hiring committee focuses on minority hiring." The firm has seen its share of success, earning the firm the Minority Corporate Counsel Association's Sager Award for its commitment to diversity in both 1999 and 2000. (The award is given for overall success in hiring, retention, and promotion of minorities.)

Arnold's results are mixed when it comes to women. "I think the firm tries very hard, and is more successful than many of its peers" in terms of recruiting and retaining women, according to one source. Insiders report the firm offers 12 weeks of maternity leave and an additional 12 weeks of personal leave, and strongly encourages new moms to take advantage. Additionally, the firm offers day care and part-time hours. However, some complain of the lack of interaction between female associates and partners. "Lots of formal programs and lunches," reports an associate. "Not a lot of informal mentoring — the kind that counts." Another contact agrees that the firm "probably could do better with regard to facilitating mentoring between senior and junior women."

Finally, Arnold associates report the firm is open with respect to gay and lesbian attorneys. "Openly gay lawyers are common here and I haven't heard from any of them that there is an issue," says one contact. Another provides a first-person account: "I am gay and could not feel more comfortable here. It either seems to be a complete non-issue or, in some cases, even seems to help — that is, people go out of their way to be even more welcoming."

Satisfied attorneys

Arnold associates generally have good things to say about their firm. Most believe the firm is one of the best in many practice areas and that Arnold has a great reputation in the legal community. "I heard about the firm even before going to law school," says one contact. "The firm has an excellent reputation for delivering the highest quality legal services," says another. "As big law firms go, I think it is the best," gushes one associate. Another gives the firm the highest possible score: "For a firm, Arnold is a 10." Attorneys report that they chose the firm because of the culture and atmosphere, the pro bono opportunities, or the compensation. "I liked the people here; I liked the pro bono commitment," says an associate. The list goes on: "I liked the work atmosphere. I liked the managing partner." The family commitment also scores big with associates.

The opportunity to work with well-regarded managing partner Jim Sandman is cited by several lawyers as one of the benefits of working with the firm. Other associates note the pay. "Arnold has an open atmosphere and the managing partner does an excellent job of keeping the associates informed about the firm," says one associate. "Great people, terrific on-site day care facility, no face time requirements," comments another contact.

When assessing the negatives, Arnold associates hit on many issues prevalent at most if not all large law firms. "The hours, the lack of autonomy, and the frustration with mind-dulling work sometimes," complains one associate. "Some of the partners here are unbearable to work for," says another. Others point to a problem with support staff. "Secretarial support is mediocre at best. Other than a small handful of people with spectacular secretaries, I think most associates learn to live with minimal secretarial support," reports one associate. Another attorney complains of "what amounts to a class system that makes staff dislike attorneys." On the whole, however, no unusually dire or telling complaints emerge — a good sign for Arnold & Porter.

Morrison & Foerster LLP

VAULT.COM PRESTIGE RANKING: 22

425 Market Street
San Francisco, CA 94105-2482
(415) 268-7000
Fax: (415) 268-7522
www.mofo.com

LOCATIONS

San Francisco, CA (HQ)
Denver, CO • Irvine, CA • Los Angeles, CA • New York, NY • Palo Alto, CA • Sacramento, CA • San Diego, CA • Walnut Creek, CA • Washington, DC • Buenos Aires • Beijing • Brussels • Hong Kong • London • Singapore • Tokyo

MAJOR DEPARTMENTS/PRACTICES

Corporate and New Media
Finance & Infrastructure
Financial Services
Investment Management
Intellectual Property, Patent, Trademark
Labor
Land Use & Environmental
Litigation
Real Estate
Tax
Technology Transactions, Internet, High Tech, Licensing

THE STATS

No. of attorneys: 844
No. of offices: 17
Summer associate offers: 40 out of 40 (San Francisco, 1999)
Chairman: Stephen S. Dunham
Hiring Attorney: James E. Hough

PAY

New York City and California offices, 2000
1st year: $125,000 + bonus
Bonus ranges from $5,000-$7,000
Summer associate (New York, Tokyo, and CA offices): $2,400/week

Denver, 2000
1st year: $105,000+ bonus
Bonus ranges from $5,000-$7,000
Summer associate: $2,000/week

Washington, DC, 2000
1st year: $110,000 + bonus
Bonus ranges from $5,000-$7,000
Summer associate: $2,400/week

NOTABLE PERKS

- Sports tickets
- Breakfast foods
- "Stressbuster awards"
- Relocation expenses
- Theme park and cultural event discounts and freebies
- Investment fund for associates
- Mortgage assistance

THE BUZZ
What attorneys at other firms are saying about this firm

- "You too can be a partner"
- "One of the most overrated institutions"
- "New economy gurus"
- "People's Republic of MoFo"

UPPERS

- Relaxed, flexible corporate culture
- Diversity
- Talented lawyers

DOWNERS

- Size can make things impersonal
- Little formal training
- Lack of support staff at some offices

KEY COMPETITORS

Brobeck, Phleger & Harrison
McCutchen, Doyle, Brown & Emerson
Orrick, Herrington & Sutcliffe
Pillsbury, Madison & Sutro
Wilson Sonsini Goodrich & Rosati

EMPLOYMENT CONTACT

Ms. Jane Cooperman
Senior Recruiting Manager
(415) 268-7665
jcooperman@mofo.com

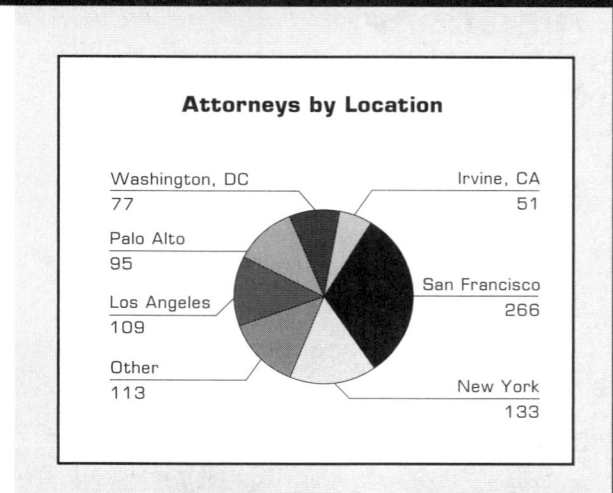

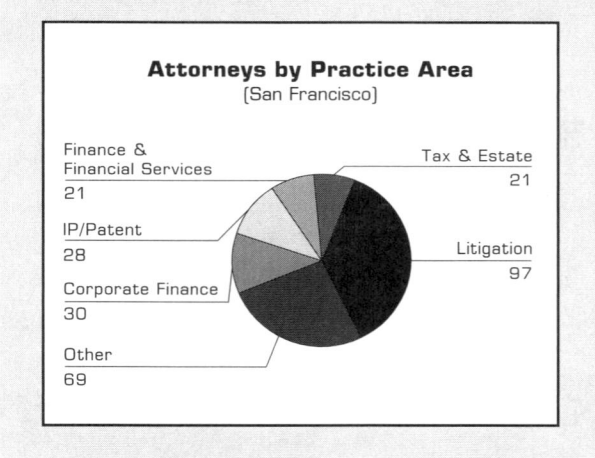

Attorneys by Location

- Washington, DC: 77
- Irvine, CA: 51
- Palo Alto: 95
- San Francisco: 266
- Los Angeles: 109
- Other: 113
- New York: 133

Attorneys by Practice Area
[San Francisco]

- Finance & Financial Services: 21
- Tax & Estate: 21
- IP/Patent: 28
- Litigation: 97
- Corporate Finance: 30
- Other: 69

QUALITY OF LIFE RANKINGS [ASSOCIATES RATE THEIR OWN FIRM]

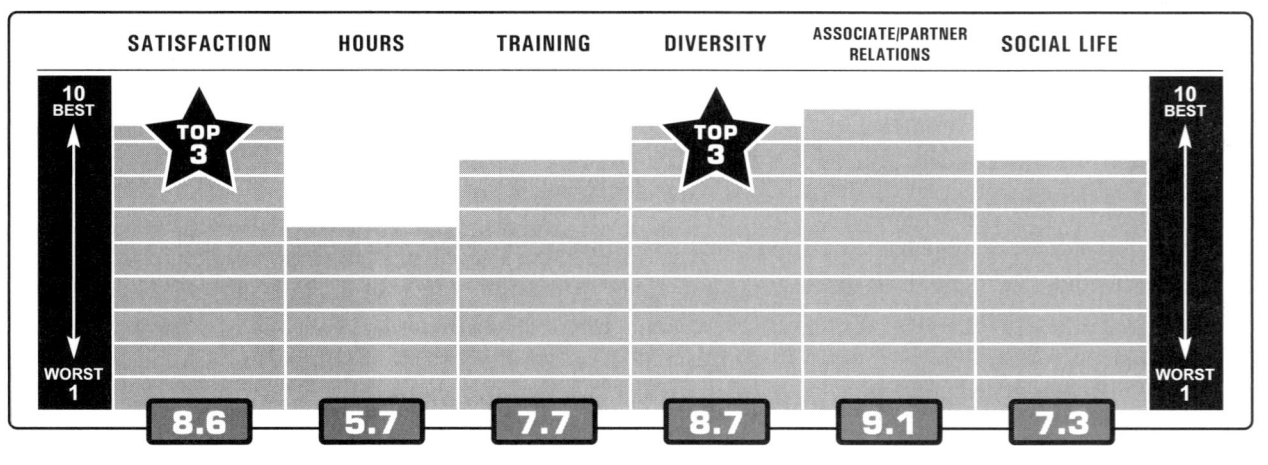

SATISFACTION	HOURS	TRAINING	DIVERSITY	ASSOCIATE/PARTNER RELATIONS	SOCIAL LIFE
8.6 (TOP 3)	5.7	7.7	8.7 (TOP 3)	9.1	7.3

(10 BEST / 1 WORST)

THE SCOOP

Based in San Francisco, Morrison & Foerster was once facetiously nicknamed "MoFo," a moniker you'd think the firm would shy away from. The firm has instead embraced the handle (its web site is mofo.com). There's a certain poetic justice in the fact that the firm's name is such an issue: MoFo has undergone 14 name changes in its 117-year history.

History: the original MoFo

Morrison & Foerster's roots can be traced back to 1883 when Thomas O'Brien and Alexander Morrison founded the firm O'Brien & Morrison. In 1890 Constantine Foerster joined the firm. Two years later, Morrison & Foerster named the firm after themselves. When Foerster died in 1898, the firm's name was changed to Morrison & Cope. In 1918 Ronald Foerster, son of Constantine, joined the practice and his family name was added back onto the sign in 1925. Fifty years later, after many deaths, arrivals, departures, and name changes, the name Morrison & Foerster was adopted for good.

Since the most recent name change, Morrison has expanded rapidly. The Los Angeles office opened in 1974, a year before the newest name was adopted, and the Washington, DC and Denver offices were added in 1979. The first international office (London) was opened in 1980 and from 1983 to 1987 seven other outposts were established, including New York, Hong Kong and Tokyo. MoFo boosted its DC practice by merging with area communications boutique Gurman Blask & Freedman in March 2000. The firm continued expanding to its present size of 844 lawyers in 17 offices.

MoFo boasts several prominent partners. James Brosnahan and Melvin Goldman each served as president of the San Francisco Bar Association and Robert Raven led the American Bar Association from 1988 to 1989. The firm added David Bayless, former head of the San Francisco office of the Securities and Exchange Commission, in May 1999.

The firm has been lauded as a great place to work by several national publications. In 1998 MoFo was the sole law firm on *Fortune*'s "100 Best Companies to Work for in America" list, placing 52nd. The firm narrowly missed making the cut the next year. *Working Mother Magazine* has included MoFo on its "100 Best Companies in America for Working Mothers" 10 times in the past 14 years.

MoFo talk radio: all law, all the time (actually, 45 minutes a quarter)

Morrison initiated an innovative marketing ploy in November 1999, launching "MoFo Talk Radio," a quarterly radio broadcast available from the firm's web site. The show, which runs approximately 45 minutes, deals with Internet issues ranging from obtaining funding to securing patents and copyrights.

Valley firm moves in on the Alley

Sensing an opportunity in the reluctance of established New York-area firms to take on risky Silicon Alley startups as clients, Morrison has gone after New York Internet companies with a vengeance. The firm's foresight has paid off: MoFo has participated in a number of Alley IPOs, including heavyweights like Razorfish and EarthWeb. Vault.com, the publisher of this book, is another Silicon Alley-based client.

Despite the sometimes speculative nature of the Internet industry, Morrison has enjoyed a healthy return on the practice. "We thought profitability would be years down the road," John Delaney, a partner at Morrison & Foerster's New York office, told *The Legal Times*. However, he said that the Internet has already proven "a successful practice." The Big Apple is just one of several areas outside of California where the firm has established a technology practice — it also has tech-focused lawyers stationed in DC, Europe, Asia, and Latin America.

All over the map

Morrison has other successful practices besides its Internet bulwark. It is perhaps best known for its work in intellectual property litigation and corporate finance. In IP the firm has represented Oracle and Fujitsu internationally. Additional clients include Chiron Corp. and Thomson Consumer Electronics. In May 1999, MoFo successfully represented the Regents of the University of California in a suit against Genentech challenging the validity of the university's patent on human growth hormone technology.

The firm has worked on hundreds of securities offerings. All-star issuers on Morrison's client list include Netscape Communications, Verio, and uBid. MoFo has also represented several investment banks including Morgan Stanley Dean Witter, Lehman Brothers, Salomon Smith Barney, Merrill Lynch, and Goldman Sachs. Additionally, the firm has represented more than 20 venture capital funds including Kleiner Perkins Caufield & Byers and H&Q Ventures on various legal matters.

Also significant is MoFo's trial and appellate practice. The firm represented 3M Corp. in over 100 national and state breast implant liability cases. Morrison also defended Dow Corning in separate breast implant cases. Additionally, it has defended General Motors in 150 cases involving safety devices such as air bags and seat belts. Finally, the firm has represented G.D. Searle in product liability cases related to the company's Copper-7 intrauterine device.

Antitrust defenders

Attorneys at Morrison have defended numerous clients against antitrust lawsuits on both national and municipal cases. MoFo has also represented firms such as Fujitsu and Compaq seeking approval of mergers.

All pro bono, all the time — even Christmas Eve

MoFo's strong pro bono service has been honored by numerous legal associations. The California State Bar presented the firm with the President's Pro Bono Service Award in October 1998. Later that year, the Bar Association of San Francisco named Morrison its Law Firm of the Year for pro bono work. Satellite offices in Denver, Los Angeles, and Orange County also received awards from local bar associations and legal groups for pro bono work. The firm has taken on several death penalty cases including that of James Lee Spencer, condemned for a murder he committed during a prison escape attempt. Spencer's sentence was changed to life after he was ruled mentally retarded by a Georgia jury. That case, among others, won Morrison the Lifetime Achievement Award from Death Penalty Focus of California. In March 2000, MoFo represented opponents of a California initiative to ban gay marriage. In another pro bono matter, the firm prepared a legal petition for a presidential pardon of Freddie Meeks, an African-American sailor convicted of mutiny during World War II. Meeks received the pardon in December 1999. MoFo lawyers also represented 23,000 Colorado students in an effort to change the state's public school financing system.

Associates at Morrison report that "the firm actively encourages pro bono work and the hours count towards the minimum billable requirement." One associate even goes so far as to say that the firm's pro bono reputation "is one of the reasons I chose this firm." A contact says that a partner worked on a pro bono case on Christmas Eve that had become urgent while the associate handling the case was travelling.

GETTING HIRED

Seeking interesting people

Insiders say that Morrison hires "interesting people who have had interesting experiences." One contact notes that foreign language skills can be especially helpful as well as "liberal leanings." "It is somewhat difficult to get in the door," one associate based outside the U.S. says. "Morrison is rather selective." Another source says that "we try to adhere to our hiring standards," which include targeting students at selected top law schools with excellent grades. However, like most law firms, growth and demand for attorney services has forced recruiters to expand their search. The foreign-based associate says that "qualified laterals have a somewhat easier time" getting into MoFo.

Interview process: to each their own

Initial interviews run for 15 to 20 minutes; callbacks are described as "relaxed." MoFo "already assumes that you've met the academic criteria" so the second round of interviews is a "matter of trying to figure out if you like the people." The firm "constructs an interview schedule that meets your interests. You can specify that you'd like to meet with a gay man, a lesbian, a Latino, a woman, someone from the labor department" or anyone else you'd like to see. One contact says that since you'll likely have a lot in common with your interviewer, "you don't need to do much preparation." Even so, it's "not a bad idea to run a Westlaw search to see if [your interviewer] has been in the news."

OUR SURVEY SAYS

We are family

One San Francisco associate says that MoFo is "very laid-back but professional. The lawyers respect each other's abilities but do not invade your space." The firm "still manages to be family in that everyone is willing to help another person out," says a real estate associate. A Palo Alto attorney says that "yellers and screamers [are] nonexistent" at MoFo. In keeping with the "relaxed" atmosphere, dress is business casual. The only qualification? "Just don't wear what you used to clean out your garage."

One contact says that "the firm's corporate culture has changed over the last few years and depending on your perspective, that may be good or bad. The law firm focuses on the bottom line more than it did a few years ago, which allows the associates to be paid more competitively." That critic concedes that "MoFo attempts to allow its associates to have a balanced life if that is what they are looking for in a job." One source says "the DC office is probably more uptight than some others but the firm seems fairly relaxed considering its size." A DC associate warns that the firm can be "a little gossipy at times."

High ratings for partners

"The majority of partners here are very good to work with," says one litigation associate. A lateral hire says that while Morrison partners are much better than those at his previous firm, he has noticed in the last year that "partners are overworked and spend less time being nice." Despite that, MoFo associates are overwhelmingly satisfied with their superiors. One Orange County lawyer says partner-associate relations are "the single most outstanding characteristic of working at Morrison & Foerster." Another attorney says that "there is great recognition by the partnership that today's associates are tomorrow's partners."

Social life makes the long hours bearable

At MoFo, "people seem to be too busy for regular happy hours but groups do go out from time to time," says a source. "I have made good friends at the firm," an associate tells Vault.com. "Although it is not extraordinarily social on a macro scale the lawyers are quite friendly and it is common for groups of friends to form and see each other socially." Contacts report that "there is no social face time or events that you must go to [in order] to succeed." "We have a nice group of lawyers at the Orange County office with diverse personalities," says one source. "Everyone is certainly not the same yet the firm provides a collegial and friendly environment. It is one of the reasons I have stayed so long and has made the long hours bearable."

Turning down work to cut back on hours

Like associates at all firms, MoFo lawyers tend to complain about the long hours required of those in the legal profession. "There's no getting around long hours in today's firm," laments one lawyer. "Last year was bad," says one source. "The partners are now making an effort to reduce everybody's hours by getting help from other offices and turning down work." Another contact reports that hours are "cyclical — one week I'll go home at 6:30 every night, the next I'm consistently here until midnight." That associate says the firm has no face time requirements and "people urge you to go home, in fact, and are honestly concerned about your work life."

Reaping the benefits of Bay Area pay raises

"My view is that I get paid a ton of money for work that is very demanding," says one associate. "It is not necessarily higher than other firms, it is comparable. You can talk all you want about the market but it is still a ton of money. Anyone who says otherwise lives in a different world." Those who live or at least work in MoFo's world receive compensation on par with other large firms. "Bay Area salaries have gone through the roof and most associates at large law firms are now very well paid," says one source. Another San Francisco lawyer reports that "associates are concerned that Bay Area attorneys do not get a cost of living adjustment to reflect how much more expensive it is to live here, as opposed to Los Angeles or other areas that are getting paid the same salary." Insiders say that the firm has a three-tier bonus structure with different financil rewards at 1,950, 2,100 and 2,200 billable hours.

Every day is casual day

Morrison attorneys receive the usual perks: cars and meals when working late, discounted gym memberships, sports and event tickets and firm social events. After 7:30, they get a $15 to $20 meal allowance. Moreover, "every day is casual day," with the usual restrictions related to client contact. "Dress ranges from flashy and hip to conservative and occasionally boring," reports one fashion maven.

Working on training, so quit bickering

MoFo insiders say that formal training, which had been below par, is improving. "The partners recognize that this is a problem but are slowly working on it," says one source. Another contact cites the text of an e-mail sent to Palo Alto associates after the firm stepped up training at that office in response to associate complaints. "The program will consist of a series of monthly seminars at noon, a deposition clinic in May and a mock trial in July," according to the electronic memo. "We are excited about the potential for this program particularly as a means of stopping associates from bickering about the lack of formal training in the office." That mole concedes that "it's only in the last few years that the Palo Alto office has become large enough to justify holding its own separate training." Most of the other offices now have formal training programs as well and the fall orientation program for new associates has recently been lengthened from two days to five. In addition, another associate says that "the informal training, feedback and communication [are] outstanding."

Palatial offices but unavailable support staff

Denver associates rave about the "fantastic mountain views" from their offices. In San Francisco "all associates have their own offices" which one associate describes as "not posh, but large and quite comfortable" and full of "nice furniture." One lawyer fell in love with the Orange County offices early on in the process, saying "I thought [it] was amazing on the day I first interviewed." Another attorney in Orange County sniffs that the digs are "a bit too post-modern for my tastes, but at least they're not stuffy." "The conference rooms are almost posh, but the offices aren't anything fancy," says a DC associate. "They're nice in a more understated way. In comparison to offices in New York, the associate offices are palatial in size."

An associate at Morrison says there's "lots of secretarial, word processing, and technical assistance and a help line. Everyone is very prompt in responding and getting the work done." In general, lawyers at MoFo say the main problem with support staff has been availability. "The patent secretaries are overworked in the DC office," says one source. Another contact claims that "there was a problem when I started here — attitude rather than insufficient staffing. I would not describe this as a problem currently as we have great staff members and a strong working relationship with them."

Retention: nobody's going anywhere, except the occasional dot-com

MoFo seems to have less of a problem with turnover than a typical law firm. "I think the turnover in the Orange County office is extremely low," says one attorney. "You'll find that most of the associates and partners have been with Morrison & Foerster for most of their careers." Another contact says that "the general feeling is that if you're going to be in a big firm, MoFo is the place to be." That doesn't mean there aren't some defectors. According to one source, "recently [turnover] has increased, which may have something to do with the environment we practice in — Silicon Valley is just crazy!" "We rarely lose associates to other comparable firms," says a different lawyer. "Usually it is to in-house or public service positions." The DC office is one location that does appear to have retention issues. "I'm not sure exactly how to calibrate this, but [my] department has almost completely turned over within the past three years."

Partnership prospects: don't call us, we'll call you

"If you do good work you will be a partner — if you want to stay and become a partner," says one source. Associates generally are considered for partner within seven to nine years, say insiders. An associate says that "quality of work really wins the day, although some junior partners with less than stellar experience have succeeded by pursuing appropriate political strategies." A contact advises associates seeking a partnership to "bill, do great work and don't piss people off too much." Sources report that "the firm is good about telling people what they need to do and providing the support they need."

Heightened diversity consciousness

One contact reports that "everyone at the firm is conscious of diversity issues." One insider charges that MoFo doesn't always "walk the talk" on minority hiring "because our emphasis on excellence sometimes leads us to ignore differences that are an asset to a practicing attorney but that don't always translate to objective criteria."

Could *Working Women* magazine have been wrong 10 out of the last 14 years? Not according to MoFo attorneys. As previously mentioned, the firm was on the publication's list of best companies for working mothers and the experiences and perceptions of associates at the firm seem to bear that out. "At Morrison & Foerster being a woman is not an issue, much less a handicap, and the firm aggressively pursues efforts to make it a better place to be a woman and a practicing attorney." The firm's maternity policy is described as "liberal" and the part-time policy is also praised. However, one female associate complains that "there is no set mentoring program for women."

For gay and lesbian attorneys, the firm reportedly offers domestic partner benefits. "[It] seems like there are a lot of gay people at the firm who are comfortably being open about their sexuality," one contact says.

Unusually satisfied

All told, MoFo insiders seem happy with firm life. "I don't think a big law firm can realistically get much better than MoFo," says one source. Another contact says, "I can honestly say that I cannot imagine working anywhere else. I don't really like big firm politics but I find the people I work with to be the best."

The people do seem to be one of the biggest plusses of working for Morrison. "They're smart but not arrogant," says one source. An associate says the firm offers "good work without completely crazy hours [and] a healthy respect for demands of personal lives." Quality of work is often praised. "The clients range from Fortune 500 to dot com companies, allowing diversity of practice." Last but not least, "the salary is great."

One associate complains that MoFo "is a big place and can be impersonal at times." Another lawyer laments the "politics of the firm," specifically the fact that partners in the Northern California and East Coast offices have little sense of the practice in Southern California. The relaxed culture also has a downside, report insiders. "Partners are so laid-back they just show up in my office without warning instead of calling to summon me to their offices."

VAULT.COM

23 PRESTIGE RANKING

Wilmer, Cutler & Pickering

2445 M Street, NW
Washington, DC 20037-1420
(202) 663-6000
Fax: (202) 663-6363
www.wilmer.com

LOCATIONS

Washington, DC (HQ)
Baltimore, MD
New York, NY
London
Brussels
Berlin

MAJOR DEPARTMENTS/PRACTICES

Antitrust & Competition
Aviation, Defense & Aerospace
Communications & Electronic Commerce
Corporate (includes the Latin American practice group)
Financial Institutions
Trade
Litigation
Securities Enforcement, Litigation and Regulatory (includes Investment Management and Broker-Dealer)
Tax

THE STATS

No. of attorneys: 344
No. of offices: 6
Summer associate offers: 34 out of 34 (Washington, 1999)
Management Committee Chair: William J. Perlstein
Hiring Partner: Mr. David P. Donovan

THE BUZZ
What attorneys at other firms are saying about this firm

- "The best in DC"
- "Good people; politically connected"
- "Snooty but without a reason to be"

PAY

Washington and Baltimore, 2000
1st year: $110,000 + $15,000 bonus
2nd year: $120,000
3rd year: $130,000
4th year: $140,000
5th year: $150,000
6th year: $160,000

$15,000 bonus for second through sixth years for 1,800 billable hours. Additional bonus (or Profit Sharing Unit) for 1,950 hours (of which 1,800 are billable and 150 may be pro bono) based upon firm profitability. Associates are eligible for a second Profit Sharing Unit at the firm's discretion and also receive one on both their second and fifth anniversary with the firm.

Summer associate: $2,400/week

New York, 2000
1st year: $125,000
2nd year: $135,000
3rd year: $150,000
4th year: $168,000
5th year: $190,000
6th year: $205,000
Bonus (or Profit Sharing Unit) for 1,950 hours (of which 1,800 are billable and 150 may be pro bono) based upon firm profitability.

NOTABLE PERKS

- Emergency child care
- On-site lactation room
- Prime tickets for the Orioles
- Year-round casual Friday; everyday casual during the summer
- Referral award

UPPERS

- Top-notch talent
- Quality clients
- Good diversity

DOWNERS

- Growth and open culture has led to chaos
- Senior associates treated the same as junior associates
- Top-notch talent can equal pretension and snobbery

KEY COMPETITORS

Arnold & Porter
Covington & Burling
Hogan & Hartson
Williams & Connolly

EMPLOYMENT CONTACT

Ms. Cheryl B. Shigo
Lawyer Recruitment Administrator
(202) 663-6368
cshigo@wilmer.com

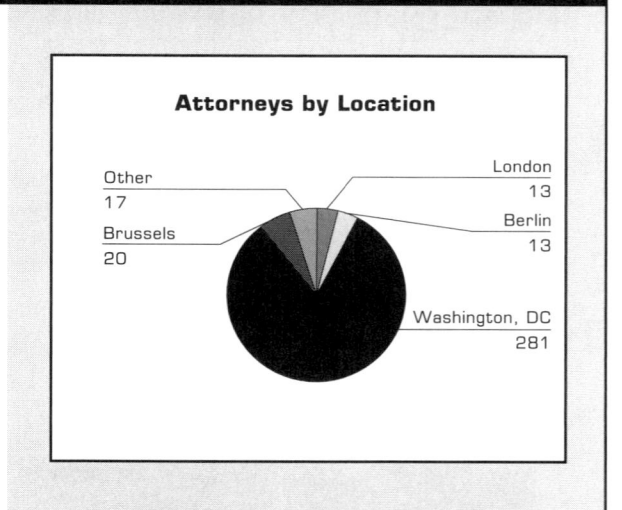

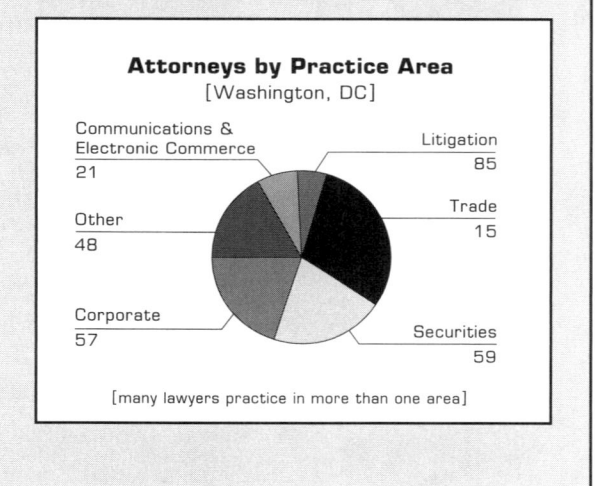

Attorneys by Location

- Other: 17
- Brussels: 20
- London: 13
- Berlin: 13
- Washington, DC: 281

Attorneys by Practice Area [Washington, DC]

- Communications & Electronic Commerce: 21
- Other: 48
- Corporate: 57
- Litigation: 85
- Trade: 15
- Securities: 59

[many lawyers practice in more than one area]

QUALITY OF LIFE RANKINGS [ASSOCIATES RATE THEIR OWN FIRM]

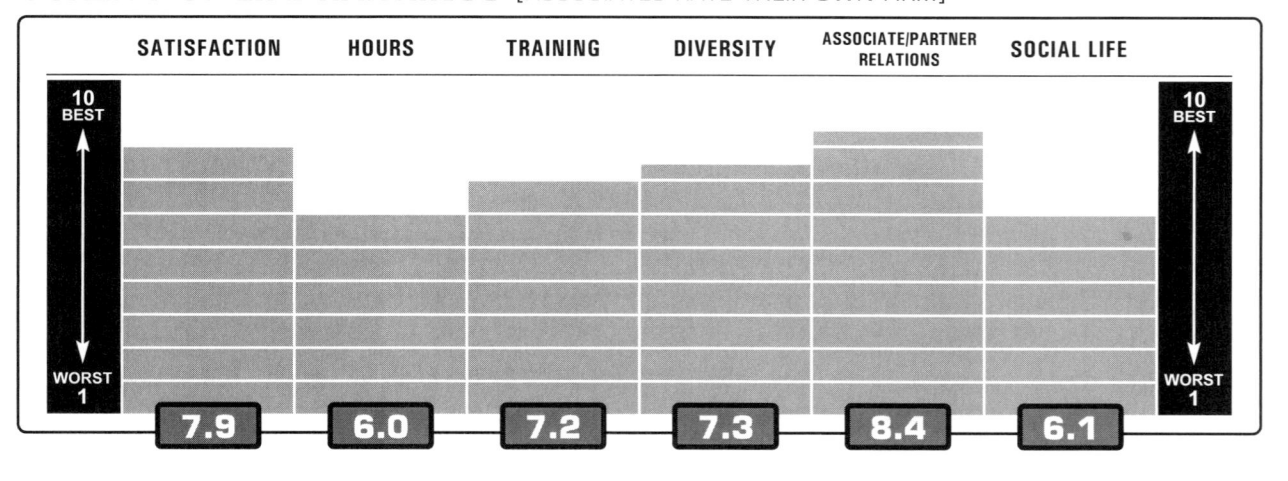

SATISFACTION	HOURS	TRAINING	DIVERSITY	ASSOCIATE/PARTNER RELATIONS	SOCIAL LIFE
7.9	6.0	7.2	7.3	8.4	6.1

THE SCOOP

Wilmer, Cutler & Pickering is a Washington, DC-based firm with strong ties to the city's power structure. The firm has represented a host of government agencies and two presidents and has an award-winning pro bono practice. Wilmer now has 350 attorneys in six offices (Washington, DC, Baltimore, New York, London, Brussels, and Berlin).

Firm history: two Democrats and a ton of government agencies

Wilmer, Cutler & Pickering was founded in 1962 in Washington with 19 lawyers. The firm soon established itself as a DC powerhouse and founding partner Lloyd Cutler has represented Jimmy Carter and Bill Clinton. Another famous Wilmer partner is Kurt Schmoke, who joined the firm in December 1999 after serving three terms as mayor of Baltimore. Wilmer attorneys have continued the government service commitment, representing the World Bank, the Federal Bureau of Investigation, the CIA, the National Security Counsel, the United States Air Force, the IRS, and the Department of the Treasury. A number of Wilmer partners have left the firm for senior positions in government agencies including the Department of Justice and the SEC.

Wilmer government contacts extend beyond the federal level. In August 1999, the city of Atlanta selected Wilmer to be one of three firms advising it on a suit brought by the Southeast Legal Foundation, which alleged that the city's affirmative action program is unconstitutional. Partner John Payton, leader of the Atlanta team, represented the city of Richmond, Virginia in a similar suit, *Richmond v. Croson*, in 1989. The Supreme Court ruled 6-3 against Richmond, a landmark decision that has paved the way for more challenges to affirmative action programs.

Corporate clients

Of course, Wilmer doesn't just represent government agencies. The firm advises companies from a variety of industries in most corporate practice areas, including antitrust, bankruptcy, electronic commerce, employee benefits, international trade, and securities law.

One antitrust client is Bayer A.G., whom Wilmer advised in the U.S. and Europe on its acquisition of Lyondell's plastics business. The firm is representing America Online in Europe in its merger with Time Warner. In another huge case, Wilmer filed a "friend of the court" brief in February 2000 on behalf of the Association for Competitive Technology, a computer industry trade group opposed to the antitrust suit against Microsoft. (The trade group has ties to Microsoft.)

Wilmer has also handled numerous bankruptcy cases. It has advised USAir, representing the company's interest in several airlines' bankruptcy proceedings. Investment bank Lehman Brothers tapped Wilmer when MCorp, a Texas bank holding company in which Lehman had invested, filed for Chapter 11. Wilmer has also represented Iridium, General Development Corp., and LTV Aerospace & Development in bankruptcies and reorganizations.

The firm has handled major securities litigation for a number of high-profile clients in investment banking as well. Among others, investment banks on the list include Donaldson Lufkin & Jenrette, Prudential Securities, PaineWebber, Salomon Smith Barney, Merrill Lynch, and Goldman Sachs.

Moral controversy

According to *The Washington Post*, in March 1999 Wilmer partners hotly debated a proposal to represent several German firms, including Siemens AG and Krupp AG, charged with using slave labor during World War II. The *Post* reported that a group of Wilmer partners and associates, including one associate whose grandfather was forced to work for one of the German companies, objected on moral grounds, saying such an association would soil the firm's name. The firm eventually decided to take the case, saying it could help broker an agreement similar to the one it had orchestrated on behalf of Swiss banks that held money belonging to Holocaust victims.

The decision to represent the German companies was most likely based on a majority decision. Wilmer was cited by *The Legal Times* for giving all partners an equal say in firm business, unlike other firms that are moving toward leadership by a managing partner or an executive board.

Swish!

Wilmer also played a significant role in bringing Michael Jordan back to basketball. The firm represented Lincoln Holdings, a holding company that owns most of the NHL's Washington Capitals and a small stake in the NBA's Washington Wizards, when the teams owners were trying to convince the basketball legend to buy a piece of the teams. Other Wilmer clients from the sports world include the NFL's Dallas Cowboys and the team's owner, Jerry Jones.

Landmark pro bono

The firm is also well known for its work in the pro bono arena. In 1982 it successfully represented the NAACP against a Mississippi hardware company which claimed that the NAACP's boycott violated antitrust laws. The Supreme Court ruled 9-0 in *NAACP v. Claiborne Hardware* that the boycott was protected speech.

Wilmer represented members of Congress challenging the constitutionality of the line-item veto as well as the League of Women Voters of Arkansas when it challenged term limits. The firm also assisted the American Civil Liberties Union and the National Association of Criminal Defense Lawyers in their challenge to mandatory drug testing for political candidates. More recently, the firm has aided a group of Bosnian refugee women, reviewed Chinese criminal proceedings for an international human rights organization, and assisted a nonprofit company in securing a loan to provide cellular phone service to residents of rural areas in Bangladesh. In addition, Wilmer has worked on behalf of World Organization Against Torture USA, Lawyers for Children America, and Stand Against Domestic Violence.

The firm's pro bono commitment has been widely recognized. Wilmer has received numerous accolades for its pro bono work, including the American Bar Association's 1998 Pro Bono Publico award. Wilmer also placed second in *The American Lawyer*'s most recent pro bono survey.

Insiders say that while pro bono work is a staple of Wilmer's business, its status in the firm is uncertain after recent pay raises in the industry. "Wilmer used to be a preeminent firm in which to do pro bono work," says one associate. "With the change in compensation structure, only a minimal pro bono involvement counts towards one's bonus."

Share the wealth

Going against the trend among DC firms of adopting discretionary pay scales for associates, Wilmer is staying fast to its policy of lockstep compensation. (Fearing competition between lawyers and between different departments, the firm organizes its partner compensation in similar lockstep fashion.) In lieu of the large bonuses offered at rival firms, Wilmer instituted a profit-sharing plan in 1999 for associates with two or more years of service. Mid-level associates were well-rewarded for their loyalty — third- and fourth-years received a bonus of $11,600 on top of their base salaries while associates with five or more years of service got twice that sum.

GETTING HIRED

Not as tough as they used to be

Wilmer has traditionally been one of the most selective firms in terms of hiring. But "because WCP is seeking to expand, it seems that it may be easier now to get hired than it once was," says one source. "In particular, we are taking more people who did not clerk. However, I still think that the associates are top-quality." Most insiders concur that while "there is a grade cutoff that slides up or down depending on where you went to school," it is much easier to get into Wilmer than in the past. Corporate attorneys specifically are in high demand. "Most associates still have very good academic credentials, but corporate associates are often an exception," says another contact. Also, "some securities associates with only so-so credentials get in if they have useful experience, like time spent at the SEC."

The interview: "it's more of a chat"

The hiring process begins with a screening interview. Those making the cut will hear within a week and move on to the next round of half-day interviews with four to six attorneys, both partners and associates. Interviews last around half an hour each and will usually connect candidates with attorneys in a substantive area of interest. Candidates can expect to hear from the firm within seven to 10 days. The firm insists that those receiving an offer are under no deadline to make a decision.

"It's more of a chat," says one Wilmer insider about the firm's interviews. "I've never heard of any questions about substantive law or anything like that." That insider explains: "Generally we'll only bring in people with superior resumés, so the interview is really just to see how they interact." Another agrees and adds that there should be "no sense of being grilled or tested."

Accordingly, Wilmer associates generally will go through the candidate's resumé and pick out things that look interesting. Laterals should expect to discuss their prior legal experiences and "what they're interested in, what they're looking for." Note that discussion of substantive issues of law will likely appear in the lunch following a morning of interviews. Says one contact: "That kind of thing frequently comes up during the lunch interview, say, if a student has just worked on a law review article or done some research for a professor. I would say there's a 50/50 chance you'll talk about something like that during lunch conversation, although it's generally pretty casual."

OUR SURVEY SAYS

Well-rounded Wilmer

Wilmer associates tend to agree on the firm's culture. The words "relaxed," "friendly," and "casual" come up repeatedly. "Lawyers at the firm are fairly well-rounded people," says one associate. "The lawyers here generally don't pigeonhole associates. Also, the firm is not competitive internally, probably because our pay scale still isn't linked that strongly to hours." Another contact says that "the firm remains an intellectual environment as opposed to a fire-breathing frat house. As a consequence of the great success of the securities enforcement and litigation practice [however], the older, genteel culture is gradually being supplanted by a more aggressive culture that requires longer hours and encourages less intellectual rumination."

Long partner memories

While Wilmer associates report a friendly environment, some criticize the firm's organizational structure. "In terms of partner-associate relations, the firm is extremely hierarchical," one insider reports. "Senior associates do not run cases and do not supervise other associates." Additionally, because of the firm's historical commitment to recruiting top candidates, Wilmer can be "nerdy" or "academic," say insiders. "Many Wilmer partners, especially the homegrown ones, see themselves as intellectuals," says one contact. "In terms of workload, they are usually attentive to detail. When an associate makes a mistake, partners remember — forever."

News flash! Partners respect associates

When discussing partner-associate relations, the hierarchy issue came up again. "Partners treat associates well in that they do not yell or insult associates, but in my book that isn't always the same thing as respect," says one insider. "The hierarchical relationship between superior and associate is always made clear in any conversation with a partner." In general, however, it seems that the relationship between partners and associates is better at Wilmer than many other large firms. One associate says that "[the] partners make every effort to treat you like a colleague or even better — no attitude problems."

No social obligations

Social interaction at Wilmer seems to be middle-of-the-road. "People do make attempts to go out socially but it does not happen on a consistent basis," reports one insider. The firm has Friday socials with moderate attendance. As one associate explains, "[you] are not obligated to be social with others."

Average hours make Wilmer "livable"

Hours at Wilmer seem to be on par with the industry, with most associates billing between 40 and 50 in a typical week. "The work here is not easy, but it is generally very interesting and the partners are great to work with [so] it is very livable." Another associate says that the problems lie not in the workload but in the way it is handled.

"Work is not well-managed and partners take on work without [regard] to staffing it properly," complains one associate. "Staffing is considered after the fact and too many matters are open at one time with conflicting deadlines. This results in an inability to focus appropriate attention on current matters and has diminished our quality of work."

Good pay, better bonus structure

Wilmer associates report being pleased with their pay. The firm avoided the bad feelings that surfaced at other firms regarding associate raises. "I like the way Wilmer handled the recent pay raises, both by seeking associate input and by keeping the billable minimum very reasonable — 1,800 hours — and including pro bono hours in the 1,950 required for a bonus," one source says. The bonus structure is especially well-received. "[Wilmer's] unique bonus structure allows high compensation with low billable requirements," says one insider. Recent bonuses were $15,000 for at least 1,800 hours and longevity bonuses can be expected after two years.

Try your luck at the raffle

"There are many opportunities for sports tickets, discounted gym membership, weekly [socials] and meals when you're here past 8 p.m.," reports a Wilmer associate. The tickets, notes one source, "are raffled off and are extremely hard to win — I have never won yet." Summer associates seem to get the best of the social events. "The summer events are fantastic," says one associate.

Well-trained associates

Wilmer's training program gets high marks. "The firm spends a lot of money on training and appears to be very dedicated to it," says one associate. A litigation attorney says that group is "making special efforts to improve training. A retired partner is in charge of the program. To a certain extent, though, every associate needs to take charge of his or her own career development." Another litigation associate reports that new associates in the department "receive weekly training on various litigation topics by partners at the firm." One insider offers this critique: "We had a series of group training lectures but there was no follow-up to see how that fit with our daily activities."

Few complaints on offices

Most associates have no problems with Wilmer's offices, calling them "comfortable" and offering "no complaints." All associates have window offices, according to insiders, and artwork at the DC office is described as "amazing." The only problems are a "weird air conditioning system" and a dearth of take-out restaurants near the building.

So-so support

Wilmer's support staff got a few complaints but most associates agree that "Wilmer is as supportive as one could ever hope for." On the other hand, one insider reveals that "some of the support staff don't do their job well — if at all — and Wilmer's non-confrontational style does not deal with this problem effectively." As in most firms, "it is clear that partners come first when it comes to secretaries and computers." Also, technical support is "inferior" and "not moving anywhere near fast enough to keep pace with our practice needs." One associate concludes that "support is good, if you know how, and whom, to ask."

Mid-level exodus

Wth regard to retention at Wilmer, "I think it's average for a large law firm," says one attorney. Apparently Internet companies are taking Wilmer associates by the truckload. "Wilmer loses a person a week to the dot coms," estimates one associate, and most agree that Wilmer associates rarely leave to go to another firm. The biggest problem seems to be mid-levels. "The firm has a lot of trouble keeping mid-level associates," reports one contact. "[They] often leave because they don't get more responsibility with time. Older associates and younger associates do much the same thing and older associates start to worry that they aren't getting good training. On the other hand, the reason mid-levels don't get more responsibility is that the firm does not distinguish very much between junior-level and more senior-level associates, so the work of junior-level associates may be more satisfying than it is at other firms."

Partnership prospects: neither rhyme nor reason

"The firm [offers] ample opportunities to make partner but the caliber of people who are partners at the firm makes it a little daunting to think that you can join them as a peer," says one lawyer. "Associates are given a good indication whether they are on track or not several years in advance of the decision." That lawyer advises prospective Wilmer partners to "work on interesting cases with a wide variety of partners — the partnership is truly a one person/one vote system." Another insider criticizes that "there does not seem to be rhyme or reason to the decisions." Sources also say the prospects are getting slimmer. "Since the new compensation system, increased hiring, and counsel system [were] put into place, it seems counsel is much more likely than partnership," one insider reports.

A diverse firm

In general, Wilmer gets good remarks for promoting diversity. One associate charges that "the firm needs to recruit more minorities" but the overall impression is positive. "Wilmer could be more aware of minority issues, though I think that the partnership does try to create an ethnically-diverse workplace," says an insider. Another lawyer comments that "there is a significant effort to mentor minority attorneys."

"The women partners are very good mentors and provide sound advice," says an insider. "The firm has a women's forum to which all of the women in the firm belong by default." That group sponsors lunches to address issues specific to women. Firm sources also applaud the maternity and part-time policies and report that the firm has an on-site day care center and a lactation room.

Associates also say that sexual preference "doesn't seem to be a problem at all in hiring, promotion, or daily life." Domestic partner benefits are available and "there are several openly gay male attorneys, including a partner."

If you're happy and you know it, you probably work at Wilmer

"No job is ideal. This one has its good and bad points but as far as law firms go it is pretty good," one insider says in what can only be construed as a compliment in the legal industry. In all seriousness, Wilmer lawyers seem to be more satisfied than those at other firms. "Big firm life does not get better," says one insider.

Wilmer insiders seem most pleased with the quality of the firm — in terms of both the clients and the attorneys. "The partners are very intelligent and very nice to associates," one contact says. "The work is also great." Another attorney raves that "I have all the benefits that I looked for in a small firm — a high level of responsibility and constant work with clients — coupled with the resources of a major firm." One associate chose Wilmer because he "wanted exposure to cases with social (rather than just monetary) consequences. I have found that at Wilmer." Another lawyer chose the firm "because I liked the people and the kind of work they do and [because] they have a 'free market' system for distributing work."

Some see the firm's rapid growth as a drawback. "It is growing too fast — Wilmer's selectivity of hiring has plummeted in the past year, especially in the corporate group," says one associate. One contact notes the firm's "strong tendency not to give substantial authority or responsibility to senior associates." Another complaint: "Wilmer's non-confrontational style permits many, many people to exploit [the firm's] culture, and when brought to the attention of management, it has more often than not chosen to do nothing about it," gripes one contact. "The partners here are very good lawyers, but not very good managers."

VAULT.COM

24 PRESTIGE RANKING

Brobeck, Phleger & Harrison LLP

One Market
Spear Street Tower
San Francisco, CA 94105
(415) 442-0900
Fax: (415) 442-1010
www.brobeck.com and www.joinbrobeck.com

LOCATIONS

San Francisco, CA (HQ)
Austin, TX • Dallas, TX • Denver, CO • Irvine, CA • Los Angeles, CA • New York, NY • Palo Alto, CA • San Diego, CA • Washington, DC • London and Oxford (joint venture with Hale & Dorr)

MAJOR DEPARTMENTS/PRACTICES

Business & Technology
Commerce and Finance
Complex Litigation
Intellectual Property
Real Estate and Land Use
Securities Litigation
Tax/Executive Compensation
Labor and Employment

THE STATS

No. of attorneys: 750
No. of offices: 12
Summer associate offers: 12 out of 13
(San Francisco, 1999)
Chairman: Tower C. Snow, Jr.
Managing Partner: James E. Burns
Hiring Attorney: Molly Moriarty Lane (San Francisco)

PAY

All Domestic Offices, 2000
1st year: $125,000 + $30,000 bonus potential
2nd year: $135,000 + $40,000 bonus potential
3rd year: $150,000 + $45,000 bonus potential
4th year: $165,000 + $50,000 bonus potential
5th year: $185,000 + $50,000 bonus potential
6th year: $195,000 + $50,000 bonus potential
7th year: $205,000 + $50,000 bonus potential
8th year: $210,000 + $50,000 bonus potential
Summer associate: $2,400/week

NOTABLE PERKS

- Home-buying assistance program for attorneys in California
- Firm-funded high tech venture fund for associates
- Associate profit sharing

THE BUZZ
What attorneys at other firms are saying about this firm

- "Riding the tech boom to great heights"
- "Disgustingly relaxed"
- "Sloppy"
- "Strong in securities offerings"

UPPERS

- Technology focus that can lead to great in-house opportunities
- Laid-back culture
- Salary and perks at the top of the market

DOWNERS

- Little training
- Brutal hours
- Lack of structure that can lead to lack of direction

KEY COMPETITORS

Cooley Godward
Gunderson Dettmer Stough Villeneuve Franklin & Hachigian
Morrison & Foerster
Orrick, Herrington & Sutcliffe
Venture Law Group
Wilson Sonsini Goodrich & Rosati

EMPLOYMENT CONTACT

Ms. Tina Shinnick
Attorney Recruiting Manager
(415) 442-1540
tshinnick@brobeck.com

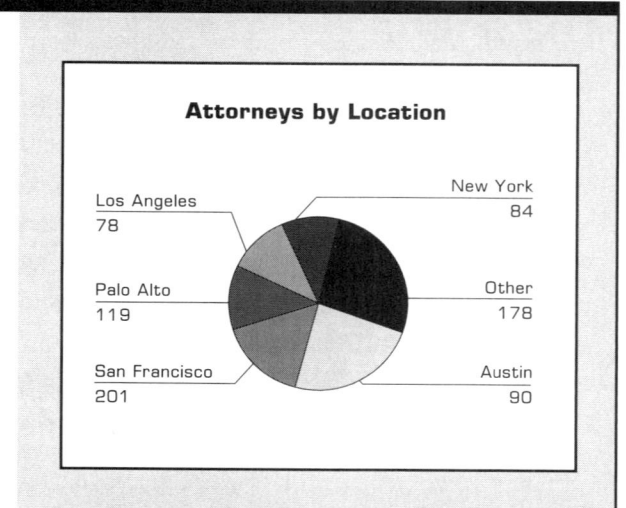

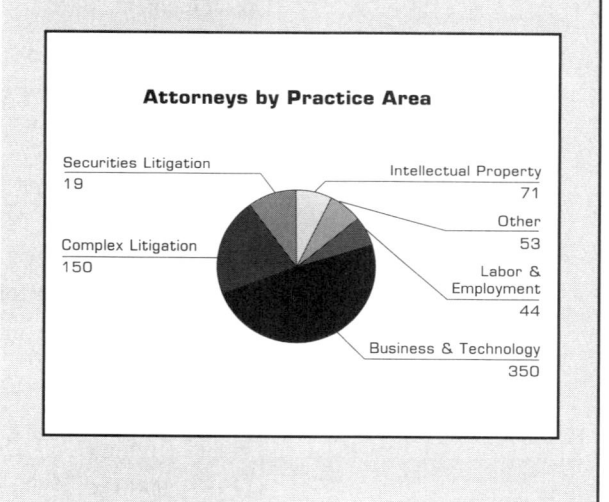

Attorneys by Location

- Los Angeles: 78
- New York: 84
- Palo Alto: 119
- Other: 178
- San Francisco: 201
- Austin: 90

Attorneys by Practice Area

- Securities Litigation: 19
- Intellectual Property: 71
- Other: 53
- Complex Litigation: 150
- Labor & Employment: 44
- Business & Technology: 350

QUALITY OF LIFE RANKINGS [ASSOCIATES RATE THEIR OWN FIRM]

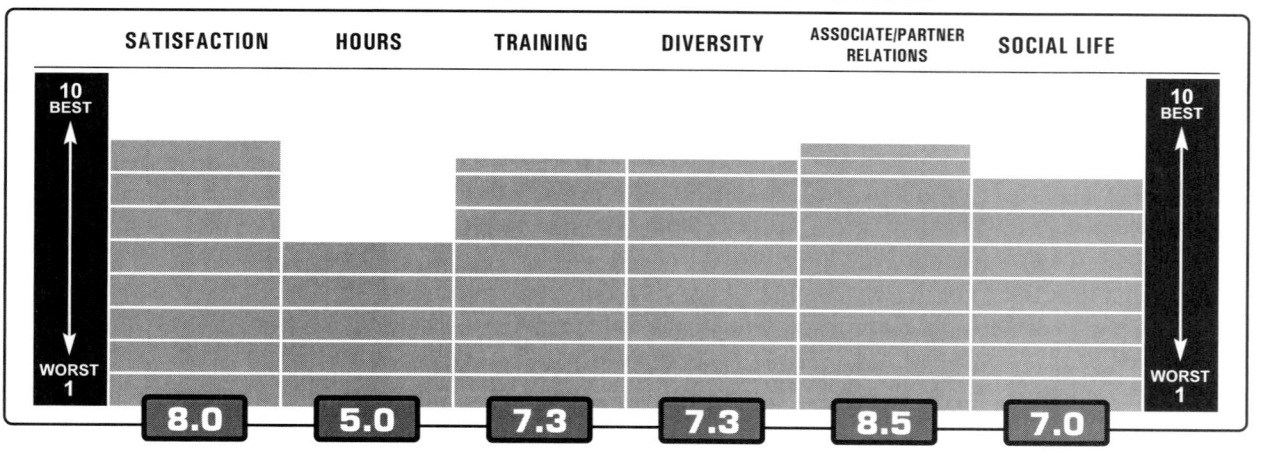

Satisfaction	Hours	Training	Diversity	Associate/Partner Relations	Social Life
8.0	5.0	7.3	7.3	8.5	7.0

THE SCOOP

Brobeck, Phleger & Harrison is one of the largest San Francisco-based firms. With approximately 750 attorneys in 10 U.S. offices and two British offices, Brobeck is a leader in technology and Internet law. As a result of the recent technology boom, the firm has experienced excellent returns over the past few years, including a 40 percent jump in profits per partner from 1998 to 1999. Much of that can be attributed to Brobeck's audacious foray into the high-stakes, high-profit world of e-business.

History: a dramatic break-up leads to West Coast success

Brobeck traces its roots to Morrison Dunne & Brobeck, a San Francisco firm prominent in the early twentieth century. That firm broke up in 1924, with some partners forming Brobeck and others moving to Morrison & Foerster (another Vault.com Top 50 firm). According to legend, Morrison partners used an axe to break down Brobeck's office door and make off with client files. Herman Phleger led the firm in the early days and later served as an advisor to President Dwight Eisenhower.

Brobeck started expanding in earnest 50 years after its founding. The Los Angeles office was founded in 1976 and now has approximately 75 attorneys. Four years after the L.A. opening, Brobeck expanded into Silicon Valley, establishing a Palo Alto office that has been among the most successful of the firm's satellites. In 1990 the firm made inroads into East Coast technology, founding a New York office that represents many of the most important companies in Silicon Alley. Other offices include Irvine (1987), San Diego (1987), Denver and Austin (1994), Washington, DC (1999), and Dallas (2000).

In February 2000, Brobeck announced plans to move its Silicon Valley offices. Brobeck will occupy one of three office buildings scheduled to be completed on January 1, 2002 in the University Circle area of Palo Alto. The San Diego office, which added 16 intellectual property attorneys in February 2000, also moved to new offices in March 2000.

IPO madness

One of Brobeck's more interesting and lucrative specialties is its corporate securities practice. The firm has represented many young dot coms that have gone public, especially in New York City's Silicon Alley. (The reason for this success? Brobeck was among the first law firms to aggressively pursue dot com business in New York, drawing on a pointed ad campaign and much leg work.) *Crain's New York Business* claimed in February 1999 that Brobeck had led more New York-area Internet IPOs than any other firm. Notable Brobeck IPO clients include online linkster About.com, web consulting firm Agency.com, online ad agency DoubleClick and free email pro Juno Online Services.

Brobeck's ties with the new media world were affirmed by rankings published in September 1999 in *The American Lawyer*. In the survey, Brobeck took top honors as the "firm mentioned most often" by new media companies and the firm "mentioned most as litigation counsel."

Brobeck partners aren't the only ones who benefit. All Brobeck associates have the option to invest in Brobeck clients — a rare (but increasingly common) perk that gives lawyers a chance to dip their hand into the golden pool of IPOs.

M&A — OK!

Mergers and acquisitions have been good to Brobeck as well. The firm advised long-time client Wells Fargo Bank on its $11.6 billion acquisition of First Interstate Bank in 1998. Brobeck also counseled GeoCities on its $4.6 billion acquisition by Yahoo!. The deal was announced in January 1999 and closed that year. In one deal famous for its swift completion, the firm represented i2 Technologies in its $9.3 billion merger with Aspect Development in March 2000. From initial negotiations to the completion of the final merger agreement, the deal took six days. Rod Howard, the Brobeck partner who led the deal, told *The Recorder* that when i2 approached Brobeck about working on a deal with such a quick target date, the firm "swallowed hard and said yes."

Securities litigation

The firm has developed a reputation for fierce litigators and its track record in securities litigation certainly bears this out. The firm has won dismissal of suits filed against clients such as Adobe Systems, BankAmerica Corp., The Gap, and Sun Microsystems and has scared away suits against 3Com, Apple Computer, and BankAmerica. (The firm likes to brag that the Apple suit, filed way back in 1991, was the largest securities class action suit voluntarily dropped since federal securities laws were enacted.) Finally, Brobeck has settled a number of securities law suits with several notable clients including John Hancock Mutual Life, Fidelity Financial, and Wells Fargo Bank.

IP practice

Intellectual property has been another noteworthy practice for Brobeck. The firm represented Matrix Pharmaceuticals in a 1997 suit by Collagen Corp. alleging that former Collagen employees who went to Matrix stole trade secrets for use in their new jobs. Brobeck also counseled Ligand Pharmaceuticals in its suit against drug giant

Pfizer. Ligand claimed Pfizer used research that the companies had collaborated on to develop a breast cancer drug. In technology cases, Brobeck represented Nomai in a case alleging that Iomega Zip Drive technology infringed on Nomai patents. In *3Com v. SynOptics Communications*, Brobeck defended Bay Networks (formerly known as SynOptics) against charges of patent infringement by 3Com.

More litigation

In the product liability area, Brobeck negotiated a $1.5 billion settlement in the early 1990s for Fibreboard Corp. in an asbestos litigation case. The firm also represented Mentor Corp. in a breast implant litigation case. Brobeck secured a $28.5 million settlement, then negotiated with Mentor's insurers to pay half the settlement.

Please don't go

Brobeck has taken steps to stem turnover among both attorneys and support staff. In October 1999, the firm allowed for 360-degree reviews and based partner compensation in part on associate feedback. At the time, *The Recorder* reported the firm had a turnover rate around 30 percent. Seeing similar problems among support staff, the firm started a $1.25 million investment pool for staff members in early 2000. And to make its support staff feel truly cherished, Brobeck gave each staff member a $1,000 bonus on Valentine's Day 2000. (Cash works better than red roses, apparently.)

Brobeck has added key laterals to its stable of top lawyers this year. Dean Kristy and Susan Samuels, formerly of Shearman & Sterling, joined the San Francisco office as securities partners in March 2000. In early April of this year, Stephen Rosenman, an IP partner from Howrey Simon Howard & White, joined Brobeck's Palo Alto office.

Investing in clients and associates

All Brobeck attorneys are automatically included in the firm's investment pool. Even with the recently seesawing Nasdaq, the profit potential is clear. Brobeck invests in its attorneys in other ways as well — in 2000 the firm finished a two-year, $37 million capital infusion program in technology. And the contribution to associate comfort? Brobeck, aping its Silicon Alley and Valley clients, was the first major law firm to shift to casual dress full-time.

GETTING HIRED

Picky, picky (at least until recently)

Traditionally, Brobeck has been very selective in hiring, recruiting almost exclusively from top national and regional law schools. Recent events, however, have apparently induced the firm to widen the scope of candidates it sees. "This used to be a fairly hard place to get an offer," says one associate. "Now, with the [economy] as hot as it is, we'll hire anybody with a pulse. I wouldn't be surprised if we hired a graduate of an unaccredited law school." While that may be a stretch, insiders do report that securing an offer at Brobeck is becoming easier. "With the really tight labor market, the firm is definitely struggling to hire people," says one source. "The firm often just hires bodies to bill." Graduates of top law schools are still coveted. "The firm tends to discriminate heavily based on law schools," reports one lawyer. "Those who attended top five or top ten schools would obviously find it very easy to get hired here."

While intellectual capacity is clearly important, personality is also taken into consideration. One attorney says that "the 'Big Three' sought-after characteristics in associate hiring seem to be (1) smart; (2) hard worker; (3) nice." "Intellect and personality fit are both important," claims one associate. The firm has a web site dedicated exclusively to recruiting (www.joinbrobeck.com) that lists openings and contact information for lawyers and support staff alike at each office.

Interview process

Callbacks for law students last half a day, including lunch. The interview can vary depending on which attorney you see. "Some are very tough," warns one contact. "Some are easy." Candidates are taken to a "nice" restaurant with two first-year associates for a lunch that lasts "about an hour and a half." After lunch candidates have an exit interview, usually with the person who conducted the on-campus interview. Lateral hires can expect a half-day of interviews with attorneys from the group matching their interests.

OUR SURVEY SAYS

Entrepreneurial culture

A firm insider describes the culture as "entrepreneurial — both for partners and associates. The hierarchy required for a firm is not oppressive here. The demeanor of the partners and associates is generally laid-back and friendly." The culture of the high tech clientele definitely has an impact. "We are very young and high-energy," says one associate. "We are kind of a cross between a high tech company and a law firm." A California-based associate says that the "San Francisco office is pretty mellow compared to Palo Alto, which can feel younger and has more of a buzz."

"The firm is managed like a business, and I mean that in a positive way," notes another attorney. "It's not that it's impersonal, it's just business-like, which I think is good in the long term. The more efficiently [firm leaders] can run the enterprise, the more money they can give to the associates." Like its dot com peers, Brobeck can't be considered a lifestyle choice. "[Brobeck] is not a lifestyle firm, nor is it necessarily a sweatshop," says one source. "While you work very hard, it's not because a partner is breathing down your neck. Rather, it's because Silicon Valley is so busy that everyone is working hard."

Partners: a mixed bag

Partner-associate relationships at Brobeck seem to be all over the scale. "Where else can you have a partner come to you at 8 p.m. with last-minute revisions to a deal and then work side-by-side with you until 2 a.m. to get the work out?" asks one Austin associate. "I have yet to meet a single pretentious partner," announces one contact. Another source says, "Partners respect my autonomy and my work but are difficult to find and communicate with."

Some associates, however, identify partner-associate problems. "The great majority of partners treat associates as mere cogs, fungible goods," says one insider. As one might imagine, not all partners are created equal. "There are partners who are known by everyone in the firm as treating associates and staff poorly and at times abusively," repines one litigation associate. "The firm does not take any action with these partners in terms of correcting the behavior or even bringing the issue to the attention of the partner who's being abusive."

Inmate social life

Associates at Brobeck are careful to point out that while the firm isn't unfriendly, there is limited social interaction outside the office, save for a few firm-sponsored events.

"People here work hard enough that they want to go home to sleep at the end of the day, not go out drinking with fellow inmates," says one Brobeck prisoner. "I think Brobeck's unusual in that associates really try to work smarter, not harder. That cuts down on the socializing during working hours and spills over into non-working hours," explains one associate. "People, I think, want a line between work and play. You don't necessarily want to see the same people 24/7."

Fun by the hour

Hours at Brobeck are lousy, but not any lousier than at other firms. "There is a ton of work here, but I do not think that the amount is much different than that at any other large law firm," reports one lawyer. "Most importantly, no one feels the obligation to put in face time. We work until the work is done, then go home." Insiders report that "workload reports are monitored by partners to ensure the even distribution of work." Obviously, different practices have different needs. For example, "the corporate practice has been extremely busy in recent years due to the boom in the Silicon Valley practice."

Some employees do seem despondent about the workload. "This is the worst aspect of the job. I don't know how much more of these hours I can take," stresses one associate. "It is affecting my health, my relationship, my attitude towards this career choice and my sanity. I have little time to do anything outside work except sleep and drive to and from the office." The beleaguered associate continues: "Friends don't even bother to call me anymore; they know where I'll be and that I can't make it. Although the new salaries make this a little more bearable, at some point the hours far outweigh the life given up."

Top-of-the-line pay

"If anyone complains about compensation at Brobeck, they should be slapped," barks one attorney. More mellow associates seem to agree. "Brobeck actually believes in providing their associates with predictable salaries commensurate with their hard work, rather than back-ending compensation with huge but miserably discretionary bonuses," says one lateral hire. "Because associate salaries are so high, morale is good. Bonuses play a minimal role in keeping associates happy." Additionally, when tallying up pay, "you have to add on the firm's investment fund. [It's] worth thousands each year." Insider report that the recent pay raises haven't caused the kind of friction between partners and associates as in other firms. "Many associates were concerned about what the impact would be on the firm culture and training. But firm management has not expressed any concern," says one source.

Typical perks

Associates at Brobeck can expect a gym discount, as well as meals and cab rides when working late. The quality of the meals is questionable — "If we bill enough hours we can get a warmed-over, soggy meal from Waiters on Wheels two hours after we ordered it" — but otherwise, complaints about perks are few. The firm provides mortgage assistance and laptops and subsidized cellular phones. If over 75 percent of calls are work-related, the firm picks up the whole bill. Finally, firm-sponsored events are few but nice, "especially the Christmas party."

Training on back burner?

One Brobeck associate reports that "because we have an overabundance of work, training tends to be pushed to the back burner. This isn't a place for any associate who needs a lot of hand-holding." "The IP partners' mantra is that our billing rates are too high to permit proper training," another associate complains.

While active training by superiors may be lacking, Brobeck does provide help electronically. "[The firm] has an intranet system called BrobeckNet which is single-handedly the greatest collection of resources for any associate on any type of deal," says one contact. There are also regularly scheduled video conferences that serve as training, which some associates find useful.

"Cramped" offices, "nonexistent" support

The downside of high growth? Cramped office space. "Brobeck's offices are generally well-decorated but the firm is suffering from over-expansion in almost all of the offices," reports one associate. However, several offices have moved or are planning to move into new digs, which should ease the overcrowding in those locations.

Brobeck offices differ by locale. An Austin associate says the offices there have a Lone Star State with a hunting lodge, Ralph Lauren-esque type décor. We even have a stuffed longhorn's head on the wall of one of our conference rooms."

There seems to be a bit more room in the Valley. "The Palo Alto office is a three-building campus which offers nice outdoor common areas," says one California insider. "The interior is a bit hodge-podge. While the associate offices are not fancy, I find them much more flexible than the sleek modular units in fashion at the big city firms." Another Valley lawyer is excited that "I get my own large office, which is great! The furniture could be a little newer but overall I can't complain."

Brobeck associates do take issue with the support staff. "The number of support staff is adequate," one lawyer says. "The issue is its quality. I am fortunate to work with an outstanding paralegal and very good secretary but several of my colleagues are not so fortunate." One San Diego associate alleges that "the firm skimps on support staff to keep the overhead costs low and partner profits high." Another lawyer seconds that, saying "the firm decided to increase partner profits a few years back and support services were the lion's share of what was eliminated to fund this." In some offices, insiders say, after-hours support is "nonexistent."

Retention: some light out for the dot coms

Attorneys at Brobeck hold the typical view of retention — that it's on par with other top firms and that those who do leave go to positions with clients. "Attrition is very high, but then so are the opportunities for attrition," says one insider. "Most of the lawyers I've seen leave have gone to clients." As an associate notes, "It's a testament to this place that we don't lose attorneys to other firms. We lose them to VCs, banks and startups."

"Mysterious" partnership prospects

Brobeck associates seem puzzled about their chances to make partner. "If that sort of thing is important to you, you may want to consider another firm," one contact warns. Another says that the partnership track is "mysterious. No one talks about it. Laterals, especially, seem to be at a loss for exactly when they'll be up for partnership. Some groups are better than others when it comes to grooming their own for partnership consideration." However, "if you're willing to put in a lot of billable hours plus a bunch of non-billable business development time, then prospects for partnership are good." One source advises potential partners to "learn to love sports, find a niche that no one else is doing [and] participate in the summer associate program."

Diversity record fairly solid

According to firm insiders, Brobeck is making an effort to support diversity but the results aren't there. "It's tough for Brobeck. We're not that ethnically diverse, and we can't seem to attract more minorities," laments one associate. "It's a vicious circle — since we don't have enough diversity, it's very difficult for us to create an environment to which ethnically diverse people wish to come." One lawyer allows that "the firm is aware and tries to hire minorities and support minority student groups at the law schools."

The firm's efforts with women seem to be more productive. "Among the firms I've worked for, Brobeck's proactive approach to lifestyle issues and the advancement of female associates knows no equal," one associate proudly states. Insiders report that maternity leave and part-time schedules are top-notch and a fair share of the partners are women. The only complaint seems to be a lack of a mentoring program for women.

Brobeck has a strong record of supporting gay and lesbian lawyers as well. "Brobeck has been very good [on gay and lesbian retention]," one associate says. "The atmosphere is simply that sexual orientation is a non-issue on a personal basis." Domestic partner benefits are offered and "the firm does support gay and lesbian groups."

No greener grass

It's a tribute to Brobeck that its associates are for the most part happy to work at the firm. "I don't wake up each day and say 'Gee! I get to go to work! Yay!' But if I have to work, I'm extremely glad it's at Brobeck," says one associate. Another attorney who evidently graduated from the same school of restraint says, "Overall I am satisfied. I am unconvinced that things would be greener anywhere else. I like the people that I work with and the work is challenging and interesting, even if stressful at times."

Salary is mentioned frequently as an upside of working at Brobeck. The "very relaxed atmosphere" is also a bonus, as are the assignments. "There is a ton of quality work," one contact says. Some attorneys also cite the firm's prestige and culture as a factor in their decision to work at Brobeck.

INTERVIEW TIP #13

DON'T concentrate your questions on perks like bonuses and cocktail hours. Your interviewer will immediately type you as someone with other things on your mind besides working toward the best interests of the firm.

Mayer, Brown & Platt

VAULT.COM PRESTIGE RANKING: 25

190 South LaSalle Street
Chicago, Illinois 60603
(312) 782-0600
Fax: (312) 701-7711
www.mayerbrown.com

LOCATIONS

Chicago, IL (HQ)
Charlotte, NC • Houston, TX • Los Angeles, CA • New York, NY • Santa Fe, NM • Washington, DC • Cologne • London

Representative Offices:
Ashgabat, Turkmenistan • Bishkek, Kyrgyz Republic • Tashkent, Republic of Uzbekistan

Correspondent Offices:
Mexico City • Paris

MAJOR DEPARTMENTS/PRACTICES

Bankruptcy & Reorganization • Corporate & Securities, Finance • Environmental • Employee Benefits • Government Relations • Labor • Information Technology • Intellectual Property • Investment Management • Litigation • Real Estate • Taxation • Trade Access • Trusts, Estates, & Foundations

THE STATS

No. of attorneys: 931
No. of offices: 9 + 5 (3 Representative and 2 Correspondent)
Summer associate offers: 61 out of 62 (Chicago, 1999)
Managing Partner: Debora de Hoyos
Hiring Partner: J. Thomas Mullen

PAY

Chicago, 2000
1st year: $125,000
2nd year: $135,000
3rd year: $150,000
Summer associate: $2,400/week

Los Angeles, 2000
1st year: $125,000
2nd year: $135,000
3rd year: $150,000
4th year: $165,000
5th year: $185,000
6th year: $195,000
7th year: $205,000
Summer associate: $1,850/week

New York, 2000
1st year: $125,000
2nd year: $135,000
3rd year: $150,000
4th year: $165,000
5th year: $190,000
6th year: $200,000
7th year: $210,000
8th year: $220,000

NOTABLE PERKS

- Emergency child care
- Domestic partner coverage

THE BUZZ

What attorneys at other firms are saying about this firm

- "Somewhat nerdy"
- "Terrific appellate work"
- "Heavy hours, strange people"
- "Youthful, aggressive, and good"

UPPERS

- Free bagels every morning
- Laissez-faire work assignment system
- Around-the-clock support staff

DOWNERS

- Associate-partner friction due to recent pay raises
- Less than primo training
- New billable hours requirement

KEY COMPETITORS

Jones, Day, Reavis & Pogue
Kirkland & Ellis
Sidley & Austin
Skadden, Arps, Slate, Meagher & Flom

EMPLOYMENT CONTACT

Ms. Kelly B. Koster
Legal Recruiting Manager
(312) 701-7002
kkoster@mayerbrown.com

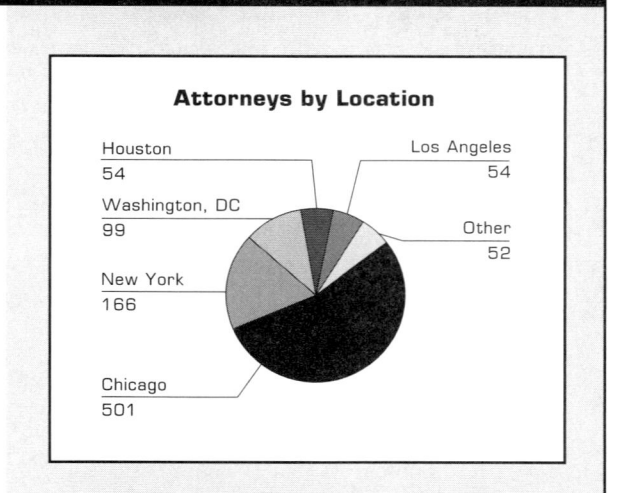

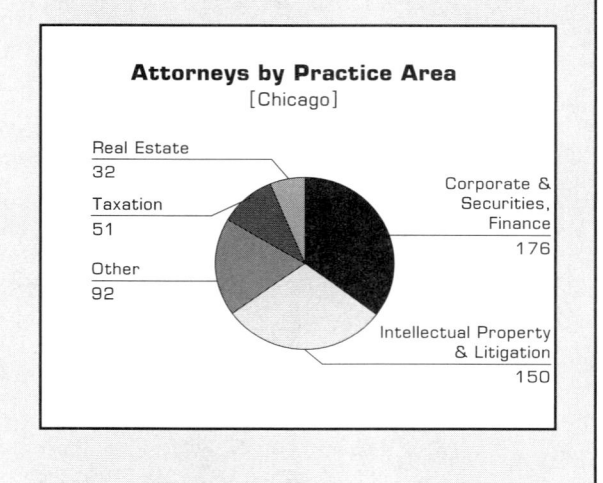

Attorneys by Location

- Houston: 54
- Los Angeles: 54
- Washington, DC: 99
- Other: 52
- New York: 166
- Chicago: 501

Attorneys by Practice Area [Chicago]

- Real Estate: 32
- Taxation: 51
- Other: 92
- Corporate & Securities, Finance: 176
- Intellectual Property & Litigation: 150

QUALITY OF LIFE RANKINGS [ASSOCIATES RATE THEIR OWN FIRM]

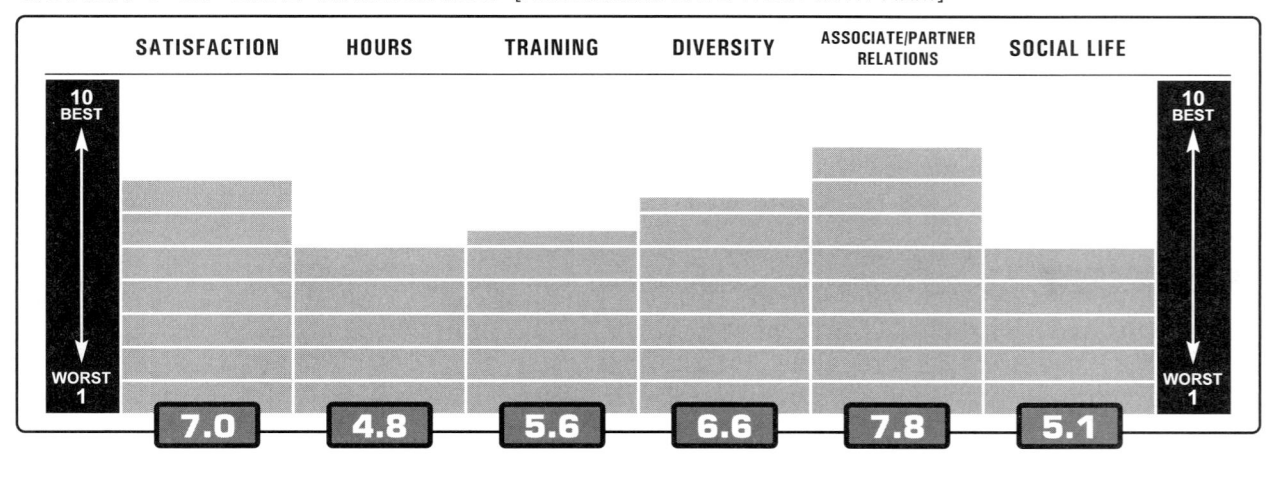

SATISFACTION	HOURS	TRAINING	DIVERSITY	ASSOCIATE/PARTNER RELATIONS	SOCIAL LIFE
7.0	4.8	5.6	6.6	7.8	5.1

(Scale: 10 BEST — 1 WORST)

THE SCOOP

With almost 120 years of history, Mayer, Brown & Platt is one of the oldest and largest firms in the world. The firm has approximately 900 attorneys in nine offices (including its Chicago headquarters). No Oscar Mayer hot dog jokes this year, Mayer Brown hits our prestige survey at 25.

Second City history

Founded in 1881, Chicago-based Mayer, Brown & Platt has become one of the largest firms in the country. Early Mayer clients included Sears Roebuck and Continental Bank, which selected Mayer when it incorporated. The firm began to branch out in the 1970s, opening offices in Washington, DC, New York, and London. Mayer became a pioneer of sorts in 1991 when Debora de Hoyos was elected managing partner. De Hoyos, a Harvard law grad, was one of the first women selected to lead a top law firm. Other top partners include former U.S. Secretary of Commerce Mickey Kantor and former Illinois Attorney General Ty Fahner. More than 10 former Supreme Court clerks now work for Mayer (including four hired in 1999) as do nine former members of the U.S. Solicitor General's office.

Steady growth (at least in most places)

With more than 500 lawyers, the Chicago practice encompasses almost half the firm's total and is well known for its government, tax, and mergers and acquisitions work. The New York office has experienced explosive growth from one attorney in 1978 to 166 in 2000 and is reportedly the most profitable non-New York-based firm operating in the city. Notable practice areas include corporate, more specifically securities law, finance, structured finance, real estate, tax, banking and bankruptcy. The London office, relatively petite at 31 lawyers, works on finance and mergers and acquisitions.

Mayer is expanding its Charlotte practice as well. The firm moved into the banking mecca in 1998, merging with local firm Blanchfield Cordle & Moore. Since then, the branch has more than tripled in size, employing 23 lawyers (including 12 partners). It has also widened its practice areas, now handling structured finance and other transactional work in addition to tax. Further expansion appears to be on the horizon as Jay Monge, architect of the firm's successful New York foray, joined the Charlotte office at the end of 1999. In spite of all this growth, Mayer Brown shut its Moscow offices in September 1999, one of many law firms to pull out of Russia after that country's economic crisis.

Merger powerhouse

Mayer's corporate practice is well-respected and the firm has advised on several high-profile mergers. For example, Mayer represented Pacific Retail Trust when it was sold to Regency Realty for $2 billion. The firm was co-counsel to Aetna when the company spent $1 billion for the health care business of Prudential Insurance, a deal completed in August 1999. The following month, Mayer Brown represented Illinois Tool Works in its $3.4 billion merger with Premark International. That December MBP served as counsel to MapQuest.com in its $1.1 billion acquisition by America Online. (The firm also advised MapQuest in its May 1999 IPO.)

Supreme Court regulars

The firm's litigation department is also top-notch. In 1999 the firm racked up five victories (with no losses) in front of the Big Nine. Mayer handled the oral arguments in four of these cases. In fact, Mayer attorneys appeared in front of the Supreme Court more than any other firm's lawyers in the 1990s. The firm's 1996 appearance in *BMW of North America v. Gore* won a reduction in a $2 million punitive damage award for the automaker. The litigation department also secured a settlement in a suit against Dow Chemical stemming from the company's breast implant liability.

Boldly into the New Economy

Mayer Brown has jumped headfirst into the Internet revolution, representing a number of firms on various issues. The firm represented startups Launch Media, Auctions.com, 3Clix.com and EDC.com on numerous issues related to their launches, from funding to incorporation. Members of senior management at Ameritrade and Apartments.com selected Mayer to negotiate compensation and employment agreements. Yesmail.com and CompUSANet.com used the firm to negotiate technology contracts and licenses. Larger, more established companies such as Ernst & Young and Dell Financial Services have used Mayer to get their own web ventures set up. The firm has represented Internet heavyweights such as America Online and Ziff-Davis in intellectual property litigation. Apartments.com and harmonycentral.com have secured venture capital funding through Mayer. Finally, Mayer has represented many companies in their exit strategies, either IPOs or mergers and acquisitions.

It's not *all* about the money

Mayer Brown's work isn't all so profitable — the firm has done substantial pro bono work has been as well. According to *The Chicago Tribune*, Mayer donates $7 million worth of time to pro bono activities per year. Mayer has set up a legal clinic in

Chicago — the Mayer, Brown & Platt Community Legal Clinic — which the firm continues to support. One pro bono effort of note involved the plight of Verneal Jimerson, whom Mayer got released from Death Row. On three occasions, Mayer associates have argued pro bono cases in front of the Supreme Court. Additionally, Mayer represented a former Washington, DC police officer who accused the Metropolitan Police Department of discriminating against her because of her disabled son. Finally, the firm unsuccessfully represented a Pentagon employee accused of espionage. In order to keep up and organize its efforts, the firm hired Marc Kadish as Director of Pro Bono and Clinical Legal Education in 1999.

Sites to see

To augment its regular web site, Mayer Brown sponsors two other sites to provide detailed information on specific practice groups. One is appellate.net, a one-stop shop for all the goings-on in the firm's Supreme Court and appellate group. In addition to a description of the practice and its attorneys, the site features Supreme Court docket reports, a selection of firm-penned articles, and a library of related legal briefs. Billed as "your free source for news and information about structured finance," the firm's other site, securitization.net, offers similar documents, along with a bulletin board, useful structured finance-oriented links, and other resources.

GETTING HIRED

You'd better study

Good news for those with great grades who may be lacking in the personality department. Mayer insiders report that the firm focuses on grades and schools and virtually ignores personalities. "MB&P tends to be quite grade focused, especially when considering students who aren't from the top five schools in the country," reports one insider. "It seems like students from so-called lesser schools have to have an almost perfect GPA to be seriously considered." Another contact says "if you have high enough grades, Mayer will hire you. If you have low grades, Mayer will not hire you. Personality is normally not an issue during the hiring process." Another source goes even further, saying "personality disorders and poor interpersonal skills are not a handicap."

Summer associates usually have it made. "It is very competitive to become a summer associate here but it is very easy to get an offer for full-time employment once you are a summer associate," reports a current Mayer lawyer and former summer associate. "Out of my class of roughly 60 summer associates, only one did not receive an offer."

The firm's web site has a section for both law school recruits and lateral hires. The law school section has facts about individual offices, including contact information. Laterals are required to have two years experience and should be admitted to the bar of the state where they apply. All applicants are encouraged to submit resumes via U.S. mail or fax, not e-mail.

Campus screening interviews

Mayer Brown conducts "screening interviews on campus with a partner or an associate," depending on who's available at the time. Applicants who cannot make a campus interview can send their resume to the office to which they are applying, where it is "reviewed by designated partners." Those who make the cut have callback interviews at the office with six attorneys (three partners and three associates). If the candidate expresses an area of interest, an interview with a partner in that area follows. Each interview "lasts a half-hour" and "sometimes includes lunch." The review committee "usually gets back to people quickly, within a week." Insiders say that "the requirements for being invited in for an interview are stiff, but once invited, many candidates are given offers."

OUR SURVEY SAYS

Corporate culture: no white shoes

Firm insiders say that Mayer is friendly but "a little stiff." But at least one associate says, "I haven't found it to be overly 'white shoe.'" "Very cold, impersonal atmosphere," complains another source. "People have strong business faces, then go out and party like fraternity boys. That might sound appealing but it's actually just immature and tedious." Another contact says associates have a lot of autonomy. "The firm is very laid-back. People are pretty friendly and helpful. You are free to do the kind of work you want as long as you meet your hours."

A wide range of partners

Associate treatment by partners varies throughout the firm, according to Mayer attorneys. "[Treatment] varies widely by individual; some treat me with the utmost respect while others have no qualms about treating me like crap," according to one Chicago associate. While some describe the partners as "friendly," there is strong sentiment to the contrary. "There is a very clear dividing line between partners and associates," reports one contact. "Partners are polite, but they will never treat associates, even senior associates, as equals. This is one of the most frustrating aspects of practice here."

Insiders report that recent developments have muddied the waters even more. "MB&P has a free market system that tends to keep partners with lousy management skills scrambling for help," says one associate. Another source adds that recent changes to the pay scale have increased friction. "The salary increase has caused the partners to resent associates, which translates into less respectful treatment of associates. It is a consensus that associates are overpaid and should expect to work considerably more than was [previously] expected."

Two types of social life

Mayer associates report that social interaction is largely up to each individual. "There are two types of associates at the firm," explains one associate. "Those who show up, close their doors and get to work so they can leave and those who work hard together and play hard together. If you are part of the first camp, you probably think that social life is non existent. If you're part of the second, you think that the best thing about MB&P is the social life."

"I have a ton of friends here who I go out to lunch with and talk to outside of work," says one social butterfly. Someone who falls into the first camp reports "MB&P is not a very social place. That isn't to say that it's unfriendly. It just means that people tend to have lives separate and apart from work."

Typical hours

Hours, insiders say, are "cyclical — some weeks are nuts, others are quiet. MB&P is not a big face time firm." The recent salary increases are expected to have an impact on workload. "Partners are very resentful of the recent salary rises," says a contact. As a result, "MB&P just raised its billable hours requirements. It remains to be seen how this will affect the quality of life at the firm."

Pay raises, grudgingly

"Although the firm has matched the salaries of other top Chicago firms and recent salary increases across the country, it wasn't without a struggle," reports one attorney. "As many of the associates pointed out, Mayer Brown was not one of the first Chicago firms to announce a salary increase." As previously noted, the jump in pay has caused problems at the firm. "Mayer has had many problems stemming from compensation — especially in the last few months," says an insider. At least one associate sided with management: "We shouldn't have made the pay jump; we are not a Silicon Valley firm and do not get the Monopoly money from taking equity in over-valued, no-asset, no-profit dot com companies."

Bonuses are unclear at this point. "The firm just trashed its old bonus program and has not yet announced the parameters of the new program," reports one source.

Chicago-specific perks

Mayer associates get most of the typical perks — meals and cabs for late nights, for example. Also, the firm gives out tickets to the Bulls and White Sox in Chicago and the Chicago Symphony. "A gym allegedly is on the way," notes one source. Also, "there is an annual associates-only party," monthly wine and cheese parties for the whole firm, and an annual event to which lawyers' families are invited. Breakfast — donuts, muffins, and bagels — is served every morning.

The invisible hand at Mayer Brown

Mayer's free market system allows associates unusual latitude in choosing the engagements on which they would like to work and the partners with whom they would like to work. This has its advantages and disadvantages, according to those in the know. While associates rave about the "tremendous opportunities" open to the proactive, others warn that "it's easy to fall through the cracks. Make sure you are willing to hustle for the good projects." "In a sense, you are truly on your own," contends one Chicago lawyer. "The system can be very effective, but it can be alienating and difficult at first." For those who master the system, the payoff is "extremely sophisticated and rewarding work."

"Sink or swim"

"Surprisingly, MB&P does not appear to pay much attention to training," says one contact. "The firm appears to want associates to learn on the job rather than through formalized training." One associate says, "'Sink or swim' seems to be the motto for certain groups. If you're lucky, a senior associate or partner will voluntarily act as your mentor." Another lawyer is even more critical: "There needs to be more structured training for first-years in basic tasks and there needs to be more training through upper levels as well." Some disagree. "The training and mentoring can be great. All you have to do is be a self-starter and take the initiative to seek it out. It won't be handed to you." Some improvement in this area should be forthcoming with the recent hiring of a former Mayer Brown partner who will work full-time training finance associates. The firm notes that Marc Kadish, Mayer's Director of Pro Bono and Clinical Legal Education, is providing training for litigation associates.

Ugly offices, beautiful support

Firm insiders are less than thrilled with their workplace habitat. "The building lobby is breathtaking but the floors are a bit shabby — it is clear that people work here and that work and storage space is at a premium." "The offices are fine," says an attorney. "The built-in furniture leaves a lot to be desired, though." It must leave an awful lot to be desired — one lawyer says, "Associate furniture is incredibly old and ugly." Associates should also be careful how they choose their space. "One office move is allowed during your time as an associate. Be sure to use it well," cautions an insider.

Associates at Mayer rave about the support staff. "Our support staff is very helpful," says one insider. "There is always help 24 hours a day." "We have a document services department available 24-7 who can help you with anything. Document service turned around a 150-page offering memorandum overnight, completely proofread," a contact gushes. The only department criticized is IT. "The computer support people are standard for the industry, which means wretched." Another associate tells this horror story: "Despite a recent upgrade, the computers are prone to crashing, and it can be hours before a technical support analyst has time to fix even major problems."

Retention: here comes the salary issue again

"Retention has been a fairly serious issue," says a contact. The salary hike has affected retention as it has everything else. "Because morale has been very low during the salary changes, I believe that more people are leaving the firm," opines an associate. "However, the amount of turnover is probably not unusual for a big firm." Insiders seem to doubt that those who jump ship at Mayer land at other firms. "There's no moving up from MB&P in the Chicago law firm market, so most people who leave do so to pursue something different, an in-house position, government, and so on." Practice area is a factor as well. "It's been a revolving door lately in the corporate and securities practice," says a corporate attorney.

Partnership prospects: did we mention the salary issue?

"I think that the prospects of making partner in litigation are very slim — especially now with the raises," reports one insider. Another associate seems to think you have to deal with the devil to get a partnership. "If you work forever, abandon your social life and outside professional pursuits and do good work (with a minimum commitment to pro bono), you might be considered for partner." That grim view isn't shared by all. "Most associates who stick around for eight years make partner and those who don't often get offered a position as counsel."

Please mentor me

Mayer's associates are critical of the firm's diversity policies in general. "I don't know if the firm is actively trying to recruit minorities and simply being unsuccessful but there don't seem to be any minorities around here," says one attorney. "The firm works at minority recruiting but needs to improve retention and mentoring, as well as lateral hiring of minorities." One associate in Chicago jokes, "I would know better if I could ask our African-American partners. Oh yeah, they don't exist!" This is not actually the case — the firm points out that there are in fact two African-American partners in the Chicago office.

The mentoring issue comes up for women as well. "I think there is gender equality with respect to hiring but not with respect to mentoring." One associate feels that Mayer uses the presence of a female managing partner as a "crutch and fails to address women's issues." Insiders do applaud the maternity leave and part-time policies but say that part-timers often have a steep hill to climb to make partner.

"Gays? Lesbians? In Chicago?" asks one associate. "I'm sure nobody minds, as long as it is never mentioned." That associate is likely speaking of the city of Chicago in general, since other insiders seem pleased with the climate for homosexuals. Domestic partner benefits are offered "and [the firm] appears very supportive of gay issues."

But we like it here

Despite the associates' complaints, most sources report being fairly satisfied at Mayer. "I think as far as law firms go this place is as good as, if not better than, most big firms," says one attorney. "I don't think working at any big firm could ever be entirely fulfilling." Another associate agrees: "The problems I have with MB&P relate primarily to the nature of the work rather than the faults of the firm. It's clients who demand Herculean feats and opposing lawyers who correct grammar in documents at 2 a.m. the night before a closing that cause me the most misery."

Other sources have a broad range of opinions. "Headhunters find fertile ground here," suggests one lawyer. "They start calling you in your first few months here because they know sooner or later you'll listen." One Chicago associate couldn't disagree more, averring, "I love this firm."

One of the main benefits of working at Mayer, say lawyers, is "the laissez-faire structure of work assignments" that allows associates to seek out the work they want to pursue and the people they enjoy working with. Associates are also pleased with the prestige that comes with working for Mayer, Brown & Platt. In fact, many Mayer associates list the firm's reputation as one of the reasons they accepted Mayer's offer. "I chose MB&P because of the reputation in the finance area and the field of securitization," says one associate. The support staff is also mentioned as a big plus.

They own you

One associate lists "the assumption that they own me" as a drawback of working at Mayer. Another lawyer complains that "it's not a meritocracy but it's promoted as one." The training is also high on the list of complaints. A Mayer insider reports "constantly feeling like you don't know what you are doing. [There's] very little training. You're supposed to know things by magic." The friction between partners and associates, exacerbated by the recent raises, also comes up. "The partners do not care about you. They just care that you get the work done."

INTERVIEW TIP #14

Afterwards, DO make notes for yourself about how the interview went. This will help you keep track of who you met with and prepare yourself for potential employment.

VAULT.COM PRESTIGE RANKING 26

Milbank, Tweed, Hadley & McCloy LLP

1 Chase Manhattan Plaza
New York, NY 10005
(212) 530-5000
Fax: (212) 530-5219
www.milbank.com

LOCATIONS

New York (HQ)
Los Angeles, CA
Washington, DC
Hong Kong
London
Moscow
Singapore
Tokyo

MAJOR DEPARTMENTS/PRACTICES

Banking & Institutional Investment • Capital Markets • Environmental • Financial Restructuring/Bankruptcy • Intellectual Property/Technology Transactions • Litigation Mergers and Acquisitions • Project Finance • Public Utilities Real Estate • Special Services • Tax • Telecommunications Transportation Finance • Trusts & Estates

THE STATS

No. of attorneys: 417
No. of offices: 8
Summer associate offers: 44 out of 45 (New York, 1999)
Chairman: Mel Immergut
Hiring Partners: Drew Fine, Daniel Mummery, and Arnold Peinado

PAY

New York, 2000
1st year: $125,000
2nd year: $135,000
3rd year: $150,000
4th year: $165,000
5th year: $190,000
6th year: $205,000
7th year: $215,000
8th year: $225,000
Summer Associate: $2,047/week

Washington, DC
1st year: $125,000
Summer Associate: $2,057/week

NOTABLE PERKS

- Cost-of-living adjustments for overseas offices
- Same-sex domestic partner benefits (first major firm to offer them)
- Free access to MoMA

THE BUZZ
What attorneys at other firms are saying about this firm

- "Still resentful of losing Chase"
- "Buoyed by Latin American work"
- "Will it bloom again?"
- "Solid, old-line NY firm"

UPPERS

- "None of the gunners I disliked from law school are here"
- Exciting and challenging work
- Significant experience early on

DOWNERS

- Partners who tend to be good lawyers but lousy managers
- Feeling dispensable
- Too much work

KEY COMPETITORS

Cleary, Gottlieb, Steen & Hamilton
Fried, Frank, Harris, Shriver & Jacobson
Sullivan & Cromwell
Simpson Thacher & Bartlett

EMPLOYMENT CONTACT

Ms. Joanne DeZego
Manager of Legal Recruiting
(212) 530-5966
JdeZego@Milbank.com

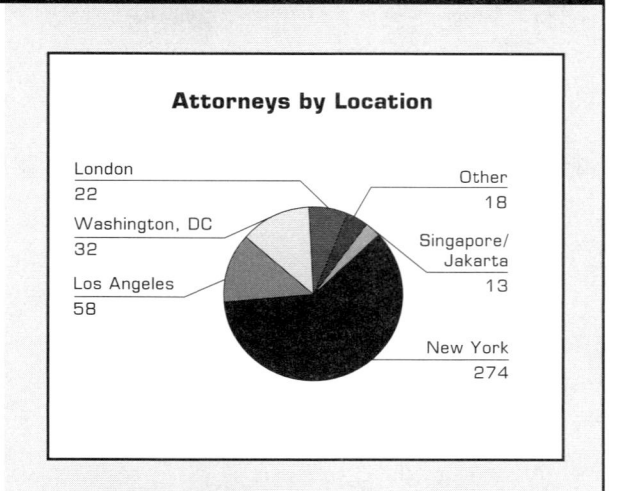

Attorneys by Location

- London: 22
- Washington, DC: 32
- Los Angeles: 58
- Other: 18
- Singapore/Jakarta: 13
- New York: 274

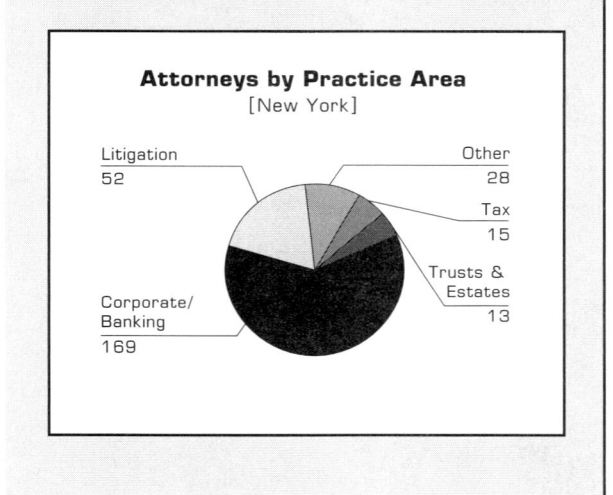

Attorneys by Practice Area [New York]

- Litigation: 52
- Corporate/Banking: 169
- Other: 28
- Tax: 15
- Trusts & Estates: 13

QUALITY OF LIFE RANKINGS [ASSOCIATES RATE THEIR OWN FIRM]

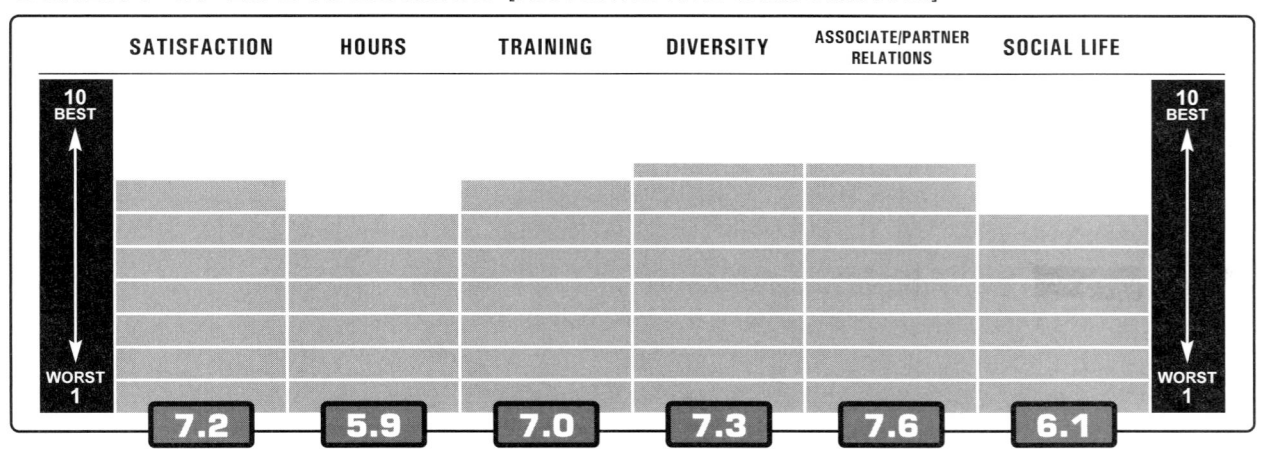

SATISFACTION	HOURS	TRAINING	DIVERSITY	ASSOCIATE/PARTNER RELATIONS	SOCIAL LIFE
7.2	5.9	7.0	7.3	7.6	6.1

THE SCOOP

Milbank, Tweed, Hadley & McCloy LLP has been a player on Wall Street since 1866, the year of its founding. Early clients included John D. Rockefeller (Junior and Senior) and various railroad barons. Milbank has since seemingly been at the forefront of every legal trend, from Depression-related issues in the late 1920s and 1930s, to helping financial clients set up investment and hedge fund mechanisms in the 1960s, 1970s and 1980s, to capitalizing on the growth of international business and finance and technology transactions in the 1990s. Today Milbank's project finance practice is considered one of the finest in the world. Milbank Tweed also boasts a strong international presence with offices in Tokyo, Hong Kong, London, Moscow, and Singapore.

Welcome to Milbank

Milbank has grown by more than 30 lawyers since 1999, including several notable lateral hires. In 1999 Milbank bolstered its bankruptcy practice by recruiting the former head of Kirkland & Ellis' bankruptcy group, Luc Despins. In February 2000, Milbank energized its Washington power and energy group by attracting of counsel Steven Kramer from Fulbright & Jaworski. In April 2000, Milbank snagged trusts and estates lawyer Hugh Jacobson from the disintegrating New Jersey firm Friedman Siegelbaum. The firm also made former Securities and Exchange Commission branch chief Orlan Johnson of counsel in November 1999. But Milbank has lost a few lawyers, too — real estate partners Mark Edelstein and John McCarthy left for Morrison & Foerster in 1999.

Oil financing and metal mergers

Milbank is perhaps best known for its project finance practice — and our insiders agree that it's a top area of the firm. The practice "is a very good place to work for a young associate. You get a lot of experience quickly," one associate reports. Drawing on its peerless expertise in transportation finance, Milbank represented Salomon Smith Barney and Lehman Brothers as lead underwriters in the 1999 aircraft lease derivative offering of $1.1 billion of enhanced equipment notes offered by AIR 2 US, a new Cayman Islands company.

Milbank has a top-notch mergers and acquisition reputation as well. Milbank lawyers took part in creating the world's largest aluminum producer. The firm advised Canada's Alcan Aluminum on the $9.2 billion three-way merger with French aluminum company Pechiney and the packaging division of Switzerland's Alusuisse Lonza Group announced in August 1999. Milbank lawyers Donald Brant Jr., Mark

Weissler, Robert Reder, Michael Goroff, William Jackson, Dale Ponikvar, Charles Westland, Brian O'Donoghue and Thomas Brenner worked on the deal.

In 1999 Milbank took part in the first-ever acquisition of a major U.S. utility by a foreign entity. The firm worked on Scottish Power's $12.6 billion acquisition of PacifiCorp, a public utility headquartered in Oregon. The firm also advised Robert Pharmaceuticals in August 1999 when it was acquired by England's Shire Pharmaceuticals for $1 billion.

Top technology practice

Milbank's technology transactions group has handled technology outsourcing deals, including a $40 billion contract between Electronic Data Systems and General Motors. In 1998 Milbank Tweed negotiated and structured on behalf of AT&T two outsourcing contracts with IBM valued at $4 billion each. The firm also served as underwriters' counsel in offerings of nearly $2 billion in bonds to help finance the Iridium global satellite project sponsored by Motorola. In late 1998, Milbank represented Nippon Telegraph & Telephone, the world's largest telephone company, in its $8 billion global share offering and in the $18.4 billion global share offering by NTT DoCoMo, its affiliated mobile telephone company (which was the largest equity offering ever at the time).

Fight for the Flatiron

The distinctive wedge-shaped Flatiron building in New York City was the site of a recent legal battle moderated by Milbank lawyers. Along the way, Milbank partner Parker Bagley and associate Keri Christ expanded the bounds of trademarks to include commercial real estate. Bagley and Christ represented Newmark & Company Real Estate in its battle to register an image of New York's famous Flatiron Building as its trademark. Newmark actually owns the Flatiron Building but venture capital firm Flatiron Partners also wanted to use the building as its symbol. The two sides worked out their differences in October 1999, with Flatiron Partners agreeing to license the image of the building from Newmark. Christ told *The New York Times* the settlement "stands as an acknowledgement of the fact that the owners of distinctive architectural works... have intellectual property rights in the designs of those buildings if they're used in connection with their business."

BT battle

Milbank partner Richard Tufaro suffered a setback in October 1999, when Milbank client Bankers Trust could not prevent four of its former investment bankers from working with Credit Suisse First Boston Corp. The Manhattan Supreme Court ruled that Bankers Trust's non-compete clause, which all BT bankers had to sign, was too broad in its applications.

Cleaning house

Along with Housing Works, Milbank lawyers Jeffrey Barist and Russell Brooks brought a class action in September 1999 against New York City. The suit alleges the city is placing 2,000 AIDS patients a month in emergency housing that is inappropriate and medically unsound for people living with AIDS. Some of the hotels the AIDS patients live in are rodent-infested and missing refrigerators that are needed for medication. The suit seeks to force the city to inspect every hotel monthly and certify that each is medically suitable for clients.

Back in bankruptcy

In November 1999, Milbank received welcome news from the New York Court of Appeals and was able to close an embarrassing chapter in its history. The firm's troubles stemmed from the misrepresentations Milbank's former bankruptcy partner John Gellene made in the District of Colorado. Federal prosecutors accused Gellene, the lead lawyer in the 1994 reorganization of Bucyrus International Inc, of concealing Milbank's representation of a main creditor of Bucyrus in an unrelated matter. Gellene was convicted on three accounts of bankruptcy fraud in March 1999.

But the New York court ruled Gellene's acts did not put the whole firm on the hook. "In a relatively large law firm, the bad acts of one partner should not be imputed to all other attorneys in the firm insofar as claims of fraudulent conduct and punitive damages are concerned," Justice Herman Cahn wrote, no doubt to the massive relief of Milbank Tweed. Chairman Mel Immergut tells Vault.com that the Gellene affair is now old news and the firm's bankruptcy practice is thriving.

A bright and bankrupt future

The addition of Luc Despins has helped the bankruptcy group's resurgence. Despins represented a committee of ICO Global Communications bondholders when that company entered Chapter 11 bankruptcy. The committee began negotiations in November 1999 with cellular phone pioneer Craig McCaw. The hyperambitious McCaw plans to take over ICO Global and, by raising $1.2 billion, make ICO solvent again. McCaw needed to show the committee the merits of his plan in order to gain approval of the bankruptcy courts in Delaware, the Cayman Islands and Bermuda without any interference from the bondholders.

In December 1999, Milbank's Michael Gottfried helped gain approval for the Southern District of New York's first online bankruptcy auction. The Southern

District bankruptcy judge allowed Milbank client AICO to sell its assets on the online auction site eBay.

Milbank's animal avenger

Milbank counts a leading animal rights crusader among its associate ranks. David Wolfson, a sixth-year litigation associate, has logged around 200 hours per year working for such animal defenders as Farm Sanctuary and animal rights magazine *The Animal's Agenda*. He also moderated a daylong conference at the New York City Bar on "The Legal Status of Non-human Animals." He has even brought in veggie burgers and more animal-friendly menus to the firm's cafeteria.

GETTING HIRED

Looking beyond the top tier

"Milbank is looking for people who have a lot of drive and are comfortable dealing with people," according to firm chairman Mel Immergut. Associates report that the firm has been responding to the tight job market by reaching out to elite students outside of the nation's top ten law schools. "I wholeheartedly agree with this approach, rather than taking anyone with a pulse from NYU or Columbia," reports one associate. A corporate attorney advises that those who are not hired from a top-tier law school tend to have the magic words "law review" on their resumé.

Mellow first rounds

Milbank's first round of interviews takes place on campus. A partner or associate conducts interviews. "Getting through the interview is not brain surgery," relates one un-operated-on associate. Some Milbank associates report that they discussed subjects unrelated to law during interviews, such as cultural events in New York City. Six interviews take place in the callback round, half with associates, the others with partners. Candidates may also be sent to lunch with one or two associates. "They try to get a sense of the kind of law you're interested in and, if you show interest in the overseas offices, you'll probably talk a lot about that too." One interviewee says that her Milbank interviewers even presented her with a few hypothetical situations and asked how she would handle them and arrive at a legal conclusion. Insiders disclose that Milbank inquisitors seek answers that show maturity, logic, and an even temperament.

OUR SURVEY SAYS

Perhaps I'll stay a while

Sources tell Vault.com that Milbank is "still a white-shoe firm in many ways but is starting to loosen up." Many associates say "work is all that matters" at Milbank and suggest that the firm "has become financially driven, bottom line oriented in the last several years." That bottom line may be that Milbank is a firm in transition.

Many Milbank lawyers report they enjoy their work and their colleagues. One attorney is even considering prolonging his stint with the firm. "I have operated under the assumption that I would not be here forever, but I'm not sure why I've always assumed that. Recently I have found myself wondering what it would be like to stay and try to become partner," he says in a display of affection and faith startling for a modern-day law firm. Associates put in their share of hours but many keep a realistic outlook about it. "Working hard is never as much fun as being at the beach, but we have good work with lots of opportunity."

Remembering the days

Insiders report Milbank has a relatively young partnership, which bodes well for the associates. "The partners are for the most part young and therefore remember their associate days," according to one lawyer. But another says, "While there are young partners seeking change, the old guard still prevents much of it." Young or old, "the partners are tremendously respectful, professional and go out of their way to be friendly, though not to be your buddies," reports a Milbanker. "It seems that many associates work with partners who fit their personality and, accordingly, are treated pretty well," observes a fourth-year. Some corporate attorneys tell Vault.com that the partnership varies widely, with some partners taking the time to go over an associates' work and others taking a hands-off approach.

Associates say there are no screamers at Milbank, with the exception of a certain partner who sometimes "just lets go." But one attorney suggests ominously that "since the pay rises earlier in the year the attitude of some partners seems to be that they are going to 'get their pound of flesh' now that we are all paid so much."

Games and parties

Milbank has a social scene for those who want it, insiders report. "There are both extremes at Milbank: people who work in their offices and never come out and those who are interested in socializing. It is not hard to find interesting people to chat with and get to know," explains one associate. Project finance and litigation are singled out as being particularly tight. "My favorite thing about Milbank is the people I have met here — they throw great parties," says a junior associate. One source admits there is even a *Jeopardy!* game circulating via email among Milbank's associates, partners, secretaries, and legal assistants. No word on the prizes.

Bonus watch

Milbank has kept up with the 2000 salary race. Most associates claim to be pleased with their new salaries, though others express concern about the amount of their bonus. Insiders say the firm is waiting to see how much its peer firms will pay out in annual bonuses. "There is no firm commitment on year-end bonuses but conventional wisdom says the firm will track the market," reports a second-year lawyer. Milbank provides a lockstep bonus by class year.

Retention on par

Milbank's associates say that the retention rate is about on par for a New York firm. Some associates tell Vault.com the project finance, T&E, and real estate departments are particularly adept at hanging onto talent. On the other hand, corporate finance and litigation have reportedly seen a lot of coming and goings. Like many other law firms, insiders say, "Milbank has recently seen a number of associates leave to join Internet start-up companies, either as attorneys or on the business side." There can be a trace of bitterness among those left behind. According to one source, "Generally morale at Milbank is quite high and it is certainly a fun place to work. But farewells for people who have worked really hard are sometimes less than friendly."

Milbank boot camp

Most associates give the formal training programs at Milbank high marks. Before beginning at Milbank, first-years attend a week-long off-site program. "The week-long training session before starting was very helpful, although it was a little like bootcamp since it was six long days of lectures and analysis," a junior associate reports.

"Milbank has a great off-site program for 1Ls which introduces them to the concepts of finance and transactional practice, which is great since most first-years have never had experience with such work. Afterwards they have a constant stream of CLE's but for the most part it is just partners zipping through an outline packed so densely with information that it is hard to follow," another source tells Vault.com.

Most attorneys feel that Milbank's informal training is very effective. "The training is good and the partners seem to be genuinely concerned with making you a better lawyer." "There is a great deal of formal training but I find the informal training in the form of feedback from partners to be the best training," says another lawyer. But one third-year suggested that "it would help to have a more hands-on experience with clients before one reaches senior associate status."

Cramming

Milbank associates' estimates of their workweeks vary wildly but many report they bill in the 60-hour range on a regular basis. A first-year associate explains, "It's basically like college. When you have a paper due or finals coming up in college, you study a lot. At Milbank, when a deal is about to close you work heavy hours." One source thinks that the work schedule is an understandable part of the job. "With great money and great cases come great responsibility and, inherently, many hours." But others don't consider the workload to be that steep. "I find that most associates exaggerate their hours. I don't see too many associates here on the weekends," sniffs one critic. Supporting this claim, the firm reports that average client billable hours number less than 40 per week per associate.

Outstanding views and lovely interior space

When arriving at Milbank's main lobby, visitors are greeted by a breathtaking view of New York Harbor with the Statue of Liberty standing in the distance. One Milbanker describes the view as "the best in New York." The attractions don't stop there. "The space and views are outstanding and comfortable. I especially like the new high tech chairs," raves one associate. "Milbank doesn't go for the old-fashioned interiors but the design of the office is quite elegant and functional," an insider reports. The firm is in the middle of renovating its entire office space. "Currently some of the floors are a little run-down but that will change," says one lawyer with great faith. Insiders report that associates share offices for no more than their first year and often less.

Thanks for all your support

Insiders are satisfied with most of the support services at Milbank. The night staff attracts special kudos. But many have problems with the level of paralegal support. One corporate lawyer says, "Milbank has a very professional word processing and support group in the evenings. But the day support group leaves much to be desired. For some reason, the firm has never taken a serious approach to training and using paralegals more comprehensively in its corporate practice." Another attorney concurs, "Secretarial, word processing and proofing are average to good. But we have a total lack of legal assistant help."

Diversity: top for gays and lesbians

Many associates praise the firm for its representation of women in the associate ranks. But several think the long hours prevents some women from rising up. A corporate associate says, "I think that any large, competitive law firm is a difficult place for women to work due to the hours and demands. However, I don't see any difference in the assignments handed to men and women in the firm." And a litigator reports, "In the litigation department, we can recruit women but we can't make them stay." The firm reports that two out of five associates promoted to partner in 1999 were women.

Insiders say the firm "bends over backwards to hire minorities" but the associate ranks are still not very ethnically diverse. One attorney opines, "At Milbank, it's a catch-22. While we want and need minorities, they are not attracted due to the amount currently in the firm, which is few." Another associate says, "Race seems to be a non-issue at the associate level, though there is not active mentoring."

Insiders claim Milbank is the first large New York firm to offer domestic partnership benefits and some call Milbank "the most gay and lesbian friendly top-tier firm in New York." "Milbank has long had a reputation for being open and receptive to gays and lesbians. That has not changed," says one attorney. Insiders also report that homosexuals are encouraged to bring their significant others to firm events.

Very odd pro bono

Insiders report that pro bono hours fall into a "strange category" of "billable-equivalent" hours. "While this category of hours will get you some credit it is definitely secondary to the real billable hours," associates argue. The firm reportedly has a program for first-years that lets them work at a pro bono organization for two months prior to their official start date. During this time the first-years get all of the firm's resources and are paid their regular salary.

"Anyone who wishes to initiate their own pro bono project is encouraged. Many associates have done just that," says a third-year lawyer. Milbank does designate one partner whose sole responsibility is to manage pro bono assignments. A source tells Vault.com that "the firm could do better at encouraging associates and partners who do not seek out pro bono work to get involved. But if you want to be involved, there is great enthusiasm and support."

VAULT.COM
27
PRESTIGE RANKING

Hale and Dorr LLP

60 State Street
Boston, MA 02109-1816
(617) 526-6000
Fax: (617) 526-5000
www.haledorr.com

LOCATIONS

Boston, MA (HQ)
New York, NY
Reston, VA
Washington, DC
London (joint international office with Brobeck)

MAJOR DEPARTMENTS/PRACTICES

Commercial
Corporate
Environmental
Intellectual Property
Labor & Employment
Litigation
Private Client
Real Estate
Tax

THE STATS

No. of attorneys: 407
No. of offices: 4
Summer associate offers: 31 out of 31 (Boston, 1999)
Managing Partner: William F. Lee
Hiring Partner: James W. Prendergast

PAY

All U.S. Offices, 2000
1st year: $125,000 + up to $30,000 bonus
2nd year: $135,000 + up to $40,000 bonus
3rd year: $145,000 + up to $50,000 bonus
4th year: $155,000 + up to $60,000 bonus
5th year: $170,000 + up to $65,000 bonus
6th year and above: $175,000 + up to $65,000 bonus
1st yr. junior partner: $180,000 + up to $65,000 bonus
2nd yr. junior partner: $190,000 + up to $65,000 bonus
3rd yr. junior partner: $200,000 + up to $65,000 bonus

Summer associate: $2,400/week

Additional bonuses paid out of returns from the Venture Capital Investment Program

NOTABLE PERKS

- Home computer
- On-site fitness center
- Emergency day care center
- Occasional Red Sox, Celtics, and Bruins tickets
- Corporate casual dress
- Maternity and paternity leave
- Palm Pilot

THE BUZZ
What attorneys at other firms are saying about this firm

- "One of Boston's best"
- "Embracing new economy"
- "Not a lot of camaraderie"
- "Brutal place to work"

UPPERS

- Cutting-edge cases and clients
- Immense pool of collective knowledge
- Great reputation

DOWNERS

- Lack of interaction among lawyers
- 24/7 work for high tech clients
- Fairly limited advancement to senior partner

KEY COMPETITORS

Goodwin, Procter & Hoar
Ropes & Gray
Testa, Hurwitz & Thibeault

EMPLOYMENT CONTACT

Ms. Evelyn M. Scoville
Director of Legal Personnel
(617) 526-6590
evelyn.scoville@haledorr.com

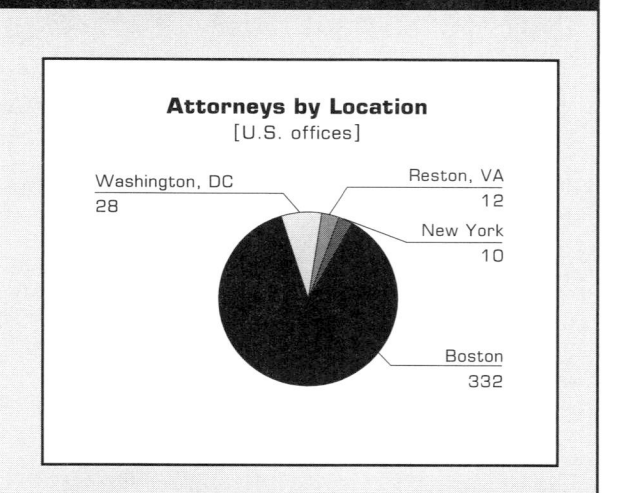

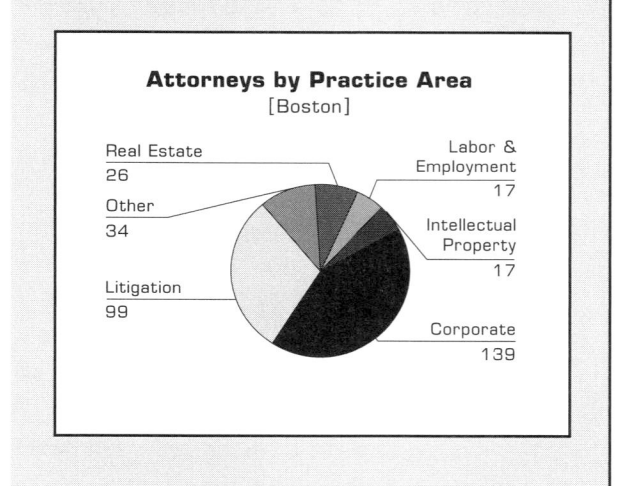

Attorneys by Location [U.S. offices]
- Washington, DC: 28
- Reston, VA: 12
- New York: 10
- Boston: 332

Attorneys by Practice Area [Boston]
- Real Estate: 26
- Other: 34
- Litigation: 99
- Corporate: 139
- Intellectual Property: 17
- Labor & Employment: 17

QUALITY OF LIFE RANKINGS [ASSOCIATES RATE THEIR OWN FIRM]

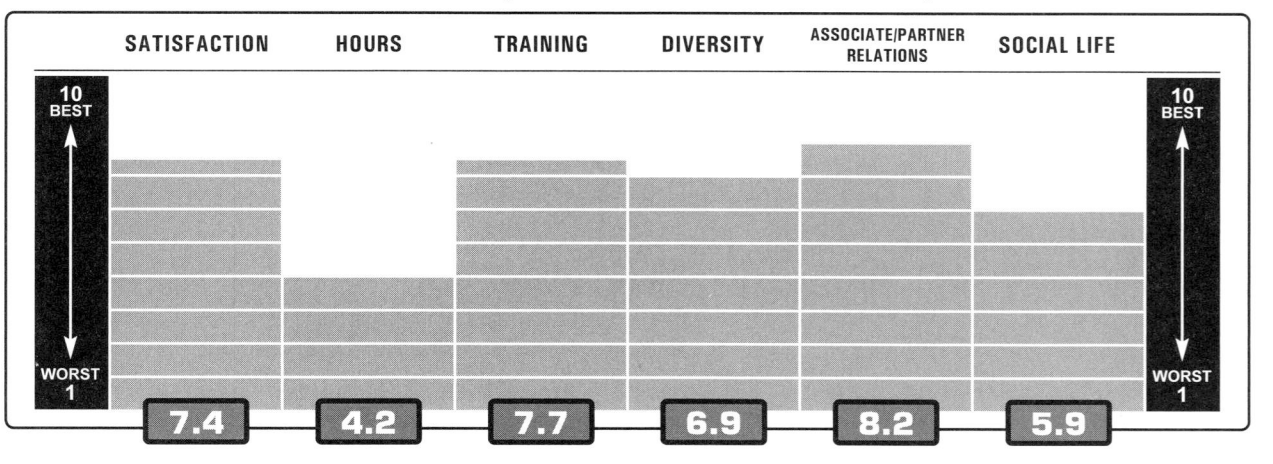

SATISFACTION	HOURS	TRAINING	DIVERSITY	ASSOCIATE/PARTNER RELATIONS	SOCIAL LIFE
7.4	4.2	7.7	6.9	8.2	5.9

THE SCOOP

Boston had a banner year in 1918. That year the Red Sox won their last World Series and Richard Hale and Dudley Dorr decided to form a new law partnership. Today, in the 21st century, Hale and Dorr is known primarily for its strong litigation practice, considered the best in New England. In recent years the ampersand-less firm has also built a strong corporate practice around the high tech industry.

Beantown history

Still headquartered in Beantown, Hale and Dorr LLP has established itself as one of the most prestigious law firms in the nation. The firm now has offices in Washington, DC, Reston, VA, New York City, and Wellesley, MA. In 1990 Hale and Dorr co-founded the independent firm of Brobeck, Hale and Dorr International in London (along with San Francisco-based Brobeck, Phleger & Harrison). Hale and Dorr seems to have as many famous lawyers as its home city has historic patriots. Litigator James St. Clair was involved in the Army-McCarthy hearings and served as Special Counsel to Richard Nixon in 1974 during the Watergate hearings. Joseph Welch also won fame in the McCarthy hearings for his famous line: "Have you no sense of decency, sir, at long last? Have you left no sense of decency?"

In addition to serving as the national chair of the 1988 Dukakis presidential campaign, partner Paul P. Brountas was named one of the "100 Most Influential Lawyers in America" by *The National Law Journal* and one of "Boston's 100 Most Powerful People" by *Boston Magazine* in 1997. Brountas pioneered the firm's corporate department. Former chief of staff to the governor of Massachusetts Karen F. Green bills at Hale and Dorr, and her one-time boss, ex-Massachusetts Governor William F. Weld (he of the showdown with North Carolina Senator Jesse Helms over the ambassadorship to Mexico), is a former partner.

William Lee, pioneer

Another major change at the firm took place in 1999 — William Lee was named managing partner of Hale and Dorr. This decision was notable not only because of Lee's national recognition as a groundbreaker in the field of IP but also because Lee is the first Asian-American in Boston to achieve the rank of managing partner. A graduate of Cornell Law School, Lee joined the firm in 1976 and was named one of the country's 10 best litigators by *The National Law Journal* in 1996. In 1999 Lee was named one of the "100 Most Influential Lawyers in America" by *The National Law Journal*.

Strong in both litigation and corporate

Hale and Dorr is best known for its prominent litigation department, the largest such department of any firm in New England, with nationally recognized intellectual property, securities, and labor groups as well as a rapidly developing international practice. The firm's emerging corporate practice has also gained renown and has been active in major M&A transactions in recent years. In late 1998, the firm represented software outfit The Learning Company in its $3.8 billion purchase by Barbie-maker Mattel. In 1999 longtime client Kenan Systems tapped Hale and Dorr to represent the software developer in its $1.5 billion acquisition by Lucent Technologies. Later that year, a team led by David A. Westerberg advised Prodigy Communications Corp. in its $900 million dollar merger with SBC Communications Inc. May 2000 brought about another high-profile deal for Hale and Dorr when the firm represented ArrowPoint Communications, Inc. in its $5.7 billion acquisition by Cisco Systems, Inc. Partner Pat Rondeau oversaw the deal and was assisted by associates Janet Rebish, Lisa Bonner, and Michael Donahue.

A-OK in IPOs

Hale and Dorr has built up a wealth of experience and a strong reputation for work on initial public offerings. In fact, the firm handled more IPOs in the 1990s than any other firm in New England. Moreover, Hale and Dorr worked on 46 different IPOs in 1999, including offerings for once-stars ZDNet, Prodigy, and iVillage. Through its joint venture with Brobeck, Phleger & Harrison in London, the firm represented Goldman Sachs and Deutsche Bank as underwriters' counsel in the $6 billion Infineon Technologies AG IPO, the largest technology IPO in history. Hale has also handled public offerings for non-tech companies, including Millennium Pharmaceuticals, West Coast Entertainment, and Boston Communications Group.

Champion of new technology

Part of the reason for Hale and Dorr's outstanding IPO practice is that the brahmin firm stands out as a champion of emerging companies — the firm's Internet practice is exploding. The firm has a long history of work in tech, having represented high tech and biotech startups for decades. Today Hale rivals many Silicon Valley law firms with its high tech client base, representing industry leaders such as Akamai, Sycamore and CMGI. One secret to Hale and Dorr's success — Boston has become a major East Coast center for high tech startups. The firm also has a strong reputation in practices that booming tech industries require: licensing, venture capital, and mergers and acquisitions.

Spankin' new offices

In order to keep pace with its growing book of high tech clients, Hale and Dorr opened two new offices in early 2000. The firm's New York office is headed by Nels Lippert, an IP lawyer lured from White & Case. The firm has already reached the double-digit mark in attorneys in the Big Apple and plans eventually to have a total of 50 lawyers in the office. The second office was opened in Reston, VA (a suburb of Washington DC) in order to tap the area's growing high tech industry, which includes America Online and MCI Worldcom.

High tech offices, too

Hale and Dorr was one of the first law firms to opt for automated back-office operations and to supply its lawyers with personal computers. Since the early 1980s, Hale and Dorr has maintained an annual technology budget of $2 million to $3 million, considerably more than most other law firms of its size. A portion of that money is used to outfit all associates with a laptop computer and a Palm Pilot. By streamlining office services, eliminating huge amounts of paper and duplicating costs, and using technology as a marketing tool, the firm believes that the capital outlay for technology more than pays for itself.

GETTING HIRED

Strong personalities wanted

If you love the law, Hale and Dorr may be for you. The firm "wants people who are interested in, and excited about, working here and being lawyers," say insiders. "People are pretty independent at Hale and Dorr so the desire for unique characters seems sincere," reports one insider. Says one litigator: "You need more than good grades to get hired at Hale and Dorr. You need a strong, engaging personality or you won't survive." However, as another associate reports, the firm's "highly selective history has been tempered somewhat by recent demand for associates." A mid-level agrees: "It seems that the booming economy of recent years and the flight of people to supposedly greener pastures in the dot com world has put pressure on recruiters not only to keep pace with the firm's expanding workload but also to replace the people accepting jobs in-house," he says. While the firm contends that its standards are as high as ever, that associate claims that Hale and Dorr is now "hiring people with credentials that it probably would have considered too lowly just a few years back."

On the other hand, Hale and Dorr has a fairly traditional interview process. The "firm sends its people on campus for a half-hour or 20-minute screening session." This is followed up with "three or four half-hour interviews" in the office. Candidates interviewed in the morning are taken out afterwards. While "you will probably interview primarily with partners," candidates go out to lunch with associates. And of course, the firm places a premium on grades and academic achievement. "You need to be from a top 10 school, in the top 10 percent from second-tier school, or clerk at a federal district court, although these standards may not be as rigorous for laterals," says one associate.

Increased lateral hiring

As at other firms, Hale and Dorr associates report increased and less selective lateral hiring recently. "For laterals, it is easier for people with expertise" in IP, ERISA, or mutual funds "than for general litigation or corporate associates," reports one who tranferred into the firm. "I am in corporate, but in a specialty field, so I probably had an easier time getting in." Says another insider: "The firm seems to be less selective with respect to laterals than first-years." Some of these specifically hired laterals get a good deal, insiders report. "The partners do not hesitate to hire laterals to fill specific needs and provide those persons with assurances of elevation to partnership," explains one mid-level associate.

OUR SURVEY SAYS

Underneath the dour Bostonian shell, an entrepreneurial firm

Hale and Dorr is "very entrepreneurial, although couched in a classic Boston style — a little reserved and dour sometimes in that craggy New England way," states an associate. Another insider elaborates, "People work hard but are tolerant of personal commitments. The members of this firm tend to be outspoken and enthusiastic. Senior partners leave their doors open and encourage contact from associates." One insider declares that "corporate casual permeates the firm, from dress code to lack of rigid social hierarchy to accessibility of senior partners to associates." Other sources reveal that "this is not the type of place that encourages a lot of hand-holding, although questions and cooperative work are encouraged."

But the New Economy may be forcing some cultural shifts. An attorney warns, "The stresses and pressures of the business are such that Hale, like other big firms, is more and more focusing on the bottom line. The old emphasis on culture and the old stress on the importance of home-grown talent is basically over. This year only one of the corporate department associates up for junior partner summered here and started with Hale as a first-year. As a result, the closeness and camaraderie that you feel existed among partners no longer does." A corporate associate agrees, "The firm doesn't deserve its reputation as a stiff, white shoe firm, but it is not very social or gregarious."

Speedy on the money

"Hale moved to raise salaries quickly before the rest of the market moved," notes an attorney. "It's comforting to see that kind of confidence and a willingness to be a leader in compensation." Another reports that in addition to salary, "Hale and Dorr has also started making a venture capital investment on behalf of associates." Moreover, as one source points out, being located in Boston has advantages other than good clam chowder. "I will be making the same actual dollars as my counterparts in New York," he notes, "yet I won't have the awful New York city tax and the cost of living in Boston is still a good notch lower than New York." Not all associates are completely enamored of the new raises. A Hale and Dorr insider observes that "many associates would rather that the firm had hired more associates (and kept the salaries somewhat lower) in order to allow associates to work fewer hours." Another critic pessimistically anticipates, "It seems like a generous package, but let's wait until the bonuses come out."

Loved associates

Partners at Hale and Dorr treat their associates well, according to our survey. "The partners I work with take every opportunity to provide feedback and involve me in all aspects of a case," declares a well-treated attorney. "I have only had good experiences." Another associates raves that the Hale partners "are excellent lawyers and mentors. They are generally considerate of personal obligations." While, as one attorney notes, "partners have all basically treated me like a peer," there are some complaints, mostly relating to availability. "Within the past 12 months, partners have become busier and less available," an ignored insider indicates. "Therefore, there is not much treatment by partners one way or the other. When one does interact with partners, they do treat us well generally." However, another insider ventures that "associates who display effort and enthusiasm are rewarded with the respect of the partners." Compared to most law firms, that's a relative love-in.

Looking for fun in all the Dorr places

One major criticism of Hale and Dorr is that social opportunities are few and far between, or as one associate states, "fun is available in limited quantities." "The firm is very busy so it can be tough to make time for work, personal time, and play," an insider reports. "That being said, there is a real effort, especially among the younger associates, to make time to go out on a somewhat regular basis." There are efforts made by the firm to promote social interaction between attorneys, one source reveals. "Associates generally attend the bi-monthly attorneys' lunch, where people gather in informal groups to eat and socialize. There are weekly Friday cocktails as well as early morning and lunch meetings for various organizations within the firm, such as the Women Associates' group."

"Although many close friendships are established within the firm," an associate explains, "people seem to work hard and play elsewhere or within different social circles." Another reports, "this is not a hopping firm for singles. The firm is kept from being a more social place not due to lack of friendliness but by the sheer volume of work and the desire to see family and friends outside of work." A fifth-year attorney wistfully contends that "it used to be better when I first got here, but now people are becoming too busy with work and as a result they have also become more boring and tired. Romance, like weeds in sidewalks, still manages to grow in the most unlikely of places and office relationships are not entirely unheard of. When do they find the time?"

Training wheels

"The formal training programs are excellent and extensive," according to a corporate insider. "Associates in the corporate department begin with two months of formal training in addition to the on-the-job training provided by working on actual assignments." A litigator agrees, noting that he "cannot imagine receiving better training than we receive in the litigation department. Some is formal, most is learn as you go, but the environment is really geared toward bringing junior associates up to speed and involving them early in all aspects of a litigation." Associates assert that there is "good availability of mentors, formal and informal," as well as a "great outside program where associates have the opportunity to work for the District Attorney's Office or the Public Defenders."

Some attorneys remain unimpressed by the formal training offered by Hale and Dorr, finding that "training seems to be done more on the job than via a program." On-the-job training becomes easier because at Hale, "the cases are staffed pretty leanly and thus give associates a chance for greater responsibility." One associate gripes that "training started off well for first-year associates but it is now almost non existent. Department meetings at which training occurs informally are now often cancelled. Associates are expected to learn solely by doing, often without any guidance." Another associate concurs that "things have been so busy that training now largely seems to be learning by doing — with or without the benefit of someone looking over your shoulder."

Keep up the pace!

"The pace varies from absolutely exhausting to pretty liveable," says an insider of the hours she works. "Everything comes in waves." Another attorney notes an early bird tendency among Hale associates. "In general, attorneys, paralegals and support staff alike tend to come in earlier (from 7:30 to 9:00 a.m.) and leave earlier (from 5:00 to 7:00 p.m.)." A mid-level associate reports that "the workload has been extremely busy for the last 12 months. Even worse, the hours have been less fun than they used to be." "There are definite highs and lows in the amount of hours I work per week," one hard-working source admits, "but as a whole, I have not been a slave to this firm, thank God." However, some attorneys have noticed "increased pressure to bill" due to "recent salary increases." A corporate associate elaborates, "While on a large matter, I definitely sense an expectation to focus first on the work. At other times, I feel that I can manage my schedule to accommodate my social and family lives."

Comfort space

One of the pleasures of working in the Boston office of Hale and Dorr is the "great view of Boston harbor from the 31st floor." In fact, one associate declares that "one of the greatest perks of the job is the office." Certain sides of the building have beautiful views of Boston harbor. Moreover, associate offices are a good size. All first-years have had their own offices from their first day (beginning in 1999) because the firm took over a new floor and "all associate offices are window offices." Sounds peachy keen.

Decency for women

Associates report that with regard to recruiting women, "the firm's efforts have been better than average. The woman-to-man ratio is pretty even at the associate level. But as with many large law firms, there are fewer senior level female attorneys than male attorneys." One source notes that "although the firm is trying very hard, the nature as well as the amount of work and client demands make it almost impossible to accommodate traditional 'mom' issues. However, the firm has equal maternity and paternity leave — and men actually take significant leave." Moreover, "the firm has tried to establish flex-time and other programs for women with young children." Another associate asserts that "the firm seems to have made a great effort over the past few years to put women in key positions."

But as usual, there's a disconnect between policy and practice. An attorney criticizes, "There is a fair amount of work to do in terms of promoting women to partner and encouraging cross-gender communication, both socially and in formal settings such as departmental meetings." Another insider cautions that "the administration drags its feet when responding to harassment complaints." The firm vehemently denies the assertion. One female associate reports that she has "never felt any disrespect or disparity in work due to my sex but at times I have sensed a boys' club mentality. This may be endemic to all large firms but is a problem when a younger female associate is trying to fit in and network within the firm structure."

Minorities still too small a minorty

Although Hale and Dorr has an Asian-American managing partner, William Lee, associates still report trouble recruiting and maintaining minority lawyers. "It seems difficult in general to attract and retain minorities in Boston law firms," explains one Hale associate. "Regardless, the firm could definitely improve its existing programs to recruit, mentor and advance minority attorneys employed by the firm." "The firm's efforts are not overly visible although I believe the firm is interested in having an ethnically diverse workplace," another reports. "However, the workforce, particularly among lawyers, is almost all white. The lack of diversity among lawyers and paralegals is even more evident when contrasted to the large proportion of minorities in clerical roles."

A slightly less critical insider observes, "H&D's heart is in the right place. Everyone feels strongly that diversity is important but the firm seems to be in a real quandary about how to go about achieving it. Percentage-wise, there are abysmally few associates of color who come to the firm and they generally leave, again on a percentage basis, more quickly than their white counterparts." Hale and Dorr argues, however, that its efforts to recruit a diverse attorney pool are paying off — the firm reports that minorities made up 29 percent of the summer associate class of 2000.

GLB open door

When asked about diversity issues with respect to gays and lesbians, an insider reports, "there are openly gay members of the firm who are given comparable benefits." A gay associate notes, "I haven't experienced any issues with it yet. I feel comfortable here. People care about work product and general well-being and not one's sexuality. I don't know what efforts are being made to increase or diversify the profile here. I was shocked at the relatively small number of gay and lesbian lawyers. However, I don't know if that's attributable to the firm's doings or not."

Corporate partnership only?

"Generally, associates are up for junior partnership after five years' employment with the firm and senior partnership two or three years thereafter," reveals an informant. "You are given indications in your evaluations early on of your prospects for partnership." While some sources believe that "prospects for making partner at either level are quite good," others characterize the chances as "extremely unlikely." Insiders report that promotions in the litigation department have been few and far between in recent years but that two litigation associates did make partner in 2000. In corporate, "you've got a pretty good shot — if you want it — but many [associates] leave well before they are up for partner." One associate gives the following heartening advice for increasing odds of making partner: "you'd better like abuse."

The long and the short of Hale

"Many associates desire more interaction and teamwork and do not want to work in isolation," critiques an insider. "This sense of isolation, not the lure of stock options at dot coms, is the primary reason a large number of lawyers are leaving the firm." Others declare, though, that Hale's work environment is "supportive and dynamic. As with complex litigation at any large firm, the work can be mundane on a day-to-day basis. However, there are many mentors looking out for each attorney's professional development and a benchmark program to ensure young associates develop certain skills." Another attorney agrees, "This is a fantastic place to be a young associate. The training and mentoring are strong, the work is challenging and interesting, and the lawyers are a great group. As at any large firm, the hours are long but if you choose to work in a large firm this is a great place to be." One associate summarizes, "If you're seeking a big-firm practice, and are willing to make all the tradeoffs that such a choice implies, it's hard to do better than Hale and Dorr."

"Romance, like weeds in sidewalks, still manages to grow in the most unlikely of places, and office relationships are not entirely unheard of. When do they find the time?."

— *Hale and Dorr associate*

VAULT.COM

28 PRESTIGE RANKING

Ropes & Gray

One International Place
Boston, MA 02110-2624
(617) 951-7000
Fax: (617) 951-7059
www.ropesgray.com

LOCATIONS

Boston, MA (HQ)
Providence, RI
Washington, DC

MAJOR DEPARTMENTS/PRACTICES

Corporate
Creditors Rights
Employee Benefits
Health Care
Labor & Employment
Litigation
Real Estate
Tax
Trusts & Estates

THE STATS

No. of attorneys: 392
No. of offices: 3
Summer associate offers: 48 out of 50 (Boston, 1999)
Managing Partner: Douglass N. Ellis
Hiring Partner: Douglas H. Meal

PAY

All offices, 2000
1st year: $125,000, plus bonus of up to $30,000
2nd year: $135,000, plus bonus of up to $40,000
3rd year: $145,000, plus bonus of up to $50,000
Summer associate: $2,400/week

NOTABLE PERKS

- Emergency child care center
- In-house gym
- Up to $1,750 subsidy for home computer and full reimbursement for Palm Pilot
- Risk-free co-investment with partners in client-advised hedge and LBO funds, as well as client-sponsored private equity investments

THE BUZZ
What attorneys at other firms are saying about this firm

- "Thick with Harvard grads"
- "Dynamic"
- "Dinosaur with attitude"
- "Very WASPy, full of would-be academics"

UPPERS

- Prestige, pay, and quality of a large New York firm, but without the hassle of living in New York
- No yelling, screaming, or freaking out as a general rule
- Strength across every practice area

DOWNERS

- Not the most social place in the world
- Lack of senior women
- Disorganized and inefficient system of assigning work

KEY COMPETITORS

Covington & Burling
Goodwin, Procter & Hoar
Hale and Dorr

EMPLOYMENT CONTACT

Ms. Joanna L. White
Director of Legal Recruitment
(617) 951-7239
jwhite@ropesgray.com

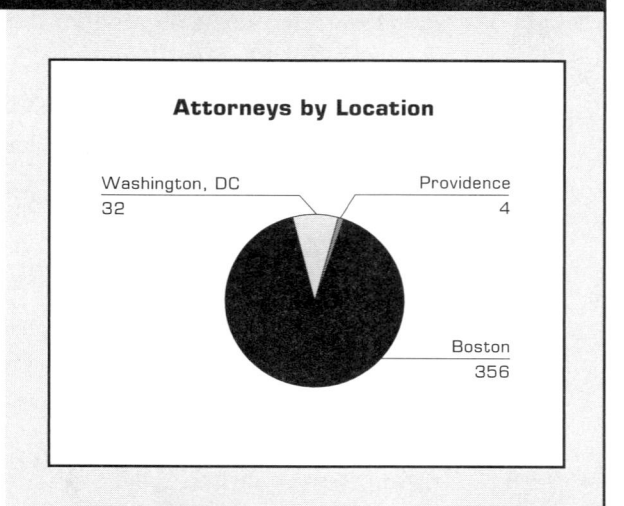

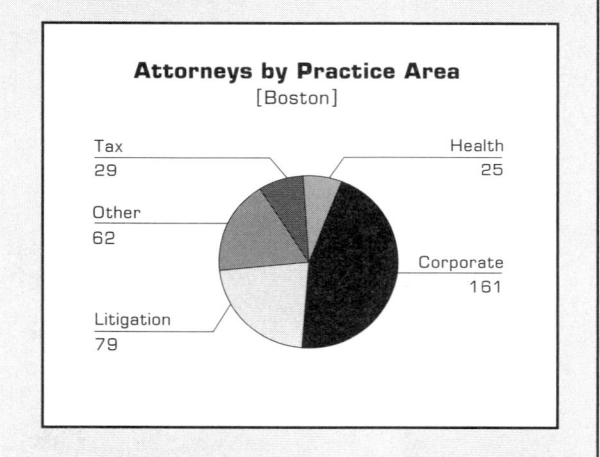

Attorneys by Location

- Washington, DC: 32
- Providence: 4
- Boston: 356

Attorneys by Practice Area [Boston]

- Tax: 29
- Health: 25
- Other: 62
- Corporate: 161
- Litigation: 79

QUALITY OF LIFE RANKINGS [ASSOCIATES RATE THEIR OWN FIRM]

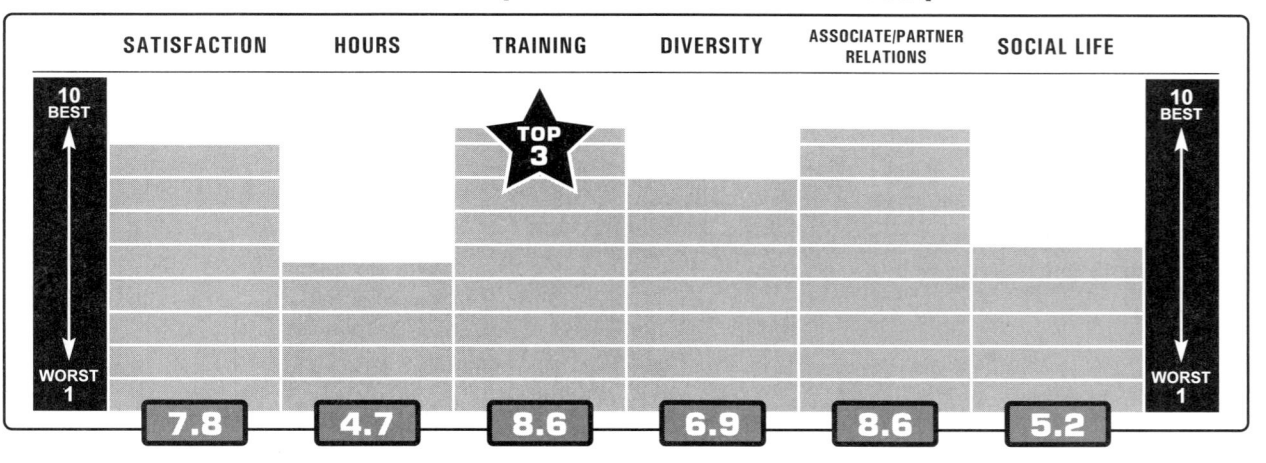

SATISFACTION	HOURS	TRAINING	DIVERSITY	ASSOCIATE/PARTNER RELATIONS	SOCIAL LIFE
7.8	4.7	8.6 (TOP 3)	6.9	8.6	5.2

THE SCOOP

Founded by Harvard Law School grads in 1865, Ropes & Gray is often considered to be one of the the top law firms in Boston. Ropes is best known for its corporate work and has well-regarded trust and estates and health care practices.

A crimson beginning

Ropes & Gray was founded in the last year of the Civil War by HLS grads John Codman Ropes and John Chipman Gray, Jr. The firm rapidly grew along with its home city of Boston and Ropes was representing banks, utilities, and railroads by the turn of the century. Despite its blue-blood background, the firm had an eye toward diversity and set an example with its progressive hiring practices. Abram Berkowitz became the firm's first Jewish partner in 1930; Mary Lennon and Blanche Quaid became the firm's first female associates in 1942. Although the firm is known for its aversion to the press, it nevertheless gained increased notoriety by representing Senator Ted Kennedy during the Chappaquiddick scandal. In 1974 Elliot Richardson, a Ropes & Gray alumnus, resigned as Attorney General when President Nixon ordered him to fire Watergate special prosecutor and fellow Ropes alum Archibald Cox.

The first firm in Boston

Ropes & Gray is arguably the preeminent firm in Boston and has a strong national reputation as well. Under the leadership of partner R. Bradford Malt, the firm has built up a strong leveraged buyout practice in addition to an impressive financial services and mutual fund practice. The firm's LBO practice includes a number of blue-chip clients, including the Butler Capital Corporation — a $1.4 billion, New York-based fund that the firm has represented in more than 40 leveraged buyouts. Other clients on the firm's leveraged buyout roster include the VC arms of Boston-based consulting firms Bain & Company and Monitor Consulting, New York-based Suez Equity Investments, and New York-based Saunders Karp & Margue.

Within the financial services and mutual fund industries, Ropes represents Fleet Financial Group and Putnam Funds. According to *The American Lawyer*, Ropes & Gray ranks No. 1 when it comes to total net assets of all funds for which the firm acts as counsel. Ropes grabbed the top spot with 77 new issues in 1999. (The firm itself also actually manages money — Ropes has an estimated $3 billion in assets under management.)

Ropes & Gray is also among the top firms in structuring IPOs, representing underwriters like Goldman Sachs. *IPO Journal* ranked partner Keith F. Higgins the No. 2 lawyer in the country in terms of acting as counsel for IPOs. Ropes is not to be counted out in the M&A arena, either — the firm represented American Heritage Life Investment Corp. (a major distributor of life, disability, and health insurance) in its $1.1 billion July 1999 sale to Allstate Corp., the nation's largest publicly-traded insurer.

Ropes clients comprise an illustrious list indeed. Clients include Bain Capital, Harvard University, Fleet Financial Group, Goldman Sachs, American Express, The Gilette Company, Ben & Jerry's Homemade (represented in its acquisition by Unilever) and Reebok International.

Strengths in other areas

In addition to its strong corporate practice, the firm is well-regarded for its trust & estates practice and its health care practice, both considered among the best in the country. While its litigation practice is not generally considered the firm's strongest, it still gets the big cases. Partner Michael Nusbaum and associate Peter Levitt of Ropes's DC office are representing April Oliver, a former CNN producer fired in the wake of controversy surrounding a CNN Vietnam documentary. After Vietnam vet Major General John Singlaub sued CNN for defaming him in the documentary, Oliver was fired. In May 1999, she sued her bosses on wrongful dismissal charges and countersued Singlaub, charging that his suit violated their confidentiality agreement to protect his identity as it related to the documentary's production. In October 2000 Ropes is scheduled to act as lead trial counsel in the L.A. Harbor cleanup case, the largest Superfund case ever brought by the United States government.

Ropes is also a leader when it comes to advising the academic world, counting both local institution (and feeder school) Harvard and Stanford University among its clients. The firm's DC office has special expertise in white collar criminal matters and intellectual property and environmental law. Although Ropes & Gray has no international branches, it is active in foreign matters, particularly in Russia and other parts of Europe.

Policy changes

In 1993 39-year-old R. Bradford Malt became the youngest person ever elected to the firm's policy committee. (Before Malt's arrival, the average age on the committee was 57.) Ropes & Gray's policy committee is powerful: it determines compensation for all partners and associates, makes partnership decisions, and largely determines the direction of the firm. Before Malt joined the committee, there was a feeling that the firm was slow to react to new trends and technologies. Things are somewhat improved now, although an insider tells Vault.com that the firm is still "somewhat slower to respond to legal marketplace trends" than its rivals. Douglass Ellis, the firm's managing partner since 1999, heads the policy committee.

Still a leader in health care?

Ropes & Gray has historically dominated the Boston health care industry's legal business, representing six downtown hospitals in the early 1990s. But the firm's stranglehold on the industry — worth more than $100 million in legal business — has been significantly loosened. Two factors account for this. First, hospitals have become more cost-conscious and consequently receptive to pitches from competing firms. Second, the firm's grip on the hospital market raised conflict-of-interest concerns from rival hospitals. Still, Ropes & Gray remains Boston's leader in this area, and has supplemented its Boston business with health care work from outside of the region. In fact, in 1999 nearly 40 percent of Ropes health care work came from outside New England. Some of this work is university-based — Ropes represented Stanford University in the dissolution of its joint venture with the University of Southern California.

Old-fashioned pro bono efforts

The firm has shown its commitment to pro bono work over the years through projects involving death penalty and prisoners' rights litigation, representation of refugees seeking political asylum, and representation of homeless individuals in civil rights actions. In April 1999, partner Joan McPhee successfully defended the State of Rhode Island against a group of teachers' union officials in a pension dispute. According to a former general treasurer of Rhode Island writing in *The Providence Journal-Bulletin*, "In this day and age of endemic cynicism about lawyers and the law, the people of Rhode Island should know that Ropes & Gray was very old-fashioned in its motivation — to make its community a better and fairer place."

Associates recognize that "pro bono work is supposedly treated like any other" and "pro bono hours are considered like billable hours in review," but claim the reality is that "the firm permits but does not encourage pro bono work." Some associates complain that there are "few opportunities and not much backup other than for litigators," which might explain why a corporate associate would say that his "department seems to have no commitment to pro bono work." According to the firm, requests for pro bono assistance are regularly e-mailed to all associates and all lawyers are actively encouraged to take pro bono assignments.

GETTING HIRED

You went to Harvard too?

Like most Top 50 law firms, Ropes & Gray "looks very closely at law school grades and appears to call back only the very top of the class at the top law schools." An insider says that the firm "seemed like the most competitive of Boston firms, and I interviewed with a lot of firms." Says an associate from a top-10 law school: "People who received callbacks from my school were on law review or close to it."

Associates agree that "it may be easier coming from Harvard." One HLS grad apologizes that "his sample is skewed, since it's not too hard for Harvard grads." Explains another associate: "They hire lots of Harvard Law School grads, [who represent] roughly a third to a half of each class — 15 of 40 my year — and maintain a very tight connection to HLS." One attorney points out that Ropes "endowed a chaired professorship for Alvin Warren, the HLS tax god, in fall 1998 and was in the million dollar club for the recent HLS library renovation." This "huge draw from Harvard" includes those who donned Crimson for either "law school or undergraduate." While the firm has recruited nationwide for a decade and a half, one associate notes that "basically, you have to have attended a Top 5 school and have a reasonably good academic record or have an outstanding academic record that includes law review at BC, BU, or a top-25 law school."

Also, "a strong Boston connection is a must and simply having attended college in the area doesn't cut it." A colleague puts it more bluntly: "If you did not go to Harvard or Yale, you had better be in the top ten percent" of your class. "You also have to come across as someone who would be OK to be stuck in a conference room with for 72 hours straight doing a closing." The firm notes that it has no class rank requirement and that in fact roughly 60 percent of its incoming 2000 summer associate class did not grow up in the Boston area. In 1999 the top five schools for summer associate origins were Harvard, Boston College, Columbia, Cornell (neither of those last two located in Beantown at last check) and Boston University. Top five alma maters of first-years were Harvard, Boston College, Georgetown, New York University, and the University of Chicago.

Extremely grade-conscious

Insiders assert that R&G has a minimum GPA requirement that candidates must meet (this varies on the mean GPA of the law school). Reports one contact: "Ropes definitely is a grades firm — B+ or higher average at Harvard Law School, higher at other places." The firm, however, maintains that it does not have a minimum GPA requirement. In any case, candidates should be prepared: "Every candidate gets interviewed by the hiring partner, who is very thorough and asks probing questions."

Others, however, say that Ropes does not ask "substantive law questions" during the interview. Says a source, "The questions I was asked were: 'Why do you want to work at Ropes & Gray?' 'Why Boston?' 'Tell me about law school.' The standard stuff." The firm asks these questions because "R&G puts a lot of effort into making sure its associates fit within its culture." With its highly academic bent, Ropes goes for "mostly law review types," according to insiders. The firm is considered "a fairly subdued place," so it would be a mistake to come across as "the hard-hitting, go-getter type." Contacts also note that "older students, [like] people attending law school after having first pursued another career, are also looked on favorably as long as they have also done fairly well academically."

OUR SURVEY SAYS

Upping the ante

Ropes & Gray has "traditionally been the leader in compensation in Boston" and has kept pace with the associate pay raises over the past year, says one associate who has been around for a while. "For example, my 1999 compensation exceeded the projected 2000 salaries and bonuses." Such candid revelations are somewhat rare, both because R&G "places a high value on the confidentiality of the compensation of both partners and senior associates" and because the new salary structure reveals the salary and bonus range only for associates in the first three years. A corporate attorney hypothesizes that "more senior associates basically have no idea what their next year's salary and bonus will be other than that it will be higher than the previous year's."

As at many of the large firms, some associates are concerned about fallout from the raises. "The partners made it clear that they were unhappy about the salary hike and I felt like some of them took it out on the associates with only slightly veiled threats about how the increased salaries were ultimately only going to result in longer hours," comments one litigator. "Based on the partners' behavior, you would have thought that the associates' pay raise was going to deprive them of the ability to feed their children." Also, the salary increase "occurred within the same week as an announcement that nonprofit clients would no longer be entitled to a charitable discount on legal services," notes a tax attorney, "which triggered accusations from other attorneys in town that local charities were bearing the cost of the salary increase."

If you can't beat 'em, leave 'em

Amidst the skyrocketing salaries, turnover at Ropes & Gray has dropped from 1998 to 1999 and looks likely to drop again in 2000. Insiders don't always see it that way. Associates "generally do not leave for other firms in Boston," although they "do leave for other business or legal opportunities." Third- and fourth-year associates are "getting offers they can't refuse from dot coms and in-house, so some turnover now is inevitable," remarks one associate. But the exodus is still distressing, highlighted by stats such as the tax department alone losing four of seven mid- to senior-level associates within two months. (One of those tax attorneys is on maternity leave and scheduled to return.) Even more troubling to some attorneys is the firm's response. Last year, the firm instituted the "widely unpopular — among both associates and partners — policy of omitting announcements of attorney departures from the daily newsletter," according to one associate. "This has contributed to a disconnect between appearance and reality on turnover."

I need my space

Those who are jumping ship might be doing so for a little breathing room — literally. Although the Boston building affords some associates their "own office with an unobstructed view of Boston, the Charles River and the Atlantic Ocean," current construction means "more junior people are doubled up and will be for the foreseeable future" — perhaps "typical for New York but unusual for Boston firms." This "temporary shortage of space" translates into an "increased use of interior offices and the off-site relocation of workrooms" until the firm can "exercise options to acquire additional floors in the building." Still, the decor is "immaculate," the views "impressive," and one litigator swears that the only thing "between us and a [rating of] 10 is better coffee and better computer monitors."

Night staff, paralegals and tech, oh my!

R&G's reportedly unreliable support services frustrate many associates, although they insist there are "good ones" out there. "There are many highly qualified secretaries but one feels oneself lucky to find one," sighs an associate. A corporate co-worker agrees that there is a "very good level of skills among support staff. However, attitude and helpfulness vary considerably" and "the night help is hit or miss." Consensus seems to reign, though, that the "paralegal staff leaves something to be desired." One attorney attests to "terrible paralegal support in the corporate department" and a litigator echoes that the "quality of the paralegal/case assistant program is below that of other comparable firms."

We love you, partners, oh yes we do

Across the board, Ropes & Gray associates seem genuinely fond of the higher-ups. Most associates say they "always feel greatly respected and appreciated by partners" and feel "they genuinely care" about associates' professional development. Partners treat associates "like their colleagues, not their employees" although at least one associate suggests that "some of the partners treat you like you're just passing through, [which can be] a self-fulfilling prophecy." And while "there are a few yellers," some associates appreciate that "partners generally regard [associates] as their peers. If you screw up, they let you know. If you do a great job, they let you know."

You gotta be strong enough

Associates seem divided on their chances of actually playing with the big boys down the road. Corporate attorneys seem to fare best, as "they've made everyone up [for it] a partner the last two years." Some of this is due to the fact that "attrition makes the classes pretty small by that point." With a nine-year track, most associates choose not to hang around, either because they have other opportunities outside R&G or because they've gotten the word from the firm, which has "a policy of letting an associate know around year five if he or she is not on partnership track." One insider breaks the process down into two key steps: "Number one: be proactive with the clients. If the clients are happy, the partners are happy. Number two: make yourself known among the partners in other departments." Of course, "being related to a member of the policy committee probably wouldn't hurt."

Litigation associates are "much more pessimistic" about their chances of making partner. "The simple fact is that there are a number of young litigation partners and right now the firm seems not to be in need of any more," avers one insider in the department. (Ropes made two new litigation partners in the fall of 1999.) Many associates say they have "no idea" or "wish [they] knew" what the magic formula is. A weary litigator suggests that you "work your ass off, be really smart and good at the law, and kiss butt when the opportunity presents itself."

Where did all the women go?

The story at Ropes & Gray sounds like that at many of its rival firms — there are "many women hired" but "it is difficult to retain good female associates." (The firm notes that in 1999, according to its statistics, attrition among male associates was double that of female associates.) While the firm "offers a generous maternity leave and permits women to work part-time on a variety of different schedules," many associates deem the policies "mostly lip service." The partnership "allows for part-time status but rarely respects it," says one corporate associate. (As of May 2000, according to the firm, Ropes had 18 woman lawyers on part-time status.)

Another insider explains that "the firm puts great pressure on women to work a 9 to 5 schedule as a part-time associate, as opposed to working a few days a week. The firm policy allows one to work a 60 percent schedule, which is based on a six-day week. Generally this ends up being difficult, as people don't respect the woman's end-of-the-day departure schedule." According to Ropes, of the 18 people currently on part-time leave as of May 2000, six work from home, nine work less than five times a week, and three work the abbreviated 9 to 5 schedule. Although an associate says, "I don't think going part-time helps your chances," the firm says that three women on part-time leave have made partner.

Won't you be my neighbor?

Many associates are "not sure if the firm's efforts to [create] diversity are sufficient" but attribute part of the struggle to hire and retain minority attorneys to circumstances external to Ropes & Gray. "I really think they try," emphasizes one lawyer, "but as is consistent with most of Boston, this place is pretty white." Several other associates agree that "part of the problem stems from Boston itself" because "it is hard to get minorities to work in Boston" due to "its reputation as a divided city, racially." Even if the city is a "tough sell for minorities," some associates question why the firm "isn't willing to compromise at all to get minority candidates — for example, by going to interview at law schools off the beaten path." "While I certainly don't think there's any proactive effort to exclude African-Americans," says an attorney, "I do think there's a passive complacency [given] the fact that this place is so overwhelmingly devoid of any, and this is disturbing." The firm points out that, according to NALP statistics, Ropes has a higher percentage of attorneys of color than its closest Boston competitors.

In contrast, a number of associates feel that "the firm is receptive to gays and lesbians and has numerous policies in place — domestic partner benefits, leaves for adoptions — that demonstrate this." One openly gay attorney observes that "there is old-fashioned embarrassment and discomfort but no open hostility" and that "the firm is growing as more of us work as openly lesbian and gay attorneys."

Firm life, family-style

First-years would be well-advised to party hard since they're the only group considered "very social." "As a whole, the firm is very 'married' and does not socialize very much," insiders say. Many associates appreciate this "family-style firm" where "people go home after work" but are aware that "the lack of pervasive social life" might be considered a negative by some of their peers.

Indeed, several attorneys voice concern that "there are very few activities outside the summer program where associates from different departments are encouraged to interact" and feel that "the firm could do much more to stimulate social interaction between associates." An out-of-towner offers this perspective: "First, many people were from here before joining the firm and second, so many people are married and having kids people tend to have full social lives outside work and aren't looking to make new friends here. This can be a little frustrating if you're moving here from somewhere else and hoping to meet new friends at work, where you spend most of your time."

'This is a working firm'

Ropes & Gray associates tend to define the firm culture as "quiet and low-key," a "professional place where everyone has a New Englandish can-do attitude regarding their work" and where "intelligence and efficiency are admired over pure effort or billables." Teamwork is of paramount importance as well. "The partnership rewards working together," insists a litigator. "This is not an 'eat what you kill' firm." A corporate colleague adds that "this is a working firm — there's no such thing as the partner getting to go home early."

The firm has occasionally suffered from the perception that it's "somewhat stodgy" but its troops insist that it is "less stuffy than one is led to believe." People are "truly nice to each other, which is pleasant when you spend long hours together. At the same time, though, it's a group of quick-witted and sharp-tongued lawyers so there's plenty of joking to go around."

Unique investments and dress code injustices

Despite not getting a meal allowance (the cafeteria is free after 7 p.m., though), Ropes & Gray associates enjoy some sweet perks above and beyond the typical gym discount or free parking. Home computers are 50 percent subsidized (up to $1,750) and Palm Pilots are 100 percent subsidized, as is ISDN or cable modem access from home. Optional laptops can be obtained at work. The firm also provides 20 days a year of emergency child care. Perhaps the most unique benefit is the opportunity for associates to participate in the profits of investment funds — the firm will "invest $10,000 a year per associate in various LBO and hedge funds. When these investments mature, the original $10,000 is returned to the firm and the associate is entitled to any gain."

These creature comforts aside, associates are pretty worked up about the dress code situation at Ropes & Gray. The firm instituted casual Fridays a while back but "late last year, the policy committee issued what appeared to be an intentionally cryptic memo announcing casual dress all summer and stating that it was difficult to determine what dress code may be appropriate for non-summer months. [The committee] said lawyers should rely on their own sartorial judgment," recalls a Boston litigator.

"The immediate impact of this was an explosion of casual dress across the firm, which has abated only in the litigation department. The litigation policy is that lawyers should dress formally unless there is a good reason for not doing so. Unfortunately, this policy was not so much announced formally as selectively insinuated by the department heads." Another associate verifies that "word from up high in the litigation department was quietly sent around that the department was not casual and that everyone should be in suits. Rather than making an official statement about the department's dress code, a senior member of the department went to an associate and asked him to spread it around. The associates were really angry about the way this was handled."

But according to Ropes, "there is some sort of misunderstanding here. The firm-wide dress code applies with full force in the litigation department."

VAULT.COM
29 PRESTIGE RANKING
Fried, Frank, Harris, Shriver & Jacobson

One New York Plaza
New York, NY 10004-1980
(212) 859-8000
Fax: (212) 859-4000
www.ffhsj.com

LOCATIONS

New York, NY (HQ)
Los Angeles, CA
Washington, DC
London
Paris

MAJOR DEPARTMENTS/PRACTICES

Bankruptcy & Restructuring
Benefits & Compensation
Corporate, Finance & Transactions
E-commerce
Litigation
Real Estate
Securities, Regulation & Enforcement
Tax
Trusts and Estates

THE STATS

No. of attorneys: 491
No. of offices: 5
Summer associate offers: 50 out of 51 (New York, 1999)
Co-Managing Partners: Peter V.Z. Cobb and Michael H. Rauch
Hiring attorneys: Howard B. Adler, Janice Mac Avoy

PAY

New York and Washington DC, 2000
1st year: $125,000 + bonus
2nd year: $135,000 + bonus
3rd year: $150,000 + bonus
4th year: $168,000 + bonus
5th year: $190,000 + bonus
6th year: $205,000 + bonus
7th year: $215,000 + bonus
8th year: $220,000 + bonus
Summer Associate: $2,400/week

(Additional discretionary bonus to be paid in New York.)

Los Angeles, 2000
1st year: $113,000 + $12,000 bonus
2nd year: $121,000 + $14,000 bonus
3rd year: $134,000 + $16,000 bonus
4th year: $147,000 + $18,000 bonus
5th year: $165,000 + $20,000 bonus
6th year: $175,000 + $20,000 bonus
7th year: $185,000 + $20,000 bonus
8th year: $190,000 + $20,000 bonus
Summer Associate: $1,750/week

(Also may include discretionary bonus)

NOTABLE PERKS

- Paid maternity and paternity leave
- Domestic partner benefits
- Emergency child care
- Free tickets galore

THE BUZZ
What attorneys at other firms are saying about this firm

- "Good M&A practice"
- "You'll never make partner"
- "Top gun and fun"

UPPERS

- Top-notch training program
- Great office locations
- Superb support staff

DOWNERS

- Tenuous partnership track
- Slow response to pay increases
- Erratic hours

KEY COMPETITORS

Cadwalader, Wickersham & Taft
Cleary, Gottlieb, Steen & Hamilton
Cravath, Swaine & Moore
Davis Polk & Wardell
Simpson Thacher & Bartlett

EMPLOYMENT CONTACT

Ms. Elizabeth M. McDonald
Director of Recruitment
(212) 859-8621
mcdonel@ffhsj.com

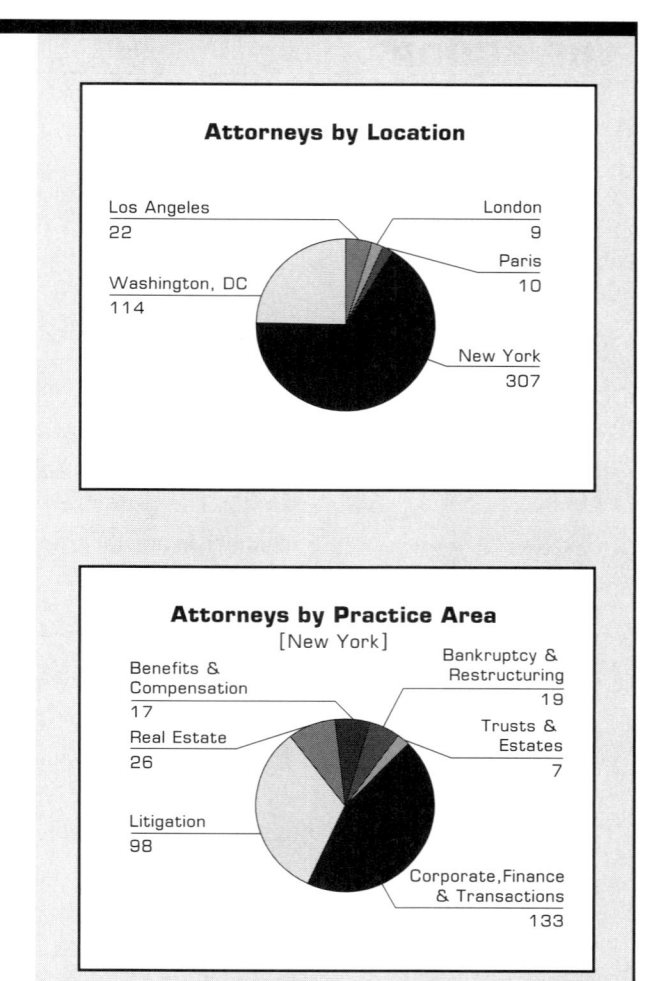

Attorneys by Location

- Los Angeles: 22
- Washington, DC: 114
- London: 9
- Paris: 10
- New York: 307

Attorneys by Practice Area [New York]

- Benefits & Compensation: 17
- Real Estate: 26
- Litigation: 98
- Bankruptcy & Restructuring: 19
- Trusts & Estates: 7
- Corporate, Finance & Transactions: 133

QUALITY OF LIFE RANKINGS [ASSOCIATES RATE THEIR OWN FIRM]

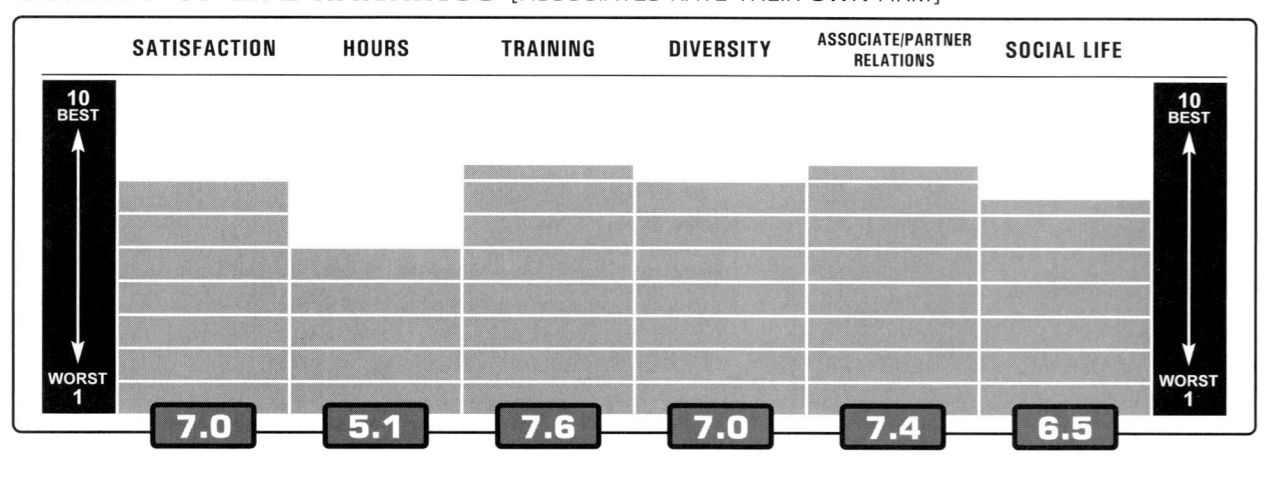

SATISFACTION	HOURS	TRAINING	DIVERSITY	ASSOCIATE/PARTNER RELATIONS	SOCIAL LIFE
7.0	5.1	7.6	7.0	7.4	6.5

(Scale: 10 BEST — 1 WORST)

THE SCOOP

If you're looking for a powerhouse M&A firm with a friendly and eclectic environment, Fried Frank might just be your firm. Fried Frank has merged everything from gigantic telecom concerns to waste companies. But lifestyle seekers be warned — Fried Frankers work hard indeed.

Fried worldwide

Fried, Frank, Harris, Shriver & Jacobson has grown over the past 30 years into a major player in the corporate practice area, especially in mergers and acquisitions. The New York-based firm opened a Washington, DC office in 1949 and a Los Angeles office in 1986. The firm also has foreign outposts in London and Paris, and in April 2000 announced an alliance with Toronto-based firm McCarthy Tetrault.

History: 1980s nostalgia

While most people would probably like to forget the 1980s-era S&L loan crisis and the antics of insider traders, Fried Frank profited handsomely from the decade famous for Michael Jackson and the pastel-clad cops of *Miami Vice*. Thomas Vartanian served as counsel for the Federal Home Loan Bank Board when the federal government was deregulating the savings and loan business in the early 1980s. When the industry crashed several years later, Vartanian was safely ensconced as a partner at Fried Frank. In his first year at the firm, he billed $12 million, mainly working on S&L bailout cases. Fried Frank also represented infamous insider trader Ivan Boesky in his criminal cases.

Since that time, Vartarian has left behind the 1980s savings and loans fad for the new trend of the 1990s and 2000 — the e-economy. Vartarian is now the chair of the ABA's Committee on Cyberspace Law and has gained recognition for his writings on the subject of e-law, particularly as the chair of a two-year ABA global project to study issues related to determining jurisdictional principles in cyberspace.

The DC nexus

Fried Frank has more than its share of connections to the Washington power structure. Sargent Shriver, one of the firm's name partners, is a member of the Kennedy clan. Fried Frank partner Thomas Christopher is the son of former Secretary of State Warren Christopher. Litigation partner Michael Bromwich served from 1994 to 1999 as Inspector General for the Department of Justice. Tax partner Martin Ginsburg is the husband of Supreme Court Justice Ruth Bader Ginsburg. Finally, there's Harvey Pitt, a corporate partner who once served as general counsel for the Securities and Exchange Commission.

M&A power players

Fried Frank's most prominent practice has been mergers and acquisitions, led by former firm chairman Arthur Fleischer, Jr. The firm represented AirTouch Communications in the company's $65.9 billion merger with Vodafone Group in February 1999. Fleischer led Fried Frank's team.

In March 1999, the firm represented Allied Waste Industries regarding its purchase by Browning Ferris Industries. The $9.1 billion deal combined the country's second-largest waste management firm (Browning Ferris) with the third-largest (Allied). The firm represented seed producer Pioneer Hi-Bred International when it sold an 80 percent stake to DuPont for $1.7 billion in April 1999.

Fried Frank kept pulling in the huge M&A deals the rest of that year. Allied Signal retained the firm for assistance with the company's $14 billion merger purchase of Honeywell International in June 1999. Two months later, Fried Frank represented Telespazio in a joint venture with Lockheed Martin Global Telecommunications Group and TRW, Inc. The venture, dubbed Astrolink, was the first global wireless broadband provider.

The firm represented Burlington Resources in its September 1999 acquisition of Canadian gas company Poco Petroleums, valued at $1.75 billion. Most recently, Fried Frank represented El Paso Energy in its purchase of The Coastal Corp. The deal, announced in January 2000, was worth $16 billion. Other top Fried Frank clients include Goldman Sachs, Andersen Worldwide, and Merrill Lynch.

Rebuilding Times Square

The firm's real estate practice celebrated a major score in 1997 when it represented publisher Condé Nast's move to new office space at 4 Times Square. The deal, completed in four and a half months, was led by Fried Frank partner Jonathan Mechanic. Condé Nast's move was influential in attracting other business to the midtown Manhattan location, which has undergone a renaissance in recent years due to the arrival of reputable businesses.

Pro bono plaudits

Fried Frank has a very strong reputation for pro bono work. For example, the firm pays half of the salary of Jennifer Friedman, a 1998 Columbia Law School graduate who works with the Courtroom Advocacy Project (CAP), a legal services program that represents victims of domestic violence. (The other half of Friedman's salary is paid by the Open Society Institute.) Other New York projects include tackling death penalty cases, discrimination cases, and aiding the Lawyer's Committe for Human Rights with asylum requests. In DC the firm has represented the Whitman Walker AIDS clinic, a death row inmate, and a 92-year-old woman with Alzheimer's seeking citizenship. In 1998 Fried Frank was named the "Pro Bono Law Firm of the Year" by the DC Bar Association. Finally, in Los Angeles the firm has handled pro bono work for the Los Angeles Legal Aid Foundation, the Alliance for Children's Rights, and the Western Center for Law and Poverty.

Many associates Vault.com contacted say that Fried Frank's pro bono programs were a major reason why they came to the firm. However, some insiders say the face of pro bono at Fried Frank has changed since the departure of Charlie King, the former of counsel head of pro bono work. "You are not allowed to take pro bono work that has not been approved" by the now scaled-down department, reports one insider. "It can take a while to get approval." Senior litigation associate Jennifer Colyer has been appointed pro bono counsel since King's departure.

GETTING HIRED

Top schools or top grades

Associates at Fried Frank rate their firm as a little more selective than most. "It is hard to get hired out of law school," says one attorney. "With the market the way it is now, I don't think it is too difficult to get hired as a lateral." The firm's search begins at top-tier national as well as regional law schools. "If you are from a top school or George Washington, your chances are very high," reports one DC lawyer. "The firm requires good grades and recruits mostly from top-tier schools, but it also values people from the top of their class at other schools and has no requirements that associates fit into a particular mold," says another source.

Look alive

One associate claims interviewers "will put pressure on you to lead the interview. They'll ask you cookie-cutter questions to keep things moving, but I recommend you have a clear picture in your head of what you want to convey; make a sort of road map for the interview and get your point across. Show you can think out of the box and motivate yourself. Don't just answer their questions." The firm likes "people with diverse interests" and "some business background is a plus."

OUR SURVEY SAYS

Friendly folks, high stress

Fried Frank associates are in agreement that the firm is "laid-back." One source says the firm's attitude is "do whatever the hell you want as long as you work hard and get it done." "People are generally nice," one source says. "There are all types — shy and quiet and loud and obnoxious. You can pretty much be yourself." The firm is "very tolerant of different personal lifestyles," according to one DC associate. "[It] does not look for stereotypical WASP or Harvard lawyers."

It's a good thing Fried Frank associates enjoy their peers — according to our inside sources, Fried Frank can be a stressful environment. "The firm has a very hierarchical feel," says a corporate lawyer. One critic harshly exclaims that Fried Frank is "a bunch of slobs who work their associates like slaves." Another angry lawyer complains the firm's partners "expect associates to jump at any whim of a partner or a client." Still, most feel the firm is making an effort to correct any problems. "The firm has done a lot to improve things," says a DC attorney. "There's not much screaming and yelling anymore but there is often a fire-alarm urgency in the air, which stems from the type of work that the firm does. People are generally good to work with and pleasant." Specifically, the firm has established an Office of Associate Affairs to field associate complaints and, when possible, rectify them.

Partners: watch out for the young ones

Partner-associate relations at Fried Frank, for the most part, are typical of those at other firms. "As with any firm, there is a broad range of partners — some are jerks and others are an absolute pleasure to work with," says one third-year associate. One insider reports that "most [partners] are great, polite, and easy to work for."

Vault.com has received conflicting reports on which partners to avoid. "There are some partners — generally older — who are rumored to treat associates badly," says one corporate lawyer. However, others say to steer clear of the new partners. "There is a group of junior partners at the firm who seem to thrive on overworking young associates," confides one source. "They laugh about our all-nighters and assign work as though hazing us. Between these junior partners, they control hiring, training, and orientation and assignments in the litigation department. If I leave the firm, it will likely be because of this new generation of partners." Fried Frank does offer recourse for wronged associates. "The firm is receptive to feedback about treatment and acts on requests not to work with certain partners," reports one New York lawyer.

I like you, you like me

Fried Frank lawyers seem to genuinely enjoy the company of their peers. Insiders report "well-attended happy hours, coffee breaks, and weekly cocktail parties. The lawyers really enjoy working and interacting together on many different levels." New associates seem to enjoy the most quality socializing time.

"First-years interact outside the firm and at the many firm events offered," says one newcomer. "Many team sports are also available and supported by the firm." On the other hand, according to one Fried associate, the social scene loses momentum after a while. "It is a chore to try to set up a Friday happy hour," he complains. "The only people who seem to socialize on a regular basis are in the first-year class."

Erratic hours

Fried Frank associates say they work very erratic hours, with the precise workload varying by department and by deal. "When a deal heats up, I'm here until midnight or later every night and working through the weekends," offers one corporate lawyer. "At other times, I'm home in time to watch *Friends*. "It is either all on or all off in terms of work pressure," according to a fifth-year associate. "We are encouraged to enjoy the downtime as much as we are encouraged to work during the difficult period." Beware of making friends with the partners, unless you want a hefty workload. "If a partner gets to know and like you, apparently you are constantly busy because that partner will go to you directly with an assignment," warns one lawyer. "First-year corporate associates are assigned to a certain group of partners and I've heard they tend to be busier for that reason."

Pay follows the leader

"No first-year associate making this much money should complain about his or her earnings — no matter how many hours they work," asserts one atypical young lawyer. That individual is clearly in the minority — the rest of his fellow Fried Frank associates leap at the opportunity to kvetch about their pay. While all concerned admit that the firm's compensation hovers around the market average in terms of pay, some criticize the firm's poky response to competitors' pay increases.

"The pay structure is completely outdated," gripes one New York lawyer who is not enamored of the lockstep pay system. "There is a lot of dead wood around here. People who barely work make the same money as people who work seven days a week." Another New Yorker regrets that "Fried Frank will always match what the other big firms do in terms of salary but is never the initiator." "The firm is always slow to match," says another attorney. "For the little amount of money they are saving, they could buy some favor with associates and simply match outright."

Even the most grasping must admit that Fried Frank has been generous in distributing bonuses. "The firm has in the last few years given an equal boom-year bonus to all associates [with increasing amounts based on seniority only] regardless of hours billed," reports a New York associate. Of course, there are some lawyers for whom that just isn't good enough. "How much is your life worth?" asks one second-year attorney rhetorically.

Go Orioles! Go Mets!

Fried Frank associates receive the "standard perks — meals and car service if you work late or on weekends, various parties and social events, [and] free sports tickets from time to time." In New York and DC, you'll get half off a gym membership, and since Sargent Shriver was once part owner of the Baltimore Orioles, choice seats at Oriole Park at Camden Yards. In New York, there's access to the Orioles' division rival New York Yankees as well as the Mets, the NBA's Knicks, the WNBA's Liberty, and the NHL's Rangers — "but partners get first dibs. They have to pay and we don't."

Graduates of FFU

One area where the firm excels is associate training. The firm sponsors "Fried Frank University," which one insider describes as "a crash course for first-years." Courses at FFU count towards Continuing Legal Education (CLE) requirements. Fried Frank also shines in the all-important informal training department. "The bulk of training comes in the form of partners trusting associates to do the work," says one New York lawyer. "The experience is invaluable." A tax attorney says that department has a "true apprenticeship" structure in its training. "We learn by doing and get a lot of responsibility." One DC associate complains that though "there are a lot of training opportunities here, sometimes it's hard to find the time to take advantage of them."

Offices: rooms with a view

The New York office has "beautiful water views on three sides," say insiders. Since the office is at the southern tip of Manhattan, attorneys with a window office can look out on the Statue of Liberty, Governor's Island, and the East River. Fried Frank is known for its top art collection. Art fans may want to look around inside, though not everyone is impressed. "According to art authorities, Fried Frank has an incredible art collection. It doesn't do much for me," sniffs one associate. When asked to comment on the décor, a New Yorker only pleads, "Can we please get rid of the ugly carpeting?"

Ugly carpet seems to be contagious. A DC Fried insider states "the carpet in the office definitely needs to be changed." Making up for the aforementioned carpeting, all Fried Frank lawyers get their own offices.

The helpful folks of Fried Frank

"People like to complain, but on the whole the support staff is usually very good," says one lawyer in the New York office. Another contact in that office goes a step further, calling the staff "outstanding." The only major complaint firm-wide is the computer system which, when it crashes, becomes a "nightmare." (The firm says that no computer crashes have plagued the Fried Frank system in 18 months, an unusual testament to compu-stability.)

Turnover: dead-on average

"We have a turnover problem especially among third- and fourth-years," reports one second-year attorney possibly on the cusp of leaving. "They mostly go to jobs other than law firms, which I guess is a good sign. Plenty go to dot coms." One insider finds that departures "seem to run in spurts." All told, while some attorneys detect unhappiness in the associate ranks, turnover is described as "dead-on average" for the industry.

Long, hard road to partner

"[It's] very hard to make partner" at Fried Frank, says one source who reports that "more lawyers are staying on as special counsel, either permanently or as a stepping stone to partnership." "The possibility is certainly there but associates can't bank on it," reports a corporate lawyer. Speaking of remote possibilities, one DC lawyer guesses that "like at any large law firm, you stand a better chance of being killed in a plane crash." [Fried Frank advises you to fly safely; the firm made 17 partners and special counsel in 1999 and 9 in 1998.]

If you still want to make partner (and you avoid a fiery death in an airline accident), insiders advise you to "find a mentor partner who likes you and your work. Work with other partners who are friends of that partner." "You must work closely and well with at least one or two senior partners in your department with big books of business who will later champion you to the firm as a whole," another associate says. One source suggests half-jokingly that an attorney seeking partnership should "move to another firm."

The laments and kudos of diversity

Fried Frank insiders say that their firm is making an effort to recruit minorities, but as at most firms, results have proven unimpressive. "The firm makes a lot of effort but these problems are so ingrained," says one second-year associate. "The firm has several fellowships with minority organizations, a person dedicated to minority hiring and retention, plenty of outreach, and a diversity committee, but it is hard to change these large institutions." Another insider reports that there are "no senior African-American associates and no partners." "It's definitely a vicious cycle," sighs a different contact. "Because there are no attorneys of color at the top, associates of color feel lost in the shuffle, consider their chances of partnership slim and tend to leave more quickly." The firm indicates that its junior workforce is "very diverse" and Fried Frank has established an annual Civil Rights Forum in honor of Fried Frank associate Michael Diehl, who died in September 1999. Diversity efforts, according to the firm, remain "on the front burner."

Fried Frank attracts criticism for its efforts toward the advancement of women lawyers — or lack thereof. Associates complain that Fried Frank's lack of official policies contributes to a difficult environment for women. "The firm makes its efforts but has trouble understanding what it needs to do to retain women," says one source. "It really needs an established, workable part-time policy that doesn't ruin one's chances for making partner." A female lawyer observes: "There are no outreach efforts to young women at the firm. Since there are so few female partners, it is easy to feel isolated as a young female associate." To be fair, another female associate claims, "I have never felt that I was treated any differently because of my gender."

One success story: Fried Frank has created a comfortable environment for gay and lesbian attorneys. "There are several openly gay or lesbian attorneys, including one partner, and they have not been treated any differently in my experience," says one contact. Another source reports that gay associates' "partners are welcome and often attend various firm functions." Fried Frank offers benefits for domestic partners.

Invigorating environment

"I think I have it pretty good here," says one DC associate. "No one micromanages my time and I try not to work weekends." Other insiders also give Fried Frank credit for high-quality work. "Because I hated law school, I feared working hard as a lawyer would be miserable," says one attorney. "I'm pleased to say the intellectual rigors of the work invigorate me every day."

Among the high points are the "quality of work and the intellect of lawyers." Additionally, "the firm makes a real effort to correct any perceived problems — it seems to listen." One attorney says, "I chose Fried Frank over a bunch of other New York firms because of the relaxed atmosphere and the eccentric and interesting people."

One common gripe is the partnership track, the perceived lack of which "is a little discouraging." Also, "you have to have a certain type of 'buddy-buddy' collegiality to do really well at this firm. In the litigation department, the people rumored to have made partner aren't necessarily more brilliant than their classmates, they just made the [right] friends." A firm insider complains about "the few partners with Rain Man-like interpersonal skills." Finally, Fried Frank "sells itself as a seven-days-a-week, 24-hours-a-day firm," according to one insider. "There's an expectation that you should always be at the office."

"No first-year associate should complain about his or her earnings — no matter how many hours they work."

— *Fried Frank associate*

VAULT.COM

30 PRESTIGE RANKING

Jones, Day, Reavis & Pogue

North Point
901 Lakeside Avenue
Cleveland, OH 44114-1190
(216) 586-3939
Fax: (216) 579-0212
www.jonesday.com

LOCATIONS

Atlanta, GA • Chicago, IL • Cleveland, OH • Columbus, OH • Dallas, TX • Irvine, CA • Los Angeles, CA • New York, NY • Pittsburgh, PA • Washington, DC • Brussels • Frankfurt • Geneva • Hong Kong • London • Madrid • Mumbai (associate firm) • New Delhi (associate firm) • Paris • Shanghai • Sydney • Taipei • Tokyo

MAJOR DEPARTMENTS/PRACTICES

Antitrust
Bankruptcy
Energy
Intellectual Property
International Finance
Labor
Litigation
Mergers & Acquisitions
Real Estate
Securities
Tax
Transactional

THE STATS

No. of attorneys: 1,289
No. of offices: 23
Summer associate offers: 113 out of 121 (Firm-wide, 1999)
Managing Partner: Patrick F. McCartan
Firm Hiring Partner: James C. Hagy

THE BUZZ
What attorneys at other firms are saying about this firm

- "Overstaffs large litigation matters — can you say 30 lawyers on a case?"
- "The leader in the industry"
- "Corporation"
- "Didn't Scalia start there?"

PAY

Cleveland, 2000
1st year: $110,000 + $4,000 stipend

Chicago, Irvine, Los Angeles, New York, and Washington, DC, 2000
1st year: $125,000 + $4,000 stipend

Dallas, 2000
1st year: $115,000 + $4,000 stipend

Salaries and merit bonuses vary by office

NOTABLE PERKS

- Home down payment assistance
- Fitness center in some offices

UPPERS

- Offices everywhere
- No back-stabbing politics
- Training for junior people

DOWNERS

- Bureaucratic due to size
- Clique mentality
- Close-mouthed about all salary decisions

KEY COMPETITORS

Clifford Chance Rogers & Wells
Kirkland & Ellis
Latham & Watkins
Skadden, Arps, Slate, Meagher & Flom

EMPLOYMENT CONTACT

Ms. Jolie A. Blanchard
Firm Director of Recruiting
(202) 879-3788
jablanchard@jonesday.com

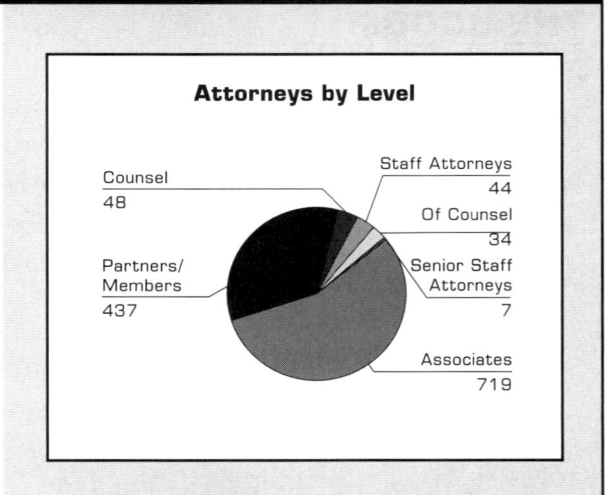

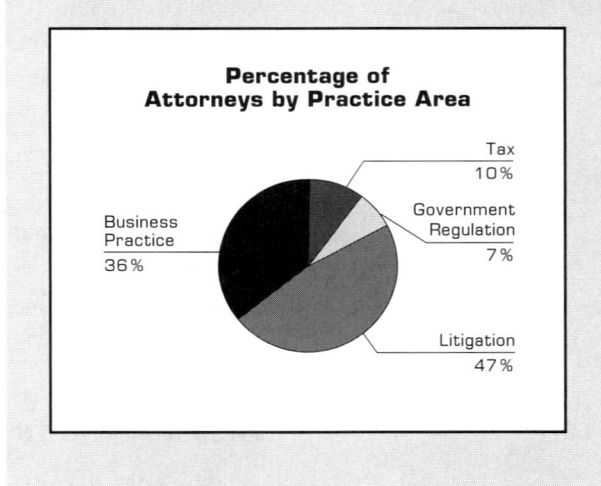

Attorneys by Level

- Counsel: 48
- Staff Attorneys: 44
- Of Counsel: 34
- Senior Staff Attorneys: 7
- Partners/Members: 437
- Associates: 719

Percentage of Attorneys by Practice Area

- Business Practice: 36%
- Tax: 10%
- Government Regulation: 7%
- Litigation: 47%

THE SCOOP

With more than 1,280 attorneys in offices worldwide, Cleveland-based Jones, Day, Reavis & Pogue takes its place among the world's largest law firms in both numbers of attorneys and gross revenues. Although Jones Day was founded in Cleveland, the firm's partners don't consider the city its headquarters in a traditional sense. No wonder: while it's true that the Cleveland office is still the firm's largest, Jones Day has six other offices with 90 attorneys or more including Washington, DC, Dallas, Chicago, New York, Los Angeles, and Atlanta (not to mention sizeable offices in Columbus, Irvine, and Pittsburgh). Speaking globally, the list of the firm's offices resembles the Sunday travel section, with operations in Brussels, Frankfurt, Geneva, London, Madrid, Paris, Sydney, New Delhi, Hong Kong, Shanghai, Taipei, Tokyo, and Mumbai.

A look at Jones Day's client list prompts the question: Who doesn't this firm represent? Jones Day provides significant representation or serves as general counsel to approximately half of the companies in the Fortune 500. According to the firm, its top five clients are Bridgestone/Firestone, Inc., RJR Nabisco, IBM, General Motors, and Texas Instruments. Other notable Jones Day clients include Amazon.com, CBS Corporation, Citigroup, Coors Brewing Company, the County of Los Angeles, Eastman Kodak Company, Goldman Sachs, J.C. Penney, Johnson & Johnson, PepsiCo, Pfizer, Procter & Gamble, the San Jose Sharks, The Tribune Company, and *The Washington Post*.

History: the firm keeps growing and growing

Established in Cleveland in 1893, Jones Day built itself up through longtime alliances with Cleveland-area manufacturing, transportation, and industrial clients. Among the firm's local mainstays are Cleveland-Cliffs, Lincoln Electric Co., M. A. Hanna, American Greetings, and The Sherwin-Williams Co. Jones Day began to creep outside Cleveland in the 1940s, establishing a Washington office in 1946. From 1960 to 1967 the firm had future U.S. Supreme Court Justice Antonin Scalia as an associate.

In the late 1980s, the firm's expansion picked up considerably. It opened 13 offices in that decade, four of which now rank among the firm's biggest: Dallas (founded in 1981), New York (1986), Chicago (1987), and Atlanta (1989). As a result, the firm tripled its number of attorneys from 1985 to 1990. Jones Day's reputation took a hit in 1993 when the firm agreed to an out-of-court settlement with the Resolution Trust Corporation for an astounding $51 million. The fine resulted from the limited role that Texas-based Jones Day lawyers played in financier Charles Keating, Jr.'s involvement with the Lincoln Savings & Loan Association. In 1993 Patrick M. McCartan took over as the firm's managing partner, succeeding Richard W. Pogue.

Spreading abroad

Jones Day's growth has not been limited to the U.S. In 1986 the firm opened offices in London, Paris, Hong Kong, and Riyadh and has continued its expansion overseas ever since. The firm opened an office in Shanghai in November 1999. Jones Day has been active in China for more than 20 years and has recently expanded its Hong Kong and Taipei offices. In 2000 Jones Day continued its global colonization by opening offices in Mumbai (formerly known as Bombay), India and Madrid. To staff the new Madrid outpost, the firm poached ten lawyers from Spain's Tena, Munoz y Asociados.

Managing CEO

Jones Day is no democracy, say insiders. Sources say the head of the firm acts more like a CEO than a managing partner. The firm's managing partner has sole power over partnership decisions, compensation, new offices, the next managing partner, and so on. Although a nine-person partnership committee can override the managing partner on compensation edicts and the firm's partners can oust a managing partner by majority vote, sources tell Vault.com that almost never happens.

Patrick McCartan took over the helm of Jones Day as managing partner in 1993. The much-admired McCartan is credited with restoring Jones Day's reputation after overexpansion in the late 1980s. McCartan has disclosed that he wants Jones Day to aggressively pursue business from the financial and capital markets, pension funds, and insurance companies, a goal that will require an even greater presence for the firm in New York and Washington.

Come together

Jones Day breaks down its practice areas into four groups: business practice, government regulation, litigation, and tax. These groups are supplemented by two specialized industry practices — energy and health care — as well as a "Technology Issues" practice.

In 1999 the firm was involved in M&A transactions totaling more than $150 billion. Jones Day lawyers Jere Thomson and Steven Guynn joined with other Jones Day lawyers from the Paris and New York offices to handle French oil company Total Fina's $48.7 billion merger with Elf Aquitane. Both companies launched hostile bids to acquire each other before officially announcing the merger in September 1999. The combination will create the world's fourth-largest oil company.

Jones Day's Chicago and Washington lawyers had a hand in creating the country's largest electric company. The firm represented Chicago-based Unicom in its $8 billion merger with Pennsylvania's Peco Energy Company announced in September 1999. Lawyers in Jones Day's Cleveland, New York, and Washington offices also helped the parent company of Macy's, Federated Department Stores, sell in cyberspace. The firm worked on Federated's $1.5 billion purchase of Fingerhut Companies. Fingerhut manages orders for Kmart, Intuit, and Quicken's web sites. And in February 1999, the firm handled Cleveland auto parts maker TRW Inc.'s purchase of British brakes and missile manufacturer Lucas Varity, a $6.6 billion transaction.

Trusty antitrust

Jones Day sports a particularly well-developed antitrust practice. Partner Joe Sims worked on the U.S. antitrust issues for the January 2000 merger between AOL and Time Warner (valued at $160 billion). Jones Day lawyers also worked on AOL's 1999 acquisition of Netscape Communications and licensing agreements with Sun Microsystems. In July 1998, Tele-Communications Inc. chose Jones Day to handle antitrust matters related to its $44 billion acquisition by AT&T.

Jones Day & the Supremes

Before taking up the top post at the firm, Patrick McCartan led the firm's litigation department. Starting in 1976, he transformed the department into a national power. In that year, Jones Day's litigation department had 25 lawyers and accounted for less than a quarter of the firm's revenues. By 1993 the department had almost 400 litigators and was responsible for 40 percent of the firm's revenues.

Jones Day lawyers have been involved in two of the most important states' rights cases in the Supreme Court's 1999-2000 season. Jones Day litigator Jeff Sutton filed an amicus brief on behalf of the state of Alabama in *Brzonkala v. Morrison*. Alabama's brief urged the Supreme Court to hold that the 1994 federal Violence Against Women Act (VAWA) is unconstitutional. The statute allows women to sue their attackers in federal court. In May 2000, the court sided with both Alabama and the defendants and held the VAWA ventured into legal areas reserved for the states.

In March 2000, Jones Day's Timothy Dyk argued that the Supreme Court should limit state power in *Natsios v. National Foreign Trade Council*. At issue is a Massachusetts law that creates barriers to winning contracts with Massachusetts for companies that do business with Myanmar, the country formerly known as Burma. Dyk contended on behalf of the trade council that the law falls into the realm of foreign policy that should be left to the federal government. This may be Dyk's last argument before the Supreme Court — he has been confirmed to the U.S. Court of Appeals for the Federal Circuit.

Bankruptcy deal maker

In April 2000, the head of Jones Day's bankruptcy department Richard Cieri became the first bankruptcy lawyer to make *American Lawyer* magazine's list of top ten deal makers. Indeed, Cieri was busy in 1999 working for the creditor's committee in the Chapter 11 bankruptcy of one of the nation's largest health care foundations, Allegheny Health. Cieri helped negotiate the sale of the foundation to Tenet Healthcare Corp. that allowed Allegheny to keep its eight hospitals and 21,000 jobs. Cieri also worked on a deal in the Purina Mills bankruptcy, allowing the company's creditors to accept newly issued stock in exchange for debt. The agreement with the creditors allowed Purina to return to relative financial health in just five months.

Working for the client

In the summer of 1999, Jones Day's Dallas office gave its summer associates some real client contact. The firm lent client Frito-Lay one summer associate per week while continuing to pay the law students' salary. No word on whether tasty corn chips were included in compensation.

GETTING HIRED

Tier two, too

If you're interested in Jones Day, don't count yourself out if you're not a graduate from a top-tier law school. "The firm is very selective but it looks at a broad range of schools," an associate says. But Jones Day can be "particular about grades." One lawyer claims that the firm usually takes from the top 15 percent of students for the top law schools and the top five percent of students for other schools.

Callback interviews at the firm usually are a series of half-hour casual chats, during which the Jones Day lawyers just try to get to know the candidate. "There are not a lot of people who want to grill you," says a Washington lawyer. A Jones Day interviewer tells us that "there are three things I'm looking for: a basic level of intelligence; a basic level of competence; and the Atlanta airport test — would I be willing to spend 10 hours on a layover in Atlanta with this person?" A source in Washington says the firm wants "fun and good-natured associates." And a Cleveland associate tells Vault.com, "Arrogance and cockiness doesn't fare well. People who are too full of themselves don't get offers."

While every interviewer will be looking for the candidate to ask questions, it's especially important at Jones Day. "I like to open questions up to the candidate," says one contact, "because there are a lot of misconceptions about Jones Day. We're often the target of those kinds of things, especially from other firms who like to paint us as a sweatshop."

OUR SURVEY SAYS

The big family machine

Lawyers describe Jones Day as everything from a "big family" to "a machine." One lawyer tells Vault.com, "I like coming here and the people I work with." Another source says, "Everything is well-managed and there is a committee for everything. The bad part is that it can feel bureaucratic and unfeeling." Many lawyers feel that an abundance of bureaucratic procedures is just part of life at such a huge firm. "It's managed like a corporation," notes another insider. But most associates feel Jones Day's size is a selling point for the firm. A contact in Dallas says: "We've got the resources to do just about anything a client could want. With a click of the mouse, or by getting on the phone, you can get the expertise you need. The strength of numbers is tremendous."

Associates say that Jones Day really does operate as one firm. "Infrastructure-wise it's one firm," comments a source. Jones Day associates get plenty of opportunities to interact with their colleagues throughout the country at the firm's training programs. Attorneys also get to work with fellow associates from around the nation because matters are often staffed in more than one office. But some attorneys feel that the DC and Cleveland offices are the "showcase offices in the firm." Another attorney thinks the L.A. office is the firm's "red-headed stepchild."

Contacts describe the firm as "conservative" and "professional." But an associate in Chicago notes, "For such a big firm it is not that formal." Many Jones Day offices feature casual Fridays and casual summers. But if you're heading to Jones Day Chicago, better hold onto your suits. That office has not officially adopted any casual days. Some associates in Cleveland feel that the office there is a bit more formal because it's seen as the headquarters. Moreover, Jones Day is certainly not casual when it comes to work. Associates claim the firm is very detailed-oriented. "The firm doesn't slide by on anything."

Partners can be pals

A Jones Day associate says the partners are "the best I've ever seen or heard of. That goes for the whole country." "There are very few yellers and I've never had anything thrown at me," says another contact. A source in L.A. describes the partners as "grandfatherly" and says, "a lot of them take it upon themselves to be mentors." A Chicago attorney reports, "They are not strict and can be your friends. Some will even show up at happy hours with associates." A Dallas associate agrees: "Even as a mere junior associate, most partners value and actively encourage my opinions and show appreciation of my hard work." But other sources say the partners "have a high opinion of themselves." "Partners don't want to be your buddy and learn about you," according to a Cleveland source. Some lawyers say that they don't have a lot of contact with the partners, mainly because of Jones Day's size.

A happy, hopping Jones Day social scene

Most of Jones Day's larger offices have an active social scene. Lawyers in Chicago say many lawyers eat lunch together and go to happy hours. "A lot of people do things outside of work and remain friends," according to an L.A. contact. "It's rare to eat lunch in your office." But L.A. associates also say the Jones Day social life is "a small group thing."

Associates in Cleveland says it's "a very married office." "Younger attorneys go out very often but it's not a great place if you're single and want to meet someone at work." Another Cleveland source says, "doors are open and there are conversations in the hallway." Every winter the Cleveland office has "The Prom" for which the firm rents a room and associates get dressed up in tuxedos. But no one asks the staff to the prom — they have a separate party.

Romantics and political hounds should enjoy the scene in Jones Day's DC office. Every Friday evening associates in Washington have an opportunity to enjoy cocktails while looking out at the capital from the firm's terrace.

Gods of Cleveland

Insiders say that Jones Day is very "hush-hush when it comes to pay." Junior attorneys receive lockstep compensation but mid-level and senior associates' paychecks vary from lawyer to lawyer. Insiders say that Jones Day decided in 2000 to pay a merit based bonuses for the first time. But the bonuses will not be tied to billables because the partnership reportedly believes such compensation schemes encourage over-billing. "The bonuses are sort of secretive," says one source. Associates say the firm has kept up with the 2000 salary race and pays the market rate at most of its offices. That's good news for associates in less pricey areas of the country. According to one well-compensated insider: "The starting salary in Cleveland is $110,000. You can live like a god in Cleveland for that money."

Shockingly extensive training

Associates say the formal training programs at Jones Day are "excellent to the point of overkill." Another source exclaims, "I am shocked by how much training there is!" New associates attend a three-day session with their fellow first-years from around the country. Moreover, Jones Day does not assign first-year associates to specific departments, but rather allows them to experiment. After trying out assignments from various practice areas, they can choose which department they want to join.

Jones Day's practice groups have annual firm-wide meetings. Each individual office also has regular training sessions throughout the year. But one associate complains that most of these training programs are geared to people who already have significant experience. The Cleveland office has a video library of training materials, but it's reportedly not very popular. "Who wants to take a video home? It's not exactly Blockbuster."

Junior attorneys say that much of their informal training comes from working with senior associates. One associate admits, "I wouldn't always feel comfortable going to partners with a question." Others claim partners "are willing to help, but getting on their schedule can be a problem." But a contact in Cleveland says the partners can be more helpful than associates. "Some [senior associates] are dedicated to training; others see you as someone to take their extra grunt work."

Insiders report the type of work given to junior associates can vary. "Sometimes the office is so busy there is no time to do exciting work. There are years when you're stuck on document reviews," according to a source in sunny Los Angeles. But another lawyer claims that the work you get depends on your own initiative. "If you knock on partners' doors you will get good work." And a lawyer in Chicago claims, "You start off slow at low levels. But by your third year, you get a lot of responsibility without a lot of supervision."

Work work work (not really)

An attorney in the Jones Day headquarters says, "The firm has a sweatshop reputation, but I don't see that. It's not a fair assessment. A sweatshop in Cleveland is closer to a lifestyle firm in New York City." A Dallas associate concurs: "The Jones, Day, Nights & Weekend rumor has not proved true here." In 1999 Jones Day's average billable hours per associate was 1,955. Most Vault.com sources find this level of commitment to be "very livable." Some even say the schedule is not a big deal. "Nobody seems to care about your hours, as long as you're available and doing your work," according to one lawyer. But an L.A. associate adds, "the partners expect you not to blink when you have to work a weekend. They want you to treat this like a career, not a job."

Gorgeous in Washington, DC

In May 1999, Jones Day's Washington, DC office relocated from the city's central business district to the Capital Hill area. The new offices feature outdoor terraces with views of the capitol dome. Most of the building has been renovated for Jones Day's arrival but much of the old marble and wood panel boardrooms have remained. Extraordinarily tall associates should be happy with the new office's 12-foot ceilings. Washington associates describe the offices as "Just gorgeous!"

In contrast, some L.A. associates feel their office is the worst in the entire firm. "There is duct tape on the carpets and the paint looks horrible. It looks like a garbage heap," according to one source. Associates in Chicago, meanwhile, rave about the good views.

Change ain't easy, even for word processing

Most larger Jones Day offices assign each secretary to two or three lawyers. A source in L.A. says the paralegals are very good but "the secretaries have an enormous amount of power because the firm won't fire them when they're bad. You have to get lucky." The computer support is reportedly improving in the L.A. office. In Washington, DC, lawyers are particularly enthusiastic about the 24-hour word processing center.

Cleveland lawyers are mostly satisfied with their support services. But some lawyers are disappointed with the availability of supplies. "Normally associates get whatever is lying around until supply staff catches up," according to one source. In addition, the firm is changing form WordPerfect to Word and apparently some secretaries in Cleveland are a bit bent out of shape about it. "It's traumatic for some people," says one source. Many Cleveland lawyers think the paralegals are excellent, although some lawyers observe the paralegals are overworked.

Support for women, sometimes

Associates say that Jones Day hires just as many (and some years more) women as men. The firm offers a woman-friendly part-time schedule in which associates can work on a reduced percentage or hourly basis. But one source says, "There is a stigma when you go part-time. Women may have other commitments to their children. But here the priority is the workplace." In contrast, an associate in the Chicago office observes that a lot of female lawyers are having children and the firm appears to be supportive. Another associate explains, "Once you go part-time then you're off the partnership track. You can get back on but it can take a year or two longer."

Jones Day also runs the "In Counsel with Women" program that helps young female attorneys learn how to bring in clients. The program features luncheons with prominent women in business and law, and helps female lawyers to develop client contacts and foster relationships. "The firm shows a commitment to helping women with getting clients," says one woman lawyer.

One minority lawyer says, "I have never felt prejudice at the firm." Associates report the firm "aggressively seeks to hire minority candidates," though other observers admit "the offices are pretty white right now." Insiders say the firm attends minority recruiting programs and makes sure minorities are represented on firm committees.

Most Jones Day lawyers say the treatment of gays and lesbians at the firm "is not really an issue." Attorneys report there are at least some openly gay lawyers at the firm. One exception is in Cleveland, though lawyers don't think that office is necessarily unfriendly to homosexuals. "It's more of a function of being in Cleveland," an associate opines.

Do as you will pro bono

When it comes to pro bono at Jones Day, "it's kind of do what you want," sources say. The firm regularly circulates messages about pro bono opportunities. The Washington, DC office, for example, does work for legal clinics for the homeless. New associates also have the option to spend a month at Legal Aid, which counts toward billable hours. "If you want to do pro bono work, you will be supported," according to one lawyer.

But some are skeptical about how pro pro bono Jones Day really is. "Partners would like to think that pro bono hours count as regular hours. But if you bill too many pro bono hours in relation to your regular billable, they will get mad at you," reports one source. "You are not encouraged to spend too much time on pro bono. They would be annoyed if billable client work slacks," says another contact. Most associates surveyed believe that there exists a limit on how many hours Jones Day associates can count towards their billing requirement, though no one could identify the precise number.

Make me a partner

Jones Day lawyers say that bringing in a lot of business is not a prerequisite to becoming partner. After all, finding new clients that won't raise conflicts of interest is pretty difficult when you have a client list as long as Jones Day. One associate says, "To make partner you're not required to have your own book of business. But you better make it up in hours." Another associate reports that those who want to make partner are supposed to demonstrate "capacity," as opposed to the approximately 2,000-hour per year average. "They don't tell you what 'capacity' is, but the general feeling is that it is somewhere around 2,400 to 2,600 hours." Another contact advises that to make partner, an associate should "be involved with the firm, both workwise and socially. The managing partner likes people who are loyal to the firm."

Making partner at Jones Day can take from nine to 11 years, insiders say. But you'll get the heads-up beforehand. One source says, "By the sixth or seventh year you know if you're on the track, and if not you leave."

31 Dewey Ballantine LLP
PRESTIGE RANKING

1301 Avenue of the Americas
New York, NY 10019
(212) 259-8000
Fax: (212) 259-6333
www.deweyballantine.com

LOCATIONS
New York, NY (HQ)
Los Angeles, CA
Silicon Valley, CA
Washington, DC
Budapest
Hong Kong
London
Prague
Warsaw

MAJOR DEPARTMENTS/PRACTICES
Bankruptcy
Corporate
Energy
ERISA/Employee Benefits
International Trade
Litigation
Project Finance
Real Estate
Securitization
Tax

THE STATS
No. of attorneys: 486
No. of offices: 8
Summer associate offers: 60 out of 60 (New York)
Managing Partner: Everett L. Jassy
Hiring attorney: Sean M. Moran

THE BUZZ
What attorneys at other firms are saying about this firm

- "Bleeding associates"
- "Tax powerhouse"
- "Brutal old-school mill"
- "Old-world charm"

PAY
All Domestic Offices, 2000
1st year: $125,000
2nd year: $135,000
3rd year: $150,000
4th year: $170,000
5th year: $190,000
6th year: $200,000
7th year: $205,000
8th year: $210,000
Summer associate: $2,403/week

NOTABLE PERKS
- Emergency child care
- Laptop computers
- Telecommuting option
- 12 weeks paid maternity leave
- Annual firm-wide formal dinner at Plaza Hotel in New York
- Complimentary private banking
- Interest-free loan for all incoming associates

UPPERS

- Strong efforts at associate retention
- Very good paralegal support staff
- Great traditional social events
- Little cutthroat competition

DOWNERS

- Limited contact with clients
- Absence of social interaction with partners
- No organized method of assigning work
- Lack of information about firm management

KEY COMPETITORS

Fried, Frank, Harris, Shriver & Jacobson
Shearman & Sterling
Skadden, Arps, Slate, Meagher & Flom
White & Case
Willkie Farr & Gallagher

EMPLOYMENT CONTACT

Mr. William H. Davis
Legal Personnel & Recruitment Manager
(212) 259-7328
williamdavis@deweyballantine.com

Attorneys by Location

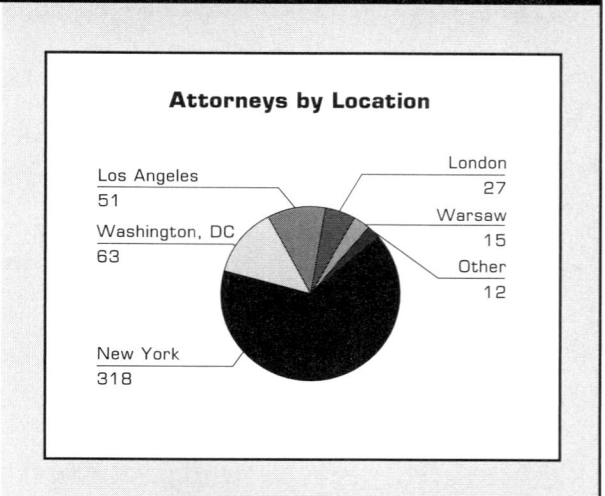

- Los Angeles: 51
- Washington, DC: 63
- New York: 318
- London: 27
- Warsaw: 15
- Other: 12

Attorneys by Practice Area [New York]

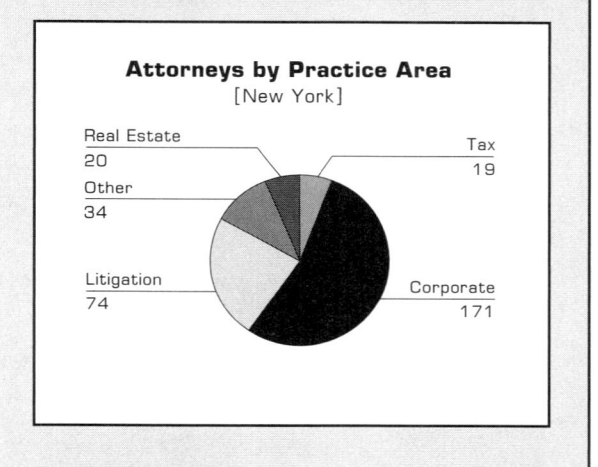

- Real Estate: 20
- Other: 34
- Litigation: 74
- Tax: 19
- Corporate: 171

QUALITY OF LIFE RANKINGS [ASSOCIATES RATE THEIR OWN FIRM]

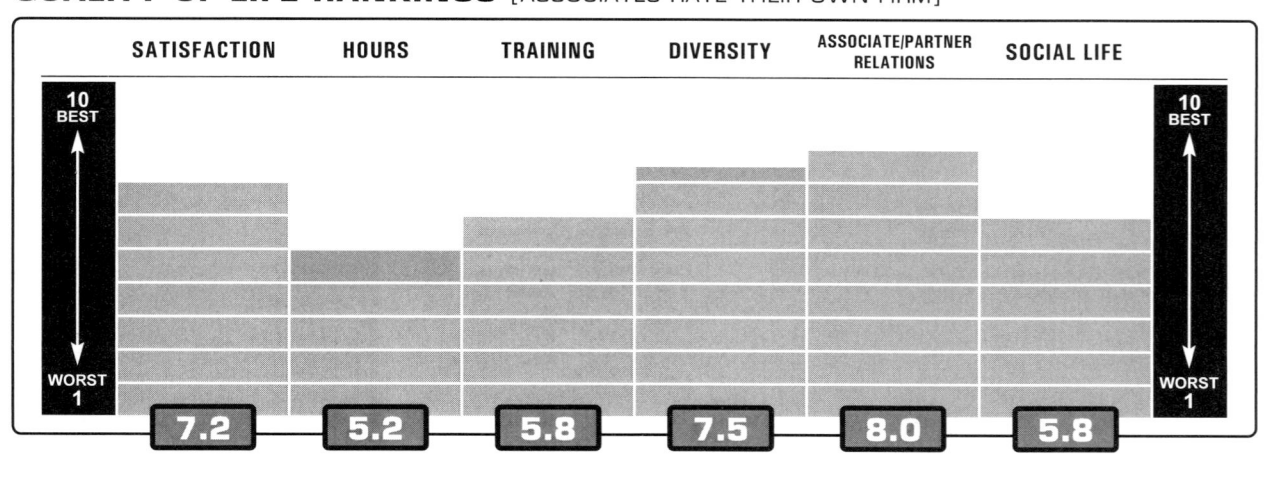

Satisfaction	Hours	Training	Diversity	Associate/Partner Relations	Social Life
7.2	5.2	5.8	7.5	8.0	5.8

THE SCOOP

Dewey Ballantine is a classic New York law firm — but that doesn't make it plain vanilla. Suer of the tobacco industry and proud counsel to Disney, Dewey Ballantine also has a strong international orientation.

History: shifting names, steady firm

Dewey Ballantine's history spans more than 90 years and is marked by a startling number of name changes. The firm was founded in 1909 as Root, Clark & Bird, and went through 12 separate name changes before settling on its current name, Dewey Ballantine LLP, in October 1997. (Incidentally, the Dewey in the firm name refers to the very same Thomas Dewey who ran unsuccessful presidential campaigns against Franklin Roosevelt and Harry Truman.)

Dewey Ballantine has proven itself to be a forward-looking firm. In 1984 it was the first tenant to agree to buy and occupy 250,000 square feet in one of the four towers of a new Times Square development. At the time, Times Square was a squalid area, a far cry from the Disneyfied tourist attraction that we know today (we'll return to the topic of Disney shortly). In the 1980s and 1990s Dewey Ballantine grew by poaching laterals from other law firms. Conquests included 16 lawyers in 1988 from the leveraged buyout firm Lane & Edson (giving Dewey excellent M&A ability); three corporate insurance specialists from LeBoeuf, Lamb Greene & MacRae in 1989, 10 securities lawyers from Winston & Strawn in 1994, and eight partners from White & Case, including that firm's former head of litigation, in 1995. Six lawyers from the now-defunct Donovan Leisure joined Dewey's M&A practice in 1998 and in June 1999, the firm lured leading tech and Internet attorney John Keitt from Rogers & Wells to its New York partnership.

The change-is-good philosophy seems to have paid off. The firm ranked 31st out of the nation's 100 top-grossing firms with gross revenue of $250 million dollars in 1998, according to *The American Lawyer*. Average compensation for Dewey partners was $805,000, fifteenth highest among New York firms.

Dewey over yonder

Dewey Ballantine hasn't neglected overseas opportunities for growth. In 1996 the firm ended its five-year association with British firm Theodore Goddard. Cutting its losses? No, Dewey Ballantine initiated the breakup, planning to expand its London office and hire both U.S. and U.K. lawyers. In February 2000, the firm sent New York-based partners Doug Getter and Louise Roman Bernstein to London to attempt to strengthen its M&A practice there (and perhaps to offset the loss of several U.K.

attorneys poached by other British firms). Dewey aims to lengthen its list of energy clients in the European market, focusing on oil and gas work on the other side of the ocean.

Dewey now maintains its own offices in Budapest, Prague, Warsaw, and Hong Kong. Several of the branches work together on international deals. The London and Prague offices advised South African Breweries on its agreement to buy Czech Republic brewers Pilsner Urquell and Radegast from Nomura International in a deal slated to closed by July 2001. It makes sense that Dewey Ballantine would have a major presence abroad; the firm's international trade practice, based in Washington, DC, is one of the largest and most prominent of its kind. More than 40 lawyers and other specialists handle a full range of legal questions attached to international commerce.

The Kodak suit

One of Dewey's biggest cases in international trade in recent years was the high-profile 1995 suit against Fuji for non-competitive practices. Dewey's client, Kodak, alleged that its main competitor, Fuji Film, controlled Japan's film market with the cooperation of the Japanese government. Dewey lawyers compiled a massive 250-page document detailing Fuji's infractions. Among other allegations, the document accused Fuji of offering rebates to the four distributors handling close to 70 percent of Japan's film and photographic paper, a disincentive to carry Kodak film. While Dewey Ballantine lawyers convinced the United States government to file a complaint with the World Trade Organization, in December 1997 the World Trade Organization ruled that Kodak, Dewey, and the U.S. government had not proven that the Japanese government had directly impaired Kodak's competitive rights. In July 1998, Dewey Ballantine sent an angry letter to the U.S. Trade Representative's office, charging that the adverse decision was made not by the WTO panel but by the WTO secretariat, who, according to Dewey, "lacked both the competence and the mandate to do so."

Dewey Ballantine continues to crusade on behalf of its clients in international trade matters in the DC office. The firm represents major U.S. manufacturers like Bethlehem Steel, USX Corp and Inland Steel Industries, who charge that Canadian and Japanese manufacturers are in cahoots to keep out of each other's markets, putting U.S. steel companies at a disadvantage.

Loving the mouse

No jokes about Mickey Mouse business! Dewey is fortunate that media empire Disney is a major client. In 1995 partner and M&A head Morton Pierce and a team of Dewey lawyers performed an amazing feat, putting together Disney's takeover of Capital Cities/ABC in three and a half days. The gigantic $19 billion deal would have normally taken months. Pierce got a call from Disney on Thursday, July 27. The company wanted a completed agreement by Monday to surprise the stock markets. As soon as the firm got the call, it turned its Midtown New York office into a veritable legal factory. Twenty lawyers took over a floor of the firm, turning out the first draft of the agreement overnight. A support staff of about 30 secretaries, receptionists and paralegals were on duty 24 hours a day, and the kitchen served breakfast, lunch and dinner to the toiling attorneys. "We became a little village unto ourselves," Pierce told *The American Bar Association Journal*. Dewey attorneys (and Cap Cities/ABC counsel Cravath) avoided the use of their cellular phones to prevent leaks. The deal went smoothly and the 51-page agreement was approved at 2:30 on Monday morning.

Since that time, Dewey has performed other tasks for Disney, such as helping the firm sell four newspapers to Knight-Ridder in 1997 and advising the Buena Vista Internet (Disney's interactive division) 60 percent purchase of the Soccer.net website. In September 1999, Sanford "Sandy" Litvack, a former member of Dewey's executive committee and chairman of the litigation department, was named vice chairman of the board of The Walt Disney Company by chairman and CEO Michael Eisner.

Cash cows

As Kodak and Disney indicate, Dewey Ballantine has more than its share of high-profile clients. Others include druggists Eli Lilly and Novartis. In recent deals, Dewey has represented Lockheed Martin in its merger with Northrop, SBC in connection with the acquisition of Ameritech, Chrysler in connection with its high highly publicized merger with Daimler Benz, and Guinness in its merger with Grand Met. The firm also served as FTC counsel to GTE in connection with its proposed acquisition of MCI; the firm's antitrust department is highly regarded.

Dewey Ballantine keeps its name in the news with a number of notable healthcare and medical products deals as well. The firm took on Cytogen Corp.'s purchase of Prostagen Inc. in June 1999. Cytogen manufactures biochemical systems for the imaging and treatment of human cancers and Prostagen is a research and technology services provider. In August 1999, Dewey represented investor General Electric in medical and breast implant manufacturer Inamed Corp.'s $142 million purchase of Collagen Aesthetics Inc., a maker of anti-aging products.

Milking startups

However, in keeping with its forward-looking tradition, Dewey represents its share of emerging growth companies. The firm has stuck its toe into the frothy Internet pool. For example, the firm handled the IPO for online music retailer N2K, Inc., and counseled Sony when it acquired (along with Time Warner Inc.) another music merchant website, CDNow Inc., in August 1999. To catch up to San Francisco firms, Dewey has even considered alternate fee agreements. "A smaller firm might be willing to accept equity in lieu of cash payments," partner Frank Morgan told *Crain's New York Business* in February 1999, adding, "It's not something historically we have done, but it is something that could be considered."

No smoking, please

Unlike several prominent NYC firms, Dewey just says no when it comes to defending big tobacco. Former co-chairperson Joseph Califano, Jr. actively campaigns against smoking and the firm won a beauty contest to represent the Coalition for Tobacco Responsibility, a group of 50 Blue Cross/Blue Shield plans suing major tobacco companies. "I don't want to paint a picture that we're high and mighty," firm chairman Everett Jassy told *The American Lawyer*, "but it was never an issue whether we would sue tobacco." In February 1999, the firm scored a victory in the battle when a senior federal judge denied a motion to dismiss the suit. A petition by the defendant to have the Second Circuit reverse the decision was denied, and the case is scheduled to go to trial in September 2000.

GETTING HIRED

Personable and smart

As with most top firms, grades are "the biggest driving force" behind the hiring of law students, though "Dewey isn't a hard grade place like other firms." Those ranking in the top "20 to 30 percent" of their classes can get a look from Dewey Ballantine. Suggests one litigator: "I think Dewey looks for very smart people who are also personable."

One contact describes the background of Dewey attorneys: "The firm would like to hire only from top-tier schools, but due to the hot job market, Dewey must hire law review types from lesser NYC and regional schools while attracting a fair number of students from Columbia, NYU, Duke, and Harvard that are not at the top of their class." Another interviewee sees the diversity of law school origins as a strength, a sign that "Dewey does a great job at recognizing talent. Although it may be a symptom of the current market, Dewey recruits and hires from schools across the country and doesn't appear to operate under the mistaken assumption that great lawyers come only from three or four schools."

First rounds with partners

First-round interviews on campus are performed solely by Dewey partners and senior associates. In the second round, candidates visit the office of interest to them and interview with Dewey lawyers. An insider suggests that prospective Deweyites take advantage of this second round to "meet with the people you will be working with." That contact opines that "the associates are generally very open and forthcoming with their descriptions of the work environment and what is expected of you. There is little cutthroat competition or backstabbing."

OUR SURVEY SAYS

Pay to stay

Although Dewey has coughed up the cash to match other New York competitors, now offering associates $125,000 their first year, a number of associates grumble about the inexact nature of the compensation packages. "We have been told that our bonus will be between 5K and 50K. Other than that, we have very little guidance about the amount or what is required of us to earn the bonus," explains a first-year tax attorney. A corporate colleague concurs that "the bonus criteria following the early 2000 salary hikes have not been announced, but it's been intimated that they will be discretionary and will be hours-based, at least in part." "The uncertainty of bonus levels is problematic because associates cannot determine beforehand whether we will be paid competitive salaries," gripes an M&A newcomer.

At the same time, some associates report high turnover at the firm, although "the flight seems to be more to companies as opposed to other firms." A litigator suggests that attrition in his department is "extremely high." Apparently "the past six months have seen a lot of junior people leave for various banking and Internet positions" and now "it seems like there are no junior associates!"

Please, sir, can I have some more?

"Some partners are great at teaching," suggests a third-year litigator, "while others just don't bother." Several colleagues criticize Dewey's training efforts as "short" and "generally a one-shot deal." In-house CLE programs are "frequent, well-attended and well done," according to a corporate associate, but feedback is given only "informally" and "semi-annual reviews are (at least for junior associates) perfunctory." Some attorneys complain that "there is very little on-the-job training" while others find that to be their only resource, with most learning in the "'sink or swim' and 'school of hard knocks'" vein. The consensus seems to be, however, that "there is a significant training deficiency."

To each his own

Dewey prides itself on office space that makes associates want to come to work. A corporate finance first-year enthuses that "Dewey's offices are probably the best I've ever seen. I got my own office after only working five months." Generally, "associates share an office for the first six months (which can be cramped) but are then moved into attractive and (relatively) large private offices." While "the carpet should probably be replaced" and "the art leaves something to be desired," a second-year says "the firm is well-maintained and attractive — it's rare to come across huge piles of documents littering a hallway or a conference room that looks like somebody has been living in there for a few years." A poor soul from the M&A sector begs for "brighter light bulbs in the hallways, please!"

Support services are said to be competent but scarce. According to a litigator, "The support staff is good, particularly the paralegals. But in terms of secretarial assistance, junior associates do not generally have full access to their own secretaries because they share them with partners and senior associates." A first-year gripes that "for some reason, secretaries believe that it is not in their job description to make copies so attorneys end up doing it themselves."

Structured socializing

In its fight to remain one of New York's power players, has Dewey Ballantine sacrificed its sense of collegiality to focus on bottom-line profits? A second-year litigator suggests that "Dewey used to have a very casual and more sociable atmosphere. In the last year or two, however, the environment has changed to the point where although it is not a stuffy environment, it definitely is not as distinct from all the other top large New York firms like it once was."

Social interaction between associates is "fairly decent during work hours" although "there is no interaction after hours and there certainly is no social interaction between partners and associates," comments an M&A observer. A corporate first-year agrees that "young associates tend to hang out a lot more than the more senior associates." The firm does host "some great social events," "traditions which occasionally make working here a lot of fun." There are those who appreciate the structured atmosphere, like the corporate second-year who finds that "there are plenty of opportunities to socialize with other lawyers. However, very few people seem to expect that colleagues are going to be their only set of out-of-the-office companions — which is probably healthy." Others chafe under the structure. "The socializing is in the form of organized firm events," assesses one insider, "as opposed to events spontaneously initiated among the lawyers."

Women and minorities are 'non-issues'

When it comes to questions of diversity, a number of Dewey associates say gender, race, and sexual orientation "seem to be non-issues." The firm "seems like a great place for women," offers a real estate associate. A litigator muses, however, that even though "I haven't really noticed a problem, I do work mostly with men and have never worked with a female partner." The same real estate first-year says, "Dewey makes a great effort" to recruit minorities, but a sixth-year colleague "would have to conclude that the firm could do more." And as for gays and lesbians, "the firm doesn't actively recruit nor discourage," leading several associates to speculate that Dewey's attitude is "neutral to receptive" on the point. At least one attorney finds "people here to bend over backwards to be accommodating," having brought his same-sex partner to all firm events and being "wonderfully received."

Sorry about the weekend

Most respondents find Dewey partners "enjoy meeting and working with associates without much concern for status" and are "generally quite nice and considerate of time and life outside the office." Some "actually apologize when work infringes on weekends." However, "some of the other partners need to take a deep breath and relax," especially the ones with "highly questionable social skills."

Associates would also appreciate it if their superiors could clue them in a little more as to the partnership process itself, since most seem to have "not a clue" or "no idea" how the anointing works. If you're looking to stick around for the long run, one new M&A teammate suggests that you "bring in or be related to clients," while a co-worker suggests you "marry an important client."

A litigator who seems to have given the question considerable thought points out that "there is a lot of turnover, so by the time you are up for partner there usually aren't that many people your year who are left. If you make it that far, I think your chances are pretty good. "Oh, come on!" snorts a first-year colleague. "Who could possibly stick around that long? Okay, okay, now some names come to mind." He suggests a three-step approach: "Work way too much. Have no life. Repeat steps 1 and 2 for a very long time."

What's next, Saville Row?

Dewey is not the only firm to have instituted a casual dress code for the summer season, but it may be one of the only ones to "negotiate corporate rates with Brooks

Brothers." If BB doesn't do it for you, don't worry — "there's a good balance of people dressing conservatively and on the trendier side." But keep in mind this is still a corporate law firm. "Trendier" may mean "typical Banana Republic or J. Crew dress;" attorney tastes "run the gamut from Homer Simpson to Beau Brummell."

We're good enough, we're smart enough, and gosh darn it, people like us

Dewey has a "very solid corporate practice, with its M&A getting the most attention," says one from that department. And "though not as high-profile as the corporate side, litigation handles many 'big' cases such as the tobacco litigation and Novartis." The firm has an "undeserved reputation for being snobby," notices a litigator, but other than that, "in all of its practice areas, DB is regarded as stellar — and rightly so."

But insecurities still nag. "I think Dewey is regarded as a top-tier firm," asserts a third-year. "Although it might not be considered by some to be the equal of Cravath or Wachtell it certainly should be." Another of the flock describes the firm as "top-flight." While "I know we are not compared to Debevoise, Cravath, and Sullivan, I'd put our work next to theirs any day."

Cooley Godward LLP

VAULT.COM 32 PRESTIGE RANKING

5 Palo Alto Square
3000 El Camino Real
Palo Alto, CA 94306-2155
(650) 843-5000
Fax: (650) 857-0663
www.cooley.com

LOCATIONS

Palo Alto, CA (HQ)
Boulder, CO
Denver, CO
Kirkland, WA
Menlo Park, CA
Reston, VA
San Diego, CA
San Francisco, CA

MAJOR DEPARTMENTS/PRACTICES

Antitrust/Trade Regulation • Corporate (Mergers & Acquisitions, International, Securities, Venture Capital) • Credit Finance • Employee Compensation & Benefits • Employment & Labor Litigation • Estate Planning • General Litigation • Immigration • Information Technology (Transactional) • Intellectual Property Litigation/Patent/Trademark • Life Sciences (Transactional) • Real Estate • Tax

THE STATS

No. of attorneys: 553
No. of offices: 8
Summer associate offers: 29 out of 31 (Palo Alto, 1999)
Managing Partner: Lee F. Benton
Hiring Attorney: Richard E. Climan (Palo Alto)

THE BUZZ
What attorneys at other firms are saying about this firm

- "Wilson Sonsini wannabe"
- "Hot in high tech"
- "A little chaotic due to growth"
- "More consistent than competitors"

PAY

All Domestic Offices, 2000
1st year: $125,000
2nd year: $135,000
3rd year: $150,000
4th year: $165,000
5th year: $185,000
6th year: $195,000
7th year: $205,000
Associates are eligible for performance bonuses
Summer associate: $2,400/week

NOTABLE PERKS

- Firm retreats (about every two years)
- Gym membership subsidy
- Up to $20 per day for meals
- Meals and taxi home if more than 10.5 hours worked in any day

UPPERS

- Commitment to maintaining "the Cooley way"
- Good balance of work and personal life
- Support for working moms
- Cutting-edge high tech and biotech clients

DOWNERS

- Too many clients = too many hours
- High turnover leaving junior associates without much leadership
- Rapid expansion threatening the "one firm" feel
- Poor people management

KEY COMPETITORS

Brobeck, Phleger & Harrison
Orrick, Herrington & Sutcliffe
Venture Law Group
Wilson Sonsini Goodrich & Rosati

EMPLOYMENT CONTACT

Ms. Jo Anne Larson
Director of Attorney Recruiting
(650) 843-5000
attorneyrecruiting@cooley.com

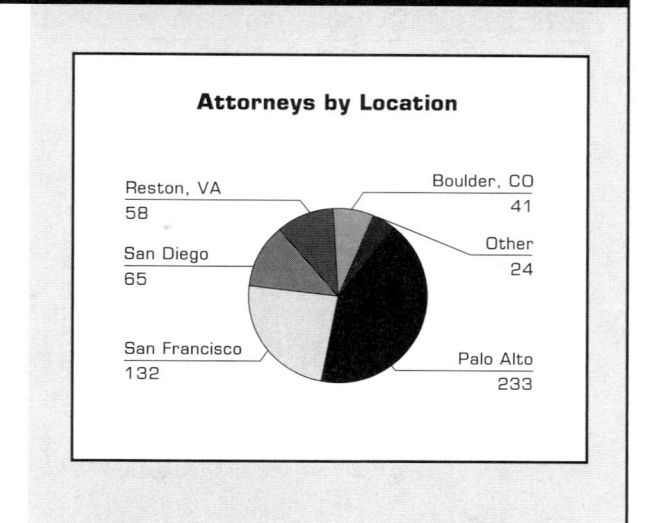

Attorneys by Location

- Reston, VA: 58
- Boulder, CO: 41
- Other: 24
- San Diego: 65
- San Francisco: 132
- Palo Alto: 233

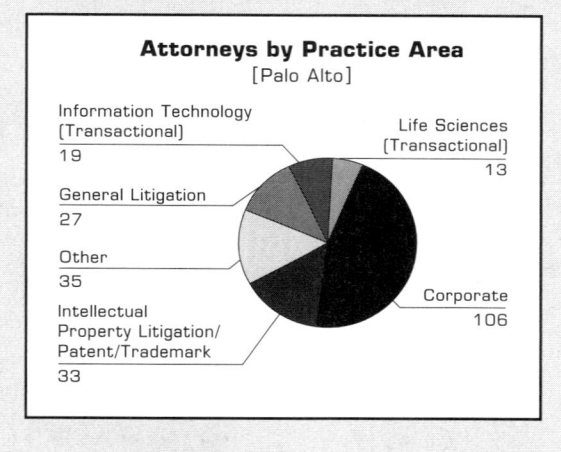

Attorneys by Practice Area [Palo Alto]

- Information Technology (Transactional): 19
- Life Sciences (Transactional): 13
- General Litigation: 27
- Other: 35
- Intellectual Property Litigation/Patent/Trademark: 33
- Corporate: 106

QUALITY OF LIFE RANKINGS [ASSOCIATES RATE THEIR OWN FIRM]

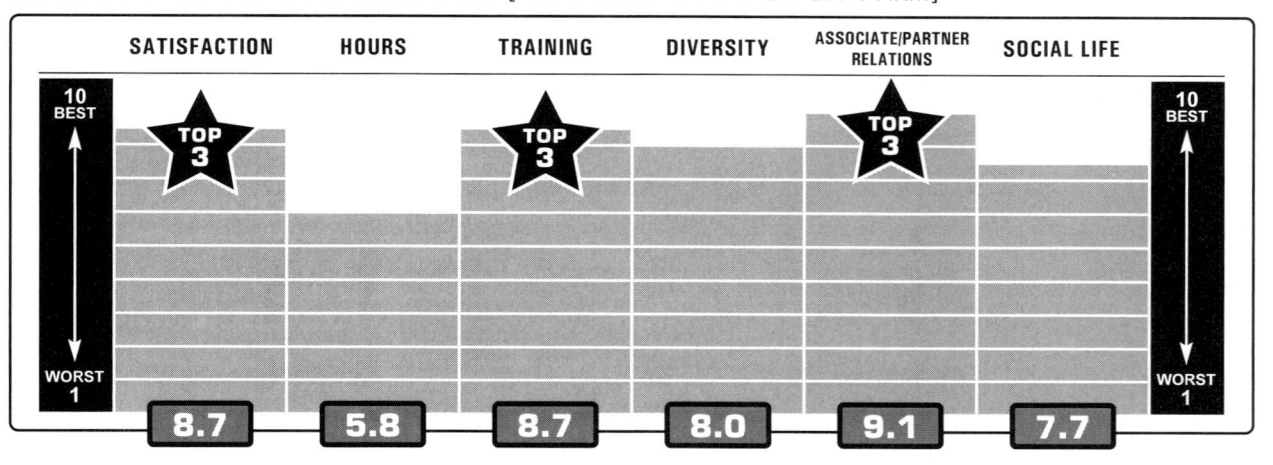

SATISFACTION	HOURS	TRAINING	DIVERSITY	ASSOCIATE/PARTNER RELATIONS	SOCIAL LIFE
8.7 (TOP 3)	5.8	8.7 (TOP 3)	8.0	9.1 (TOP 3)	7.7

THE SCOOP

Cooley Godward, a firm boasting strong corporate and litigation departments, is known primarily for its work in the high tech and biotech industries. Dubbed a lifestyle firm by many of its associates, Cooley faces the challenges of rapid expansion — including how to continue offering a high quality of life to its associates.

Good times at Cooley

Under the management hand of Kenneth Guernsey (who stepped down as acting manager in 1996) and his successor Lee Benton, Cooley Godward has grown along with Silicon Valley. Despite some problems at the beginning of the decade that necessitated the shutdown of the Newport Beach office, the 1990s have been wonderful for Cooley. Since 1990 the firm has more than doubled in size to over 500 lawyers. Cooley has changed with the times, even moving its base of operations from scenic San Francisco to booming Silicon Valley and Palo Alto. The firm has established offices in San Diego, Denver, Boulder, Kirkland, WA, and Reston, VA.

Corporate work plows ahead

Nor does Cooley show much sign of slowing down. Leading the way into the sunny land of profits is the firm's corporate department; the Palo Alto M&A attorneys have kept particularly busy. Notable deals in 1999 included representing Gilead Sciences Inc. in its March agreement to buy NeXstar Pharmaceuticals in a $550 million transaction. In the software industry, Cooley ushered Pennsylvania's SunGard Data Systems through its acquisition of Sterling Wentworth in February 1999.

In February 2000, Cooley represented Wind River Systems Inc. in its $930 million stock-for-stock acquisition of Integrated Systems Inc., icing the company's hat trick after it acquired DIAB-SDS, Doctor Design and Takefive Software. The same team handled the acquisition of Embedded Support Tools for 6.3 million shares of Wind River stock (valued at $300 million).

The firm acted as outside counsel to Signio Inc. in its January 2000 acquisition by VeriSign, an e-commerce tech company that verifies the identity of buyers and sellers on the Internet, in a roughly $840 million stock swap. Signio's services will allow VeriSign to check an e-commerce customer's ability to pay, in addition to identifying said customer. That same month, another team from the same office advised Saraide (the top wireless Internet service provider in Canada, Europe and Japan) when it was bought by Infospace.com (a leading provider of infrastructure services for consumers, merchants and wireless devices) in a more than $1 billion stock swap. The deal facilitated the formation of the largest global alliance in the wireless Internet services market. Finally, in March 2000 the firm represented Aspect Development in its $9.3 billion merger with i2 Technologies, the largest deal at that point in the software industry.

Litigation: play ball!

Cooley litigators have also stayed busy with high-profile suits such as *Sun Microsystems v. Microsoft* and Qualcomm's dispute with Ericsson Inc. (Cooley has a longstanding relationship with Qualcomm, having taken the San Diego-based cell phone systems company public in 1995.) In the litigation-happy biotech industry, Cooley represents industry giants Amgen (the firm also took Amgen public) in licensing and trade secrets suits. In fact, Cooley won the first trade secret suit in biotech when it successfully protected Genentech's proprietary information against use by former employees. (The firm no longer represents Genentech.)

While it might seem otherwise, Cooley Godward isn't just about tech. In December 1998, the firm did its part for baseball in the Bay Area. Partners Kenneth Adelson and Christopher Westover, representing the owners of the Oakland A's in an arbitration proceeding with the city and county, successfully negotiated an agreement to keep the A's in Oakland until at least 2004 — a major victory for all true baseball lovers.

Growing by leaps and bounds

The good times at Cooley mean expansion. The firm has grown to eight offices in various high tech corridors around the country and has enjoyed particular success in Palo Alto, San Diego (where the firm snagged two information technology partners in May 2000 from McCutchen, Doyle, Brown & Enersen and Shaw Pittman), and Colorado. Cooley opened an outpost in the Seattle suburb of Kirkland, Washington in July 1998 with three partners hired laterally. Host to 15 total attorneys, the Washington office services the needs of Northwestern clients such as F5 Labs, Molecumetics, Vixel, Sun Systems, Coinstar, and TriNet Services.

In April 1999, the firm announced it would throw its hat into the increasingly crowded Washington, DC market and serve the city's sizzling tech industry by opening a Reston, VA office. The new office integrated some Cooley lawyers with 12 lawyers poached from McLean, VA's Hunton & Williams, bringing the new office's total to 58 attorneys by 2000. Cooley has also managed to assure its expansion in the extremely tight confines of Silicon Valley. In December 1998, the firm signed a long-term lease for a 129,000-square-foot expansion space in Stanford's Research Park. The new "campus" was in session by February 2000 and has room for 200 attorneys. One Palo Alto real estate broker told *The Business Journal*: "There was a lot of competition for this space. It was a real coup for Cooley to secure it."

Check your head at Cooley

Like some of its "touchy-feely" Bay Area competitors, Cooley has made efforts to develop its reputation as a progressive workplace. However, the firm currently falls short of its diversity ideals. Of 120 partners, only four are minority group members and only 27 are women. Nevertheless, the firm seems to be making a good faith effort to diversify. Of the 14 lawyers who made partner in 1998, eight were women and two counted themselves as members of a minority group.

Cooley has taken extraordinary steps to reduce friction between its employees. In January 1999, *The Recorder* reported that for the past three years Cooley has made use of industrial psychologists to help with issues such as intergroup communications and getting people to "talk in a non-threatening way." Of all the top Bay Area firms, Cooley alone has turned to organizational behavior professionals to resolve its internal issues.

GETTING HIRED

"Selectivity seems to vary..."

The seemingly insatiable market demand for attorneys has forced Cooley's hiring hand, according to insiders, as it has at many other prestigious firms. A San Francisco associate concedes that the firm has been "hiring a lot of people lately, as have most Bay Area firms, so I think it is harder to be as selective as the firm would like to be given the demand for associates." In Boulder, say associates, the firm is "attempting to expand and might be less selective than we'd otherwise like to be." A second-year opines that "San Francisco may be a little more selective than Palo Alto in that San Francisco hires about 15 summer associates, whereas Palo Alto hires more than 50."

"The selectivity depends on the department," insists an IP attorney from the Bay Area. "The IP department is extremely selective based on a multitude of criteria, including whether an associate will fit in. If any one interviewer doesn't approve of hiring a candidate, the candidate cannot be hired. Many highly qualified candidates with personality problems (such as a superiority complex or failure to be a team player) have not been successful." An international associate in Silicon Valley echoes that "Cooley wants to hire nice people. Problematic characters and arrogant associates even from the best schools are not welcome here." Interviewers "don't really care where you went or how you did," points out another IP lawyer. "We look for intelligence (shown in conversation, not by grades) and, of vastly greater importance, we look for people we'll like working with." As a result, "the interview process is long" and candidates should "expect to be interviewed by everyone in the relevant practice group." If you want to brush up, the recruiting area of Cooley's web site offers a chance to review the firm's recruiting schedule and browse openings indexed according to office location, approximate class year, practice group, and background/experience.

OUR SURVEY SAYS

Well-compensated efforts

Come payday, it sounds like Cooley Godward associates are downright delighted. The firm's commitment to paying its associates top dollar was evidenced by its move to be the first Bay Area firm to follow Gunderson Dettmer Stough Villeneuve Franklin & Hachigian's pay raises in January 2000. A corporate fourth-year boasts that the firm works to keep "the compensation structure simple: no multi-tiered salary or bonus system like many of the other firms have instituted to pay for associate pay raises through disguised billable hour increases." Indeed, "the bonus structure does not focus on billable hours and at the same time is very equitable." In addition to sky-high salaries, "investment funds offer additional bonus opportunities," according to a sixth-year securities associate in Palo Alto, and "spot bonuses are sometimes given in particularly busy times or for exceptionally hard work and strong performance on a deal."

High turnover, but we're not worried

Attrition rates at Cooley are "astronomical," but associates don't seem overly concerned, mostly because of the reasons behind attorney turnover. "We lose great people to dot coms," shrugs a fourth-year in IP. "We rarely lose them to other firms." In other words, the firm accepts that it will lose some of its troops "due to successful clients" who lure them away. As long as lawyers aren't leaving for other firms, then Cooley is doing its job. "The firm pays incredible attention to associate and staff retention," compliments a DC fifth-year, "and it makes everyone feel privileged to work here." It's all about perspective. "Compared to most Bay Area firms, our retention seems to be much better, but compared to firms in areas that rely less on the tech sectors and dot coms, it may seem quite volatile." A first-year suggests that "turnover seems to have slowed a bit now that instant dot com riches are less likely." A colleague agrees that while "dot coms have had a great impact here, a lot of associates are coming back to Cooley."

We love our partners, oh yes we do

Cooley associates fairly burst with enthusiasm when asked about the firm's partners. They are described as "relaxed," "professional," "collegial," "generally very respectful," and "appreciative." Although there are the "occasional temper tantrums," most partners "follow a true open-door policy and are not tied to any titles or hierarchies," boasts an IP senior associate in the Valley. Cooley's fearless leaders "aren't social misfits," says another in the same practice area. "We go drinking together. We go for coffee together. Doors are always open." Others agree, citing partners' lunches with associates and "wonderful mentoring" as reasons to laud their superiors. "Everyone has their moments — partners, associates and staff alike — but people here are respectful and act like human beings," declares a content corporate first-year.

The enthusiasm extends to assessing partnership prospects for associates themselves. "With the attrition caused by the dot com exodus, there's a lot of head room," judges a third-year in Colorado. "At this point, if you make it to year eight, you're probably in." In fact, "partners would love it if more associates stuck around to make partner." A sixth-year litigator in San Diego finds that "the partners believe that they are stewards of the firm who have an obligation to prepare the institution to be strong for the future. Partnership does not depend on the number of clients that one has. Instead, it depends on the ability to be a team player and solve problems in an efficient and effective way." Advice for would-be players? "Do good work. Focus on quality of work, not quantity of hours," according to one source. "Find good mentors and consistently strive to learn and produce," suggests another. Bottom line: "Don't be a prima donna" and "schmooze, schmooze, schmooze."

Enroll at Cooley College

The training at Cooley draws raves from its attendees. Every fall and winter, a multi-session program offers new attorneys training from the most senior attorneys in the firm on all major areas of practice. A corporate fourth-year explains that "the firm flies everyone to the Bay Area for five sessions, which are typically two days at a time," adding up to a total of approximately 80 to 100 hours of training. A SF first-year wonders "how associates at other law firms survive without such training." Down in Palo Alto, a second-year terms Cooley College "the best training of any firm in the Bay Area and perhaps the country."

The firm makes enormous investments in training, according to associates. Over thirty binders containing the collected wisdom of the firm line the shelves of each attorney. In addition, each practice group has a monthly conference call meeting to discuss current issues in that particular area as well as periodic lunches to "revisit fundamentals." And even though "at more senior levels, learning is mostly by doing," the firm has "recently instituted a yearly 'senior seminar,' which is excellent." A West Coast fourth-year specifically came to Cooley for its training: "Cooley is committed to training its associates and that is one of the reasons that I came to this firm. It values its lawyers and its lawyers' knowledge and understanding of not only the law but the business of being a well-rounded, savvy, and business-oriented lawyer."

Beautiful views and great furniture

Even if Cooley offices aren't "posh," they often afford associates a "fantastic location with great views." According to one unpampered associate, "[Offices are] not 'posh,' but I don't consider 'posh' a good thing." In Reston, "the offices are new and are still being finished. Lots of desk space." The Palo Alto branch just opened a new office so some attorneys are housed in the "brand-new complex on Hanover Street, complete with cafe and courtyard fountain" while others remain in the old, dingier digs. A sixth-year labor associate in the Valley laments that "those of us who are still in the old building are feeling a bit poorly done by, since the new space is so nice."

In San Francisco "the offices are plain beige — utilitarian but not flashy." Others have less praise. One insider says that "the office decor recalls the set on *Sanford & Son*. Updating is needed." A colleague concurs that the SF office is "great space-wise but absolutely the ugliest, darkest 1970s decor in downtown's ugliest building." (Haven't these people heard about the 1970s nostalgia revival?) A first-year can live with the "standard office," though, in light of the "gorgeous view of the city and the Golden Gate Bridge." And hey, at least "the furniture for associates is exceptional."

'Spotty' support services

"Cooley's not a factory and you can tell by the support," admits a San Francisco associate. "The services (mail and fax rooms especially) are understaffed compared to firms with which I have worked in the past." A co-worker adds that "Palo Alto is generally pretty good but San Francisco still likes to pretend it is a small office by refusing to retain adequate paralegal, secretarial, and word processing support, especially during peak hours." Services are available — "everything but a personal trainer and a concierge," in the words of a corporate fifth-year — but are often "overteamed." The reality is that "chronic low unemployment rates and the high cost of housing in Silicon Valley make it exceedingly difficult to retain a qualified support staff."

Women on top

Across the board, Cooley associates back up the firm's commitment to promoting women in its ranks. "Women are here at all levels, including partner levels," comments a second-year IP associate. "There are lots of female attorneys with children whose needs outside the offices are respected. Many parents, mostly women, work reduced schedules with great success." A fourth-year in the same department adds that the firm has "women who have taken maternity leave and made partner on time. That's pretty unusual for what I've seen. I haven't seen anything remarkable in the world of part-time, however."

Several associates give personal testimony to the firm's efforts. "I am the best example of this," offers a San Diego litigator. "I work 50 percent and get paid 50 percent of the salary of a regular associate. I recognize that this is not an option for everyone, from both the firm and the attorney's perspective, but the fact that Cooley did this for me (and hired me with this schedule) is a huge indication of the firm's willingness to be flexible if they perceive that you can fill a need it has."

Of course, not all offices are created equal. The retention, promotion and mentoring of women "varies a lot from office to office," cautions a third-year in San Francisco. "San Francisco is decent; Palo Alto is so-so (but no worse than other Silicon Valley firms); Reston is reportedly very male." An important "caveat is that you must be your own gatekeeper," warns a labor associate. "The women who are careful not to schedule appointments on their days off and who carefully monitor their time seem to do great and the firm supports them. But if you continue to work full-time hours on a part-time schedule, no one is going to say no for you, although they will adjust your compensation accordingly."

Minorities: 'efforts are substantial, but not substantial enough'

In terms of recruiting and promoting minorities, attorneys seem to feel that Cooley does "as well or better than most Silicon Valley firms, but overall that's a pretty low standard." There are especially few minorities in the partnership; while "Cooley consistently recruits and hires a diverse group of attorneys, the problem is retention." As a senior San Diego litigator puts it, "I think [firm leaders] are trying, but they have a lot of ground to cover. It's a difficult subject because there is so much competition for the minority attorneys who meet Cooley's standard profile."

Gays and lesbians at Cooley: 'Like nowhere else in the world'

A number of associates point out that "Cooley has a large number of gay and lesbian attorneys." A third-year in San Francisco says that "all of the gay and lesbian attorneys [I know] are openly out and vocal. The firm is very supportive of gay and lesbian issues." Another source in the same office asserts that "in San Francisco the ratio of gay men to straight is probably close to 40/60 and there are several lesbian women. This is true among partners as well as associates. Domestic partner benefits are given broadly." A fourth-year woman sighs that "frankly, it's hard to find a straight, single man here."

Pro bono is up to you

Associates seem divided as to the firm's support of pro bono work. A mid-level associate in San Francisco says he has "several pro bono clients" and finds the firm to be "supportive of any idea" he brings to the table. "The transactional pro bono opportunities need to be made by us, but once we have the ideas, the firm's 100 percent behind us." A Silicon Valley second-year adds that "Cooley participates in the East Palo Alto Volunteer Attorney program," whereby "Cooley attorneys provide pro bono services to the members of the East Palo Alto community. Cooley does not impose any limits on pro bono hours after which they don't count toward the billable target."

"Let's be honest," argues a litigator in San Diego. "You can't pay the salaries Cooley is paying if people are spending a lot of time on pro bono and any firm that tries to convince you otherwise is lying. If you want to spend your own time on it, no problem. Otherwise, you will find it hard to fit in pro bono work." A first-year on the same team suggests that "there is great lip service for pro bono work, but the general sense is that we are all too busy to adequately take on pro bono cases. We are very busy with all of our paying clients."

Balancing act

Even though it sometimes means turning away high-profile clients (one Colorado source estimates that the firm "turns away 75 percent or more of potential clients"), Cooley takes seriously its promise to make its lawyers' lives livable. An IP fourth-year asserts that "currently our corporate department is doing whatever it takes" to cut back on associate burnout. "Litigation and IP are already there. I have been impressed with the commitment to reduce billables at the partner level. The firm has set up a screening process for new clients and for significant projects from existing clients." While "it's the volatility of the schedule that is exhausting," a first-year knows that he has it "better than any of my friends who went to big firms" and still manages "to find time to enjoy living in the Bay Area."

This respect for attorneys' personal lives extends to the attitude about socializing at the firm. An M&A second-year in the Valley finds that Cooley "recognizes the importance of family by inviting them to events" but also by "respecting the decision of lawyers to decline social invitations in order to spend free time with family." The firm "genuinely strives to allow its attorneys to reach a good balance between life inside and outside the firm," stresses one source. "The commitment is real and not mere lip-service," emphasizes another.

Work and play the Cooley way

Maybe "it's not *Animal House*," but Cooley associates do seem to love to socialize together. In terms of formal events to facilitate colleague carousing, the firm sponsors weekly firm-wide lunches, monthly pizza parties, birthday celebrations, and cocktail parties affectionately referred to as "TGI Cooley's." An international fourth-year mentions the "all-firm, all-attorney outing in LaQuinta (Palm Springs). It is an experience like this that makes the firm so human. Social interaction between lawyers is encouraged and is actually a Cooley trait." A corporate second-year enthuses that it "feels like I joined a firm where all my best friends worked. [There is an] unbelievable social support system for junior lawyers." A classmate employs a similar metaphor, feeling like he's "part of a big team."

It makes sense then that "there's virtually no competition between associates" because "advancement takes place by being a contributor to the team and not by having a book of business," according to a sixth-year litigator in San Diego. The team mentality means that "any attorney will stop what he or she is doing to help or teach. None of the partners or associates are territorial and the expertise of other departments is often sought and freely given." A fourth-year patent attorney agrees that there are "no traditional firm 'kingdoms' under one or two partners."

One contact tells us that "high tech clients represent the lion's share of our business and Cooley reflects much of that sector's dynamic qualities." That reflection carries through in the "laughter [that] is one of the most common things you will hear as you walk the halls of our office," according to a corporate lawyer, and the possibility of "jeans five days a week." "To think it is a law firm is nearly impossible," exults a Valley second-year.

Why we're here

Most associates say they chose Cooley Godward over other firms because of its "prestige," "quality lawyers," and "excellent reputation" as a firm that "does high quality work without being hierarchical or a sweatshop." Others had more specific criteria such as "practice areas, particularly in biotech patent litigation," "a strong information technology practice" and "its burgeoning dot com practice." Location came into play as well — a Boulder associate mentions the "14,000-foot mountains" he can see from his office and a San Francisco second-year "chose Cooley because it has the best Silicon Valley practice in the city — I did not want to go to Shallow Alto." A number of female attorneys mention the firm's "commitment to working flexibility during the recruiting process and afterward." A fourth-year associate chose Cooley "because I can be a good mom and a good lawyer."

A fourth-year patent attorney comments that he's "not into the old-boy network of law firms and Cooley is a very un-law firm law firm" — a compliment, obviously, since it made accepting his offer "an easy choice." A DC colleague writes that "simply stated, the laid-back atmosphere makes it easy to come to work every day."

Words to the wise

"Cooley is a unique place," according to many associates, and so if you're considering coming here you should "talk to as many people as you can and ask honest questions. You will get honest answers." You have to "enjoy being in a fluid, fast-paced environment," insists a senior IP associate in DC. If you do, "this place is great. The long hours are very tolerable because you are working with good people (nice, funny, bright, and so on)." The firm is "very much for independent, self-starter types." Also bear in mind that "many attorneys here go in-house to technology companies and dot coms, so if that's your ultimate goal, this firm is a good place to start."

As for the daily grind, "live close. A long commute will kill you." On the West Coast, "beware of the real estate market in the Bay Area!" "If you don't want to live in the boonies of Palo Alto, and want the work, this is your only (and conveniently, best) choice," declares a possibly biased San Francisco associate. If you choose the Valley, "don't even dream about owning a nice home in the Palo Alto area until you're a mid-level partner."

Clifford Chance Rogers & Wells

VAULT.COM PRESTIGE RANKING: 33

200 Park Avenue
New York, NY 10166
(212) 878-8000
Fax: (212) 878-8375
www.cliffordchance.com

LOCATIONS

New York, NY • Washington, DC • Amsterdam • Bangkok • Barcelona • Beijing • Berlin • Brussels • Budapest • Dubai • Dusseldorf • Frankfurt • Hong Kong • Leipzig • London • Luxembourg • Madrid • Milan • Moscow • Munich • Padua • Paris • Prague • Rome • Sao Paulo • Shanghai • Singapore • Tokyo • Warsaw

MAJOR DEPARTMENTS/PRACTICES

Antitrust • Bankruptcy • Corporate Finance/Securities • Cross-Border Finance • Debt & Equity Capital Markets • Derivatives and Structured Products • E-Commerce • Intellectual Property • International Banking • Litigation & Dispute Resolution • Media/First Amendment • Mergers & Acquisitions • Private Equity • Project Finance • Real Estate • Tax, Trusts & Estates • Technology • White Collar Crime

THE STATS

No. of attorneys: 2,531
No. of offices: 29
Summer associate offers: (New York, 1999)
100% of summer class received an offer
Managing Partner: Laurence E. Cranch
Hiring attorney: David L. Taub

PAY

New York and Washington, DC, 2000
1st year: $125,000
2nd year: $135,000
3rd year: $150,000
4th year: $165,000
5th year: $185,000
6th year: $195,000
7th year: $205,000
8th year: $210,000
Summer associate: $2,404/week

NOTABLE PERKS

- Back-up child care
- $2,000 subsidy for technology equipment
- Ft. Lauderdale and Ponte Vedra Beach vacation facilities available for associate use
- Sign-on bonuses for clerkships
- Accelerated seniority for relevant advanced degrees

THE BUZZ
What attorneys at other firms are saying about this firm

- "Londoners"
- "An 800-kilogram gorilla"
- "International practice is first-rate"
- "Two mediocres don't make a great"

UPPERS

- Big firm means tremendous clout
- Travel to exotic locales
- Unusually reasonable hours

DOWNERS

- New merger means uncertain culture
- Poor diversity
- Associates can get lost in huge firm

KEY COMPETITORS

Simpson Thacher & Bartlett
Cleary, Gottlieb, Steen & Hamilton
Shearman & Sterling
Linklaters

EMPLOYMENT CONTACT

Carolyn S. Older
Manager of Legal Recruiting
(212) 878-8252
carolyn.older@cliffordchance.com

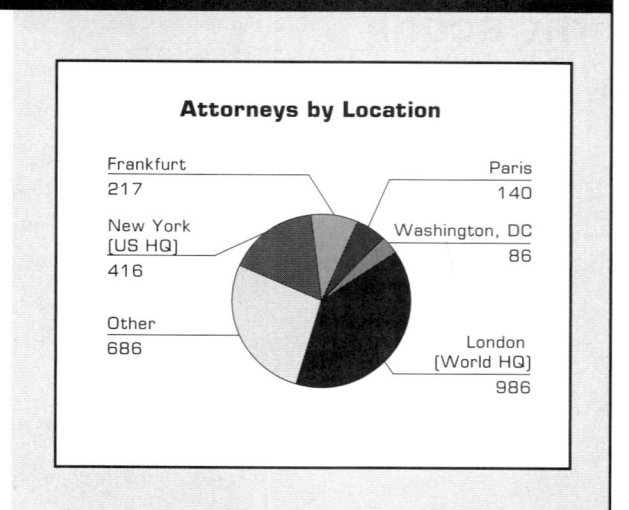

Attorneys by Location
- Frankfurt: 217
- Paris: 140
- New York [US HQ]: 416
- Washington, DC: 86
- Other: 686
- London [World HQ]: 986

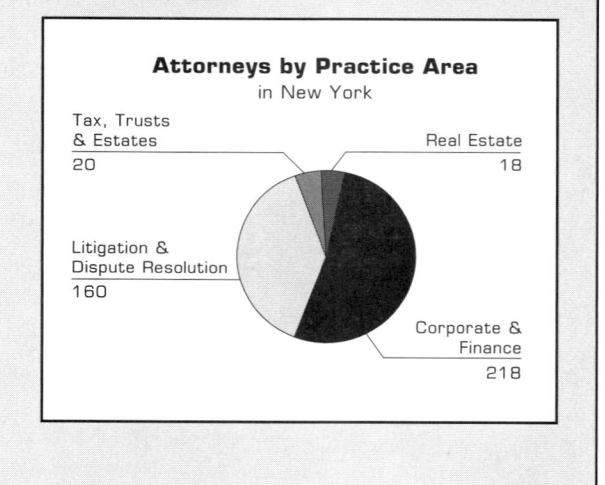

Attorneys by Practice Area in New York
- Tax, Trusts & Estates: 20
- Real Estate: 18
- Litigation & Dispute Resolution: 160
- Corporate & Finance: 218

QUALITY OF LIFE RANKINGS [ASSOCIATES RATE THEIR OWN FIRM]

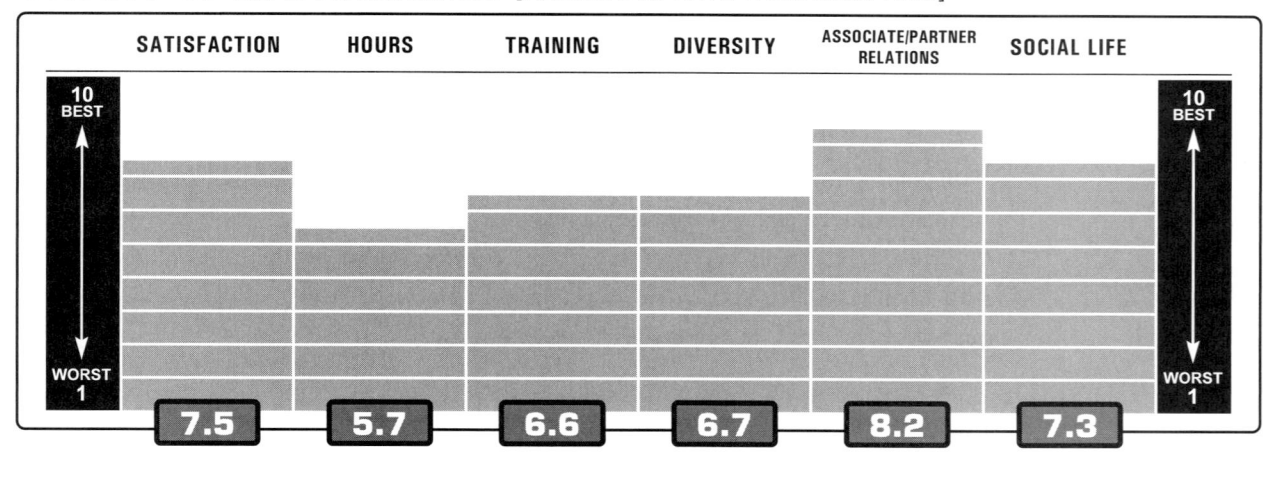

Satisfaction	Hours	Training	Diversity	Associate/Partner Relations	Social Life
7.5	5.7	6.6	6.7	8.2	7.3

THE SCOOP

Clifford Chance Rogers & Wells is the American name of international law firm Clifford Chance LLP, which was formed in January 2000 by the merger of British firm Clifford Chance, U.S.-based Rogers & Wells, and Germany's Punder, Volhard Weber & Axster. The firm is known internationally as Clifford & Chance, except in some European locations, where it's called Clifford Chance & Punder. No matter what you call it, the firm as is the world's largest international legal practice, with 2,500 lawyers in 29 offices worldwide.

Before the merger: an impressive resume

Rogers & Wells traces its history to 1871 when attorney Walter Carter established an office in the New York Life Building to represent insurance companies bankrupted by the Great Chicago Fire. The firm took the name Rogers & Wells in 1973 when William Rogers and Jack Wells took control of the firm. Rogers is as big as they come in the legal profession. He served as Attorney General under President Dwight Eisenhower and Secretary of State under Richard Nixon. In between, he was appointed by Lyndon Johnson as the U.S. representative to the United Nations General Assembly and argued two landmark First Amendment cases, *New York Times v. Sullivan* and *The Associated Press v. Walker*. If that's not enough to impress you, note that he also served as chief counsel to the Permanent Senate Investigations Committee (originally known as the Senate War Investigating Committee or the Truman Committee) and as chairman of the commission that investigated the tragic 1986 explosion of the space shuttle Challenger.

Intellectual property heavyweights

In the U.S., Rogers & Wells has established a top-of-the-line intellectual property practice. The firm is DuPont's primary IP counsel and has represented the company in several cases, including a patent infringement case against Molecular Biosystem in Wilmington, Delaware. The firm also represented Genentech in a jury trial involving human growth hormones. Later, in *National Baseball Hall of Fame v. All Sports Promotion*, Rogers & Wells represented the Cooperstown, NY baseball museum against an alleged infringement on its trademark. In addition to *AP v. Walker*, Rogers & Wells represented the news organization in a fair use copyright case, *Matheson v. AP*. Finally, the firm successfully represented Honda against charges that it infringed on patents covering fuel-control systems.

Speaking of mergers

In addition to dealing with its own merger, Rogers & Wells has advised many other firms through the process. One example is the firm's representation of Siemens in its $1.53 billion acquisition of Westinghouse's power generation business. R&W was also counsel to the Hearst Corp. in the $1.2 billion merger of its broadcast group with Argyle Television and a later merger of Hearst-Argyle with Pulitzer Publishing Company, which was valued at $1.85 billion. Additionally, the firm represented Caterpillar in the $1.33 billion purchase of Perkins Engines, a unit of Lucas Varity. Internationally, it represented Swedbank in a $1.6 billion merger with Foreningsbanken, and is currently advising Amsterdam's United Pan-Europe Communications NV in its $2.8 billion purchase of SBS Broadcasting SA.

Sleeping with the enemy?

Clifford Chance's antitrust practice is headed by Kevin Arquit, who was once on the other side of the fence as Director of the Bureau of Competition of the Federal Trade Commission where he was responsible for antitrust enforcement. The firm has represented MasterCard International on two separate antitrust matters: a suit by 4 million retailers against MasterCard and Visa and a lawsuit filed against the two companies by the Department of Justice. Another client, Philadelphia-based options and brokerage firm Susquehanna Investment Group, was hit with an antitrust class suit alleging a conspiracy to fix the spreads on options traded on the American Stock Exchange. Rogers also successfully defended NYNEX and its subsidiary, New England Telephone & Telegraph, in an antitrust action in the District of Massachusetts.

Securities litigation

Another successful practice area for Clifford Chance's American partner is securities litigation. The firm represented American Honda Motor in a 1998 shareholder suit regarding a bribery and kickback scheme involving Honda employees. (The suit was dismissed.) It also successfully defended Merrill Lynch against a suit filed by bond investors that claimed the investment bank failed to adequately disclose the risks associated with the bonds. R&W saved the bank again when a lawsuit alleged that Merrill Lynch analysts inflated the price of Ann Taylor stock by hiding excess inventory.

Other litigation: abracadabra

Rogers & Wells has established a reputation for defending media organizations against libel claims. In addition to the two First Amendment cases argued by the firm's star partner, the firm has represented *Time* magazine, *Newsday*, and Univision and has been dubbed the "Houdini of libel law" by *American Lawyer*. In one case, *Time* was sued for publishing photos of Brazilian prostitutes and Rogers & Wells won a favorable judgment for the magazine. The firm also won the dismissal of a federal case filed by an adult telephone "900" line whose practices were investigated by television journalists. Though it's not quite as exciting, Rogers & Wells runs a phone line of its own; the firm's libel hotline allows publications to seek advice on editorial and advertising content before pieces are printed.

GETTING HIRED

Be nice

Insiders say that Clifford Chance has historically been fairly selective in hiring, while Rogers & Wells was slightly more flexible. After the merger, the firm's standards are closer to those at Clifford Chance. "The firm has become more competitive since the merger," one New York associate says. "However," that source adds, "if you are nice, polite and have a good personality you have a better chance than if you are just number one in your class somewhere." "We are looking for people who will enjoy working here and match the personality of the work area," says a contact. One lawyer says that "demand for our international practice and expanded international M&A practice has increased the number of applicants enormously." Another associate says that the firm "is usually looking for additional language skills, bar admissions, international experience [and] business background." The firm contends that, given its vast amount of domestic work, applicants need not have international experience.

Attending a top law school is definitely an asset. "Getting hired at this firm is especially competitive if you are coming from an out-of-state second-tier school," notes a corporate attorney. "The firm pretends to be selective, but will hire just about anyone with a pulse from a top law school," fumes one lawyer.

OUR SURVEY SAYS

A tale of two cultures

Whenever there's a merger, especially one where the participants are considered equals, there's bound to be a culture clash. The combination of the Brits at Clifford Chance and the Americans at Rogers & Wells hasn't led to a reenactment of the Battle of Bunker Hill — not yet at least — but firm insiders say the two firms have noticeably different cultures that haven't quite melded yet. One corporate associate says that as it currently stands, the firm is "schizophrenic" in the culture department. Another lawyer adds that the firm has indicated a "strong sense of trying to build cohesion with the merger."

"The old white shoe Rogers & Wells mentality is quickly losing ground to the more worldly, intellectual approach of CC," observes one New York lawyer. "Changes in partner compensation have [led to] people actually helping each other across disciplines." A former R&W associate remarks that "this used to be a family-type place where Bill Rogers still came to work every day. Now, since the merger, it has a rather British lilt to it and it is a very different workplace." Another ex-Rogers & Wells attorney ventures that "the very strong 'eat what you kill' culture that prevailed in the last few years may change with the merger."

Not everyone coming from Rogers & Wells is upset by the change. "I find Clifford Chance easy to work for," says an attorney, "as firm politics and bureaucracy take a back seat to client service. I rarely waste time on non-work matters, which means I do not spend more time here than necessary to complete my billable work."

Lawyers from the old Clifford Chance seem upbeat about the post-merger culture. Says one contact: "Speaking for the former CC employees, it's a hard-working, entrepreneurial environment where everyone is treated like they have a stake in the firm and an effort is made to minimize the petty bureaucratic headaches that poison other New York firms." One example of the lack of bureaucracy: "Rather than writing multi-page legal memos about the acceptable parameters of casual dress for Fridays, the firm issues short general guidelines and otherwise trusts the attorneys' discretion." But the firm still has a ways to go — "Clifford Chance was a very, very collegial and informal place," summarizes a source. "Rogers & Wells [was] much more bureaucratic, hierarchical and generally colder." Still, says one gung-ho insider, "it's exciting being at ground zero of the first big law mega-merger.

Partners: a tale of two age groups

Associates at Clifford Chance Rogers & Wells give firm partners fairly good marks. "[They] are respectful and expect hard work but have had realistic expectations of what I can and can't do at this point in my career," says a junior-level associate. "It's the upper- and mid-level associates who sometimes can use a slap upside the head for their treatment of first-years." Adds another contact, "barring one or two abnormalities, the partners treat associates with great respect, both professionally and personally. Much of this is due to the young age of the partners."

Social life proves a major plus

Firm associates report a healthy social life at Clifford Chance Rogers & Wells. "The firm has well-attended monthly socials during the year and a handful of other events," says one New York lawyer, adding that "in the summer there are many firm events." "Beyond that, more junior associates seem to socialize fairly regularly and there is a general air of congeniality at the firm." Another associate agrees, saying the social life at Clifford Chance Rogers & Wells is "one of the strongest aspects of the firm." A firm insider admits, however, that lateral hires have difficulty breaking into social groups. "If you weren't a summer associate here, forget about a social life unless you meet up with other laterals."

Wobbly hours

"The work load is quite heavy, but I have never been asked to stay in the office any longer than necessary to complete billable work," reports one associate. "There is no such thing as face time here and clients' needs completely dictate my work schedule." Another lawyer says that "the firm is demanding but probably not as much so as some other large firms," adding that "my schedule has been easier to balance as I've grown more senior, but I certainly continue to spend my fair share of weekends in the office."

"The impression that I get is that the hours of corporate first-year associates can vary widely for one's first few months, while first year litigators have a steadier amount of work from day one," says one corporate lawyer. "But after a few months things steady out somewhat and eventually everyone gets as much work as they can handle."

Required hours at the new Clifford Chance are in flux. "The firm originally had a 2,000 hour target for bonuses when I started," says one lawyer. "That was raised to 2,100 last year. After the merger, the firm eliminated this target, and bonuses are now based on quality of work rather than hours."

Pay: keeping pace

"I am overpaid," admits one DC attorney, "but I am not giving any back." While most Clifford Chance Rogers & Wells attorneys don't consider themselves overpaid, they do believe the firm is trying to pay on par with other large law firms, with mixed results. "The firm tells associates it's committed to remaining competitive with top-tier firms but in reality, they lag behind those firms," complains one lawyer. "In the senior classes [especially], they seem to really drop the ball." Not surprisingly, the firm maintains that associate compensation at all levels is and will continue to be competitive.

A source reports that Clifford & Chance is keeping an eye on the market, noting that "as salaries skyrocketed last fall, the firm raised our salaries to compete with other large firms." Don't count on Clifford & Chance being a leader, though. Says one contact: "[The] firm always waits for other firms to raise their associates' salaries first. In terms of associate compensation, the firm is not a leader but a follower." Given the recent turmoil both within the firm (the merger) and in the industry as a whole (in terms of salary growth), bonuses are as yet unclear. "The firm has stated numerous times that the bonuses would be large enough so that the associates' total package will be competitive with the remainder of the market," says one contact. But one experienced lawyer notes that "the firm seems to be penalizing its senior associates in order to fund the junior raises."

Free Florida vacation

Firm associates can expect cars and meals for working late, event tickets, and gym privileges — in other words, the typical large-firm perks. "We also have two condos in Florida which are available for a week per year for free to each attorney that signs up," reports one source. Additionally, in what insiders say may be a test for year-round casual, the firm recently announced a move to an all-casual summer (complete with discounts at local clothing stores). That, of course, brings the usual Mr. Blackwell-type critique of colleagues' dress. "They dress like the average inhabitants of Darien, CT dress on a Saturday," says one New York lawyer of his comrades. Another associate reports that "some [attorneys], even partners, dress more slovenly than one might expect." A Washington lawyer zings his colleagues, saying "people in DC can't dress; it's conservative highlighted by boring."

Training by fire

Clifford Chance Rogers & Wells lawyers report little formal training and a "jump-right-in mentality." "Given our workload, some of our training is by fire," says one source. "Now that we are so busy, sometimes training falls through the cracks and there is more focus on just getting the job done," adds an associate. Another contact complains that "the firm lacks an associate mentoring program, which would be helpful. We do have regular 'associate training luncheons,' but I would not say that they are valuable." The firm does offer a number of other programs, including weekly instruction sessions on topics like legal writing and ethics as well as courses covering technical skills useful for the litigation and corporate practices. Individual practice groups also provide their own training programs and the firm is now developing a global curriculum of technical and business skills training.

Offices and support

Firm insiders say the office space is "classy," if a bit cramped in some cases. "Because of the layout of the Met Life building [in New York], many of the associate offices are internal, non-window offices. [Thus], while you spend your first two years in a shared window office, you are then moved to an internal office without a window where you might stay until your fifth year." Actually, 75 percent of associates get a windowed office by their fourth year, with the remaining 25 percent getting one by the end of that year. Still, a former Clifford Chance associate feels he's getting the shaft as a result of a forced move to Rogers's mid-town Manhattan digs. "[Office space] will definitely change once we move to Rogers & Wells offices, which, in my opinion, are hellish. I am moving from a huge office with windows over New York Harbor to a windowless inside cell. The space and décor at Rogers & Wells are just plain bad."

The quality of support service at Clifford also seems to be lacking. "Support staff acts like they can not be bothered and there is an 'us against them' mentality," fumes one associate. "Word processing and computer departments are laughably incompetent," another lawyer complains. One attorney remarks that, "[because] Clifford Chance stresses congeniality, this results in our support staff getting away with things they never could at other law firms. They take too much advantage of our non-confrontational, congenial environment." Yet another contact rips into support staff, saying they're "not in the supporting business. My secretary makes my life more difficult every day. Only partners are assigned competent secretaries."

After the merger, some jumping ship

According to firm insiders, the Clifford Chance/Rogers & Wells merger resulted in the typical round of turnover as those unsure about life in the new firm looked for greener pastures. "People are generally apprehensive about the merger and there is a lot of talk about leaving," says one New York lawyer. "Moreover, the billing requirement is leading to people leaving in droves. How can someone sustain working 13-14 hour days (including weekends) for more than a few months? They can't pay us for the time we are putting in." Another contact says that while post-merger departures may be on the rise (Clifford Chance claims that turnover remains similar to pre-merger levels), "I expect it to be low to very low in the future."

Post-merger partnerships unclear

As with many other things in the post-merger Clifford Chance Rogers & Wells, partnership prospects in the firm are unclear. "With the merger I think partnership prospects have greatly increased," says one lawyer. Former Rogers & Wells associates, on the other hand, seem displeased. "Making partner is akin to winning a seat in the U.S. Senate. What's worse, the new system they reject you with is terrible." That contact says that after the required eight years, "you go over to London and participate in a week-long festival of psychological testing. They make you role play, take an IQ test, a math test, and other ridiculous things." The results are then sent to

Clifford Chance partners in London "whom you have never met, and they decide whether you are fit to be a partner." Associates are still nominated by the partners they have worked with, as was the case before the merger. All told, the aggressive plans of the new firm may require them to add more partners. "If this firm is serious about growth projections, they're going to need a lot more partners," says one associate.

Diversity: last bastion of WASPishness?

One CCR&W associate criticizes the firm's diversity efforts, noting that "the firm actively recruits but makes little effort to retain minorities, and there is no minority representation at partner level." Another lawyer is much more vehement in his criticism: "What minorities? You mean the ones that won't be partners? Most of them are on their way out." To be fair, most associates say the firm is "trying to change its reputation as one of the last bastions of WASPishness, but it seems to be an uphill battle." Insiders note that the firm has formed an ethnic diversity group that works with an outside consultant on diversity issues.

Associates report that female associates are in a similar position to minorities. "The firm seems to be proactively trying to promote more women and to get them involved in more deals," says an associate, while a female lawyer adds that Clifford Chance is "leaps and bounds better than when I started here." On the downside, "there is very little effort to allow someone to be a lawyer and a parent who is involved in her children's lives," says one contact. "Most women leave after having children." On the other hand, the firm points out that two of the three women elected to partner in 2000 had children during their careers at Clifford Chance. And in attempt to become more woman-friendly, the firm passed a new initiative in January 2000 allowing associates the option to work part-time for three years.

Gays and lesbians seem to have it easier at the firm. One gay attorney says that he does not think his sexuality would be an issue in a partnership decision and most associates back that statement up, saying that gays and lesbians experience no discrimination at Clifford Chance Rogers & Wells.

No sweat

Insiders are enthusiastic about the lack of a "sweatshop mentality" at Clifford Chance. The people and culture get high marks from many, as do pay and benefits. Says one insider: "We strike a nice balance for corporate associates who want to do high-level transaction work without being subjected to insufferable working conditions." Though the merger has created a level of uncertainty, at least one associate seems enthusiastic about the opportunities at the new firm. "I chose Rogers & Wells because of the excellent antitrust practice group and the impending merger with Clifford

Chance," reveals a recent hire. Another contact notes, "It had the most compatible people that I met — there wasn't a culture of 'everything's a crisis.'"

Some woes

Some, however, point to the merger as a drawback to working for the firm. "There is some uncertainty about pay, corporate culture, and partnership prospects. On the plus side, those issues will likely be resolved one way or the other over the next year." Others mention the lack of diversity as a source of contention. The firm's size is also an issue. "You can get lost and people will forget you exist (but they'll keep sending you paychecks)," says one lawyer. Speaking of paychecks, the new billing requirements are causing some angst. One associate says that between having an office on the interior of the building and the hours he works, "I figure I haven't seen the sun in about a year." Finally, one attorney gripes that "associates are generally viewed as fungible until they've stuck around two years. After two years, partners may try to remember your name."

Looking forward to the post-merger future

Despite the uncertainty surrounding the merger, attorneys at Clifford Chance Rogers & Wells seem satisfied with their firm — most complaints are typical of the law profession. "[I] love the job and the people," says one lawyer. "I am learning a lot about what it is like to be a big city lawyer but not getting killed by the hours or finding that I am limited to the office," adds another source. "A lot of the work seems pretty menial but I have come to accept that as part of the learning process. Overall, as long as I am at a big New York law firm, I will be at this one."

"The old white shoe Rogers & Wells mentality is quickly losing ground to the more worldly, intellectual approch of CC."

— *Clifford Chance associate*

Morgan, Lewis & Bockius LLP

VAULT.COM PRESTIGE RANKING: 34

1701 Market Street
Philadelphia, PA 19103-2921
(215) 963-5000
Fax: (215) 963-5299
www.morganlewis.com

LOCATIONS

Harrisburg, PA • Los Angeles, CA • Miami, FL • New York, NY • Philadelphia, PA • Pittsburgh, PA • Princeton, NJ • Washington, DC • Brussels • Frankfurt • London • Singapore • Tokyo

MAJOR DEPARTMENTS/PRACTICES

Antitrust
Business and Finance
Employee Benefits
Energy
Environmental
FDA
Intellectual Property
Investment Management
Labor and Employment
Litigation
Personal Law
Real Estate
Tax

THE STATS

No. of attorneys: 1,010
No. of offices: 12
Summer associate offers: 99 out of 102
Firm Chair: Francis M. Milone
Hiring Partners: Joseph J. Costello (Philadelphia); Gregory L. Needles (Washington, DC); Robert G. Robison (New York); Peter Wallace (Los Angeles); Mark E. Zelek (Miami); David A. Gerson (Pittsburgh)

THE BUZZ
What attorneys at other firms are saying about this firm

- "Needs to figure out HQ"
- "Very prestigious in Philly"
- "Too youthful and eager"
- "Overall solid firm"

PAY

Philadelphia and Pittsburgh, 2000
1st year: $110,000
2nd year: $110,000 + minimum bonus of $5,500
3rd year: $110,000 + minimum bonus of $16,500
4th year: $120,000 + minimum bonus of $18,000
5th year: $120,000 + minimum bonus of $24,000
6th year: $130,000 + minimum bonus of $26,000
7th year: $130,000 + minimum bonus of $26,000
8th year: $131,000 + minimum bonus of $26,200
Summer associate: $1,900/week

New York, 2000
1st year: $125,000 + bonus
2nd year: $125,000 + bonus
3rd year: $135,000 + bonus
4th year: $147,000 + bonus
5th year: $167,000 + bonus
6th year: $177,000 + bonus
7th year: $187,000 + bonus
8th year: $190,000 + bonus
Summer associate: $2,405/week

Washington, DC, 2000
1st year: $110,000 - $125,000 + bonus
2nd year: $120,000 - $135,000 + bonus
3rd year: $130,000 - $150,000 + bonus
4th year: $140,000 - $165,000 + bonus
5th year: $150,000 - $180,000 + bonus
6th year: $160,000 - $195,000 + bonus
7th year: $170,000 - $205,000 + bonus
Summer associate: $2,000/week

NOTABLE PERKS

- Concert and sports tickets
- Exercise room
- Interoffice summer softball tournament
- Weekly happy hours
- "Extensive" recruiting budget for meals and social events

UPPERS

- Good maternity leave program
- Strong teamwork atmosphere
- Strong ethics
- Reasonable hours, no face time
- Great labor practice

DOWNERS

- Long partnership track (10 to 12 years)
- Part-time policy needs work
- Bureaucratic firm management

KEY COMPETITORS

Jones Day, Reavis & Pogue
Sidley & Austin
Latham & Watkins
Kirkland & Ellis

EMPLOYMENT CONTACT

Mr. Eric Kraeutler
Chair, Professional Recruiting Committee
(215) 963-4840

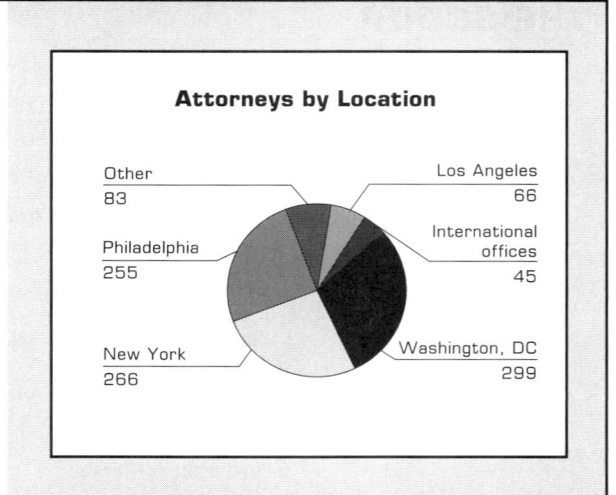

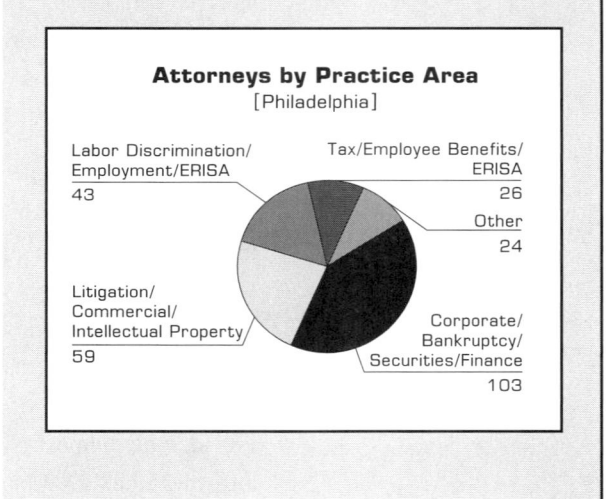

Attorneys by Location

- Other: 83
- Los Angeles: 66
- International offices: 45
- Philadelphia: 255
- Washington, DC: 299
- New York: 266

Attorneys by Practice Area [Philadelphia]

- Labor Discrimination/Employment/ERISA: 43
- Tax/Employee Benefits/ERISA: 26
- Other: 24
- Litigation/Commercial/Intellectual Property: 59
- Corporate/Bankruptcy/Securities/Finance: 103

QUALITY OF LIFE RANKINGS [ASSOCIATES RATE THEIR OWN FIRM]

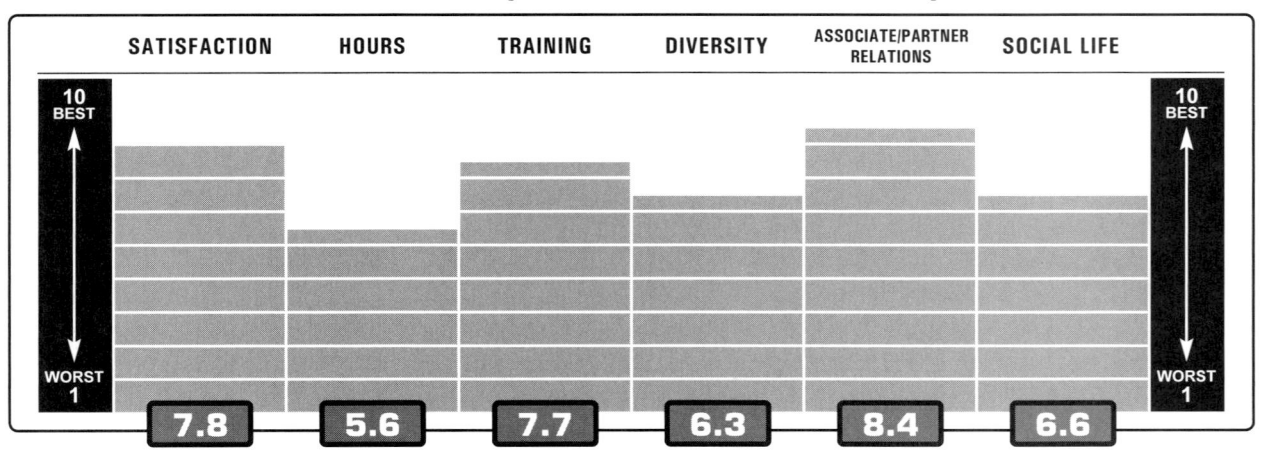

SATISFACTION	HOURS	TRAINING	DIVERSITY	ASSOCIATE/PARTNER RELATIONS	SOCIAL LIFE
7.8	5.6	7.7	6.3	8.4	6.6

THE SCOOP

Morgan, Lewis & Bockius has turned a nice triple play: the firm is one of the oldest, largest, and most respected law firms in the country. Although founded in Philadelphia, the firm maintains large offices in Washington, DC and New York and has no official headquarters. (All three offices have between 250 and 300 lawyers.) All told, the firm has more than 1,000 lawyers in a dozen offices worldwide.

History: long way from Philly

Morgan Lewis was founded in March 1873 by Civil War veterans Charles Eldridge Morgan Jr. and Francis Draper Lewis. The firm took a long time to start seriously growing — it wasn't until the 1970s that the firm expanded into major markets such as New York (1972) and Los Angeles (1976). It expanded internationally in the next decade, adding London (1981), Tokyo (1988), Brussels and Frankfurt (1989) offices. Though growth was slow for the first 100 years, the next 20 were explosive, seeing the firm quintuple in size.

In October 1999, Morgan made changes in its management structure intended to streamline and centralize the decision-making process. These changes included giving more authority to the chair of the firm and creating new positions of managing partner for practice (filled by Philip Werner, an M&A partner in New York), managing partner for operations (Thomas Sharbaugh, a DC antitrust lawyer), and managing partner for legal personnel (Michael Kelly, a corporate lawyer in Philadelphia). Francis Milone was elected chair. In February 2000, Howard Meyers was named head of the Philadelphia outpost after 27 years with the firm. One week later, Gerald Freedman, a partner since 1984, was picked to lead the New York office.

SEC invasion

Morgan's business and finance section, with over 300 lawyers, is the largest in the firm. (The business and finance section correlates to what most firms would call their corporate practice.) Business and finance breaks down into eight practice areas: banking, bankruptcy and reorganization, corporate finance, emerging business investment management, lease and project finance, mergers and acquisitions, public finance, real estate, and securities regulation.

The firm has 45 lawyers in the antitrust area, where they have won numerous high-profile victories. One notable success was a "bet the company" case where Morgan won a reversal of a verdict of hundreds of millions of dollars, ending a case that had been looming over the client for five years.

In February 2000, Morgan expanded their securities practice in New York and DC. Four new partners were added, including Thomas Lemke, former chief counsel at the SEC's Division of Investment Management and David Sirignano, former associate director for international corporate finance in the SEC's corporate finance division. Additionally, Frank Zarb, special counsel in the SEC's corporate finance division, joined Morgan Lewis as of counsel. The firm also poached four associates from the SEC.

M&A wheeling and dealing

One of Morgan's largest practice areas is M&A. The firm represented Bell Atlantic in its $33 billion merger with NYNEX, its $1.5 billion purchase of Metro Mobile CTS, and its $70 billion merger with Vodafone AirTouch PLC. U.S. Foodservice was represented by Morgan when it merged with Rycoff-Sexton. CoreStates Financial picked the firm to represent it in its $730 million merger with First Pennsylvania. Finally, the firm represented Pearson PLC when the British media company purchased Simon & Schuster for $4.3 billion and later when the company sold $1 billion worth of Simon & Schuster to investment firm Hicks, Muse, Tate & Furst.

Strong labor practice

Led by Mark Dichter, Morgan Lewis' labor law practice is one of the best in the world. The firm has argued a number of labor cases in front of the Supreme Court including *Faragher v. City of Boca Raton*, *East Texas Motor Freight Systems v. Rodriguez* and *Building and Construction Trades Council v. Associated Builder and Contractors, et al*. In employee discrimination, the firm successfully defended Kidder Peabody against EEOC claims. Major League Baseball (whose fans accidentally frequented Morgan's former web site, mlb.com) has tapped the firm to represent it in its collective bargaining agreements and individual teams have used Morgan lawyers in salary arbitration cases. M&A client Bell Atlantic was represented by Morgan in a challenge to Bell Atlantic's early retirement window program. More recently, Morgan won an injunction barring Bell Atlantic workers from mass picketing during a strike. The ruling was upheld by the Superior Court of Pennsylvania.

Defend thyself, criminals

Morgan has taken part in numerous criminal prosecutions, but the firm's web site says that it hopes to resolve criminal matters before an indictment is handed down. The firm successfully represented a Federal Aviation Administration official charged with conspiracy to defraud the United States in a Department of Transportation contract. Morgan also defended a senior employee of a Fortune 500 company charged with customs fraud in connection with importing company products into the U.S. Finally, a medical device and products manufacturer charged with improperly testing its products by the Federal Drug Administration chose Morgan to represent it.

Award-winning IP

The firm's intellectual property practice has been growing quickly, both in terms of size and prestige. *The National Law Journal* named Morgan's successful defense of Adobe Systems a "Major Defense Verdict" in 1997. Morgan also successfully defended Prince PLC, whose registration of the domain name prince.com was challenged in October 1997 by the maker of Prince tennis rackets.

More recent successes include the representation of a prominent New York restaurant in a challenge against the unauthorized use of the restaurant's name in the U.K. and the international trademark protection of two of the world's most popular computer games.

Pro bono awards, too

Morgan Lewis has been honored many times for its pro bono work, including several awards from the Philadelphia Bar Association as well as from other local bar associations and lawyers' groups. The firm represented a newsletter publisher who was jailed for 33 months without a hearing after being charged with transmitting classified information. Additionally, Morgan represents the interests of abused children through the Children's Rights Project. Another example is the firm's representation of the Dunbar Economic Development Corp., a Los Angeles organization devoted to revitalizing a jazz-era district on Los Angeles' Central Avenue. In 2000 Morgan lawyers Michael Banks and Gordon Cooney Jr. managed to secure a dramatic last-minute reprieve for a death row inmate convicted more than 15 years earlier. They discovered that crucial blood evidence in a related case had been concealed.

The firm makes an effort to encourage their associates to do pro bono work. "Not only does it count toward billing time, at our annual ball several attorneys are recognized for their pro bono efforts," says one contact. "There are a couple of partners who are extremely dedicated to pro bono work and who actively encourage associates to take on pro bono representations," says a Morgan lawyer.

Play ball

Looking for the latest Red Sox scores? You might find Morgan instead. The firm's web site, www.mlb.com, has attracted a lot of baseball fans. Morgan has a link to Major League Baseball's web site on the firm's home page to redirect those seeking scores, highlights, and game analysis. This minor fun will end in June 2000, however — Morgan Lewis is taking the domain name morganlewis.com, leaving mlb.com to Major League Baseball (also a longstanding client of the firm).

GETTING HIRED

Broad recruiting effort

Any firm with 1,000 attorneys is going to have to do a lot of recruiting. Firm insiders say that each office does its own recruiting and generally focuses on local law schools. The firm lists Columbia University, the University of Virginia, Georgetown, Harvard, the University of Pennsylvania, NYU, Stanford, Yale, Michigan, and Duke as the main targets.

The firm's growth, coupled with a booming economy, has made recruitment more challenging for Morgan Lewis. Some associates fear this has led to a lower quality of hires. "I think it used to be more difficult [to work at Morgan Lewis], but now the volume of people interested in working in Philadelphia seems to have dropped at the same time that a large number of associates have left the firm," reports one associate. "As a result, while there are still some schools that Morgan will not recruit from, I think more candidates get offers than used to be the case." Another contact charges that Morgan has "hired a slew of under-qualified laterals in the last year." Morgan Lewis reportedly had to stretch a little bit in the most recent recruiting season. "We were being turned down by candidates that wouldn't have gotten offers [in the past]," says one insider. The firm says that while it focuses on the quality of law schools for entry-level applicants, it gives equal weight to experience when hiring laterals.

Interview process: social rejects need not apply

Morgan Lewis recruits can expect an initial on-campus interview, usually conducted by a partner. If they like what they see and hear, callbacks visit their office of choice to "meet with four to six partners and associates" for a half a day. "You have to be able to come into the interview and speak about your interests," says one lawyer. Some offices cap off your visit with lunch or cocktails depending on when you come in. Academic credentials are generally checked during the campus interview, so office interviews are "looking for a personality fit." "They don't hire social rejects," says one source.

OUR SURVEY SAYS

Everybody's happy

Firm insiders paint a fairly rosy picture of the corporate culture. "[Morgan] is a very high-energy place, teeming with clients, prominent partners and interesting work," says one Philadelphia associate. "It is also incredibly collegial. I can go to any associate's office to discuss one of my assignments and without exception or hesitation that associate will take the time to help. Lawyers here know each other's spouses or significant others and children and seem to genuinely enjoy each other's company." Insiders use the words "relaxed", "team", and "collegial" often. One contact seems to have changed his mind about the firm. "I had a negative preconception about the firm's culture but came here anyway for the professional opportunities," says that contact. "One of the pleasant surprises is that it's a pleasant place to work."

In March 2000, Morgan went business casual full-time in all offices. The change "has been well-received and has only improved an already good working environment."

The culture is not without its critics, though. "Generally, I have found that the firm's culture has retained some of the 'white shoe' reputation of years past," one associate complains. That contact concedes that "coupled with that is a general attitude of congeniality among associates and partners who work together."

Little hierarchy

Naturally, partners vary in their treatment of associates. At Morgan, the treatment tends to be positive. "I have had very positive interactions with partners here who respect me and my work and who treat me as if I am far more senior than I am," one Philadelphia associate states proudly. "Partners [include] me on strategy sessions and in some instances, [allow] me to take the lead in cases and to be responsible for day-to-day dealings with the clients, local counsel and opposing counsel." "There is very little sense of hierarchy here," one source says. "Partners and associates are on the same team." Of course, not all partner-associate relationships are perfect. "My direct supervisor treats me like an idiot," one Philadelphia associate says. "Other partners treat me well."

The New York office reports more specific problems. While one insider notes that "we have no yellers or screamers — wouldn't be tolerated," others say the partners get into the habit of seeing associates as "billing units." "The firm's business model has been set up to take on very big cases," explains one New Yorker. The firm favors "big, gravy-train type cases" that don't allow for associate development. The firm notes that the litigation and labor and employment practice groups tend to handle a large number of small cases.

Firm romance

In keeping with the happy atmosphere, firm associates report a healthy social life at Morgan. There are "many social events and a fair number of romances," one associate notes. "Familiarity does not seem to breed contempt here!" Events include a Friday happy hour, softball, shared shore houses and a formal dinner dance. One associate feels the need to point out that despite the active social life, "this is a highly professional business, not a college dorm."

Typical hours

"The workload is comparable to other big firms," says one contact of the hours at Morgan. Another reports that "hours have become increasingly important in recent months" as salaries have risen with the industry. A business and finance associate claims that "we have a transactional practice" so hours can vary widely. That associate says that during a busy month, his peers can expect to bill between 260-340 hours; during a slow month, 170-190. "One of the best things about ML&B's Philadelphia office is that you get the opportunity to handle interesting work but do not have to work killer hours on a consistent basis," says one source.

Pay: you got some 'splainin' to do!

Morgan attorneys seem fairly satisfied with their pay, saying it's at or near the top of the market. "The firm has indicated in the past that it wants its associates to be the most highly compensated in this market" says a Philadelphia source, "and it has responded to market pressure recently to confirm that this is the case." Still, some associates, especially those who watch *Nick at Nite*, seem perplexed by Morgan Lewis' pay scale. "There are more harebrained schemes when it comes to ML&B's compensation practices than an 'I Love Lucy' marathon," says one contact. Another worries that if the firm's business ever suffers, layoffs will be necessary to keep the firm in the black. "I just hope that when the music stops, everyone still has a chair."

Insiders report that Morgan Lewis was slow to match the recent salary increases. The firm's excuse was that it "wanted to sit down and look at the best way of approaching the raises." Insiders charge that Morgan Lewis only matched the increases because they were afraid not doing so would hurt recruiting efforts. Additionally, the most significant raises went to recent law school graduates. "There's really no significant raise for third-years and above," reports one New Yorker. Attorneys at ML&B feel management was only "doing what they absolutely had to in order to put a good face on recruiting."

Perks are appreciated

Those working late at Morgan Lewis can expect the usual dinner and a ride home at the firm's expense. One contact warns incoming associates to "cancel your local gym membership." The Philly branch has a fully stocked gym replete with "stair-masters, rowing machines, treadmill, free weights, two televisions (with cable) and towel service." Tickets for sports, charity, and civic events are distributed frequently. The firm also features a "very inexpensive cafeteria — eggs & toast breakfast for under $1" in Philadelphia. (What, no cheese steaks?) Each associate gets a firm credit card and calling card. "Nobody's ever questioned any receipt I submitted," says one contact. The business casual dress is appreciated — "Suits are so 20th century!" However, casual and creative aren't the same thing; one insider cites his fellow associates' casual style as "drab."

Firm-supported training

Like the military, Morgan features "good basic training," says an associate who points out that "the best training comes from the extensive opportunities given to associates to actually do things." One source reports "you learn by doing at ML&B, there is no formal professional training. You are exposed to complex transactional problems early on in your career and you are expected to solve them with guidance and input from senior associates and partners." "I have found senior ML&B lawyers to be helpful and instructive as long as I take the initiative to ask the questions." Others blast the firm's training initiatives. "Right now training is probably our biggest problem in litigation," says one insider. "It's trial by fire. That's usually not a good thing."

Utilitarian offices

"We just moved into these offices within the year and are already bursting at the seams," one Philadelphia lawyer notes. "Little effort has been made to make them 'homey.'" Another Philly associate calls the move "tumultuous" and the office décor "eclectic." "The Philadelphia office is OK on the inside," according to a contact. "The outside is nasty." "Some of the real pluses of our new digs are the rooftop terrace for lunch and cocktail parties, a big cafeteria with wraparound windows, a great conference center and mock courtroom, and large associate offices," another says.

In the New York office, a space crunch has caused some friction. "They keep us doubled up through the third year," reports one source, despite the fact that there are some open offices. This may be avoided in the future, as sources say the firm is expanding to another floor in New York, which may provide more space.

Support services take a new turn

Morgan Lewis militants complain that there often isn't enough support to go around. "Young associates often do their own typing, so support services are not as necessary as they may be for older associates and partners," one contact reports. When available, support is generally good. "You drop off dictation or copying at night and presto, it is back first thing in the morning, no matter how big the job," one associate reports. "Our secretarial, word processing and copying staff are hard working and dedicated," one attorney says, despite the fact that "our technology sucks." Morgan notes that it is one of the first large law firms to use eRoom technology, a sort of intranet that allows Morgan lawyers, clients and other parties to access any work undertaken in eRoom.

Out the door

Turnover at Morgan Lewis seems to be an issue. A hot market means all firms are losing associates, but for various reasons Morgan associates seem to be leaving at a slightly higher rate. "The Philadelphia office has lost a number of senior associates and has replaced them with groups of less-qualified junior associates," one insider reports. Part of the problem is related to the opportunities Morgan associates encounter. "Due to the great training here and the incredibly sophisticated work, only a few years is required to become a hot commodity in the market," says one attorney. "Many associates leave for a huge options package to go in-house for a better lifestyle." Another contact says that while "traditionally the turnover rate has been higher in business and finance, [it] has spread to virtually all sections." One of the biggest factors in turnover has been the lack of responsibility, say insiders. One litigation associate reports that a lawyer was hired laterally into that department only to leave after soaking up the culture for a whole three months.

The stress of growth

One attorney says that the recent turnover has led to "increased lateral hirings [which] means many new faces and perhaps a bigger challenge to gel." One associate gripes that "the fact that the firm has high expectations and more work than one can handle may create some pressure." An angry business and finance associate says that a big drawback to working at Morgan is "enduring the whiners in sections other than the corporate department who think they should get paid a lot of money based on the fact that law firms in general are raising their salaries to retain corporate attorneys."

Two tiers don't make a partner

"The firm announced a two-tier partnership this year," a contact reports. After seven years, associates can become an income (read: non-equity) partner. After two more years, full partnerships are available. Even with this newly diluted partner system, Morgan associates see their chances of making partner as "slim to none." One insider advises would-be partner to "work seven million hours a year for ten years straight with no vacation." More serious advice would be to "focus on producing work of the highest quality, on being a positive influence within the firm, and on getting involved in committee work." In litigation, "an associate must be able to handle all aspects of a case (including writing and advocacy), must be able to handle multiple matters, must be able to effectively mentor and supervise more junior attorneys, and must have the potential to attract and develop business." As of June 2000, 35 partnership nominations were under consideration.

Reasonable diversity

According to Morgan Lewis associates, the firm is better than average in promoting diversity. "The firm does a good job attracting and retaining a diverse group of associates but needs to do a better job of mentoring and retaining minorities," says one lawyer. "I am a minority and I feel very supported but I have seen few minority attorneys and I don't yet know to what I can attribute that fact," says one associate.

Female lawyers seem to fare a little better at Morgan. As with minorities, the firm "needs to do a better job mentoring and retaining women." "I think the firm is trying but there just hasn't been a critical mass of women who have stayed to help transform the firm into a more female-friendly environment," critiques one associate. Another lawyer complains that "women tend to give work to women. I believe this sends the wrong message of a desire to form cliques and to isolate oneself."

Happy, happy Morgan: some love it, some chase their friends away

"If you would like to do highly sophisticated work with a variety of companies from the multitude of start-up dot coms to the world's largest companies, then this place is for you," says an associate who might make a promising copywriter. That cheerleader continues: "If you enjoy being the leader on projects and handling as much responsibility as you can, you can get it here." In general, "everyone here seems to be happy and I can't say that about friends who work at other firms." Another source reports that "in my five years at ML&B I've been stressed, exhausted, overworked and panicked — but never bored or unchallenged."

One associate claims that a plus of working at Morgan is the "responsiveness of management to associate concerns. Examples of this are the biannual state of the firm meetings that provide information on firm performance and the firm's vision for the future. Most associates are stunned by the scope of information that is provided." Another lawyer brags that "the quality and level of sophistication of the work is superior. The prestige level of the firm is also rewarding." Still another lawyer offers what is probably the worst comment you can make about your job: "It's not a firm that I recommend to my friends. Headhunters tell them to try Morgan Lewis, but when they call me, I tell them to stay where they are."

Atmosphere, prestige, and quality of work are the biggest factors in choosing Morgan. One lateral hire says, "I voluntarily left my previous firm when I was told that ML&B was looking to hire a new associate. My decision was very easy simply because we are number one in the state and [have] an outstanding national reputation."

King & Spalding

VAULT.COM PRESTIGE RANKING: 35

191 Peachtree Street
Atlanta, GA 30303
(404) 572-4600
Fax: (404) 572-5100
www.kslaw.com

LOCATIONS

Atlanta, GA (HQ)
Houston, TX
New York, NY
Washington, DC

MAJOR DEPARTMENTS/PRACTICES

Banking & Finance
Bankruptcy
Contracting
Corporate
Employee Benefits
Employment
Environmental
Food & Drug
Government Affairs
Intellectual Property
Litigation
Public Finance
Real Estate
Tax
Trusts & Estates

THE STATS

No. of attorneys: 558
No. of offices: 4
Summer associate offers: 45 out of 45 (Atlanta, 1999)
Managing Partner: Walter W. Driver, Jr.
Hiring Partner: Jon R. Harris, Jr.

THE BUZZ
What attorneys at other firms are saying about this firm

- "The best the South has to offer"
- "Way out of touch with associates"
- "Will never have a casual day"
- "Woman-unfriendly"

PAY

Atlanta, 2000
1st year: $100,000 + $10,000 signing bonus
2nd year: $105,000
3rd year: $110,000
4th year: $115,000
5th year: $122,500
6th year: $130,000
7th year: $137,500
All associates receive bonuses after 2,050 hours
Summer associate: $1,750/week

New York, 2000
1st year: $125,000 + relocation and bar expenses
2nd year: $135,000
3rd year: $150,000
4th year: $165,000
5th year: $185,000
6th year: $200,000
7th year: $210,000
All associates receive bonuses after 2,050 hours
Summer associate: $2,400/week

Washington, 2000
1st year: $125,000 + relocation and bar expenses
2nd year: $135,000
3rd year: $145,000
4th year: $155,000
5th year: $165,000
6th year: $175,000
7th year: $185,000
All associates receive bonuses after 2,050 hours
Summer associate: $2,150/week

NOTABLE PERKS

- Emergency child care services
- Pretax flexible spending account

UPPERS

- Access to high-profile clients
- Highly qualified and highly intelligent attorneys
- Most prestigious firm in the South

DOWNERS

- No casual dress
- Lack of commitment to pro bono
- Near impossibility of making partner

KEY COMPETITORS

Altson & Bird
Long Aldridge
Sutherland, Asbill & Brennan
Troutman Sanders

EMPLOYMENT CONTACT

Ms. Patty Blitch Harris
Recruiting Manager
(404) 572-4990
pbharris@kslaw.com

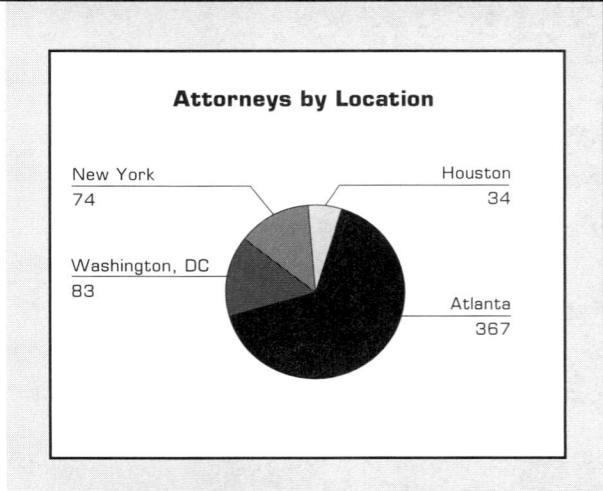

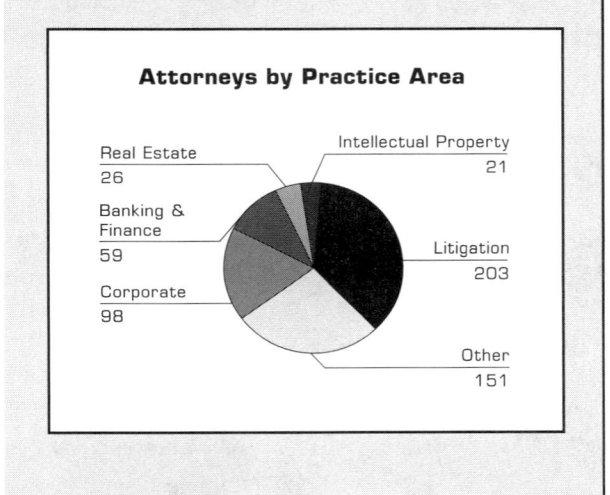

Attorneys by Location

- New York: 74
- Houston: 34
- Washington, DC: 83
- Atlanta: 367

Attorneys by Practice Area

- Real Estate: 26
- Intellectual Property: 21
- Banking & Finance: 59
- Litigation: 203
- Corporate: 98
- Other: 151

QUALITY OF LIFE RANKINGS [ASSOCIATES RATE THEIR OWN FIRM]

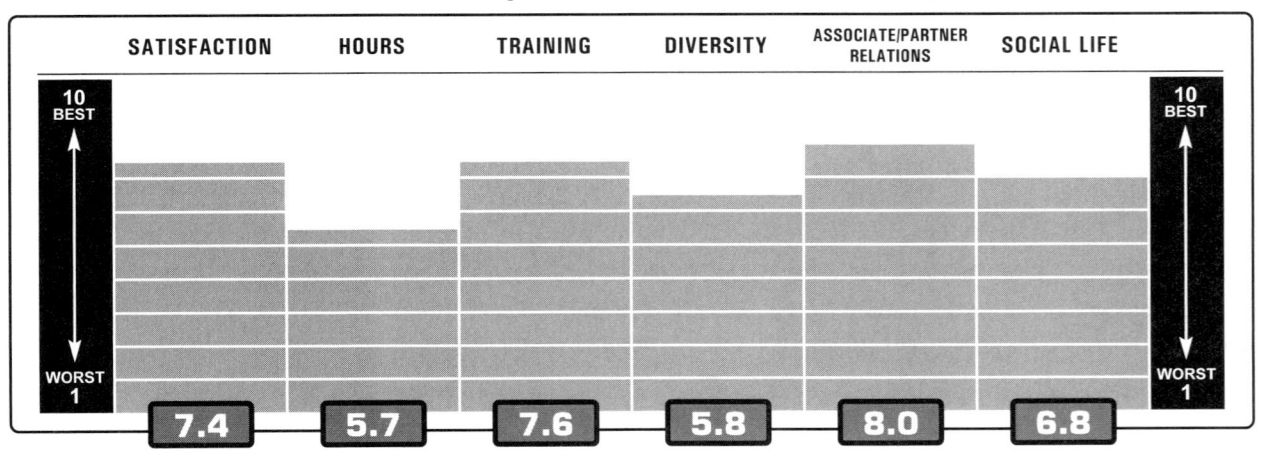

SATISFACTION	HOURS	TRAINING	DIVERSITY	ASSOCIATE/PARTNER RELATIONS	SOCIAL LIFE
7.4	5.7	7.6	5.8	8.0	6.8

THE SCOOP

Soon after Sherman burned Atlanta, King & Spalding rose from its ashes to become the city's top law firm. Over a century later, the firm still rules the South. You may not be able to wear your khakis here, but you'll do well-regarded and sophisticated legal work.

History: two judges and a senator

Atlanta-based King & Spalding was founded on January 1, 1885 by Alex C. King and Jack J. Spalding. King would later become the Solicitor General of the United States as well as a judge on the United States Court of Appeals for the Fifth Circuit. In 1979 the firm opened up its first branch office, in Washington, DC. Also in that year, Griffin B. Bell rejoined the firm after stints as the Attorney General of the United States and as a judge on the Fifth Circuit Court of Appeals. In 1990 the firm opened up a New York office, concentrating on corporate matters. The firm's newest office, in Houston, was established in 1995. Two years later, former United States Senator Sam Nunn, Atlanta's most revered ex-politician, joined the firm after 24 years in the U.S. Senate.

King of the Stone Mountain

As Atlanta's biggest, richest, and most prestigious firm, King & Spalding is a firmly entrenched member of the city's establishment. The firm has made headlines for its work in the world of athletics, serving as general counsel to the Atlanta Committee for the Olympic Games. In 1999 K&S defended the Georgia Amateur Athletics Foundation against claims that the GAAF had won the bid from the International Olympic Committee with gifts, money, and other shady perks. Moreover, King & Spalding represents Atlanta's most prominent company, Coca-Cola — a bubbly fountain of reverence.

After the soft-drink juggernaut, the firm's second-most important client is beleaguered tobacco titan Brown & Williamson. Other clients on the its list include Home Depot, SunTrust Banks, United Parcel Service, General Electric, General Motors, Lockheed Martin, Texaco, Prudential, and Sprint. The firm's headquarters are located in Atlanta's prestigious 191 Peachtree Building. Attorneys hail the offices as being "the sweetest associates' offices in the country, bar none." Along with its headquarters in the capital of the Peach State, the firm has offices in New York, Houston, and Washington, DC, each of which is rapidly expanding.

Litigation is king

Litigation, the firm's largest practice area, has a royal record of court victories for big-name clients. The beverage industry has historically been a major focus of King & Spalding's practice and in 1999 the firm defended The Coca-Cola Company against a class-action racial discrimination suit. K&S is also The Real Thing to companies besides Coke. The firm defended General Motors in a 1999 product liability suit involving a fatality caused by the ruptured fuel tank of a Chevrolet Chevette.

Sprinting to the top

Although King & Spalding is best known for its litigation, perhaps the firm's biggest splash of 1999 came courtesy of its corporate group. K&S advised Sprint in its proposed merger with MCI WorldCom, Inc. The deal, valued at $115 billion when bid, could possibly be the largest ever, depending on stock prices at closing. The firm has represented clients in a number of other big-money M&A deals as well, including serving as co-counsel to Union Texas Petroleum Holdings in its $3.3 billion sale to ARCO and working on Suntrust Banks' $9.5 billion takeover of Crestar Financial Corp. Suntrust is just one of many banking clients. King & Spalding is among the top five most used firms by commercial banks, according to *The National Law Journal*.

Comings and goings

K&S underwent some changes in personnel in 1999, including its managing partner post. After a successful seven-year reign, litigator Ralph B. Levy stepped down to make room for policy committee chairman Walter W. Driver. Driver will serve a three-year term, while Levy will return to his trial practice at King & Spalding. Meanwhile, the firm's tax practice suffered a blow when several lawyers from that group defected to join a law firm being formed by Big Five accountancy Ernst & Young.

King is so money

In spite of these defections, King & Spalding enjoyed a banner year financially in 1999. Once again, K&S ranked as the highest-grossing law firm in Atlanta by a wide margin. Associates enjoyed some of the benefits of that success, seeing their compensation increase considerably during the year. The firm raised first-year associates' salaries in its headquarters office by $25,000 to a cool $100,000 per year and threw in a $10,000 signing bonus to boot. It also followed the scale increases in other cities and reportedly is contemplating offering discretionary bonuses for associates making "extraordinary non-billable contributions." A $40,000 associate retention bonus has been rumored as well.

GETTING HIRED

Dinner before callbacks

When it comes down to it, claims an associate, "selectivity is based on grades. After that, if you breathe, you can get hired." One insider offers the following as a guideline: "If you had a 3.2 at a tier-one or tier-two law school, you'll get a job." Many attorneys speak of regional recruiting problems. "We have more trouble recruiting in New York than in Atlanta," reports one source. Another continues, "King & Spalding seems to be hiring more students from local and regional law schools. I think K&S undersells itself at the Top 15 law schools." Most aspects of the interview process are described as "pretty standard," including the on-campus screening interview and expenses-paid trip to Atlanta. The firm tries to make candidates feel comfortable by "bringing [them] down the night before for dinner with two or three associates."

More interviews than at most firms

Where K&S's interviews diverge from most is in their sheer number. Candidates undergo "eight to 10 interviews with a mixture of partners and associates," most of whom "are on the hiring committee." If the candidate indicates certain areas of interest, the firm attempts to get interviewers from that area. Each interview lasts roughly half an hour. The interview day includes lunch with "two or three associates." The tone of interviews "depends on the individual" interviewer, but in general, "no one's playing games or hiding the ball."

The pressure is not as great as it might seem, though, says one insider: "If you make it to a second interview, you've really got to annoy people not to get an offer." Indeed, "it seems to be a seller's market" as "lately the firm has been digging deeper into the pool of recruits." This is good for applicants but perhaps not ideal for the overall health of the firm. Says one source, "There's been a dramatic downward spiral in the past few years in terms of selectivity."

OUR SURVEY SAYS

Southern comfort

"The best word to describe K&S is 'Southern,'" claims one insider in King & Spalding's New York office. Others prefer terms such as "traditional," "old-school," and "conservative." While some might perceive this environment as negative, most insiders see it as an asset. "I believe, and I also believe few would argue otherwise, that King & Spalding sits at the apex of the legal community in Atlanta." Therefore, attorneys "constantly have quality work for big-league clients." An insider continues, "K&S is a great place to work. You do first-rate work, work with first-rate lawyers, and there is a great deal of respect for the fact that you have a life outside the office."

We work hard for the money

"The general consensus among associates is that the Atlanta market as a whole underpays," begins one source. "However, everyone was generally pleased with the salary structure (adopted March 1, 2000) placing starting salaries at $100,000." The pay increase and its consequences were felt in other firm locations as well. "K&S recently matched the salaries that the other top Houston firms are paying. With this increase, however, came an enormous pressure to up billable hours." While associates generally approve of the pay increase, some still find room for criticism. "This is where K&S really whiffed this year," an insider argues, voicing a popular opinion. "It continues to position itself as a national law firm with national clients and certainly national partner pay. However, when it came time to match the pay of those other national law firms, K&S copped out and said they would only pay what the Atlanta market was paying. K&S had the chance to really claim [to be] the leader in every respect, including pay, but when it came time to pay what our peers are making, K&S took the cheap route. It is so unbecoming of a national law firm." Associates are also split as to whether the bonus target, set at 2,050 billable hours, is overly ambitious. Some find the target "entirely reasonable," while others assert, "I try never to work that hard."

Fresh lawyers

All the King's men (and women) must enroll at K&S University, the firm's "in-house training program." Graduates describe it as "a great training program the firm offers with lots of hands-on experience." An insider reports that "the training here is excellent, especially in comparison to other large firms. Equally important, the partners at K&S really expect the associates to participate fully in all training events, even to the point where it may reflect negatively upon you if you decide to blow off the events." Moreover, many associates find "individual mentoring provided by partners is unique and highly valuable."

"In some cases," one source retorts, "the partners seem to be cramming this stuff [training] down associates' throats. What associates really want is on-the-job training in real cases — either through small matters or pro bono work — but there is precious little of that to go around." "The one-on-one just is not there," another attention-starved associate comments. "There is not time, and the billing pressures are too high."

Time is not on our side

Like most large firms, King & Spalding places a heavy emphasis on billable hours. "We are also encouraged to bill hours in a category listed as 'total productive hours.' This entails bar activities, client development, and so on," notes one source. "I have no idea when they expect us to do these activities, given the workload." Indeed, most insiders find that "the hours are extremely intense and stressful." A first-year associate warns prospective employees to be prepared to work until "8 or 9 on most nights, and work at least two weekends out of a month." While one content attorney insists that he's "never found it unbearable" and that "the firm makes an effort to permit a workload to balance with family life," another argues that "it is difficult to impossible to make plans for after work, as I will end up canceling 80 to 90 percent of the time." Moreover, "pro bono is encouraged, but we're not really rewarded for it and we're still expected to bill, bill, bill."

Long-distance partners mean little camaraderie

"There is no great divide here between the partners and the associates as one finds at other firms," reports an insider. "In my opinion, the partners really do value the associates and treat them well." Associates take pleasure in being treated as "resources to build for the future" rather than "resources to be used up." Furthermore, "[partners at K&S] go out of their way to solicit my advice and be exceedingly gracious." One particularly well-fed source reports that he goes "to lunch with partners regularly and finds them to be good guys to hang out with." A Washington associate who has had experience dealing with partners at the firm's headquarters notes, "treatment by partners within the Washington office is terrific. Treatment by long-distance partners in Atlanta is much more big-firm."

Complaints about the partners at King & Spalding are as widespread as compliments. "[Partners] have no clue as to what work associates are doing for other partners. Additionally, they think nothing about setting artificial and unrealistic deadlines," one source grouses. Others report that "there are some partners who could use some training in people skills." An insider observes that "there is very little camaraderie with most partners. There are rumors that they think the junior associates don't work hard enough, [which] produces animosity between partners and associates." In spite of these reports, many attorneys note that there is "no screaming" at the firm and that "disrespectful behavior by a partner would not be looked upon favorably by team or firm management."

Social opportunity without social desire

King & Spalding attorneys enjoy the company of their peers — that is, when they're not too tired. "The firm provides a great deal of opportunity for socializing — from lavish holiday parties to monthly birthday celebrations to occasional happy hours," a fifth-year associate states. "The firm also tries to acclimate new associates by linking them with a more senior associate and a junior partner who get an entertainment budget to spend on that new associate." However, while attorneys at the firm seem to get along, many agree with the question voiced by one source: "I spend all day with these people. Why spend more?" Another gripes, "I find it difficult to have much of a social life between the hours of 10 p.m. to midnight during the week. On the weekends, when I happen to get at least one day off, I am usually too tired to do anything." A lateral hire in the New York office finds that "people are very professional. They come to work, [and they] do the job well but there is not a lot of the 'rah rah' social aspect that one finds in firms where most of the lawyers came through an established summer program." Perhaps the social life at King & Spalding is best summarized by the lawyer who notes that "the lawyers here tend to maintain very busy lives outside the office and generally go their separate ways after hours."

Crowning new kings?

Partnership seems an elusive goal to many associates at King & Spalding. One finds his chances of making partner to be "poor at best. No one comes here with this as a goal. It would be too unrealistic." Attorneys who do attain that position "work themselves to death, have no life outside the firm, and do not take vacations." One source reports, "It requires more than just a lot of billable hours [to make partner]. You must be well-known and well-liked throughout the firm, contribute to the community, and either have some of your own clients or regularly service existing firm clients. It is important to recognize that the partnership track is a marathon, not a sprint. Consistent performance over the years, combined with a strong performance in the year or two before consideration, are likely to get you further than one or two outrageous years at a pace you can't sustain." Another insider believes the formula is simpler: "look and think like everyone else here — and [do] not be a woman."

Kings without queens

King & Spalding is most often taken to task for its treatment of women. "There are very few women with families here," begins one Houston associate, "and the firm does not promote or encourage any kind of alternative work program." Although the firm "recently started offering part-time," female associates note that "generalizations regarding women and marriage and/or childbirth still exist. Also, being a young woman often works to your disadvantage because people — usually older men —

mistake you for a paralegal or secretary." Others note that K&S is "a tough place to balance a family, especially [if you are] recently married. Most of the divorces in the past year involve young female associates." Moreover, "there is no mentoring by female partners, as far as I can tell. Counsel are much better mentors. The part-time options are practically non-existent and not discussed. The lack of communication on these issues is deplorable. The of counsel position is now almost entirely women and the non-equity partner position almost entirely men. I have also noticed that it is absolutely possible to telecommute, yet it is not an open option. This would be a great opportunity for K&S to better accommodate lawyers with families, at least a few days a week."

Diversity: a numbers game

When questioned about minority issues at the firm, an associate notes simply, "Look at the numbers." Another reports, "I do not think we have even one corporate partner here who is of a racial minority. The minority associates I know talk about the disparity and the overall lack of a mentoring program with respect to racial minorities at our firm and how they believe it serves as a limitation to their advancement here." A DC attorney finds the "number of minority attorneys in the office to be embarrassingly low." Insiders concur that "efforts to recruit more minority associates could be stronger."

Similar attitudes are apparent in K&S's treatment of gays and lesbians. "There is, unfortunately, little in the way of acceptance here," says one source. An Atlanta-based attorney observes that "most of the gay attorneys remain very much in the closet. Other firms in town have more gay attorneys — many more."

Long live the King

All in all, associates at K&S are reasonably satisfied with their experience at the firm. "The work can be very stimulating. An associate also has some control over her destiny," states one insider. Another sums up by stating, "Overall, I find the work to be challenging and interesting and I enjoy the people I work with. It is really a nice place to come every day."

"I spend all day with these people. Why spend more?"

— *King & Spalding associate*

Willkie Farr & Gallagher

VAULT.COM PRESTIGE RANKING: 36

The Equitable Center
787 Seventh Avenue
New York, NY 10019-6099
(212) 821-8000
Fax: (212) 728-8111
www.willkie.com

LOCATIONS

New York, NY (HQ)
Washington, DC
London
Milan
Paris
Rome

MAJOR DEPARTMENTS/PRACTICES

Bankruptcy
Corporate/Finance
Employee Benefits and Relations
Intellectual Property
Litigation
Real Estate
Tax
Trusts and Estates

THE STATS

No. of attorneys: 424
No. of offices: 6
Summer associate offers: 54 out of 54 (New York, 1999)
Chairman: Jack Nusbaum
Hiring attorneys: Michael Kelly, Christine Kim, T. Golden, and J. Poss

PAY

All Domestic Offices, 2000
1st year: $125,000
2nd year: $135,000
3rd year: $150,000
4th year: $170,000
5th year: $190,000
Summer associate: $2,000/week

NOTABLE PERKS

- Emergency day care center
- Occasional baseball tickets
- Monthly informal cocktail party
- Attorney lounge

THE BUZZ

What attorneys at other firms are saying about this firm

- "Fraternity/sorority culture among associates"
- "People waste a lot of time litigating cases"
- "Good lawyers but wouldn't want to have a drink with any of them"
- "Good old-line firm"

UPPERS

- "Non-white shoe firm with sassiness"
- Beautiful offices
- High quality of associate existence

DOWNERS

- Indifferent training
- Tenuous partnership track
- Problems with support staff

KEY COMPETITORS

Dewey Ballantine
Fried, Frank, Harris, Shriver & Jacobson
Milbank, Tweed, Hadley & McCloy
Weil, Gotshal & Manges

EMPLOYMENT CONTACT

Ms. Patricia Langlade
Recruiting Coordinator
(212) 728-8469
tlanglade@willkie.com

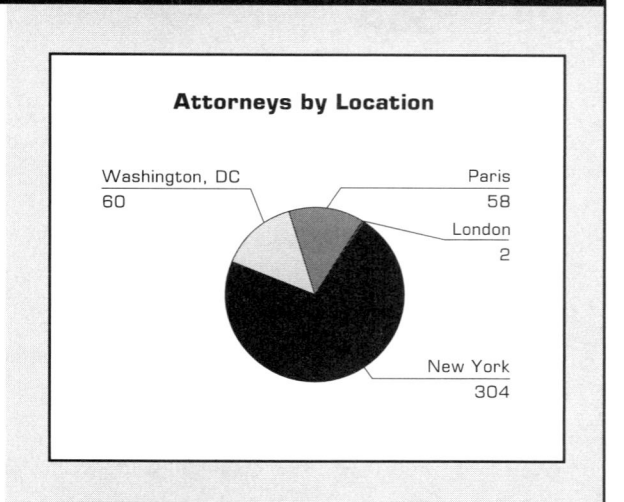

Attorneys by Location
- Washington, DC: 60
- Paris: 58
- London: 2
- New York: 304

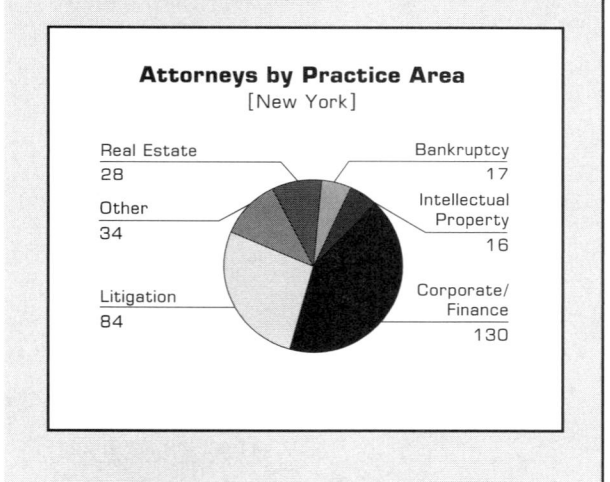

Attorneys by Practice Area [New York]
- Real Estate: 28
- Bankruptcy: 17
- Other: 34
- Intellectual Property: 16
- Litigation: 84
- Corporate/Finance: 130

QUALITY OF LIFE RANKINGS [ASSOCIATES RATE THEIR OWN FIRM]

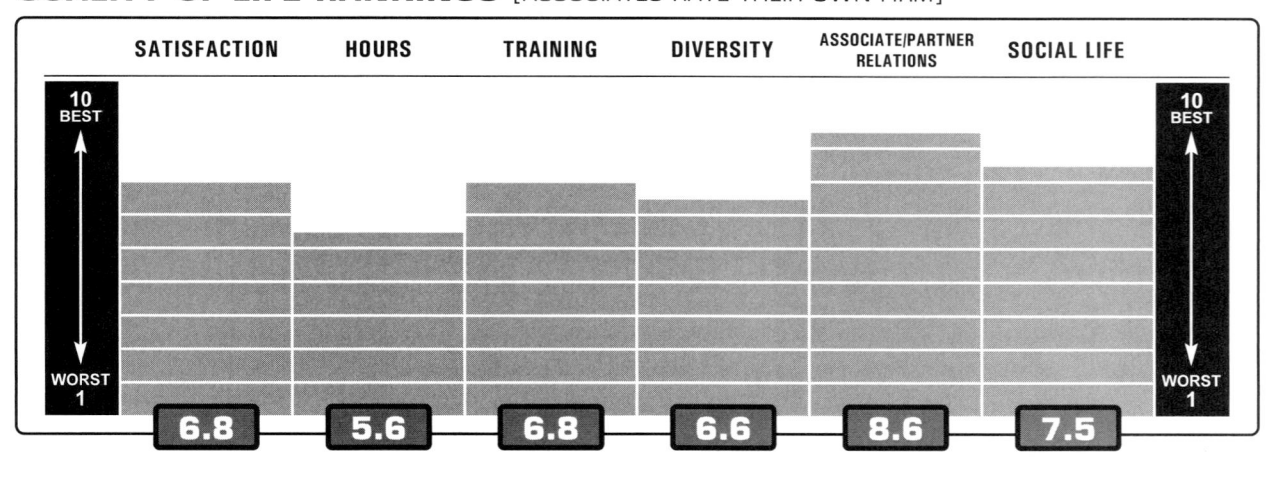

SATISFACTION	HOURS	TRAINING	DIVERSITY	ASSOCIATE/PARTNER RELATIONS	SOCIAL LIFE
6.8	5.6	6.8	6.6	8.6	7.5

THE SCOOP

Willkie Farr may not get the notice of a Cravath or Skadden, but it's a quietly effective firm. With signficant strengths in bankruptcy (clients include "The Trump" himself), corporate practice and intellectual property, those who know Willkie — especially those in the inside — regard it highly.

History: politicians everywhere

Willkie Farr & Gallagher was founded in 1889 in New York and now has more than 400 attorneys in six offices. (Besides New York, the firm has operations in Washington, DC, Paris, Rome, Milan, and London.) The Willkie in Willkie Farr is Wendell Willkie, the 1940 Republican presidential candidate who lost to Franklin Roosevelt. Willkie is not the only politician connected with the firm — former governor of New York Mario Cuomo became a partner after leaving office in 1995. More recently, Craig Johnson, an associate in Willkie's bankruptcy department, was elected to the Nassau County (NY) Legislature in May 2000, taking the place of his mother who died of breast cancer in March 2000. Johnson's bankruptcy experience will come in handy; Nassau County was facing a deficit of $178 million when he took office. Another prominent Willkie lawyer is Chester Straub, a former partner named a Circuit Court judge.

With client departure, a major restructuring

Perversely, perhaps the best thing that happened to Willkie Farr was the sale of Shearson Lehman. The broker had been a major client of Willkie's in the 1980s, at one time accounting for as much as one-third of the firm's business. When Shearson Lehman was sold to the Traveler's Companies in 1993, that business disappeared. The firm suffered, laying off approximately 20 associates, but learned its lesson. Willkie rebuilt and reorganized and no client is now responsible for more than five percent of the firm's business — a much sounder policy.

We merge for you

One of Willkie Farr's best-known practices is mergers and acquisitions. The firm represented the National Association of Securities Dealers (the parent company of the Nasdaq stock market) when it acquired a controlling interest in the American Stock Exchange in 1999. Willkie represented CalEnergy Company in its $5.5 billion acquisition of MidAmerican Energy Holding Company. In investment banking, Willkie lawyers represented Cowen & Co in its sale to Societe Generale. J. Crew used Willkie when the clothing company was sold to TGP Partners. More recently, the firm represented Nextlink Communications regarding its $2.9 billion merger with

Concentric Network in February 2000. Later that month, Willkie was tapped by CompUSA to represent it in its acquisition by Grupo Sanborns, a Mexican retail company.

Big on bankruptcy

While M&A has been good to Willkie, many in the firm think Willkie has "one of the best bankruptcy departments around." The firm's most famous reorganization case involved the Trump Organization. Willkie helped Donald Trump, the New York-based real estate tycoon, restructure his hotel and casino holdings, including the Plaza Hotel, Taj Mahal, Trump Plaza Hotel and Casino and Trump Castle. No doubt the firm will be working with the perpetually financially troubled zillionaire in the future. The firm also represented high-profile Chapter 11 filers like the Grand Union Company, Days Inn of America, Orion Pictures, and Harvard Industries.

Glam securities

One of the major growth engines of the New Economy has been the omnipresent IPO and Willkie has participated fully. The firm has been active in public securities offerings, participating in 40 IPOs since January 1997 as well as 50 debt offerings. One such offering was for Level 3 Communications, one of the largest high-yield offerings of the 1990s. Other Willkie IPOs include Nextlink Communications, Globalstar Communications, Panavision and Knoll.

If you've had the chance to buy a piece of Ziggy Stardust, you can thank Willkie. Perhaps the most famous Willkie securities offerings have been its "Bowie bonds," securities backed by song royalties. The firm participated in the first such song offering, structured for rock star David Bowie. That association led to some legal troubles for the firm. Willkie was one of several defendants named in a lawsuit by David Pullman, one of the creators of the bonds. Pullman claims Willkie played a role in cutting his company out of a joint venture with Prudential Insurance to sell additional royalty-backed bonds. Prudential and a handful of other companies were also named in the suit, filed in December 1999.

Venture capital is a strong component of Willkie's corporate practice. The firm represented Warburg Pincus in its $100 million investment in a Czech pharmaceutical company. Additional clients include startups and venture capital funds in various transactions, including incorporation, funding issues, and public offerings.

A smart intellectual property practice

Willkie has been active in intellectual property, counseling companies on trademark, Internet and licensing transactions. The firm has represented Bloomberg in establishing a network for broadcasting and publishing. Willkie has also advised organizations such as the American Institute of Certified Accountants and the Trustees of St. Patrick's Cathedral in New York in setting up web ventures.

A tidy little litigation practice

Willkie's litigation department consists of over 90 lawyers. The firm successfully defended Donald Trump in a lawsuit filed by bondholders of the Taj Mahal casino. Willkie has represented Major League Baseball on several matters, including its discipline of Hall of Famer Pete Rose and the colorful former Cincinnati Reds owner Marge Schott, known for her Saint Bernard "Schottzie" and her racist and anti-Semitic remarks. The Willkie litigation team conducted an investigation into the accounting practices at computer giant Cendant after irregularities caused a 40 percent drop in the company's stock price.

All delight in pro bono

The firm's pro bono work has earned several awards, notably the New York Bar Association's Pro Bono Service Law Firm Award in 1996 and the President's Award from the Puerto Rican Legal Defense and Education Fund in 1998. "We are absolutely wonderful in this area," raves one insider. "I brought in a pro bono matter which was supported by significant resources from more than one department. Pro bono hours count as billable hours." Pro bono clients include Women in Need, City Harvest, and the Westside Cluster of Centers and Settlements. The firm also works closely with the Volunteer Lawyers for the Arts, the Network for Women's Services, and the Lawyers Alliance for New York.

GETTING HIRED

Better get on law review

Willkie "seems to be looking for a particular kind of personality" in its candidates, says one lawyer. That personality is "nice and very diligent." Additionally, the firm "looks heavily on whether the applicant is on law review," especially in the case of candidates from second-tier schools. While candidates from top-tier schools are preferred, students from other schools still have a decent shot. Willkie's selectivity "has changed a lot, in my view, in the recent strong market," reports one associate — more grads than ever have a chance to join the Willkie club.

Casual callbacks

The firm's web site (www.willkie.com) has a recruiting section that includes contacts and a campus recruiting schedule. The firm visited 18 schools in 1999, a majority of which were in the New York or Washington, DC areas.

Insiders describe callbacks as "very, very casual," with partners trying to start a conversation with questions like "What did you do last summer?" as opposed to grilling interviewees. After you study for the law review, brush up on your people skills. One contact reports that "students with good grades from good schools often get rejected after call-back."

OUR SURVEY SAYS

Culture: a clear hierarchy, but unusually supportive

Willkie associates generally describe the firm as relaxed and friendly. "Overall, it is not a competitive environment," says one lawyer. "Partners' doors are always open to ask questions or to socialize. Associates are usually more than eager to help one another out." That doesn't mean there isn't a separation based on experience. "There is a clear hierarchy, observed and obeyed by everyone," says one first-year associate. "However, those at the upper end of the hierarchy are highly accessible to us peons." Despite that rather backhanded compliment, it appears good feelings abound. "People here are outgoing and have very distinct personalities," says one corporate attorney. "The people here are ones that you would notice (and would hear) in a crowd."

Underlying all of this is the reality that Willkie Farr, like all large firms, maintains a corporate environment. "The firm is very corporate, obviously," notes a first-year lawyer, "but the partners seem to have some iota of a sense of humor about that fact. This makes life a little more palatable."

The firm gets high marks for its partner-associate relationships. "Like any other firm, it depends on the partner," observes one attorney. "Most whom I work with treat me with respect and with the same level of courtesy as they expect to see from me." A first-year associate notes, "Most partners have nice personalities, but they expect you to sacrifice your free time without complaint." Several associates note that they appreciate the exposure they get to many "substantive areas, resulting from having a single corporate department without groups."

Social butterflies

One associate says that since "my colleagues are generally pretty friendly and down-to-earth," getting together socially isn't a problem. "Willkie is a very sociable firm," reports a second-year associate. "I have some of my closest friends at the firm. I enjoy going out after work with Willkie lawyers because most are laid-back and know how to have a good time." As always, though, different people and different departments have different atmospheres. "[It] depends on the individual and the group they associate with. [It] also depends on how busy the firm is," says one lawyer. "It is difficult to do a happy hour when people are working until midnight."

Hours: welcome to the club

A sixth-year associate admits that "at times [the hours] are overwhelming. Willkie does its best to ameliorate this realistic condition of our work by not requiring face time, not condoning busy work, and respecting and encouraging vacations." But not everyone is strong enough to maintain perspective. "Associates who can't say no work very long hours," says one contact. "If you attempt to manage your schedule, you can have a reasonable lifestyle." Another insider says that hours worked "depend on the deal you are on and how well you manage your time. People try to respect your right to a life outside the firm." One associate complains that "it's not so much the amount of time worked but the lack of predictability as to when I will be free that makes the job overwhelming." However, that first-year lawyer concludes, "that's just a part of corporate life." Insiders say partners are sensitive to their hours. One New York associate claims to have "been taken to task for not planning a vacation yet."

Pay's fine — but complaints persist

"I am vastly overpaid compared to teachers, medical residents and many others who contribute more to society than I [do]," says one philosophical lawyer. "However, I am underpaid compared to investment bankers, venture capitalists and other participants in the markets for which I toil." That lawyer adds, "I should note that I am confident that Willkie is committed to match or exceed the New York City market."

Willkie lawyers do complain about a perceived disparity in pay with other markets. "When I started work at Willkie, New York firms were paying more than firms in other cities. Now they pay the same salary," says one corporate attorney. "Effectively, I make less than my peers in other cities and see no reason to work the long hours or put up with the high cost of living if those factors are not going to be calculated into my salary." Another associate agrees: "Given the cost of living in Manhattan, our salary should be higher than our peers in less expensive cities such as Houston. This is not the case right now."

Plenty of booze

Meals, cars and sports tickets — the usual lush law perks — are abundant at Willkie Farr. Potential summer interns take note: "The summer program is the most opulent in the country," claims one first-year lawyer, "and associates get to utilize it to their advantage as well. Once a month there is an informal gathering with hors d'oeuvres and booze." Associates get "tickets to baseball and basketball games" (not surprising considering the firm represents Major League Baseball). However, one contact warns that "unless the partner who guards the tickets knows you and likes you, he'd rather give them to clients." There are other complaints. "We have a gym in the building, but Willkie has not offered to foot the tab, which would make spending all day and night here much more bearable."

Learning from your mistakes

Associates at Willkie seem split on the quality of training. "The training is hands-on," says one first-year associate. "There are no seminars or the like. You learn by doing, making mistakes, and learning from those who make mistakes." A more senior associate says, "I think we do our best and we do more than most." Finally, one corporate associate reports that "the partners with whom I work directly make an effort to train me, which I appreciate."

Beautiful offices, if you take care of them

One New York lawyer says he goes to work in "beautiful new offices in a modern, attractive building." Other contacts describe the space as "airy, modern, not stuffy at all." "The firm has the most beautiful offices I've ever seen," says one first-year associate with an admittedly limited frame of reference. "I love the office space." It seems the only way to get stuck with an ugly office is to do it to yourself. "Mine isn't well-decorated," confesses one corporate attorney, "but that is my fault."

It's a secretary! Run!

The support staff at Willkie is often termed subpar. "I feel like I'm constantly sucking up to support services to help me with my work, and the quality is often quite lacking," grouses one associate. "It can be really stressful, especially when I'm very busy." There seems to be a rift between lawyers and support staff. "I hear a lot of grumbling from the support staff that we're ungrateful," says one first-year associate. "On the other hand, they fail to realize that they should help us, particularly when the client has an urgent matter. I think it's a matter of miscommunication and mutual grievances. One odd thing about this firm is that attorneys seem afraid of the support staff."

Retention: the familiar refrain

Willkie associates share the opinion of those at other firms — lawyers rarely leave for lateral positions. "I have been here a year and do not recall hearing about anyone leaving to go to another law firm," says one contact. Another reports that "people leave for interesting jobs." That opinion is echoed by a corporate associate who says that "we generally don't lose quality people to other large New York City firms. We have lost some talent recently to dot coms and banks."

"It's a long shot"

Don't get too excited about becoming a partner, Willkie insiders say. Associates describe partnership prospects as "slim to none." "It would be nice to know what the process is. At our retreat this year, an associate asked Jack Nusbaum, our chairman, what it took to make partner. He answered, 'You make partner when you become a partner.' What does that mean?"

For those who still harbor hopes, expect a political process punctuated by a lot of hours. "Don't even think about having a family — unless you plan on not spending much time with them," advises one source. Another attorney claims making partner is "really a matter of personality, less about pure smarts." One lawyer says you get to be partner "just by doing a good job and avoiding angering people." Department assignment also plays a role. "The firm makes a handful of partners each year and they are primarily from corporate and litigation," says one associate. "The chances of making partner in a specialty department are slim."

The sad and familiar diversity story

Willkie Farr has made an effort to increase diversity, associates say, but the results have been lacking. "I think we're good in this regard," one lawyer says, although "we seem underrepresented at the partner level. I don't believe any member of a minority group has been up for partner during my tenure. I'm not sure what more we can do." "They try, but there is no real strong presence at the firm — especially at the top," says another source. "We need to get more diversity," says one attorney critical of the firm's results. "There are plenty of qualified people of color who would flourish here if only we would seek them out."

The firm's efforts with women also seem to be yielding few results. "The firm tries to do programs but they never seem to work," complains one insider. "There isn't a strong female presence at the firm. Some senior male members of the firm have expressed this concern but we haven't been able to come up with a solution yet." One associate has a solution: "We need more women partners. We have fewer than 10 and among those, only one has a child. It's pathetic."

The climate for gays and lesbian seems a little better. "One of our partners is openly gay and no one makes an issue of it," reports one attorney. "However, I know of few other openly gay associates." That contact says the issue "is never discussed." Another associate says, "I don't want to classify the firm as not receptive, but rather not focused on targeting gay and lesbian recruits. The firm does have domestic partner benefits."

For New York in particular, a comfortable haven

In general, Willkie attorneys are satisfied with the firm. "Whatever problems I have with working here are based on a general desire to work in the public sector," says one attorney who's going places. "As far as I'm concerned, this is as good as it gets in the private sector." "As far as big New York firms go this is a great place," another lawyer says. "People are interesting and smart and there's no mold to fit into. Clients have told me that Willkie attorneys don't have a lot of attitude but produce great work."

Willkie associates seem pleased with the people and culture. The firm "encourages associates to go out and play — for example, my mentor/partner has taken me to task for not planning a vacation yet. I am supposed to present her with unbreakable vacation plans by the end of the month and then take them." In summary, an associate says, "I chose this firm over others because it's a comfortable place to work."

Venture Law Group

VAULT.COM PRESTIGE RANKING: 37

2800 Sand Hill Road
Menlo Park, CA 94025
(650) 854-4488
Fax: (650) 233-8386
www.vlg.com

LOCATIONS

Menlo Park, CA (HQ)
Kirkland, WA

MAJOR DEPARTMENTS/PRACTICES

Corporate & Securities
Intellectual Property
Tax & Employee Benefits

THE STATS

No. of attorneys: 97
No. of offices: 2
Summer associate offers: 18 out of 19 (Menlo Park, CA 1999)
Chairman of Executive Committee: Craig Johnson
Hiring Attorney: Mike Morrissey

PAY

All Domestic Offices, 2000
1st year: $125,000 plus bonus
Summer associate: $2,400/week

NOTABLE PERKS

- Home computer with high-speed connection
- Annual retreat to Pebble Beach
- Stocked fridges
- Cell phone plan reimbursed by firm
- On-site massages and car washes

THE BUZZ

What attorneys at other firms are saying about this firm

- "Entrepreneurial"
- "Will it last?"
- "A new model for the business of law"
- "Venture, not law"

UPPERS

- Individual sense of being part of the firm's direction
- VLG's brand-name recognition
- Potentially lucrative equity investments

DOWNERS

- Relentless pace
- Commute from San Francisco
- Cyclical, market-based nature of work

KEY COMPETITORS

Brobeck, Phleger & Harrison
Cooley Godward
Gunderson Dettmer Stough Villeneuve Franklin & Hachigian
Wilson Sonsini Goodrich & Rosati

EMPLOYMENT CONTACT

Ms. Donna Tavenner
VP, Human Resources
(650) 854-4488
jobs@vlg.com

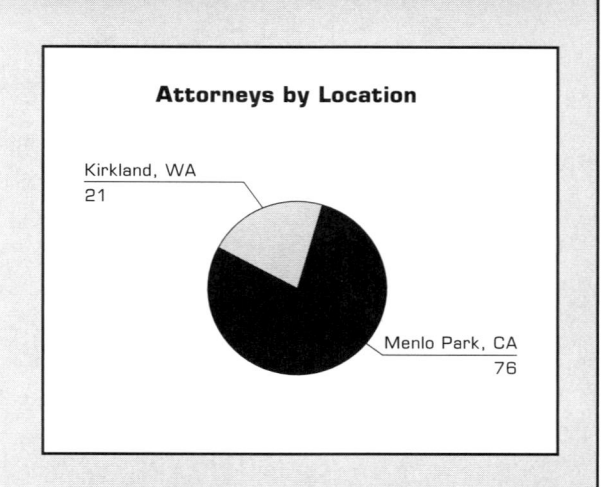

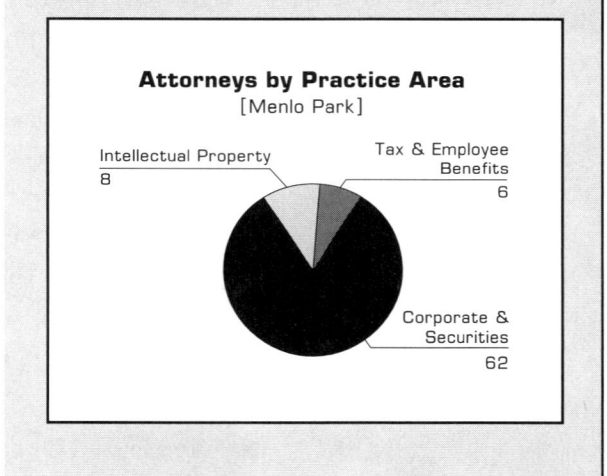

Attorneys by Location
- Kirkland, WA: 21
- Menlo Park, CA: 76

Attorneys by Practice Area [Menlo Park]
- Intellectual Property: 8
- Tax & Employee Benefits: 6
- Corporate & Securities: 62

THE SCOOP

Like venture capital? Wish you could join a startup? Went to law school? Never fear — just point yourself towards Venture Law Group. This tiny (under 100 lawyers) law firm has an appeal that outweighs its numbers; the law-cum-VC-firm hits our Top 50 survey for the first time at an impressive No. 37.

Dream firm

Craig Johnson's colleagues at Wilson, Sonsini, Goodrich & Rosati must have thought he was crazy when he left the partnership of the revered Silicon Valley firm in 1993 to open Venture Law Group. Johnson said he had a dream on a Friday night, climbed out of bed and wrote it all down, still in his pajamas. He envisioned a cross between a venture capital firm and a traditional law firm. By dawn, the attorney had filled fifteen pages of a notebook with details of a new kind of law firm, which would concentrate on "helping tech companies get started, find financing, and structure and grow their businesses," according to VLG literature. He gave his notice the next day and took 13 other attorneys from Wilson with him. Today, Venture Law Group is a tiny firm that has an influence much greater than its numbers in the VC-fevered atmosphere of California and Washington.

Upstarts in startups

The VLG pioneers aspired to a new business model entirely different from the big law firms in the Valley at the time. Their name said as much, passing up the typical string of founder names in order to evoke the nature of the practice they envisioned in their Menlo Park office. In 1994 and 1995, two other groups of lawyers from San Francisco's Brobeck, Phleger & Harrison and Morrison & Foerster joined them. They haven't looked back since.

Describing his brainchild to *Inc.* in 1998, Johnson suggested that readers "think of [Venture Law Group] as a McKinsey or a Boston Consulting Group for start-ups, with the added value that we can actually do the deals." VLG bills itself as a law firm focused on startups, helping launch new clients, and then leading them through the legal labyrinth that follows. When VLG takes on new clients, it behaves much like a VC firm at the outset, picking and choosing start ups that promise the most potential success. VLG doesn't actually finance its proteges, but does purchase a limited amount of equity (usually less than one percent) through a venture fund called VLG Investments. The firm positions itself as a lead player in defining client companies' business plans, providing strategic advice intended to build the select clients it represents into ultimately productive investments down the road. Firm policy dictates that clients are not charged for initial strategic planning — the bills kick in later, once the client company has secured funding.

Star Wars tactics

VLG's initial success depended heavily on Johnson's personal experience with startups and his extensive circle of contacts, built in his eighteen years at Wilson Sonsini. He developed strong relationships with the venture-capital community, which brought him recognition immediately when he embarked on his VLG journey. He says he can identify business plans that stand out from the pack, describing that moment of recognition as "target lock." Johnson made a "slightly scary analogy" in an April 2000 *Fortune* interview, describing his "mission as akin to that of Darth Vader trying to get target lock on Luke Skywalker as he maneuvers through the trenches of the Death Star." It's not about luck or having a great idea, he insisted in the interview. "Instead, it's all about striking the right partnerships, establishing a brand name and becoming big first. If you do those things right, you create huge barriers for potential competitors."

The few and the proud

From its inception, VLG has been downright picky in terms of clients, although by Valley VC standards it still takes on a lot of risky business. Even the most aggressive venture capital firms only back about ten to 20 new companies a year. Between 1993 and 1998, Venture Law Group invested in over 200 companies. Johnson has struggled to limit the growth of the firm, keeping the California office to under 100 lawyers and pledging to maintain the same cap in the new Washington branch. In order to promise clients that senior partners will be closely involved with each and every deal, VLG has limited its lawyers to counseling no more than 25 companies at a time (at other firms, each partner often counts 30 to 50 companies as clients). Johnson himself accepted only five of the 2,000 companies that sent him business plans in 1999 — the firm claims to turn away more than 95 percent of the work it is offered. Potential clients hoping for litigation assistance are out of luck at VLG; the firm, proud of its narrowcasting, refers those clients not seeking corporate, securities, tax, licensing and employment law services to other specialists.

The strategy has brough rewards in the form of heavy-duty clients and profits. The firm reaped $41 million in 1998 revenues and $53 million in 1999 — no doubt assisted by the $2 billion in IPOs VLG handled in 1999. VLG lists Hotmail Corporation, Intel Corporation, Cerent, Drugstore.com, garage.com, eToys, Oracle Corporation, WebTV and Yahoo! Inc. among its superstars. The demand for services has far outstripped VLG's supply of attorneys as well as the firm's commitment to intimate attention for each client. Associates averaged 11 billable hours a day in the early years. Craig

Johnson told *The National Law Journal* in October 1998 that the firm was "running the risk of burning out our associates," who started leaving despite sumptuous pay packages and profit-sharing plans. That year the firm took the right to accept new matters away from its 21 partners, passing the decisions to a new-business committee. Acceptance depends on whether a proposal falls into an area that interests VLG-affiliated VCs, if the firm has the resources to handle it, and how much risk is associated with the project.

eDeals

The fine-tooth-comb method of representation has resulted in some high-profile deals. In the fall of 1999, VLG represented Cerent in its $7.0 billion acquisition by Cisco, the largest acquisition of a private firm in history. The firm also headed up Yahoo!'s January 1999 purchase of GeoCities Inc. (the fifth most popular portal on the web — Yahoo! is the third) for $4.6 billion and Yahoo!'s April 1999 buy of Broadcast.com for $5.7 billion. Nortel Networks' grab of Clarify for $2.1 billion was another big M&A deal in 1999. That same year, the firm handled IPOs for Phone.com ($891.0 million raised), eTOYS ($166.4 million) and Drugstore.com ($90 million). Over the course of the year, VLG worked on 18 deals valued at more than $100 million and another 31 valued at less than $100 million. The firm tallied $30 million in paper profits in 1999 and expects to earn more than $100 million this year — impressive considering that VLG's revenue from legal fees (about $53 million in 1999) is only a fifth of the average New York firm's revenues.

Growing pains

Despite phenomenal financial success, VLG has begun to experience some of the internal struggles that it had hoped to avoid when establishing its niche. Turnover in Silicon Valley is notoriously high; associates and even partners are hard-pressed to turn down multi-million dollar offers to become in-house counsel at some of the very startups they counsel regularly at VLG. The firm has raised its compensation again and again and offers equity in potentially lucrative investments, making its associates some of the best-compensated in the country. Still, the dot com siren song is too strong for some lawyers who relish the opportunity to get in with a new company at ground level.

More ominous, however, may be the reminders that an innovative law firm might fall victim to its own philosophy of investment. In November 1998, partners James Brock Jr. and Robert Zipp proposed a plan to their colleagues that would have diluted their partnership draws and their involvement with VLG in exchange for larger equity stakes in their clients. The firm balked, afraid that the two powerful attorneys had inside information they were keeping from VLG. Brock and Zipp were offered two choices: cut all client ties and head out on their own terms after the next partnership draw or be fired immediately. They weren't willing to walk away from their client relationships, and in an acrimonious split with the firm, quit that very day. At that time, Brock and Zipp were the first partners ever to leave Venture Law Group.

Since then, a number of other associates have left "for business development or dot coms." Some have even headed to more traditional firms, seeking structure that VLG couldn't provide. While the base numbers of defectors might not be impressive, the impact is profound in a firm as small as this one and "the firm is a little concerned about this," ventures a corporate contact. As a result, the firm has restructured its pay plan several times, working to entice attorneys to stay with the firm without sacrificing the unique structure of Venture Law Group. VLG offers financial incentives to lawyers who start their own companies without leaving the firm. Craig Johnson has founded three: Grassroots.com, an online political action and fundraising service; garage.com, an Internet matching service for business plans and "angels" financiers which is expected to go public later this year; and Financial Engines, Inc., an online investment advisor.

Equity for all

As part of VLG's partnership approach to its clients, the firm asks its startup clients for the opportunity to buy into their businesses, purchasing common stock first and preferred stock after a company receives financing. All senior lawyers and partners turn over a pro rata portion of their profits to VLG Investments; that fund then takes a limited equity position in the firm's startup clients. Each partner responsible for bringing in a particular client also invests in that company. As a rule, VLG partners must take from 10 to 20 percent of the equity available to VLG, with the other 80 or 90 percent held for the firm's fund.

VLG also prides itself on offering unique compensation plans to all of its employees, not just attorneys. At the end of every quarter, VLG adds up its costs and overhead, deducts the total from its receipts and splits up the leftover money among everyone at VLG, from the secretaries and file clerks to the senior directors. Partners receive the biggest slice of the profits as a nod to their greater responsibility for bringing in business.

Outsourcing other work

As a result of the recent tech market boom, VLG has been besieged by requests for legal services that the firm doesn't have the capability to offer. Rather than shifting its focus and risking the loss of its original goals, VLG has found another solution. In March 1999, the firm teamed up with San Francisco's Orrick, Herrington & Sutcliffe to help clients who need work in practice areas like real estate, labor or intellectual property law. Orrick jumped at the opportunity to capitalize on VLG's client base and expand its tech company experience. The relationship has been such a success that Orrick opened a Seattle branch in response to prodding from VLG's Pacific Northwest office. When VLG takes on a new client, the firm gives strategic advice on the company's business model and on teaming with other industry contacts; Orrick lawyers then generate the supporting documentation that lock in the company's decision. By March 2000, Orrick had taken on about 115 of VLG's clients.

GETTING HIRED

Prepare for your closeup

Since VLG is still such a young firm, many of its new hires are laterals, so the reputation of a candidate's previous firm carries as much weight as his or her law school pedigree and grades. Still, "grades and schools are very important," according to a Valley corporate securities attorney and "you have to be in the top five to ten percent of a non-top-tier school — it's not that much different from other top firms" in that respect. VLG interviews on-campus at Boalt Hall, Chicago, Columbia, Harvard, Hastings, NYU and Stanford, among other schools. The firm is "extremely selective, especially in Menlo Park," states a Seattle associate, and is "pretty focused on brand-name schools as well as people skills and interaction with clients. We want people who present well and inspire confidence in clients."

JD/MBA nirvana

VLG's unique approach to law and business makes a difference in its hiring practice. The firm looks for more than the typical law school grad. "Since we view ourselves not only as a law firm but also as a consulting firm and an investment bank," explains a corporate associate, "we tend to gravitate towards business types," leading to a "disproportionate number of JD/MBAs." Also, VLG maintains "stringent standards" because the firm is so small — in 1999 14 laterals and six first-years came aboard, although in 2000 five to eight laterals and 15 first-years are expected. As a result, "people make an effort to get a sense of personality — it matters" in a firm with less than 100 attorneys in the Menlo Park office and just over 20 outside Seattle.

OUR SURVEY SAYS

Our partners are not like your partners

In keeping with efforts to design an entirely different kind of firm, Venture Law Group's partnership structure is unique to the firm. After four to five years, associates are promoted to senior attorney, then a few years later moved up to director. While it is "hard to gauge" directorship prospects "because we're still so young" (in Seattle, "all directors right now were laterals"), associates agree that "it seems making director is easier than at other firms due to demand in the Valley." As a corporate lawyer puts it, "no one really is here after seven years without making director."

The effects of redefining the hierarchy trickles down to general sentiment about directors' treatment of associates. Directors "treat us well," compliments a Menlo Park source. It's a "young firm, not a traditional, white-shoe firm — there is more parity and respect between directors and attorneys." The "concern with retaining associates" translates into a strong "open-door policy" and a "pretty egalitarian" atmosphere, suggests a Washington associate. All attorneys work for two directors. Several associates express that their directors have given them "a lot of space" and allow them to "hit the ground running — but always with a safety net." And since clients are banging down VLG's door these days, "attorneys are a more scarce resource than clients."

Collegial if not particularly social

Although VLG prides itself on a "family" atmosphere, the real family focus is outside of work. While everyone is "friendly and nice," there is "not a lot of outside socializing." The firm is "very family-oriented" and "attracts people who know what they want to do." Some attribute the atmosphere to the fact that "it's a niche firm" and so it "attracts a different type — more focused and serious." Others cite logistics as a reason that the social life comes down to "lots of lunching." Hanging out with other attorneys often "depends on who lives near each other" since many associates commute from San Francisco to Menlo Park. A Seattle associate swears that the newest VLG branch is "less stiff than Menlo Park" and is "pretty sociable within limitations of how hard we work." The firm notes that its artwork on the walls consists of pictures of VLG lawyers and their families — a nice way to show appreciation and save money on Picassos and Lichtensteins at the same time.

Associates consistently use the words "innovative," "dynamic," and "progressive" to describe this iconoclastic law firm. VLG is "creative" and "outside the mold." The "collegial," "West Coast sort of approach" means that "if you have a question you can always get an answer from anyone." A Washington respondent asserts that "people here have enough confidence in themselves that they can be normal people — they don't have to be stiff."

On top of the (tech) world

VLG associates can't say enough good things about their offices. The "best location in the Valley," boasts one lawyer. VLG headquarters are located on Sand Hill Road — the only principal law firm on the famed block that's home to numerous heavy-hitting VC firms and banks. A corporate contact waxes a tad hyperbolic in describing the "idyllic" site as "the most expensive real estate in the country, if not the world." In terms of practicality, the office is "accessible to people on the peninsula and San Francisco" — perfect for sundry commuters. Up north, Seattle associates "have decks around all the offices, overlooking the marina." One happy camper compares Venture Law Group to a country club, with fully-stocked refrigerators at all times.

Word processing support services are reportedly "adequate." Some associates seem hesitant to lavish praise since "we don't have 24-hour support due to the small number of associates and no litigation needs." While VLG may have less assistance than a large firm, "it does what it needs to do" and "you can always arrange help if you need it."

Since it opened, VLG has placed a premium on automation. To that end, the firm has developed a program that maintains a standard form of every document used in the practice, available in the computer database. Director of automation Jackson Ratcliffe has designed a system which allows every lawyer desktop access to all firm financial data. Attorneys can read up on current billings and collections, as well as detailed information on all of the firm's clients. About 80 percent of the legal staff have desktop scanners that can convert documents into the firm's word processing language so lawyers can edit and save their work into the firm's document management system. Associates rave about how much easier these programs make their professional lives.

Diversity: time will tell

While other law firms have been grappling with questions of diversity for years, VLG is "only beginning to encounter these issues, because it's a young firm." In terms of recruiting, "the firm makes no distinction between genders" and is "as progressive as any other firm around here," declares a California source, although the tech community is a "very male-dominated culture." A Seattle colleague adds that "one of our three directors is a female" and that "one of our senior attorneys took nine months off for maternity (three paid, six unpaid) and is venturing to director rank."

In terms of sheer numbers, minorities face the same challenges as women — there just aren't very many of them. "On the whole, Silicon Valley is pretty white bread," sighs a corporate associate. "The firm does try to recruit, but the end result is that our numbers are pretty low." With one Latino and "not many African-Americans" in the Washington branch, the place "feels pretty white," though at least one minority associate feels the wan hue of VLG has "never had any impact on my career. This is a young firm so the ideology of equality is pretty palpable." When asked about gays and lesbians at the firm, attorneys are even more nonchalant — one in Menlo Park says that "we would never think to ask" about sexual orientation. A co-worker in Seattle figures that the community is "so ahead of the curve here and in the Bay area that [sexuality] is a non-issue."

Glad to be here

Many interviewees say they "came for the business model" or because they "wanted to specialize in startups." Most are glad they made the move. While satisfaction "totally depends on the hours," the firm offers "very exciting work with exciting clients — it's somewhat scary how smart everyone is," enthuses a contented Valley employee. There is "a lot of responsibility early on" and lawyers "learn a lot quickly," leading to an "incredibly strong sense of culture that gives you a sense of being part of something significant, rather than just another associate at another law firm." More than one insider boasts that "this is the best corporate law job in America." Those irritated by the commute to Menlo Park will be happy to hear that VLG is considering opening new offices in Los Angeles and San Francisco.

How do we look?

How do other firms view Venture Law Group? VLG associates hazard a few guesses. "Until a few years ago, we were considered elitist, but now everyone is turning away work so that's changed," hypothesizes one who has watched the firm grow. "We were pioneers in taking equity in our clients," explains another source, and were perhaps "the most aggressive." Even if "some think we are too money-focused," VLG associates take comfort in the cliche that "imitation is the most sincere form of flattery." VLG associates may be considered "mavericks" who "don't abide by any rules," suggests a Valley insider, who says the image is a misperception, as is the idea that VLG is "not a law firm as much as a VC shop."

Keep that in mind and "be sure you want to be a corporate lawyer," because "this is a law firm, not VC." VLG-seekers would be well-advised to "be aggressive in asking questions" and "know that you want to specialize in startup work" because it involves "a lot of hand-holding" for clients. "Don't just get the dollar signs in your eyes," warns one Washington worker. "Be sure you know what you want."

Gunderson Dettmer Stough Villeneuve Franklin & Hachigian

VAULT.COM PRESTIGE RANKING: 38

155 Constitution Drive
Menlo Park, CA 94025
(650) 321-2400
Fax: (650) 321-2800
www.gunder.com

LOCATIONS

Menlo Park, CA (HQ)
Austin, TX
Boston, MA
New York, NY

MAJOR DEPARTMENTS/PRACTICES

Corporate
Employment
Executive Compensation
Intellectual Property
Tax

THE STATS

No. of attorneys: 110
No. of offices: 4
Summer associate offers: 14 out of 14 (Menlo Park, CA 2000)
Hiring Attorneys: Gregory Lemmer, Daniel E. O'Connor, Anthony J. McCusker

PAY

All Domestic Offices, 2000
1st year: $125,000 + $20,000 guaranteed bonus
2nd year: $135,000 + $25,000 guaranteed bonus
3rd year: $150,000 + $30,000 guaranteed bonus
4th year: $165,000 + $30,000 guaranteed bonus
5th year: $185,000 + $30,000 guaranteed bonus
6th year: $195,000 + $30,000 guaranteed bonus
7th year: $205,000 + $30,000 guaranteed bonus
Summer associate: $2,400/week

NOTABLE PERKS

- $2,000 home computer allowance
- Vending machines — quarter an item
- Pool and foosball tables
- Pretzels and chocolates and socials on Fridays

THE BUZZ
What attorneys at other firms are saying about this firm

- "God bless Bob"
- "Frat house"
- "The platinum standard for corporate"
- "Flash in the pan — won't survive when Nasdaq craters"

UPPERS

- Can wear jeans to work every day
- All tech work, all of the time
- Market leader in pay

DOWNERS

- Unpredictable work
- Hours sometimes "really crappy"
- Corporate practice for VC community very intense

KEY COMPETITORS

Cooley Godward
Venture Law Group
Wilson Sonsini Goodrich & Rosati

EMPLOYMENT CONTACT

Ms. Corinne Dritsas
Director of Legal Recruiting
(650) 463-5248
cdritsas@gunder.com

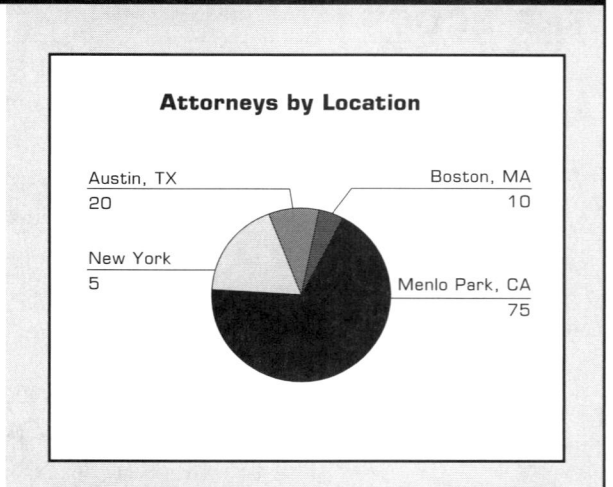

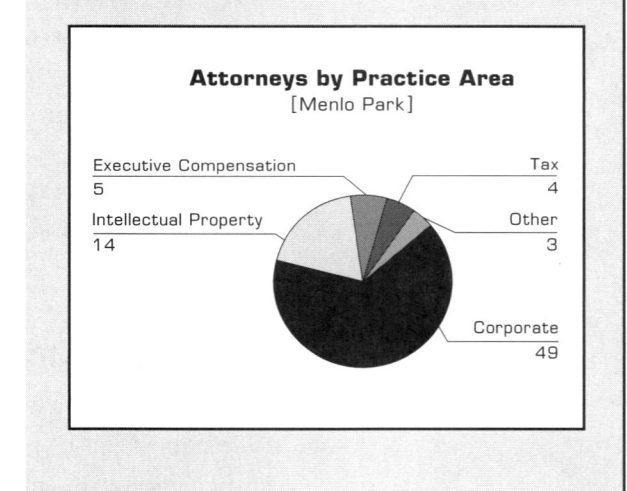

Attorneys by Location

- Austin, TX: 20
- Boston, MA: 10
- New York: 5
- Menlo Park, CA: 75

Attorneys by Practice Area
[Menlo Park]

- Executive Compensation: 5
- Tax: 4
- Intellectual Property: 14
- Other: 3
- Corporate: 49

THE SCOOP

In five short years, Gunderson Dettmer Stough Villeneuve Franklin & Hachigian has grown from one office with 18 lawyers to four offices with a total of 110 lawyers. The firm has received rave reviews on its summer associate program and grabbed national headlines for its huge salary hike. Now Gunderson has put the finishing touches on its astounding ascent by breaking into the Vault.com Top 50.

Gigantic Gunderson growth

From the time of its founding in 1995, the story of Gunderson Dettmer has followed a script of constant expansion. In September of that year, a group of six partners and over twenty associates abandoned Brobeck, Phleger & Harrison's technology group to start a different type of firm focusing on the rapidly expanding technology sector. A year and a half later, Gunderson opened its first office in the South's tech mecca, Austin, Texas. The Austin office now boasts 20 lawyers. In September 1999, Gunderson became one of the first high tech Northern California firms to take on the Boston market. The outpost has 17 lawyers in its ranks headed by firm founder Jay Hachigian. In March 2000, the firm launched a new office in the Big Apple. The firm returned to its roots to help staff its New York office, taking Kenneth McVay and Babak Yaghmaie from Brobeck, Pleger & Harrison in early 2000.

The Gunderson effect

The firm takes recruiting seriously and even makes being the "employer of choice" in the legal marketplace part of its mission statement. Since ranking at the top of *The America Lawyer's* summer associate survey in 1997, Gunderson has been a hot destination for legal job seekers. Gunderson offers its associates a focus on the cutting-edge tech economy and a relaxed atmosphere. Gunderson has a year-round casual dress policy — and casual means casual. Jeans are completely acceptable for all Gundersonians.

While quality summer programs and casual dress have their allure, nothing attracts talent like money. Gunderson grabbed national attention in December 1999 when the firm raised starting salaries 50 percent to an unprecedented $125,000. It also threw in a guaranteed $20,000 bonus for good measure. In addition, the firm offers its associates shares in an investment pool. The raises touched off a wave of salary hikes that started in Silicon Valley but quickly spread east to New York and Washington. The so-called Gunderson effect marked the first times pay hikes have originated on the left coast (the traditional originator of pay hikes being New York's Cravath, Swaine & Moore.) But unlike some of the salary followers, the firm leaders say they do not peg the new salaries or bonuses to hours billed, "never have, never will."

"The purpose of raising the salaries was to help in attracting top talent, to beat the ferocious struggle for talent, and to work fewer hours," one insider explains. The firm says that its focus on the tech sector sparked the raises. "If there are to be emerging growth company lawyers in the future they will be compensated at levels that are competitive with alternative emerging growth company career paths (in-house counsel, business development, venture capital, investment banking)." Gunderson Dettmer also claims that it can afford the raises because it focuses on the areas of the market that generate "superior financial returns." (For the time being, that's the tech market.)

Not a legal department store

Despite its reputation for high pay and high-quality work, Gunderson is not for everyone. The firm prides itself on not being a "legal department store," pointing out that it does not have "vast armies of lawyers offering a smorgasbord of legal services. We operate with focus and efficiency." Those young legal hopefuls interested in litigation, prosecuting patents or T&E work would be wise to give Gunderson a pass.

Gunderson specializes in doing corporate work such as corporate formation, financing, and public offerings for startups and other tech companies. Gunderson counts B2B services provider Ariba, e-consulting firm Scient, and Internet caching appliance maker Cacheflow among its technology clients. The firm has also done work for many star venture capital firms, such as Accel Partners, Redpoint Ventures, eBay investor Benchmark Capital, and Hummer Windblad Venture Partners. Gunderson has also catered to investment banks including Morgan Stanley, Goldman Sachs and CS First Boston. In addition Gunderson does work for medical and health care companies.

Gunderson Dettmer divides its practice into four basic areas: (1) corporate securities; (2) IP; (3) executive compensation and employment; and (4) tax. But the firm does not handle its workload in the traditional department-centered manner. Instead, Gunderson Dettmer relies on what it calls a "client-centric" approach. The firm creates small teams of lawyers from different practice areas to build a relationship with the client and handle that particular client's needs.

Crazy for IPOs

Gunderson Dettmer and its tech clients were kept very busy in 1999. The firm worked on twenty-four IPOs that year. Robert Gunderson, Jeffrey Higgin, Jonathan Noble, David Davis, and Tabetha Nakasone worked on PlanetRx.com's October 1999 IPO. In February 1999, the managing partner of Gunderson's Austin office, Brian Beard, handled the IPO of software firm Vignette, which raised $75 million. The firm has also helped Heartport Inc, a manufacturer of medical supplies, and software developer Check Point Software Technologies Ltd. go public.

Lots of merging going on

Gunderson's corporate lawyers have had plenty to do in the M&A area as well. In January 2000, Scott Dettmer, Steven Franklin and Daniel Niehans advised DSL tech company Promatory Communications in its purchase by Nortel Networks for $778 million. The previous April, Gunderson helped in the sale of another of its clients, Shasta Networks, to Nortel. Gibson, Dunn & Crutcher worked with Nortel on both acquisitions.

In December 1999, partners Robert Gunderson and Daniel Niehans, as well as associates Renee Lanam, David Davis, and Heather Shane advised Redback Networks on its $4.3 billion merger with software company Siara Systems. In January 1998, Robert Gunderson and Steven Spurlock helped software maker Avant! Corp. acquire Technology Modeling Associates for $95 million in stock. And the previous year, Jay Hachigian, Daniel Niehans and Thomas Villeneuve advised MDL Information Systems when the software maker was acquired by Reed Elsevier (the owner of Lexis-Nexis) for $320 million in cash.

Son of Wal-Mart

In January 2000, Gunderson Dettmer helped Wal-Mart give birth to a new online presence. The retailer launched Wal-Mart.com, a separate company owned by both Wal-Mart and venture capital firm Accel Partners. Wal-mart had an online presence since 1996 which had been generating less than stellar sales. By creating a separate company specifically for the Internet, Wal-mart hopes to make a dent in the e-commerce world. Robert Gunderson, Thomas Villeneuve, Michael Taviss and Anthony McCusker served as counsel to Wal-Mart.com, while lawyers from Weil, Gotshal & Manges advised the parent company.

GETTING HIRED

"We are not school snobs"

Insiders at Gunderson say the firm looks at the usual hiring criteria: personality, school, and grades. Gunderson recruits from top schools such as Michigan, Harvard, Stanford, Berkeley, UVA, NYU, Columbia, and the University of Texas. But some associates say you don't have to necessarily be in the top tier of law schools to enjoy the Gunderson effect. "We are not school snobs. There is no cutoff when it comes to your school."

Similarly, Gunderson takes laterals from the nationally recognized law firms or distinguished regional firms. For laterals the firm looks closely for applicable experience working with startups or doing IP work. Associates say the firm has taken litigators into its ranks but they usually will drop a few levels in pay. The firm also values people with an MBA, accounting degree or business background. But Gunderson lawyers say that a technical background is not necessarily a prerequisite to getting hired. Gunderson's corporate group reportedly went through a big lateral hiring phase in late 1999 and early 2000.

Those who get callbacks at Gunderson can expect a full day of interviews, around half of which will be with partners. At least one interviewer will be on the hiring committee. Insiders say the interviews are casual. In fact, applicants are not even expected to show up in a suit, according to sources. The interviewers usually won't test your legal knowledge. Rather they are interested in finding out if you are a "good fit" for the firm. "We put a high premium on personality," says one attorney.

Associates say that candidates should show that they understand the firm and its place in the market. In other words, expressing an interest in the firm's litigation practice won't fly too well at Gunderson interviews. Another contact advises, "Show why you want to do this stuff."

OUR SURVEY SAYS

The freewheeling startup feeling

Associates call Gunderson Dettmer "a very friendly place where people take their work but not themselves too seriously." Insiders report the atmosphere at Gunderson is not unlike that of Gunderson's startup clients. One associate says that although Gunderson still has an entrepreneurial feel, as Gunderson gets bigger "it is becoming more [like a regular] firm." Some describe the atmosphere at the firm as "freewheeling" and "loose." "The firm is very hard-working but casual and laid-back at the same time," raves another source.

The casual atmosphere is evidenced by the dress code at Gunderson. It's nonexistent. Jeans are acceptable all year round. One source says, "Issues like what you are wearing are kind of like — who cares?" Of course when meeting clients, lawyers have to dress appropriately. But one Austin lawyer says that isn't usually much of a restriction, because the clients are often wearing shorts and sandals.

Insiders also praise Gunderson Dettmer's "team approach" to work, and they wax particularly enthusiastic about their fellow lawyers. "Gunderson has the cream of the crop as far as attorneys and experience," boasts one lawyer. "I'd hang out with the people here even if I weren't working with them," claims another. "The sort of individual we seek to attract to the firm is one who could as easily step into an in-house counsel or business development role at an emerging growth company or, alternatively, become a venture capitalist or investment banker," explains a Gunderson lawyer. But associates do emphasize that the Gunderson lawyers "work hard to satisfy our clients." Another lawyer summed up the Gunderson experience this way: "If you're going to practice law in a law firm, it doesn't get any better in terms of pay, work, and great clients."

The flat firm

Vault.com sources say they have a good relationship with their bosses. "Partners treat associates well. They don't talk down to them or scream. Those who have been at other firms will see the difference," one source claims. "No one is ever criticized or chastised for the work they're doing," agrees another Gundersonian. Associates also say the partners keep themselves accessible. "The firm is open door, with the exception of Bob Gunderson, who is just not in the office that much," observes an attorney. "When associates have issues, partners listen and weigh in discussions," says another source.

Associates claim that Gunderson Dettmer does not have a hierarchical atmosphere. "It is a very flat firm. No one gets any special privileges," notes a lawyer. Another concurs, "The partners are the best I have ever seen. The attitude is that no person at the firm is any more valuable than anyone else." In fact, insiders say partners offices are the same size as the associates' digs and that there are no corner offices, just corner conference rooms. Lawyers in the Austin office recall that before the firm moved into its new offices, space was running out. The partners were reportedly the first ones to offer to double up. Gunderson lawyers also say that the firm's system of partner compensation limits internal competition. Partners are not compensated based on the work they bring to the firm. "It is not an 'eat what you kill' system," explains one lawyer.

The married firm

Insiders say Gunderson Dettmer endeavors to balance associates' work life with their social life. Sources also tell Vault.com that many Gunderson associates have spouses waiting for them at home. "There are not a lot of single people. Some say people used to go out together more in the early days of the firm. But now a lot of them have gotten hitched — sometimes to each other," says one source. Another attorney claims, "[Gunderon is] an extremely married firm. But the unmarried groups are very, very social." "People come in early and try to get home and see their families. But we always have lunch together," notes another contact.

Gunderson Dettmer features twice-monthly socials for partners and staff. One associate reports that the associates always throw a happy hour when the partners are away at a retreat. "But the partners know about it," he explains sheepishly. Gunderson Dettmer sponsors a yearly retreat for both attorneys and paralegals which in 2000 featured sea kayaking. In October there is a firm-wide anniversary party — costumes required. In addition, Gunderson's partners will throw dinner parties at their houses for new attorneys.

Sure, we'll show you the money

Gunderson's pay scale has been well-publicized. But in case you've missed the lucrative news, the firm pays $125,000, $135,000, $150,000, $165,000, $185,000, $195,000 and $205,000 for first- through seventh-years respectively. This pay scheme has become the new gold standard in the legal industry and the source of grief for lawyers whose firms will not match. In addition Gunderson offers first-years a guaranteed bonus of $20,000, second-years a guaranteed bonus of $25,000 and all other associates a $30,000 bonus.

Although associates expected to get a raise they didn't expect the whopping fifty percent hike. "I was floored — totally blown away," says one attorney. Indeed, after the initial announcement some attorneys believed they had heard the figure incorrectly. "People think it's extremely generous — no one gripes," claims one lawyer. Associates say the raises were "deserved but appreciated." "The partners have acknowledged the value associates bring to the law firm. They also recognize that competition is intense," according to one contact. One lawyer was particularly thankful that his bonus was not attached to hours. "It's all about the guaranteed bonus."

Working like it was 1999

Associates say Gunderson Dettmer doesn't want its associates to be slaves to the firm. "The firm recognizes that we went to law school to improve our lives, not to find a substitute for them," say one associate. Insiders say even when the raises were announced, "the firm wanted to make sure people knew they were not trying to get people to work harder." Despite the firm's intentions, many lawyers say they have been working longer hours. "The hours on a prolonged basis can really take it out of you," complains another lawyer. "We have a lot of work and we still need to get some more people," says one lawyer. Another source admits, "[My schedule] could be better but it is by no means crushing."

Although Gunderson does not have any billing requirements, the firm sets a yearly "target" at 1,975 hours. But lawyers say most attorneys in 1999 billed anywhere from 2,100 to 2,500 hours or more. "The hours in 1999 were really crappy," states one source. Some say the work load has eased a bit in 2000. "This may change if the market pops back up or there are consolidations," opines an associate.

Better than average retention

Most insiders feel that Gunderson's retention rate is "better that average. "There are still people leaving for other opportunities, but the tide is stemming," according to one associate. "Since the [April 2000 Nasdaq] market crash, [the retention rate] has been great," rejoices another insider. Few if any leave to go to another law firm. Associates report that those who do leave aren't going to other firms but usually to startups. "The ones who leave get the types of offers that you'll kick yourself if you don't take," explains one attorney. As of spring 2000, the Austin office had only lost one associate in its history.

Assignment system

Gunderson Dettmer does not have a traditional assignment system with one assigning partner. Instead, every week associates at Gunderson attend a work-flow meeting. They sit around the table and see who has time on his or her hands and who has too much work. All the partners then get a work-flow report and will seek out associates for new assignments based on their availability. Eventually Gunderson lawyers essentially become assigned to a client and will handle that client's needs as they arise. Associates seem pretty happy with this set-up and rave about the "broad mix" of work to which it exposes them.

Sharing the grunt work

Insiders tell Vault.com that the grunt work is also evenly spread out. "There is not a cherry-picking mentality where senior people get all of the good stuff," says a Gundersonian. "Everybody does due diligence, including the partners," according to another contact. Associates say they get "a ton of responsibility" early in their careers. "The firm is geared to people who want to take on responsibility early. If there is something you don't know you have to go out and find the answer." In addition, associates say they benefit from the firm's tech emphasis. "The practice is focused, so you get expertise quickly." "From the second year on, you're running most of the deals by yourself," boasts a contact. To help newcomers along, each associate is assigned a partner mentor and the partners are reportedly efficient in getting lawyers a quick answer to their questions. "Partners will take as much time as needed to explain things," one source tells Vault.com.

Associates attend weekly training sessions during their first year at the firm. The firm also sponsors periodic training sessions for the rest of the associates as well — many of which are coordinated with all of the offices through teleconferencing. The firm has also assigned one senior associate to be in charge of attorney development full time. "He puts together menus of legal updates and makes sure everyone is getting the training they need," an insider explains.

Light and airy offices

Gunderson has two offices in Menlo Park. One of the offices is a converted warehouse while the other "looks sort of like an ad agency." "They try to make the offices look like our clients' offices," one source explains. "It is not your formal, red-carpet type of place," says another contact. The warehouse office has "a light and airy feeling." The space features exposed brick and drop down ceilings. Gunderson lawyers should be careful about falling asleep at their desks, because the walls of the office are glass. The firm's Texas lawyers moved into new offices in February 2000. The new digs have essentially the same look and feel as the Menlo Park branch. That is no coincidence. The same architect designed both offices.

Attorneys say the individual lawyers' offices are very modest and "don't have a lot of decorations." "Everybody shows up, does work, and gets out of there. There is no need to decorate extravagantly or put in a couch," one insider says.

Gunderson lawyers also rave about the support staff. "We have top-notch people," one contact says. Associates report that the firm gives paralegals a lot of responsibility and practically treats them like first-year associates. But Gunderson attorneys say the firm is short-staffed on paralegals: "Everybody needs help, so we wish had more." Attorneys at the Gunderson satellite office tell Vault.com that much of their computer support and word processing work is done out of the Menlo Park office.

Improving situation for women

In the early days of Gunderson the firm had very few women. But insiders say the firm has made great strides to rectify the situation. "Two years ago, it was bad. Now it's about 50 percent women," according to one source. But associates report there are few female lawyers in mid- to senior-level positions. Many lawyers believe as time goes by the situation will even itself out. "The firm is getting there now. Many women associates are around the third-year level now," an attorney reports. Although associates report the firm has been supportive of new families, there is no official flex-time policy.

As far as recruiting minorities, Gunderson lawyers feel the firm needs to do better. "We wish we had more minorities. I haven't even seen any African-American candidates," one source reports. The firm appears to be improving in this area as well, however. In spring 2000 it hired two African-American attorneys and reports having a very diverse summer class. Associates say they don't think Gunderson has a hostile environment for minorities. "We don't care about your sex or race. We care about your qualifications. We are a performance-based office," insists a Gundersonian.

Not a pro bono leader

While Gunderson may be the place to be for tech work, it is far from a leader in pro bono. The firm does not have any formal procedures for giving out pro bono assignments and Vault.com sources at Gunderson say that pro bono assignments have been few and far between. Most insiders seem to attribute the lack of pro bono hours to the firm's tech focus. "Because of the type of work that we do there are fewer pro bono opportunities for which we are qualified," explains one associate. "The firm doesn't discourage pro bono but it is harder as a corporate firm," concurs another source. One associate confesses, "We are very busy but should do more [pro bono]."

You can be a partner too

The partnership track at Gunderson Dettmer is six to eight years long (relatively short). Most associates feel their chances of making partner are reasonably good. "The firm doesn't hire summer clerks unless it plans on making them associates, and it doesn't hire associates unless it thinks they will make partner," one source explains. Insiders report that in 1999 five attorneys were up for partner and all five got the promotion. Associates don't necessarily have to bring in business to make partner. Perhaps more vital is developing existing client relationships. "The question, is do they keep clients happy? That is where referrals come from," explains a contact. "You control your own destiny at a fairly young age. At some point you should start acting like a partner," advises another lawyer.

"The firm recognizes that we went to law school to improve our lives, not to find a substitute for them."

— *Gunderson associate*

39 PRESTIGE RANKING

Hogan & Hartson LLP

555 13th Street, NW
Washington, DC 20004-1109
(202) 637-5600
Fax: (202) 637-5910
www.hhlaw.com

LOCATIONS

Washington, DC (HQ)
Baltimore, MD • Boulder, CO • Colorado Springs, CO • Denver, CO • Irvine, CA • Los Angeles, CA • McLean, VA • Miami, FL • New York, NY • Rockville, MD • Brussels • London • Moscow • Paris • Prague • Tokyo • Warsaw

MAJOR DEPARTMENTS/PRACTICES

Antitrust • Communications • Community Services • Corporate & Securities • Education • Energy • Environmental • Financial Transactions • FDA • Franchise • Government Contracts • Health • Intellectual Property • International Trade • Internet • Labor • Legislative • Litigation (Trial & Appellate) • Private Equity/Venture Capital • Project Finance • Public Finance • Real Estate • Tax • Technology • Transportation

THE STATS

No. of attorneys: 737
No. of offices: 18
Summer associate offers: 45 out of 45 (Firm-wide, 1999)
Managing Partner: Bob Glen Odle
Hiring Partners: Robert J. Waldman, Robert B. Duncan, & Donna A. Boswell

PAY

Washington, DC, Baltimore, and McLean, 2000
1st year: $125,000
2nd year: $135,000
3rd year: $150,000
4th year $165,000
5th year: $180,000
6th year: $190,000
7th year: $200,000
8th year: $210,000
Summer associate: $2,400/week

Boulder and Denver, 2000
1st year: $110,000
2nd year: $120,000
3rd year: $130,000
4th year: $145,000
5th year: $155,000
6th year: $165,000
7th year: $175,000
8th year: $185,000
Summer associate: $1,900/week

New York, 2000
1st year: $125,000
2nd year: $135,000
3rd year: $150,000
4th year: $165,000
5th year: $180,000
6th year: $195,000
7th year: $210,000
8th year: $225,000

NOTABLE PERKS

- Paid moving expenses
- Laptop subsidy ($2,000)
- Back-up day care
- "Plenty of cocktail parties"

THE BUZZ
What attorneys at other firms are saying about this firm

- "DC meat-and-potatoes practice"
- "Overrated"
- "If I needed a lawyer I'd call them"
- "Won't be in New York in seven years"

UPPERS

- Equity investments for associates
- Excellent communication from management
- "Humane" and flexible billable hours system

DOWNERS

- "Crummy" coffee in firm vending machines
- Cramped DC offices
- Slow adaptation to casual dress

KEY COMPETITORS

Akin, Gump, Strauss, Haver & Feld
Arnold & Porter
Covington & Burling
Skadden, Arps, Slate, Meagher & Flom
Williams & Connolly
Wilmer, Culter & Pickering

EMPLOYMENT CONTACT

Ms. Ellen M. Swank
Director of Recruitment
(202) 637-8601
EMSwank@hhlaw.com

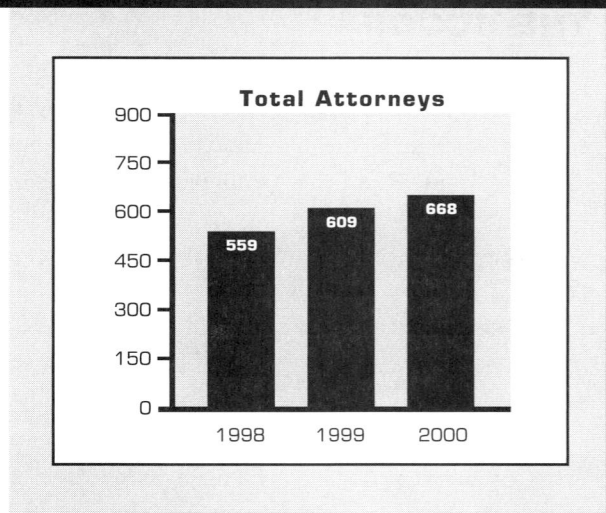

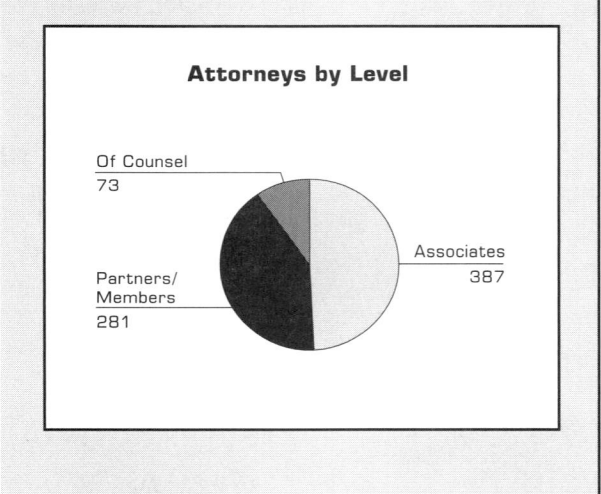

Total Attorneys
- 1998: 559
- 1999: 609
- 2000: 668

Attorneys by Level
- Of Counsel: 73
- Partners/Members: 281
- Associates: 387

QUALITY OF LIFE RANKINGS [ASSOCIATES RATE THEIR OWN FIRM]

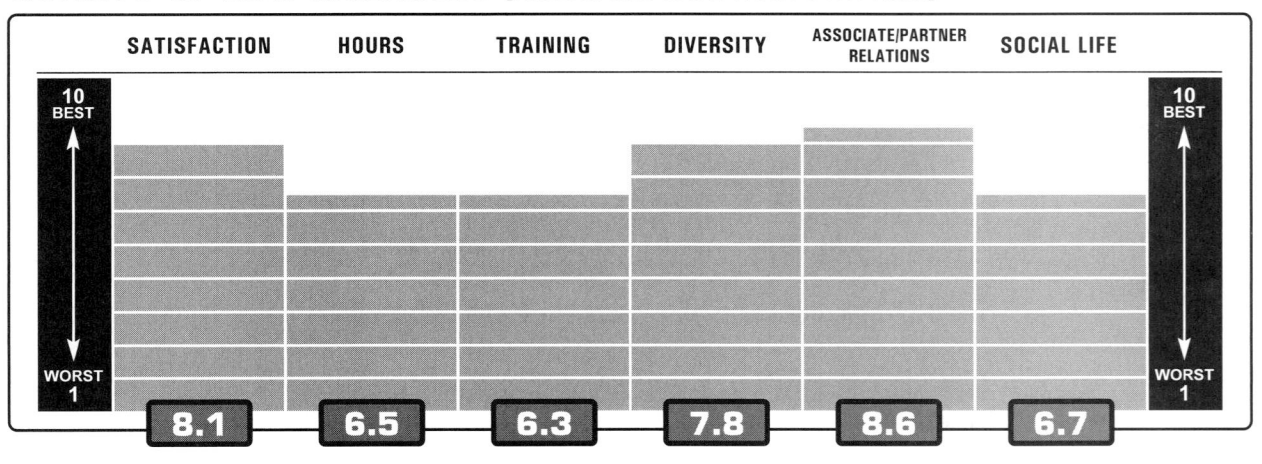

SATISFACTION	HOURS	TRAINING	DIVERSITY	ASSOCIATE/PARTNER RELATIONS	SOCIAL LIFE
8.1	6.5	6.3	7.8	8.6	6.7

THE SCOOP

Hogan & Hartson traces its roots back to 1904 when Frank Hogan, a respected trial attorney, founded a firm in Washington, DC. In 1925, Nelson Hartson, an attorney with the Internal Revenue Service, joined the firm to boost its tax practice. Thirteen years later, Hartson became a full partner and the name Hogan & Hartson was adopted. The firm now has approximately 730 attorneys in 18 offices worldwide.

Hogan's hero

Hogan is now run by Bob Odle, a University of Texas alum who has been with the firm since 1966 and once served as an aide to former House of Representatives Speaker Sam Rayburn. Odle managed the firm's expansion after his 1989 appointment as managing partner. In 1990 the firm opened its London office and added shops in Brussels, Belgium, Paris, Warsaw, Poland and Prague in 1991. Three years later, H&H opened a Moscow post, followed by a Budapest office in 1996. Surprisingly, it wasn't until 1998 that the firm set up shop in New York. That office handles corporate, litigation, M&A, and health regulatory matters. The firm supplemented the New York practice by merging with local firm Davis Weber & Edwards in April 2000. H&H also absorbed Davis' Miami office. All told, the firm added 35 lawyers as a result of the merger. Despite the rapid expansion, the DC office continues to be the cornerstone of the practice; approximately 440 lawyers, or two-thirds of the firm's total, practice in the capital.

Lobby lawyers

Considering that the firm has such a large DC presence, it's not surprising that lobbying and legislative issues are one of Hogan's strengths. The firm counts several Washington insiders among the fold. David Skaggs joined the firm as of counsel after serving 12 years in the House of Representatives for Colorado. Robert Michel acts as an advisor to the firm; he served 28 years as a representative from Illinois, including 14 years as House Minority Leader. Firm attorneys have counseled numerous government officials and political endeavors at various levels, including Bob Dole and the 1992 George Bush/Dan Quayle presidential campaign. In fact, Hogan has, with admirable even-handedness, counseled both Republican and Democratic candidates in the 1992, 1996 and 2000 Presidential campaigns.

H&H's lobbying efforts have influenced several important issues. Partner Agnes Dover, formerly with the Department of Energy, has been involved in Year 2000 legislative issues. Lance Bultena, counsel at Hogan, worked on the Product Liability Fairness Act as well as tobacco settlement legislation. The firm also successfully represented the Business Coalition for U.S.-China Trade, which, unsurprisingly, favored the passage of a bill permanently normalizing trade relations with China.

M&A proves triumphant

Hogan's mergers and acquisitions practice has worked on some formidable deals as well. The firm represented Jacor Communications in its $4.4 billion acquisition by Clear Channel Communications in 1998. In 1999 H&H represented Williams Communications when SBC Communications invested $500 million in the Oklahoma communications company.

Additionally, the firm has worked on the antitrust aspect of several deals. Hogan represented General Dynamics in its merger with Gulfstream Aerospace. Hogan lawyers also counseled Mobil on that company's $81 billion union with Exxon — one of the largest mergers ever. The merger was completed in November 1999. ISP enthusiasts should note that Hogan represented MindSpring Enterprises in a "merger of equals" with Earthlink to form the second largest Internet access provider in the United States in 2000.

Another notable deal was Hogan's involvement in the MediaOne-Deutsche Telekom deal — the largest M&A transaction to date in Central and Eastern Europe. Hogan represented MediaOne in the disposition of its wireless telephone interests in Poland, Hungary and Russia to Deutsche Telekom for $2 billion. The agreement was executed in October 1999. The deal called upon Hogan attorneys from the firm's Washington, Brussels, London, Warsaw, Budapest and Moscow offices.

Practiced litigation

The firm's litigation team is quite impressive — it argued 12 cases in front of the U.S. Supreme Court between 1997 and 2000. The appellate practice is headed by John Roberts, named one of the top 10 civil litigators by *The National Law Journal* in 1999.

Several cases have earned the firm headlines recently. In January 1999, the firm negotiated a settlement on behalf of Downey Communications and Marketing Management & Information. They had been sued by a woman who claimed the companies rescinded a job offer after discovering she was pregnant. One month later, client DaimlerChrysler was hit with a $60 million jury verdict in connection with problems with air bags in certain automobiles.

That same month, the Supreme Court ruled in favor of the National Collegiate Athletic Association (NCAA) in a Title IX case. The court ruled that the NCAA, the firm's client, was not subject to the federal law governing gender equality in college athletics. In November 1999, the firm represented Intergraph Corp., a computer workstation manufacturer, against Intel Corp. in a suit claiming Intel had violated an antitrust injunction requiring Intel to supply Intergraph with microprocessor information. The absence of the information crippled Intergraph's business, the suit charged, and forced the company to lay off over 200 employees. In January 2000, the firm represented Cinergy in a pollution suit filed by the Department of Justice and the Environment Protection Agency.

Bunny ears

Lovers of mildly racy daytime TV will applaud Hogan & Hartson's First Amendment victory before the Supreme Court on behalf of Playboy Entertainment Group, the cable television programming subsidiary of Playboy Enterprises. The Court affirmed, 5 to 4, a permanent injunction against Section 505 of the Communications Decency Act of 1996. What this effectively means is that Playboy is free to transmit its fleshy broadcasts 24 hours a day instead of confining them to hours of the day when children are less likely to view them. This is the first Supreme Court decision affirming that even the most trashy cable television is entitled to the highest level of First Amendment protection.

So pro bono

Hogan & Hartson has a firm commitment to pro bono practice. In 1970 the firm established a Community Services Department responsible for staffing and managing pro bono cases. The firm has worked with a number of public interest groups, including the American Civil Liberties Union and the National Association for the Advancement of Colored People (NAACP). One major victory was in *Mainstream Loudoun v. Board of Trustees of the Loudon County Public Libraries,* a celebrated First Amendment case where the public libraries in Loudon County, Virginia banned certain web sites from library computers. A federal judge banned the ban, equating the practice with book burning. The firm also won the release of Victor Henderson, who was arrested and jailed due to a change in the Maryland law that was enacted after his initial release from prison. In a segregation case that dragged on for 25 years, Hogan (along with the NAACP) secured an agreement from the state of Maryland to build more schools in African-American communities in Prince Georges County.

According to insiders, the firm stands behind their stated commitment to pro bono work. Up to 100 hours of donated legal services count towards the bonus requirement and one lawyer says H&H has the "preeminent commitment of any large firm towards pro bono." "Many of the partners are heavily involved and most associates do genuinely substantive pro bono as a matter of course," reports one source.

GETTING HIRED

Focused search

Like all top firms, Hogan tries to focus their search on top law schools and outstanding performers at lower-tier schools. The firm's web site (www.hhlaw.com) says H&H interviewed students at 29 law schools in the fall of 1999. "Top law schools are significant but not a prerequisite," one insider says. One litigation associate feels the firm has its favorites, even among top schools. "The firm is unfortunately too selective with respect to certain schools that have not historically sent enough associates here (such as NYU or Columbia) and takes too many, too easily from schools that are represented highly here — Georgetown, for example."

"Hogan hires not just on pure academic and professional achievement (although those two areas are critical), but also on personality, interest and character," says one lawyer. Selectivity seems to vary by department. "Corporate associates seem to have an easier time gaining employment," says one source, "while litigation associates seem to have a tougher row to hoe."

Interview process: know your cases

Those campus interviewees who make the cut can expect half-day interviews at the firm's offices with about five or six lawyers, including one from the recruiting committee. Questions, naturally, vary by interviewer. "At one extreme, there are people who will ask substantive questions about recent Supreme Court cases," warns one lawyer. "Personally, I don't like to ask about someone's activities at school. I want to hear about their personal interests, why they are interested in Hogan and why they are interested in Washington. I want to see how serious they are about staying."

OUR SURVEY SAYS

Arrogant not appreciated, but friendly is

When describing the firm's corporate culture, many associates resort to the word "friendly." One Washington associate says that "Hogan places heavy emphasis on personality in hiring decisions — arrogance is definitely not appreciated." Despite the firm's size, don't worry about getting lost in the shuffle. "Hogan is truly a big firm, but it does its very best to make sure associates are not simply cogs in the wheel," says one lawyer. "The overall atmosphere is serious yet collegial." "Hogan's focus is on quality work, which means having people who are honest, smart, friendly and willing to go the extra mile when necessary to meet a client's needs," reports one attorney.

That's not to say the firm doesn't have its problems. "[Hogan] is conservative and slow-moving, as is to be expected of a firm of its size," says one source. "Associates must be proactive about locating the kind of work that they want to do or the people they want to work with and pursuing them." Overall, "Hogan likes to think of itself as a more humane firm that cares about its attorneys but the push for money and the hours are encroaching."

Happy together

Insiders report excellent partner-associate relationships. "I have never been mistreated by a partner, and the partners I work for are consistently pleasant to me and understanding of my desire to spend more time at home with my family," says one associate. "I have only worked directly with one partner so far as an associate," reports a recent hire. "That partner gives me a lot of responsibility but also expects me to be available for anything at whim." There are a few bad apples that the firm tries to rein in. "I've heard some stories of a few screamers," says one lawyer but another contact reports "any time a partner has not treated me with respect (and those times are few), the other partners have immediately shown their support for me and their intolerance for disrespectful behavior."

The social butterflies of Hogan

Firm insiders say that "weekly happy hours sponsored by Hogan keep associates in touch" and that social life is generally active. "If you're young, single and want to hang out at a lot of cocktail parties, there is plenty of that," says one DC lawyer. You'd better make friends fast, though. Lateral associates report difficulty developing peer relationships. "My impression is that Hogan is very social among junior folks, although it appears a bit high-school and cliquish," says one lateral hire. "It's just not a very friendly place for laterals, in the sense that most mid- to senior-level people are not super-interested in socializing at the office."

Hours appropriate to human beings

Hogan & Hartson seems to allow for hours that are slightly more tolerable than at most other firms. Most associates report the usual 50 to 60 hours per week billed, with five to 10 extra hours on occasion. "I have not worked too hard, but my schedule is sporadic," says one new associate. "There does not seem to be any extensive oversight of my billable hours at this point. The firm stresses that billable hours are not a concern during a new associate's first year at the firm, though I do not know if that will prove true at the end of the year." Insiders report that the firm sets a target of 1,950 billable hours a year.

Face time, apparently, is not an issue. "The partners I work for care more about the end result than face time," says one contact. "If I want to read cases at home, I usually can without any worries about being absent from the office." A Denver associate agrees, saying at that location "if you are busy, you are working; if you aren't, you are expected to take advantage of the slow times and enjoy yourself. I never come in a weekend or stay late just to show my face."

Two-tier salary

In keeping with their commitment to reduced hours, Hogan "just instituted a two-tiered salary for associates based on different levels of billable hours: $120,000 for 1,800 minimum and $135,000 for 1,950 minimum." That policy allows associates "to decide whether to go for the extra compensation or take a reasonable trade-off of lower required billables for a lower salary. It is, I think, the best way to handle the escalating salary pressures in the current market," says one lawyer. Reportedly, those who opt for the 1,800 hour plan but wind up hitting 1,950 get a hefty bonus; exact bonuses in general have not yet been hammered out.

The salary structure as a whole has been very well-received by the asssociates Vault.com associated. "I can't believe how much they pay me to do this stuff," exclaims one attorney. A more reserved colleague says, "I consider myself extremely lucky to be an associate at a large firm during this time of unprecedented salaries. I'd have no credibility if I complained about any aspect of associate compensation."

All the usual perks — and more

As at most large firms, associates at Hogan get meals and cars when working late and some access to sports and event tickets. Insiders also report a laptop subsidy and monthly attorney socials and breakfasts. These bimonthly breakfasts feature a speaker discussing a notable case or transaction (usually a Hogan attorney, though outsiders are also sometimes invited) over morning munchies. Situational perks in DC include discounted Metro tickets and access to Orioles tickets. Associates can also use MCI Center box tickets — if clients haven't nabbed them first. The firm also sponsors monthly galas "with gourmet food and lots of liquor" for the social and indulgent.

"We have casual Fridays," reports one associate, "and there is a rumor that we might go casual summer." This rumor, like so many, proves to be true — the firm has adopted casual dress all summer long. This policy still lags behind other firms, which have already instituted a policy of year-round khakis. In the works: an associate investment fund.

So-so training

"Training is not a highlight, although there are clear signs that the firm is moving to address this problem," reports one contact. A litigation associate claims that his department is leading the charge. "The firm is making an effort under Barrett Prettyman to revamp and improve its associate training, which has always been somewhat lacking." Another contact says that "informal training can be excellent [at Hogan] although not all supervising attorneys are good at it." A senior associate complains that "the partners give you the [case] and don't really want to deal with it much. Some are there to answer questions but others are not." In response to such concerns, the firm recently established the "H&H Academy," a training program that addresses issues of interest and importance to all lawyers regardless of experience level or practice. From mid-2000 through 2001, the emphasis on the curriculum is on client service.

I need air

The aspect of Hogan life that draws the most criticism is the "dank," "overcrowded," "windowless" offices. One DC associate complains that there are "not enough window offices. Some fourth-year associates still don't have windows." There is a "serious office space shortage. First-year associates are really mad about their office conditions," says another contact. "Junior associates have internal, windowless offices, if they are lucky," says another source who reports that those young lawyers are often "stuck in legal assistant offices." Insiders say the wait for a window office is at least two years.

On the plus side, associates report that support services are better than average. "If I need help, it is there," says one lawyer. One displaced New Yorker says "support is probably quite good by DC standards, [but by New York standards] the support level here seems pretty lame. Then again, there aren't enough folks here working late at night to justify New York City levels of support." There does seem to be a question of numbers. "The firm needs to hire more secretaries and support them better," one lawyer complains. "I have a wonderful secretary," raves an associate. "But with two busy associates and a partner, she is often overworked."

Gone to government, every one

"A fair number of litigation and regulatory associates leave for jobs with the Department of Justice, the U.S. Attorney's office, and various House and Senate committees and subcommittees," reports one DC contact. "The opportunity to move into interesting government jobs — legal or non-legal — was a factor that influenced my decision to come here." Most at Hogan seem to share the opinion that turnover is on par with other large firms, with few lateral departures. "The Baltimore office has unusually high turnover of associates," says one lawyer in that city, though the firm begs to differ. Another associate complains that "there does not seem to be a good level of cooperation at the firm in allocating our workload evenly among associates," leading to burned-out and ultimately ex-Hogan & Hartson associates. To curb associate burnout, the firm says that it has hired a number of new attorneys, enabling it to reduce the number of hours required.

The road to partner

"[Partnership prospects] appear to be pretty decent," according to one firm insider. "As of this past fall, associates are considered for partner seven years after graduation from law school. Obviously, billing a lot of hours helps. But they're also looking for people who they think will represent the firm well and who have made efforts to make Hogan a better place to work — like getting involved in firm committees. I'm sure potential for client development helps a lot, too."

"They tell us that any associate who stays for a few years and makes the minimum 1800 hour target has a very good chance of making partner," says a DC lawyer. "An associate up for partner might also be made counsel for the first few years. Almost all new partners become non-equity partners, which doesn't seem to have any advantages over counsel." One disadvantage of non-equity partnership, continues that DC contact, is that "they are the last to benefit from the firm's good fortune." Another lawyer offers that "I don't think that any associate at any firm really knows" what the chances for a partnership are. At Hogan, say insiders, partnership prospects aren't discussed in earnest until "at least the fifth year."

Satisfying diversity

Hogan associates seem satisfied with the firm's efforts on diversity. "Hogan appears to have a strong commitment and a good recruiting track record," says one lawyer. Another source says the firm "seeks a diverse workplace and works very hard to interview and make offers to qualified minority candidates." At least one associate is more critical. "They make an effort to mentor, but I feel like the recruiting effort is not very strong. The numbers are poor for a firm with an interesting and diverse practice and clientele."

"The firm seems like a good place for women," says one contact. "The female associates I know have never complained to me about the environment. The firm also appears to be flexible and encouraging regarding maternity leave." On the whole, Hogan is a comfortable environment for women, and one associate calls this area "a big strength" for the firm.

In keeping with the firm's general atmosphere, gays and lesbians are reportedly welcome at the firm. Although one associate says that there are "not many" openly gay lawyers, "those who are seem very happy and [are] recruiting."

Who could ask for anything more?

Hogan & Hartson seems to breed contentment. "My work is interesting, my colleagues are nice to me, my hours are manageable and I'm grossly overpaid. What more could I want?" asks one associate. One lawyer is looking to the future. "I'm not yet doing exactly what I came here to do but I'm still optimistic that I will be able to at some point," says that litigation attorney. "The only reason I do not find working at Hogan entirely fulfilling is that I do not want to be a lawyer," says one who appears to have wasted three years in law school. "As firms go, however, I think Hogan is a wonderful place to work."

Prestige, quality of work and compensation are frequently cited as advantages of working at Hogan. "The quality of practice is very high and there is a sense of pride in performing high-quality legal work for clients," says one happy associate. Another cites "the people," explaining "you can't go to work everyday in a demanding environment if you don't feel your teammates are good people who you can count on to stay friendly under stress."

"My work is interesting, my colleagues are nice to me, my hours are manageable, and I'm grossly overpaid. What more could I want?"

— *Hogan & Hartson associate*

VAULT.COM
40 PRESTIGE RANKING
Munger, Tolles & Olson LLP

355 South Grand Avenue
35th Floor
Los Angeles, LA 90071-1560
(213) 683-9100
Fax: (213) 687-3702
www.mto.com

LOCATIONS

Los Angeles, CA (HQ)
San Francisco, CA

MAJOR DEPARTMENTS/PRACTICES

Bankruptcy
Environmental
Intellectual Property & Entertainment
Labor
Litigation
Real Estate
Transactional
Tax

THE STATS

No. of attorneys: 133
No. of offices: 2
Summer associate offers: 30 out of 32 (Los Angeles, 1999)
Co-Managing Partnesr: Ruth Fisher and Bob Johnson
Hiring Partners: Jeffery A. Heintz and Marc A. Becker (Los Angeles)

PAY

Los Angeles and San Francisco, 2000
1st year: $125,000
2nd year: $135,000
3rd year: $150,000
4th year: $165,000
5th year: $185,000
6th year: $195,000
Summer associate: $2,400/week

NOTABLE PERKS

- "Parking in San Francisco, dude — can't beat it"
- Annual three-day resort retreat
- Lunch catered three days a week, donuts and bagels every Thurday morning and Friday afternoon happy hour

THE BUZZ
What attorneys at other firms are saying about this firm

- "Brain trust"
- "Supreme Court clerk hang-out"
- "Holier than thou"
- "Eccentric but bright attorneys"

UPPERS

- Democratic firm governance
- Lack of an old-boys' network
- More reasonable hours than most peer firms

DOWNERS

- No dinner reimbursement for working late
- Outdated technology ("Phones are over ten years old!")
- More work than attorneys to do it

KEY COMPETITORS

Gibson Dunn & Crutcher
Irell & Manella
Latham & Watkins
O'Melveny & Myers

EMPLOYMENT CONTACT

Ms. Kevinn Villard
Director of Legal Recruiting
(213) 683-9242

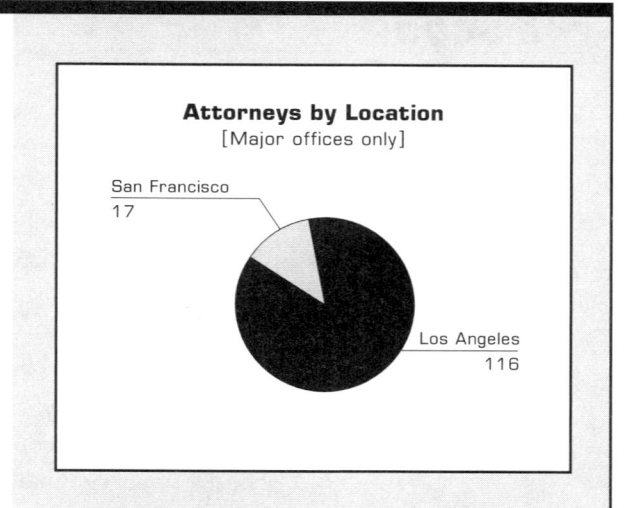

Attorneys by Location
[Major offices only]

- San Francisco: 17
- Los Angeles: 116

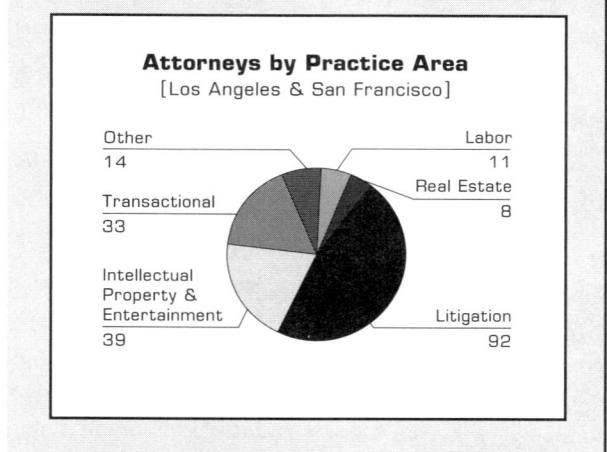

Attorneys by Practice Area
[Los Angeles & San Francisco]

- Other: 14
- Labor: 11
- Real Estate: 8
- Transactional: 33
- Intellectual Property & Entertainment: 39
- Litigation: 92

QUALITY OF LIFE RANKINGS [ASSOCIATES RATE THEIR OWN FIRM]

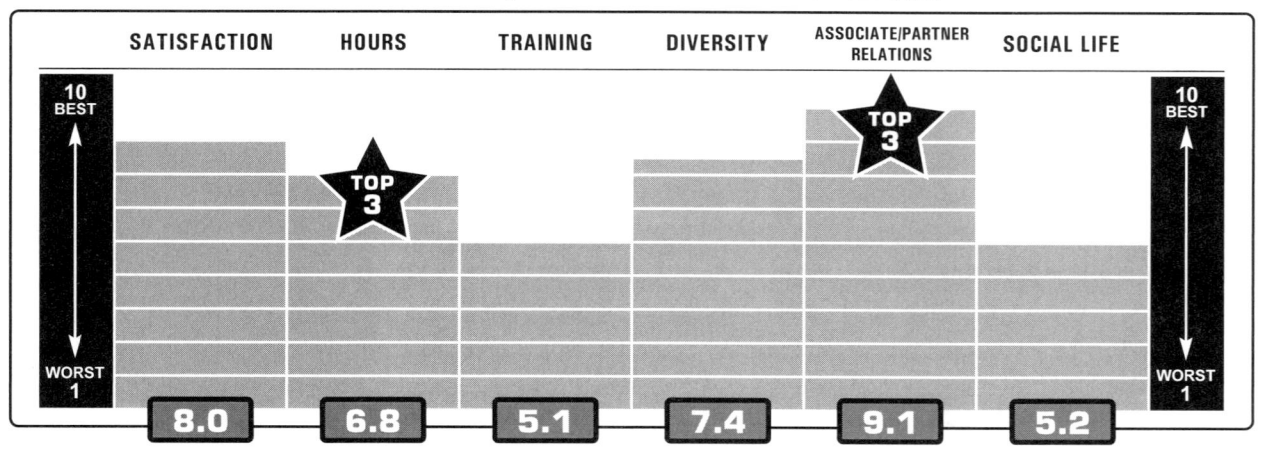

Satisfaction	Hours	Training	Diversity	Associate/Partner Relations	Social Life
8.0	6.8 (TOP 3)	5.1	7.4	9.1 (TOP 3)	5.2

(Scale: 10 Best – 1 Worst)

THE SCOOP

Although not one of the best-known or largest of law firms, Munger, Tolles & Olson is one of the most prestigious among those in the know. Like its East Coast and Midwest analogues, Williams & Connolly in Washington, DC and Jenner & Block in Chicago, Munger bases its reputation on high-end litigation work.

A short but sweet history

Though not a household name, Munger, Tolles & Olson has a distinguished, if not terribly long, history. Seven lawyers founded the firm in 1962. One of them, Charles T. Munger, is a longtime friend of billionaire investment guru Warren Buffett. Munger left the firm to go into the business world (he owns the Daily Journal Corp., which publishes *The Los Angeles Daily Journal* and *The San Francisco Daily Journal*), eventually becoming Buffett's partner and vice chairman of Berkshire Hathaway, Buffett's investment company. The name partner, however, still maintains an office at the firm's Los Angeles headquarters.

Another of the founding members, Harvard Law professor Roderick Hills, recruited one of his students, Robert Denham, to join the firm in 1971. Denham served as managing partner of the firm, and then joined Buffett's management team at Salomon Brothers, helping to rescue the firm from allegations that it had rigged the market in certain U.S. Treasury securities markets. Denham became CEO of Salomon, overseeing its 1997 acquisition by Travelers Group, Inc. before heading back to the cozy confines of partnership at Munger in 1998. In January 1999, the firm turned an historical corner when it selected Ruth Fisher and Robert Johnson as the firm's first co-managing partners.

The few, the proud, the Munger

While certain Munger partners like Denham — and especially name partner Ronald Olson — have gained fame as superlawyers, the physical size of the firm hasn't kept pace with its reputation. With only two offices (in Los Angeles and San Francisco) Munger is a small but powerful player in the legal world. As of January 2000, the firm claimed only 150 attorneys. Munger, Tolles & Olson is an elitist shop in virtually every sense of the word. Tough to crack as an associate, Munger Tolles is even tough to hire — the firm is choosy when it comes to taking on work. The two types of selectivity, of course, go hand in hand. Unlike large firms that have gone on hiring sprees in the superheated legal economy of the late 1990s and early 2000, Munger has chosen to remain ultra-selective when bringing in new lawyers, and has said "thanks, but no thanks" to other firms interested in merging. "I've been hearing for 20 years that a mid-size firm can't make it. I say, 'You do your thing, and we'll do ours,'"

Ronald Olson, a name partner at the firm, told *The Recorder* in 1999. "For us, it's pretty simple. We believe the best people will get the best results, hence the best clients." So far, the Munger philosophy is working just fine.

Star litigators

Most of Munger's highly publicized work comes from litigation and more than two-thirds of its attorneys are litigators. The department is led by name partner Ronald Olson, who brings the firm well over $10 million a year and whose book of business includes companies such as Universal Studios, Atlantic Richfield Company (ARCO) and Merrill Lynch. Widely admired, Olson was voted California's most influential lawyer in a 1997 poll of 200 attorneys conducted by *California Law Business*. In 1998 Olson won recognition for arranging a $400 million bankruptcy settlement between Merrill Lynch and Orange County. Though hardly pocket change, the $400 million settlement was considered a triumph by many, given that the county was seeking $2 billion in damages. Merrill Lynch perhaps heeded the experience of another of Ron Olson client, Alyeska Pipeline Service Co. In disputes related to the Exxon Valdez spill, Alyeska settled for $98 million. Exxon chose to fight and got hit with $5 billion in punitive damages.

Headline grabbers

As Olson's work indicates, Munger has handled many highly publicized lawsuits. The firm defended lawsuits against client Vons Markets after a 1993 E. coli outbreak among customers of Jack In The Box restaurants, to which Vons supplied meats. And through its connection to Warren Buffett, Munger has handled high-stakes litigation for Salomon Brothers (now Salomon Smith Barney).

The firm also brings in plenty of revenue from two oft-sued entities: big oil and big tobacco. Phillip Morris tapped Munger to represent it in connection with the class-action suits against the industry. On the oily end, Munger has defended Shell Oil in a statewide California antitrust action relating to gasoline pricing. The firm also defended Unocal Corp when 15 members of an indigenous Burmese group sued the oil company for alleged human rights abuses resulting from a partnership between Unocal and a state-owned oil and gas company in Myanmar (the former Burma).

Lights, camera, lawsuit!

Munger doesn't neglect its hometown's snazziest industry, the film business. The firm serves as the regular outside counsel for Universal Studios. In April 1998, the firm suffered a setback when it was bumped on conflict grounds from defending Gary Shandling's former manager in a $100 million lawsuit brought by the actor/comic. A

Munger partner, Alan Friedman, had previously represented Shandling in a sexual harassment suit. The disqualification didn't affect Munger's participation in other matters, however, notably representing Michael Ovitz in litigation over his breathtaking but apparently legal $140 million severance package from Walt Disney. In March 1999, Munger also played a role in negotiating the settlement between Sony and MGM regarding the exclusive right to produce James Bond movies.

Oh yeah, they do corporate work too

Because Munger is best known for its star litigators, its corporate and other departmental work is often unfairly overlooked, associates say. The firm represents Berkshire Hathaway, Universal Studios, and Kaufman and Broad in M&A work and has advised Southern California Edison in connection with the restructuring of California's electric utility industry, including the diversiture of its various power generation facilities. Munger is also counsel to new economy companies including Broadband Sports and Salus Media as well as tech-focused investors such as The Yucaipa Companies and Michael Ovitz. The firm built up a respectable real estate practice in the 1980s through the efforts of former partner Dan Garcia, a top advisor to the mayoral administrations of Tom Bradley and Richard Riordan. The still-thriving department is now led by Dick Volpert and O'Malley Miller.

Impressive pro bono

Munger also has an excellent reputation for public service. Accolades include the American Bar Association's Pro Bono Publico Award (Munger is the only California firm to have won this award) and the State Bar of California's law firm pro bono award. Attorneys have been recognized for their efforts in proposing zoning changes that would benefit L.A. homeless shelters and in launching the Skid Row Housing Trust to buy and renovate residential hotels. The firm's pro bono undertakings include providing legal services to AIDS Project L.A., the Alliance For Children's Rights, the American Civil Liberties Union, the Constitutional Rights Foundation, the Federal Indigent Defense Panel, the Lambda Legal Defense and Education Fund, and the League of Women Voters, among others. Pro bono hours are "recorded and considered for bonuses and evaluations" (the firm has no billing requirements) and such work "can be very important to a lawyer's success at the firm," suggests one contact. Another adds that the firm has been "immensely supportive" in offering "support services" for "very fulfilling pro bono work."

Munger has attracted attention for its commitment to many sides of pro bono issues, some more controversial than others. For instance, some partners who are personally opposed to abortion have struggled to accept the firm's long-standing relationship with Planned Parenthood, one of founder Charles Munger's favorite charities and a regular beneficiary of Munger Tolles' pro bono assistance. A few years ago, pro-lifers at the firm argued to support litigation work that would seek to end federal funding for family planning clinics that offer abortion counseling, including Planned Parenthood offices. "It was a position with which not all of us agreed," Bradley Phillips, the firm's pro bono coordinator, told *The Recorder*. "But we felt that those lawyers should be able to do that."

GETTING HIRED

High-caliber candidates, lots of clerks

Becoming a Munger attorney isn't easy. Our contacts universally acknowledge that getting hired at the firm is extremely competitive and that hiring is based largely on top schools and grades. Munger interviews at the usual first-string names: Boalt, Chicago, Columbia, Duke, Harvard, NYU, Michigan, Penn and Yale as well as USC, Texas and UCLA, among others. One third-year tells us that "being near the top of the class and a clerkship or some other special experience is almost mandatory." Another thinks that "the firm views recruitment of outstanding attorneys as its most important task. The firm looks for top graduates of the best law schools and people who have had prestigious clerkships." This repeated emphasis on clerkships isn't just for show. As a corporate associate points it, "with almost one out of every eight lawyers here being a former Supreme Court clerk, the selectivity bar is quite high."

The whole firm has a say in hiring

Candidates with Munger suffer through the regular rigmarole of on-campus interviews and half-day or full-day callbacks. But Munger's hiring process becomes interesting behind the scenes after callbacks. "Everyone who met that candidate writes up a review and sends it to the recruiting committee," explains one associate. The committee meets and makes recommendations to the membership at large. Each candidate is then discussed and voted on by the firm as a whole. "Generally what happens is that people put up the resume and the grades on the overhead projector," says one associate. A discussion about the candidate, usually led by members of the committee, ensues and then a vote is taken. "A 10 percent dissent means a no," says one insider.

OUR SURVEY SAYS

Where do you think you're going?

The firm's stringent hiring standards seem to pay off, since many associates seem to agree that "no one leaves Munger to go to another law firm." As at many other top-tier firms, turnover has "increased somewhat in the past year as people take jobs at Internet companies" or "go in-house or to the government." A sixth-year litigator seems unfazed by the defections, taking them in stride: "The lawyers at Munger, Tolles have sterling credentials, and thus have myriad opportunities available to them."

Keeping pace with competitor firms' salaries has kept attorneys from abandoning ship as well, as "Munger has matched the highest going rates for associate salaries," according to a third-year litigator. But some are concerned about the bottom-line impact of the new bonus structure, part of which "gives first- and second-year associate bonuses, whereas previously they did not receive bonuses until their third year." "Consequently, all we know about bonus size is that it will keep the firm competitive with compensation packages at other comparable firms and that it will reflect quality of work (as opposed to any pure hours-based component)." A fourth-year translates: "I don't know how the new base package is going to effect the bonus numbers. It might bring them down from my expectations."

I think I can, I think I can, I think I can make partner

While associates at other firms normally say prospects of making partner are slim, Mungerians think they've got a fair shot. A second-year cites the odds: "Seven new partners were made at the end of 1999. There are now more partners than associates." The "firm's attitude when associates are hired is that they are potential partners and that if they perform well, they will make partner." Not only that, but the "partnership track is extremely short — four to six years" and "you do not have to be a rainmaker."

Many associates seem to look forward to the partnership parade for reasons other than financial windfall — they plan on treating attorneys under them as well as they have been treated. A litigation source comments that "one of the distinguishing features of this firm is the respect accorded the associates by the partners." A colleague adds that "Munger's reverse leverage and free-agent system for associates' work assignments mean that partners must treat associates with respect."

Good enough for us

Associates seem content with their offices as well as their officers. While the Los Angeles and San Francisco may be "no frills," the offices are "comfortable." A third-year litigator suggests that the firm "would rather spend money on things other than fancy office space."

Support services are satisfactory, too. While the San Francisco "satellite office does not have the full array of support services," the "ratio of attorneys to secretaries is never more than two to one." An M&A intellectual exults that "support services are available and associates are encouraged to use them so as to devote their time to thinking through legal issues."

It's all about initiative

Training opportunities are available at Munger Tolles, but associates need to seek them out because "formal training sessions are essentially nonexistent." If you do want formal training, "the firm will support you in going to outside seminars," paying for associates "to attend just about any off-site training course anywhere in the country."

Several contacts praise "outstanding informal training." According to a third-year litigator, "partners by and large try to ensure that associates get good practical experience." More importantly, chimes in an officemate, "actual responsibility comes early, and there are plentiful opportunities to learn by doing. I have found partners and senior associates very willing to teach and guide me through unfamiliar territory."

Same story, different firm

Munger attorneys admit they struggle with the same recruiting and retention problems with women and minorities as many of their competitors. While "the firm is committed to gender equality" and is "very conscious of the issue," it has "not yet found a successful formula for retaining enough women lawyers," says a SF litigator. An L.A. "working mom," though, insists that "the firm has been more than willing to accommodate my requests for a flexible schedule." A second-year sums up the sentiments of several when she says there are simply "too few women associates at the moment."

There is "little if any mentoring for minority associates," comes a cry from the M&A department. "Retention is an issue and new hiring is not reflective of the population at elite law schools." It's true, laments a Los Angeles litigator. "We have put much effort into this area" and the firm "has some terrific role models" but "unfortunately, our numbers don't yet reflect the efforts." A San Francisco insider declares that he "does not believe that there is any discrimination (overt or covert) but the firm is less conscious of affirmatively recruiting gays and lesbians than it is with women and minorities."

Nonetheless, the firm has "many openly gay partners and associates" and has had "openly gay lawyers in positions of power at the firm throughout the firm's history," according to a sixth-year. "It is truly a non-issue at the firm."

Family fun

Survey respondents emphasize that "lawyers at this firm are very collegial and friendly" and that there is "good camaraderie and social interaction" but "Munger is a firm where most people want to spend their free time with their families or significant others," opines one insider. "Social activities together are primarily at organized firm functions (which are pretty frequent)." The culture of the firm itself might be described as "slightly buttoned-down — the attorneys here are serious about doing high-quality work, which makes for a focused work environment." One associate suggests that "the firm leans towards quiet intellectuals although there are more outgoing, gregarious people as well."

Take a vote

Munger is unique among law firms for its democratic culture — many major firm decisions are put to a vote. This "intellectually stimulating" band of "self-motivated individuals" who are "more brainy than practical" work to make the firm "very democratic, with both partners and associates taking part in various firm decisions such as hiring." Indeed, several attorneys insist that the firm is "committed to minimizing (although not eliminating) distinctions between partners and associates." A labor lawyer adds that "although there are firm votes on many issues, for many important decisions a consensus is reached or majority garnered through informal means (walking the halls, canvassing attorneys, one-on-one meetings) prior to the formal vote."

"You get to work with some of the best and the brightest on the thorniest and toughest legal issues. You get a lot of responsibility very soon, but you also get the support you need," declares an L.A. litigator. "Most of the lawyers here really enjoy wrestling with difficult legal problems, and you can easily find people to bounce ideas off of," chimes in another L.A. associate.

Forewarned is forearmed

Munger players do think that potential candidates should consider seriously what they want before deciding on Munger because "some of the things that make it unique have side effects." One associate warns that although "you get a lot of responsibility and thus more interesting work," with "responsibility comes additional pressure. Additionally, the open culture and democratic governance means that if you want to change something, you can, but that means that you will spend time and energy (including emotional energy) trying to make those changes."

"If you are looking for a place where you will socialize a great deal with your co-workers, Munger is not the place for you. People do their work and then go home," cautions a litigator. "At the same time, you will know most of the other lawyers here because the firm is relatively small and you do have interaction with people at the firm lunches and at the weekly Friday evening gathering." Those contemplating Munger should also "realize this is an intense place full of perfectionist, smart attorneys," points out a corporate newcomer. "This doesn't mean you'll work long hours, but it does mean your work will be scrutinized and people will have high expectations."

Bottom line? "You really have to know that you want to practice law or you will probably not be happy. Most people here are into law intrinsically and aren't very good at talking about much else." But when it comes to choosing Munger over other firms, a third-year litigator echoes many of his colleagues: "The choice was easy. The average Munger associate was both brighter and happier. The partnership prospects seemed better at Munger. The responsibility came much more quickly at Munger. And Munger's pay was at least as high as its competition."

VAULT.COM
41 PRESTIGE RANKING
Paul, Hastings, Janofsky & Walker LLP

555 South Flower Street
Twenty-third Floor
Los Angeles, CA 90071
(213) 683-6000
Fax: (213) 627-0705
www.phjw.com or www.paulhastings.com

LOCATIONS

Los Angeles, CA (HQ)
Atlanta, GA
Costa Mesa, CA
New York, NY
San Francisco, CA
Stamford, CT
Washington, DC
London
Tokyo

MAJOR DEPARTMENTS/PRACTICES

Corporate
Employment
Litigation
Real Estate
Tax

THE STATS

No. of attorneys: 729
No. of offices: 9
Summer associate offers: 57 out of 67 (Firm-wide, 1999)
Chairman: John S. McGeeney
Hiring Partner: Mary Dollarhide

THE BUZZ
What attorneys at other firms are saying about this firm

- "Good for employment law"
- "Getting moldy from lack of use"
- "Continuing on course to shake up the L.A. 'Big Three'"
- "Too spread-out"

PAY

All California Offices and Washington, DC, 2000
1st year: $125,000
2nd year: $135,000
3rd year: $150,000
4th year: $165,000
5th year: $185,000
6th year: $195,000
7th year: $205,000
8th year: $210,000
$9,000 bar stipend in CA offices
$5,000 bar stipend in Washington, DC office
Summer associate: $2,400/week

Atlanta, 2000
1st year: $100,000 + $7,000 bar stipend
2nd year: $105,000
3rd year: $110,000
4th year: $115,000
5th year: $122,500
6th year: $130,000
7th year: $137,500
8th year: $144,000
Summer associate: $1,750/week

New York, 2000
1st year: $125,000 + $3,000 bar stipend
2nd year: $135,000
3rd year: $150,000
4th year: $170,000
5th year: $190,000
6th year: $200,000
7th year: $210,000
8th year: $215,000
Summer associate: $2,400/week

NOTABLE PERKS

- Free parking (L.A.)
- Attorney dining room (L.A.)
- Corporate casual dress year-round
- $10,000 and one year credit for clerkships at U.S. District Court or Appeals Court
- $20,000 and two years' credit for U.S. Supreme Court clerks

UPPERS

- "The best employment work available"
- High-quality lawyers
- Battle Fowler merger notoriety

DOWNERS

- Pressure to bill more hours
- Slim chance of making partner
- Lack of communication between partners and associates

KEY COMPETITORS

Gibson, Dunn & Crutcher
King & Spalding
Latham & Watkins
Milbank, Tweed, Hadley & McCloy
Weil, Gotshal & Manges

EMPLOYMENT CONTACT

Ms. Joy McCarthy
Director of Attorney Programs
(213) 683-6000
recruit@phjw.com

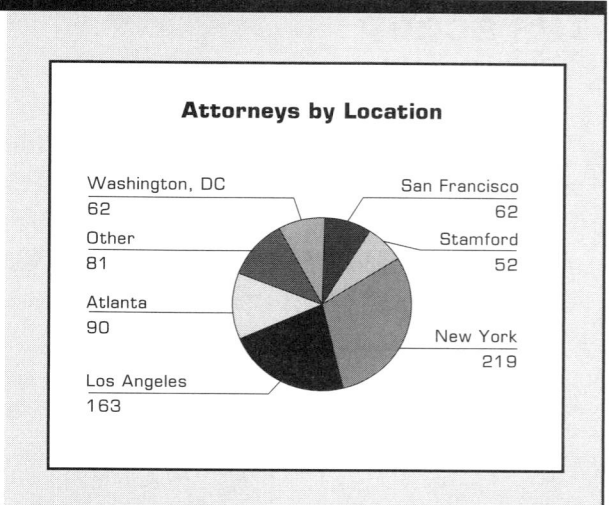

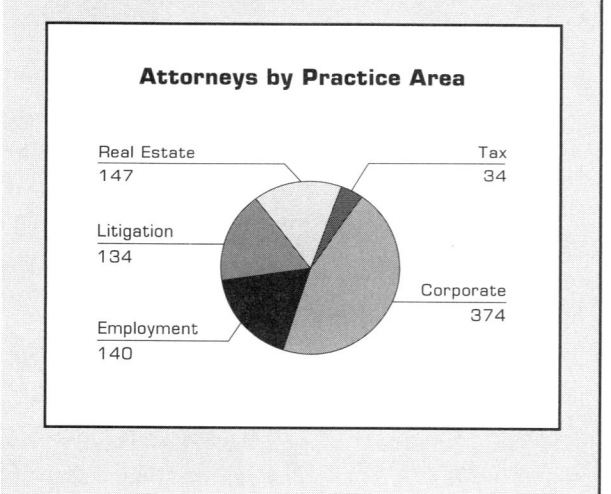

Attorneys by Location

- Washington, DC: 62
- San Francisco: 62
- Other: 81
- Stamford: 52
- Atlanta: 90
- New York: 219
- Los Angeles: 163

Attorneys by Practice Area

- Real Estate: 147
- Tax: 34
- Litigation: 134
- Corporate: 374
- Employment: 140

QUALITY OF LIFE RANKINGS [ASSOCIATES RATE THEIR OWN FIRM]

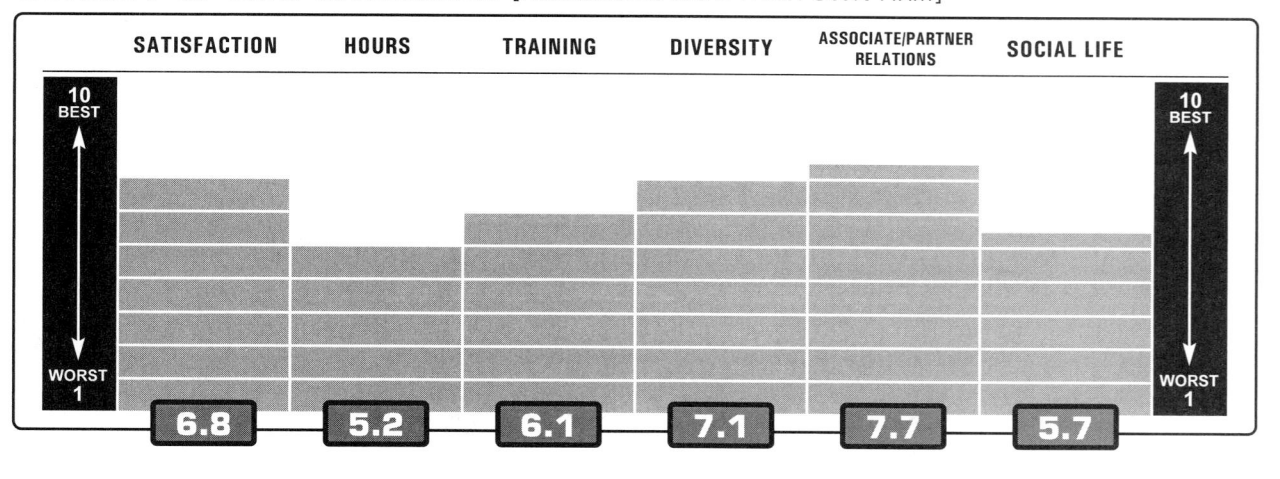

SATISFACTION	HOURS	TRAINING	DIVERSITY	ASSOCIATE/PARTNER RELATIONS	SOCIAL LIFE
6.8	5.2	6.1	7.1	7.7	5.7

THE SCOOP

Paul Hastings is a Los Angeles powerhouse, albeit not yet one of the so-called L.A. "Big Three," comprised of Latham & Watkins, O'Melveny & Meyers, and Gibson, Dunn & Crutcher. The firm is well known for its all-star labor and employment practice, and over the last decade the corporate practice has developed its own reputation of excellence. We'll see if the recent merger with Battle Fowler will help Paul Hastings make the Big Three a foursome.

West coast history

In 1946 friends Robert Hastings, Lee Paul and Warner Edmonds formed Paul, Hastings & Edmonds in Los Angeles. Edmonds left in 1950 to establish a practice in nearby Santa Barbara; the next year, Hastings and Paul were joined by Leonard Janofsky. The firm's last name partner, Charles Walker, joined in 1962. The employment law department, for which the firm is best known, was led at the outset by Janofsky, who later served as president of the American Bar Association. In the 1970s, Paul Hastings began moving into the Asia-Pacific region, gaining a foothold by helping Japanese clients set up U.S. operations, distribution and joint ventures. The following decade the firm opened its Tokyo office, performing M&A and financing work for clients in the region as well as picking up new Japanese, Korean, and Taiwanese clients. Back in the good old U.S.A., the firm expanded eastward beginning in the early 1980s, setting up offices in Atlanta, Washington, DC, Stamford, CT, and New York City.

Paul Hastings, like most of its Los Angeles-based competitors, suffered through its share of financial and other troubles in the early 1990s. In May 1993, then-managing partner Robert DeWitt abruptly quit his post, voicing his dissatisfaction with the firm's management structure. The loss followed on the heels of other defections — three key partners, including litigation head William Campbell, decamped for the Los Angeles office of Orrick, Herrington & Sutcliffe. Despite the losses, the firm continued to grow, adding attorneys and opening new offices in Tokyo, San Francisco, and London.

In June 2000, Paul Hastings swallowed up 130 attorneys from New York real estate gurus Battle Fowler. The move greatly boosts Paul's Hasting's East Coast presence. Despite its wide reach, the firm confidently proclaims that it has the technological tools to run the entire firm on "a geography-blind basis."

No more sitting at the kiddie table

Has Paul Hastings joined the big leagues? For the past two decades, the firm has scrambled to take its place among the top firms based in Los Angeles, and in 2000, the gap seems to be closing. With nine offices and 729 lawyers, the firm stacks up, at least in terms of size, to L.A. rivals O'Melveny & Myers (752 attorneys) and Gibson, Dunn & Crutcher (749 attorneys). (All three firms have a ways to go to catch 935-lawyer Latham.) The firm certainly compares in terms of partner compensation — 1999 figures hit $675,000 in profits per partner with revenues of $285 million, up seven percent from 1998.

Corporate: stealth strength

While Paul Hastings has built its reputation on the strength of its litigators, particularly in the field of employment law, the firm's corporate department is in fact its largest. Among the firm's major corporate clients are The General Electric Company, Lend Lease Corp., and Bank of America. The firm also has close relationships with investment banks Bear Stearns, Morgan Stanley Dean Witter, and Donaldson, Lufkin & Jenrette. In November 1999, the firm represented Charter Communications in its $3.2 billion public offering, the third-largest IPO in history. The company also tapped Paul Hastings for help with its $3.6 billion high-yield financing. The firm worked on other IPOs as well in 1999, including representing Autobytel.com in its $103.5 million offering and DLJ as lead underwriter for a $90 million offering of Network Access Solutions.

By the numbers

In 1999 Paul Hastings saw the exodus of real estate hotshot Paul Walker and two other partners from the department, who defected to New York-based Dewey Ballantine. Despite gaining six attorneys from McCutchen, Doyle, Brown & Enersen, other departures brought the firm's grand total of attorneys down to 615, 14 fewer than the previous year's total. However, the addition of attorneys from Battle Fowler has vastly increased the firm's numbers. In fact, Paul Hastings's New York office in June 2000 is now bigger than its L.A. home.

Got wrongful discharge problems? Call Paul Hastings

Paul Hastings has traditionally been known as a litigator's firm — the firm's first managing partner and many subsequent managing partners have been litigators, bucking the standard law firm trend toward supposedly cool-headed corporate department heads. Notable cases for 1999 include defending client Toyota against a recall order and successfully representing Oglethorpe Power Corp. in an arbitrated contract dispute with LG&E Energy Corporation. Employment law, led by department chair Nancy Abell, remains a strength for Paul Hastings. The firm has taken on notable engagements for Hughes Aircraft as well as UPS. For the latter client, the firm negotiated a $12.14 million settlement with a group of African-American employees claiming the company had systematically denied them opportunities for advancement and extra hours.

GETTING HIRED

Casting a broader net

While continuing to actively recruit at the nation's top law schools, Paul Hastings seems to be expanding the range of schools at which it recruits. In the words of one associate, "We've lately broadened our criteria for entering associates beyond the top-tier schools to look at noteworthy candidates from second-level schools." However, an insider explains that there may be ulterior motives behind this broadening of horizons. "Normally, the firm is fairly picky in a pseudo-intellectual, snotty sort of way," he notes. "Lately, however, we have become desperate enough to lower our lofty standards." Moreover, some associates worry that "the merger with Battle Fowler will further lower these standards."

As for what constitutes a "noteworthy" candidate, insiders suggest only those from the top 25 percent of their class need apply. "If you can make the grade cut-off," one contact opines, "it's not too hard to get an offer as long as you have a personality, some confidence and you act genuinely interested in the firm."

Centralized hiring process

Insiders warn that the hiring process at Paul Hastings may take longer than at other firms, as satellite offices need to go "through Los Angeles to make decisions." (The firm asserts that this is part of its effort to maintain uniform standards of quality across all of its offices.) Each on-campus recruiter makes recommendations to the firm's recruiting committee regarding final call-backs for students. Call-backs to Paul Hastings involve a half-day of interviews. Associates say that the firm is generally looking for personality fit during the interviews. "I think that we don't fly people back who don't have pretty good grades," reports one insider. "We just try not to take real jerks — we had somebody who whipped out a cell phone in the middle of an interview." The cell phone enthusiast did not get an offer. Technology enthusiasm aside, "it's a question of whether a person can handle themselves well," maintains a contact. Says one associate who has had a hand in interviewing candidates, "We're looking for leaders, so I look at what they have done in the past to try to see if they've had responsibility for running things." Another associate adds, "Paul Hastings takes very seriously performance in law school as an indicator of how well one will do in practice. However, we have hired students from schools not traditionally on our recruiting schedule if they can establish the ability to excel in other ways."

The firm's summer associate committee, which is composed mainly of associates, has the primary responsibility for coordinating the summer program. At the end of the summer, they will make recommendations to the recruiting committee based on their interaction with and knowledge of the summer associates. The recruiting committee is responsible for reviewing all work assignments and evaluations and ultimately making final offer decisions. Summer associates have an extremely high probability of receiving offers at the end of their experience. One of our contacts observes, "Of the five summer classes that have come through beginning with mine, all but one or two members each year received offers. And the 'rejections' are carefully and painfully deliberated."

OUR SURVEY SAYS

Culture clash

Paul, Hastings, Janofsky, & Walker has nine major offices worldwide. It is not surprising, therefore, that associates report that the firm has a bit of an identity problem. Many associates claim that the firm has a distinctively Californian flair and "a fairly laid back approach. There is no intimidation factor when you start work here — people are very supportive." Others note, however, that "Paul Hastings has turned into a typical New York law firm in terms of work and hours." Another declares, "the firm is committed to being one of the top 25 firms in the country. That focus is causing a shift in culture to the New-York-big-firm style — billing hours is the focus." An insider, apparently in agreement with the previous comment, explains that Paul Hastings is "very conservative — in dress, socially, and financially."

However, dissenters to this opinion claim that, "Paul Hastings does not camouflage individuals with corporate clothes. While every attorney here is a professional, he or she is also an individual and not forced to fit into a certain mold in order to succeed here." A third opinion emerges in the culture war. "We have no culture," one dissenter admits. "The office consists of numerous small groups that make lots of money for the group heads and try to stay away from each other."

Bonus anxiety

A San Francisco-based attorney observes that at Paul Hastings, "the base salary meets the market rate, but the firm has been lax in determining the associate bonus structure.

Since a large part of associate compensation depends on bonuses, our pay could easily go from market rate to below market if the bonus structure doesn't match the bonus structure of other firms." An insider warns, "If they try to cheat us on bonuses, there will be trouble. If I am going to bill 2,400 hours this year, I expect to be compensated accordingly." However, a source in the DC office exults that "Paul Hastings finally got off its rear and came out with a progressive bonus plan ahead of the rest of the market [in May 2000] that continues to reward excessive hours quite handsomely. The first-year grinder who wants to bill 3,000 hours will bring home over $200,000." Another source doesn't feel like the firm has been quite that generous. "They'll pay as little as possible to maintain a 'national' image. Locally, we match the other big firms. Bonuses are low, with the explanation that salaries are high."

Partners are OK

While some insiders at Paul Hastings are satisfied with their treatment by partners, complaints are widespread and come from nearly every office of the firm. As an Atlanta-based source remarks of his relationship with partners, "The term 'fungible commodity' comes to mind." An associate in Los Angeles insists that "there haven't been any screamers, but the partners here could definitely be more positive, encouraging, and motivating towards associates." One attorney notes that "partners are usually polite in a formal way, but one never gets the impression there is much interest behind the courtesies." Another insider offers a suggestion to foster good relations with the partnership: "Keep your hours up to expectations and you will always be on the firm's good side."

Other associates react very positively to partners. As an attorney based in the District of Columbia states, "The partners here are exceptionally concerned and involved in associate development." A fourth-year elaborates: "Generally, associates are treated as equals but that also requires associates to act like equals." Another insider explains, "The respect with which all attorneys in my department treat each other was evident to me in my interviews and is one of the primary reasons I determined that this is the appropriate firm for me." A litigator supplies, "The partners understand that the key to success is constructive criticism that is well-founded and delivered with respect and understanding. For me, this has been the perfect environment for developing my skills and abilities."

Lawyers who lunch

If it's a party you're looking for, look somewhere that's not Paul Hastings. "This is not a big party firm," indicates an insider. "Most lawyers are married and have kids." One source reports that "it is a friendly and collegial working environment, but most attorneys make an effort to have their own lives outside of the office and the work."

Complaints range from mild ("the social events are sometimes dull") to harsh ("back-stabbing, finger-pointing group of people who live for the weekend and time away from each other"). A mid-level associate frets, "[Paul Hastings] is not a very social place, particularly between departments." Another associate agrees, adding that the firm hosts "little partner/associate interaction."

A New York-based attorney has a different opinion of the social life at the firm, speaking admiringly of "lots of opportunity to socialize outside the office. People always eat lunch (and dinner if they have to) together. Several extra-office athletic teams bring the associates close together." An associate concurs, "We do a lot of things together that are firm events, like monthly associate luncheons, which allow us to interact in a relaxed setting. Combining this with our busy schedules, I think that's the most people can do." One lateral hire thinks that social life is not an issue at Paul Hastings, observing, "I can work with people I don't like — not that I don't like the people here, but I can't work with people whose work I don't respect."

Workingman's blues

An unwelcome side effect of the recent salary raise at Paul Hastings was a corresponding increase of the billable hours requirement to 2,000 hours (a level that the firm says remains close to the average that associates have billed historically). Moreover, an insider reports, "the firm is very clear about the 2,000 billable hours requirement. Unlike many firms, they calculate exactly how many hours per day you have to average in order to make the minimum and still get all your vacation time — and they send out reports comparing your performance to the budget." Attorneys also note that "there is an expectation that you will work harder than the minimum" — this minimum is cited as 2,100 hours. Many associates find the results of this increased pressure to bill to be overwhelming; one attorney in Atlanta cites pressure to come in on weekends to assist other overworked associates. One exasperated source grumbles, "The phrase 'work-life balance' is routinely tossed about, but I'm not real sure what it means."

Some do not find the hours as overbearing as others. A fifth-year remarks, "I'm here, I do my work, I may take work home, but no one is watching my clock." A lateral also notes, "I haven't slept in my office, which was a regular occurrence at my old firm."

Training: such a variety

Training at Paul Hastings is just as variable as its culture. One corporate attorney describes his experience as "training on the fly," with firm leaders "too busy to hold anyone's hands." A litigator, on the other hand, finds that "the formal training classes here are great and very useful. However, the level of work that is assigned is uneven. Some litigation associates have only done legal research assignments while others have done more advanced things. It's rare for any to have done depositions, appeared in court, or even drafted legal motions."

Those without much formal training report, "Most of the training comes from the hands-on work and interaction with senior associates, of counsel and partners, who always seem eager to explain difficult concepts. However, the formal training program is mostly ineffective." Another raves, "I just changed practice areas, and as a result I need a lot of training. I'm given every opportunity I need to ask questions, to try things on my own, and to seek review of any work product that I have produced."

A seventh-year associate explains that "although there is no formal training at any level, the expectation is that if you are a certain year, you should know it by now." Nevertheless, an insider reveals that change seems imminent: "The new Paul Hastings management team has spent significant time over the last year working out a training program focused on real experiences. They have developed lists of experiences for associates to receive (depositions, court appearances, summary judgment motions) by certain levels and have put in place a mentoring program that will ensure the goals are met. I am very excited about this plan."

Staffing problems

Associates at Paul Hastings report widespread support staff problems. One attorney identifies support staff as "probably the area which offers the most significant room for improvement. However, the new office management recognizes this and is already putting in place incentives to attract and retain better support staff. The litigation group, although it has holes, probably enjoys the most reliable support staff." Many complain about management problems regarding staffing. "Some associates have a long wait before getting a secretary assigned to them," supplies a source. Another declares that "secretarial assignments have no rhyme or reason. One associate has his secretarial assignment on another floor."

A San Francisco associate observes, "Associates are not provided adequate or qualified support staff. There is extensive use of temporary employees. Providing associates permanent qualified secretarial support is a very low priority with the firm. When there is a secretary out ill, the desk is rarely covered. If there is coverage it is because of a specific request and some kind of emergency. With the increase in hours the lack of adequate support causes many problems."

An Atlanta associate gripes, "Paul Hastings allows incompetent and subpar assistants to abuse associates and make the same amount of money as better-trained, skilled assistants." Another Georgian offers up the following reasons for the less than spectacular support: "The firm is far below market with pay for secretaries and paralegals. As a result, morale is low, turnover is high, support is minimal, and the burden falls on the associates." Help is on the way though; the firm reports that it has recently adjusted paralegals' compensation by an average of 14 percent and is reviewing other staff compensation issues.

Paulina Hastings

Because one of Paul Hastings' major areas of focus is employment law, some attorneys point out that when it comes to diversity, the firm "has to maintain a good image." As a female associate notes, "The women in the firm support each other. I think the firm needs to do better in mentoring and retaining women as we become more senior." Another reports that "there are female partners here, and the first-year class is composed primarily of women, but there isn't anything actively done to mentor or meet the special needs of women." One insider allows the facts to speak for themselves: "The head of my department is a woman. Of the five associates in my department in this city, three are women and one of the managing partners of this office is a woman. I am treated by all persons working for the firm in terms of general office demeanor as a person and not as a sex." A third-year observes, "A women was promoted to of counsel just one day before she was scheduled to go on a six-month maternity leave."

Other women find some constraints to success at the firm, stating that the firm "does not have subsidized day care, does not allow partners to work part-time, and does not have many of the programs that other firms have in place to support women with families. Therefore, there are very few female partners who have families. Personally, I have already decided that I'm not going to be able to be a partner because I plan to have children, and the firm does not allow part-time partners. With the demands of the work schedule, my children would be getting the short end of the stick."

Minorities wanted

Although the firm has succeeded in attracting female attorneys, a source observes that "the number of minorities working here is extremely low. Nothing, to my knowledge, is done to actively recruit or retain minority candidates. However, I think a minority person would feel comfortable working here." Others report that the "firm appears to be trying hard to diversify the office — but, with the exception of strong representation of Asian-Americans, it isn't reflected yet in the associate ranks." One source simply points out that "the proof is in the pudding. This firm is very white."

The firm does seem to be accepting of gay attorneys. An associate reveals, "Domestic partner benefits are available. I note with pleasure that no one seems to care at all what anyone's sexual preference is." Others indicate that "there are a large number of openly gay attorneys who work at Paul Hastings." "We have several openly gay attorneys and staff. The atmosphere is open and refreshing."

Partnership prospects that rhyme with "Jim"

When questioned regarding the chance of making partner, associates at Paul Hastings reveal that prospects look "grim," "dim," and "slim." Only four attorneys were promoted to partner last year. According to associates, some events that are more probable than making partner at Paul Hastings include: "winning Powerball" "the Detroit Tigers winning the World Series during the next few years," and "getting struck by lightning." Moreover, "the of counsel position used to be used sparingly. Now it seems that the firm is making every non-lateral pay his or her dues as an of counsel before he or she can make partner. Of course, the associates have heard that the firm has instituted a non-equity status for certain partners though they haven't told us this — it figures." Some hopes remain intact. One source speculates, "Perhaps as profits per partner increase, the partners will loosen their death grip on the pie. In the meantime, the of counsel ranks are swelling. This firm is truly approaching a diamond structure."

All in all, satisfied

"There is no doubt that in the past the firm was one of the top at balancing lifestyle with salary and prestige," supplies an associate. "However, the firm has made a conscious decision to join the 'Big 3' at all costs — it has succeeded to its credit, but quality of life has suffered as a result. The recent salary hikes changed the collegial atmosphere between the partners and associates to an 'us against them' mentality, as if the associates were picketing to get these raises."

Still, many at Paul Hastings are satisfied. "As far as law firms go, there are very few things to change, and I doubt that I could find as good a combination elsewhere," reports a New York-based source. "The people are great and although the deal flow is heavy, the associates have the opportunity to gain much more responsibility here than at other big firms." A Los Angeles associate agrees, stating, "This place has its problems like any large firm, but overall I think I am happier than any of my friends at the other big firms in L.A. The pay is at the top of the market, the partners are decent and friendly, and the work is interesting."

"Normally, the firm is fairly picky in a pseudo-intellectual, snotty sort of way."

— *Paul Hastings associate*

Orrick, Herrington & Sutcliffe LLP

VAULT.COM PRESTIGE RANKING: 42

The Old Federal Reserve Bank
400 Sansome Street
San Francisco, CA 94111
(415) 392-1122
Fax: (415) 773-5759
www.orrick.com

LOCATIONS

San Francisco, CA (HQ)
Los Angeles, CA • New York, NY • Sacramento, CA • Menlo Park, CA • Washington, DC • Seattle, WA • London • Singapore • Tokyo

MAJOR DEPARTMENTS/PRACTICES

Commercial Transactions, Banking & Bankruptcy
Company Practice
Compensation & Benefits
Employment
Intellectual Property
Litigation
Market Regulation
Project Finance
Public Finance
Real Estate
Structured Finance
Tax

THE STATS

No. of attorneys: 540
No. of offices: 10
Summer associate offers: 12 out of 12 (San Francisco, 1999)
Chairman: Ralph H. Baxter, Jr.
Hiring Attorney: Peter A. Bricks (East Coast)
Michael McAndrews (West Coast)

THE BUZZ
What attorneys at other firms are saying about this firm

- "Great securities practice"
- "A bad experiment waiting to fall apart"
- "Grew too fast"
- "Very solid firm, both in CA and NY"

PAY

All Domestic Offices except Sacramento, 2000
1st year: $125,000
2nd year: $135,000
3rd year: $150,000
4th year: $165,000
5th year: $185,000
6th year: $195,000
7th year: $205,000
8th year: $210,000
Summer associate: $10,400/month

Sacramento, 2000
1st year: $95,000
2nd year: $100,000
3rd year: $115,000
4th year: $125,000
5th year: $140,000
6th year: $145,000
7th year: $155,000
8th year: $165,000
Summer associate: $7,900/month

NOTABLE PERKS

- Free lunch (San Francisco)
- Annual firm-wide retreat

UPPERS

- High-quality work and attorneys
- Atmosphere of mutual respect fostered by the partners
- Free lunch at "trough"

DOWNERS

- High expectations for billable hours
- Not a particularly attainable partnership
- Bicoastal schizophrenia of firm management

KEY COMPETITORS

Brobeck, Phleger & Harrison
Milbank, Tweed, Hadley & McCloy
Morrison & Foerster
Pillsbury, Madison & Sutro
Wilson Sonsini Goodrich & Rosati

EMPLOYMENT CONTACT

Karen M. Sucre (San Francisco)
(415) 773-5588; ksucre@orrick.com

Carrie Marker (New York)
(212) 506-3551; cmarker@orrick.com

(See www.orrick.com for other employment contacts)

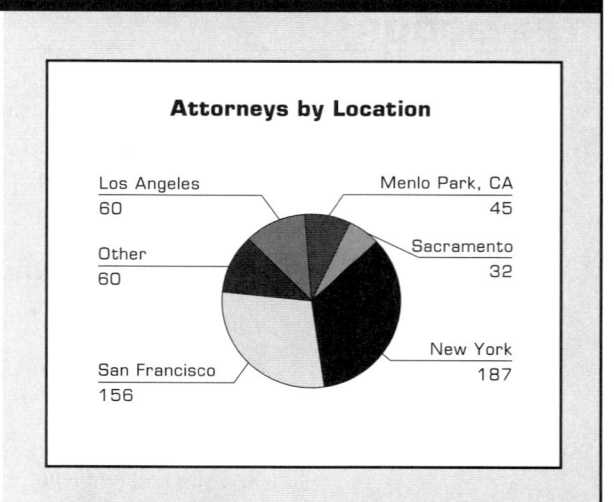

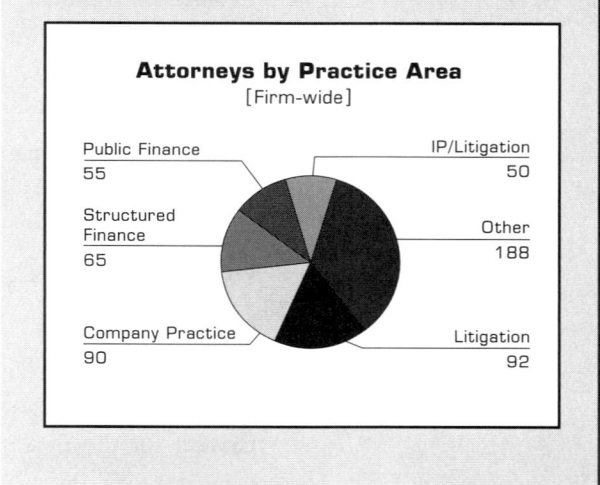

Attorneys by Location
- Los Angeles: 60
- Menlo Park, CA: 45
- Other: 60
- Sacramento: 32
- San Francisco: 156
- New York: 187

Attorneys by Practice Area [Firm-wide]
- Public Finance: 55
- IP/Litigation: 50
- Structured Finance: 65
- Other: 188
- Company Practice: 90
- Litigation: 92

QUALITY OF LIFE RANKINGS [ASSOCIATES RATE THEIR OWN FIRM]

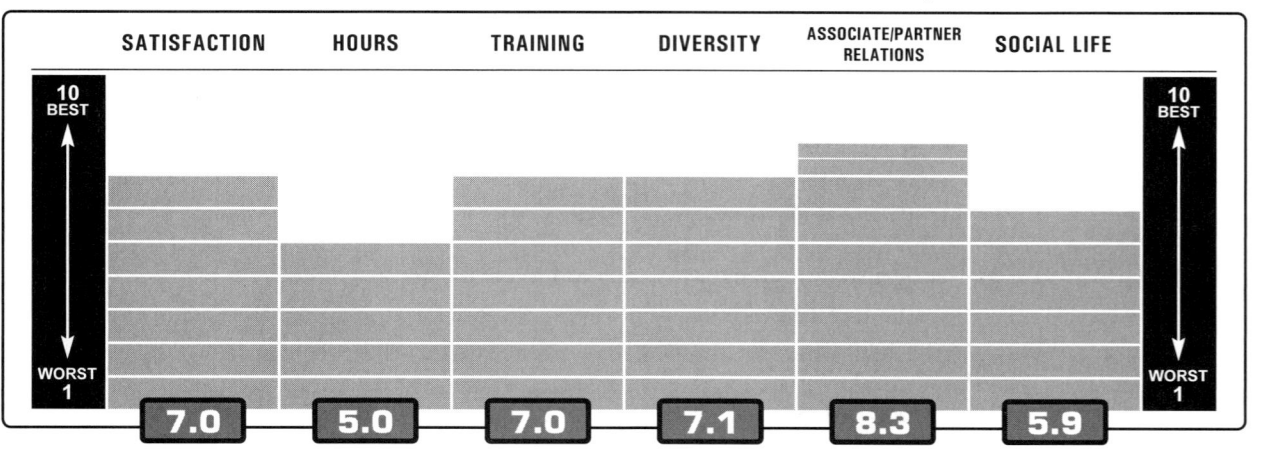

SATISFACTION	HOURS	TRAINING	DIVERSITY	ASSOCIATE/PARTNER RELATIONS	SOCIAL LIFE
7.0	5.0	7.0	7.1	8.3	5.9

THE SCOOP

Although Orrick, Herrington & Sutcliffe's roots run from laid-back San Francisco, the pace at this dynamic firm is anything but relaxed. With its largest office now located in New York City, Orrick represents movers and shakers on both coasts.

History: building the Bay Area

Orrick traces its roots back 137 years to when its predecessor firm was organized to represent the San Francisco Bank. The firm helped put together the Pacific Gas & Electric Company, which today remains one of the firm's top clients. Orrick also helped reorganize the Fireman Fund's Insurance Company after the 1906 earthquake and fire and lent a helping hand to the financing of the Golden Gate Bridge, the former Candlestick Park, and BART (the Bay Area Rapid Transit system). Orrick took a hit to its core public finance business in the mid- and late-1980s because of changes to bond tax law. In 1987 profits per partner slumped to $220,000. Chairman Ralph Baxter took over the firm in 1990 and began pushing the firm toward ambitious expansion goals, in particular by building up Orrick's New York office. In 1996 the firm opened its first overseas office in Singapore.

Public finance star

Orrick is known best for its public finance work. The firm, which according to its web site "handles over 500 to 600 public offerings of municipal securities, aggregating $30 to $40 billion" in a typical year, was named Top Bond Counsel and Top Underwriters counsel for the first quarter of 2000 by *The Bond Buyer*. Public finance work generates over $50 million dollars annually in revenue for the firm. In March 2000, Orrick was chosen by Orange County, California, as transactional counsel for a $900 million class-action suit settlement between tobacco companies and forty-six states. The firm had also served as counsel for New York City in a 1999 tobacco settlement. Particular areas of expertise include: general obligation bonds; school finance; redevelopment agency financing; public power finance; water and wastewater finance; industrial development; pollution control and solid waste financing; transportation finance; health care finance; housing finance; higher education and student loan financing; and derivative products/swaps.

The firm's other strengths — such as project finance and structured finance — flow from the firm's public finance prowess. Most of the firm's top clients are investment banks, with whom the firm works on finance deals. These include heavy hitters such as Credit Suisse First Boston, J.P. Morgan, Merrill Lynch, Chase Manhattan, Goldman Sachs, and Bear Stearns. Orrick's public power practice boasts clients like the Tennessee Valley Authority, the largest electric utility in the country.

Techlaw.com

Although Orrick showed up late to the Silicon Valley frenzy, making its first Valley deals in 1995, it has thus far tapped successfully into the world's greatest generator of wealth. Orrick took steps to deepen its involvement with the high tech world in 1999 by forming an innovative strategic partnership with the Venture Law Group, a boutique technology firm (also featured on Vault.com's Top 50 list for 2000). The partnership offered Orrick access to Venture Law Group's high-profile clients by contributing services that the boutique does not. More recently, the firm opened a new office in tech center Seattle in order to further focus on e-business. The firm has also concentrated on the hot field of intellectual property litigation. In fact, Orrick has opened a "trial center" in downtown San Jose, which serves as a war room for several of Orrick's high-profile cases, including *Sun Microsystems v. Microsoft Corp*, *AMD v. Hyundai*, and *Storage Tech v. EMC*. IP attorneys at the firm had the Force with them while aiding Lucasfilms in its attempt to keep pirated versions of *Star Wars Episode I — The Phantom Menace* off the Web (the film is now available at your local video store).

West Coast litigants, however, haven't been Orrick's only high tech clients. Both Virginia-based America Online and New Jersey-based Lucent Technologies have tapped the firm's attorneys. Orrick has also formed a strategic partnership with Lucent in order to enhance training and recruiting of both firm and in-house attorneys. In May 1999, Orrick attorneys based in Los Angeles helped craft a marketing partnership for three companies: Life Bank, Prodigy Communications, and Austin, Texas-based Recompute International. Under the terms of the deal, client Life Bank agreed to finance consumer purchases of Prodigy's iLife program, pre-installed on new and refurbished computers from Recompute.

The rise of the bicoastal firm

Do you have a BHAG — a Big, Hairy, Audacious Goal? Orrick chairman Ralph Baxter, Jr. says he does. Baxter's BHAG is to take Orrick to the same level as legal elite firm Cravath, Swaine & Moore or at least that of California rival Latham & Watkins (both Vault.com Top 10 firms). The buildup of the firm's New York presence has been a key part of Baxter's strategy. The New York office was opened in 1984 with six defectors from Brown & Wood. Rather than transfer attorneys from other offices or gradually bring newly minted associates into the branch, Orrick chose to build the New York office through lateral hires. The firm actually had the nerve to place advertisements in *The Wall Street Journal* for New York litigation partners (needless to say, uncommonly bold for top firms). Playing on its strengths as a municipal financier, the firm built relationships with the Port Authority of New York and New Jersey, Newark, Kennedy and LaGuardia airports, and cultural institutions such as the Museum of Modern Art, Carnegie Hall, and the American Museum of Natural History. Nevertheless, the rapid growth strategy prompted some observers to suggest that the firm risked instability in expanding its New York offices so quickly.

Miracle grow

Orrick is growing more quickly than a well-watered Chia pet. The firm has more than doubled its size in the last decade. The firm's Los Angeles office, opened in 1985 with two attorneys, now has more than 50 lawyers, and the firm expects the office to double in size in the next five years. In the summer of 1998, the firm set up shop in London after hiring U.K. project finance specialist Ian Johnson in April. Johnson and another Orrick partner, Michael Volstad, opened the office with two associates, and by 2000 it had grown to 10 lawyers. Orrick's presence in England would have increased significantly if a proposed merger with London-based Bird & Bird had not fallen through. The newly opened Seattle office is expected to grow to 20 attorneys by the end of 2000.

GETTING HIRED

Serious about recruiting

Orrick "almost always sends partners" to do on-campus interviews. According to an insider, "The firm only picks from a few select law schools. If you come from one of those law schools, it's easy to get hired; otherwise, it's pretty difficult." Moreover, sources report that while "Orrick is perhaps not as selective as some other big firms," it is "getting progressively more competitive." Callback interviews last a half-day, involving four or five interviews with both associates and partners from the groups in which an associate has expressed interest as well as a member of the office's hiring committee. Then it's off to a two-hour lunch with two junior associates, "usually at a chi-chi place." Each office handles its own recruiting, although contacts from different offices report using the same procedure. Although some offers are given the day of the second round, this is not always the norm, our contacts tell us. "San Francisco and Silicon Valley are more selective than New York," reports one New York-based associate. "It is much easier to lateral in than to get a position as a summer associate," states an attorney. "Lateral hires are actively pursued, and as long as there are no 'landmines' in prior experience and background, an offer is likely."

Serious about interviewing

Orrick interviewees shouldn't expect a walk in the park. One of our contacts recalls a vigorous on-campus interview. "My experience was that it was more than just talking," that contact notes, adding that the interviewer "had definitely looked at my resumé. It was more formal than what some of my friends went through." How did that insider manage to impress? "I really showed my interest in the firm and why I wanted to go to Orrick as opposed to just getting a job."

Serious about diversity hiring

Given the firm's documented struggles to improve its diversity, women and minority candidates can expect to be courted assiduously. One contact recalls efforts to hire a diverse summer associate class: "The diversity committee made extra sure to do interviews. We did huge follow-up campaigns with minority and women candidates that we liked. We called them relentlessly."

OUR SURVEY SAYS

Movin' on up

Orrick, Herrington & Sutcliffe associates characterize the firm as one that is "definitely on the upward slope and planning to have a bigger presence in the Valley. [Orrick] is dominated by an irreverent, often coarse sense of humor. The attorneys, including the partners, want to have fun while they succeed." Another insider notes that Orrick is "an upbeat, exciting place to work, and most attorneys share in the enthusiasm." Many credit the growth of the firm to Ralph Baxter, Orrick's CEO, whom an associate likens to a "benevolent dictator." The growth has created identity problems for the firm, one attorney reports. "It wants to be an old 'white shoe' firm when it's a really a high-quality, young, brash startup." One source sums up the firm by simply stating that "most of the Silicon Valley/California cliches apply here."

Money makes the world go 'round

Orrick had drawn some heat from associates by being among the last of San Francisco firms to raise associates wages. Once the raises were given, Orrick "kept pace with the market on base salaries," reports one associate. "However, its bonus structure requires slightly higher billables than other San Francisco and Silicon Valley firms." An attorney remarks, "Most of the salary is now built into the base. I will get a bonus if I bill 1,950 hours — which I will likely do. The amount is so small compared to the base, however, that it's not worth thinking about. It's kind of odd, it almost works to remove the billable hour requirement." However, we hear that "Orrick is willing to go beyond the stated number for exceptional effort or hours."

While generally satisfied with the pay raise, insiders note that there is a downside to the windfall. "We just joined the income spiral — it is bad for law firm economics, and it will eventually only result in more hard work for associates," observes a source. Not all Orrick offices are pleased with their pay raises. Attorneys at the Sacramento office received a smaller raise and feel snubbed. "Although other national firms decided to pay their Sacramento associates the same as at all other offices, Orrick chose not to," sighs a Sacramento source. "We have a 25% differential from SF and all of the other locations. Morale is low due to the differential."

Pro bono or no bono?

The pay increases have also affected lawyers who wish to work on pro bono cases. "There are rumblings about the demise of pro bono in the wake of salary increases," an insider reports, "but I have not seen concrete evidence of this yet." Another observes that "the pressure to increase billable hours has decreased the emphasis on pro bono work." A second-year associate states that while "unlimited pro bono counts toward billable hours, very little emphasis is placed on doing pro bono. The firm is only as committed as any individual lawyer may be."

Nice partners

Associates give very good reviews to the "down-to-earth" partners at Orrick. "Though there is a growing expectation that I will work longer hours, the partners always treat me with respect for my ideas and work," states a second-year attorney. "The partners are very vested in the well-being of the firm which translates into mentoring and retaining the associates," another reports. Moreover, "they are open with praise and ready to confer responsibility upon associates who can handle it." Associates are "impressed with the complexity of tasks that they are trusted with" by partners. "Partners at Orrick don't just treat associates well," reports an informant in the Silicon Valley office. "They also take an active interest in my life outside of the office and my family." While most associates were overwhelmingly positive in their attitudes towards partners, there were some critics among the ranks at Orrick. "They have no respect for an associate's outside commitments or values, like spending time with family, resting, or staying healthy."

Busy bees

An Orrick associate is a busy associate. When asked about the social opportunities available at the firm, one attorney simply asked, "Social life, what's that?" Despite the obvious time crunch, others report that, "associates frequently hang out together and have happy hours together. Certain partners are often involved. [Orrick is] a very warm and genial place that encourages interaction." Even corporate associates have been known to get in on the action. "We try as much as possible to interact socially; and so far the results have been superb. We are even very close to the litigators." Imagine that! One source believes that the negative aspects of the firm's social life can be traced to socializing by "level of seniority. Partners do not socialize with junior associates." Overall, though, an insider observes that "people here are very nice and easy to be with, but we have our own lives. We don't feel a need to spend 100 percent of our time with our colleagues."

It's training men (hallelujah)

"I have never received and benefited from training as much as I have at Orrick," a Silicon Valley-based attorney declares. "The firm has found the ability to train associates on the essential elements needed to be a good lawyer." Orrick encourages associates to go to the ten-day National Trial Advocacy Program and offers a three-month volunteer program at the Santa Clara County District Attorney's office. A graduate of the program recalls that "during that time, I collected my Orrick salary, contributed toward earning my bonus as if I were billing as an associate, and had the moral support of the attorneys in the office while I was away." Some associates gripe that "after the first year there is virtually no formal training program for litigation associates." Moreover, "on the corporate side, the firm has never managed to produce a formal training program despite paying lip service to it for years. The result is occasional lunches (with stale handouts) that are cancelled and rescheduled as often as they are held."

They keep going and going and going...

Orrick associates have found that success has its downside in ever-increasing hours. "The quantity of hours has grown like the Internet company stocks," supplies a simile-fond source. Another agrees, stating, "The hours are extremely erratic and unpredictable. You never know whether you are going home or going away for the weekend until the minute you walk out the door. Long weekends have taken on a new meaning; instead of going away, we just work longer hours than usual." As one overworked Orrickian orates, "When it is bad, it is very, very bad. Some months you feel as if you'll drop dead from exhaustion." While the grind definitely wears associates down, one source who is pretty convinced that the cup is half full offers the opinion that "having a cordial, respectable, and supportive work environment makes [the hours] more bearable."

The extraordinary road to partner

"It takes an extraordinary effort to make partner here," reports a San Francisco associate. "The firm line of partnership consideration within eight years is a joke — it is more of a 10 to 12 year track, and then you are made a non-equity partner for the first three years of partnership." Moreover, an insider observes, "it seems as though Orrick hires more lateral partners than it promotes from its associate pool. Thus, the best way to become a partner is to leave and then come back." One well-informed source reveals, "The magic number is 2000 hours consistently." Other suggestions to increase one's chances are to "work all the time and love it," "bill, bill, bill," and "don't say no to work." Furthermore, "kissing the right asses doesn't hurt." Those willing to fulfill these requirements for partnership may find partnership is not the plum it used to be. As one attorney states, "most associates are not interested in becoming a partner here. The partners seem very unhappy with their lives and few associates have any desire to emulate them."

Looking for lateral women

"Sure, the firm hires an equal amount of female and male associates, but there are extraordinarily few female partners," criticizes an insider in the New York office. "If the firm were truly interested in having more women partners, it could make it a priority to hire lateral women. It has not done so." An associate notes that Orrick "could do a lot better in mentoring, part-time programs, and other work-family issues. They simply aren't discussed." Many female attorneys feel that "the underlying sense is that they do not like part-time associates and are looking for ways to do away with the program altogether or pay part-time associates less." A DC resident states, "This firm has crappy maternity leave policies and very little real (as opposed to on-paper) support for working mothers. The senior woman partner in the office is hostile to parenting issues generally (and not generally supportive of women)."

Efforts for ethnic diversity fruitless so far

An attorney at Orrick relates that there is "very little diversity among associates here." Furthermore, as a San Francisco source observes, "there are virtually no minority partners. The firm takes steps to recruit minority associates but has not found a way to attract significant minority attorneys and has done nothing to recruit lateral minority partners." Some believe that "there is a conscious effort to make the firm reflect the diversity of our Silicon Valley clients; unfortunately, it has not resulted in a significant minority presence yet."

Gay OK

Orrick is a "San Francisco-based firm and therefore is very receptive to diversity issues" with respect to gays and lesbians, associates say. "The associates and partners seem very open and accepting."

According to one attorney, "The firm is great on gay and lesbian issues. Orrick supports gay and lesbian groups as pro bono counsel and makes all benefits available to same-sex partners. At social gatherings, same-sex couples are treated no differently than heterosexual couples. There are a number of openly gay and lesbian partners as well as associates."

And, in the end

"No job is entirely fulfilling, but I am generally quite satisfied," states an Orrickian. Another finds some "dissatisfaction in the number of hours I am sometimes required to dedicate to work. It's hard to find a balance between personal life and professional life." However, the positive aspects of working at Orrick — "exciting clients, challenging work, fulfilling environment, and excellent preparation for many opportunities" — makes it a firm that at least one associate finds "about as good as it gets for a big law firm."

VAULT.COM 43 PRESTIGE RANKING
Akin Gump Strauss Hauer & Feld, L.L.P.

Robert S. Strauss Building
1333 New Hampshire Avenue, NW
Washington, DC 20036
(202) 887-4000
Fax: (202) 887-4288
www.akingump.com

LOCATIONS

Washington, DC • Austin, TX • Dallas, TX • Houston, TX • Los Angeles, CA • New York, NY • Philadelphia, PA • San Antonio, TX • Brussels • London • Moscow • Riyadh (affiliate)

MAJOR DEPARTMENTS/PRACTICES

Antitrust • Bankruptcy • Communications • Corporate • Energy/Environmental • Entertainment • Food and Drug • Health Industry • Intellectual Property • International • Litigation • Labor and Employment • Public Law and Policy • Real Estate • Tax • Technology

THE STATS

No. of attorneys: 908
No. of offices: 12
Summer associate offers: 43 out of 46 (Washington, DC, 1999)
Chairman: R. Bruce McLean
Hiring Partner: Dennis M. Race (Washington, DC)

THE BUZZ
What attorneys at other firms are saying about this firm

- "Good political connections"
- "Faded glory"
- "Lobbying group is very prestigious and very hard to get into"
- "Achin' Rump"

PAY

Washington, DC, 2000
1st year: $125,000 + bonus
2nd year: $135,000 + bonus
3rd year: $150,000 + bonus
4th year: $160,000+ bonus
5th year: $170,000+ bonus
6th year: $185,000+ bonus
Salaries based on 2,000 hours
Bonuses based on hours and merit; additional bonus for associates billing more than 2,400 hours
Summer associate: $2,400/week

Austin, Dallas, Houston, 2000
1st year: $115,000 + bonus
2nd year: $125,000 + bonus
3rd year: $135,000 + bonus
4th year: $150,000 + bonus
5th year: $160,000 + bonus
6th year: $175,000 + bonus
7th year: $180,000 + bonus
8th year: $185,000 + bonus
Salaries based on 2,000 hours
Bonuses based on hours and merit; additional bonus for associates billing more than 2,400 hours
Summer associate: $1,750/week

New York, 2000
1st year: $125,000 + bonus
2nd year: $135,000 + bonus
3rd year: $150,000 + bonus
4th year: $170,000 + bonus
5th year: $190,000 + bonus
Salaries based on 2,000 hours
Bonuses based on hours and merit; additional bonus for associates billing more than 2,400 hours
Summer associate: $2,400/week

NOTABLE PERKS

- Emergency child care
- Frequent sports tickets, especially in New York
- $60,000 longevity bonus when promoted to counsel after 6 years of service
- Investment plan
- Discount movie tickets

UPPERS

- Vibrant associate social life
- Casual dress every day
- Counsel program

DOWNERS

- Poor support staff (but improving)
- Some friction between partners and associates
- "Less than posh" offices

KEY COMPETITORS

Arnold & Porter
Covington & Burling
Hogan & Hartson
Verner Lipfert Bernhard McPherson & Hand

EMPLOYMENT CONTACT

Ms. Mary G. Beal
Recruitment Administrator
(202) 887-4181
mbeal@akingump.com

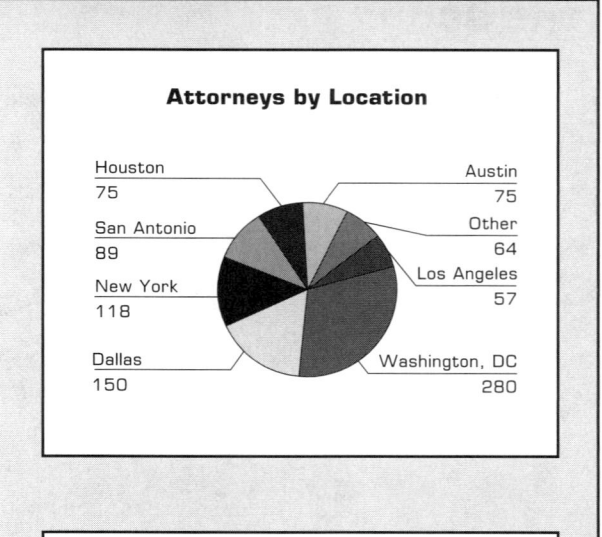

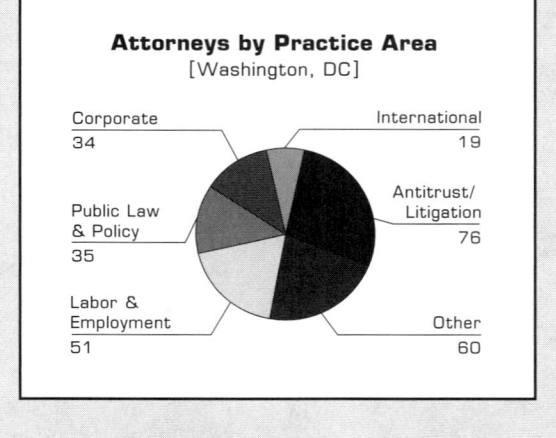

Attorneys by Location

- Houston 75
- Austin 75
- San Antonio 89
- Other 64
- New York 118
- Los Angeles 57
- Dallas 150
- Washington, DC 280

Attorneys by Practice Area [Washington, DC]

- Corporate 34
- International 19
- Public Law & Policy 35
- Antitrust/Litigation 76
- Labor & Employment 51
- Other 60

QUALITY OF LIFE RANKINGS [ASSOCIATES RATE THEIR OWN FIRM]

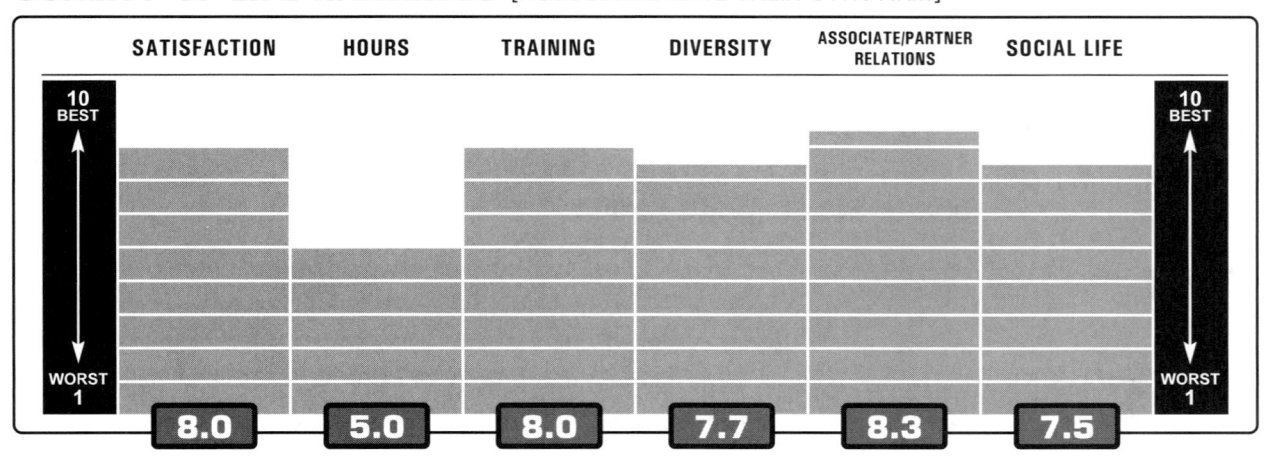

SATISFACTION	HOURS	TRAINING	DIVERSITY	ASSOCIATE/PARTNER RELATIONS	SOCIAL LIFE
8.0	5.0	8.0	7.7	8.3	7.5

THE SCOOP

Though its birthplace is Dallas, Texas, Akin Gump is widely known as the quintessential Washington, DC law firm. Akin Gump is poised not only to reap the benefits that come from a steady stream of white collar (alleged) criminals but to capitalize on the burgeoning tech corridor of Northern Virginia.

History: the legacy of Akin

When Robert Strauss and Richard Gump started their law firm in Dallas in 1945, they might not have gotten very far if Henry Akin hadn't been practicing down the hall. After providing them with invaluable advice during their start-up years, Akin joined as a partner in 1966. After his name was appended to the title, the firm quickly grew into a major national and international legal entity. The firm now has approximately 900 lawyers in 11 offices worldwide.

In early 2000, one week after his 100th birthday, Akin passed away, leaving Akin Gump Strauss Hauer & Feld as his legacy. "We didn't think Henry was ever going to die," remarked founding partner Robert Strauss to *The Legal Times* after Akin's death. "We thought he was going to live forever. And he will, with us."

One of the president's men

The firm tries to be true to its Texas roots, but it has been labeled as the ultimate Washington, DC insider firm. With President Clinton's golf buddy Vernon Jordan, Jr. as the firm's most recognized attorney, it's not surprising that it has earned that reputation. (Jordan changed his role at Akin from partner to senior counsel in December 1999 when he accepted a position at Wall Street i-bank Lazard Freres & Co.) Akin Gump's Washington, DC office, with nearly 300 lawyers, is the firm's largest and most influential outpost. Jordan isn't the firm's only high-profile lawyer, however. Former U.S. Representative Bill Paxon has joined the DC office, and Randy Levine, counsel in the firm's labor and employment practice in New York, is also president of the fabulous New York Yankees.

Expansion through merger

While just about every major law firm has hopes of cashing in on the Internet economy, few firms have the institutional resources of Akin Gump. The firm is pursuing a dual strategy of opening new offices in hot areas for tech interests and developing an extensive technology infrastructure of its own. It recently announced plans to open a Northern Virginia office along the so-called Dulles corridor, where technology companies are springing up like techno dandelions. Meanwhile, the firm has assembled a 200 lawyer multi-disciplinary tech team called Akin Gump Technology Ventures. Akin Gump intends to expand its office infrastructure to include extranets with clients and virtual closing rooms, where all parties can virtually review information pertinent to transactions.

In June 1999, Akin Gump announced an affiliation with the law office of Abdulaziz Fahad in Riyadh, Saudi Arabia. "We determined that our clients' needs would best be served by establishing a presence in the Middle East," announced Vernon Jordan and Robert Strauss in a release at the time of the merger. "A Riyadh office is an important part of our strategic plan as we continue to serve our clients' international needs."

Patently high IP growth

Several recent mergers have burnished the lustre of Akin's intellectual property group. In January 1999, the firm merged with the Houston IP boutique Pravel Hewitt. To solidify its position in Philadelphia's relatively competitive IP market, Akin Gump also combined with Philadelphia IP powerhouse boutique Panitch Schwarze Jacobs & Nadel in July 1999. As of June 2000, 28 of the 31 attorneys in the Philadelphia office are working exclusively for IP clients. The expansion has paid off: in May 2000, *Intellectual Property Today* ranked the firm No. 2 in the number of trademarks registered in 1999.

Black eye

Akin Gump suffered a minor embarrassment in 1999 when it was revealed that founding partner Robert Strauss was connected to rogue money manager Martin Frankel. The devious Frankel misrepresented himself to a slew of investors, claiming he had contacts in the Roman Catholic Church and inside major insurance companies. As it turns out, the Greenwich, Connecticut-based money manager was a fraud who left the country with hundreds of millions of dollars in ill-gotten gains. Frankel was referred to Akin by Strauss, and the firm represented trusts that Frankel used to manage his money before his exposure. It is important to note that while Frankel, who was eventually caught and extradited to the U.S., is facing a host of indictments, the firm has not been accused of any wrongdoing.

Corporate practice pulls its weight

The corporate practice has been important to Akin Gump's business, with operations ranging from mergers and acquisitions to bankruptcy to securities. In April 1999, the firm advised Clear Channel Communications in its $4.4 billion acquisition of SFX Entertainment. Four months later, Akin assisted with the merger between Dynegy, Inc., a Texas corporation that markets energy products and services, and Illinova

Corp., an electric and gas utilities company headquartered in Decatur, IL. Dynegy owns and operates 47 gasoline processing plants, with a paid staff of 2,500 people. In 1998 the firm's bankruptcy practice took part in the restructuring of the Caspian Pipeline consortium, a $2.2 billion project bringing oil from Russia to the Black Sea.

White collar defendants

Akin Gump has also made a name for itself defending alleged white collar criminals. The firm's white collar defense team is led by William Hundley, formerly chief of the Department of Justice's Organized Crime and Racketeering department and an assistant to Robert Kennedy when he was attorney general. Another well-known partner in criminal defense is John Dowd, famous for conducting the investigation that got Pete Rose banned from baseball. The firm has also represented defendants in the investigation of Agriculture Secretary Michael Espy, the Iran-Contra scandal, the Whitewater investigation and Watergate.

The lion of litigation

Some of Akin Gump's best work has come from its litigation team. The firm successfully represented supermarket chain Food Lion against ABC, arguing that an undercover story for the network's Primetime Live program, exposing unsanitary conditions, was unfair and employed sneaky journalistic tactics, including hidden cameras. (Akin Gump notes pointedly on its web site that ABC journalist Diane Sawyer has since used hidden cameras on ABC staffers, to the distress of those employees.)

Good deeds really rewarded

In June 1999, the DC Bar named Akin Gump litigation associate Michael L. Converse its Pro Bono Lawyer of the Year. Showing the softer side of the huge corporate law firm, the next month Akin Gump launched the Washington Lawyer's Committee for Civil Rights and Urban Affairs' 30th anniversary fund drive with a generous gift of $200,000. The organization's mission is to encourage the private bar to address the pervasive problems of discrimination and poverty in the DC metropolitan area. The firm's other pro bono commitments include the Lawyers for Human Rights, Parents for Autistic Children, the Legal Counsel for the Elderly, and the Washington Area Lawyers for the Arts, as well as a newly-formed partnership with volunteer organization DC Cares. In one pending case, Akin Gump is representing DC officials against a religious discrimination suit brought by a former firefighter.

GETTING HIRED

A stringent process

Getting hired at Akin is no walk in the proverbial park. "Hiring standards are stringent," says one contact. "The firm hires primarily out of its summer program. A hiring committee manages the recruitment of summer associates each year. The committee looks primarily for students near the top of their class from the top 25 law schools and the DC area schools." Another associate concurs, noting that Akin Gump is "very selective for new associates — only a handful of Ivies and top schools are targeted."

"Exceptional academic qualifications alone are not sufficient to guarantee being hired," warns a source. "The firm also looks equally at whether the interviewee is well-rounded and personable."

After campus interviews, candidates are flown to their office of interest for a round of interviews starting promptly at 9 a.m. local time ("So don't be late!") and wrapping up in the early afternoon. The firm also springs for lunch with two associates from different practice areas. Don't expect to get grilled on law topics. Interviewers will more likely ask about interesting things on your resume. Says one associate, "If [the candidate] went to my school, I'll ask about professors that we might have had." If you survive the questioning, expect a decision from Akin in a week to 10 days.

OUR SURVEY SAYS

Changing culture

Insiders' descriptions of the firm's corporate culture vary significantly. Apparently, while the firm is generally relaxed, there is a movement toward a more rigid structure and a focus on the bottom line. One DC lawyer says that Akin Gump is "very upbeat and social. [It's a] great collection of people who are intelligent, funny, and sociable." A New York associate adds that "it's not uncommon to see young partners in the litigation group throwing a football or swinging a golf club in the hallway."

That said, one contact claims that while Akin Gump has historically been "laid-back, relaxed and easy going," there has been a visible shift in the Akin atmosphere in recent months. "Recently, there has been much more of a focus on hours and billables," says one associate. Adds a Los Angeles attorney, "For years, Akin has held itself out as one big family. I think that remains true to a certain extent, at least as compared to other firms of its size. But certainly, perhaps because of the rapid growth over the past few years — and the rise in salaries — there is a more contentious atmosphere here. It's like the firm has reached its teenage years and is experiencing some angst and growing pains as it tries to figure out exactly who it is and who it wants to be."

Growth has also been an issue in New York. "The office has grown significantly in the last few years," remarks one corporate associate. "It's morphed from a place where you used to know everyone to one where there are now plenty of faces without names associated with them." Culture can vary by department, too. Says another insider, "Akin culture" completely depends upon who you work with — part of the [firm] is fun and functions as a team; another part is competitive and only concerned with the bottom line."

There might be some help on the way, however. A Houston associate reports that partners there "are making a concerted effort to improve associate morale." Another lawyer is confident the firm will improve with time and seasoning. "It's a young partnership and has a lot of potential."

Partners: Some bitterness?

Says one Akin Gump associate: "Partners, for the most part, treat associates well." While many colleagues agree, some call the partnership "a mixed bag." Pay is an issue, as it always is. Reports one DC associate, "Since the salary hike, partners are visibly bitter at paying associates as much as the market demands." (The firm disputes this notion.) Another lawyer feels that "communication between [partners] could be improved with respect to assigning work to associates." Don't get too negative an impression, however. According to one Dallas lawyer, "The partners' treatment of non-partners is one of the best aspects of Akin Gump. An associate typically feels like a productive member of the team, rather than a cog in a wheel."

Akinly affection

Despite some disagreements with their superiors, Akin Gump associates seem to get along with each other. "There is a tremendous amount of social interaction among attorneys in my group," says a lawyer from the Houston office. "Additionally, there appears to be much social interaction among the more junior associates in all groups: lunches, softball, fantasy football, parties, etc." Similarly, in Washington, insiders report that "after work on Friday, you can always find a group of attorneys at Buffalo Billiards," a bar in the basement of the building housing Akin offices.

The usual (long) hours

"The average number of billable hours can range tremendously," reports one litigation associate. "It's dictated by the amount of work within the section or the dictates of a particular case, rather than a sweatshop mentality." That source goes on to add: "I guess the more important question is whether the firm appreciates the billable effort when you're dog-paddling and still taking in water, and the answer is yes." Other sources confirm the "wide discrepancies in hours. It really depends on the luck of the draw. Most associates seem to hit a particularly busy spell at some point in their first couple of years and they get busier and busier the more senior they become." Akin Gump acknowledges that about 25 associates (5 percent of the firm's total) billed more than 2,400 hours in 1999, and the few that reached that level received an extra bonus of an undisclosed amount. The firm also reports that for the year, associates averaged a more reasonable 1,900 billable hours.

At least one lawyer feels the workload is fair. "If you're working at a large law firm and getting paid over $100,000, don't be crying about long hours," growls one DC associate. "If you want short hours, go work for the government or an association and earn that wage. You can't have your cake and eat it too, unless, of course, you're a dot com millionaire."

Pay fails to thrill

While Akin Gump is paying their associates the market rate, some of that pay is in the form of deferred compensation. Under a new system, associates earn bonuses on a point system — similar to that used for partners' compensation — which is based in part on the firm's profitability. The firm claims that deferred compensation is the best way to reward associates for hours billed and that they can potentially earn more than at other firms. Not all associates buy it. "Deferred compensation is awarded only to associates who meet 2,000 billable hours in a year," explains one lawyer. "Akin's deferred payment plan was a major disappointment," confides one insider. "Rather than simply follow suit with our competitors, Akin chose a compensation plan that left associates questioning management's intentions."

Another associate is similarly displeased: "Akin has belatedly and begrudgingly come up to the bare minimum necessary to stay competitive with the DC market. I expect to see attrition on the rise as the Silicon Valley firms with Northern Virginia offices keep raising salaries." Another associate concurs, commenting that pay "is the most contentious issue at Akin these days, as it is at most firms." According to the firm, the bonus system has addressed most lawyers' needs and concerns, and no increase in compensation-related departures is expected.

Perks: an inside track on the Bronx Bombers

Akin Gump associates can pick from the usual array of perks. Meals and cars are paid for by the firm when associates works late; there is no official cut-off time for free meals, and associates can use their judgement about how much to spend. A well-stocked kitchen is also available in the Houston office. "We have Starbucks coffee, free canned sodas, crackers, soup, and aspirin and the like," says one associate in appreciation. All offices have access to discount movie tickets and free sports tickets, but "there is a hierarchy to who receives such tickets." If you like baseball, especially the Yankees, the New York office is probably the best place for you. Partner Randy Levine is the team's president and his access to tickets thus as good as you would expect. In the Washington office, the firm's gym is being remodeled, and there is also a discount on memberships at a local gym. Additionally, the firm recently started an investment fund for associates and moved to a casual dress code every day.

Graduates of "Lawyer College"

Lawyers at Akin Gump seem split over the quality of the firm's training. For Dallas litigators and corporate attorneys, the firm offers "Lawyer College." "Lawyer College seeks to teach what law school typically does not," explains one associate. That includes deposition, motion, and trial skills [as well as transactional skills]. "There's a great emphasis on informal training," says an insider. "I feel the partners in litigation have made a substantial commitment of their personal time to my professional training." One third-year associate notes that during his first year, training was minimal. However, "my second and third years have been a quantum leap forward, both in the amount of responsibility I'm given and the support I've received in learning how to do the transactions." One contact warns that "the [litigation] section takes a learning by doing approach, which is fine, unless you get stuck doing document review for any length of time." Associates firm-wide can receive training in time management, financial management, and Internet research as well as department-specific instruction.

Comfortable but ugly offices

DC associates were relieved when the firm's offices underwent an overhaul in early 2000. "Akin's pre-renovation offices were a disgrace," says one contact. "The post-renovation offices are somewhat better," that source notes, adding that "this firm will never spend the money required for truly first-class space." Others are unhappy with the remodeling. According to one insider, "there have been several complaints regarding the quality of the work that was done" in DC. One associate calls the space "comfortable but ugly," while another terms the artwork "horrific." Despite such sentiments, the firm is extremely proud of its new conference center, opened in May 2000, and looks forward to a new gym and cafeteria.

In New York, "the firm's rapid growth has ensured that the space is never quite sufficient," though only first-year associates are currently sharing offices. Texas offices are graded high, and a renovation in Dallas has gone much better than the one in DC (or at least associates there are less discriminating). Says a source: "The office got new paint, carpet and wall fixtures, and added an entire floor for a conference center."

Creaky support

Akin Gump associates aren't delighted with their luck in support staff, though they concede the situation could be worse. One associate calls support staff "a soft spot that is gradually improving." Another lawyer complains' "I find the support to be poor and many secretaries to be below average in technical operations." A DC associate reports that Akin Gump is "currently reorganizing and improving the computing department and personnel." Additionally, the DC office has hired more staff, including a professional executive director and a chief technology officer.

Sticking around

At Akin Gump, "people start leaving around their fourth or fifth year, but it's not a mass exodus and it's definitely better than it is at other firms." As with all firms, Akin Gump associates feel that few associates leave for other firms. Rather, "they go to dot-coms or other in-house jobs. It says a lot about the firm that people do get such great opportunities after working here," boasts one associate. The government is another popular destination. "This is a last stop for people practicing in the firm environment," says another source.

Partnership track: room at the inn

In September 1998, Akin Gump adopted a new policy that promotes associates to counsel in their sixth year of service with the firm. The counsel position serves as a training ground for partnership — responsibility increases, and mentoring and client development are stressed.

When it comes to the process of making partner, decisions seem less mysterious at Akin Gump than at other firms, according to insiders. "In my time here, I've only been surprised by a couple of the partnership decisions," says one associate. "I think predictability is a good thing." Another lawyer agrees, remarking, "I know associates who are a mortal lock for partner, and I know associates who don't stand a chance."

"If you stay for eight or nine years, consistently bill 2,000 hours and turn out high-quality work product," says one source, "your chances of making litigation partner are better than at a lot of other places — where you can do all of the above and still be told 'Sorry, no room at the inn.'"

One attorney says that outstanding written work is the key to making partner. "The partnership game is about instilling confidence in the partners. You want them to think 'OK, this is someone who the clients will like, will trust and will send more business to.' At least for your first year or so, most of your work will involve submitting a written product to a partner. Nothing kills the partner's confidence like a sloppy work product."

Commitment to diversity

"The firm is clearly committed to finding and keeping a racially diverse workforce," says a source. "However, minority recruiting and retention still present significant challenges. The firm still needs to do better, but it appears to recognize that need." Insiders say that Akin "makes an effort to recruit minority candidates through various avenues, including minority job fairs." The firm as a whole is "far more diverse than the average law firm." In 1999 Akin Gump won the Thomas L. Sager Award for diversity.

Akin Gump is also doing a commendable job of job hiring, promoting, and mentoring women, associates say. Notes one female associate: "Not only are the women well-respected and well-represented in the partnership ranks, they also hold firm management positions and [serve] on firm-wide committees." "In short," she adds, "it's a true meritocracy from a gender standpoint." Not so in some other offices: "[There's] definitely equality in hiring," says a DC lawyer, "but virtually no mentoring, part-time programs or other programs to even provide a forum to discuss the issue."

With respect to "alternative lifestyles," sources say "the firm is very receptive." Akin Gump offers domestic partner benefits, and insiders report a few "out" partners and associates. While this hasn't created any problems, some insiders say that when it comes to a few of the older partners, the "less known about a gay attorney, the better off that attorney is."

Hard to beat

Despite the "sub-par office space and support," and the firm's growing focus on "the bottom line or end result," insiders concede that all law firms have their problems.

In general, however, Akin Gump associates report a high degree of satisfaction. "I get frustrated because the firm is incredibly cheap on issues like salary and office space," says one source, "but I can't argue with my training, experience, partnership prospects or interpersonal relationships." "It comes down to this: there's more to life and work than money and on just about every front other than money, I have found Akin Gump hard to beat." A lateral hire calls his stint at Akin Gump "the first law job I have enjoyed. It sounds pretty goofy, but I credit Akin Gump with making me like practicing law."

Winston & Strawn

VAULT.COM PRESTIGE RANKING: 44

35 West Wacker Drive
Chicago, Illinois 60601
(312) 558-5600
Fax: (312) 558-5700
www.winston.com

LOCATIONS

Chicago, IL (HQ)
Los Angeles, CA
New York, NY
Washington, DC
Geneva
Paris

MAJOR DEPARTMENTS/PRACTICES

Contracts
Corporate (Mergers & Acquisitions/Securities Offerings)
Employment & Labor
Energy
Government Relations
Intellectual Property & Technology
Litigation
Real Estate
Trusts and Estates

THE STATS

No. of attorneys: 725
No. of offices: 6
Summer associate offers: 32 out of 33 (Chicago, 1999)
Managing Partner: James M. Neis
Hiring Partner: Paul H. Hensel (Chairman)

PAY

All Domestic Offices, 2000
1st year: $125,000 + discretionary bonus
2nd year: $135,000 + discretionary bonus
3rd year: $150,000 + discretionary bonus
Summer associate: $2,400/week

NOTABLE PERKS

- Emergency day care for children
- All attorneys receive a laptop
- New part-time policy
- Skyboxes at Comiskey Park and United Center
- Highly praised subsidized firm dining room in Chicago

THE BUZZ

What attorneys at other firms are saying about this firm

- "Very Republican"
- "Good lawyers, great offices"
- "Mean to its associates"
- "Gained strength under Jim Thompson"

UPPERS

- Open to intra-firm transfers
- Top-notch litigation practice
- Pro bono powerhouse

DOWNERS

- Decision-making process leaves associates out
- Fear that salary increases = more billable requirements
- "No gym in Chicago office"

KEY COMPETITORS

Kirkland & Ellis
Mayer, Brown & Platt
McDermott, Will, & Emery
Sidley & Austin

EMPLOYMENT CONTACT

Ms. Paulette R. Kuttig
Legal Recruiting Manager
(312) 558-5742

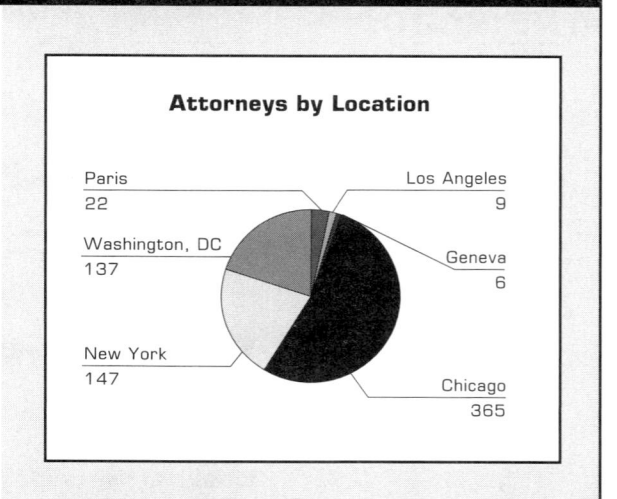

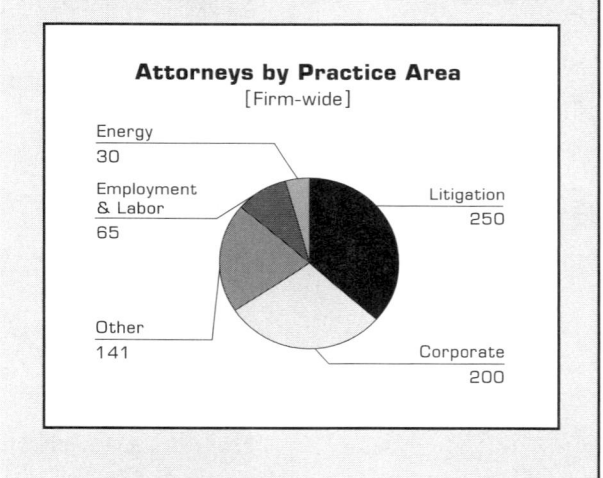

Attorneys by Location

- Paris: 22
- Washington, DC: 137
- New York: 147
- Los Angeles: 9
- Geneva: 6
- Chicago: 365

Attorneys by Practice Area [Firm-wide]

- Energy: 30
- Employment & Labor: 65
- Other: 141
- Litigation: 250
- Corporate: 200

QUALITY OF LIFE RANKINGS [ASSOCIATES RATE THEIR OWN FIRM]

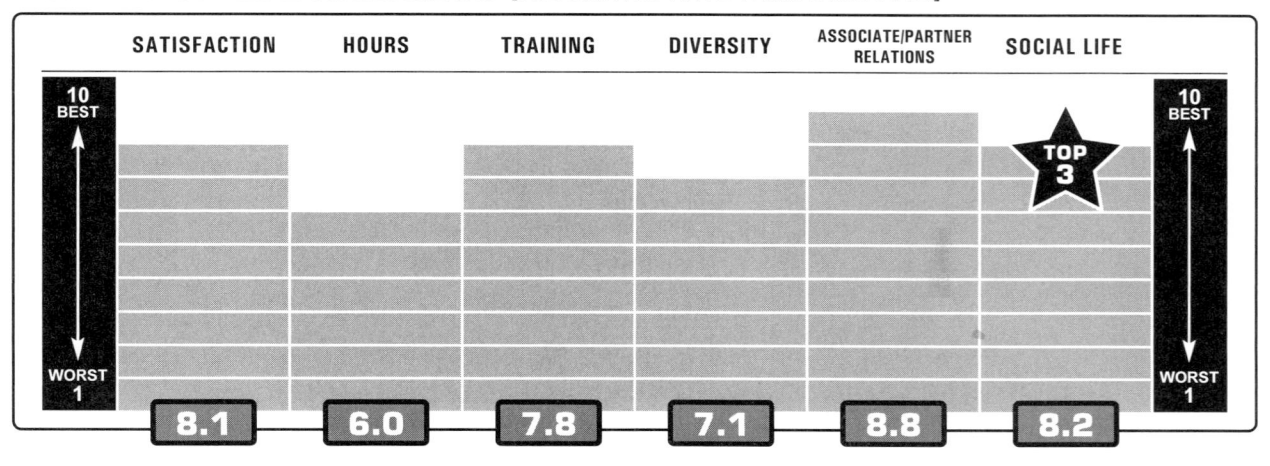

SATISFACTION	HOURS	TRAINING	DIVERSITY	ASSOCIATE/PARTNER RELATIONS	SOCIAL LIFE
8.1	6.0	7.8	7.1	8.8	8.2 (TOP 3)

THE SCOOP

Winston is a Chicago firm with attitude. This top-tier firm is noted for representing unpopular clients like the tobacco industry — and doing a darn good job of it too. Other top Illinois-area clients include Sears and Abbott Laboratories. Winston's prowess in both litigation and corporate matters, however, ensure it's not just a regional firm.

History: old-timers — and we mean that as a compliment

Chicago-based Winston & Strawn was founded in 1853 by Frederick Winston; in 1892 Silas Strawn, the firm's other name partner, was added. Over the years, the firm added offices in New York, Washington, DC, Los Angeles, Paris, France, and Geneva, Switzerland. Growth through merger has been popular. In 1989, the firm merged with New York-based Cole & Deitz; the next year, it was DC's Bishop, Cook. The merging has continued into the new millennium. *The Lawyer* reported in March 2000 that Winston was in talks to merge with New York firm Whitman Breed Abbott & Morgan. That would increase the number of Winston attorneys to 850 — up from approximately 700 — and boost the New York office to 250 from 145.

As impressive as Winston's history has been, the firm was embarrassed in 1994 when then-managing partner Gary Fairchild pleaded guilty to embezzling almost $800,000 from the firm and five clients. But the ironically named Fairchild's peccadillos are outweighed by Winston's stable and strong leadership. James Thompson, former governor of Illinois and U.S. Attorney, joined the firm in 1991 as a partner (he had been of counsel prior to taking office in 1977). The firm is led by James Neis, a DePaul Law graduate who has been with the firm since 1977.

Acrobatic litigation

Winston's known for hard-hitting litigation — a reputation that associates echo gleefully. "In litigation, we are considered to be a big firm," one Chicago-based associate boasts to Vault.com. "We do not cut corners and we will make you jump through every hoop. You won't outspend us." Indeed, litigation is probably the firm's shining strength. The 200-member litigation team is led by Dan Webb, a Loyola Law School graduate who has been with the firm since 1985. Webb's profile on Winston's web site (www.winston.com) includes a link to a 17-page document detailing his greatest hits. Why does Webb need that much storage space on the Winston server? He's famous, mostly for prosecuting General John Poindexter, the National Security Advisor to President Ronald Reagan, in the Iran-Contra affair of the 1980s.

More recently, Webb represented Philip Morris in several lawsuits brought against tobacco companies, taking the role of lead counsel for the cigarette maker and even serving as lead courtroom counsel on common issues for all the tobacco companies named in the suit. Webb relishes his role as the representative of unpopular clients such as Big Tobacco. "The companies are accused of a lot of misconduct, but when it gets in front of a jury, jurors realize the allegations are not true and that individuals have to be held accountable for the decisions they make," Webb told *The Illinois Legal Times*. Webb sometimes has time to handle clients not enmeshed in controversy. For example, he served as lead counsel for Bell Atlantic in several cases, including an antitrust suit against AT&T and Lucent Technologies.

Webb does let other lawyers litigate cases. Winston attorneys successfully represented Abbott Laboratories in a negligence suit filed by an HIV-infected plaintiff. The firm also represented Cleveland law firm Baker & Hostetler in a malpractice suit.

Corporate needs no practice

Winston's corporate practice spans the entire spectrum from mergers and acquisitions to bankruptcy to securities. In M&A, Winston represented concert promoter SFX Entertainment when they were purchased for $3.3 billion by Clear Channel Communications in March 2000. That same month, the firm represented Royal Numico when the Netherlands nutritional products maker purchased Pittsburgh-based General Nutrition for $1.77 billion.

GETTING HIRED

School doesn't matter

Firm insiders report that Winston puts little weight on school attended. "We're a Chicago firm, not an East Coast firm, so you don't need an Ivy League school on your resume," reports one source. While the most prestigious law schools in the Midwest — Chicago, Northwestern, and Michigan — are prevalent, Notre Dame, Illinois, and Loyola are also represented. "Winston prides itself on hiring the best talent in the market," says one associate. That means that grades are important, no matter what school you attended, and a spot on the law review is key. Clerkships are also looked upon favorably.

Some at Winston claim to detect a recent drop in the quality of lateral hires. "As the firm has expanded, I've noticed the quality of associates hired, particularly laterals, has gone down somewhat," says one source. "I think, however, that the firm intends to tighten its criteria going forward, given new salary and associate performance considerations."

Good cop, good cop

Besides grades, personality is a key Winston criteria during the hiring process. Winston does "not want a gunner mentality," says one source. The interviews, therefore, are designed to be low-stress. "We're very friendly," says a Chicago associate. "At other places some people try to play the bad cop. We don't." One piece of advice: try to stand out. "[Since] lawyers at Winston interview many candidates each year, it's crucial to distinguish yourself — in terms of personality and interests — from all the other candidates," says one contact. "Winston looks for well-rounded people who are team players," summarizes one insider.

OUR SURVEY SAYS

We're not stuffy! (But we do work hard)

If you thought a law firm (and Winston in particular) might be a staid place to work, Winston insiders encourage you to reconsider. "Contrary to popular opinion, Winston is not a stuffy place to work," bristles one first-year associate. Most insiders echo that opinion, calling Winston "very professional, exciting, and rewarding. A great place to develop one's legal career." Most of the comments Vault.com hears about Winston culture, in fact, are rosy. "Many people here are very laid-back and fun to work with," says one observer. Other sources call the firm "very professional and somewhat formal — but not in a bad way."

Nothing's perfect, and a complaint associates share is the hierarchical structure that shapes Winston's decision-making process. "The firm is bureaucratic," complains one lawyer. "Decisions are made by a small group of powerful partners, and there is almost never any solicitation of associate feedback. It is possible to have a good time here, but there is always a political undertone that one must be aware of — you never know when something you do is going to create a reputation for you." A first-year associate agrees with that perception, stating that "an elite few make the rules and let everyone know after the fact."

While the environment is as stressful as any other firm, "the pressure on Winston associates is from the work, not the people," according to one associate. "Client service is paramount. A Winston partner will never tell you to work a weekend because of how much you are paid. Instead, a partner is more likely to reference the client's needs and say something like 'the client needs us to get this done and we'll get it done.'" Subtle or direct though the plea may be, Winston associates end up working many weekends.

Partners who say "please" and "thank you"

Winston associates note that "other than the occasional jerk partner, most partners here are very kind and very wonderful to work for." "The relationships between associates and partners seems to be largely left up to the individuals — respect goes both ways," says one source. "Additionally, there exist few or no barriers in the communications between partners and associates." Politeness reigns. "It says a lot about people when they pay you a boatload of money, yet still say please and thank you," says a litigation lawyer. Another associate relates a similar experience, saying "I am thanked for my help more often than I would expect." "Overall, the firm is a meritocracy, and treatment by partners seems to reflect this," reports one source.

Winstonites do admit to the presence of tyrannical partners at Winston. "There are a few partners that treat us like fungible warm bodies and have no respect for us as people," says one second-year associate. Fortunately, "it is relatively easy to maneuver yourself so that you don't work with them again."

Hot social life in the Second City

Insiders say that "once you have established yourself, Winston can be a friendly environment." Better look for a place in the city if you want an active social life. "Winston is a very enjoyable place to work because of its associates," says one Chicago associate. "There is a great deal of social interaction between attorneys outside the firm, particularly those who live in Chicago, as opposed to the suburbs." "I regularly hang out with a group of about 10 lawyers in my class — we are constantly getting together outside of work. We have arranged group trips, dinners, and parties," says one busy attorney.

Can you really determine your hours?

"To a certain degree, you can determine how many hours you work" says a fourth-year associate. "Obviously, the more you work, the more value you provide the firm and the higher your bonus." Another associate contends that "hours pressure is mostly self-imposed here. [Hours] clearly matter for bonuses, but it is rare to have someone mention it to you, even though it is clear it is being followed. In my class, 2,100 to 2,200 hours is the norm — those who get sent away on trial end up with significantly more, but otherwise it is rare to hear of someone with more than 2,400." Winston is making an effort to make it easier for associates to work fewer hours. "The firm has invested heavily in technology that makes my work more efficient, and also makes it easy to work remotely if necessary."

Pay flap

Winston's pay structure excites interest in most associates Vault.com surveyed. "Several firms set a new pay scale. Winston was not among the leader firms and it was noticed," reports one litigation associate. "The firm finally announced that it would match these numbers for those with acceptable hours and evaluations. Approximately one month later, each associate received a memo with his or her new salary." And what did that memo say? "This salary was determined by dividing each class into three tiers — only the top tier received the numbers that match the rest of the market." Not everyone makes the same. The result, that contact says, was that "many associates feel betrayed and misled by the way in which these raises were handed out."

Pro bono issues prove a bone of contention for many lawyers. "For purposes of base compensation, the top tier of the structure for each class does not take pro bono or firm committee matters into account," grumbles one associate. Another frets that "while pro bono hours have always counted towards your yearly billable total, they were not included when determining whether an associate billed enough to make it to tier one for salary."

Winston points out that associates themselves were not divvied up into three categories by the new pay structure. Rather, the hours were divided into three levels. All associates billing 1,950 hours and above will receive the highest level of compensation. Tier two associates are those billing between 1,850 and 1,950 hours. According to the firm, the only tier three associates "are those with utilization issues" — and the vast majority of associates are already comfortably in tier one. Pro bono hours do not count towards salary, but do count towards bonus.

May I take your order?

Associates at Winston rave about the subsidized attorney dining room which is open for lunch and a Friday cocktail hour. "The attorney dining room is fabulous," says one associate. "Winston attorneys get to have an hour away from work to have lunch with friends and socialize at a central location. Not everyone takes advantage of it, but it is a major perk." Another lawyer rattles off the menu: "For $7.75, you can get all you can eat, or you can buy per item. There are plenty of choices for main courses, plus a salad bar, two soups, etc." Not only that, the food is reportedly "decent."

Additionally, the firm pays for meals after 7 p.m., as well as transportation subsidies. If you like sports, "the firm has tickets to luxury boxes for the White Sox and the

United Center. Most associates end up going to one or two events per year." Finally, it pays to get involved with the summer associate program. "If you are a summer associate advisor, you get to go to plenty of summer events," says one contact.

Training for juniors

Insiders say that "training opportunities are offered not only within one's professional field, but in areas which assist an individual generally in his or her practice, such as computer training," says one contact. "They make a decent effort to have formal training programs," reports a source. "For a while, they held morning meetings about once a month to cover different areas. They had a deposition training session where they flew in the associates from DC and New York and we met for three days." Obviously, the training is geared towards newer lawyers. "There is a formal training program that affects junior associates more than mid-levels," says one attorney. "The firm spends both money and time on deposition training, legal writing training, and marketing training for junior associates."

Beautiful skyline views

One attorney at Winston describes the offices as "spectacular. The Chicago office is absolutely beautiful with lovely views over Lake Michigan and the Chicago skyline." Another lawyer calls the offices "classic but understated." Other Chicago associates say Winston has "without a doubt, the most beautiful offices in the city," and that "only a visit could do Winston justice."

Support staff: too respectful?

Winston associates rave about the support staff, saying the firm provides "support services for just about every attorney need." Another lawyer worries that support staff treats associates "almost with too much respect. I have to go out of my way to have support staff call me by my first name." Over-respectful staff — an uncommon complaint indeed!

One associate offers this criticism. "We tend to invest in computer programs — word processing, document imaging and retrieval, e-mail — that are cumbersome and that occasionally sag under the weight of all their bells and whistles, most of which are entirely irrelevant to the average associate."

Low turnover

"Most associates are satisfied with their employment and turnover is extremely low in comparison to other firms," reports one lawyer. Another insider says "not only does it seem relatively rare for people to leave (as large firms go), but it is not uncommon for people to return." Insiders also claim that associate turnover has risen along with the market. "Turnover has increased recently given greater salary stratification within associate classes," says one lawyer.

Get on the partnership track (and make friends with the right people)

Insiders say that "hours are the crucial factor in making partner," and income partners are elected after eight years; equity partnership is awarded four to five years later. The cut off for hours appears to be about 2,100 to 2,200, and, clearly, doing good work is important. There are other factors to consider. "The key is latching onto a partner who will go to bat for you," reports one lawyer. "After a year or two here, you end up working with one or two partners more often than others — they end up being, in many respects, your sponsor once you are up for partner. Obviously, some partners are better than others at marketing you." Another associate concurs, saying that "partnership prospects can be improved by working for powerful attorneys who will push your name." One source advises potential prospects to "make a concerted effort to gain as much experience and responsibility on cases as possible."

Diversity efforts soldier on

On the whole, Winston & Strawn associates say their firm is making an effort to encourage diversity in hiring, mentoring, and promotion. "The firm has made significant efforts to create and support a diverse workplace," reports one insider. Another adds that "Winston makes a real effort to recruit minorities."

"I have the sense from several female colleagues who are mothers and work part-time that they feel they are accorded second-class citizenship on certain matters," says one source about the state of gender diversity at Winston. There is disagreement on that point, however. "It is my view that women are treated with the utmost respect and equality within the firm, and that significant efforts have been made to continue doing so," remarks one associate. In general, most insiders hold the opinion that "many partners are aware of gender diversity issues, though there are still areas which are less sensitive than others. Fortunately, there are partners whose commitment to gender equality is outstanding and who take an active role in mentoring women."

For gays and lesbians, one associate says that Winston offers a "level playing field." Another counters that "the firm offers domestic partner benefits, but [I'm] still under the impression that it is a 'don't ask, don't tell' environment." But, the firm continues to try to improve its diversity in all areas. In 1998, it created the Women's Initiative — later expanded into the Diversity Initiative — aimed at stepping up its recruitment, training, mentoring, and other programs.

The 24-partner committee in charge of the Diversity Initiative has seen its work pay off: according to *Chicago Lawyer*, as of May 1999 Winston & Strawn had the most minority lawyers of any large firm in the city. In February 2000, the firm was presented with The Minority Corporate Association's Sager Award for diversity for the second straight year.

Pro bono is popular, but compensation changes loom

As opposed to some other firms that officially encourage pro bono work, but rarely allow attorneys to take the time to perform it, Winston & Strawn has associates who devote 50 percent of their time to pro bono activities. One such Winstonite is Ilene Bloom, an associate who joined the firm in 1996. Bloom's passion is child welfare; she is involved in several children's legal organizations, including the Chicago Bar Association Adoption Assistance Program, and has represented abused and neglected children in Cook County (Illinois) Juvenile Court. When speaking about Winston's pro bono program, Bloom told *The Recorder* that she feels she is on equal footing with other Winston associates.

Her sense of her status is supported, for the most part, by Winston insiders. "The firm has an outstanding commitment to pro bono work," says one associate. But changes to compensation for pro bono work seem to have riled some Winston attorneys. While pro bono hours count towards the 1,950 minimum billable hours requirement, the 2000 salary hikes have brought with them a minimum hourly requirement where none existed before. This policy is new, having been put in place after the 2000 salary hikes, and has met with some confusion and dismay by attorneys. "Associates are very upset about this new attitude toward pro bono, especially the fact that the policy was changed with little fanfare or discussion," one insider reports. "Many associates have told me that they will not take on any more pro bono work." Other associates contend that pro bono hours should count toward both minimum billable requirements and bonus consideration.

Attorney satisfaction remains high

"This is the best firm to work at," says one boastful Winston & Strawn associate. "The partners are respectful, the work is high quality, and the associates make the work entertaining." "For a big firm, it would be difficult to imagine things being significantly nicer," says one third-year associate. "There will always be pressure to work, and there will always be pressure by nature of the work we do. This is not a place to work if you are interested in being home for dinner, or never having to worry before making weekend plans. But generally we get good work and work with smart people." Not everyone is that thrilled. One associate who apparently is unsatisfied with the level of support grouses, "it is hard to be fulfilled by making copies, proofreading, and distributing documents, but that is the price associates pay."

Some Winstonites cherish both the work and the co-workers, stating they are excited that they "get to do interesting work for partners and associates I enjoy spending time with." Another associate notes, "We are paid well, we have access to virtually any resources we need, the people are generally friendly, and the work is high profile."

Potential trouble

That doesn't mean all is — or will remain — idyllic in Winstonville. Like associates at other firms, Winstonites are nervous about the impact of increased hours pressure on their quality of life. On the downside, "some partners do not acknowledge that you have a life outside the firm and regularly make demands that are not really necessary," according to one associate. "For example, requiring research immediately on a Friday afternoon, when they're not going to look at it until Tuesday." Another insider reports: "The mood here changed after the raises — there is a bit of latent hostility by the partners toward the associates. [The partners] definitely do not have qualms about making us sweat for the extra money." Stay tuned.

"We're a Chicago firm, not an East Coast firm. So you don't need an Ivy League school on your resume."

— *Winston & Strawn associate*

Baker & McKenzie

VAULT.COM PRESTIGE RANKING: 45

International Executive Offices
One Prudential Plaza
130 E. Randolph Street, Suite 2500
Chicago, IL 60601
(312) 861-8000
Fax: (312) 861-2898
www.bakernet.com

LOCATIONS

Chicago, IL • Dallas, TX • Houston, TX • Miami, FL • New York, NY • Palo Alto, CA • San Diego, CA • San Francisco, CA • Washington, DC • Toronto • 50 other offices world-wide

MAJOR DEPARTMENTS/PRACTICES

Banking & Finance
Corporate & Securities
E-Commerce
Information Technology/Communications
Intellectual Property
International Dispute Resolution
International Trade (WTO)
Labor, Employment, and Employee Benefits Law
Litigation
M&A
Major Projects/Project Finance
Tax
Venture Capital

THE STATS

No. of attorneys: 2,700
No. of offices: 60
Chairman of Executive Committee: Christine Lagarde

THE BUZZ
What attorneys at other firms are saying about this firm

- "Influential; great internationally"
- "McDonald's of law firms"
- "International behemoth"

PAY

Chicago, 2000
1st year: $125,000
2nd year: $130,000
3rd year: $140,000
4th year: $150,000
5th year: $170,000
6th year: $180,000
7th year: $185,000

Dallas, 2000
1st year: $110,000 (for 1,850 billable hours)
2nd year: $114,000 (for 2,000 billable hours)
3rd year: $121,000 (for 2,000 billable hours)
4th year: $130,000 (for 2,000 billable hours)
5th year: $140,000 (for 2,000 billable hours)
6th year: $145,000 (for 2,000 billable hours)
7th year: $155,000 (for 2,000 billable hours)
(bonuses after 2,100 billable hours)

New York, 2000
1st year: $125,000
2nd year: $135,000
3rd year: $150,000
4th year: $165,000
5th year: $185,000
6th year: $193,000

Washington, DC, 2000
1st year: $125,000
2nd year: $135,000
3rd year: $145,000
4th year: $165,000
5th year: $180,000
6th year: $190,000
7th year: $200,000

Average summer associate pay in 2000 (North American offices): $1,520/week

NOTABLE PERKS

- Court registration fees and association dues
- Relocation allowance
- Great opportunities for travel
- Financial awards for graduate legal study

UPPERS

- Exposure to international clients
- Reasonable hours expectations
- Opportunity for overseas exchange program

DOWNERS

- Unclear partnership track
- Perks scant
- International nature of firm leads to disorganization

KEY COMPETITORS

Clifford Chance Rogers & Wells
Jones, Day, Reavis & Pogue
Sidley & Austin
Skadden, Arps, Slate, Meagher & Flom
White & Case

EMPLOYMENT CONTACT

Ms. Vivian Maine
Director of International Administration
(312) 861-8800

Attorneys by Level [globally]
- Partners: 580
- Associates: 2,120

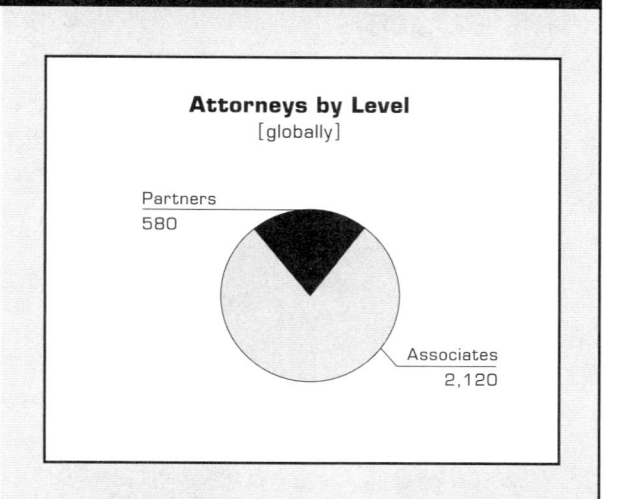

Attorneys by Practice Area [U.S.]
- Litigation: 69
- International Trade: 70
- Corporate Securities: 83
- Other: 124
- Tax, Trusts & Estates: 97
- Labor & Employment: 90

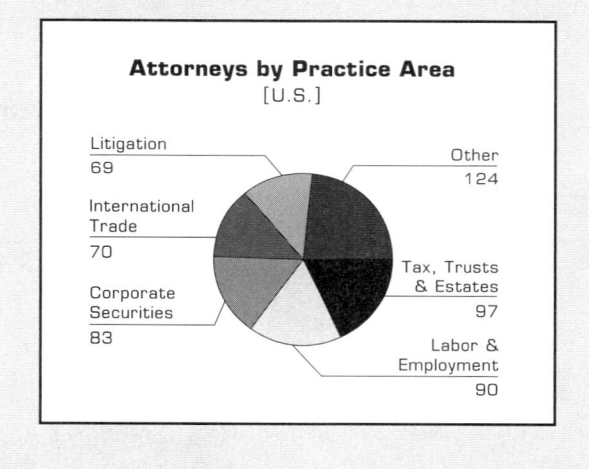

QUALITY OF LIFE RANKINGS [ASSOCIATES RATE THEIR OWN FIRM]

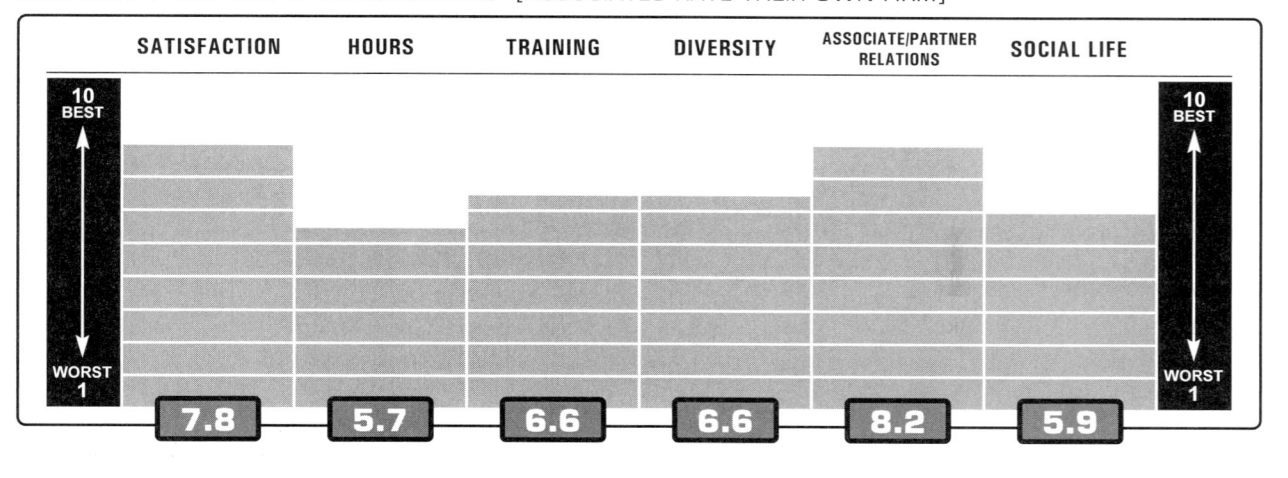

Satisfaction	Hours	Training	Diversity	Associate/Partner Relations	Social Life
7.8	5.7	6.6	6.6	8.2	5.9

THE SCOOP

If the old adage, "size matters," is true, then Baker & McKenzie matters a lot. The firm has approximately 2,700 attorneys in more than 60 offices spread out over 35 countries, making it the largest law firm in the world (just edging the newly-formed Clifford Chance Rogers & Wells).

"One firm or no firm"

Baker's stated strategy is "one firm or no firm." Offices are staffed mostly with local lawyers, and all outposts are viewed as equals. Close to 80 percent of the firm's lawyers are based outside of the United States. While Baker's size and reach are impressive, some within the legal industry have derided the firm's affinity for expansion. Baker & McKenzie obviously objects to the criticism it has received. "We're a single global partnership," Baker executive committee chairman Christine Lagarde told *The Economist* in February 2000. "We've built the infrastructure and we have a genuinely international culture." The firm audits about one-quarter of its offices every year to ensure the quality of their legal services, and boasts that "no other law firm maintains such a dynamic, cooperative organization so singularly invested in the well-being of its attorneys and clients and committed to the building of lasting relationships."

History: rapid expansion

The firm's roots can be traced back to 1949, when Russell Baker, a University of Chicago law graduate, opened up a law practice in the Windy City. Sensing the potential of the global economy, Baker devoted his practice to international law. Litigator John McKenzie's tax practice served as the foundation upon which the firm would begin to help clients expand overseas.

The first Baker & McKenzie outpost was in Caracas, Venezuela in 1955. (It was also the first U.S. law office in Latin America.) Two years later, the firm opened up offices in Washington, DC, Amsterdam, and Brussels. New York came on in 1958; Manila was the first Asian office in 1963. Other openings of note: Sydney (1964), San Francisco (1970), Tokyo (1972), Hong Kong (1974), and Palo Alto (1987). The London office, opened in 1961, is currently the firm's largest. Today, Baker truly spans the world. Indeed, it took home "Best Global Law Firm" at the 1999 Lawyer Awards in London.

Gender equality: the good news

Christine Lagarde was elected leader of the firm in October 1999, succeeding John Klotsche. Lagarde, a Parisian practicing since 1981, was one of the first women chosen to lead a large law firm. Lagarde's title was a source of lighthearted debate; she told *The New York Times* she deliberated for days and solicited numerous opinions before deciding to call herself "chairman," rather than the more politically correct "chairwoman" or the awkward "chairperson" or "chair." When asked by the *Times* what advice she would give a female lawyer trying to make it to the top, she replied, "Grit your teeth, because it is a matter of resilience, stamina, and energy. And never try to imitate what the boys do."

Gender equality: the bad news

As welcome as the news of Ms. Lagarde's election was, the firm suffered a setback on gender issues in 1999. In April, the firm's appeal of a $3.5 million punitive damage award was upheld by the California Supreme Court. Legal secretary Rena Weeks alleged in 1992 that Martin Greenstein, a former partner at the firm, had harassed her and other female staffers. Weeks further alleged that the firm knew of Greenstein's conduct but took no action because he was a major rainmaker. Greenstein resigned from the firm in October 1993, and the case wound its way through the appeals process for six more years. Putting the incident behind it, Baker & McKenzie announced after the California court's decision that it would not seek a review of the decision in the U.S. Supreme Court. The firm has also shown its dedication to forging a more woman-friendly reputation by initiatives including the sponsorship of Women.future, a gathering of thousands of women in business at over 300 locations in April 2000.

Comings and goings

While departures are fairly common in the law industry, Baker's fine tax practice was subject to an unusual amount of poaching in 1999: the firm lost nine lawyers from the department to Big Five accounting firms. According to some insiders, the defections were a result of Baker's desire to grow other practices. Phillip Morrison, a former partner at Baker who previously served as international tax counsel for the Department of Treasury under President George Bush, told *The National Law Journal* that "some might say Baker has spent too much energy building up its corporate and securities practice at the expense of tax." Morrison left the firm's DC office for Deloitte & Touche in February 1999.

While such high-level departures are never good for a firm, no one expects Baker & McKenzie's DC practice to fold. Joseph Andrews, a former Baker partner who served in the Reagan administration and left for PricewaterhouseCoopers, told the *Law*

Journal, "These defections aren't helpful to Baker's DC office, but I'm not of a view that it's going to eliminate the ability of Baker's 100 tax lawyers nationwide to carry on. Baker will be just fine."

Tax wasn't the only practice area hit by departures. Three partners in the Houston office went to King & Spalding in January 2000. The four were in the international transactions department and represented more than half of the partnership in the Houston satellite office.

Although it has experienced a talent drain in some areas, the firm points out that it has actually grown by 10-20 partners in 2000. Baker has recently attracted several impressive lateral hires. For example, in June 1999 the firm hired Antoinette Konski as a partner in the intellectual property department in San Francisco; Konski had been a partner at Morrison & Foerster. Two attorneys were added to that office in of counsel positions: Richard Walker, a former entertainment partner at Bronson, Bronson & McKinnon, and J. Michael Goulding, ERISA/executive compensation counsel at Silver, Freedman & Taff. Bronson, Bronson & McKinnon IP associate Aimee Arost also joined Baker & McKenzie's branch in the Bay Area. The tax department made some additions as well — in August of that year, tax lawyers David Tillinghast and Klas Holm joined the firm in New York, while Peter M. Daub moved to the DC office in January 2000. Four months later, a noted eight-member litigation team, led by Kerry Blair and Brendan Cook, signed on with Baker's Houston office.

Baker brings Mickey and Minnie to China

Considering the firm's international presence, it's no surprise that representing companies overseas is a major Baker strength. Baker represented The Walt Disney Company in a January 2000 agreement to build a Hong Kong Disneyland. Partners David Fleming, Cole Capener, and Maurice Emmer served as Disney's advisors on the $1.8 billion deal. Baker worked on another China vacation destination, representing China Resorts International in the company's efforts to build a ski resort in Manchuria that backers hope will one day help attract the Winter Olympics. The $150 million project was announced in November 1999. Outside of Asia, Baker beat out several prominent firms in November 1999 (including international competitor Clifford Chance) to represent the Croatian government in privatizing that country's telecommunications network. Partners Clive Cook, Peter Strivens, and Joachim Scherer led the deal, valued at $875 million.

Big deals

Baker's mergers and acquisitions practice has pulled in several deals of impressive size. Partners Michael Kunstler and Christopher Saxon represented Texas Utilities in its $1 billion purchase of Australian gas companies Kinetik Energy and Westar in February 1999. That November, the firm represented Cygnus Solutions, a technology company purchased by software developer Red Hat. Partners Michael Madda, Andre Saltoun, Michael Bumbaca, Virginia Gibson, and John Hentrich, and associates Nicholas Spyros and Stewart Lipeless worked on various aspects of the $674 million deal. During the same month, partners Tim Gee, Alison Flood, and Ian Jack, along with associates Helen Bradley, Helen Goldberg, and George Brady advised SFX Entertainment on its $275 million acquisition of the Apollo Leisure Group and the MCP Group.

Gaseous litigation

Like all firms, Baker stands ready to defend its clients if a dispute should go to trial. Baker is handling, for example, a breach of contract dispute for Union Pacific Resources filed in March 2000. The plaintiffs, natural gas suppliers to Union Pacific, alleged that UPR sold gas at a reduced rate to entities it controlled; the UPR entities then sold the gas at market value to third parties, thus cheating the suppliers out of royalties they collect on the first transactions. Attorneys for the suppliers allege that the damages could total as much as $100 million.

GETTING HIRED

Different folks for different offices

According to firm insiders, Baker & McKenzie's hiring practices and standards can vary according to office or practice group. "People with good educational backgrounds" are universally valued, and one source says there's a "significant emphasis on Harvard, Stanford, and Boalt as sources of first-year hires." "Applicants who have graduated from a top-tier law school or [who are] at the top of their class will find the application process to be easy," according to one Chicago associate. "Other applicants will encounter significant hurdles obtaining even a screening interview." Of course, grades aren't the only criteria. "The standards are pretty high, but I can honestly say that it isn't just about grades," says one lawyer. "We are looking for unique, bright, and outgoing people. Fluency in other languages also gets noticed," though insiders report that English is spoken at all offices and by most clients.

The Baker crap shoot

Since hiring is up to individual offices and practice areas, getting into the firm can be a "crap shoot" depending on where one applies. Candidates should know to which office they want to apply and what practice area they will focus on since "each office establishes its own hiring criteria and procedures and there is considerable variation among them." Lateral hires have an edge if they have significant experience in their practice area.

When in doubt, talk sports

Interviews can run from a half-day to a full day, depending on the office. At the Chicago office, there's a "20-minute on campus screening interview." Those who fare well can expect a callback in two to three days. Callback interviews include both partners and associates and last a half hour. Interviewees describe the process as "casual." "They just wanted to know if I was enjoying school and talked about [my alma mater's] football team," reports one associate.

OUR SURVEY SAYS

Different culture for different offices

Baker's worldwide reach also affects the firm's culture. "Each office is different," states one New York associate. "Chicago is the largest and most social. New York has more of a work-and-go-home attitude." There are some aspects of the culture that can be found at all offices. "The firm's culture demands a significantly greater independent effort by associates to develop their own career," observes one third-year Baker attorney. "The international network of offices and the international nature of the work does provide a global perspective. The firm's financial model had produced a culture that emphasizes individual effort over group problem solving, to the point that group efforts to retain clients, develop clients, or develop associates are extremely disadvantaged. On the other hand, for the aggressive, assertive attorney, there are a number of opportunities for interesting work and a lucrative career." There is a downside to the firm's international network. "Baker is extremely decentralized, which makes for little organization," complains one lawyer. "Oftentimes, the firm operates not as a single entity, but as a massive number of small firms banded together."

"Historically, the culture was terrible — a total boys club environment that was exclusionary to women and minorities," says one longtime associate. "The culture has improved significantly." Now, according to another associate, "there are a few frat boy types who are shunned by other associates. They probably will not last in the firm."

Little interaction with partners

Baker & McKenzie associates report an interesting dichotomy when it comes to partner-associate relationships. "In [the tax] department, the partners seem to be fairly respectful with the associates," says one lawyer. "However, there is little interaction." Another associate agrees with that assessment, saying "partners generally do not develop close relationships with associates and some are simply not approachable." Another lawyer says age is a factor. "I find the more senior the partner, the more they feel you're capable of doing simple things without review," says one fourth-year associate. "The younger the partner, the more likely they seem to revise every cover letter you draft." However, the partner horror stories are rare. "There is no intimidation, yelling, or unpleasantness from partners," reports one first-year associate.

No forced socializing

Sources at Baker report a fairly active social life. "Social interaction among associates is reasonably good," says one Palo Alto attorney. "Among partners and associates, however, it is very limited." Most support that opinion. "The associates have several regular social events, including dinners and baseball games," says a Chicago associate. "For example, last year, when the partners were at the annual partners' meeting, the tax associates organized a paintball outing." Social misfits and wallflowers, take heart. "There is no forced socializing," says one attorney. "You are not expected to socialize."

Hours: this is why you're paid that much

"There is a reason why associates are paid so much," says one DC lawyer. "Anybody who complains about the hours should not be in a large, private firm." Of course, some do complain. "The grace period is over — I now have to have my time filled constantly and taking an entire weekend off is a luxury," gripes one Chicago associate. "We are now expected to earn our salaries by increased hours." Indeed, this sentiment is fairly common. "The nature of the law will always require a large time commitment," says one tax lawyer. "If we do not love what we do, then there is no reason to work this hard and we should be off doing something else."

Progressive pay

Suprisingly, compensation seems to be a non-issue at Baker. Says one DC lawyer simply, "We are all paid way too much." Another attorney goes a step further, saying "At some point, associates will realize that the money we make is far more than the money we earn and far exceeds that which we contribute to society." While their colleagues might disagree, everyone seems satisfied with their paychecks. "Baker & McKenzie's new associate compensation structure is very progressive in the legal market," claims one Chicago attorney. "Associates are able to earn a bonus on non-billable contributions to the firm." Additionally, at Baker "you become a second-year associate after only nine months, instead of 15 like at other firms, which means earlier raises."

Perks: find a summer associate

Though pay may be top-notch, Baker offers fewer perks than most firms, according to associates. There are the typical meal and car service arrangements, and "occasional tickets and social events." According to one DC attorney, if you want anything else, "you'll need to have a summer associate around." At some offices, there are child care arrangements, gym memberships, and discounts. As Baker is a worldwide entity, the opportunities to travel are generally greater than at most large law firms. "A few associates," according to a tax lawyer, "have traveled to Amsterdam, Hong Kong, and Santiago, Chile. A larger number attended a training session in Vail, Colorado." Dwellers in Baker's Chicago headquarters have the special opportunity to enjoy "free soup luches." Even if the firm does offer more perks, however, it's tough for some associates to tell. "The firm can't keep the Employee Manual updated. It's a big shame."

Ad hoc training

Baker associates report that there is "very little in the way of formalized training. Almost everything seems to be on the job or ad hoc." "There is no hand-holding here," warns a Chicago attorney. A San Francisco lawyer says the firm has displayed "only a superficial commitment to training in this office. Other offices in the firm differ." Similarly, some departments are more committed to training than others. For example, "In the tax department we have weekly training sessions and associates are encouraged to attend seminars on tax topics." The firm also offers a six- to 24-month "Associate Training Program" in which selected associates may transfer to another Baker office — domestic and international — to work on their skills and build relationships with clients.

Scenic views

A DC associate says the offices there have "pretty nice décor — but it's probably more British than our London offices. Lots of dark wood and pictures of fox hunting." Partners can look over the commander-in-chief's shoulder. "Some of the offices have an amazing view of the White House." A bonus for the cramped — "no one has to share offices."

Washington isn't the only office with amazing views. In Chicago, "the South Side views [are of] Grant Park, the Loop, and Lake Michigan." A drawback is the "dingy, built-in furniture. In San Francisco, the offices are "cramped for space," but senior associates in most locations don't have to share offices.

Support needs work

"Associates work very hard, putting in long hours," fumes one lawyer. "But the secretary and word processing support has not expanded to keep up with our increased productivity." The quality of secretaries can vary widely, and you're usually stuck with what you have. "[It's] very hard to get rid of a bad secretary," says an associate. Another reports that "who you get is largely a matter of seniority and the secretaries that work in your department." Library services, like most aspects of associate life, can vary by office. A DC contact raves that "the library staff is very good," while a Chicago lawyer complains "we have one of the worst libraries and library staff I have ever seen." Baker & McKenzie partners might have some complaints of their own about the firm's staff: in June 2000, Dennis Masellis, a former accounting department employee in Baker's New York office, pleaded guilty to stealing more than $7 million from the firm since 1993.

Retention: after the Big 5, some stability

A New York associate says that turnover "was quite high in 1998 and 1999 but has tapered off quite a bit." Another source concurs, saying departures "seen to have stabilized since the Great Big Five Exodus of 1999." One lawyer remarks: "The firm responded to the mass exodus by addressing certain quality-of-life issues." "The turnover is average," concludes a co-worker in the tax department.

Partnership prospects: don't hold your breath

The road to partner is longer and harder at Baker & McKenzie than at most firms; worse, insiders say the firm isn't always clear on where an associate stands. One New York associate frets that "many partners are relatively young and many don't have the business to support and nourish a junior partner." "The firm is not good at communicating partnership opportunities," says one source. "Perhaps one of the worst [firms at doing so]. Partnership is effectively controlled by practice groups." As for timing, it "looks like a seven-year track for the superstars and a 10 to 12 year track for everyone else," according to one insider. "The good thing is that there is no 'up-or-out' policy, so you can stay on as a senior associate if you are doing good work."

Diversity efforts not met with startling results

Overall, Baker associates feel that while an effort is made to recruit minorities, the results aren't noticeable. "The firm is trying hard to hire more diverse staff but has not been very successful yet," says one source. Others are more critical. "It is not clear that the office is particularly focused on diversity issues, although working at the firm can be a diverse experience because of the extensive interaction with foreign lawyers," comments one third-year associate.

Considering the firm's history — both the high-profile harassment suit and the election of a female leader — Baker today has a good environment for women. One associate says the presence of a female managing partner means there's "no glass ceiling." "The firm is trying to work hard on these issues and does not deserve its sometimes bad reputation from the past," remarks one associate. Still, there are some criticisms. While part-time and maternity leave policy has been praised, "women who have children are not treated the same when they return."

Homosexuals are cautioned to be careful at Baker & McKenzie. (It's rumored that the film "Philadelphia" is based in part on a gay ex-Baker attorney dismissed because he had AIDS.) "As a closeted gay associate, the firm is simply not ready to deal with having openly gay associates," says one source. "It is very much a 'don't ask, don't tell' kind of a firm. Discretion is the key." Another lawyer says, "I would say that it is a very uninviting place to be openly gay." The firm does offer domestic partner benefits, but one associate points out that, at least in San Francisco, those benefits are required by law.

Globetrotters are satisfied

One associate reports "mixed emotions" working at Baker. "[I] love the people, but the quality of work, poor training, and nonexistent method of work distribution hurts." Other associates are more positive. "This is the best place to work in DC," raves one lawyer. "I think this is a positive example of firm life overall," states one contact. "I work with very skilled and intelligent people," adds one attorney. "The work is quite challenging. You are given the appropriate amount of independence and client contact from the minute you set foot in the door."

Associates report that the "global client base allows you to interact with a wide range of diverse people." One globetrotter says, "there is nowhere else that I can work on matters involving disputes and transactions in Russia, Japan, Argentina, and Chicago, and still not miss my kids' soccer games or swimming lessons."

There are negatives to being so large, of course. One source says there are "perpetual conflicts due to the breadth of the firm internationally." "Baker & McKenzie is run like an Athenian democracy, where decisions are made by consensus," says one insider. "While that has its advantages, it also means that the firm is sometimes slow to react to certain developments in the marketplace." Naturally, there are those whose complaints are about the law life in general. One lawyer's biggest complaint is "working at a firm. If I never have to bill another minute, it will be too soon."

Vinson & Elkins LLP

Prestige Ranking: 46

2300 First City Tower
1001 Fannin
Houston, TX 77002-6760
(800) 833-1594
www.velaw.com

LOCATIONS

Houston, TX (HQ)
Austin, TX
Dallas, TX
New York, NY
Washington, DC
Bejing
London
Moscow
Singapore

MAJOR DEPARTMENTS/PRACTICES

Administrative & Environmental Law
Business & International
Corporate Finance & Securities
Energy
Employment Litigation & Labor
Intellectual Property/Technical Litigation
Litigation/Appellate/Insolvency & Reorganization
Public Finance
Tax/TEC

THE STATS

No. of attorneys: 658
No. of offices: 9
Summer associate offers: 59 out of 63 (Houston, 1999)
Managing Partner: Harry M. Reasoner
Hiring Partner: James A. Reeder

THE BUZZ
What attorneys at other firms are saying about this firm

- "Growing fast — soon to be premier"
- "They are Texas — yee haw!"
- "Too much work, not enough sympathy from partners"
- "Has tried everything to stop the bleeding but direct pressure"

PAY

All Texas Offices, 2000
1st year: $110,000 + $5,000
2nd year: $114,000 + $10,000
3rd year: $121,000 + $15,000
4th year: $130,000 + $20,000
5th year: $140,000 + $20,000
6th year: $145,000 + $25,000
7th year: $155,000 + $25,000
8th year: $160,000 + $25,000
Summer associate: $1,700/week

New York, 2000
1st year: $120,000 + $5000
2nd year: $125,000 + $10,000
3rd year: $135,000 + $15,000
4th year: $150,000 + $20,000
5th year: $165,000 + $25,000
6th year: $175,000 + $25,000
7th year: $180,000 + $30,000
8th year: $190,000 + $30,000
Summer associate: $2,100/week

Washington, DC, 2000
1st year: $120,000 + $5,000
2nd year: $130,000 + $5,000
3rd year: $140,000 + $10,000
4th year: $150,000 + $15,000
5th year: $160,000 + $20,000
6th year: $170,000 + $20,000
7th year: $175,000 + $25,000
8th year: $185,000 + $25,000
Summer associate: $2,000/week

NOTABLE PERKS

- Medical coverage, including coverage between graduation and arrival at the firm
- Unlimited recruiting expenditures
- Subsidized parking

UPPERS

- Great compensation compared to cost of living
- Freedom in clients and cases represented
- Attorneys have interests outside of their practice areas

DOWNERS

- Few trial opportunities for young lawyers
- Still fighting for high tech work
- Move toward "New York" hours

KEY COMPETITORS

Andrews & Kurth
Baker Botts
Fulbright & Jaworski

EMPLOYMENT CONTACT

Ms. Patty H. Calabrese
Director of Attorney Employment
(713) 758-4544
pcalabrese@velaw.com

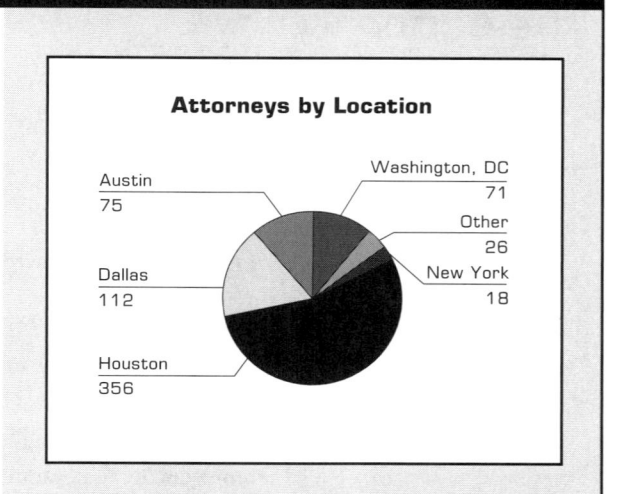

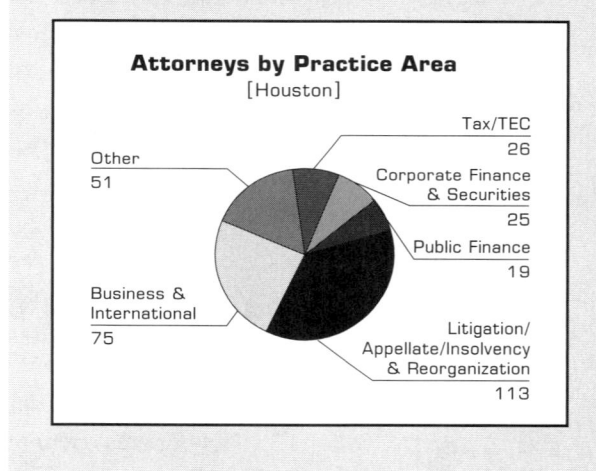

Attorneys by Location

- Austin: 75
- Washington, DC: 71
- Other: 26
- New York: 18
- Houston: 356
- Dallas: 112

Attorneys by Practice Area [Houston]

- Other: 51
- Tax/TEC: 26
- Corporate Finance & Securities: 25
- Public Finance: 19
- Litigation/Appellate/Insolvency & Reorganization: 113
- Business & International: 75

THE SCOOP

Vinson & Elkins is not the lone star firm of the Lone Star State, but it is one of the brightest. Having opened a New York office in 1998 and now possessing five domestic and four foreign offices, Vinson is hoping to extend its influence.

History: first Texas, then the world

If J.R. Ewing needed a law firm (and actually, he probably does), he'd call in Vinson & Elkins. Founded in 1917 by Texas Judge James A. Elkins and William Ashton Vinson, the firm has historically relied on oil and gas industry-related litigation. Vinson opened its first international office in 1971 in London. The firm also represented clients active in the Soviet Union beginning in the early 1970s — although the firm did not set up an office in Russia until 1991. In 1979, the firm opened its second Texas office in the state's capital, Austin, followed by a Dallas branch in 1986. The Dallas office has since grown into the firm's largest outside Houston. In 1994, the firm's London office established a multi-national partnership (MNP) under the rules of the English Law Society and can now practice English as well as U.S. law. In that same year, the Moscow office relocated to 16 Ulitsa Spirodonovka, putting it within strolling distance of the Kremlin and Red Square.

A Texas-sized practice

Vinson & Elkins is one of the few Southern firms that can compare with the New York powerhouses. The firm has gained recognition as a leading law firm in the South in a variety of areas, representing more Texas-headquartered Forbes 500 companies than any other firm. In addition to its Houston home, the firm has offices in Austin, Dallas, Washington, DC, London, Moscow, Singapore, and Beijing. (Our insiders tell us that foreign assignments are reportedly hard to come by, however.) In 1998, Vinson decided to start rubbing elbows with Yankees, opening a 13-lawyer office in New York City (which the firm intends to build to a headcount of 50 by 2000).

Boom!

Business is booming at Vinson & Elkins. The firm's client list continues to swell, its workload continues to accelerate, and its revenues continue to skyrocket. Some Vinson insiders feared that the boom years would level off with the collapse of overseas markets in 1998, but recent indications suggest this won't happen for some time. While some lawyers have had to change their field or geographic region of concentration, the economic crisis has barely affected Vinson. The downside of all this success — tremendously overworked attorneys (at least in some areas). To ease associate pain, the firm has taken the lead in the Texas associate-salary market with offers of $110,000 ($125,000 in DC and NYC) for first-years in 2000, edging out big-name Southern competitor Andrews & Kurth.

Practice areas get lots of practice

Litigation is the largest practice area at Vinson & Elkins. No longer just centered around oil and gas, the practice now handles antitrust, intellectual property, medical and professional malpractice, securities law, and a host of other specialties. Two of the firm's 1997 cases, the libel trial of *Kastrin v. CBS, Inc.* and the personal injury suit *Ainsworth v. Colonial Pipeline Co.*, were ranked among the top 15 defense victories in 1997 by *The American Law Journal*. The next year, the firm won a reversal of a jury verdict for client Randall's Food Markets Inc. in a major lawsuit against John Paul Mitchell Systems, Inc. and Ultimate Salon Services, Inc. Last year, the firm represented NEC Electronics, Inc. in a suit filed against Toshiba Corporation and NEC (one of three Toshiba subsidiaries named) in which the plaintiffs accused the computer companies of selling faulty floppy-disk drives that could potentially corrupt user data. A $2.1 billion settlement was negotiated; as part of that settlement, claims against NEC were dropped.

Strapping practices

Vinson's corporate practices are robust as well. Vinson's health care practice is one of the largest in the nation. The firm is a leader in corporate work such as information technology, project development and finance, and real estate transactions. The energy industry has always been a gusher of revenue for Vinson & Elkins. The M&A group has been active lately, representing regular Vinson client Enron Corporation in its $2.1 billion sale of Portland General Electric (and assumption of $1 billion in debt) to Sierra Pacific Resources in November 1999. The department advised the directors of Kinder Morgan Energy Partners in their January 2000 acquisition of KN Interstate Gas Transmission Co. from Kinder Morgan Inc. for $735 million. The energy industry loves and appreciates Vinson — Vinson was named the best firm in the industry at the semi-significant 1998 Energy Finance Awards, the same year that the firm advised on more than 100 mergers and acquisitions in the industry.

GETTING HIRED

Bright southerners welcome

If you're smart, diligent, and a graduate of the University of Texas, you fit Vinson's target profile dead-on. But plenty of other candidates have a shot at joining Vinson.

Recruiters first and foremost "expect you to be bright, a self-starter, kind of independent, hard working," and have "good communication skills." Vinson looks for less generic attributes as well. For instance, according to the firm literature, "individuality, not conformity, is looked upon as an asset" and "foreign language proficiency" is given consideration. Our sources add that the firm tends to "mostly hire from Texas." This is true in terms of academics, as well. In addition to the usual line-up from Harvard, Yale, Chicago and Stanford, Vinson "looks to the University of Texas" and the "University of Houston somewhat." The ol' college tie is a boon to those grads with some holes in their transcript, as Vinson will "take the top quarter or top third at UT" but usually only the "top five percent at other schools." Regardless, Vinson recruitment is a "grade-driven" process, and even though there is "a whole lot of the 'good old boy network'" in place, there are still "particular grade cutoffs, although not as stringent as at some New York firms," according to a Houston office associate.

It's all about you

Once a potential candidate does get in the door, each of his or her interviews is conducted by both a partner and an associate and lasts about 30 minutes. Lateral candidates may have a two-day session. Interviewers are not chosen based on practice area, but "if you indicate an interest, you'll talk to at least one person from that group." This focus on getting to know the individual permeates the interview process. One recruiter explains that when he interviews candidates, he wants to know "what they enjoy doing. If they indicate interest in a particular area, I want to know why. It doesn't have to be a profound, deeply thought-out answer, just basic characteristics."

OUR SURVEY SAYS

Staying out of the fray

Vinson associates report that turnover at the firm is "average for this size Texas firm." The firm's geographic distance from San Francisco and New York's Internet feeding frenzy seems to have kept the firm from hemorrhaging of its attorneys to hard-charging dot coms. Nonetheless, Vinson does "constantly have people leaving for other opportunities." Some are worried that "pretty high turnover" is becoming a "problem," with at least one associate reporting a loss of "about ten percent of the firm each year." A colleague reminds worriers that "actual attrition is different than life change" decisions that take associates to employment outside of the corporate law firm world. Let's see if Vinson's recruiting staff agrees.

Women and minorities: in and out

"Compared to other local firms," Vinson's "got to be near the tip-top" of gender sensitivity, muses a Houston insider. The firm reportedly boasts "very sensitive management emphasis on gender in hiring" and "variations of pretty flexible maternity/part-time policies." Nonetheless, associates seem a bit resigned to the fact that "female associates get to a certain age and they leave. The firm may be "very receptive" and "actively recruit female lawyers," but some attorneys suggest that Vinson leaders "talk a better game than they play" and that "'Mommy tracking' for associates" leads to only a "little bit improved retention." Others insist, though, that the firm is "not only accommodating but wants people to use" different flex plans.

Could a name be enough to bolster minority recruiting and retention efforts? An associate finds that Vinson is "very aware of the issues" pertaining to recruitment and retention of minority lawyers but doesn't "know of any special formal mentoring programs." "Our name attracts minorities, but not because we've done anything special — it's almost happenstance." A Dallas contact argues that "it doesn't seem like this is a firm issue as much as an issue of there not being enough candidates." A Houston colleague concurs that recruiting opportunities at local law schools have dropped, particularly as a result of recent Texas rulings against affirmative action for university funding. While "not specific to this firm," many attorneys think the overall situation is "still a problem — [Vinson's] not a bad place, but not for minorities."

Vinson associates point out that the firm offers benefits for same-sex domestic partners and was "the first firm in Texas to do so." The firm "tries to be progressive," according to a corporate teammate. "We tend to be a vanguard firm." There is "definitely a handful of out attorneys," some of whom "say that they feel supported" at the office and some who "say they don't." One source suggests that it's a "non-isssue" to come out at Vinson, but "if you are out when you're coming in [to the firm] it's a problem."

Pro bono weighs in

Rare is the associate who dismisses the firm's pro bono efforts as "lip service," even if "the pressure is to bill" steadily in addition to undertaking public service work. Vinson & Elkins donated "about two or three million dollars'" worth of time to represent the University of Texas in a controversial case, which in March 1996 stripped the public university system of affirmative action funding. Another high-profile effort found lawyers doing much of the legwork behind the U.S. Consumer Product Safety Commission's action in December 1999 to create a federal safety standard for multipurpose lighters. The firm became involved after representing the parents of a four-year-old girl who died from burns suffered as a result of playing with a multipurpose lighter.

Attorneys undertake "about 50 family law cases each year" as well; luckily for associates, all the work all "counts towards billable hours" and receives "a lot of encouragement from partners," which is "rare for a law firm." A New York litigator says he has "spent more than 10 percent of my time on pro bono work." A Houston peer raves that "if there's one thing this firm is committed to, it's pro bono."

So you wanna be a partner?

While partners' relationships with associates "vary by department" and may not offer "much in the way of mentoring," a number of associates recount tales of "very good treatment" at the hands of their fearless leaders. The "vast majority [of partners] are people with friendly attitudes toward associates," offers a Houston litigator, and "they don't pass along grunt work." An officemate finds that partners are "considerate of my own personal life and my work load. They give credit where credit is due, especially in front of clients."

But how to join their ranks? Grabbing the brass ring remains a mysterious process to most associates, however. "Who knows?" wonders a Houston attorney. "I have no clear understanding — I know what I should be doing, but I also know that doesn't guarantee anything." On the other coast, a New York insider echoes his confusion: "I wish I knew — at this point in my career, I should know." Another in that office declares that there is "no formula." Make or break factors cited by associates "billing records for the three years prior to the partnership decision being made, quality of work, general rep at the firm, and client comfort." But remember "it's not just about hours."

Another insider adds that "intensive evaluations are important — it all depends on partners' perceptions of how good you are as a lawyer and your ability to bring in clients." Bearing that in mind, "it's always sort of been that if you stick around the eight years and people like you, chances are good."

Marathon training

More than one associate uses the word "outstanding" to describe Vinson's training opportunities. The firm is "loaded with training — constantly bombarding us with CLE training" and offering formatting software programs that annotate various agreements and other documents to assist new attorneys. One Houston associate enthuses that "partners look out for the development of my practice" and another mentions "five or six workshops for first-year litigators — lots of money, time and effort put into it." Another litigator explains that there are "one to three CLEs each week" and for first-years in his department, "workshops on depositions, motions, and trial advocacy." The only sour note may be the informal training — some associates criticize a "complete 'sink or swim' mentality" with "partners who abandon you completely."

Big offices and competent staff

Vinson's main asset, it's safe to say, is not its office staff. "There are nicer buildings in Houston," according to a litigator in said city, and one might be "a little envious of the Dallas office," overall the firm has "nice offices — good-sized and good facilities." The Dallas building is "very user-friendly" with "built-in storage and plenty of space" and the New York office is a "little industrial" with "dated decor" but is also "very big."

The availability of support services is "huge and amazing," exults a litigator who says his "secretary can do pretty much anything." A co-worker describes her secretary as "incredible" as well, even considering that "usually an associate and a partner share. Sometimes word processing is overloaded, but everyone is competent. People work out priority schedules." A New Yorker states that "central support services are excellent;" a counterpart in Houston says there is "always plenty of help at night."

Socializing your way to the top

The social life at Vinson is alive and well, "better than other Texas firms," in the words of a Houston litigator, with a "traditional 'party' reputation." The scene is "fairly good," with "lots of social events — arts, sports — especially in the summer," although there is "less associate/partner mixing than there should be. "If you want to spend your time hanging out with people from the office, there's a lot there," advises another associate in the same office. "There is a premium on 'company bonding.'"

Perhaps too much so, grumble some non-party animals. "Playing internal politics is very important here," gripes a corporate associate in Houston. "The firm is a sharp pyramid — I would not describe it as a meritocracy." A New York colleague sums up some of his co-workers as "excessively collegial in an insincere kind of way." It seems to help if you're a Longhorn, too — a litigator sighs that "if you didn't go to UT, then you might be happier elsewhere." The atmosphere encourages some self-described "pretty big cheerleaders" who feel that "Vinson sticks out as a firm where it's fun to work;" others who "don't love it here" wonder if "big raises lately bought loyalty."

The stuff that Vinson's made of

Advice abounds for those considering making Vinson a professional home. The firm's reputation is as "strong as any" and "this is a good place to start your practice, regardless of your long-term goals." Those weighing the decision "should ask what sort of people, training, and work experience," may be gained, "plus consider the cost of living in Texas." (Hint: lower than San Francisco and New York.) Along the same lines, a New York litigator counsels that you "see if you like the people and consider the benefits of the practice at a larger firm. This is a 'self-starter' place — if you'd rather be assigned to one partner, this is probably not the best place."

From Houston comes the warning to "watch your back — don't believe everything you are told" and be aware that "there will be some very large tradeoffs. Find good work and partners you can tie in with, and be very cognizant of what the atmosphere here is like compared to other firms." Finally, "be very sure of what is important to you." A quality-of-life corollary from Dallas reminds candidates not to be "afraid to take time off and do things outside the office — I think that's a hard thing for an associate to keep in mind."

"If you want to spend your time hanging out with people from the office, there's a lot there. There is a premium on company bonding."

— *Vinson & Elkins associate*

Cadwalader, Wickersham & Taft

47 PRESTIGE RANKING

100 Maiden Lane
New York, NY 10038
(212) 504-6000
Fax: (212) 504-6666
www.cadwalader.com
cwtinfo@cwt.com

LOCATIONS

New York, NY (HQ)
Charlotte, NC
Washington, DC
London

MAJOR DEPARTMENTS/PRACTICES

Banking & Finance
Capital Markets
Corporate/Mergers & Acquisitions
Financial Restructuring
Healthcare/Not for Profit
Litigation
Real Estate
Tax & Private Client

THE STATS

No. of attorneys: 411
No. of offices: 4
Summer associate offers: 48 out of 50 (New York, 1999)
Management Committee Chair: Robert O. Link, Jr.
Hiring Partner: Robert O. Link, Jr.

PAY

New York, 2000
1st year: $125,000 + $35,000 potential bonus
2nd year: $135,000 + $40,000 potential bonus
3rd year: $150,000 + $45,000 potential bonus
4th year: $170,000 + $45,000 potential bonus
5th year: $190,000 + $45,000 potential bonus
6th year: $200,000 + $45,000 potential bonus
7th year: $205,000 + $50,000 potential bonus
Summer associate: $2,400/week

NOTABLE PERKS

- Flexible spending account
- Paid moving expenses
- Gym subsidy
- $40 meal allowance for summer meals
- Beer-and-pretzel Thursdays
- Sabbatical program for associates with five full years of service at the firm
- In-house CLE training

THE BUZZ
What attorneys at other firms are saying about this firm

- "An old firm trying to be hip"
- "Dennis Block helps"
- "Maybe if it were 1880"
- "Moving toward being high-powered"

UPPERS

- Billable hour requirements still below many New York firms
- Year-round casual policy
- Interesting and high-profile work; firm on upswing

DOWNERS

- Many complaining lawyers
- Conflicting assignments
- Uncertain job security

KEY COMPETITORS

Davis Polk & Wardwell
Fried, Frank, Harris, Shriver & Jacobson
Sullivan & Cromwell

EMPLOYMENT CONTACT

Ms. Virginia L. Quinn
Manager of Legal Recruitment
(212) 504-6290
vquinn@cwt.com

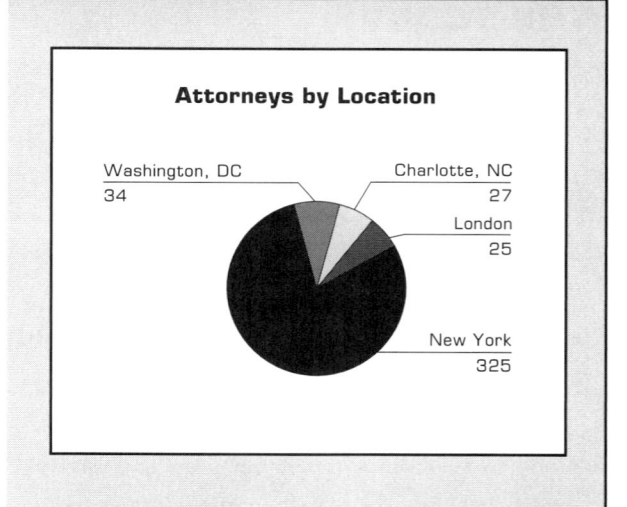

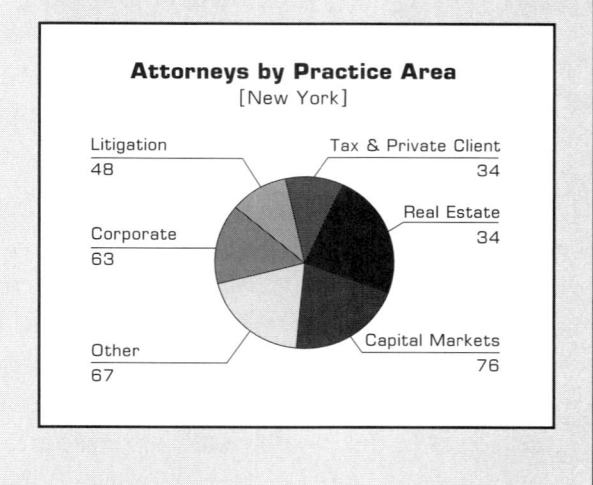

Attorneys by Location

- Washington, DC: 34
- Charlotte, NC: 27
- London: 25
- New York: 325

Attorneys by Practice Area [New York]

- Litigation: 48
- Tax & Private Client: 34
- Real Estate: 34
- Corporate: 63
- Capital Markets: 76
- Other: 67

QUALITY OF LIFE RANKINGS [ASSOCIATES RATE THEIR OWN FIRM]

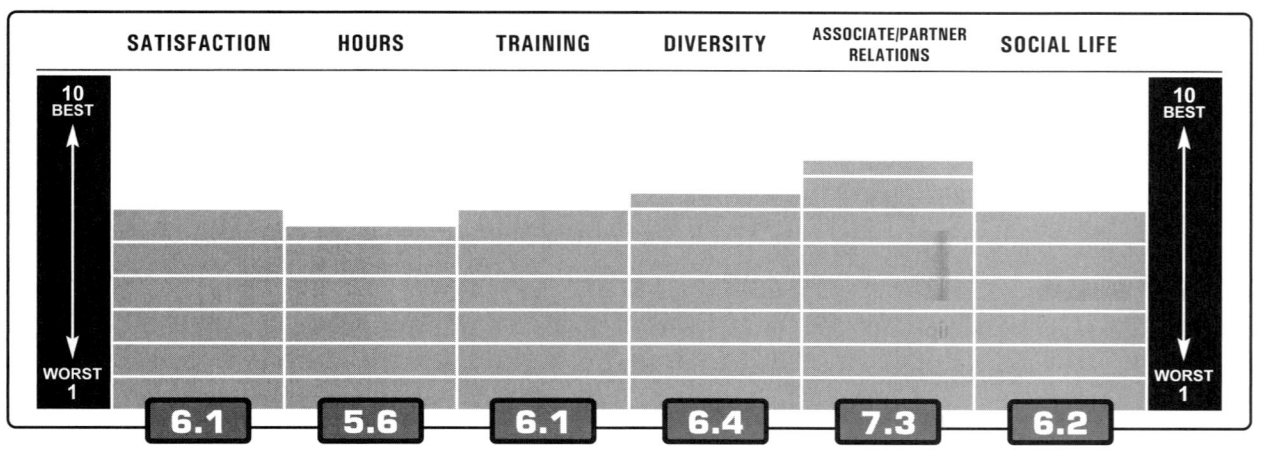

SATISFACTION	HOURS	TRAINING	DIVERSITY	ASSOCIATE/PARTNER RELATIONS	SOCIAL LIFE
6.1	5.6	6.1	6.4	7.3	6.2

THE SCOOP

Cadwalader, Wickersham & Taft is a storied Wall Street firm determinedly developing a younger, more aggressive image. The firm has already attracted some welcome publicity by creating new departments and shifting to a decidedly non-fusty year-round casual dress code. Others are watching to see if Cadwalader, with the help of hard-charging new partner Dennis Block, can complete the transition.

History: an old dog's new tricks

Founded in 1792, Cadwalader boasts that it is the oldest firm in New York. But age isn't always an asset. By the early 1990s the firm had a reputation for being a bit too relaxed (read: slow) in the aggressive world of New York law. In 1994, however, a group of rainmaking younger partners, including current chairman Robert Link, initiated an upheaval that ousted the firm's senior management. In that coup, dubbed "Project Rightsize," 17 of the firm's partners were cast out and the firm's Palm Beach office was closed. Two of the former partners brought suit against the firm claiming the firm's partnership agreement did not allow the firm to get rid of them. Cadwalader settled the cases.

British invasion

In the spring of 1998, the firm opened its London office with a splash, luring some of London's star attorneys to the office, including Clifford Chance's Andrew Wilkinson, who had headed that British firm's bankruptcy practice. Cadwalader's new office (which also poached leading partners from Freshfields and Simmons) is a full-service shop focusing on English and European Community law. In October 1998, Cadwalader landed a major client when it was appointed to advise bondholders in the restructuring of troubled U.K. telecom company Ionica. Cadwalader also advised the Crest Group on a successful hostile takeover of engineering company Forward Technology plc, a transaction that raised unusual issues under the Takeover Code and Companies Act.

In April 2000 Cadwalader's London office snagged banking litigation partner Michelle Duncan from Weil, Gotshal & Manges. The switch was Duncan's second major move. She left Clifford Chance for Weil in 1996. In addition, Cadwalader moved two partners from New York to the London office in 1999: Jim Croke, a partner whose specialty is asset-backed securities, and Alan Lawrence, a real estate finance pro.

A capital office

Cadwalader's Washington, DC location was created as a "convenience office" in 1963 and converted to a full-service office in 1967. The Washington branch focuses on environmental, white collar, regulatory, trade, and legislative matters. The firm's Charlotte office has thrived since opening in 1996, serving financial services clients such as First Union and the former NationsBank (now Bank of America). The Charlotte office specializes in capital markets, banking and finance, and real estate finance.

The new kid is Block

In July 1998, Cadwalader beat out the likes of Latham & Watkins and Simpson Thacher in the battle to woo Weil Gotshal defector Dennis Block. The M&A guru left Weil because of disagreements over that firm's business strategy. Qualified as both a litigator and a corporate attorney, Block joined Cadwalader as co-chairman of both the firm's corporate and litigation groups.

Many insiders complain that Block is extremely demanding and expects associates to be at his disposal 24/7. However, he's brought plenty of business to the firm. In September 1998, General Motors Pension Trust hired Cadwalader and Block to help handle the trust's $1.43 billion sale of its stake in Taubman Realty Group, which owns properties such as the Short Hills Mall in New Jersey and the Stamford Town Center in Connecticut. In early 1999, the firm was tapped to represent NAC Re, a seller of business insurance and reinsurance, in its $1.25 billion acquisition by Bermuda-based XL Capital.

Star lawyer Block was involved in three of the top M&A deals of 1999. In April Cadwalader handled Colorado-based MediaOne Group's proposed $40 billion acquisition by Philadelphia-based Comcast Corp. Block worked with former colleagues at Weil Gotshal in representing MediaOne. The next month, Block worked with Louis Bevilacqua, advising Baby Bell US West on its proposed $37 billion merger with Bermuda-based Global Crossings and its subsequent merger with Qwest Communications. And in February 2000, Block advised Pfizer Inc. on its $90 billion merger deal with Warner-Lambert.

Restructuring and reinsuring

Block is not the only attorney Cadwalader has lured away from another top firm. In September 1998, Bruce Zirinsky, a reorganization specialist from Weil Gotshal, came over to Cadwalader to join the firm's financial restructuring practice group. Then, in April 2000, Cadwalader captured the reinsurance dispute resolution practice from Rosenmann & Colin. The new Cadwalader lawyers include group leader Lawrence Brandes and partners Clifford Schoenberg, Harry Cohen, and John Finnegan.

Finding a future in a banking model

Cadwalader put together a "Strategic Solutions Team" in May 2000, using an investment bank management model to tackle the problems of high-tech firms as well as more traditional clients. The new group brings together lawyers from the Capital Markets, Corporate, Tax, and Financial Restructuring groups for open group discussions on client matters. Partners Ira Schacter and Brian Hoffmann serve as co-chairs. The team also advises Internet-oriented clients, including entrepreneurs, venture capitalists, and startups, on legal issues stemming from the growth of the Web and e-commerce. Clients include fashionmall.com, killerinfo.com, and BroadBand Services.

In January 2000, Cadwalader organized talent from its Capital Markets, Corporate, and Project Finance departments into a new Banking & Finance Group. Partners Steven Cohen and Robert Vitale will co-chair the new department, which focuses on lending and project finance transactions.

CMBS maestro

Even before the creation of the new groups, Cadwalader was a big player in the corporate arena. Commercial Mortgage Alert has consistently ranked Cadwalader one of the most active law firms on commercial mortgage-backed securities deals. Cadwalader was the No. 1 firm in the area for 1999, representing underwriter's counsel on 11 of the 47 public and Fannie Mae offerings.

Casual Cadwalader

In March 2000, CWT made the leap to a year-round casual dress policy. To celebrate the new policy, the firm sponsored the hilariously-named "Casual Walader Day" during which lawyers donated suits to Career Gear and Dress for Success, two nonprofits that provide business attire to low-income-people. In April 2000, Polo Ralph Lauren and *Esquire* hosted a cocktail party at Polo Ralph Lauren's flagship Madison Avenue store and held a seminar on how to put together a sharp business casual wardrobe. Some lucky attorneys even got fashion makeovers at the event.

GETTING HIRED

Alma mater matters

According to Vault.com's sources, Cadwalader puts a lot of emphasis on candidates' alma maters. "The firm is overly concerned about whether candidates came from a top-tier school," says one insider. "It will decline offers to otherwise strong candidates based on school attended." But some lawyers tell Vault.com that the firm does take students from other schools. "I am very pleased that the firm does consider local New York City law schools and does not recruit exclusively from [the] Ivy League," says a contact.

Some associates at Cadwalader say the firm may once again be sharpening its selectivity after a brief dip in admission standards. "The firm is becoming more selective," one attorney reveals, "But during 1998, anyone who applied and didn't screw up the interview would have probably gotten an offer." Still, another Cadwalader insider points out, "With today's hot job market, hiring standards must necessarily fall."

Financial background a plus

"Once the on-campus interview is passed, and the candidate is from a good school, getting an offer is not too difficult," reports an associate. One source notes that the firm "likes older students with work experience or financial background." Says a recent Cadwalader addition with confidence: "If you're hired as a summer associate, you will get an offer."

Candidates should know that "interviewing as a lateral is more rigorous," according to one associate. "The process involved two callbacks." Interested laterals should keep in mind that "the firm has seen a large increase in lateral hires, both as a result of turnover and internal growth."

OUR SURVEY SAYS

Competitive culture

Although insiders say Cadwalader is laid-back, many sources also describe the firm as "competitive." "Overall, it's relaxed, but with a competitive edge. It is not an uptight or formal place. But despite the casual atmosphere, work is taken very seriously," explains one associate. Adds a corporate attorney, "It has become more competitive in the last year. There is not always enough good work to go around."

Happy partners — and notorious exceptions

Although associates say the vast majority of their bosses treat them well, "some are just downright nasty." "Most are respectful — with some notable, and notorious, exceptions," says one Cadwalader lawyer. But other partners were described as "eager to relate to associates," and are "younger and happier than most." "The partners with whom I've worked are considerate of family matters, don't expect you to come in if you're sick, try to minimize weekend hours, and let you step out to catch a baseball game without hesitating," reports another lawyer.

Socializing in the bunker

Insiders note the firm sponsors many events, including monthly mixers. Cadwalader's Associates Development Committee throws parties for associates "that usually turn into a night of bar-hopping." The firm even has a travel club, organized by library director Rissa Peckar, to discuss vacation destinations. At the first meeting the club talked about Bali while lunching on fried bananas in peanut sauce.

One source tells Vault.com, "People in general know how to have a good time — partners included — and don't hesitate to do so." But some contacts paint a less idyllic picture of Cadwalader: "People are generally antisocial and pissed off." "Everyone puts on a smile, but very few mean it," according to another lawyer. Still others say that social interaction is limited to work hours. "We pal around at work, but there's not much after-work socializing." A corporate attorney says he gets along very well with his colleagues because they have a "bunker mentality."

Non-retro raises

In April 2000, Cadwalader raised salaries to the new starting base of $125,000. But associates grumble that the firm was slow in boosting pay and did not make the raises retroactive. "The firm attempted to play games when New York salaries increased, only to give in. By not making the raise retroactive, they disappointed a lot of people," gripes one Cadwalader attorney.

Gently undulating hours

Associates say that the hours vary greatly from associate to associate. Some lawyers say they put in a 9:30 a.m. to 8:00 p.m. day, while others report working much longer hours. "I have been luckier than many of my fellow associates who work past midnight on a regular basis," gloats one attorney. But a corporate attorney claims, "If you leave before 10 p.m. [partners] ask why you are working a half day." Lawyers say there is a partner known for calling associates at 5 p.m. for a surprise double all-nighter. Another contact tells Vault.com, "I work less than my peers at other big New York firms. However, the recent salary increase has been accompanied by an increased emphasis on billable hours."

See you later

Insiders report a "disturbingly" high turnover rate at Cadwalader. Some go as far as to say there is a "void" in the mid-level ranks. "Look to your left. Look to your right. Neither of these people nor you will be here in a year," predicts one lawyer. Some lawyers say many of the defectors go to investment banks.

Mold me

"There are regular firm-wide training seminars on various areas of our practice, but the real training comes from the work," associates say. The mentoring provided by the partners "ranges from micromanagement to almost total lack of guidance," according to insiders. "It's a get-up-and-go place to work. If you have to ask questions you will be tagged as brainless," one source claims. On the bright side, some lawyers tell Vault.com that the older associates help the younger attorneys "learn the ropes." [The firms says it offers more than 80 in-house CLE classes.]

A building that makes you proud

Cadwalader associates get their own offices after their first year. First-years share interior offices but then move up to their own private office with a window. One insider describes the décor at Cadwalader as "classy and old-school." Insiders in New York think the offices are nice and rave particularly about the building. "The building, highlighted by the atrium, is gorgeous. It makes you feel proud to work in such a distinctive environment." In April 2000, Cadwalader's Washington outpost left its home of more than 20 years on Dupont Circle and moved to the capital's F Street corridor.

Associates exult that the library staff and word processing center are "outstanding," though some junior associates feel they are not getting the help they need from their secretaries.

Diversity: an acceptable record

Associates say women are well represented among the associate ranks and the firm has "amazing child care." But some associates report that it can be hard to make it to partner and make time for a family. "Women are expected, like all associates, to put in the work to get promoted. The firm has part-time work options, but pursuing those options, even for a short time, takes you off the partner track entirely." The firm offers flex-time options as well. In 2000 Cadwalader formed the Cadwalader's Women's Initiative, a quarterly forum designed to address women's issues.

There is a dearth of minority lawyers at Cadwalader, sources say. But lawyers emphasize that it is not because the firm has a "racist thing going on." "I don't know if [the lack of minority attorneys] results from a lack of receptivity, or rather a lack of active recruitment among minority candidates." It's worth noting that in January 2000 Derrick Cephas became the first African-American to be elected to Cadwalader's management committee.

There are no barriers to gays and lesbians getting hired at CWT, and insiders report there are openly gay lawyers at the firm. "I think the firm is hospitable, but I think [gays] are very low profile," says one lawyer.

It's no dream world

Some insiders attack the firm with vigor: "Nice surroundings, but vicious partners and burned out mid-levels make coming to work every day a fearful experience." Some just wish they worked fewer hours. "The work is very interesting and partners and senior associates are helpful and generally nice. But the expectations are high as to billable hours." Others gripe about the griping: "If everyone would stop complaining about how miserable they are and suck it up, I'd be happy. I think most people were totally shocked to find out that lawyering isn't as cool as it looks on TV."

Limited support for pro bono

As of June 2000, pro bono work at Cadwalader does not count toward billing requirements. But insiders report the firm is contemplating changing that policy. Associates say that the firm only gives lip service to pro bono work. "Talk, talk, talk. That's what Cadwalader does about pro bono. But the action part is very weak," one lawyer says. Another contact was more blunt: "It doesn't happen. Forget it."

A long road to partnership

Insiders say that it takes nine to ten years to become a partner and the firm strictly adheres to that timetable. Some sources say partnership chances are "a crapshoot." "If the timing is right and you are working at the time for a partner who has business, then you have a chance. Otherwise, the firm simply strings associates along," says one source. Another associate suggests, "You have to put in the hours, be considered brilliant and be able to attract clients." A corporate associate had this advice for prospective partners: "Work for Dennis Block and bill."

"Overall it's relaxed with a competitive edge. It is not an uptight or formal place. But despite the casual atmosphere, work is taken very seriously."

— *Cadwalader associate*

Proskauer Rose LLP

VAULT.COM 48 PRESTIGE RANKING

1585 Broadway
New York, NY 10036
(212) 969-3000
Fax: (212) 969-2900
www.proskauer.com

LOCATIONS

New York, NY (HQ)
Boca Raton, FL
Los Angeles, CA
Newark, NJ
Washington, DC
Paris

MAJOR DEPARTMENTS/PRACTICES

Bankruptcy Creditors' Rights
Corporate Securities International
Employee Benefits/ERISA
Entertainment/Sports/Intellectual Property
Estates/Trusts/Wills/Probate
Health
Labor/Employment
Litigation/Appellate/Arbitration
Real Estate/Environmental/Zoning
Tax

THE STATS

No. of attorneys: 501
No. of offices: 6
Summer associate offers: 27 out of 27 (New York, 1999)
Chairman: Alan S. Jaffe
Hiring Partner: Michael E. Foreman

THE BUZZ
What attorneys at other firms are saying about this firm

- "Great work product in labor and employment law"
- "Billable hell"
- "Union busters and ex-jocks"
- "Strong sports law"

PAY

New York, 2000
1st year: $125,000
2nd year: $135,000
3rd year: $150,000
4th year: $165,000
5th year: $185,000
6th year: $195,000
7th year: $205,000
8th year: $210,000
Summer associate: $2,404/week

Los Angeles, 2000
1st year: $125,000
2nd year: $135,000
3rd year: $150,000
4th year: $165,000
5th year: $185,000
6th year: $195,000
7th year: $205,000
8th year: $210,000
Summer associate: $2,404/week

Washington, DC, 2000
1st year: $110,000 +$15,000 for 2,000 hours
2nd year: $120,000 +$15,000 for 2,000 hours
3rd year: $130,000 +$15,000 for 2,000 hours
4th year: $140,000 +$15,000 for 2,000 hours
5th year: $150,000 +$15,000 for 2,000 hours
6th year: $160,000 +$15,000 for 2,000 hours

NOTABLE PERKS

- Paid disability leave
- Paid child care leave, followed by unpaid leave
- Emergency child care
- "Awesome" chocolate chip cookies

UPPERS

- A great deal of independence for associates
- Very cool clients
- Cookies

DOWNERS

- Attorneys on call all the time
- Wednesdays in Times Square fighting tourists
- Overemphasis on billables

KEY COMPETITORS

Milbank, Tweed, Hadley & McCloy
Morgan, Lewis & Bockius
Paul, Weiss, Rifkind, Wharton & Garrison
Weil, Gotshal & Manges
Wilkie Farr & Gallagher

EMPLOYMENT CONTACT

Ms. Diane M. Kolnik
Manager of Associate Recruiting
(212) 969-5071
dkolnik@proskauer.com

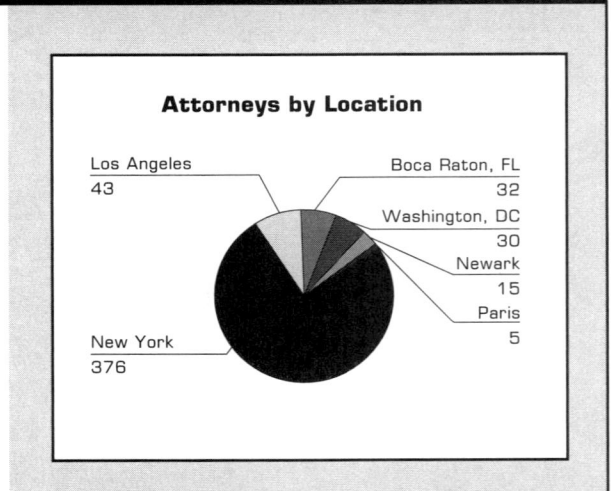

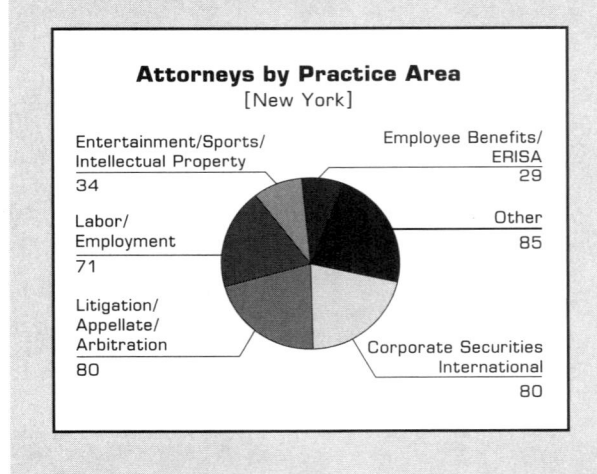

Attorneys by Location

- Los Angeles: 43
- New York: 376
- Boca Raton, FL: 32
- Washington, DC: 30
- Newark: 15
- Paris: 5

Attorneys by Practice Area [New York]

- Entertainment/Sports/Intellectual Property: 34
- Labor/Employment: 71
- Litigation/Appellate/Arbitration: 80
- Employee Benefits/ERISA: 29
- Other: 85
- Corporate Securities International: 80

THE SCOOP

Proskauer Rose, a New York firm with a high-profile sports law practice, caters to clients such as the NBA, the NHL, and the ATP tour. While the Proskauer Rose name may be known among the general public for the firm's sports practice, it is probably best known among legal brethren for its leading labor and employment law practice.

A vibrant history

Founded by Alfred Rose in 1875, Proskauer Rose truly blossomed after Judge Joseph Proskauer joined the firm in 1930. From that point on, Proskauer's litigation department grew to world-class status. Unfortunately for Proskauer, it was on the losing side of perhaps its most famous case, the Oscar Robertson antitrust suit, which established free agency in basketball. Although lead litigator David Stern lost, the NBA was clearly impressed with Proskauer's representation: The basketball league hired Stern as its in-house counsel in 1978 and later promoted him to NBA commissioner. Also in the late 1970s, the firm opened up three domestic branch offices in Boca Raton, Florida, Washington, DC, and Los Angeles, CA.

In the past decade, the firm has seen major growth, boosting its number of attorneys more than 50 percent. In 1994, Proskauer plumped up its real estate department by hiring 20 attorneys from disintegrating rival firm Shea & Gould. In 1997 the firm's name of Proskauer Rose Goetz & Mendelsohn was truncated to Proskauer Rose, proving that a Proskauer Rose by any other name would still be as sweet.

A slam-dunk practice

Ever dream of being the commissioner of a sports league? If so, joining Proskauer Rose wouldn't be a bad start. Both David Stern and Gary Bettman, commissioners of the National Basketball Association and the National Hockey League, respectively, started out at Proskauer. The firm is outside counsel to the NBA, the NHL and Major League Soccer and has dominated the area of sports law (along with its fierce rival Weil, Gotshal & Manges) since the mid-1970s. Proskauer's sports practice brought the firm into the spotlight in 1998 when its New York headquarters served as the site of the grueling negotiations surrounding the six-month lockout of the NBA players that threatened to shut down the pro basketball season. Proskauer partners Howard Ganz and Neil Abramson represented the league in the negotiations. In 1999, Proskauer attorneys Joseph M. Lecese and Bradley I. Ruskin represented ATP Tour, Inc. in a $1.2 billion marketing deal with Swiss based ISL Marketing AG. The firm also represented Robert Wood Johnson IV, heir to the Johnson & Johnson fortune, in his $635 million purchase of the New York Jets in early 2000.

That's entertainment!

Proskauer Rose has also taken steps to expand its entertainment practice, most notably in L.A. The firm attracted over 15 new lateral entertainment attorneys to its California office in 1999 and 2000, including prominent litigators Bert Deixler, Larry Rappaport, and Charles Ortner. Deixler, Rappaport, and eight others came to Proskauer in a merger with the litigation practice of McCambridge, Deixler and Marmaro in April 2000. McCambrudge also brought with him a large roster of high-profile clients including NBC, Elektra Entertainment, Beck, Smashing Pumpkins, Dr. Dre, and Snoop Dog. Charles Ortner brought his five-partner litigation practice (as well as clients including Madonna, Lauryn Hill, and the National Academy of Recording Arts and Sciences) to Proskauer Rose in 1999.

Labor and employment is the leader

But Proskauer serves more than just those in sports and entertainment. In fact, the firm's top department is labor and employment law — arguably the best department of its kind anywhere. In a newsworthy case in 1997, the firm represented Yale University against an unfair labor practice suit. The case, filed by disgruntled graduate student teaching assistants, was argued before the National Labor Relations Bureau. (The charges were dismissed.) Alan Jaffe, who was elected in 1999 to a three-year term as Proskauer's chairman, leads the esteemed practice. Among Jaffe's clients are Madison Square Garden, Radio City Music Hall, the New York City Ballet, and the New York City Opera.

Proskauer also has a strong litigation practice, with more than 140 lawyers. The firm is known for its liberal application of computer technology, including the use of animation in presenting cases to juries. Recently, in a highly publicized case, Proskauer Rose represented BDO Seidman, Deloitte & Touche, and Ernst & Young (along with their predecessor firms) in major securities lawsuits and in administrative proceedings before the Securities and Exchange Commission.

Improving corporate practice

Industry insiders say Proskauer Rose's corporate practice is not at the level of the top New York law firms, although the firm's investment/finance, real estate, and bankruptcy practices are growing. The firm has worked hard in the past few years to improve its corporate department by enhancing its international practice (Asia, South America, Israel, and Europe), hospitality group, technology group, M&A, bankruptcy, and intellectual property groups, as well as by adding a patent group. The firm has had a hand in several noteworthy mergers and acquisitions in recent years. In 1998, the firm represented Superior Telecom in its purchase of Essex International for $1.4 billion, solid waste disposal company American Disposal Services in its $1.2 billion acquisition by Allied Waste Industries, and Charter Communications' in its $4.5 billion acquisition by Microsoft co-founder Paul Allen. The firm's corporate clients represent a variety of industries. Other major clients include health care products supplier Henry Schein, investment bank J.P. Morgan, and private equity fund Charterhouse Group International.

iPractice, uPractice, we allPractice...

Proskauer Rose took steps in 1999 to increase its attractiveness to Internet companies. The firm mirrored law firms in California by creating a new pricing policy for new media companies, including lower hourly rates and a willingness to take a company's stock instead of fees. The firm also created a new division, iPractice, in order to better serve its Internet clients. Proskauer's major new media clients include e-retailer dELiA*s, online advertising leader 24/7 Media (which Proskauer helped take public), and teen site iTurf Inc.

We do get out of the city sometimes

Although the firm is firmly entrenched in its New York headquarters (more than 70 percent of its lawyers are housed there), it has branches in the legal hot spots of Los Angeles, Paris, and Washington, DC along with offices in less common locations like grandparent-haven Boca Raton, FL and reviving Newark, NJ.

Fashionable practices

Although Proskauer does not typically handle humongous deals, it is second to none in snaring quirky cases. Three of the firm's more interesting practice groups are media (officially called "libel, copyright, and first amendment"), sports, and fashion. Cases the media group has tried range from persuading the Supreme Court to unanimously strike down on First Amendment grounds New York's Son-of-Sam law (preventing criminals from profiting from their memoirs) to representing *The Washington Post* against a libel suit filed by the Church of Scientology. Moreover, the firm has represented titans in the retail fashion business for decades. Among its clients are Barney's New York, Hermes of Paris, and Bed Bath & Beyond.

GETTING HIRED

Looking for hires in corporate

In hiring, Proskauer focuses on two factors more than anything else: grades and prestige of the law school. "Personality only plays a role if you are a borderline candidate," a source says. Other factors that insiders suggest play a role are "undergraduate performance" and "demonstrated leadership abilities." A contact tells us that the litigation department is "looking primarily for people who can write." Some say that candidates who express an interest in corporate work have a better chance of getting hired. Remarks one associate: "The firm does not have the best corporate department, but it's trying to make it better." Notes another, "Most people who are interested in corporate work don't think of Proskauer. So if you want to do corporate work at Proskauer, you have a really good shot."

We like Cornell

According to insiders, the firm's "favorite school" is Cornell. "We have a relationship with them, since they have a labor and employment school," explains a source. "There is a classroom up there that is named after us because we paid them a lot of money to name it after us." (The firm informs Vault.com that it did not give money to Cornell, but rather a group of partners who are Cornell alumni did so on their own.) Although associates interview candidates, we were told that "associate opinion does not count for a lot" in hiring decisions. The firm recruits at "top-15 ranked schools," as well as two local New York schools — "Brooklyn Law School and Fordham".

A popular summer hangout

The 2000 summer class was the firm's "largest ever," bursting at the seams with 80 law students. High attrition rates in the legal industry, as well as the recent economic boom, have made more aggressive hiring methods necessary. Not only has the size of the summer associate class grown, but in 1999 every law student in the program received an offer.

Proskauer tries to make its summer program "very realistic," say insiders. "The firm is quite busy," adds a source. "There is enough work to do." Two partners handle assignments during the summer, which are distributed according to the preferences of summer associates. There is no formal rotation system in the summer — associates must simply request work of interest to them. "Now that the firm will give you a department when they give you an offer, it is very important to impress the people in the department that you want to work in," an insider explains. "For example, in the labor and employment practice, which is what the firm is most known for, there may be 20 summer associates who want to work there, but only eight spots available. Thus, assignments will be made based on whether you made a favorable impression in the department." Among the firm's organized social activities in New York are bowling at Chelsea Piers and a pool party at a partner's home. The firm also organizes an "alumni sports law lunch," during which former Proskauer attorneys working for major sports leagues like the NBA and NHL talk about their practices and relationship to the firm.

OUR SURVEY SAYS

Relaxed yet productive atmosphere

Insiders describe Proskauer as a laid-back place to work. "For a law firm, it's relaxed and not stuffy — with real people," reports one corporate associate at Proskauer. Another insider is more specific: "The firm, as it was founded, is a Jewish firm, so we have lots of personalities, a casual atmosphere, and an open-door policy."

Laid-back hours and dress

While Proskauer associates have worried in recent years whether a minimum billable guideline of 2,000 hours would change its culture, insiders report that they still enjoy a relatively manageable schedule. "Most associates here work less than at virtually all other big New York firms," one associate says. "It's all relative," says another. "The hours are livable compared to other attorneys, but still unreasonable by normal standards." Most associates report billing about 50 hours a week. And Proskauer associates, unlike many of their industry compatriots, seem more inclined to accept their hours as part of the package. "It's a New York firm," reports one associate. "I didn't come here to slack off." Says another: "We work hard, but that's the job. They don't pay you this kind of money to hang out."

The firm is also not as buttoned-up as some of its conservative New York competitors when it comes to dress, associates say. Says one litigation associate: "The people here are more 'hip' than conservative but still wear business attire." Another associate reports that the firm does not have an "enforced dress code. Pants are OK for women. Men do not wear their jackets in the office." This laid-back approach to the dress code is confirmed by other associates. "There are some rumblings when people overdo it on casual day," reports one insider, "but there's generally no fashion police."

A unique assignment system, below average feedback

Associates get their assignments from a centralized assignment system the first nine months. After that period, Proskauer employs a unique system: The firm has one non-practicing attorney in the corporate group, one in labor, and another in litigation who create a customized assignment system for associates.

Associates are reviewed formally "about once a year." The reviews, which can last as little as five minutes, are viewed by most associates as "unsatisfying" and "subpar." "[The reviews] are not a very detailed thing," an associate says. "A partner will say, 'You did a good job on this. You could have done better on that.'" We are told, however, that some partners "make an effort to give more feedback" on an informal basis.

A venerable institute

A senior associate recalls, "Five years ago, when I arrived, training wasn't good, but now it's gotten better." A more recent hire elaborates that "in the past couple of years Proskauer has put a lot of effort into its training programs, such as instituting a several-day training session ("Proskauer Institute") for first-years upon arrival and developing periodic departmental training programs throughout the year. Other than that, it's learning by doing. In our department cases are often staffed with one partner and one associate, which gives the associate opportunities to participate in the case and to see how a partner runs a matter." The firm also allows associates to bill up to 125 hours as training (200 for first-years) and to charge the firm up to $1,000 a year for training expenses.

OK, OK we'll pay

Proskauer met the most recent round of industry-wide salary increases. However, some associates feel as if the partners gave the raises grudgingly. "The raise was not retroactive, and I feel like the partners believe that it was undeserved," reports one associate. Others complain that the "bonus structure is a little iffy, especially with the new salary increase." One New York-based associate elaborates, "Prior to this year, associates got at least 10% of salary as a bonus at year-end.

This year, Proskauer matched the citywide raises by giving us approximately the bonus amount in salary raises, but now guarantees no bonus whatsoever unless one works more than 2,100 hours. Above 2,100 hours, no specific amount has been mentioned. 2,300 hours triggers a higher (but again undisclosed) amount." Another attorney gripes, "I work pretty hard, but because of lots of non-billable work and difficult clients, it is not so easy to convert all the time into billables. In its effort to try to meet the market, Proskauer has definitely increased pressure to raise billables." Most associates do agree that the pay is sufficient. "Not only does the salary meet market prices, but when considering the average number of hours a Proskauer associate works, the pay is actually quite good."

The grind

Associates at Proskauer are not exempt from arduous workweeks. "People work hard here, because they know everybody else is working hard," a Proskauer attorney reports. "People don't have a problem hitting 2,000 hours." A New York associate adds, "For a large New York firm, the hours are fairly reasonable. If you reach 2,000 hours then you're in good standing." Moreover, many attorneys characterize the amount of hours worked by a Proskauer associate as being "self-selected." Associates don't hesitate to complain: "Corporate associates have been busier than litigators," one begins. "Moreover, more dedicated associates end up working a lot more." Another source reveals that at Proskauer "billable targets understate total hours significantly. While I find I can succeed with 2,000 or 2,100 billable hours, I must do at least 400 to 500 mandatory but 'nonbillable' hours each year, such as recruiting or writing articles for others."

The career climb

First-year associates say they feel like "mercenaries." "Someone always needs something done quickly, so you do it," a source says. In litigation, the firm's largest department, associates generally start out doing "mostly research." Though it's "not unheard of for first-year associates to be in court by themselves" on smaller matters, "it's not common." Litigators generally begin taking depositions in their second or third year. "The on-the-job training is pretty good," reports one litigator. "I'm doing briefs, depositions, and court appearances, and I'm only a second-year."

In the firm's specialty, labor and employment law, associates start off conducting research and "gradually begin writing motions" later in their first year. In the second year, "associates begin doing more discovery work." It is not until the fifth or sixth year that labor/employment associates get court time."

Obscure partnership path

"Are you kidding?" asks one associate when asked about partnership prospects at Proskauer. "These days it takes a 10+ year miracle or a substantial client portfolio." Says a slightly more optimistic associate: "The odds are not very high; I think in the last few years around three people per class firm-wide made partner, with around the same number of new senior counsel." In truth, the firm actually made four partners and six senior counsel in 1999. Regardless of the numbers, "the vast majority of associates have already left for other places by the time those decisions are made."

Another source is more analytical. "Each case is complicated," says this senior associate. "I believe that the firm does not want to make anyone a partner and will do so only when they have to. To 'have to' is a combination of how big a loss someone would be multiplied by the chance they will leave if not made a partner. It's very tough to figure." While the partnership track is generally eight to 12 years, associates note that "you don't really come here expecting to be partner."

Associates say that it's "hard to determine what the criteria for making partner at Proskauer are," save for the minimum of seven years of experience. Although the firm distributes a manual to all new associates detailing the criteria for success, insiders are still at a loss. "No one knows what's important," a source says. Says another: "It's a long, slow, and obscure promotion process. I have no idea how to improve my chances of making partner other than to do exceptional work and hope for growth in my department."

Retention: a hidden gem

As for most large firms, turnover is an issue for Proskauer Rose. Prior to 1999-2000, "turnover felt normal" to associates, but "now it seems like between three and seven attorneys leave every week, especially during the period of January to May 2000." The perception may not meet reality — the firm contends that the turnover rate is no higher than it has been in the past, and that it is actually low for New York. Proskauer attorneys note that the class of 1996 has "more than half of its associates," and that "retention of laterals has been great." However, many also notice that "firm morale hasn't been the highest lately." Associates leave Proskauer for various reasons, an insider reveals: "Associates will often leave after a few years to go to in-house positions (usually at our clients). Others leave because of 'lifestyle changes' (e.g., different career, smaller firm), but it's rare in our firm for an associate to go to another big firm from here."

Professional treatment

Proskauer associates say that their partners are "friendly" and "very professional," although most concede that there are exceptions. Says one source: "We have a handful of yellers but much less than at other firms." Reports an associate: "Treatment by partners varies. There is definitely a 'my time is more valuable than yours' attitude. For example, some partners will take calls while you are sitting in their office and schedule meetings without consulting your calendar." Another declares that "while partners are very nice, they don't have the time to deal with associates. When you need help the partners are not around." Despite these occasional complaints, most associates believe they are treated well. "Partners at Proskauer roll up their sleeves and work alongside associates," reports one insider. One source raves that at the firm there is "no distinction" between how partners and associates are treated. Says the source: "If you walked in a room, you wouldn't be able to tell who is the partner and who is the associate, except by age, possibly."

Selective prestige

Although associates admit that Proskauer Rose is "not in the top echelon" of law firms, most feel that the firm is "very prestigious." The firm's most highly regarded practice is labor and employment, which "is one of the best in the country if not the best." The litigation department also has a strong, "well-deserved" reputation. The real estate department is "very good" and the health care practice is "growing by leaps and bounds." Of course, associates enjoy the firm's reputation in sports. Says one insider: "This is the best, biggest sports law firm in the country." Another reports that during the negotiations over the NBA lockout, "[New York Knicks star] Patrick Ewing walked by my office. He's a big man." Admittedly, Proskauer "is not known as a top corporate place, although the firm is trying to build up corporate to a premier practice," insiders say. Explains one corporate associate: "The corporate work is more corporate counsel than big deal-oriented. The firm is moving more toward big deals and would like our corporate department to be seen as a force."

Social life: boat builders

One associate in the Washington DC office reports that "people genuinely like each other here." Another notes, "Due to the long working hours of a large firm lawyer's life, it is a necessity that an associate like the people he or she works with. I feel that my fellow attorneys are part of my extended family, which makes the long hours tolerable, if not enjoyable." Many disagree, stating that while "there are cool people, and they are not afraid to be individuals, people do not really socialize outside of work." Litigation associates at Proskauer do enjoy well-attended cocktail parties every other Friday. In terms of formal events, Proskauer hosts an annual firm ball for attorneys and their significant others. Proskauer also has a firm-wide Christmas party at a hotel in Times Square (no dates allowed). In addition, once every two or three years, the firm sponsors a "bonding" retreat in upstate New York. At the retreat, attorneys engage in golf, canoeing, and "teamwork workshops — we all work together to build a boat." Says one corporate associate: "The associates in the corporate department are great. I find I have many people to lunch with." Othrt associates cite plenty of door-to-door chatter."

Committed to pro bono

Many associates view Proskauer as being "quite committed" to pro bono work. An insider reveals that "there is a partner in charge of assigning pro bono options."

Another attorney elaborates, "Pro bono counts only toward bonus-related 'billable' targets. It is considered 'legal nonbillable' for all other purposes (i.e., it is not reported to department heads for performance purposes and is otherwise not counted). The firm's commitment to pro bono seems to have decreased rapidly in the past few months since the latest salary hikes." A corporate associate reports that litigation associates are more likely to be encouraged to take part in pro bono work than their corporate counterparts. He recalls that the head of the department once asked, "Who gives a damn about poor people?" "He was joking, but the impression I got was that I would not be assisted, and it would not be looked upon well."

Good firm for gays

Proskauer insiders say the firm is welcoming to gays and lesbians. "We have many openly gay associates who are very well regarded in the firm," reports one associate. Says another: "Gay attorneys here are out, welcomed, and appear to be entirely comfortable." Says yet another: "The firm is great in this area. Being out is not a hindrance at all."

The firm is "great on advancement" with respect to minority attorneys, insiders add. One notes that "two [minorities] have been made partner in the last few years." However, notes that associate, "the firm is not so good in hiring." As for the environment for women, one associate reports: "I think they're very receptive. But there aren't many female partners." "The firm has been incredibly supportive of my decision to work part-time," reveals a female attorney. "They have never stopped talking about advancing me."

Centrally located offices

Proskauer's New York headquarters is located in Times Square, which the firm's associates describe as one of the advantages of working at the firm. "I like the fact that the place is always busy," a source says. "I feel safe if I'm leaving at 10 p.m." Associates share an office for their first year but get their own after that. Offices come equipped with a computer, a printer, and "always a window." Reports one insider: "There's a great river view from my office." The firm's cafeteria, although not subsidized, serves "very good" food and is "still cheaper than eating outside."

Although associate offices in its headquarters are described as large, the firm is not intent on creating a posh environment, insiders point out. "If I were a client, I'd be happy. I'd know my money was used for stellar legal advice and not for froufrou office artwork or decadent furniture."

Baker Botts LLP

VAULT.COM PRESTIGE RANKING: 49

One Shell Plaza
910 Louisiana
Houston, TX 77002-4995
(713) 229-1234
www.bakerbotts.com

LOCATIONS

Houston, TX (HQ)
Austin, TX • Dallas, TX • New York, NY • Washington, DC • Baku • London • Moscow

MAJOR DEPARTMENTS/PRACTICES

Corporate and Securities
Energy
Environmental
Government Contacts/Regulatory
Intellectual Property
International
Labor & Employment
Tax
Trial
Technology

THE STATS

No. of attorneys: 546
No. of offices: 7
Summer associate offers: 95% (Firm-wide 1999)
Managing Partner: Richard C. Johnson
Hiring Partner: James Edward Maloney (Houston)

PAY

All Texas Offices, 2000
1st year: $110,000 + $5,000 potential
2nd year: $114,000 + $10,000 potential
3rd year: $121,000 + $15,000 potential
4th year: $130,000 + $20,000 potential
5th year: $140,000 + $20,000 potential
6th year: $145,000 + $25,000 potential
7th year: $155,000 + $25,000 potential
8th year: $160,000 + $25,000 potential
Summer associate: $1,700/week

New York, 2000
1st year: $125,000 + $10,000 potential
2nd year: $135,000
3rd year: $150,000
4th year: $165,000
5th year: $180,000
6th year: $190,000 + $45,000 potential
7th year: $200,000
8th year: $205,000 + $50,000 potential
Summer associate: $2,400/week

Washington, DC, 2000
1st year: $120,000 + $10,000 potential
2nd year: $130,000 + $10,000 potential
3rd year: $140,000 + $20,000 potential
4th year: $150,000 + $25,000 potential
5th year: $160,000 + $30,000 potential
6th year: $170,500 + $35,000 potential
7th year: $175,000 + $40,000 potential
8th year: $185,000 + $50,000 potential
Summer associate: $2,300/week

NOTABLE PERKS

- Three months maternity leave
- Free parking
- Tickets to sporting events when available
- Free sodas and coffee

THE BUZZ

What attorneys at other firms are saying about this firm

- "Probably the best Texas firm"
- "Lobbyist firm, schmoozefestarony"
- "Can't break the regional mold"
- "Tops in energy"

UPPERS

- Partners very accomplished, fair and likeable
- Associates given significant responsibility early in careers
- High-quality clients

DOWNERS

- Lawyers don't socialize much at the office
- Training could be more formalized
- Conservative management

KEY COMPETITORS

Fulbright & Jaworski
Gibson, Dunn & Crutcher
Vinson & Elkins
Weil Gotshal & Manges

EMPLOYMENT CONTACT

Ms. Melissa O'Neal (Houston office only)
(713) 229-2056
melissa.o'neal@bakerbotts.com

(See web site for additional contacts)

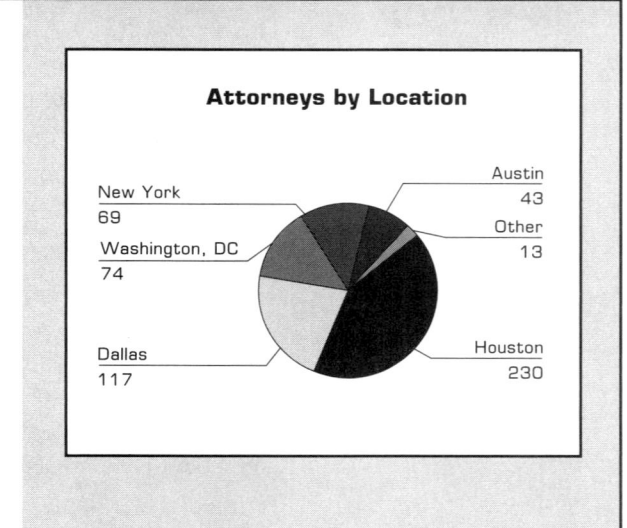

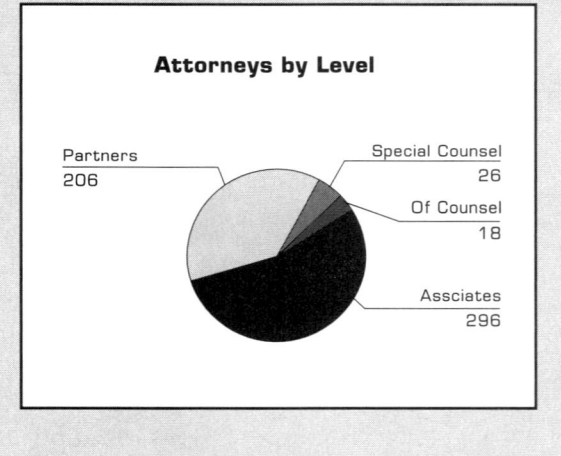

Attorneys by Location

- New York: 69
- Washington, DC: 74
- Dallas: 117
- Houston: 230
- Austin: 43
- Other: 13

Attorneys by Level

- Partners: 206
- Special Counsel: 26
- Of Counsel: 18
- Associates: 296

QUALITY OF LIFE RANKINGS [ASSOCIATES RATE THEIR OWN FIRM]

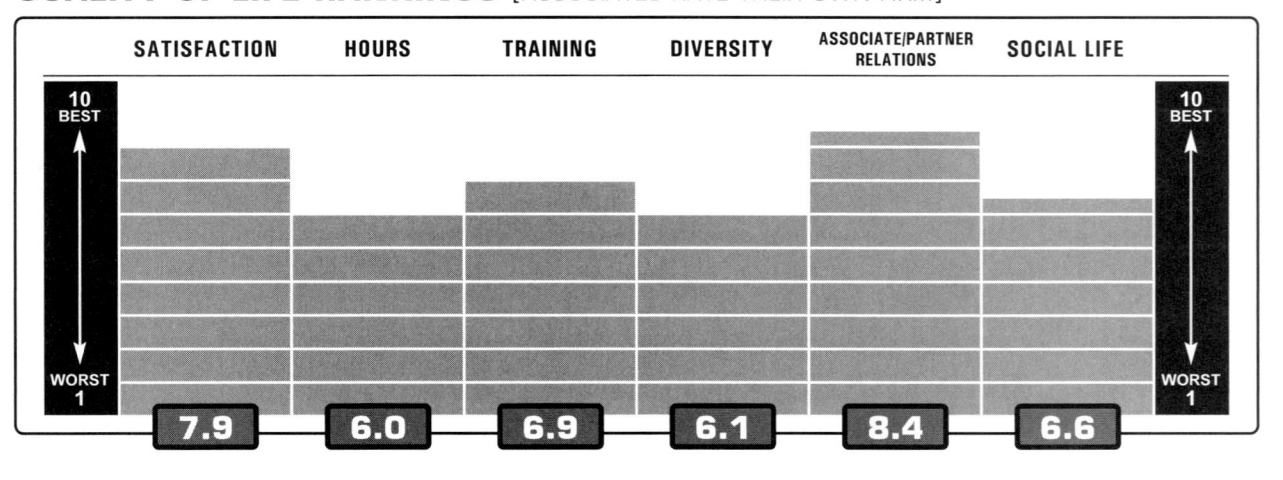

SATISFACTION	HOURS	TRAINING	DIVERSITY	ASSOCIATE/PARTNER RELATIONS	SOCIAL LIFE
7.9	6.0	6.9	6.1	8.4	6.6

THE SCOOP

Although Baker Botts LLP has been around for 160 years, 1999 saw this good ol' Texas firm taking steps to modernize its image for the new millenium. With strong energy and international practices, Baker Botts proudly claims the 49th slot on this year's Vault.com Top 50.

They almost remember the Alamo

Baker Botts was a fixture in the Houston area before the United States annexed the Republic of Texas. Its 1840 founding makes it the oldest law firm in the Lone Star State. In the nearly 160 years since, the firm has managed to keep up with the times, and today employs about 550 lawyers. Baker Botts began expanding outside the Houston market in the 1972 with the establishment of an office in Washington, DC, and furthered its Texas presence by opening branches in Austin and Dallas during the 1980s. It took on the Big Apple in 1992, and five years later merged its New York office with intellectual property specialists Brumbaugh, Graves, Donohue & Raymond.

In the ensuing years, the branch offices have flourished, many of them growing from just a handful of lawyers at their inception to become large, full-service legal operations. (For example, the firm's Dallas office, originally a 10-lawyer outfit, now has 115 attorneys and continues to grow.) Major policy decisions (such as compensation and election of new partners) are made based upon a vote of the entire partnership, as is election to the nine-person executive committee.

Baker Botts went global in the 1990s, opening offices in Moscow in 1993 and London in 1998. Baker Botts also moved into Baku in 1998 in order to take advantage of Azerbaijan's lucrative oil business. (The firm has been handling matters in the region for clients like Pennzoil since the early 1990s.)

The new guy

Baker Botts welcomed another Baker into the fold in 1993: James A. Baker III, former U.S. Secretary of State and Secretary of the Treasury. Baker, whose great-grandfather was also a member of the firm, is a senior partner working in the Houston office. Could there be more Texan politicians in Baker Bott's future?

Freshly punctuated with raises and perks

2000 has been a year of change for this Texas stalwart. Baker Botts had a notable departure in January 2000: the ampersand in the firm's name was dropped in order to project a sleeker, more modern image for a firm often characterized as "old-line." The firm's Houston office also decided to allow associates to dress business casual year-round (this policy, generous for offices mired in Southern heat, varies from office to office.) Perhaps the most important change, as far as associates are concerned, was the raising of associates' salaries. All Texas first-years had their base salaries raised to $110,000, and associates at the same level in the New York office will receive $125,000. The new perks have been well received by Baker Botts' attorneys. In a 1999 quality of life poll conducted by *Texas Lawyer*, the firm was ranked fifth in the state, up five spots from the previous year.

Oily lawyers

To play with the big boys of the Texan legal world, a law firm must be a major player in energy work. Baker Botts does not disappoint. In 1999, the firm represented Conco Inc. in its $4.4 billion IPO and its subsequent $12 billion split-off divestiture by parent E.I. du Pont. That same year, a team led by corporate partner J. David Kirkland, Jr. represented Schlumberger Ltd. in a $3.2 billion merger of its offshore drilling business, Sedco Forex Offshore, with Transocean Offshore Inc. The new company, Transocean Sedco Forex is now the world's largest offshore drilling company. Also in 1999, the firm advised PennzEnergyCo. in its $2.3 billion acquistion by Devon Energy Corp. Furthermore, partner Joe Poff assisted Reliant Energy Inc. in its $2.4 billion acquisition of N.V. UNA and the $2.1 billion acquisition of power plants from Sithe Energies.

In 1998, Baker Botts advised Baker Hughes in its $5.5 billion takeover of Western Atlas, Lyondell Petrochemical in its $5.6 billion acquisition of ARCO Chemical, and, again, Schlumberger Ltd. when it bought Camco International for $2.3 billion. These days, the firm is extending its energy practice across the globe. Baker Botts recently hired Tony Higginson, previously the head of Lovell White Durant's energy department, to head up the firm's energy practice in London.

Those other practices

Energy is not the only area in which Baker Botts' M&A lawyers have been busy. Other major transactions last year include representing Tele-Communications, Inc. when it was acquired by AT&T for $55 billion. Baker Botts' also assisted Electronic Data Systems Corp. in its $1.65 billion acquisition of MCI Systemhouse from MCI Worldcom. In addition, Baker Botts represented TV Guide Inc. in its $8.9 billion acquisition by Gemstar International.

The firm's litigation practice has been involved in a number of high-profile matters as well. In early 2000, IP partner John A. Fogarty, Jr. was invaluable in helping DYMO CoStar Corporation in a patent infringement suit against Seiko Instruments USA. The firm also successfully represented Procter & Gamble against a claim that the company had been negligent in its product labeling. A Texas woman took Aleve painkillers for a longer period of time than recommended and sued PRC.

GETTING HIRED

Local focus

Baker Botts likes to homegrow its hires. In 1998, the University of Texas was the top law school from which the firm drew both summer and first-year associates. The University of Houston, Baylor, and Southern Methodist University were also near the top of the list. Additionally, insiders say, "We get a lot of candidates from Harvard and Chicago." In all, the firm recruits at more than 30 schools but appears unwilling to spend the money to widen the student pool. "When I first came, we went to more schools," says a senior associate. "We go to fewer now. It's a budgetary issue. We've been less successful at Yale and Stanford, so we make fewer recruiting efforts there now." Another insider notes, "we generally only consider law students from reputable law schools whose grades are above a minimum cut-off, which varies by school. We generally only consider lateral candidates whose school and grades would have qualified them for consideration as a law student."

Dinner with associates

The firm requires no specific credentials "unless you're interested in a particular area. [For example], IP lawyers need more specialized backgrounds." Prospective summer associates are given the standard 30-minute interviews on campus, "generally with one partner and one associate," followed by dinner. "We tell people quickly, inside of a week" if they make the second round, insiders report. Those who make the cut "get called back for a day of interviews and another dinner." Dinner is usually the night before, but the schedule is not set in stone, as Baker Botts realizes that out-of-towners "typically look at three to four firms." On the big day, "people come in at 9 or 10, and [the interview session] takes until early into the afternoon." There are usually "six office interviews with one person each — both partners and associates — and lunch with two to three people who are almost always associates."

The interviewers represent "a cross section [of different groups] to the extent people are interested. If you say 'I'm interested in trial and only trial,' you'll meet with predominantly trial lawyers." In general, says one associate, "they do a good job of matching you up with people you'd like. There is [usually] some similarity in background." Some formal elements of organization are missing from the hiring process, insiders report. For instance, "there has never been any kind of instruction" for interviewers. Adds one interviewer: "The evaluation we fill out is very open-ended. There are no guidelines." Interviews are "more of a chat. Your numbers are on paper, so they're trying to get a sense of you." Regardless of the tone of the interviews, the odds of success are good. "Once you get a callback, you're pretty much there," says an insider. "The presumption is that the people we bring in for callbacks are people we want to hire. It's not a big hurdle."

The "committee of eight or 10 partners meets every week or every other week," and tries to "get back to people within two weeks." The legal payola begins once the offer is given, as the firm will try to sell itself through lunches, phone calls, and the ever-mysterious "care packages." Moreover, as one ex-summer associate reports, "getting a summer associate position may be difficult, but most summer associates are hired."

OUR SURVEY SAYS

Completely aerated

Baker Botts "has a reputation of being stuffy," but associates claim that this is simply "not true." Insiders report that the firm is "very professional without being stiff or overly formal. People are friendly and respectful," adding that "the 'S.O.B. factor' is very low." An attorney in Houston notes that the firm is "generally conservative, but in that compassionate conservative sort of way. People are very friendly and not at all difficult to get to know. [They] do tend to be very polite — and that may come across as overly formal or stuffy to some people." Associates note that "Baker Botts is proud of its long history," and that "the younger offices (like Dallas) are considerably more dynamic and entrepreneurial than others (like Houston)." However, even Houstonians find Baker to be "relatively laid back compared to other firms of this size." As one source observes, "Quality is king. The firm will do everything possible to make you the best lawyer you can be. If you demonstrate your competence, you'll be rewarded. There is a very professional and mutually respectful relationship between partners and associates."

Love the COLA (not the drink)

Texans are notorious for their deep-rooted pride, in the state's expansive size and unique nature. BB's Texas based associates are no exception — and frequently boast about the low cost of living they enjoy. One resident of the Longhorn State says of the firm's pay: "When considering cost-of-living, hours worked, and quality of work, it is probably the best in the U.S." Most Texas-based attorneys don't even mind that they are paid less than their counterparts in New York. One lawyer notes: "While my pay may be a little behind the New York and California firms in absolute numbers, it definitely far outstrips what they are paying when cost of living is factored in." Many Baker insiders did, however, cook up suggestions to improve the pay structure. "Profit sharing would be nice," offers one source. "So would an hours-based bonus for good performers." Because many associates feel the "bonus structure is vague and not guaranteed," another insider proposes "providing a bonus or a percentage of billing for clients that were brought in by an associate. This would provide an incentive for an associate to grow his or her practice, and to expand the client base of the firm."

Genuine respect for partners

"If I had to name my top reason for working here," reports an insider, "it would be the partners in our office. I respect them, and genuinely like them." Most associates at the firm agree with this opinion. One states that there are "no 'screamers' here. Partners deal with associates with a great deal of respect." Moreover, as a Houston-based source indicates, "partners give a lot of responsibility," even to first-years. A pro-partner attorney states that "every project is a cooperative effort among the associates and partners. The partners are open to questions and proposed solutions." Others disagree, however, complaining that some partners "often criticize in front of peers, and either give contradictory instructions or none at all." Another associate allows that, "there are a few partners who treat associates poorly, but they are the exception."

Social but not yee-haw crazy

Baker Botts may not be the wildest firm in Texas, but associates still manage to have a good time. "I came to work here because everyone that I met was very nice, genuine and intelligent," an attorney recalls. A fifth year reports, "Most of my best friends work at the firm, both because I have made great friends here and because I have recruited my existing friends to come practice here." An IP specialist reveals that Baker even hosts "monthly card games." There is still some trouble regarding social interaction, mostly due to a lack of interdepartmental socializing. "While there is a lot of social interaction between the lawyers in my section," an associate explains, "there is only modest social interaction with lawyers from other sections." A Houston-based attorney notes, "The corporate and trial departments use different elevator banks, which creates more of a social division between the departments than there might be otherwise." There also seem to be social rifts caused by rank at Baker Botts. A senior associate remembers that there "used to be more interaction between partners and associates socially. This has tapered off some — it may have something to do with higher salaries of late." One lawyer points out that, "our social contact is pretty much limited to summer or recruiting functions, in part, because we are all very busy and, in part, because we would prefer to go home to our other lives whenever possible."

The matter of mentors

Associates at Baker Botts quickly learn that most of their training will be "on the job. Partners attach a lot of importance to the quality of work, so associates are rarely left on their own to work without guidance." There is an extensive mentoring program in place at Baker Botts. An insider explains the process: "I was assigned a senior associate as a mentor when I joined the firm. The mentor was responsible for finding me work, monitoring my workload, and making sure I progressed. In addition, the mentor was responsible for reviewing my assignments and being a general sounding board." Another adds that "anyone other than your mentor is [also] willing to help." On-the-job training works well at Baker Botts, an associate speculates, because "partners like to play professor and help with technical issues. The firm cultivates partners rather than merely churning billable hours using associates." Some associates do complain about negligent mentors, specifically noting that, "there is little formal training, even less informal training, and the approach to CLE is stingy."

Efficiency experts?

Associates warn Baker Botts recruits to "be prepared to commit to long hours. With the recent salary increases, the firm is monitoring work even more diligently." Moreover, insiders note that "the culture puts a high priority on delivering superior quality work and, where possible, exceeding client expectations. That can create additional stress for associates who can't control their time as well as partners can." Baker Botts is an environment in which "everyone is expected to work hard, but I don't feel people sit around counting up their hours." "We have a lot of deals," a source reports, "and the partners work just as hard, if not harder, than the associates. But, in general, I find it to be rewardingly intense." Senior associates add some historical perspective to the picture. A New York associate says, "The current work load is above the norm compared to my first two and a half years at the firm." A Houstonian continues, "traditionally, the firm has never been openly focused on hours and the bottom line and has been concerned that associates have a life. The dramatic increases in associate salaries will (and is) put pressure on the firm to become more focused on hours and the bottom line. It will be interesting to see where Baker Botts is 5 and 10 years from now." And an overworked first-year speculates hopefully, "Once I learn to be more efficient, the hours should be no problem."

Not too supportive

Baker Botts associates were unenthusiastic when asked about support staff. While some problems are due to the general quality of support, "understaffing and poor supervision are big problems." While associates share secretaries with more senior attorneys, "there is always word processing to fall back on if a secretary is not available." Attorneys also note that the firm "could use more after-hours help and more floater attention." Insiders do say that the firm is taking steps to correct these problems.

Pro bono flexibility

Baker Botts was recently recognized for "Outstanding Contribution to the Houston Volunteer Lawyer Programs" by a large firm. Baker Botts associates seem puzzled by this fact. In spite of this performance, attorneys find that pro bono work is "accepted, but not encouraged." Other insiders claim that "you can do as much or as little pro bono work as you can afford to do." According to one associate, "doing pro bono work is certainly recognized as providing a valuable contribution, but it does not count as 'billable' time." Another associate continues, stating, "The current workload from paying clients doesn't allow much time for pro bono." An eighth year disagrees, explaining that "although pro bono hours are not credited toward expected billing levels, a significant pro bono matter is generally viewed as a valid, acceptable reason for lower billable hours, provided that it doesn't occur year after year. The firm encourages pro bono activity, but looks down on an associate that consistently fails to meet budgeted billing levels for any reason."

That brass ring

Baker Botts attorneys believe they have a good chance of making partner. It just takes a willingness "to work hard, consistently bill 2000+ hours per year and demonstrate judgment and either very strong technical capability or strong interpersonal skills." One associate indicates that "most people who stick it out through their fifth year as an associate will make partner in their eighth year unless there is an obvious problem." Other associates explain the high probability of partnership as part of the firm's "commitment to growing. Making associates into partners is a big part of the growth plan." A source notes that "the vast majority of associates have left and gone on to other things by the time their partnership year arrived. However, most of those who are still around end up making partner." But while chances are good, an insider cautions that "loyalty and hard work isn't enough. They have to need you. That usually means clients, unless you are a trial associate, and IP is heavily leveraged with a small group at the top." A source who is also pessimistic about prospects of making partner reports: "if you are male, bill boatloads of hours, and work in an area considered desirable by the powers that be, your prospects are pretty good. If you do not meet all three of these criteria, you may have a problem."

Wanting women

Numerous Baker Botts associates report that "women are treated in a very professional manner, with a great deal of respect, and in all respects equally as men in our firm." Several female associates, however, have a different take on the firm's efforts — especially when it comes to working mothers. "While a reduced hour option is offered, it is not very attractive," one begins. "First, it requires a departure from the partner track, unlike other comparable firms (Vinson & Elkins to name one). Second, there is absolutely no internal support for the reduced hour lawyer. That is, you are required to police your own hours and make up for busy weeks when and if you can. Also, you are told that you should always appear available to help, rather than simply explain your reduced hour schedule. In sum, Baker Botts' attempt at a part-time program fails in comparison to other comparable firms." Another female source indicates that "there are no senior women to mentor in several sections, including trial, corporate, and intellectual property. Most important, the management does not seem to be the least bit concerned about this issue."

A more content female associate observes: "Although the firm as an institution has no formal program to mentor female associates, I have found that certain partners will make extra efforts to mentor women. There are female attorneys with families who work reduced hours. However, the firm's policies about alternative work arrangements are not very clear."

No official diversity policy

Some attorneys are displeased with the firm's lack of diversity. Insiders note that Baker Botts' "lack of African-Americans is questionable." Another agrees, saying, "I just don't see the efforts." In regards to hiring of gay and lesbian attorneys, a source relays, "It is our firm's policy not to base employment decisions on the basis of sexual orientation." Another continues, "I'm not aware of any special programs for gay/lesbians. The firm has discussed a domestic benefits program, but I don't know if one has been implemented." That source adds that "there are several openly gay/lesbian lawyers at the firm, at both partner and associate level." A third characterizes the firm as being "very friendly," but emphasizes that there are "no official policies regarding antidiscrimination and domestic partner benefits."

Not perfect, but pretty good

Attorneys do have complaints about Baker Botts: bureaucracy that often slows important decision-making processes, lack of diversity, and long hours. Most attorneys, however, find themselves content at the firm. As one contact summarizes, "I believe it would be difficult to find another large firm that meets, much less exceeds, working at Baker Botts from the view of quality of work, hours, and treatment by the majority of the partners (at least the ones I work for). That is not to say it is perfect — it is still a large firm, with both the advantages and disadvantages that any large firm has due to size, which makes it slow to react sometimes. But if you are going to a large firm, then I think Baker Botts is a good place to work."

> "Quality is King. The firm will do everything possible to make you the best lawyer you can be."
>
> — *Baker Botts associate*

Cahill Gordon & Reindel

VAULT.COM 50 PRESTIGE RANKING

80 Pine Street
New York, NY 10005
(212) 701-3000
Fax: (212) 269-5420
www.cahill.com

LOCATIONS

New York, NY (HQ)
Washington, DC
London

MAJOR DEPARTMENTS/PRACTICES

Antitrust
Corporate
Litigation
Mergers & Acquisitions
Real Estate
Securities
Tax
Trusts & Estates

THE STATS

No. of attorneys: 219
No. of offices: 3
Summer associate offers: 36 out of 37 (New York, 1999)
Chairman of Executive Committee: Ike Kohn
Hiring Partner: W. Leslie Duffy

PAY

New York, 2000
1st year: $125,000 + indeterminate bonus
2nd year: $135,000 + indeterminate bonus
3rd year: $150,000 + indeterminate bonus
4th year: $170,000 + indeterminate bonus
5th year: $190,000 + indeterminate bonus
6th year: $210,000 + indeterminate bonus
7th year: $220,000 + indeterminate bonus
8th year: $230,000 + indeterminate bonus
Summer associate: $2,400/week

NOTABLE PERKS

- Luxury sedans for car service
- Three gala social events a year (one with staff, the other two with attorneys and significant others)
- Daily cookie tray
- Emergency child care

THE BUZZ
What attorneys at other firms are saying about this firm

- "Ugliest law offices in America"
- "Aggressive and surprisingly, not too white shoe"
- "Snowball's chance in hell of making partner"
- "Premier First Amendment firm"

UPPERS

- Very high pay without any strict billing requirements
- Incredibly interesting work
- Lots of flexibility
- Positive, non-stuffy atmosphere

DOWNERS

- Complete lack of any structure whatsoever
- Pathetic office space
- Virtually no chance of making partner as a litigator
- Poor communication between partners and associates

KEY COMPETITORS

Cleary, Gottlieb, Steen & Hamilton
Davis, Polk & Wardell
Paul, Weiss, Rifkind, Wharton & Garrison
Simpson Thacher & Bartlett
Sullivan & Cromwell

EMPLOYMENT CONTACT

Ms. Joyce A. Hilly
Hiring Coordinator
(212) 701-3901
jhilly@cahill.com

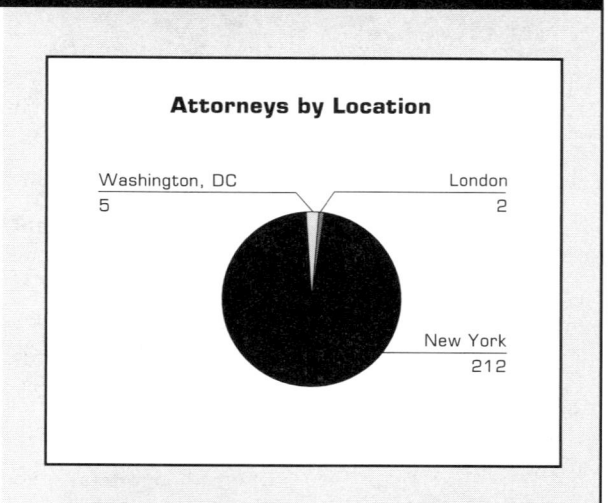

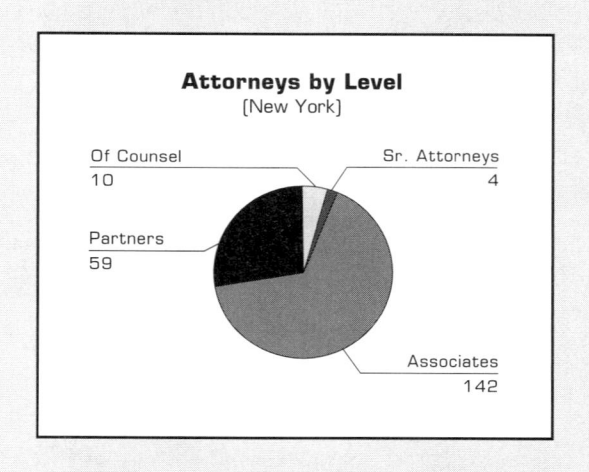

Attorneys by Location
- Washington, DC: 5
- London: 2
- New York: 212

Attorneys by Level (New York)
- Of Counsel: 10
- Sr. Attorneys: 4
- Partners: 59
- Associates: 142

QUALITY OF LIFE RANKINGS [ASSOCIATES RATE THEIR OWN FIRM]

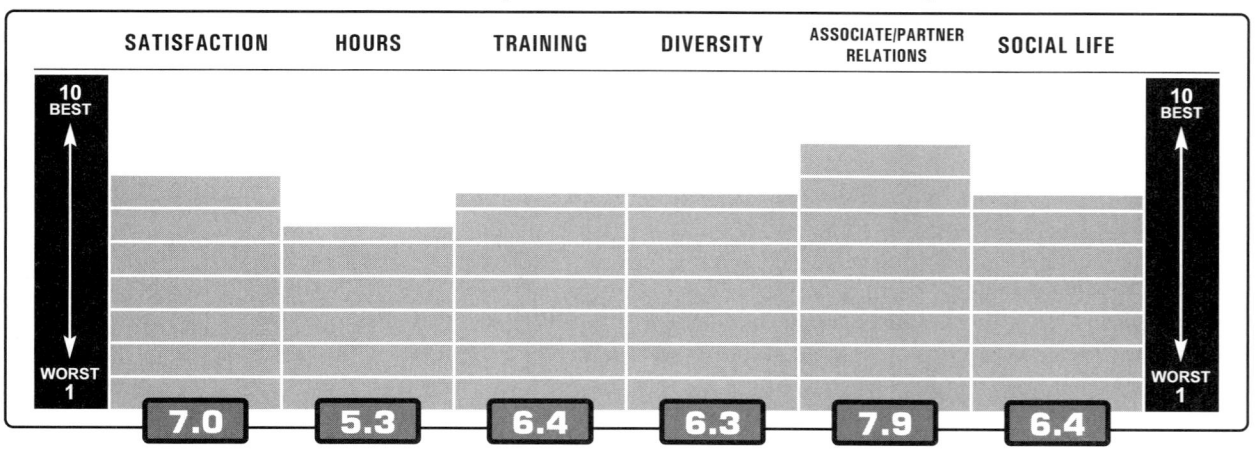

Satisfaction	Hours	Training	Diversity	Associate/Partner Relations	Social Life
7.0	5.3	6.4	6.3	7.9	6.4

THE SCOOP

Cahill Gordon & Reindel may be smallish and less high-profile than some of its competitors, but that hasn't impacted its success or very healthy profits ($1.7 million per partner in 1999). Cahill isn't just about the money — the firm also boasts a Constitution-crusading First Amendment practice, headed by the renowned Floyd Abrams.

History: strength in litigation

Founded in 1919, Cahill Gordon & Reindel has long been celebrated for its litigation practice, which was built up by former U.S. Attorney John Cahill. Cahill Gordon was tapped as special litigation counsel for *The New York Times* in its 1973 decision to publish the Pentagon Papers. Since the early 1980s, however, the firm has emphasized corporate finance and this specialization has fueled its growth — the firm has doubled in size to over 200 lawyers since 1988. When Wall Street went bust in the late 1980s, the firm lost two of its major clients to bankruptcy — E.F. Hutton and Drexel Burnham Lambert. (Drexel, the junk bond firm led by Michael Milken, accounted for an estimated 25 to 30 percent of firm billings in 1988 and 1989.) But Cahill rebounded, gobbling up investment bank business as the economy improved in the mid-1990s.

We're in the money

You can bank on Cahill, and many of the most prestigious investment banks in New York do just that, including J.P. Morgan, Donaldson, Lufkin & Jenrette, Merrill Lynch, Wit Capital, CIBC World Markets Corp., UBS Warburg, Salomon Smith Barney, and Goldman Sachs. In addition to these cash-cow clients, Cahill represented the underwriters in the $3.5 billion financing for Paul Allen's Charter Communications. The firm also represented the underwriters in offerings of over $7 billion of common stock of Genentech. It's no wonder, therefore, that the mid-sized firm is flush with funds. From 1996's $130.5 million, firm revenues rose to $137 million in 1997 to $148 million in 1998 to $155.5 million in 1999.

The sensational Floyd Abrams

Cahill is more than just a money machine. The firm also has a high-profile First Amendment practice, led by the venerable Floyd Abrams. In one of 1999's most publicized cases, Abrams and Susan Buckley successfully defended the Brooklyn Museum against an eviction notice from the New York City government. The notice was delivered after New York Mayor Rudolph Giuliani became displeased with the museum's housing of the controversial exhibit "Sensation: Young British Artists from the Saatchi Collection," which included a portrait of the Virgin Mary bedecked with elephant dung.

In February 2000, Abrams once again made headlines. After Court TV was prevented from filming the controversial Amadou Diallo murder trial of four New York City police officers, Abrams proved successful in removing a 48-year-old ban on cameras and recording devices in New York courtrooms.

In an earlier case, Abrams successfully defended client CBS against a closely watched copyright action brought by the descendants of Dr. Martin Luther King, Jr. in July 1998. The suit, filed in federal court in Georgia, sought to prevent CBS from reproducing 62 percent of Dr. King's "I Have a Dream" speech. The district court found that Dr. King had encouraged the coverage and rebroadcast of the speech, thus rendering it a "general publication" unprotected by copyright laws. The plaintiffs appealed and in May 1999 the Eleventh Circuit heard oral arguments on the case. Before several members of the King family sitting in the hearing room, including Coretta Scott King, Abrams insisted that "there were no limits whatsoever" on coverage and accordingly none on reproduction rights.

Wheelin' and dealin'

Despite Cahill's modest size, some rather large corporations have turned to the firm for big business deals. Notable deals in 1999 include representing Consolidated Natural Gas in its merger with Dominion Resources, a deal that was valued at $6.3 billion and created a $25 billion energy concern. In February of that year, the firm helped LucasVarity, a London-based producer of auto brake systems and aerospace equipment in its $6.5 billion acquisition by Cleveland's TRW, Inc. Cahill also was the main advisor to British drug company Shire Pharmaceuticals in its $1 billion dollar acquisition of US company Roberts Pharmaceuticals. At the turn of the millennium, (for those pendants out there, we mean 2000) the firm represented Olsten in its $13.7 billion merger with Adecco to create the world's largest personnel company. Cahill also handled the split-off of Olsten's health care services business as a public company.

And now for something completely different...

Cahill has decided to try something new in the year 2000. Yes, Cahill is moving its European office from Paris to trendy law hotspot London, England. Cahill has had only two offices besides its New York office — the one in Paris, opened in 1928, as well as one in Washington, DC, which opened in 1935. Due to pressure from its notable banking clients, the firm has announced its intent to establish a presence in the UK by moving its Paris operations to London in order to be better equipped to deal with the demands of a growing European market. Cheerio!

GETTING HIRED

Not hung up on pedigree

Cahill isn't particularly elitist, although coming from a top school won't hurt your chances of getting hired. One insider explains: "Cahill does not hesitate to hire graduates from smaller schools, so long as they meet one essential criterion — willingness to work hard. In this industry, Cahill's is a refreshing approach — it is not steeped in snobbery which so afflicts its competitors." However, another associate reveals that candidates from "lesser schools have to shine bright." Reports one litigation associate: "Cahill seeks associates who fit in to the unstructured firm culture." A colleague has a less positive take on Cahill's willingness to broaden its candidate search, lamenting that "Cahill's best days are behind it; what once was a firm that was highly selective has become a firm desperate to find bodies to do the work." Foolish associate! A majority of new associates at Cahill come from three excellent law schools: Columbia, Harvard, and NYU. The firm also regularly draws on Fordham, Georgetown, Penn, and Cornell.

Show you can handle responsibility

"While the standards are high, most of the screening takes place before the initial interview," a contact tells us. "Most people who reach the call-back stage will get offers, as long as they have personalities and aren't offensive." So what is Cahill looking for? Since the firm is leanly staffed and devoid of formal structure, says one associate, "it's a good idea to show that you can handle substantial responsibility with little supervision." A recent hire notes that "if candidates want a year or two to ease into a job and want formality, Cahill is not the place." The firm also reportedly "adores" clerkships, "especially on the litigation side."

OUR SURVEY SAYS

Say it loud — we're unstructured and we're proud

"Can we please get rid of the phrase 'loosey goosey' to describe Cahill?" one associate asks, referring to a description of the firm from the *1999 Vault Top 50 Guide*. "The firm culture is not stuffy or rigid, but it's not like we're practicing out of the back of a Volkswagen bus either." Consider it done. However, we should point out that insiders at Cahill Gordon & Reindel do describe the firm as both "unstructured" and "kind of a free-for-all." "There's less pretense here than elsewhere," another continues, "and

[Cahill] is very open to different personalities and ways of doing things." While "self-motivators thrive, those who want direction and formality become turnover statistics." However, most Cahill cadets look at this lack of structure as an asset. "As long as your work product is good and timely," one reports, "no one cares about bullshit that is considered important at other places, like face time or dress." A liberated lawyer elaborates, "The firm is pretty fond of its 'dysfunctionalism.' It's a culture of individuals. Partners strongly defend the historic lack of a system."

The (bonus) suspense is killing Cahill

"Cahill always pays at the city's top rate," reveals an insider. However, there has been some controversy regarding the firm's decision not to reveal the guidelines for 2000 bonuses. "The major concern for current associates is the indeterminate nature of the bonus this year," an associate reports. "We deserve better given the explosive profits at this firm." Although the firm indicates that the "bonus will be competitive with bonuses other New York firms will end up paying," associates are still upset. "We are in wait-and-see mode," explains a fourth-year associate, "which some people find frustrating, since it gives the appearance that our bonuses are contingent on the hours billed by associates at other NY firms." Moreover, some associates feel that the bonus scale illustrates that associates are not "sharing in the partners' wealth to the extent we should. It is like we are given little credit for the firm's success." However, as an enthusiastic real estate specialist points out, "Cahill will be sharing the profits of investments in IPOs with associates. GO CAHILL!"

Shut the door — you're letting the associates out!

"Turnover [at Cahill] has historically been high, in part due to dim partnership prospects," states an insider. "Most people do not come with the intention of staying for the long haul. Recently, turnover has been higher, with more people going into non-traditional situations." A litigator observes that "associates are fleeing like mad, particularly in litigation. There are almost no senior litigation associates left." Another associate states, "It feels like there is a going-away party for a different associate every week." "There has not been an exodus of this size at any time in the firm's history," announces an insider dramatically, though he offers no evidence to back his assertion. Many attribute the relatively high rate of attrition in 2000 to the fact that "turnover has been lower than one might have expected during each of the past two years" and to the existence of "an incredibly hot job market." One attorney, who could not be bothered to list the factors that have caused Cahill's poor retention rate, notes simply that "people are running out the door right now."

Courtly partners

A majority of associates at Cahill have positive things to say about the firm's well-compensated partnership. An associate states, "If you work hard, you will be treated as a junior colleague." An attorney concurs, reporting that "as a general rule, partners give associates a great deal of responsibility and the freedom to handle the work however the associate sees fit, without a lot of breathing down your neck. Partners are available for and welcome questions, but for the most part do not micromanage." The responsibility given to Cahill associates is not treated lightly. "I find my input is not only appreciated, but it is also required," notes a source. "I am never asked a question as a test. Instead, when a partner comes to me with a question it is for an answer that will be used."

Criticism of the Cahill partners also lies in the independence given to the associates. One indicates that "few have any idea about what other work I have other than the work I do for them." Another asserts that "they're not deeply interested in our development and usually are pretty eager to get associates out of their offices." While some partners have been "known to treat associates with great disrespect, if you do not want to work with a partner you can generally avoid them." A corporate finance attorney agrees with this statement warily: "Avoiding all problem partners limits partnership chances."

Forecast: cloudy, with a slight chance of partnership

Rumor has it that "Cahill is notorious for not making partners." Associates agree, describing their chances to attain the position (which in 1999 paid an average of $1.7 million) as being "dismal" and "bleak." Insiders report that Cahill has an eight-year partnership track, and report that "due to the relative strength of the firm's corporate and litigation practices, litigation associates have a much-reduced chance of making partner." One associate reports that "no litigation associate has made it since 1997." (The firm points out that litigator Michael Weiss made partner in early 2000.) An associate's chance of making partner is "worse than at some comparable firms," an attorney states, offering the following as an example: "A very senior associate recently left after being passed up for partner here to become a partner at Shearman." One Cahillian attributes the low number of associates promoted to partner to the firm's retention problems — "it appears that very few associates stay until they are up for partner."

No geeks

A first-year asserts, "I can not imagine a more social environment. These aren't the geeks I went to law school with." Another associate notes that "there are a lot of characters at this firm. Unlike most large law firms, Cahill has a history of hiring lawyers with a lot of 'personality'. My class has some great personalities. It makes Cahill a much more enjoyable place to work at." Moreover, "the firm has started to have monthly happy hours to encourage social interaction; however, these events seem to be thinly attended with nary a partner in sight." A social detractor declares, "I'm sure plenty of people have many friends at the firm, but in general people are not very social. People are generally lacking in social skills. A newly hired associate would find that very few people would say hello and introduce themselves."

Social interaction is not required at the firm, an associate with a family reports. "Cahill has its share of people who socialize, but also has a fair contingent of people with families. Because there are no 'face time' requirements or expectations at Cahill, it is strictly up to the associate how much they socialize. The atmosphere is conducive to friendships." As a superbly sentimental source says, "Although we all will not end up Cahill partners together, we all will remain friends."

Just enough rope

Cahill is not the place elaborate training programs. When asked about training, a second-year asserts that "Cahill gives you enough rope to hang yourself. Formal training is basically nonexistent. However, self-starters can really take the ball and run with it. As a result, you get a lot of deal experience at an early stage of your career." Another associate elaborates, "Anyone yearning to spend hours in a dark room watching a movie about how to conduct a deposition should look elsewhere. At Cahill you'll spend those hours assisting a skilled attorney at an actual deposition. And after not too much longer, you'll be doing your own." "There is no formal training beyond weekly seminars given on specific topics," an attorney concurs. "However, it has been my experience that many attorneys here, particularly more senior associates and some partners, are enthusiastic about working intensively and directly with junior associates on aspects of transactions and teaching and training junior associates, to the extent there is time, in that context." There are some drawbacks to the hands-on system. "Some associates are very willing to take the time to explain things to you and make sure you're learning while you're working," remarks one of Cahill's finest. "Other associates just want to make sure you're getting their crap work done for them." Another associate allows, "the firm has made some good strides in lunchtime seminars that qualify for CLE credit. But it needs more practical skills stuff."

No firm policy on hours

Haters of billable hours requirements, rejoice "Cahill does not have any minimum billing requirement, so there is some flexibility" in the number of hours an associate must work. Some report that "weekend work is required only in an emergency." As one associate points out, "How much you work at Cahill is pretty much up to you. If you're interested in developing your skills, though, you will find it hard to pass up the incredibly interesting work that is always abundant." Another reveals, "As long as you're on par with your class [which takes billing about 2,000 hours yearly] at the end of the year, no one cares."

But all is not idyllic at Cahill. The firm's high rate of attrition has had an impact on hours. "Work has piled up on mid-level associates. Many associates have departed; and laterals have not been hired to replace them," reports one beleaguered attorney. "In addition, in litigation there have not been sufficient levels of new junior associates to take on the burden. Thus, mid-level litigation associates have felt a significant crunch on their time." One fourth-year associate notes that "the Cahill un-system for work assignments leads to huge disparities in associate workload." Another attorney agrees: "If you have a reputation for being good, or are otherwise popular, you will have tons of work. Others, often for no good reason, slip through the cracks."

"Hovel"

Cahill is well-known for its parsimonious nature, Perhaps the most obvious outward sign of this thrift is the tatty state of Cahill offices. "The offices are not uncomfortable, but not particularly attractive," reports a New Yorker. "Cahill is sort of the 'Sprite' of law firms, 'image is nothing'. The prevailing attitude [towards decor] is, 'Who cares, as long as you get good work and are paid well.' The good news is that you tend to get your own office rather quickly." Other associates are not quite as kind, referring to the office as "a dump — but not really uncomfortable. Only uncomfortable when it is too hot or too cold, but we're obviously not in a hovel. The worst are the conference rooms, which are abominable."

Women's issues not an issue

"Promotion of gender equality through hiring is self-evident," reports an associate. "Off-site child care and individualized part-time arrangements are available. However, there are no specific mentoring programs." A different source observes that "the firm recently made two women partners. But even by Wall Street standards, the firm is disproportionately male." A female lawyer doesn't feel hampered by the environment. "I don't feel that the men in my class have any advantage over me by being male. I think that associates get work and the quality of that work is evaluated irrespective of gender."

Women have an advocate in power. Partner Helene Banks "takes a great interest in the other corporate women to make sure they get to know each other. She plans an event exclusively for women, twice a year. It is really nice because we get to meet each other in a social setting, which makes it easier to approach each other in the work setting if we need help with something. The women here tend to stick together because of this." While "part-time status must be requested and approved on a case-by-case basis," a mother who takes part in the program notes that her "experience as a part-time lawyer has been excellent."

Minority record not the best

Cahill seems to be suffering a whiteout in the area of minority hiring. As one informant notes, "efforts are certainly being made, but Cahill's statistics on minority hiring (while improving) remain pretty bad." Another source states that "the results are dismal." "We've not had a good track record retaining African-Americans, and I think that may be an unfortunate self-perpetuating pattern. But there are and have been a number of well-respected minority associates (including African-Americans)."

Welcoming to gay attorneys

While the firm has "no formal policy" regarding the treatment of gays and lesbians (other than a general anti-harassment policy and the Workplace Environment Committee), "there are a number of highly successful openly gay lawyers at Cahill." Associates report that the firm possesses "a very open and relaxed atmosphere." One states, "I think Cahill is very welcoming, as we have a few openly gay associates and I'm sure a few more who are not so openly gay. We also have an openly gay partner. I think it also says a lot that some of the gay associates feel comfortable bringing their partners to firm functions."

Forget that pro bono

Many associates complain about pro bono opportunities at Cahill. "While it counts toward billing, it is hardly encouraged," a source reveals. "The firm does very little to facilitate associates looking for pro bono work." A well-informed insider explains, "The firm has done some big projects in the past that some felt got out of hand. But the firm has been sending a clear message in recent years that it doesn't want people to spend too much time on pro bono." Another continues, "The rumor is that the current partner in charge of pro bono is more interested in screening out pro bono cases than promoting them."

Cahill niceties

"Cahill can provide a fabulous experience for some, and be a complete nightmare for others," explains an associate. "A lot depends on how your own personality fits with the unstructured environment and the particular people you work with here. I've been fairly happy on both counts." "At Cahill," comments one satisfied associate, "if you work in your pajamas, and if you do good work, no one will even notice." Another associate remarks, "I believe that I am getting better legal experience than the majority of my counterparts at other big law firms. And I'm having fun while I do it. I do not think I could have picked a better firm at which to start my career, especially in New York."

WILLKIE FARR & GALLAGHER

WILLKIE FARR & GALLAGHER is one of the nation's oldest and most distinguished law firms. We practice at a level of sophistication matched by few firms. Our clients' activities in the areas of investment banking, mergers and acquisitions, venture capital and financial services make our corporate, tax and real estate practices highly transaction-oriented and involve our litigators in leading securities, corporate takeover and commercial cases. Our bankruptcy department is involved in major reorganizations and sophisticated debt restructurings. Our trusts and estates department is active in will contests as well as traditional planning and counseling, and our employee relations and benefits department works closely with the corporate department on acquisitions and financings.

The firm recruits individuals who not only demonstrate, through their academic performance, the ability to practice law at its highest level, but who also have the character and personality that will make them friends and valued colleagues. We also consider achievements that demonstrate individual initiative, such as involvement with law journals, moot court and clinical programs, prior work experience and public interest activities.

If you are interested in learning more about our firm and our summer program please contact our Director of Legal Personnel and Recruiting, Billie L. Kelly, at (212) 728-8468.

787 Seventh Avenue • New York, NY 10019-6099
New York • Washington, DC • Paris • London

PLEASE VISIT OUR WEBSITE AT WWW.WILLKIE.COM

Amazon.com was young once too.

We've helped Amazon.com, Yahoo! and hundreds of other growing companies.

Whether you're planning your career, or starting a company, join the action!

legalminds@internet**speed**℠

Contact: K.A. Tuohy, Esq.   E-mail: tuohk@perkinscoie.com

PERKINS COIE LLP

ANCHORAGE BELLEVUE BOISE DENVER HONG KONG LOS ANGELES MENLO PARK OLYMPIA
PORTLAND SAN FRANCISCO SEATTLE SPOKANE TAIPEI WASHINGTON, D.C.

www.**perkinscoie**.com

NEARLY AND NOTABLE

Alston & Bird

VAULT.COM NEARLY & NOTABLE

1201 West Peachtree Street
Atlanta, GA 30309-3424
(404) 881-7000
Fax: (404) 881-7777
www.alston.com

LOCATIONS

Atlanta, GA (HQ)
Charlotte, NC
Raleigh, NC
Washington, DC

MAJOR DEPARTMENTS/PRACTICES

Adversarial
Transactional
Intellectual Property
Tax

THE STATS

No. of attorneys: 469
No. of offices: 4
Summer associate offers: 44 out of 49 (Atlanta, 1999)
Managing Partner: Ben F. Johnson III
Hiring Attorney: Joseph V. Myers, Jr.

PAY

Atlanta, 2000
1st year: $100,000
2nd year: $105,000
3rd year: $110,000
4th year: $115,000
5th year: $122,000
6th year: $130,000
7th year: $137,000
Summer associate: $1,750/week

Washington, 2000
1st year: $120,000
Summer associate: $2,000/week

Charlotte, 2000
Summer associate: $1,750/week

Raleigh, 2000
Summer associate: $1,750/week

NOTABLE PERKS

- Partnership credit for passing the patent bar
- Firm contributes to associate investment pool

THE BUZZ
What attorneys at other firms are saying about this firm

- "Still trading on overblown 'happy firm' image"
- "Grinds up & spits out associates"
- "Among the best... in Atlanta"
- "Extremely-well regarded firm, reputation for diverse attorneys"

UPPERS

- Cordial working environment
- "High-quality people"
- Good balance of work and personal life

DOWNERS

- Young associates get less exciting work
- Bottom line looms
- Firm discourages women from working reduced hours

KEY COMPETITORS

Kilpatrick Stockton
King & Spalding
Troutman Sanders

EMPLOYMENT CONTACT

Ms. Chamblee Abernethy
Recruiting Coordinator
(404) 881-7994
cabernethy@alston.com

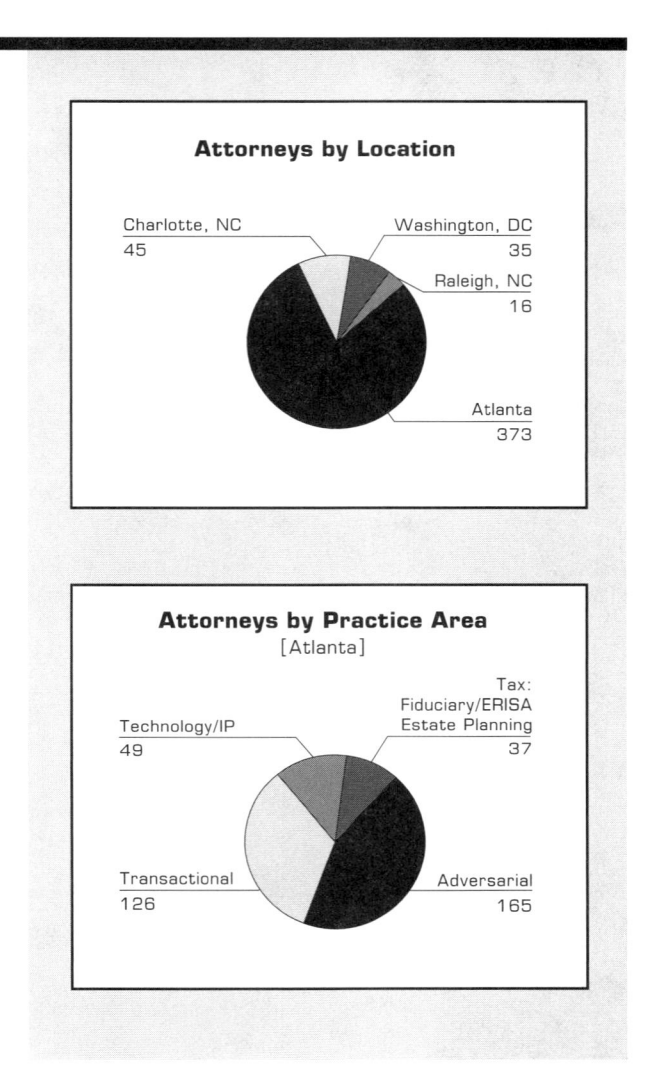

Attorneys by Location
- Charlotte, NC: 45
- Washington, DC: 35
- Raleigh, NC: 16
- Atlanta: 373

Attorneys by Practice Area [Atlanta]
- Technology/IP: 49
- Tax: Fiduciary/ERISA Estate Planning: 37
- Transactional: 126
- Adversarial: 165

QUALITY OF LIFE RANKINGS [ASSOCIATES RATE THEIR OWN FIRM]

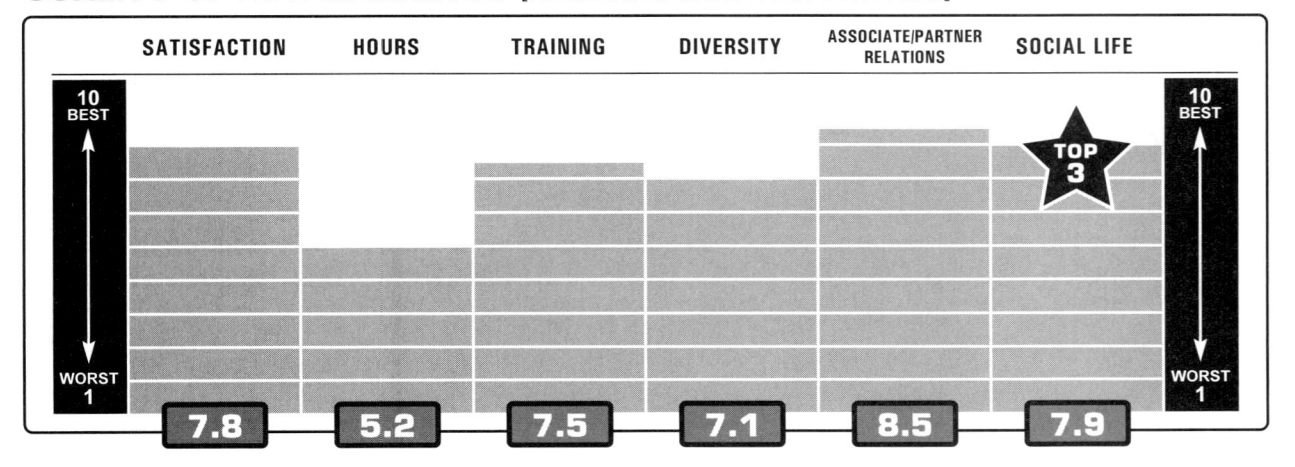

SATISFACTION	HOURS	TRAINING	DIVERSITY	ASSOCIATE/PARTNER RELATIONS	SOCIAL LIFE
7.8	5.2	7.5	7.1	8.5	7.9 (TOP 3)

THE SCOOP

A November 1999 article in *The New York Times* reported the Atlanta region's population grew no less than 70 percent between 1980 and 1999. Observers expect that the fabled Southern city will add an additional one million more people by 2025. Riding the population wave is Atlanta's Alston & Bird, one of the city's top law firms.

Alston & Bird takes wing

Judge Augustus Holmes Alston once told his son, Robert C. Alston: " I know of no one who has a brighter future before them than you have. The world is open to you, and you can be anything that an honorable ambition may aspire to." The younger Alston went on, of course, to become a lawyer, and in 1893 founded the firm that would be Alston & Bird. The firm is one of the oldest — and largest — firms in the southeast, employing about 470 lawyers in Atlanta, GA, Washington, DC, Charlotte, NC, and the Research Triangle Area of North Carolina. Moreover, the firm's Atlanta branch has grown so quickly that it is rapidly running out of office space. Recognizing this, Alston signed a 12-year lease for a new building located directly across the street from their current offices, which they will continue to occupy.

Put another notch on their lipstick case

Alston & Bird has attracted many accolades in its recent history. In 1998 Alston & Bird shared first place with Wachtell, Lipton, Rosen, & Katz on *AmLaw Tech Magazine's* list of the top 100 firms for technological prowess. The firm also placed highly on *The American Lawyer*'s 1998 "Corporate Scorecard" (particularly for its work as counseling both issuers and underwriters of initial public offerings) and has won recognition in rankings compiled by industry watchers such as Securities Data, *American Banker*, the *International Tax Review*, and MergerStat. January 2000 saw *Fortune* magazine include the firm on its closely watched list of "The 100 Best Companies to Work For in America." Alston, ranked 36th, was one of only two law firms to make the list.

E-commerce for everyone

The jewel in Alston & Bird's crown is its high tech and intellectual property practice. In fact, 50 lawyers at the firm are members of the patent bar, a number that sets Alston & Bird well apart from its Georgia-based competitors and puts it in the same class as IP heavyweights such as Baker Botts and Howrey & Simon. The firm particularly touts its e-commerce practice group and its three-pronged strategy for growth: helping established companies with e-commerce efforts; catering to startups; and leveraging the firm's expertise in venture capital. Alston partner David Stewart represented

Umbro International Inc. in its bid against a cyber-squatter who registered the domain name umbro.com. While Umbro prevailed in getting the domain name, it wasn't satisfied with later developments in the case. In May 2000, the Virginia Supreme Court ruled that Umbro could not garnish the other domain names held by the defendant, a Canadian company that held no other available assets.

Big news, big deals, and big clients

Alston & Bird attorneys have been involved in some high-profile cases recently. In a rare move, partner Joe D. Whitley (a federal prosecutor under both Reagan and Bush) was hired by a judicial panel in May 2000 to investigate U.S. District Judge Norma Holloway Johnson. Johnson, the chief federal judge in Washington, DC, personally assigned half a dozen cases involving the President's friends to judges President Clinton appointed, circumventing the normal randomized selection procedures. Upon completion of his investigation, Whitley will make recommendations to the judicial council of federal appeals and district judges who must then decide whether or not to discipline Johnson.

Alston represented the Georgia-based mobile communications software provider LHS Group Inc. earlier in 2000 in its $4.7 billion merger with Sema Group plc, a London-based telecommunications software concern. (The merger is subject to traditional closing conditions and approvals.) At the time of the merger, the creation of the telecommunications giant was the second-largest software acquisition ever announced, creating a 2,600 employee sector with revenues of $400 million.

Alston's litigation department has also been in the press. Bernard Taylor, a partner in the Atlanta office, represented Michelin North America in the settlement of a $43.6 million judgement over a tire defect case filed in 1990. And NationsBank chose Alston to defend them in *Canadyne-Georgia Corp v. NationsBank N.A. et al*, a case alleging the bank was negligent as a trustee in the release of hazardous wastes.

Getting involved

Business isn't the only way that Alston & Bird has made a national name for itself. Alston was the only Atlanta-based firm to appear on *The American Lawyer*'s 1998 "Pro Bono Honor Roll," a list of the top 100 U.S. law firms for pro bono activity. Alston & Bird lawyers have volunteered their time across the country for a variety of causes, from chairing the Trust for Public Land (based in San Francisco) to serving on the board of Brown University. In fact, the firm has set up an entire committee to keep track of how and where Alston & Bird lawyers get involved in both the public and nonprofit sectors.

GETTING HIRED

Top grades expected

Alston & Bird associates report that the firm's hiring "seems like it used to be more competitive." Nevertheless, insiders state that the firm "usually hires applicants from the top 10 to 15 percent of graduates." One contact notes that grades are not the only criteria used by the hiring committee: "The firm is highly competitive in its selection process, but not in an arbitrary or unfair manner." Another associate elaborates, "For associates being hired directly out of law school, the firm expects top grades. The firm also continues to place significant emphasis on the personality fit between the firm and the student. Great grades alone are not enough if the student's attitude or conversational skills don't measure up." Insiders disclose that the type of law one plans to practice is also vital to the decision-making process: "Some practice groups really focus on personality mix, others just really need the bodies." Most summer associates are given offers, according to associates. In fact, "it seems that the weeding out of associates occurs later on." The firm recruits at most top-tier law schools as well as large law schools throughout the South.

OUR SURVEY SAYS

Green Atlanta

Alston & Bird associates maintain that they are very well compensated. Notes one Atlantan, "The recent raises have exceeded the expectations of 90 percent of the associates." A litigator reports (no doubt to the distress of Alston partners) that the firm's "pay is tremendous, really extraordinarily generous. I feel that I am overcompensated for the work I perform." The bonus system is "based on percentage of billable hours over a certain amount plus other intangibles," according to an attorney. A first-year elaborates, "The firm has instituted a program by which associates who attain 2,100 billable hours will receive an automatic 10 percent bonus. Those who do not attain the 2,100 billable hours will receive a bonus only on a discretionary basis [for what the firm calls an 'extraordinary contribution']. The firm has, however, decided not to offer this bonus program to first-year associates." A content attorney remarks that "the bonus potential is great — depending upon your billable hours — but is not guaranteed. Because of the recent salary increase, I am pleased with this system. If you work very hard, you get a big bonus. Otherwise you just get a great salary — not bad."

Not everybody is pleased with the new bonus structure, however. Insiders report that the "dramatic restructuring of the bonus system will result in more billable hours for associates, but not necessarily more reward." Others have problems with the base compensation as well. A third-year associate states: "When I think how much an average partner makes, and what my billing rate is, I know I am being compensated below what I'm worth." Mid-level associates are also concerned about salary raises as attorneys gain seniority: "Initial salary is very competitive, but increases for mid-level associates are relatively small. Overall, the pay 'ramp' for associates is not very steep."

Stand by me, please?

Retention has become a big issue for every law firm; Alston & Bird is no exception. "We suffer some turnover like any other big firm," notes an associate, "but we've had no large-scale departures and our retention rate is better than most." A first-year reports that associates "tend to stay at Alston & Bird unless they get an incredibly good in-house offer that they simply can't resist." One attorney based in Washington, DC supplies a reason why turnover rates may be rising: "With the new salary increases, there has been increased pressure on billable hours. The tendency now seems to be to focused less on quality of life and family and more on billing those hours." A fifth-year associate disagrees with this statement, placing the blame on the strong economy. "Turnover has been historically low," he notes, "but within the past one and a half years, it has risen in key sectors such as technology and securities work." Indeed, an attorney in the firm's Intellectual Property group states that in his department, "it's a revolving door." Attorneys explain that turnover is generally not to other Atlanta firms. One insider states that "seldom, if ever, do associates leave to go to other law firms within the same city. Quite frankly, why would they?"

Solid partner treatment

Alston & Bird partners bring home a solid "B" on their report card this year. While many associates are very pleased with their treatment, others pointed out areas in which their superiors could improve. A real estate attorney reports, "No one yells or throws things — nothing like that. There does, however, seem to be a dichotomy between partners and associates. The partners treat me well, but we are not friends." An ERISA specialist remarks, "The atmosphere is collegial and professional. However, it is not clear that partners expect associates to advance to partnership someday." A mid-level source has more serious gripes: "Partners give little feedback. They expect you to be a slave and give up any free time to devote to their irrational deadlines." Other reports are more positive. A fifth-year associate says that "the best feature of this firm is the way associates are treated. Firm management is very open, approachable, and helpful. In addition, firm information, including financial results, is widely shared with associates." Another insider also gives the partners a "thumbs up," stating that "the partners are the number one reason I came to this firm, as they are an impressive group of talented, highly motivated, bright, and kind people with whom I hope to work the rest of my life."

Make me a big Bird

Associates at the firm report that chances of making partner at the firm are "pretty good." However, many associates also note that the ascent to partnership seem to be "getting harder every day." An attorney elaborates, "Although the opportunity for partnership is greater than at a New York firm, there is an increasing perception that associates generally will not make partner and will choose to leave." Alston & Bird has a seven-year track in order to be considered for a non-equity partner position. After being promoted, it usually "takes a few more years in order to make equity partner." An associate who was hired in 1993 reports that this position, which was once intended to be a one year trial period, "is now a four- or five-year stay (this is unwritten) in the non-equity pool until you can make equity, and then only if you have clients. But non-equity partners are paid very well."

A litigation associate sketches out the effort necessary to reach the brass ring. "The firm requires about 2,200 billable and 800 non-billable hours to make equity partner, about 2,000 billable and 500 non-billable to make non-equity." Associates are still optimistic. "I think as long as an associate does good work and is willing to invest the time necessary to make partner," one declares, "he or she will make it." While a labor/employment source states that "making non-equity seems common," he points out that "equity opportunities are anemic." Attorneys are well informed of their status. A third-year reveals, "annual reviews give you a very good idea of your partnership prospects. Reviews given at the beginning of your sixth and seventh year are labeled 'green' (keep up the good work and you'll be partner), 'yellow' (you need to do X over the next year) or 'red' (go ahead and look for another job)."

Fraternity firm

The social life at Alston is active, to say the least. One corporate party animal raves that "there is more social interaction between the lawyers than there was in my college fraternity" (a statement which might reflect more on his fraternity than it does on the firm). A mergers and acquisition specialist reports that Alstonians know how to have fun, and it's not due diligence: "Associates often spend a fair amount of time together after hours and on weekends. The camaraderie is very high at Alston." Another associate gleefully notes, "Some of my best friends are lawyers here." Firm-sponsored events include a popular Friday night happy hour.

Not all associates are quite as enthusiastic regarding the firm's social atmosphere. An Atlanta associate declares, "At work people are very social and friendly, and firm functions are pretty fun. However, people usually don't hang out with other people from work outside of the office besides firm functions, retreats, and so on." A seventh-year points out that the firm is also suitable for family types: "Not everyone is active socially. It is perfectly acceptable to just do your work and find social outlets outside the firm. That said, most people are interested in social interaction with other associates and partners. As a result, it's a very social firm." A sixth-year is nostalgic for the old days, when Alston & Bird really rocked: "While social interaction still remains a strong suit of the firm, the culture has shifted sharply away from it in the past few years."

Hearts in right place, training not present

The associates give very mixed reviews to the firm's training program. A fifth-year explains, "Training depends in great part upon your practice group's dedication to the cause. As for mine, their hearts are clearly in the right place, but the swirl of practice sometimes places training on a back burner." Another associate agrees, reporting that at Alston "it's sink or swim. I have basically trained myself with very little guidance from partners." An ERISA specialist notes that training is "probably the firm's weakest area. Partners no longer believe that most associates will make partner. The lack of formal training leaves associates at the whims of the partner they work for."

Some associates report more favorably on the firm's training programs. A senior associate declares that "there are as many in-house training sessions on various areas of the law as you would want to attend. Partners seem to take an active role in ensuring you receive a varied and different workload." One source notes, "The partners I work with are very willing to stop and explain things." Another continues, "The experience of working with the partners in this firm is unparalleled and I have had excellent mentors." An insider points out that "associates are the commodity of the firm." Therefore, he notes, "the level of training and mentoring of associates is extremely high."

Time, time, time

Alston associates work harder than some would like. An insider who has been around for six years predicts that the "restructuring of the bonus system is bound to put more billable hour pressure on associates." However, another associate responds that "the hours are not all that unreasonable, given the profession and the client demand. I just wish they were less. The hours are definitely not driven by the firm, though. It's the clients that are demanding." A litigator agrees: "There is a lot of work here and the final product must be good. It's rewarding but hard at times." An Alstonian who has been burning the midnight oil for seven years tells Vault.com, "I have been encouraged to take it easy, though I enjoy working so much it is tough to slow down."

Other Alston attorneys don't believe that they are overworked. One comments that "2,000 billable hours a year is the stated and followed goal. The average is always less, however. Under the new bonus structure, an automatic bonus of 10 percent of salary is paid at 2,100 billables, but thus far the new bonus target has not had any effect on the firm's 2,000 hour goal." Another associate continues, "I'd say we work no harder than associates in any other firm. The firm is devoted to allowing time for family and community commitments. The number one complaint given by the firm to associates last year was that we had too many billable hours and not enough community involvement. Anyone can bill 2,500 hours in a year and become increasingly dull. It takes a lot more to make a well-rounded lawyer and person. The firm realizes and promotes that." Insiders point out that "non-billable time can add up" but also note that "the management really does care about it."

Associates need space

Alston & Bird's Atlanta offices are reported by some to be "a very comfortable working environment" with "phenomenal art and offices." Others are not as fortunate, noting that "windowless offices are the standard for junior associates in some departments (Intellectual Property, Technology) — very dreary and depressing." Moreover, "the firm has outgrown its space expectations. Some attorneys find themselves in lavish surroundings, while others feel crammed into coat closets." Keep the faith — the firm plans to expand its office space very soon.

Most attorneys characterize the support staff as being "quite able." "We have 24-hour support services that are beyond exceptional," raves a contact. "You can drop work off at 5:00 p.m on your way out and pick it up when you come in the next morning. They also check citations, grammar and formatting for all briefs and legal documents." Associates do report some secretarial problems: "The secretaries believe that they work for partners and do not intend to perform anything more than minimum work for even mid-level associates."

Mix it up

The firm receives mixed reviews for its treatment of women associates. An insider writes, "Our summer classes are typically 50 percent women and the firm has a wide variety of part-time arrangements." Another continues, "The firm devotes considerable resources to mentoring women and encouraging part-time and other creative work solutions for working mothers." However, a fifth-year reports that "there is no gender equality. The partners have made it clear that this is a business and there is no special treatment for anyone, other than with respect to short-term special instances."

Attorneys see "a real effort to attract and retain minority associates." These attempts have not been entirely successful, as a fifth-year Alstonian reveals: "The effort seems to be there in the hiring phase. However, retention and promotion are places where improvement is needed."

Alston & Bird is reported to be relatively receptive to gay and lesbian issues. "The firm and its management are socially liberal and very receptive to gays and lesbians," states a source. Another continues, "I know a number of gay and lesbian associates and believe them all to be more than comfortable here." A third associate summarizes that "the firm is very open to all lifestyles."

Pro pro bono?

Alston & Bird's commitment to pro bono work is a controversial subject. Some associates are upset because the firm does not count pro bono work towards billing requirements. Others note that "it is considered during the review process." A fifth-year elaborates, "The firm counts pro bono commitments in its evaluations of 'other contributions' which go toward earning a bonus (in lieu of 2,100 billable hours). The theory is yet untested since the bonus structure is brand new, however. In practice, I have received a lot of support from my practice group to continue pro bono work." Another fifth-year continues, "Pro bono does not count toward billing, but it is an expected contribution and those who participate minimally or not at all are asked to step it up." Moreover, the firm assists associates in finding pro bono work: "There is a pro bono committee in place to help associates who want to do pro bono work. Many of the partners are visibly committed to doing pro bono work."

Chadbourne & Parke LLP

Chadbourne Parke LLP
30 Rockefeller Plaza
New York, NY 10112
(212) 408-5100
Fax: (212) 541-5369
www.chadbourne.com

LOCATIONS

New York, NY (HQ)
Los Angeles, CA
Washington, DC
Hong Kong
London
Moscow

MAJOR DEPARTMENTS/PRACTICES

Bankruptcy
Corporate & Corporate Finance
E-Practice
Employment
Environmental
Insurance/Reinsurance
Intellectual Property
Litigation
Project Finance
Real Estate
Tax
Trusts & Estates

THE STATS

No. of attorneys: 312
No. of offices: 6
Summer associate offers: 18 out of 18 (New York, 1999)
Operations Partner: Charles K. O'Neill
Hiring attorney: Vincent Dunn

THE BUZZ
What attorneys at other firms are saying about this firm

- "Smoker's paradise"
- "Project finance machine"
- "Middle of the pack"

PAY

All Domestic Offices, 2000
1st year: $125,000
2nd year: $135,000
3rd year: $150,000
4th year: $170,000
5th year: $190,000
6th year: $205,000
7th year: $210,000
8th year: $215,000
Summer associate: $2,403/week

NOTABLE PERKS

- Emergency alternative day care center
- Subsidized gym membership
- Discounts at Rockefeller Center stores
- Maternity/paternity leave policy

UPPERS

- Caring, brilliant partners
- Year-round casual dress
- Cappuccino machines on every floor

DOWNERS

- Characterized as "wannabe" firm
- Think ahead, guys — it's the Internet
- Not top-tier brand name

KEY COMPETITORS

Dewey Ballantine
Milbank, Tweed, Hadley & McCloy
White & Case
Willkie Farr & Gallagher

EMPLOYMENT CONTACT

Ms. Bernadette L. Miles
Director of Legal Recruiting
(212) 408-5338

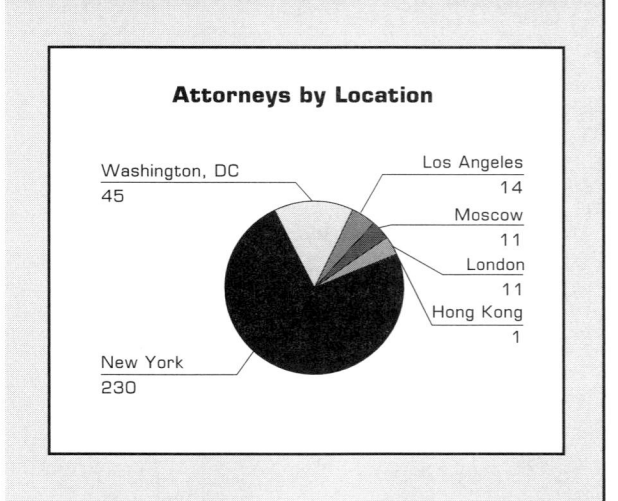

Attorneys by Location

- Washington, DC: 45
- Los Angeles: 14
- Moscow: 11
- London: 11
- Hong Kong: 1
- New York: 230

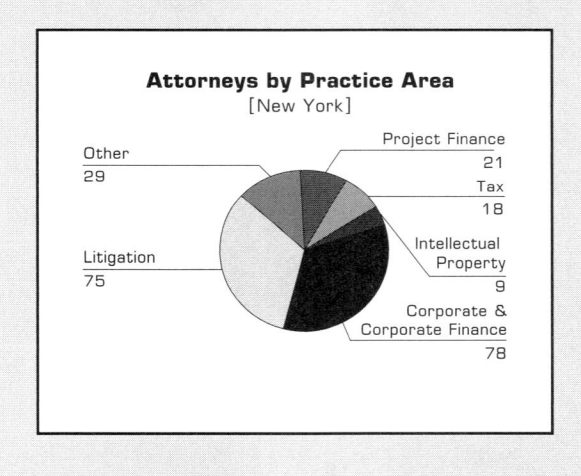

Attorneys by Practice Area
[New York]

- Other: 29
- Project Finance: 21
- Tax: 18
- Intellectual Property: 9
- Corporate & Corporate Finance: 78
- Litigation: 75

QUALITY OF LIFE RANKINGS [ASSOCIATES RATE THEIR OWN FIRM]

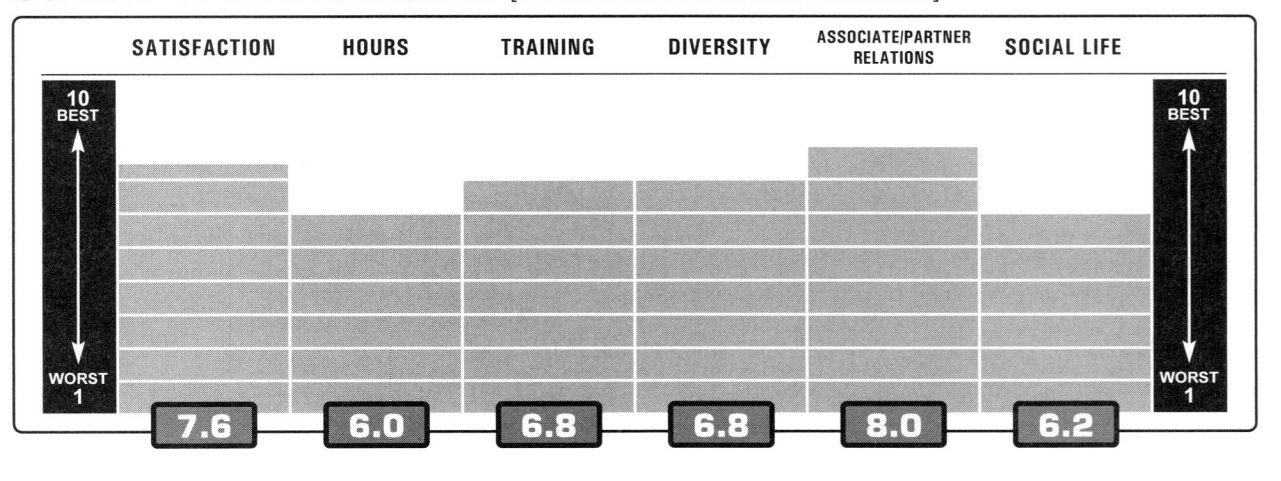

SATISFACTION	HOURS	TRAINING	DIVERSITY	ASSOCIATE/PARTNER RELATIONS	SOCIAL LIFE
7.6	6.0	6.8	6.8	8.0	6.2

THE SCOOP

From tobacco companies to golfers to Russian firms, Chadbourne & Parke has an eclectic and profitable client portfolio. Not content to rest on its laurels, Chadbourne is steadily pushing itself in the legal spotlight.

A smoky, international history

Chadbourne & Parke, founded in 1902, historically relied on a few bedrock clients for its bread and butter — American Brands, the Rockwell International Corporation, Sperry Corporation, Trans World Airlines, and Anaconda Minerals. It's worth noting that Chadbourne's intimate relationship with Big Tobacco began early on. In 1932 Chadbourne partner Louis S. Levy was disbarred for procuring a $250,000 loan for Second Circuit Judge Martin T. Manton. Manton drafted the majority opinion in favor of the American Tobacco Company at about the same time as the suspicious loan. American Tobacco was owned by Chadbourne client American Brands at the time.

For most of its history, Chadbourne was known for catering to the needs of its corporate clients and staying out of the limelight. But in the early 1980s, sleepy Chadbourne found itself at a crossroads. Most of the firm's institutional client base was crumbling — the Sperry Corporation, Trans World Airlines, and Anaconda Minerals either folded or were acquired. The firm needed help fast and found it in the fightin' form of Rigdon Boykin. Boykin joined the firm (then known as Chadbourne, Parke, Whiteside & Wolff) in 1980 as a senior associate and built Chadbourne into a leader in the energy industry. Boykin also led the campaign to reform Chadbourne's management, replacing its ineffective 12-member executive committee with a sleeker five-member crew. In addition, he influenced a revamp of the partner compensation system, introducing more incentives for performance. The rejuvenated firm required more manpower and in 1984 embarked on a successful lateral partner hiring program building its insurance, intellectual property, tax, and corporate finance practices.

In 1996 Chadbourne & Parke was stung by a *Presumed Equal* survey indicating that the firm was unfriendly to women. Chadbourne decided to hire a management consultant, Freada Klein, to assess its working environment. Klein conducted focus groups and distributed a survey, in which about 90 percent of Chadbourne lawyers took part. In response to the survey findings, Chadbourne formalized a part-time policy — attorneys are now permitted to work 60 to 80 percent of a full-time schedule for prorated pay and benefits. The firm also put into place a strengthened anti-harassment policy and ran discrimination-sensitivity training sessions for lawyers and staff. Finally, Chadbourne hired an ombudsman (or what it calls a "ombuds," with exquisite gender neutrality).

The specter of personnel problems re-appeared at Chadbourne in 1998. In March of that year, Boykin left after differences over the firm's overseas strategy emerged. He now heads O'Melveny & Myers' global project finance practice group. Other major partners left the firm in spring 1998 due to various client conflicts and took with them several associates from their teams. Chadbourne's London office was similarly hard-hit. By May 1998, the firm had lost two of its U.K. partners to defections. On the bright side, in early 1999 Chadbourne's DC office gained Kenneth Hansen, formerly general counsel of the Export-Import Bank of the United States. And in March 2000, former Mayer, Brown & Platt partner Denis Petkovic joined the project finance team in Chadbourne's London office.

From Russia with chocolate

Chadbourne has had a longstanding commitment to Russia and in 1990 became one of the first foreign law firms to set up an office there. It also represented the first Russian company to be listed on the New York Stock Exchange. Despite the current rampant corruption and wobbly state of the Russian economy, Chadbourne refuses to give up on the region. Quite the opposite — in October 1999, it added five corporate, banking, and litigation attorneys to its 16-lawyer Moscow office and relocated two Russian associates from its New York office. Chadbourne has worked extensively with Nestle in its Russian expansion, participating in Nestle's first acquisition in Russia in 1994 — a majority interest in a chocolate factory. In 1999 the firm assisted Nestle in its acquisition of a confectionery company in Samara, Russia by winning an investment competition for state-held shares and acquiring shares in the secondary market.

Chadbourne around the world

Beyond Moscow, the firm has representative offices in Almaty, Minsk, Kiev, and Baku. Chadbourne has affiliations with Kazakhstan's top law firm (Zanger), Belarus's top firm (Borotsov & Salei), the Ukraine's Grischenko Partners, and the BM Law Firm in Azerbaijan. It also has affiliations with Chambers & Company in Melbourne, as well as Watanabe, Nakamori, Nishida & Sugiura in Tokyo. Although the firm has no official offices there, Chadbourne & Parke is extensively engaged in Latin America, particularly in project finance, power generation, privatization, capital markets, and mergers and acquisitions. In September 1999, Chadbourne's Lynne Gedanken represented PSE&G Global when the company sponsored a $480 million plan to construct a power station in Tunisia.

Project finance: all for one

Chadbourne lost Boykin, the leader of its project finance group, in 1998 after Chadbourne decided to cut back on its Asian practice. Despite the loss, the department's revenues rose 40 percent in 1999 and *Project Finance Magazine* ranked Chadbourne as one of its top ten firms. In October of that year, the firm handled the legal work for the construction of the Cross-Israel Highway, the largest-ever privately-financed infrastructure project in that country. It also advised Credit Suisse First Boston and Citibank N.A., the lead arrangers on *Institutional Investor's* Project Finance Deal of the Year, a $675.4 million natural gas project in Argentina.

The firm's ability to weather Boykin's defection can perhaps be attributed to its all-for-one philosophy — the group awards billing credit to the project finance group as a whole rather than to individual lawyers. Group leader Chaim Wachsberger has said that this system encourages attorneys to help each other out with the bigger assignments.

Products liability maestro

Led by Thomas Bezanson, Chadbourne's litigation practice employs 72 attorneys, 21 of whom are partners or counsel. The firm engages in a wide range of litigation areas: antitrust and trade regulation; securities and derivative litigation and shareholder disputes; intellectual property; insurance/reinsurance litigation; creditors' rights/lender liability; government contracts; commercial litigation; mergers & acquisitions; employment; international; trusts & estates litigation; corporate and governmental investigations; and environmental.

Perhaps Chadbourne's best-known specialty is its products liability group. The group has particular experience in matters involving the alcoholic beverage industry, winning a 1989 verdict for Jim Beam Brands in the first fetal alcohol syndrome case ever brought to trial. Chadbourne also touts its work in automotive components, agricultural products, and telecommunication equipment cases, as well as its defense of a nuclear bomb manufacturer in a suit resulting from the first hydrogen bomb test. (You mean those things are dangerous?)

Chadbourne & Parke is ssssssssmokin'!

Of all the industries Chadbourne services, tobacco has been the kindest to the firm's fortunes. The litigation department represented American Brands, which owned American Tobacco for over 50 years. When American Brands sold American Tobacco to Brown & Williamson's parent company in 1995, Chadbourne began to represent B&W as well.

In 1996 Chadbourne took on representation of B&W in *Carter v. American Tobacco Co.* In that case, plaintiff Grady Carter sued Brown & Williamson, seeking to hold the tobacco company liable for his lung cancer. Carter, a 66-year-old retired air traffic controller, smoked for 44 years until quitting in 1991 when a cancerous growth was removed from his left lung. After a two-week trial, a Duval County, Florida jury awarded Carter and his wife $750,000 in damages. The verdict stunned the industry, as it was only the second damage award ever levied against Big Tobacco. (The first was a $400,000 award given to the family of Rose Cipollone in 1988, but that assessment was overturned on appeal and eventually the suit was dropped.) A deciding factor in the Carter verdict was the introduction of B&W documents revealing that past executives had acknowledged the addictive nature of cigarettes but had not come forward with the findings.

B&W spokespeople predicted a reversal on appeal, and they were proven right. In a major triumph for Chadbourne and B&W, Florida's First District Court reversed the $750,000 award in 1998, agreeing with defense counsel that Carter's suit exceeded the four-year statute of limitations by five days. The court concluded that Carter should have known that he had a smoking-related illness on Feb. 5, 1991, when his doctor diagnosed a pulmonary condition. Carter did not file his action, however, until February 10, 1995. In March 1999, the Florida Court went on to anull the $1.78 million fee for Carter's attorneys as well.

Good sports

Sports lovers have Chadbourne to thank for continued ESPN baseball access. Chadbourne represented the Disney-owned sports network ESPN in its suit against Major League Baseball (*ESPN Inc. v. The Office of the Commissioner of Baseball*). The dispute began in 1998, when ESPN sought to move three September Sunday night baseball games to its sister network, ESPN2, in order to make room for football games on ESPN. Not only did the league refuse to shift channels, but MLB Commissioner Bud Selig decided to terminate the league's $40 million per year deal with ESPN. ESPN struck back by filing suit, represented by Chadbourne partners Eric Lobenfeld and Robert Schwinger as well as associates Jonathan Sobel and Romy Berk. But hours before trial was to begin, both sides made up and extended their contract to 2005. As part of the new compromise, ESPN agreed to televise two games for every baseball game moved from the Sunday night slot. ESPN will also fork over around $133 million per season for the next three years.

The firm represented golf equipment maker Acushnet Co. when it brought suit against Nike for its use of Tiger Woods in television advertising. Chadbourne argued that Nike had overstepped the bounds of Acushnet's assignment of rights regarding the use of Woods in promoting shoes and apparel. Acushnet dropped the suit in October 1999 as part of its new deal with the golf star. Tiger's part of the bargain? Using Acushnet's Titleist clubs.

Outside the field of play

Chadbourne's Russel Frye stood behind Stone Container Corp. in its fight with the Montana Coalition for Health, Environmental and Economic Rights (CHEER) and the EPA. CHEER brought a citizen suit against the company and also intervened in the U.S. Environmental Protection Agency Clean Air Act action against Stone Container Corp. Stone Corp. negotiated a consent decree with both the EPA and CHEER. In November 1999, Chadbourne cut Stone Corp.'s losses though by successfully arguing before the Ninth Circuit that CHEER was not entitled to collect attorneys' fees for joining in the government's suit.

In May 1999, Chadbourne settled one of its largest-ever cases, *Allard v. Arthur Andersen & Co*. Chadbourne represented David Allard, who became the trustee of the DeLorean Motor Company when it went bankrupt in 1983. In his role as trustee, Allard alleged that DMC's bankruptcy stemmed from the questionable financial practices of founder and owner John DeLorean and sued accounting giant Arthur Andersen for malpractice. Arthur Andersen, Allard claimed, should not have issued DeLorean a clean report when it audited the company in 1979 and 1980. A Manhattan jury agreed and in March 1998 awarded Allard a whopping $110 million. Arthur Andersen immediately filed an appeal. The parties agreed to an undisclosed out-of-court settlement in May 1999.

Playing the ponies

One of Chadbourne's partners, Stuart A. Rosenthal, came under investigation in 1992 for unlawful currency transfers in connection with his Atlantic City gambling winnings. Chadbourne claims that Rosenthal orally agreed to leave the firm in exchange for the firm representing him in the investigation. But Rosenthal saw things differently, and sued Chadbourne for firing him without the requisite full partnership vote. Rosenthal also brought an ill-fated legal malpractice action, claiming Chadbourne had a conflict of interest because it failed to advise Rosenthal of his possible claim against the firm. The court threw out the malpractice action because the alleged malpractice had nothing to do with the criminal investigation.

The firm settled the rest of the suit for $460,000 in February 2000. Rosenthal was never charged with any wrongdoing, and in fact helped federal officials convict an Atlantic City executive who manipulated deposits in order to avoid reporting sizeable currency transfers.

GETTING HIRED

Choosier than Cravath?

Unlike many other firms (which reportedly are loosening their standards for new hires), insiders report that it is actually getting harder to get hired at Chadbourne. "It has gotten more difficult since I was hired. I probably could not get a first interview today," a litigator confesses with bracing honesty. Another contact reports that Chadbourne is limiting its incoming classes to graduates from the top 15 law schools. "There was traditionally a greater emphasis on the personality of the candidate, and this allowed them to take good people without first-rate grades. When it comes to work, these people often outperform their 'gunner' peers. Now, however, there is a greater emphasis on the numbers, which makes it a bit tougher to find these diamonds in the rough," one contact explains.

Personality does still count during the selection process, though. "Recruits must be people you will be able to deal with at 3 a.m.," says one lawyer. In fact, associates claim the firm has rejected candidates who had the academic credentials to get hired at Skadden, Simpson, and Cravath.

OUR SURVEY SAYS

Chadbourne cares

Insiders say Chadbourne has a "live and let live" culture where associates enjoy a great deal of autonomy. "Overall [Chadbourne] is a very humane environment where people care about each other, the development and learning curve of the associates, and consistently improving the interaction of staff," says one lawyer. Another contact describes Chadbourne as "a white shoe firm which is going casual all year long." "This is as good as it's gonna get for big-firm life in New York City. Our clients aren't as sophisticated and big as they once were, but they are still solid," states another insider.

A corporate attorney claims the firm has a decentralized organizational structure. "The firm has informal groupings within departments, so it seems potluck to get work from interesting groups or to get stuck with not-so-interesting work," he explains. "Everyone's doors are open and information on the firm is readily available," says another attorney.

"Normal people"

Insiders feel they are treated well by their bosses. "We are not a yell-at-you or beat-you-down kind of firm," one associate explains. "For better or worse, our partners can't afford to mistreat us because our retention rate is so bad." A New York attorney says, "I have no complaints except for the occasional oblivious partner." Adds a litigator, "I have never been treated poorly by a partner. In fact, my only real complaint is a lack of feedback." And a source in the DC office claims the partners are "one of the main reasons I love working here." The partners in Washington are reportedly "normal people with lives" who make an effort to be good mentors.

Whooping it up

"If Chadbourne was any more social, I wouldn't get any work done," muses an attorney in the New York office. New Yorkers say that firm functions are "plentiful and enjoyable." But enjoying the social offerings at Chadbourne is an individual choice, explain others. "You can get in with a good group of friends and enjoy it or you could just as easily toil in anonymity." Insiders say they get along well with their colleagues and will drop by each other's offices to talk. One associate says it's sometimes hard to find time to get together after work. "However, when we do get together, it's usually a raucous affair. Associates at Chadbourne definitely like to get a few drinks in them and whoop it up," he says. As at many firms, social events are particularly prominent in the summer. "The summer recruiting season is always a great time at Chadbourne. Summer events are legendary for the debauchery!"

A source in the Washington office paints a different picture: "The office is very businesslike. People come in, do their work, and go home. Most people eat lunch at their desk — not because they don't have time to eat but because they want to get home to families as soon as possible." Associates attribute the lack of a social scene in the Washington office to its smaller size and to the abundance of lawyers who are married with children.

Keeping pace with the big boys

Chadbourne has been a good soldier in the 2000 salary wars, keeping pace with recruiting adversaries. "Hey, we'll always take more money, but you can't argue at all with what we get paid after the recent pay raises," one associate enthuses. "The firm has done a good job keeping pace with the big boys. In general, Chadbourne meets the top firms in the lower classes and lags slightly behind in the more senior classes," an associate reports. Although most associates are happy with their newfound wealth, one attorney wishes he had another option. "I would rather have foregone the recent pay hikes for less pressure about hours," he says. Associates appreciate that "Chadbourne has paid boom-year bonuses every year since the trend began."

Associates do not yet know what the bonus structure will be for 2000," but "reportedly it will be based on the firm's profits and individual performance."

CLE in abundance

Sources say there are well-run CLE classes once a week at Chadbourne. The Washington litigation department reportedly meets every Monday for breakfast to discuss its cases, which one lawyer finds very helpful. Although they recognize that the firm is trying to implement more formal training sessions, many associates describe training at Chadbourne as "trial by fire." "Due to the lean staffing, if you can handle the work, you will get as much responsibility as you want. Consequently, there's a lot of on-the-job training," comments one source. "If you luck out with a good partner who teaches, you will learn a lot," comments another associate.

Billing for Uncle Chaddy

When it come to hours, "Uncle Chaddy is the place to be," one lawyer says. Chadbourne sets a billing goal of 1,900 hours. Associates report they work from as little as 40 hours per week to more than 70. Chadbourne lawyers don't seem too distressed by their workload and have accepted a certain number of late nights as a natural part of a lawyer's life. "Of course there are the occasional late nights or long weeks, but on the whole, this place has very livable hours, at least for a large New York law firm," says a contact. "There is no such thing as face time here. We have a lot of work, but when it's done there is no need to hang around just to bill," according to a DC lawyer.

Plain and spacious offices

New York associates describe their offices as "relatively plain" but "spacious and well-equipped." One lawyer observes that "associate offices are actually larger than some partner offices I've seen at other firms." "My view is so nice that I've photographed it at night," boasts one attorney. In the New York branch, associates get their own offices by the second year. First-years reportedly get their own office in DC, and most attorneys there believe that they have nicer digs than their New York counterparts.

Reduced support services

Associates report that Chadbourne has cut support services in recent years in an effort to lower operating costs. "In terms of technology, which is everything nowadays, we are starting to scrape the bottom," moans one lawyer. Associates also complain about not having quick access to laptops.

Comments on the support staff situation range from "it sucks" to "pretty awesome." One lawyer observes, "They really do go out of their way to help you out so long as you treat them with respect and courtesy." A contact in the New York office tells Vault.com, "The firm doesn't hesitate to whack secretaries who go around with a bad attitude and work ethic." But another associate opines, "The amount and quality of the services available are first-rate. The real problem is that, all too often, the people staffing these services are surly and unhelpful. It's tough to get your work done when you have to negotiate to get someone to do their job." And some junior attorneys believe they are at the bottom of the pecking order. "As a junior associate, your work always comes last. You end up doing everything yourself."

Hiring the most qualified

Associates believe that Chadbourne treats women well. One lawyer raves, "I work almost exclusively with women on security offerings. Barbara Becker is the main partner on those deals and she does a great deal to help the women's agenda — not the least of which is the excellent example that she sets." And a litigator claims, "There are more women attorneys than men in my practice group. I don't think there are any special efforts to hire women. They hire the most qualified. It just turns out to be more women!" Insiders say the firm has made great efforts to accommodate lawyers who wish to balance work and motherhood but remain unsure if part-timers will qualify for partnership.

Sources also say Chadbourne is a comfortable place for minority attorneys. Many associates say the ethnic diversity in the firm has been weak in the past but that the firm is making it a priority. "The efforts are certainly there. I think it will take time before the statistics meaningfully change." Others say race is simply not an issue at the firm. "To the best of my knowledge, they hire the most competent person, regardless of race — which is how it should be," says one lawyer.

Associates believe the firm does not have a problem accepting gays and lesbians. Comments one source, "There are openly gay associates at our firm, and I haven't seen anything to indicate that one's sexual orientation makes any difference here."

Mixed signals on pro bono

Chadbourne has taken on death penalty cases and other work on a pro bono basis, and the Washington office has an internship programs for associates at local nonprofit legal aid providers. But associates say the firm gives mixed signals when it comes to pro bono work. "The official line is that pro bono work is highly encouraged. That being said, the firm is not entirely satisfied if your pro bono hours occupy the majority of your time," explains one source. Some attorneys complain that pro bono work does not count toward the 1,900 hour billing requirement. "The firm — like most big firms — claims to be committed to pro bono, but if the hours spent on pro bono projects don't count toward your yearly total, one must question that commitment," declares an associate. However, others note that the firm does take associates' pro bono hours into account when handing out bonuses.

Choate, Hall & Stewart

VAULT.COM NEARLY & NOTABLE

Exchange Place
53 State Street
Boston, MA 02109
(617) 248-5000
Fax: (617) 248-4000
www.choate.com

LOCATIONS

Boston, MA (HQ)
Manchester, NH

MAJOR DEPARTMENTS/PRACTICES

Bankruptcy
Corporate
Environmental & Land Use
Health
Labor
Litigation
Patent
Real Estate
Tax
Trusts & Estates

THE STATS

No. of attorneys: 176
No. of offices: 2
Summer associate offers: 27 out of 27 (Boston, 1999)
Co-Managing Partners: William P. Gelnaw, Jr. and John A. Nadas
Hiring Partner: Lyman G. Bullard, Jr.

PAY

Boston, 2000
1st year: $125,000 + $30,000 bonus potential
2nd year: $135,000 + $40,000 bonus potential
3rd year: $145,000 + $50,000 bonus potential
4th year: $155,000 + $60,000 bonus potential
5th year: $170,000 + $65,000 bonus potential
6th year: $175,000 + $65,000 bonus potential
7th year: $175,000 + $65,000 bonus potential
8th year: $175,000 + $65,000 bonus potential
Summer associate: $1,730/week

NOTABLE PERKS

- Parental leave
- Moving expenses

THE BUZZ
What attorneys at other firms are saying about this firm

- "Social, strong local firm; hard-working"
- "Old-school firm that has fallen behind the times"
- "Stuffy, stuffy, stuffy"
- "In transition"

UPPERS

- Tons of responsibility and client contact
- Easy to get interesting work
- Dynamic and growing practice

DOWNERS

- Failure to share workload equally among associates
- Unpredictable hours
- Inefficient work assignment system

KEY COMPETITORS

Foley, Hoag, & Eliot
Goodwin Procter & Hoar
Hale and Dorr
Ropes & Gray

EMPLOYMENT CONTACT

Ms. Robin Carbone
Director of Recruiting
(617) 248-5000
rcarbone@choate.com

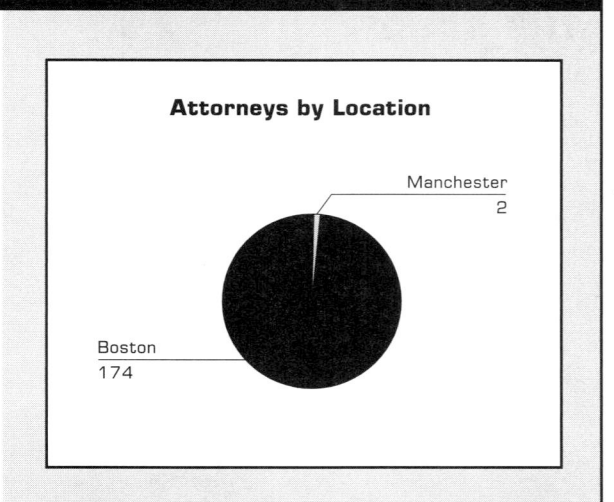

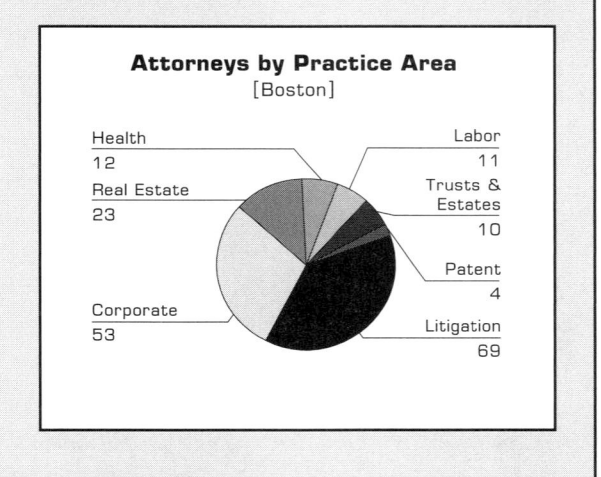

Attorneys by Location

- Boston: 174
- Manchester: 2

Attorneys by Practice Area [Boston]

- Health: 12
- Real Estate: 23
- Corporate: 53
- Litigation: 69
- Patent: 4
- Trusts & Estates: 10
- Labor: 11

QUALITY OF LIFE RANKINGS [ASSOCIATES RATE THEIR OWN FIRM]

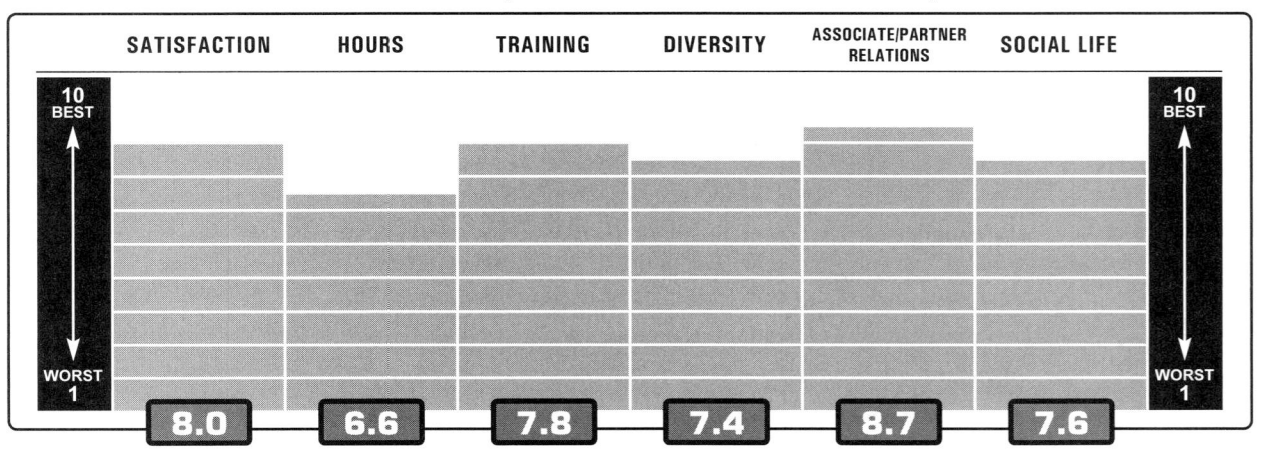

SATISFACTION	HOURS	TRAINING	DIVERSITY	ASSOCIATE/PARTNER RELATIONS	SOCIAL LIFE
8.0	6.6	7.8	7.4	8.7	7.6

THE SCOOP

Did you know that Massachusetts' Supreme Judicial Court is the oldest continuously running legal tribunal in the United States? Better yet, did you know that Margaret Marshall, a Choate, Hall & Stewart alumna, now serves as that court's highest officer? While the date of the firm's founding (1899) doesn't stretch back quite as far of that of the court (1692), Choate, Hall & Stewart can nevertheless boast of a rich history as a New England stalwart.

Litigation first and foremost

Firm literature doesn't hesitate to describe Choate's 70-person litigation department, the firm's largest, as "one of the preeminent litigation practices in New England." A glance at Choate's client list tends to suggest that the firm isn't exaggerating. Notable names on the roster include Bayer Corporation, Citigroup, Deloitte & Touche, Ernst & Young, Hewlett-Packard, IBM, John Hancock, Liberty Mutual, Microsoft, The Starwood Companies, Teradyne, Inc., and Transkaryotic Therapies, among others.

Choate divides its litigators among several subgroups, including Intellectual Property Litigation, Complex Financial Litigation, Government Enforcement & Compliance, Antitrust, Employment Litigation and Agency Proceedings, Insurance and Reinsurance Litigation, and Significant Tort Litigation. The firm's IP litigation team has won particular recognition — *The National Law Journal* named one partner from that group, Robert S. Frank, as one of New England's top litigators. Frank's win list runs long, including multi-million dollar victories on behalf of Data General and New England Reinsurance. In 1998 Frank won summary judgment for Cambridge, MA-based Transkaryotic Therapies (TKT), the target of a patent suit filed by biotech giant Amgen.

Business: Palladino at the helm

More than 50 lawyers devote themselves to Choate's business department, which the firm characterizes as its fastest-growing. The group subdivides into the following practice areas: Internet and New Media; Venture Capital & Buyouts; Mergers, Acquisitions and Joint Ventures; International Transactions; Specialty Finance; Energy & Telecommunications; and Workout & Bankruptcy. In September 1999, corporate finance specialist Peter Palladino was named chairman of the group.

As Palladino's appointment suggests, commercial and institutional finance is a traditional Choate strength and the firm draws business from such New England heavyweights as John Hancock, Mass Mutual, Fleet Bank, and Citizens Bank. Other areas also deserve mention. Choate's Venture Capital & Buyout expertise has attracted a sparkling clientele, and the firm serves as general counsel to high-flying private equity funds such as Boston Ventures and Heritage Partners. Stephen Cohen has developed a national reputation for heading up this area. Another key partner in this area is Harry Hanson, who also heads up efforts in Choate's newly-formed Internet and New Media practice group.

Finally, Choate has racked up an impressive record in energy and telecom. In 1999 Choate worked on $2.5 billion in debt transactions for utility giants such as Sierra Pacific Power Company, Maine Yankee Power Company, and Nevada Power Company.

High-profile health care

Like Beantown competitor Ropes & Gray, Choate, Hall & Stewart offers a highly-developed health care practice. Choate's clientele list tends is impressive, listing a wide variety of physician organizations (HMOs, and so on) and industry groups such as the Massachusetts Hospital Association, the Massachusetts Association of Health Maintenance Organizations, and the Massachusetts Medical Society. In March 2000, Choate attorneys Edward C. Kenna, Brian A. Davis, and Raymond A. O'Brien represented pharmaceutical concern Interneuron in a suit alleging fraud, misrepresentation, and breach of contract on the part of American Home Products.

Choate's substantial expertise hasn't protected it entirely from the convulsions affecting the health care business. Partner Charles Glerum, appointed by a Massachusetts court to oversee the closure of home health care provider Optimum Health Care, came under fire in September 1999 for shutting down the company's operations without giving social services agencies adequate time to arrange replacement care for patients. "I truly thought arrangements were made," Glerum told *The Boston Globe*, "and I regret if there were any oversights."

Lateral moves

Though confined to two offices, Choate, Hall & Stewart doesn't want for business. In fact, the firm has enjoyed a streak of record-breaking profits since 1996. But Choate, Hall & Stewart hasn't escaped talent ebb and flow. In spring 1999, two partners quit the firm for bigger, if not necessarily greener, pastures; one tax partner defected to professional services giant Ernst & Young, while the head of Choate's labor practice headed for 800-lawyer McDermott, Will & Emery. The losses had many industry observers wondering whether Choate, Hall & Stewart would take the merger plunge to boost its platform and profile. For its part, the firm points out that as of January 2000, Choate qualified as a "net beneficiary" of lateral moves, having added nine lateral partners and counsel over an 18-month period.

The multi-layered tableau of public service

As evidenced by Margaret Marshall's appointment as chief justice of the Massachusetts Supreme Judicial Court, Choate, Hall & Stewart has a strong tradition of public service on many levels. For example, a Choate partner was a founding director of the Massachusetts chapter of the Lawyers Committee for Civil Rights, and another serves on its Board of Advisors. On a sporting level, partner Frank B. Porter is president of the Boston Athletic Association, the organization in charge of the Boston Marathon. Golfers will be pleased to know that Partner John M. Cornish was tapped to be general chairman of the 1999 Ryder Cup, held at The Country Club in Brookline, MA. And in July 2000, Martin E. Levin, the head of the Massachusetts Environmental Strike Force (a division of the attorney general's office), will be joining the firm. Choate, Hall & Stewart has also been known to dip its toe into the frothy pool of Massachusetts politics. In August 1999, lawyers at the firm raised $8,000 for Massachusetts Governor Paul Celucci.

The Choate one-stop shop

Like other litigation powerhouses, Choate, Hall & Stewart offers clients considerable in-house resources. For example, the firm's Business Information Services boasts a network of "experienced investigators with substantial federal and state government service" including former FBI agents. The firm also leverages its expertise for its Fiduciary & Investment Services division, which offers an investment advisory service. Here again, Choate's government ties make themselves felt — partner Dennis J. Kearney, who leads the firm's government relations practice, has 12 years of experience as a member of the Massachusetts Legislature and as Sheriff of Suffolk County.

GETTING HIRED

Alumni connections count

The recruiting area of Choate's web site provides good information about the firm's management structure, assignment system, and pro bono efforts. It also lists a schedule of on-campus recruiting efforts, which in 1999 took place at the following schools: Boalt, BU, Chicago, Columbia, Cornell, Duke, George Washington, Georgetown, Harvard, Michigan, Northeastern, Northwestern, NYU, Penn, Stanford, Suffolk, BC, UT, UVA, and Yale.

As for the insider perspective on selectivity, one litigator explains: "If you went to a first-tier school and were in the top third of your class, it's easy. If not, you need something distinctive on your resume or several terrific interviews. For certain Boston-area schools with a strong alumni presence, such as BU and BC, grades seem to matter a little bit less." Another litigator adds: "I believe law students come from the top 15 percent of their class and are drawn from the top 20 law schools."

Insiders also insist that Choate isn't just about the numbers. Says one associate: "A huge amount of time and effort is spent on trying to find good, friendly, collegial people. Most of the people who are interviewed could do the work at Choate. Those that are hired typically offer something more." Another insider expounds on that "something more" by reporting that the firm looks "for substantial writing or advocacy experience, and wants people with a history of leadership and outside activities."

The laid-back interview process

"Laid-back" seems to be the buzzword for Choate interviews. On-campus candidates can expect junior or mid-level associates to conduct the screening interview. "They know you're intelligent when you walk in the door," says an insider, "so they really want to see that you can communicate."

Candidates who make the screening cut are brought to the firm for a half day of second-round interviews, split between mid- and senior-level associates and partners. Sources reveal that one of the partners is usually from the senior ranks. Candidates can also expect lunch with one or two junior associates, an "easygoing thing."

Consistent with the mood of the interview, one insider describes a fairly mellow interviewing M.O. That contact explains, "I read their resume, and I'll highlight things in my mind I want to find out about. We'll just get to talking, and usually the questions I want to ask come out during the conversation."

Sought-after candidates can expect intense follow-up. Choate circulates a firm-wide e-mail listing through which candidates have received offers, and encourages attorneys to call their prospective colleagues.

OUR SURVEY SAYS

Pretty sprightly for a hundred-year-old

Our insiders insist that, in spite of its age, Choate, Hall & Stewart has kept a youthful esprit. "It is a very nimble, fun place for a large, 100-year-old firm," says one mid-level attorney. A litigator agrees: "Despite being a 100-year-old firm, the partnership is young, and the mix of the two translates into a professional, low-key culture." Still another litigator describes Choate as "a white-shoe, prestigious Boston firm that has enough personality and genuine concern for individuals to make it a pleasant place to work, even considering the high-pressure environment of big-firm law." From the business group, an attorney muses that "there are still a number of people with old-school attitudes," but notes that "for the most part, the people that I work with are friendly, accessible, and willing to answer questions."

Pretty hard-working, too

In a free association psychological test, if you said "Choate's culture," most associates at the firm would answer "hard-working." An IP contact reveals that the firm puts "emphasis on quality of product, which is both exciting, in terms of more responsibility and your sense of importance, and daunting — you had better be good!" A corporate associate concurs, suggesting that the "firm really tries to promote the concept of lawyers as entrepreneurs" and "intentionally stays smaller than it could be, which gives associates a lot of responsibility early." "It can be sink or swim," that contact sighs.

Others point out the firm's warmer, fuzzier qualities. A health care associate finds co-workers to be "hardworking lawyers who are intelligent and sociable." "Superior work product is expected," says a litigator, but "it's an easy-going and laid-back place." "Open, friendly, not uptight," offers a colleague, adding: "People pride themselves on turning out top-notch work and on remaining sane while they do it."

Thumbs up for partners

"The partners are the nicest, most cordial bunch you could imagine," says one smiley corporate associate. Do we detect a hint of sarcasm? Judging from other responses in this category, not at all. Explains a senior litigator: "Aside from one or two people, the partners here are extremely courteous and respectful. I don't always get all the feedback I'd like, but I've never had anyone raise his or her voice at me. In general, no one expects you to spend face time in the office. If you don't have to stay late to get something finished, people expect you to go home and have a life." A colleague agrees, noting that "the hierarchy at Choate is not evident. I have felt part of a team." In the firm's corporate department, an associate raves that "the corporate partners are great — you get lots of responsibility early on, and they are really committed to see that you learn on the job." Another agrees: "Most of the partners that I work with have been great. There is a good open-door environment that allows a lot of contact with partners. I have not heard of any occasions where someone was openly berated for making a mistake. The typical response is 'How do we fix the mistake?'" Finally, one contact offers some revealing commentary: "I have found the partners to be extremely supportive of my part-time status and willing to accommodate my schedule."

Are there any complaints in this category? A litigator voices some discontent: "The partners always treat associates with basic respect appropriate for a business. Nonetheless, one always has the feeling that most partners have their own, sometimes hidden, agendas. Also, there is an unfair propensity to blame associates when things go wrong on a case, regardless of whether the associate really is responsible."

Strong on gender issues

Associates nearly all register satisfaction with the firm's handling of gender issues. As one corporate contact notes, "[Choate] was the first Boston firm to name a woman partner." A T&E insider reveals that "one of the main reasons I joined the firm is how well women and family issues are treated and respected." "Fourteen out of the 19 attorneys in my class are women," says a litigator, adding that "several attorneys I know are currently part-time. The firm seems to be very supportive of these issues."

Others confirm this assertion. Says a litigator, "I have never encountered a situation within this firm where I felt that I was receiving less favorable treatment because I am female." Another explains that "there are a number of other women working 60 percent or 80 percent schedules. So far, no one has made partner while keeping up a 60 percent schedule. We do have a number of women partners who work 80 percent." Still another litigator, who notes that "Choate has about an even split between male and female associates," applauds "a very real part-time program that allows men and women to structure their work in order to stay home with children."

Ethnic diversity: a ways to go

Choate associates consistently cite the need for greater diversity among their ranks. "There are very few minorities here," admits a health care contact. Another calls the firm "very receptive," but notes that "action plans still need to be honed."

Other contacts emphasize the firm's efforts. "The firm is trying hard to recruit and retain minority attorneys," says a litigator. A colleague agrees that "our record so far is not great, but the firm is working to improve in this area." A third adds: "The firm has a ways to go. While I think its heart is in the right place, the numbers definitely are not. The firm is actively working on this issue, though." Choate says that the firm has placed increasing its diversity on its "Priority Agenda" for the year, and has retained a Boston-based consulting firm to conduct a workplace assessment.

Pay happiness

It's always nice to see lawyers who admit to being decently compensated. "We're overpaid," quips a litigator, "but we're overworked as well, so it evens out." Many Choate associates supply both good scores and positive commentary in this category.

"It's not New York," says another litigator, "but I'm still paid far more than I am worth — and I don't have to practice in New York." "There is always room for improvement in the area of pay," a colleague chimes in, "but I am very happy with my current salary."

Associates aren't quite as chipper when it comes to bonuses. According to our contacts, Choate offers yearly bonuses to associates, beginning in their second year. To be eligible for a bonus, an associate must bill a minimum of 2,000 hours, including pro bono work. "After that," an insider reveals, "bonuses are based mostly on merit and not the number of hours billed." As noted, the bonus situation doesn't sit well with everyone. "They don't give a bonus until the third year here," moans a second-year attorney, "which is terrible and compares very poorly to other firms in Boston." The situation has since been rectified with Choate's new salary structure and we await the input of mollified Choate associates.

Not fratty

Choate Hall associates give their firm high marks for its social life, but tend to play down firm-related social activity. "Choate is not really a social firm," says a litigator, who adds, "people are friendly and groups may get together after work, but largely people come here to work and then go home to their social life." Another litigator agrees that "contrary to some of those law firm guides, it is not a 'work hard/play hard, frat-like' firm." Indeed, the slow social pace gives cheer to some. Explains one insider: "There's less after-hours socializing than at many firms. I take that as a good thing — it means we all still have friends and significant others who don't work here."

"Basic" training

Junior associates at Choate enjoy considerable training, although contacts describe the level of that training as "pretty basic." A corporate informant points out that "the better training has come from the attorneys who have been very patient in explaining how to do something if I have not done it before." "Most of the training for new associates is incredibly basic," a junior litigator confirms. "The training focuses on a general understanding of how things work, rather than at developing substantive skills. On the other hand, there is some form of a training seminar at least once a week, and in the litigation department there are mock depositions, which are conducted early on. Associates also have the opportunity to attend various proceedings and have their time billed as on-the-job training. Thus, they get credit for the hours spent attending a deposition, trial, or closings, but the client does not get charged."

Nice views, not-so-nice furniture

At the generous end of the spectrum, Choate associates describe their firm's office space as "classy" and stress that "you can't beat the views of Boston Harbor." Impeccable office space, however, doesn't seem to be Choate's forte. "The building is lovely," notes a litigator, "but the décor is a bit drab and the furniture is old. Recently, we were forced to rent space in a separate building to accommodate all of our attorneys, which is inconvenient." Another contact sighs that "space is at a premium here, so first-year offices are pretty small and not nicely furnished." A colleague in T&E confides that "first-years get the crappy furniture" but assures Vault.com that "the rest of the office is lovely."

The support pecking order

Choate's "team-oriented" workplace atmosphere seems to break down a bit when it comes to support. "Support staff is fantastic," notes one insider, "but the pecking order is clear — partner work comes first." A corporate contact also picks up on the pecking order theme, explaining: "Very few, if any, attorneys have their own secretaries. Most younger associates share with an upper-level attorney or a partner, or both. This can lead to younger attorneys' work being put off for a while, but it gets done eventually, either by your secretary or by a number of secretaries that come in at night. Choate could use some more quality secretaries, and should look to see if its compensation and benefits are on par with other firms in the city."

Hours: ebb and flow

As with associates at other litigation-heavy firms, Choate associates often bemoan the unpredictability of their schedule. Says one mid-level: "The number of hours doesn't usually get to me, although my non-lawyer fiancé thinks I am nuts. What bugs me is the unpredictability of my schedule, which I think is a function of having chosen litigation. I don't think the problem is Choate-specific." A health care associate reveals that hours "can vary widely. Some weeks I'm out the door by 6:30 every night. Other weeks it is 1:00 a.m. before I leave." And in the firm's business department, an insider reveals that "it can be crazy busy on a deal for a while, but then the deal closes and the ebb part of deal flow kicks in for a while. You just have to take advantage of the more normal times."

As for cold, hard numbers, Choate has a yearly recommendation of 1,900 billable hours, but according to insiders, "you are always at work more hours than that represents." A litigator muses that "on average, associates seem to work from 8 or 8:30 to 6:30 or 7."

Partnership prospects — don't get too excited

Choate litigators don't exactly keep their hopes up for their partnership prospects. While one sees chances as "fair," others remain glum. "Tough," says a junior litigator. "Weak," says a more senior colleague. Still another litigator puts odds at "1 in 10. At best." (Odds-players should note that in 1999, Choate elected five new partners.)

Contacts on the corporate side tend to rate their chances of partnership somewhat higher. "Decent," offers a tax attorney. "Reasonable," opines another. "It's hard to say," admits a corporate contact, adding: "The firm recently made a big group of partners, after several dry years. The firm swears that it wants to expand, but it has stayed basically the same size for at least five years."

In 1999 Choate switched from a straight nine-year track to a "multi-tiered" system. A corporate contact elaborates that "the partnership track has recently been changed to add a second tier. There is still some confusion about how this is going to work, but it generally means consideration for the first tier of partnership around your sixth year and then consideration for the next tier three to four years later." This is, in fact, an accurate depiction of how the system works. After six years, lawyers at Choate can become non-equity partners, a position which involves such great perks as attending partner meetings, participating in the business planning process, and accessing exciting business and financial information about the firm.

Choate reputation

Choate, Hall & Stewart associates generally agree that they work for a "very prestigious" firm, although many concede the regional scope of the firm's prestige. "One of the top firms in the Northeast," says a litigator. Another casts Choate "as a top-tier firm, maybe not with a huge national presence, but definitely with a New England presence. Our litigation, T&E, and health care practices are among the best in Boston."

The firm takes care to promote its "national practices in certain areas" and associates also frequently comment on the stature of individual practice groups. A litigator mentions that "as a rule, we don't practice win-at-all costs litigation. Plus, the partners stress the importance of doing the right thing in terms of our ethical obligations. You are not going to be asked to bury a bad document here." As for the firm's corporate capabilities, an insider observes that "the business department, while becoming well-known in the venture capital, LBO fund arena, is not understood to be actively involved in other areas." Another associate sees "a growing and innovative corporate practice, especially in private equity and emerging technology," and "the best traditional trust practice in the East." Still another corporate insider describes a "good corporate department, strongest in M&A and financing transactions, weaker in international and securities." That contact also comments that Choate possesses "arguably the best" bankruptcy department in Boston, "solid" real estate and environmental groups, and a "weak labor practice."

Dechert Price & Rhoads

VAULT.COM NEARLY & NOTABLE

4000 Bell Atlantic Tower
Philadelphia, PA 19103-2793
(215) 994-4000
Fax: (215) 994-2222
www.dechert.com

LOCATIONS

Philadelphia, PA (HQ)
Boston, MA
Harrisburg, PA
Hartford, CT
New York, NY
Princeton, NJ
Washington, DC
Brussels
London
Paris

MAJOR DEPARTMENTS/PRACTICES

Business
Employee Benefits
Government
Litigation
Private Client
Tax

THE STATS

No. of attorneys: 496
No. of offices: 10
Summer associate offers: 33 out of 33 (Philadelphia, 1999)
Managing Partner: Bartin J. Winokur, Esq.
Hiring Partners: Glenn D. Blumenfeld, Esq. and David M. Howard, Esq.

PAY

Philadelphia and Princeton 2000
1st year: $105,000 + $5,000 bonus
2nd year: $110,000 + $5,000 bonus
3rd year: $117,500 + $7,500 bonus
4th year: $125,000 + $10,000 bonus
5th year: $132,500 + $12,500 bonus
6th year: $140,000 + $12,500 bonus
Bonus based on 1,950 billable hours and satisfactory performance; discretionary bonuses are also offered
Summer associate: $2,000/week

Boston, New York, Washington, DC, 2000
1st year: $125,000
Summer associate (Boston and New York): $2,400/week
Summer associate (Washington): $2,250/week

Harrisburg, 2000
1st year: $85,000

Hartford, 2000
1st year: $85,000
2nd year: $90,000
3rd year: $95,000
4th year: $102,000
5th year: $109,000
Summer associate: $1,625/week

NOTABLE PERKS

- Emergency child care center in Philadelphia
- Dependent care assistance
- Black-tie dance every other year
- Cookies on Fridays in New York
- Free breakfast on Mondays in DC
- Pre-tax mass transit and parking program
- Investment pool

THE BUZZ
What attorneys at other firms are saying about this firm

- "Good place to get worked to death, but sophisticated practice and large institutional clients"
- "Solid Philadelphia firm but a little arrogant"
- "Not a happy place to work"
- "Nerdy but the most solid firm in the city"

UPPERS

- Quality and diversity of work and clients
- Associates are given a real role in deals
- New York pay without New York hours

DOWNERS

- Very difficult to determine partnership prospects
- Salary anxiety
- Poor associate/partner communication

KEY COMPETITORS

Ballard, Spahr, Andrews & Ingersoll
Morgan, Lewis & Bockius

EMPLOYMENT CONTACT

Ms. Carol S. Miller
Director of Associate Administration
(215) 994-2147
carol.miller@dechert.com

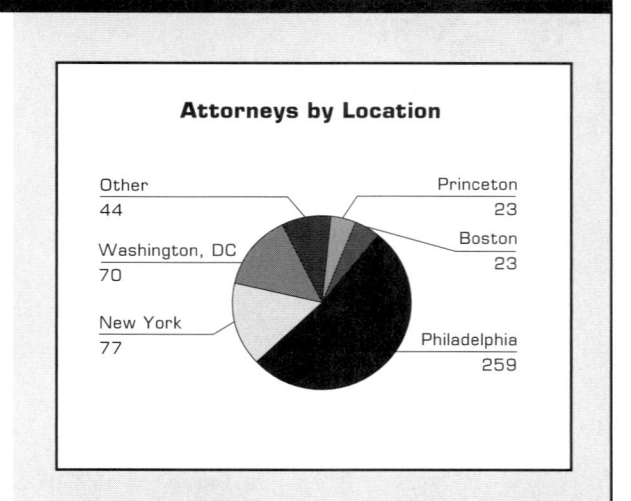

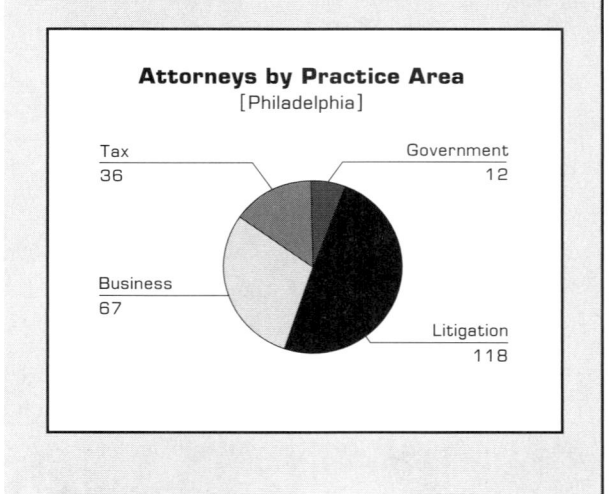

Attorneys by Location

- Other: 44
- Princeton: 23
- Washington, DC: 70
- Boston: 23
- New York: 77
- Philadelphia: 259

Attorneys by Practice Area [Philadelphia]

- Tax: 36
- Government: 12
- Business: 67
- Litigation: 118

QUALITY OF LIFE RANKINGS [ASSOCIATES RATE THEIR OWN FIRM]

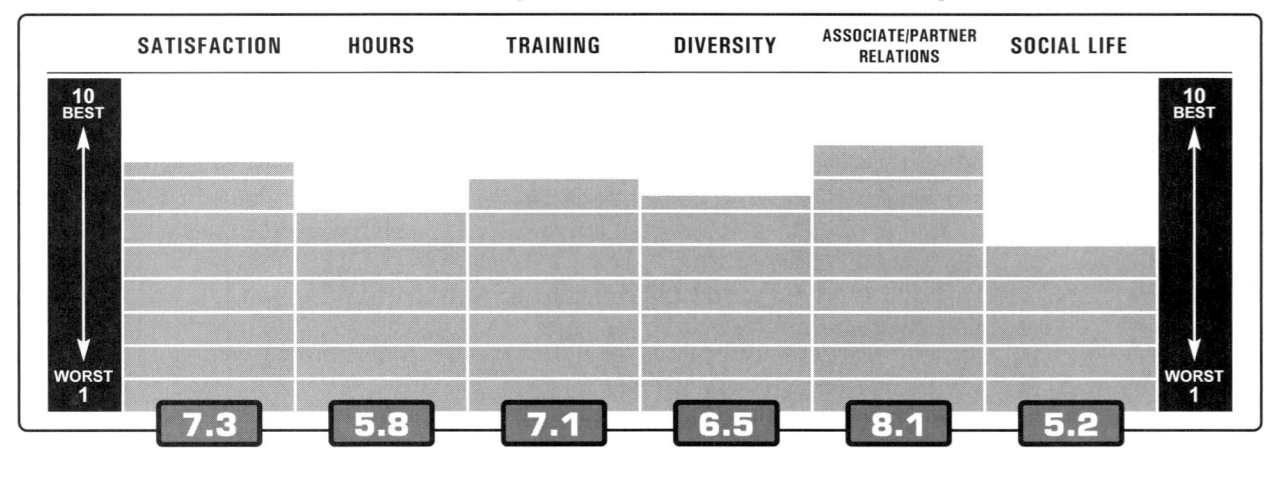

SATISFACTION	HOURS	TRAINING	DIVERSITY	ASSOCIATE/PARTNER RELATIONS	SOCIAL LIFE
7.3	5.8	7.1	6.5	8.1	5.2

THE SCOOP

Led by a nationally renowned litigation department, Dechert Price & Rhoads is Philadelphia's second-largest law firm. With Morgan, Lewis & Bockius disavowing Philly as its headquarters, Dechert is the top-ranked firm based in the City of Brotherly Love.

History: a Philadelphia story

Founded in 1875, Dechert Price & Rhoads remained a purely Philadelphian firm until the late 1960s, when the firm began to expand aggressively. In 1968 Dechert established a branch in Brussels, joining the few American law firms opening offices in Europe at this time. In 1969 the firm opened offices in Washington, DC and Harrisburg, its first domestic offices outside Philadelphia. The firm now boasts seven U.S. offices — Philadelphia, New York, Washington, DC, Princeton, Boston, Harrisburg, and Hartford. Its two largest offices outside of Philadelphia are in New York and DC. From 1995 to 1997, the firm experienced extraordinary growth: in 1995 the firm had 355 lawyers, but by 1998 the ranks had ballooned to 442.

In 1972 Dechert opened its London branch. The firm's London presence was bolstered in 1994 when Dechert formed an alliance with British firm Titmuss Sainer & Webb, now called Titmuss Sainer Dechert. The combined practices of Dechert Price & Rhoads and Titmuss Sainer Dechert now have more than 550 lawyers. Dechert's most recent international office opening came in 1995, when the firm set up shop in Paris.

Distinguished figures

One of Dechert's two original partners, Wayne MacVeagh, served as U.S. Attorney General and Ambassador to Italy, and thus began a proud firm tradition of involvement in public affairs. In 1951 former partner Joseph S. Clark was elected Mayor of Philadelphia. Clark won election to the U.S. Senate in 1956. A second alumnus of the firm, well-known Pennsylvania Senator Arlen Specter, won his seat in 1980. More recently, former hiring partner Mary McLaughlin served as chief counsel to the Senate subcommittee investigating the Ruby Ridge incident. McLaughlin received a presidential nomination for a judiciary position on Philadelphia's federal trial court in March 2000. The nomination was confirmed two months later. Judge McLaughlin joins two other former partners, Norma L. Shapiro and Harvey Bartle III, who are both judges in the U.S. District Court for the Eastern District of Pennsylvania.

Philadelphia lawyers are in demand

Dechert is a solid member of the legal elite. The firm's litigation department is nationally renowned. The firm has quietly built its M&A practice into a powerhouse as well. Dechert also boasts some strong niche practices, most notably in the mutual fund industry. Among the firm's clients in the asset management industry are Capital Research & Management and Goldman Sachs Asset Management. The firm offers other strengths as well; its corporate department represented Internet Capital Group in its $150 million IPO in 1999, as well as ICG's $1.4 billion follow-up offering. And Dechert's tax practice, with more than 20 partners, was named one of the top tax advisors on the East Coast by *International Tax Review* in 1998.

Although the firm represents its hometown's two daily newspapers, *The Philadelphia Inquirer* and *The Philadelphia Daily News*, as well as other Pennsylvania manufacturers, the majority of the firm's business comes from national and international clients based outside of the city. Over the past decade, Dechert's litigation department has developed a reputation for excellence, due at least in part to department head Robert Heim. Dechert has developed national-level product liability, antitrust, and general commercial litigation practices.

Among the top-line clients the firm has attracted are Baxter Healthcare Corporation, Gerber Products Company, US Airways, and Pfizer Inc. In late 1999, Martin J. Black and Christopher J. Culleton represented McNeill PPC, the manufacturer of Tylenol, in a patent suit against the Bayer Corp. The firm also represented Gerber in a price-fixing suit originally dismissed by a New Jersey judge. That decision was later upheld in January 1999 by the 3rd Circuit Court of Appeals. Among the firm's most important (and most lucrative) work in litigation has been its national representation of embattled tobacco giant Philip Morris.

Deals, deals, deals

Dechert's M&A practice has also been gaining attention recently. Dechert was tapped in September 1998 to advise Dyckerhoff A.G., a German cement and building materials company, on its $1.2 billion acquisition of Lone Star Industries Inc. In June 1998, Dechert represented Viagra manufacturer Pfizer in the $2.1 billion sale of its medical device manufacturing operations to Boston Scientific Corporation. The deal represented Pfizer's largest transaction ever. Dechert's other recent transactional work includes representation of AlliedSignal in its $9.8 billion August 1998 takeover bid of AMP and Campbell Soup's $1.4 billion divestiture of Swanson Foods. The firm also did work for Crown Cork & Seal when it acquired Carnaud Metalbox for $5.2 billion, the largest acquisition ever of a European company by an American company.

GETTING HIRED

Bank on law school prestige

Sources say that the law schools from which Dechert recruits have become increasingly more prestigious. "It's changing," an insider tells Vault.com of Dechert's recruiting. "We used to get a lot of people from Penn, Villanova, and Temple. Now we're still getting people from Penn — but also Harvard and Yale." While the firm has always hired from Harvard and Yale, associates report a significant increase in hiring from those schools. The firm also reportedly attracts a lot of students from Michigan and Berkeley. A contact reports, "Even in this market, Dechert really demands stellar credentials from its candidates. Your credentials really have to demonstrate that you are capable of superior work."

Some associates feel that the firm is becoming too focused on school names. Says one associate in Boston: "The firm puts too much weight on big name schools like Harvard and often overlooks excellent candidates from lesser-named schools." Reports an associate in Philadelphia: "If you're at a top 10 national school, you've got a good shot. If you're otherwise local, getting on a journal is key." Dechert reports that its top three schools in 1999 full-time hiring were Penn, Harvard, and Villanova, both in Philadelphia and firm-wide. The firm also reports that it has recently broadened the base of law schools from which it hires — in the Philadelphia office, 19 different schools were represented in the 2000 summer associate class.

Highly academic

Sources admit that "personality matters less than grades." An associate gripes that "they seem to place a high emphasis on grades. From what I have seen, this has resulted in hiring mostly drones with no personalities."

Sums up a contact: "Dechert is very focused on law school grade point average and pedigree of school (law school and undergraduate). No writing sample is required, and the interview process is not difficult at all. If you have the GPA and pedigree, it's fairly easy to get hired. Even for lateral associates, law school GPA and pedigree are essential."

OUR SURVEY SAYS

Dechert dips into its pockets

After the most recent round of raises for associates, Dechert Price & Rhoads raised the salary for its first-years in Philadelphia to $105,000. "The partners waited to see what other players in the Philadelphia market were doing and then put together a package far superior to that offered by any other firm in Philadelphia," says an associate. "Dechert was very open in informing associates about the salary deliberations and even asked for associate input. So as not to penalize associates for the length of the salary deliberations, the firm made the salary increase retroactive to February 1, 2000. I am not aware of any other firm in Philadelphia which made its salary increases retroactive."

Philadelphia-based associates are pleased with the new salary structure, noting that "the first-year salaries are obscene." There are guaranteed bonuses for meeting the "reasonable" target of 1,950 billable hours. "In addition to the guaranteed bonus," a source cites "discretionary bonuses that are independent of the 1,950-hour target." Some associates worry about the vague criteria for reaching these bonuses. "Many associates suspect that the discretionary bonuses operate as a way of rewarding corporate associates more than litigation associates. The fact that pay is not simply lockstep as it is in the major New York firms creates a lot of bad feeling among associates." Other complaints about the bonus structure exist, as a fifth-year contact reports. "The bonus system does not compensate associates for working substantial hours or for producing exceptional work." The firm counters, however, that it has a discretionary bonus program in place to reward attorneys based on their quality and quantity of work.

Dot coms talk, associates walk

While the firm made salaries retroactive to February 1, 2000, Dechert's sluggishness in setting new salaries did, according to many attorneys, have one pronounced effect among the ranks of associates: higher attrition rates. As one source reveals, "Many associates left prior to the salary increase announcements." Another contact indicates that "while Dechert makes wonderful recruitment efforts and provides active mentoring for summer associates and first-years, I think it really falls down on retention. Dechert needs to take a much more active interest in the careers of its individual associates, and to create a better sense of collegiality among the higher-level associates." A Philadelphia-based attorney believes that the high turnover of late is somewhat misleading. "You can pretty much lateral anywhere from Dechert —

from specialty boutique to 1,000-lawyer firm — so turnover has always been relatively high. The dot coms have just exacerbated the situation."

The firm has taken steps to improve retention, including appointing Steve Brown to serve as associate development partner. Brown is in charge of creating initiatives to promote the professional growth and satisfaction of the firm's young lawyers. Additionally, "Dechert has recently made some investments that will be held as retention bonuses," a source states. "The value of those bonuses is indeterminate because they are in volatile startups." Keep watching Nasdaq for more news.

Congenial partners

Dechertites harbor warm and fuzzy feelings toward the partners at the firm. An associate declares, "I have had extremely favorable treatment by the partners, who are down-to-earth and easy to talk to. They are an invaluable source and are willing to mentor you through the process." Another associate describes the firm as having a "remarkably congenial atmosphere. I have yet to either experience or hear of anything that approaches associate abuse." A DC-based lawyer elaborates, "I have great respect for the expertise each partner possesses. Partners at Dechert can be demanding but are always accommodating. Lately, I've been working for people who give me responsibility and earnestly seek my thoughts and advice."

But Dechert partners shouldn't sign up for sainthood yet. Associates do have issues. A Philadelphia-based source complains, "Most treat us very well, but the few that are allowed by their fellow partners to treat other people badly (associates and partners and support staff alike) make a significant impression." Many report a lack of social contact between partners and associates: "Partners seem unwilling to take social time with associates (lunches, dinners, and so on), while they are happy to do these things when it comes to recruitment." A third-year continues, "There are a few partners that I enjoy working for, but many could care less about your development and happiness and solely care about their work getting done. Also, many routinely put you in a time bind by not bothering to forward assignments and revisions in a timely manner." To combat such practices, in 2000 Dechert instituted a upward feedback program in which associates can anonymously evaluate the partners with whom they work.

Friendly, not social

Dechert associates report that, while most attorneys are "pleasant," there is not much of a social life at the firm. Contacts report that "younger, non-married associates do socialize together," but most tend to work and go home. An associate elaborates, "Besides events that occur during the work day, many lawyers seem to forgo these opportunities in favor of spending time with their families." Another source characterizes

Dechert as a "very married firm. At quitting time, people flee to their families. Large size makes it feel like a corporation full of people whose only contact is during work hours and people are satisfied with that."

Not everyone joins the caravan out the door. A first-year notes, "I enjoy social relationships with a large number of attorneys and other workers here. While mostly confined to lunches, having dinner with a number of associates and their significant others is not uncommon. In my short time here, I have probably been to at least seven parties thrown by attorneys here that were not firm functions. These have been well-attended." Another enthuses, "I have made most of my best social friends through the firm. There is a regular happy-hour crowd among young and mid-level associates. Softball also spurs some interaction."

This training's bound for glory

Attorneys find that "Dechert provides excellent formal training programs (yes, there are several) and extensive informal training opportunities." An eighth-year reveals, "The firm is paying a lot more attention to training now than when I started." Another associate elaborates, "Partners and senior associates work closely with mid-level and junior associates, and in my experience are almost as interested in training as they are in completing the project. Dechert offers a wide variety of interesting projects. The firm has an assignment system in place through which associates can request (and in my experience generally receive) projects that match their particular interest." Litigators have the opportunity to attend a "trial team training program" which "high-level partners attend" and which provides associates with "common sense information regarding our roles as attorneys." As a second-year notes, the partners "keep us grounded and tell us their horror stories. They appear to be open to questions for advice."

Not every associate is pleased with the training at Dechert. A senior associate explains, "Training is spotty, with an excellent first-year program, then a lapse before a deposition training program and trial training (modified NITA-type courses)." A corporate attorney is also critical: "The training for my practice group is sporadic and scheduled training sessions are cancelled more often than not. I think an intensive training program for new associates in my practice group would be very useful to give new lawyers some context about what we do." A Philadelphia-based attorney observes, "There is virtually no formal training — it's all on-the-job. No one has time for it, though, so it's just as well."

You work hard for the money

While associates at Dechert definitely put in their hours, many note that "Dechert associates are paid very well and are expected to work very hard." While long, the hours are not oppressive, as one associate explains. "In the abstract, I feel like I spend a lot of time at work. Compared to other young lawyers I know in other firms, and also to some other associates at my own firm, I have a great life in terms of hours." Another contact says, "A good thing about Dechert is that no one expects face time. If you're done, you go home. At the same time, with the new salaries I think new associates should expect to work hard here." Attorneys at the firm also have the ability to manage their own work schedule, according to one associate: "You have no problem keeping your hours lower if that is what you want, but you will have to refuse some very tempting projects."

A third-year notices a recent change in lifestyle: "Dechert truly lived up to the promise that there were no minimum billing requirements here. This has changed somewhat with the new bonus system, where the bonus is tied to the billings. Still, the volume of work, especially on the corporate side and within the M&A group, means that you're working long hours regardless of expectations. There are capacity issues in the outlying offices, though, leaving some associates to beg for work."

Veteran staff (but could they come in on weekends?)

While attorneys in the Philadelphia office report that "Dechert has support staff that have been with the firm for over 25 years," many have trouble with their secretaries and assistants. One exasperated Philadelphian explains, "Dechert does not pay the best going rate for secretaries in town and it is starting to show. Unless you have a secretary who has been at Dechert for a while, it can be very hit or miss. With the longer hours we also need much better after-hours services. Twenty-four-hour support at some level would be great. And how about someone to answer the phone on weekends?"

Other associates complain of an "incredible amount of attitude from the secretaries. The latest associate raises have only exacerbated the problem." Many still find "a lot of quality people here at all levels. Secretaries range from mediocre to superb. Paralegals and project assistants are generally very helpful." One source notes that "in particular, the litigation secretaries are extremely qualified." Attorneys in the DC office also complain of support problems, noting "most secretaries are not dependable and are poor performers. The word processors and paralegals are horrendous."

A convoluted path to partner

The partnership track at Dechert is "at least eight years — realistically, nine or 10 years," and associates complain that "the criteria are very opaque." A sixth-year explains, "Prospects used to be good and were a big selling point for Dechert. However, Dechert has recently introduced a two-tier partnership structure (equity and non-equity partners). This is clearly a way of partnering fewer people and keeping partnership profits high. Those associates who came to Dechert before this happened feel cheated by what's happened. It's dispiriting." Many others believe the non-equity track, which one associate calls "some sort of ambiguous purgatory," will hamper their chances of making partner. Another associate notes: "Laterals with something special to offer have a better shot than people who came straight up the Dechert chain." This issue, however, may not be as important as it once was to attorneys, as "many associates no longer focus on this and have different career paths in mind."

Brotherly love

Dechert attorneys in the Philadelphia office say the firm strongly encourages them to participate in pro bono activities. An associate notes, "I have always had the full resources of the firm available for my pro bono work, and have received nothing but encouragement." Another states, "I honestly think you could book a quarter of your billing time in a year to a pro bono matter or matters and not have that count against you, either in advancement or bonus terms." Some insiders assert that pro bono work is "strongly encouraged if you are a litigator and not really discussed if you are a corporate associate." However, a corporate attorney notes that while "there is not quite as natural a fit for pro bono work as there would be for litigation associates, I have already worked on two pro bono assignments since I have been here and enjoyed both of them." Attorneys in the DC office complain that the emphasis placed on pro bono work in Philadelphia is not found in the nation's capital. A senior associate in that office frets, "I want to do some pro bono work but have been discouraged from doing so by partners."

Part-time work is welcomed

Dechert is a comfortable place for women to practice law. A source asserts, "I do not feel I've been treated differently as a woman." Moroever, associates are "very surprised how supportive the firm has been of women who wish to work part-time." The firm's part-time policy allows any Dechert lawyer — male or female — to work 60 percent or more of a full-time schedule. Those electing this option in order to spend time as a caregiver need not obtain the firm's approval; those who want to move to part-time for other reasons must get the OK from the chair of the Professional Resources Committee. One associate comments that the firm provides "excellent flexibility in terms of part-time, but what that really means in terms of advancement is an open question. Part of the problem is that it is so hard to be part-time — not because of Dechert, but because of the profession. Many women give up before the firm has the opportunity to show what it would do if they stayed. Dechert's policies are as enlightened as they come."

Powerhouse minority efforts, minor results

When questioned about diversity at Dechert, an associate responds, "As a minority, it has not been an issue. I don't feel an emphasis has been placed on my status. Instead, I'm treated as an attorney without respect to gender or minority status." Others report that "we try hard, but can't seem to get many minority lawyers. I do not believe there is discrimination, but there do not appear to be any determined efforts to recruit minorities." One contact disagrees with the previous statement. "It may not yet be reflected in the statistics, but I am convinced Dechert is beginning to make great strides here. I know the firm cares about these things."

When it comes to gays, silence

While many law firms have rushed to ensure a comfortable working environment for gay and lesbian lawyers, according to insiders at Dechert silence reigns on gay and lesbian issues at the firm. "Dechert has been completely silent on this issue, despite the good example set by New York firms such as Milbank Tweed," indicates one associate. "I cannot think of one associate who is openly gay at Dechert — although, at the same time, I have never heard any anti-gay remarks while I have been here. Someone in the partnership should take the lead on this." One associate notes that while there are "very few, if any, out attorneys, relatively out summer associates have done fine and gotten offers."

"I honestly think you could book a quarter of your billing time in a year to pro bono matters and not have that count against you."

— *Dechert Price & Rhoads associate*

Fulbright & Jaworski LLP

VAULT.COM NEARLY & NOTABLE

1301 McKinney St., Suite 5100
Houston, TX 77010-3095
(713) 651-5151
Fax: (713) 651-5246
www.fulbright.com

LOCATIONS

Houston (HQ)
Austin
Dallas
Los Angeles
Minneapolis
New York
San Antonio
Washington, DC
Hong Kong
London

MAJOR DEPARTMENTS/PRACTICES

Admiralty
Corporate
Energy & Real Property
Environmental
Health Law Administration & Litigation
Intellectual Property & Technology
Labor & Employment Law
Litigation
Public Law
Tax, Trusts, Estates, & Employee Benefits

THE STATS

No. of attorneys: 737
No. of offices: 10
Summer associate offers: 47 out of 57 (Houston, 1999)
Chairman of Executive Committee: A.T. Blackshear, Jr.
Hiring Partner: Christopher E. H. Dack

THE BUZZ
What attorneys at other firms are saying about this firm

- "Litigation powerhouse"
- "Old-boy culture"
- "Not a good place for women"
- "Good Texas firm"

PAY

All Texas Offices, 2000
1st year: $110,000 + $1,000 bonus
Summer associate: $1,700/week

Washington, DC, Los Angeles, 2000
1st year: $112,000 + bonus
Summer associate: $1,800/week

Los Angeles, 2000
1st year: $120,000 + bonus
Summer associate: $2,400/week

New York, 2000
1st year: $120,000 + bonus
Summer associate: $2,400/week

NOTABLE PERKS

- Free parking downtown in Houston
- Health club in DC office
- Lavish summer program
- Generous client development budget

UPPERS

- Compensation generous, especially for Texas firm
- Early responsibility and experience
- Social life unusually lively

DOWNERS

- Lots of bureaucracy leads to slow decisions
- Partnership chances growing slimmer
- Noticeable lack of diversity

KEY COMPETITORS

Baker Botts
Vinson & Elkins

EMPLOYMENT CONTACT

Ms. Leslie S. Rice
Manager of Attorney Employment
(713) 651-5518
lrice@fulbright.com

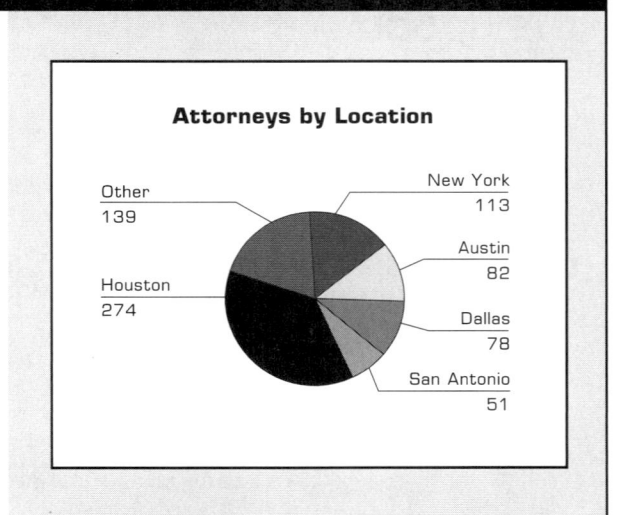

Attorneys by Location
- Other: 139
- Houston: 274
- New York: 113
- Austin: 82
- Dallas: 78
- San Antonio: 51

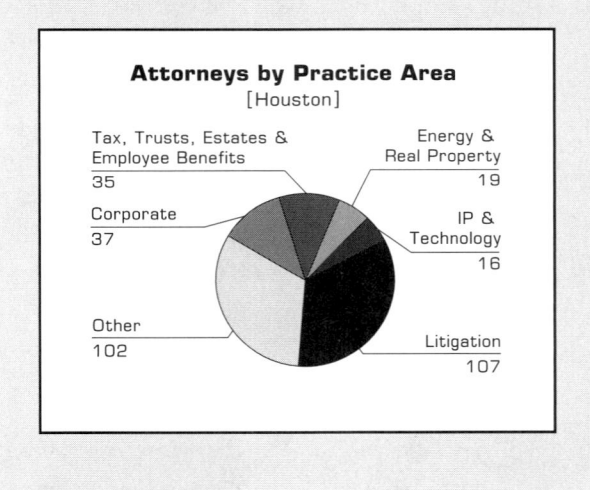

Attorneys by Practice Area [Houston]
- Tax, Trusts, Estates & Employee Benefits: 35
- Corporate: 37
- Other: 102
- Energy & Real Property: 19
- IP & Technology: 16
- Litigation: 107

QUALITY OF LIFE RANKINGS [ASSOCIATES RATE THEIR OWN FIRM]

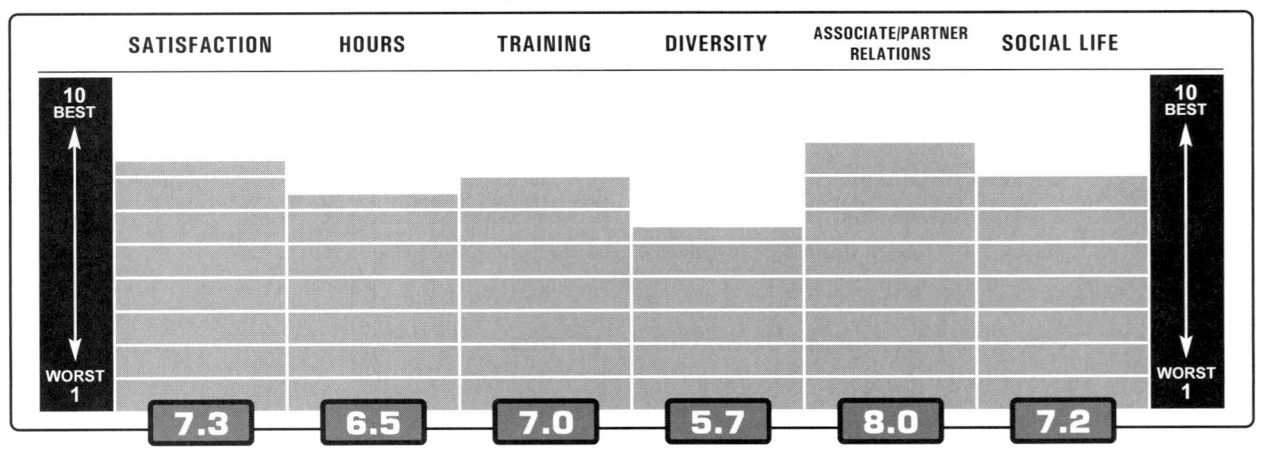

SATISFACTION	HOURS	TRAINING	DIVERSITY	ASSOCIATE/PARTNER RELATIONS	SOCIAL LIFE
7.3	6.5	7.0	5.7	8.0	7.2

THE SCOOP

From deep in the heart of Texas comes Fulbright & Jaworski LLP, a hard-workin', free-spendin', two-steppin' legal juggernaut. Fulbright is a renowned legal powerhouse in both corporate finance and litigation.

History: a bright star shining in Lone Star country

Fulbright & Jaworski has been an important figure in the history of the legal profession in Texas. Founded in 1919, Fulbright, Crooker & Freeman took its current name after Leon Jaworski joined in 1932. Jaworski, after an illustrious law career, rose to national prominence in the 1970s as the special prosecutor in the Watergate hearings. A 1981 merger with Dumas, Huguenin, Boothman & Morrow enabled Fulbright to open a branch office in Dallas, and another merger with Reavis & McGrath (one of the largest law firm mergers ever) moved the firm into New York in 1989. Fulbright has crossed the oceans in its zeal to expand as well — the firm now has satellite offices in London and Hong Kong. Within the U.S., Fulbright & Jaworski is active in a number of professional organizations. Five of its lawyers have become president of the Texas State Bar, and a sixth, Otway B. Denny, was a candidate for the position in the spring of 2000. On the national level, more members of the American Bar Association's House of Delegates have come from Fulbright than from any other firm in the nation.

Fitting Texas to a T

They grow them big in Texas, and Fulbright & Jaworski is certainly no exception, weighing in at approximately 670 attorneys. The firm has grown recently through strategic mergers and lateral hiring. It also recently expanded its public finance and administrative law group by adding a number of lawyers and staff to its Los Angeles office. The partner ranks are also increasing from within. Fulbright promoted seven lawyers, representing three different offices, in both February 1999 and 2000. Fulbright also increased the number of associates hired in 1999 to 64, up from 56 in 1998. Yet as the number of attorneys hired by the firm has risen, the attrition rate has dropped, to only 7 percent annually. Tactics credited with keeping associates happy include Fulbright chair Gus Blackshear meeting with every associate in small groups, as well as a new mentoring program for litigation attorneys.

Across-the-board leadership

The firm is among the Lone Star State's leaders in initial public offerings representing issuers, equity offerings representing issuers, underwriter's counsel deals, environmental law, and in ERISA and pensions. Mergers & acquisitions is another area of expertise.

Fulbright handles deals for some of the larger companies in the country, as well as some of its neighbors. One client that fits both descriptions is Cogen Technologies, which the firm recently represented in its $1.1 billion sale of three power plants to Enron Corp. Fulbright also advised Fort Worth's Union Pacific Resources Group when it sold its natural gas operations to Duke Energy Field Services for $1.35 billion. In 2000, the firm assisted Voxware of Princeton to acquire the wireless assets of InRoad, Inc., for $8.1 million.

As might be expected in Texas, much of Fulbright's business comes from the oil and energy industry. At the 1998 Energy Finance Awards, the firm placed ninth for knowledge of international energy law. Fulbright services oil and energy barons not just through IPOs, but also in the preparation and negotiation of contracts, advising foreign corporations investing in American oil operations, and in the financing of gas properties. Fulbright also features a thriving environmental practice, dealing with oversight and enforcement of government programs, pollution case litigation, and environmental auditing.

Modern times

In order to keep up with the recent economic boom linked to information technology, Fulbright has beefed up its IP department. Early in 2000, Fulbright brought over 30 attorneys, including 11 partners, from the Austin office of IP law firm Arnold White & Durkee, expanding a group that had already been enhanced through a merger with Felfe & Lynch during the summer of 1998. The firm now boasts of having "one of the largest concentrations of intellectual property attorneys in any full-service law firm." Other efforts to keep up with the new economy include the formation of the firm's Technology and Emerging Companies group, which is based in the Austin office. Headed by former corporate securities partner Howard Wolf, the new group's mission is to attract techie clients and capitalize on the ascendancy of e-commerce.

Legendary litigators

Despite the firm's strong transactional practices, litigation remains the Fulbright mainstay. Fulbright attorneys are, according to insiders, "very well respected in litigation throughout the country." The firm puts its litigators through the paces of a "rigorous training program," including "seminars on all aspects of trial advocacy," as well as "simulated trials in the firm's own courtroom." Not surprisingly, the litigation practice excels in areas as diverse as oil and gas law and breach of contract cases.

In past years, the firm has represented 3M in silicone breast implant litigation and Coca-Cola in the defense of widely publicized litigation brought on as the result of a truck and school bus collision in South Texas. More recently, Fulbright represented native Texan and notable actor Matthew McConaughey, as well as Creative Artists, in a dispute with the makers of *The Return of the Texas Chainsaw Massacre*. They also advised Toshiba of America in a class action suit in which the company was accused of selling faulty floppy disk drives. The parties reached a $2.1 billion settlement. In a major criminal case, partner Brian Grieg and Mary Hogan Greer aided death row occupant Jose Santellan Sr. in having his capital murder charge overturned.

GETTING HIRED

Why Texas, indeed!

Fulbright "has placed increasing emphasis on recruiting at Top 10 schools, but it is still a place where students from lower tier schools have a shot to be competitive," reports a source who made it through Fulbright's hiring process. Furthermore, another associate asserts that "the better the law school, the lower in the class Fulbright will consider a candidate," though "if there is some sort of real need, the firm will go outside these parameters." In any case, however, "grades and school reputation are important" to get the initial interview.

After that, in the second interview, "the important thing is the impact you make on, and how well you get along with, the attorneys you meet. The personality component holds a great deal of weight." Because of Fulbright's litigation emphasis, Fulbright puts a "premium on hiring personalities who would sway a jury, and who are good, fun people to have around." While "an emphasis is placed on getting a socially capable person," this focus "may be declining as Fulbright works on larger commercial matters." For now, an "outgoing personality [is] more of a requirement here than at other firms." It is also key for a "recruit [to] appreciate the importance of everyone on the team."

Fulbright "typically interviews about 20 people and calls back two or three, except at Texas schools. We interview 80 to 100 people at the University of Texas. A higher proportion gets called back, since it's less expensive to bring them in." The firm clearly is intent on maintaining the local pipeline. "We do look for someone with ties to the area," reveals an insider. Those who think that the Alamo is a rental car company "can expect a question like, 'Why do you want to go to Texas?'" Among 1998 summer associates, the most frequently represented law school was UT, followed by the University of Houston.

Advice for lateral applicants

Insiders warn of many potential stumbling blocks to getting hired as a lateral. "Generally, everyone gets concerned if there are unexplained gaps in work experience," warns one insider, predictably. Similarly, "having failed a bar exam doesn't go over well. If you haven't taken one yet, work hard to make sure you pass. It's not fatal, but it's better not to have that strike against you." Preparation is of paramount importance in getting a foot in the door. "If you can talk to someone in the section you are interested in, you stand a better chance of getting an interview," says an associate. "You need to know what it is you want to do — nobody wants to hire an attorney that doesn't know what kind of law they want to practice, since that indicates a lack of desire, interest, and aggressiveness."

Candidates must undergo a "pretty formal" hiring process. An attorney "will weed out resumes that just don't fit (if the candidate's interested in a practice area that's not hiring), and forward the remaining resumes to the heads of the appropriate practices. If this person is interested, there will generally be a phone interview and then an office interview. The office interview will include time with attorneys from the section and attorneys on the recruiting committee."

OUR SURVEY SAYS

All roads lead to Houston

Associates credit Fulbright's "Texas charm" as a defining factor in the firm's culture, claiming that "you feel right at home from the first day." While insiders note that the atmosphere of the firm is "fairly conservative," the reputation that "it is the kind of place where attorneys put their jackets on to go to the food court," may be overstated. One source reports that "it's open, relaxed, social, friendly, and welcoming." An attorney with an especially fond view of the firm states that "Uncle Fulbright really seems to care."

Easy money?

"Fulbright's compensation is not the highest in town, but it is competitive." states a Washington DC based associate. Most lawyers in the Houston office agree. "Other firms have higher base salaries than Fulbright, but the difference is more than made up by very reachable incentive bonuses." Moreover, "when you take into consideration the cost of living here," asserts a content Houston attorney, "I am making out so much better than my friends in New York, Chicago, and DC." The aforementioned bonuses, which are based on billable hours, "can be attained with very little extra effort. The first bonus is at 1,850 hours." Some complain that the firm "is very late to react," "definitely a follower in salaries," and "does not tell if the bonus is discretionary or guaranteed." "Even with these gripes ," acquiesces one critic, "I still feel my salary is superior." There seems to be some negative consequences of the high wages. "The more money they give us, the more we have to work," one overworked associate wistfully declares. "I wish they would take some of the money back so I could have a life."

Show me the hours

"The main driving force behind the number of hours worked is the amount of client work to be done, not partner pressure. It is nice to be needed," notes an insider. However, many Fulbright attorneys refer to an overwhelming workload as a negative aspect of working at the firm. Fulbright & Jaworski "only recently began having billable hours targets associated with bonuses. Previously there were no minimum hours and attorneys were encouraged to use vacation time." "This is supposed to be a lifestyle firm," grumbles an associate in the Washington office, "but I have yet to experience that." Escalating pressure to bill more is also felt by attorneys wishing to work on pro bono cases. One source states that, "pro bono counts toward billing requirements, but this has essentially meant billing requirements have been increased to cover this area." An associate notes, however, that "regardless of the increasing hours worked by attorneys, the impression that the firm wants associates to have lives outside of the office" still exists.

Social as we wanna be

In regards to the social life of its attorneys, Fulbright tends to take an open stance. A superb social environment exists for those who wish to take part. "Even those silly *Ally McBeal* folks with their martinis every evening don't have much on us," insists a Fulbright socialite. "There is a very friendly, welcoming, social atmosphere here." Furthermore, "monthly firm sponsored happy-hours are generally well attended." In spite of generally positive reviews of the firm's social environment, one source complains that "it's like high school in some respects. Some associates treat each other well, while others create cliques and try to decide who deserves respect and who doesn't."

The amount of social events sponsored by Fulbright & Jaworski increases greatly during the summer, when the firm's summer associates arrive. Associates recall their summer at the firm as being "an absolute blowout." One former summer associate remembers being "treated like a queen." Another associate complains (unsympathetically) that the summer program can "become exhausting after a couple of months. You are taken to lunch every day and dinner or some other event most nights." Nevertheless, many cite the experience of having been a summer associate at Fulbright as the deciding factor in accepting a position at the firm.

Training by department

"Some departments or sections receive more real training than others," reports an associate. Insiders are wild about the litigation program, giving it such compliments as "Fulbright's litigation program is extensive and comprehensive," and "probably the best litigation program out there." However, corporate associates have been more critical of the firm's training programs, stating that the "corporate training program has been less focused," and even claiming that there is "no formal training whatsoever for most transactional associates." Real estate specialists find the training available to them to be even more problematic, saying that "any training we get is irrelevant to our work."

Kindly partners

"Overall, partners treat associates with respect," one associate states, "and give them high levels of responsibility. "Furthermore, while insiders report, "partners will give you as much responsibility as you show you can handle," they "are also quite aware that we have lives away from the office." Moreover, many partners illustrate their respect for associates by, "frequently [soliciting their] ideas in even the most difficult and technical matters." Not all associates at Fulbright & Jaworski feel quite as warm towards their superiors, stating that "they seem to be in their own world a lot of the time" and "there is little to no mentoring and no apparent interest in our professional development." As one source remarks, "Some partners are friendly and others are stand-off-ish. Like anywhere else, some partners choose their favorites early, and it's not easy to change that. It's sort of like *Animal Farm*: Some associates are more equal than others."

Don't try this at home, kids

"Since I have been here the partnership track has gone from 8 to 10 years and they have greatly reduced the number of partners they make each year," states an associate. However, "if you stay for 10 years, there's a chance, [which is] better than at most firms." Some insiders disagree. "This past year many deserving associates were overlooked. I believe this is primarily because the firm made too many partners in the eighties. Now some of the really shining stars are passed over because an older partner is (essentially) taking up a new partner's potential spot." "Prospects are better for young associates," adds another associate, "because many partners will have retired by the time young associates are up for partner." According to one source, attorneys will increase their chances of becoming a partner by abiding by the philosophy of "bill, bill, bill and bring in lots of business." Becoming "a respected member of the community" is also helpful. However, a disenchanted Fulbrightian suggests that the best way to increase his chances of making partner would be to "kill off one of the partners."

Bring us the women

"The firm is actively recruiting women," notes an insider. "[Also, it] has recently implemented a part-time policy that allows associates to go part-time and then come back on partnership track." However, others claim that "part time is frowned upon," and "the firm makes no effort to promote gender equality through mentoring, part-time or other programs." A female associate reports, "what we see once we are here is that female partners have no life — i.e. no kids, not married, or they had their kids prior to coming to the firm." "The problem, however, is that [the firm has] no clue as to how to retain females," another attorney continues, "How many other law firms would permit a male partner to hang something on his office wall that says 'cunnilingus'?"

In spite of this attempt, one attorney voices a popular opinion among his peers by stating, "despite the firm's obvious attempts to hire and retain minorities, I would like to see more diversity within the workplace." When questioned regarding diversity issues with respect to gays and lesbians, one insider states, "It is not discussed." The firm does not offer domestic partner benefits.

Everyone's happy

In spite of complaints by associates, reviews of the firm as a whole are overwhelmingly positive. "The people and work are top notch," states one attorney. Another continues, "overall, it is one of the friendliest and most open firms in the city. I don't think that any other major firm would offer a better lifestyle." "If you are going to practice law, this a great place to do it," summarizes an insider. "You are paid well, get treated with respect, and [are given] a lot of responsibility early in your career."

"Even those silly *Ally McBeal* folks with their martinis every evening don't have much on us."

— *Fulbright associate*

Gray Cary Ware & Freidenrich

VAULT.COM NEARLY & NOTABLE

401 B Street, Suite 1700
San Diego, CA 92101
(619) 699-2700
Fax: (619) 236-1048
www.graycary.com

400 Hamilton Avenue
Palo Alto, CA 94301
(650) 833-2000
Fax: (650) 327-3699

LOCATIONS

Palo Alto, CA (HQ)
Austin, TX
Golden Triangle (No. San Diego), CA
La Jolla, CA
Seattle, WA
Sacramento, CA
San Diego (Downtown), CA
San Francisco, CA

MAJOR DEPARTMENTS/PRACTICES

Bankruptcy/Commercial Law
Corporate & Securities
Employment Services
Environmental, Land Use & Real Estate
Intellectual Property — Licensing and Litigation
Patent & Trademark
Litigation
Tax & Trust

THE STATS

No. of attorneys: 398
No. of offices: 8
Summer associate offers: 19 out of 19 (Palo Alto, 1999); 19 out of 22 (San Diego, 1999)
Regional Managing Partners: Bob Shuman, Jr. (Northern region) and Jeff Shohet (Southern region)
Hiring Partner: Richard Yankwich

PAY

All Offices, 2000

1st year: $125,000 + $30,000 bonus potential
2nd year: $135,000 + $40,000 bonus potential
3rd year: $150,000 + $45,000 bonus potential
4th year: $165,000 + $50,000 bonus potential
5th year: $185,000 + $50,000 bonus potential
6th year: $195,000 + $50,000 bonus potential
7th year: $205,000 + $50,000 bonus potential
Summer associate: $2,200/week

NOTABLE PERKS

- Moving expenses
- Free parking
- Attorney equity incentives
- Mortgage assistance (California offices)

THE BUZZ
What attorneys at other firms are saying about this firm

- "High tech Brobeck follower"
- "Not a top California firm, but close"
- "Trying hard to reinvent"
- "Up and coming in the Valley"

UPPERS

- Extremely bright colleagues
- Relatively good hours
- At the forefront of technology law

DOWNERS

- Cultural differences between the Palo Alto and San Diego offices
- Lousy office furniture
- Intense work load

KEY COMPETITORS

Brobeck, Phleger & Harrison
Cooley Godward
Fenwick & West
Wilson Sonsini Goodrich & Rosati

EMPLOYMENT CONTACT

Ms. Leslie Colvin
Director of Recruitment (Northern region)
(650) 833-2133
lcolvin@graycary.com

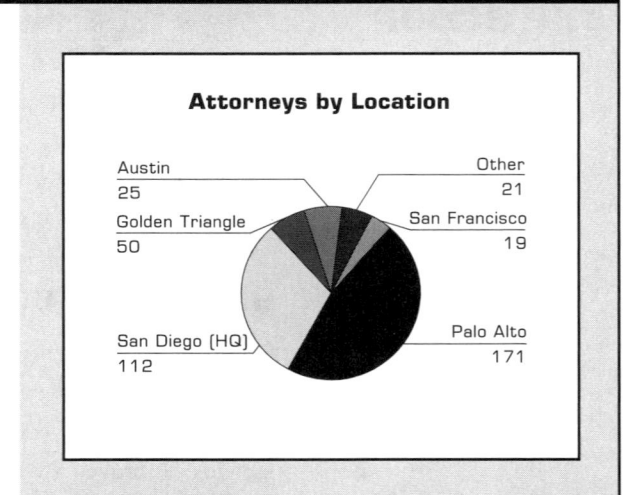

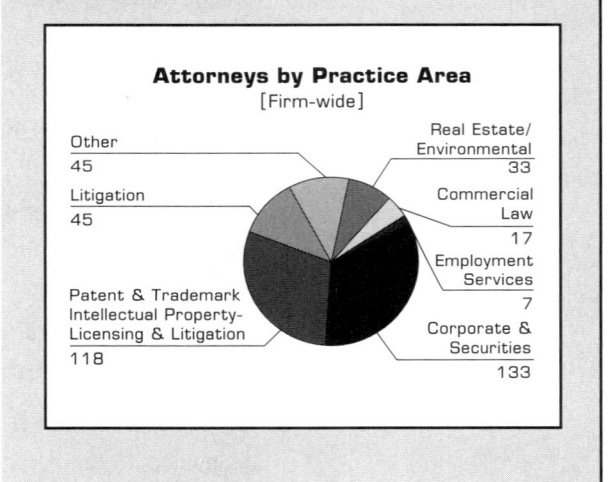

Attorneys by Location

- Austin: 25
- Golden Triangle: 50
- San Diego (HQ): 112
- Palo Alto: 171
- San Francisco: 19
- Other: 21

Attorneys by Practice Area [Firm-wide]

- Other: 45
- Litigation: 45
- Patent & Trademark Intellectual Property- Licensing & Litigation: 118
- Real Estate/Environmental: 33
- Commercial Law: 17
- Employment Services: 7
- Corporate & Securities: 133

QUALITY OF LIFE RANKINGS [ASSOCIATES RATE THEIR OWN FIRM]

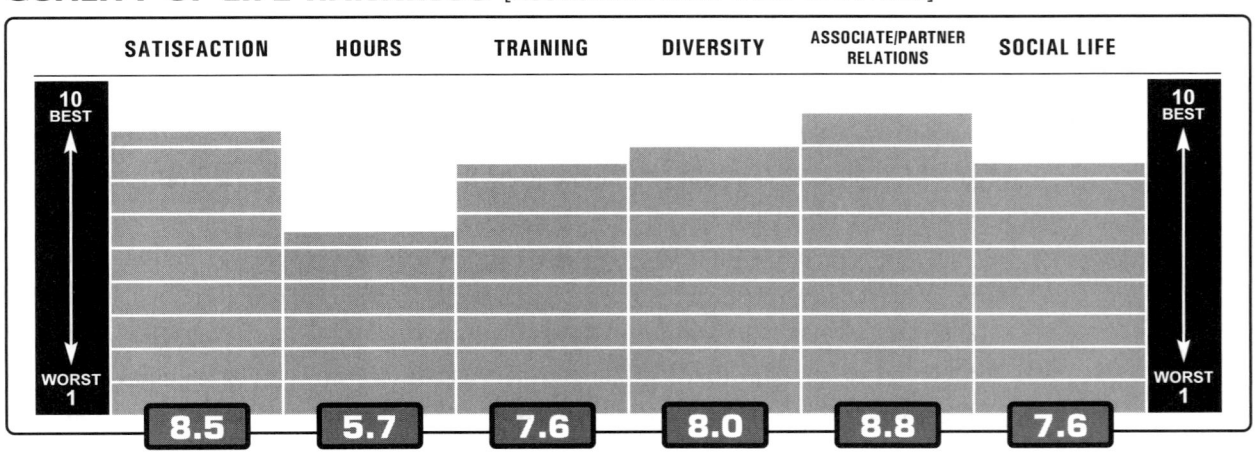

SATISFACTION	HOURS	TRAINING	DIVERSITY	ASSOCIATE/PARTNER RELATIONS	SOCIAL LIFE
8.5	5.7	7.6	8.0	8.8	7.6

THE SCOOP

Gray Cary Ware & Freidenrich is headquartered in Palo Alto, holy ground for tech-oriented law firms. Gray Cary's recent aggressive growth has made this firm impossible to ignore — it's put down roots in both Northern and Southern California. Is an East Coast expansion in the future of this up-and-coming firm?

History: San Diego (and Silicon Valley) diary

Gray, Cary, Ames & Frye opened its doors in San Diego in 1927. In 1993 the firm was already San Diego's largest law firm (168 lawyers) when the decision was made to merge with Silicon Valley-based Ware & Freidenrich, a 24-year-old firm with 108 lawyers. It proved a wise business decision, as tech deals continue to stream in from Silicon Valley.

The superheated high tech market in Silicon Valley induced Gray Cary to build out that location. The Palo Alto and San Francisco offices have over 200 lawyers with the San Diego and Golden Triangle offices lagging behind at approximately 145 lawyers. In addition, the firm has expanded to other tech hot spots. In January 1998, the firm followed the large Silicon Valley firms to Austin, opening its first office outside of California. The firm continued its expansion in 1999 and 2000, opening offices in both Sacramento (not that Sacramento is particularly hot for tech) and Seattle.

Dot com culture and cases

Gray Cary has been fighting tooth and nail with Silicon Valley law firms and other contenders to carve out a niche for itself in the high tech market. Gray Cary was one of the first firms in the country to match fellow California firm Gunderson Dettmer's 2000 associate pay raise. Proactive Gray Cary has offered its associates the option of business casual dress since 1993. Associates enjoy the excitement of dot com work in San Diego as well as the Valley and Austin; in 1998 14 of 22 IPOs the firm handled were in San Diego.

Gray Cary took part in two high profile IPOs in May 1999, advising LAUNCH Media, Inc. in an offering valued at $74.8 million and representing Extreme Networks, Inc. in a $137 million IPO. In 1998 the firm represented AtWeb, Inc. in a merger with Netscape Communications Corporation which was valued at $204.3 million and assisted Network Associates, an enterprise network security and mangement solutions supplier, in a $130 million acquisition of CyberMedia. In November 1999, Gray Cary served as counsel to Zhone Technologies in connection with its $500 million equity financing, perhaps the largest financing ever for a communications equipment startup.

Ageless lawsuit

In a somewhat unusual case, Gray Cary engaged in a high-stakes legal battle with babyfaced guru, New Age author, spiritualist, and San Diego resident Deepak Chopra. After Gray Cary attorneys represented a client in a sexual harassment case against Chopra, the bestselling author of *How to Know God* and *Ageless Body, Timeless Mind* accused the firm of attempting to blackmail him for $1 million. All claims against the firm, with the exception of an invasion of privacy charge, were thrown out of court.

Big and getting bigger

Gray Cary has been expanding aggressively since its merger. Since mid-1996, the firm has grown from 235 attorneys to over 390 and gone from two offices to eight. Gray Cary has also increased the number of attorneys that make partner. In 1998 only nine associates were promoted, while in 1999 12 reached the position. The firm has also reported astounding growth in revenue. In 1999 the firm took in $140 million, an increase of 27 percent from the previous year.

GETTING HIRED

Increasingly selective

Tech sells in the hiring world. When asked about Gray Cary's hiring practices, associates note, "This firm is growing fast and becoming a first-tier entity. Its hiring is becoming increasingly more selective." The firm pays a great deal of attention to academics, but other factors are also important. Reports an insider: "Law school performance is important, but equally important is being well-rounded and sociable. Also, grades and school reputation aren't as important for laterals."

Nontraditional lawyers: enter here

One contact elaborates, "Gray Cary really cares about the caliber of people who work for the firm, so the hiring process is geared at determining whether the prospective associate would be a good fit with the other people who work here." Insiders reveal that the formula for getting hired by Gray Cary is merely "excellent grades and a personable demeanor." Another associate is pleased with the diversity of her co-lawyers, praising Gray Cary's "highly talented but unusually offbeat and eclectic mix. I think that reputation is recognized in the Valley, and consequently we may be a self-selecting group." "The firm is much more open than others to the non-traditional candidate," announces a Palo Alto associate.

The invisible hand of the legal market

An insider points out that since the firm has become more prominent, the demand for talented attorneys is currently much larger than the supply. "While the firm tries to be selective, the job market is so tight, I get the sense that it's hard to be as selective as you'd like to be." Another attorney notes, "some practice groups are more selective than others. For instance, if you're a strong candidate, especially in the area of IP, it's probably very easy to be hired. Corporate finance is a bit more competitive." The firm recruits separately for its San Diego and Silicon Valley offices, but representatives from both offices recruit at major colleges throughout California, as well as other top-tier schools.

OUR SURVEY SAYS

Give me money

Gray Cary was among the first large California firms to meet the pay raises initiated by Gunderson Dettmer. Associates at the firm are, understandably, pretty content with their wages. A San Diego associate raves: "Salaries have recently become on par with the highest-paying firms in the nation, with the added bonus that you get to live and work in San Diego, perhaps the best place to live in the U.S." Even non-San Diego fans have a reason to check out Gray Cary. Another associate agrees that "the pay is excellent, especially if you are living in a city with a lower cost of living, such as Sacramento, Austin, or San Diego."

A Silicon Valley attorney notes that "associates also have opportunities, both individually and through the firm's investment partnerships, to take equity in companies during private rounds of financing. Similarly, they frequently receive directed shares when they work on IPOs. The current market seems to require that corporate firms make both types of opportunities available to their associates." One associate is so happy, he even admits that he and his fellow associates are "ridiculously overpaid. I feel guilty all the time. The firm is losing money on its first-, second-, and third-year associates." Many insiders applaud the "bonus structure — it's great. It recognizes the big billers (up to 40K for billing) and also recognizes other contributions to the firm (up to 10K)." Moreover, an associate reports, "the salary is at the top of the market, but the real work requirements are not." According to another insider, "the bonus is largely based on hours. I'd rather work less and have a smaller bonus and I feel that I can do that here." Why not, when you're making a top salary? But there are shortcomings to the bonus structure, as a San Diego associate warns,

"The new bonus structure measures billed hours in 100-hour increments. Be careful you don't just miss the next increment."

Turnover differences

Retention can be a problem at Gray Cary, especially in the Silicon Valley office, where the attraction of dot com in-house positions is omnipresent and persistent. (Despite the siren song of stock and low strike prices, Gray Cary indicates that turnover overall for the firm has averaged under 15 percent over the past 10 years.) A Palo Altan defends the attrition rate, explaining, "Most attorneys leaving are going out of big firm practice altogether, not leaving to competitors." A third-year states, "The lure of the huge IPO money is still irresistible. But I've only seen lawyers in my group jump to a startup, never to a competitor." Another resident of Silicon Valley reports that while the turnover is high, "I believe it is one of the lowest for this area of the country doing this type of work."

Their firm-mates to the South, however, seem to have very little reason to leave the firm. Perhaps the weather keeps the San Diego associates satisfied. A junior associate reveals, "I have been with the firm for almost two years and only one person from my class is no longer with the firm." A fourth-year elaborates, "It seems that each month one to four lateral attorneys arrive and one to two attorneys leave. In the San Diego office, most of the attorneys who leave the firm go in-house or to cities outside of San Diego. Most do not leave our firm for other firms in San Diego."

Partners just want to be your friends

Partners at the firm attract overwhelmingly sunny feedback from associates. One source declares, "There are the notable exceptions, but on the whole, the partners are as nice as the associates." Another associate asserts, "The partners are very respectful. Even the biggest guns take time to get to know people personally and to thank you for your efforts." A senior associate reports that there is a "very low tolerance for jerky people here. I've been with a whole lot of firms, and while Gray Cary has its problems, partners are pretty nice." A wide-eyed first-year with a startlingly optimistic tone gushes that "the partners are so nice! I love these guys!"

A more temperate Gray Caryan explains that "given the number of opportunities available to associates, partners have to treat the associates well, and they know it. Some of them don't like it, but they are rather respectful nevertheless." Most agree that Gray Cary possesses "very, very few hierarchy issues. Nearly all of the partners are approachable, understanding, supportive. Lots of bantering and many true friend relationships exist between associates of all levels and partners."

A jaunty social scene

Associates at Gray Cary are satisfied with the social life at the firm. A lawyer from the San Francisco office reveals that "[there are] Wednesday socials and Friday high-end scotch-tastings; occasional ski jaunts or baseball games — it's a beautiful thing." According to a third-year, Gray Cary is "not party central, but a fair number of the lawyers in my group are actually fun people! Everyone seems to get along very well with no huge egos or political battles." Another continues, "I've been at other major law firms and I find people here are genuinely friends, especially the partners." As a senior associate explains, Gray Cary attorneys have little choice but to be social. "If folks spend 18 hours a day here, they really don't socialize with anyone else." A fourth-year disagrees slightly, claiming "this is a firm that attracts people who like to have a life outside the office, but many of us choose to spend our free time with our friends from the office. The firm also hosts a lot of parties that make it easy to get together."

Learn as you go

Associates note that there is very little formal training at the firm. However, as a lateral hire reports, the informal training is very helpful: "The mentoring I've found here at Gray Cary is truly incredible and exists on all levels. Mentoring is taken very seriously and done extremely well." A Silicon Valley-based associate with a gift for drama states, "The corporate training I get here is analogous to the kind of medical training a doctor gets when working in the emergency ward." Another Gray Cary attorney says, "We're very busy — there are lots of opportunities to learn by doing progressively more advanced work, but sometimes it can feel like trial by fire. If you're a competent, confident person, it's actually a great thing because you get to do a lot more than you might in some other firms." However, one senior associate cautions, "People don't always have enough time to give good feedback."

Hours: severe but controlled

"Who isn't working long hours?" questions an overworked Gray Caryan rhetorically. Well, some associates aren't. Most associates find the hours at Gray Cary to be reasonable. An associate remarks, "The rumors about big firm hours don't seem to apply as much here." Indeed, the average attorney at Gray Cary bills about 2,000 hours a year, with the minimum being slightly more reasonable, at 1,950 billable hours. A Silicon Valley associate reports that Gray Cary attorneys still work hard: "Hours are pretty severe, but controllable. The new centralized assignment system appears to permit a more even spreading of workloads." A fifth-year asserts, "It's very busy here — the hours come from the amount of work, not any pressure to put in face time. I do feel like I spend too much time at work, but I also feel that Gray Cary does respect your personal life." An attorney in the firm's brand new Seattle office doesn't really mind the long hours: "Again, we're very busy, but it's good, fun work. I usually take weekends off, but I tend to work 12-hour days during the week."

Good chance for partnership

Unlike some other firms, many associates find partnership to be an attainable goal at Gray Cary. In fact, an associate predicts that even merely "'competent' associates will likely make partner." One attorney reports, "They say making partner is tough, but since I have been here I have seen virtually everyone who was up make it. I can only count on one hand the people I know of who were up for partner but did not make it in the last five years."

The partnership is divided into an income level and a capital level. An insider explains the firm's partnership track: "The firm has a six-year track. Generally, making it after six years is difficult if you're in the right practice group (one with few junior partners) and impossible if you're in the wrong group (one with many junior partners). Making it after seven years is more merit based and prospects are good if you are hard-working, have outstanding judgment, and have shown the ability to develop solid client relationships — all of which Gray Cary associates have plenty of opportunities to learn along the way." One reason partnership prospects are so sunny at Gray Cary, according to a Silicon Valley-based associate, is that "the ranks of mid-levels are so thinned out from defections to dot coms." Indeed, one associate hints that the issue is not whether an associate will make partner, but rather "whether an associate can resist stock options to stay with the firm."

Womanly influence

Associates report that Gray Cary is a relatively comfortable place for women. "There are lots of women partners with power here and it is totally acceptable to work part-time and still remain on track [for partnership]," notes an insider. A Silicon Valley source asserts, "The firm has a very high percentage of women in comparison to other firms. Many, if not most, of the department chairs are women." Another associate adds, "Gray Cary is one of the best firms I've seen for women. There are lots of women in very influential positions in the firm, and the atmosphere is extremely supportive." A San Diego-based lawyer agrees: "We have had women as managing partners in the past. We have several women equity partners and income partners. My summer associate class in 1995 had more women than men." However, a female associate does not feel that the workplace is a paradise of equality: "Don't expect to make partner as a female in the litigation department. You'll have to be 10 times better than any of the males to make it."

Try, try, try for minority representation

On the subject of diversity issues with respect to minorities, a contact reports, "I think they're trying. They're definitely committed." However, success has been elusive, and the firm remains "pretty white." While an attorney notes that the "numbers could be much better," he also explains that "San Diego is sometimes a difficult place to recruit minorities." Another associate supplies, "I think the firm has really tried to create an ethnically diverse workplace. For some reason, however, our firm has not attracted a lot of minorities."

An open closet door

The firm is better with recruiting and hiring of gays and lesbians. There are, according to sources, "several openly gay partners and associates." One contact declares that "openly gay attorneys feel comfortable bringing significant others to firm social functions." One such attorney indicates that sexual preference is "not an issue at all. I feel more comfortable here than in any previous work or school environment." Another lawyer supplies, "I would say Gray Cary is not a place intolerant people would last very long. It is not so much promoted, encouraged, or made a huge issue, it is just accepted. I guess that is another great benefit of working here."

Pro bono for first-years

Associates have had mixed experiences regarding pro bono work at the firm. A second-year states, "Pro bono is probably rewarded in some way, but I've never heard the words 'pro bono' mentioned." Another reports that "Gray Cary is one of the leading providers of pro bono legal assistance through the East Palo Alto Volunteer Project," and that the "firm regularly staffs pro bono clinics and projects." Moreover, the firm makes an effort to promote pro bono activities, having established a committee which sends out regular e-mails regarding pro bono opportunities. A San Diego associate comments that "the less experienced, cheaper associates like me are definitely strongly encouraged to take at least one pro bono case each year. Additionally, I often get asked to help others with their pro bono cases, so on the whole I've ended up doing a lot for pro bono clients." However, one attorney asserts that "only certain types of pro bono work are approved for billable credit. These tend to be services offered to clients who don't really need pro bono services."

"[We are] ridiculously overpaid. I feel guilty all the time. The firm is losing money on its first-, second-, and third-year associates."

— *Gray Cary associate*

Irell & Manella LLP

VAULT.COM NEARLY & NOTABLE

1800 Avenue of the Stars
Suite 900
Los Angeles, CA 90067
(310) 277-1010
Fax: (310) 203-7199
www.irell.com

LOCATIONS

Century City, CA (HQ)
Los Angeles, CA
Newport Beach, CA

MAJOR DEPARTMENTS/PRACTICES

Corporate & Tax
Creditor's Rights & Insolvency
Environmental
Intellectual Property & Insolvency
Litigation, Intellectual Property Litigation & Labor
Personal Planning
Real Estate & Banking
White Collar Crime

THE STATS

No. of attorneys: 202
No. of offices: 3
Summer associate offers: 27 out of 27
(Los Angeles, 1999)
Co-Managing Partners: Morgan Chu and Kenneth R. Heitz
Hiring Partner: Bruce A. Wessel, Esq.

PAY

All Offices, 2000
1st year: $130,000
2nd year: $135,000
3rd year: $150,000
Summer associate: $2,400/week

NOTABLE PERKS

- Five weeks' salary while studying for the bar
- Paid maternity and paternity leave
- Free parking
- Fitness center
- Weekend meals
- Free sodas
- $500 decorating allowance for the office

THE BUZZ

What attorneys at other firms are saying about this firm

- "IP powerhouse"
- "Aloof, brainy nerds"
- "The West Coast Wachtell"
- "Hires only Order of the Coif"

UPPERS

- No commute downtown
- Early responsibility
- Pay not tied to billable hours

DOWNERS

- Poor formal training
- Very, very difficult to get hired
- "Geeky" culture can be a turnoff to some

KEY COMPETITORS

Gibson, Dunn & Crutcher
Latham & Watkins
Munger Tolles & Olson
O'Melveny & Myers
Wilson Sonsini Goodrich & Rosati

EMPLOYMENT CONTACT

Ms. Robyn Steele
Recruiting Administrator
(310) 277-1010
rsteele@irell.com

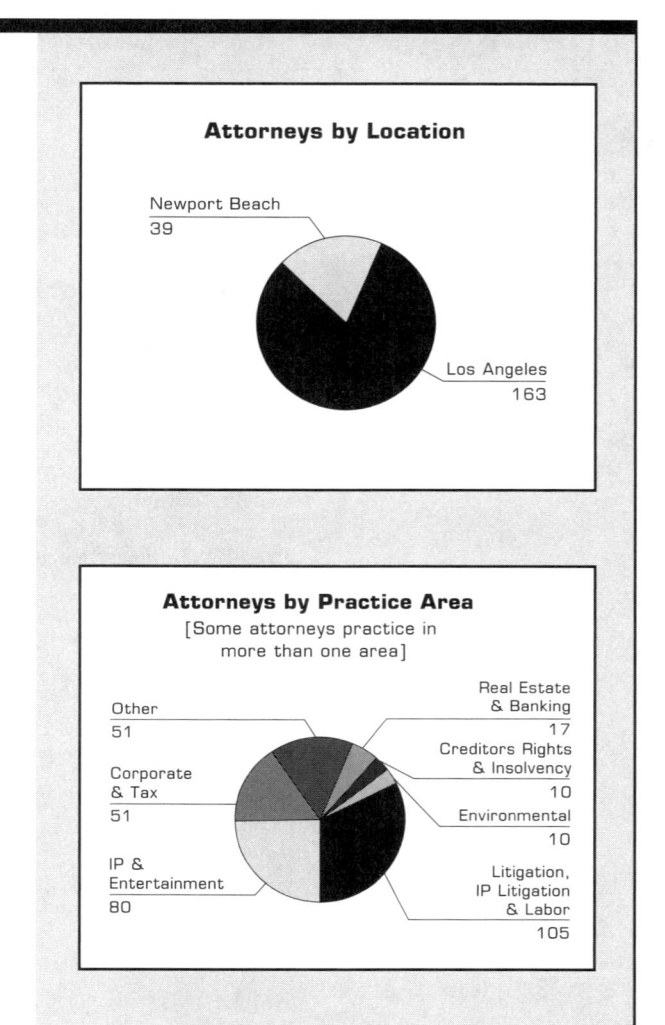

Attorneys by Location

- Newport Beach: 39
- Los Angeles: 163

Attorneys by Practice Area
[Some attorneys practice in more than one area]

- Other: 51
- Corporate & Tax: 51
- IP & Entertainment: 80
- Real Estate & Banking: 17
- Creditors Rights & Insolvency: 10
- Environmental: 10
- Litigation, IP Litigation & Labor: 105

QUALITY OF LIFE RANKINGS [ASSOCIATES RATE THEIR OWN FIRM]

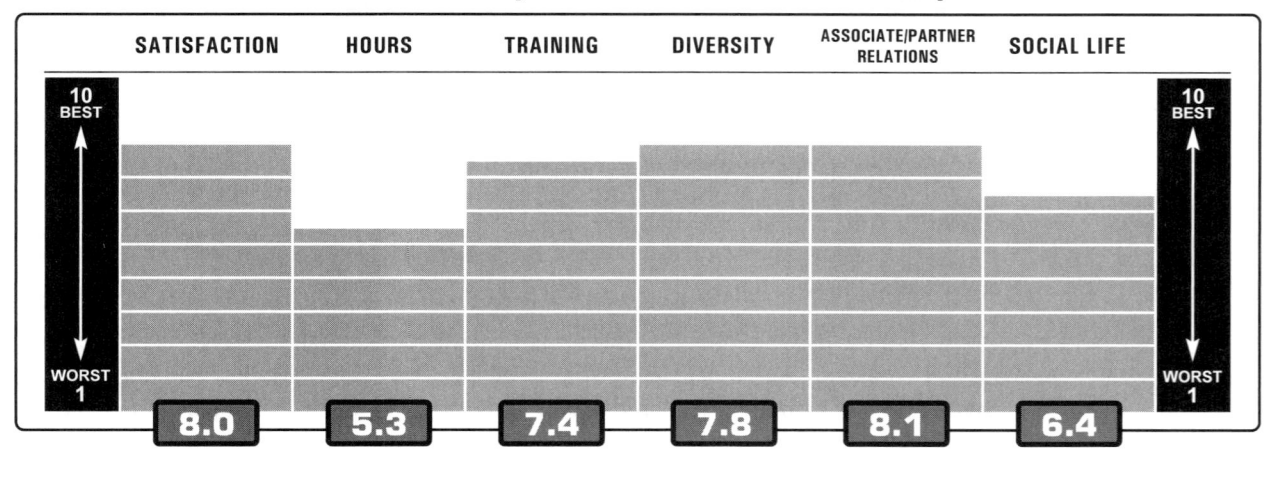

SATISFACTION	HOURS	TRAINING	DIVERSITY	ASSOCIATE/PARTNER RELATIONS	SOCIAL LIFE
8.0	5.3	7.4	7.8	8.1	6.4

THE SCOOP

It's small, it's almost impossible to get a job there, it's a great place for intellectuals (or at least intellectual property.) We're talking abou Irell & Manella, a quirky and very successful California-based firm.

A taxing history

Irell & Manella was founded as a tax boutique by Lawrence Irell and Eugene Berger in Century City, California in 1941. In 1944, Arthur Manella joined the firm and was made partner in 1945. He aggressively grew the tax practice, which early on included celebrities such as Lucille Ball, Desi Arnaz, Frank Sinatra, Dean Martin and Elizabeth Taylor.

In 1979, Irell opened its second office, in Newport Beach, California, just an hour away from the home base. Nine years later, the firm expanded into downtown Los Angeles. (That office, however, is currently being consolidated into the Century City headquarters.) Irell & Manella now has over 200 lawyers.

Learning IP the hard way

Morgan Chu and Kenneth Heitz are co-managing partners of Irell & Manella. Soon after joining the firm, Chu was thrust into a case that would change the focus of the firm. In 1977, Chu's first year with the firm, long-time Irell client Mattel approached the firm with a problem. The toy maker was involved in a patent dispute regarding hand-held video games they were producing and their intellectual property counsel had been dismissed from the case due to a conflict of interest. Irell, who had represented Mattel in their 1960 IPO, accepted the case, despite the fact that no one at the firm had any significant IP litigation experience. Chu, who holds a PhD from UCLA and an MSL from Yale in addition to a Harvard law degree, acted as lead counsel despite his inexperience. "I can remember the evening before the first day of the trial, thinking 'Gee, I don't know where I'm supposed to stand for the opening,'" Chu recalled to *California Law Business* in 1999. Despite his jitters, Chu and Mattel prevailed in a decision that was later upheld on appeal.

Chu's victory led to a new practice for Irell. Now, the firm is perhaps best known for its intellectual property work. In November 1997, Irell counseled Intel on a settlement of a patent infringement dispute with Digitial Equipment. The Irell team consisted of Chu, partners Elliot Brown and Jonathan Steinberg and associate Harry Mittleman. The firm represented publisher Matthew Bender in a copyright suit filed by West Publishing challenging Bender's use of "star pagination" which linked users of Bender's CD-ROM products to West's summaries of legal opinions. A decision for

Bender was upheld on appeal in November 1998. Representing Bender for Irell were firm superstar Chu as well as Brown, of counsel David Nimmer and associate Perry Goldberg. Another noteworthy IP client was Lucas Digital, whom Irell successfully represented in a patent dispute involving technology used in *Forrest Gump*.

Hollywood litigators

The glamour of California's TV industry has descended upon Irell & Manella — the firm has represented a slew of entertainment industry clients. These include television shows such as *Dynasty*, *Star Trek: The Next Generation*, and *L.A. Law*, as well as big-screen clients Walt Disney, Sony, and Paramount. Musicians Stevie Wonder, Smashing Pumpkins and Third Eye Blind have retained Irell as well.

The firm's most significant litigation work involves a technology company that seems pedestrian by comparison. Irell represented Stac Electronics in a patent infringement suit against computer giant Microsoft. The firm won a $120 million verdict (one that was partially offset by a $13.7 million finding against Stac) in 1994. The case was later appealed and settled for $83 million. Other clients include directors of First Interstate Bancorp, whom Irell successfully defended against shareholder suits related to the company's merger with Wells Fargo, and the Cable News Network, whom the firm represented regarding the sale of CNN programming.

Celebs come to corporate

In addition to their famous tax practice, mergers and acquisitions work has made up the core of Irell's strong corporate practice. In 1998, the firm represented Green Equity investors in their $1 billion purchase of Thrifty Corp. and United Merchandising from Pacific Enterprises. Thrifty later bought the Payless Drug Store chain, which was then snapped up by Rite Aid.

In keeping with the firm's tradition of famous clients, Irell represented Microsoft co-founder Paul Allen in his investment in America Online, Ticketmaster, Dreamworks SKG and Charter Communications. The firm assisted Charter with its $3.45 billion IPO, completed in November 1999. The Irell team consisted of partners Scott Epstein, Kevin Finch, Elliot Freier, Milton Hyman, Alvin Segel and associate Richard Kim.

Disaster reversed on appeal

The firm faced a legal battle of its own when a California state lawyers union sued to reclaim fees paid to Irell for work done on behalf of the California State Department of Transportation. The state lawyers claimed the work should have been handled by union members instead of outside counsel. The California Court of Appeal crushed the motion, claiming it was so baseless it should have been dismissed with prejudice by the trial court.

GETTING HIRED

A little too selective?

Firm associates agree that school and grades are key to landing a position at Irell. "Irell has stringent GPA requirements, and it's hard to get an interview if you're not from a top law school," says one source. According to another associate, getting into Irell is a breeze. "If you attend a top ten law school and have a GPA of 3.6 or better, then it's not difficult." What could be easier?

In fact, insiders say the firm may focus on grades too much, perhaps to their detriment. "Irell is perhaps a little too selective," says one lawyer. "Strong candidates anywhere else are routinely dinged here because of grades or a second-tier law school," says one sixth-year lawyer.

OUR SURVEY SAYS

Eclectic culture

Irell associates describe the firm as "totally diverse. You have all types of people here, jocks, devout Jews, Christians, Hindus, law review geeks, techies, whatever." Another lawyer says that at Irell, "competence and intelligence are valued above all else, promoting a meritocracy and, some might say, a rather 'law-geeky' environment." And how long do those lawyers geek out? "There is a strong sense of competence and trust in the associates — you are free to work as many or as few hours as required to turn in excellent quality work," says one litigation associate. "The firm tolerates many different types of people and lifestyles." A second-year associate claims that Irell "has more of an academic environment than other firms." "Everyone seems to feel comfortable being themselves, no matter how wacky that may be," says one associate.

The diversity of personalities may make for a interesting crowd — but not necessarily a compatible one. "Irell hires only the best and the brightest, but not the most socially adept," critiques one second-year lawyer. "The associates are uniformly pleasant to work with, but people don't barbecue together on weekends." Finally, one third-year associate offers that "the face of the firm is changing. It used to be kind of academic, even geeky. Some of the younger faces are more hip, more West L.A." Or maybe that's just him.

No great divide between partners and associates

Associates at Irell & Manella report that the partners generally treat them well. "The partnership is generally very respectful to the associates," reports one insider. Attitude is important to them. "The partners here are more comfortable with confident (not cocky) associates," says a litigation associate. "Those with fragile egos do not do so well." Of course, treatment "varies from partner to partner." One associate says that "like anywhere, there are a few bad apples who should be — and can be — avoided." In general, though, "there is no sense of a great divide between partners and associates."

No party firm

"This is not a party firm," says one litigation associate. "On the other hand, the summer associate program is an excuse for the associates to wine and dine themselves on the firm's tab. Just don't expect lots of people going out during the rest of the year." That opinion is echoed by other contacts. "We socialize greatly during lunch hours, occasionally at the firm happy hour and more rarely after hours," says one IP lawyer. "Most of us work pretty hard during the day and want to see our loved ones at night. Irell is not a party firm," that lawyer continues, echoing his colleague. "Maybe we're all geeks, but it seems to suit most people just fine. People here are warm and approachable. They just have other lives outside of the firm." For those who don't have lives outside the firm, "associate ski trips and weekend parties are common."

Hours range from mellow to insane

As at most firms, associates at Irell & Manella are expected to put in a great deal of hours, especially at deal time. "The hours range from mellow to insane, on a week-to-week basis," says one IP associate. "There is never a middle ground. Stretches of killer 80 plus hour work weeks happen, and then there are stretches of 30 hour weeks. There is not a perception that one must come in on the weekends to show one's value. No one cares about that — they do care that you get the work done."

How's 2000 been so far? Crazy. A corporate attorney reports that "the year 2000 started with a bang. We are so busy we don't know what to do with ourselves. Generally, Irell associates work hard, but it is certainly manageable." "I'm in litigation, so it's feast or famine," says one lawyer. "The nice part is that face time is looked down upon here. If you're not busy, go skiing. No one expects you to show up when you don't have to work. Trust me, you'll be here enough when you're busy." One older associate is sick of hearing the young 'uns complain. "Hour claims are exaggerated by younger associates. We average a couple hundred less than some of the other big firms," growls the curmudgeonly veteran.

Still, the workload, an issue at all firms, can be especially tricky at Irell — partially due to the firm's elitism and ambition. "The firm often takes on complex matters that are of great urgency to the clients, and the attorneys here are the sort of people who want to win," says a litigation associate. "The resulting pressure and stress can be difficult at times."

L.A. pay

According to one contact, "Irell provides lockstep compensation for all associates, regardless of hours billed." That means associates "don't have to forgo that vacation in December if we are 50 hours below a bonus threshold." "After their third year, associates participate in profit-sharing," says one attorney. The downside is that attorneys in those classes aren't guaranteed to be paid the same as colleagues at other firms. If the firm has a bad year, fourth-years and above are guaranteed at least $151,000-$157,000. If the firm has a good year, of course, pay can wind up much higher than industry average.

Notably, the recent pay raises didn't cause the resentment at Irell that they did at other law firms. Unlike other firms, "the partners here do not express irritation or anger at the current very large increases recently passed on to junior associates," says one first-year associate. "Irell associates weren't very concerned about the recent salary wars," says one lawyer. "Irell associates have always known that the partners would take care of them and ensure that Irell's associates are at the top of the market."

However nice it may sound, the compensation plan is not without its critics. "The associate investment pool is a pittance," says one corporate lawyer. "Associates are not permitted (except on rare occasions) to purchase directed shares in a client IPO."

Perks: better with a summer associate

Irell may be small, but it's hardly perk-free. "All after-hours meals are paid for," by Irell & Manella, says one associate. Additionally, "there is an on-site gym with weights, treadmills, exercise bikes, and televisions," says a fourth-year attorney. The real fun, however, comes in the summer. "You can go out to eat, to concerts, and to sporting events as much as you want" during the summer, according to one litigation associate. "[There's] no limit as long as a summer associate comes along." The firm "organizes periodic social events such as golf tournaments, formals, and holiday parties which are fun," says one IP lawyer. "We also have two or three all-expenses-paid weekend retreats a year at various luxury resorts. Irell regularly has the best tables at fund-raisers, which are often attended by politicians and celebrities. I sat 10 feet away from Al Gore at one dinner." Other perks include a $500 decorating allowance for offices, free parking, bar dues, and a clerkship bonus.

Training: just do it

Insiders say the firm is great for informal training but doesn't offer a lot of formal opportunities. "The firm's official motto is 'you learn by doing, so go do it,'" says one source (apologies to Nike). A first-year associate reports that "much of the training is trial-by-fire." "This place is best for those who can figure things out for themselves, although everyone is very open to answering questions and sharing information and experience." Sink or swim might be fine with some, but there are those at Irell that are critical of the practice. "With all the responsibility piled on Irell associates at an early age, there could certainly be more training," gripes a third-year associate. Another lawyer feels the firm doesn't stack up to others. "You'll get the same level of training as your peers at other firms, but at Irell, it's insufficient due to the intense early responsibility that associates are given." An IP associate reports the firm is making an effort to improve formal training opportunities. "The firm has recently been beefing up weekly meetings for the different work groups for additional training," reports that source.

Paint the office red

One associate says that at Irell, "junior associates' offices are a little small, but the furniture is nice, the computers are good, and you get a $500 decorating budget." The Century City office underwent a remodeling in the spring of 2000 and "all of the offices will be great before summertime," says a lawyer in that location. Lawyers in Century City sound like real estate agents, raving about location, location, location. "One great thing about our Century City office is its location in Century City — very convenient to some of the best places for young people to live in L.A.," gushes one associate there.

Superb support

The support staff at Irell & Manell seem to be on the ball. "Irell has an outstanding support staff and support is readily available for associates," reports one source. "You can get help 24 hours a day, seven days a week." The obligatory complaints are there. "The support staff is skilled individually, but the overall organization of the support staff is a bit haphazard," complains one lawyer. Another worries that "the firm seems to be cutting back in this area."

The well-paved road to dot com

Lawyers at Irell tell the same retention story as those at other firms. "It is my impression that we rarely lose associates to other large law firms," says one litigation attorney. "Associates who leave tend to join dot coms or boutique law practices." There are "lots of dot com defections due to the firm's high-tech IP practice," says one lawyer. "Even the litigators are getting offers to go in-house at dot coms." According to one Irell insider, "people leave because they can. Even those who are driven out find good jobs. There is a nearly 90 percent turnover among young corporate lawyers over every five-year period. Two corporate associates made partner two years ago. Other than them, none of the people who were corporate associates three or four years ago are still here." However, one associate notes that the hot market for ex-Irellians could dry up "with the recent stock market corrections."

Partnership track: stick around

Partnership decisions are usually made starting in an attorney's seventh year. According to insiders, anyone who stays around that long has an excellent shot at making partner. "I wouldn't say [it's] easy," says one lawyer, "but if you consistently do very good work, you have an excellent shot." "When you start, you are treated as a future partner, not as an asset to be depreciated over five to seven years," reports a third-year associate. The good news is that "partnership decisions appear to be based on merit, not politics." The quietly competent should note that "a book of business is not a requirement" for partnership.

Too small for diversity?

Irell associates are mixed on the firm's diversity. While most admit the firm has made a good-faith effort to recruit minorities, there are some who feel that, like at many law firms, the results haven't been there. "We really need to find a way to recruit more African-Americans and Hispanics," admits one source. Another contact concurs, saying "although we appear relatively diverse in some ethnic groups (Asian groups especially), we are very low in numbers as far as other groups (African-Americans, Indians and Hispanics.)" One lawyer ventures that because of the firm's commitment to excellence in all attorneys, there is less likely to be any "outreach" programs targeting specific groups.

The firm's efforts with respect to women are also criticized. "There are simply too few women at the firm, which makes mentoring difficult, if not impossible," says one contact. "Although I do not think the atmosphere is unwelcoming toward women, for some reason the numbers here are low." One insider reports that "there are strong women partners here, even a part-time partner. But recently part-time women have not been happy here." "Irell does try to promote gender equality, but between the hours and the type of practice, it's tough to retain women," says another lawyer.

No matter what issues the firm has with other minority groups, Irell undeniably maintains a positive work environment for homosexuals. "This is a very gay-friendly place to work," says one source. "Quite a few associates and partners are openly gay, and same-sex partners are more than welcome at firm events." Insiders also point out that the firm represented gay high schools students who were banned by their school from forming a club.

Irell's eclectic style can have its drawbacks. "There is a certain lack of unity that comes with the diversity," says one contact. "It is hard to get a sense of the firm as a whole. You have to work hard to do well and sometimes it seems like nobody cares."

"A great place to work"

In general, Irell associates have few complaints about life at the firm. "I genuinely look forward to going to work in the morning, and I hope to be at Irell for a long time," gushes a third-year attorney. "The firm has an individualistic, quirky culture (check out the bow ties), and I feel very comfortable just being myself here." Another lawyer is a little less enthusiastic but no less satisfied. "I'm not fond of practicing law, but Irell is about the best place to do it." A mid-level associate doles out the following back-handed compliment. "Irell is a very good place to work, provided one is prepared to dedicate a substantial amount of one's life to work."

Attorneys at Irell rave about the "large amounts of responsibility for young associates." "Don't let other firms toss this cliché around," says one Irell lawyer. "No one in my law school class comes close to me in terms of the level of responsibility I've seen." Quality of work is also looked upon favorably. "I'm nearly always positively impressed by our work product and often shocked and disappointed by the quality of work done by many of our purported competitors," brags one source.

Jenner & Block

VAULT.COM NEARLY & NOTABLE

One IBM Plaza, Suite 3800
Chicago, Illinois 60611
(312) 222-9350
Fax: (312) 527-0484
www.jenner.com

LOCATIONS

Chicago, IL (HQ)
Lake Forest, IL
Washington, DC

MAJOR DEPARTMENTS/PRACTICES

Commercial
Corporate & Securities
Environmental
Estate Planning & Probate
Government, Health Care & Association
Insurance Coverage Litigation
Labor & Employment
Litigation
Real Estate
Tax/ERISA
Technology Law Group

THE STATS

No. of attorneys: 391
No. of offices: 3
Summer associate offers: 31 out of 41 (Chicago, 1999)
Chairman: Jerold Solovy and Theodore R. Tetzlaff
Hiring Partner: John H. Mathias, Jr.

PAY

Chicago and Washington, 2000
1st year: $125,000
Summer associate: $2,400/week

NOTABLE PERKS

- Dinner buffet (Chicago)
- Free gym (DC)
- Cocktail hour on Fridays

THE BUZZ
What attorneys at other firms are saying about this firm

- "Hard-edged street litigators"
- "Lots of morale problems"
- "Maybe the best firm in Chicago"
- "Way overrated"

UPPERS

- "Quite decent" shot at partnership
- Complex and exciting work
- Great emphasis on pro bono work

DOWNERS

- Distracting internal politics
- Occasionally repetitive and unchallenging work
- Less than pleasing bonus structure

KEY COMPETITORS

Jones, Day, Reavis & Pogue
Mayer, Brown & Platt
McDermott, Will & Emery
Sidley & Austin

EMPLOYMENT CONTACT

Ms. Linda J. Maremont
Manager of Legal Recruiting
(312) 923-2616
lmaremont@jenner.com

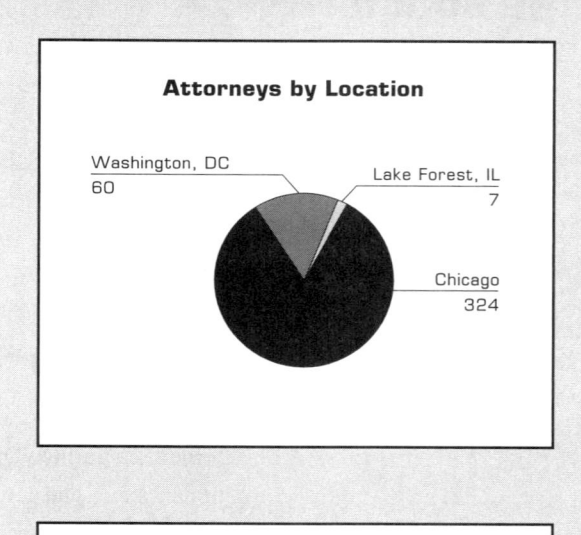

Attorneys by Location

- Washington, DC: 60
- Lake Forest, IL: 7
- Chicago: 324

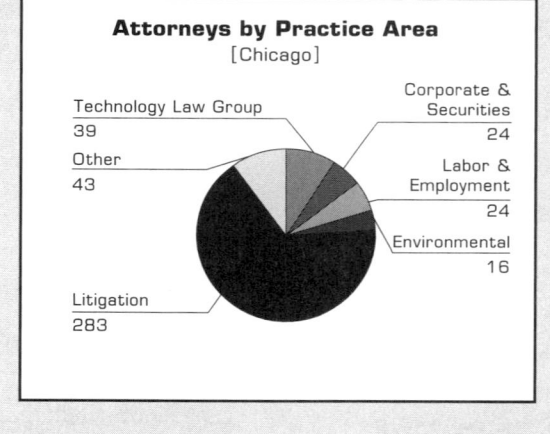

Attorneys by Practice Area
[Chicago]

- Technology Law Group: 39
- Other: 43
- Corporate & Securities: 24
- Labor & Employment: 24
- Environmental: 16
- Litigation: 283

QUALITY OF LIFE RANKINGS [ASSOCIATES RATE THEIR OWN FIRM]

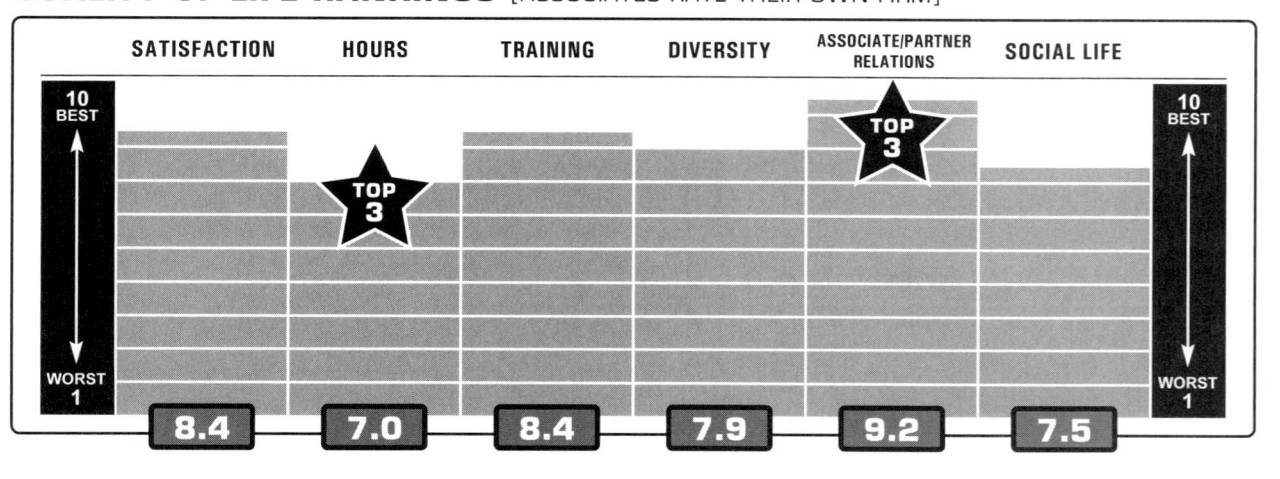

Satisfaction	Hours	Training	Diversity	Associate/Partner Relations	Social Life
8.4	7.0 (TOP 3)	8.4	7.9	9.2 (TOP 3)	7.5

(Scale: 10 Best – 1 Worst)

THE SCOOP

Those who like their litigation tough and their Internet uncensored will appreciate Jenner & Block. Since 1912 the firm has developed a reputation as one of Chicago's top firms, up for just about any challenge. Jenner even helped defeat the ill-fated (and ill-conceived) Communications Decency Act, struck down by the Supreme Court in 1997. Lifestyle firm seekers should note that Jenner is the No. 2 "Best Firm to Work For" in the 2000 Vault.com survey.

High-powered history

Jenner offers its share of high-powered attorneys, including two former United States Attorneys, a former Deputy Assistant Attorney General, and "numerous leaders of national, state, and local bar associations," according to the firm. In August 1999, Chicago litigation associate Daniel Hurtado made headlines for being sworn in as the president of the Hispanic National Bar Association. Corporations such as American Airlines, Dell Computer, General Dynamics, GE Capital, Hitachi, MCIWorldcom, Motorola, People's Energy, Sara Lee and Tenneco turn to Jenner & Block for litigation and transactional work. The firm has offices in Chicago, IL, Lake Forest, IL, and Washington, DC.

No shying away from complex litigation

Of Jenner & Block's 400 attorneys, over half are litigators and the firm, eschewing modesty, proudly recognizes itself as "one of the nation's preeminent litigation firms," capable of handling the "most complex and challenging" civil and criminal cases. A glance at some of Jenner's recent engagements shows that in fact the firm places its money where its mouth is. Jenner offers a wide variety of expertise, including complex commercial litigation, securities and antitrust matters, white-collar crime and internal investigations, and civil rights cases.

A sure indicator of Jenner's litigation capabilities is provided by the firm's ability to navigate the byzantine complexities of telecommunications law, particularly the Telecommunications Act of 1996. In March 1999, for example, Jenner litigators went before the Seventh Circuit on behalf of client MCI Telecommunications. They successfully argued that defendant Illinois Commerce Commission and its members subjected themselves to federal jurisdiction when they arranged for telephone interconnection agreements between long-distance companies and local carriers.

But the fun doesn't stop with telecom. Jenner has been retained by food purveyor Sara Lee on all matters, including class action litigation arising out of nationwide recall of food products. American Airlines turned to Jenner to defend it in airplane crash litigation. In the great state of Illinois, Commonwealth Edison chose the firm to represent it in all matters related to a series of Chicago-area power outages, and the City of Chicago retained the firm to litigate hundreds of commercial claims stemming from a major Chicago flood. The firm also offers a significant transactional practice that features practice groups such as Associations, Bankruptcy, Securities, Estate Planning & Probate, Government Contracts, Health Care, Environmental, Real Estate, Tax, and Patent & Technology law. Notably, the firm's Association practice group represents over 250 national trade associations, professional societies, and non-profit groups.

Jenner's corporate client list ranges from "multinational corporations to small family-owned business and individuals." A notable source of business has been General Dynamics. In July 1999, Jenner helped the defense giant acquire three units of GTE Corp. for $1.05 billion. Los Angeles' O'Melveny & Myers sat across the table on the deal.

Aggressive amicus

Jenner insiders regularly comment on the firm's reputation for "aggressive" and "hard-nosed" litigators. Jenner filed a "friend of the court" brief on behalf of a large group of lawyers from various firms throughout the city in support of certain positions advocated on appeal by Miriam Santos, the former city Treasurer. A three-judge panel of the 7th U.S. Circuit Court of Appeals threatened to sanction the firm for filing the brief without disclosing the fact that Jenner had previously represented Santos and her campaign in several matters. Jenner voluntarily withdrew the brief and was not sanctioned. The court ultimately ruled for Santos on various issues, including some Jenner's brief had supported.

The annals of Ennis

One of Jenner's most celebrated attorneys is Washington-based litigator Bruce J. Ennis. Once an ACLU lawyer, Ennis joined forces with his former employer to defeat the Communications Decency Act, Congress' first attempt to police the Internet. Ennis' case, *American Library Association v. United States*, worked itself all the way to the U.S. Supreme Court, requiring no less than 5,300 hours of work and $1.1 million in fees. Ennis appeared again before the Supreme Court in December 1998, this time representing MCI in connection with the 1996 Communications Act. Ennis argued against Eighth Circuit rulings striking FCC provisions beneficial to long-distance carriers and won glowing reviews from *The American Lawyer* for his performance, particularly his ability to "move the Court out of the bog of detail into some of the real-world consequences of the circuit court ruling against the FCC."

Pro bono pride

When it comes to pro bono, Jenner doesn't hesitate to declare that "no tradition is of greater pride to Jenner & Block than its commitment to providing legal assistance to those who are in critical need but unable to pay for legal services." Here again, it seems that Jenner puts its time and money where its PR organs are. For example, in 1999 the firm chalked up 51,778 hours of pro bono time, and won the "Leadership Vision Award" from Leadership Greater Chicago. This year Jenner's DC office won the DC Bar Association's large firm pro bono award. The firm's pro bono engagements range widely, from defending victims of racially motivated attacks and helping those seeking political asylum to defending indigent criminal defendants and representing homes for neglected children.

GETTING HIRED

Elite schools but no elitism

For recruiting purposes, Jenner targets the following schools: Boalt Hall, University of Chicago, Columbia, Duke, Georgetown, Harvard, Howard, Illinois, Indiana, Iowa, Loyola, Michigan, North Carolina, Northwestern, Notre Dame, Stanford, Texas, Virginia, Washington University, William & Mary, Wisconsin, and Yale. As the above list indicates, Jenner & Block sets its standards high, a proposition supported by many insiders. "The firm has always had the highest hiring standards," says an associate. "Even in this incredibly employee-friendly job market, the firm has resisted the urge to lower those standards."

Others, however, stress the importance of other factors. A litigator explains: "Jenner is very selective in its hiring decisions, but does not get caught up in law school elitism. The firm recruits top students from a variety of schools and the mix of associates' backgrounds and life experiences is quite rich." A DC source agrees, noting that "the office hires almost exclusively people who have clerked in the federal courts of appeals or the Supreme Court. My sense is that the 'for whom did you clerk' question is paramount." Note also that the firm's litigation focus will inform the hiring process. The firm even explicitly states that it looks for those with a "firm commitment to the fair administration of justice."

Rounds one and two

Jenner candidates can expect "a myriad of social events" to kick off the hiring process, including campus presentations, social dinners, and receptions. "It's a chance to chat with people," says one insider, who adds, "I've had some students give me resumes or just express their interest in the firm." A 20 minute first-round interview conducted by a partner and an associate follows these "meet the employee" events. "Usually all the people that you're seeing make our grade cutoff and other paper requirements," an associate informs Vault.com. "Thus the interview is to answer questions like 'Is this person articulate?' and 'Are they interesting?'" The firm reports that 60 percent generally make it past the first round.

For the second round, candidates will have four to five interviews, plus a lunch, typically with two associates. Again, Jenner seeks to provide a suitable mix of gender and level. Interviews will take place with a senior partner, a mid- or junior-level partner, an upper-level associate, and a mid-level associate. The lunch interview will be with first- to third-years. Jenner reassures Vault.com that it evaluates each candidate "as a whole," focusing on "performance in law school, past experience, activities, legal and non-legal skills, personality and demeanor." Thus a "candidate's opportunity is never determined solely on the basis of her or his response to questions during an on-campus interview."

Tough-as-nails questions

When asked to comment on the mood of those interviews, one insider explains: "We have all the resumes and credentials beforehand, so we've had a chance to look at a person's experiences, whether in the past or at law school, like moot court or trial practice programs. We really want to see what the person is like and how they present themselves. Sometimes the questions can be a little tough." As an example, that contact warns that candidates claiming proficiency in a certain language might be asked to have a brief conversation in the language (presumably with an equally proficient interviewer). "Sometimes we get people who refuse to do it," that contact marvels, adding, "We had that happen twice last year."

Interviewers will also want to discuss any challenging work or extracurricular experiences that an individual may have. The reason? To probe how he presents himself. Candidates who express a particular practice interest can expect to have interviews with attorneys working in the field. For example, those interested in environmental law will usually interview with three attorneys specializing in environmental work. "However," a contact explains, "even though someone may express an interest in litigation, that doesn't preclude them from interviewing with someone doing transactional work."

OUR SURVEY SAYS

Cultural openness

Associates generally enjoy working at Jenner & Block, characterizing the firm as "open and dynamic." It is a place where, according to one Chicago resident, attorneys are "very serious about the work that we do but not overly serious about themselves." One attorney reports, "The culture at Jenner is very diverse. Being a firm that is somewhat dominated by litigators, there are some big egos, but most everyone is charismatic and outgoing. This can be a fun group at a party. It is definitely not a 'white shoe' firm." Another satisfied source notes, "It's okay to be quirky and to disagree with partners" and calls the firm "a very, very comfortable place."

A large part of attorney satisfaction at Jenner is rooted in the firm's dedication to pro bono work. "The firm prides itself on its pro bono work and commitment to providing legal services to those who cannot afford it," states an attorney. "The firm seems reluctant to exchange its pro bono commitment for a more profit-driven culture, although the firm places a strong emphasis on profits and manages to pay its associates salaries that are among the highest in the city." Moreover, the same contact continues, "associates are not cut throat with one another at all." While some attorneys note that the firm does have a "slight liberal bent," be sure to note that "all views are welcome." While "standards are high, partnership is not as unattainable as it is at many other comparable firms" — also important in keeping lawyers happy.

Salary cleared up

Jenner has matched the latest round of raises, an associate notes. "We have always paid at market and I expect that to continue. The increases are retroactive to Jan. 1, 2000." The firm is making an important change in its salary structure. Senior associates salary will be discretionary, based on performance rather than lockstep, and the bonus structure has also changed. Jennerians complain about the unclear nature of the new salary structure. A DC attorney reports, "We are unsure of our actual salaries beyond the first three years and it appears that bonuses are available only for those who bill 2,200 or more hours, excluding pro bono." [The figure is actually 2,150 hours.] Another source gripes: "Apparently, associates who bill a very high number of billable hours may qualify for a significant bonus." Most are still pleased with the pay. A second-year says that "Jenner has designed a new compensation structure that rewards individual achievement and work. I never thought that I would be making so much money this early in my career."

Surprisingly good partnership prospects

For a firm of its size, Jenner offers its associates an unusually high chance of making partner. Indeed, one contact states that at Jenner, the "presumption is that you will make partner." Others reveal that "any associate who receives good reviews and meets minimum billing requirements (recently modified to 2,000 billable hours and no non-billable requirement) for the majority of his or her career will make partner." An associate with an interest in Zen notes, "The mantra is, if you do good work and bill your time, you will make partner." However, many associates see trouble ahead. "Under the new compensation system," one explains, "everything is in question. Under the former system, if you stayed for 7.5 years and you did good work, you were pretty much guaranteed to make equity partner. Now things don't seem as certain." Another insider posits, "I have to believe that the latest shake-up in the market will change this and it will become more selective." At least one associate has been able to view the decrease in partnership prospects in a favorable manner. "When I started, prospects were good. Making partner is becoming more difficult. Hopefully this will make the firm more profitable."

Partner affection

Associates in both Chicago and DC are relatively enamored of Jenner's partners. As a Windy City inhabitant asserts, "Partners treat me like a partner. They have solicited my input regarding not only substantive matters, but also firm and departmental governance issues. On a global scale, the firm holds frequent meetings of associates, both to keep associates informed of firm policy and to obtain input and reactions from the associates." Members of the firm located in DC agree. "This is perhaps the principal selling point of our office. It is very — I mean VERY — non-hierarchical. Partners and associates alike get along astonishingly well and are very respectful of each other." Another attorney elaborates, "The partners in the DC office are the best part of practicing. They are young, smart, and very good to associates." A second-year chimes in, "I am on a first-name basis with all partners that I work with. My experience has been that they give credit when it is due and when I make mistakes no one has ever yelled at me or thought any less of me. In fact, in such circumstances the partners I have worked for have taken the time to help me learn from my mistakes." A sixth-year associate is not quite as enthusiastic, noting that "in a firm with approximately 200 partners, there are certainly a few whom I try to avoid. Most of the partners, however, are decent people to work for. In particular, I have rarely encountered a partner who does not respect the fact that personal plans and obligations sometimes conflict with work."

Come together — then go home

Jennerians reveal that "various groups of lawyers frequently socialize [at] both firm-related and unrelated events." A fourth-year indicates "the laid-back atmosphere fosters interaction between attorneys from all different practice groups." A Chicago resident reports, "Social life at Jenner is terrific. The firm's Friday happy hour is well-attended. Individual practice groups often have both formal and impromptu social outings. Finally, there are lots of opportunities for associates to join in summer program events." Moreover, a former summer associate notes that "friendships made among summer associates tend to last after they join the firm full-time."

Though socializing is appreciated by many, it's not a requisite of Jenner life. "There is a no-pressure feeling with regard to social activities," a contact contributes. "There is always something to do but attorneys respect each other's private lives as well." Another source indicates that there is "not a huge amount of socializing at Jenner & Block, but some. The culture of the firm remains 'work hard and go home.'"

Decent marks for training

Jenner & Block generally receives good marks for its training. "The firm conducts in-house legal writing and NITA deposition training and pays for associates to attend outside NITA training as well," says an attorney. "In addition, the firm encourages associates to attend (and compensates reasonable expenditures related to) outside seminars related to the associate's area of practice. On top of all of this, the partners and senior associates at the firm provide extensive, informal training both on particular matters and through in-house CLE-type programs." Others note that "to the extent good training opportunities are available, the firm tries very hard to make sure associates are able to take advantage of those opportunities." An associate in Washington comments: "There is little formal training, but partners are very willing to throw associates to the wolves early on — the learning curve is fairly steep." In spite of this, the attorney notes, "I believe that both my skills and my judgment have improved significantly in the time I have been at Jenner, much of which I attribute to working closely with outstanding attorneys rather than to any formalized training program."

No sweat

"Contrary to some of the myths I have heard, Jenner is not a sweatshop. I work no harder than friends at other Chicago firms. This has been the case for the past five years," declares a senior associate. It depends how you define sweatshop. A fifth-year associate states, "Jenner doesn't attract people who are willing to work in a sweatshop and the culture of the place doesn't resemble a sweatshop, but people work very hard. This is by no means a lifestyle firm, and associates almost uniformly feel that we work too hard — and the firm just raised our billable hour requirement by another 100 hours."

The billables may pile up at Jenner but, as an associate explains, attorneys are rewarded for their time. "Although Jenner has a billable hours requirement, it has always been seen as both a 'floor' and a 'ceiling.' Thus, people who just make their billables requirement routinely make partner." A contact describes his experience at the firm: "In one and a half years at Jenner, I have only come in on the weekend twice, I have never pulled an all-nighter or stayed past 9:00. Working at home is fine. Face time is not a requirement."

Robust pro bono

Many associates are attracted to Jenner & Block by its pro bono program. Indeed, attorneys at the firm note that pro bono work is not just "strongly encouraged" but rather "expected." An associate notes, "Almost everyone does some pro bono work, including (especially) partners." Another raves, "Jenner & Block has the best pro bono program in the country without any doubt. We try lots of pro bono cases. This is a great public service and it is a great opportunity for young litigators to get real courtroom experience. If there is one thing that makes Jenner unique and special among the big firms, this is it." A lawyer in the DC office continues, "Four associates in the 60-person DC Office, for example, spent half their year on a pro bono case last year and received full bonuses and lots of encouragement."

Some attorneys wonder whether the firm's commitment to pro bono work will wane in the face of market pressures. A Chicago-based associate elaborates, "In this office, it is not unusual for lawyers to do more than 400 hours annually of pro bono, and the firm is 100 percent supportive of that effort. This may change in light of the shifting market. The firm has never required pro bono, and has never counted it in the billable hour requirement. Before the year 2000, however, the firm required 1,900 billable hours and 350 'other' hours (billable, pro bono, CLE, and so on). Because this place has attracted the type of people who love to do tons of pro bono work, most people billed exactly 1900 hours and spent the rest of their time doing pro bono work — and the firm was happy. For 2000, however, the firm has apparently raised our billables to 2,000 and abolished the 'other hours' requirement (and instituted a bonus for billing 2,150 hours). I worry about the type of people the firm will likely attract in the future. The firm's rhetoric is otherwise, but its actions indicate that given the choice between making more money and doing more good for society, they want the money."

Jenner is for women

Jenner also scores well with respect to women's issues. Associates note that Jenner "has a part-time program for both associates and partners. There are extremely favorable parental leave benefits. Both the firm and individual departments organize meaningful women's lunches for female associates, who are encouraged to engage in frank discussions about advancement issues, business development issues, and balancing issues." A female source comments, "I don't feel like gender is an issue here, at least not in my department. I don't feel like I'm treated like a 'woman lawyer,' I feel like I'm just treated like a lawyer, like everyone else." Another explains that treatment of females is "sort of a mixed bag here. The office has made efforts to increase the numbers, and the associate and summer associate ranks are increasingly populated by women. And the part-time associate/part-time partner program is exceptional, allowing people to become a part-time partner without ever having been a full-time associate. On the other hand, none of the top-level partners in DC are women and there's a general resistance (led by several female partners) to 'women-only' programs or mentoring, which is unfortunate. Overall, this office is very sensitive (in a good way) to women's issues, and perhaps it is this sensitivity that breeds whatever dissatisfaction there may exist. But generally speaking, at least among the associate ranks, there is a feeling that everything is fine."

Vague disquiet about minority recruitment

Many associates at Jenner are concerned by the firm's lack of success in recruiting minority attorneys. "We have very few minority attorneys," declares a source. "This office is overwhelmingly populated with old school liberals who appear highly aware of race issues and are deeply troubled by our lack of success in minority recruiting. I do know that the desire is universal to have more minority lawyers and nothing about the environment here seems to be detrimental to minority hiring." Many report that "Jenner has been and is committed to increasing the level of diversity in the firm, although those efforts have not to date resulted in a workplace that is as diverse as I (and the other attorneys at the firm) would prefer."

Forward-looking GLB policy

When asked about diversity issues with respect to gays and lesbians, a gay attorney reports, "Jenner implemented same-sex domestic partner benefits as part of its recruitment efforts for gay attorneys. In fact, Jenner received an award from the Illinois Human Rights Commission recognizing Jenner as a leader in its commitment to gays and lesbians. Also, several openly gay associates have worked their way to partnership. I have had no problem keeping a picture of my partner on my desk or bringing my partner to firm events. The only problem I have is the firm no longer discloses this information on its NALP form." Others add, "We have several openly gay and lesbian associates and partners and the firm is extremely welcoming. Partners are invited and expected to attend all firm events."

A satisfied crew

Overall, attorneys at the firm are very satisfied. Many characterize the firm as being "an outstanding place to work." Some still voice complaints: "We work too many hours for my taste and too much of our work in this office is for one or two key clients namely, MCI Worldcom and General Dynamics. People come here with very high expectations and are rattled by the fact that, at bottom, this is still a law firm and not a branch of the ACLU." Most, however, agree with the following associate's opinion: "I think that Jenner is a tremendous place to practice law. The people I work with are personable, dedicated, public service-oriented, highly intelligent, and above all, excellent lawyers. At this point in my career, I cannot imagine working anywhere else."

Kilpatrick Stockton LLP

1100 Peachtree Street, Suite 2800
Atlanta, GA 30309-4530
(404) 815-6500
Fax: (404) 815-6555
www.kilstock.com

LOCATIONS

Atlanta, GA • Augusta, GA • Charlotte, NC • Miami, FL • Raleigh, NC • Washington, DC • Winston-Salem, NC • Brussels • London • Stockholm

MAJOR DEPARTMENTS/PRACTICES

Bankruptcy
Business Transactions/Securities/Finance
Environmental
Employee Benefits
Financial Restructuring
Healthcare
Intellectual Property
Labor & Employment
Litigation
Real Estate
Tax
Technology

THE STATS

No. of attorneys: 470
No. of offices: 10
Summer associate offers: 45 out of 45 (Firm-wide, 1999)
Managing Partner: Tim Carssow
Hiring Attorneys: Paul V. Lalli, Richard J. Keshian, and Ben Barkley

PAY

Atlanta, Miami, and Washington, DC, 2000
1st year: $100,000 + $5,000 bonus (for 2,000 hours)
Bonus of up to 20 percent of base salary for outstanding contribution

Augusta, 2000
1st year: $75,000 + $5,000 bonus (for 2,000 hours)
Bonus of up to 20 percent of base salary for outstanding contribution

Salaries for North Carolina offices under review at time of publication

NOTABLE PERKS

- Subsidized attorney dining room
- Annual beach trip
- Weekly happy hour
- 401(k) matching

THE BUZZ
What attorneys at other firms are saying about this firm

- "Progressive and entrepreneurial"
- "Strange marriage"
- "Strong but unique"
- "Lacks an identity"

UPPERS

- Flexibility of hours, including telecommuting options
- Big-firm benefits and pay without the bureaucracy
- Lots of autonomy
- Importance of family community

DOWNERS

- Growing obsession with billable hours
- Poor supervision and feedback for associates
- Inconsistent assignment system
- Not enough mentoring

KEY COMPETITORS

Alston & Bird
Hunton & Williams
King & Spalding

EMPLOYMENT CONTACT

Mr. Jaden K. Jones
Recruiting Coordinator
(404) 815-6344
jadjones@kilstock.com

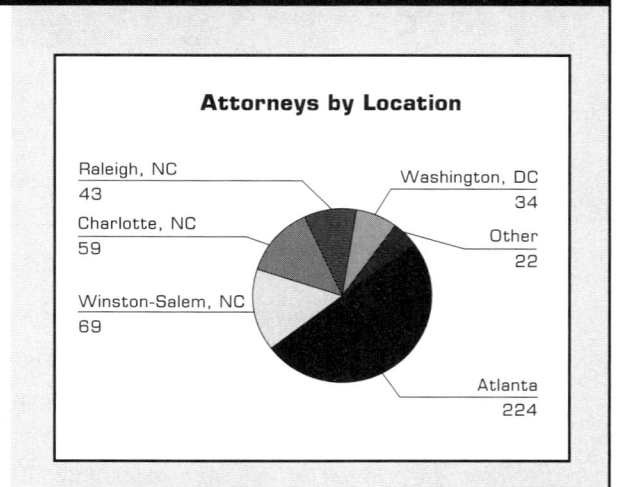

Attorneys by Location

- Raleigh, NC: 43
- Charlotte, NC: 59
- Winston-Salem, NC: 69
- Washington, DC: 34
- Other: 22
- Atlanta: 224

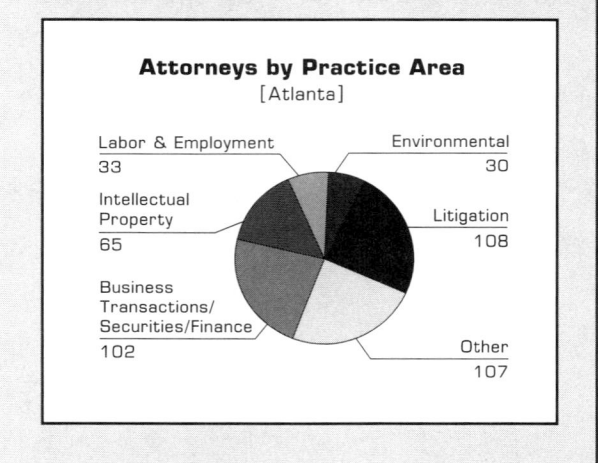

Attorneys by Practice Area [Atlanta]

- Labor & Employment: 33
- Intellectual Property: 65
- Business Transactions/Securities/Finance: 102
- Environmental: 30
- Litigation: 108
- Other: 107

QUALITY OF LIFE RANKINGS [ASSOCIATES RATE THEIR OWN FIRM]

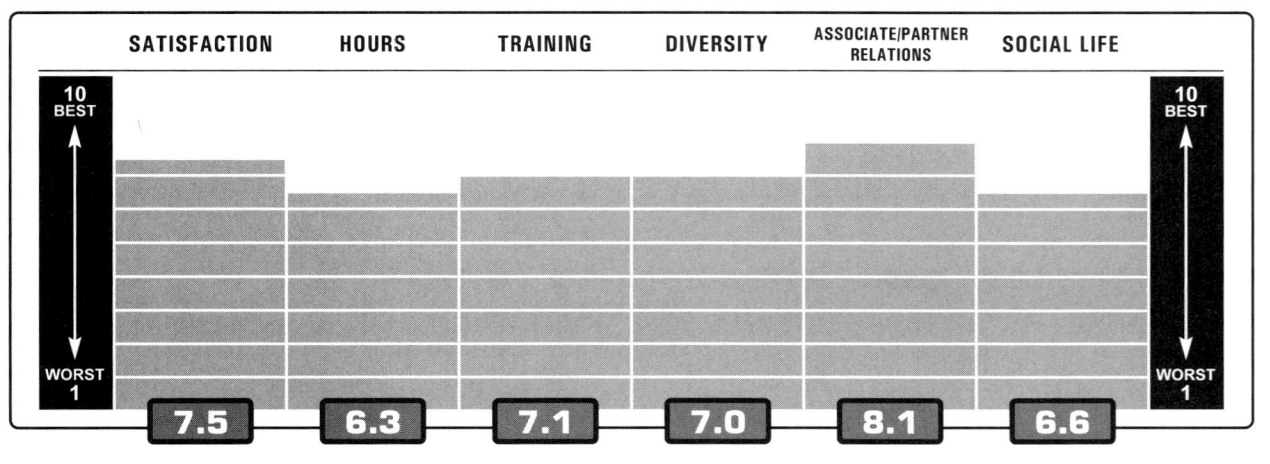

SATISFACTION	HOURS	TRAINING	DIVERSITY	ASSOCIATE/PARTNER RELATIONS	SOCIAL LIFE
7.5	6.3	7.1	7.0	8.1	6.6

THE SCOOP

The South has already risen again — at least as far as Kilpatrick Stockton is concerned. Kilpatrick is one of the Atlanta region's top law firms and hopes to build an even stronger legal reputation nationwide.

History: and the law firms said, let there be a merger

Kilpatrick Stockton LLP debuted onto the legal scene in early 1997, the result of the merger of two distinguished Southern firms. Kilpatrick & Cody was founded in Atlanta in 1874; Petree Stockton opened its doors in 1918 in Winston-Salem, North Carolina. Forty percent of Kilpatrick partners remain in the firm's three North Carolina offices, although the firm's single largest office is in Atlanta. The firm now employs over 475 lawyers in those cities as well as Augusta and Washington, DC, distinguishing it as one of the nation's 50 largest law firms. Kilpatrick has maintained an overseas presence since 1980 and currently operates offices in London, Brussels, and Stockholm.

Building a practice

Since Kilpatrick Stockton's birth, the firm has continued to grow by leaps and bounds. In July 1998, the firm catapulted onto *The American Lawyer*'s list of the country's 100 top revenue-producing law firms for the first time, generating $125 million in revenues that year. The firm has continued to trawl for outside talent as well, with reasonable success. Kilpatrick raided rival law firm Smith, Currie & Hancock for lawyers with construction expertise, luring 10 lawyers from that unfortunate firm by May 1999. The new arrivals handle disputes and litigation related to large infrastructure projects. Clients include the Massachusetts Water Resources Authority in connection with a $3.5 billion cleanup of Boston Harbor and the Carolina Hurricanes (a local hockey team) in its construction of an arena in Raleigh, North Carolina.

At the end of October 1999, the firm hired three securities attorneys, two focusing on commercial mortgage-backed securities businesses and one specializing in structured finance and servicing matters related to asset-backed securities and commercial mortgage-backed securities businesses. The addition of the three handy lawyers has proved a boon to Kilpatrick's 2000 deal volume.

Losing a 'Renaissance lawyer'

In July 1999, the whole firm mourned the passing of senior partner Harry Baxter — "Mr. Baxter" to most of the younger whippersnappers. The 83-year-old Baxter pursued a lengthy and active legal career in Atlanta. He joined the legal profession as an associate in 1941 after serving in the Army's counterintelligence division and went on to lead the Atlanta Legal Aid Society, the Georgia Board of Bar Examiners, the University of Georgia Foundation and the Judicial Qualifications Commission over the next several decades, in addition to joining the Atlanta Bar Association, the American Bar Association, the Lawyers Club of Atlanta and the Old War Horse Lawyers Club.

The talented attorney was mourned by his colleagues. One partner commented to *The American Lawyer* that Baxter "could dictate a brief in final form. He had great control of the English language." Another colleague said that if he had ever been wrongly accused of a crime in his younger days, he wouldn't have wanted anybody but Harry Baxter to represent him.

Gateway to Latin America

For the past several years, the firm has represented Central and South American companies in U.S.-related transactions, such as stock and bond offerings and other financings. U.S. clients retain Kilpatrick to handle commercial transactions and acquisitions in Latin America as well. Kilpatrick has seized the opportunity to establish itself in Miami, which has become a center for technology practice in Latin America. The firm merged with Concepcion Sexton in January 2000, naming founding partner Carlos F. Concepcion (who will continue to run the Florida branch) a Kilpatrick Stockton partner.

Kilpatrick advised Atlanta's BellSouth, a participant in a 22-member consortium purchasing cellular telephone rights in Sao Paulo for $1.8 billion. The transaction was named by Latin Finance as the syndicated loan of the year. Kilpatrick handled a similar deal in northeastern Brazil for $850 million as well as the $300 million privatization of Argentina's national mortgage bank. As of April 1999, eight to 10 of Kilpatrick's attorneys were working full-time in the Latin American practice. The firm is considering opening a Sao Paulo or Buenos Aires branch to handle its South American business.

Of homeland and football

In a suit filed against the city of Atlanta in 1997, land developer TAP Associates and Larry Kelly sought to overturn a City Council decision that denied Kelly permission to rezone a residential area as "mixed use," which would permit commercial development. Wyck Knox, Jr., the Kilpatrick attorney who represented the plaintiffs, won a January 2000 ruling that decreed city-imposed boundaries between commercial and residential development in the contested area were no longer needed to protect neighboring communities.

In a sexier deal, Kilpatrick entertainment and business lawyer Terry Aronoff represented recently retired Denver Broncos quarterback John Elway in an October 1999 investment and five-year endorsement contract with Florida's JWGenesis Financial Corp., parent company of fitness, finance and football site MVP.com. Elway serves as co-chairman of the venture. Kilpatrick also hosted the big NFL consumer-protection news conference in January 2000, where NFL executives displayed "counterfeit Super Bowl merchandise" and provided "tips for fans to distinguish between authentic and bogus items."

A Rosa by any other name

Kilpatrick partner Joseph Beck found himself in a curious position last year. In November 1999, Beck successfully defended rap group Outkast and its recording companies against a suit brought by civil rights icon Rosa Parks, who claimed Outkast had not sought her permission to use her name as the title of one of its songs on its double-platinum album *Aquemini*. At the same time, Beck was arguing that CBS had wrongfully failed to obtain authorization from Martin Luther King, Jr.'s family before selling videotapes that include a large segment of King's "I Have a Dream" speech. In one case, he sought to establish that Parks has no right to prevent her own name being used; in the other, he insisted on the King family's right to control the speeches of MLK, Jr. Although he was criticized by his opponents (and initially even by some of his colleagues) for defending Outkast in the Parks case, Beck stands by his argument that no celebrity can keep his or her name from being used in the title of a song or other work protected by the First Amendment.

Political conscience

South Carolina's affection for the flying of the Confederate flag has sparked heated discussion in the corridors of Kilpatrick Stockton. In February 2000, the firm e-mailed all of its attorneys to inform them that the annual associate's weekend would be moved from its traditional South Carolina site to Sandestin, Florida. The e-mail said the retreat locale was changed "because we, as a firm, are committed to diversity and mutual respect" and "to ensure that participation will be comfortable for all our associates and partners and recruitment guests." The firm did not join the state tourism boycott led by the NAACP, and no particular person or group at Kilpatrick had protested the planned locale of the retreat. Rather, Kilpatrick's Attorney Resources Committee made the decision based on its commitment "to creating and maintaining an environment that's comfortable for everyone involved," according to hiring partner Evelyn Coats in *The Fulton County Daily Report*.

Public service commitment

The firm has made a very firm commitment to pro bono work, encouraging all associates and partners to devote a minimum of 50 hours per year to public service work. Kilpatrick represents indigent clients through the Atlanta Volunteer Lawyers Foundation Saturday Lawyers Program and the Volunteer Lawyer's Program in North Carolina. That state's bar association recently honored the firm for "Outstanding Pro Bono Service by a Law Firm" for spending 5,730 hours in one year on pro bono efforts.

In addition to volunteer programs, each office is involved in local community programs, such as Habitat for Humanity and the Legal Aid Society's Grandparents Adoption Program in Atlanta. Attorneys have represented low-income tenants with housing disputes through various legal services offices in Charlotte, Winston-Salem, Raleigh and Augusta. Augusta lawyers plan fundraisers and sit on the board of the Ronald McDonald House. The DC office is a member of the Civil Pro Bono Panel and assist in evaluating cases and represent litigants on issues concerning prisoners' rights cases and Freedom of Information Act cases.

Despite Kilpatrick's very public commitment to pro bono service, many associates dismiss it as "lip service." Many of the transactional associates find themselves "at a loss as to how to meet the new requirement" of 50 hours per year of public service work.

GETTING HIRED

Sizzling job market

You might find yourself employed at Kilpatrick without even showing up. Since it's a "hot market," summer associates are generally "given full-time offers prior to joining the summer program," according to a corporate fifth-year. Most recruits are from "top 20 law schools, plus the University of Georgia." A fifth-year Atlanta litigator says "it's easy to get hired if you have excellent grades. If not, you should try to get an inside contact in the firm to spread your name around."

Several associates admit that while the firm doesn't "pay enough to be highly selective," Kilpatrick "tends to make offers to candidates who are looking for more than a paycheck." A first-year IP associate in DC finds that Kilpatrick's selectivity is "not necessarily in the traditional sense. Instead of relying on the traditional elitist notion of what constitutes a qualified applicant, Kilpatrick looks closely for individuals who are perfect matches."

The firm prides itself on its activities for summers, intended to lure them back permanently after graduation. The Atlanta office takes its new attorneys-in-training "up on the roof" for a welcoming house party. In North Carolina, summer associates and their mentors canoe through the lovely back country of that state. The interview process is cozy and intimate. Prospective associates interview with attorneys in the Kilpatrick office on Friday and are invited to dinner in the homes of two of the firm's lawyers on Thursday and Friday nights.

OUR SURVEY SAYS

Raise the roof

Kilpatrick's big recruiting news in 2000 was the pay hike for first-year lawyers. As of February 2000, Atlanta and DC first-year associates were pulling down $100,000, while North Carolina associates earned $85,000 and Augusta, GA newcomers netted $75,000. In addition, associates are eligible for a $5,000 bonus for producing 2,000 billable hours and for meeting "personal development plans," according to the firm. To top it off, the firm will pay another 20 percent of an associate's salary for those who "make an outstanding contribution to the firm, the profession, or the community."

Some associates still gripe that there is "no signing bonus" and that the "billing bonus is negligble." Even more frustrating to some associates is the sense that "the firm touts that it no longer has a salary scale," complains a second-year labor specialist in Atlanta. "This is just a way to pay second- and third-year lawyers the same as a new law school graduate." Also, the salary differences between offices "sometimes leads to hard feelings."

Partners are a mixed bag

Some associates say they have "always been treated as part of a team" and that firm partners "treat [associates] as professionals, with respect and an interest in assuring" each associate that he or she is a good attorney. A patent lawyer insists that even when "things get a little too bumpy," the firm management does get involved and "surprisingly enough, has taken the side of an associate over that of a partner on more than one occasion." Still, comments arise about "major caste systems;" a fifth-year hates that at "group lunches, each partner is asked to talk about his or her current work while associates are not. Similarly, associates are rarely included in client development work."

The task of becoming a partner at Kilpatrick is increasingly difficult. The partnership path recently broke into two tiers — income partners and equity partners. Would-be partners must "develop the ability to retain a strong book of business or have some other value to the firm." "Historically, chances were good as long as an associate stuck around long enough," explains a corporate fifth-year. "Now it is becoming more selective. A significant contribution to the firm's business prospects is necessary." Although the process may be an arduous one, many Kilpatrick associates declare that the "firm is clear about communicating what's expected and how an associate is proceeding towards that goal."

'This firm is preoccupied with gender equality'

There is a curious gendered phenomenon at Kilpatrick. Insiders say that while there are few part-time working mothers in the associate ranks, the partnership is loaded with them. An employment associate in Atlanta explains that in that practice group, "there are three female associates for every one male. The partners are the opposite ratio, but one of the most powerful partners in the group is a female who works a reduced-hours schedule. We have two reduced-hours partners and three reduced-hours associates."

Others paint a less rosy picture. "There is definitely a penalty for women who take time to have children — slowing them down at least a year on the partnership track," claims a mid-level associate. "It is, hands down, the most unattractive feature of the firm for me. Then again, I don't know that any firm really has a positive take on motherhood."

Minorities and gays: a long way to go

"The efforts are there" for minority recruitment at Kilpatrick, "especially with new associates," but there's "still a long way to go at the senior associate and partner levels," say insiders. While many associates sense that "the firm's decision to switch its associates' weekend from South Carolina showed particular sensitivity to these issues," they still wonder how to attract and retain minorities.

As for gays and lesbians at the firm, "the general policy seems to be 'don't ask, don't tell,'" one contact observes. "In the Southern offices, where there are some very conservative individuals," the issue is "not spoken about," leading a third-year attorney to assess the environment as "average" in its reception of homosexuals. In terms of pure practicality, the firm has "no domestic partner benefits," which, according to a first-year Atlanta associate, "hurts heterosexual cohabitants as well as gays and lesbians."

Renovated offices and scant secretarial staffing

An Atlanta associate brags that "the firm's new associate offices are much, much nicer than some that I've seen in New York City." A colleague agrees that "on the whole, the firm is nicely furnished and decorated" although "some of the associate offices have older, more scuffed furniture." A first-year in DC anticipates that "we will be moving into new office space within the next year. This should improve things significantly."

While the quality of secretaries and word processors may be "great," there just aren't enough of these fine professionals. A second-year labor associate "went for three months with decent secretarial help" in Atlanta. "The firm doesn't jump on these needs for associates."

'Not exceptionally social' but 'very warm and open'

While some associates lament what they see as a "transition to the adoption of a management that places great emphasis on efficiency and profitability," Kilpatrick Stockton has a long way to go before turning into a sweat-soaked billing factory. While most concur the firm is "conservative," few go so far as to call it "stuffy;" one insider points out that in the Raleigh tech practice, jeans are common.

As a matter of fact, most associates credit Kilpatrick with careful attention to individual needs. "After lunch I take a nap," says one associate. "That's considered my business. No one bothers me." The more family-oriented associates find Kilpatrick to be a welcoming haven as well. "A children's soccer game is just as important as a client meeting," says one Atlanta parent and associate. This attitude feeds on itself; as one associate states, "Being nice and playing nice are key to getting ahead at Kilpatrick."

"After lunch I take a nap. That's considered my business. No one bothers me."

— *Kilpatrick associate*

LeBoeuf, Lamb, Greene & MacRae, LLP

125 West 55th Street
New York, NY 10019-5389
(212) 424-8000
Fax: (212) 424-8500
www.llgm.com

LOCATIONS

New York, NY (HQ)
Albany, NY • Boston, MA • Denver, CO • Harrisburg, PA • Hartford, CT • Houston, TX • Jacksonville, FL • Los Angeles, CA • Newark, NJ • Pittsburgh, PA • Salt Lake City, UT • San Francisco, CA • Washington, DC • Almaty • Bejing • Bishkek • Brussels • Johannesburg • London • Moscow • Paris • Riyadh • Tashkent

MAJOR DEPARTMENTS/PRACTICES

Bankruptcy
Corporate
Energy/Utilities
Insurance
Intellectual Property/e-commerce
International/Project Finance
Litigation
Tax

THE STATS

No. of attorneys: 750+
No. of offices: 24
Summer associate offers: 23 out of 23 (New York, 1999)
Co-Chairmen: Peter R. O'Flinn and Steven H. Davis
Hiring attorney: John M. Aerni
Head of corporate department: Peter R. O'Flinn
Head of litigation department: Charlie C. Platt

THE BUZZ
What attorneys at other firms are saying about this firm

- "Great insurance practice, but who wants to work on insurance all the time?"
- "Quality of life firm"
- "Traditional but not stuffy"
- "Past its prime"

PAY

New York, 2000
1st year : $125,000
2nd year: $135,000
3rd year: $150,000
4th year: $170,000
5th year: $190,000
6th year: $200,000
7th year: $205,000
8th year: $210,000
Summer associate: $2,403/week

Washington, DC, 2000
1st year: $112,500 +$12,500 bonus potential
2nd year: $112,500 +$12,500 bonus potential
3rd year: $121,500 +$13,500 bonus potential
4th year: $130,500 +$14,500 bonus potential
5th year: $135,000 +$15,000 bonus potential
6th year: $144,000 +$16,000 bonus potential
7th year: $144,000 +$16,000 bonus potential
Summer associate: $2,163/week

Summer associate (Denver): $1,700/week
Summer associate (Houston): $1,635/week
Summer associate (Jacksonville): $1,150/week
Summer associate (Newark): $1,635/week
Summer associate (Pittsburgh): $1,654/week
Summer associate (Salt Lake City): $1,442/week

NOTABLE PERKS

- Gym subsidy
- Same-sex domestic partner benefits
- $2,500 relocation bonus

UPPERS

- More "livable" hours than at many competitor firms
- Flexibility in practice areas for corporate associates
- Top-shelf insurance practice

DOWNERS

- Unclear assignment structure
- Limited client base due to extreme focus on certain industries
- Lack of "sexy" clients

KEY COMPETITORS

Debevoise & Plimpton
Dewey Ballantine LLP
White & Case
Wilkie Farr & Gallagher

EMPLOYMENT CONTACT

Ms. Deborah M. Gustafson
Manager of Recruiting and Pro Bono Administration
(212) 424-8267
dgustafs@llgm.com

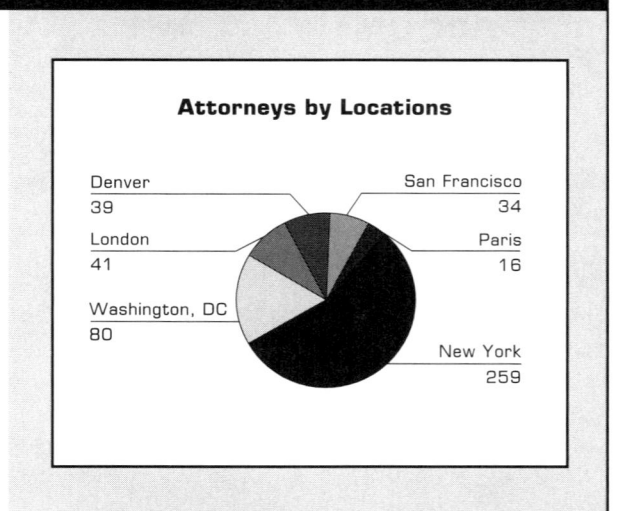

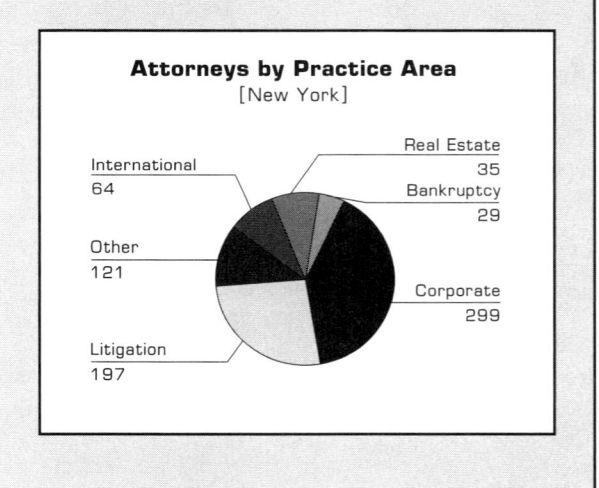

Attorneys by Locations

- Denver: 39
- London: 41
- Washington, DC: 80
- San Francisco: 34
- Paris: 16
- New York: 259

Attorneys by Practice Area [New York]

- International: 64
- Other: 121
- Litigation: 197
- Real Estate: 35
- Bankruptcy: 29
- Corporate: 299

QUALITY OF LIFE RANKINGS [ASSOCIATES RATE THEIR OWN FIRM]

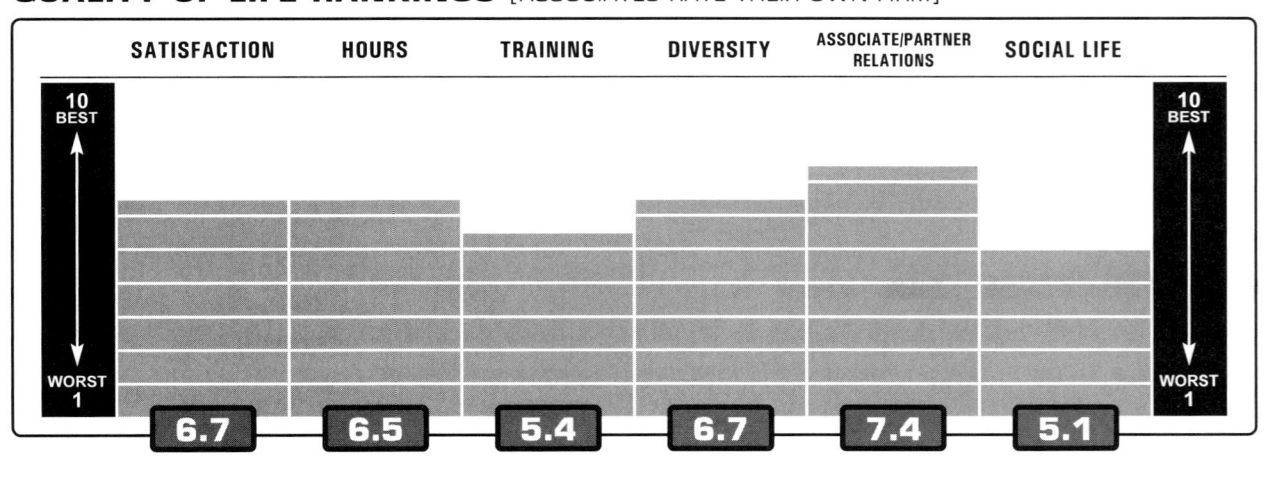

SATISFACTION	HOURS	TRAINING	DIVERSITY	ASSOCIATE/PARTNER RELATIONS	SOCIAL LIFE
6.7	6.5	5.4	6.7	7.4	5.1

THE SCOOP

You can bet on LeBoeuf — the firm has a strong background in insurance practice. To continue the bad puns, you may also find working at LeBoeuf electrifying, due to the firm's extensive work in energies and utilities. Read on to find out more about this strong niche player.

LeBoeuf's energetic history

A leading firm in the insurance and energy/utility industries, LeBoeuf, Lamb, Greene & MacRae, LLP was founded in 1929 by Randall LeBoeuf, who had been the Assistant Attorney for New York on water power matters from 1925 to 1927. Consequently, LeBoeuf has been fully engaged in energy matters from its inception; its energy practice continues to be a mainstay of the firm today. In the 1960s, LeBoeuf became one of the first top law firms to represent substantial corporate plaintiffs in antitrust litigation. The firm represented a large group of utilities in connection with the alleged price fixing of electrical equipment by the nation's turbine manufacturers. In the early 1970s, the firm established its insurance practice, which soon rose to national prominence. Today the firm boasts 14 domestic offices and 10 overseas branches, occupied by a total of 750 attorneys.

Place a bet on LeBoeuf

Today, New York-based LeBoeuf is the preeminent firm in the insurance area, with more than 150 insurance attorneys worldwide. Recently, the firm represented Lloyd's of London as its U.S. general counsel in the insurance company's settlement with its "names" (partners of the firm) as well as AXA in its purchase of Equitable Life Insurance. The firm also represented AXA in its subsequent demutualization, an area in which LeBoeuf is among the leading firms internationally.

With merger mania affecting the insurance industry, LeBoeuf has been busy in the past few years. Insurance giant Provident Companies tapped the firm in December 1998 for its $5 billion acquisition by Unum Corp. And in February 1999, LeBoeuf advised Dutch insurance giant Aegon on its $10.8 billion merger with Transamerica. That deal represented the second-largest merger in the U.S. life insurance industry at the time.

The firm says its top clients are ALCOA, Columbia Energy Group, energy peddler Enron, Lloyd's of London, U.S. Filter Corporation, and United Technologies Corporation.

Leader in energy & utilities

LeBoeuf has been a leader in energy law since its founding in 1929. With about 75 lawyers, the firm's energy & utilities practice is engaged in nearly all aspects of the operations of the electric, gas, telecommunications, and water industries. The firm has been involved in more electric and gas M&A deals than any other firm — including M&A kings Skadden and Wachtell — and is especially active in electric utility mergers. In 1998 LeBoeuf worked on the first-ever successful acquisitions of U.S. utlities by foreign purchasers, representing British utility National Grid Group plc in its $3.2 billion acquisition of Massachusetts-based New England Electric System, as well as PacifiCorp's $7.0 billion deal with Scottish Power plc. The firm remained active in energy deals in 1999, representing Dominion Resources in its $8.3 billion takeover of Consolidated Natural Gas in February, New Century Energies Company in its $7.9 billion merger with Northern States Power in March, and Florida Progress Corp. in its $8 billion deal with Carolina Power & Light in August

To further target potential clients, the firm opened an office in oil-slicked Houston, Texas in 1998. The Houston office primarily focuses on representing the energy industry although insurance and international project finance work, especially in Latin America, are fast becoming mainstays of the office as well. The firm made its first foray into southeast Asia when it opened a branch in Beijing in March 1999. LeBoeuf plans to concentrate its practice there on energy, environment and insurance, three areas managing partner James Woods believes are essential to countries still in the throes of conversion to a free market.

The other departments: it's all good

Although best known for its insurance and energy work, LeBoeuf also has active bankruptcy, corporate, litigation, real estate, tax, and trusts & estates practices. Litigation is the largest of these. The firm benefited from the absorption of boutique law firm's Werner & Kennedy's litigation, insurance and reinsurance practices in May 1999, adding three new partners and several associates from the New York- and Connecticut-based firm. The firm has captured recent attention in the legal community for occasionally taking on a client's litigation on a flat-fee basis instead of the traditional billable hours method. For instance, LeBoeuf struck a flat-fee deal with Alcoa, Inc., a Pittsburgh-based aluminum company, to handle all of its litigation.

LeBoeuf has made efforts to expand its technology practice by keeping its finger on the pulse of the industry through its San Francisco office and by opening a branch in Salt Lake City, a city that has exploded as a high tech center outside of Silicon Valley. In April 2000, however, Dorsey & Whitney LLP raided LeBoeuf's Utah office, taking Nolan Taylor and Thomas Taylor (no relation) back to its Minneapolis lair to direct the corporate markets practice. Two months earlier, final negotiations for a merger between the British firm Rakisons and the London arm of LeBoeuf fell apart, possibly as a result of the departure of Rakisons' telecom head Chris Hoyle. LeBoeuf was reported to have been looking for a telecoms and IP/IT practice at the time.

LeBoeuf has successfully taken on several recent pro bono cases. One notable case involved a team of first-year associates, supervised by a litigation partner which succeeded in winning asylum for a gay couple from Colombia.

In-house entrepreneurs

It's not particularly surprising that LeBoeuf has worked with a smallish Internet startup that vends something called "joybucks." What is unusual is that the startup was founded by two former LeBoeuf associates — who headquartered their fledgling company in LeBoeuf's New York office.

According to the *New York Law Journal*, associates Anil Aggarwal and Ray Iglesias conceived the idea for joybucks.com while working at LeBoeuf. After discussions with the firm, LeBoeuf agreed to do legal work for the startup (the bills to be deferred until the company closes a round of financing) and allowed joybucks.com to take space on the 12th floor of LeBoeuf offices. David Grimes, a partner at LeBoeuf who works with joybucks.com, told the *New York Law Journal* that he was pleased that Iglesias and Aggarwal were "living out that [Internet] dream."

GETTING HIRED

Looking for pedigree, asking for writing samples

LeBoeuf recruits from the top law schools, and it's quantitative in its approach to hiring. "The older people on the hiring committee really want grades," an insider says. "They are looking for a certain type of pedigree." The firm is also reportedly a bit more thorough than some of its competitors in doing its due diligence on candidates. Associates report that the firm always asks for a writing sample from its candidates, which a member of the hiring committee supposedly actually reads. Sources also report that LeBoeuf is very thorough and does extensive reference checks. Popular schools at the firm are NYU, Columbia, Fordham, Harvard, Yale, Georgetown, and UVA.

Know the firm's practice strengths

Interviewers often test if the applicant can differentiate LeBoeuf from other firms. (For instance, can a candidate point out that LeBoeuf does a lot of insurance and utilities work?) Rumor has it that the firm seems to prefer work experience and special interest in the industries LeBoeuf serves.

But just a grasp of insurance law won't get you in the door. At least one interviewer looks for "someone who I feel like I wouldn't mind hanging out with at three in the morning." Another contact says that the firm is not looking for the "super-aggressive, obnoxious" type, as the firm is a "gentlemanly place." Also, bear in mind that in the corporate department "many [associates] are laterals with a year or more experience obtained from work with other firms."

OUR SURVEY SAYS

The pay is terrific, but bonuses are a mystery

Most associates agree that the firm "is very focused on ensuring that associates' salaries are competitive with other NYC firms." From what associates tell us, LeBoeuf can be proud that "management has been very responsive in recent years in this regard" and is "moving to be proactively competitive, rather than just reacting as in the past." This "whole new attitude that [LeBoeuf] is really a top firm now" is "much appreciated." While LeBoeuf "is not a leader in salaries or year-end bonuses," "it does tend to follow the pack."

Recent incoming classes seem more comfortable with the salary structure than more senior associates. One such attorney points out that "those associates senior to eighth-year are subject to individual determination for salary. I currently make less than an eighth-year although I am senior, and I do not know whether the firm will increase my salary based on recent raises."

Bonuses are another story. LeBoeuf associates are not happy about the fact that "the firm is not setting bonuses until the end of the year." A second-year associate in New York complains that "last year the firm didn't handle bonuses very well. Having set forth 2,000 hours as the target all year, come bonus time you had to bill 2,100 to get more than the $5,000 per class bonus. This was especially insulting to the senior people, who, if they billed around 2,000, got the same bonus as second-years, when obviously the senior people are worth more to the firm." Another "crappy thing the firm did was overcompensate first-years relative to second-years, which angered a lot of second-years. Every class in the firm got a standard bonus of $5,000 and then the 2,100-hour amount differed by class, except for first-years, who got a standard $3,000 for working only three months!"

According to LeBoeuf, the firm paid two bonuses in 1999. One bonus, comparable to other deferred compensation bonuses at New York law firms, was paid to all New York associates regardless of hours. The range was $5,000 for the class of 1998 to $40,000 for the class of 1992. The second bonus was a boom-year bonus, and seems to be the bonus to which the dissatisfied associates refer. All New York associates in good standing who had billed under 2,100 hours received $5,000, while those billing over 2,100 hours received $5,000 through $20,000, based on seniority. Incoming associates in the class of 1999 received $3,000.

A few bad apples

By and large, LeBoeuf partners are "generally a nice bunch of people who realize that their associates are human." Most of these perceptive partners seem to "appreciate and acknowledge the hard work of the associates," assesses a corporate second-year. While the firm does have "several quirky folks," most of the "quirks are learnable and livable." That doesn't mean all is well in Partnerville. A disgruntled first-year finds that "some [partners] are too old-school and think that just because they got treated badly as a first-year in 1954 they get to do the same to you now. A little more thinking as to when to distribute assignments that have been sitting on their desks all week, like not on Friday afternoon, would go a long way." And while "seniority breeds respect to some degree," partners tend to "hoard work, and thus the senior associates get less interesting work."

Joining the exalted ranks of partners

Associates looking to climb the ranks themselves stand a better chance if they "practice in corporate or insurance, stick around long enough and are 'in' with the right people," guesses one insider. "In other departments, it is really hard to make it because of the small size." According to LeBoeuf, in 1999 two associates made partner in New York and seven made it firmwide. Sources say that "chances of partnership are declining" and that "partnership is very difficult to obtain," especially if "a woman has had children as an associate."

If you're still determined to make partner, say associates, there are a few ways to increase your odds. A senior associate gives her breakdown of the necessary steps to making partner. First of all, "work on big cases or deals with the partners who have clout," and then make sure to "work in a department that makes partners — [like] insurance — and not one that hires from outside." For example, Real Estate "hasn't made a partner in years," she says, and "ditto Trusts & Estates."

Inconsistent with women and minorities

Of course, that's not to say that women don't make it to the top. While there are "not many formal structures in place," in the words of one of the corporate corps, "women do make partner here and some are quite visible and powerful." Many "male partners mentor women as well as men." What's lacking, according to woman associates, is "any emphasis on issues that an average female associate might care about, like how to balance legal practice with children." Despite "committees galore," the firm has "no central policy on its quality-of-life type programs. Depending on the department, one could conceivably work a three-day part-time schedule and have both an office and a secretary or take the same schedule and be considered a 'contract attorney' working out of a conference room with no secretary. Not every department even offers part-time schedules."

LeBoeuf "really does get a diverse class in the door" but "retaining associates of color, for whatever reason, is a real problem." In the New York office, there is "only one black partner," counts one associate, and "no Asians that I can think of." A first-year demurs, insisting that although "the majority of lawyers are white, many ethnicities are represented."

The firm has introduced some "new initiatives" in terms of its reception of gays and lesbians at the New York office and associates know of "many gay associates and partners here." One attorney laments that there are "out" lawyers at the firm "but they have not self-identified on the NALP [National Association for Law Placement] form. I think if they did, it would go a long way in making prospective gay and lesbian attorneys more excited about the firm."

"Watch and learn"

Training at LeBoeuf is pretty much on-the-job, to the dismay of some associates and pleasure of others. "There is virtually no training here," sighs one insider. "It's catch as catch can. Some partners here are good and willing teachers, but the burden is on the associate to seek them out." The firm "has had occasional seminars on certain areas of law" and has implemented a new associate training progam. But since there is only "formal training in some departments," associates find that to "watch and learn is the best way."

Shared offices and support services

First-years at LeBoeuf share offices, but "generally you receive your own office in your second year." While the decor usually gets approval from LeBoeuf's denizens, most "wish there was a little more space," citing a "lack of adequate work-room and conference space." Even if "the offices are not beautifully appointed," shrugs a second-year, "they are comfortable and functional." And you can bring your own throw rugs.

Sharing secretaries is more problematic. "Associates share a secretary with usually one partner and another associate," explains one interviewee. A colleague complains that "the secretaries do not pay attention to junior associates" because the opinions of the sharing senior associates and partners "count more than junior-levels for review purposes." Another finds that because his secretary works for a partner, he is "clearly second fiddle." A bankruptcy first-year cautions that "there are always complaints about secretaries." However, "the firm has recently implemented a new program of assigning secretaries to only lower-level associates, removing any hierarchy issues among the assigned lawyers."

Reactions to word processing services run from "not bad" to "usually good" to "top-rate," although the information technology department "is a problem that is supposedly getting better but still isn't great." The final assessment of one associate is that "basically, LeBoeuf needs to give more support in general to younger people in sheer numbers."

Culture in transition

LeBoeuf seems to be undergoing a change from a more sedate, lifestyle-based firm to a fast-paced, top-tier player. The change has both positive and negative aspects for current insiders. So what's the beef at LeBoeuf? The culture at LeBoeuf is "confused," says a corporate first-year, "laid-back and very conservative at the same time." This description seems to sum up a firm that is "old, but getting younger quickly" as a result of a "young management" which is "more willing to take risks in terms of expanding the client base and marketing the firm." LeBoeuf is "slowly making the transition from a 'lifestyle' firm to a competitive, top-25 NYC firm," with the "clients, hours and salaries to match," according to a real estate associate. Some associates find it "incredibly political," particularly in terms of making partner. Others counter that "hard work pays off" and that the firm is a "pull-yourself-up-by-the-bootstraps kind of place."

All quiet on the social front

The social front is relatively quiet. "A lot of people just go home to the spouse and kids, which is understandable," acknowledges a second-year. "But it would be nice if more people made the effort to go out for a drink or two every now and then, especially for people's going-away parties." The firm has recently instituted bowling nights and monthly cocktail hours but it seems understood that "the lawyers at LeBoeuf have lives outside of the office. When work is done, people go home to their families and friends." For those who crave social contact, along with the previously mentioned social activities, the firm is home to a co-ed sofball team and men's and women's basketball teams.

Insurance means status — but other areas strong too

Insurance is the first thing that comes to LeBoeuf lawyers' minds when asked about the firm's reputation in the legal industry. It is "the premier insurance firm in the U.S.," declares one first-year. Another insider clarifies that LeBoeuf is "best known for its insurance and public utilities practices." LeBoeuf's "innovative rates" keep "large, established clients and their investment banks in the energy and financial services sector" and has led to "increasing international transactions capability."

While some share sentiments that LeBoeuf has a "weak general corporate department," other associates term LeBoeuf a "solid all-around firm" with "up-and-coming corporate and litigation practice areas." The stats are in LeBoeuf's favor — in 1999 LeBoeuf ranked fourth among all financial services legal advisors on M&A deals, behind only Wachtell, Sullivan & Cromwell and Skadden Arps.

Getting the assignments you want

It "may take time to develop a working relationship with a department," cautions a first-year in bankruptcy. "If a new associate is interested in a specific department, he or she should work hard to get involved with that department early on, especially if it is a specialty department such as tax or real estate." A senior associate seconds that emotion: "While the firm provides some support, it takes a self-starter to succeed here." And unfortunately, "the people who don't get work are not necessarily incompetent or have some character flaw," adds a second-year in the corporate department. "They just weren't lucky enough to get into some 'pipeline.'"

Advice for newcomers

Associates remind those considering offers at the firm that LeBoeuf "probably still has the best quality of life for attorneys of any firm its size and stature in NYC." Associates "are treated well" and it's a good place "for older people or second-career people," asserts a corporate third-year. Another positive is that "you can stand out more easily at LeBoeuf, as opposed to at billable hours-obsessed firms, by working hard at the appropriate times, showing initiative at all times and having a good attitude with all employees."

McDermott, Will & Emery

VAULT.COM NEARLY & NOTABLE

227 West Monroe Street
Chicago, Illinois 60606-5096
(312) 984-2000
Fax: (312) 984-7700
www.mwe.com

LOCATIONS

Chicago, IL (HQ)
Boston, MA
Irvine, CA
Los Angeles, CA
Miami, FL
Menlo Park, CA
New York, NY
Washington, DC
London
Moscow
Vilnius, Lithuania

MAJOR DEPARTMENTS/PRACTICES

Corporate/Real Estate
Employee Benefits
Estate Planning/Probate
Health Law
Intellectual Property
Regulation & Government Affairs
Trial
Tax

THE STATS

No. of attorneys: 834
No. of offices: 11
Summer associate offers: 52 out of 55 (Firm-wide, 1999)
Chairman: Lawrence Gerber
Hiring Partner: Jeffrey E. Stone

THE BUZZ
What attorneys at other firms are saying about this firm

- "Bigger is not always better"
- "Growing legislative practice"
- "Social climber for the first tier"
- "Unknown winner"

PAY

Chicago, Boston, Washington, 2000
1st year: $125,000
2nd year: $135,000
3rd year: $145,000
4th year: $155,000
5th year: $170,000
6th year: $175,000
Summer associate: $2,400/week

Los Angeles, Menlo Park, Irvine, 2000
1st year: $125,000
2nd year: $135,000
3rd year: $150,000
4th year: $165,000
5th year: $185,000
Summer associate: $2,400/week

New York, 2000
1st year: $125,000
2nd year: $135,000
3rd year: $150,000
4th year: $165,000
5th year: $185,000
6th year: $195,000
7th year: $205,000
Summer associate: $2,400/week

NOTABLE PERKS

- Four weeks paternity leave
- Emergency child care
- Free coffee, tea and instant oatmeal; free bagels on Friday in NY
- Monthly cocktail parties
- Attorney lunches every other Friday

UPPERS

- Manageable hours
- Opportunity to work in different areas
- Responsibility comes early for associates

DOWNERS

- Lack of firm unity
- Poor secretarial support
- "Lateral heaven"

KEY COMPETITORS

Jones, Day, Reavis & Pogue
Kirkland & Ellis
Mayer, Brown & Platt
Sidley & Austin
Skadden, Arps, Slate, Meagher & Flom

EMPLOYMENT CONTACT

Ms. Karen K. Mortell
Legal Recruiting & Development Manager
(312) 984-7784
kmortell@mwe.com

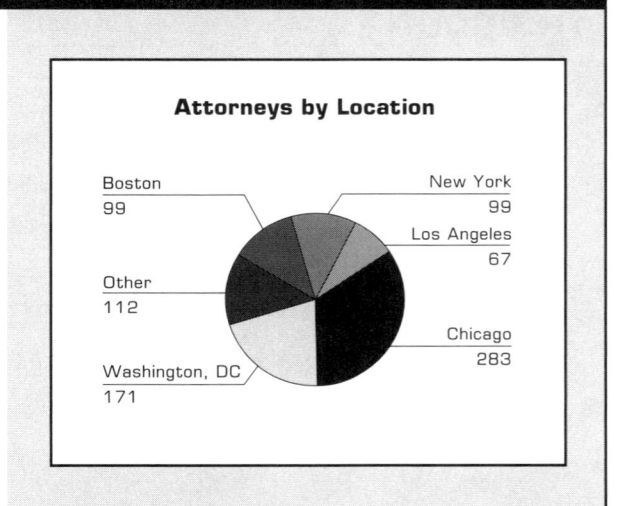

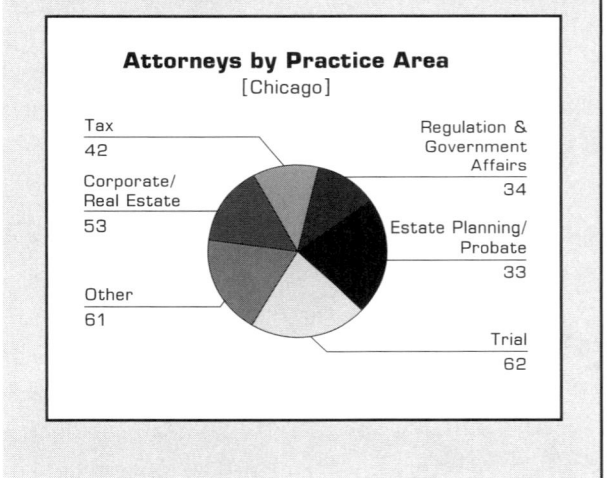

Attorneys by Location

- Boston: 99
- New York: 99
- Los Angeles: 67
- Chicago: 283
- Washington, DC: 171
- Other: 112

Attorneys by Practice Area [Chicago]

- Tax: 42
- Corporate/Real Estate: 53
- Other: 61
- Regulation & Government Affairs: 34
- Estate Planning/Probate: 33
- Trial: 62

QUALITY OF LIFE RANKINGS [ASSOCIATES RATE THEIR OWN FIRM]

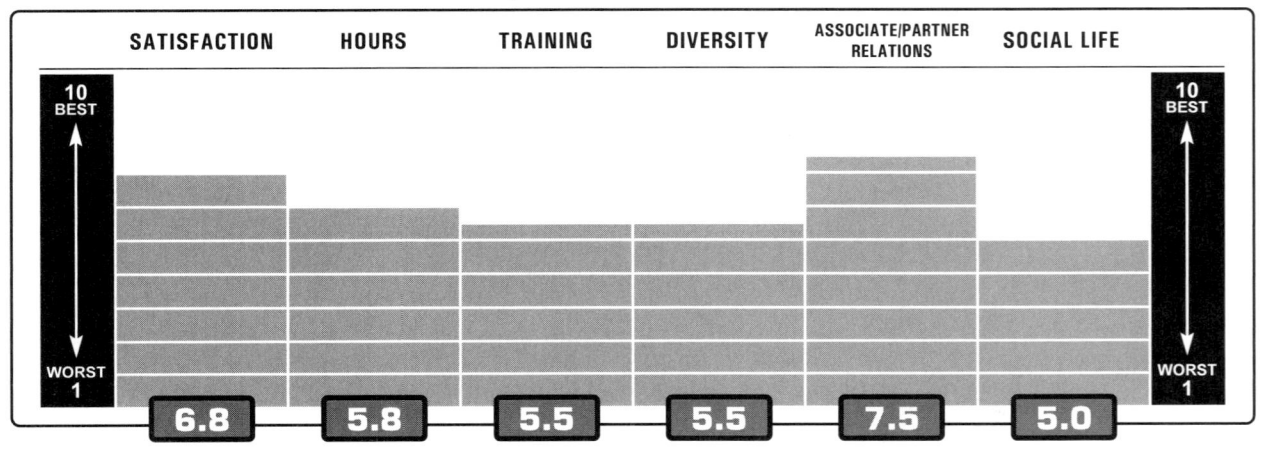

SATISFACTION	HOURS	TRAINING	DIVERSITY	ASSOCIATE/PARTNER RELATIONS	SOCIAL LIFE
6.8	5.8	5.5	5.5	7.5	5.0

THE SCOOP

The Chicago-based firm of McDermott, Will & Emery has a history dating back to its founding by E.H. McDermott in 1934, but in the 1970s, the firm really began making news. Since 1972, McDermott has tripled in size. Today, the firm is home to more than 800 lawyers worldwide.

History: growth spurts

McDermott has grown mainly through mergers with other smaller firms, mostly to bolster specific practice groups. Recent mergers have strengthened the firm's already well-established tax practice, as well as its intellectual property practice in Washington, DC. McDermott's growth efforts have also included numerous lateral hiring sprees such as absorbing Loeb & Loeb's labor practice in Los Angeles and hiring several estate planning attorneys in New York from Donovan Leisure Newton & Irvine. With so many high-profile practices, McDermott counts a few stars amidst its firmament of lawyers. Former Massachusetts governor William Weld now calls the firm home, as does former Illinois attorney general Neil Hartigan.

Large and in charge

Though associates in other branches joke about their "stealth firm" reputation, no discussion of the major players on the Chicago law scene would be complete without mentioning McDermott, Will & Emery. Through its program of mergers and lateral hires, McDermott has become the ninth-largest law firm in the country. McDermott's expansion shows no sign of slowing. From 1993 to 1998, 126 associates made income partner and 120 income partners were elected to capital partner status. Nearly half of Fortune's largest 500 companies in America are McDermott clients. The firm's financial success is commensurate with its size. McDermott ranks among the top law firms in the entire country in terms of gross revenues and profits per partner.

I see London, I see Lithuania

McDermott, Will & Emery was founded as a tax firm and still houses the nation's largest tax practice. The firm has added other areas of specialty in recent decades, such as international and health law. To better handle its thriving international law business, McDermott opened an office in Moscow in March 1997. In March 2000, the Lithuanian government chose a consortium that included legal adviser McDermott and was led by investment bank CIBC Wood Gundy, as its financial counsel on the restructuring and privatization of Lietuvos Energija (Lithuanian Energy) to non-Lithuanian speakers.

In 1998 McDermott moved into London, where the firm has established a thriving full-service office that has grown from three lawyers to 44. (It recently picked up two department heads and a senior banking partner from Simmons & Simmons.) Brits have lavished praise on the newcomer. The UK-based *Legal Business* awarded McDermott, Will & Emery second place in the magazine's "U.S. Firm of the Year" award and named William Charnley, London's partner-in-charge, to its short list for "Managing/Senior Partner of the Year."

IP in the house

McDermott has targeted growth in its intellectual property group by opening offices in Silicon Valley (both Menlo Park and San Jose), hoping to better serve its high-tech clients. The firm's clients in the industry already include National Semiconductor Corporation, Pioneer-Standard Electronics and Analog Devices, and Micro Unity. However, the fate of the San Jose office is in doubt as a result of an exodus of partners. In March 2000, San Jose-based Brian Hickman, Christopher Palermo and Edward Becker left McDermott to return to their IP boutique roots in that city, opening a new firm in their names (along with Bobby Truong). They were joined by three associates, leaving McDermott's office with just two remaining associates. According to David Slaby, MWE's managing partner in San Jose and Menlo Park, the firm hasn't decided whether to maintain a San Jose presence. He told *California Law* that "it depends on whether we can find additional appropriate people and space."

Growth at McDermott's Boston branch has helped to balance out San Jose's loss, though. A group of lawyers from the IP boutique Lappin & Kusmer LLP joined McDermott's office in February 2000. Intellectual property is, of course, just one specialty of the firm's litigation department. With more than 300 lawyers located around the country, litigation stands out as McDermott's largest practice group, covering areas as varied as environmental law, product liability, and occupational safety and health.

Healthy McDermott

Health law is, aside from tax, McDermott's best-known and most widely respected practice. It is also among the largest health law practices in the country, with more than 100 McDermott lawyers. McDermott health law attorneys serve in a range of functions, such as insuring compliance with government regulations, finding new revenue sources, and preparing employee compensation and benefit plans. Health law subpractices include managed care, product regulation, physician practice management, health product regulation groups, mergers and acquisitions, reimbursement, tax exemption, sub-acute/long-term care, information systems, and captive insurance.

Litigation and corporate catching up?

McDermott's strong tax, healthcare and IP practices have in the past overshadowed its litigation and corporate work. Although several associates in McDermott's various offices lament that the firm does "mediocre litigation and corporate work," others insist that "MWE is thought to be in a 'building phase.'"

Regardless, McDermott has handled some interesting cases. On the litigation side, McDermott's litigation practice grabbed headlines in December 1999, when it helped to clear Castle Rock Entertainment's name in a Florida copyright infringement case. University of Miami student Karen Herzog alleged that John Sayles, author of the movie "Lone Star," had gained access to her copyrighted screenplay, "Concealed," without her permission and had based its movie script on it. The federal appeals court upheld a lower court ruling that there was insufficient evidence that Sayles gained such access or that the works were substantially similar.

The corporate department has picked up some high-profile deals lately as well. Dutch publishing firm Verenigde Nederlandse Uitgeversbedrijven NV announced in August 1999 that it would purchase McDermott's client Nielsen Media Research Inc. (responsible for the Nielsen book, the compilation of program ratings that make or break television programs) for $2.5 billion. The firm is representing Whittman-Hart, Inc. in its $5.9 billion (in stock) acquisition of USWeb/CKS Inc. to create the largest Internet professional services firm in the world, announced in December 1999.

Attempts to be progressive

McDermott has a proud history of progressive policies for women. It was the first firm in the city to elect a woman to partnership (back in the June Cleaver days of 1957) and since then has maintained a "woman-friendly atmosphere." Today, women constitute about 30 percent of the firm's lawyers and almost half of its associates. In line with its commitment to diversity, McDermott offers family-friendly policies such as reduced time commitment arrangements to lawyers with at least two years of service at the firm.

At least one woman chose McDermott because she felt "the firm has an excellent reputation for hiring and promoting women" and felt "that gender equality was an important goal for a firm."

But other insiders are less impressed with the day-to-day situation of women at McDermott, especially working mothers (whom one Boston associate suggests the "firm seems to view as kin to aliens"). "Very few women become capital partners," argues a DC associate. "They are punished for having families, and the firm is not responsive to alternatives such as telecommuting and part-time employment." A Chicago comrade agrees and thinks that it's "not as much because we 'don't get it' as because we're choosing other priorities. There are extremely knowledgeable and obsessively hardworking women who spend very long days at the office, even though it's absolutely clear that they'll reach retirement without becoming capital partners."

Hope is on the horizon. "The firm has recently increased its maternity benefits, and signs seem to suggest that women can and will make equity partners in the future," asserts a fourth-year New York litigator. "Some of the slowness is simply a pipeline issue. There are a number of women who are getting closer to the time that equity partnership decisions are made, and only time will tell whether they make it or not."

Pro bono deemphasized

McDermott has a shaky history of encouraging the pursuit of pro bono work. The firm has consistently failed to meet the minimum requested by the ABA's Law Firm Pro Bono Challenge, a mere three percent of billable hours. However, the firm seems to recognize the situation and is taking steps to increase pro bono billing. In one notable pro bono case, McDermott took on the cause of Vietnam vet George Skypeck, whose poem titled "Soldier" was published in a calendar commemorating the war without his permission. As a token of his thanks, Skypeck gave each member of his litigation team an autographed lithograph of "Soldier," which now hang in McDermott offices.

In addition, MTE helped an elderly couple whose life insurance policy was cancelled due to their failure to pay premiums — except that they had been paying, for twenty years. A former insurance agent had been coming to their house and collecting the premiums — and putting them straight into his own pocket. After McDermott's intervention, the insurance company agreed to reinstate the couple's policy.

Still, when asked about the firm's commitment to public service work, more than one associate responds by asking, "What pro bono?" With a few exceptions, scoffs a NYC litigator, "the firm wouldn't know a pro bono matter if it bit them in the ass." The problem is that "pro bono counts towards billing, but is not given the same weight as regular billables. Therefore, while you're not prohibited from doing it, there's no great push towards it either." A corporate colleague admits that he doesn't "know anyone who is working on any pro bono projects." The unspoken message is clear: "Although the firm professes its commitment to pro bono," suggests a Boston associate, "the culture views the work as second-class work. The is especially true when people are busy with paying clients."

McDermott specialization

McDermott is, by any standards, a large organization. The firm tries to increase its operating efficiency by divvying up its lawyers into specialized practice groups, a management technique the firm has followed for 65 years. McDermott Chairman

Lawrence Gerber told the *Illinois Legal Times* that the firm maintains dedicated practice groups, which "build knowledge and experience that gives them a competitive advantage." The firm is divided into national departments, most of which (tax, litigation, corporate, and so on) focus on a practice. The other, health law, zeroes in on the health care industry. Each department contains several small subpractices, "which cross office lines and may cross departments." Gerber claims that lawyers prefer the tight, semi-independent practices at McDermott, as opposed to the more general departments of other firms.

GETTING HIRED

Academic performance not the sole factor

Like every other law firm in this book, McDermott "looks for people who have performed well academically." But its lawyers emphasize that "the great thing about McDermott is that it is not solely your grades that matter, although top ten percent [of your law school class] is expected." What really matters is "the prospective candidate's personality and their fit within the overall culture of the firm," stumps a New York corporate associate. "Positive, upbeat, can-do attitudes will go far!"

Some insiders wonder if McDermott's standards are high enough. "McDermott has only recently decided (in New York, at least) to go after students at the top schools. This summer's class looks to be more competitive (with respect to schools represented, not personalities) than previous classes," confides a fourth-year New Yorker. A blunt shot comes from Chicago: "Beggars can't be choosers."

Serious process, casual interviews

McDermott employs the standard screening interview ("20 minutes on campus"), followed by callback interviews at a nearby McDermott office. These interviews vary in number "depending on the department, though there are a minimum of three interviews." Both partners and associates interview candidates. Prospective "summer associates interview with people on the recruitment committee and often others." Lateral candidates interview solely within their intended department and must undergo "a longer process," interviewing with many more people, up to "everyone in the department." The "recruitment process is taken seriously, but it is fairly casual." "No one is grilled," says a former interviewee. In fact, there are reports of "several very fun interviews" in which candidates are asked about "enjoyable things — books, music, and how [they] liked law school." Of course, didn't everyone love law school?

OUR SURVEY SAYS

Mirror, mirror on the wall, what's the bonus after all?

McDermott "matched the market rate within two weeks" of the salary competitions of 2000, and nearly every associate received a bonus in 1999, ranging from $3,000 to $30,000. Nonetheless, McDermott seemingly seethes with malcontents, mainly due to the "extremely subjective" nature of the bonus system, which makes it "impossible to predict what your bonus will be." The firm "would not commit to a fixed bonus amount," snarls a New York litigator. "Instead, the firm advertises that associates can expect a bonus range of roughly zero to 22 percent of their base salaries." The "current party line" in Chicago "is that you need to bill 2,000 hours to keep your job, but you don't get a bonus until you bill 2,250." With "no nice grids like other firms," it is "difficult to assess whether the firm is competitive until after the fact." Another Chicago caveat: "Early classes are paid consistently with our competitor large law firms, but the compression is such that after the third year, our associates make less than peers at other firms in Chicago."

Turn, turn, turn

"Lately the corporate department in this place has been like a revolving door," complains a New York first-year. Although the level of exodus seems to vary by department — in Boston, "the turnover in litigation is virtually non-existent" — the refrain sounds the same. "McDermott, Will & Emery has no interest in retaining associates," accuses a Chicago lawyer. "McDermott uses them for a few years and then replaces them with laterals at the income partner level." A DC litigator estimates that the firm "has lost 50 percent of its associates in the span of a year. People do not feel that they are valued — in fact, the firm makes it clear that they are easily replaced." While perhaps "McDermott's turnover is similar to that at other law firms," associates are concerned. An Orange County litigator explains that "people have left this office complaining of the way they were treated. This is the weak link that hurts everything here. It needs fixing."

Frustration with partners

Some associate frustration stems from partners who "seem ready to exact their pound of flesh from the associates ever since the increase in associate salaries," according to a Chicago trust and estates lawyers. "Although there are some fantastic partners who take the time to work with associates, the overwhelming majority view associates as a necessary evil — a way to get their work done," assesses a corporate third-year in New York. A colleague expresses more bitterness: "McDermott long ago adopted a 'noasshole' rule in its recruitment of lateral partners. New York has been a stunning failure in implementing that rule. The most striking example of this is that partners seem to feel absolutely no collegiality with the associates, which shows up in silly rules, condescending lectures about professional behavior and, more troubling, an unwillingness to treat associates as full-fledged, albeit less-experienced, members of the same team."

A Chicago bankruptcy attorney has no patience for such assertions. "I don't know of any large firm where a third-year associate is treated with great respect. Respect for what? Your three long years of experience? The most important thing is that the partners at McDermott treat associates like adults. If you are continuing to get assignments at McDermott, then you are doing good work. The partners are real people and not unapproachable. They recognize that everyone has a life and that the firm is NOT your life."

An Orange County litigator offers some advice, suggesting that "the problems I have seen could be easily remedied by training partners, especially from the moment they make income partner, on how to treat others to maximize their performance and job satisfaction."

Two-step partnership process

McDermott's partnership has two tiers, equity and non-equity (also called income). Most insiders agree that "the prospects are good for an associate to make income partner (in practice for at least five and a half years, with the firm at least two years)," but that making "capital partner is a lot tougher." "You are not eligible until you've been an income partner for four years," according to a sixth-year Miami litigator. The process may be a little longer these days, though. "Promotion to non-equity partner was, until recently, considered a fait accompli when you completed your fifth year," explains an associate of said year in New York. "Recently, however, the firm has pushed back the consideration date by a year." On the positive side, "if you are willing to stop at the income partner level, there does not seem to be an up-or-out mentality," a sixth-year Chicago associate comments. "Income partners seem to be able to stay as long as they want."

What's the magic password to the upper echelon? To make equity partner, "it's not clear that you have anything to do with it. A lot is luck, and a lot is politics." Besides following the mantra of "bill, bill, bill and rain, rain, rain," you might want to try a DC sixth-year's three-step program. "(1) Work 2,200+ billable hours; (2) Establish yourself as an expert in some important area — whether you're an expert on some section of a statute or regulation, or can churn out a great brief in 24 hours, or can always be counted on to take a great deposition; and (3) be visible. Be nice. Talk to people. Play golf and tennis. Have a social and charming spouse who will come to the occasional firm event." A New York colleague emphasizes that "McDermott is an 'eat what you kill' firm, so you must bring in a decent amount of business if you aspire to be an equity partner."

Won't you be my trainer?

Partners aren't the only ones who could use a little training — associates count themselves among the needy as well. There is "no formal and very little informal training. Associates receive information on a 'need to know' basis," states a second-year. A newcomer hates that "there is no structured method of training at MWE. I have no goals or sign posts established by the firm. Instead, I am at the mercy of randomness."

According a New York corporate associate, though, "partners actually take the time to teach, from the big picture lessons to the subtle nuances that will make you a better lawyer. Numerous training programs and video-conferencing make access to knowledge on a national level an every day event." A litigator in the same office remains distressed that "although the associates are sometimes given high levels of responsibility, they are permitted to run until they fall. No attempt is made either to guide the associates as they try something new or treat mistakes as learning experiences." Attempts to include associates in their evaluation processes have reportedly spurred "I love me" memos, performance reviews associates write about their own contributions to the firm.

Hours are 'livable'

In contrast to most associates at big law firms, McDermott lawyers think they work "generally reasonable hours." Or at least they did. An L.A. litigator says that "prior to January 1, this office had the reputation of offering competitive salaries at livable billing hours. In the last few months, however, this has changed dramatically. Time will tell if this is just because the office is extremely busy and we are understaffed or if it is a sea change in firm mentality. Still, a Chicago sixth-year continues "to be amazed that associates are not here on weekends. Generally speaking, this is not a tough place in terms of hours and expectations." Perhaps "the hours expectation is unreasonable in terms of bonuses," but "you do have a choice of whether you want to work the outrageous hours or not."

How progressive are we?

While associates recognize the policy efforts (if not results) regarding the recruitment, retention and promotion of women at McDermott, the same cannot necessarily be said for minority recruitment and retention. "From outward appearances the firm has done a good job of recruiting minority attorneys," judges a New York litigator. "There is no formal mentoring, and very few partner role models, but there is a fair amount of informal mentoring by more senior minority lawyers to more junior ones." But in that same office, a colleague points out, "there are no black partners. Additionally, there has been for the last few years only one black male attorney." A government regulation associate in Chicago suggests part of the problem may be that "the firm is not attractive enough to hire minority candidates with the type of educational background they consider necessary. It may be unfair to criticize efforts to diversify, which I don't know much about, but the results are startlingly homogenous."

Several associates with an opinion on the subject say that treatment of gays and lesbians at McDermott is "not an issue, really." There "have been some openly gay and lesbian lawyers at McDermott's New York office," although other branch associates say they "don't really know" of out attorneys or the policies that might affect them. A Boston litigator sets the record straight (so to speak): "I do know there are not domestic partner benefits."

Great view, lousy furniture

Every McDermott office is a different world — at least as far as the decor is concerned. The Chicago branch attracts the most praise for its "great view of Lake Michigan" and "beautiful reception area," but still, the "offices could use painting — they look tired." More specifically, "the furniture is reminiscent of the public sector," gripes one associate. "The general issue attorney chair is extremely uncomfortable and fits few. There's no clear process for requesting a chair that fits."

A New York litigator announces approvingly that "fashionable office design is one of McDermott's strengths. We could use more war-rooms and file storage space, but overall, the offices are well-appointed." Well, when you've got good-looking offices, who needs file storage? Last year, DC firm leaders signed a 15-year lease in a brand-new building downtown. The building was designed as another lure in the ongoing battle to attract new associates in a fiercely competitive hiring market. The new site features ergonomically advanced furniture, special compressed shelving for greater accessibility and a large conference center with high-tech audio/visual capabilities. Other perks include coffee stations and a roof terrace with seating for daily use and social events.

But as an Orange County litigator points out, not all McDermott offices are created equal. "No one will ever accuse McDermott of overspending. 'Posh' is not a word I would ever use for the offices I have seen." Another point of interest is "the fact that the assignment of offices is a game played with such pettiness than I am surprised the decision is actually made by adults. One thing is certain, I had no input whatsoever in the choice of office space I received. This is especially surprising in a building where there is a surplus of space."

Understaffed support services

A number of associates are vociferous in their denigration of support services available to them. While the "library staff is outstanding," the "mail room/copy center is competent, but barely so" and secretarial help "is the single worst thing about working at McDermott." "The biggest problem at McDermott is that your secretary believes that she works for the firm and not for the lawyers," laments one third-year in Chicago. "If you complain about a secretary at McDermott there is a good chance you will get black-balled and you will end up with an even more worthless secretary." Associates should "be prepared to do [their] own photocopying, faxing, word processing, and so on. And that of the income partner. And that of the capital partner," warns a Los Angeles litigator.

But even the most strident critics fault the firm, as opposed to individual staff members, for these deficiencies. "We do not have enough support from the firm in this area," says one Chicago source. "For example, if your secretary is out, you are on your own to use a 'floater' who handles floor overflow rather than being assigned a secretary for the day. There is no coordination by the firm on this critical issue." The DC office is getting "tighter and tighter with money" and so "not only are the secretaries underpaid by industry standards, but they are overextended in the number of attorneys they are expected to support."

'Generally non-existent' social life

"McDermott does not do 'social,'" declares an unsocialized Chicago bankruptcy associate. Another associate in the same office says that "lawyers tend to eat lunch alone in their offices with the door shut" and in DC "it is rare to see attorneys from the same floor, much less other floors." People seem "to value their life away from the office more than socializing with their co-workers." Exactly, says a sixth-year from Chicago. "Do you really want to spend any more time with the people you spend ten hours a day with?"

Efforts are still made, however. "There is definitely an 'us vs. them' mentality between partners and associates, but among associates, the social interactions are invariably pleasant and enjoyable," argues a fourth-year litigator in New York. "For example, the Associates Committee at the firm has recently revived the monthly cocktail party (the so-called 'Booze & Schmooze'), and the attendance is always good." In addition, "many attorneys (mostly male) are involved with McDermott sports teams" in Chicago and "small groups (primarily associates) tend to go out for drinks after work every now and then."

Corporate culture clash

In a firm of McDermott's size, it's not surprising to read conflicting assessments of office culture, especially in different offices. Attorneys in Los Angeles and Miami mention a "relaxed, casual atmosphere" where "people work hard while at work, but everyone has, and is expected to have, an outside life." The culture is "formal" and "generally conservative" across the country, and while there has been "a little more pressure regarding hours than in the past and turnover has increased recently," the firm still maintains a "pretty laid-back environment."

A pervasive sense that the firm is "a little tight-fisted when it comes to parties and such" leads at least one New York litigator to dub McDermott: "'What have you done for me lately?' meets 'Do it cheaper'." The focus is on "getting quality work done and out the door. There is little training or nurturing of associates," suggests a Boston fourth-year. "You must be able to take initiative if you need anything, whether it is questions about an assignment or staff help or workload. No one will come around to see how you are doing." In other words, "complainers need not apply."

Another concern is the impact of the lateral influx. In the New York office, "there is a sense among some [of the laterals] that their prior firms still turn out better lawyers," sighs a second-year litigator. "I'm not sure I can handle one more litigation group meeting where I hear about how Weil, Sullivan and Skadden do things." A first-year in that office asks "What corporate culture? Everyone comes from another firm — the corporate culture depends on the partner you are working for."

Things to keep in mind

McDermott can be "a great place to get an education working on genuinely interesting projects with very talented attorneys," cheers a DC sixth-year. A New York associate agrees that the firm "is a good place to come to if you did not get an offer from another national firm," but thinks you should "stay for two years and then lateral to another firm. If you stay for more than two years, you will learn that associates at other firms might be more advanced than you are, and they will have a significant advantage not only negotiating transactions but interviewing for in-house positions as well."

Another thing to consider is the firm's two-tier partnership. "The first-tier income partner is viewed by most to be simply another way in which the firm saves money," assesses a DC litigator. "The income partner has no equity in the firm, yet is self-employed for tax purposes. Hence, they actually make less money than they did as an associate. The benefits to the firm far outweigh any benefit realized by the income partner.

Despite intermittent bitching, incoming associates still choose McDermott for quality-of-life factors. For laterals, it can offer "the opportunity for junior associates to be on the front lines, and to get basic litigation skills" in the "small offices of a large firm" where "cases are staffed leanly." In the Big Apple, some chose it because "it was supposed to be a lifestyle firm." While "that doesn't really seem to have turned out to be quite accurate, it does seem to be a little more life-friendly than some other New York firms."

Perkins Coie LLP

VAULT.COM — NEARLY & NOTABLE

1201 Third Avenue
48th Floor
Seattle, WA 98101-3099
(206) 583-8888
Fax: (206) 583-8500
www.perkinscoie.com

LOCATIONS

Seattle, WA (HQ)
Anchorage, AK • Bellevue, WA • Boise, ID • Denver, CO • Los Angeles, CA • Menlo Park, CA • Portland, OR • San Francisco, CA • Spokane, WA • Washington, DC • Hong Kong • Taipei

MAJOR DEPARTMENTS/PRACTICES

Business/Tax
Commercial Transactions
Corporate/SEC
Energy
Environmental/ Natural Resources and Land Use
General Litigation
Intellectual Property
Labor & Employment
Patent
Product Liability

THE STATS

No. of attorneys: 500
No. of offices: 14
Summer associate offers: 20 out of 22 (Seattle, 1999)
Managing Partner: Robert E. Giles
Hiring Partner: Mr. Steven Y. Koh

PAY

Seattle, 2000
1st year: $100,000-$125,000
2nd year: $87,000-$135,000
3rd year: $90,000-$150,000
4th year: $93,000-$165,000
5th year: $96,000-$185,000
6th year: $100,000-$195,000
7th year: $105,000-$205,000
Bonus for billing 1,850 hours

Summer associate, 2000:
Los Angeles: 1,673/week
Menlo Park/SF: $2,400/week
Portland: $1,300/week
Seattle: $1,635/week
Washington, DC: $1,650/week

THE BUZZ
What attorneys at other firms are saying about this firm

- "Unlikely player, great e-commerce"
- "Sloppy with recruiting process"
- "Hot tech clients"
- "Boeing LLP"

UPPERS

- Commitment to quality of life
- High levels of individual responsibility at junior levels
- Partners willing to take time to mentor associates

DOWNERS

- Competition from California firms
- Associates could be friendlier
- Orange carpet reminiscent of Burger King

KEY COMPETITORS

Cooley Godward
Davis Wright Tremaine
Preston Gates & Ellis
Venture Law Group
Wilson Sonsini Goodrich & Rosati

EMPLOYMENT CONTACT

Ms. Kari Anne Tuohy, Esq.
Director of Lawyer Personnel
(206) 583-8888
tuohk@perkinscoie.com

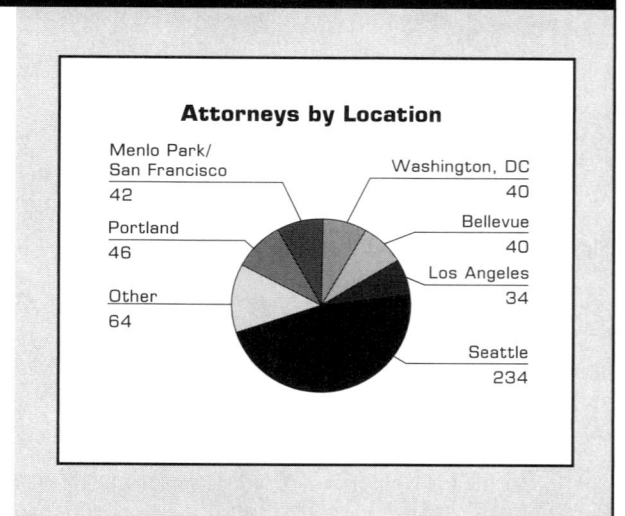

Attorneys by Location

- Menlo Park/San Francisco: 42
- Portland: 46
- Other: 64
- Washington, DC: 40
- Bellevue: 40
- Los Angeles: 34
- Seattle: 234

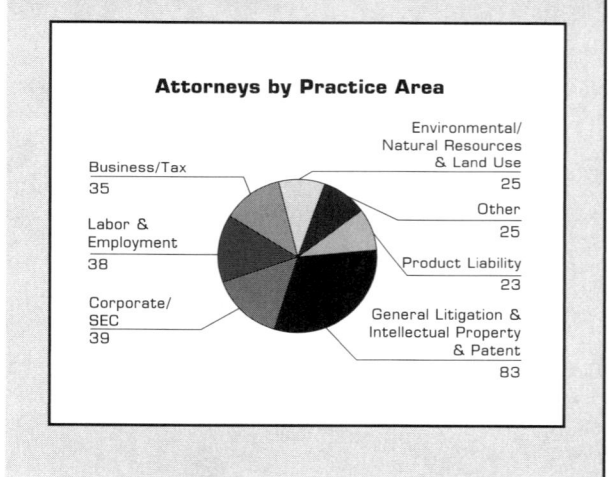

Attorneys by Practice Area

- Business/Tax: 35
- Labor & Employment: 38
- Corporate/SEC: 39
- Environmental/Natural Resources & Land Use: 25
- Other: 25
- Product Liability: 23
- General Litigation & Intellectual Property & Patent: 83

QUALITY OF LIFE RANKINGS [ASSOCIATES RATE THEIR OWN FIRM]

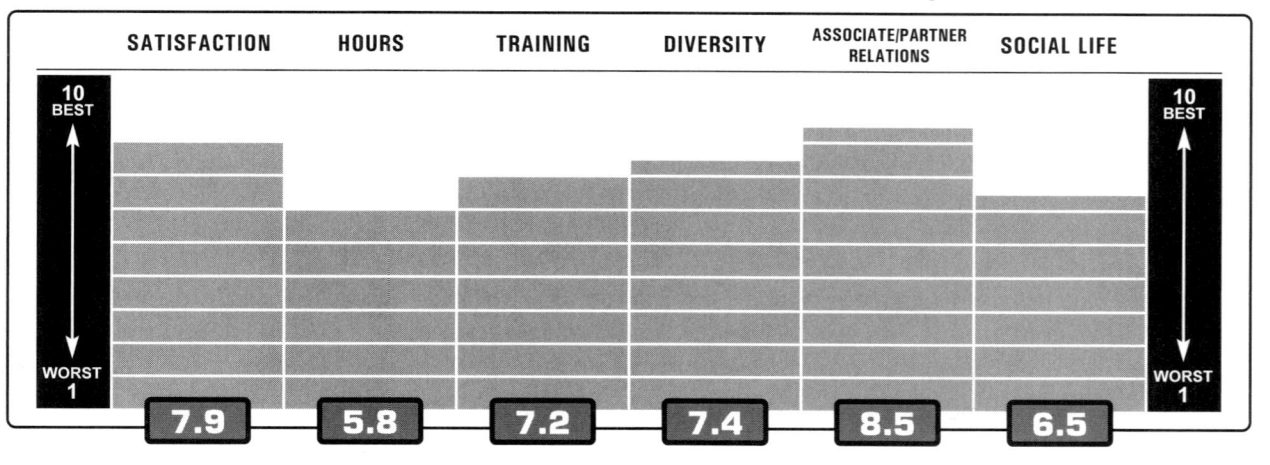

Satisfaction	Hours	Training	Diversity	Associate/Partner Relations	Social Life
7.9	5.8	7.2	7.4	8.5	6.5

THE SCOOP

Perkins Coie hails from that haven of fleece vests, cappuccino, and rainy days that we call Seattle. Insiders characterize it as being a firm that "pays market rates but still feels that lifestyle (seeing the sunset) is as important as work." This "laid-back," "casual" firm is known throughout the West for its high tech practice.

A rain-soaked Northwestern

Pacific Northwest mainstay Perkins Coie traces its history back to the spring of 1912, when Federal Judge George Donworth and U.S. Attorney Elmer Todd founded their partnership with "a handshake on a Seattle sidewalk." Donworth & Todd, as the firm was then known, opened its doors on May 1, 1912 and began acquiring major clients. Only two years after opening, the firm picked up perhaps its most important client, William Boeing, who manufactured the newfangled machines called airplanes. By 1969 the firm's name had evolved to Perkins, Coie, Stone, Olsen and Williams, which was shortened to Perkins Coie in 1985. In March 1988, the firm became the first law firm from the Pacific Northwest to open a branch in L.A. by merging with the 17-lawyer boutique Johnsen, Manfredi & Thorpe. Perkins' California expansion continued in 1998 when the firm opened San Francisco and Silicon Valley offices. The firm established its first overseas office in Taipei in 1992, followed shortly by an office in Hong Kong (1993). Attorneys from the firm have served in many high level positions including President of the American Bar Association and Chief Justice of the Washington Supreme Court. The firm also has two retired partners serving as judges on the Ninth Circuit Court of Appeals.

Flying high

Perkins Coie is the undisputed heavyweight champion of the Seattle region, weighing in at 500 lawyers and having offices in every state on the West Coast. Furthermore, the firm has over 100 more attorneys in Seattle (286) than its closest competitors, Davis Wright Tremaine (171), and Microsoft counsel Preston Gates & Ellis (166). The firm's position as the largest firm in Seattle is due in part to its biggest client — Boeing. However, the firm is not dependent on Boeing. In the area of aviation alone, clients include heavy hitters Alaska Airlines and Delta Airlines. Indeed, the firm's clients include close to 100 of the Fortune 500 companies. Perkins Coie's clients come from such varied industries as investment banking (CS First Boston, Goldman Sachs, Salomon Smith Barney), manufacturing (General Motors, Toshiba), and consumer products (Sears Roebuck, Starbucks). The firm handled more than 100 public offerings throughout the 1990s. According to the firm, Perkins Coie litigators generally handle more than 750 cases per year. While the firm continues to offer a full range of services to traditional clients, the firm has also made an effort to be at the forefront of high tech law.

High tech clientele

With high-profile clients including Amazon.com, Yahoo!, RealNetworks, Egghead.com, and US West, Perkins Coie is decidedly a force in the world of high tech law. As early as 1996, high tech clients already accounted for close to one quarter of the firm's revenues. In 1999 Perkins Coie was placed on *Red Herring* magazine's "Top 10 High Tech Law Firms." In early 2000, Perkins Coie defended Amazon.com in a highly publicized patent suit against Barnesandnoble.com. In the controversial suit, which was satirized in *The New York Times Magazine*, attorneys from Perkins Coie argued that Barnes and Noble's Express Lane feature, which allowed consumers to purchase an item with a single click of a mouse, violated Amazon's patent on the "1-Click" method for Internet purchases. The judge found in favor of Amazon, and Barnesandnoble.com had to add an additional step to their process. The firm also had to defend the online retailer in a high-profile case the previous year. In April 1999, partner Susan Foster caught attention for her work on behalf of Amazon.com in *Amazon Bookstore Inc v. Amazon Inc.*, a suit brought by a Minneapolis-based women's bookstore against the online giant.

Perkins Coie vs. Silicon Valley

In 1998 Perkins Coie opened its Silicon Valley office by merging with 13-lawyer high tech boutique Hosie, Wes, Sacks & Brelsford. Next, lured lateral lawyers from Palo Alto's Venture Law Group, Menlo Park's high-paying Gunderson, Dettmer, Stough, Vinnenueve, Franklin & Hachigan, Los Angeles' Troop Steuber Pasich Reddick & Tobey, and Palo Alto's prestigious Fenwick & West. At the same time, large Silicon Valley firms including the Venture Law Group, Orrick, and Brobeck moved up to Seattle in an effort to expand their high tech departments, a move which chased many Seattle firms out of the market. Perkins Coie continues to duke it out with the California giants.

Springing up in SoMa

In spite of the competition with Silicon Valley firms, Perkins Coie has continued to grow. The L.A. office, which opened in 1988 with 17 lawyers, now has more than 35 lawyers and moved to new offices in order to create room for more expansion. Perkins Coie's Silicon Valley offices have found new digs as well. The new offices, which are already almost full, are located on swanky Commonwealth Drive in Menlo Park and in the trendy SoMa district of San Francisco.

GETTING HIRED

Academic focus

Perkins Coie has a "high focus on academic achievement," notes an insider. However, high grades alone will not get you a position at the firm. Another associate reports that "Perkins Coie generally seeks applicants with strong academic backgrounds and ties to the Pacific Northwest (or any other markets where they intend to work), who are well-rounded and have additional interests aside from the law." Moreover, the associate continues, "Perkins will interview countless candidates for only one slot." Another contact reveals: "Summer associates are likely to do all right, once they get that position, but the firm is very, very picky about lateral candidates." One attorney has noticed a drop in selectivity in recent years, stating that "hiring at the firm is generally very competitive, though in recent boom times it has been less so." Many of Perkins Coie's favorite law schools include University of Washington, University of Michigan-Ann Arbor, Berkeley, Georgetown University, George Washington University, and Duke. Attorneys also come from Harvard, Stanford, and NYU.

Summers are freebie heaven

Summer associates report that the Perkins program "was a very good summer experience and certainly has a big impact on one's decision." Another elaborates: "The summer is phenomenal. Every day's another event, and you have to remind yourself to get work done. More freebies than you can shake a stick at — there's even a summer associate pool of rental cars, which can be signed out to enjoy the city and surrounding area. The firm also helps you set up your housing. They even assemble a list of potential apartments, which someone in personnel has visited and reviewed!"

OUR SURVEY SAYS

Jackpot!

"Perkins Coie's salary structure is outstanding," an associate reports. "All associates make a good wage, especially considering Seattle's cost of living and the absence of state or local income taxes." Other associates note that "the firm responded quickly to match the new salaries but has not yet formalized the bonus process. I expect that it will be competitive with other Silicon Valley firms, although this has not been formalized yet." A considerably compensated contact comments, "The compensation structure at Perkins Coie is complicated but fair. California and New York firms may offer more money but, after working at a large New York firm, I expect my per hour pay to be better here. Certainly, my life outside of work is better because I have one now." Many agree with this assumption, adding that "the minimum billable hours for full-time associates is very reasonable — 1,850 hours per year." One laywer recalls how lucky his co-law students thought him after he landed a job "at a firm that pays well and expects far fewer hours."

Flexibility seems to be the key of Perkins Coie's pay scale. "It allows associates to differ in terms of the hours they choose to work. I can work more hours if I'd like to increase my pay, or I can choose to give up some pay in exchange for lower hours." First-year bonuses are guaranteed. Moreover, there is an associate equity pool to further compensate associates. Associates are given points of the "seven-digit" pool based on seniority. [Perkins honestly points out, to its credit, that the portion of the pool allocated to associates is actually six-digit.]

Some associates do have gripes with the compensation. An associate based in the capital city declares, "Perkins Coie DC associate salaries are currently way below the DC market for firms with which we supposedly compete. We are in the process of salary adjustments now, but we don't know how much we'll be receiving. I do not expect to be competitive with the rest of the market, even after the adjustments." A Seattle source has a similar complaint: "The Seattle market is lower than other parts of the country even though the cost of living is rapidly rising." Listening to such complaints, Perkins has raised its DC salaries retroactive to February 2000; productivity bonuses now start at 1,850 hours.

Laid-back partners

Partners at Perkins Coie are generally well-regarded by the associates. "Perkins Coie has a very progressive atmosphere that tends to favor the mentoring relationship between partners and associates," notes a Seattle-based source. "There quite simply are no barriers between partners and associates either socially or in the work environment." An associate in Silicon Valley adds, "The partners in our Menlo Park office are very supportive and treat the associates as equals." Associates at Perkins Coie observe that "partners freely share firm information such as expansion plans, partner and associate salary levels, and firm profitability with associates. Associates are included in the management of the firm and are generally treated with a high level of respect." A second-year adds, "I have a great working relationship with the partners; there is very much a team mentality to the work done here." A senior associate agrees, "Partners are uniformly down-to-earth and approachable. There is very little sense of hierarchy."

Others characterize the partners as being very gracious, reporting that "partners thank secretaries, paralegals, and associates for their work." There are some associates who are slightly critical of partners, however. A source elaborates, "The only concern anyone has is that partners are so busy that they don't have time to supervise adequately. They do expect new associates to ramp up quickly and treat us as equals." Another attorney reports a similar problem. "There is currently more demand for our services than associates can provide, so partners (particularly from other offices) are unhappy when associates cannot take on new work for their clients."

No crazy party

While many associates at Perkins Coie define the firm as being a lifestyle firm, most do not characterize that lifestyle as being based *around* the firm. An attorney based in Seattle reveals, "The social interaction between lawyers at Perkins Coie may not be as high as at other firms, because the attorneys here have extremely varied interests and substantial lives outside the firm." Another source agrees, "There tends not to be a ton of after-hours social interaction, but chalk that up to the fact that people have (or are trying to have) a life outside of work."

Although the social life may not be incredibly active, at least one contact insists that Perkinites do like each other. "The people here, across the board, are very friendly — it's one of the things which drew me to the firm." A Seattle third-year declares, "Social interaction among young associates is common, welcome, and probably aided by the fact that Perkins tries very hard to hire only friendly and interesting folks." There do seem to be some divisions within the firm. As one DC-based attorney indicates: "There does not appear to be much social interaction between partners, and with a few exceptions, there is not much social interaction between partners and associates." Another critical lawyer complains, "Perkins has not done a very good job of integrating me and my group of laterals into the firm."

Mentors: the freshmaker

"Structured training programs and informal mentoring create a terrific environment for practice development at Perkins Coie," reports an attorney. Another reveals, "Training is good, though, as always, the informal training one receives from partners is more valuable than the formal training one gets from firm programs. Still, the latter are often pretty valuable." A San Franciscan states: "The partners try to put on regular training sessions but they get canceled more often than not for scheduling reasons. The training is very much 'on the job' and 'learn by doing.' I have learned an incredible amount during my time here." "There's an official training program, but the bulk of training is still on-the-job," an insider offers. "Partners are good about getting associates involved early on with significant tasks, though. Three weeks after arriving I did my first solo deposition. It's worth noting, though, that whenever I feel as if I need some guidance, I can approach the partner involved relatively easily.

It's not a sink-or-swim atmosphere." A senior associate warns, however, that "with a few exceptions, I don't think training or mentoring are adequate for the more junior associates."

Bonus mininum below competitors, business persists

The 1,850 hour billable minimum is an important indicator of the firms' attitude towards work. A litigator elaborates, "In Perkins Coie's litigation department, the work comes in waves. Generally, when an attorney's cases are in a lull, he or she is encouraged to take advantage of the free time." Moreover, another associate adds, "the compensation structure minimizes pressure to bill. The number of hours an associate is expected to bill is built into her salary. It's a fair and rational system." Another insider notes, "The firm is good in that it allows a relatively low number of hours as truly acceptable (1,850, or in some cases even less), but increases bonuses for those who want to work more. In addition, the firm is pretty supportive of part-time policies."

Associates are expected to work as many hours as are necessary to complete the job at hand. One attorney reports, "As with any big law firm, there can be times when you're busier than you'd like to be (i.e., night or weekend work). I've found this to balance out well, though, with days when I can leave the office early and take advantage of a long weekend. It's also worth noting that partners are great about vacation time. I took more than three weeks off my first year when I wanted to, and I plan on taking a full month this year." Another declares that "work has been overwhelming in the past. But we have recently added attorneys to the department, which has helped a great deal."

East side, West side, all-around reputation

Perkins Coie attorneys wax thoughtful about the firm's reputation in the legal industry at large. No one doubts that Perkins is "the premier firm in the Pacific Northwesst," even in light of the move of many prominent California firms to the Seattle area. "The firm has responded and remained competitive," assesses one Seattle associate, who adds "Perkins has definitely responded better than other Seattle firms." Arriviste Seattle competitors include Wilson Sonsini, Venture Law Group, Cooley Godward and Orrick. The firm's reputation in the Bay area is "expanding," especially in the arena of Internet law. One Alaska insider says that office is particularly well-known for labor and employment law.

If you're betting on partnership…

Perkins associates are happy about their relatively high chances of making partner. A Seattle-based associate estimates there is "about 50 percent chance of making it." One associate supplies, "If an associate continues to do good work, his or her prospects for partnership are all but guaranteed." A senior associate explains the structure of the partnership track: "The seven-year partnership track is firmly established. Associates are apprised of their partnership status beginning their fifth year. My sense is that during the two years leading up to the final partnership decision, the associate and the evaluation committees involved mutually agree on promotion status — either partner or of counsel. I have heard no stories of associates who felt they were passed over for partner."

Another associate reveals, "If you produce good quality work and contribute to the positive atmosphere, it seems your chances are very good. You don't have to be a rainmaker to make partner. The firm realizes that there are those people who bring in lots of business and there are others who are masters at servicing clients' needs once clients are with the firm. The firm rewards both types of attorneys." An Anchorage-based attorney indicates that even Alaskan associates can count on pretty good prospects for partnership: "We have had several associates come up through the ranks in Anchorage and make partner, although I'm not sure if it was done within the tight seven-year period."

Many associates report that the chances of making partner may not be as high as reported: "With the raises and all the lateral partner hiring, there's a perception that it'll be harder, but not enough time has passed to tell." Others report that part-time work can be a hindrance to the partnership, stating that "while part-time associates can make partner, it still seems to be based significantly on the number of hours worked here. In addition, bringing in work seems to be another big factor."

Quality but not quantity

The support staff at Perkins Coie receives mixed reviews from the associates. Negative reviews generally have more to do with availability of resources than quality of support. A source based at the firm's headquarters raves, "Excellent and vast resources are at your command as an associate, from library, copying, messengers, paralegals, secretaries, and word processing." An associate from the Bay Area is not quite as enthusiastic: "Support services have dramatically improved over the past year, but we still have a ways to go." A Seattle-ite critiques, "Secretaries don't have enough time, but in general the support is pretty dedicated and skilled." A lateral hire notes that the lack of support resources can keep Perkins attorneys from working overwhelming hours like their counterparts. "We do not have the same evening and night support as a large New York firm, but that is also a blessing."

Good for women, but where are the women partners?

The firm receives good marks when questioned regarding diversity issues with respect to women. A female associate states, "Generally, the firm enjoys great parity between the genders. There are still too few male assistants or secretaries, and the firm is struggling to make compensation equitable for those who choose to participate in the part-time program." Another associate reports that firm policies are "generally very strong. Part-time policies for care givers are excellent." One associate cautions that while "the firm's intent is good, and I'm not sure what it's doing wrong; it just can't seem to retain women. Perhaps if there were a woman partner it might send a healthier message."

Wonderfully diverse

"Compared to many law firms, Perkins Coie attorneys are a wonderfully diverse group," notes an associate, when questioned about minority issues at the firm. "However, the law profession has a long way to go yet, and the firm reflects that fact." Others assert that "the proof is in the pudding, and there haven't been very good results to date." While one associate believes that "efforts have been very good, there has been less success" than expected. Another indicates that "the firm is trying hard to hire minorities, but the partnership (firm-wide) is overwhelmingly white."

Gay in Perkins

A Bay Area associate notes, "In San Francisco any firm is foolish not to recognize the value of the gay community. Many of the attorneys and staff here are openly gay and are welcomed with open arms." According to one attorney, the firm provides "full benefits to the extent permitted by federal tax laws and a very supportive and welcoming environment." A gay associate reports, "I was openly gay when they hired me. They've been very comfortable with it and I've felt very welcome to be out here."

Pro bono, really?

Attorneys at the firm are divided regarding their firm's commitment to pro bono work. While an associate notes, "I have always received encouragement from partners in my representation of pro bono clients," many feel the firm's attitude towards counting pro bono hours towards billable requirements is stifling. "There is no incentive to do more pro bono work, because only 50 hours of pro bono work counts towards billables," reports a senior associate. Another attorney continues, "The policies regarding 'marginal' hours such as pro bono and training have been getting more and more unintelligible, and since the latest raises, no one knows if anything other than pure billables counts." Corporate attorneys notice differences between departments.

"Some of the litigators do pro bono work, but the corporate finance people have never seen a pro bono case cross their desk."

C'mon, get happy

Associates at Perkins Coie are generally very happy. "I don't think I would be as happy anywhere else. In fact, I was not nearly as happy at the first large firm I worked for in San Francisco. This firm has a great outlook on work and lifestyle," explains one source. Another states, "For those who love the Internet and the law, this is the perfect place to practice. There is no better place in the U.S. to do this kind of work — fast-paced, interesting deals with great people and great clients." A Seattle-based Perkinite reports that "for a big firm, I think this is about as good as it gets. It's not perfect, but I've heard very few complaints. For the most part, I've been able to choose the kind of work I do, and take on challenging and significant responsibilities in the process. The people here, from staff to partners, are also great. I really enjoy the people I work with. The flexibility hours-wise has also been key. I've been able to really enjoy the Seattle area, and there's a lot to enjoy."

"The summer is phenominal. Every day's another event, and you have to remind yourself to get work done. More freebies than you can shake a stick at."

— *Perkins Coie associate*

Pillsbury Madison & Sutro LLP

Pillsbury Madison & Sutro LLP
50 Fremont Street
San Francisco, CA 94105
(415) 983-1000
Fax: (415) 983-1200
www.pillsburylaw.com

LOCATIONS

San Francisco, CA (HQ)
Los Angeles, CA • New York, NY • Orange County, CA • Palo Alto, CA • Sacramento, CA • San Diego (Downtown), CA • San Diego (North County), CA • Washington, DC • Vienna, VA • Tokyo

MAJOR DEPARTMENTS/PRACTICES

Bankruptcy and Creditors' Rights
Class Actions and Complex Litigation
Commerce and Technology
Corporate, Securities, Banking and Emerging Companies
Employment and Labor Relations
Environmental and Land Use
Executive Compensation and Employee Benefits
Intellectual Property
International Transactions and Project Finance
Life Sciences and Technology
Political Law
Real Estate, Project Development & Construction
Tax Planning and Litigation

THE STATS

No. of attorneys: 554
No. of offices: 11
Summer associate offers: 43 out of 46 (Firm-wide, 1999)
Firm Chair: Mary B. Cranston
Chair Firmwide Recruitment: William S. Waller

THE BUZZ
What attorneys at other firms are saying about this firm

- "Can you say 'dinosaur'? I knew you could."
- "Making a comeback"
- "Rough last couple of years but still a SF mainstay"
- "Just discovered Silicon Valley"

PAY

All Domestic Offices except Sacramento, 2000
1st year: $125,000 (Bonus of $5,000 for 2,100 hours; $7,500 for 2,250 hours; $12,500 for 2,400 hours)
2nd year: $135,000 (Bonus of $7,500 for 2,100 hours; $10,000 for 2,250 hours; $15,000 for 2,400 hours)
3rd year: $150,000 (Bonus of $8,500 for 2,100 hours; $11,500 for 2,250 hours; $16,500 for 2,400 hours)
4th year: $165,000 (Bonus of $10,000 for 2,100 hours; $12,500 for 2,250 hours; $17,500 for 2,400 hours)
5th year: $180,000 (Bonus of $10,000 for 2,100 hours; $12,500 for 2,250 hours; $17,500 for 2,400 hours)
6th year: $185,000 (Bonus of $10,000 for 2,100 hours; $12,500 for 2,250 hours; $17,500 for 2,400 hours)
7th year: $185,000 (Bonus of $12,500 for 2,100 hours; $17,500 for 2,250 hours, $10,000 for 2,400 hours)
8th year: $185,000 (Bonus of $12,500 for 2,100 hours; $17,500 for 2,250 hours, $10,000 for 2,400 hours)
sixth- through eighth-year associates share in firm profits and associates who reach 2,100 hours also participate in the firm's venture fund.

Summer associate (San Francisco, Palo Alto, San Diego, 1999): $1,650/week

Summer associate (Los Angeles, Orange County, 1999): $1,825/week

Summer associate (Washington, DC, 1999): $1,700/week

Sacramento, 2000
1st year: $90,000 (Bonus of $5,000 for 1,950 hours; $5,000 for 2,150 hours; $7,500 for 2,250 hours; $12,500 for 2,400 hours)

NOTABLE PERKS

- Dinner served nightly at 7 p.m.
- Loan guarantee program to help associates purchase residences
- Retreat for first- and second-year associates
- Back-up child care (in S.F, L.A., DC, and Orange County)
- Discounted gym membership
- Venture fund participation for associates

UPPERS

- Casual dress every day
- Interesting cutting-edge matters
- Good money and appealing bonuses

DOWNERS

- Lack of support services
- Not yet a truly global firm
- Incredible hours pressure
- Scaled-down pro bono policy

KEY COMPETITORS

Brobeck, Phleger & Harrison
Heller Ehrman White & McAuliffe
Latham & Watkins
Morrison & Foerster
Orrick, Herrington & Sutcliffe
Wilson Sonsini Goodrich & Rosati

EMPLOYMENT CONTACT

Mr. William S. Waller
Chair, Firm-wide Recruitment
(213) 488-7163
waller_ws@pillsburylaw.com

Ms. Mary Ellen Hatch
Firmwide Attorney Recruitment Manager (Los Angeles)
Pillsburyrecruit_LA@pillsburylaw.com

Attorneys by Location

- Other: 61
- Washington, DC: 77
- Palo Alto: 80
- Los Angeles: 97
- San Diego: 37
- San Francisco: 202

Attorneys by Practice Area [San Francisco]

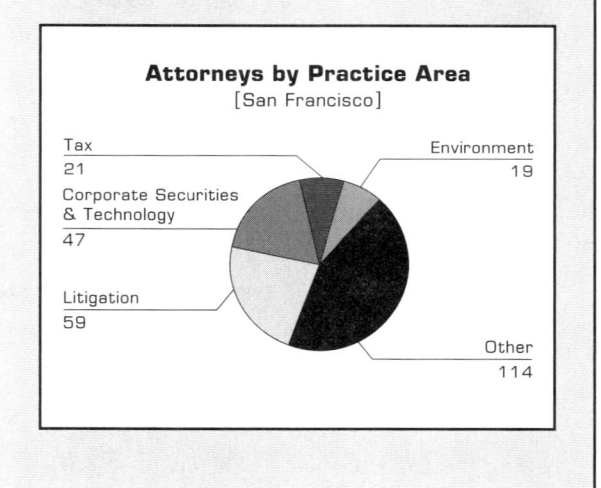

- Tax: 21
- Corporate Securities & Technology: 47
- Litigation: 59
- Environment: 19
- Other: 114

QUALITY OF LIFE RANKINGS [ASSOCIATES RATE THEIR OWN FIRM]

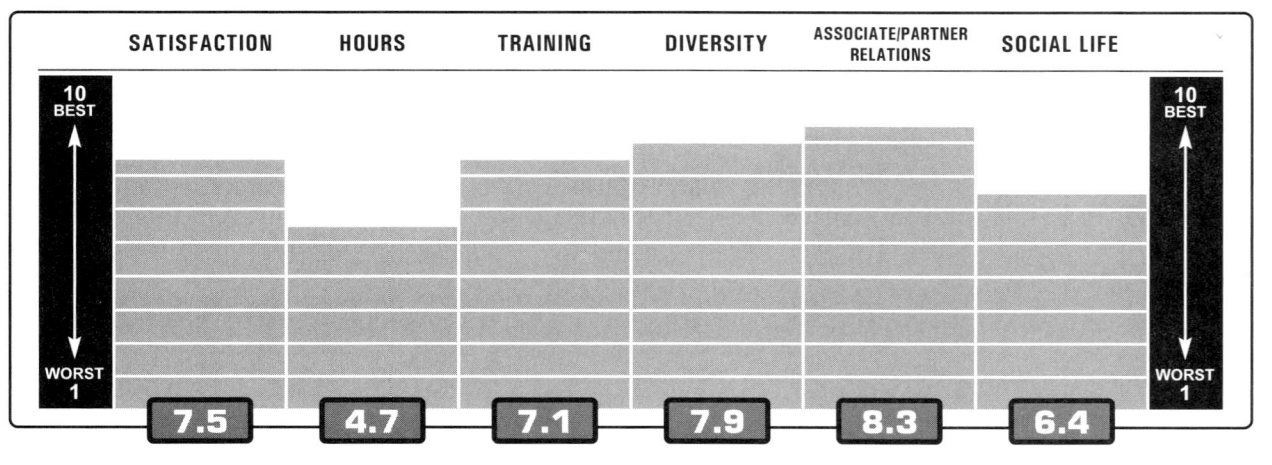

SATISFACTION	HOURS	TRAINING	DIVERSITY	ASSOCIATE/PARTNER RELATIONS	SOCIAL LIFE
7.5	4.7	7.1	7.9	8.3	6.4

THE SCOOP

Pillsbury Madison & Sutro is a firm in transition. After earning a reputation as a firm lacking in direction during the 1980s and much of the 1990s, Pillsbury has been making dramatic efforts under the leadership of Mary Cranston and Marina Park to straighten its course. Pillsbury has put renewed emphasis on its intellectual property, capital markets, complex litigation, and international markets practices. The firm has also tried to be more open and communicative. "I would watch Pillsbury very carefully over the next year, to see how the firm changes," advises one associate.

Pillsbury days of yore

Pillsbury Madison & Sutro celebrated its 125th Anniversary in July 1999 with an extravaganza in San Francisco that was brought to all of Pillsbury's other offices via the wonder of the Web. As proof of the firm's prominence in the Bay Area, San Francisco Mayor Willie Brown dubbed the date "Pillsbury, Madison & Sutro Day." (Mark it on your calendars.)

The firm began in 1874, when Evan S. Pillsbury set up shop in San Francisco. The name of the firm became Pillsbury, Madison & Sutro in 1905 to reflect the addition of partners Frank D. Madison and Alfred Sutro. A year later, Pillsbury suffered the complete loss of its offices and records in the great San Francisco earthquake and fire of 1906 but weathered the traumatic event to become one of San Francisco's enduring institutions.

In 1991 Pillsbury was part of what was then the largest law firm merger in history when it joined with Lillick & McHose. Lillick & McHose, a Los Angeles-based firm, had 171 lawyers. Pillsbury's LA office jumped from a 42-attorney operation to 160 in one fell swoop. In 1996 Pillsbury combined with Washington, DC firm Cushman, Darby & Cushman, adding 65 intellectual property attorneys.

Pillsbury's challenges

In 1997 Pillsbury's profits per partner plunged 20 percent to $300,000, a stark contrast to the rising profits at other tech-happy Bay Area firms. Firm leaders and industry watchers attributed the fall to the settlement of an age discrimination suit against the firm that same year, an extremely expensive computer overhaul (upwards of $8 million), merger-related costs, and a cyclical fall in business from the firm's largest clients: Chevron, AirTouch, Bank of America and Pacific Telesis.

Perhaps the most striking sign of Pillsbury's hard times has been fleeing personnel. In March 1999, *The American Lawyer* reported that the firm had lost no less than 40 partners since 1997. The firm's Los Angeles office witnessed a virtual exodus of lawyers, as many members of the firm's corporate, securities and technology group (many of whom moved to fast-expanding Orrick Herrington & Sutcliffe) left the firm. By summer 1998, only one corporate attorney remained in L.A. Orrick struck again in April and May 1999 when it lured four benefits partners and two other attorneys from Pillsbury. The firm claims that it has stemmed the tide of departures, but it has done its own poaching to help offset these losses. In April 2000, Pillsbury bolstered its presence in Northern Virginia, a new area of growth for high tech, by grabbing six lawyers from Washington, DC's Reed Smith Shaw & McClay. The addition of partners Frederic Spindel, Jay Halpern, and Stanley Jutkowitz and associates Jeffrey Lobb, Paul Mamalian, and George Thomas nearly doubled the size of the firm's outpost in the area. In addition, the firm added four partners in Silicon Valley and one partner in Orange County. Also among its prizes is George Howard, a top employment and labor attorney now in the firm's San Diego office.

From pyramids to diamonds

In the fall of 1998, Pillsbury announced it would scrap its "one partner, one vote" process for electing management, a system that many felt was unwieldy and inefficient. In its stead, the firm instituted a "slate election system," in which a nominating committee chooses seven to nine partners to run the firm, including a chairperson and managing partner. Commenting on the new changes, Alfred Pepin, then chairman, told *The Recorder*: "I may have very well put in motion my own demise." Pepin, now retired, couldn't have been more correct.

In what one associate described as "a coup against the old guard," Pillsbury's partners elected Marina H. Park as managing partner and Mary Cranston as chair of the firm. Cranston thus became the first woman in the country to lead a firm of Pillsbury's size. She quickly set the tone of her leadership by circulating summaries of board meetings to personnel, announcing more autonomy and responsibility for local offices, raising salaries and letting the rest of her partners know they were expected to contribute 2,500 hours annually.

The firm also changed its partnership structure from a so-called "pyramid" system to a "diamond" system. Pillsbury now has two types of partners: full-equity partners and partners who get a salary with a partial equity stake in the firm. The new system increases Pillsbury's profits per partner numbers and also makes the firm more merger-friendly. (Rumors have circulated in the legal press that it is in the market for a dance partner.) The extra step now needed to become a full-equity partner also may serve as an incentive for partners to perform. Some partners have not been pleased with these changes, and around 12 percent of Pillsbury's partners hit the road in 1999 for other competitors or in-house jobs.

The changes at Pillsbury have not been limited to the partnership. Pillsbury has doubled its bonus pool and the diamond structure gives senior associates an equity stake in the firm. In fact, associates at the sixth-year level and above are now called "senior attorneys I, II or III." Cranston instituted a 1,950-hour minimum billing requirement. Mid- and junior-level associates now operate on a three-tiered bonus system, which is tied to billable hours.

No-door policy

In 1999 the L.A. office got a new leader in the person of Michael Meyer. In keeping with Cranston's new direction for the firm, Meyer had the door to his office physically removed to promote the firm's open-door policy.

In February 2000 three Sacramento partners, Cary Boyden, J. Cleve Livingston and John Cooluris, pulled out of Pillsbury, essentially reforming the boutique practice they had had before joining the firm. They now work in the same building as Pillsbury's Sacramento office. Sounds like they left on good terms; Cooluris told *The Recorder* that the new firm will be passing on a lot of work to Pillsbury. The head of the Sacramento office, Benjamin Webster, describes the firm's relationship with the upstarts as a "strategic alliance."

Teaming up with Pillsbury

The firm counts many of California's most prominent companies as clients including Bank of America, Chevron, Ford Motor Company, Pacific Telesis, AirTouch Communications, Qualcomm, Abovenet Communications, Toshiba, and Xerox. Of course, the firm has more than blue-chip companies as clients. It often does work for the area's numerous startups and the San Francisco Giants baseball club.

Vodafone calling

Pillsbury's M&A lawyers had a record year in 1999, working on $1.3 billion in deals. The firm has also been busy putting together joint ventures for its clients. Pillsbury attorneys worked for 18 days and nights on behalf of Britain's Vodafone AirTouch in the fall of 1999 to finalize a $70 billion deal with Bell Atlantic. The new joint venture will serve around 20 million wireless customers in the United States, making it the biggest wireless business in the country. Pillsbury has seen the wireless company through many incarnations. In February 1999 the firm helped put Vodafone AirTouch together by advising San Francisco-based AirTouch on its merger with Vodafone.

Techie Pillsbury

Pillsbury has been making efforts to increase its reputation for corporate high tech work. Pillsbury's Jorge Del Calvo, Marina Park and Collin Morris helped Chevron negotiate a deal with business-to-business software company Ariba to set up Petrocosm.com, a marketplace for energy-related products and services. Chevron and Ariba are taking a minority stake in Petrocosm and allowing the rest of the equity to be divided among other energy players. And when Wells Fargo decided to team up with online auctioneer eBay in March 2000 to offer online person-to-person payments, it tapped Pillsbury for the deal.

Pillsbury works on attention-getting IPOs as well. In February 2000 attorneys from the firm's Northern Virginia and Silicon Valley offices worked on the IPO of Network Solutions, the leading registrar of Internet domain names. The $2.2 billion public offering was one of the largest at the time.

Pillsbury's emphasis on its intellectual property practice may also be bearing fruit. The firm filed 2,123 patents in 1999 and ranked fifth in *Intellectual Property Today*'s annual Top Patent Firm Survey.

Plentiful litigation, especially in IP

Litigation at Pillsbury is split into four areas: (1) antitrust, trade regulation and complex business litigation; (2) securities, financial institutions, creditors' rights, construction, real estate, commercial and appellate; (3) products liability, maritime/admiralty, insurance and commercial; and (4) employment and labor. The first group includes Pillsbury's busy IP practice. In 1996 Qualcomm Inc. brought in Pillsbury for its suit against Motorola over flip-top wireless telephones. The parties successfully negotiated an agreement in the spring of 2000. The IP department also won one of the largest patent infringement awards in history in connection with its representation of Haworth, Inc., a maker of cubicle steel frames.

GETTING HIRED

Still selective?

Some Pillsbury lawyers observe that admission standards have sunk in the last few years and the firm is now taking more candidates from lower-tier schools. But in spite of the tight job market and the expansion of the firm, Pillsbury officials contend that standards are as high as ever. One contact supports this contention, warning, "If you don't belong to a top five school, then you have to be in the top five to ten percent of your class to even get noticed by this firm." Although many associates emphasize that "solid grades are a must," some say it takes a little more than that to get hired at Pillsbury. "The person needs to be nice and well-rounded in addition to having solid grades."

One lawyer says that lateral corporate candidates are in extremely high demand at the firm. "As far as lateral hiring is concerned, the firm seems more interested in valuable experience rather than relying on old-school elitism of specific law schools and grades," says a lawyer in the San Francisco office.

Connect with Pillsbury

Those interviewing for Pillsbury's summer programs, take note: "The thing that we look for in an interview for the summer is a connection to the community," says a member of the firm's recruiting committee. "Especially in this market, we want to make sure that you're not coming to the firm to have a vacation for the summer. People need to demonstrate a connection — whether it's family, or having gone to school there, or something else." The firm reports that the schools from which it draws most heavily include Boalt, Hastings, Stanford, UCLA and Santa Clara as well as Harvard and Yale. It also recruits heavily at Duke, Virginia, Georgetown, and Howard.

OUR SURVEY SAYS

Relaxed billing machine

The changes at Pillsbury have had their impact on the insiders Vault.com spoke with. "The corporate culture is in flux," says one associate. While many attorneys seem pleased with the new open management structure, others fear the firm's new emphasis on billable hours. "It's moving from a great place to work to a billing machine," frets one associate.

But insiders still see Pillsbury as a "laid-back" and "relaxed" firm. Perhaps the full-year casual dress policy contributes to that atmosphere. Attorneys can even wear jeans on Fridays. The San Diego office has casual wine socials on Fridays and provides breakfast one day per week.

Others say Pillsbury lawyers are "smart as hell but not hung up on old-fashioned conceptions of the business world." "Pillsbury does not seem to promote the type of self-aggrandizing loud mouths that have a way of dominating the legal profession," raves another contact. Although some say Pillsbury is hierarchical, an attorney in the

San Francisco disagrees. "To the extent Pillsbury is portrayed as having a peculiarly hierarchical structure, I believe that is a myth or at least a relic of the past."

Those fun-loving partners

A source in the San Francisco office boasts, "At all times, I feel I have been treated with great respect as a person by the partners." And a tax attorney tells Vault.com, "The partners I work with strive to make sure that I have interesting work and an enormous amount of client contact." A lawyer in the Sacramento office even said the partners were "upbeat" and "fun-loving." But another source gripes, "Partners sometimes forget how hard you're working for them." One contact says the "jock mentality" of the L.A. office is "symbolized by a senior partner with two offices — one crammed with sports memorabilia." Some associates suggest that there may just be a few bad apples at Pillsbury offices who have given the firm a "bad rap." "A few partners have not learned how to deal professionally with associates, but the other partners tolerate them if they are big rainmakers."

Social life — it's out there

Insiders report that there is a social life at many of Pillsbury offices for those who want it and participation in baseball teams and other firm activities is relatively high. A contact in L.A. says, "Partners and associates often play basketball during lunch or golf on the weekends. Others go to area clubs and bars together on a regular basis." A San Diego attorney comments: "Associates tend to get along well and spend time together outside the office as time permits."

But some contacts don't draw their social circles from the firm. A San Francisco associate observes, "Most people find that work creates enough interaction. After that we prefer to live our own lives. However, there are several groups that go out every Friday night after work." "I don't come to work to find friends; if I did, I could," concurs another contact. One insider explains, "There is a very devoted social contingent among the younger associates. Among more senior associates, this level of activity drops off. But I attribute a lot of that to marriage."

Three levels of compensation

The money-conscious have found happiness at Pillsbury in recent months. "PM&S has kept its pledge to pay top-of-the-market salary!" one associate exclaims. The firm was one of the first firms to raise starting salaries. In addition, the firm has adopted a three-tier bonus structure. First-years who bill 2,100, 2,250 or 2,400 hours will get a bonus of $5,000, $7,500, or $12,500, respectively. In addition, associates can earn a merit bonus ranges from $5,000 for first-years up to $10,000 for fourth- and fifth-years. Senior associates can earn a profit-sharing component to their salary that ranges from $10,000 to $30,000. Although the $125,000 starting salary has reached San Diego, San Francisco, Palo Alto and Washington, DC, it has not come to all of Pillsbury's offices. "The firm is paying associates in the Sacramento office less than every other office in the firm, despite the fact that we are doing the same work at the same rates," carps one attorney at that office.

Associates seem generally pleased with the flexibility of the new compensation plan. "Although the pay increases do entail a certain increased emphasis on billable hours, the three-tier bonus structure arguably allows an associate to pick his or her own lifestyle." "Sometimes I wish I worked less hours, but then I acknowledge that my hours are a function of my own ambitions," confesses an associate.

But some believe the new salaries come with a price. "Under the new salary structure it is quite clear that not making the minimum of 1,950 hours is not acceptable," explains a wary source. Some attorneys believe that "the billable hour requirement is excessive compared to the pay." One contact points out a mixed message: "As a general policy, the firm does not want associates to burn out and move on. Still, the nature of the economy right now is leading to attorney exhaustion."

No hand-holding

Pillsbury allows its first-year associates to count up to 100 hours of training or pro bono towards their billing requirement. The firm also sponsors National Institute of Trial Advocacy (NITA) advanced trial training for upper-level litigators. While some describe the formal training programs as "superior" at Pillsbury, others suggest that regular training sessions are "somewhat lacking." One source tells Vault.com, "Training programs are abundant at Pillsbury. However, many associates are too concerned with their billable hours and bonus potential to take advantage of these opportunities." A lawyer in San Diego comments pointedly, "This is an office for self-starters who do not need hand-holding."

But most lawyers seem to agree that they are getting good on-the-job training. "I think the partners I work for are exceedingly concerned with our professional development," opines one lawyer. "The opportunities here are incredible for those that seek them out. Those who are afraid to ask for them appear to be the most disenchanted with their experience here," a litigator says. But another Pillsbury attorney contends that "partners do not have much time to explain the practice of law. You have to figure that out for yourself."

Temptations

Opinions on the retention rate at Pillsbury vary, with some insiders saying the firm has "an extremely high turnover rate" and others asserting that "the retention rate has improved substantially over the past two years." A source in the San Francisco office says that "retention levels are somewhat unclear at the moment, but I would say that this is an area in which the firm is improving." Another associate adds, "Despite the many opportunities for qualified attorneys elsewhere, associates feel a certain sense of loyalty to the firm." For its part, the firm says that its attrition rate for both associates and partners is on par with the industry. It has passed several policies, including offering senior asociates an equity stake in the firm, to further reduce departures. The Internet continues, however, to sing its siren song: "No one can resist the temptation of dot coms," admits one associate (who's still with Pillsbury for now). For those who manage to resist the Internet allure, associates report there is a pretty good chance of making partner "if you bring in clients and stick around for seven to 10 years."

Offices are oh-so-chic

Pillsbury's San Francisco office has relocated to the trendy SoMa area of San Francisco. The new offices have put Pillsbury's attorneys and staff under the same roof for the first time since the 1970s. Pillsbury's new home is reportedly "spacious and comfortable with modern design throughout." One source describes the new offices as "a gorgeous mix of industrial surfaces and Asian detailing." Vault.com sources explain that the offices are designed for greater social interaction. "Partners no longer have the big desk to sit behind. Each partner has a circular table at which he or she speaks with associates." But some associates aren't thrilled with their new views — the offices occupy the lower floors of the building.

Most associates at other offices express satisfaction with their surroundings, too. A San Diego lawyers states, "Our offices are beautiful and fairly large, but space is always at a premium." The nation's capital attracts less praise. One source grumbles, "Not a great location in the DC area." Fortunately, the firm has plans to move most of the DC and Northern Virginia offices into a brand-new space.

Entitled support staff

"I would not say support is one of Pillsbury's strong points," one source tells Vault.com. "It is often difficult to earn the respect of the staff, which translates into poor levels of assistance." "The sense of entitlement of some of the staff members is mind-boggling," gripes a junior lawyer. Pillsbury associates note there has been a large turnover in secretarial staff. The staff is probably overworked — insiders note Pillsbury usually has around three attorneys to a secretary.

Insiders say the library staff at the San Francisco office is excellent and there is 24-hour word processing support "which, for the most part, manages to get all projects done on schedule." (Other offices do not enjoy round-the-clock word processing.) The firm also has the capability for attorneys to dial into its network via the Internet, "which is a big plus for those who wish to work off-site."

The women are running the firm!

One associate describes Pillsbury as "undoubtedly one of the best law firms in the world for women." Associates note that there are many women in senior management positions at the firm, including firm chair Mary Cranston. Eighteen percent of the firm's partners are women and four out of the seven associates promoted to partner in 1999 were women. "It is fair to say our firm is currently run by women. There is no lack of gender equality here," says a San Francisco lawyer. A female lawyer reports, "I don't feel that being a woman is any sort of impediment here." "Gender has become a non-issue," concurs another source.

Big effort, little results

Associates claim the firm tries hard to recruit minorities but so far its efforts have not paid off. "Ethnic minorities are not too visible, but I don't think there is an effort to exclude," says one source. "I'm disappointed that we don't have more minority attorneys," sighs another lawyer. Pillsbury reports that 18 percent of its total attorneys and 26 percent of its associates are people of color, figures it feels compare favorably with most of its competitors.

No gay issue

Associates report that openly gay and lesbian attorneys are in prominent positions throughout the firm. "I feel that there simply is no gay issue at Pillsbury," states an attorney in the San Fran office. Not only do insiders claim the firm is comfortable for homosexual attorneys, but gay lawyers' partners are also openly accepted at firm events.

Pro bono no mo'?

In the past Pillsbury has received accolades for its pro bono work. But many fear the new salary structure has forced many associates to forego pro bono work for billable work. "The increase in salaries and the fact that pro bono work no longer is included in billing requirements will effectively kill pro bono work," predicts one source. First-years are able to count up to 100 hours of pro bono or training toward their billing requirements. One mid-level associate complains, "I do a lot of pro bono work, and since Pillsbury no longer allows associates beyond their first year to count pro bono work toward the billable hours requirement, I have been working very tiring hours to make ends meet here."

Preston Gates & Ellis LLP

NEARLY & NOTABLE

5000 Columbia Center
701 Fifth Avenue
Seattle, WA 98104-7078
(206) 623-7580
Fax: (206) 623-7022

LOCATIONS

Seattle, WA (HQ)
Anchorage, AK
Coeur d' Alene, ID
Los Angeles, CA
Orange County, CA
Palo Alto, CA
Portland, OR
San Francisco, CA
Spokane, WA
Washington, DC
Hong Kong

MAJOR DEPARTMENTS/PRACTICES

Corporate/Business
Environmental/Land Use
Intellectual Property and Technology
Labor & Employment
Litigation
Municipal
Real Estate/Bankruptcy

THE STATS

No. of attorneys: 349
No. of offices: 11
Summer associate offers: 13 out of 14 (Seattle, 1999)
Managing Partner: B. Gerald Johnson
Hiring Partner: Ramona M. Emerson

PAY

Seattle, 2000
1st year: $100,000 + bonus after 1,900 billable hours + discretionary bonus
Summer associate: $1,650/week

NOTABLE PERKS

- Wills drafted by firm attorney
- Parental leave
- Free parking after three years
- $100 bonus for submitting time sheets on time

THE BUZZ
What attorneys at other firms are saying about this firm

- "Microsoft-dependent"
- "Great for Seattle (if you don't mind working for the Evil Empire)"
- "Quality life, quality work."

UPPERS

- Microsoft
- Flexibility to work for many partners and practice areas
- Associate practice development

DOWNERS

- Low percentage of minorities
- Lack of information shared with associates
- Stinginess with laptops

KEY COMPETITORS

Cooley Godward
Perkins Coie
Venture Law Group
Wilson Sonsini Goodrich & Rosati

EMPLOYMENT CONTACT

Ms. Kristine Immordino
Manager Legal Recruitment and Development
(206) 623-7580
krisi@prestongates.com

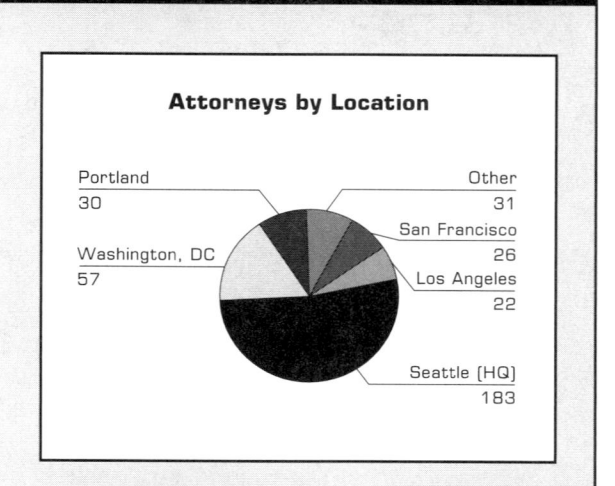

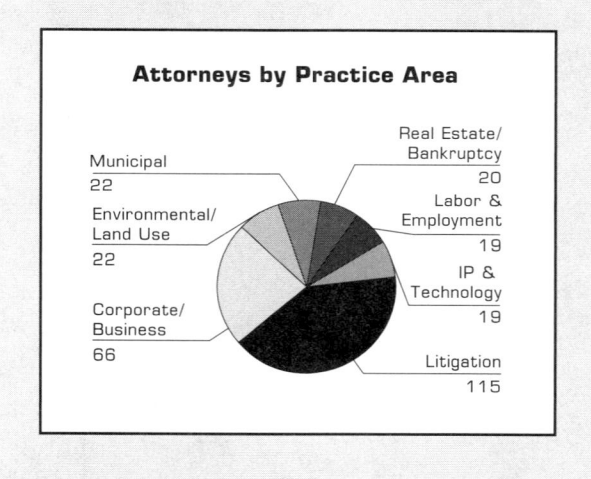

Attorneys by Location

- Seattle (HQ): 183
- Washington, DC: 57
- Portland: 30
- Other: 31
- San Francisco: 26
- Los Angeles: 22

Attorneys by Practice Area

- Litigation: 115
- Corporate/Business: 66
- Municipal: 22
- Environmental/Land Use: 22
- Real Estate/Bankruptcy: 20
- Labor & Employment: 19
- IP & Technology: 19

QUALITY OF LIFE RANKINGS [ASSOCIATES RATE THEIR OWN FIRM]

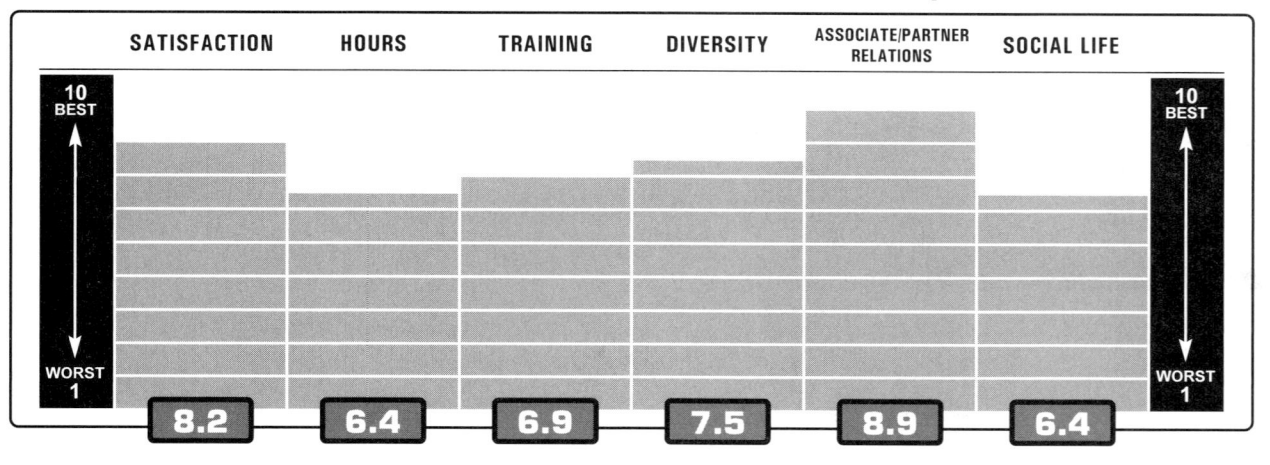

Satisfaction	Hours	Training	Diversity	Associate/Partner Relations	Social Life
8.2	6.4	6.9	7.5	8.9	6.4

THE SCOOP

Seattle. Gates. Seattle. Gates. Get it? The Gates in Preston Gates & Ellis refers to none other than Bill Gates' daddy, William H. Gates. Talk about rainmaking! This Seattle mainstay has been around for far longer than Microsoft, however, and while the perhaps soon-to-be split software company is the firm's largest client, it only accounts for about 10 percent of the firm's total billing.

Old faithful in Seattle

Preston Gates & Ellis, Seattle's oldest continuously operating firm, can trace its family tree back to 1883, when 25-year old Harold Preston, fresh from the cornfields of Iowa, arrived in Seattle to hang out his shingle. Preston would become a major force in Washington politics, even drafting the state's first workers' compensation law in 1911. In 1990 a new chapter in the firm's history began when the firm merged with another Seattle-based firm, 63-year-old Shidler, McBroom, Gates & Lewis. Shidler, McBroom brought into the deal alumni including a former State Supreme Court Justice and more importantly, a client list that included a certain software company. In 2000 the firm counts almost 350 lawyers practicing throughout five states, Washington, DC, and Hong Kong.

Business at the firm breaks down into the following areas: business, technology and intellectual property, real estate, environmental and land use, municipal, litigation and public policy. Municipal finance is a particular strength. According to industry-watcher Securities Data Company, the firm ranked tenth nationally in 1999 for the number of bond issues (243) and 10th in the nation in terms of dollar value of issues ($4.04 billion).

L.A. office reshuffles the deck

In June 2000, Preston Gates announced that its Los Angeles office would undergo a change in business strategy, abandoning several practice areas in order to focus on technology-oriented litigation. Opened in 1994, the 20-lawyer office dropped its environmental, general litigation, business, and public finance practices. While the the office's 12 associates will remain, five to six partners — including environmental lawyer David Sadwick, the managing partner of the office — were expected to leave at the time of the announcement.

"Big Bill" and Microsoft

William H. Gates, Bill Gates' father, was a well-known Seattle resident before his son became the richest man in the world. "Big Bill," as his friends call him, was president of the State Bar Association as well as an active participant in Seattle civil life and the Republican party. While the senior Gates, now retired, was the most visible lawyer at the firm, he never involved himself with the Microsoft account.

These days Microsoft keeps the firm busy. Along with Sullivan & Cromwell, Preston Gates attorneys helped the computer giant battle a private antitrust suit brought by Caldera, Inc. Caldera claimed Microsoft prevented Caldera's development of a potential competitor of Microsoft's MS-DOS operating system. The two sides settled the suit in January 2000.

Microsoft and Preston Gates suffered a bit of a setback in May 2000 when a federal judge in California issued a preliminary injunction stopping Microsoft from distributing Sun Microsystem's Java Technology. Sun Microsystems claimed Microsoft had violated a license agreement by modifying Java so it would run only on Windows and Internet Explorer. However, the Ninth Circuit Court of Appeals vacated the injunction shortly thereafter and the lower court dismissed Sun's copyright infringement claim.

I'll have a latte

The firm has kept true to its policy of not accepting tobacco clients for over 20 years, refusing to represent the tobacco companies that have generated millions of dollars of revenues for other firms. Moreover, the firm represented the City of Los Angeles in a 1998 suit against 16 tobacco companies. The city charged the companies with failing to warn consumers about the dangers of secondhand smoke. Despite the anti-tobacco stand, one of Preston's biggest clients provides the legal vice that is Seattle's prime addiction: coffee. The firm took Starbucks public in 1992 and the company has remained a client since.

Bond work

A large percentage of Preston Gates & Ellis' practice is bond work. In fact, the firm does more bond work than any other firm in Washington. PG&E has served as bond counsel to clients ranging from the Washington State Housing Finance Commission to the Seattle Mariners. The firm was involved in the 1999 bond financing of the Mariners' new stadium, the beautifully named Safeco Field.

Lobbying love

Preston has also attracted considerable notice for its Federal/Regulatory/Legislative practice, which offers a variety of services including direct lobbying, monitoring legislative activities, drafting legislation, representing clients in congressional and executive branch investigations, and organizing grassroots and constituent support. In

1999 the firm's Washington, DC office was ranked among the top five firms in terms of lobbying revenues. While the group pulls in plentiful fees, the PR hasn't always been terrific. The firm drew criticism for its lobbying on behalf of The Northern Marianas Islands, a South Pacific U.S. territory with no member in Congress. Hired by the Northern Marianas to fight proposals in Congress to extend U.S. minimum wage and immigration laws to the territory, the firm was blasted by Interior Secretary Bruce Babbitt, who accused the firm of orchestrating "a massive campaign of intimidation" against federal officials seeking to clean up the territory's unsavory working conditions.

GETTING HIRED

Choosy Northwesterners

"For a native Northwest firm, we are very selective," reports a Preston Gates insider. Another notes that "the hiring committee has very high standards for law school, grades, and writing ability." Indeed, the firm recruits at all the top-tier schools, as well as major law schools throughout the Northwest, including University of Washington, Seattle University, and University of Oregon. After meeting with either the recruiting manager or a member of the hiring committee, "students invited for call-back interviews meet seven to 10 attorneys from a range of departments." Candidates can also expect to be treated to lunch or dinner at one of "Seattle's most enjoyable restaurants." But these chosen ones should be on their best behavior — the hiring committee is watching.

Laterals ease in

According to the firm, "candidates are evaluated and rated in the following areas: intellect, traits befitting an attorney, personality, and compatibility with the firm's needs." (There is no swimsuit competition.) While the competition for first-year associate positions at the firm is fierce, many laterals have had a much easier time getting hired. One transfer elaborates, "I had a very difficult time trying to get a job here while I was in law school. However, once I had been in practice in a specialty that was needed by the firm, I had no trouble. Timing was everything."

OUR SURVEY SAYS

An almost matchless reputation

Associates point out that in the Pacific Northwest, Preston Gates & Ellis' reputation is pristine. One declares, "It is the oldest firm in Seattle and it has represented Microsoft for most of Microsoft's lifetime. The fact that the partners at the firm have been doing large-scale transactions for many years puts them in a league above any other Seattle law firm." Attorneys in the firm feel the reputation is for the most part justified. The firm creates a "casual atmosphere full of incredibly smart, experienced attorneys," reports one. Many note that Preston is "very big on process and fairness. It is striving to maintain a balance between working hard and having a life." A third-year associate indicates that change is in the air: "The firm was previously very committed to municipal and government service — the culture now is leaning toward the dot com and IPO attitude of fast action and fast money." Another points out that the firm's future culture is to some extent "up for grabs. As we grow rapidly, there will be tension between those motivated by cash and those motivated by other values."

Precious Preston pay

While Preston Gates has not matched the salary raises set by Gunderson, associates are nevertheless content with the salary raise the firm gave in 2000. First-year associates receive a base salary of $100,000. The Seattle office has a billable hour target of 1,800 hours and the firm gives out productivity bonuses at 1,900, 2,000, and 2,100 billable hours. An associate reports, "The salaries here are extremely competitive, especially given the billable hours requirement. The bonus compensation plan is aggressive, although as currently structured it does not fairly compensate laterals on a pro rata basis for fractional years."

Live well, work here

Attorneys at PG&E reveal that while there is pressure to bill a lot of hours, "this firm is very committed to quality of life." A lateral continues, "In comparison to my stint at a large Manhattan firm, the hours here are very livable." Indeed, many characterize the firm's billable target of 1,800 to 2,000 hours per year as very reasonable. A third-year attorney relates his schedule to Vault.com: "I have been billing about 40-55 hours per week. I usually work from about 8 a.m. to 7 p.m." It is not overwhelming work, therefore, that causes turnover at the firm. Retention of attorneys is nevertheless an issue at Preston Gates & Ellis, especially considering the fact that the firm is located in tech mecca Seattle. While attorneys do leave, a first-year observes that "people rarely leave for other firms. Rather, they go in-house, often at a dot com startup."

Another associate elaborates that "every month or so you hear about another associate leaving to go in-house. I haven't really heard of associates leaving for other firms."

A diversity of partners — and partner opinions

The partners at Preston are a very large and diverse group; the ratio of partners to associates at the firm's Seattle headquarters is nearly two to one. It is no surprise, then, that opinions regarding the partners vary. A third-year states that "Preston is a very non-hierarchical firm. Associates are treated as individuals and with respect. I would even say that associates are pampered by the firm." Another associate concurs, "The vast majority of the partners treat me with great respect and are very friendly [although] I had one horrible experience with one partner in particular."

Other Prestonites have had negative experiences. "Except for the partners for whom I work, I feel ignored," explains an attorney, "but I suppose this is just related to each individual partner's personality." One informant supplies that firm politics get in the way of associate/partnership relations: "Firm politics are prevalent. You have to watch what you say to whom very, very closely here." Moreover, another declares, relationships between the two tiers "sometimes suffer from lack of information being shared with associates." Because most of the training at the firm is on the job, much of the responsibility falls on the shoulders of the partners. A public finance attorney notes that "my partners are helpful and patient, but there is no formal training program." One associate, not as enamored of the efforts by partners, cautions that "training is weak, as is mentoring."

Make me a partner

Associates say chances of making partner are very good. "The partnership track is six to nine years generally." Indeed, many note that the "firm still subscribes to the policy that every new associate is intended to be a partner." A second-year explains that the "general expectation is that everyone who starts here will make partner if they stick it out." Furthermore, while the track is six to nine years, the "average is seven years, and this year a fifth- and sixth-year were both made partner." One complaint made by a senior associate is that while partners generally provide "pretty good feedback at annual evaluation about chances for partnership, they do not give much information on when a decision will be made." However, an environmental attorney states that there is little reason to worry: "I cannot remember any associate being let go since 1994 or 1995, but lots of folks decide that firm life is not for them and so bail of their own accord. Those small numbers who stay stand a very good chance of becoming partner."

Social life transpires outdoors

Preston Gates & Ellis is located in Seattle, a lovely, if rain-soaked, city only a short distant from the mountains and offering opportunities to take part in a vast array of outdoor activities. When work is over PG&E associates disappear. A first-year writes, "At work the contact between attorneys is great — outside of work it is nonexistent." Another source gives a different hypothesis for the lack of after work interaction: "There is not a tremendous amount of after-hours socializing as the firm is quite family-oriented." A litigator agrees, "The social life could be better, but part of the issue is that a lot of us have families and would rather get our work done and get home than hang around socializing." A bankruptcy attorney feels that socializing is "not really encouraged or required by the firm. I think people focus more on their families. Most of the social events I've been to recently are for departing associates!"

Looking out at the mountains and Puget Sound

PG&E's Seattle office offers a "great view" with "terrible decor." A third-year notes that the "high floors of the Bank of America Tower have stellar views of the Puget Sound, the Cascade Mountains and the Olympic Mountains." Another Seattle-ite describes his office as "comfortable but unattractive." One widespread complaint is of outdated, uncomfortable furniture. One source notes, "I think eventually I will become a hunchback. The furniture is terrible!" Many wait hopefully for the "new office space expected in two or three years" and pray for better furniture, as well as cutting-edge high tech equipment.

Associates give mixed reviews to the support staff. Many attorneys note that the "staff, especially the paralegals, are top-notch" and rave about the two-to-one lawyer-secretary ratio. Others gripe that "word processing is terrible and secretaries are luck of the draw." One associate notes that the "firm needs document management software." A laptopless lawyer laments, "I wish the firm was a little more liberal about providing laptops."

So pro bono

The firm counts 50 hours of pro bono work towards its billable targets. Beyond 50 hours, pro bono work may be counted at the discretion of the compensation committee. Moreover, an associate notes, "pro bono work is one of the factors for receiving discretionary bonuses." Associates state that the firm's commitment to pro bono work is fair. According to insiders, "the firm is committed to pro bono as long as it doesn't interfere with paying work." Another continues: "The last five years saw a significant retreat from pro bono commitment at this firm while we focused on financial stability and then pure profit. How we resurrect our pro bono program will be a key indicator of the direction of firm culture."

Impressive women, looking for minorities

When questioned about women's issues, associates cite "an impressive number of women partners, including women on the executive committee, department chairs and branch directors." One source reports that "several department heads have been or are women. Part-time is possible but sometimes has been an issue." A seventh-year points out that the firm has problems with retention of women: "We've lost a lot of new mothers to other places or to stay at home, but it is something the firm seems genuinely interested in addressing."

When addressing issues with respect to minorities, attorneys state simply that "unfortunately, we are a very white firm" and the firm "needs more effort to attract minorities." However, gay attorneys seem to find the firm "very welcoming." A Prestonite states that the firm is home to "a large number of openly gay attorneys and staff." Another reports, "We continue to make progress in this area. In 1993 I would have given us a much lower mark on this."

"Candidates are evaluated and rated in the following areas: intellect, traits benefitting an attorney, personality, and compatibility with the firm's needs."

— *Preston Gates associate*

HUNTON & WILLIAMS

"...high quality work, high quality colleagues"

—www.vault.com

www.hunton.com

Atlanta Bangkok Brussels Charlotte Hong Kong
Knoxville London McLean Miami New York
Norfolk Raleigh Richmond Warsaw Washington

THE BEST OF THE REST

Arent Fox Kintner Plotkin & Kahn, PLLC

1050 Conneticut Avenue, NW
Washington, DC 20036-5339
(202) 857-6000
Fax: (202) 857-6395
www.arentfox.com

LOCATIONS

Washington, DC (HQ)
New York, NY
Bucharest
Riyadh

MAJOR DEPARTMENTS/PRACTICES

General Business
Internatonal
Litigation and Dispute Resolution
Regulatory and Public Policy
Technology

THE STATS

No. of attorneys: 285
No. of offices: 4
Summer associate offers: 9 out of 10 (Washington, DC 1999)
Managing Attorney: Christopher Smith
Hiring Attorney: Elliot I. Portnoy

NOTABLE PERKS

- $10,000 judicial clerkship bonus
- Domestic partner benefits
- "Dress for the day" every day

EMPLOYMENT CONTACT

Ms. Amber Winsberg
Attorney Recruitment/Development Manager
(202) 857-6146
winsbera@arentfox.com

PAY

Washington, DC, 2000
1st year: $110,000
Summer associate: $1,925/week

New York, 2000
Summer associate: $1,925/week

THE BUZZ
What attorneys at other firms are saying about this firm

- "DC oldie"
- "Washington firm that wants to play with the NYC big boys"
- "Good regional firm"

Ballard Spahr Andrews & Ingersoll, LLP

1735 Market Street
Philadelphia, PA 19103-7599
(215) 665-8500
Fax: (215) 864-8999
www.ballardspahr.com

LOCATIONS

Philadelphia, PA (HQ)
Baltimore, MD
Camden, NJ
Denver, CO
Salt Lake City, UT
Voorhees, NJ
Washington, DC

MAJOR DEPARTMENTS/PRACTICES

Business & Finance
Employee Benefits
Estates
Litigation
Public Finance
Real Estate
Tax

THE STATS

No. of attorneys: 341
No. of offices: 7
Summer associate offers: 18 out of 19 (Philadelphia, 1999)
Chairman, Management Committee: David L. Cohen
Hiring Partner: Rhonda R. Cohen and Mark S. Stewart

THE BUZZ
What attorneys at other firms are saying about this firm

- "Cult of personality"
- "Good litigation and real estate department"
- "Watch out on those interviews"
- "Political powerhouse"

NOTABLE PERKS

- Profit sharing
- Sports and orchestra tickets

EMPLOYMENT CONTACT

Lateral Attorney Employment:
Ms. Bonnie Bell
Director of Personnel
(215) 864-8163
bellb@ballardspahr.com

Philadelphia Summer Associate Employment:
Ms. Alberta Bertolino
Professional Personnel Administrator
(215) 864-8167
bertolino@ballardspahr.com

PAY

Philadelphia, 2000
1st year: $100,000 + bonus
Summer associate: $1,900/week

Baltimore, 2000
1st year: $95,000 + bonus
Summer associate: $1,800/week

Denver, 2000
1st year: $90,000 + bonus
Summer associate: $1,700/week

Salt Lake City, 2000
1st year: $90,000 + bonus
Summer associate: $1,700/week

Vorhees, 2000
1st year: $95,000 + bonus

Washington, 2000
1st year: $104,000 + bonus
Summer associate: $2,000/week

Bingham Dana LLP

150 Federal Street
Boston, MA 02110
(617) 951-8000
Fax: (617) 951-8736
www.bingham.com

LOCATIONS

Boston, MA (HQ)
Hartford, CT
Los Angeles, CA
New York, NY
Washington, DC
London
Singapore

MAJOR DEPARTMENTS/PRACTICES

Corporate/Technology • Estate Planning • Finance/Financial Restructuring/Project Finance/Private Equity/Real Estate • Litigation • Tax

THE STATS

No. of attorneys: 400
No. of offices: 7
Summer associate offers: 31 out of 31 (Boston, 1999)
Managing Partner: Jay S. Zimmerman
Hiring Attorney: Marijane Benner Browne

THE BUZZ
What attorneys at other firms are saying about this firm

- "Rising star"
- "Old-fashioned but excellent firm"
- "Intellectual"
- "Parochial but trying to branch out"

NOTABLE PERKS

- Full-time casual dress
- Emergency child care center
- PCs for home use
- Judicial clerkship bonus
- Domestic partner benefits

EMPLOYMENT CONTACT

Ms. Maris L. Abbene, Esq.
Director of Recruitment
(617) 951-8556
abbeneml@bingham.com

PAY

Boston, 2000
1st year: $125,000 + discretionary bonus
2nd year: $130,000 + discretionary bonus
3rd year: $135,000 + discretionary bonus
4th year: $160,000 + discretionary bonus
5th year: $180,000 + discretionary bonus
6th year: $190,000 + discretionary bonus
7th year: $200,000 + discretionary bonus
Summer associate: $2,400/week

Hartford, 2000
1st year: $85,000 + discretionary bonus
2nd year: $90,000 + discretionary bonus
3rd year: $95,000 + discretionary bonus
4th year: $105,000 + discretionary bonus
5th year: $115,000 + discretionary bonus
6th year: $120,000 + discretionary bonus
7th year: $125,000 + discretionary bonus
Summer associate: $1,635/week

New York, 2000
1st year: $125,000 + discretionary bonus
2nd year: $130,000 + discretionary bonus
3rd year: $140,000 + discretionary bonus
4th year: $165,000 + discretionary bonus
5th year: $190,000 + discretionary bonus
6th year: $200,000 + discretionary bonus
7th year: $210,000 + discretionary bonus
Summer associate: $2,400/week

Blank Rome Comisky & McCauley LLP

One Logan Square
Philadelphia, PA 19103-6998
(215) 569-5500
Fax: (215) 569-5555
www.blankrome.com

LOCATIONS

Philadelphia, PA (HQ)
Allentown, PA
Baltimore, MD
Boca Raton, FL
Cherry Hill, NJ
Media, PA
New York, NY
Trenton, NJ
Washington, DC
Wilmington, DE

MAJOR DEPARTMENTS/PRACTICES

Bankruptcy • Civil & White Collar Crime • Corporate & Securities • Creditor's Rights • Environmental • Finance • Government • Health Care • Intellectual Property • International • Labor, Employment & Employee Benefits • Litigation • Matrimonial • Municipal • Public Finance • Real Estate • Tax • Trusts & Estates

THE STATS

No. of attorneys: 385
No. of offices: 10
Summer associate offers: 14 out of 14 (Philadelphia, 1999)
Managing partner: David F. Girard-diCarlo
Hiring Partner: Mark I. Rabinowitz

THE BUZZ
What attorneys at other firms are saying about this firm

- "Wired to the Republican party"
- "A lot to offer"
- "Cutthroat"

NOTABLE PERKS

- Dependent care spending account
- On-site fitness center

EMPLOYMENT CONTACT

Ms. Donna Branca
Manager of Attorney Relations
(215) 569-5751
branca@blankrome.com

PAY

Philadelphia and Washington, DC, 2000
1st year: $105,000 + discretionary bonus
Summer associate (Philadelphia): $2,000/week

New York, 2000
1st year: $120,000 + discretionary bonus

Bonus includes business generation component.

Bracewell & Patterson, LLP

711 Louisiana, Suite 2900
South Tower Penzoil Place
Houston, TX 77002-2781
(713) 223-2900
www.bracepatt.com

LOCATIONS

Houston, TX (HQ)
Austin, TX
Corpus Christi, TX
Dallas, TX
Fort Worth, TX
San Antonio, TX
Washington, DC
Almaty
Astana, Kazakhstan
London

MAJOR DEPARTMENTS/PRACTICES

Corporate and Securities • Energy and Finance • Environmental • Financial Services • Government Regulations/Strategy • Intellectual Property • Labor and Employment • Real Estate • Regulated and Restructured Industries • School and Public Law • Tax • Trial • Wills, Trusts & Estates

THE STATS

No. of attorneys: 295
No. of offices: 11
Summer associate offers: 25 out of 28 (Houston, 1999)
Managing Partner: Kelly Frels
Hiring Partner: Mr. Jeffery J. Horner (entry-level)

THE BUZZ
What attorneys at other firms are saying about this firm

- "Decent, litigation-oriented Texas firm"
- "Conservative"
- "Second-tier, but growing practice"

NOTABLE PERKS

- Sabbaticals for partners
- Free parking

EMPLOYMENT CONTACT

Ms. Melanie G. Beck
Manager of Attorney Employment
(713) 221-1296
mbeck@bracepatt.com

PAY

Houston, Austin, and Dallas, 2000
1st year: $105,000 + $5,000 potential
2nd year: $105,000 - $115,000 + $10,000 potential
3rd year: $107,000 - $120,000 + $20,000 potential
4th year: $110,000 - $125,000 + $25,000 potential
5th year: $113,00 - $135,000 + $30,000 potential
6th year: $121,00 - $145,000 + $30,000 potential
7th year: $131,000 - $155,000 + $30,000 potential
Summer associate: $1,650/week

Corpus Christi and San Antonio, 2000
1st year: $95,000 + $9,000 potential
2nd year: $95,000 - $104,000 + $9,000 potential
3rd year: $97,000 - $108,000 + $18,000 potential
4th year: $99,000 - $113,000 + $23,000 potential
5th year: $102,00 - $122,000 + $27,000 potential
6th year: $110,00 - $131,000 + $27,000 potential
7th year: $115,000 - $140,000 + $27,000 potential

Washington, DC, 2000
1st year: $110,000 + $10,000 potential
2nd year: $110,000 - $120,000 + $10,000 potential
3rd year: $112,000 - $125,000 + $20,000 potential
4th year: $115,000 - $130,000 + $25,000 potential
5th year: $118,000 - $140,000 + $30,000 potential
6th year: $127,000 - $150,000 + $30,000 potential
7th year: $136,000 - $160,000 + $30,000 potential

Signing bonus for entry-level associates and judicial clerks.

Drinker Biddle & Reath, LLP

One Logan Square
18th and Cherry Streets
Philadelphia, PA 19103-6996
(215) 988-2700
Fax: (215) 988-2757
www.dbr.com

LOCATIONS

Philadelphia, PA (HQ)
Berwyn, PA
Florham Park, NJ
New York, NY
Princeton, NJ
Washington, DC

MAJOR DEPARTMENTS/PRACTICES

Business and Finance
Litigation
Personal Law

THE STATS

No. of attorneys: 355
No. of offices: 6
Summer associate offers: 22 out of 23 (Philadelphia, 1999)
Chairman & Chief Executive, Management Committee: James M. Sweet
Hiring Partner: Seamus C. Duffy

NOTABLE PERKS

- Bar membership dues paid
- $5,000 stipend for all first-year associates

EMPLOYMENT CONTACT

Maryellen Wyville Altieri
Director of Professional Recruitment
(215) 988-2663
wyvillem@dbr.com

PAY

Philadelphia, Berwyn, and Princeton, 2000
1st year: $105,000 + $5,000 bonus at 1,950 hours and additional bonus at 2,000 billable hours
Summer associate: $2,019/week

Washington, DC, 2000
1st year: $110,000 + $5,000 bonus at 1,900 hours and additional $5,000 bonus at 2,000 billable hours
Summer associate: $2,115/week

Florham Park, 2000
1st year: $95,000 + $5,000 stipend
Summer associate: $1,827/week

THE BUZZ
What attorneys at other firms are saying about this firm

- "Good regional firm"
- "Old-line Philly firm"

Duane, Morris & Heckscher LLP

One Liberty Place, Suite 4200
1650 Market Street
Philadelphia, PA 19103-7396
(215) 979-1000
Fax: (215) 979-1020
www.duanemorris.com

LOCATIONS

Philadelphia, PA (HQ)
Allentown, PA • Bangor, ME • Boston, MA • Cherry Hill, NJ • Chicago, IL • Harrisburg, PA • Houston, TX • Miami, FL • New York, NY • Newark, NJ • Palm Beach, FL • Pleasantville, NY • Princeton, NJ • San Francisco, CA • Washington, DC • Wayne, PA • Wilmington, DE

MAJOR DEPARTMENTS/PRACTICES

Administrative
Bankruptcy
Corporate
Environmental
Health Care
Intellectual Property
Labor & Employment & ERISA
Litigation
Real Estate
Tax
Trusts & Estates

THE STATS

No. of attorneys: 390
No. of offices: 18
Summer associate offers: 11 out of 13 (Philadelphia, 1999)
Chairman, Management Committee: Sheldon M. Bonovitz
Hiring Partner: Thomas G. Servodidio, Esq.

THE BUZZ
What attorneys at other firms are saying about this firm

- "Spasmodic, curious growth"
- "Big name in the banking and insurance world"
- "Nice offices"

NOTABLE PERKS

- Bar study stipend
- Domestic partner benefits

EMPLOYMENT CONTACTS

Mr. Pedro J. Rivera
Director of Legal Recruiting
(215) 979-1279
pjrivera@duanemorris.com

PAY

Philadelphia, 2000
1st year: $100,000 + discretionary bonus
Summer associate: $1,730/week

Fenwick & West LLP

Two Palo Alto Square
Palo Alto, CA 94306
(650) 494-0600
Fax: (212) 494-1417
www.fenwick.com

LOCATIONS

Palo Alto, CA (HQ)
San Francisco, CA
Washington, DC

MAJOR DEPARTMENTS/PRACTICES

Corporate
Employment & Labor
Intellectual Property
Licensing & Technology
Litigation
Mergers & Acquisitions
Patent
Securities
Tax
Trademark
Venture Capital

THE STATS

No. of attorneys: 259
No. of offices: 3
Summer associate offers: 32 out of 33
Chair, Management Committee: Gordon K. Davidson
Hiring attorneys: John Steele, Esq. and Jeff Vetter, Esq.

NOTABLE PERKS

- Mortgage assistance
- Auto insurance
- Pet insurance
- Associate investment program
- Use of firm condo in Maui or Park City
- Clerkship bonus

EMPLOYMENT CONTACT

Ms. Karen Amartangelo-Block
Attorney Recruiting Manager
(650) 858-7141

PAY

All offices, 2000
1st year: $125,000 + bonus
2nd year: $135,000 + bonus
3rd year: $150,000 + bonus
4th year: $165,000 + bonus
5th year: $185,000 + bonus
6th year: $195,000 + bonus
7th year: $205,000 + bonus
Summer associate: $2,400/week

THE BUZZ
What attorneys at other firms are saying about this firm

- "Gracefully transitioning to big firm/high tech practice"
- "Always a bridesmaid, never a bride"
- "Another cool Valley lifestyle firm"

Fish & Neave

1251 Avenue of the Americas
New York, NY 10020
(212) 596-9000
Fax: (212) 596-9090
www.fishneave.com

LOCATIONS

New York, NY (HQ)
Palo Alto, CA

MAJOR DEPARTMENTS/PRACTICES

Intellectual Property
Patents and Trademarks Litigation
Patents and Trade Secrets

THE STATS

No. of attorneys: 167
No. of offices: 2
Summer associate offers: 20 out of 20 (New York, 1999)
Managing Partner: Jesse J. Jenner
Hiring attorneys: John M. Hintz and Frances M. Lynch

NOTABLE PERKS

- Occasional Friday afternoon keg parties
- Reduced rates for local gym and cellular phones
- Discounts at some Rockefeller Plaza stores
- Tickets to sports events and concerts

EMPLOYMENT CONTACT

Ms. Heather C. Fennell
Legal Recruitment Manager
(212) 596-9121
hfennell@fishneave.com

PAY

New York and Palo Alto, 2000
1st year: $125,000
2nd year: $135,000
3rd year: $150,000
4th year: $165,000
5th year: $185,000
6th year: $200,000
7th year: $215,000
8th year: $230,000
Summer associate: $1,925/week

THE BUZZ
What attorneys at other firms are saying about this firm

- "IP Kings"
- "Patent law geeks"

Fish & Richardson P.C.

225 Franklin Street
Boston, MA 02110
(617) 542-5070
Fax: (617) 542-8906
www.fr.com

LOCATIONS

Boston, MA
Dallas, TX
Menlo Park, CA
Minneapolis, MN
New York, NY
San Diego, CA
Washington, DC
Wilmington, DE

MAJOR DEPARTMENTS/PRACTICES

Intellectual Property
Litigation
Patent Prosecution
Trademark

THE STATS

No. of attorneys: 170
No. of offices: 8
Summer associate offers: 21 out of 23 (Firm-wide, 1999)
President, Executive Committee: Peter J. Devlin
Chair, Executive Committee: Robert E. Hillman
Hiring Attorney: Richard J. Anderson

NOTABLE PERKS

- Ability to work from home
- Periodic socials
- Relocation expenses
- Maternity and paternity leave
- Firm-wide video conference forum every Thursday

EMPLOYMENT CONTACT

Ms. Jill E. McDonald
Director of Attorney Hiring
(858) 678-5070
jobs@fr.com

PAY

All Offices, 2000

1st year: $125,000 + $45,000 bonus potential
2nd year: $135,000 + $47,800 bonus potential
3rd year: $140,000 + $59,200 bonus potential
4th year: $150,000 + $72,000 bonus potential
5th year: $160,000 + $82,300 bonus potential
6th year: $165,000 + $88,700 bonus potential
7th year: $175,000 + $91,500 bonus potential
8th year: $180,000 + $92,900 bonus potential
Bonuses are partly based on billable hours.
Summer associate (1999): $2,400/week

THE BUZZ

What attorneys at other firms are saying about this firm

- "Prestigious niche player"
- "IP boutique, well-respected"
- "One-dimensional"

Foley, Hoag & Eliot LLP

One Post Office Square
Boston, MA 02109
(617) 832-1000
Fax: (617) 832-7000
www.fhe.com

LOCATIONS

Boston, MA (HQ)
Washington, DC

MAJOR DEPARTMENTS/PRACTICES

Administrative
Business
Environmental
Intellectual Property
Labor
Litigation
Real Estate
Tax
Trusts & Estates

THE STATS

No. of attorneys: 210
No. of offices: 2
Summer associate offers: 28 out of 28 (Boston, 1999)
Co-Managing Partners: Mark F. Clark & Barry B. White
Hiring Attorney: Anthony D. Mirenda

NOTABLE PERKS

- Child care
- Profit sharing
- Moving expenses

EMPLOYMENT CONTACT

Ms. Dina M. Wreede
Director of Legal Recruiting & Professional Development
(617) 832-7060
dwreede@fhe.com

PAY

Boston, Washington, DC, 2000
1st year: $125,000 + bonus potential
2nd year: $135,000 + bonus potential
3rd year: $145,000 + bonus potential
4th year: $155,000 + bonus potential
5th year: $170,000 + bonus potential
6th year: $175,000 + bonus potential
7th year: $180,000 + bonus potential
8th year: $190,000 + bonus potential
Summer associate (1999): $1,730/week

THE BUZZ
What attorneys at other firms are saying about this firm

- "Geeky academic"
- "Quiet but powerful"
- "Intellectual"
- "Old-school"

Foley & Lardner

Firstar Center
777 E. Wisconsin Avenue
Milwaukee, Wisconsin 53202-5367
(414) 271-2400
Fax: (414) 297-4100
www.foleylardner.com

LOCATIONS

Milwaukee, WI (HQ)
Chicago, IL • Jacksonville, FL • Los Angeles, CA • Madison, WI • Orlando, FL • Sacramento, CA • San Diego, CA • San Francisco, CA • Tallahassee, FL • Tampa, FL • Washington, DC • West Palm Beach, FL

MAJOR DEPARTMENTS/PRACTICES

Employment
Environmental/Regulatory
Finance/Public Finance
Health
Insurance
Intellectual Property
Litigation
Real Estate
Securities
Tax, Trusts and Estates, Benefits

THE STATS

No. of attorneys: 802
No. of offices: 14
Summer associate offers: 69 out of 77 (Firm-wide, 1999)
Chairman: Michael W. Grebe
Hiring Partner: E. Robert Meek

NOTABLE PERKS

- Child care leave available after one year of service
- Loan guarantee for purchase of residence (WI, IL, FL offices)
- Household goods moving fee (up to $5,000)
- One-time interest-free loan of up to $5,000 available to first-years prior to start date

EMPLOYMENT CONTACT

Ms. Alice Hanson-Drew
Director of Recruitment
(414) 297-5452
ahansondrew@foleylaw.com

PAY

Milwaukee, 2000
1st year: $100,000
2nd year: $105,000
3rd year: $110,000
4th year: $115,000
5th year: $125,000
6th year: $135,000
7th year: $145,000
8th year: $155,000
Summer associate: $1,925/week

Chicago, 2000
1st year: $125,000
2nd year: $130,000
3rd year: $145,000
4th year: $160,000
5th year: $175,000
6th year: $185,000
7th year: $195,000
8th year: $200,000
Summer associate: $2,000/week

THE BUZZ
What attorneys at other firms are saying about this firm

- "Big, but no one knows it"
- "Respectable growing health practice"
- "Trying to build a national practice"

Gardere & Wynne, L.L.P.

1601 Elm Street, Suite 3000
Dallas, TX 75201
(214) 999-3000
Fax: (214) 999-4667
www.gardere.com

LOCATIONS

Dallas, TX (HQ)
Houston, TX
Tulsa, OK
Mexico City

MAJOR DEPARTMENTS/PRACTICES

Banking & Creditors' Rights
Corporate
Employee Benefits & Insurance
Healthcare
Intellectual Property
Labor
Real Estate
Tax
Trial

THE STATS

No. of attorneys: 302
No. of offices: 4
Summer associate offers: 17 out of 24 (Dallas, 1999)
Managing Partner: Larry L. Schoenbrun
Hiring Partner: Paul S. Leslie

NOTABLE PERKS

- Moving expenses
- Paid parking for first-years
- Bar exam and review expenses

EMPLOYMENT CONTACT

Ms. Tammy Tremont
Director of Recruiting & Associate Development
(214) 999-4177
ttremont@gardere.com

PAY

Dallas and Houston, 2000
1st year: $86,000 + bonus

THE BUZZ
What attorneys at other firms are saying about this firm

- "Connected to local politics"
- "Diverse"

Goodwin, Procter & Hoar LLP

Exchange Place
Boston, MA 02109
(617) 570-1000
Fax: (617) 523-1231
www.gph.com

LOCATIONS

Boston, MA (HQ)
Roseland, NJ
New York, NY
Washington, DC

MAJOR DEPARTMENTS/PRACTICES

Corporate
Environmental
ERISA
Labor
Litigation
Probate
Real Estate
Tax

THE STATS

No. of attorneys: 414
No. of offices: 4
Summer associate offers: 42 out of 42 (Boston, 1999)
Chairman: Regina M. Pisa
Hiring Partner: Lawrence R. Cahill

NOTABLE PERKS

- Elder care assistance
- Child care resource and reference

EMPLOYMENT CONTACT

Ms. Maureen A. Shea
Director of Legal Personnel
(617) 570-1288
mshea@gph.com

PAY

Boston, 2000
1st year: $110,000
Summer associate (1999): $1,730/week

Washington, DC, 2000
1st year: $125,000
Summer associate: $2,400/week

THE BUZZ
What attorneys at other firms are saying about this firm

- "All their eggs in one basket: REITs"
- "One of the top Boston firms"
- "The area's #1 sweatshop but they do crank out cutting-edge work"

Haynes and Boone, LLP

901 Main Street, Suite 3100
Dallas, TX 75202-3789
(214) 651-5000
Fax: (214) 651-5940
www.haynesboone.com

LOCATIONS

Dallas, TX (HQ)
Austin, TX • Fort Worth, TX • Houston, TX • Richardson, TX • San Antonio, TX • Washington, DC • Mexico City

MAJOR DEPARTMENTS/PRACTICES

Antitrust
Appellate
Bankruptcy
Business Planning
Corporate
Employee Benefits
Employment & Labor/Immigration
Energy
Environmental
Financial Transactions
Government Contracts
Intellectual Property & Technology
International
Litigation: Business, Insurance, Securities, and IP
Real Estate
Tax
White Collar Defense

THE STATS

No. of attorneys: 356
No. of offices: 8
Summer associate offers: 19 out of 27 (Dallas, 1999)
Managing Partner: Robert E. Wilson
Hiring Partner: Ronald W. Breaux

THE BUZZ
What attorneys at other firms are saying about this firm

- "Up-and-comer"
- "Touchy-feely liberal place"

NOTABLE PERKS

- Dependent care account

EMPLOYMENT CONTACT

Ms. Melanie Kraft
Fall Recruiting Coordinator
(214) 651-5362
kraftm@haynesboone.com

PAY

All Texas Offices, 2000
1st year: $110,000 + $5,000 guaranteed bonus
2nd year: $110,431 + $5,000 guaranteed bonus
3rd year: $111,569 + $10,000 guaranteed bonus
4th year: $118,333 + $15,000 guaranteed bonus
5th year: $127,059 + $20,000 guaranteed bonus
6th year: $136,863 + $20,000 guaranteed bonus
7th year: $144,667 + $25,000 guaranteed bonus
Summer associate: $1,700/week

Heller Ehrman White & McAuliffe LLP

333 Bush Street
San Francisco, CA 94104-2878
(415) 772-6000
Fax: (415) 772-6268
www.hewm.com

LOCATIONS

San Francisco, CA (HQ)
Anchorage, AK • Los Angeles, CA • Menlo Park, CA • New York, NY • Palo Alto, CA • Portland, OR • San Diego, CA • Seattle, WA • Washington, DC • Hong Kong • Singapore

MAJOR DEPARTMENTS/PRACTICES

Antitrust and Trade Regulation • Business • Corporate Securities/M&A/Securities Litigation • Energy • Environmental • Financial Services • Information Technology • Insurance Coverage • Intellectual Property Litigation • Labor & Employment • Life Sciences • Litigation • Patents/Trademarks/Licensing • Product Liability • Professional Liability • Real Estate • Tax

THE STATS

No. of attorneys: 465
No. of offices: 12
Summer associate offers: 24 out of 26 (San Francisco, 1999)
Firm Chair: Barry S. Levin
Hiring Attorneys: Robert L. Gibney, Jr. and Renata M. Sos (San Francisco); James E. Torgerson (Anchorage); Jon L. Rewinski (Los Angeles); Derek P. Freyberg and Hope L. Hudson (Menlo Park and Palo Alto); Peter Di Iorio and Rosemary Fanelli (New York); Michael C. Dotten (Portland); Susan S. Gonick (San Diego); Frederic P. Corbit (Seattle); Kit A. Pierson (Washington, DC); Simon Luk (Hong Kong); Richard Cassin (Singapore)

THE BUZZ
What attorneys at other firms are saying about this firm

- "Trying to foster a friendly, family-like atmosphere"
- "Touchy-feely firm"
- "Great litigation but not as well known for corporate work"

NOTABLE PERKS

- Dependent care referral system
- Moving expenses
- Associate retention bonus
- Associate results-based counseling program

EMPLOYMENT CONTACT

Ms. Melissa E. Katz
Professional Recruitment Manager
(415) 772-6047
mkatz@hewm.com

PAY

San Francisco, Los Angeles, Menlo Park, New York, Palo Alto, and San Diego, 2000
1st year: $125,000 base
Summer associate: $2,400/week

Seattle, 2000
1st year: $92,500 base
Summer associate: $1,525/week

Washington, DC, 2000
1st year: $104,000 base

Howrey Simon Arnold & White, LLP

1299 Pennsylvania Street, NW
Washington, DC 20004
(202) 783-0800
Fax: (202) 383-6610
www.howrey.com

LOCATIONS

Washington, DC (HQ)
Houston, TX
Los Angeles, CA
Menlo Park, CA (Silicon Valley)
San Diego, CA (La Jolla)

MAJOR DEPARTMENTS/PRACTICES

Antitrust
Commercial Trial
Environmental
Government Contracts
International Trade
Intellectual Property
White Collar Crime

THE STATS

No. of attorneys: 395
No. of offices: 5
Summer associate offers: 23 out of 24 (Washington, 1999)
Managing Partner: Robert F. Ruyak
Hiring Partner: Richard A. Ripley

THE BUZZ
What attorneys at other firms are saying about this firm

- "Big IP and antitrust firm"
- "Smart merger"
- "Merger has decimated its talent base"

NOTABLE PERKS

- Health club stipend
- Year-round business casual

EMPLOYMENT CONTACT

Ms. Sarah M. Ford
Recruitment Coordinator
Washington, DC
(202) 783-0800
fordsarah@howrey.com

PAY

Washington, 2000
1st year: $125,000
2nd year: $135,000
3rd year: $145,000
4th year: $155,000
5th year: $165,000
6th year: $175,000
7th year: $185,000
8th year: $195,000
Summer associate: $2,000/week

Los Angeles, San Diego, and Menlo Park, 2000
1st year: $125,000
2nd year: $135,000
3rd year: $150,000
4th year: $165,000
5th year: $185,000
6th year: $195,000
7th year: $205,000
Summer associate: $2,000/week

Houston, 2000
1st year: $115,000
2nd year: $123,000
3rd year: $132,000
4th year: $142,000
5th year: $152,000
6th year: $163,000
7th year: $175,000
Summer associate: $1,700/week

Hunton & Williams

Riverfront Plaza
East Tower
Richmond, VA 23219-4074
(804) 788-8200
Fax: (804) 788-8218
www.hunton.com

LOCATIONS

Richmond, VA (HQ)
Atlanta, GA • Charlotte, NC • Knoxville, TN • McLean, VA • Miami, FL • New York, NY • Norfolk, VA • Raleigh, NC • Washington, DC • Brussels • Bangkok • Hong Kong • London • Warsaw

MAJOR DEPARTMENTS/PRACTICES

Administrative
Antitrust
Bankruptcy
Business Practice
Corporate & Finance
Energy & Telecommunications
Environmental
Labor & Employment
Litigation
Patent
Project Development, Finance and Leasing
Securities
Tax

THE STATS

No. of attorneys: 696
No. of offices: 15
Summer associate offers: 61 out of 71 (Firm-wide, 1999)
Managing Partner: Thurston R. Moore
Hiring Chair: R. Hewitt Pate

THE BUZZ
What attorneys at other firms are saying about this firm

- "Steadily rising star"
- "Big Tobacco"
- "Old South trying to become global"

NOTABLE PERKS

- Fee reimbursement for real estate closings
- Child care leave

EMPLOYMENT CONTACT

Ms. Christine Tracey
Legal Recruiting Manager
(212) 309-1000
ctracey@hunton.com

PAY

Richmond, Charlotte, Raleigh, Knoxville, and Norfolk, 2000
1st year: $90,000
Summer associate: $1,500/week

Atlanta, 2000
1st year: $100,000 + $5,000 bonus
Summer associate: $1,500/week

Miami, 2000
1st year: $105,000
Summer associate: $1,500/week

New York, 2000
1st year: $125,000
Summer associate: $2,200/week

McLean and Washington, 2000
Summer associate: $1,800/week

Jenkens & Gilchrist, P.C.

1445 Ross Avenue, Suite 3200
Dallas, TX 75202
(214) 885-4500
Fax: (214) 885-1300
www.jenkins.com

LOCATIONS

Dallas, TX (HQ)
Austin, TX
Chicago, IL
Houston, TX
Los Angeles, CA
San Antonio, TX
Washington, DC

MAJOR DEPARTMENTS/PRACTICES

Bankruptcy/Reorganization • Construction • Corporate & Securities • ERISA/Labor/Immigration • Financial Institutions • Financial Services • Franchise and Distribution • Health • Intellectual Property • International • Litigation • Real Estate/Land Use • Tax/Estate Planning

THE STATS

No. of attorneys: 437
No. of offices: 7
Summer associate offers: 63 out of 85 (All cities, 1999)
Chairman, Management Committee: David M. Laney
Hiring Partner: Jeffery W. Giese

THE BUZZ
What attorneys at other firms are saying about this firm

- "Grew too fast; suffering growing pains"
- "They speak Texas-friendly"

NOTABLE PERKS

- All-attorney lunch and happy hour every Friday
- Judicial clerkship bonus
- Relocation expenses

EMPLOYMENT CONTACT

Ms. Amy Troup
Manager of Recruiting
(214) 885-4217
atroup@jenkens.com

PAY

Dallas, Austin, & Houston, 2000
1st year: $110,000 + Bonus
2nd year: $114,000 + Bonus
3rd year: $121,000 + Bonus
4th year: $130,000 + Bonus
5th year: $140,000 + Bonus
6th year: $145,000 + Bonus
7th year: $155,000 + Bonus
Summer associate: $1,650/week

Chicago, 2000
1st year: $125,000 + Bonus
2nd year: $135,000 + Bonus
3rd year: $150,000 + Bonus
4th year: $165,000 + Bonus
5th year: $185,000 + Bonus
6th year: $195,000 + Bonus
Summer associate: $1,700/week

Los Angeles, and Washington, DC, 2000
1st year: $115,000 + Bonus
2nd year: $121,000 + Bonus
3rd year: $127,000 + Bonus
4th year: $135,000 + Bonus
5th year: $145,000 + Bonus
6th year: $155,000 + Bonus
7th year: $160,000 + Bonus
Summer associate: $1,700/week

Katten Muchin Zavis

525 West Monroe Street, Suite 1600
Chicago, Illinois 60601-3693
(312) 902-5526
Fax: (312) 577-8937
www.kmz.com

LOCATIONS

Chicago, IL (HQ)
Los Angeles, CA
New York, NY
Washington, DC

MAJOR DEPARTMENTS/PRACTICES

Corporate
Customs & International Trade
Employee Benefits
Estates & Trusts & Tax
Finance & Bankruptcy
Health Care
High Tech
Labor
Litigation
Private Equity
Public Finance
Real Estate/Environmental

THE STATS

No. of attorneys: 450
No. of offices: 4
Summer associate offers: 28 out of 29 (Chicago, 2000)
Managing Partner: Vince Sergi
Hiring Attorney: David Schmitt

NOTABLE PERKS

- Credit union
- Paid sabbatical program for fifth-year associates

EMPLOYMENT CONTACT

Ms. Kelley Lynch
Director of Legal Recruiting
(312) 902-5200
klynch@kmz.com

PAY

Chicago and Los Angeles, 2000
1st year: $125,000
2nd year: $135,000
3rd year: $150,000
4th year: $165,000
5th year: $175,000
6th year: $185,000
7th year: $195,000
2,000 minimum billable hours; bonuses at 2,200 and 2,400 hours
Summer associate: $2,400/week

THE BUZZ
What attorneys at other firms are saying about this firm

- "Very aggressive"
- "Entrepreneurial attitude"

Kaye, Scholer, Fierman, Hays & Handler

425 Park Avenue
New York, NY 10022
(212) 836-8000
Fax: (212) 836-8689
www.kayescholer.com

LOCATIONS

New York, NY (HQ)
Los Angeles, CA
Washington, DC
West Palm Beach, FL
Hong Kong
Shanghai

MAJOR DEPARTMENTS/PRACTICES

Bankruptcy
Computer/Internet/E-commerce
Corporate/Finance
Labor
Latin America/Emerging Markets
Litigation/Antitrust
Intellectual Property
Real Estate
Tax
Trusts & Estates

THE STATS

No. of attorneys: 361
No. of offices: 6
Summer associate offers: 31 out of 31 (New York, 1999)
Executive Committee Chairman: David Kingsberg
Hiring Partner: James Herschlein

NOTABLE PERKS

- Friday night cocktails
- Subsidized cafeteria

EMPLOYMENT CONTACT

Ms. Lara Schecter
Legal Recruiting Administrator
(212) 836-8000
lschecter@kayescholer.com

PAY

New York and Washington, DC, 2000
1st year: $125,000
2nd year: $135,000
3rd year: $150,000
Summer associate: $2,400/week

THE BUZZ
What attorneys at other firms are saying about this firm

- "Good for litigation"
- "Never quite recovered from S&L scandal"
- "Solid, hard-working"

Kelley Drye & Warren LLP

101 Park Avenue
New York, NY 10178
(212) 808-7800
Fax: (212) 808-7897
www.kelleydrye.com

LOCATIONS

New York, NY (HQ)
Chicago, IL
Los Angeles, CA
Parsippany, NJ
Stamford, CT
Washington, DC
Brussels
Hong Kong

MAJOR DEPARTMENTS/PRACTICES

Bankruptcy/Creditors' Rights
Corporate
Employee Benefits
Environmental
Labor
Litigation
Real Estate
Tax
Private Clients
Telecommunications

THE STATS

No. of attorneys: 329
No. of offices: 8
Summer associate offers: 16 out of 17 (New York, 1999)
Managing Partner: Merrill B. Stone
Hiring attorney: Jonathan K. Cooperman

NOTABLE PERKS

- Transit vouchers
- Corporate charge cards
- Clerkship bonus
- Emergency child care

EMPLOYMENT CONTACT

Ms. Megan C. Clouden
Recruiting Coordinator
(212) 808-7510
recruiting@kelleydrye.com

PAY

All offices, 2000
1st year: $125,000
2nd year: $135,000
3rd year: $150,000
4th year: $165,000
5th year: $180,000
6th year: $195,000
7th year: $205,000
Summer associate: $2,403.85/week

THE BUZZ
What attorneys at other firms are saying about this firm

- "Good diversity of practice"
- "80s relic"
- "Nice working environment"

Loeb & Loeb LLP

1000 Wilshire Boulevard
Suite 1800
Los Angeles, CA 90017
(213) 688-3400
Fax: (213) 688-3460
www.loeb.com

LOCATIONS

Los Angeles, CA (HQ)
Century City, CA
Nashville, TN
New York, NY
Rome
Tokyo

MAJOR DEPARTMENTS/PRACTICES

Bankruptcy
Corporate
Entertainment
Financial Services
Intellectual Property
Labor
Litigation
Real Estate
Tax Law
Trusts & Estates

THE STATS

No. of attorneys: 202
No. of offices: 6
Summer associate offers: 9 out of 9 (Los Angeles, 1999)
Co-chairs, Management Committee: David H. Carlin and John T. Frankenheimer
Hiring Partner: Paul D. Tosetti

NOTABLE PERKS

- Moving expenses
- One-month bar stipend
- Paid parking

EMPLOYMENT CONTACT

Ms. Cecilia Toll
Recruiting Administrator
(213) 688-3512
ctoll@loeb.com

PAY

Los Angeles, 2000
1st year: $125,000
Summer associate: $1,700/week

New York, 1999
Summer associate: $1,923/week

THE BUZZ
What attorneys at other firms are saying about this firm

- "Fallen entertainment firm of the 80s"
- "Good entertainment firm"

Long Aldridge & Norman LLP

303 Peachtree Street, Suite 5300
Atlanta, GA 30308
(404) 527-4000
Fax: (404) 527-4198
www.lanlaw.com

LOCATIONS

Atlanta, GA (HQ)
Washington, DC

MAJOR DEPARTMENTS/PRACTICES

Administrative/Regulatory/Government
Bankruptcy
Commercial Real Estate
Corporate and Government Finance
Environmental
Financial Restructuring
Intellectual Property
Litigation
Mergers & Acquisitions
Sports & Entertainment
Tax & Employee Benefits
Technology
Trusts & Estates

THE STATS

No. of attorneys: 147
No. of offices: 2
Summer associate offers: 17 out of 18 (Firm-wide, 1999)
Chairman, Management Committee: Clay C. Long
Hiring Partner: David Dantzler

NOTABLE PERKS

- Compensation credit for judicial clerks
- Moving and bar stipend

EMPLOYMENT CONTACT

Ms. Jennifer Queen/ Ms. Aimee Black
Director Attorney Recruitment/Recruiting Coordinator
(404) 527-4000
jqueen@lanlaw.com / ablack@lanlaw.com

PAY

Atlanta, 2000
1st year: $100,000
All other years: Base salary + $10,000 bonus at 1,900 billable hours, an additional $7,500 at 2,000 hours, and an additional $2,500 at 2,200 hours
Summer associate: $1,500/week

Washington, DC, 2000
Summer associate: $1,900/week

THE BUZZ
What attorneys at other firms are saying about this firm

- "Decent litigation"
- "Very quiet, but a good firm"

Manatt, Phelps & Phillips, LLP

11355 W. Olympic Boulevard
Los Angeles, CA 90064-1614
(310) 312-4000
Fax: (310) 312-4224
www.manatt.com

LOCATIONS

Los Angeles, CA (HQ)
Palo Alto, CA
Sacramento, CA
Washington, DC
Mexico City
Monterrey

MAJOR DEPARTMENTS/PRACTICES

Business, Finance & Real Estate
Entertainment & Media
Government & International
Litigation & Employment

THE STATS

No. of attorneys: 219
No. of offices: 6
Summer associate offers: 12 out of 12 (Los Angeles, 1999)
Managing Partner: Paul H. Irving

NOTABLE PERKS

- Investment fund for senior associates
- Private health club
- Parking
- Year-round business casual

EMPLOYMENT CONTACT

Ms. Kimberly A. Firment
Recruiting Manager
(310) 312-4187
kfirment@manatt.com

PAY

All Domestic Offices, 2000
1st year: $115,000 + $40,000 deferred base/bonus potential
2nd year: $120,000 + $55,000 deferred base/bonus potential
3rd year: $130,000 + $65,000 deferred base/bonus potential
4th year: $135,000 + $80,000 deferred base/bonus potential
5th year: $145,000 + $90,000 deferred base/bonus potential
6th year: $150,000 + $95,000 deferred base/bonus potential
Deferred base is based partially on billable hours.
Summer associate: $2,200/week

THE BUZZ
What attorneys at other firms are saying about this firm

- "Great political connections"
- "Rebuilding"
- "Major West Side firm"
- "Friends of Bill"

Mintz, Levin, Cohn, Ferris, Glovsky and Popeo, P.C.

One Financial Center
Boston, MA 02111
(617) 542-6000
Fax: (617) 542-2241
www.mintz.com

LOCATIONS

Boston, MA
New York, NY
Reston, VA
Washington, DC

MAJOR DEPARTMENTS/PRACTICES

Business & Finance
Commercial
Communications
Employment, Labor, Benefits, & Immigration
Environmental
Federal
Health Care
Intellectual Property & Patent
Litigation
Real Estate
Tax
Trusts & Estates

THE STATS

No. of attorneys: 345
No. of offices: 4
Summer associate offers: 20 out of 20 (Boston, 1999)
Chairman, Executive Committee: R. Robert Popeo
Hiring Attorneys: Rosemary M. Allen and Charles Carey (Boston and New York); James Kirkland (DC and Reston)

NOTABLE PERKS

- Events tickets
- Associate stock investment plan

EMPLOYMENT CONTACT

Ms. Julie E. Zammuto (Boston and New York)
HR Manager - Attorney Recruitment
(617) 348-4929
jzammuto@mintz.com

Ms. Sharon Simmons (DC and Reston)
Recruitment Coordinator
ssimmons@mintz.com

PAY

Boston, 2000
1st year: $125,000 + $30,000 bonus potential
2nd year: $135,000 + $40,000 bonus potential
3rd year: $145,000 + $50,000 bonus potential
4th year: $155,000 + $60,000 bonus potential
5th year: $170,000 + $65,000 bonus potential
6th year: $175,000 + $65,000 bonus potential
7th year: $180,000 + $65,000 bonus potential
8th year: $190,000 + $65,000 bonus potential
Summer associate: $2,400/week

THE BUZZ
What attorneys at other firms are saying about this firm

- "May be growing too fast"
- "Hands down, the best firm in Boston"
- "Very friendly, cutting-edge, dynamic practice"
- "Growing firm with bright talent"

Montgomery, McCracken, Walker & Rhoads, LLP

123 South Broad Street
Philadelphia, PA 19109-1030
(215) 772-1500
Fax: (215) 772-7620
www.mmwr.com

LOCATIONS

Philadelphia, PA (HQ)
Cherry Hill, NJ
Newark, DE

MAJOR DEPARTMENTS/PRACTICES

Bankruptcy
Corporate
Environmental
Estates & Trusts
Government
Health & Education
Labor & Employment
Nonprofit
Real Estate
Tax & Employee Benefits
Transactional

THE STATS

No. of attorneys: 155
No. of offices: 3
Summer associate offers: 4 out of 6 (Philadelphia, 1999)
Chair, Management Committee: David H. Marion
Hiring Attorney: Thomas H. Suddath, Jr.

NOTABLE PERKS

- Judicial clerkship bonus
- Business casual Fridays and all summer

EMPLOYMENT CONTACT

Ms. Jennifer D. Moore
Recruitment Coordinator
(215) 772-7506
jmoore@mmwr.com

PAY

Philadelphia, 2000
1st year: $100,000 + $5,000 stipend
Summer associate: $1,730/week

THE BUZZ
What attorneys at other firms are saying about this firm

- "Old-boy network"
- "Litigation, labor & employment strength"
- "Cultivates future U.S. Attorneys"
- "Locally connected"

Palmer & Dodge LLP

One Beacon Street
Boston, MA 02108
(617) 573-0100
Fax: (617) 227-4420
www.palmerdodge.com

LOCATIONS

Boston, MA (HQ)

MAJOR DEPARTMENTS/PRACTICES

Business
Corporate
Labor
Litigation
Public Finance
Public Law
Real Estate
Probate Trusts

THE STATS

No. of attorneys: 196
No. of offices: 1
Summer associate offers: 18 out of 20 (Boston, 1999)
Managing Partner: Jeffery F. Jones
Hiring Attorney: Daryl J. Lapp

NOTABLE PERKS

- Credit union

EMPLOYMENT CONTACT

Ms. Katy von Mehren
Director of Associate Recruitment
(617) 573-0172
kvonmehren@palmerdodge.com

PAY

Summer associate (2000): $1,730/week

THE BUZZ
What attorneys at other firms are saying about this firm

- "Old-school but trying to become more modern"
- "Three words: bonds, bonds, bonds. Oh yeah, they also do good corporate work"
- "Family-friendly"

Pepper Hamilton LLP

3000 Two Logan Square
18th and Arch Streets
Philadelphia, PA 19103-2799
(215) 981-4000
Fax: (215) 981-4750
www.pepperlaw.com

LOCATIONS

Philadelphia, PA (HQ)
Berwyn, PA
Cherry Hill, NJ
Detroit, MI
Harrisburg, PA
New York, NY
Pittsburgh, PA
Wilmington, DE

MAJOR DEPARTMENTS/PRACTICES

Bankruptcy • Construction • Corporate & Securities • Employee Benefits • Environmental • Finance • Intellectual Property • Labor and Employment • Litigation • Real Estate • Tax • Trusts and Estates

THE STATS

No. of attorneys: 370
No. of offices: 9
Summer associates: 38 (Firm-wide, 2000)
Chairman of Executive Committee: Barry M. Abelson
Executive Partner: James L. Murray
Hiring Attorney: Scott D. Godshall

NOTABLE PERKS

- Maternity and paternity leave
- Transportation reimbursement program
- Short-and long-term disability insurance
- Emergency child care (Philadelphia)
- Fitness center and cafeteria (Philadelphia)

EMPLOYMENT CONTACT

Ms. Sharon R. Buckingham
Director of Associate Development
(215) 981-4265
buckinghams@pepperlaw.com

PAY

Philadelphia, 2000
1st year: $100,000 + stipend and bonus opportunity

THE BUZZ
What attorneys at other firms are saying about this firm

- "Competitive"
- "Good local firm but not a national player"

Piper Marbury Rudnick & Wolfe

203 N. La Salle Street, Suite 1800
Chicago, Illinois 60601-1293
(312) 368-4000
Fax: (312) 236-7516
www.piperrudnick.com

LOCATIONS

Baltimore, MD
Chicago, IL
Dallas, TX
Easton, MD
New York, NY
Philadelphia, PA
Reston, VA
Tampa, FL
Washington, DC

MAJOR DEPARTMENTS/PRACTICES

Corporate & Securities • Environmental Law • Franchise • Information Technology • Intellectual Property • Labor & Employment • Litigation • Patent • Real Estate • Tax

THE STATS

No. of attorneys: 790
No. of offices: 9
Summer associate offers: 53 out of 61 (Firm-wide, 1999)
Chairmen, Management Committee: Francis B. Burch, Jr. and Lee Miller
Hiring Attorneys: Sally J. McDonald (Chicago); James D. Thias (Baltimore); Jeff Keitelman and David Clarke (Washington, DC); Danal Abrams (New York); Joe Kernen (Philadelphia); Ron Holliday (Tampa); and Michael Santa Maria (Dallas)

THE BUZZ
What attorneys at other firms are saying about this firm

- "Probably a 9 out of 10 for real estate alone"
- "Associates are happy there"

NOTABLE PERKS

- MBA tuition reimbursement
- Full-time business casual

EMPLOYMENT CONTACT

Ms. Marguerite E. Strubing
Director of Legal Recruiting
(312) 368-8928
marguerite.strubing@piperrudnick.com

PAY

Chicago, 2000
1st year: $125,000
2nd year: $135,000
3rd year: $145,000
4th year: $155,000
5th year: $170,000
6th year: $180,000
7th year: $190,000
Summer associate: $1,850/week

Baltimore, 2000
1st year: $115,000
Summer associate: $1,800/week

New York, 2000
1st year: $125,000
Summer associate: $2,000/week

Philadelphia, 2000
1st year: $100,000
Summer associate: $1,750/week

Tampa, 2000
1st year: $95,000 + $5,000 bonus
Summer associate: $1,500/week

Dallas, 2000
1st year: $111,000
Summer associate: $1,500/week

Washington, DC, Reston, 2000
1st year: $125,000
Summer associate: $1,950/week

Saul, Ewing, Remick & Saul LLP

Centre Square West
1500 Market Street, 38th Floor
Philadelphia, PA 19102
(215) 972-7777
Fax: (215) 972-1822
www.saul.com

LOCATIONS

Philadelphia, PA (HQ)
Baltimore, MD
Berwyn, PA
Harrisburg, PA
Princeton, NJ
Wilmington, DA

MAJOR DEPARTMENTS/PRACTICES

Bankruptcy
Business
Environmental
Estates
Health Law
Intellectual Property
Labor
Litigation
Public Finance
Real Estate
Tax

THE STATS

No. of attorneys: 232
No. of offices: 6
Summer associate offers: 16 out of 17 (Philadelphia, 1999)
Managing Partner: John F. Stoviak
Hiring Attorneys: Paul D. Shaffner & Gary B. Eldelman

NOTABLE PERKS

- Savings program
- 12 weeks maternity leave
- Business casual

EMPLOYMENT CONTACT

Ms. Donna J. Nolan
Recruitment Coordinator
(215) 972-7991
dnolan@saul.com

PAY

Wilmington, Philadelphia, Princeton, and Berwyn, 2000
1st year: $100,000 + discretionary bonus
Summer associate: $1,925/week

Baltimore, 2000
1st year: $95,000 + discretionary bonus
Summer associate: $1,830/week

Harrisburg, 2000
1st year: $85,000 + discretionary bonus
Summer associate: $1,635/week

THE BUZZ
What attorneys at other firms are saying about this firm

- "Wonderful people, a joy to work with"
- "Sleepy Philadelphian"

Schiff Hardin & Waite

6600 Sears Tower
233 S. Wacker Drive
Chicago, Illinois 60606
(312) 258-5500
Fax: (312) 258-5700
www.schiffhardin.com

LOCATIONS

Chicago, IL (HQ)
Merrillville, IN
New York, NY
Washington, DC
Dublin

MAJOR DEPARTMENTS/PRACTICES

Antitrust • Class Action • Commodities & Regulated Industries • Construction • Corporate & Securities • Environmental Law • Estate Planning • Finance • Intellectual Property • Labor & Employment • Litigation • Municipal • Product Liability • Real Estate • Tax

THE STATS

No. of attorneys: 226
No. of offices: 5
Summer associate offers: 20 out of 22 (Chicago, 2000)
Managing Partner and Chair: Peter V. Fazio, Jr.
Hiring Attorney: Carol R. Prygrosky and Steven D. Friedland

NOTABLE PERKS

• Domestic partner benefits

EMPLOYMENT CONTACT

Ms. Lilly Beltran
Law Student Recruitment Coordinator
(312) 258-4832
lbeltran@schiffhardin.com

PAY

Chicago, 2000
1st year: $125,000
2nd year: $135,000
3rd year: $145,000
Summer associate: $2,000/week

THE BUZZ
What attorneys at other firms are saying about this firm

• "Lifestyle firm or one of the big boys?"
• "Comfortable, traditional"
• "Not competitive with the top firms"

Schulte Roth & Zabel LLP

900 Third Avenue
New York, NY 10022
(212) 756-2000
Fax: (212) 593-5955
www.srz.com

LOCATIONS

New York, NY (HQ)

MAJOR DEPARTMENTS/PRACTICES

Bankruptcy/Creditors' Rights
Corporate
Employment & Employee Benefits
Environmental Law
Individual Client Service
Litigation
New Media and Intellectual Property
Real Estate
Tax

THE STATS

No. of attorneys: 240
No. of offices: 1
Summer associate offers: 28 out of 28 (New York, 1999)
Members of Executive Committee: Burton Lehman, Paul Roth, Irwin Sugarman, Alan Waldenberg, and Paul Weber
Hiring attorneys: Stephanie R. Breslow and Kurt F. Rosell

NOTABLE PERKS

- Dinner served in office
- Casual dress on Fridays and all summer

EMPLOYMENT CONTACT

Susan R. Galligan, Esq.
Director of Professional Development
(212) 756-2218
wwwmail@srz.com

PAY

New York, 2000
1st year: $125,000
2nd year: $135,000
3rd year: $150,000
4th year: $170,000
5th year: $190,000
6th year: $205,000
7th year: $215,000
8th year: $220,000
Summer associate: $2,403/week

THE BUZZ
What attorneys at other firms are saying about this firm

- "Getting better all the time but cutthroat"
- "Aggressive and high-energy"

Shaw Pittman

2300 N Street, NW
Washington, DC 20037
(202) 663-8000
Fax: (202) 663-8007
www.shawpittman.com

LOCATIONS

Washington, DC (HQ)
Los Angeles, CA
New York, NY
Tysons Corner, VA
London

MAJOR DEPARTMENTS/PRACTICES

Bankruptcy
Corporate
Diversity & Government Contracts
Employee Benefits & Health
Energy & Environment
Financial Institutions
Government Relations & Transportation
Litigation
Real Estate
Securities
Tax
Technology

THE STATS

No. of attorneys: 388
No. of offices: 5
Summer associate offers: 34 out of 34 (Firm-wide, 1999)
Managing Partner: Paul F. Mickey, Jr.
Hiring Attorney: D. Craig Wolff, Esq.

NOTABLE PERKS

- Domestic partner benefits
- On-site gym
- Moving and travel expenses paid

EMPLOYMENT CONTACT

Ms. Kathleen A. Kelly
Director, Human Resources
(202) 663-8394
kathy.kelly@shawpittman.com

PAY

All offices, 2000
1st year: $125,000
2nd year: $135,000
3rd year: $145,000
4th year: $155,000
5th year: $175,000
6th year: $185,000
Bonuses partially based on hours
Summer associate: at least $2,000/week

THE BUZZ
What attorneys at other firms are saying about this firm

- "Strong technology firm"
- "Cutting-edge"
- "Meathead corporate"

Sheppard, Mullin, Richter & Hampton LLP

333 So. Hope Street, 48th Floor
Los Angeles, CA 90071
(213) 620-1780
Fax: (213) 620-1398
www.smrh.com

LOCATIONS

Los Angeles, CA (HQ)
Costa Mesa, CA (Orange County)
San Diego, CA
San Francisco, CA

MAJOR DEPARTMENTS/PRACTICES

Banking & Finance
Corporate & Securities
Intellectual Property
Labor & Employment
Litigation
Real Estate & Land Use
Tax & Estate Planning

THE STATS

No. of attorneys: 306
No. of offices: 4
Summer associate offers: 21 out of 22 (Los Angeles, 1999)
Chairman, Executive Committee: Richard W. Brunette, Jr.
Hiring Partner: Anthony R. Callobre (Los Angeles)

NOTABLE PERKS

- Paid parking
- Full-time business casual

EMPLOYMENT CONTACT

Ms. Sally C. Bucklin
Manager of Attorney Hiring
(213) 617-4101
sbucklin@smrh.com

PAY

All Offices, 2000
1st year: $110,000 + $5,000 for 2,100 billable hours + $20,000 discretionary bonus potential
2nd year: $120,000 + $5,000 for 2,100 billable hours + $20,000 discretionary bonus potential
3rd year: $130,000 + $10,000 for 2,100 billable hours + $25,000 discretionary bonus potential
4th year: $140,000 + $10,000 for 2,100 billable hours + $30,000 discretionary bonus potential
5th year: $145,000 + $10,000 for 2,100 billable hours + $35,000 discretionary bonus potential
6th year: $150,000 + $15,000 for 2,100 billable hours + $35,000 discretionary bonus potential
7th year: $150,000 + $15,000 for 2,100 billable hours + $40,000 discretionary bonus potential
8th year: $150,000 + $15,000 for 2,100 billable hours + $45,000 discretionary bonus potential
Summer associate: $2,000/week

THE BUZZ
What attorneys at other firms are saying about this firm

- "Fun and young"
- "Not cutting-edge"

Sonnenschein Nath & Rosenthal

8000 Sears Tower
Chicago, IL 60606
(312) 876-8000
www.sonnenschein.com

LOCATIONS

Chicago, IL (HQ)
Kansas City, MO
Los Angeles, CA
New York, NY
St. Louis, MO
San Francisco, CA
Washington, DC
London

MAJOR DEPARTMENTS/PRACTICES

Bankruptcy
Corporate
Employee Benefits
Environmental
Intellectual Property and Patent
Labor
Litigation/Antitrust
Real Estate
Tax
Trusts and Estates

THE STATS

No. of attorneys: 462
No. of offices: 7
Summer associate offers: 20 out of 21 (Chicago, 1999)
Managing Partner: Errol L. Stone
Hiring Partner: Jacqueline M. Vidmar

THE BUZZ
What attorneys at other firms are saying about this firm

- "Friendly Midwestern firm"
- "Quality, solid"
- "Plodding"

NOTABLE PERKS

- Maternity leave paid up to 17 weeks
- Paternity leave paid up to 5 weeks
- Moving expenses

EMPLOYMENT CONTACT

Ms. Barbara Petrie
Recruitment Coordinator
(312) 876-8000
rlp@sonnenschein.com

PAY

All Domestic Offices except St. Louis and Kansas City, 2000
1st year: $125,000
2nd year: $135,000
Summer associate (Chicago): $1,865/week
Summer associate (L.A. & San Francisco): $1,825/week
Summer associate (New York): $2,076/week
Summer associate (Washington, DC): $1,942/week

Squire, Sanders & Dempsey LLP

4900 Key Tower
127 Public Square
Cleveland, OH 44114-1304
(216) 479-8500
www.ssd.com

LOCATIONS

Cleveland, OH (HQ)
Cincinnati, OH • Columbus, OH • Houston, TX • Jacksonville, FL • Miami, FL • New York, NY • Phoenix, AZ • Washington, DC • Almaty • Bratislava • Brussels • Budapest • Hong Kong • Kyiv • London • Madrid • Moscow • Prague • Taipei

MAJOR DEPARTMENTS/PRACTICES

Corporate
Environmental
Federal Regulatory
Labor and Employment Law
Litigation
Public Law
Taxation

THE STATS

No. of attorneys: 538
No. of offices: 20
Summer associate offers: 24 out of 29 (Firm-wide, 2000)
Management Committee Chairman: R. Thomas Stanton
Hiring Attorneys: Susan C. Hastings (Cleveland); Daniel M. Maher (Columbus); Christopher D. Thomas (Phoenix); and Charles F. Donley III (Washington, DC)

NOTABLE PERKS

- Heath care spending account
- Housing loan guarantee

EMPLOYMENT CONTACT

Ms. Morgan L. Smith
Legal Personnel Manager
(216) 802-7571
msmith@ssd.com

PAY

Cleveland, 2000
1st year: $110,000 + stipend
Summer associate: $8,250/month

Columbus and Phoenix, 2000
1st year: $110,000 + stipend
Summer associate: $6,750/month

Washington, 2000
1st year: $125,000 + stipend
Summer associate: $2,200/week

THE BUZZ
What attorneys at other firms are saying about this firm

- "Good in telecom"
- "Good rep in Cleveland"
- "Old-school"

Steptoe & Johnson LLP

1330 Connecticut Avenue, NW
Washington, DC 20036-1795
(202) 429-3000
Fax: (202) 828-3661
www.steptoe.com

LOCATIONS

Washington, DC (HQ)
Los Angeles, CA
Phoenix, AZ

MAJOR DEPARTMENTS/PRACTICES

Business Solutions (includes Tax, Transactions, and ERISA/Employment)
Energy and Natural Resources
International
Litigation
Technology (includes E-commerce, Intellectual Property, and Telecommunications)

THE STATS

No. of attorneys: 280
No. of offices: 3
Summer associate offers: 18 out of 19 (Washington, DC, 2000)
Managing Partner: J.A. (Lon) Bouknight, Jr.
Hiring Attorneys: Antonia B. Ianniello and Edmund W. Burke

THE BUZZ
What attorneys at other firms are saying about this firm

- "Merger bait"
- "Nice people"
- "Steady"

NOTABLE PERKS

- Moving expenses
- Associate referral bonus
- Judicial clerkship bonus

EMPLOYMENT CONTACT

Ms. Rosemary Kelly Morgan
Director of Attorney Services & Recruiting
(202) 429-8036
legal_recruiting@steptoe.com

PAY

Washington, 2000
1st year: $110,000 + $15,000
2nd year: $116,000 + $15,000
3rd year: $123,000 + $15,000
4th year: $130,000 + $15,000
5th year: $140,000 + $15,000
6th year: $150,000 + $15,000
7th year: $157,000 + $15,000
8th year: $165,000 + $15,000
In addition, firm provides annual work effort bonuses (starting at 2,100 hours), tenure awards that range from $12,500 to $57,500, and discretionary bonuses.
Summer associate (1999): $2,000/week

Phoenix, 2000
1st year: $90,000 + $10,000
2nd year: $94,000 + $10,000
3rd year: $08,000 + $10,000
4th year: $103,000 + $10,000
5th year: $108,000 + $10,000
6th year: $113,000 + $10,000
7th year: $118,000 + $10,000
8th year: $123,000 + $10,000
Summer associate: $1,600/week

Los Angeles, 2000
1st year: $92,000

Stroock & Stroock & Lavan LLP

180 Maiden Lane
New York, NY 10038-4982
(212) 806-5400
Fax: (212) 806-6006
www.stroock.com

LOCATIONS

New York, NY (HQ)
Los Angeles, CA
Miami, FL
Washington, DC

MAJOR DEPARTMENTS/PRACTICES

Corporate & Structured Finance
E-commerce and Technology Entertainment
ERISA
Health Care
Insolvency
Insurance
Intellectual Property
Labor/Employment
Litigation
Real Estate
Tax
Trusts & Estates

THE STATS

No. of attorneys: 331
No. of offices: 4
Summer associate offers: 22 out of 22 (New York, 1999)
Managing Partner: Thomas E. Heftler
Hiring Partner: James R. Tanenbaum

THE BUZZ
What attorneys at other firms are saying about this firm

- "Nicest people on earth"
- "Good at bankruptcy"
- "Brontosaurus"

NOTABLE PERKS

- Banking services
- Home computer subsidy

EMPLOYMENT CONTACT

Ms. Diane A. Cohen
Director of Legal Personnel & Recruiting
(212) 806-5406
dcohen@stroock.com

PAY

New York, 2000
1st year: $125,000 + bonus
2nd year: $135,000 + bonus
3rd year: $150,000 + bonus
4th year: $170,000 + bonus
5th year: $190,000+ bonus
6th year: $200,000 + bonus
7th year: $205,000 + bonus
Summer associate: $2,400/week

Los Angeles, 2000
1st year: $125,000 + bonus
2nd year: $135,000 + bonus
3rd year: $145,000 + bonus
4th year: $160,000 + bonus
5th year: $175,000+ bonus
6th year: $190,000 + bonus
Summer associate: $2,400/week

Miami, 2000
1st year: $105,000 + bonus
2nd year: $110,000 + bonus
3rd year: $115,000 + bonus
4th year: $120,000 + bonus
5th year: $125,000 + bonus
Summer associate: $1,300/week

Swidler Berlin Shereff Friedman, LLP

3000 K Street, NW
Suite 300
Washington, DC 20007-5116
(202) 424-7500
Fax: (202) 424-7643
www.swidlaw.com

LOCATIONS

Washington, DC (HQ)
New York, NY

MAJOR DEPARTMENTS/PRACTICES

Antitrust
Bankruptcy
Corporate
Energy
Environmental
Financial Services
Insurance Coverage
Intellectual Property
Legislation
Litigation
Real Estate/Structured Finance
Securities
Tax/ERISA
Telecommunications
Trust & Estates

THE STATS

No. of attorneys: 310
No. of offices: 2
Summer associate offers: 9 out of 9 (Washington, 1999)
Managing Partner: Barry Direnfeld
Hiring Attorney: David M. Martin

NOTABLE PERKS

- Counseling
- Moving expenses
- Reduced work schedules
- 12 weeks of maternity leave
- On-site fitness center
- Domestic partner benefits

EMPLOYMENT CONTACT

Ms. Katherine M. White
Director of Professional Development
(202) 424-7739
kmwhite@swidlaw.com

PAY

Washington, 2000
1st year: $125,000 + $40,000 bonus potential
2nd year: $135,000 + $40,000 bonus potential
3rd year: $145,000 + $40,000 bonus potential
4th year: $160,000 + $40,000 bonus potential
5th year: $170,000 + $40,000 bonus potential
6th year: $185,000 + $40,000 bonus potential
7th year: $200,000 + $40,000 bonus potential
8th year: $205,000 + $40,000 bonus potential
Summer associate: $2,115/week

New York, 2000
1st year: $130,000 + $40,000 bonus potential
2nd year: $145,000 + $40,000 bonus potential
3rd year: $155,000 + $40,000 bonus potential
4th year: $170,000 + $40,000 bonus potential
5th year: $190,000 + $40,000 bonus potential
6th year: $200,000 + $40,000 bonus potential
7th year: $215,000 + $40,000 bonus potential
8th year: $225,000 + $40,000 bonus potential
Summer associate: $2,310/week

THE BUZZ
What attorneys at other firms are saying about this firm

- "Strong telecom practice"
- "Cutthroat environment"
- "Associates can't leave fast enough"
- "Hard-working"

Testa, Hurwitz & Thibeault, LLP

125 High Street
Boston, MA 02110
(617) 248-7000
Fax: (617) 248-7100
www.tht.com

LOCATIONS

Boston, MA (HQ)

MAJOR DEPARTMENTS/PRACTICES

Bankruptcy & Creditors' Rights
Business
Environmental
Labor, Employment & Immigration
Litigation
Patent & Intellectual Property
Probate, Trusts & Estates
Real Estate
Tax & ERISA

THE STATS

No. of attorneys: 298
No. of offices: 1
Summer associate offers: 38 out of 38 (Boston, 1999)
Managing Partner: Richard J. Testa
Hiring Attorney: Mark D. Smith

NOTABLE PERKS

- Concierge service
- Equity investment policy

EMPLOYMENT CONTACT

Ms. Judith A. St. John
Recruiting Administrator
(617) 248-7401
stjohn@tht.com

PAY

Boston, 2000
1st year: $140,000
2nd year: $155,000
3rd year: $167,500
4th year: $180,000
5th year: $192,500
6th year: $205,000
7th year: $217,500
8th year: $230,000
Summer associate: $2,600/week

THE BUZZ
What attorneys at other firms are saying about this firm

- "Excellent in its VC, high tech niche; not well-rounded"
- "Show me the $$$$!!!"
- "Bold mover"
- "Exponential growth but unclear what will happen when the dot com craze ends"

Thelen Reid & Priest LLP

40 West 57th Street
New York, NY 10019
(212) 603-2000
Fax: (212) 603-2001
www.thelenreid.com

101 Second Street, Suite 1800
San Francisco, CA 94105
(415) 371-1200
Fax: (415) 371-1211

LOCATIONS

New York, NY (Co-HQ)
San Francisco, CA (Co-HQ)
Los Angeles, CA
San Jose, CA
Washington, DC

MAJOR DEPARTMENTS/PRACTICES

Business & Finance
Commercial Litigation
Construction & Government Contracts
Government Affairs
Insurance
Labor & Employment
Project & Asset Finance
Real Estate
Tax, ERISA, Trusts & Estates
Technology & Intellectual Property

THE STATS

No. of attorneys: 400
No. of offices: 5
Summer associate offers: 9 out of 9 (New York, 1999); 14 out of 14 (San Francisco, 1999)
Managing Partner: Richard N. Gary
Hiring Attorneys: Michele Jawin (New York) and Richard Lapping (San Francisco)

THE BUZZ
What attorneys at other firms are saying about this firm

- "Bulldogs, but they know their construction work"
- "Much healthier post-merger"
- "Middle of the road"
- "Up-and-coming, quality work"

NOTABLE PERKS

- Domestic partner benefits
- Associate merit bonus

EMPLOYMENT CONTACT

Ms. Sandra Persaud (East Coast)
(212) 603-2292
spersaud@thelenreid.com

Ms. Marilee Stone (West Coast)
(415) 369-7316
mstone@thelenreid.com

PAY

All California Offices, 2000
1st year: $125,000 + $5,000 @ 2,000 hours and $15,000 @2,200 billable hours
2nd year: $125,000 - $135,000 + $10,000 @ 2,000 hours and $20,000 @2,200 billable hours
3rd year: $130,000 - $150,000 + $10,000 @ 2,100 hours and $20,000 @2,250 billable hours
4th year: $135,000 - $165,000 + $15,000 @ 2,100 hours and $30,000 @2,250 billable hours
5th year: $140,000 - $185,000 + $15,000 @ 2,100 hours and $30,000 @2,250 billable hours
6th year: $145,000 - $195,000 + $20,000 @ 2,100 hours and $40,000 @2,250 billable hours
Counsel: $150,000-$205,000 + $20,000 @ 2,100 hours and $40,000 @2,250 billable hours
Additional discretionary bonus given to all associates based on merit
Summer associate: $2,400/week

New York and Washington, DC, 2000
1st year through 6th year: same as California offices
7th year: $150,000 - $205,000 + $20,000 @ 2,100 hours and $40,000 @2,250 billable hours
8th year: $155,000 - $210,000 + $20,000 @ 2,100 hours and $40,000 @2,250 billable hours
9th year: $160,000 - $215,000 + $20,000 @ 2,100 hours and $40,000 @2,250 billable hours
Additional discretionary bonuses given to all associates based on merit

Summer associate: $2,400/week

Thompson & Knight, LLP

1700 Pacific Avenue, Suite 3300
Dallas, TX 75201
(214) 969-1700
Fax: (214) 969-1751
www.tklaw.com

LOCATIONS

Dallas, TX (HQ)
Austin, TX
Fort Worth, TX
Houston, TX
Monterrey, Mexico

MAJOR DEPARTMENTS/PRACTICES

Business Transactions
Creditors' Rights/Bankruptcy
Corporate
Environment
Estates/Probate/ERISA
Healthcare
Intellectual Property
International
Labor & Employment & Immigration
Litigation
Oil & Gas
Regulatory Affairs
Tax

THE STATS

No. of attorneys: 245
No. of offices: 5
Summer associate offers: 47 out of 51 (Firm-wide, 1999)
President, Board of Directors: James L. Irish III
Hiring Partner: Dennis J. Grindinger

NOTABLE PERKS

- Moving expenses
- Judicial clerkship bonus

EMPLOYMENT CONTACT

Courtney Bankler
Recruiting Coordinator
(214) 969-1379
recruit@tklaw.com

PAY

All Texas Offices, 2000
1st year: $100,000 + signing bonus
Summer associate: $1,650/week

THE BUZZ
What attorneys at other firms are saying about this firm

- "Best Dallas law firm but no match for the Houston 'Big 3'"
- "Friendly people"

Troutman Sanders LLP

Bank of America Plaza, Suite 5200
600 Peachtree Street, N.E.
Atlanta, GA 30308-2216
(404) 885-3000
Fax: (404) 885-3900
www.troutmansanders.com

LOCATIONS

Atlanta, GA (HQ)
Washington, DC
Hong Kong

MAJOR DEPARTMENTS/PRACTICES

Corporate
Litigation
Public Law (Regulatory)
Real Estate

THE STATS

No. of attorneys: 267
No. of offices: 3
Summer associate offers: 38 out of 41 (Atlanta, 1999)
Managing Partner: Robert W. Webb
Hiring Attorney: Larry E. Gramlich

NOTABLE PERKS

- Gym

EMPLOYMENT CONTACT

Ms. Betsy Hatcher
Recruiting Manager
(404) 885-3000
betsy.hatcher@troutmansanders.com

PAY

Atlanta, 2000
1st year: $100,000 + $6,000-$18,000 bonus potential
Salary after first year is merit-based
Summer associate: $1,400/week

Washington, DC, 2000
1st year: $120,000 + $9,000-$21,000 bonus potential
Summer associate: $1,600/week

THE BUZZ
What attorneys at other firms are saying about this firm

- "Great lifestyle firm, but perceived as economically unsound"
- "Seems to be one step behind"
- "Great place to work; doesn't pay enough"
- "Good people, second-rate work"

Winstead Sechrest & Minick, PC

5400 Renaissance Tower
1201 Elm Street
Dallas, TX 75270
(214) 745-5400
Fax: (214) 745-5390
www.winstead.com

LOCATIONS

Dallas, TX (HQ)
Austin, TX
Fort Worth, TX
Houston, TX
Mexico City

MAJOR DEPARTMENTS/PRACTICES

Bankruptcy
Corporate & Finance
Environmental & Energy
Financial Institutions
Intellectual Property
Labor & Employment
Litigation
Real Estate
Tax

THE STATS

No. of attorneys: 260
No. of offices: 5
Summer associate offers: 42 out of 58 (Firm-wide, 1999)
President, Board of Directors: W. Mike Baggett
Hiring Partner: J. Richard White

THE BUZZ
What attorneys at other firms are saying about this firm

- "Good reputation"
- "Fungible Dallas clone"
- "Trying to grow"

NOTABLE PERKS

- Paid parking

EMPLOYMENT CONTACT

Ms. Dominique Anderson
Recruitment Administrator
(214) 745-5306
danderson@winstead.com

PAY

All Texas Offices, 2000
1st year: $96,000 - $105,000
Bonus: $0-10K @1,800 hours; $10-12K @2,050; $11-13K @2,200; $12-15K @2,400
2nd year: $98,700 - $115,200
Bonus: $0-10K @1,800 hours; $10-13K @2,050; $12-14K @2,200; $13-17K @2,400
3rd year: $102,000 - $126,000
Bonus: $0-16K @1,800 hours; $16-18K @2,050; $17-19K @2,200; $18-20K @2,400
4th year: $103,500 - $132,500
Bonus: $0-25K @1,800 hours; $25-28K @2,050; $26-29K @2,200; $27-32K @2,,400
5th year: $131,000 - $145,000
Bonus: $0-25K @1,800 hours; $25-29K @2,050; $27-30K @2,200; $28-34K @2,400
6th year: $134,500 - $148,500
Bonus: $0-25K @1,800 hours; $25-30K @2,050; $28-32K @2,200; $29-38K @2,400
7th year: $148,000 - $155,000
Bonus: $0-25K @1,800 hours; $25-31K @2,050; $29-33K @2,200; $30-40K @2,400
Summer associate: $1,700/week

Winthrop, Stimson, Putnam & Roberts

One Battery Park Plaza
New York, NY 10004-1490
(212) 858-1000
Fax: (212) 858-1500
www.winstim.com

LOCATIONS

New York, NY (HQ)
Palm Beach, FL
Stamford, CT
Washington, DC
Hong Kong
London
Singapore
Tokyo

MAJOR DEPARTMENTS/PRACTICES

Bankruptcy
Corporate & Capital Markets
Employee Benefits & ERISA
Finance
Individual Client Services
International Trade & Business
Labor & Employment
Litigation
Real Estate
Tax

THE STATS

No. of attorneys: 256
No. of offices: 8
Summer associate offers: 23 out of 24 (New York, 1999)
Chairman, Management Committee: John F. Pritchard, Esq.
Hiring attorney: Craig M. Scully, Esq.

NOTABLE PERKS

- Subsidized health club
- Flexible spending accounts (child care and medical)
- 3 months paid maternity leave
- Leave of absence for public service

EMPLOYMENT CONTACT

Ms. Dorrie Ciavatta
Director of Legal Employment
(212) 858-1526
ciavattad@winstim.com

PAY

New York, 2000
1st year: $120,000 + $5,000 signing bonus
2nd year: $127,000 + $8,000 for billing 2,000 hours
3rd year: $135,000 + $15,000 for billing 2,000 hours
4th year: $152,000 + $18,000 for billing 2,000 hours
5th year: $170,000 + $20,000 for billing 2,000 hours
6th year: $175,000 + $25,000 for billing 2,000 hours
7th year: $185,000 + $25,000 for billing 2,000 hours
8th year: $190,000 + $28,000 for billing 2,000 hours
Summer associate: $2,404/week

THE BUZZ
What attorneys at other firms are saying about this firm

- "Hear less about them these days"
- "Remarkably distinguished"
- "Decidedly mixed"
- "Good working environment"

Wolf, Block, Schorr and Solis-Cohen, LLP

1650 Arch Street, 22nd Floor
Philadelphia, PA 19103-2097
(215) 977-2362
Fax: (215) 405-3962
www.wolfblock.com

LOCATIONS

Philadelphia, PA (HQ)
Camden, NJ
Harrisburg, PA
New York, NY
Norristown, PA
Wilmington, DE

MAJOR DEPARTMENTS/PRACTICES

Bankruptcy
Corporate & Finance
Employment Services
Estates & Trusts
Family Law
Health Law
Intellectual Property/Information Technology
Litigation/Complex Liability/Surety
Real Estate & Environmental
Tax

THE STATS

No. of attorneys: 237
No. of offices: 6
Summer associate offers: 16 out of 16 (Philadelphia, 2000)
Co-chairs: Mark L. Alderman & Matthew H. Kamens
Hiring Attorney: Jodi T. Plavner, Esq.

NOTABLE PERKS

- Homeowners and auto group insurance
- Credit union

EMPLOYMENT CONTACT

Ms. Eileen M. McMahon
Director, Legal Personnel & Recruitment
(215) 977-2362
emcmahon@wolfblock.com

PAY

Philadelphia, 2000
1st year: $100,000 + discretionary bonus
Summer associate: $1,725/week

THE BUZZ
What attorneys at other firms are saying about this firm

- "Fun, friendly, hard-working"
- "Competitive, miserable atmosphere"
- "Doing better work than many know"

■ OUR LAWYERS HAVE DEGREES IN: CLASSICAL STUDIES, ASIAN STUDIES, ECONOMICS, ARCHITECTURE & SOCIETY, POLITICAL SCIENCE ■

High-tech law @ Fenwick & West — it's not just for geeks.

If you are a superb law student or attorney and your VCR isn't flashing 12:00, Fenwick & West wants you.

Fenwick & West is the ONLY law firm on Fortune's 1999 and 2000 listings of the "100 Best Companies to Work For." We do cutting-edge legal work for high-technology clients from our offices in Palo Alto, San Francisco and Washington DC, but we do not require technical degrees. In fact, fewer than 15% of our over-200 lawyers have technical degrees.

CONTACT
KAREN AMATANGELO-BLOCK
ATTORNEY RECRUITING MANAGER
650.494.0600
RECRUIT@FENWICK.COM

FORTUNE 100 BEST COMPANIES TO WORK FOR 1999
100 BEST COMPANIES TO WORK FOR FORTUNE 2000

FENWICK & WEST LLP
LAWYERING FOR THE INFORMATION AGE
PALO ALTO SAN FRANCISCO WASHINGTON DC
WWW.FENWICK.COM

APPENDIX

Alphabetical Index of Law Firms

Akin Gump Strauss Hauer & Feld	554
Alston & Bird	648
Arent Fox Kinter Plotkin & Kahn	807
Arnold & Porter	308
Baker Botts	622
Baker & McKenzie	578
Ballard Spahr Andrews & Ingersoll	808
Bingham Dana	809
Blank Rome Comisky & McCauley	810
Bracewell & Patterson	811
Brobeck, Phleger & Harrison	340
Cadwalader, Wickersham & Taft	600
Cahill Gordon & Reindel	634
Chadbourne & Parke	658
Choate, Hall & Stewart	670
Cleary, Gottlieb, Steen & Hamilton	142
Clifford Chance Rogers & Wells	444
Cooley Godward	432
Covington & Burling	226
Cravath, Swaine & Moore	60
Davis Polk & Wardwell	104
Debevoise & Plimpton	274
Dechert Price & Rhoads	682
Dewey Ballantine	422
Drinker Biddle & Reath	812
Duane, Morris & Heckscher	813
Fenwick & West	814
Fish & Neave	815
Fish & Richardson	816
Foley, Hoag & Eliot	817
Foley & Lardner	818
Fried, Frank, Harris, Shriver & Jacobson	398
Fulbright & Jaworski	694
Gardere & Wynne	819
Gibson, Dunn & Crutcher	262
Goodwin, Procter & Hoar	820
Gray Cary Ware & Freidenrich	704

ALPHABETICAL INDEX OF FIRMS (cont'd)

Gunderson Dettmer Stough Villeneuve Franklin & Hachigian 498

Hale and Dorr 374

Haynes and Boone 821

Heller Ehrman White & McAutliffe 822

Hogan & Hartson 510

Howrey Simon Arnold & White 823

Hunton & Williams 824

Irell & Manella 714

Jenkens & Gilchrist 825

Jenner & Block 724

Jones, Day, Reavis & Pogue 410

Katten Muchin Zavis 826

Kaye, Scholer, Fierman, Hays & Handler 827

Kelley Drye & Warren 828

Kilpatrick Stockton 736

King & Spalding 468

Kirkland & Ellis 194

Latham & Watkins 170

LeBoeuf, Lamb, Greene & MacRae 746

Loeb & Loeb 829

Long Aldridge & Norman 830

Manatt, Phelps & Phillips 831

Mayer, Brown & Platt 352

McDermott, Will & Emery 756

Milbank, Tweed, Hadley & McCloy 364

Mintz, Levin, Cohn, Ferris, Glovsky and Popeo 832

Montgomery, McCracken, Walker & Rhoads 833

Morgan, Lewis & Bockius 456

Morrison & Foerster 320

Munger, Tolles & Olson 522

O'Melveny & Myers 284

Orrick, Herrington & Sutcliffe 544

Palmer & Dodge 834

Paul, Hastings, Janofsky & Walker 532

Paul, Weiss, Rifkind, Wharton & Garrison 236

Pepper Hamilton 835

Perkins Coie 770

ALPHABETICAL INDEX OF FIRMS (cont'd)

Pillsbury Madison & Sutro	782
Piper Marbury Rudnick & Wolfe	836
Preston Gates & Ellis	794
Proskauer Rose	610
Ropes & Gray	386
Saul, Ewing, Remick & Saul	837
Schiff Hardin & Waite	838
Schulte Roth & Zabel	839
Shaw Pittman	840
Shearman & Sterling	156
Sheppard, Mullin, Richter & Hampton	841
Sidley & Austin	250
Simpson Thacher & Bartlett	130
Skadden, Arps, Slate, Meagher & Flom	116
Sonnenschein Nath & Rosenthal	842
Squire, Sanders & Dempsey	843
Steptoe & Johnson	844
Stroock & Stroock & Lavan	845
Sullivan & Cromwell	90
Swidler Berlin Shereff Friedman	846
Testa, Hurwitz & Thibeault	847
Thelen Reid & Priest	848
Thompson & Knight	849
Troutman Sanders	850
Venture Law Group	488
Vinson & Elkins	590
Wachtell, Lipton, Rosen & Katz	76
Weil, Gotshal & Manges	214
White & Case	298
Williams & Connolly	204
Willkie Farr & Gallagher	478
Wilmer, Cutler & Pickering	330
Wilson Sonsini Goodrich & Rosati	182
Winstead Sechrest & Minick	851
Winston & Strawn	566
Winthrop, Stimson, Putnam & Roberts	852
Wolf, Block, Schorr and Solis-Cohen	853

Firms by Main Offices

Atlanta

Alston & Bird	648
Kilpatrick Stockton	736
King & Spalding	468
Long Aldridge & Norman	830
Troutman Sanders	850

Boston

Bingham Dana	809
Choate, Hall & Stewart	670
Fish & Richardson	816
Foley, Hoag & Eliot	817
Goodwin, Procter & Hoar	820
Hale and Dorr	374
Mintz, Levin, Cohn, Ferris, Glovsky and Popeo	832
Palmer & Dodge	834
Ropes & Gray	386
Testa, Hurwitz & Thibeault	847

Chicago

Baker & McKenzie	578
Jenner & Block	724
Katten Muchin Zavis	826
Kirkland & Ellis	194
Mayer, Brown & Platt	352
McDermott, Will & Emery	756
Piper Marbury Rudnick & Wolfe	836
Schiff Hardin & Waite	838
Sidley & Austin	250
Sonnenschein Nath & Rosenthal	842
Winston & Strawn	566

Cleveland

Jones, Day, Reavis & Pogue	410
Squire, Sanders & Dempsey	843

FIRMS BY MAIN OFFICES (cont'd)

Dallas

Akin Gump Strauss Hauer & Feld	.554
Gardere & Wynne	.819
Haynes and Boone	.821
Jenkens & Gilchrist	.825
Thompson & Knight	.849
Winstead Sechrest & Minick	.851

Houston

Baker Botts	.622
Bracewell & Patterson	.811
Fulbright & Jaworski	.694
Vinson & Elkins	.590

Los Angeles

Gibson, Dunn & Crutcher	.262
Irell & Manella	.714
Latham & Watkins	.170
Loeb & Loeb	.829
Manatt, Phelps & Phillips	.831
Munger, Tolles & Olson	.522
O'Melveny & Myers	.284
Paul, Hastings, Janofsky & Walker	.532
Sheppard, Mullin, Richter & Hampton	.841

Menlo Park

Gunderson Dettmer Stough Villeneuve Franklin & Hachigian	.498
Venture Law Group	.488

Milwaukee

Foley & Lardner	.818

New York

Cadwalader, Wickersham & Taft	.600
Cahill Gordon & Reindel	.634
Chadbourne & Parke	.658
Cleary, Gottlieb, Steen & Hamilton	.142
Clifford Chance Rogers & Wells	.422

FIRMS BY MAIN OFFICES (cont'd)

Cravath, Swaine & Moore 60
Davis Polk & Wardwell 104
Debevoise & Plimpton 274
Dewey Ballantine 444
Fish & Neave 815
Fried, Frank, Harris, Shriver & Jacobson 398
Kaye, Scholer, Fierman, Hays & Handler 827
Kelley Drye & Warren 828
LeBoeuf, Lamb, Greene & MacRae 746
Milbank, Tweed, Hadley & McCloy 364
Morgan, Lewis & Bockius 456
Paul, Weiss, Rifkind, Wharton & Garrison 236
Proskauer Rose 610
Schulte Roth & Zabel 839
Shearman & Sterling 156
Simpson Thacher & Bartlett 130
Skadden, Arps, Slate Meagher & Flom 116
Stroock & Stroock & Lavan 845
Sullivan & Cromwell 90
Thelen Reid & Priest 848
Wachtell, Lipton, Rosen & Katz 76
Weil, Gotshal & Manges 214
White & Case 298
Willkie Farr & Gallagher 478
Winthrop, Stimson, Putnam & Roberts 852

Palo Alto
Cooley Godward 432
Gray Cary Ware & Freidenrich 704
Fenwick & West 814
Wilson Sonsini Goodrich & Rosati 182

Philadelphia
Ballard Spahr Andrews & Ingersoll 808
Blank Rome Comisky & McCauley 810
Dechert Price & Rhoads 682
Drinker Biddle & Reath 812
Duane, Morris & Heckscher 813

FIRMS BY MAIN OFFICES (cont'd)

Montgomery, McCracken, Walker & Rhoads 833
Morgan, Lewis & Bockius 456
Pepper Hamilton 835
Saul, Ewing, Remick & Saul 837
Wolf, Block, Schorr and Solis-Cohen 853

Richmond

Hunton & Williams 824

San Diego

Gray Cary Ware & Freidenrich 704

Seattle

Perkins Coie 770
Preston Gates & Ellis 794

San Francisco

Brobeck, Phleger & Harrison 340
Heller Ehrman White & McAuliffe 822
Morrison & Foerster 320
Orrick, Herrington & Sutcliffe 544
Pillsbury, Madison & Sutro 782
Thelen Reid & Priest LLP 848

Washington, DC

Akin Gump Strauss Hauer & Feld 554
Arent Fox Kinter Plotkin & Kahn 807
Arnold & Porter 5
Covington & Burling 226
Hogan & Hartson 510
Howrey Simon Arnold & White 823
Shaw Pittman 840
Steptoe & Johnson 844
Swidler Berlin Shereff Friedman 846
Williams & Connolly 204
Wilmer, Cutler & Pickering 330

People Index

Abell, Nancy	535
Abramson, Neil	612
Acheson, Dean	228
Adelson, Kenneth	435
Aggarwal, Anil	750
Akin, Henry	556
Allen, Maurice	218
Alston, Robert C.	650
Andrews, Joseph	581
Aquila, Frank	98
Aronson, Virginia L.	254
Arquit, Kevin	447
Baer, William	310
Bagley, Parker	367
Baker III, James A.	624
Baker, Russell	580
Ball, George W.	144
Ball, Lucille	716
Ball, Stephen	264
Bangs, Francis	106
Banks, Michael	460
Barist, Jeffrey	368
Barnett, Robert	207
Bartle III, Harvey	684
Baxter, Harry	738
Baxter, Jr., Ralph	546, 547
Bayless, David	322
Beard, Brian	501
Beattie, Richard	133
Beck	613
Beck, Joseph	740
Becker, Edward	759
Beisner, John	287
Belichick, Bill	302
Bell, Griffin B.	470
Bender, Matthew	121
Benny, Jack	286
Benson, Douglas	159
Benton, Lee	434
Berger, Eugene	716
Berk, Romy	663
Berkowitz, Abram	388
Berlin, Peter	96
Bernstein, David	278
Bernstein, Louise Roman	424
Bettman, Gary	612
Bezanson, Thomas	662
Birnbaum, Sheila	121
Black, Martin J.	685
Blair, Kerry	582
Blaskic, Tihomir	173
Block, Dennis	216, 217, 602, 603, 608
Bloom, Ilene	575
Boesky, Ivan	400
Boies, David	95, 287
Bonner, Lisa	377
Born, Brooksley	310
Boutrous Jr., Theodore	265
Boyden, Cary	786
Boykin, Rigdon	660
Bradbury, Steven	198
Bradley, Donald	186
Bradley, Helen	583
Brady, George	583
Brandes, Lawrence	603
Brant Jr., Donald	366
Brenner, Thomas	367
Brock Jr., James	492
Bromwich, Michael	400
Brooks, Russell	368
Brosnahan, James	322
Brountas, Paul P.	376
Brown, Elliot	716
Brownstein, Andrew	81

PEOPLE INDEX (cont'd)

Brummel, Sally	107
Buckley, Abrams	636
Buckley, Susan	636
Buffet, Warren	524
Bultena, Lance	512
Bumbaca, Michael	583
Burling, Edward	228
Byowitz, Michael	81
Cahill, John	636
Cahill, William	120
Califano, Joseph	206, 427
Camahort, Steve	187
Campbell, William	534
Capener, Cole	582
Caplan, Lincoln	118
Cappuccio, Paul	198
Carlton, Richard	95
Carter, Jimmy	332
Carter, Walter	446
Cartwright, David	289
Cephas, Derrick	608
Charnley, William	759
Chen, Peter	186
Christ, Keri	367
Christopher, Thomas	400
Christopher, Warren	288
Chu, Morgan	716
Cicero Jr., Frank	197
Cieri, Richard	414
Clark, Joseph S.	684
Claussen, Olof	174
Cleary, George	144
Clifford, Clark	109
Clinton, Bill	80, 81, 93, 121, 206, 332
Coates, John	80
Coats, Evelyn	740
Cogut, Charles	133
Cohen, H. Rodgin	92, 93, 98
Cohen, Harry	603
Cohen, Jerome	239
Cohen, Stephen	673
Cohen, Steve	604
Cohen, Steven	81
Cole, Thomas	253
Collins, Dale	161
Concepcion, Carlos F.	739
Condon, Creighton	160
Connolly, Paul	206
Converse, Michael L.	558
Conway, Georger	80
Cook, Brendan	582
Cook, Clive	582
Cooluris, John	786
Cooney Jr., Gordon	460
Cooper, Gary	286
Cooper, Mike	101
Cornish, John M.	674
Covington, J. Harry	228
Cox, Archibald	388
Craig, Gregory	207
Cranston, Mary	784, 785
Creighton, Susan	186
Croke, Jim	602
Crompton III, Charles	174
Cromwell, William	92
Crosby, Bing	286
Culleton, Christopher J.	685
Cuomo, Mario	480
Currie, Frank	106
Curry, Christian	109
Cutler, Lloyd	332
Dannhauser, Stephen	216, 217
Daub, Peter M.	582
Davis, Brian A.	673

PEOPLE INDEX (cont'd)

Davis, David	501
Davis, Evan A.	147
Davis, John	106
de Hoyos, Debora	354
Dean, Arthur	92
Debevoise, Eli Whitney	276
DeFranco, Michael	160
Deixler, Bert	613
Delaney, John	323
Denham, Robert	524
Denny, Otway B.	696
Despins, Luc	366, 368
Dettmer, Scott	502
Dewey, Thomas	424
DeWitt, Robert	534
Dogg, Snoop	613
Dolan, Lawrence	276
Dole, Bob	512
Donahue, Michael	377
Donaldson, Sam	207
Donworth, George	772
Dorr, Dudley	376
Douglas, Charles W.	253
Dover, Agnes	512
Dowd, John	558
Dr. Dre	613
Driver, Walter W.	471
Dulles, John Foster	92
Duncan, Michelle	602
Dwyer, Cornelius	162
Dyk, Timothy	414
Earp, Wyatt	198
Edelman, Theodore	101
Edelstein, Mark	366
Edmonds, Warner	534
Edwards, Lucy	96
Elkins, James A.	592

Ellis, Douglas	390
Elwin Jr., J. William	167
Emmer, Maurice	582
Epstein, Scott	717
Ettinger, John	110
Evanich, Kevin	196
Ewing, Patrick	208
Fahner, Ty	354
Fairchild, Gray	568
Faulkner, Shannon	162
Field, David Dudley	158
Filardi, Edward	302
Finch, Kevin	717
Finkelson, Allen	65
Finnegan, John	603
Fisher, Ora	180
Fisher, Ruth	524
Fiske, Robert	108
Fleischer, Jr, Arthur	401
Fleming, David	172, 582
Flom, Joseph	118
Flood, Alison	583
Foerster, Constantine	322
Fogarty, Jr., John A.	625
Forester, Ronald	322
Fortas, Abe	310
Francies, Mike	218
Frankel, Martin	557
Franklin, Steven	502
Freier, Elliot	717
Friedman, Alan	526
Friedman, Andrew	230
Friendly, Henry J.	144
Frye, Russel	663
Ganz, Howard	612
Garcia, Dan	526
Garrison, Lloyd	238

PEOPLE INDEX (cont'd)

Gates, William H.	796
Gee, Tim	583
Gellene, John	368
Gerber, Lawrence	762
Getter, Doug	424
Gibson, Virginia	583
Ginsburg, Martin	400
Giuliani, Rudy	264, 300
Glerum, Charles	673
Glover, Stephen	264
Goldberg, Helen	583
Goldberg, Perry	716
Goldman, Melvin	322
Goldschmid, Harvey	217, 310
Gonzalez, Juan Miguel	207
Gooden, Lisa	289
Goroff, Michael	367
Gottfried, Michael	368
Gottlieb, Leo	144
Gottschalk, Tom	197
Gould, Jay	158
Goulding, J. Michael	582
Graves, Jackson A.	286
Gray Jr., John Chipman	388
Green, Karen F.	376
Greenstein, Martin	581
Greer, Mary Hogan	698
Grieg, Brian	698
Grimes, David	750
Gruber, Joseph	159
Guernsey, Kenneth	434
Gunderson, Robert	501
Guynn, Steven	413
Hachigian, Jay	500
Hale, Richard	376
Hall, Richard	65
Halpern, Jay	785
Hansen, Kenneth	661
Hanson, Harry	673
Hartigan, Neil	758
Hartson, Nelson	512
Hatchard, Michael	120
Hayman, Russell	173
Heim, Robert	685
Hein, Peter	80
Heitz, Kenneth	716
Helmsley, Leona	206
Helwick, Timothy	95
Hentrich, John	583
Herbst, Jeff	186
Herlihy, Edward D.	81, 82
Hickman, Brian	759
Higgin, Jeffrey	501
Higginson, Tony	625
Hill, Grant	208
Hill, Lauryn	613
Hills, Roderick	524
Hoffmann, Brian	604
Hogan, Frank	512
Holdclaw, Chamique	208
Holm, Klas	582
Horowitz, Gary	133
Howard, George	785
Howard, Rod	342
Hundley, William	558
Hurlock, James B.	300
Hurtado, Daniel	726
Huston, DeVerille A.	254
Hutton, E.F.	636
Hyman, Milton	717
Icahn, Carl	78
Iglesias, Ray	750
Immergut, Mel	368, 369
Immordono, Michael	174

PEOPLE INDEX (cont'd)

Irell, Lawrence 716
Jack, Ian 583
Jackson, Andrew 62
Jackson, Thomas Penfield 95, 96
Jackson, Michael 400
Jackson, William 367
Jacobson, Hugh 366
Jaffe, Alan 613
Jaffe, Helene 219
Janofsky, Leonard 534
Jaworski, Leon 696
Jimerson, Verneal 356
Johnson, Craig .184, 480, 490
Johnson, Ian 548
Johnson, Karen Silverman 174
Johnson, Orlan 366
Johnson, Robert 524
Jones, Jerry 79, 333
Jones, Paula 80, 121
Jordan, Jr., Vernon 556
Jordan, Michael 82, 333
Jutkowitz, Stanley 785
Kadish, Marc 356
Kaelin, Kato 288
Kantor, Mickey 354
Karasz, Peter 145
Karmazin, Mel 65
Kattan, Joseph 265
Katz, George 78
Kearney, Dennis J. 674
Keating Jr., Charles 412
Keitt, John 424
Kelley, Bill 106, 107
Kelly, Larry 739
Kelly, Michael 458
Kendall, David 208
Kenna, Edward C. 673

Kennedy, Michael 186
Kennedy, Raoul 121
Kessler, Jeffrey 218
Kim, Richard 717
Kindler, Robert A. 64
King, Alex C. 470
King, Charlie 402
Kinmonth, G. Frederick 240
Kirkland, Jr., J. David 625
Klain, Ronald 288
Klein, Calvin 239
Klein, Freada 660
Klotsche, John 581
Knight, Adrian 159
Knox, Jr., Wyck 739
Konski, Antoinette 582
Kramer, Steven 366
Kristy, Dean 344
Krueger, Karen 81
Kunstler, Michael 582
Lacovara, Michael 101
Lagarde, Christine 580, 581
Lanam, Renee 502
Latham, Dana 172
Lawrence, Alan 602
LeBoeuf, Randall 748
Lecese, Joseph M. 612
Lee, Spike 239
Lee, William 376
Lennon, Mary 388
Levin, Jack 196
Levin, Martin E. 674
Levin, Richard 121
Levine, Randy 556
Levitt, Peter 389
Levy, Louis S. 660
Levy, Ralph B. 471

PEOPLE INDEX (cont'd)

Lewinsky, Monica	.121
Lewis, Francis Draper	.458
Lincoln, Abraham	.62
Link, Robert	.602
Lipeless, Stewart	.583
Lippert, Nels	.378
Lipton, Martin	.78, 79, 81
Litvack, Sanford "Sandy"	.426
Livingston, J. Cleve	.786
Llewelyn, David	.301
Lobb, Jeffrey	.785
Lobenfeld, Eric	.663
London, Martin	.241
Luethke, Charles	.110
Lynch, Gary	.109
Lyons, James	.120
MacFarlance, Helen	.162
MacVeagh, Wayne	.684
Madda, Michael	.583
Madison, Frank D.	.784
Madonna	.613
Mallen, Ronald	.185
Malt, Bradford	.388, 389
Malt, R. Bradford	.388
Mamalian, Paul	.785
Manella, Arthur	.716
Manton, Martin T.	.660
Marshall, Margaret	.672, 674
Martin, Dean	.716
Martin, Katherine	.186
Martin, R. Eden	.253
Mastro, Randy	.264
Maurer, Robert	.66
McBryde, John	.109
McCartan, Patrick M.	.412, 413, 414
McCaw, Craig	.368
McCusker, Anthony	.502
McDermott, E.H.	.758
McDermott, James	.109
McKenzie, John	.580
McLaughlin, Mary	.684
McNally, Laura	
McPhee, Joan	.390
McVay, Kenneth	.500
Mechanic, Jonathan	.401
Meeks, Freddie	.324
Mendelson, Alan	.174
Mestres, Ricardo	.92
Milken, Michael	.172, 206, 239, 240
Miller, Harvey	.217
Miller, O'Malley	.526
Millstein, Ira	.219
Miner, Judson	.727
Mitchel, Robert	.512
Mittleman, Harry	.716
Monge, Jay	.354
Morgan Jr., Charles Eldridge	.458
Morgan, J. Pierpont	.106
Morris, Collin	.787
Morrison, Alexander	.322
Morrison, Phillip	.581
Muller, Scott	.109
Munger, Charles T.	.524
Myerson, Toby	.239
Nabozny, Jamie	.121
Nakasone, Tabetha	.501
Neis, James	.568
Niehans, Daniel	.502
Nimmer, David	.716
Noble, Jonathan	.501
Norris, Kandance Weems	.101
North, Oliver	.206
Nunn, Sam	.470
Nussbaum, Bernard	.80

PEOPLE INDEX (cont'd)

Nussbaum, Michael	.389
O'Brien, John Lord	.228
O'Brien, Judith	.185
O'Brien, Mark	.110
O'Brien, Raymond A.	.673
O'Brien, Thomas	.322
O'Donnell, Terrence	.206
O'Donoghue, Brian	.367
Oliver, April	.389
Olson, John	.264
Olson, Ronald	.525
Olson, Theodore	.265
O'Melveny, Henry	.286
O'Melveny, Jack	.286
Ortner, Charles	.613
Osborn, Charles	.158
Palermo, Christopher	.759
Park, Marina H.	.784, 785, 787
Pataki, George	.101
Paul, Lee	.534
Paul, Rudolph	.238
Paxon, Bill	.556
Payton, John	.332
Pearlstein, Debra	.219
Peckar, Rissa	.606
Pepin, Alfred	.785
Petkovic, Denis	.661
Philips, Bradley	.527
Phleger, Herman	.343
Pickens, T. Boone	.78
Pickford, Mary	.286
Pierce, Morton	.425
Pillsbury, Evan S.	.784
Pitofsky, Robert	.310
Pitt, Harvey	.400
Plapinger, William	.94
Plimpton, Francis T.P.	.276
Poff, Joe	.625
Pogue, Richard W.	.412
Polk, Frank	.106
Pomerantz, Mark F.	.240
Ponikvar, Dale	.367
Porter, Frank B.	.674
Porter, Paul	.310
Preston, Harold	.796
Proskauer, Joseph	.612
Quaid, Blanche	.388
Quayle, Dan	.206
Quinn, James	.218
Raines, Mark	.159
Rappaport, Larry	.613
Raven, Robert	.322
Reardon, Roy	.134
Rebish, Janet	.377
Reder, Robert	.367
Redstone, Summer	.65
Rice, Thomas	.134
Richardson, Elliot	.388
Rifkind, Simon	.238
Robbins, Barbara	.80
Roberts, Cokie	.207
Robertson, Oscar	.612
Rogers, William	.446
Rondeau, Pat	.377
Ropes, John Codman	.388
Roppel, Mark	.160
Rosati, Mario	.184
Rosen, Leonard	.78
Rosenman, Stephen	.344
Rosenthal, Stuart A.	.664
Rothenberg, Alan	.172
Rublee, George	.228
Ruegger, Philip	.133
Rule, Charles (Rick)	.228

PEOPLE INDEX (cont'd)

Ruskin, Bradley I.	.612	Spencer, James Lee	.324
Sack, Robert	.266	Spindel, Frederic	.785
Sadwick, David	.796	Sporkin, Stanley	.217
Saltoun, Andre	.583	Springer, David	.121
Samuels, Susan	.344	Spurlock, Steven	.502
Sanders, Barry	.172	Spyros, Nicholas	.583
Sandman, James	.310	St. Clair, James	.376
Saper, Jeffrey	.185	Steen, Mel	.144
Saxon, Christopher	.582	Stein, Eugene	.162
Schacter, Ira	.604	Steinberg, Jonathan	.716
Scherer, Joachim	.582	Steinberg, Michael	.95
Schindler, David	.174	Steinhart, William	.265
Schmoke, Kurt	.332	Stellabotte, John	.95
Schoenberg, Clifford	.603	Sterling, John	.158
Schwinger, Robert	.663	Stern, David	.612
Segel, Alvin	.717	Stetson, Francis	.106
Servan-Screiber, Pierre	.94	Stevenson, William	.276
Seward, William	.62	Stewart, David	.650
Shane, Heather	.502	Stewart, Jimmy	.286
Shapiro, Norma L.	.684	Stiles, Ned	.145
Sharbaugh, Thomas	.458	Straub, Chester	.480
Shearman, Thomas	.158	Strauss, Robert	.556, 557
Sheehan, Robert C.	.119	Strawbridge, James	.186
Sheppard, Matthew	.95	Strawn, Silas	.568
Shorb, Paul	.228	Strivens, Peter	.582
Shriver, Sargent	.400	Sullivan, Algeron	.92
Simpson, Scott	.120	Sullivan, Brendan	.206, 207
Sims, Joe	.414	Sutro, Alfred	.784
Sinatra, Frank	.716	Sutton, Jeff	.414
Singlaub, Maj. Gen. John	.389	Swaine, Robert	.62
Skaggs, David	.512	Taviss, Michael	.502
Smith, Donald	.158	Taylor, Bernard	.651
Smith, George	.158	Taylor, Elizabeth	.716
Smith, Jeffrey	.62, 312	Taylor, Nolan	.749
Sobel, Jonathan	.663	Taylor, Thomas	.749
Sonsini, Larry	.184	Terwilliger, George	.301
Spalding, Jack J.	.470	Teynier, Eric	.159

PEOPLE INDEX (cont'd)

Thomas, George	785	Wells, Jack	446
Thome, Jonathan	158	Werner, Philip	458
Thompson, James	568	Westerberg, David A.	377
Thomson, Jere	413	Westland, Charles	367
Tillingshast, Davis	582	Westover, Christopher	435
Todd, Elmer	772	Wharton, John	238
Treuhold, Bob	160	Whitley, Joe D.	651
Tufaro, Richard	367	Wickes, Paul	161
Tweed, William	106	Wilkinson, Andrew	602
Urowsky, Richard	95	Will, George	207
Vardaman, Jack	206	Williams, Edward Bennett	206, 207
Vartanian, Thomas	400	Williams, Natalie	278
Villeneuve, Thomas	502	Willkie, Wendell	480
Vinson, William Ashton	592	Wilson, John	184
Vitale, Robert	604	Wing, Rusty	219
Volk, Stephen	160	Winston, Frederick	568
Volpert, Dick	526	Winters, Vernon	174
Volstad, Michael	548	Wolf, Howard	697
Vullo, Maria T.	241	Wolfson, David	369
Wachsberger, Chaim	662	Wright, Judge	121
Walker, Diana	286	Yaghmaie, Babak	500
Walker, Richard	582	Youngwood, Alfred	238
Wall, Daniel	174	Youngwood, Jonathan	135
Wardwell, Allen	106	Zarb, Frank	459
Watchell, Herbert	79, 80, 82	Zipp, Robert	492
Watkins, Paul	172	Zirinsky, Bruce	603
Wayland, Joseph F.	135		
Weaver, Sigourney	239		
Webb, Dan	568		
Webster, Benjamin	786		
Weeks, Rena	581		
Weiss, Louis	238		
Weissler, Mark	366		
Welch, Joseph	376		
Weld, William	758		
Weld, William R.	376		
Wells Jr., Theodore V.	240		

Company/Organization Index

24/7 Media	.614
3Clix.com	.355
3Com	.343
3M Corp.	.323, 697
Abbott Laboratories	.569
ABC	.80
About.com	.343
Abovenet Communications	.786
Accel Partners	.174, 501
Acushnet Co.	.663
Adobe Systems	.343, 460
Aegon	.748
Aetna	.355
Agency.com	.343
AICO	.369
AIDS Legal Counsel, The	.254
AIDS Project, L.A.	.526
AIR 2 US	.366
AirTouch Communications	.401, 784, 786
Akamai	.377
Alaska Airlines	.772
Alcan Aluminum	.366
Alcoa	.81, 748
Alliance for Children's Rights, The	.526
Allied Waste Industries	.401
AlliedSignal	.401, 685
Alyeska Pipeline Service Co.	.525
Amazon.com	.412, 773
America Online	.64, 120, 133, 312, 332, 355, 173, 378, 414
American Airlines	.276, 726
American Bar Association	.526
American Brands	.660, 662
American Civil Liberties Union	.254, 334, 514
American Disposal Services	.613
American Express	.389
American Greetings	.412
American Heritage Life Investment Corp.	.389
American Home Products	.134, 207
American Honda Motor	.447
American Institute of Certified Accountants	.482
American Red Cross	.312
Ameritrade	.355
Amsterdam's United Pan-Europe Communications NV	447
Anaconda Minerals	.660
Analog Devices	.759
Andersen Worldwide	.401
Animals Agenda, The	.369
Apartments.com	.355
appelate.net	.356
Apple Computer	.288, 343, 173
Archer Daniels Midland	.207
Argentaria Caja Postal	.108
Ariba	.787
ArrowPoint Communications, Inc.	.377
Asian Development Bank	.147
Ask Jeeves	.185
Aspect Development	.343, 435
Association for Competitive Technology	.332
Association of American Medical Colleges	.229
AT&T	.81, 253, 277, 367
Atlantic Richfield Company (ARCO)	.65, 525
ATP tour, The	.612
AtWeb, Inc.	.706
Auctions.com	.355
Autobytel.com	.535
Avant! Corp.	.502
Avon Products	.219
AXA	.748
B.A.T. Industries	.134
Bain & Company	.388
Bain Capital	.389
Baker & Hostetler	.569
Baker Hughes	.625

COMPANY/ORGANIZATION INDEX (cont'd)

Banc One	79, 81
Banco Bilbao Vizcaya	108
Banco de Credito Hispanoamerica	108
Banco Hipotecario	108
Banco Nacional de Panama	300
Banco Santander	108
Bank of America	81, 603, 535, 652, 784, 786
Bank of New York	96
BankAmerica	81, 343
Bankeast Corp.	311
Bankers Trust	81, 368
Barclays	134
BASF	160
BAT Industries	66
Baxter Healthcare Corp.	685
Bayer A.G.	66, 332
Bayer Corporation	672
BDO Seidman	613
Bear Stearns	535,546
Beenz	174
Bell Atlantic	277, 287, 312, 459, 569
BellSouth	739
Belmont Learning Complex	289
Ben & Jerry's Homemade	389
Benchmark Capital	501
Berkshire Hathaway	526
Bethlehem Steel	425
beyond.com	162
Black Panthers	310
Blanchfield Cordle & Moore	354
Bloomberg	481
Boeing	772
Boston Communications Group	377
Boston Ventures	673
BP Amoco	196, 93, 311
Bridgestone/Firestone, Inc	412
Bristol Technologies	288
Bristol-Myers Squibb	66
British Airways	94
BroadBand Services	604
BroadcastSports.com	253
Brown & Williamson	134, 470, 662
Browning Ferris	401
Bucyrus International Inc.	368
Buena Vista Internet	426
Burlington Northern Santa Fe Corp.	108
Burlington Resources	401
Business Coalition for U.S.-China Trade	513
Butler Capital Corporation	388
Cable News Network	717
CalEnergy Company	480
Campbell Soup	685
Canadian National Railway Company	108
Capital Research & Management	685
Carolina Hurricanes	738
Caspian Pipeline Consortium	558
Castle Rock Entertainment	760
Caterpillar	447
Caulfield & Byers	174
CBS Corporation	65, 160, 161, 286, 412, 637
Cendant	482
Champion International	120
Chancellor Broadcasting	219
Charter Communications	535, 614, 636, 717
Charterhouse Group International	614
Chase Manhattan Corp.	546
Chemical Bank	93
Chevron	784, 786, 787
Children's Rights Projects	460
China Resorts International	582
Chiron Corp.	323
Chrysler (DaimlerChrysler)	277, 426, 513
CIA	332
CIBC World Markets Corp.	636,134

COMPANY/ORGANIZATION INDEX (cont'd)

CIGNA Corp.	.286
Cinergy	.514
Cisco Systems, Inc	.377, 492
Citibank	.134
Citicorp	.253
Citigroup	.161, 286, 412, 672
Citizens Bank	.672
City Harvest	.482
Clear Channel Communications	.557
Cleveland Indians	.276
Cleveland-Cliffs	.412
CMGI	.377
CNA Financial Corp.	.78
Coalition for Tobacco Responsibility	.427
Coastal Corp.	.120
Coca-Cola Company, The	.145, 146, 470, 471, 698
Cogen Technologies	.697
Coinstar	.435
Collagen Corp.	.343
Colombia Energy Group	.748
Comcast	.81
Compaq	.324
CompUSA	.355, 481
Computer Associates International	.120, 230
Computer Science Corp	.265
Comsat Corporation	.287
Conco Inc.	.625
Conde Nast	.401
Consolidated Natural Gas	.637
Constitutional Rights Foundation, The	.526
Continental Airlines	.217, 311
Continental Bank	.354
Cooperstown, NY Baseball Musuem	.446
Coors Brewing Company	.412
CoreStates Financial	.459
Cowen & Co.	.480
Creative Artists	.698
Credit Lyonnais	.160
Credit Suisse First Boston Corp.	.546
Crest Group	.602
Crown Cork & Seal	.685
CS First Boston	.501, 772
Cygnus Solutions	.583
Cytogen Corp.	.426
DaimlerChrysler	.277, 426, 513
Dallas Cowboys	.333
Days Inn of America	.481
dELIA*s	.614
Dell Computer	.726
Dell Financial Services	.355
Deloitte & Touche	.613, 672
Delta Airlines	.772
Democratic National Committee	.206, 276, 277
Department of Justice	.332
Department of Treasury	.332
Deutsche Bank	.145, 301, 377
Deutsche Telekom AG	.146
Dewar's Scotch Whisky and Bombay Gin	.229
Digital Cities	.312
DigitalCars.com	.253
Dominion Resources	.749
Donaldson, Lufkin & Jenrette	.333, 535, 636
DoubleClick	.343
Dow Chemical	.355
Dow Corning	.196, 217, 229, 323
Drexel Burnham Lambert	.217
Drugstore.com	.491, 492
Dunbar Economic Development Corp.	.460
DuPont	.446
Dyckerhoff A.G.	.685
DYMO CoStar Corporation	.625
Dynegy, Inc.	.557
EarthWeb	.323
Eastern Airlines	.217

COMPANY/ORGANIZATION INDEX (cont'd)

eBay	.161
EDC.com	.355
Edison's General Electric Company	.92
Edmunds.com	.253
Egghead.com	.773
El Paso Energy	.120, 401
Electronic Data Systems Corp.	.367, 625
Elektra Entertainment	.613
EM.TV	.277
EMI Group	.108
EMI Music	.64
Empire Blue Cross/Shield	.217
Enel	.94, 120
Enron Corporation	.593
Ernst & Young	.355, 613, 672
ESPN	.663
eTOYS	.491, 492
Euratom	.66
European Bank of Reconstruction and Development	.147
European Community, The	.66
European Investment Bank	.66
Extreme Networks	.706
Exxon	.109
F5 Labs	.435
Farm Sanctuary	.369
fashionmall.com	.604
Federal Bureau of Investigation	.332
Federal Home Loan Bank Board	.400
Federal Home Loan Mortgage	.146
Federal Trade Commission	.186
Federated and Allied Department Stores	.217
Federated Department Stores	.414
Fibreboard Corp.	.344
Fidelity Financial	.343
Financial Securities Data	.133
Fingerhut Companies	.414
Firestone	.196
First Chicago	.79, 81
First Data Corporation	.253
First Empire State Bank	.311
First Family	.206
First Interstate Bancorp	.287, 343
First Union	.603
Flatiron Partners	.367
Fleet Bank	.672
Fleet Financial Group	.388, 389
Florida Progress Corp.	.749
Food Lion	.558
Ford Motor Company	.286, 786
Four Seasons Hotel	.293
Fox Inc.	.286
Fred Meyer, Inc.	.311
Frito Lay	.415
FTC Counsel	.426
Fujitsu	.323, 324
G.D. Searle	.324
Gap, The	.343
Gay Men's Health Crisis	.95
Genentech	.636
General Development Corp.	.333
General Dynamics	.513, 726, 727
General Electric	.207, 310, 311, 426, 470, 535,
General Electric Capital	.134, 726
General Instruments Corp.	.81
General Motors	.197, 323, 367, 412, 470, 471, 772
General Motors Pension Trust	.603
Genetech	.323
GeoCities	.343
George Bush/Dan Quayle Presidential Campaign	.512
Georgia Amatuer Athletics Foundation	.470
Gerbert Products Company	.685
Gilead Sciences Inc.	.434
Gilette Company, The	.389
Glaxo SmithKline	.160

COMPANY/ORGANIZATION INDEX (cont'd)

Globalstar Communications	481
GM Hughes Electronic Corp.	172
Golden Eagle	119
Goldman Sachs	94, 146, 161, 173, 276, 377, 388, 389, 401, 412, 501, 546, 333, 636, 685, 772
Goodyear Tire & Rubber	286
Government of Colombia	303
Government of Panama	300
Grand Union Company	481
Green Bay Packers	302
Green Equity Investors	717
Greyhound	217
GTE Corp.	287
Guiness PLC.	311, 426
Gulf & Western	132
Gurman Blask & Freedman	322
H & Q Ventures	323
Habitat for Humanity	741
harmonycentral.com	355
Harvard Industries	481
Harvard University	389
Hasbro, Inc.	276
Hearst Corp., The	447
Hearst-Argyle	447
Heartport Inc.	502
Henry Schein	614
Heritage Partners	673
Hewlett-Packard	672
Hitachi	726
Home Depot	470
Homestore.com	174
Honda	446
Hotmail Corporation	491
Housing Works	368
HSBC Holdings	145
Hughes Aircraft	535
Hummer Windblad Venture Partners	501
i2 Technologies	343
IBM	66, 367, 672
ICO Global Communications	368
idealab!	174
Illinois Tool Works	355
Illinova Corp.	557
Infoseek	286
Inland Steel Industries	196, 425
Intel	265, 310, 491, 716
Intergraph Corp.	513, 514
International Bank for Reconstruction and Development (the World Bank)	147
International Harvester	196
International Paper	106
Internet Capital Group	685
Iriduim	333
IRS	332
ITT	79, 106
iTurf	614
iVillage	377
J. Crew	480
J.P. Morgan	106, 276, 546, 614 636
Jack In The Box Restaurants	525
Jacor Communications	513
Jim Beam Brands	662
Jim Henson Company, Inc., The	277
John Hancock Mutual Life Insurance	277, 343, 672
Johnson & Johnson	412
Joybucks.com	749
Juno Online Services	343
Kajima Corp	289
Keepe, Bruyette & Woods, Inc.	109
Kenan Systems	377
killerinfo.com	604
Kinder Morgan Energy Partners	593
Knoll	481
Kodak	425

COMPANY/ORGANIZATION INDEX (cont'd)

Kohlberg Kravis Roberts & Co 79, 132, 286, 172
Kraft 79
Kroger Co. 311
Krupp AG 333
Lamda Legal Defense and Education Fund 147
LAUNCH Media 706
Launch Media 355
Lawyers for Children America 334
Lawyers for Human Rights .558
League of Women Voters 526
League of Women Voters (Arkansas) 334
Learning Company, The 377
Legal Aid Society's Grandparents Adoption Program . .741
Lehman Brothers 132, 323, 333, 366
Lend Lease Corp 535
Level 3 Communications 481
Lever Brothers 277
Lexis-Nexis 161
LHS Group Inc. 651
Liberty Mutual 672
Life Bank 547
Ligand Pharmaceuticals 343
Lincoln Electric Co. 412
Lincoln Holdings 333
Lloyd's of London 748
Lockheed Martin 207, 287, 401, 426, 470
Lockheed Martin Global Telecommunications Group . .401
Looksmart 162
Los Angeles Dodgers 286
LTV Aerospace & Development 333
Lucas Digital 717
LucasVarity 637
Lucent Technologies 197, 252, 377
Lyondell Petrochemical 625
M. A. Hanna 412
Macy's 217
Madison Square Garden 613

Maine Yankee Power Company 673
Major League Baseball 435, 459, 460, 482
Mannesmann AG 120
Manufacturers Hanover Trust 132
MapQuest.com 355
Marriott 286
Marshall Field 196
Maryland Deposit Insurance Fund 311
Mass Mutual 672
Massachusetts Hospital Association 673
Massachusetts Medical Society 673
Massachusetts Water Resource Authority 738
Matrix Pharmaceuticals 343
Mattel, Inc. 377, 716
Mayfield Fund 174
MCI Center 82
MCI WorldCom 65, 726
McNeill PPC 685
Mcorp 333
MDL Information Systems .502
MediaOne Group Inc. 81, 218, 513, 603
Mellon Bank 93
Mentor Corp. 344
Merchandising AG 277
Merrill Lynch 160, 323, 333, 401, 447, 525, 636, 546
MetLife 276
Metropolitan Life Insurance 277
MGM Grand Hotel Theme Park 173
Michelin North America 651
Micro Unity 759
Microsoft 64, 66, 95, 96, 288, 332, 672, 797
Millennium Pharmaceuticals 377
MindSpring 513
Mission Insurance 311
Mobil 513
Molecular Biosystem 446
Molecumetics 435

COMPANY/ORGANIZATION INDEX (cont'd)

Monitor Consulting 388
Morgan Stanley Dean Witter . .106, 160, 239, 323, 501, 535,
Motorola 81, 198, 367, 726
N2K 426
NAC Re 603
NAFTA 160
National Academy of Recording Arts
and Sciences, The 613
National Association for the Advancement
of Colored People, The 333, 514
National Association of Criminal
Defense Lawyers, The 334
National Association of Securities
Dealers, The 480
National Basketball Association, The 230, 612
National Basketball Players Association, The 216
National Collegiate Athletic
Association, The 513
National Football League, The 230, 276
National Grid Group 749
National Hockey League, The 230, 276, 612
National Property Fund of Czech
Republic, The 302
National Security Counsel, The 332
National Semiconductor Corporation 759
National Veterans Legal Services
Project, The 254
NationsBank (now Bank of America) 81, 603, 535,
652, 784, 786
NBC 613
Nestle 66, 661
Netscape Communications 323, 414
Network Solutions 108
Nevada Power Company .673
New Century Energies Company 749
New York City Ballet, The .613
New York City Opera, The 613
New York Musuem of Modern Art 147, 219
New York Times, The 276

Newmark & Company Real Estate 367
Newsday 447
NextCard 253
Nextlink Communications .480
NextWave Telecom 266
NFL Properties 302
Nippon Telegraph & Telephone 367
Nomai 344
Norelco 95
Nortel Networks 492
Northwest Corp. 93
Norwest Corp. 81
Ogleghorpe Power Corp. 535
Oracle Corporation 323, 491
Orion Pictures 481
Oxygen Media 276
Pacific Mutual Life Insurance 286
Pacific Retail Trust 355
Pacific Telesis 784, 786
PacifiCorp 367, 749
PaineWebber 333
Panavision 481
Paramount 132, 286, 717
Parents for Autistic Children 558
Park Place Entertainment Corp. 173
Pearson 459
Pechiney 366
Peco Energy 65
PennzEnergy Co. 625
Pennzoil 624
People's Energy 726
PepsiCo 412
Pfizer 81, 344, 603, 685
Philadelphia Daily News, The 685
Philadelphia Inquirer, The .685
Philip Morris 66, 79, 80, 106, 228, 310, 311, 525, 569
Phillips Petroluem 78

COMPANY/ORGANIZATION INDEX (cont'd)

Phone.com 492
Pioneer Hi-Breed International 401
Pioneer-Standard Electronics 759
Playboy Entertainment Corp. 514
PNC Bank 311
Premark International 355
Preview Travel Inc. 133
Priceline.com 66, 120
PricewaterhouseCoopers 65, 276, 277
Prince 460
Procter & Gamble 625
Prodigy Communications 377, 547
Product Liability Fairness Act 512
Professional Golfer's Association of America 312
Provident Companies 748
Prudential Securities 333, 355, 470
PSE&G Global 661
Public School Reform Project 110
Purina Mills 415
Putnam Funds 388
Qualcomm 786
QVC 79
Radio City Music Hall 613
RadioWave.com 253
Randall's Food Markets 593
Raychem 162, 173
Razorfish 323
RealNetworks 773
Recording Industry Association of America 311
Redback Networks 502
Reebok International 389
Regent of the University of California, The 323
Republic National Committee, The 206
Resolution Trust Corporation 412
Revlon 239
Reynolds Metal Co. 81
RJR Nabisco 106, 132, 286, 412

Robert Pharmaceuticals 367
Rockwell International Corp., The 660
Royal Ahold 302
Royal Numico 569
Salomon Brothers 66, 144
Salomon Smith Barney .. 66, 144, 323, 333, 366, 636, 772
San Francisco Bank 546
San Francisco Giants 786
Santa Fe Industries 196
Sara Lee 726
Saraide 434
Saunders Karp & Margue 388
SBC Communications 377
Schering-Plough Corp. 197
Schlumberger Ltd. 625
Scient 501
Scottish Power 367
Sears, Roebuck 354, 772, 568
Securities and Exchange Commission 322
Security Pacific National Bank 287
Sedco Forex Offshore 625
SFX Entertainment 569,583
Shasta Networks 502
Shell Oil 525
Shire Pharmaceuticals 636
Siemens AG 333, 447
Sierra Pacific Power Company 673
Signio Inc. 434
Silicon Graphics 173, 186
SkyTel 65
Smashing Pumpkins 613
Societe Generale 93
Sony 426, 717
South African Breweries 425
Southeast Legal Foundation 332
Sperry Corporation 660
Sprint Corp. 65, 470

COMPANY/ORGANIZATION INDEX (cont'd)

Stac Electronics	.717
Stand Against Domestic Violence	.334
Stanford University	.389, 390
Star, The	.208
Starbucks	.772
Starwood Companies, The	.672
State Bar of California	.526
Stone Container Corp.	.664
Suez Equity Investments	.388
Sun Microsystems	.343, 414, 435
SunGuard Data Systems	.434
SunTrust Banks	.470
Superior Telecom	.613
Swedbank	.447
TAP Associates	.739
TCI	.81
Telecom Italia	.277, 289
Tele-Communications Inc.	.414, 625
Tenet Healthcare Corp.	.415
Tenneco	.726
Teradyne, Inc.	.672
Texaco	.217, 470
Texas Instruments	.412
Texas Utilities	.582
Thomson Consumer Electronics	.323
Time Magazine	.288, 447
Time Warner	.64, 120, 133, 288
Tobacco Institute	.435, 459, 460
Toshiba	.698, 772, 786
Total Fina	.413
Toyota	.535
Trans World Airlines	.660
Transkaryotic Therapies	.672
Travelocity	.133
Treuhandanstalt	.144
Tribune Co.	.252
TriNet Services	.435

Trump Organization	.481
Trust for Public Land	.651
Trustees of St. Patrick's Cathedral	.482
TRW, Inc.	.401, 414
TV Guide Inc.	.625
TWA	.78
U.S. Census Bureau	.289
U.S. Filter Corporation	.748
U.S. Steel	.106
uBid	.323
UBS Warburg	.636
Umbro International Inc.	.651
Unicom	.413
Unilever	.66
Union Carbide	.93
Union Pacific Resources Group	.583, 697
Union Texas Petroleum Holdings	.471
United Arab Emirates	.160
United Parcel Service	.470
United States Steel Corporation	.92
United Technologies Corporation	.748
Universal Studios	.525, 526
Univision	.447
Unocal Corp.	.525
UPM-Kymmene	.120, 302
Uptown Hull House Legal Clinic	.254
US Air Force	.332
US Airways	.333, 685
US West	.603, 773
USX Corp	.425
VA Linux	.185
Vault.com	.323
Velox Retail Holdings	.302
Verbund	.302
Verenigde Nederlandse Uitgeversbedrijven NV	.760
Verio	.323
VeriSign	.108

COMPANY/ORGANIZATION INDEX (cont'd)

Viacom 65, 160, 161
Vignette 501
Vixel 435
Vodafone 93, 120, 401
Vons Markets 525
Voxware 697
Wal-Mart 502
Walt Disney Company, The 286, 425, 426, 582, 717
Walt Disney Productions 286
Warburg Pincus 481
Warner-Lambert 81
Washington Bancorporation 311
Washington Post, The .412
Washington Wizards 82
Waste Management, Inc. 277
WebTV Networks Inc. .491
Webvan 185
Wells Fargo 81, 343
West Coast Entertainment 377
Westside Cluster of Centers and Settlements 482

Whittman-Hart 760
Williams Communications 513
Wind River Systems 434
Wit Capital 636
Witman Walker AIDS Clinic 402
Wizards of the Coast 276
Women in Need 482
World Bank 332
World Organization Against Torture USA 334
Xerox 310, 311, 786
Yahoo! .343, 491, 492, 773
Yesmail.com 355
ZDNet 355, 377
Zhone Technologies 706
Ziff - Davis 355, 377

About the Authors

Steven Gordon has a JD from the University of Pennsylvania Law School and a BA from Rutgers University. Before coming to Vault.com, he was a litigator at the New York City law firm Patterson Belknap, Webb & Tyler. Prior to law school, Steven worked for Voter News Service, the news media's primary source for election results.

Hussam Hamadeh is co-founder and managing director of Vault.com. He holds a BA in economics from UCLA and a JD/MBA from the Wharton School of Business and the University of Pennsylvania Law School, where was an editor on Law Review. He has worked at the law firms Cravath Swaine & Moore and Skadden Arps and at the investment banks Goldman Sachs and Morgan Stanley. He has authored numerous books on career-related subjects. He is a member of the New York Bar.

Mark Oldman is co-founder and managing director of Vault.com. He graduated Phi Beta Kappa from Stanford University with a BA and MA in English and JD from Stanford Law School. He designed and taught a course on the U.S. Supreme Court at Stanford University and has authored numerous books on career-related subjects. He is a member of the New York Bar.

Douglas Cantor is the content manager at Vault.com. He is a graduate of Vanderbilt University. Previously, he worked for the New York Yankees.

Catherine Cugell is a law writer at Vault.com. She graduated from Amherst College with a BA in English, French and Women's and Gender Studies. She has taught English in Athens, Greece and worked with the law firm Simpson Thacher & Bartlett.

Michael Erman is a writer at Vault.com. He graduated from Columbia University with a BA in Political Science. Previously, he toiled at the law firm Reboul, MacMurray, Hewitt, Maynard & Kristol. This is the first book he has authored for Vault.com.

Marcy Lerner is the director of content at Vault.com. She graduated from the University of Virginia and Yale University.

Chris Prior is a graduate of Queens College of the City University of New York. Before joining Vault.com, he was a staff reporter at Treasury and Risk Management Magazine, a financial trade publication based in New York City.

Design and Layout: Robert Schipano and Clarissa Londis

[trying to decide whether to make him partner]

[trying to decide between I-banking and e-Commerce]

AOL Keyword: Vault.com

Industry Channels
Insider Research >
Message Boards
News
Find a Job

Hot Topics:
Alternative Careers

Insights and resources designed to help you guide your career in any direction you choose.

VAULT.COM
[The truth is in the VAULT]

> **Just got a new billable target for hours?**

> **Don't agree with the Top 50 rankings?**

Talk it over on the Vault.com message boards

- Share late-breaking bonus news
- Compare working conditions at your firm to others
- Discuss the latest salary increases
- Talk about summer associate events

Vault.com's Legal Electronic WaterCooler™

Stop by for a refreshing drink of truth today!

Vault.com is the most vibrant community for career discussion on the Web. Visit us at http://www.vault.com and check out our LAW channel to start talking!

VAULT.COM
> the insider career network

HR VAULT

HUMAN RESOURCES FOR THE NEW ECONOMY

HR Vault is the only web site you need for comprehensive HR news, articles and resources. Talk to your peers and other HR professionals and managers on our message boards, or head to Vault.com's industry and company message boards to hear the inside word on your own firm and the legal industry. Attract qualified candidates with Vault.com's recruiting services, including our free job board and convenient 1-Click Job Posting Marketplace.

HR Vault cuts across all industries to deliver the inside track to hot HR issues, such as recruiting and retention, employee relations and training, and compensation and benefits. You'll find that HR Vault's 'insider' tools and resources are key to managing your HR career more effectively.

RECRUITING TOOLS

All the tools you need to effectively recruit the best talent for your organization.

Vault.com Job Board

- Post jobs FREE
- Advertise as many jobs as you like

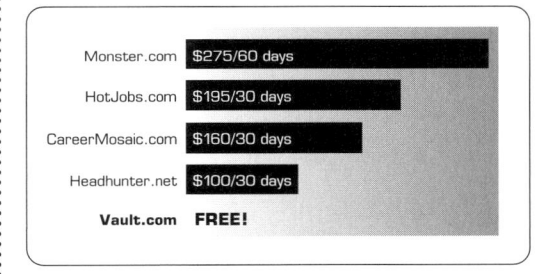

Monster.com	$275/60 days
HotJobs.com	$195/30 days
CareerMosaic.com	$160/30 days
Headhunter.net	$100/30 days
Vault.com	FREE!

One Click Service

- Cross post your jobs to leading sites on the Internet with one simple click
- Receive 1 invoice for all your listings
- Pay no extra service fee

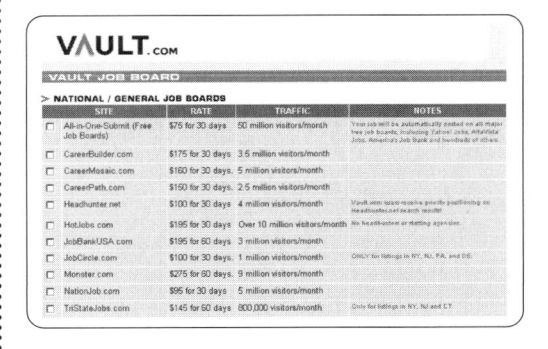

HR INSIDER CONTENT

HR Vault offers extensive career research and news.

- Insider career profiles
- The latest HR news from AIRS, HR Next, Nolo, and Kennedy Information
- Expert moderators for fast advice for your most pressing HR issues.

COMMUNITY

Networking, mentoring, and benchmarking opportunities abound on HR Vault's message boards.

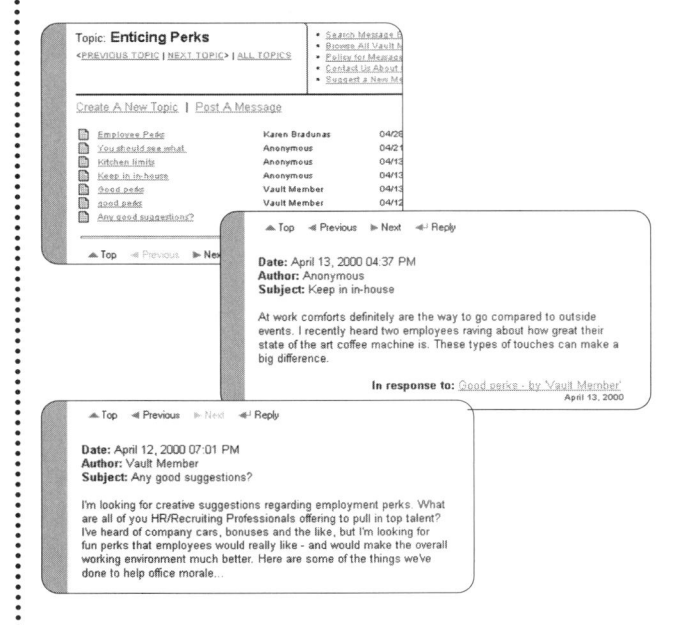

> Visit the HR Vault at http://www.vault.com

VAULT.COM
> the insider career network

Attract qualified candidates and...

...convince them to accept your offer. Appeal to potential hires before they even consider making a career move. As a highly-respected and trusted source for objective employer information, the content created by Vault.com's award-winning editorial department will highlight your company's positive attributes.

Sponsorships

Place your company's banner on any Industry and/or Career Channel. Build brand awareness and direct traffic to your recruiting site.

Recruiting Video

Post your recruiting video or CD-ROM on our site. You'll give candidates immediate, unique and interactive access to your most effective marketing tool.

Highlights

Highlights are an excellent 3rd party endorsement: a great way to show off your company's positive attributes and differentiate you from your competition.

Q&A

Speak directly to your recruiting demographic. Discuss corporate programs, policies, initiatives and strategies. Address issues and topics pertinent to your company, in your own words. The Vault.com Q&A filters the best and most interested candidates to your company.

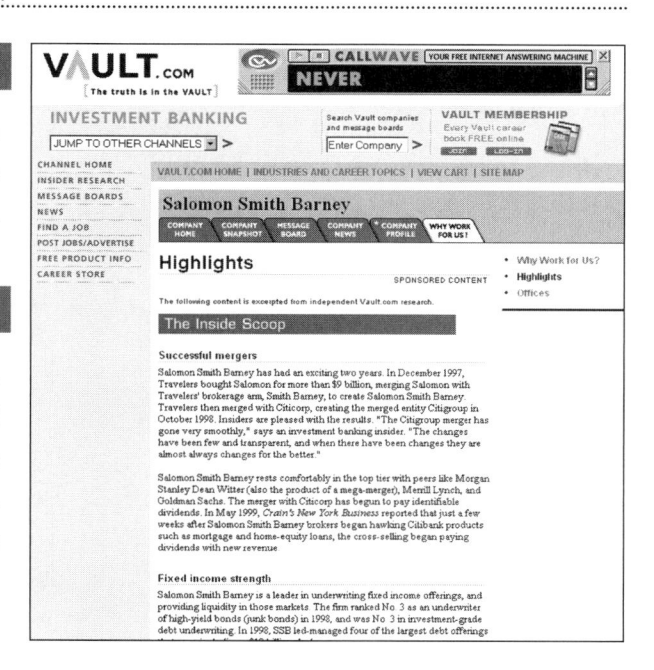

For more information on Vault.com's recruitment marketing services, please call (212) 366-4212 x257 or e-mail recruitingsales@staff.vault.com

VAULT.COM
> the insider career network